Africa 68-69

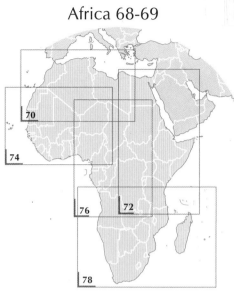

Europe 80-81

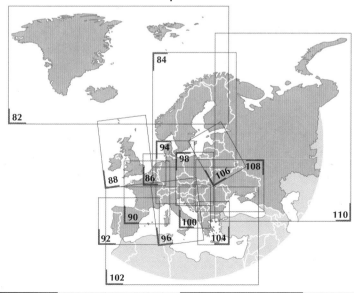

WORLD ATLAS

ESSENTIAL

LONDON, NEW YORK, MELBOURNE, MUNICH, DELHI

LONDON, NEW YORK, MELBOURNE, MUNICH, DELHI

FOR THE EIGHTH EDITION

SENIOR CARTOGRAPHIC EDITOR Simon Mumford
CARTOGRAPHY Encompass Graphics Ltd., Brighton, UK
PRODUCTION CONTROLLER Mandy Inness   PRODUCER, PRE-PRODUCTION Rebekah Parsons-King
INDEX DATABASE David Roberts   JACKET DESIGNER Mark Cavanagh
PUBLISHER Jonathan Metcalf   ART DIRECTOR Philip Ormerod
ASSOCIATE PUBLISHER Liz Wheeler

DORLING KINDERSLEY CARTOGRAPHY
PROJECT CARTOGRAPHY AND DESIGN
Julia Lunn, Julie Turner

CARTOGRAPHERS
James Anderson, Roger Bullen, Martin Darlison,
Simon Mumford, John Plumer, Peter Winfield

DESIGN
Katy Wall

INDEX-GAZETTEER
Natalie Clarkson, Ruth Duxbury, Margaret Hynes, Margaret Stevenson

PRODUCTION
Hilary Stephens, David Proffit

EDITORIAL DIRECTION
Andrew Heritage

ART DIRECTION
Chez Picthall

First American edition 1997. Second edition 1998. Third edition 2001. Fourth edition 2003.
Fifth edition 2005. Sixth edition 2008. Seventh edition 2011. Eighth edition 2013.

Published in the United States by DK Publishing,
375 Hudson Street, New York, New York 10014
A Penguin Company.

13 14 15 16 17 10 9 8 7 6 5 4 3 2 1

001—188128—May/2013

A catalog record for this book is available from the Library of Congress.

ISBN: 978-1-4654-0228-8

Printed and bound by Hung Hing, Hong Kong.

Discover more at **www.dk.com**

Key to map symbols

Physical features

Elevation

	6000m/19,686ft
	4000m/13,124ft
	3000m/9843ft
	2000m/6562ft
	1000m/3281ft
	500m/1640ft
	250m/820ft
	0
	Below sea level

△ Mountain

▽ Depression

△ Volcano

)(Pass/tunnel

▦ Sandy desert

Drainage features

──── Major perennial river

──── Minor perennial river

- - - Seasonal river

──── Canal

| Waterfall

⬭ Perennial lake

⟨⟨⟨⟩ Seasonal lake

▦ Wetland

Ice features

▢ Permanent ice cap/ice shelf

▢ Winter limit of pack ice

▢ Summer limit of pack ice

Borders

━━━ Full international border

- - - - Disputed de facto border

· · · · · Territorial claim border

✕━✕━✕ Cease-fire line

━ ━ ━ ▪ Undefined boundary

──── Internal administrative boundary

Communications

──── Major road

──── Minor road

──── Railway

✈ International airport

Settlements

▣ Above 500,000

◉ 100,000 to 500,000

○ 50,000 to 100,000

○ Below 50,000

● National capital

◉ Internal administrative capital

Miscellaneous features

+ Site of interest

ⅿⅿⅿ Ancient wall

Graticule features

──── Line of latitude/longitude/Equator

- - - Tropic/Polar circle

25° Degrees of latitude/longitude

Names

Physical features

Andes

Sahara Landscape features

Ardennes

Land's End Headland

Mont Blanc
4,807m Elevation/volcano/pass

Blue Nile River/canal/waterfall

Ross Ice Shelf Ice feature

PACIFIC
OCEAN

Sulu Sea Sea features

Palk Strait

Chile Rise Undersea feature

Regions

FRANCE Country

JERSEY
(to UK) Dependent territory

KANSAS Administrative region

Dordogne Cultural region

Settlements

PARIS Capital city

SAN JUAN Dependent territory capital city

Chicago

Kettering Other settlements

Burke

Inset map symbols

▢ Urban area

⬭ City

▢ Park

▪ Place of interest

▫ Suburb/district

Contents

The World Today

Flags of the World.................................6-7
The Political World...............................8-9
The Physical World.............................10-11
Time Zones.......................................12-13
Geology & Structure..........................14-15
World Climate....................................16-17
Ocean Currents..................................18-19
Life Zones...20-21
Population..22-23
Languages..24-25
Religion..26-27
The Global Economy..........................28-29
Politics and Conflict...........................30-31

The World's Regions

North & Central America

North & Central America.....................34-35
Western Canada & Alaska....................36-37
Eastern Canada..................................38-39
USA: The Northeast.............................40-41
USA: The Southeast.............................42-43
  Bermuda
USA: Central States.............................44-45
USA: The West...................................46-47
  Los Angeles & Hawaii

USA: The Southwest.............................48-49
Mexico...50-51
Central America..................................52-53
The Caribbean...................................54-55
  Jamaica, St. Lucia, & Barbados

South America

South America....................................56-57
Northern South America.......................58-59
Western South America.........................60-61
  Galapagos Islands
Brazil...62-63
Southern South America.......................64-65
The Atlantic Ocean.............................66-67

Africa

Africa...68-69
Northwest Africa.................................70-71
Northeast Africa.................................72-73
West Africa..74-75
Central Africa.....................................76-77
  Sao Tome & Principe
Southern Africa..................................78-79

Europe

Europe...80-81
The North Atlantic..............................82-83
Scandinavia & Finland.........................84-85
The Low Countries..............................86-87
The British Isles.................................88-89
  London

continued....

Europe *continued*

France, Andorra, & Monaco 90-91
  Paris, Andorra, & Monaco
Spain & Portugal 92-93
  Azores & Gibraltar
Germany & the Alpine States 94-95
  Liechtenstein
Italy 96-97
  San Marino & Vatican City
Central Europe 98-99
Southeast Europe 100-101
  Bosnia & Herzegovina
The Mediterranean 102-103
  Malta & Cyprus
Bulgaria & Greece 104-105
The Baltic States & Belarus 106-107
Ukraine, Moldova,
  & Romania 108-109
European Russia 110-111

North & West Asia

North & West Asia 112-113
Russia & Kazakhstan 114-115
Turkey & the Caucasus 116-117
The Near East 118-119
  West Bank
The Middle East 120-121
Central Asia 122-123

South & East Asia

South & East Asia 124-125
Western China & Mongolia 126-127

Eastern China & Korea 128-129
  Hong Kong (Xianggang)
Japan 130-131
  Tokyo & Nansei-Shoto
South India & Sri Lanka 132-133
North India, Pakistan,
  & Bangladesh 134-135
Mainland Southeast Asia 136-137
Maritime Southeast Asia 138-139
  Singapore
The Indian Ocean 140-141

Australasia & Oceania

Australasia & Oceania 142-143
The Southwest Pacific 144-145
Western Australia 146-147
Eastern Australia 148-149
  Sydney
New Zealand 150-151
The Pacific Ocean 152-153
Antarctica 154
The Arctic Ocean 155

Index– Gazetteer

Overseas Territories
  & Dependencies 156-159
Glossary of Geographical
  Terms 160-161
Continental Factfiles 162-163
Geographical Comparisons 164-166
Index-Gazetteer of Places
  & Countries 167-256

Flags of the World

NORTH & CENTRAL AMERICA

CANADA PAGES 36-39 · UNITED STATES OF AMERICA PAGES 40-49 · MEXICO PAGES 50-51 · BELIZE PAGES 52-53 · COSTA RICA PAGES 52-53 · EL SALVADOR PAGES 52-53 · GUATEMALA PAGES 52-53 · HONDURAS PAGES 52-53

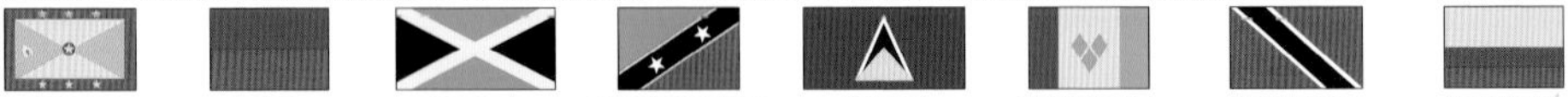

GRENADA PAGES 54-55 · HAITI PAGES 54-55 · JAMAICA PAGES 54-55 · ST KITTS & NEVIS PAGES 54-55 · ST LUCIA PAGES 54-55 · ST VINCENT & THE GRENADINES PAGES 54-55 · TRINIDAD & TOBAGO PAGES 54-55

SOUTH AMERICA

COLOMBIA PAGES 58-59

URUGUAY PAGES 64-65 · CHILE PAGES 64-65 · PARAGUAY PAGES 64-65

AFRICA

ALGERIA PAGES 70-71 · LIBYA PAGES 70-71 · MOROCCO PAGES 70-71 · TUNISIA PAGES 70-71 · BURUNDI PAGES 72-73

SUDAN PAGES 72-73 · TANZANIA PAGES 72-73 · UGANDA PAGES 72-73 · BENIN PAGES 74-75 · BURKINA FASO PAGES 74-75 · CAPE VERDE PAGES 74-75 · CÔTE D'IVOIRE (IVORY COAST) PAGES 74-75 · GAMBIA PAGES 74-75 · GHANA PAGES 74-75

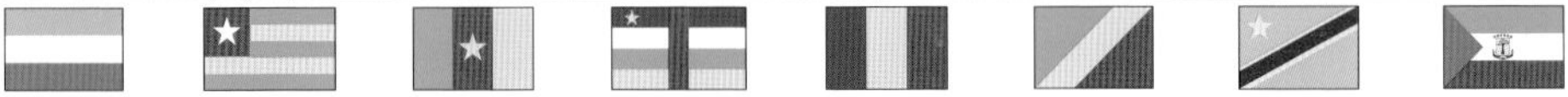

SIERRA LEONE PAGES 74-75 · TOGO PAGES 74-75 · CAMEROON PAGES 76-77 · CENTRAL AFRICAN REPUBLIC PAGES 76-77 · CHAD PAGES 76-77 · CONGO PAGES 76-77 · DEM. REP. CONGO PAGES 76-77 · EQUATORIAL GUINEA PAGES 76-77

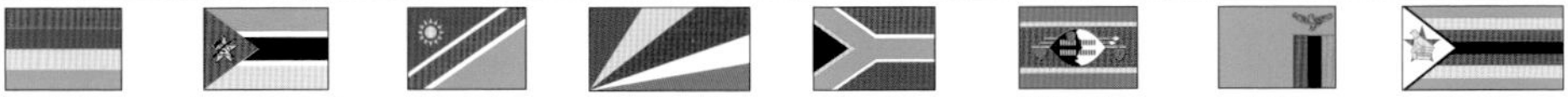

MAURITIUS PAGES 78-79 · MOZAMBIQUE PAGES 78-79 · NAMIBIA PAGES 78-79 · SEYCHELLES PAGES 78-79 · SOUTH AFRICA PAGES 78-79 · SWAZILAND PAGES 78-79 · ZAMBIA PAGES 78-79 · ZIMBABWE PAGES 78-79

UNITED KINGDOM PAGES 88-89 · FRANCE PAGES 90-91 · MONACO PAGES 90-91 · ANDORRA PAGES 90-91 · PORTUGAL PAGES 92-93 · SPAIN PAGES 92-93 · AUSTRIA PAGES 94-95 · GERMANY PAGES 94-95

POLAND PAGES 98-99 · SLOVAKIA PAGES 98-99 · ALBANIA PAGES 100-101 · BOSNIA & HERZEGOVINA PAGES 100-101 · CROATIA PAGES 100-101 · KOSOVO PAGES 100-101 · MACEDONIA PAGES 100-101 · MONTENEGRO PAGES 100-101

MOLDOVA PAGES 108-109 · ROMANIA PAGES 108-109 · UKRAINE PAGES 108-109 · RUSSIAN FEDERATION PAGES 110-115

ASIA

KAZAKHSTAN PAGES 114-115 · ARMENIA PAGES 116-117 · AZERBAIJAN PAGES 116-117 · GEORGIA PAGES 116-117

KUWAIT PAGES 120-121 · OMAN PAGES 120-121 · QATAR PAGES 120-121 · SAUDI ARABIA PAGES 120-121 · UNITED ARAB EMIRATES PAGES 120-121 · YEMEN PAGES 120-121 · AFGHANISTAN PAGES 122-123 · KYRGYZSTAN PAGES 122-123

JAPAN PAGES 130-131 · INDIA PAGES 132-135 · SRI LANKA PAGES 132-133 · MALDIVES PAGES 132-133 · PAKISTAN PAGES 134-135 · BANGLADESH PAGES 134-135 · BHUTAN PAGES 134-135 · NEPAL PAGES 134-135 · CAMBODIA PAGES 136-137

PHILIPPINES PAGES 138-139 · SINGAPORE PAGES 138-139

AUSTRALASIA & OCEANIA

FIJI PAGES 144-145 · KIRIBATI PAGES 144-145 · MARSHALL ISLANDS PAGES 144-145 · MICRONESIA PAGES 144-145 · NAURU PAGES 144-145 · PALAU PAGES 144-145

NICARAGUA
PAGES 52-53

PANAMA
PAGES 52-53

ANTIGUA &
BARBUDA
PAGES 54-55

BAHAMAS
PAGES 54-55

BARBADOS
PAGES 54-55

CUBA
PAGES 54-55

DOMINICA
PAGES 54-55

DOMINICAN
REPUBLIC
PAGES 54-55

GUYANA
PAGES 58-59

SURINAME
PAGES 58-59

VENEZUELA
PAGES 58-59

BOLIVIA
PAGES 60-61

ECUADOR
PAGES 60-61

PERU
PAGES 60-61

BRAZIL
PAGES 62-63

ARGENTINA
PAGES 64-65

DJIBOUTI
PAGES 72-73

EGYPT
PAGES 72-73

ERITREA
PAGES 72-73

ETHIOPIA
PAGES 72-73

KENYA
PAGES 72-73

RWANDA
PAGES 72-73

SOMALIA
PAGES 72-73

SOUTH
SUDAN
PAGES 72-73

GUINEA
PAGES 74-75

GUINEA-BISSAU
PAGES 74-75

LIBERIA
PAGES 74-75

MALI
PAGES 74-75

MAURITANIA
PAGES 74-75

NIGER
PAGES 74-75

NIGERIA
PAGES 74-75

SENEGAL
PAGES 74-75

GABON
PAGES 76-77

SAO TOME &
PRINCIPE
PAGES 76-77

EUROPE

ANGOLA
PAGES 78-79

BOTSWANA
PAGES 78-79

COMOROS
PAGES 78-79

LESOTHO
PAGES 78-79

MADAGASCAR
PAGES 78-79

MALAWI
PAGES 78-79

ICELAND
PAGES 82-83

DENMARK
PAGES 84-85

FINLAND
PAGES 84-85

NORWAY
PAGES 84-85

SWEDEN
PAGES 84-85

BELGIUM
PAGES 86-87

LUXEMBOURG
PAGES 86-87

NETHERLANDS
PAGES 86-87

IRELAND
PAGES 88-89

LIECHTENSTEIN
PAGES 94-95

SLOVENIA
PAGES 94-95

SWITZERLAND
PAGES 94-95

ITALY
PAGES 96-97

MALTA
PAGES 96-97

SAN MARINO
PAGES 96-97

VATICAN CITY
PAGES 96-97

CZECH REPUBLIC
PAGES 98-99

HUNGARY
PAGES 98-99

SERBIA
PAGES 100-101

CYPRUS
PAGES 102-103

BULGARIA
PAGES 104-105

GREECE
PAGES 104-105

BELARUS
PAGES 106-107

ESTONIA
PAGES 106-107

LATVIA
PAGES 106-107

LITHUANIA
PAGES 106-107

TURKEY
PAGES 116-117

ISRAEL
PAGES 118-119

JORDAN
PAGES 118-119

LEBANON
PAGES 118-119

SYRIA
PAGES 118-119

BAHRAIN
PAGES 120-121

IRAN
PAGES 120-121

IRAQ
PAGES 120-121

TAJIKISTAN
PAGES 122-123

TURKMENISTAN
PAGES 122-123

UZBEKISTAN
PAGES 122-123

CHINA
PAGES 126-129

MONGOLIA
PAGES 126-127

NORTH KOREA
PAGES 128-129

SOUTH KOREA
PAGES 128-129

TAIWAN
PAGES 128-129

LAOS
PAGES 136-137

MYANMAR
(BURMA)
PAGES 136-137

THAILAND
PAGES 136-137

VIETNAM
PAGES 136-137

BRUNEI
PAGES 138-139

EAST TIMOR
PAGES 138-139

INDONESIA
PAGES 138-139

MALAYSIA
PAGES 138-139

PAPUA NEW
GUINEA
PAGES 144-145

SAMOA
PAGES 144-145

SOLOMON
ISLANDS
PAGES 144-145

TONGA
PAGES 144-145

TUVALU
PAGES 144-145

VANUATU
PAGES 144-145

AUSTRALIA
PAGES 146-149

NEW ZEALAND
PAGES 150-151

The Political World

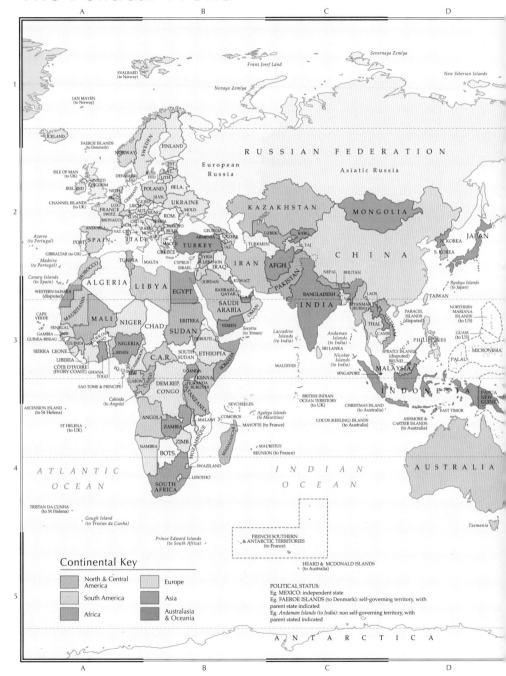

Continental Key

- North & Central America
- South America
- Africa
- Europe
- Asia
- Australasia & Oceania

POLITICAL STATUS:
Eg. MEXICO: independent state
Eg. FAEROE ISLANDS (to Denmark): self-governing territory, with parent state indicated
Eg. *Andaman Islands (to India)*: non self-governing territory, with parent stated indicated

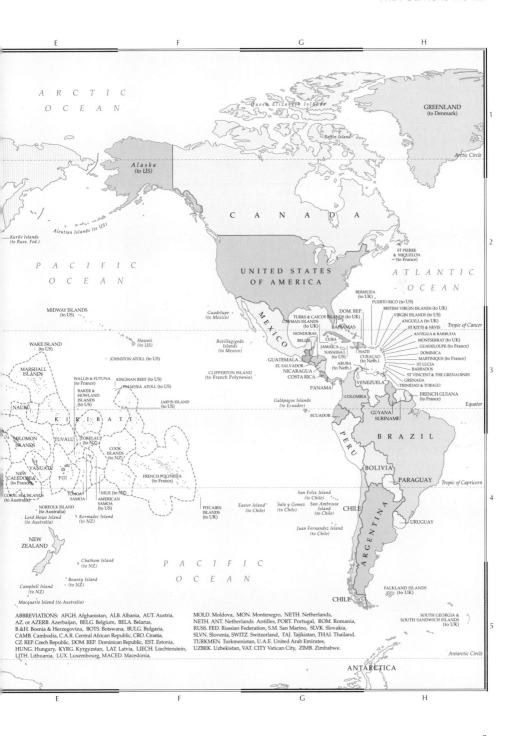

ABBREVIATIONS: AFGH. Afghanistan, ALB. Albania, AUT. Austria, AZ. or AZERB. Azerbaijan, BELG. Belgium, BELA. Belarus, B.&H. Bosnia & Herzegovina, BOTS. Botswana, BULG. Bulgaria, CAMB. Cambodia, C.A.R. Central African Republic, CRO. Croatia, CZ. REP. Czech Republic, DOM. REP. Dominican Republic, EST. Estonia, HUNG. Hungary, KYRG. Kyrgyzstan, LAT. Latvia, LIECH. Liechtenstein, LITH. Lithuania, LUX. Luxembourg, MACED. Macedonia,

MOLD. Moldova, MON. Montenegro, NETH. Netherlands, NETH. ANT. Netherlands Antilles, PORT. Portugal, ROM. Romania, RUSS. FED. Russian Federation, S.M. San Marino, SLVK. Slovakia, SLVN. Slovenia, SWITZ. Switzerland, TAJ. Tajikistan, THAI. Thailand, TURKMEN. Turkmenistan, U.A.E. United Arab Emirates, UZBEK. Uzbekistan, VAT. CITY Vatican City, ZIMB. Zimbabwe.

The Physical World

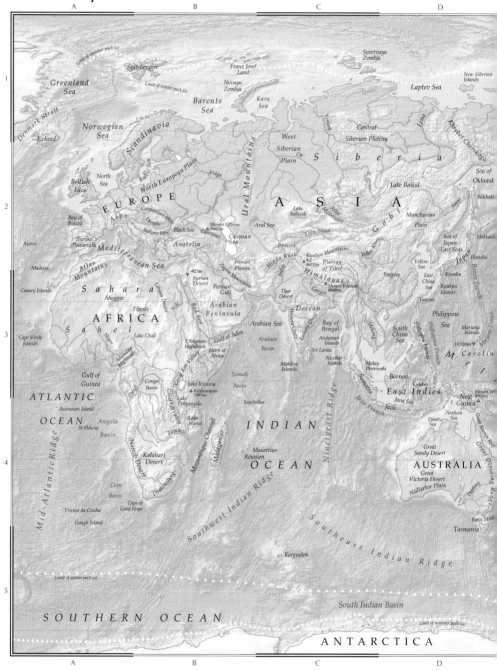

Greenland
Sea

Limit of summer pack ice

Spitsbergen

Franz Josef
Land

Severnaya
Zemlya

New Siberian
Islands

Limit of winter pack ice

Novaya
Zemlya

Barents
Sea

Kara
Sea

Laptev Sea

Denmark Strait

Iceland

Norwegian
Sea

Scandinavia

West
Siberian
Plain

Yenisey

Central
Siberian Plateau

Lena

Kolyma

Verkhoyansk

British
Isles

North
Sea

Baltic Sea

North European Plain

Volga

Ural Mountains

Ob'

S i b e r i a

Sea of
Okhotsk

EUROPE

Alps

Carpathian Mts

Danube

Balkans Mts

A S I A

Lake
Balkash

Altai
Mountains

Gobi

Manchurian
Plain

Amur

Sakhalin

Bay of
Biscay

Azores

Madeira

Iberian
Peninsula

Black Sea

Mount Elbrus
△5642m

Caucasus

Aral Sea

Tien Shan

Sea of
Japan
(East Sea)

Hokkaido

Mediterranean Sea

Anatolia

Caspian
Sea

Pamirs

Hindu Kush

Kunlun Mountains

K2
△8611m

Plateau
of Tibet

Yellow River

Yangtze

Yellow
Sea

East
China
Sea

Honshu

Kyushu

Kyukyu
Islands

Japan

Canary Islands

Atlas
Mountains

S a h a r a

Libyan Desert

Nile

△423m
Syrian
Desert

Zagros Mountains

Iranian
Plateau

Indus

Persian
Gulf

Thar
Desert

Ganges

Himalayas

Mount Everest
8848m

Deccan

Taiwan

Philippine
Sea

Mariana
Islands

Mariana Trench

Ahaggar

AFRICA

S a h e l

Niger

Tibesti

Lake Chad

Red Sea

Ethiopian
Highlands

Gulf of Aden

Arabian
Peninsula

Arabian Sea

Western Ghats

Eastern Ghats

Bay of
Bengal

Andaman
Islands

Sri Lanka

Mekong

South
China
Sea

Philippine Islands

Philippine Trench

-10,920m ▽

M   Carolin

Cape Verde
Islands

Adamawa
Highlands

Horn of
Africa

Arabian
Basin

Maldive
Islands

Nicobar
Islands

Malay
Peninsula

Borneo

Celebes

e   l

Gulf of
Guinea

Congo

Congo
Basin

Great Rift Valley

Lake Victoria
△Kilimanjaro
5895m

Somali
Basin

Seychelles

Sumatra

Java Trench

East Indies

Java

Java Sea

New
Guinea

Mount
△4509m

Arafura
Sea

ATLANTIC

OCEAN

Ascension Island

St Helena

Angola
Basin

Lake
Tanganyika

Great Rift Valley

Lake
Nyasa

I N D I A N

Mauritius
Réunion

Timor
Sea

Great
Sandy Desert

Great Barrier Reef

Great Dividing Range

Mid-Atlantic Ridge

Namib Desert

Zambezi

Kalahari
Desert

Mozambique Channel

Madagascar

O C E A N

Ninetyeast Ridge

AUSTRALIA

Great
Victoria Desert

Nullarbor Plain

Darling

Cape
Basin

Drakensberg

Cape of
Good Hope

Southwest Indian Ridge

Bass Strait

Tristan da Cunha

Tasmania

Gough Island

Southeast Indian Ridge

Kerguelen

Limit of winter pack ice

S O U T H E R N   O C E A N

South Indian Basin

Limit of summer pack ice

A N T A R C T I C A

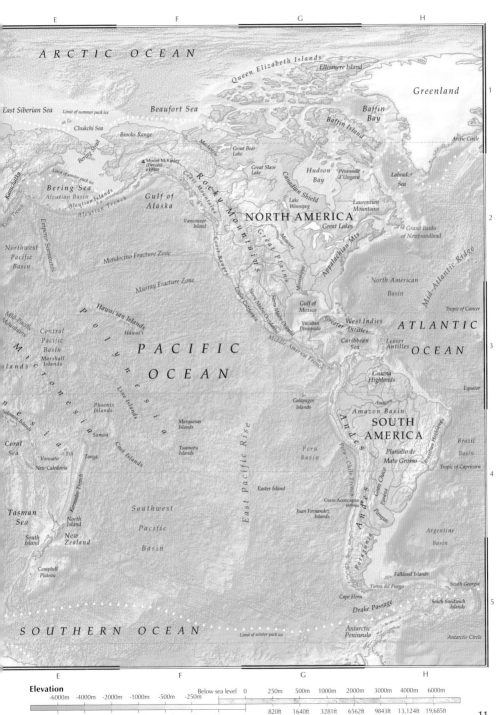

ARCTIC OCEAN

Queen Elizabeth Islands
Ellesmere Island

Greenland

East Siberian Sea   Limit of summer pack ice   Beaufort Sea

Baffin
Bay

Chukchi Sea

Baffin Island

Brooks Range

Arctic Circle

Mackenzie

Great Bear
Lake

Bering Strait

Mount McKinley
(Denali)
6194m

Great Slave
Lake

Hudson
Bay

Péninsule
d'Ungava

Labrador
Sea

Bering Sea

Kamchatka

Aleutian Basin
Aleutian Islands

Gulf of
Alaska

Kuril Trench

Limit of winter pack ice

Aleutian Trench

Coast Mountains

Rocky Mountains

Vancouver
Island

NORTH AMERICA

Canadian Shield

Lake
Winnipeg

Great Lakes

Laurentian
Mountains

Grand Banks
of Newfoundland

Emperor Seamounts

Northwest
Pacific
Basin

Mendocino Fracture Zone

Great Plains

Missouri

Appalachian Mts

North American
Basin

Mid-Atlantic Ridge

Murray Fracture Zone

Coast Ranges

Mississippi

Tropic of Cancer

Mid-Pacific
Mountains

Hawai'ian Islands

Hawai'i

Sierra Madre Occidental

Sierra Madre Oriental

Gulf of
Mexico

Yucatán
Peninsula

Greater Antilles

West Indies
Lesser
Antilles

ATLANTIC

Central
Pacific
Basin

PACIFIC

Sierra Madre del Sur

Caribbean
Sea

OCEAN

Micronesia

Marshall
Islands

Gulf of California

Middle America Trench

Islands

OCEAN

Polynesia

Line Islands

Guiana
Highlands

Equator

Solomon Islands

Phoenix
Islands

Marquesas
Islands

Galápagos
Islands

Amazon

Amazon Basin

SOUTH
AMERICA

Brazilian Highlands

Brazil
Basin

Coral
Sea

Samoa

Tuamotu
Islands

Peru
Basin

Planalto de
Mato Grosso

Tropic of Capricorn

Vanuatu   Fiji   Tonga

Cook Islands

East Pacific Rise

Peru-Chile Trench

Gran Chaco

Andes

New Caledonia

Easter Island

Paraná

Tasman
Sea

Kermadec Trench

North
Island

Southwest

Pacific

Cerro Aconcagua
6959m

Juan Fernández
Islands

Pampas

Patagonia

Argentine
Basin

South
Island

New
Zealand

Basin

Campbell
Plateau

Andes

Falkland Islands

South Georgia

Tierra del Fuego

Cape Horn

SOUTHERN   OCEAN

Limit of winter pack ice

Drake Passage

Antarctic
Peninsula

South Sandwich
Islands

Antarctic Circle

Elevation

| -6000m | -4000m | -2000m | -1000m | -500m | -250m | Below sea level | 0 | 250m | 500m | 1000m | 2000m | 3000m | 4000m | 6000m |

| -19,658ft | -13,124ft | -6562ft | -3281ft | -1640ft | -820ft | -328ft/-100m | 0 | 820ft | 1640ft | 3281ft | 6562ft | 9843ft | 13,124ft | 19,685ft |

Time Zones

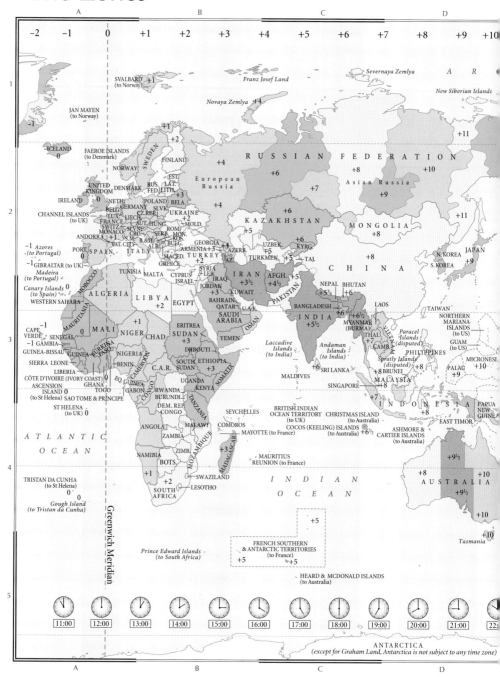

The numbers represented thus; +2/-2, indicate the number of hours each time zone is ahead or behind UCT (Coordinated Universal Time)

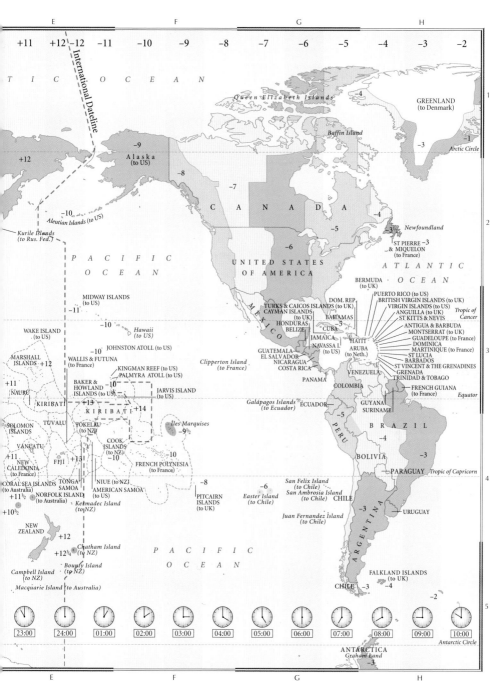

The clocks and 24-hour times given at the bottom of the map show time in each time zone when it is 12.00 hours noon UCT

Geology & Structure

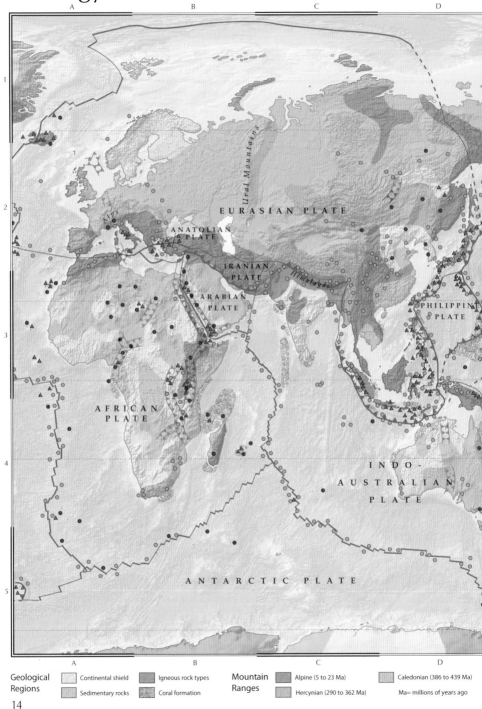

Geological
Regions

Continental shield		Igneous rock types
Sedimentary rocks		Coral formation

Mountain
Ranges

Alpine (5 to 23 Ma)	Caledonian (386 to 439 Ma)
Hercynian (290 to 362 Ma)	Ma= millions of years ago

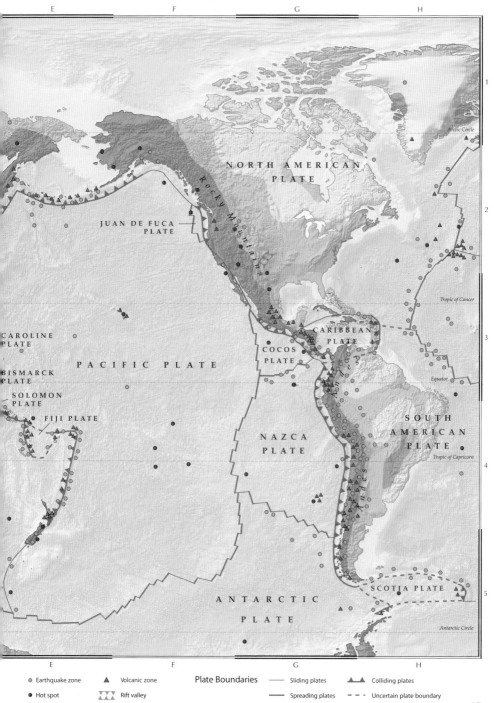

ANTARCTIC
PLATE

| E | F | G | H |

Earthquake zone   ▲ Volcanic zone   **Plate Boundaries**   —— Sliding plates   ▲▲ Colliding plates

● Hot spot   ▼▼▼ Rift valley   —— Spreading plates   - - - Uncertain plate boundary

World Climate

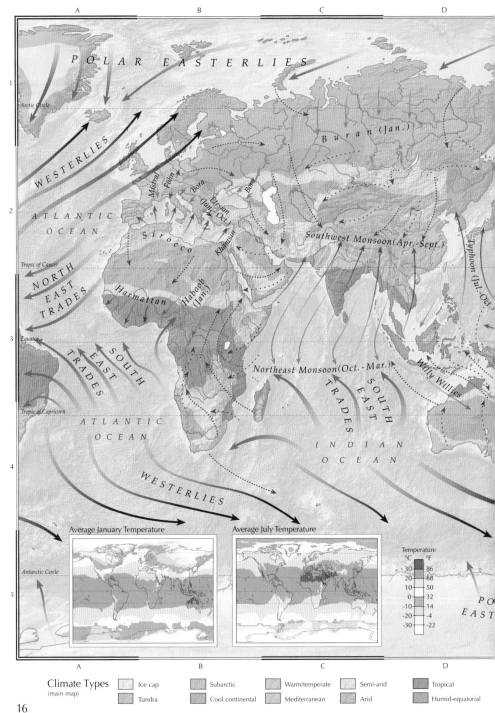

Average January Temperature

Average July Temperature

Temperature	
°C	°F
30	86
20	68
10	50
0	32
-10	14
-20	-4
-30	-22

Climate Types
(main map)

Ice cap · Subarctic · Warm/temperate · Semi-arid · Tropical

Tundra · Cool continental · Mediterranean · Arid · Humid-equatorial

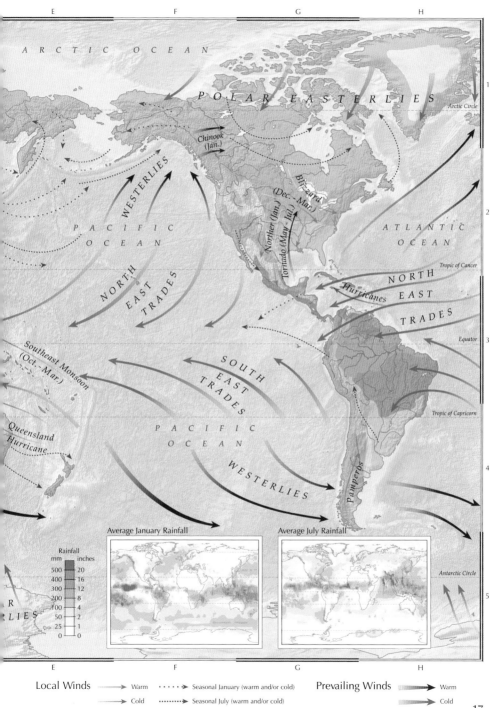

ARCTIC OCEAN

POLAR EASTERLIES

Arctic Circle

Chinook
(Jan.)

Blizzard
(Dec. - Mar.)

Norther (Jan.)

Tornado (May - Jul.)

WESTERLIES

PACIFIC
OCEAN

ATLANTIC
OCEAN

Tropic of Cancer

NORTH
EAST
TRADES

NORTH
EAST

TRADES

Hurricanes

Equator

Southeast Monsoon
(Oct - Mar.)

SOUTH
EAST
TRADES

Tropic of Capricorn

Queensland
Hurricane

PACIFIC
OCEAN

WESTERLIES

Pamperos

WESTERLIES

Antarctic Circle

Average January Rainfall

Average July Rainfall

Rainfall
mm	inches
500	20
400	16
300	12
200	8
100	4
50	2
25	1
0	0

R

LIES

Local Winds   ⟶ Warm   •••••⟶ Seasonal January (warm and/or cold)   Prevailing Winds ⟶ Warm

⟶ Cold   ••••••⟶ Seasonal July (warm and/or cold)   ⟶ Cold

17

Ocean Currents

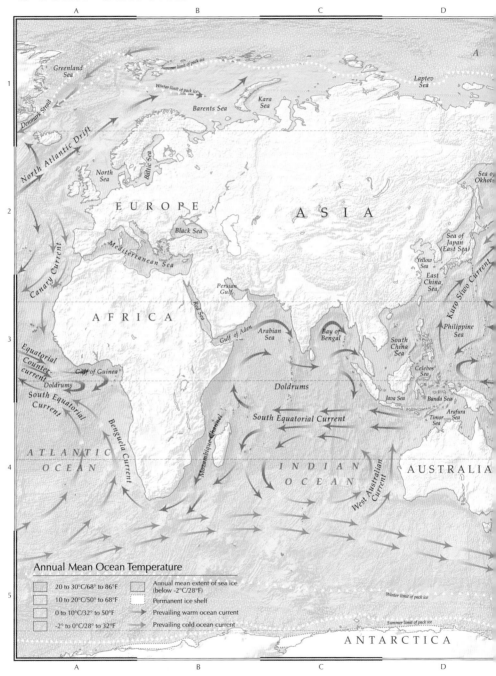

A

Greenland
Sea

Summer limit of pack ice

Laptev
Sea

Winter limit of pack ice

Kara
Sea

Barents Sea

Denmark Strait

North Atlantic Drift

North
Sea

Baltic Sea

Sea of
Okhotsk

EUROPE

ASIA

Black Sea

Sea of
Japan
(East Sea)

Canary Current

Mediterranean Sea

Yellow
Sea

Red Sea

Persian
Gulf

East
China
Sea

Kuro Siwo Current

AFRICA

Gulf of Aden

Arabian
Sea

Bay of
Bengal

South
China
Sea

Philippine
Sea

Equatorial
Counter-
current

Gulf of Guinea

Celebes
Sea

Doldrums

Doldrums

South
Equatorial
Current

South Equatorial Current

Java Sea

Banda Sea

Benguela Current

Mozambique Channel

Timor
Sea

Arafura
Sea

ATLANTIC
OCEAN

INDIAN
OCEAN

AUSTRALIA

West Australian Current

Annual Mean Ocean Temperature

	20 to 30°C/68° to 86°F	Annual mean extent of sea ice (below -2°C/28°F)
	10 to 20°C/50° to 68°F	Permanent ice shelf
	0 to 10°C/32° to 50°F	Prevailing warm ocean current
	-2° to 0°C/28° to 32°F	Prevailing cold ocean current

Winter limit of pack ice

Summer limit of pack ice

ANTARCTICA

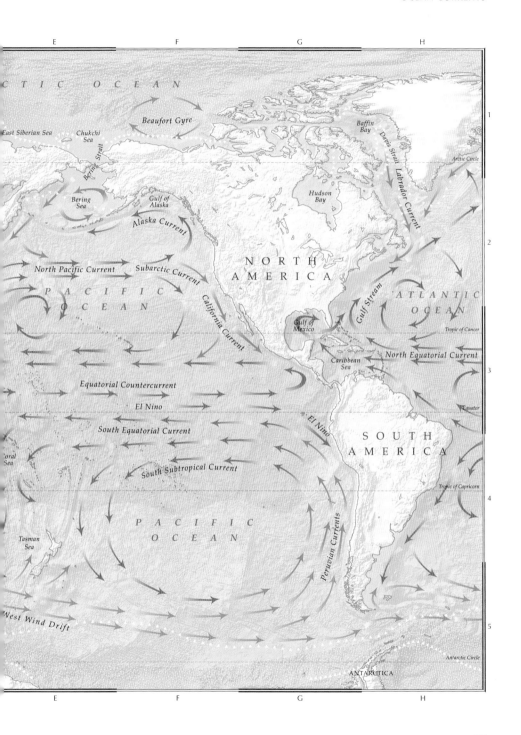

Life Zones

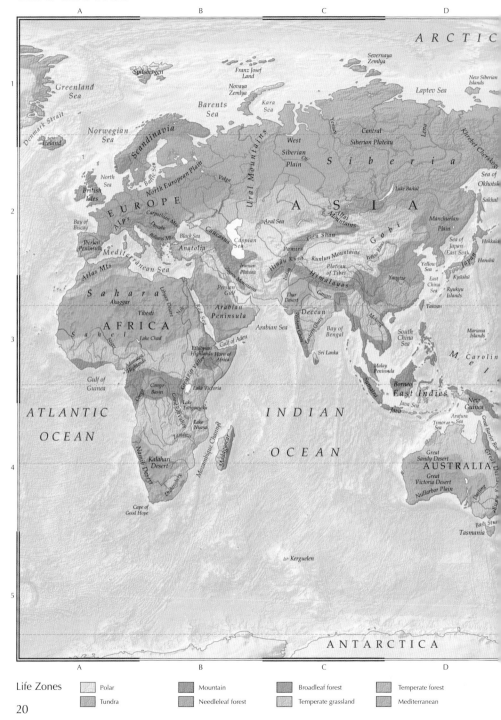

ARCTIC

Spitsbergen
Franz Josef Land
Severnaya Zemlya
New Siberian Islands
Greenland Sea
Novaya Zemlya
Laptev Sea
Denmark Strait
Norwegian Sea
Iceland
Barents Sea
Kara Sea
Scandinavia
West Siberian Plain
Ob
Yenisey
Central Siberian Plateau
Lena
Kolyma
Kolyma Range
Cherskiy
North Sea
Baltic Sea
Volga
Ural Mountains
Siberia
Sea of Okhotsk
British Isles
North European Plain
EUROPE
ASIA
Sakhalin
Bay of Biscay
Alps
Carpathian Mts.
Aral Sea
Altai Mountains
Gobi
Manchurian Plain
Sea of Japan (East Sea)
Hokkaido
Iberian Peninsula
Balkans Mts.
Danube
Black Sea
Caucasus
Caspian Sea
Tien Shan
Kunlun Mountains
Yellow River
Honshū
Japan
Atlas Mts.
Mediterranean Sea
Anatolia
Pamirs
Hindu Kush
Plateau of Tibet
Yellow Sea
Kyūshū
Libyan Desert
Iranian Plateau
Zagros Mountains
Indus
Himalayas
Yangtze
East China Sea
Ryukyu Islands
Sahara
Ahaggar
Persian Gulf
Thar Desert
Ganges
Deccan
Mekong
Taiwan
AFRICA
Tibesti
Nile
Red Sea
Arabian Peninsula
Western Ghats
Eastern Ghats
Bay of Bengal
South China Sea
Mariana Islands
Sahel
Lake Chad
Gulf of Aden
Arabian Sea
Sri Lanka
M a r s h a l l   I s l a n d s
Caroline
Niger
Adamawa Highlands
Ethiopian Highlands
Horn of Africa
Malay Peninsula
Gulf of Guinea
Congo
Congo Basin
Great Rift Valley
Lake Victoria
Sumatra
Borneo
East Indies
New Guinea
ATLANTIC
Lake Tanganyika
Java Sea
Java
Arafura Sea
OCEAN
Lake Nyasa
INDIAN
Timor Sea
Zambezi
Mozambique Channel
Madagascar
Great Sandy Desert
Great Barrier Reef
Great Dividing Range
Namib Desert
Kalahari Desert
OCEAN
AUSTRALIA
Great Victoria Desert
Darling
Drakensberg
Nullarbor Plain
Cape of Good Hope
Murray
Bass Strait
Tasmania
Kerguelen

ANTARCTICA

Life Zones

Polar	Mountain	Broadleaf forest	Temperate forest
Tundra	Needleleaf forest	Temperate grassland	Mediterranean

20

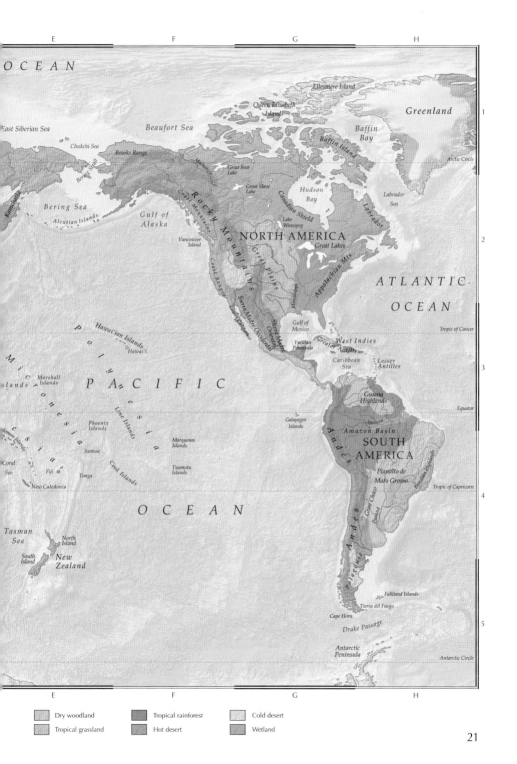

OCEAN

East Siberian Sea

Chukchi Sea

Bering Strait

Kamchatka

Bering Sea

Aleutian Islands

Brooks Range

Beaufort Sea

Mackenzie

Great Bear Lake

Great Slave Lake

Queen Elizabeth Islands

Ellesmere Island

Baffin Island

Greenland

Baffin Bay

Arctic Circle

Hudson Bay

Canadian Shield

Labrador Sea

Labrador

Gulf of Alaska

Coast Mountains

Rocky Mountains

Coast Range

Vancouver Island

Lake Winnipeg

Great Lakes

NORTH AMERICA

Great Plains

Appalachian Mts

ATLANTIC
OCEAN

Mississippi

Sierra Madre Occidental

Sierra Madre Oriental

Baja California

Gulf of Mexico

Yucatán Peninsula

Greater Antilles

West Indies

Tropic of Cancer

Hawaiian Islands

Hawai'i

Caribbean Sea

Lesser Antilles

Polynesia

Micronesia

Marshall Islands

Islands

PACIFIC

Phoenix Islands

Line Islands

Marquesas Islands

Galapagos Islands

Guiana Highlands

Amazon

Equator

Solomon Islands

Samoa

Cook Islands

Tuamotu Islands

Amazon Basin

SOUTH AMERICA

Coral Sea

Fiji

Tonga

New Caledonia

Andes

Planalto de Mato Grosso

Brazilian Highlands

Tropic of Capricorn

OCEAN

Gran Chaco

Pampas

Tasman Sea

North Island

South Island

New Zealand

Andes

Patagonia

Tierra del Fuego

Falkland Islands

Cape Horn

Drake Passage

Antarctic Peninsula

Antarctic Circle

E   F   G   H

| | Dry woodland | | Tropical rainforest | | Cold desert |
| | Tropical grassland | | Hot desert | | Wetland |

Population

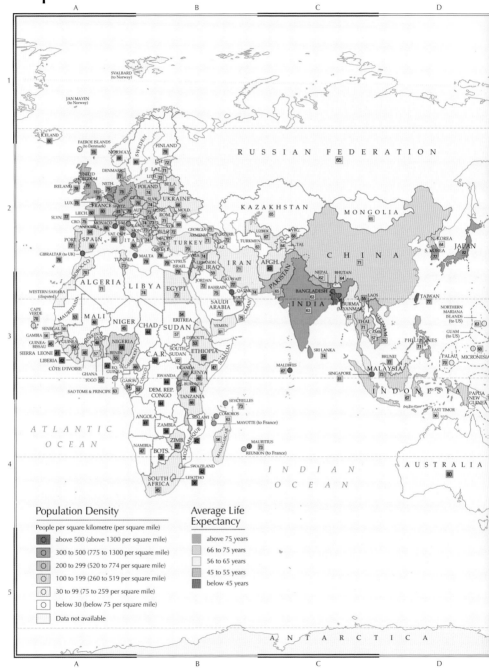

Population Density

People per square kilometre (per square mile)

- above 500 (above 1300 per square mile)
- 300 to 500 (775 to 1300 per square mile)
- 200 to 299 (520 to 774 per square mile)
- 100 to 199 (260 to 519 per square mile)
- 30 to 99 (75 to 259 per square mile)
- below 30 (below 75 per square mile)
- Data not available

Average Life Expectancy

- above 75 years
- 66 to 75 years
- 56 to 65 years
- 45 to 55 years
- below 45 years

ARCTIC
OCEAN

Arctic Circle

Alaska
(to US)

GREENLAND
(to Denmark)
67

C A N A D A
80

PACIFIC
OCEAN

UNITED STATES
OF AMERICA
77

ATLANTIC
OCEAN

Tropic of Cancer

Hawai'i
(to US)

BERMUDA
(to UK)
75

PUERTO RICO (to US)
74
DOM. REP.
68
CAYMAN ISLANDS
(to UK)
77
BAHAMAS
75

ST KITTS & NEVIS
72

ANTIGUA & BARBUDA
75

GUADELOUPE (to France)
75

DOMINICA
77

MARTINIQUE (to France)
76

ST LUCIA
77

BARBADOS
75

ST VINCENT &
THE GRENADINES
71

GRENADA
73

TRINIDAD & TOBAGO
70

HONDURAS
CUBA
70
BELIZE
72
JAMAICA
71
HAITI
52
CURAÇAO
(to Neth.)
76
ARUBA
(to Neth.)
73
GUATEMALA
68
EL SALVADOR
71
NICARAGUA
70
COSTA RICA
79
PANAMA
75
VENEZUELA
74
COLOMBIA
73
ECUADOR
75

MEXICO
75

GUYANA
SURINAME
64 69
FRENCH GUIANA
(to France)
75

Equator

PERU
70

BRAZIL
71

BOLIVIA
65

PARAGUAY
71

Tropic of Capricorn

MARSHALL
ISLANDS
70

NAURU
63

KIRIBATI
63

TUVALU
68

TOKELAU
(to NZ)

SOLOMON
ISLANDS
63

COOK
ISLANDS
(to NZ)
70

WALLIS & FUTUNA
(to France)

VANUATU
69

NEW
CALEDONIA
(to France)
74

FIJI
68

TONGA
72

NIUE (to NZ)
SAMOA
AMERICAN
SAMOA
(to US)

FRENCH POLYNESIA
(to France)
70

PITCAIRN
ISLANDS
(to UK)

CHILE
78

ARGENTINA
75

URUGUAY
75

NEW
ZEALAND
79

PACIFIC
OCEAN

CHILE

FALKLAND ISLANDS
(to UK)
76

SOUTH GEORGIA &
SOUTH SANDWICH ISLANDS
(to UK)

Antarctic Circle

ANTARCTICA

E   F   G   H

1

2

3

4

5

Languages

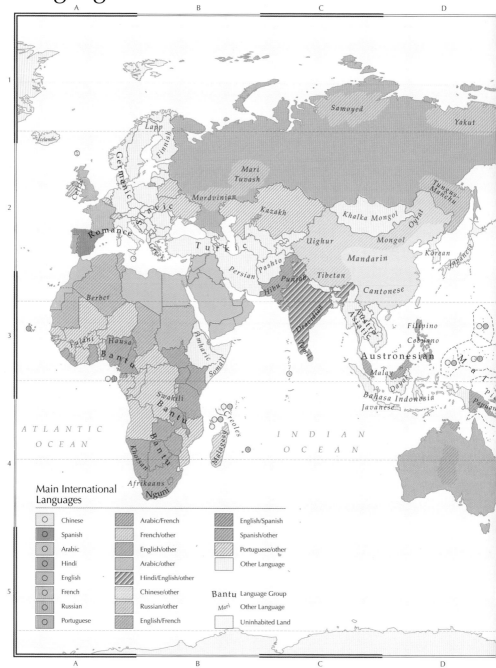

Main International Languages

○ Chinese	Arabic/French	English/Spanish
○ Spanish	French/other	Spanish/other
○ Arabic	English/other	Portuguese/other
○ Hindi	Arabic/other	Other Language
○ English	Hindi/English/other	
○ French	Chinese/other	**Bantu** Language Group
○ Russian	Russian/other	Mari Other Language
○ Portuguese	English/French	Uninhabited Land

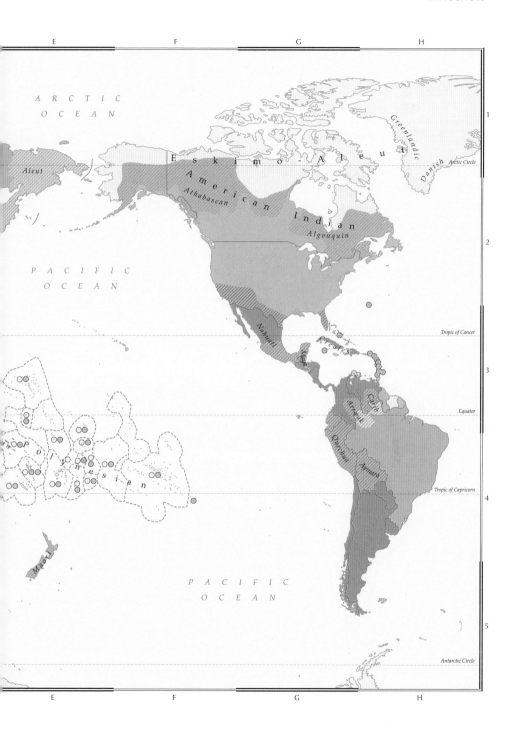

Religion

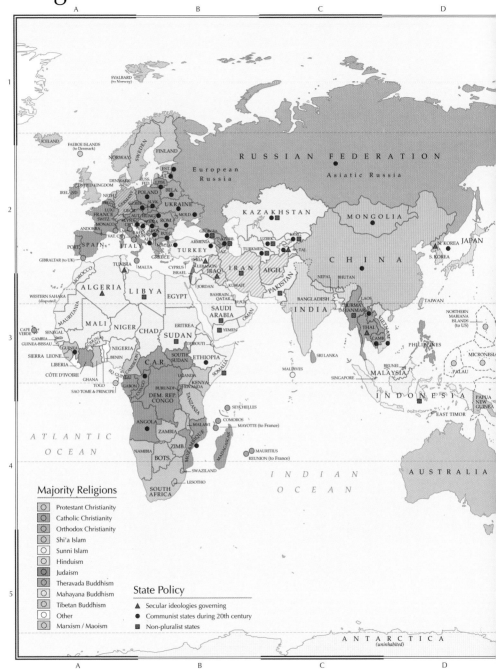

Majority Religions

- Protestant Christianity
- Catholic Christianity
- Orthodox Christianity
- Shi'a Islam
- Sunni Islam
- Hinduism
- Judaism
- Theravada Buddhism
- Mahayana Buddhism
- Tibetan Buddhism
- Other
- Marxism / Maoism

State Policy

- ▲ Secular ideologies governing
- ● Communist states during 20th century
- ■ Non-pluralist states

The Global Economy

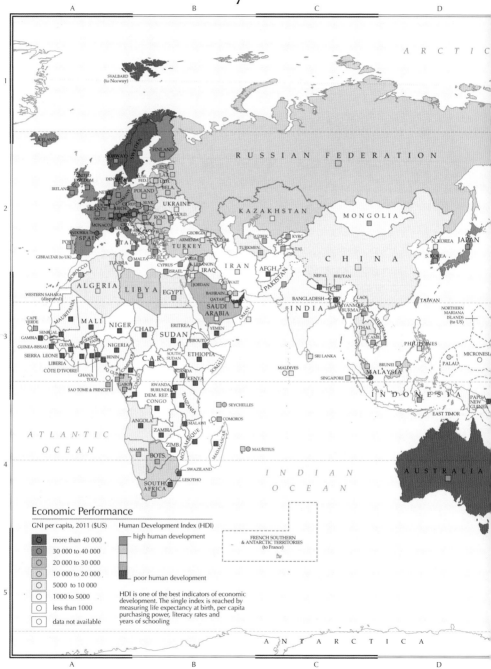

Economic Performance

GNI per capita, 2011 ($US)

- more than 40 000
- 30 000 to 40 000
- 20 000 to 30 000
- 10 000 to 20 000
- 5000 to 10 000
- 1000 to 5000
- less than 1000
- data not available

Human Development Index (HDI)

- high human development
- poor human development

HDI is one of the best indicators of economic development. The single index is reached by measuring life expectancy at birth, per capita purchasing power, literacy rates and years of schooling

FRENCH SOUTHERN & ANTARCTIC TERRITORIES (to France)

Politics and Conflict

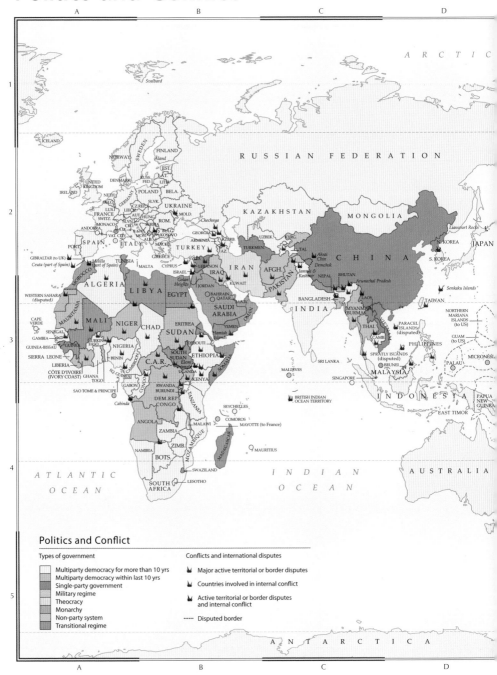

Politics and Conflict

Types of government

- Multiparty democracy for more than 10 yrs
- Multiparty democracy within last 10 yrs
- Single-party government
- Military regime
- Theocracy
- Monarchy
- Non-party system
- Transitional regime

Conflicts and international disputes

- Major active territorial or border disputes
- Countries involved in internal conflict
- Active territorial or border disputes and internal conflict
- ······ Disputed border

O C E A N

GREENLAND
(to Denmark)

Arctic Circle

Alaska
(to US)

— *Kurile Islands*
(part of Russ.Fed.)

C A N A D A

P A C I F I C

O C E A N

ST PIERRE
& MIQUELON
(to France)

A T L A N T I C

O C E A N

UNITED STATES
OF AMERICA

Hawai'i
(to US)

Tropic of Cancer

BAHAMAS

M E X I C O

GUANTANAMO BAY
(to US)
BELIZE
GUATEMALA
EL SALVADOR
HONDURAS
NICARAGUA
COSTA RICA
PANAMA

CUBA
JAMAICA

DOM. REP.

HAITI

ST KITTS & NEVIS
ANTIGUA & BARBUDA
DOMINICA
ST LUCIA
BARBADOS
ST VINCENT & THE GRENADINES
GRENADA
TRINIDAD & TOBAGO
FRENCH GUIANA
(to France)

MARSHALL
ISLANDS

NAURU

K I R I B A T I

TUVALU

SOLOMON
ISLANDS
VANUATU

SAMOA

COOK
ISLANDS
(to NZ)

FIJI
TONGA

FRENCH POLYNESIA
(to France)

VENEZUELA

COLOMBIA

ECUADOR

GUYANA

SURINAME

Equator

P E R U

B R A Z I L

NEW
CALEDONIA
(to France)

PITCAIRN
ISLANDS
(to UK)

BOLIVIA

PARAGUAY

Tropic of Capricorn

NEW
ZEALAND

P A C I F I C

O C E A N

CHILE

URUGUAY

A
R
G
E
N
T
I
N
A

CHILE

FALKLAND ISLANDS
(to UK)

Antarctic Circle

ANTARCTICA

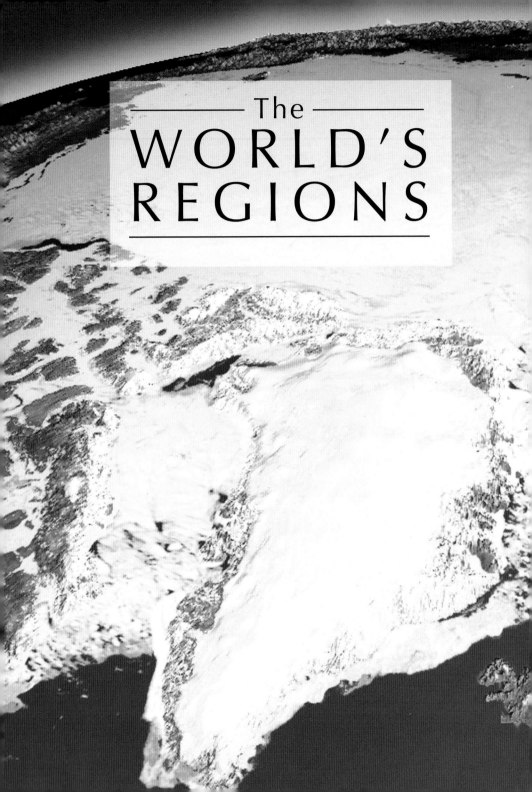

The ——
WORLD'S
REGIONS

North & Central America

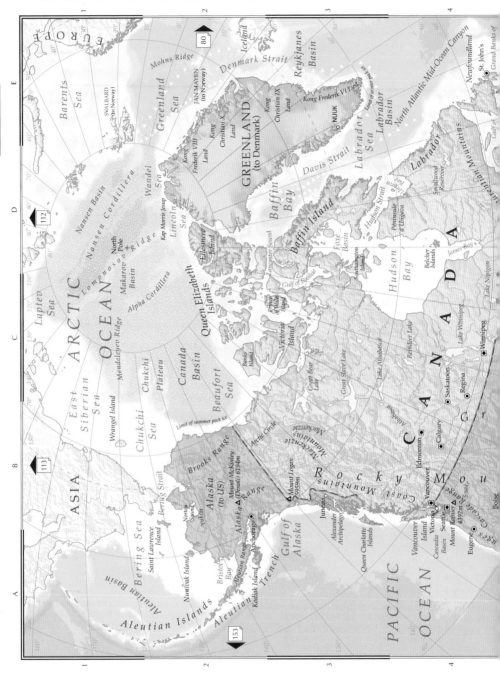

0 km · 1000
0 miles · 1000

Population　● National capital

o below 50,000　　o 50,000 to 100,000　　◉ 100,000 to 500,000　　■ above 500,000

Western Canada & Alaska

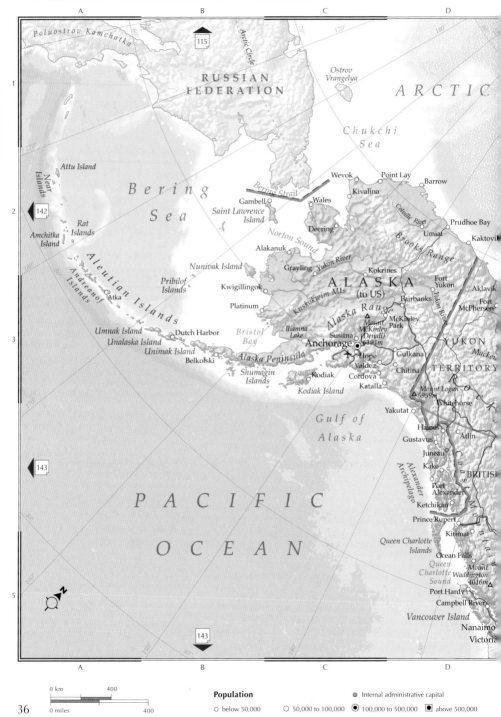

115

142

143

143

Poluostrov Kamchatka

Arctic Circle

RUSSIAN FEDERATION

Ostrov Vrangelya

A R C T I C

Chukchi Sea

Bering Sea

Attu Island

Near Islands

Rat Islands

Amchitka Island

Andreanof Islands

Aleutian Islands

Atka

Wevok
Point Lay
Barrow

Bering Strait
Wales
Kivalina

Gambell
Saint Lawrence Island
Deering

Colville River

Prudhoe Bay

Umiat
Kaktovik

Brooks Range

Norton Sound
Alakanuk

Nunivak Island

Pribilof Islands

Kwigillingok

Platinum

Grayling
Yukon River
Kokrines

Kuskokwim Mts

A L A S K A
(to US)

Fort Yukon

Fairbanks

Yukon River

Aklavik

Fort McPherson

Iliamna Lake

Alaska Range

McKinley Park

Mount McKinley
(Denali)
6194m

McKinley

Y U K O N

Umnak Island
Unalaska Island
Dutch Harbor

Unimak Island

Belkofski

Bristol Bay

Susitna
Anchorage

Hope
Valdez
Cordova

Gulkana

Chitina

T E R R I T O R Y

Mackenz

Alaska Peninsula

Shumagin Islands

Kodiak

Katalla

Kodiak Island

△ Mount Logan
5959m

Whitehorse

R O C K

Yakutat

Gulf of Alaska

Haines

Gustavus

Atlin

Juneau

Kake

BRITISH

Port Alexander

Ketchikan

Prince Rupert

Kitimat

Queen Charlotte Islands

Ocean Falls

Queen Charlotte Sound

Mount Waddington
4016m △

Port Hardy

Campbell River

Vancouver Island

Nanaimo

Victoria

Alexander Archipelago

P A C I F I C

O C E A N

N

Population

0 km 400
0 miles 400

○ below 50,000 ○ 50,000 to 100,000 ◉ 100,000 to 500,000 ■ above 500,000

● Internal administrative capital

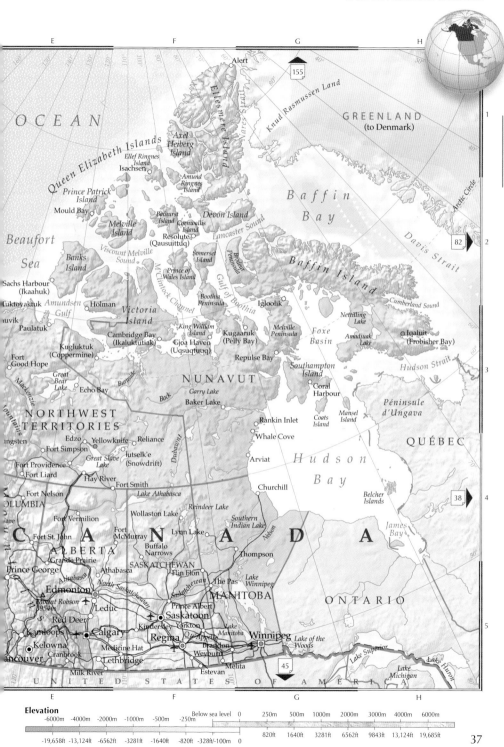

O C E A N

Alert

155

Knud Rasmussen Land

GREENLAND
(to Denmark)

Ellesmere Island

Queen Elizabeth Islands

Axel
Heiberg
Island

Ellef Ringnes
Island
Isachsen

Amund
Ringnes
Island

Baffin
Bay

Prince Patrick
Island

Mould Bay

Bathurst
Island

Devon Island

Melville
Island

Cornwallis
Island

Lancaster Sound

Arctic Circle

Davis Strait

82

Beaufort
Sea

Banks
Island

Viscount Melville
Sound

Resolute
(Qausuittuq)

Somerset
Island

Brodeur
Peninsula

Baffin Island

Cumberland Sound

Sachs Harbour
(Ikaahuk)

Prince of
Wales Island

Gulf of Boothia

Boothia
Peninsula

Igloolik

Nettilling
Lake

Tuktoyaktuk

Amundsen
Gulf

Holman

McClintock Channel

Melville
Peninsula

Foxe
Basin

Amadjuak
Lake

Iqaluit
(Frobisher Bay)

uvik

Paulatuk

Victoria
Island

King William
Island

Cambridge Bay
(Ikaluktutiak)

Gjoa Haven
(Uqsuqtuuq)

Kugaaruk
(Pelly Bay)

Fort
Good Hope

Kugluktuk
(Coppermine)

Repulse Bay

Southampton
Island

Hudson Strait

Great
Bear
Lake

Echo Bay

Burnside

N U N A V U T

Coral
Harbour

Péninsule
d'Ungava

NORTHWEST
TERRITORIES

Back

Garry Lake

Baker Lake

Dubawnt

Coats
Island

Mansel
Island

ngsten

Edzo

Yellowknife

Reliance

Rankin Inlet

QUÉBEC

Fort Simpson

Great Slave
Lake

Lutselk'e
(Snowdrift)

Whale Cove

Fort Providence

Hay River

Fort Liard

Fort Smith

Arviat

H u d s o n

B a y

Fort Nelson

Lake Athabasca

Churchill

38

OLUMBIA

Fort Vermilion

Wollaston Lake

Reindeer Lake

Belcher
Islands

James
Bay

are

Fort St. John

C

Fort
McMurray

A

Lynn Lake

N

Southern
Indian Lake

A

Nelson

D

A

Prince George

ALBERTA

Grande Prairie

Athabasca

Buffalo
Narrows

SASKATCHEWAN

Flin Flon

Thompson

Edmonton

Mount Robson
3954m

North Saskatchewan

Athabasca

The Pas

Lake
Winnipeg

MANITOBA

ONTARIO

Kamloops

Leduc

Red Deer

Calgary

Kindersley

Prince Albert

Saskatoon

Yorkton

Saskatchewan

Lake
Manitoba

Qu'Appelle

Winnipeg

Lake of the
Woods

Kelowna

Cranbrook

Medicine Hat

Regina

Brandon

Lake Superior

Lake
Michigan

Lake Huron

ancouver

Lethbridge

Milk River

Weyburn

Estevan

Melita

45

U N I T E D   S T A T E S   O F   A M E R I C A

37

Elevation

-6000m	-4000m	-2000m	-1000m	-500m	-250m	Below sea level	0	250m	500m	1000m	2000m	3000m	4000m	6000m

-19,658ft -13,124ft -6562ft -3281ft -1640ft -820ft -328ft/-100m 0 820ft 1640ft 3281ft 6562ft 9843ft 13,124ft 19,685ft

Eastern Canada

NORTHWEST
TERRITORIES

NUNAVUT

SASKATCHEWAN

Charles
Island

Ivujivik

Coats
Island

Mansel
Island

Péninsule
d' Ungava

Hudso

Southern
Indian Lake

Churchill

Nelson

H u d s o n

Rivière aux
Feuilles

Lac
Minto

Inukjuak
(Port Harrison)

B a y

MANITOBA

Hayes

Severn

Fort Severn

Belcher
Islands

La
Bienvill

Cedar
Lake

Lake
Winnipeg

Peawanuk

Lake
Winnipegosis

Sandy Lake

Winisk

J a m e s
B a y

Akimiski
Island

QUÉ

Lake
Manitoba

C A N

Attawapiskat

Attawapiskat

A

O N T A R I O

Albany

Fort
Albany

Eastmain

Lac Seul

Moosonee

Rivière de Rupert

Lac
Mistassini

Moose

Harricana

Kenora

Dryden

Armstrong

Chibougamau

Lake of
the Woods

Lake
Nipigon

Longlac

Hearst

Kapuskasing

Réservoir
Gouin

Fort Frances

Atikokan

Nipigon

Marathon

Cochrane

Amos

NORTH
DAKOTA

Rainy
Lake

Thunder Bay

Tip Top Mountain
△ 640m

Timmins

Rouyn-Noranda

Val-d'Or

L a k e   S u p e r i o r

Wawa

Foleyet

Kirkland
Lake

MINNESOTA

MICHIGAN

Sault Ste.Marie
Sudbury

North
Bay

Pembroke

Gatineau
Hull

Lav

SOUTH
DAKOTA

Manitoulin
Island

Georgian
Bay

OTTAWA

NEBRASKA

U N I T E D   S T A T E S

WISCONSIN

Lake
Michigan

Lake
Huron

Midland

Peterborough

Kingston

Lake
Ontari

O F   A M E R I C A

I O W A

Brampton
Kitchener
Hamilton

Oshawa
Toronto
St.Catharines

NEW YORK

Sarnia

Mississippi River

ILLINOIS

Windsor

London

Niagara
Falls

Leamington

Lake Erie

INDIANA

OHIO

PENNSYLVANIA

0 km   300

0 miles   300

Population
O below 50,000
● National capital
○ 50,000 to 100,000
◉ 100,000 to 500,000
○ Internal administrative capital
■ above 500,000

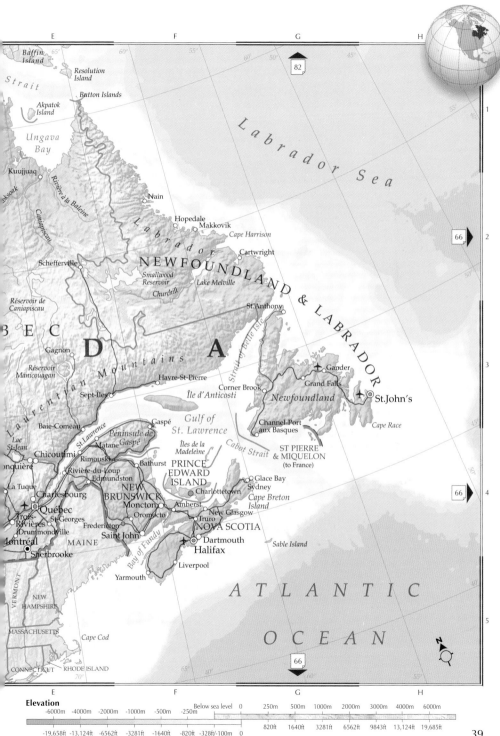

Baffin
Island
Strait
Resolution
Island
Button Islands
Akpatok
Island
*Ungava
Bay*

Kuujjuaq

Nain

Hopedale
Makkovik
Cape Harrison

Cartwright

Schefferville

*Smallwood
Reservoir*
Lake Melville
Churchill

St.Anthony

Réservoir de
Caniapiscau

Gagnon

Réservoir
Manicouagan

Sept-Îles

Havre-St-Pierre

Île d'Anticosti

Corner Brook

Newfoundland

Gander

Grand Falls

St.John's

Cape Race

Baie-Comeau

Gaspé

*Gulf of
St. Lawrence*

Île de la
Madeleine

Channel-Port
aux Basques

ST PIERRE
& MIQUELON
(to France)

Chicoutimi
Rimouski
Matane
Rivière-du-Loup
Bathurst
PRINCE
EDWARD
ISLAND

Glace Bay
Sydney

Edmundston
Charlottetown
Cape Breton
Island

La Tuque

Charlesbourg
NEW
BRUNSWICK
Moncton
Amherst
New Glasgow

Québec
Oromocto
Truro

Trois-
Rivières
St-Georges
Fredericton
NOVA SCOTIA

Montréal
Saint John
Dartmouth

Drummondville
MAINE
Halifax

Sherbrooke
Liverpool

Bay of Fundy
Sable Island

Yarmouth

VERMONT

NEW
HAMPSHIRE

MASSACHUSETTS

Cape Cod

CONNECTICUT
RHODE ISLAND

L a b r a d o r   S e a

82

66

66

66

L a b r a d o r

N E W F O U N D L A N D   &   L A B R A D O R

Laurentian Mountains

Péninsule de
Gaspé

Strait of Belle Isle

Cabot Strait

A T L A N T I C

O C E A N

Elevation

-6000m	-4000m	-2000m	-1000m	-500m	-250m	Below sea level	0	250m	500m	1000m	2000m	3000m	4000m	6000m
-19,658ft	-13,124ft	-6562ft	-3281ft	-1640ft	-820ft	-328ft/-100m	0	820ft	1640ft	3281ft	6562ft	9843ft	13,124ft	19,685ft

USA: The Northeast

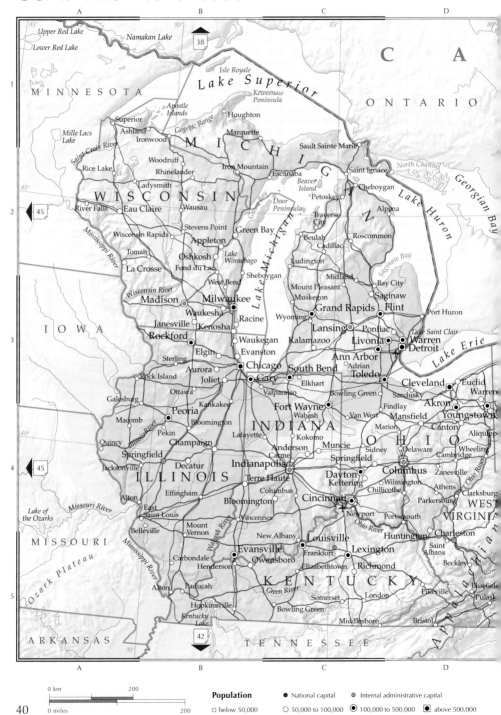

0 km · 200
0 miles · 200

Population
● National capital · ◉ Internal administrative capital
○ below 50,000 · ○ 50,000 to 100,000 · ◉ 100,000 to 500,000 · ■ above 500,000

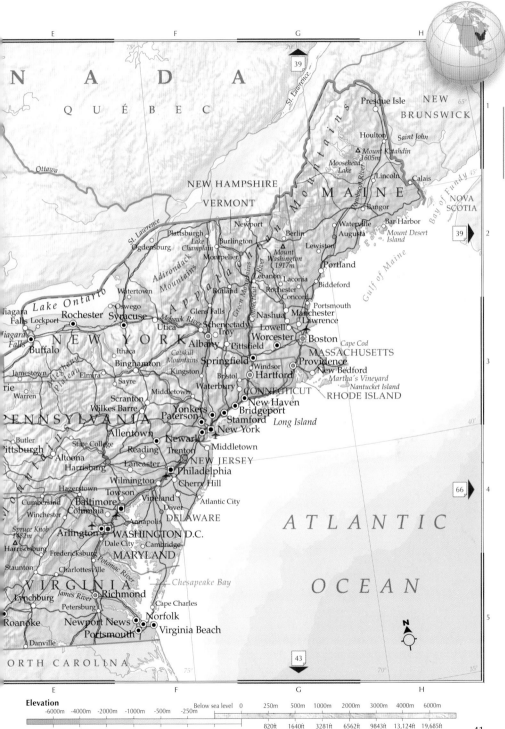

USA: The Southeast

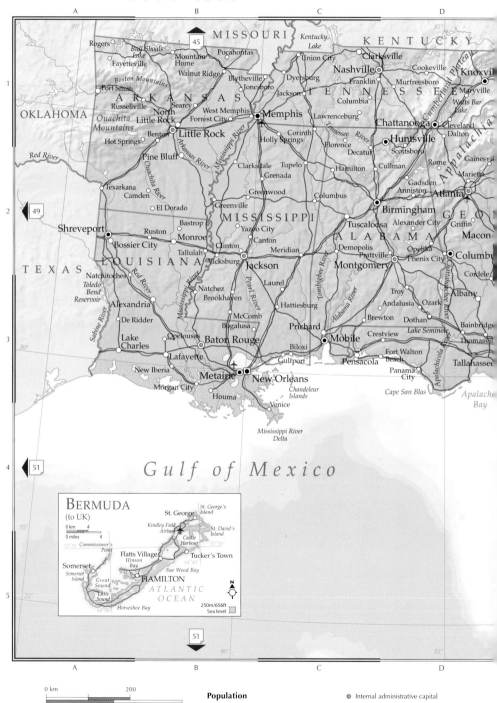

NORTH & CENTRAL AMERICA

MISSOURI

Rogers
Bull Shoals
Lake
Mountain
Home
Pocahontas
Kentucky
Lake
K E N T U C K Y
Fayetteville
Walnut Ridge
Union City
Clarksville
Cookeville
Knoxvil
Boston Mountains
Blytheville
Dyersburg
Nashville
Franklin
Murfreesboro
Maryville
Fort Smith
Jonesboro
Jackson
T E N N E S S E E
Watts Bar
Lake
A R K A N S A S
West Memphis
Columbia
OKLAHOMA
Russellville
Searcy
Memphis
Lawrenceburg
Chattanooga
Cleveland
North
Forrest City
Dalton
Ouachita
Little Rock
Little Rock
Corinth
Holly Springs
Huntsville
Mountains
Benton
Florence
Scottsboro
Gainesvil
Hot Springs
Decatur
Pine Bluff
Clarksdale
Tupelo
Hamilton
Cullman
Rome
Marietta
Red River
Grenada
Gadsden
Anniston
Atlanta
Greenwood
Columbus
Texarkana
Greenville
Birmingham
G E O
Camden
MISSISSIPPI
Montgomery
El Dorado
Bastrop
Yazoo City
Tuscaloosa
Alexander City
Griffin
Shreveport
Ruston
Monroe
Canton
A L A B A M A
Macon
Bossier City
Tallulah
Clinton
Meridian
Demopolis
Opelika
Columbu
T E X A S
L O U I S I A N A
Vicksburg
Jackson
Prattville
Phenix City
Cordele
Natchitoches
Laurel
Troy
Albany
Toledo
Bend
Reservoir
Natchez
Brookhaven
Hattiesburg
Andalusia
Ozark
Alexandria
McComb
Brewton
Dothan
Bainbridge
De Ridder
Bogalusa
Prichard
Crestview
Lake Seminole
Thomasvil
Lake
Charles
Opelousas
Baton Rouge
Mobile
Fort Walton
Tallahassee
Lafayette
Biloxi
Beach
Pensacola
Panama
New Iberia
Metairie
Gulfport
City
Morgan City
New Orleans
Chandeleur
Islands
Cape San Blas
Apalache
Bay
Houma
Venice

Mississippi River
Delta

Gulf of Mexico

Population

0 km   200
0 miles   200

○ Internal administrative capital
○ below 50,000   ○ 50,000 to 100,000   ◉ 100,000 to 500,000   ■ above 500,000

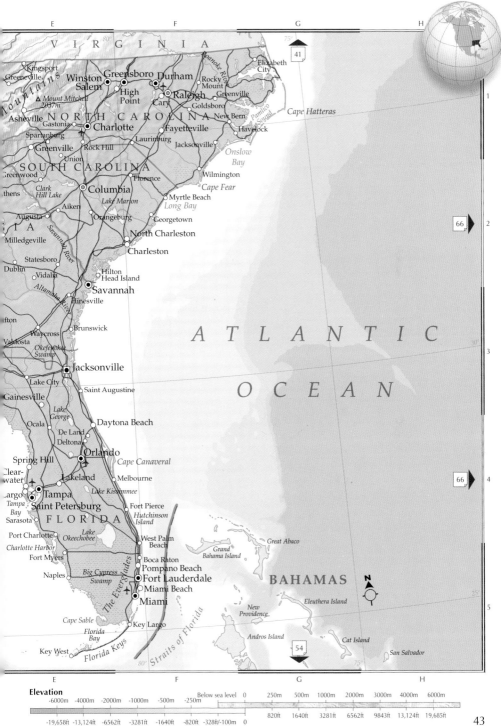

Elevation

-6000m	-4000m	-2000m	-1000m	-500m	-250m	Below sea level	0		250m	500m	1000m	2000m	3000m	4000m	6000m
-19,658ft	-13,124ft	-6562ft	-3281ft	-1640ft	-820ft	-328ft/-100m	0		820ft	1640ft	3281ft	6562ft	9843ft	13,124ft	19,685ft

USA: Central States

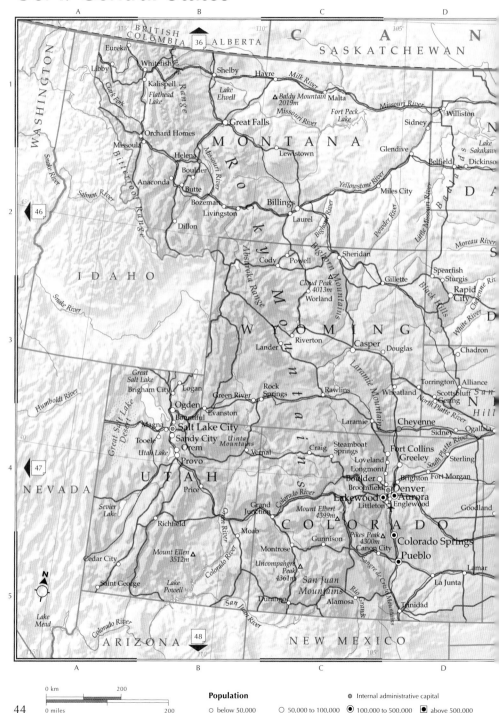

0 km 200

0 miles 200

Population

○ below 50,000 ○ 50,000 to 100,000 ◉ 100,000 to 500,000 ■ above 500,000

◉ Internal administrative capital

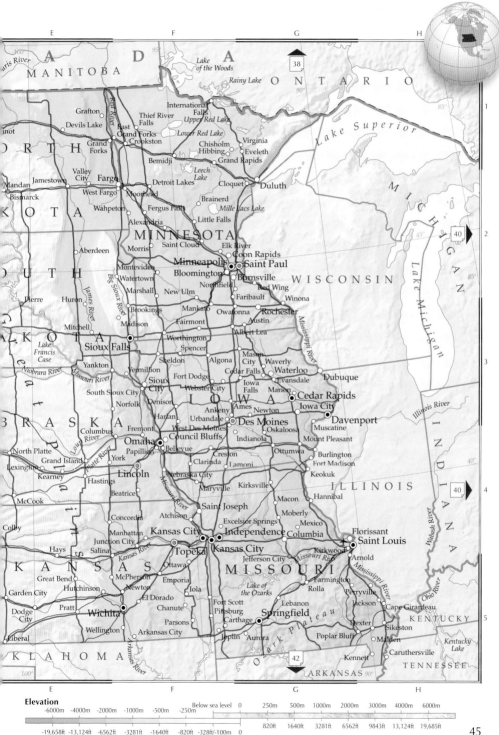

Elevation

-6000m	-4000m	-2000m	-1000m	-500m	-250m	Below sea level	0	250m	500m	1000m	2000m	3000m	4000m	6000m
-19,658ft	-13,124ft	-6562ft	-3281ft	-1640ft	-820ft	-328ft/-100m	0	820ft	1640ft	3281ft	6562ft	9843ft	13,124ft	19,685ft

45

USA: The West

Population

- ○ below 50,000
- ○ 50,000 to 100,000
- ◉ 100,000 to 500,000
- ■ above 500,000
- ● Internal administrative capital

0 km 200
0 miles 200

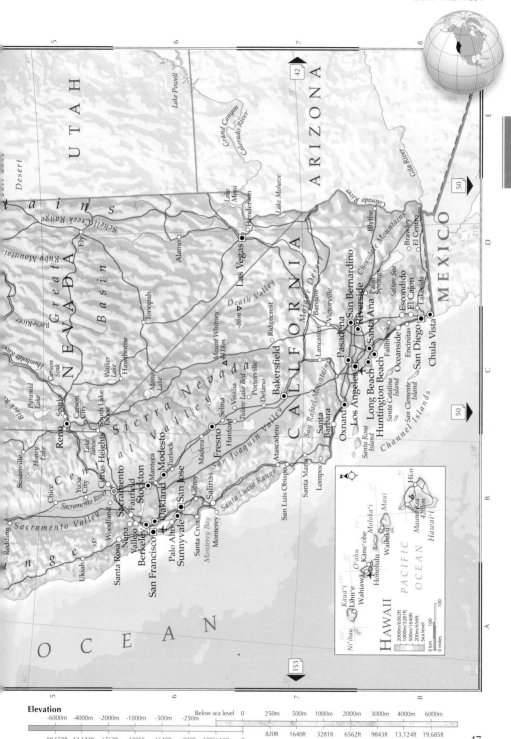

42

50

50

153

UTAH

NEVADA

ARIZONA

MEXICO

CALIFORNIA

Great Basin

Sierra Nevada

Central Valley

Desert

Lake Powell

Grand Canyon

Colorado River

Schell Creek Range

Ruby Mountains

Reese River

Humboldt River

Black R.

Ely

Alamo

Las Vegas

Henderson

Lake Mohave

Colorado River

Oviedo River

Gila River

Blythe

Chocolate Mountains

Brawley

El Cajon
Lakeside

El Centro

San Diego

Chula Vista

Lake Mead

Tonopah

Death Valley

-86m ▽

Mount Whitney
△4418m

Ridgecrest

Mojave Desert

Barstow

Victorville

San Bernardino
Riverside
Santa Ana

Palm
Springs

Salton Sea

Escondido

Oceanside

Encinitas

Fallbrook

Pasadena

Los Angeles

Long Beach

Huntington Beach

Lancaster

Bakersfield

Delano

Porterville

Visalia
Hanford

Fresno
Selma
Madera

Tulare Lake Bed

San Joaquin Valley

Atascadero

San Luis Obispo

Santa Maria

Lompoc

Santa
Barbara

Oxnard

San Rafael Mountains

Santa Rosa Island

Santa Catalina Island

San Clemente Island

Channel Islands

Sparks
Reno

Carson City

Walker Lake

Hawthorne

Mono Lake

Susanville

Honey Lake

Pyramid Lake

Carson Sink

South Lake Tahoe

Lake Tahoe

Citrus Heights

Sacramento
Fairfield
Stockton
Napa
Vallejo
Oakland
Berkeley
San Francisco
Palo Alto
Sunnyvale
San Jose

Manteca
Modesto
Turlock

Gilroy

Salinas

Santa Lucia Range

Santa Cruz

Monterey Bay

Monterey

Woodland

Chico
Yuba City

Sacramento River

Sacramento Valley

Redding

Ukiah

Santa Rosa

Honey Lake

O C E A N

P A C I F I C   O C E A N

HAWAII

Ni'ihau
Kaua'i
Lihu'e
Wahiawā
Kāne'ohe
O'ahu
Honolulu
Moloka'i
Wailuku
Maui
Hilo
Mauna Kea 4205m
Hawai'i

2000m/6562ft
1000m/3281ft
500m/1640ft
200m/656ft
Sea level

0 km   100
0 miles   100

Elevation

-6000m	-4000m	-2000m	-1000m	-500m	Below sea level	0	250m	500m	1000m	2000m	3000m	4000m	6000m
					-250m								

| -19,658ft | -13,124ft | -6562ft | -3281ft | -1640ft | -820ft | -328ft/-100m | 0 | 820ft | 1640ft | 3281ft | 6562ft | 9843ft | 13,124ft | 19,685ft |

USA: The Southwest

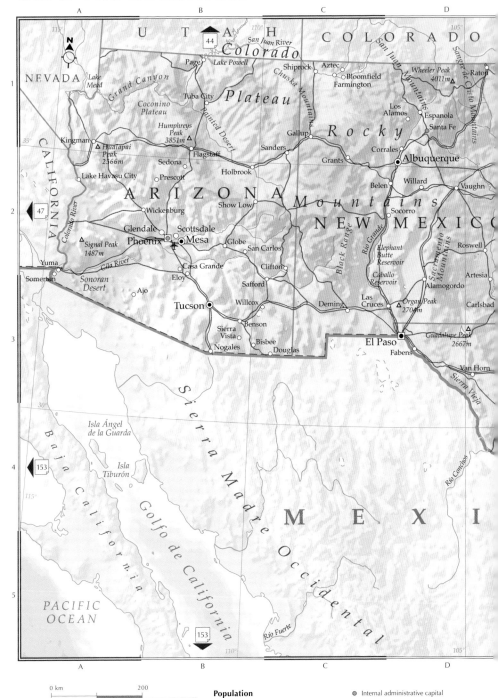

UTAH

NEVADA

COLORADO

44

San Juan River

Colorado

Page

Lake Powell

Shiprock

Aztec

Wheeler Peak
4011m

Raton

Lake
Mead

Grand Canyon

Tuba City

Plateau

Bloomfield
Farmington

Los
Alamos

Espanola

Santa Fe

Coconino
Plateau

Painted Desert

Chuska Mountains

San Juan Mountains

Sangre de Cristo Mountains

Humphreys
Peak
3851m

Gallup

Rocky

Kingman

Hualapai
Peak
2566m

Flagstaff

Sanders

Corrales

Albuquerque

CALIFORNIA

Sedona

Holbrook

Grants

Belen

Willard

Vaughn

Lake Havasu City

Prescott

A R I Z O N A

Mountains

47

Wickenburg

Show Low

NEW MEXICO

Socorro

Roswell

Colorado River

Glendale

Scottsdale

Globe

Black Range

Rio Grande

Elephant
Butte
Reservoir

Sacramento Mountains

Signal Peak
1487m

Phoenix

Mesa

San Carlos

Roswell

Yuma

Casa Grande

Clifton

Caballo
Reservoir

Alamogordo

Artesia

Somerton

Gila River

Eloy

Safford

Sonoran
Desert

Ajo

Willcox

Deming

Las
Cruces

Organ Peak
2706m

Carlsbad

Tucson

Benson

Sierra
Vista

Nogales

Bisbee

Douglas

El Paso

Fabens

Guadalupe Peak
2667m

Van Horn

Sierra Vieja

Isla Ángel
de la Guarda

Sierra Madre Occidental

153

Isla
Tiburón

Baja California

Golfo de California

M E X I C I

Río Conchos

Río Fuerte

PACIFIC
OCEAN

153

Population

⊙ Internal administrative capital

0 km   200

0 miles   200

○ below 50,000   ◉ 50,000 to 100,000   ◉ 100,000 to 500,000   ■ above 500,000

48

K A N S A S
MISSOURI

Boise City
Guymon
Woodward
Perryton
Dumas
Borger
Pampa

Dalhart

Amarillo
Canyon
Hereford
Tulia
Childress
Muleshoe
Plainview
Vernon

Littlefield
Levelland
Lubbock
Llano
Estacado
Brownfield

Hobbs
Lamesa
Snyder
Sweetwater
Abilene
Andrews
Big Spring
Seminole
Colorado City
Stephenville
Cleburne
Midland
Odessa
Ballinger
Coleman
Brownwood
Monahans
San Angelo
Pecos
McCamey
Brady
Copperas Cove

Fort Stockton
Stockton
Plateau
Alpine

Amistad
Reservoir
Del Rio
San Antonio
Hondo
Uvalde
Pearsall
Eagle Pass
Kenedy
Beeville

Emory Peak
△2385m

Laredo

Alva
Ponca City
Bartlesville
Miami
Table Rock
Lake
Enid
Sand Springs
Tulsa
Vinita
Claremore
Broken Arrow
Beaver
Lake
Stillwater
Sapulpa
Tahlequah
Taloga
Okmulgee
Muskogee
The Village
Oklahoma City
Warner
Clinton
El Reno
Moore
Shawnee
Eufaula
Lake
Elk City
Norman
Chickasha
Ada
McAlester

O K L A H O M A

Altus
Lawton
Duncan
Hugo
Idabel
Ardmore
Lake
Texoma
Durant
Burkburnett
Wichita River
Denison
Paris
Texarkana
Wichita
Falls
Gainesville
Sherman
Atlanta
Denton
Greenville
Sulphur Springs
Plano
Garland
Marshall
Mineral Wells
Fort Worth
Dallas
Lake Tawakoni
Longview
Arlington
Tyler
Henderson
Ennis
Athens
Jacksonville
Corsicana
Nacogdoches
Toledo
Bend
Reservoir
Waco
Lufkin
Pineland

T E X A S

Killeen
Temple
Belton
Huntsville
Livingston
Neches River
Sabine River
Taylor
Bryan
Round Rock
College Station
Conroe
Brenham
Lake Travis
Austin
Houston
Baytown
Beaumont
Port Arthur
Kerrville
Pasadena
New
Braunfels
San Marcos
Seguin
Rosenberg
Alvin
Galveston
Schertz
El Campo
Angleton
Lake Jackson
Victoria
Bay
City
Freeport
Robstown
Alice
Port Lavaca
Port O'Connor
Kingsville
Portland
Corpus
Christi

Gulf of
Mexico

Norias
Laguna Madre
Padre
Island
Edinburg
Mission
Harlingen
McAllen
San Benito
Brownsville

Sierra Madre Oriental

C O

Red River
Canadian River
Lake
Meredith
Beaver River
Arkansas River

Rio Grande
Pecos River
Edwards Plateau
Brazos River
Trinity River
Colorado River
Guadalupe River
San Antonio River

A R K A N S A S
L O U I S I A N A

45
42
54
51

100°
95°
100°
95°
35°
30°

Elevation

-6000m -4000m -2000m -1000m -500m   Below sea level 0   250m 500m 1000m 2000m 3000m 4000m 6000m
                                        -250m

-19,658ft -13,124ft -6562ft -3281ft -1640ft -820ft -328ft/-100m 0   820ft 1640ft 3281ft 6562ft 9843ft 13,124ft 19,685ft

49

Mexico

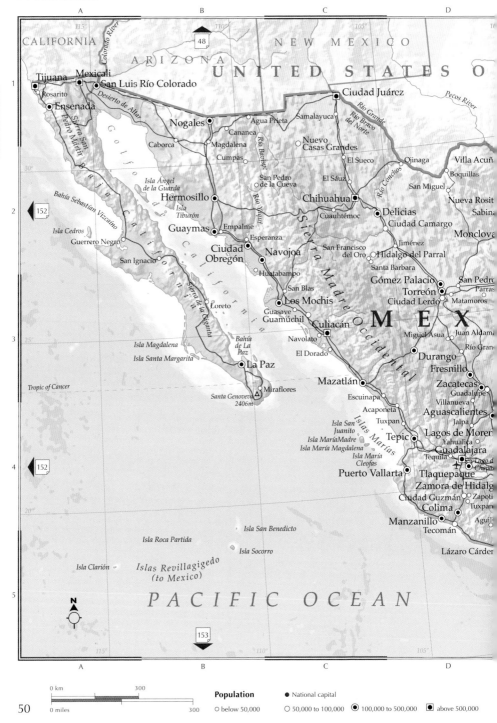

CALIFORNIA

Tijuana
Rosarito
Mexicali
San Luis Río Colorado
Ensenada

ARIZONA

UNITED STATES O

NEW MEXICO

Ciudad Juárez
Pecos River

Samalayuca
Río Grande
del Norte

Colorado River

Desierto de Altar

Nogales
Agua Prieta
Cananea
Magdalena
Caborca
Cumpas
San Pedro
de la Cueva
El Sueco
El Sáuz
Nuevo
Casas Grandes
Ojinaga
Villa Acuñ
Boquillas

Sierra San Pedro Mártir

Golfo

de

California

Río Bavispe

Bahía Sebastián Vizcaíno

Isla Ángel
de la Guarda

Hermosillo
Isla
Tiburón

San Pedro
de la Cueva

Chihuahua
Cuauhtémoc

San Miguel

Delicias
Ciudad Camargo

Nueva Rosit
Sabina

Río Conchos

Isla Cedros

Guerrero Negro
San Ignacio

Guaymas
Empalme
Esperanza
Ciudad
Obregón
Navojoá
San Francisco
del Oro
Jiménez
Hidalgo del Parral
Santa Barbara

Monclova

San Pedr
Parras

Río Yaqui

Sierra Madre

Huatabampo
San Blas
Los Mochis
Guasave
Guamúchil
Culiacán
Navolato
El Dorado

Gómez Palacio
Torreón
Ciudad Lerdo
Matamoros

M E X

Loreto
Bahía
de La
Paz

Isla Magdalena
Isla Santa Margarita

Occidental

Miguel Asua
Juan Aldam
Río Gran

Sierra de la Giganta

La Paz

Durango
Fresnillo
Zacatecas
Guadalupe
Villanueva
Aguascalientes
Jalpa

Tropic of Cancer

Santa Genoveva
2406m
Miraflores

Mazatlán
Escuinapa
Acaponeta
Tuxpan

Isla San
Juanito
Isla MaríaMadre
Isla María Magdalena
Isla María
Cleofas

Islas Marías

Tepic
Yahualica
Lagos de Morer
Guadalajara
Tequila
Lago d
Chapa

Puerto Vallarta

Tlaquepaque
Zamora de Hidalg
Ciudad Guzmán
Zapotl
Tuxpan
Colima
Manzanillo
Tecomán
Aguil
Lázaro Cárder

Isla San Benedicto
Isla Roca Partida
Isla Socorro

Isla Clarión

Islas Revillagigedo
(to Mexico)

N

P A C I F I C   O C E A N

0 km   300
0 miles   300

Population   ● National capital

○ below 50,000   ○ 50,000 to 100,000   ◉ 100,000 to 500,000   ▣ above 500,000

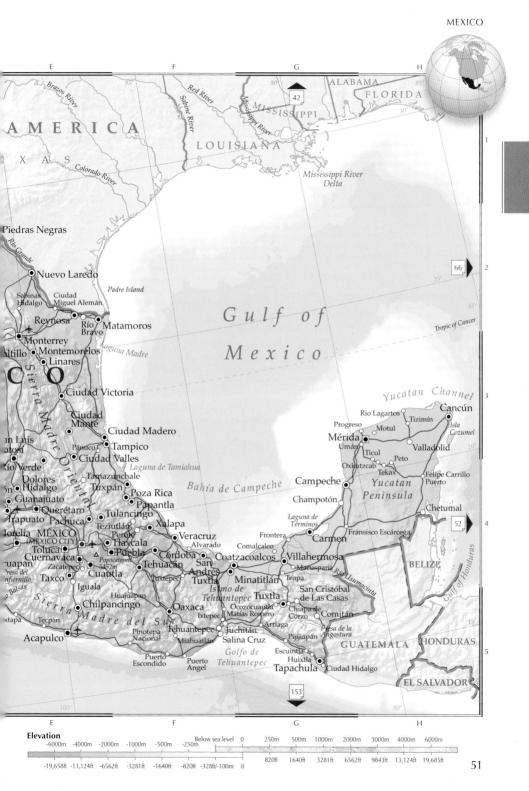

Central America

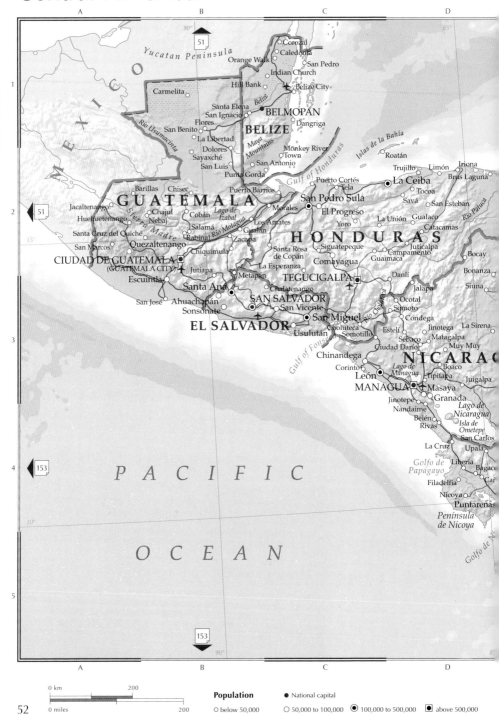

Population   ● National capital
○ below 50,000   ○ 50,000 to 100,000   ◉ 100,000 to 500,000   ◼ above 500,000

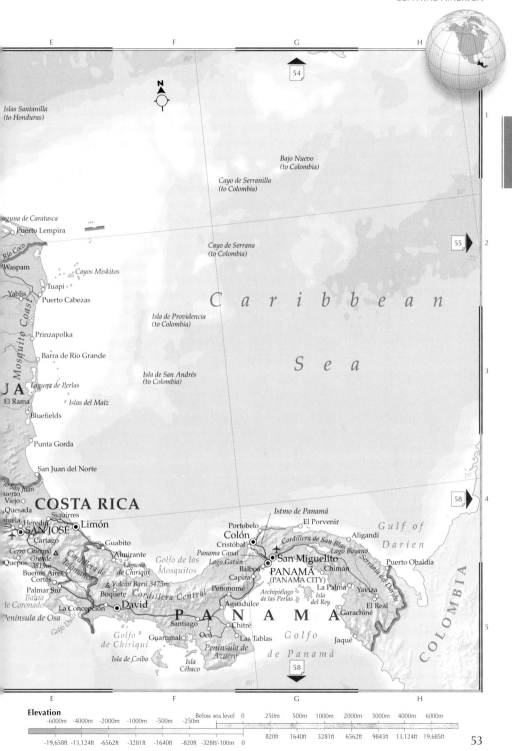

Islas Santanilla
(to Honduras)

N

Laguna de Caratasca

Puerto Lempira

Río Coco

Waspam

Cayos Miskitos

Tuapi

Yablis

Puerto Cabezas

Mosquito Coast

Prinzapolka

Barra de Río Grande

JA

El Rama

Laguna de Perlas

Islas del Maíz

Bluefields

Punta Gorda

San Juan del Norte

54

Bajo Nuevo
(to Colombia)

Cayo de Serranilla
(to Colombia)

Cayo de Serrana
(to Colombia)

55

Isla de Providencia
(to Colombia)

Isla de San Andrés
(to Colombia)

Caribbean

Sea

Río San Juan
Puerto
Viejo
Quesada
ajuela
Heredia
Siquirres
Cartago
SAN JOSÉ
Limón

COSTA RICA

Cerro Chirripó
Grande
3819m
Quepos
Buenos Aires
Cortés
Palmar Sur

Cordillera de Talamanca

Guabito

Almirante

Laguna
de Chiriquí

Volcán Barú 3475m

Boquete

La Concepción

David

Península de Osa

Bahía
de Coronado

Golfo Dulce

Golfo
de Chiriquí

Isla de Coiba

Golfo de los
Mosquitos

Cordillera Central

Santiago

Guarumal

Ocú

Isla
Cébaco

Península de
Azuero

Portobelo

Colón
Cristóbal
Panama Canal
Lago Gatún
Balboa
Capira

PANAMA
(PANAMA CITY)

San Miguelito

Penonomé

Aguadulce

Chitré

Las Tablas

P A N A M A

El Porvenir

Istmo de Panamá

Cordillera de San Blas

Aligandí

Lago Bayano

Chimán

La Palma

Isla
del Rey

Archipiélago
de las Perlas

Golfo
de Panamá

Jaqué

Gulf of
Darien

Serranía del Darién

Puerto Obaldía

Yaviza

El Real

Garachiné

C O L O M B I A

58

58

1

2

3

4

5

80°

85°

75°

15°

10°

Elevation

| -6000m | -4000m | -2000m | -1000m | -500m | -250m | Below sea level | 0 | 250m | 500m | 1000m | 2000m | 3000m | 4000m | 6000m |

-19,658ft -13,124ft -6562ft -3281ft -1640ft -820ft -328ft/-100m 0 820ft 1640ft 3281ft 6562ft 9843ft 13,124ft 19,685ft

The Caribbean

UNITED STATES
OF AMERICA

Gulf of Mexico

The Everglades

Grand Bahama
Island

Freeport

Marsh Harbour
Great Abaco

Bimini
Islands

Berry
Islands

Nicholls
Town

NASSAU

New
Providence

Eleuthera Island

Rock Sound

Northeast Providence Channel

Andros Town

Florida Keys

Tropic of Cancer

Straits of Florida

Cay Sal

Andros Island

Exuma
Cays

Exuma
Sound

Cat Island

San Salvador

LA HABANA
(HAVANA)

Guanabacoa

B A H A M A S

Anguilla Cays

George Town

Rum Cay

Artemisa

Cárdenas

Great Exuma Island

Long Island

Pinar del Río

Matanzas

Sagua la Grande

Santa Clara

Placetas

Archipiélago
de Camagüey

Clarence
Town

Crooked Island

Consolación
del Sur

Cienfuegos

Crooked Island Passage

La Fé

Ragged Island
Range

Acklins
Island

Mayaguana

Nueva Gerona

Isla de
la Juventud

Cayo Largo

Sancti
Spíritus

Morón

Ciego de Ávila

C U B A

Mayaguana Passage

Caicos Passage

Little
Inagua

Archipiélago de los Canarreos

Bahía de Cochinos

Camagüey

Nuevitas

Las Tunas

Holguín

Lake Rosa

Matthew
Town

Great Inagua

Archipiélago de
los Jardines de la Reina

Manzanillo

Bayamo

Palma Soriano

Cap-
Haïtien

Little Cayman

Cayman Brac

Santiago de Cuba

Guantánamo

Guantánamo Bay
(to US)

Windward Passage

Gonaïves

GEORGE
TOWN

Grand Cayman

CAYMAN ISLANDS
(to UK)

NAVASSA
ISLAND
(to US)

Île de la Gonâve

Jérémie

HAITI

PORT-AU-
PRINCE

Montego Bay

Spanish Town

Portmore

KINGSTON

Jamaica Channel

Cayes

Jacmel

JAMAICA

Pedro Cays

HONDURAS

C a r i b b e a n

NICARAGUA

52

JAMAICA

Montego Bay

Lucea

Falmouth

Discovery
Bay

St Ann's Bay

*Caribbean
Sea*

The Cockpit
Country

Ocho Rios

Annotto Bay

Cambridge

Christiana

Ewarton

Buff Bay

Port Antonio

Savanna-
La-Mar

Mandeville

Spanish
Town

Blue Mountain Peak
△ 2258m

Black River

May Pen

Old Harbour

Portmore

KINGSTON

Morant Bay

Portland Bight

Caribbean

Sea

0 km   20
0 miles   20

2000m/6562ft
1000m/3281ft
500m/1640ft
200m/656ft
Sea level

COSTA
RICA

COLOMBIA

0 km   200
0 miles   200

Population

● National capital

○ below 50,000   ○ 50,000 to 100,000   ◉ 100,000 to 500,000   ◼ above 500,000

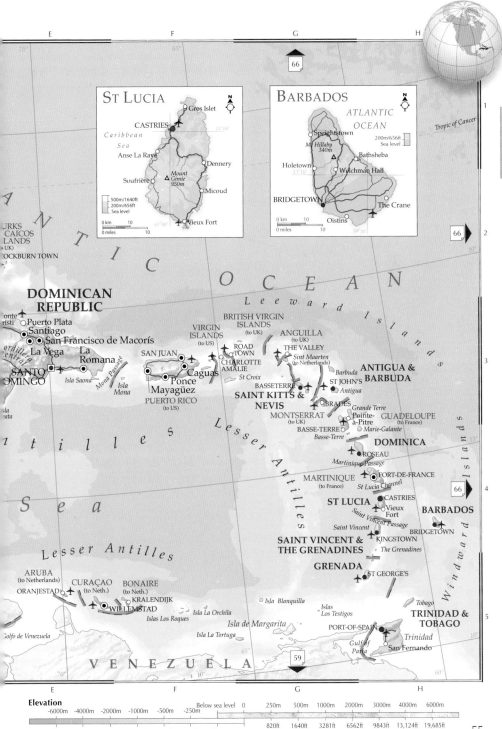

ST LUCIA

N

Gros Islet

CASTRIES

Caribbean Sea

Anse La Raye

Dennery

Soufrière

△ Mount Gimie 950m

Micoud

500m/1640ft
200m/656ft
Sea level

0 km   10
0 miles   10

Vieux Fort

BARBADOS

N

ATLANTIC OCEAN

Speightstown

Mt Hillaby 340m △

Bathsheba

Holetown

Welchman Hall

200m/656ft
Sea level

BRIDGETOWN

The Crane

0 km   10
0 miles   10

Oistins

Tropic of Cancer

URKS
CAICOS
LANDS
(to UK)

OCKBURN TOWN

DOMINICAN REPUBLIC

Leeward Islands

onte
risti

Puerto Plata
Santiago
San Francisco de Macorís
La Vega
La Romana

SANTO
OMINGO

Isla Saona

Isla Mona

Mona Passage

SAN JUAN

Caguas

Ponce

Mayagüez

PUERTO RICO
(to US)

VIRGIN
ISLANDS
(to US)

BRITISH VIRGIN
ISLANDS
(to UK)

ROAD
TOWN

CHARLOTTE
AMALIE

St Croix

ANGUILLA
(to UK)

THE VALLEY

Sint Maarten
(to Netherlands)

Barbuda

ST JOHN'S

ANTIGUA & BARBUDA

Antigua

BASSETERRE

SAINT KITTS & NEVIS

BRADES

MONTSERRAT
(to UK)

Grande Terre

Pointe-à-Pitre

Marie-Galante

GUADELOUPE
(to France)

BASSE-TERRE

Basse-Terre

DOMINICA

ROSEAU

Martinique Passage

MARTINIQUE
(to France)

FORT-DE-FRANCE

St Lucia Channel

ST LUCIA

CASTRIES

Vieux
Fort

BARBADOS

Saint Vincent Passage

Saint Vincent

SAINT VINCENT & THE GRENADINES

KINGSTOWN

BRIDGETOWN

The Grenadines

GRENADA

ST GEORGE'S

Windward Islands

Lesser Antilles

Sea

Lesser Antilles

ARUBA
(to Netherlands)

ORANJESTAD

CURAÇAO
(to Neth.)

BONAIRE
(to Neth.)

KRALENDIJK

WILLEMSTAD

Islas Los Roques

Isla La Orchila

Isla Blanquilla

Islas
Los Testigos

Tobago

TRINIDAD & TOBAGO

Isla La Tortuga

Isla de Margarita

PORT-OF-SPAIN

Trinidad

San Fernando

Gulf of Paria

Golfo de Venezuela

V E N E Z U E L A

Elevation

						Below sea level	0	250m	500m	1000m	2000m	3000m	4000m	6000m
-6000m	-4000m	-2000m	-1000m	-500m	-250m									
-19,658ft	-13,124ft	-6562ft	-3281ft	-1640ft	-820ft	-328ft/-100m	0	820ft	1640ft	3281ft	6562ft	9843ft	13,124ft	19,685ft

South America

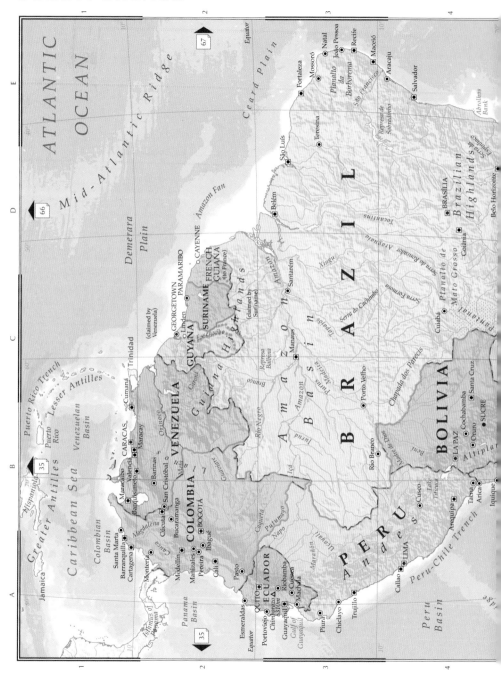

Population

● National capital

o below 50,000 o 50,000 to 100,000 ◉ 100,000 to 500,000 ■ above 500,000

0 km   500

0 miles   500

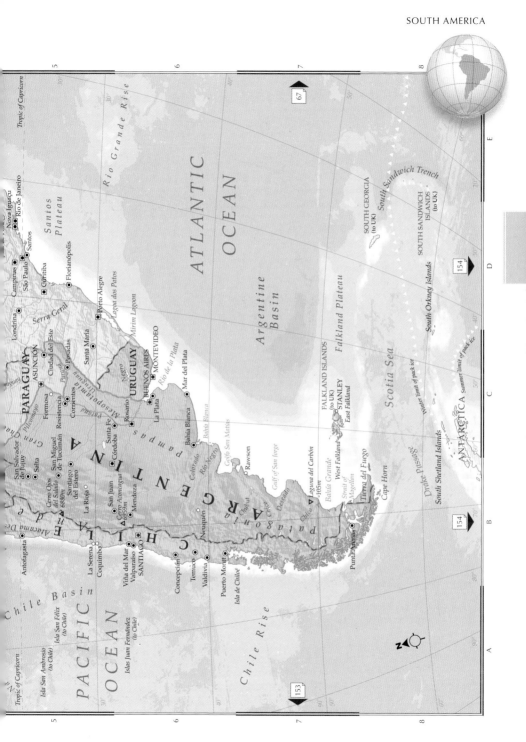

ATLANTIC

OCEAN

PACIFIC

OCEAN

Northern South America

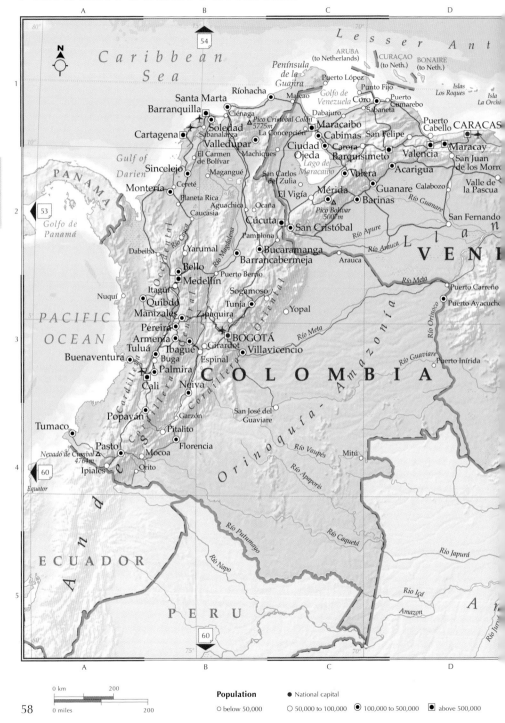

Caribbean Sea

54

N

Península de la Guajira

ARUBA (to Netherlands)

CURAÇAO (to Neth.)

BONAIRE (to Neth.)

L e s s e r   A n t

Puerto López

Islas Los Roques

Isla La Orchi

Golfo de Venezuela

Punto Fijo

Ríohacha

Maicao

Coro

Puerto Cumarebo

Sabaneta

Dabajuro

Puerto Cabello

CARACAS

Santa Marta

Barranquilla

Soledad

Ciénaga

Pico Cristóbal Colón 5775m

Maracaibo

San Felipe

Puerto

Cartagena

Sabanalarga

La Concepción

Cabimas

Carora

Valencia

Maracay

Valledupar

El Carmen de Bolívar

Machiques

Ciudad Ojeda

Barquisimeto

Acarigua

San Juan de los Morro

Sincelejo

Magangué

San Carlos del Zulia

Valera

Valle de la Pascua

Gulf of Darien

Montería

Cereté

Lago de Maracaibo

Mérida

Guanare

Calabozo

PANAMA

Planeta Rica

El Vigía

Barinas

Río Guanare

53

Aguachica

Ocaña

Pico Bolívar 5000m

San Fernando

Golfo de Panamá

Caucasia

Cúcuta

San Cristóbal

Río Apure

Dabeiba

Yarumal

Pamplona

Bucaramanga

Río Arauca

L a n

V E N I

Bello

Barrancabermeja

Arauca

Puerto Berrío

Medellín

Itagüí

Sogamoso

Río Meta

Puerto Carreño

Nuquí

Quibdó

Tunja

Yopal

Puerto Ayacucho

PACIFIC

Manizales

Zipaquira

Río Orinoco

OCEAN

Pereira

Río Meta

Amazonía

Armenia

BOGOTÁ

Tuluá

Ibagué

Girardot

Villavicencio

Río Guaviare

Puerto Inírida

Buenaventura

Buga

Espinal

Palmira

C O L O M B I A

Cali

Neiva

Popayán

Garzón

San José del Guaviare

Tumaco

Pitalito

Orinoquía

Pasto

Mócoa

Florencia

Río Vaupés

Mitú

Nevado de Cumbal 4764m

Río Apaporis

A

60

Ipiales

Orito

Equator

ECUADOR

Río Napo

PERU

Río Putumayo

Río Caquetá

Río Japurá

Río Icá

Amazon

A

60

0 km   200

0 miles   200

Population   ● National capital

○ below 50,000   ○ 50,000 to 100,000   ◉ 100,000 to 500,000   ◼ above 500,000

ATLANTIC

OCEAN

SAINT VINCENT & THE GRENADINES

BARBADOS

GRENADA

Isla Blanquilla

Isla de Margarita

Islas Los Testigos

Tobago

La Asunción

Porlamar

umaná

Carúpano

Güiria

TRINIDAD & TOBAGO

Gulf of Paria

Trinidad

Tortuga

Cariaco

Puerto La Cruz

Barcelona

San Mateo

Anaco

Maturín

Zaraza

Cantaura

Tucupita

El Tigre

Río Orinoco

Ciudad Guayana

Ciudad Bolívar

Upata

Embalse de Guri

El Callao

ZUELA

Matthews Ridge

Charity

Spring Garden

El Dorado

Aurora

Parika

GEORGETOWN

Río Paragua

Río Caroní

Salto Ángel

Peters Mine

Rockstone

Bartica

New Amsterdam

PARAMARIBO

Nieuw Amsterdam

St-Laurent-du-Maroni

Kamarang

Linden

Totness

Sinnamary

Río Caura

Mount Roraima 2810m

GUYANA

Nieuw Nickerie

Kaaimanston

Kourou

Orealla

Apoera

CAYENNE

Pakaraima Mountains

Kurupukari

SURINAME

W. J. van Blommesteinmeer

Grand-Santi

Ouanary

St-Georges

Guiana

Essequibo River

Juliana Top 1230m

FRENCH GUIANA

(to France)

Camopi

(Venezuela claims all of Guyana west of Essequibo River)

Lethem

Courantyne River

Tumuc-Humac Mountains

(claimed by Suriname)

Río Orinoco

Highlands

Acarai Mountains

(claimed by Suriname)

Equator

Río Negro

BRAZIL

zon Basin

Amazon

Amazon

Amazon

Amazon

Río Purús

Río Tapajós

55

67

5

62

62

Elevation

-6000m	-4000m	-2000m	-1000m	-500m	-250m	Below sea level 0	250m	500m	1000m	2000m	3000m	4000m	6000m

-19,658ft -13,124ft -6562ft -3281ft -1640ft -820ft -328ft/-100m 0   820ft   1640ft   3281ft   6562ft   9843ft   13,124ft 19,685ft

Western South America

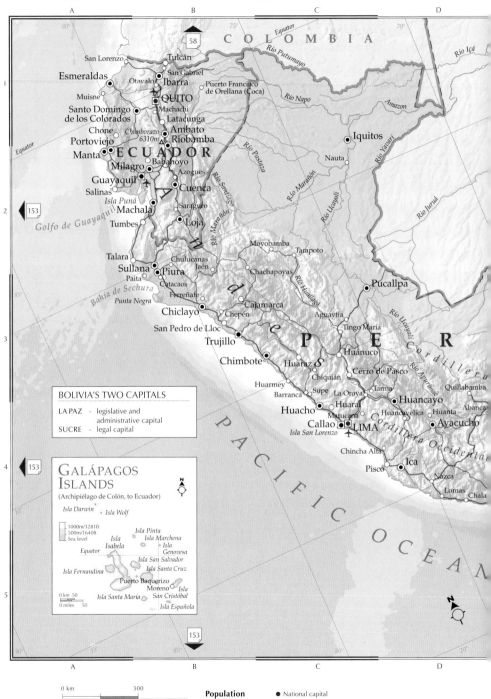

BOLIVIA'S TWO CAPITALS

LA PAZ - legislative and administrative capital

SUCRE - legal capital

GALÁPAGOS ISLANDS

(Archipiélago de Colón, to Ecuador)

Isla Darwin · Isla Wolf

1000m/3281ft
500m/1640ft
Sea level

Isla Pinta
Isla Isabela   Isla Marchena
Isla Genovesa
Equator
Isla San Salvador
Isla Fernandina   Isla Santa Cruz
Puerto Baquerizo Moreno   Isla San Cristóbal
Isla Santa María
Isla Española

0 km 50
0 miles 50

Population

● National capital

○ below 50,000 ○ 50,000 to 100,000 ◉ 100,000 to 500,000 ■ above 500,000

0 km 300

0 miles 300

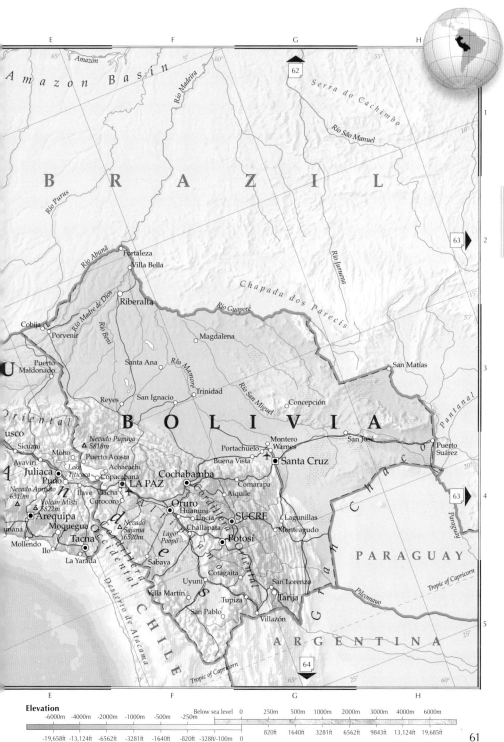

Elevation

-6000m	-4000m	-2000m	-1000m	-500m	-250m	Below sea level	0	250m	500m	1000m	2000m	3000m	4000m	6000m
-19,658ft	-13,124ft	-6562ft	-3281ft	-1640ft	-820ft	-328ft/-100m	0	820ft	1640ft	3281ft	6562ft	9843ft	13,124ft	19,685ft

Brazil

VENEZUELA

COLOMBIA

Cordillera Occidental
Cordillera Oriental

Andes

ECUADOR

Río Putumayo

Río Napo

Equator

Galapagos Islands
(Archipiélago de Colón)
(to Ecuador)

58

Guiana Highland

Uraricoera
Boa Vista
Caracaraí

Roraima

△ Pico da Neblina
3014m

Río Negro
Represa Balbi

Río Japurá

Río Içá

Tefé
Amazon
Manaus
Coari

Río Juruá

Río Purus

Humaitá

B Porto Velho **R**

153

Río Marañón

Río Yavari

Japiim
Feijó

Acre

Río Abuná

Río Ucayali

PERU

Andes

Lake
Titicaca

Cordillera

BOLIVIA

Cordillera Oriental

Río Guaporé
Vilhena

Rondônia
Chapada dos Parecis

Río Mamoré

Lago
Poopó

153

Desierto de Atacama

Cordillera Occidental

P A C I F I C   O C E A N

Tropic of Capricorn

Andes

CHILE

ARGENTINA

Pilcomayo
Río Bermejo

Gran

Chaco

PARAG

Río Salado

153

N

0 km   600
0 miles   600

Population

● National capital
○ below 50,000
○ 50,000 to 100,000
◉ 100,000 to 500,000
▣ above 500,000

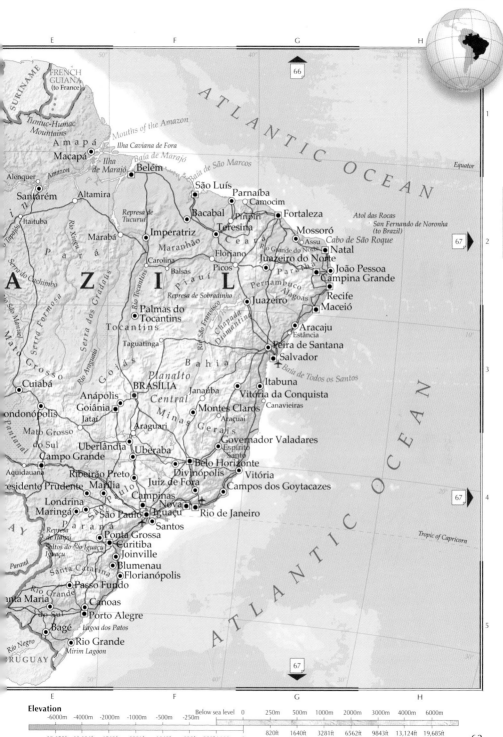

BRAZIL

Elevation

-6000m -4000m -2000m -1000m -500m -250m Below sea level 0 250m 500m 1000m 2000m 3000m 4000m 6000m

-19,658ft -13,124ft -6562ft -3281ft -1640ft -820ft -328ft/-100m 0 820ft 1640ft 3281ft 6562ft 9843ft 13,124ft 19,685ft

63

Southern South America

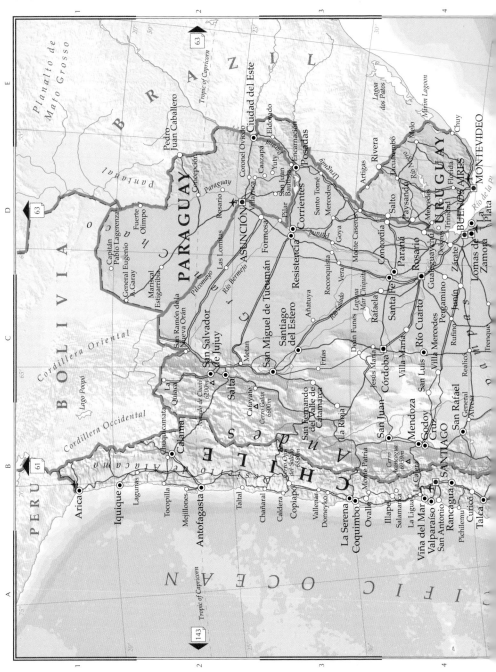

Population

● National capital

○ below 50,000 ○ 50,000 to 100,000 ◉ 100,000 to 500,000 ■ above 500,000

0 km 200

0 miles 200

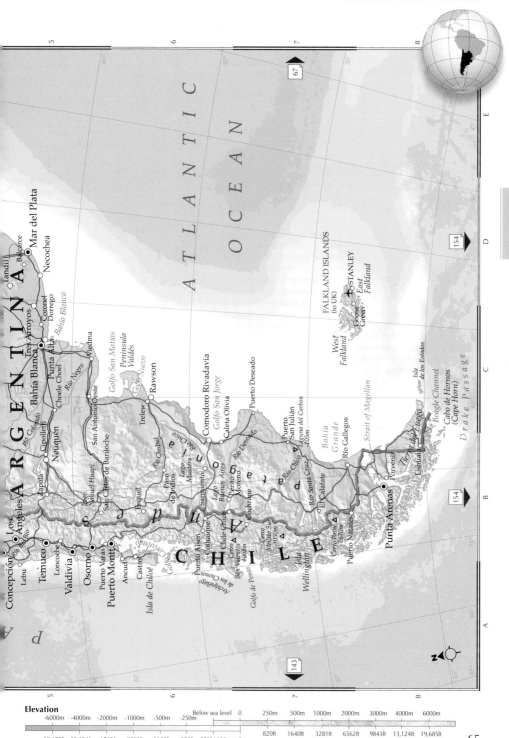

ATLANTIC

OCEAN

A R G E N T I N A

Jandil
Balcarce
Mar del Plata
Necochea
Coronel
Dorrego
Tres Arroyos
Bahía Blanca
Punta Alta
Choele Choel
Río Colorado
Río Negro
Viedma
Bahía Blanca

Golfo San Matías
Península
Valdés
Golfo Nuevo
Rawson
Trelew
Golfo San Jorge
Comodoro Rivadavia
Caleta Olivia
Puerto Deseado

FALKLAND ISLANDS
(to UK)
Goose
Green
West
Falkland
STANLEY
East
Falkland

San Antonio Oeste
Neuquén
Cipolletti
Zapala
San Carlos de Bariloche
Lago
Nahuel Huapi
Esquel
Paso
de Indios
Río Chubut
Río Chico
Río Senguer
Lago
Musters
Sarmiento
Río Deseado
Río Chico
Puerto
San Julián
Laguna del Carbón
-105m
Río Chico
Río Santa Cruz
Río Gallegos
Bahía
Grande
Isla
de los Estados
Beagle Channel
Cabo de Hornos
(Cape Horn)
Drake Passage

Los
Angeles
Concepción
Lebu
Temuco
Loncoche
Valdivia
Osorno
Puerto Varas
Puerto Montt
Ancud
Castro
Isla de Chiloé
Golfo Corcovado
Archipiélago
de los Chonos
Golfo de Penas

C H I L E

Puerto Aisén
Coihaique
Chile Chico
Cochrane
Cerro
San Valentín
4058m
Isla
Wellington
Lago
Buenos Aires
Perito
Moreno
El Calafate
Cerro
Mellizo Sur
3050m
Cerro Paine
2670m
Puerto Natales
Punta Arenas
Porvenir
Ushuaia
Tierra del Fuego
Strait of Magellan

N

Elevation

-6000m	-4000m	-2000m	-1000m	-500m	-250m	Below sea level	0	250m	500m	1000m	2000m	3000m	4000m	6000m
-19,658ft	-13,124ft	-6562ft	-3281ft	-1640ft	-820ft	-328ft/-100m	0	820ft	1640ft	3281ft	6562ft	9843ft	13,124ft	19,685ft

67
154
154
143

65

The Atlantic Ocean

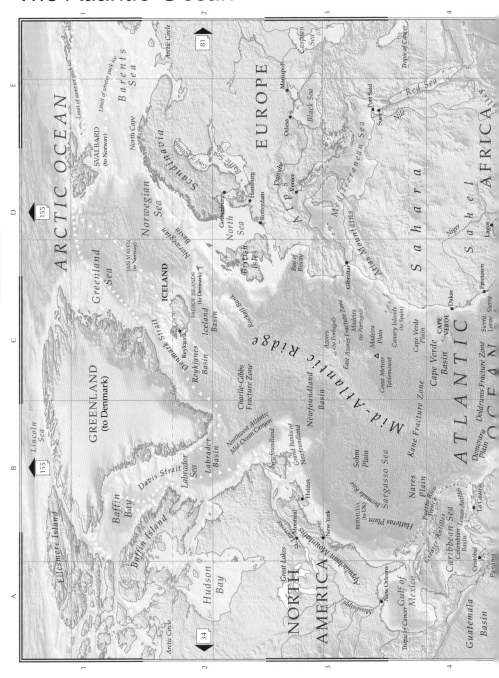

81

155

155

34

ARCTIC OCEAN

Limit of summer pack ice
Limit of winter pack ice

Barents Sea

Arctic Circle

North Cape

SVALBARD
(to Norway)

Scandinavia

Gulf of Bothnia

Caspian Sea

EUROPE

Mariupol

Odesa

Black Sea

Port Said

Red Sea

Suez

Nile

AFRICA

Sahel

Lagos

Niger

Sahara

Atlas Mountains

Mediterranean Sea

Bosporus, Sea

Venice

Alps

Danube

Hamburg

Rotterdam

Gothenburg

North Sea

Baltic Sea

British Isles

Bay of Biscay

Gibraltar

Rockall Bank

Norwegian Sea

Norwegian Basin

Greenland Sea

JAN MAYEN
(to Norway)

ICELAND

Reykjavik

Denmark Strait

FAEROE ISLANDS
(to Denmark)

Iceland Basin

Reykjanes Basin

Charlie–Gibbs Fracture Zone

Mid-Atlantic Ridge

Azores
(to Portugal)

East Azores Fracture Zone

Madeira
(to Portugal)

Madeira Plain

Great Meteor Tablemount

Canary Islands
(to Spain)

Cape Verde Plain

CAPE VERDE

Dakar

Sierra Leone

Freetown

ATLANTIC OCEAN

Cape Verde Basin

Kane Fracture Zone

Doldrums Fracture Zone

Demerara Plain

GREENLAND
(to Denmark)

Lincoln Sea

Labrador Sea

Davis Strait

Baffin Bay

Baffin Island

Ellesmere Island

Labrador Basin

Northwest Atlantic Mid-Ocean Canyon

Newfoundland

Grand Banks of Newfoundland

Newfoundland Basin

Halifax

Sohm Plain

Sargasso Sea

BERMUDA
(to UK)

Bermuda Rise

Nares Plain

Hatteras Plain

Puerto Rico Trench

La Guaira

Greater Antilles

Lesser Antilles

Caribbean Sea

Colombian Basin

Cristobal

Panama

Guatemala Basin

NORTH AMERICA

St. Lawrence

Montreal

New York

Appalachian Mountains

Great Lakes

New Orleans

Mississippi

Gulf of Mexico

Tropic of Cancer

Arctic Circle

ATLANTIC OCEAN

0 km   1000
0 miles   1000

• Major port

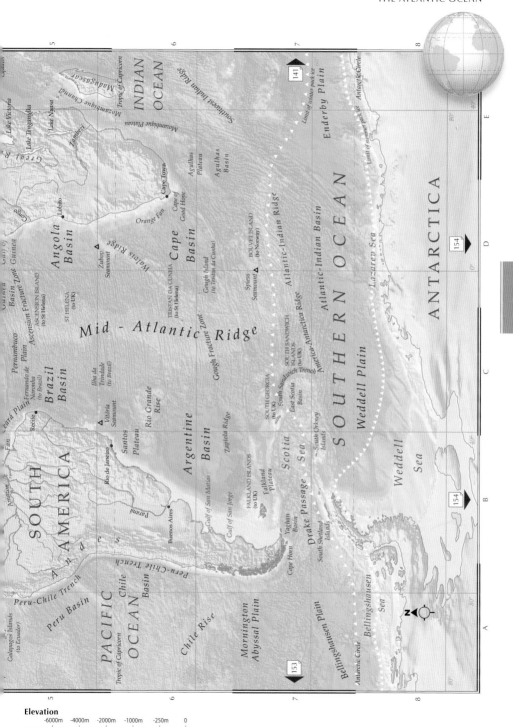

INDIAN OCEAN

Tropic of Capricorn

Madagascar

Mozambique Channel

Lake Victoria
Lake Nyasa
Lake Tanganyika
Zambezi

Great R.

Southwest Indian Ridge

Limit of winter pack ice

Antarctic Circle

Enderby Plain

Mozambique Plateau

Agulhas Plateau

Agulhas Basin

Cape Town

Limit of summer pack ice

Gulf of Guinea

Congo

Lobito

Angola Basin

Guinea Basin

Walvis Ridge

Zaboy Seamount

Orange Fan

Cape of Good Hope

Cape Basin

SOUTHERN OCEAN

Lazarev Sea

141

154

ANTARCTICA

Pernambuco Plain

Ascension Fracture Zone

ASCENSION ISLAND (to St Helena)

ST HELENA (to UK)

Gulf of Guinea

Atlantic-Indian Ridge

BOUVET ISLAND (to Norway)

Atlantic-Indian Basin

Gough Island (to Tristan da Cunha)

Spiess Seamount

Mid - Atlantic Ridge

TRISTAN DA CUNHA (to St Helena)

Gough Fracture Zone

Fernando de Noronha (to Brazil)

Brazil Basin

Recife

Ilha da Trindade (to Brazil)

Vitória Seamount

Rio Grande Rise

Santos Plateau

SOUTH AMERICA

Amazon

Ceará Plain

Rio de Janeiro

Paraná

Buenos Aires

Argentine Basin

Zapiola Ridge

SOUTH GEORGIA (to UK)

SOUTH SANDWICH ISLANDS (to UK)

South Sandwich Trench

East Scotia Basin

Weddell Plain

Andes

Gulf of San Matías

Gulf of San Jorge

FALKLAND ISLANDS (to UK)

Falkland Plateau

Scotia Sea

South Orkney Islands

Weddell Sea

Cape Horn

Yaghan Basin

Drake Passage

South Shetland Islands

Peru-Chile Trench

Chile Basin

Chile Trench

Peru-Chile Trench

PACIFIC OCEAN

Tropic of Capricorn

Peru Basin

Galapagos Islands (to Ecuador)

Chile Rise

Mornington Abyssal Plain

Bellingshausen Plain

Bellingshausen Sea

Antarctic Circle

154

153

Elevation

-6000m	-4000m	-2000m	-1000m	-250m	0
-19,658ft	-13,124ft	-6562ft	-3281ft	-820ft	0

67

Africa

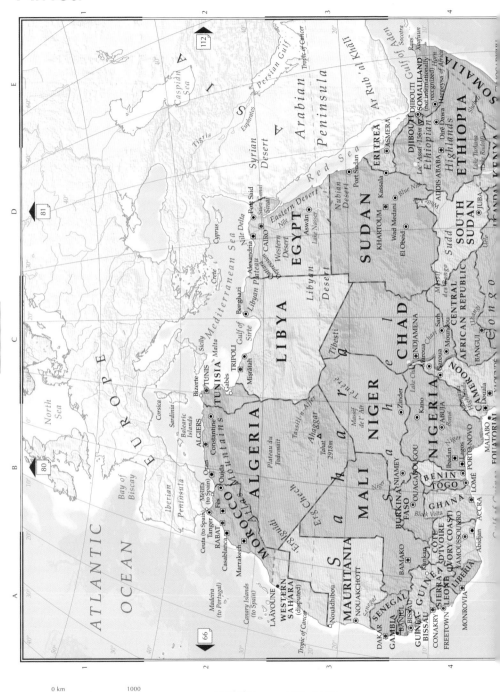

Population ● National capital

○ below 50,000 ○ 50,000 to 100,000 ◉ 100,000 to 500,000 ■ above 500,000

0 km 1000
0 miles 1000

Kisimaayo

Somali
Basin

Aldabra
Group

MAYOTTE
(to France)

COMOROS
MORONI

MADAGASCAR

ANTANANARIVO

Fianarantsoa

Madagascar
Basin

Tropic of Capricorn

Madagascar
Plateau

INDIAN

OCEAN

Southwest Indian Ridge

Crozet
Plateau

Prince Edward Islands
(to South Africa)

141

154

Kisumu
Lake Victoria
NAIROBI
Mombasa
Kilimanjaro
5895m
Masai
Steppe

RWANDA
KIGALI
BUJUMBURA
BURUNDI

TANZANIA
DODOMA

Pemba
Tanga
Zanzibar
Dar es Salaam

Lake Nyasa

MALAWI
LILONGWE
Blantyre

Mahajanga
Nacala
Nampula

Toliara

Mozambique Plateau

MOZAMBIQUE

Beira

DEM. REP.
CONGO

Bukavu

Lake Tanganyika

Great Rift Valley

Lake Rukwa

Kalemie

Ilebo

Kananga

Kasai

Matadi

KINSHASA

BRAZZAVILLE

GABON

Port-Gentil

SÃO TOMÉ & PRÍNCIPE

Cabinda
(to Angola)

LUANDA

Cuango

Cuanza

Lubango

Namibe

Móco 2619m
Huambo
Plateau

Bié
Plateau

ANGOLA

Cunene

Cubango

Cuito

Okavango
Delta

Etosha
Pan

Namib Desert

NAMIBIA
WINDHOEK

Lake Mweru

Lualaba

Luapula

Lubumbashi

Kitwe
Ndola

ZAMBIA
LUSAKA

Lake Kariba

Kariba

Victoria Falls

Zambezi

HARARE
ZIMBABWE
Bulawayo

Francistown

BOTSWANA
GABORONE

Kalahari
Desert

Johannesburg

Mozambique Channel

PRETORIA
TSHWANE
Limpopo

MAPUTO
MBABANE
SWAZILAND

Durban

MASERU
LESOTHO

BLOEMFONTEIN

SOUTH
AFRICA

Orange River

Nossob

Vaal

Drakensberg

Great Karoo

East London

Port Elizabeth

Stanger

CAPE TOWN
Cape of
Good Hope

Orange Fan

Cape
Basin

Agulhas
Plateau

Agulhas
Basin

Mozambique Plateau

Walvis Ridge

Angola
Basin

ATLANTIC

OCEAN

SAINT HELENA
(to UK)

ASCENSION ISLAND
(to Saint Helena)

Ascension Fracture Zone

Guinea
Basin

TRISTAN DA CUNHA
(to Saint Helena)

Gough Island
(to Tristan da Cunha)

Mid-Atlantic Ridge

Tropic of Capricorn

Atlantic-Indian Ridge

Winter limit of pack ice

67

154

69

Northwest Africa

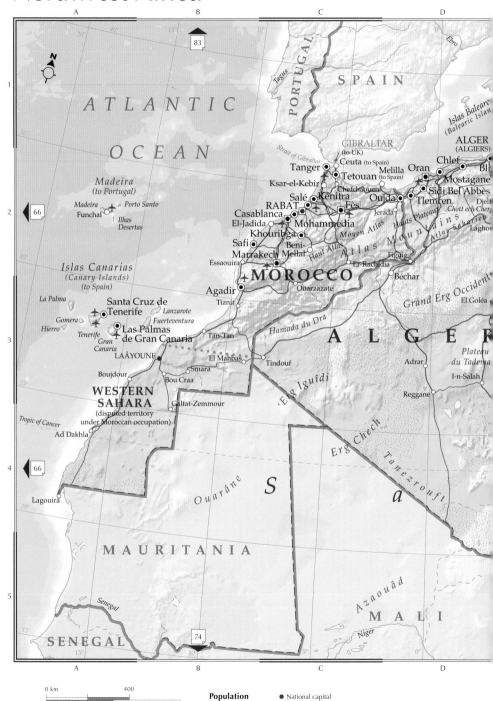

ATLANTIC

OCEAN

PORTUGAL

SPAIN

GIBRALTAR
(to UK)

ALGER
(ALGIERS)

Islas Baleare
(Balearic Islan

Tanger
Ceuta (to Spain)
Tetouan
Melilla
(to Spain)
Oran
Chlef
Bli
Mostagane

Ksar-el-Kebir
Chefchaouen
Sidi Bel Abbès

Salé
Kenitra
Oujda
Tlemcen
Djel

RABAT
Fès
Jerada
Chott ech Cher

Casablanca
Laghor

El-Jadida
Mohammedia

Safi
Khouribga
Moyen Atlas
Hauts Plateaux
Atlas Saharier

Beni-
Mellal
Haut Atlas
Atlas Mountains
Figuig

Marrakech
Er-Rachidia

Essaouira
MOROCCO
Ouarzazate
Béchar

Agadir
Grand Erg Occident

Tiznit
El Goléa

ALGER

Madeira
(to Portugal)

Madeira
Porto Santo
Funchal
Illhas
Desertas

Islas Canarias
(Canary Islands)
(to Spain)

La Palma
Santa Cruz de
Tenerife
Lanzarote
Fuerteventura

Gomera
Hierro
Tenerife
Gran
Canaria
Las Palmas
de Gran Canaria

LAÂYOUNE

Tan-Tan
Hamada du Dra
Plateau
du Tadema

Adrar
I-n-Salah

Boujdour
Smara
El Mahbas
Tindouf
Reggane

Bou Craa

WESTERN
SAHARA
(disputed territory
under Moroccan occupation)
Galtat-Zemmour

Tropic of Cancer

Ad Dakhla

Lagouira

S
'Erg Iguîdi
Erg Chech
Tanezrouft

Ouarâne

a

MAURITANIA

Azaouâd

MALI

Senegal
Niger

SENEGAL

Population
National capital
below 50,000
50,000 to 100,000
100,000 to 500,000
above 500,000

0 km   400
0 miles   400

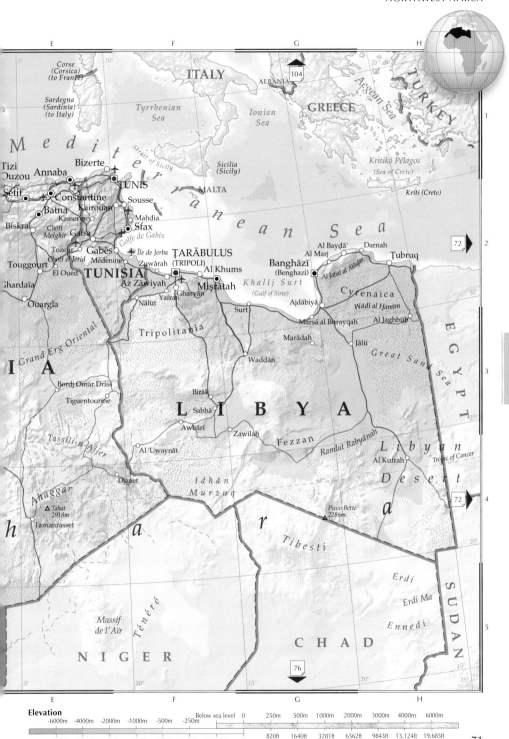

Elevation

-6000m	-4000m	-2000m	-1000m	-500m	-250m	Below sea level	0	250m	500m	1000m	2000m	3000m	4000m	6000m
-19,658ft	-13,124ft	-6562ft	-3281ft	-1640ft	-820ft	-328ft/-100m	0	820ft	1640ft	3281ft	6562ft	9843ft	13,124ft	19,685ft

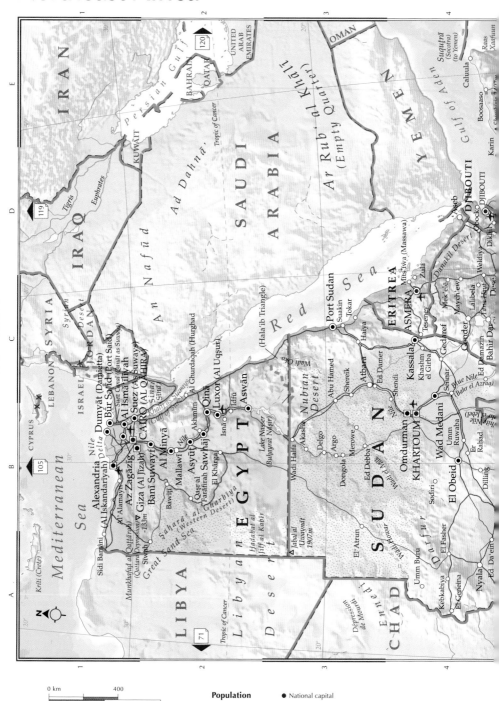

Population

○ below 50,000   ○ 50,000 to 100,000   ◉ 100,000 to 500,000   ▣ above 500,000

● National capital

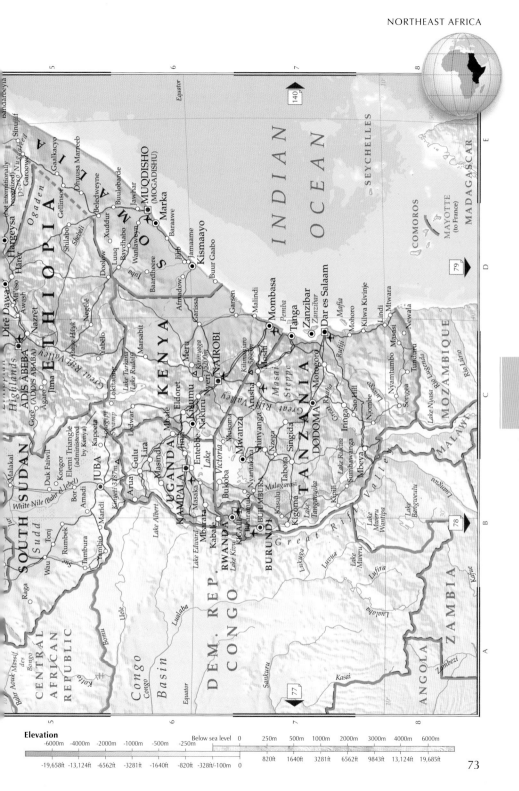

SEYCHELLES

INDIAN OCEAN

COMOROS

MAYOTTE
(to France)

MADAGASCAR

79

ETHIOPIA

Hargeysa
Harēr
Dirē Dawa
Afdeso
Awash
Nazrēt
ADIS ABEBA
(ADDIS ABABA)
Gorē
Agaro
Jima
Highlands
Awash Hayk'
Abaya Hayk'
Negēlē
Yabelo

Ogaden

Not internationally
recognized border

SOMALIA

Sinujiif
Garoowe
Gaalkacyo
Dhuusa Marreeb

bandarbeyla

Burdarbeyla

Xuddur
Baydhabo
Doolow
Luuq
Wanlaweyn
Baraawe
Marka
MUQDISHO
(MOGADISHU)
Jawhar

Buulobarde
Beledweyne
Cellinsor
Shiilabo
Shabeelle

Garissa
Afmadow
Baardheere
Buur Gaabo
Kismaayo
Jamaame
Jilib

SUDAN
SOUTH
Malakal
Duk Faiwil
Kongor
Bor
Raga
Wau
Toni
Rumbek
Tambura
Amadi
Maridi
Yambio

Sudd
White Nile (Bahr el Jebel)
Bahr el Ghazal

CENTRAL
AFRICAN
REPUBLIC
Bahr Aouk Massif
des Bongo
Kotto
Bomu

DEM. REP.
CONGO

Congo Basin

Equator

Uele
Lualaba
Kasai
Sankuru
Congo

KENYA
Great Rift Valley
Lokichoggio
Lodwar
Lokitaung
Lake Turkana
(Lake Rudolf)
Marsabit
Meru
NAIROBI
Kirinyaga
5199m
Nyeri
Nakuru
Kisumu
Eldoret
Mbale
Kitale
Garsen
Malindi

UGANDA
KAMPALA
Gulu
Lira
Masindi
Arua
Kapoeta
Duk Faiwil
Jinja
Entebbe
Masaka
Mbarara
Kabale
Eleni Triangle
(administered
by Kenya)
Kibish
3187m
Lake Albert
Lake Edward
Lake Kivu
Lake
Victoria

RWANDA
KIGALI
Butare
Gitarama

BURUNDI
BUJUMBURA
Bubanza

TANZANIA
Mwanza
Bukoba
Nyantakara
Shinyanga
Nzega
Singida
Tabora
Kasulu
Kigoma
Sumbawanga
Mbeya
DODOMA
Moshi
Kilimanjaro
5895m
Arusha
Masai
Steppe
Morogoro
Iringa
Njombe
Songea
Kilwa Kivinje
Mtwara
Masasi
Tunduru
Sao Hill
Great Ruaha
Mafia
Dar es Salaam
Zanzibar
Tanga
Pemba
Mombasa
Kirinyaga

Lake Rukwa
Lake Tanganyika
Lake Malagarasi
Kirifi
Lukuga
Luvua
Lake
Mweru
Malagarasi
Ruvuma
Rufiji
Great Ruaha
Great Rift Valley
Lake Nyasa (Lake Nyasa)

MALAWI
MOZAMBIQUE
Rio Lúrio
Newala
Lindi
Mohoro
Nyamtumbo

ZAMBIA
ANGOLA
Zambezi
Kafue
Lualaba
Lufira
Lake Bangweulu
Lake
Mweru
Wantipa
Lake
Mweru

Equator

77

78

Elevation

					Below sea level	0	250m	500m	1000m	2000m	3000m	4000m	6000m
-6000m	-4000m	-2000m	-1000m	-500m	-250m								

| -19,658ft | -13,124ft | -6562ft | -3281ft | -1640ft | -820ft | -328ft/-100m | 0 | 820ft | 1640ft | 3281ft | 6562ft | 9843ft | 13,124ft | 19,685ft |

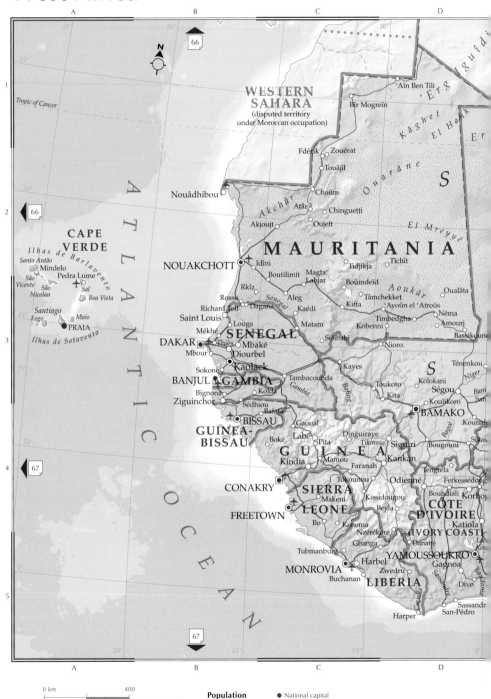

WESTERN
SAHARA
(disputed territory
under Moroccan occupation)

Aïn Ben Tili

Bir Mogreïn

'Erg Iguïdi

Kâghet

El Hamk

Er

Fdérik   Zouérat

Touâjil

Nouâdhibou

Choûm

Akchâr   Atâr   Chinguetti

Ouarâne

S

Akjoujt   Oujeft

El Mreyyé

MAURITANIA

Idîni   Boutilimit   Magta'   Lahjar   Tidjikja   Tîchît

Rkîz   Aleg   Boûmdeïd   Aoukâr   Oualâta

NOUAKCHOTT

Rosso   Senegal   Kaédi   Kiffa   Tâmchekket   Ayoûn el 'Atroûs   Néma

Richard Toll   Dagana   Timbedgha   Amourj

Saint Louis   Matam   Kobenni   Bassikoune

Mékhé   Louga   Sélibabi   Nioro   S

DAKAR   Thiès   Mbaké   Kayes   Ténénkou   Niger

Mbour   Diourbel   Kolokani   Ségou   Bani   San

Sokone   Kaolack   Toukoto   Kita   Koulikoro   Koutiala

BANJUL   GAMBIA   Tambacounda   Gambia   BAMAKO

Bignona   Kolda   Gaoual   Dinguiraye   Tikinsso   Siguiri   Bougouni   Sikasso

Ziguinchor   Sédhiou   Bafata   Boké   Labé   Pita   Bani

BISSAU   GUINEA   Kindia   Mamou   Faranah   Kankan   Tengréla   Ferkessédougou

GUINEA-   Gaoual
BISSAU

CONAKRY   Tokounou   Odienné   Boundiali   Korhogo

Makeni   Kissidougou   Beyla   CÔTE   Katiola

FREETOWN   SIERRA   Bo   Koïnadou   Nzérékoré   IVORY COAST   Kos

LEONE   Gbanga   Danané   Kos

Tubmanburg   YAMOUSSOUKRO

MONROVIA   Harbel   Gagnoa

Buchanan   Zwedru   LIBERIA   Divo

Sassandra

Harper   San-Pédro

CAPE
VERDE

Ilhas de Barlavento

Santo Antão   Mindelo
São   Pedra Lume
Vicente   São   Sal
Nicolau   Boa Vista

Santiago   Maio
Fogo
PRAIA

Ilhas de Sotavento

ATLANTIC OCEAN

Population

● National capital

○ below 50,000   ○ 50,000 to 100,000   ◉ 100,000 to 500,000   ■ above 500,000

0 km   400
0 miles   400

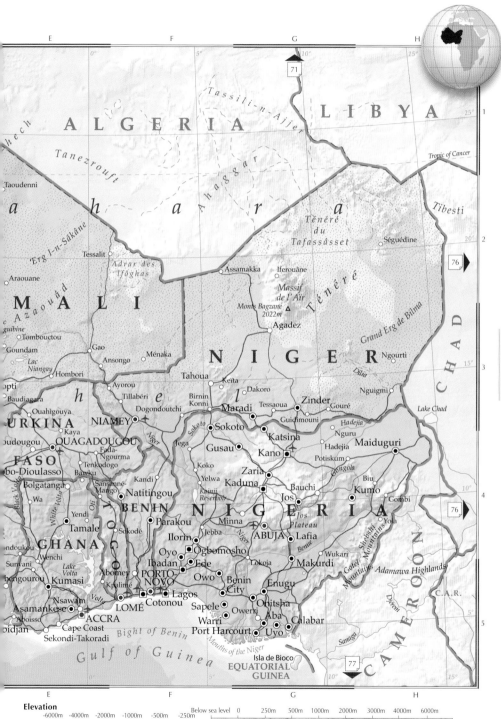

Elevation

					Below sea level	0	250m	500m	1000m	2000m	3000m	4000m	6000m
-6000m	-4000m	-2000m	-1000m	-500m	-250m								

| -19,658ft | -13,124ft | -6562ft | -3281ft | -1640ft | -820ft | -328ft/-100m | 0 | | 820ft | 1640ft | 3281ft | 6562ft | 9843ft | 13,124ft | 19,685ft |

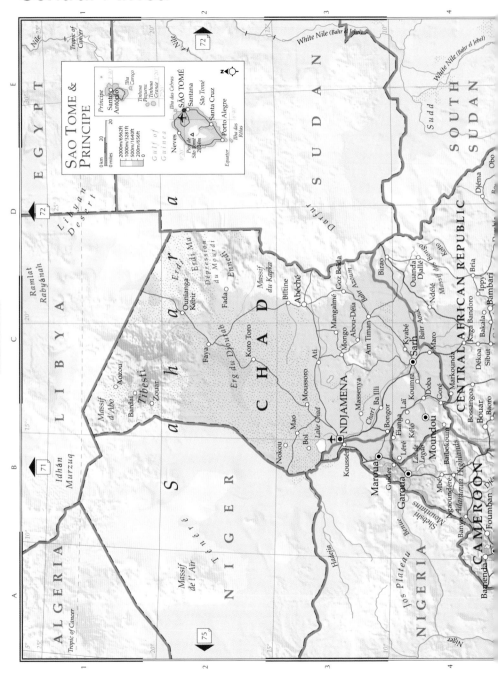

SAO TOME & PRINCIPE

Príncipe
Santo
António

Tiribosa
Pequeni
Tinibosa
Grande

Neves
SÃO TOMÉ
Santana
São Tomé
Santa Cruz

Pico de
São Tomé
2024m

Porto Alegre

Ilha das Cabras

Ilha do
Carreço

Ilha das
Rólas

Gulf of
Guinea

Equator

0 km   20
0 miles   20

2000m/6562ft
1000m/3281ft
500m/1640ft
200m/656ft

EGYPT

LIBYA

Libyan Desert

Ramlat Rabyānah

Idhān Murzuq

ALGERIA

Tropic of Cancer

NIGER

Massif de l'Air

Ténéré

S a h a r a

Massif d'Abo

Bardaï

Tibesti

Zouar

Aozou

Erdi Ma

Erdi

Ounianga Kébir

Fada

Dépression du Mourdi

Enneri

Massif du Kapka

Bitkine

Abéché

Goz Beïda

Faya

Kono Toro

Erg du Djourab

Ati

Mongo

Mangalmé

Abou-Déïa

Am Timan

Bahr Azoum

CHAD

Moussoro

Mao

Nokou

Bol

Lake Chad

Kousséri

NDJAMENA

Massenya

Chari

Ba Illi

Bongor

Lagé

Lagdo

Léré

Guidér

Lai

Kélo

Fianga

Kyabé

Sarh

Maro

Bahr Aouk

Markounda

Koumra

Doba

Goré

Bossangoa

Bouar

Baoro

Bossembélé

Dékoa

Bakala

Bambari

Bria

Tippy

Ndélé

Naga Bandoro

Ouanda Djallé

Birao

Bozoum

Massif des Bongo

Kaga Bandoro

CENTRAL AFRICAN REPUBLIC

Djéma

Obo

SOUTH SUDAN

SUDAN

Darfur

White Nile (Bahr el Jebel)

White Nile (Bahr el Jebel)

Sudd

Nile

Tropic of Cancer

Maroua

Garoua

Mbé

Ngaoundéré

Banyo

Adamawa Highlands

Foumban

Bamenda

Bafoussam

CAMEROON

Benue

Shebshi Mountains

Jos Plateau

NIGERIA

Niger

Hadejia

0 km   400
0 miles   400

Population

● National capital

○ below 50,000   ○ 50,000 to 100,000   ◉ 100,000 to 500,000   ▣ above 500,000

Elevation

-6000m	-4000m	-2000m	-1000m	-500m	-250m	Below sea level	0	250m	500m	1000m	2000m	3000m	4000m	6000m
-19,658ft	-13,124ft	-6562ft	-3281ft	-1640ft	-820ft	-328ft/-100m	0	820ft	1640ft	3281ft	6562ft	9843ft	13,124ft	19,685ft

Southern Africa

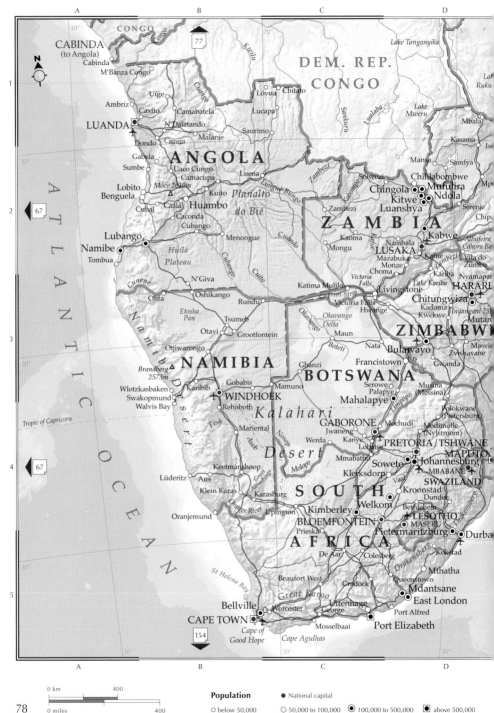

Population

- National capital

○ below 50,000 ○ 50,000 to 100,000 ◉ 100,000 to 500,000 ▣ above 500,000

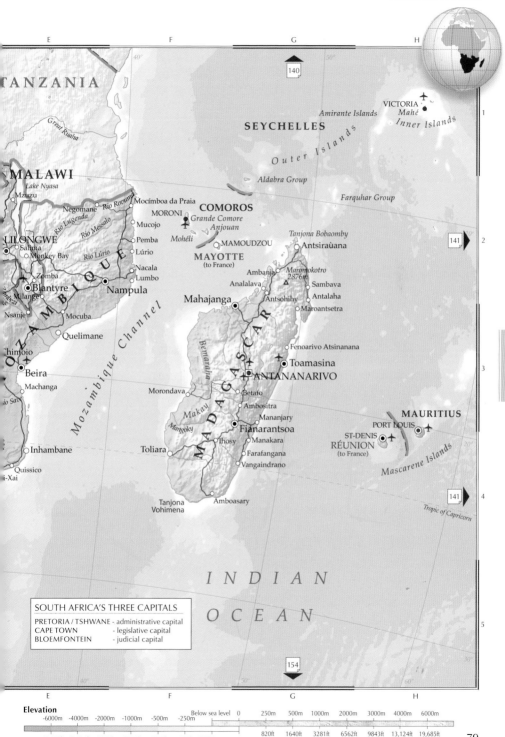

SEYCHELLES

VICTORIA
Mahé
Inner Islands

Amirante Islands

Outer Islands

Aldabra Group

Farquhar Group

TANZANIA

Great Ruaha

MALAWI

Lake Nyasa

Mzuzu

Negomane
Rio Rovuma

Mocímboa da Praia

MORONI
Grande Comore
COMOROS

Mucojo

Rio Lugenda

Pemba

Mohéli
Anjouan

LILONGWE
Sahna
Monkey Bay
Rio Messalo

Lúrio

MAMOUDZOU

Rio Lúrio
Nacala

MAYOTTE
(to France)

Zomba
Milange
Blantyre

Nampula

Lumbo

Tanjona Bobaomby

Antsiraùana

Nsanje

Mocuba

Mahajanga

Ambanja
Maromokotro
2876m

Sambava

Analalava

Antalaha

Quelimane

Antsohihy

Maroantsetra

himoio

Beira

Machanga

Fenoarivo Atsinanana

io Sav

Morondava

Toamasina

ANTANANARIVO

Betafo

MAURITIUS

Ambositra

Mananjary

PORT LOUIS

Inhambane

Toliara

Fianarantsoa

Ihosy

Manakara

ST-DENIS
RÉUNION
(to France)

Quissico
i-Xai

Farafangana

Vangaindrano

Mascarene Islands

Tanjona
Vohimena

Amboasary

Tropic of Capricorn

I N D I A N

O C E A N

Mozambique Channel

Bemaraha

MADAGASCAR

Makay

Mangoky

SOUTH AFRICA'S THREE CAPITALS

PRETORIA / TSHWANE - administrative capital
CAPE TOWN - legislative capital
BLOEMFONTEIN - judicial capital

Elevation

| -6000m | -4000m | -2000m | -1000m | -500m | -250m | Below sea level | 0 | 250m | 500m | 1000m | 2000m | 3000m | 4000m | 6000m |

| -19,658ft | -13,124ft | -6562ft | -3281ft | -1640ft | -820ft | -328ft/-100m | 0 | 820ft | 1640ft | 3281ft | 6562ft | 9843ft | 13,124ft | 19,685ft |

Europe

Charlie - Gibbs Fracture Zone

Reykjanes Ridge

REYKJAVÍK

ICELAND
Vatnajökull

Arctic Circle

Limit of winter pack ice

Faeroe-Iceland Ridge

Iceland Basin

Hatton Ridge

FAEROE ISLANDS
(to Denmark)

Norwegian Basin

Norwegian Sea

Trondheim

Lofo

Mid - Atlantic Ridge

Rockall Bank

Rockall Trough

Outer Hebrides

Shetland Islands

Faeroe-Shetland Trough

Orkney Islands

Bergen

Stavanger

OSLO

Vä

66

Porcupine Plain

British Isles

Glasgow

Edinburgh

Gothenburg

Aalborg

Jönköpir

A T L A N T I C

Ireland

Belfast

UNITED KINGDOM

North Sea

IRELAND

ISLE OF MAN
(to UK)

DUBLIN

Liverpool

Manchester

Britain

Birmingham

DENMARK

Odense

COPENHAC

Jutland

Malmö

O C E A N

Celtic Sea

Cardiff

LONDON

NETHERLANDS

THE HAGUE

AMSTERDAM

Rotterdam

Hanover

Hamburg

Elbe

N O

Celtic Shelf

English Channel

CHANNEL IS.
(to UK)

le Havre

BELGIUM

Liège

BRUSSELS

Düsseldorf

Bonn

BERLIN

Pozr

Charcot Seamounts

Biscay Plain

Rennes

Seine

PARIS

LUXEMBOURG

LUXEMBOURG

GERMANY

Frankfurt am Main

Wrocław

PRAG

Azores-Biscay Rise

Iberian Plain

Nantes

Loire

Orléans

Strasbourg

Stuttgart

CZECH REPUBL

FRANCE

Munich

BRATISL

Bay of Biscay

A Coruña

Galicia Bank

Bordeaux

Bilbao

Lyon

SWITZERLAND

BERN

Zurich

Innsbruck

LIECH

VIENNA

Salzburg

AUSTRIA

Porto

Cordillera Cantábrica

Duero

Garonne

Massif Central

Rhône

Mont Blanc
4807m

Milan

Turin

Venice

LJUBLJANA

SLOVENIA

ZAGE

Trieste

66

PORTUGAL

Iberian Peninsula

Zaragoza

MADRID

Ebro

Toulouse

Pyrenees

ANDORRA

Nice

MONACO

Marseille

Bologna

SAN MARINO

Adriatic Sea

BOS & HI

SARAJ

Mosti

Horseshoe Seamounts

Tagus Plain

LISBON

Tagus

SPAIN

Guadalquivir

Duero

Barcelona

Corsica

Pisa

VATICAN CITY

ROME

Naples

Bari

Madeira
(to Portugal)

Seville

Valencia

Palma

Balearic Islands

Sardinia

Algerian Basin

Cagliari

Tyrrhenian Sea

Cosenza

GIBRALTAR
(to UK)

Málaga

Ceuta
(to Spain)

Strait of Gibraltar

Melilla
(to Spain)

Palermo

Mount Etna
3340m

Catania

Sicily

Ion Bas

Canary Islands
(to Spain)

N

Atlas Mountains

68

AFRICA

M e d i t e r r a n e

MALTA

VALLETTA

Ion a

0 km   500
0 miles   500

Population

● National capital

○ below 50,000

◉ 50,000 to 100,000

◉ 100,000 to 500,000

■ above 500,000

Barents Sea

North Cape

Ostrov Kolguyev

Arctic Circle

Ob'

Irtysh

Murmansk
Kola
Peninsula

White
Sea

Archangel

Northern Dvina

Ural Mountains

R U S S I A N

Perm'

FINLAND

Tampere

Lake Onega

F E D E R A T I O N

Turku HELSINKI

Lake Ladoga

Vologda

Saint Petersburg

Ufa

TALLINN

ESTONIA

Yaroslavl'

Kazan'

STOCKHOLM

Nizhniy
Novgorod

Ul'yanovsk

LATVIA

MOSCOW

Samara

Orenburg

RIGA

Ural

LITHUANIA

Vitsyebsk

Kaunas

Ural

VILNIUS

Central
Russian
Upland

Aral
Sea

KALININGRAD
(to Russ.Fed.)

MINSK

Syr Darya

BELARUS

Babruysk

Homyel'

Voronezh

Volga Uplands

WARSAW

Brest

Don

Amu Darya

Pripet
Marshes

Dnieper Lowlands

Volgograd

POLAND

Kraków

L'viv

KIEV

Kharkiv

Dnieper

Astrakhan'

Caspian Sea

UKRAINE

Dnipropetrovs'k

Volga Delta
-28m

Chernivtsi

Donets'k

Rostov-na-Donu

SLOVAKIA

Dniester

MOLDOVA

BUDAPEST

Cluj-Napoca

CHIŞINĂU

Stavropol'

HUNGARY

ROMANIA

Sea of
Azov

A

 ROMANIA

Braşov

Odesa

Crimea

BELGRADE

BUCHAREST

Simferopol'

Caucasus

Elbrus 5642m

SERBIA

Constanţa

Black Sea

S

KOSOVO

BULGARIA

Varna

Danube

PRISTINA

Balkan Mountains

Burgas

I

SOFIA

SKOPJE

MACED.

TURKEY

A

ALBANIA

Aegean
Sea

Anatolia

GREECE

ATHENS

Piraeus

Zagros Mountains

Peloponnese

Tigris

Irákleio

Cyprus

Euphrates

Crete

Sea

The North Atlantic

A B C D

Arctic Circle

37

Gulf of Boothia

Devon
Island

Ellesmere Island

N U N A V U T

Nares Strait

Qaanaaq

Knud Rasmussen La

Hudson
Bay

Southampton
Island

Innaanganeq

Savissivik

Qimusseriarsuaq

1

Foxe
Basin

Baffin
Bay

Kullorsuaq

2

38

C A N A D A

Baffin Island

Upernavik

Péninsule
d'Ungava

Limit of summer pack ice

Uummannaq

Qeqertarsuaq

Qeqertarsuaq

G R E E N L A N D

(to Denmark)

QUÉBEC

Hudson Strait

Davis Strait

Qeqertarsuup Tunua

Qasigiannguit

Arnaud

Frobisher Bay

Cumberland Sound

Sisimiut

Kong Frederik IX
Land

3

Ungava
Bay

George

Maniitsoq

Kong Christian IX Land

Gunnbjørn Fj

370

Mont Forel
3360m

NUUK

4

39

Paamiut

Ammassalik

N E W F O U N D L A N D
& L A B R A D O R

Ivittuut

Kong Frederik VI Kyst

Denmar

Labrador
Sea

Qaqortoq

Nanortalik

Limit of winter pack ice

Reykjanes Basin

ATLANTIC

Nunap Isua
(Kap Farvel)

5

OCEAN

66

A B C D

0 km   400

0 miles   400

Population   ● National capital

○ below 50,000   ○ 50,000 to 100,000   ◉ 100,000 to 500,000   ▣ above 500,000

Lincoln
Sea

ARCTIC
OCEAN

Kap Morris Jesup

Wandel
Sea

SVALBARD
(to Norway)

Zemlya
Frantsa-Iosifa

Kvitøya

Novaya
Zemlya

Independence Fjord

Nord

Nordaustlandet

Kong Karls Land

Kong Frederik VIII Land

Spitsbergen

Barentsøya

Edgeøya

Barents
Sea

LONGYEARBYEN
Barentsburg

Storfjorden

Limit of winter pack ice

Greenland
Sea

Bjørnøya
(to Norway)

Kong Christian X
Land

Limit of summer pack ice

Daneborg

Nordkapp
(North Cape)

△ Petermann Bjerg
2940m

Mohns Ridge

FINLAND

Kong Oscar Fjord

Ittoqqortoormiit

JAN MAYEN
(to Norway)

Arctic Circle

Kangertittivaq
Kangikajik

Norwegian
Sea

Vestfjorden

trait

Norwegian Basin

S
W
E
D
E
N

Gulf
of
Bothnia

ICELAND

Bolungarvík
Siglufjördhur
afjördhur
Raufarhöfn

Húsavik

Akureyri

Stykkishólmur
Seydhisfjördhur

caflói
REYKJAVÍK
Neskaupstadhur

Selfoss
Vatnajökull
Djúpivogur

horlákshöfn
Hvannadalshnúkur
2119m

Surtsey
Vestmannaeyjar

FAEROE ISLANDS
(to Denmark)

N
W   E
S

NORWAY

TÓRSHAVN

Shetland
Islands

Elevation

-6000m	-4000m	-2000m	-1000m	-500m	-250m	Below sea level 0	250m	500m	1000m	2000m	3000m	4000m	6000m
-19,658ft	-13,124ft	-6562ft	-3281ft	-1640ft	-820ft	-328ft/-100m 0	820ft	1640ft	3281ft	6562ft	9843ft	13,124ft	19,685ft

Scandinavia & Finland

RUSSIAN FEDERATION

FINLAND

Barents Sea

ARCTIC OCEAN

Norwegian Sea

Nordkapp
(North Cape)

Lapland

Arctic Circle

Population

0 km   200
0 miles   200

● National capital

O below 50,000   O 50,000 to 100,000   ◉ 100,000 to 500,000   ▣ above 500,000

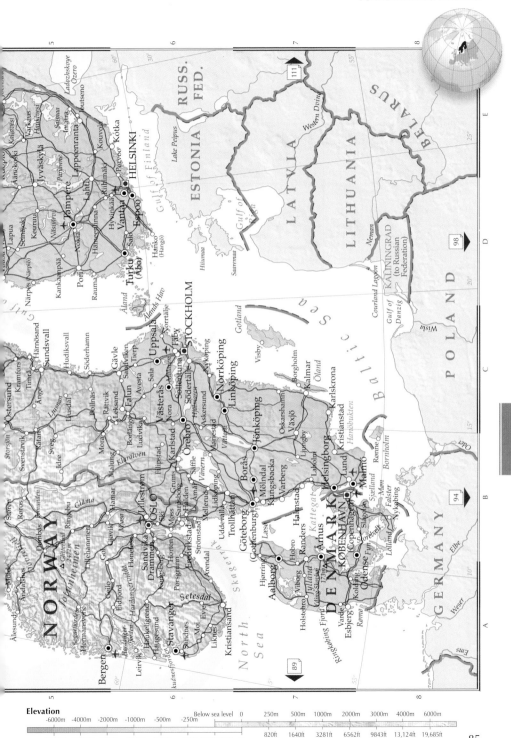

Elevation

						Below sea level	0	250m	500m	1000m	2000m	3000m	4000m	6000m
-6000m	-4000m	-2000m	-1000m	-500m	-250m									

| -19,658ft | -13,124ft | -6562ft | -3281ft | -1640ft | -820ft | -328ft/-100m | 0 | 820ft | 1640ft | 3281ft | 6562ft | 9843ft | 13,124ft | 19,685ft |

The Low Countries

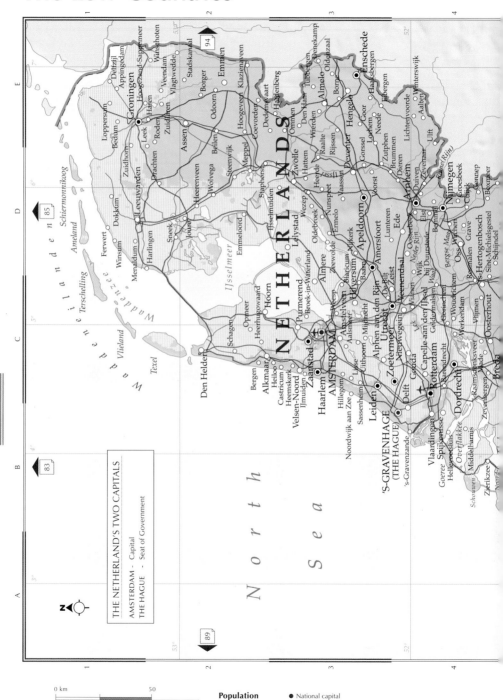

THE NETHERLAND'S TWO CAPITALS

AMSTERDAM - Capital
THE HAGUE - Seat of Government

Population

● National capital

○ below 50,000   ○ 50,000 to 100,000   ◉ 100,000 to 500,000   ▣ above 500,000

0 km   50
0 miles   50

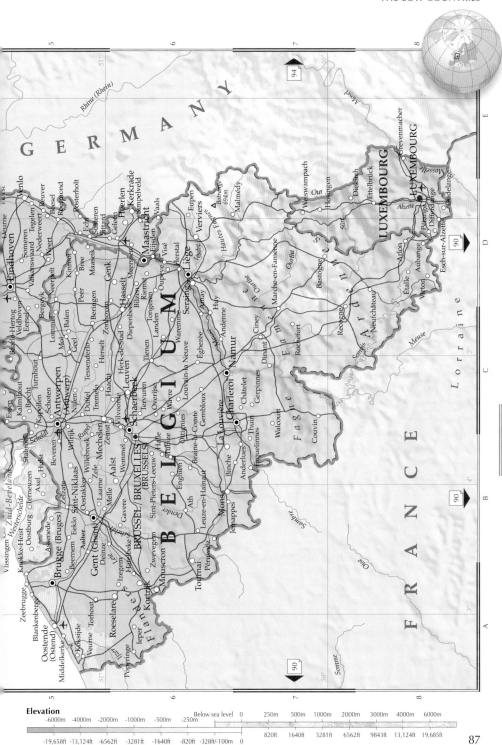

Elevation

-6000m	-4000m	-2000m	-1000m	-500m	-250m	Below sea level	0	250m	500m	1000m	2000m	3000m	4000m	6000m
-19,658ft	-13,124ft	-6562ft	-3281ft	-1640ft	-820ft	-328ft/-100m	0	820ft	1640ft	3281ft	6562ft	9843ft	13,124ft	19,685ft

The British Isles

North Sea

ATLANTIC OCEAN

Shetland Islands
Unst
Fetlar
Yell
Mainland
Lerwick

Fair Isle

Orkney Islands
Sanday
Mainland
Kirkwall
Hoy
John o'Groats
Thurso

The Minch

North West Highlands
Ben Hope 927m △
Ullapool
Loch Ness
Inverness
Aviemore

Isle of Lewis
Stornoway
Harris
The Little Minch
Isle of Skye
Kyle of Lochalsh
Mallaig

North Uist
South Uist
Barra
Rhum
Eigg
Coll
Tiree
Isle of Mull
Firth of Lorn
Jura
Islay

St Kilda

Outer Hebrides
Inner Hebrides

SCOTLAND
Grampian Mountains
Dee
Fraserburgh
Peterhead
Aberdeen
Elgin
Spey
Montrose
Forfar
Arbroath
Dundee
St Andrews
Firth of Forth
Tay
Perth
Dunfermline
Ben Nevis 1343 △
Fort William
Loch Lomond
Forth
Stirling
Edinburgh
Glasgow
Hamilton
Clyde
Paisley
Greenock
East Kilbride
Prestwick
Kilmarnock
Ayr
Isle of Arran
Kintyre
Coleraine

NORTHERN

Berwick-upon-Tweed
Galashiels
Hawick
Cheviot Hills
Tyne
Newcastle upon Tyne
South Shields

Southern Uplands

N

Population

● National capital   ● Internal administrative capital

○ below 50,000   ○ 50,000 to 100,000   ◉ 100,000 to 500,000   ◼ above 500,000

0 km   100

0 miles   100

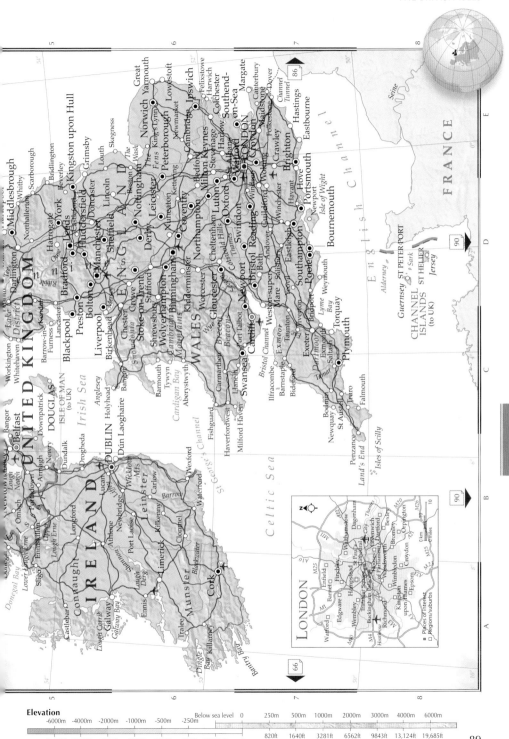

Elevation

-6000m	-4000m	-2000m	-1000m	-500m	-250m	Below sea level	0	250m	500m	1000m	2000m	3000m	4000m	6000m

| -19,658ft | -13,124ft | -6562ft | -3281ft | -1640ft | -820ft | -328ft/-100m | 0 | 820ft | 1640ft | 3281ft | 6562ft | 9843ft | 13,124ft | 19,685ft |

France, Andorra & Monaco

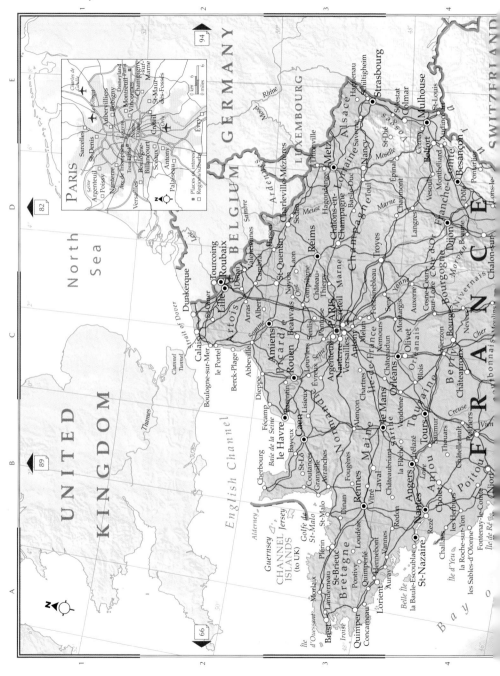

Population

● National capital

○ below 50,000   ○ 50,000 to 100,000   ◉ 100,000 to 500,000   ▣ above 500,000

0 km   100
0 miles   100

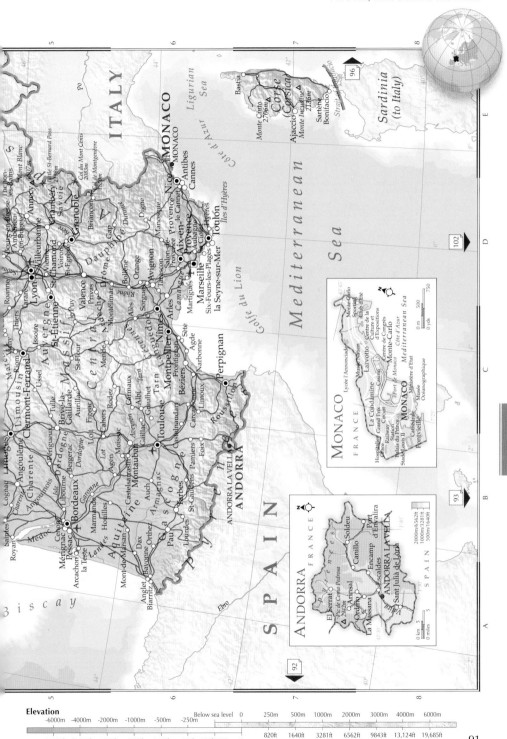

ITALY

MONACO

Ligurian Sea

Bastia
Monte Cinto
2706m▲
Corse
Corsica
Ajaccio ▲Monte Incudine
2136m
Sartène
Bonifacio

*Sardinia
(to Italy)*

Mont Blanc
4807m
Col du Mont Cenis
Col du Grand-St-Bernard Pass
2083m
Chamonix
le Fayet
Pont
Lac du Bourget
Thonon-les-Bains
Annecy
Aix-les-Bains
Chambéry
Savoie
Voiron
Grenoble
Briançon
Gap
Dauphiné
Digne
Drôme
Manosque
Orange
Aubagne
Salon-de-Provence
Aix-en-Provence
Provence
Nice
Antibes
Cannes

Côte d'Azur

MONACO

Bourg-en-Bresse
Villeurbanne
Lyon
St-Étienne
le Puy
Privas
Montélimar
Valence
Romans
St-Chamond
Roanne
Ardèche
Avignon
Sorgues
Arles
Camargue
Nîmes
Marseille
Martigues
Six-Fours-les-Plages
la Seyne-sur-Mer
Toulon
Hyères
Îles d'Hyères

Thiers
Vichy
Riom
Clermont-Ferrand
Issoire
Ussel
Aurillac
St-Flour
Auvergne
Massif Central
Mende
Alès
Sète
Agde
Béziers
Narbonne
Montpellier
Frontignan
Lodève

Golfe du Lion

Mediterranean Sea

Limoges
Tulle
Brive-la-Gaillarde
Périgueux
Bergerac
Dordogne
Lot
Figeac
Rodez
Cahors
Moissac
Agen
Montauban
Albi
Tarn
Gaillac
Carmaux
Castres
Castelsarrasin
Toulouse
Gaillac
Pamiers
Foix
Mazamet
Limoux
Carcassonne
Castelnaudary
Perpignan
Roussillon

ANDORRA LA VELLA
ANDORRA

Cognac
Angoulême
Charente
Angoulins
Royan
Libourne
Bordeaux
Marmande
Garonne
Houilles
Castelsarrasin
Condom
Auch
Mont-de-Marsan
Dax
Pau
Tarbes
St-Gaudens
Lourdes
Anglet
Bayonne
Biarritz

Biscay

S P A I N

Ebro

96
102
93

MONACO

Lycée l'Annonciade
Musée National
Monte-Carlo
Sporting Club d'Été
Larvotto
Centre de la Culture et d'Expositions
Casino
Centre de Congrès
Monte-Carlo
La Condamine
Grand Prix
Port de Monaco
Côte d'Azur
Mediterranean Sea
Musée Océanographique
Ministère d'État
Palais du Prince
Cathédrale
Stade Louis II
Hospital Centre
Railway

FRANCE

MONACO

0 m   500   750
0 yds   500   750

ANDORRA

FRANCE

Pyrenees
El Serrat
Pic de Coma Pedrosa
2942m
Arinsal
Ordino
La Massana
Soldeu
Canillo
Encamp
Escaldes
ANDORRA LA VELLA
Sant Julia de Loria
Port
d'Envalira

S P A I N

2000m/6562ft
1000m/3281ft
500m/1640ft

0 km   5
0 miles 5

Elevation

					Below sea level	0	250m	500m	1000m	2000m	3000m	4000m	6000m
-6000m	-4000m	-2000m	-1000m	-500m	-250m								
-19,658ft	-13,124ft	-6562ft	-3281ft	-1640ft	-820ft	-328ft/-100m	0	820ft	1640ft	3281ft	6562ft	9843ft	13,124ft	19,685ft

Spain & Portugal

12°   10°   8°   44°   6°   4°
Bay of Biscay

N

A Coruña
(La Coruña)   Ferrol   Luarca   Avilés   Gijón   *Costa Verde*
                                      (Xixón)
Laracha   Betanzos   Tineo   Pravia   Villaviciosa   Santander
                                        Oviedo   Llanes
Santa Cataliña de Armada   Vilalba   **Asturias**   Torrelavega
Cabo Fisterra   Mieres del Camín   *Cantabri*
Oues   Galicia   Lugo   La Pola   Cabanaquinta   Reinosa
Muros   Cordillera Cantábrica
Santiago de Compostela   Chantada   Monforte   Ponferrada   León   Burgo
Santa Uxía de Ribeira   Lalín   de Lemos   Astorga   **Castilla-León**
Pontevedra   O Carballiño   Benavente   Palencia
Marín   Lerma
Vigo   Ourense (Orense)   Valladolid   Aranda
Ponteareas   Xinzo de Limia   Zamora   de Duero
                         Toro   Duero
Viana do Castelo   Ponte da Barca   Bragança   *Embalse de*   Medina del Campo
                    Braga   Chaves   *Ricobayo*   Salamanca   Segovia   *Sierre*
Póvoa de Varzim   Guimarães   **S**   **P** *Guadarr*
Vila do Conde   Vila Real   *Embalse*   Ávila   **Central**
Matosinhos   *de Almendra*   MADRID
Porto (Oporto)   Lamego   Douro   Getafe
Vila Nova de Gaia   Ovar   São João da Madeira   Ciudad-Rodrigo   *Sistema*   Talavera   Aranj
    Albergaria-a-Velha   Béjar   *Sierra de Gredos*   de la Reina
Aveiro   Viseu   Guarda   *Sistema Central*   Toledo
Ílhavo   *Alto da Torre*   Plasencia   Coria
    T1993m
Coimbra   Cáceres
Figueira da Foz   *Embalse de*   *Embalse de*   Herrera
PORTUGAL   Tagus   *de Alcántara*   *Valdecañas*   del Duque   Daim
Leiria   Castelo Branco   Coria   Trujillo
Entroncamento   Tomar   Abrantes   Mérida   **Extremadura**   Ciudad Real
Peniche   Caldas da Rainha   Portalegre   Villanueva de la Serena   Puertollano
Torres Vedras   Santarém   Don Benito   Pozoblanco
Sintra   Coruche   Estremoz   Elvas   Badajoz   Almendralejo   La Caroli
Cascais   **LISBOA** (LISBON)   Castuera   Bailén
Almada   Barreiro   Évora   Zafra   Villafranca de los Barros
Setúbal   Alcácer do Sal   *Barragem*   Azuaga   Linar
    do Alqueva   Jerez de los Caballeros   **Morena**   Montoro   Ja
Baía de Setúbal   Beja   Córdoba   Bujalance   Martos   Alcaude
Sines   Ourique   Cortegana   *Sierra*   Palma del Río   Lucena
    Nerva   La Algaba   Carmona   Ecija   **Andalucia**   Granat
    Valverde del Camino   Sevilla   Osuna   Archidona   *Sistem*
Algarve   Ayamonte   Lepe   (Seville)   Antequera   *Sierr*
Portimão   Faro   Huelva   Dos   Lucena   Málaga
Lagos   Isla   Hermanas   Alora   *Costa del S*
    Tavira   Cristina   Olvera   Ronda   Fuengirola
Cabo de   Olhão   *Golfo de Cádiz*   Lebrija   Marbella
São Vicente   Sanlúcar de Barrameda   Ubrique   Estepona
    El Puerto de Santa María   Jerez de la Frontera
    Cádiz   Com   **GIBRALTAR**
    San Fernando   Vejer de la Frontera   Algeciras   (to UK)
    Barbate de Franco   *Strait of Gibraltar*   Ceuta (to Spain)
Costa de la Luz   **MOROCCO**

ATLANTIC

OCEAN

AZORES (to Portugal)

Corvo   **N**
Flores   São   Graciosa
    Jorge   Terceira
Faial   Pico   São Miguel
Ponta Delgada
    Santa Maria

0 km   100
0 miles   100   200m/656ft
Sea level

Population   ● National capital
○ below 50,000   ○ 50,000 to 100,000   ◉ 100,000 to 500,000   ▣ above 500,000

FRANCE

Golfe du Lion

redo
Bermeo
Zarautz
Donostia/San Sebastián
ilbao
Eibar
Irun
Tolosa
País Vasco
Bergara
Pamplona
(Iruña)
Vitoria-Gasteiz
Miranda
de Ebro
Estella
Logroño
Navarra
Jaca
Arnedo
Calahorra
Huesca
La Rioja
Tudela
Ejea de
los Caballeros
Barbastro
Soria
Monzón
Tarazona
El Burgo
de Osma
Zaragoza
Lleida
(Lérida)
Fraga
Calatayud
Medinaceli
Aragón
Daroca
Alcañiz
Cuenca
Teruel
Tortosa
Tarancón
Amposta
Sant Carles de la Ràpita
Guadalajara
Alcalá de Henares
Vinaròs
rrejón de Ardoz
Javalambre
2020m
Castilla-La Mancha
Onda
Castellón de la Plana
Mota del Cuervo
Borriana
Campo de Criptana
Vall d'Uxó
Sagunto
Socuéllamos
Burjassot
(Sagunt)
La Roda
Valencia
Tomelloso
Torrent
Catarroja
Manzanares
Albacete
Algemesí
Sueca
La Solana
Almansa
Xàtiva
Cullera
depeñas
Ontinyent
Gandia
Villanueva de los Infantes
Oliva
Alcoy
Dénia
Hellín
Villena
Benidorm
Jumilla
Elda
Villajoyosa (La Vila Joíosa)
Beas de Segura
Monóvar
Sant Joan d'Alacant
Moratalla
Elche
Alicante (Alacant)
Villacarrillo
Cieza
(Elx)
beda
Mula
Callosa de Segura
Cazorla
Murcia
Orihuela
Murcia
Huéscar
Totana
La Unión
Baza
Lorca
Cartagena
Guadix
Aguilas
Madhacén
3481m
Mojácar
Nevada
Berja
Almería
Adra

Sistema Ibérico

País Valenciano

Costa del Azahar

Golfo de Valencia

Costa Blanca

Béticos

Mediterranean Sea

ALGERIA

La Seu d'Urgell
ANDORRA
Monte Perdido
3348m
Ripoll
Figueres
Berga
Girona
(Gerona)
Banyoles
Manlleu
Palafrugell
Palamós
Cataluña
Vic
Balaguer
Blanes
Cervera
Arenys de Mar
Tàrrega
Sabadell
Terrassa
Mataró
Vilafranca del Penedès
Valls
Barcelona
Reus
L'Hospitalet de Llobregat
El Vendrell
Sitges
Tarragona

Costa Brava

90
96
97

Ciutadella
Menorca
(Minorca)
Pollença
Maó
Sa Pobla
Palma
Manacor
Llucmajor
Felanitx
Illa de
Cabrera
Mallorca
(Majorca)
Eivissa (Ibiza)
Ibiza
Formentera

Islas Baleares
(Balearic Islands)

GIBRALTAR (to UK)
N
SPAIN
Gibraltar
Airport
North Mole
Gibraltar
Harbour
Catalan Bay
Catalan
Bay
The Rock
Bay of Gibraltar
Rosia
Sandy
Bay
Summit
Buena Vista
Rosia
Bay
Little
Bay
200m/656ft
Sea level
Europa Point
0 km
1
0 mile
1
Strait of Gibraltar

Elevation

						Below sea level	0	250m	500m	1000m	2000m	3000m	4000m	6000m

-6000m -4000m -2000m -1000m -500m -250m

-19,658ft -13,124ft -6562ft -3281ft -1640ft -820ft -328ft/-100m 0   820ft 1640ft 3281ft 6562ft 9843ft 13,124ft 19,685ft

Germany & the Alpine States

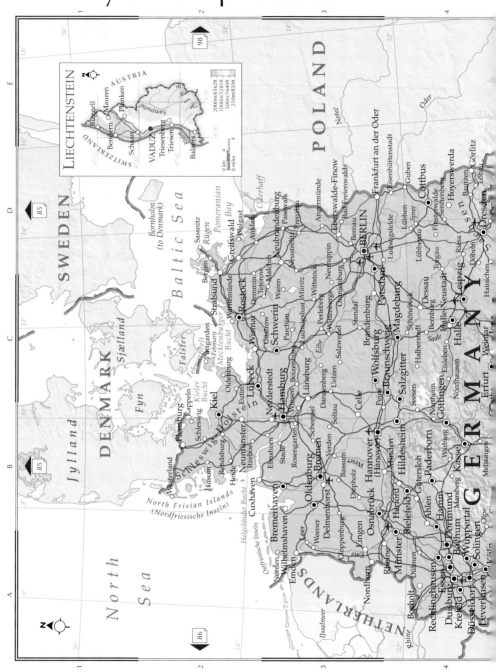

Population

● National capital
○ below 50,000
○ 50,000 to 100,000
◉ 100,000 to 500,000
■ above 500,000

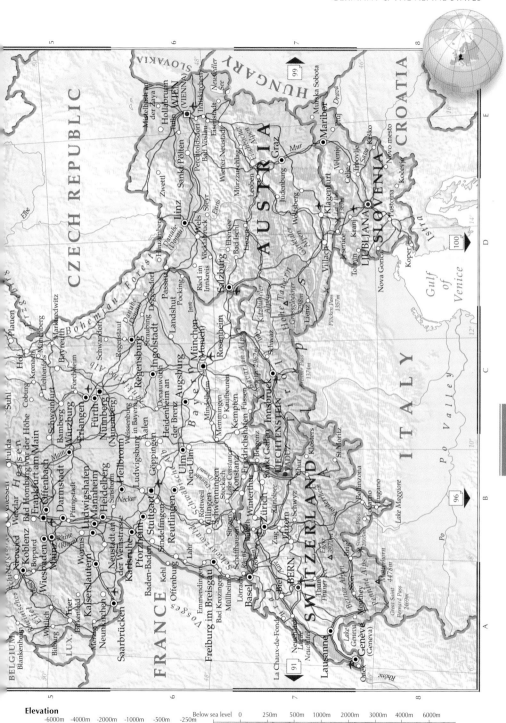

Elevation

-6000m	-4000m	-2000m	-1000m	-500m	Below sea level	0	250m	500m	1000m	2000m	3000m	4000m	6000m
					-250m								

| -19,658ft | -13,124ft | -6562ft | -3281ft | -1640ft | -820ft | -328ft/-100m | 0 | | 820ft | 1640ft | 3281ft | 6562ft | 9843ft | 13,124ft | 19,685ft |

SAN MARINO

Dogana
Fiorina
Cailungo
Gaetano
ITALY
Serravalle
Montegiardino
Monte Titano 739m
Murata

SAN MARINO
Borgo Maggiore
SAN MARINO
ITALY
Gualdicciolo
Chiesanuova
ITALY

500m/1640ft
200m/656ft
100m/328ft

SLOVAKIA
HUNGARY
Drava
Sava
SLOVENIA
CROATIA
Dalmatia
Adriatic Sea
BOSNIA &
HERZEGOVINA

Istra

GERMANY
AUSTRIA
Brenner Pass 1374m
Inn

LIECHTENSTEIN
SWITZERLAND
FRANCE
MONACO

Lake Constance
Lake Geneva
Rhône
Lake Maggiore
Lago di Como

Mont Blanc 4807m
Little St-Bernard Pass
Great St-Bernard Pass 2469m
Gran Paradiso 4061m

Susa
Rivoli
Moncalieri
Savigliano
Cuneo
Mondovi
Ventimiglia
San Remo
Imperia
Finale Ligure
Savona
Cecina

Torino (Turin)
Asti
Alessandria
Vercelli
Novara
Pavia
Casteggio
Mondovi
Piemonte
Appennino
Golfo di Genova
Genova (Genoa)
La Spezia
Massa
Carrara
Viareggio
Pisa
Livorno
Piombino
Portoferraio Isola d'Elba
Corse (Corsica) (to France)

Milano (Milan)
Monza
Como
Bergamo
Sesto San Giovanni
Brescia
Cremona
Mantova
Lombardia
Lago di Garda
Arco
Edolo
Merano
Bolzano
Trento
Bressanone
Dolomitiche
Alpi
Cortina d'Ampezzo

Tarvisio
Udine
Gemona del Friuli
Pordenone
Monfalcone
Trieste
Portogruaro
Conegliano
Treviso
Venezia (Venice)
Mestre
Chioggia
Gulf of Venice
Foci del Po

Verona
Vicenza
Padova
Monselice
Bassano del Grappa
Ostiglia
Rovigo
Adige
Po
Ferrara
Comacchio
Ravenna
Rimini
SAN MARINO
SAN MARINO
Pesaro
Fano

Piacenza
Parma
Reggio nell'Emilia
Modena
Carpi
Bologna
Imola
Faenza
Forlì
Cesena
Emilia-Romagna
Appennino Tosco-Emiliano

Pistoia
Lucca
Prato
Firenze (Florence)
Arno
Chianti
Siena
Toscana
Lago Trasimeno
Arezzo
Sansepolcro
Perugia
Umbria
Appennino Umbro-Marchigiano
Foligno
Todi
Terni

Grosseto
Orbetello
Civitavecchia
Viterbo
VATICAN CITY
ROME

Marche
Falconara Marittima
Ancona
Civitanova Marche
Fermo
Ascoli Piceno
Giulianova
Teramo
L'Aquila
Avezzano
Tivoli
Appennino
Abruzzese
Pescara
Ortona
Chieti
Lanciano
Termoli

Ligurian Sea
Archipelago Toscano

0 km   100
0 miles   100

Population   ● National capital
○ below 50,000   ◎ 50,000 to 100,000   ◉ 100,000 to 500,000   ■ above 500,000

5   6   7   8

E

71

D

C

71

B

71

A

Strait of Otranto

Brindisi
Maglie
Lecce
Manfredonia
Foggia
Molfetta
Barletta
Bari
Campobasso
Cerignola
Bitonto
Andria
Altamura
Puglia
Matera
Taranto
Manduria
Gallipoli
Golfo di Taranto

Ciro Marina
Crotone
Catanzaro
Rossano
La Sila
Siderno
Reggio di Calabria

Ionian Sea

38°

18°

16°

E

Benevento
Avellino
Casoria
Napoli (Naples)
Torre del Greco
Vesuvio 1277m
Campania
Salerno
Battipaglia
Agropoli
Golfo di Salerno
Isola di Capri
Gaeta
Golfo di Gaeta
Terracina
Isole Ponziane

Appennino Lucano
Sala Consilina
Potenza
Sapri
Castrovillari
Cosenza
Amantea
Lamezia Terme
Palmi
Paola

Stretto di Messina
Messina
Catania
Siracusa
Medica
Ragusa
Pozzallo

Isole Eolie
Isola Stromboli
Isola Lipari
Isola Vulcano
Cefalù
Palermo
Isola d'Ustica
Alcamo
Monte Etna 3340m
Simeto
Caltanissetta
Gela
Vittoria
Agrigento

Sicilia (Sicily)

Strait of Sicily

Trapani
Isole Egadi
Marsala
Castelvetrano

Isola di Pantelleria

Isole Pelagie

Malta Channel
Gozo
MALTA
VALLETTA
Malta

Tyrrhenian Sea

Mediterranean Sea

Sardegna (Sardinia)
Siniscola
Olbia
Ozieri
Nuoro
Macomer
Oristano
Villacidro
Iglesias
Carbonia
Cagliari
Quartu Sant' Elena
Punta La Marmora 1834m
Alghero

TUNISIA

Elevation

					Below sea level	0	250m	500m	1000m	2000m	3000m	4000m	6000m
-6000m	-4000m	-2000m	-1000m	-500m	-250m								
-19,658ft	-13,124ft	-6562ft	-3281ft	-1640ft	-820ft	-328ft/-100m	0	820ft	1640ft	3281ft	6562ft	9843ft	13,124ft	19,685ft

Central Europe

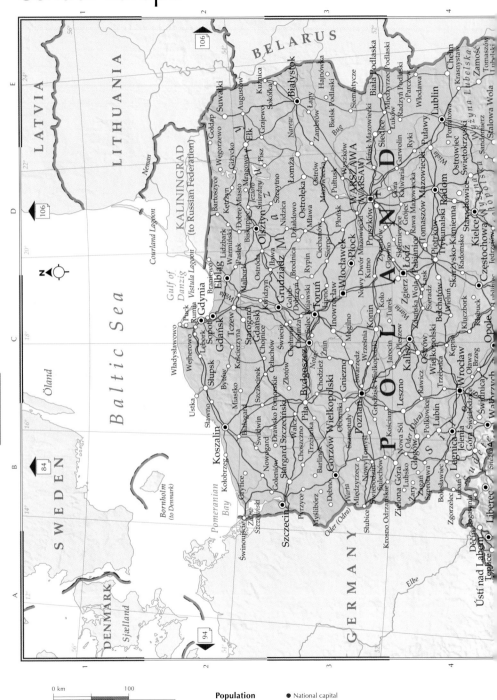

Population			
● National capital			
○ below 50,000	○ 50,000 to 100,000	◉ 100,000 to 500,000	◼ above 500,000

0 km 100

0 miles 100

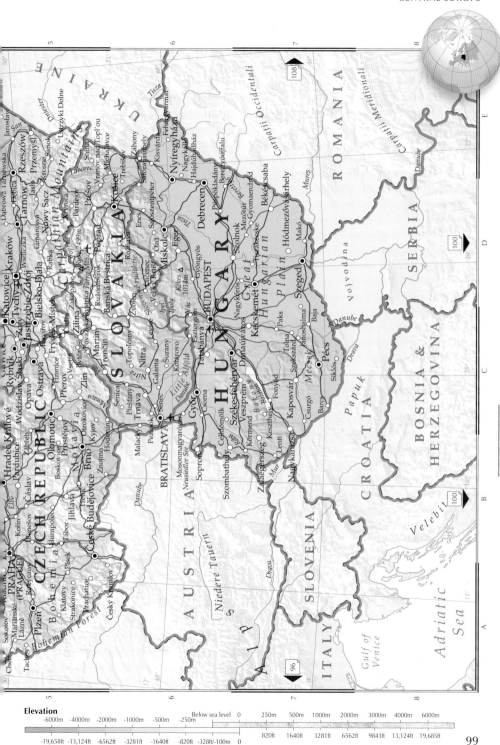

Elevation

-6000m	-4000m	-2000m	-1000m	-500m	Below sea level 0	250m	500m	1000m	2000m	3000m	4000m	6000m

-19,658ft -13,124ft -6562ft -3281ft -1640ft -820ft -328ft/-100m 0   820ft   1640ft   3281ft   6562ft   9843ft 13,124ft 19,685ft

Southeast Europe

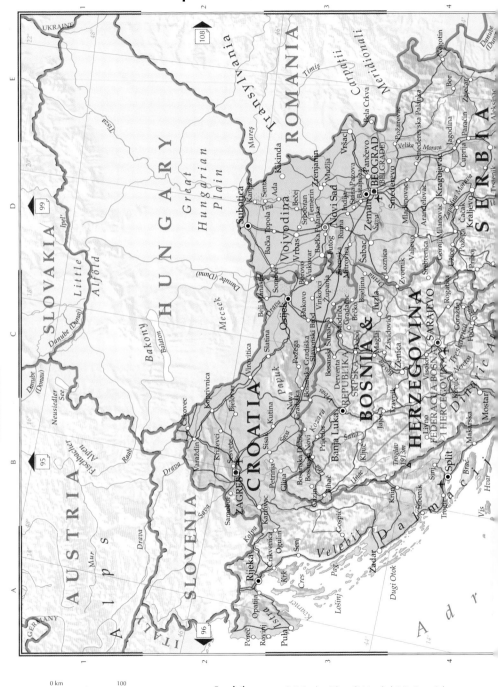

0 km 100

0 miles 100

Population

● National capital   ○ Internal administrative capital

○ below 50,000   ○ 50,000 to 100,000   ◉ 100,000 to 500,000   ◼ above 500,000

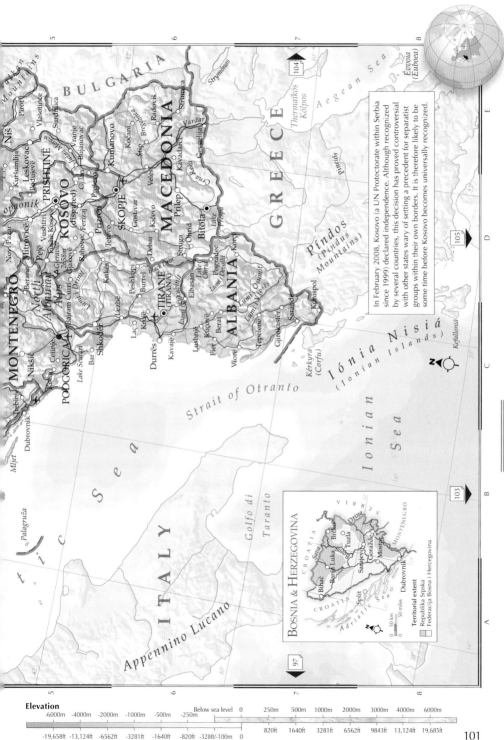

In February 2008, Kosovo (a UN Protectorate within Serbia since 1999) declared independence. Although recognized by several countries, this decision has proved controversial with other states wary of setting a precedent for separatist groups within their own borders. It is therefore likely to be some time before Kosovo becomes universally recognized.

BULGARIA

MACEDONIA

GREECE

KOSOVO
(disputed)

MONTENEGRO

ALBANIA

ITALY

Aegean Sea

Thermaïkós Kólpos

Thermaïkós Kólpos

Évvoia (Euboea)

Níš
Pirot
Vlasotince
Surdulica
Leskovac
Bujanovac
Kuršumlija
Bači Lužević
Kopaonik
Novi Pazar
Berane
Mitrovicë
Vushtrri
PRISHTINË
Pejë
Gjilan
Preševo
Kratovo
Kumanovo
Radoviš
Kočani
Breşa
Štip
Strumica
Vardar
Veles
Gevgelija
SKOPJE
Tetovo
Gostivar
Kičevo
Prilep
Prizren
Ferizaj
Kavadarci
MACEDONIA
Crna Reka
Ohrid
Bitola
Lake Prespa
Korçë
Lake Ohrid
Debar
Struga
Pogradec
Berat
Elbasan
Burrel
Lezhë
TIRANË (TIRANA)
Durrës
Kavajë
Lushnjë
Fier
Vlorë
Nepelenë
Tepelenë
Gjirokastër
Konispol
Sarandë
Kërkyra (Corfu)

Pindos (Pindus Mountains)

Pēneiōs

Strait of Otranto

Ióna Nisiá (Ionian Islands)

Ionian Sea

Golfo di Taranto

Appennino Lucano

Adriatic Sea

Palagruža

Mljet

Dubrovnik
Trebinje
Nikšić
Cetinje
PODGORICA
Bar
Shkodër
Lake Scutari

BOSNIA & HERZEGOVINA

SERBIA
CROATIA
MONTENEGRO
Sava
Drina
Brčko
Tuzla
Goražde
Bihać
Banja Luka
Bijeljina
Sarajevo
Mostar
Split
Dubrovnik

Adriatic Sea

Territorial extent
Republika Srpska
Federacija Bosna i Hercegovina

50 km
50 miles

Elevation

-6000m	-4000m	-2000m	-1000m	-500m	-250m	Below sea level 0	250m	500m	1000m	2000m	3000m	4000m	6000m
-19,658ft	-13,124ft	-6562ft	-3281ft	-1640ft	-820ft	-328ft/-100m 0	820ft	1640ft	3281ft	6562ft	9843ft	13,124ft	19,685ft

The Mediterranean

Population

- National capital

○ below 50,000 ○ 50,000 to 100,000 ◉ 100,000 to 500,000 ■ above 500,000

In 1974 Turkey occupied the northern part of Cyprus while Greek Cypriots remained in control of the south. Cyprus was effectively partitioned and a UN buffer zone currently divides the two areas. In 1983 the north of the island proclaimed itself the Turkish Republic of North Cyprus. It was only recognized by Turkey.

Elevation

					Below sea level	0		250m	500m	1000m	2000m	3000m	4000m	6000m
-6000m	-4000m	-2000m	-1000m	500m	-250m									

| -19,658ft | -13,124ft | -6562ft | -3281ft | -1640ft | -820ft | -328ft/-100m | 0 | 820ft | 1640ft | 3281ft | 6562ft | 9843ft | 13,124ft | 19,685ft |

Bulgaria & Greece

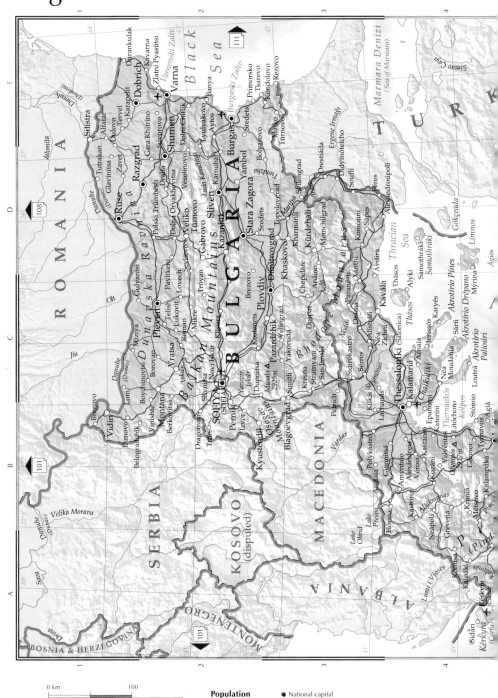

0 km 100

0 miles 100

Population   ● National capital

○ below 50,000   ○ 50,000 to 100,000   ◉ 100,000 to 500,000   ■ above 500,000

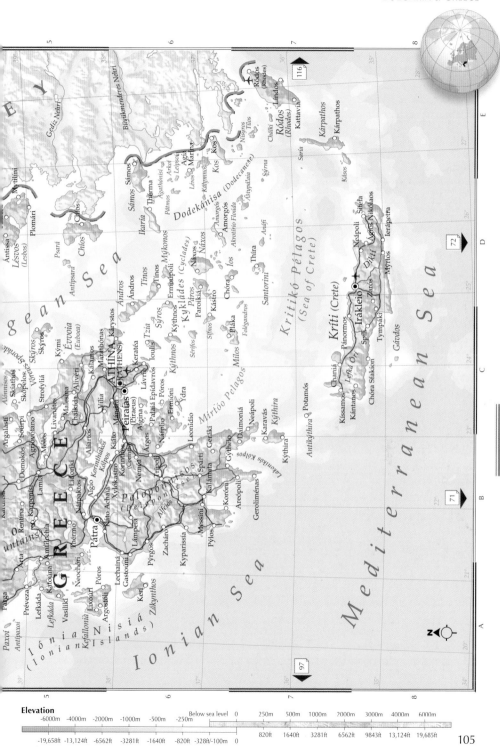

116

72

71

97

Elevation

						Below sea level	0	250m	500m	1000m	2000m	3000m	4000m	6000m
-6000m	-4000m	-2000m	-1000m	-500m	-250m									
-19,658ft	-13,124ft	-6562ft	-3281ft	-1640ft	-820ft	-328ft/-100m	0	820ft	1640ft	3281ft	6562ft	9843ft	13,124ft	19,685ft

The Baltic States & Belarus

Population

- National capital
- ○ below 50,000
- ○ 50,000 to 100,000
- ◉ 100,000 to 500,000
- ▣ above 500,000

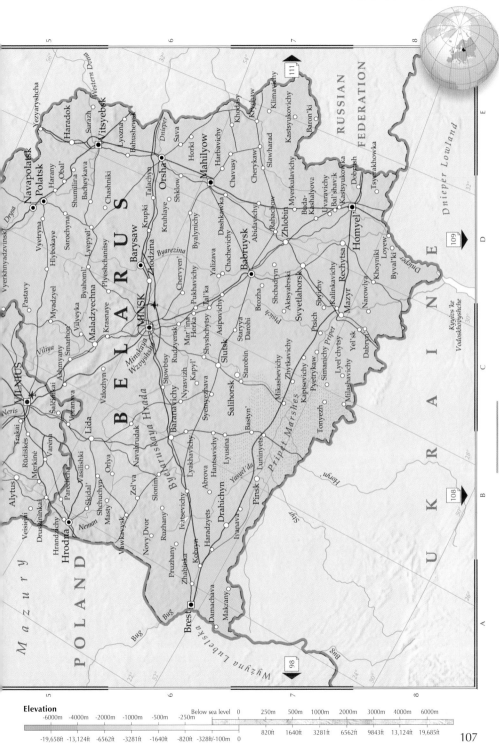

109

108

98

RUSSIAN FEDERATION

U K R A I N E

P O L A N D

M a z u r y

B E L A R U S

Dnieper Lowland

Navapolatsk
Polatsk
Vitsyebsk
Haradok
Surazh
Lyozna
Bahushewsk
Obal'
Shumilina
Bacheykava
Chashniki
Orsha
Talachyn
Mahilyow
Horki
Shklow
Sava
Khislavichy
Khodasy
Klimavichy
Krychaw
Kastsyukovichy
Slawharad
Cherykaw
Harbavichy
Chavusy
Myerkulavichy
Bluda-Kashalyova
Baron'ki
Uvaravichy
Bal'shavik
Kastsyukowka
Dobrush
Tsvetakhowka
Homyel'
Barysaw
Hrodzina
MINSK
Babruysk
Zhlobin
Rahachow
Abidavichy
Shchadryn
Brozha
Aktsyabrski
Svyetlahorsk
Rechytsa
Mazyr
Kalinkavichy
Narowlya
Loyew
Khoyniki
Byval'ki
Brahin

Elevation

-6000m -4000m -2000m -1000m -500m Below sea level 0 250m 500m 1000m 2000m 3000m 4000m 6000m
                                        -250m
-19,658ft -13,124ft -6562ft -3281ft -1640ft -820ft -328ft/-100m 0 820ft 1640ft 3281ft 6562ft 9843ft 13,124ft 19,685ft

Ukraine, Moldova & Romania

BELARUS

POLAND

Małopolska

Wyżyna Lubelska

Wisła

Kovel'
Sarny
Olevs'k
Ovru

Volodymyr-Volyns'kyy
Novovolyns'k
Kivertsi
Korosten
Luts'k
Rivne
Malyn
Sokal'
Dubno
Novohrad-Volyns'kyy
Radomyshl'

Carpathian Mountains

Zhovkva
Chervonohrad
Slavuta
Shepetivka
Zhytomyr
Yavoriv
L'viv
Zolochiv
Kremenets'
Izyaslav
Polonne
Berdychiv

Tatra Mountains

Horodok
Zbarazh
Starokostyantyniv
Kozyat

SLOVAKIA

Sámbir
Drohobych
Khodoriv
Berezhany
Ternopil'
Khmel'nyts'kyy
Vinnytsya

Slovenské Rudohorie

Boryslav
Stryy
Zhydachiv

U K R

Kalush
Chortkiv
Lypovets'

Uzhhorod
Dolyna
Ivano-Frankivs'k
Zhmerynka

Tisza

Nadvirna
Kam"yanets'-Podil's'kyy
Haysyn

Mukacheve
Kolomyya
Mohyliv-Podil's'kyy
Tul'chyn

Berehove
Chernivtsi

Podil's'ka Vysochina

Vynohradiv
Khust
Hora Hoverla 2061m
Negreşti-Oaş
Darabani

HUNGARY

Satu Mare
Dorohoi
Soroca
Balta

Carei
Baia Mare
Rădăuţi
Botoşani
Bălţi
Ribniţa
Koto

Marghita
Baia Sprie
Borşa
Solca
Suceava
Streţ

Şimleu Silvaniei
Zalău
Năsăud
Fălticeni
MOLDOVA

Great Hungarian Plain

Oradea
Aleşd
Dej
Bistriţa
Toplita
Târgu-Neamţ
Paşcani
Iaşi
Călăraşi
Orher

Salonta
Beiuş
Reghin
Bicaz
Roman
Ungheni
Strásent

Curtici
Ineu
Cluj-Napoca
Gheorgheni
Piatra-Neamţ
CHIŞINĂU
Tighin

Muntii Apuseni
Turda
Ludus
Bacău
(KISHNEV)
(Bender)

Sânnicolau Mare
Arad
Abrud
Târgu Mureş
Hincesti
Tiraspol

Mures
Lipova
Alba Iulia
Aiud
Mediaş
Cristuru Secuiesc
Miercurea-Ciuc
Vaslui

Jimbolia
Timişoara
Deva
Rupea
R O M A N I A
Târgu Ocna
Bârlad
Comrat
Basarabeas

Lugoj
Hunedoara
Sibiu
Făgăraş
Târgu Secuiesc
Adjud
Cahul
Cădir-Lunga

Bocşa
Oţelu Roşu
Cisnădie
Vârful Moldoveanu 2544m
Codlea
Sfântu Gheorghe
Taraclia
Artsyz

Reşiţa
Petroşani
Câmpulung
Braşov
Focşani
Tecuci
Bolhrad

Anina
Moldova Nouă
Carpaţii Meridionali
Râşnov
Râmnicu Sărat
Galaţi
Ozero Yalpuh
Kiliya

Oraviţa
Târgu Jiu
Călimăneşti
Sinaia
Câmpina
Brăila
Izmayil

Orşova
Motru
Curtea de Argeş
Moreni
Buzău
Măcin
Isaccea
Tulcea

Drobeta-Turnu Severin
Strehaia
Piteşti
Titu
Ploieşti
Urziceni
Babadag

Filiaşi
Drăgăşani
Târgovişte
Mizil
Lacul Razim

SERBIA

Wallachia

Craiova
Slatina
Buftea
BUCUREŞTI (BUCHAREST)
Slobozia
Feteşti
Lacul Sinoie

Balş
Caracal
Alexandria
Olteniţa
Călăraşi
Medgidia

Velika Morava

Calafat
Roşiori de Vede
Turnu Măgurele
Ţăndărei
Hârşova

Corabia
Zimnicea
Giurgiu
Techirghiol
Constanţa

Danube (Dunărea)

Jiu
Olt
Ialomiţa

Dunavska Ravnina

Eforie-Sud
Mangalia

BULGARIA

0 km 100
0 miles 100

Population ● National capital

○ below 50,000 ○ 50,000 to 100,000 ◉ 100,000 to 500,000 ▣ above 500,000

E F G H

Horodnya
Shchors   Shostka
Hlukhiv
Chernihiv   Krolevets'
Konotop
Nizhyn   Bakhmach
Oster   Romny   Sumy
Nosivka
KYIV   Brovary   Pryluky   Lebedyn
Yahotyn   Pyryatyn   Okhtyrka   Zolochiv
Vasyl'kiv   Hrebinka   Lubny   Derhachi
astiv   Myrhorod   Lyubotyn   Kharkiv
Bila Tserkva   Kaniv   Kaniv'ke
Vodoskhovyshche   Mereta
Bohuslav
Horodyshche   Hlobyne   Poltava
Zvenyhorodka   Cherkasy   Starobil's'k
Tal'ne   Smila   Kremenchuts'ke   Izyum   Kreminna
Shpola   Chyhyryn   Vodoskhovyshche   Rubizhne
Oleksandrivka   Svitlovods'k   Kremenchuk   Slov"yans'k   Syeverodonets'k
Mala Vyska   Znam"yanka   Dniprodzerzhyns'ke   Kramators'k   Lysychans'k
han   Holovanivs'k   Zhovti Vody   Dnioprodzerzhyns'k   Vodoskhovyshche   Novomoskovs'k   Zolote
Ulyanivka   Kirovohrad   Dnipropetrovs'k   Pavlohrad   Kostyantynivka   Luhans'k
Vil'shanka   Dolyns'ka   P"yatykhatky   Horlivka   Slakhanov
Pervomays'k   Bobrynets'   Kryvyy Rih   Synel'nykovo   Yenakiyeve   Krasnodon
Kryve Ozero   Arbuzynka   Pokrovs'ke   Makiyivka   Krasnyy Luch
Inhulets'   Nikopol'   Zaporizhzhya   Donets'k   Torez
Novyy Buh   Ordzhonikidze   Orikhiv   Volnovakha   Dokuchayevs'k   Amvrosiyivka
Voznesens'k   Marhanets   Dniprorudne   Polohy   Novoazovs'k
Kam"yanka-Dniprovs'ka   Tokmak
Kakhovs'ka   Molochans'k   Mariupol'
Mykolayiv   Vodoskhovyshche
Zhovtneve   Dnieper   Melitopol'
Ochakiv   Kherson   Kakhovka   Yakymivka   Gulf of Taganrog
Odesa   Hola Prystan'   Tsyurupyns'k   Novotroyits'ke   Prymors'k   Berdyans'k
Illichivs'k   Chaplynka   Heniches'k
Kalanchak   Armyans'k   Sea of Azov
Krasnoperekops'k
Karkinits'ka Zatoka   Rozdol'ne   Dzhankoy
Krasnohvardiys'ke   Zatoka   Kerch   Kerch Strait
Chornomors'ke   Nyzhn'ohirs'kyy   Syvash   RUSSIAN
Yevpatoriya   Kryms'kyy   Lenine   FEDERATION
Saky   Pivostriv   Feodosiya   Kuban'
Simferopol'
Bakhchysaray   Kryms'ki Hory
Sevastopol'   Alushta
Yalta
Alupka

RUSSIAN
FEDERATION

Dnieper
(Dnipro)
Desna
Desna
Psel
Oskil
Donets
Don
Srednerusskaya
Vozvyshennost'
Don
Yeya

Black Sea

Dnieper Lowland

Black Sea

E F G H

Elevation

| -6000m | -4000m | -2000m | -1000m | -500m | -250m | Below sea level 0 | 250m | 500m | 1000m | 2000m | 3000m | 4000m | 6000m |

| -19,658ft | -13,124ft | -6562ft | -3281ft | -1640ft | -820ft | -328ft/-100m 0 | | 820ft | 1640ft | 3281ft | 6562ft | 9843ft | 13,124ft | 19,685ft |

European Russia

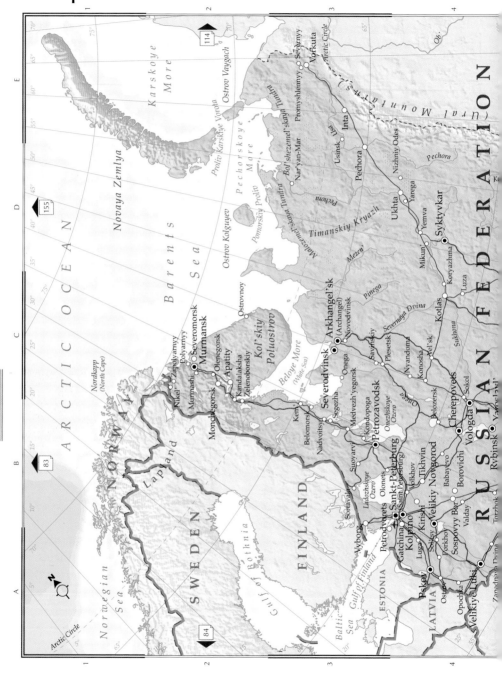

0 km 300

0 miles 300

Population

● National capital

○ below 50,000 ○ 50,000 to 100,000 ◉ 100,000 to 500,000 ▣ above 500,000

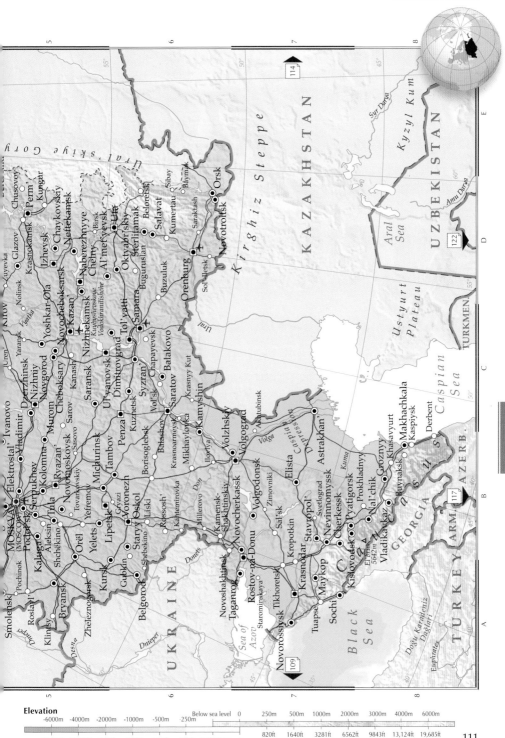

114

122

117

109

Ural'skiye Gory

KAZAKHSTAN

Kirghiz Steppe

UZBEKISTAN

Aral Sea

Kyzyl Kum

Syr Darya

Amu Darya

TURKMEN.

Ustyurt Plateau

Caspian Sea

TURKEY

ARM.

AZERB.

GEORGIA

Doğu Karadeniz Dağları

Euphrates

Black Sea

Sea of Azov

UKRAINE

Dnieper

Desna

Dnieper

Smolensk

Roslavl'

Klintsy

Bryansk

Zheleznogorsk

Kursk

Belgorod

Pochinok

Kaluga

Shchëkino

Gubkin

Shebekino

Staryy Oskol

Rossosh'

Liski

Kalach

MOSKVA
(MOSCOW)

Elektrostal'

Ivanovo

Vladimir

Podol'sk

Serpukhov

Aleksin

Tula

Tovarkovskiy

Yefremov

Yelets

Lipetsk

Gryazi

Voronezh

Orël

Chusovoy

Perm'

Kungur

Kizel

Guyevka

Glazov

Krasnokamsk

Izhevsk

Chaykovskiy

Neftekamsk

Nolinsk

Yaransk

Vyatka

Kirov

Uren'

Yoshkar-Ola

Dzerzhinsk

Nizhniy
Novgorod

Novocheboksarsk

Cheboksary

Kazan'

Kanash

Sarov

Sasovo

Murom

Kolomna

Ryazan'

Novomoskovsk

Michurinsk

Tambov

Kanash

Saransk

Nizhnekamsk

Naberezhnyye
Chelny

Birsk

Ufa

Oktyabr'skiy

Al'met'yevsk

Sterlitamak

Belebey

Beloretsk

Salavat

Meleuz

Kumertau

Sibay

Baymak

Orsk

Novotroitsk

Saraktash

Sol'-Iletsk

Orenburg

Buzuluk

Buguruslan

Kuybyshevskoye
Vodokhranilishche

Tol'yatti

Samara

Chapayevsk

Balakovo

Dimitrovgrad

Ul'yanovsk

Syzran'

Kuznetsk

Vol'sk

Penza

Saratov

Krasnyy Kut

Kamyshin

Mikhaylovka

Krasnoarmeysk

Balashov

Kamensk-
Shakhtinskiy

Millerovo

Morozovsk

Volgodonsk

Tsimlyansk

Sal'sk

Zimovniki

Elista

Akhtubinsk

Volzhskiy

Volgograd

Volga

Volga

Caspian
Depression

Astrakhan'

Kuma

Khasavyurt

Makhachkala

Kaspiysk

Derbent

Groznyy

Buynaksk

Nal'chik

Prokhladnyy

Pyatigorsk

Kislovodsk

Nevinnomyssk

Cherkessk

Svetlograd

Stavropol'

Budënnovsk

Vladikavkaz

El'brus
5642m

Maykop

Krasnodar

Tikhoretsk

Kropotkin

Armavir

Novorossiysk

Sochi

Tuapse

Novoshakhtinsk

Taganrog

Rostov-na-Donu

Novocherkassk

Shakhty

Staurominskaya

Don

Donets

Kakhtemirovka

Voronezh

Borisoglebsk

NOLINSK

55°

50°

45°

45°

50°

55°

60°

40°

45°

40°

5

6

7

8

E

D

C

B

A

Elevation

-6000m	-4000m	-2000m	-1000m	-500m	-250m	Below sea level	0	250m	500m	1000m	2000m	3000m	4000m	6000m
-19,658ft	-13,124ft	-6562ft	-3281ft	-1640ft	-820ft	-328ft/-100m	0	820ft	1640ft	3281ft	6562ft	9843ft	13,124ft	19,685ft

111

North & West Asia

A   B   C   D

ARCTIC

Franz Josef Land

155

Severnaya Zem.

Ostrov Komsomolets

Ostrov Oktyabr'skoy Revolyutsii
Ostrov Bol'shevik

Summer limit of pack ice

Winter limit of pack ice

Norwegian Sea

North Cape

Barents Sea

Ostrov Kolguyev

Novaya Zemlya
East Novaya Zemlya Trench

Kara Sea

Poluostrov Yamal

Poluostrov Taymyr

Oze Tayr

North Siberi

Kheta

Murmansk

Kola Peninsula

White Sea

RUSSIAN **FE**

Noril'sk

Central Siberian Plateau

Kurejka

81

Arctic Circle

Archangel

Lake Onega

Northern Dvina

Lake Ladoga

Saint Petersburg

Vologda

Yaroslavl'

Nizhniy Novgorod

MOSCOW

Central Russian Upland

Ul'yanovsk

Kazan'

Ufa

Samara

Perm'

West Siberian Plain

Ob'

Yekaterinburg

Irtysh

Ob'

Chelyabinsk

Omsk

Novosibirsk

Tomsk

Lower Tunguska

Stony Tunguska

Angara

Chulym

Yenisey

Si

Krasnoyarsk

Irkutsl

Novokuznetsk

KALININGRAD
KALININGRAD (to Russ. Fed.)

Kaliningrad

Baltic Sea

Gulf of Bothnia

Voronezh

Saratov

Volga

Orenburg

Ural'sk

Ural

ASTANA

Kirghiz Steppe

Karagandy

Kazakh Uplands

Semipalatinsk

Sayanskiy Khrebet

A

S

Altai Mountains

G

E U R O P E

Rostov-na-Donu

Don

Volgograd

Astrakhan'

Stavropol'

El'brus
5642m

Caucasus

Black Sea

Danube

Istanbul

Aktau

Ustyurt Plateau

Aral Sea

Syr Darya

Aral'sk

KAZAKHSTAN

Kyzyl Kum

Kyzylorda

Lake Balkhash

Ozero Zaysan

Il'

Almaty

Tien Shan

Pik Pobedy 7443m

GEORGIA

Küre Dağları

ARMENIA

TBILISI

BAKU

AZERB.

Daşoguz

UZBEKISTAN

Amu Darya

TURKMENISTAN

TASHKENT

KYRGYZSTAN

BISHKEK

ANKARA

YEREVAN

TURKEY

Adana

Gaziantep

Van

Tabriz

Lake Van

ASGABAT

Garagum

TAJIKISTAN

DUSHANBE

CYPRUS

SYRIA

IRAQ

DAMASCUS

BAGHDAD

Aleppo

Mosul

Qom

Isfahan

IRAN

TEHRAN

Iranian Plateau

KABUL

Herat

AFGHANISTAN

Jalalabad

Hindu Kush

Kunlun Mountains

Khyber Pass

Himalayas

LEBANON

BEIRUT

ISRAEL

AMMAN

JORDAN

JERUSALEM

*Dead Sea
- 423m*

An Nafud

Tigris

Euphrates

Syrian Desert

Basra

Shiraz

Zahedan

Zagros Mountains

Bandar-e 'Abbas

Thar Desert

Ganges

Ganges Fan

103

KUWAIT

KUWAIT

SAUDI ARABIA

MANAMA

BAHRAIN

RIYADH

QATAR

DOHA

Dubai

U.A.E.

MUSCAT

Persian Gulf

ABU DHABI

Sur

Gulf of Oman

Indus Fan

Murray Ridge

Tropic of Cancer

Jedda

At Ta'if

Arabian Peninsula

Red Sea

Ar Rub' al Khali

OMAN

A F R I C A

Nile

SANA

YEMEN

Ta'izz

Aden

Gulf of Aden

Socotra
(to Yemen)

Arabian Sea

Bay of Bengal

69

A   B   C   D

0 km   800
0 miles   800

Population

● National capital

○ below 50,000   ○ 50,000 to 100,000   ◉ 100,000 to 500,000   ■ above 500,000

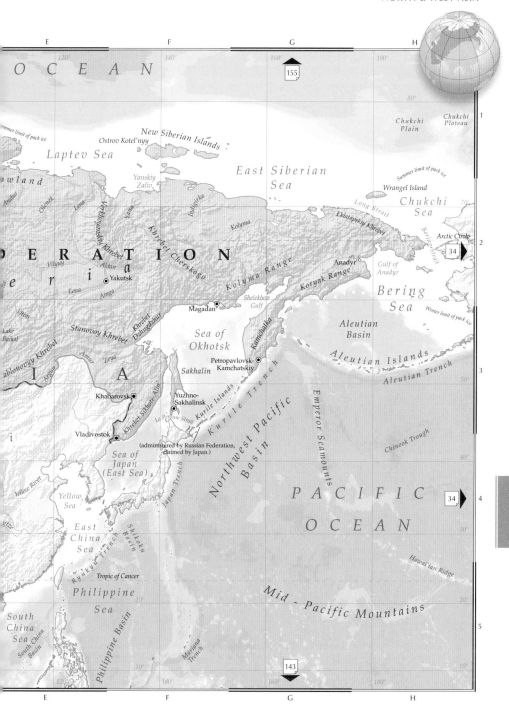

OCEAN

155

Chukchi
Plain

Chukchi
Plateau

1

Summer limit of pack ice

New Siberian Islands

Ostrov Kotel'nyy

Laptev Sea

East Siberian
Sea

Summer limit of pack ice

Wrangel Island

Chukchi
Sea

Yanskiy
Zaliv

Indigirka

Kolyma

Long Strait

Ekiatapskiy Khrebet

Bering Strait

Arctic Circle

34

Olenek

Lena

Verkhoyanskiy Khrebet

Khrebet Cherskogo

Kolyma Range

Koryak Range

Anadyr

Gulf of
Anadyr

2

Vilyuy

Aldan

Yakutsk

Shelekhov
Gulf

Bering
Sea

Winter limit of pack ice

Lena

Amga

Magadan

Kamchatka

Aleutian
Basin

Vitim

Stanovoy Khrebet

Khrebet Dzhugdzhur

Sea of
Okhotsk

Petropavlovsk-
Kamchatskiy

Aleutian Islands

Aleutian Trench

3

Lake
Baikal

Yablonovyy Khrebet

Amur

Zeya

Sakhalin

Kurile Islands

Kurile Trench

Emperor Seamounts

Chinook Trough

Khabarovsk

Yuzhno-
Sakhalinsk

Khrebet Sikhote-Alin

Argun

Vladivostok

La Pérouse Strait

(administered by Russian Federation,
claimed by Japan.)

Northwest Pacific
Basin

PACIFIC

34

4

Sea of
Japan
(East Sea)

Japan Trench

OCEAN

Yellow River

Yellow
Sea

Shikoku
Basin

East
China
Sea

Hawaiian Ridge

Ryukyu Trench

Tropic of Cancer

Philippine
Sea

Mid - Pacific Mountains

5

South
China
Sea

Philippine Basin

South China
Basin

Mariana
Trench

E   F   G   H

143

Russia & Kazakhstan

Population

● National capital

○ below 50,000 ○ 50,000 to 100,000 ◉ 100,000 to 500,000 ◼ above 500,000

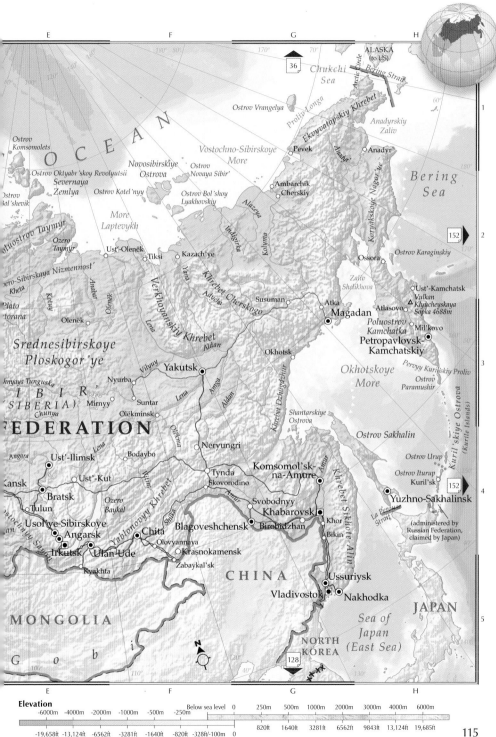

36

ALASKA
(to US)

*Chukchi
Sea*

Bering Strait

Ostrov Vrangelya

Prolip Longa

Ekvyoatapskiy Khrebet

Anadyrskiy
Zaliv

1

OCEAN

*Vostochno-Sibirskoye
More*

Pevek

Anadyr'

60°

Ostrov
Komsomolets

Novosibirskiye
Ostrova

Ostrov
Novaya Sibir'

Ambarchik
Cherskiy

*Bering
Sea*

Ostrov Oktyabr'skoy Revolyutsii
Severnaya
Zemlya

Ostrov Kotel'nyy

Ostrov Bol'shoy
Lyakhovskiy

Alazeya

Koryakskoye Nagor'ye

Ostrov
Bol'shevik

*More
Laptevykh*

Indigirka

Kolyma

Ossora

Ostrov Karaginskiy

152

2

Poluostrov Taymyr

Ozero
Taymyr

Ust'-Olenëk

Tiksi

Kazach'ye

Yana

Adycha

Zaliv
Shelikhova

Ust'-Kamchatsk
Vulkan
Klyucheyskaya
Sopka 4688m

Severo-Sibirskaya Nizmennost'

Kheta

Anabar

Olenëk

Verkhoyanskiy Khrebet

Khrebet Cherskogo

Susuman

Atka

Atlasovo

*Poluostrov
Kamchatka*

Mil'kovo

Plato
Putorana

Kotuy

Olenëk

Lena

Aldan

Magadan

Petropavlovsk-
Kamchatskiy

50°

*Srednesibirskoye
Ploskogor'ye*

Vilyuy

Yakutsk

Okhotsk

*Okhotskoye
More*

Pervyy Kuril'skiy Proliv
Ostrov
Paramushir

3

Nizhnyaya Tunguska

Nyurba

Amga

Aldan

Khrebet Dzhugdzhur

Chunya

Mirnyy

Suntar

Olëkminsk

Lena

Olëkma

Shantarskiye
Ostrova

Ostrov Sakhalin

*SIBIR'
(SIBERIA)*

FEDERATION

Neryungri

Ostrov Urup

Kuril'skiye Ostrova
(Kurile Islands)

Angara

Ust'-Ilimsk

Bodaybo

Vitim

Tynda

Komsomol'sk-
na-Amure

Amur

Khrebet Sikhote-Alin'

Ostrov Iturup
Kuril'sk

152

4

Kansk

Ust'-Kut

Skovorodino

Amur

Svobodnyy

Khabarovsk

La Perouse Strait

Yuzhno-Sakhalinsk

Bratsk

Tulun

Ozero
Baykal

Shilka

Blagoveshchensk

Birobidzhan

Khor

(administered by
Russian Federation,
claimed by Japan)

Vostochnyy Sayan

Usol'ye-Sibirskoye

Angarsk

Chita

Olovyannaya

Bikin

Yablonovyy Khrebet

Irkutsk

Ulan-Ude

Krasnokamensk

Ussuriysk

Kyakhta

Zabaykal'sk

CHINA

Vladivostok

Nakhodka

5

MONGOLIA

G o b i

N

**NORTH
KOREA**

*Sea of
Japan
(East Sea)*

JAPAN

128

Elevation

					Below sea level	0	250m	500m	1000m	2000m	3000m	4000m	6000m
-6000m	-4000m	-2000m	-1000m	-500m	-250m								
-19,658ft	-13,124ft	-6562ft	-3281ft	-1640ft	-820ft	-328ft/-100m	0	820ft	1640ft	3281ft	6562ft	9843ft	13,124ft	19,685ft

Turkey & the Caucasus

ROMANIA
Lacul Sinoie

UKRAINE
Kryms'kyy
Pivostriv

BULGARIA

Varnenski
Zaliv

Burgaski
Zaliv

B l a c k   S e a

Maritsa

Kırklareli
Edirne
Çorlu
Tekirdağ
Bandırma
Çanakkale

Ergene Çayı

İstanbul Boğazı
(Bosporus)

Zonguldak
Cide
İnebolu
Sinop
Gerze
Bartın
Küre Dağları
Kastamonu
Bafra
Karabük
Samsun
Devrek
Çerkeş
Kargı
Ünye
Ord

Marmara Denizi
(Sea of Marmara)
İstanbul
İzmit
Adapazarı
Yalova
İznik Gölü
Bursa
Bilecik

Bolu
Gerede
Çankırı
Kızıl Irmak
Merzifon
Çanik Dağları
Çorum
Tokat
Yıldızeli

Çanakkale
Boğazı
(Dardanelles)
Balıkesir
Edremit
Ayvalık

Bozüyük
Eskişehir
ANKARA
Kalecik
Alaca
Sorgun
Sivas

Lésvos
Akhisar
Manisa
Menemen
Chíos
İzmir
Ödemiş
Sámos

Kütahya
Simav
Gediz
Uşak
Afyon

Polatlı
Kırıkkale
Hirfanlı
Barajı
Kulu
Tuz Gölü
İncesu
Şarkışla
Bozağlıyan
Bünyan
Gürün

T U R K

Aydın
Nazilli
Alaşehir
Dinar
Denizli
Burdur
İsparta

Büyükmenderes Nehri
Anatolia
Beyşehir
Gölü
Cihanbeyli
Akşehir
Aksaray
Nevşehir
Niğde
Kayseri
Göksun
Gü n

Söke
Milas
Tavas
Burdur
Gölü
Konya
Ereğli
Kahramanmar

Bodrum
Muğla
Dalaman
Sugla Gölü
Karaman
Toros Dağları
Tarsus
Ceyhan
Gazian

Marmaris
Fethiye
Kaş
Finike
Antalya
Manavgat
Alanya
Mut
Mersin (İçel)
Silifke
İskenderun
Adana
Osmaniye
Kilis
Antakya
Kırıkhan

GREEC

Dodekánisa
(Dodecanese)
Ródos
(Rhodes)
Kárpathos

Antalya
Körfezi
Anamur

Orontes

TURKISH REPUBLIC OF
NORTHERN CYPRUS
(recognized only by Turkey)

CYPRUS

M e d i t e r r a n e a n
S e a

LEBANON

0 km   200

0 miles   200

Population   ● National capital

○ below 50,000   ○ 50,000 to 100,000   ◉ 100,000 to 500,000   ◙ above 500,000

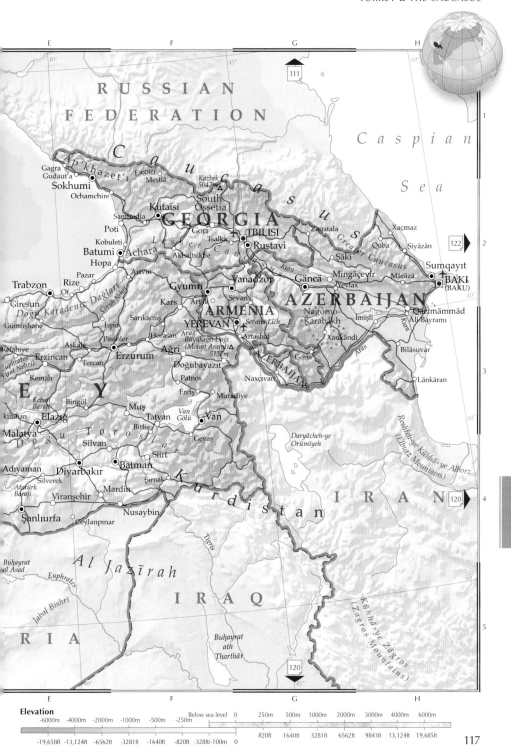

RUSSIAN FEDERATION

Caspian Sea

Caucasus

Gagra
Gudaut'a
Sokhumi
Ochamchire
Ap'khazet'i
Enguri
Mestia
Kazbek
5047m △
Kutaisi
South Ossetia
GEORGIA
Samtredia
Gori
Poti
Tsalka
TBILISI
Zaqatala
Xaçmaz
Kobuleti
Akhaltsikhe
Rustavi
Quba
Siyäzän
Batumi
Achara
Lesser Caucasus
Şäki
122
Hopa
Artvin
Kura
Mingäçevir
Märäzä
Sumqayıt
Pazar
Rize
Gyumri
Vanadzor
Gäncä
Yevlax
BAKI
(BAKU)
Trabzon
Of
Ani
Sevan
AZERBAIJAN
Giresun
Doğu Karadeniz Dağları
Kars
Çoruh Nehri
Sevana Lich
Nagorno-
Karabakh
Qazimämmäd
Gümüşhane
İspir
ARMENIA
YEREVAN
Imişli
Ali-Bayramı
Refahiye
Askale
Pasihler
Sarıkamış
Horasan
Artashat
Xankändi
Biläsuvar
Erzincan
Tercan
Ağri
Doğubayazıt
Büyükağrı Dağı
(Mount Ararat) △
5137m
Goris
Aras
Naxçıvan
Länkäran
Kemah
Patnos
AZERBAIJAN
E Y
Bingöl
Erciş
Muradiye
Keban Barajı
Elazığ
Muş
Tatvan
Van Gölü
Van
Daryācheh-ye Orūmīyeh
Malatya
Bitlis
Reshteh-ye Kūhhā-ye Alborz (Elburz Mountains)
kımlan
Silvan
Gevaş
Adıyaman
Toroslar
Siirt
I R A N
120
Diyarbakır
Batman
Silverek
Şırnak
Atatürk Barajı
Viranşehir
Mardin
Kurdistan
Nusaybin
Kūhhā-ye Zagros (Zagros Mountains)
Şanlıurfa
Ceylanpınar
Tigris
Buhayrat al Asad
Al Jazīrah
Euphrates
Jabal Bishrī
I R A Q
RIA
Buhayrat ath Tharthār

Elevation

-6000m	-4000m	-2000m	-1000m	-500m	-250m	Below sea level	0	250m	500m	1000m	2000m	3000m	4000m	6000m

| -19,658ft | -13,124ft | -6562ft | -3281ft | -1640ft | -820ft | -328ft/-100m | 0 | 820ft | 1640ft | 3281ft | 6562ft | 9843ft | 13,124ft | 19,685ft |

The Near East

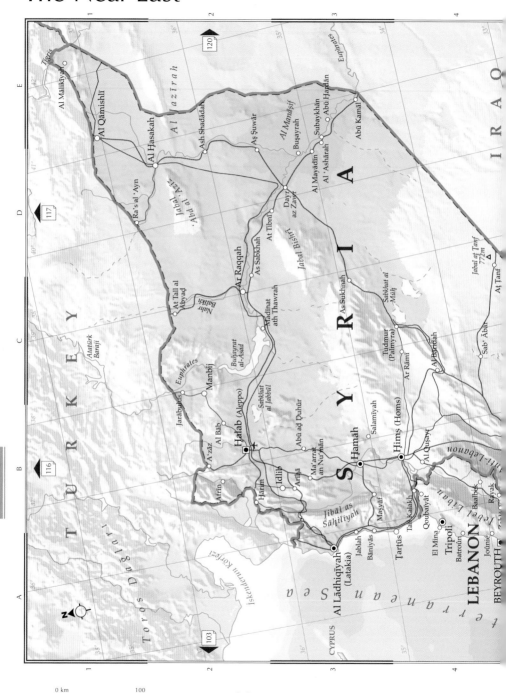

Population ● National capital

○ below 50,000 ○ 50,000 to 100,000 ◉ 100,000 to 500,000 ■ above 500,000

0 km 100
0 miles 100

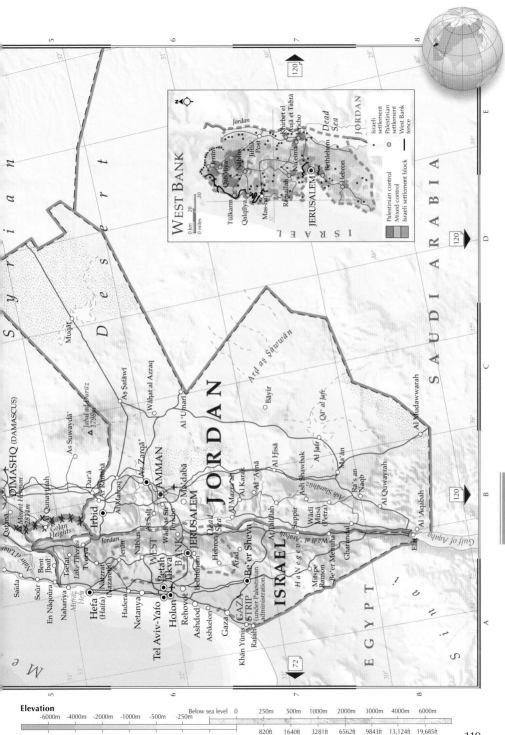

WEST BANK

Túlkarm
Qalqílya
Mas'ha
Jenin
Qabâtiya
Nãblus
Post
Ariha/
Jericho
Khirbet el 'Auja et Tahtã
Nu'eima
Ramallah
JERUSALEM
Bethlehem
Hebron

Jordan

Dead Sea

JORDAN

ISRAEL

Israeli settlement
Palestinian settlement
West Bank fence

Palestinian control
Mixed control
Israeli settlement block

0 km   20
0 miles   20

Elevation

Below sea level													
-6000m	-4000m	-2000m	-1000m	-500m	-250m	0	250m	500m	1000m	2000m	3000m	4000m	6000m
-19,658ft	-13,124ft	-6562ft	-3281ft	-1640ft	-820ft	-328ft/-100m	0	820ft	1640ft	3281ft	6562ft	9843ft	13,124ft	19,685ft

The Middle East

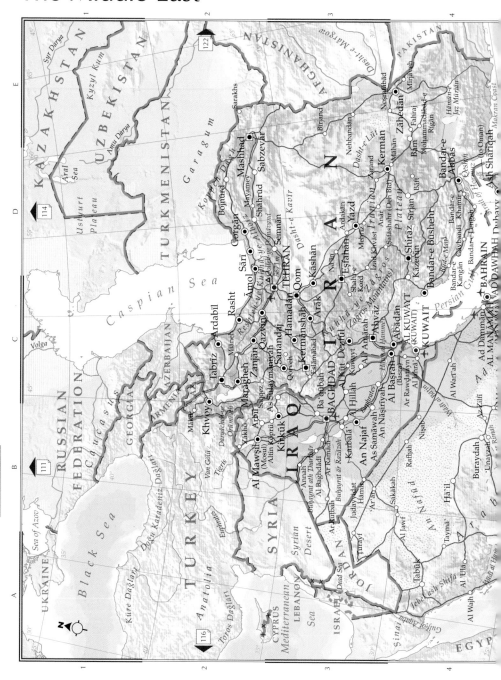

122

Population

● National capital

○ below 50,000

○ 50,000 to 100,000

◎ 100,000 to 500,000

■ above 500,000

0 km   400

0 miles   400

140

140

73

73

(MUSCAT)
Sūr
Ar Rustāq
Ramlat
Al Ghābah
Jazīrat
Maṣīrah
Al Ghābah
Khalīj
Maṣīrah
Al Ghābah
Duqm
Sawqirah

O M A N

Thamarīt
Ṣalālah
Damqawt

U N I T E D   A R A B
E M I R A T E S
ABU ẒABI
(ABU DHABI)

Arabian
Sea

INDIAN

OCEAN

Raas Xaafuun

Suqutrā
(Socotra)
(to Yemen)

S A U D I   A R A B I A

Ar Rub' al Khālī
(Empty Quarter)

Al Mahrah

Sayḥūt

Sanāw

Y E M E N

Hadramawt

Ash Shiḥr
Al Mukallā

Tarīm
Sayʼūn

Gulf of Aden

S O M A L I A

SOMALILAND
(not internationally
recognized)

Ogaden

AR RIYAḌ
(RIYADH)

Jabal Ṭuwayq

Laylá

As Sulayyil

Wudayʼah

Ramlat
Dahm

Ramlat
as Sabʼatayn

Najrān

Khamis Mushayt
Tathlīth
Qal'at Bīshah
Abhā
Al Bāḥah
Shuqrah

Adan
(Aden)

SAN'Ā'
(SANA)

 Taʼizz

Peninsula

Zalim
Turabah
Aṭ Ṭāʼif

Jabal Sawda'

Shabwa
Jizān
Sa'dah

Zabid

Al Hudaydah
(Hodeida)

D J I B O U T I

Turabah

Ḥarrat Raḥaṭ

(Medina)

Al Lith
Makkah
(Mecca)
Jiddah
(Jedda)

Jazāʼir
Farasān

E R I T R E A

E T H I O P I A

Ethiopian
Highlands

Great Rift Valley

Danakil Desert

Red
Sea

S U D A N

Yambu' al Baḥr

Nubian
Desert

Bāb el Mandeb

Elevation

-6000m	-4000m	-2000m	-1000m	-500m	-250m	Below sea level 0	250m	500m	1000m	2000m	3000m	4000m	6000m
-19,658ft	-13,124ft	-6562ft	-3281ft	-1640ft	-820ft	-328ft/-100m	0	820ft	1640ft	3281ft	6562ft	9843ft	13,124ft	19,685ft

121

Central Asia

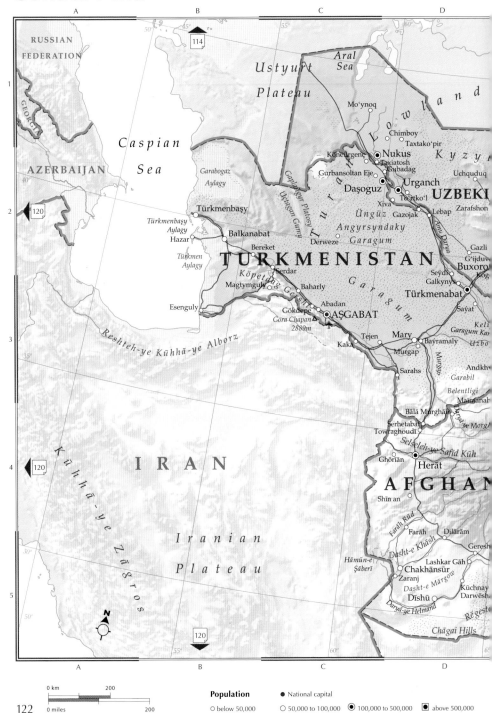

RUSSIAN
FEDERATION

GEORGIA

Caspian

Sea

AZERBAIJAN

Garabogaz
Aylagy

Türkmenbaşy

Türkmenbaşy
Aylagy
Hazar

Türkmen
Aylagy

Balkanabat

Bereket

TURKMENISTAN

Köpetdag Gersh

Magtymguly   Serdar

Baharly

Esenguly

Gökdepe
Gora Chapan △
2889m

Abadan

AŞGABAT

Kaka

Tejen

Mary

Murgap

Sarahs

Ustyurt

Plateau

Aral
Sea

Mo'ynoq

Chimboy
Taxtako'pir

Küneürgenç   Nukus
Taxiatosh   Qubadag
Gurbansoltan Eje

Daşoguz   Urganch

Xiva   To'rtko'l   UZBEKI

Üngüz   Gazojak   Lebap   Zarafshon

Angyrsyndaky   Amu Darya

Garagum   Gazli

G'ijduv

Buxoro
Seýdi   Kog
Galkynyş

Türkmenabat   Saýat

Garagum   Keli
Garagum Kan

Uzbo

Baýramaly   Andkh
Garabil
Belentligi
Mainjanal

Bālā Murghāb

Serhetabat   Murgāb-ye Morgl
Towraghoudī

Selseleh-ye Safid Küh

Ghōrīān   Herāt

IRAN   AFGHAN

Reshteh-ye Kūhhā-ye Alborz

Kūhhā-ye Zāgros

Iranian

Plateau

Shīn an

Farah Rūd

Farāh   Dilārām

Dasht-e Khāsh   Geresh

Hāmūn-e   Lashkar Gāh
Şāberi   Chakhānsūr
Zaranj   Küchnay
Dasht-e Mārgow   Darwēsh

Dīshū

Darya-ye Helmand   Régest

Chāgai Hills

Gaplañgyr Platosy

Turan Lowland

Kyzy

Uchquduq

Zarafshon

Mo'ynoq

114

120

120

120

0 km   200
0 miles   200

Population   ● National capital

○ below 50,000   ○ 50,000 to 100,000   ◉ 100,000 to 500,000   ▣ above 500,000

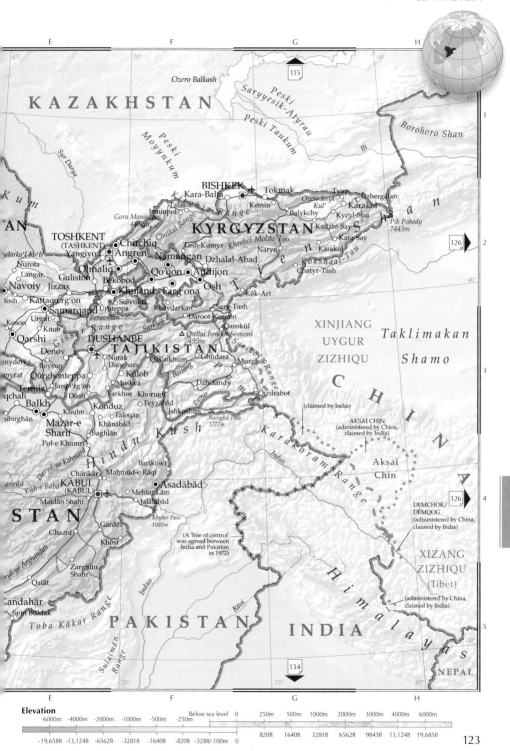

KAZAKHSTAN

Ozero Balkash

Peski Saryyesik-Atyrau

Peski Taukum

Peski Moýynkum

Borohoro Shan

Syr Darya

Ili

BISHKEK Tokmak
Kara-Balta *Ozero Issyk-* Tyup Dzhergalan
Íteninpol Kemin *Kul'* Karakol
Talas Balykchy Kyzyl-Suu
Gora Manas Kadzhi-Say Kara-Say **Pik Pobedy**
4482m K_yr_gyz Range **7443m**

TOSHKENT
(TASHKENT) Chirchiq **KYRGYZSTAN** *Chatkal Range*
Yangiyo'l Angren Namangan *Khrebet Moldo-Too*
Olmaliq Qo'qon Andijon Naryn Karakol
Bekobod *Kokshaal-Tau*
Nurota Guliston Osh Chatyr-Tash
Langar Jizzax **Khujand** Farg'ona
Navoiy Kök-Art
tosh Kattaqo'rg'on Uroteppa Sulyukta
Koson **Samarqand** *Zeravshan* Khaydarkan Sary-Tash
Urgut *Range* Daroot-Korgon
Kitob Qarokül

Qarshi *Gissar* **DUSHANBE** △ *Qullai Ismoili Somoni* **XINJIANG**
Denov **TAJIKISTAN** **7495m** **UYGUR** *Taklimakan*
myderya Norak Qal'aikhum Ghüdara **ZIZHIQU** *Shamo*
Boysun Danghara Murghob
myrat Qürghonteppa Külob Moskva *Sarikol Range*
Jarqo'rg'on Dûsti Farkhor *Bartang* Dzhelandy
qchah Termiz Khorugh Feyzäbad Qizilrobot **C**
Balkh Kongduz Täloqan *Pamir* **H**
nibirghän Khulm Khänäbäd Ishkoshim *Indus* (claimed by India) **I**
Mazar-e Baghlän *Baroghil Pass* **AKSAI CHIN** **N**
Sharif Pol-e Khumri 3777m (administered by China,
Hindu Barikowt claimed by India) **Aksai**
Darya-ye Kahmard Charikar Mahmūd-e Räqi **Chin** **A**
arirüd *Küh-e Bäbä* **KĀBUL** **Asadābād**
Kush (KABUL) **DEMCHOK/**
Maïdän Shahr Mehtaṛ Läm **DÉMQOG**
STAN Jaläläbäd (administered by China,
Ghazni *Khyber Pass* (A 'line of control' claimed by India)
Gardêz 1080m was agreed between **XIZANG**
Khôst India and Pakistan *Karakoram Range* **ZIZHIQU**
Zarghūn in 1972) **(Tibet)**
Qalät Shahr *Indus* (administered by China,
claimed by India)
andahar *Ravi*
Spin Buldak *Toba Kākar Range* **PAKISTAN** **INDIA** *Himalayas*

Sulaimān Range **NEPAL**

Elevation

-6000m	-4000m	-2000m	-1000m	-500m	-250m	Below sea level	0	250m	500m	1000m	2000m	3000m	4000m	6000m
-19,658ft	-13,124ft	-6562ft	-3281ft	-1640ft	-820ft	-328ft/-100m	0	820ft	1640ft	3281ft	6562ft	9843ft	13,124ft	19,685ft

South & East Asia

A B C D

Black Sea
Caspian Sea
Aral Sea
Syr Darya
Lake Balkash
40°
50°
60°
70°
80°
90°
100°
110°

112

1

Irtysh
Yenisey
Lake Baikal
Uvs Nuur
Hovsgol Nuur
Altai Mountains
Yablonovyy Khrebet
Erdenet
ULAN BATOR
Choybalsa
Kerulen
MONGOLIA
Plateau of Mongolia
Gobi
Baotou
Ordos Desert
Dator
Yellow River
Taiyuan

Iranian Plateau
A S I A
Tien Shan
Ürümqi
Turpan Pendi -154m
Tarim He
Tarim Basin
Takla Makan Desert
Altun Shan
Qilian Shan
Qaidam Pendi
Xiqing Shan
Lanzhou
Xi'an
Sichuan Pendi
Yangtze

112
2

20°

Hindu Kush
K2 8611m
Kunlun Mountains
Aksai Chin (administered by China claimed by India)
Denchok/Demqog (administered by China claimed by India)
Plateau of Tibet
C H I N A
Chengdu
Chongqing
Dong

Peshawar
ISLAMABAD
Gujranwala
Lahore
Jammu and Kashmir
Quetta
Faisalabad
Multan
Ludhiana
PAKISTAN
Indus
Bolan
Thar Desert
Himalayas
Brahmaputra
Salween
Mekong

Guiyang
Kunming
Nanning
Xi Ji

Arabian Peninsula
Persian Gulf
Gulf of Oman
Murray Ridge
Mouths of the Indus

Hyderabad
Karachi
Delhi
Jaipur
NEW DELHI
Kanpur
Yamuna
Ganges
NEPAL
KATHMANDU
Mount Everest 8850m
THIMPHU
BHUTAN
Guwahati
Imphal
Chindwin

Ahmadabad
Rann of Kachchh
Vindhya Range
Indore
Narmada
Satpura Range
Nagpur
Godavari
Patna
BANGLADESH
DHAKA
Khulna
Chittagong
Mandalay
VIETNAM
HANOI
Har Phon
Gulf of Tongking

3

Gulf of Khambhat
Mumbai (Bombay)
Pune
Solapur
Hyderabad
Hubli
INDIA
Deccan
Kolkata (Calcutta)
Mouths of the Ganges
MYANMAR (BURMA)
NAY PYI TAW
Bago
LAOS
Loungphabang
Vinh
VIENTIANE
Da N.

Arabian Sea
Arabian Basin
Laccadive Islands (to India)
Carlsberg Ridge
Owen Fracture Zone
Western Ghats
Eastern Ghats
Vijayawada
Bangalore
Chennai (Madras)
Mysore
Bay of Bengal
Andaman Islands (to India)
Rangoon
Pathein
Mouths of the Irrawaddy
Chiang Mai
THAILAND
BANGKOK
Tonle Sap
CAMBODIA
PHNOM PENH
Pakxe
Gulf of Thailand
Mekong
Hô Chi M
Mouths of the Mekong

4

69

Equator
Mid-Indian Ridge
Chagos-Laccadive Plateau
Jaffna
Gulf of Mannar
SRI LANKA
COLOMBO
SRI JAYEWARDENAPURA KOTTE
MALDIVES
MALE
Ceylon Plain
Nicobar Islands (to India)
Andaman Sea
Strait of Malacca
Malay Peninsula
Kota Bharu
Natuna Islands
Medan
Dumai?oba
MALA
KUALA LUMPUR
PUTRAJAYA
SINGAPORE
Pekanbaru
Pontianak
Sumatra
Greate
Bangka

INDIAN OCEAN
Cocos Basin
Padang
Ja

Mascarene Plateau
BRITISH INDIAN OCEAN TERRITORY (to UK)
Mid-Indian Basin
Ninetyeast Ridge
Palembang
JAKAR
Semar
Bandung
Jac
Java Trene

5

141

A B C D

N

0 km 1000
0 miles 1000

Population

• National capital

○ below 50,000
◎ 50,000 to 100,000
◉ 100,000 to 500,000
■ above 500,000

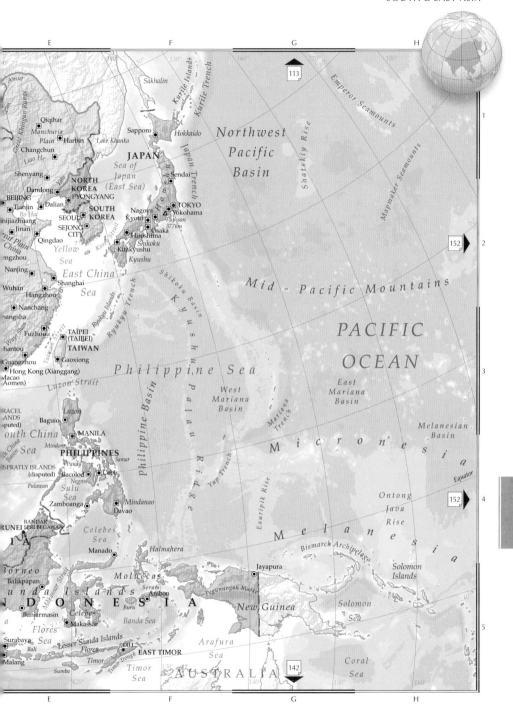

Western China & Mongolia

Population

- National capital
- Internal administrative capital
- ○ below 50,000
- ○ 50,000 to 100,000
- ◉ 100,000 to 500,000
- ■ above 500,000

0 km 400

0 miles 400

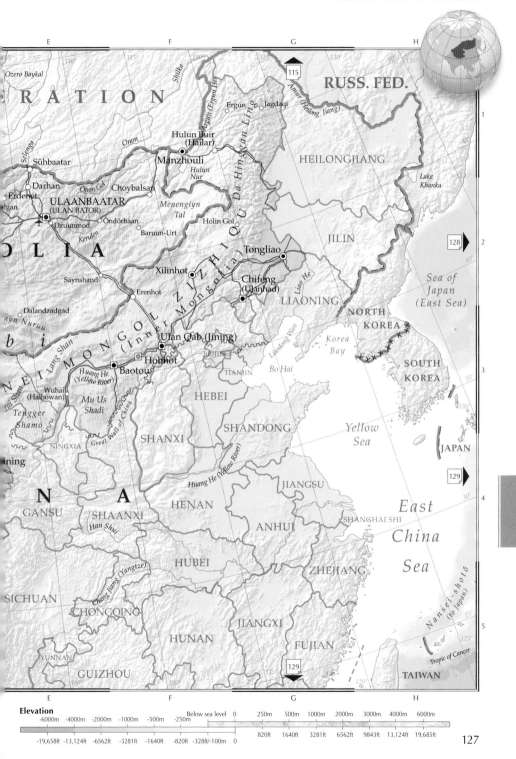

RUSS. FED.

Ozero Baykal

RATION

Shilka

Amur (Heilong Jiang)

Argun (Ergun He)

Ergun

Jagdaqi

HEILONGJIANG

Lake Khanka

Onon

Hulun Buir (Hailar)

Manzhouli

Sühbaatar

Selenga

Hulun Nur

Darhan

Onon Gol

Choybalsan

Erdenet

Menengiyn Tal

Kerulen

Dzuunmod

Öndörhaan

Holin Gol

JILIN

ULAANBAATAR (ULAN BATOR)

OLIA

Baruun-Urt

Tongliao

Saynshand

Xilinhot

Chifeng (Ulanhad)

Erenhot

Dalandzadgad

Liao He

LIAONING

NORTH KOREA

Sea of Japan (East Sea)

Dzavhan Nuruu

Ulan Qab (Jining)

BEIJING

SOUTH KOREA

bi

NEI Lang Shan MONGOL ZIZHIQU (Inner Mongolia)

Hohhot

TIANJIN

Bo Hai

Korea Bay

Huang He (Yellow River)

Baotou

JAPAN

Wuhai (Haibowan)

Mu Us Shadi

Great Wall of China

HEBEI

SHANDONG

Yellow Sea

Tengger Shamo

NINGXIA

SHANXI

ining

GANSU

N A

SHAANXI

Han Shui

Huang He (Yellow River)

HENAN

JIANGSU

East China Sea

SHANGHAI SHI

ANHUI

SICHUAN

Chang Jiang (Yangtze)

HUBEI

ZHEJIANG

Nansei-shotō (to Japan)

CHONGQING

JIANGXI

HUNAN

FUJIAN

Tropic of Cancer

YUNNAN

GUIZHOU

TAIWAN

Elevation

-6000m	-4000m	-2000m	-1000m	-500m	-250m	Below sea level	0	250m	500m	1000m	2000m	3000m	4000m	6000m
-19,658ft	-13,124ft	-6562ft	-3281ft	-1640ft	-820ft	-328ft/-100m	0	820ft	1640ft	3281ft	6562ft	9843ft	13,124ft	19,685ft

Eastern China & Korea

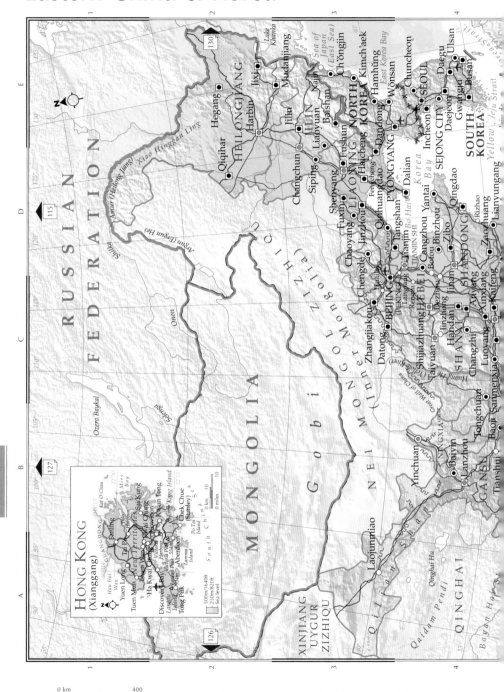

Population

● National capital   ● Internal administrative capital

○ below 50,000   ○ 50,000 to 100,000   ◉ 100,000 to 500,000   ◼ above 500,000

0 km   400

0 miles   400

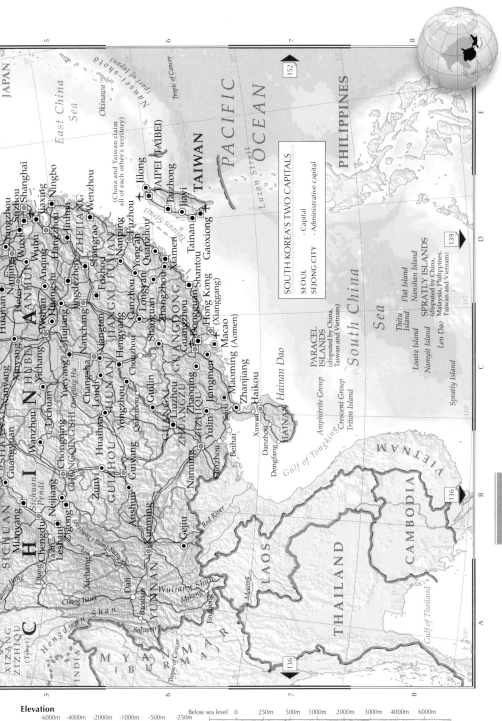

SOUTH KOREA'S TWO CAPITALS

SEOUL — Capital
SEJONG CITY — Administrative capital

Elevation

-6000m	-4000m	-2000m	-1000m	-500m	-250m	Below sea level	0	250m	500m	1000m	2000m	3000m	4000m	6000m
-19,658ft	-13,124ft	-6562ft	-3281ft	-1640ft	-820ft	-328ft/-100m	0	820ft	1640ft	3281ft	6562ft	9843ft	13,124ft	19,685ft

Japan

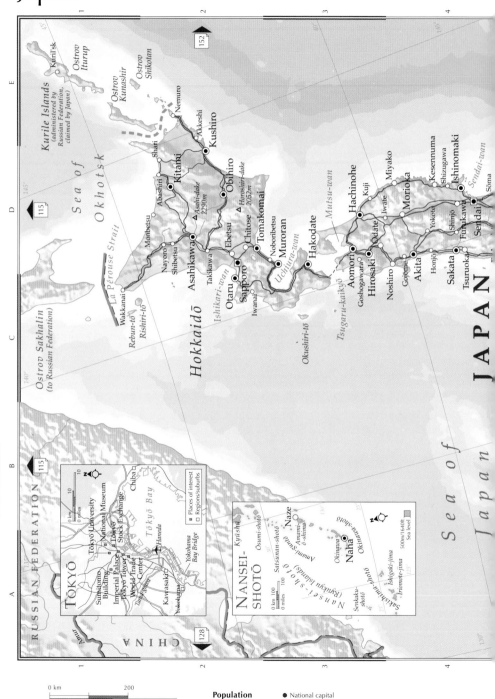

152

115

115

115

128

Kuril'sk
Ostrov Iturup

Kurile Islands
(administered by
Russian Federation,
claimed by Japan)

Ostrov Shikotan

Ostrov Kunashir

Nemuro

Akkeshi

Shari

Kushiro

Sea of
Okhotsk

Kitami

Abashiri

Monbetsu

Asahi-dake
2290m

Obihiro

Horoshiri-dake
2052m

Nayoro

Shibetsu

Takikawa

Ebetsu

Chitose

Tomakomai

Noboribetsu

Muroran

Uchiura-wan

Hakodate

Mutsu-wan

Hachinohe

Kuji

Miyako

Morioka

Kesennuma

Shizugawa

Ishinomaki

Sendai-wan

Soma

Sendai

La Pérouse Strait

Wakkanai

Rebun-tō
Rishiri-tō

Asahikawa

Ishikari-wan

Otaru

Sapporo

Iwanai

Takikawa

Hokkaidō

Oshushiri-tō

Tsugaru-kaikyō

Aomori

Goshogawara

Hirosaki

Noshiro

Gojōme

Honjō

Yokote

Ōdate

Iwate

Shinjō

Funakawa

Akita

Sakata

Tsuruoka

Ostrov Sakhalin
(to Russian Federation)

Sea of
Japan

JAPAN

Amur

RUSSIAN FEDERATION

Amur

CHINA

TŌKYŌ inset

Chiba

Tōkyō Bay

Tōkyō University

National Museum

Tōkyō
Stock Exchange

Tōkyō Tower

Sumitomo
Building

Imperial Palace

World Trade
Center

Tōkyō Tower

Haneda

Yokohama
Bay Bridge

TŌKYŌ

Kawasaki

Yokohama

■ Places of interest
□ Regions/suburbs

0 km   10
0 miles   10

NANSEI-SHOTŌ inset

Kyūshū

Ōsumi-shotō

Satsunan-shotō

Amami-shotō

Naze

Amami-
ō-shima

Okinawa

Naha

Okinawa

Nansei-shotō (Ryukyu Islands)

Tokara-rettō

Shigaki-jima

Sakishima-shotō

Iriomote-jima

Senkaku-shotō

**NANSEI-
SHOTŌ**

500m/1640ft
Sea level

0 km   100
0 miles   100

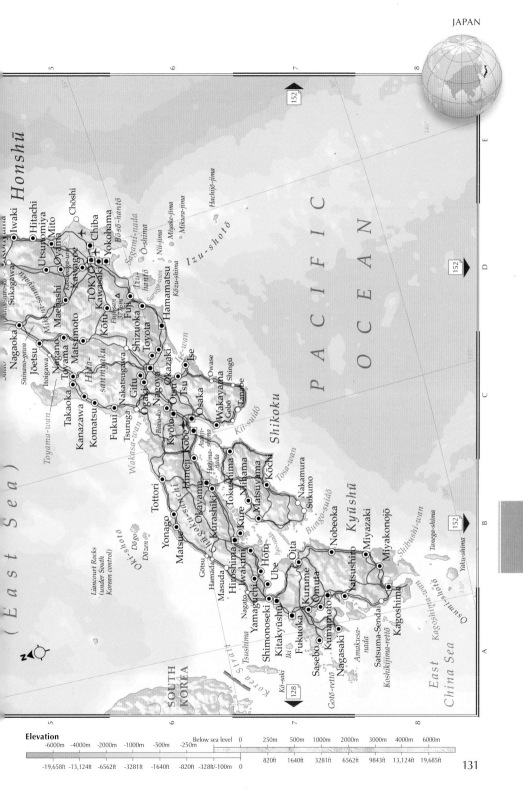

Southern India & Sri Lanka

Mumbai (Bombay)
Kalyān
Pune
Ahmadnagar
Bārāmati
Nizāmābād
Nānded
Jagdalpur
Karīmnagar
Vizianagaram
Solāpur
Sāngli
Secunderābād
Visākhapatna
Rājahmund
Kolhāpur
Gulbarga
Hyderābād
Kākinād
Belgaum
Rāichūr
Vijayawāda
Machilīpatnan
Panaji
Gadag
Kurnool
Andhra
Chirāla
Ongole
Hubli
Nandyāl
Pradesh
Kāvali
Tungabhadra
Reservoir
Tādpatri
Dāvangere
Anantapur
Nellore
Shimoga
Cuddapah
Bhadrāvati
Udupi
Tumkūr
Vellore
Chennai
(Madras)
Mangalore
Bangalore
Kānchīpuram
Kāsaragod
Mandya
Krishnagiri
Tiruppattūr
Kannur
Mysore
Salem
Pondicherry
Kozhikode
Erode
Neyveli
Coimbatore
Tamil Nādu
Tiruchchirāppalli
Thrissur
Ernākulam
Dindigul
Madurai
Kochi
Alappuzha
Rājapālaiyam
Jaffna
Kollam
Tuticorin
Mannar
Vavuniya
Thiruvananthapuram
Trincomalee
Nāgercoil
Gulf of
Mannar
Puttalam
Anuradhapura
Batticaloa
Negombo
Matale
Kandy
COLOMBO
SRI JAYEWARDENAPURA
KOTTE
Kalutara
Ratnapura
Galle
Matara

Arabian

Sea

*Amīndīvi
Islands*

*Lakshadweep
(Laccadive Islands)
(to India)*

*Kavaratti
Island*

*Kalpeni
Island*

*Nine Degree
Channel*

Minicoy Island

Eight Degree Channel

*Ihavandhippolhu
Atoll*

MALDIVES

*Faadhippolhu
Atoll*

*Horsburgh
Atoll*

Ari Atoll

Male'Atoll
MALE'

Felidhu Atoll

Mulakatholhu

Kolhumadulu

Hadhdhunmathi Atoll

North Huvadhu Atoll

*South Huvadhu
Atoll*

Equator

Addu Atoll
Gan

SRI LANKA

I N D I A N

SRI LANKA'S TWO CAPITALS

COLOMBO   - Capital
SRI JAYEWARDENAPURA KOTTE   - Administrative capital

Population		National capital
0 km 300		
0 miles 300	O below 50,000	● 100,000 to 500,000
	O 50,000 to 100,000	■ above 500,000

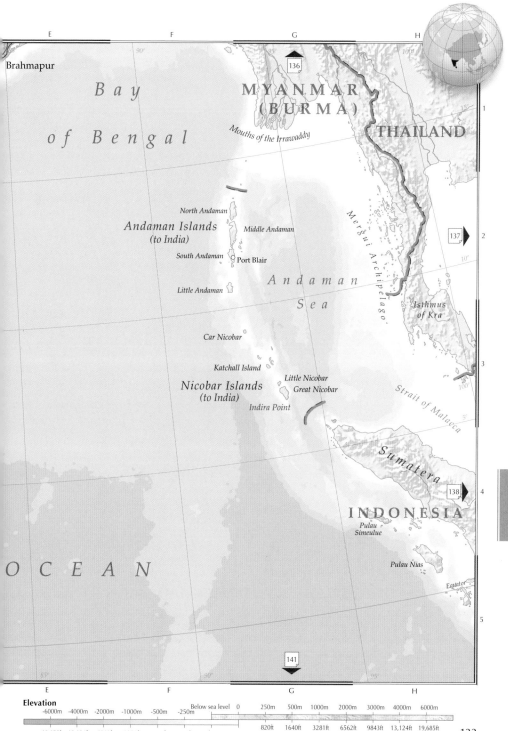

Brahmapur

B a y

o f   B e n g a l

M Y A N M A R
(B U R M A)

Mouths of the Irrawaddy

THAILAND

North Andaman

Andaman Islands
(to India)

Middle Andaman

South Andaman

Port Blair

A n d a m a n

S e a

Little Andaman

Merghi Archipelago

Isthmus
of Kra

Car Nicobar

Katchall Island

Nicobar Islands
(to India)

Little Nicobar

Great Nicobar

Indira Point

Strait of Malacca

S u m a t e r a

I N D O N E S I A

Pulau
Simeulue

O C E A N

Pulau Nias

Equator

Elevation

-6000m	-4000m	-2000m	-1000m	-500m	Below sea level	0	250m	500m	1000m	2000m	3000m	4000m	6000m
					-250m								
-19,658ft	-13,124ft	-6562ft	-3281ft	-1640ft	-820ft	-328ft/-100m	0	820ft	1640ft	3281ft	6562ft	9843ft	13,124ft	19,685ft

Northern India, Pakistan & Bangladesh

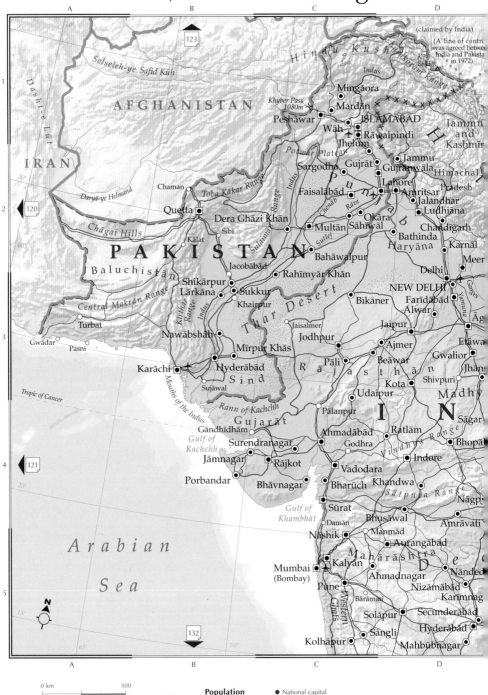

(claimed by India)

(A "line of contro
was agreed betwee
India and Pakista
in 1972)

A · **B** · **C** · **D**

123

Selseleh-ye Safid Kūh

Hindu Kush

K2
8611m

Karakoram Range

Indus

Mingaora

AFGHANISTAN

Khyber Pass
1080m

Mardān

Peshāwar

ISLĀMĀBĀD

Jammu
and
Kashmir

Wāh

Rāwalpindi

Jhelum

Jammu

IRAN

Dasht-e Lut

Himachal
Pradesh

Potwar Plateau

Sargodha

Gujrāt

Gujrānwāla

Daryā-ye Helmand

Chaman

Toba Kākar Range

Faisalābād

Lahore

Amritsar

Jalandhar

Ludhiāna

120

Quetta

Dera Ghāzi Khān

Chenāb

Rāvi

Okāra

Sāhīwāl

Chandīgarh

Chāgai Hills

Sibi

Multān

Bathinda

Haryāna

Karnāl

PAKISTAN

Kālat

Sulaimān Range

Sutlej

Bahāwalpur

Delhi

Meer

Baluchistān

Jacobābād

Rahīmyār Khān

NEW DELHI

Farīdābād

Shikārpur

Sukkur

Bīkaner

Alwar

Āg

Central Makrān Range

Lārkāna

Khairpur

Thar Desert

Jaipur

Turbat

Kīrthar Range

Nawābshāh

Jaisalmer

Jodhpur

Ajmer

Beāwar

Etāwa

Gwalior

Gwādar

Pasni

Indus

Mīrpur Khās

Pāli

Rājasthān

Kota

Jhan:

Karāchi

Hyderābād

Shivpuri

Mouths of the Indus

Sujāwal

Sind

Udaipur

Madhy

Tropic of Cancer

Rann of Kachchh

Pālanpur

I

N

Gāndhīdhām

Gujarāt

Ahmadābād

Godhra

Ratlām

Sāgar

Gulf of
Kachchh

Surendranagar

Bhopā

Jāmnagar

Rājkot

Vadodara

Indore

Porbandar

Bhāvnagar

Bharūch

Khandwa

Nāgp

Satpura Range

Arabian

Sūrat

Bhusāwal

Amrāvati

Daman

Manmād

Nāshik

Aurangābād

Sea

Mumbai
(Bombay)

Kalyān

Mahārāshtra

De

Nānded

Ahmadnagar

Nizāmābād

Pune

Karīmnag

N

Bārāmati

Solāpur

Secunderābād

Western Ghats

Sāngli

Hyderābād

Kolhāpur

Mahbūbnagar

132

0 km   300

0 miles   300

Population   ● National capital

○ below 50,000   ◎ 50,000 to 100,000   ◉ 100,000 to 500,000   ■ above 500,000

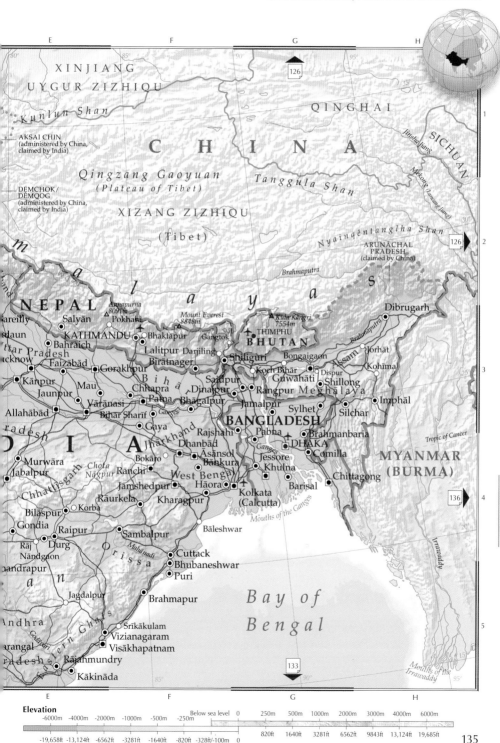

XINJIANG
UYGUR ZIZHIQU

Kunlun Shan

AKSAI CHIN
(administered by China,
claimed by India)

C H I N A

QINGHAI

SICHUAN

Jinshajiang

Qingzang Gaoyuan
(Plateau of Tibet)

Tanggula Shan

Mekong (Lancang Jiang)

DEMCHOK /
DÊMQOG
(administered by China,
claimed by India)

XIZANG ZIZHIQU

(Tibet)

Nyainqêntanglha Shan

ARUNACHAL
PRADESH
(claimed by China)

Brahmaputra

m
a
l
a
y
a
s

NEPAL

Annapurna
8091m▲

Pokhara

Salyān

Mount Everest
8848m▲

Gangtok

▲Kula Kangri
7554m

Dibrugarh

Brahmaputra

areilly

KATHMANDU

Bhaktapur

Bahrāich

Lalitpur

Darjiling

Biratnager

Shiliguri

THIMPHU

BHUTAN

Bongaigaon

Assam

Jorhat

daun

Faizābād

Gorakhpur

Koch Bihar

Guwāhāti

Dispur

Shillong

Kohīma

icknow

Uttar Pradesh

B i h
a
r

Chhapra

Saidpur

Dinajpur

Rangpur

Meghālaya

Imphāl

Kānpur

Jaunpur

Mau

Patna

Bhāgalpur

Jamālpur

Sylhet

Silchar

Vārānasi

Bihar Sharif

Ganges

BANGLADESH

Allahābād

Gaya

Rajshahi

Pabha

Brahmanbaria

MYANMAR
(BURMA)

Jharkhand

Dhanbād

Ganges

DHAKA

Tropic of Cancer

Murwāra

Bokaro

Āsānsol

Jessore

Comilla

Jabalpur

*Chota
Nāgpur*

Ranchi

Bankura

Khulna

Chhattisgarh

Jamshedpur

West Bengal

Hāora

Barisal

Chittagong

Bilāspur

Korba

Rāurkela

Kharagpur

Kolkata
(Calcutta)

Irrawaddy

Gondia

Raipur

Sambalpur

Bāleshwar

Mouths of the Ganges

Rāj
Nāndgaon

Durg

Mahānadi

Orissa

Cuttack

a
n

Jagdalpur

Bhubaneshwar

Puri

*Bay of
Bengal*

Brahmapur

Andhra

Eastern Ghats

Srikākulam

Vizianagaram

Visākhapatnam

arangal

Pradesh

Rājahmundry

Kākināda

Godavari

*Mouths of the
Irrawaddy*

Elevation

| -6000m | -4000m | -2000m | -1000m | -500m | -250m | Below sea level 0 | 250m | 500m | 1000m | 2000m | 3000m | 4000m | 6000m |

| -19,658ft | -13,124ft | -6562ft | -3281ft | -1640ft | -820ft | -328ft/-100m | 0 | 820ft | 1640ft | 3281ft | 6562ft | 9843ft | 13,124ft | 19,685ft |

135

Mainland Southeast Asia

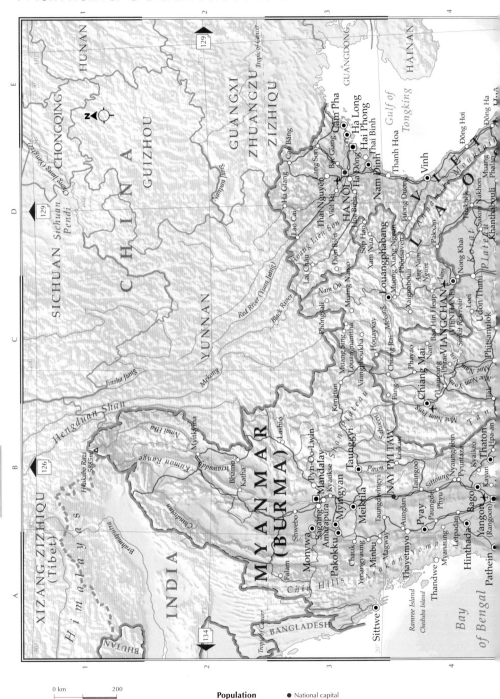

0 km 200

0 miles 200

Population

● National capital

○ below 50,000

○ 50,000 to 100,000

◉ 100,000 to 500,000

◼ above 500,000

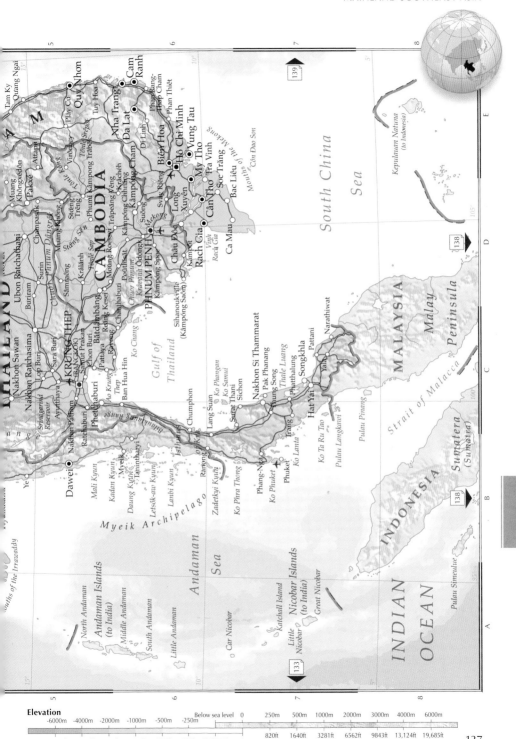

Elevation

-6000m	-4000m	-2000m	-1000m	-500m	-250m	Below sea level 0	250m	500m	1000m	2000m	3000m	4000m	6000m

| -19,658ft | -13,124ft | -6562ft | -3281ft | -1640ft | -820ft | -328ft/-100m | 0 | 820ft | 1640ft | 3281ft | 6562ft | 9843ft | 13,124ft | 19,685ft |

Maritime Southeast Asia

SINGAPORE

0 km   10
0 miles   10

Johore Strait

Causeway
Lim Chu
Kang
Bukit Panjang   Hougang   Pulau
Choa Chu   New Town   Ubin   Pulau
Kang   City   Tekong
Queenstown   Changi
Jurong   City   Bedok
Industrial   Telok Blangah   New Town
Estate   Sentosa
Selat Pandan
Pulau Sudong
Pulau Pawai

Bukit Timah 176m

Strait of Singapore

Urban areas
Open areas
Nature reserves

MYANMAR
(BURMA)

137

THAILAND

LAOS

VIETNAM

Gulf of
Tongking

Hainan Dao
(to China)

PARACEL ISLANDS
(disputed by China, Taiwan
and Vietnam)

South China

Sea

133

CAMBODIA

Mekong

Mouths of
the Mekong

SPRATLY ISLANDS
(disputed by China, Malaysia,
Philippines, Taiwan and Vietnam)

Andaman
Sea

Isthmus of Kra

Gulf of
Thailand

Nicobar Islands
(to India)

Banda Aceh   Sigli

Meulaboh

Langsa

George   Kota Bharu
Town   Butterworth
Pulau   Kuala Terengganu
Pinang   Taiping   Dungun
Ipoh   Cukai
Kuantan   Kepulauan
Natuna

Guning Kinabalu
4101m

Kota Kinabalu
BANDAR SERI
BEGAWAN
BRUNEI
Miri   Tawa

Medan
Tebingtinggi
Pematangsiantar
Kepulauan   Danau   Klang   KUALA LUMPUR   M A L A Y S I A   Bintulu
Banyak   Toba   PUTRAJAYA   Melaka   Selat Serasan
Sibolga   Muar   Keluang   Sibu   Batang Rajang   Sarawak   Pegunungan
Pulau Nias   Batu Pahat   Johor Bahru   Kuching   Sri Aman   Muller
Pulau Simeulue   SINGAPORE   Singkawang   Sidas   Sungai Kapuas   Borneo
Equator   Pekanbaru   Kepulauan   Pontianak   Sampit   Samarinda
Solok   Lingga   Kalimantan   Balikpapan
Padang   Rengat   Selat Karimata   Sungai Barito
Pulau Siberut   Batang Hari   Kualatungkal   Sungai Mahakam
Jambi   Bangka   Amuntai
Kepulauan   Sungaipenuh   Pangkalpinang   Pulau   I   N   D   Kandangan
Mentawai   133   Palembang   Belitung   Banjarmasin
Bengkulu   Lahat   Pulau
Kotabumi   Java   Sea   Laut

Sumatera
(Sumatra)

Pulau
Madura

INDIAN

OCEAN

Bandar Lampung   Cirebon   Tegal
Serang   JAKARTA   Pekalongan   Semarang   Pulau
Bogor   Kudus   Madura   Surabaya
Sukabumi   Probolinggo
Bandung   Tasikmalaya   Malang   Jember Matara
Jawa   Cilacap   Kediri   Denpasar   N
(Java)   Magelang   Madiun   Bali
Yogyakarta   Pulau
Surakarta   Lombok

Balabac

Palaw

Sabah

Tawa

Butterworth
Tapanuli

Sungai Kayan

Makass

141

133

MALAYSIA'S TWO CAPITALS

KUALA LUMPUR   - Capital
PUTRAJAYA   - Administrative capital

0 km   200
0 miles   200

Population   ● National capital
○ below 50,000   ○ 50,000 to 100,000   ◉ 100,000 to 500,000   ◼ above 500,000

E   F   G   H

Luzon Strait
Babuyan Island
Babuyan Channel
Baguio
Tuguegarao
Ilagan
Cordillera Central
Luzon
ngeles
Dagupan
Cabanatuan
ANILA
Lucena
PHILIPPINES
Batangas
Naga
Legazpi City
Mindoro
Mindoro Strait
Sibuyan Sea
Calbayog
Roxas City
Samar
Cadiz
Tacloban
Panay Island
Iloilo
Leyte
Bacolod City
Cebu
Palawan
Puerto Princesa
Negros
Bohol Sea
Butuan
Iligan
Cagayan de Oro
Bislig
Sulu Sea
Zamboanga
Moro Gulf
Mindanao
Davao
adakan
Basilan
Lebak
Davao Gulf
General Santos
Sulu Archipelago

Philippine Sea

NORTHERN MARIANA ISLANDS (to US)

GUAM (to US)

Yap
144

MICRONESIA

P A C I F I C

Babeldaob

PALAU

O C E A N

Equator

Kepulauan Talaud

Celebes Sea

Manado
Bitung
Gorontalo
Molucca Sea
Kepulauan Sangir
Pulau Morotai
Pulau Halmahera
Pulau Waigeo
Sorong
Jazirah Doberai
Manokwari
Pulau Biak
Pulau Yapen
Jayapura
Laut Halmahera
Selat Dampir
Pulau Misool
Teluk Berau
Pulau Seram
Laut Seram
Wahai
Waflia
Tifu
Ambon
Pulau Buru
Pulau Seram
Teluk Cenderawasih
Puncak Jaya 5030m
Pegunungan Maoke
Sungai Mamberamo
PAPUA
Papua (Irian Jaya)
New Guinea
NEW GUINEA
Sungai Digul

144

Palu
Tomini Teluk
Sulawesi (Celebes)
Danau Poso
Pegunungan Quarles
Teluk Bone
repare
N
Kendari
Pulau Buton
Kolaka
Watampone
Pulau Buton
Maluku (Moluccas)
Pulau Misool
I
A
ngkang
E
S
Makassar
Bulukumba
Banda Sea
Kepulauan Kai
Kepulauan Aru
Kepulauan Banggai
Kepulauan Sula

Flores Sea
a Tenggara
Flores
Kepulauan Alor
Pulau Wetar
Pulau Yamdena
Kepulauan Tanimbar
Kepulauan Leti
DILI
Timor
EAST TIMOR
Arafura Sea
Nikiniki
Kupang
Pulau Sumba
lores Sea
lat Sumba
Savu Sea
Torres Strait
AUSTRALIA

Timor Sea

148

E   F   G   H

Elevation

					Below sea level	0	250m	500m	1000m	2000m	3000m	4000m	6000m
-6000m	-4000m	-2000m	-1000m	-500m	-250m								
-19,658ft	-13,124ft	-6562ft	-3281ft	-1640ft	-820ft	-328ft/-100m	0	820ft	1640ft	3281ft	6562ft	9843ft	13,124ft	19,685ft

The Indian Ocean

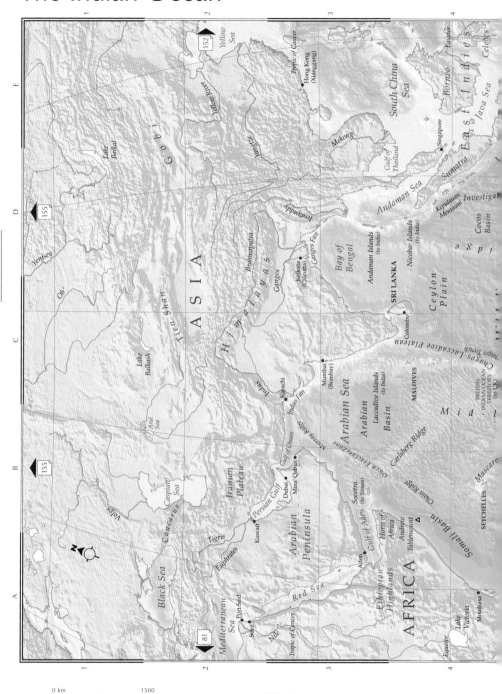

0 km   1500

0 miles   1500

● Major port

Elevation

-6000m	-4000m	-2000m	-1000m	-250m	0
-19,658ft	-13,124ft	-6562ft	-3281ft	-820ft	0

Australasia & Oceania

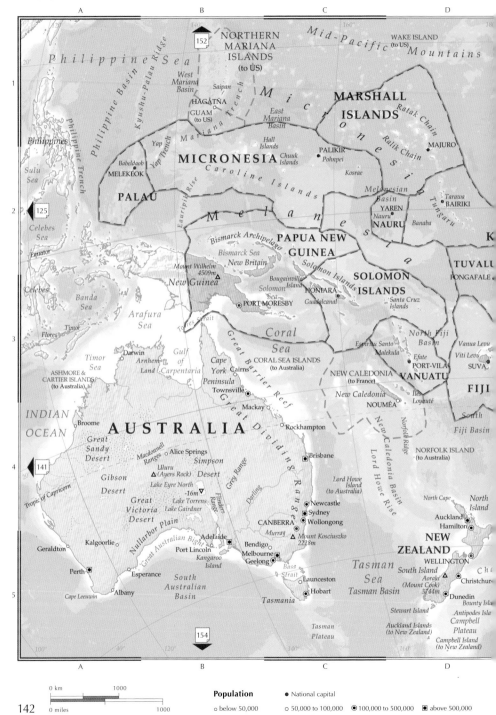

A   B   C   D

NORTHERN MARIANA ISLANDS (to US)

Mid-Pacific WAKE ISLAND (to US) *Mountains*

Philippine Sea

West Mariana Basin

Saipan

HAGÅTÑA
GUAM (to US)

Mi

MARSHALL ISLANDS

East Mariana Basin

Ratak Chain

Philippine Basin Ridge

Kyushu-Palau Ridge

Yap

Mariana Trench

Yap Trench

Hall Islands

Ralik Chain

MAJURO

Philippines

Philippine Trench

Babeldaob
MELEKEOK

MICRONESIA

Chuuk Islands

PALIKIR
Pohnpei

Caroline Islands

Kosrae

c
r
o
n
e
s
i

Tarawa
BAIRIKI

Sulu Sea

PALAU

Eauripik Rise

Melanesian Basin

YAREN
Nauru

NAURU

Banaba

Tungaru

K

Celebes Sea

Equator

M
e
l
a
n
e

PAPUA NEW GUINEA

Bismarck Archipelago

Bismarck Sea
New Britain

Solomon Islands

SOLOMON ISLANDS

s
i
a

TUVALU
FUNAFUTI

Celebes

Banda Sea

Mount Wilhelm
4509m

New Guinea

Bougainville
Island

Solomon
Sea

HONIARA
Guadalcanal

Santa Cruz
Islands

North Fiji Basin

Vanua Levu

Timor

Flores

Arafura Sea

Torres Strait

PORT MORESBY

Coral Sea

Espiritu Santo
Malekula

Efate

Viti Levu

SUVA

Timor Sea

Darwin

Arnhem Land

Gulf of Carpentaria

Cape York
Peninsula

CORAL SEA ISLANDS
(to Australia)

Cairns

PORT-VILA

VANUATU

Iles Loyauté

FIJI

ASHMORE & CARTIER ISLANDS (to Australia)

Townsville

Great Barrier Reef

NEW CALEDONIA (to France)

New Caledonia
NOUMÉA

South Fiji Basin

INDIAN OCEAN

Broome

AUSTRALIA

Mackay

Rockhampton

New Caledonia Ridge

NORFOLK ISLAND
(to Australia)

Great Sandy Desert

Macdonnell Ranges

Alice Springs

Simpson

Brisbane

Lord Howe Basin

Norfolk Ridge

Tropic of Capricorn

Gibson Desert

Uluru
(Ayers Rock)

Desert

Lake Eyre North
-16m

Grey Range

Lord Howe
Island
(to Australia)

North Cape

North Island

Kalgoorlie

Great Victoria Desert

Lake Torrens
Lake Gairdner

Flinders Range

Darling

Newcastle
CANBERRA
Sydney
Wollongong

Auckland
Hamilton

Geraldton

Nullarbor Plain

Adelaide

Port Lincoln

Bendigo
Melbourne
Geelong

Murray

Mount Kosciuszko
2228m

NEW ZEALAND
WELLINGTON

Perth

Esperance

Great Australian Bight

Kangaroo Island

South Australian Basin

Cape Leeuwin

Albany

Bass Strait

Launceston

Hobart

Tasman Sea

Tasmania

South Island

Aoraki
(Mount Cook)
3744m

Christchur

Dunedin
Bounty Isla

Tasman Basin

Tasman Plateau

Stewart Island

Auckland Islands
(to New Zealand)

Antipodes Isla

Campbell Plateau

Campbell Island
(to New Zealand)

A   B   C   D

0 km   1000
0 miles   1000

Population

o below 50,000   o 50,000 to 100,000   ◉ 100,000 to 500,000   ■ above 500,000

● National capital

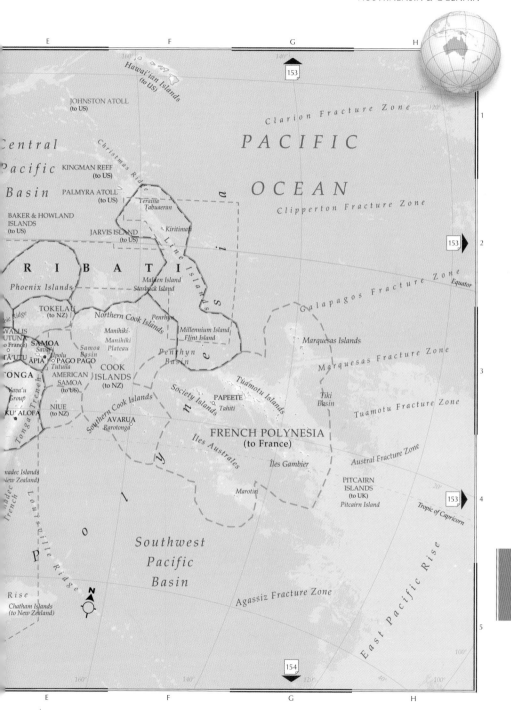

Hawaiʻian Islands
(to US)

JOHNSTON ATOLL
(to US)

Central

Pacific

Basin

KINGMAN REEF
(to US)

PALMYRA ATOLL
(to US)

Teraina
Tabuaeran

BAKER & HOWLAND
ISLANDS
(to US)

JARVIS ISLAND
(to US)

Kiritimati

Christmas Ridge

Clarion Fracture Zone

P A C I F I C

O C E A N

Clipperton Fracture Zone

K I R I B A T I

Phoenix Islands

Malden Island
Starbuck Island

Line Islands

Galapagos Fracture Zone

Equator

TOKELAU
(to NZ)

Northern Cook Islands

Penrhyn

Millennium Island
Flint Island

Marquesas Islands

WALLIS
& FUTUNA
(to France)

SAMOA

Savaiʻi

Upolu

Samoa
Basin

Manihiki
Manihiki
Plateau

Penrhyn
Basin

Marquesas Fracture Zone

ridge

TAʻU

APIA
Tutuila

PAGO PAGO

COOK
ISLANDS
(to NZ)

Tuamotu Islands

Tiki
Basin

TONGA

AMERICAN
SAMOA
(to US)

Society Islands

PAPEETE
Tahiti

Tuamotu Fracture Zone

Kava'u
Group

Southern Cook Islands

NUKU'ALOFA

NIUE
(to NZ)

AVARUA
Rarotonga

FRENCH POLYNESIA
(to France)

Îles Australes

Îles Gambier

Austral Fracture Zone

Kermadec Islands
(to New Zealand)

Louisville Ridge

Marotiri

PITCAIRN
ISLANDS
(to UK)
Pitcairn Island

Tropic of Capricorn

Southwest
Pacific
Basin

Agassiz Fracture Zone

East Pacific Rise

Rise

Chatham Islands
(to New Zealand)

N

153

153

153

153

154

The Southwest Pacific

MARSHALL ISLANDS

Saipan
Tinian
Rota
NORTHERN MARIANA ISLANDS
(to US)
GUAM (to US)
HAGÅTÑA

152

Enewetak Atoll
Bikini Atoll
Rongelap Atoll
Ailuk Atoll
Ujelang Atoll
Wotje Atoll
Kwajalein Atoll
Maloelap Atoll
Namu Atoll
Majuro
Ailinglaplap Atoll
Jaluit Atoll
Mili Atoll

Ratak Chain
Ralik Chain

Yap

Babeldaob
MELEKEOK
PALAU

139

MICRONESIA

Chuuk Islands
PALIKIR
Pohnpei

Caroline Islands

Kosrae

Ebon Atoll

Makir

Tarawa
BAIRIKI

Abemama

YAREN
NAURU
Nonou
Banaba

Equator

Admiralty Islands
St.Matthias Group
Bismarck Archipelago
Bismarck Sea
New Ireland

New Guinea

Madang
PAPUA NEW GUINEA
△ Mount Wilhelm 4509m
Central Range
Lae
Owen Stanley Range

INDONESIA

New Britain

Solomon Sea

Bougainville Island

Choiseul

Santa Isabel

New Georgia Islands

Malaita

HONIARA
Guadalcanal

SOLOMON ISLANDS

Melanesia

Arafura Sea

Gulf of Papua

PORT MORESBY
Torres Strait

D'Entrecasteaux Islands

Louisiade Archipelago

San Cristobal
Rennell

Santa Cruz Islands

Arnhem Land
Groote Eylandt
Gulf of Carpentaria

Coral Sea

Banks Islands

Espíritu Santo
Maéwo
Pentecost
Malekula
Ambrym
Epi
Efate
PORT-VILA

146

Cape York Peninsula

Barkly Tableland

CORAL SEA ISLANDS
(to Australia)

NEW CALEDONIA
(to France)

VANUATU
Erromango
Tanna
Aneityum

NORTHERN

TERRITORY

Tropic of Capricorn

Macdonnell

Ranges

QUEENSLAND

Great Barrier Reef

Great Dividing Range

New Caledonia

Ouvéa
Lifou
Maré
Îles Loyauté

NOUMÉA

AUSTRALIA

149

Population   ● National capital

○ below 50,000   ○ 50,000 to 100,000   ◉ 100,000 to 500,000   ◼ above 500,000

0 km   750
0 miles   750

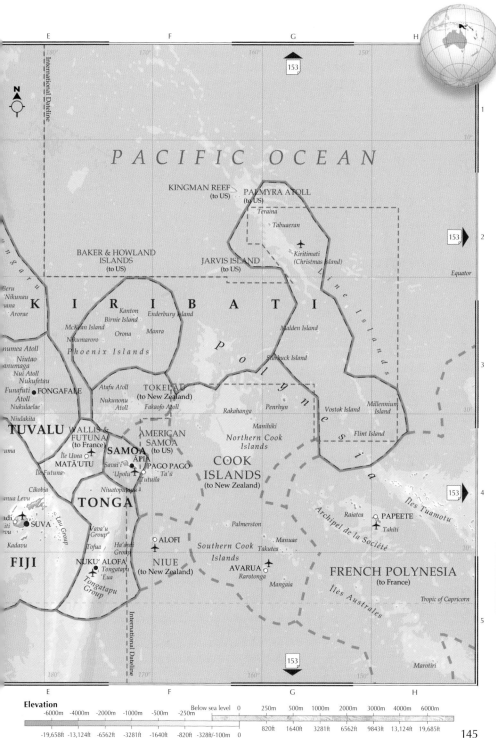

Western Australia

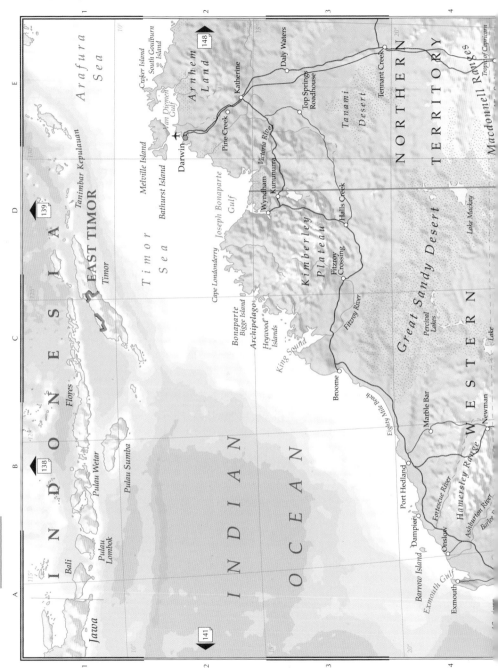

Arafura Sea

Tanimbar Kepulauan

Arnhem Land

148

Coker Island
South Goulburn Island

Katherine

Daly Waters

Tennant Creek

NORTHERN   TERRITORY

Macdonnell Ranges

Tropic of Capricorn

EAST TIMOR   139

Timor

Melville Island

Bathurst Island

Van Diemen Gulf

Darwin

Pine Creek

Top Springs Roadhouse

Tanami Desert

I N D O N E S I A

Timor Sea

Cape Londonderry

Joseph Bonaparte Gulf

Wyndham
Kununurra

Victoria River

Halls Creek

Lake Mackay

Flores

Bonaparte Archipelago
Bigge Island
Heywood Islands

Kimberley Plateau

Fitzroy Crossing

Fitzroy River

Great Sandy Desert

Percival Lakes

W E S T E R N

138

Pulau Wetar

Pulau Sumba

King Sound

Broome

Lake

Marble Bar

Newman

I N D I A N

Eighty Mile Beach

Port Hedland

Hamersley Range

Fortescue River

Ashburton River

Barlee

Pulau Lombok

Bali

O C E A N

141

Barrow Island
Dampier
Onslow

Exmouth Gulf

Exmouth

Jawa

0 km   300

146   0 miles   300

Population

○ below 50,000   ○ 50,000 to 100,000   ◉ 100,000 to 500,000   ■ above 500,000

● Internal administrative capital

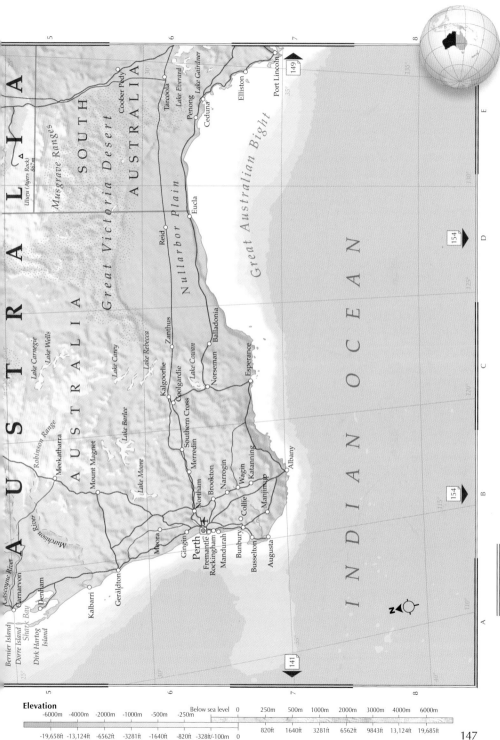

Elevation

-6000m	-4000m	-2000m	-1000m	-500m	-250m	Below sea level	0	250m	500m	1000m	2000m	3000m	4000m	6000m
-19,658ft	-13,124ft	-6562ft	-3281ft	-1640ft	-820ft	-328ft/-100m	0	820ft	1640ft	3281ft	6562ft	9843ft	13,124ft	19,685ft

Eastern Australia

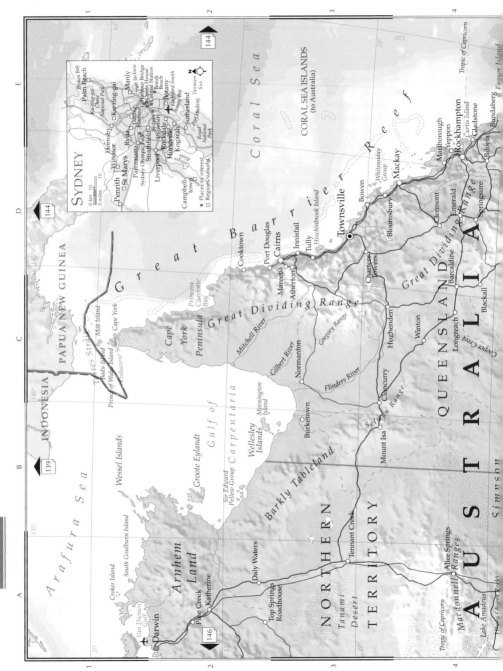

Population

● National capital   ● Internal administrative capital

○ below 50,000   ○ 50,000 to 100,000   ◉ 100,000 to 500,000   ◼ above 500,000

0 km   300

0 miles   300

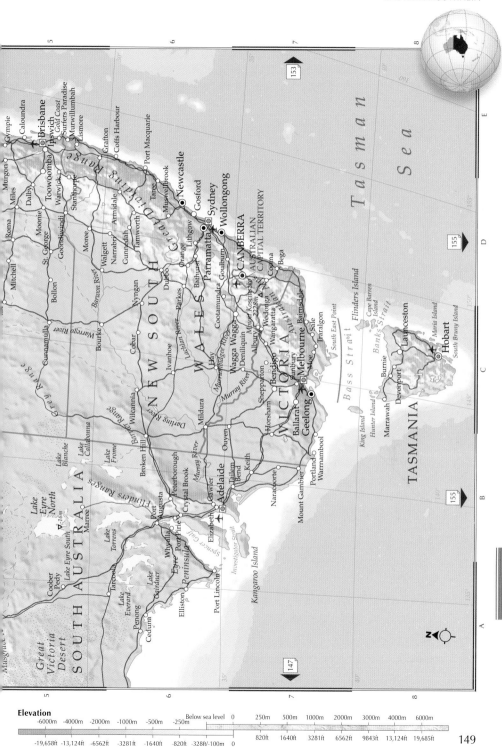

Elevation

-6000m	-4000m	-2000m	-1000m	-500m	-250m	Below sea level	0	250m	500m	1000m	2000m	3000m	4000m	6000m
-19,658ft	-13,124ft	-6562ft	-3281ft	-1640ft	-820ft	-328ft/-100m	0	820ft	1640ft	3281ft	6562ft	9843ft	13,124ft	19,685ft

New Zealand

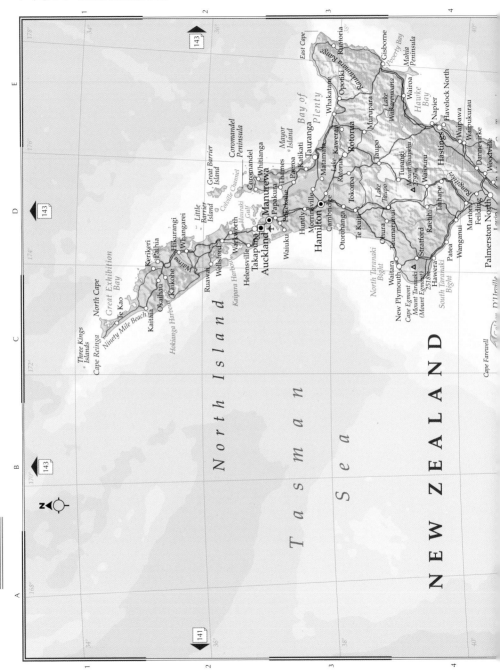

Three Kings Islands
Cape Reinga
North Cape
Great Exhibition Bay
Ninety Mile Beach
Te Kao
Kaitaia
Okaihau
Kaikohe
Hokianga Harbour
Kerikeri
Paihia
Hikurangi
Whangarei
Waitara
Ruawai
Wellsford
Helensville
Warkworth
Takapuna
Auckland
Manurewa
Waiuku
Papakura
Huntly
Morrinsville
Hamilton
Cambridge
Te Awamutu
Otorohanga
Te Kuiti
Coromandel Peninsula
Coromandel
Great Barrier Island
Little Barrier Island
Kaipara Harbour
Hauraki Gulf
Cabbage Channel
Whangaparaoa Harbour
Mayor Island
Whitianga
Whangamata
Thames
Paeroa
Katikati
Tauranga
Matamata
Bay of Plenty
Whakatane
Opotiki
East Cape
Ruatoria
Gisborne
Poverty Bay
Mahia Peninsula
Raukumara Range
Oporiki
Wairoa
Lake Waikaremoana
Hawke Bay
Napier
Havelock North
Waipawa
Waipukurau
Danneirke
Woodville
Hastings
Murupara
Rotorua
Lake Rotorua
Lake Kaweray
Taupo
Lake Taupo
Turangi
Mount Ruapehu 2797m
Ohura
Taumarunui
Waitara
North Taranaki Bight
New Plymouth
Cape Egmont
Mount Taranaki (Mount Egmont) 2518m
South Taranaki Bight
Hawera
Stratford
Patea
Wanganui
Marton
Feilding
Palmerston North
Takapane
Raetihi
Taihape
Rangitikei
Cape Farewell

North Island

Tasman Sea

NEW ZEALAND

N

Population

0 km 100
0 miles 100

● National capital

○ below 50,000
○ 50,000 to 100,000
◉ 100,000 to 500,000
◼ above 500,000

143

154

154

154

142

South Island

Cook Strait
Lower Hutt
WELLINGTON
Cape Palliser
Cape Campbell
Seddon
Blenheim
Picton
Nelson
Clarence
Kaikoura
Kaikoura Peninsula
Richmond
Mount Owen
1875m
Richmond Range
Tasman Mts
Motueka
Wairau
Clarence
Waiau
Hanmer
Springs
Springs
Junction
Waipara
Rangiora
Kaiapoi
Christchurch
Lyttelton
Pegasus
Bay
Banks
Peninsula
Lake
Ellesmere
Canterbury
Bight
Reefton
Lake
Brunner
Otira
Arthur's Pass
920m
Oxford
Darfield
Canterbury Plains
Mayfield
Ashburton
Hinds
Seddonville
Westport
Runanga
Greymouth
Hokitika
Ross
Cape Foulwind
Karamea
Bight
Rakaia
Geraldine
Temuka
Timaru
Studholme
Oamaru
Hampden
SOUTHERN
ALPS
Aoraki
(Mount Cook)
3744m
Mount Cook
Fairlie
Rangitata
Waitaki
Waimate
Otago Peninsula
Dunedin
Mosgiel
Milton
Balclutha
Abut Head
Fox Glacier
Whataroa
Lake
Pukaki
Lake
Hawea
Cromwell
Alexandra
Taieri
Clutha
Gore
Mataura
Tokanui
Molyneux Bay
Haast
Jackson Head
Lake
Wanaka
Lake
Wanaka
Lake
Wakatipu
Queenstown
Lumsden
Mataura
Winton
Invercargill
Riverton
Ruapuke
Island
Toetoes Bay
Eyre Mts
Te Anau
Lake
Te Anau
Lake
Manapouri
Waiau
Oreti
Foveaux Strait
Milford Sound
Milford
Sound
Livingstone Mts
George Sound
Cassell Sound
Fiordland
Lake
Te Anau
Lake
Hauroko
Te Waewae Bay
Resolution
Island
West
Cape
Codfish Island
Halfmoon Bay
Muttonbird
Islands
Stewart Island
South West
Cape

P A C I F I C

O C E A N

42°

44°

46°

48°

178°

176°

174°

172°

170°

168°

166°

5

6

7

8

A

B

C

D

E

Elevation

-6000m	-4000m	-2000m	-1000m	-500m	-250m	Below sea level	0	250m	500m	1000m	2000m	3000m	4000m	6000m

| -19,658ft | -13,124ft | -6562ft | -3281ft | -1640ft | -820ft | -328ft/-100m | 0 | 820ft | 1640ft | 3281ft | 6562ft | 9843ft | 13,124ft | 19,685ft |

151

The Pacific Ocean

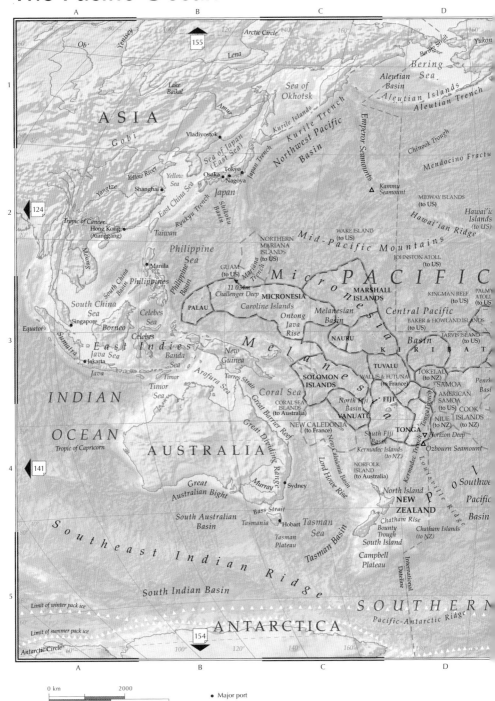

155

124

141

154

ASIA

Ob'
Yenisey
Arctic Circle
Lena
Yukon
Bering Strait
Bering Sea
Aleutian Basin
Aleutian Islands
Aleutian Trench
Lake Baikal
Sea of Okhotsk
Amur
Gobi
Kurile Islands
Kurile Trench
Northwest Pacific Basin
Chinook Trough
Mendocino Fracture
Vladivostok
Japan Trench
Emperor Seamounts
Kammu Seamount
Sea of Japan (East Sea)
Yellow River
Yellow Sea
Tokyo
Osaka
Nagoya
Japan
Shikoku Basin
Hawai'ian Ridge
MIDWAY ISLANDS (to US)
Hawai'i Islands (to US)
Yangtze
Shanghai
East China Sea
Ryukyu Trench
Tropic of Cancer
Hong Kong (Xianggang)
Taiwan
Mid-Pacific Mountains
WAKE ISLAND (to US)
Philippine Sea
NORTHERN MARIANA ISLANDS (to US)
JOHNSTON ATOLL (to US)
Mekong
Manila
Philippine Basin
GUAM (to US)
Mariana Trench
Micronesia
PACIFIC
MARSHALL ISLANDS
KINGMAN REEF (to US)
PALMYRA ATOLL to US
South China Basin
11 034m Challenger Deep
MICRONESIA
Caroline Islands
Melanesian Basin
Central Pacific
BAKER & HOWLAND ISLANDS (to US)
South China Sea
PALAU
Ontong Java Rise
NAURU
Central Pacific Basin
JARVIS ISLAND (to US)
Singapore
Borneo
Celebes Sea
Celebes
K I R I B A T I
Equator
Sumatra
East Indies
New Guinea
Melanesia
TUVALU
TOKELAU (to NZ)
Penrhyn Basin
Java Sea
Jakarta
Banda Sea
SOLOMON ISLANDS
WALLIS & FUTUNA (to France)
SAMOA
AMERICAN SAMOA (to US)
Java
Timor
Arafura Sea
Torres Strait
VANUATU
North Fiji Basin
FIJI
NIUE (to NZ)
COOK ISLANDS (to NZ)
INDIAN
Timor Sea
Coral Sea
CORAL SEA ISLANDS (to Australia)
NEW CALEDONIA (to France)
South Fiji Basin
TONGA
Horizon Deep
OCEAN
Great Barrier Reef
Kermadec Islands (to NZ)
Ozbourn Seamount
Tropic of Capricorn
Great Dividing Range
New Caledonia Basin
Louisville Ridge
AUSTRALIA
NORFOLK ISLAND (to Australia)
Southwest
Great Australian Bight
Murray
Sydney
Lord Howe Rise
North Island
NEW ZEALAND
Pacific Basin
Bass Strait
South Australian Basin
Tasmania
Hobart
Tasman Sea
Chatham Rise
Bounty Trough
Chatham Islands (to NZ)
Tasman Plateau
Tasman Basin
South Island
Campbell Plateau
International Dateline
Southeast Indian Ridge
South Indian Basin
SOUTHERN
Limit of winter pack ice
Pacific-Antarctic Ridge
Limit of summer pack ice
Antarctic Circle
ANTARCTICA

0 km 2000
0 miles 2000

• Major port

E F G H

155

Arctic Circle

Anchorage

Hudson
Bay

Labrador
Sea

**NORTH
AMERICA**

1

Rocky Mountains

Vancouver

Cascadia
Basin

Great Lakes

ATLANTIC

Colorado

Appalachian Mountains

OCEAN

San Francisco

ilf of
aska

Murray Fracture Zone

Long Beach

Mississippi

Tropic of Cancer

66

2

olokai Fracture Zone

Gulf of
California

Gulf of
Mexico

Greater Antilles

Lesser Antilles

Clarion Fracture Zone

O C E A N

Clipperton Fracture Zone

CLIPPERTON ISLAND
(to France)

Middle America Trench

Caribbean Sea

Guatemala
Basin

Panama City

Cocos Ridge

N

Galapagos Fracture Zone

Gallego Rise

Galápagos Islands
(to Ecuador)

Amazon

Equator

3

Marquesas
Islands

Marquesas
Fracture Zone

Bauer
Basin

Galapagos
Rise

Peru Basin

Peru-Chile Trench

**SOUTH
AMERICA**

East Pacific Rise

Callao

Tahiti

FRENCH
POLYNESIA
(to France)

Tiki
Basin

Mendaña Fracture Zone

Nazca Ridge

Íles Gambier

Austral
Fracture Zone

Sala y Gomez
(to Chile)

Sala y Gomez Ridge

Chile Basin

Tropic of Capricorn

les Australes

PITCAIRN ISLANDS
(to UK)

Easter Island
(to Chile)

Easter Fracture Zone

Isla San Félix
(to Chile)

Isla San Ambrosio
(to Chile)

67

4

Andes

Paraná

Islas Juan Fernández
(to Chile)

Valparaíso

Agassiz Fracture Zone

Challenger Fracture Zone

Chile Rise

ATLANTIC

Eltanin Fracture Zone

Mornington
Abyssal
Plain

OCEAN

Cape Horn

5

O C E A N

Southeast Pacific Basin

Bellingshausen Plain

Drake Passage

154

Amundsen Plain

PETER I OY
(to Norway)

Antarctic Circle

E F G H

Elevation

-6000m -4000m -2000m -1000m -250m 0
-19,658ft -13,124ft -6562ft -3281ft -820ft 0

Antarctica

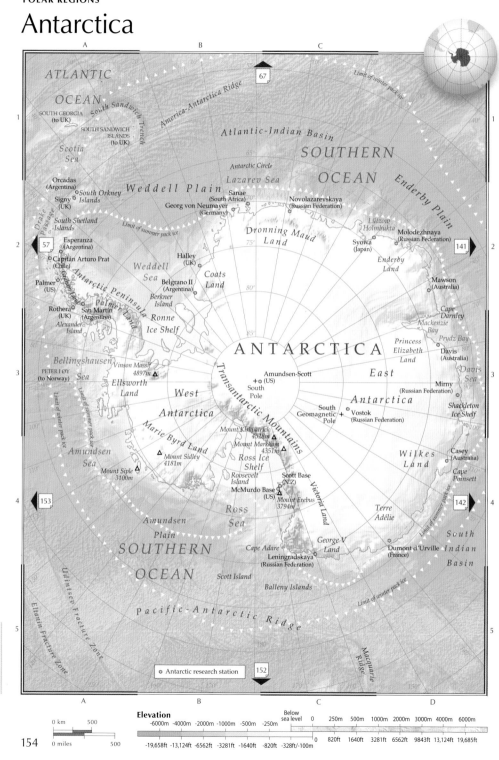

ATLANTIC

OCEAN

SOUTH GEORGIA
(to UK)

SOUTH SANDWICH
ISLANDS
(to UK)

*Scotia
Sea*

South Sandwich Trench

America-Antarctica Ridge

Atlantic-Indian Basin

SOUTHERN

OCEAN

Enderby Plain

Antarctic Circle

Lazarev Sea

Orcadas
(Argentina)

*South Orkney
Islands*

Signy
(UK)

Weddell Plain

Sanae
(South Africa)

Georg von Neumayer
(Germany)

Novolazarevskaya
(Russian Federation)

*Dronning Maud
Land*

Lützow
Holmbukta

Molodezhnaya
(Russian Federation)

*South Shetland
Islands*

Limit of summer pack ice

Syowa
(Japan)

*Enderby
Land*

Esperanza
(Argentina)

Capitán Arturo Prat
(Chile)

Palmer
(US)

Rothera
(UK)

San Martín
(Argentina)

*Weddell
Sea*

Halley
(UK)

*Coats
Land*

Belgrano II
(Argentina)

*Berkner
Island*

*Ronne
Ice Shelf*

Mawson
(Australia)

Cape
Darnley

*Mackenzie
Bay*

Prydz Bay

*Princess
Elizabeth
Land*

Davis
(Australia)

ANTARCTICA

*Alexander
Island*

Antarctic Peninsula

Graham Land

Palmer Land

*Bellingshausen
Sea*

Vinson Massif
4897m △

*Ellsworth
Land*

*West
Antarctica*

Transantarctic Mountains

Amundsen-Scott
(US)

⊕ South
Pole

East

Antarctica

Mirny
(Russian Federation)

*Davis
Sea*

PETER I ØY
(to Norway)

*Amundsen
Sea*

Marie Byrd Land

Mount Sidley
4181m △

△ Mount Siple
3100m

Mount Kirkpatrick
4528m △

Mount Markham
4351m △

*Ross Ice
Shelf*

*Roosevelt
Island*

McMurdo Base
(US)

South
Geomagnetic
Pole

Vostok
(Russian Federation)

Scott Base
(NZ)

△ Mount Erebus
3794m

Victoria Land

*Wilkes
Land*

Casey
(Australia)

Cape
Poinsett

*Shackleton
Ice Shelf*

Shelf

*Amundsen
Plain*

SOUTHERN

OCEAN

*Ross
Sea*

Cape Adare

Leningradskaya
(Russian Federation)

*George V
Land*

Scott Island

Balleny Islands

Dumont d'Urville
(France)

*Terre
Adélie*

*South
Indian
Basin*

Udintsev Fracture Zone

Eltanin Fracture Zone

Pacific-Antarctic Ridge

*Macquarie
Ridge*

○ Antarctic research station

Elevation

-6000m -4000m -2000m -1000m -500m -250m | Below sea level | 0 | 250m 500m 1000m 2000m 3000m 4000m 6000m

-19,658ft -13,124ft -6562ft -3281ft -1640ft -820ft -328ft/-100m | 0 | 820ft 1640ft 3281ft 6562ft 9843ft 13,124ft 19,685ft

0 km   500

0 miles   500

Arctic Ocean

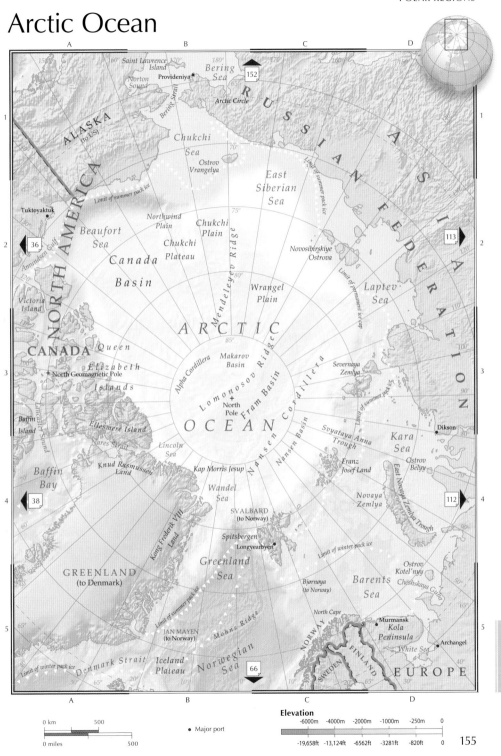

Elevation

-6000m	-4000m	-2000m	-1000m	-250m	0
-19,658ft	-13,124ft	-6562ft	-3281ft	-820ft	0

0 km   500

0 miles   500

● Major port

Overseas territories & dependencies

Despite the rapid process of global decolonization since the Second World War, around 8 million people in more than 50 territories around the world continue to live under the protection of France, Australia, the Netherlands, Denmark, Norway, New Zealand, the UK, or the USA. These remnants of former colonial empires may have persisted for economic, strategic or political reasons and are administered in a variety of ways.

AUSTRALIA

Australia's overseas territories have not been an issue since Papua New Guinea became independent in 1975. Consequently there is no overriding policy toward them. Norfolk Island is inhabited by descendants of the H.M.S Bounty mutineers and more recent Australian migrants.

Ashmore & Cartier Islands
Indian Ocean
Status: External territory
Claimed: 1931
Capital: Not applicable
Population: None
Area: 2 sq miles
(5.2 sq km)

Christmas Island
Indian Ocean
Status: External territory
Claimed: 1958
Capital: The Settlement
Population: 1403
Area: 52 sq miles
(135 sq km)

Cocos Islands
Indian Ocean
Status: External territory
Claimed: 1955
Capital: No official capital
Population: 596
Area: 5.5 sq miles
(14 sq km)

Coral Sea Islands
South Pacific
Status: External territory
Claimed: 1969
Capital: None
Population: 8 (meteorologists)
Area: Less than 1.2 sq miles
(3 sq km)

Heard & McDonald Is.
Indian Ocean
Status: External territory
Claimed: 1947
Capital: Not applicable
Population: None
Area: 161 sq miles
(417 sq km)

Norfolk Island
South Pacific
Status: External territory
Claimed: 1774
Capital: Kingston
Population: 2141
Area: 13 sq miles
(34 sq km)

DENMARK

The Faeroe Islands have been under Danish administration since Queen Margreth I of Denmark inherited Norway in 1380. The Home Rule Act of 1948 gave the Faeroese control over all their internal affairs. Greenland first came under Danish rule in 1380. Today, Denmark is responsible for the island's foreign affairs and defense.

Faeroe Islands
North Atlantic
Status: External territory
Claimed: 1380
Capital: Tórshavn
Population: 48,917
Area: 540 sq miles
(1399 sq km)

Greenland
North Atlantic
Status: External territory
Claimed: 1380
Capital: Nuuk
Population: 56,452
Area: 840,000 sq miles
(2,175,516 sq km)

FRANCE

France has developed economic ties with its *Territoires d'Outre-Mer,* thereby stressing interdependence over independence. Overseas *départements,* officially part of France, have their own governments. Territorial *collectivités* and overseas *territoires* have varying degrees of autonomy.

Clipperton Island
East Pacific
Status: Dependency of French Polynesia
Claimed: 1935
Capital: Not applicable
Population: None
Area: 2.7 sq miles
(7 sq km)

French Guiana
South America
Status: Overseas department
Claimed: 1817
Capital: Cayenne
Population: 229,000
Area: 32,253 sq miles
(83,534 sq km)

French Polynesia
South Pacific
Status: Overseas territory
Claimed: 1843
Capital: Papeete
Population: 264,000
Area: 1608 sq miles
(4165 sq km)

Guadeloupe
West Indies
Status: Overseas department
Claimed: 1635
Capital: Basse-Terre
Population: 405,500
Area: 687 sq miles
(1780 sq km)

Martinique
West Indies
Status: Overseas department
Claimed: 1635
Capital: Fort-de-France
Population: 397,000
Area: 425 sq miles (1100 sq km)

Mayotte
Indian Ocean
Status: Territorial collectivity
Claimed: 1843
Capital: Mamoudzou
Population: 194,000
Area: 144 sq miles (374 sq km)

New Caledonia
South Pacific
Status: Overseas territory
Claimed: 1853
Capital: Nouméa
Population: 249,000
Area: 7374 sq miles (19,100 sq km)

Réunion
Indian Ocean
Status: Overseas department
Claimed: 1638
Capital: Saint-Denis
Population: 827,000
Area: 970 sq miles (2500 sq km)

St. Pierre & Miquelon
North America
Status: Territorial collectivity
Claimed: 1604
Capital: Saint-Pierre
Population: 7063
Area: 93 sq miles (242 sq km)

Wallis & Futuna
South Pacific
Status: Overseas territory
Claimed: 1842
Capital: Matá'Utu
Population: 15,289
Area: 106 sq miles (274 sq km)

NETHERLANDS

The country's remaining overseas territories were formerly part of the Dutch West Indies. The Netherlands Antilles dissolved in 2010 leaving the constituent islands with varying degrees of autonomy, but the Netherlands remains responsible for their security.

Aruba
West Indies
Status: Autonomous part of the Netherlands
Claimed: 1643
Capital: Oranjestad
Population: 103,065
Area: 75 sq miles (194 sq km)

Bonaire
West Indies
Status: Special municipality of the Netherlands
Claimed: 1816
Capital: Kralendijk
Population: 14,006
Area: 113 sq miles (294 sq km)

Curaçao
West Indies
Status: Autonomous part of the Netherlands
Claimed: 1816
Capital: Willemstad
Population: 141,766
Area: 171 sq miles (444 sq km)

Sint Maarten
West Indies
Status: Autonomous part of the Netherlands
Claimed: 1816
Capital: Philipsburg
Population: 40,917
Area: 13 sq miles (34 sq km)

NEW ZEALAND

New Zealand's government has no desire to retain any overseas territories. However, the economic weakness of its dependent territory Tokelau and its freely associated states, Niue and the Cook Islands, has forced New Zealand to remain responsible for their foreign policy and defense.

Cook Islands
South Pacific
Status: Associated territory
Claimed: 1901
Capital: Avarua
Population: 19,596
Area: 91 sq miles (235 sq km)

Niue
South Pacific
Status: Associated territory
Claimed: 1901
Capital: Alofi
Population: 1398
Area: 102 sq miles (264 sq km)

Tokelau
South Pacific
Status: Dependent territory
Claimed: 1926
Capital: Not applicable
Population: 1416
Area: 4 sq miles (10 sq km)

NORWAY

In 1920, 41 nations signed the Spits-bergen Treaty recognizing Norwegian sovereignty over Svalbard. There is a NATO base on Jan Mayen. Bouvet Island is a nature reserve.

Bouvet Island
South Atlantic
Status: Dependency
Claimed: 1928
Capital: Not applicable
Population: None
Area: 22 sq miles (58 sq km)

Jan Mayen
North Atlantic
Status: Dependency
Claimed: 1929
Capital: Not applicable
Population: None
Area: 147 sq miles (381 sq km)

Continued on page 158

Overseas territories & dependencies

Peter I. Island
Southern Ocean
Status: Dependency
Claimed: 1931
Capital: Not applicable
Population: None
Area: 69 sq miles (180 sq km)

Svalbard
Arctic Ocean
Status: Dependency
Claimed: 1920
Capital: Longyearbyen
Population: 2572
Area: 24,289 sq miles
(62,906 sq km)

UNITED KINGDOM

The UK still has the largest number
of overseas territories. These are
locally-governed by a mixture
of elected representatives and
appointed officials, and they
all enjoy a large measure of internal
self-government, but certain powers,
such as foreign affairs and defense,
are reserved for Governors
of the British Crown.

Anguilla
West Indies
Status: Dependent
territory
Claimed: 1650
Capital: The Valley
Population: 13,600
Area: 37 sq miles
(96 sq km)

Ascension Island
South Atlantic
Status: Dependency
of St. Helena
Claimed: 1673
Capital: Georgetown
Population: 940
Area: 34 sq miles
(88 sq km)

Bermuda
North Atlantic
Status: Crown colony
Claimed: 1612
Capital: Hamilton
Population: 67,837
Area: 20 sq miles (53 sq km)

**British Indian
Ocean Territory**
Status: Dependent
territory
Claimed: 1814
Capital: Diego Garcia
Population: 4000
Area: 23 sq miles
(60 sq km)

British Virgin Islands
West Indies
Status: Dependent territory
Claimed: 1672
Capital: Road Town
Population: 27,000
Area: 59 sq miles
(153 sq km)

Cayman Islands
West Indies
Status: Dependent territory
Claimed: 1670
Capital: George Town
Population: 60,456
Area: 100 sq miles (259 sq km)

Falkland Islands
South Atlantic
Status: Dependent territory
Claimed: 1832
Capital: Stanley
Population: 3140
Area: 4699 sq miles
(12,173 sq km)

Gibraltar
Southwest Europe
Status: Crown colony
Claimed: 1713
Capital: Gibraltar
Population: 29,286
Area: 2.5 sq miles (6.5 sq km)

Guernsey
Channel Islands
Status: Crown dependency
Claimed: 1066
Capital: St. Peter Port
Population: 65,573
Area: 25 sq miles (65 sq km)

Isle of Man
British Isles
Status: Crown dependency
Claimed: 1765
Capital: Douglas
Population: 80,085
Area: 221 sq miles (572 sq km)

Jersey
Channel Islands
Status: Crown dependency
Claimed: 1066
Capital: St. Helier
Population: 91,626
Area: 45 sq miles (116 sq km)

Montserrat
West Indies
Status: Dependent territory
Claimed: 1632
Capital: Plymouth *(de jure)*,
Brades *(de facto)*
Population: 4655
Area: 40 sq miles (102 sq km)

Pitcairn Islands
South Pacific
Status: Dependent territory
Claimed: 1887
Capital: Adamstown
Population: 50
Area: 18 sq miles (47 sq km)

St. Helena
South Atlantic
Status: Dependent territory
Claimed: 1673
Capital: Jamestown
Population: 4255
Area: 47 sq miles (122 sq km)

**South Georgia & The
South Sandwich Islands**
South Atlantic
Status: Dependent territory
Claimed: 1775
Capital: Not applicable
Population: No permanent
residents
Area: 1387 sq miles
(3592 sq km)

Tristan da Cunha
South Atlantic
Status: Dependency
of St. Helena
Claimed: 1612
Capital: Edinburgh
Population: 276
Area: 38 sq miles (98 sq km)

Turks & Caicos Islands
West Indies
Status: Dependent territory
Claimed: 1766
Capital: Cockburn Town
Population: 36,605
Area: 166 sq miles
(430 sq km)

UNITED STATES
OF AMERICA

America's overseas territories
have been seen as strategically
useful, if expensive, links with its
"backyards." The US has, in most
cases, given the local population a
say in deciding their own status.
A US Commonwealth territory, such
as Puerto Rico, has a greater level
of independence than that of a US
unincorporated or external territory.

American Samoa
South Pacific
Status: Unincorporated
territory
Claimed: 1900
Capital: Pago Pago
Population: 65,628
Area: 75 sq miles (195 sq km)

Baker &
Howland Islands
South Pacific
Status: Unincorporated
territory
Claimed: 1856
Capital: Not applicable
Population: None
Area: 0.5 sq miles (1.4 sq km)

Guam
West Pacific
Status: Unincorporated
territory
Claimed: 1898
Capital: Hagåtña
Population: 178,000
Area: 212 sq miles
(549 sq km)

Jarvis Island
South Pacific
Status: Unincorporated territory
Claimed: 1856
Capital: Not applicable
Population: None
Area: 1.7 sq miles (4.5 sq km)

Johnston Atoll
Central Pacific
Status: Unincorporated
territory
Claimed: 1858
Capital: Not applicable
Population: Not applicable
Area: 1 sq mile (2.8 sq km)

Kingman Reef
Central Pacific
Status: Administered territory
Claimed: 1856
Capital: Not applicable
Population: None
Area: 0.4 sq mile
(1 sq km)

Midway Islands
Central Pacific
Status: Administered
territory
Claimed: 1867
Capital: Not applicable
Population: None
Area: 2 sq miles
(5.2 sq km)

Navassa Island
West Indies
Status: Unincorporated
territory
Claimed: 1856
Capital: Not applicable
Population: None
Area: 2 sq miles (5.2 sq km)

Northern
Mariana Islands
West Pacific
Status: Commonwealth
territory
Claimed: 1947
Capital: Saipan
Population: 86,616
Area: 177 sq miles (457 sq km)

Palmyra Atoll
Central Pacific
Status: Unincorporated
territory
Claimed: 1898
Capital: Not applicable
Population: None
Area: 5 sq miles (12 sq km)

Puerto Rico
West Indies
Status: Commonwealth
territory
Claimed: 1898
Capital: San Juan
Population: 4.0 million
Area: 3515 sq miles
(9104 sq km)

Virgin Islands
West Indies
Status: Unincorporated
territory
Claimed: 1917
Capital: Charlotte Amalie
Population: 108,448
Area: 137 sq miles
(355 sq km)

Wake Island
Central Pacific
Status: Unincorporated
territory
Claimed: 1898
Capital: Not applicable
Population: 200
Area: 2.5 sq miles
(6.5 sq km)

Glossary of geographical terms

The following glossary lists all geographical terms occuring on the maps and in the main-entry names in the Index–Gazetteer. These terms may precede, follow or be run together with the proper elements of the name; where they precede it the term is reversed for indexing purposes – thus Poluostov Yamal is indexed as Yamal, Poluostrov.

A
À *Danish, Norwegian,* River
Alpen *German,* Alps
Altiplanicie *Spanish,* Plateau
Álv(en) *Swedish,* River
Anse *French,* Bay
Archipiélago *Spanish,* Archipelago
Arcipelago *Italian,* Archipelago
Arquipélago *Portuguese,* Archipelago
Aukštuma *Lithuanian,* Upland

B
Bahía *Spanish,* Bay
Baía *Portuguese,* Bay
Baḥr *Arabic,* River
Baie *French,* Bay
Bandao *Chinese,* Peninsula
Banjaran *Malay,* Mountain range
Batang *Malay,* Stream
-berg *Afrikaans, Norwegian,* Mountain
Birket *Arabic,* Lake
Boğazı *Turkish,* Strait
Bucht *German,* Bay
Bugten *Danish,* Bay
Buḥayrat *Arabic,* Lake, reservoir
Buḥeiret *Arabic,* Lake
Bukit *Malay,* Mountain
-bukta *Norwegian,* Bay
bukten *Swedish,* Bay
Burnu *Turkish,* Cape, point
Buuraha *Somali,* Mountains

C
Cabo *Portuguese,* Cape
Cap *French,* Cape
Cascada *Portuguese,* Waterfall
Cerro *Spanish,* Hill
Chaîne *French,* Mountain range
Chau *Cantonese,* Island
Cháy *Turkish,* Stream
Chhâk *Cambodian,* Bay
Chhu *Tibetan,* River
-chôsuji *Korean,* Reservoir

Chott *Arabic,* Salt lake, depression
Ch'ün-tao *Chinese,* Island group *Cambodian,* Mountains
Cordillera *Spanish,* Mountain range
Costa *Spanish,* Coast
Côte *French,* Coast
Cuchilla *Spanish,* Mountains

D
Dağı *Azerbaijani, Turkish,* Mountain
Dağları *Azerbaijani, Turkish,* Mountains
-dake *Japanese,* Peak
Danau *Indonesian,* Lake
Đao *Vietnamese,* Island
Daryá *Persian,* River
Daryácheh *Persian,* Lake
Dasht *Persian,* Plain, desert
Dawḥat *Arabic,* Bay
Dere *Turkish,* Stream
Dili *Azerbaijani,* Spit
-do *Korean,* Island
Dooxo *Somali,* Valley
Düzü *Azerbaijani,* Steppe
-dwíp *Bengali,* Island

E
Embalse *Spanish,* Reservoir
Erg *Arabic,* Dunes
Estany *Catalan,* Lake
Estrecho *Spanish,* Strait
-ey *Icelandic,* Island
Ezero *Bulgarian, Macedonian,* Lake

F
Fjord *Danish,* Fjord
-fjorden *Norwegian,* Fjord
-fjørdhur *Faeroese,* Fjord
Fleuve *French,* River
Fliegu *Maltese,* Channel
-fljór *Icelandic,* River

G
-gang *Korean,* River
Ganga *Nepali, Sinhala,* River
Gaoyuan *Chinese,* Plateau
-gawa *Japanese,* River

Gebel *Arabic,* Mountain
-gebirge *German,* Mountains
Ghubbat *Arabic,* Bay
Gjiri *Albanian,* Bay
Gol *Mongolian,* River
Golfe *French,* Gulf
Golfo *Italian, Spanish,* Gulf
Gora *Russian, Serbian,* Mountain
Gory *Russian,* Mountains
Guba *Russian,* Bay
Gunung *Malay,* Mountain

H
Ḥadd *Arabic,* Spit
-haehyôp *Korean,* Strait
Haff *German,* Lagoon
Hai *Chinese,* Sea, bay
Ḥammádat *Arabic,* Plateau
Hámún *Persian,* Lake
Hawr *Arabic,* Lake
Háyk' *Amharic,* Lake
He *Chinese,* River
Helodrano *Malagasy,* Bay
-hegység *Hungarian,* Mountain range
Hka *Burmese,* River
-ho *Korean,* Lake
Hô *Korean,* Reservoir
/olot *Hebrew,* Dunes
Hora *Belorussian,* Mountain
Hrada *Belorussian,* Mountains, ridge
Hsi *Chinese,* River
Hu *Chinese,* Lake

I
Île(s) *French,* Island(s)
Ilha(s) *Portuguese,* Island(s)
Ilhéu(s) *Portuguese,* Islet(s)
Irmak *Turkish,* River
Isla(s) *Spanish,* Island(s)
Isola (Isole) *Italian,* Island(s)

J
Jabal *Arabic,* Mountain
Jál *Arabic,* Ridge
-järvi *Finnish,* Lake
Jazírat *Arabic,* Island
Jazíreh *Persian,* Island

Jebel *Arabic,* Mountain
Jezero *Serbian/Croatian,* Lake
Jiang *Chinese,* River
-joki *Finnish,* River
-jökull *Icelandic,* Glacier
Juzur *Arabic,* Islands

K
Kaikyó *Japanese,* Strait
-kaise *Lappish,* Mountain
Kali *Nepali,* River
Kalnas *Lithuanian,* Mountain
Kalns *Latvian,* Mountain
Kang *Chinese,* Harbor
Kangri *Tibetan,* Mountain(s)
Kaôh *Cambodian,* Island
Kapp *Norwegian,* Cape
Kavír *Persian,* Desert
K'edi *Georgian,* Mountain range
Kediet *Arabic,* Mountain
Kepulauan *Indonesian, Malay,* Island group
Khalíg, Khalíj *Arabic,* Gulf
Khawr *Arabic,* Inlet
Khola *Nepali,* River
Khrebet *Russian,* Mountain range
Ko *Thai,* Island
Kolpos *Greek,* Bay
-kopf *German,* Peak
Körfäzi *Azerbaijani,* Bay
Körfezi *Turkish,* Bay
Kõrgustik *Estonian,* Upland
Koshi *Nepali,* River
Kowtal *Persian,* Pass
Kúh(há) *Persian,* Mountain(s)
-kundo *Korean,* Island group
-kysten *Norwegian,* Coast
Kyun *Burmese,* Island

L
Laaq *Somali,* Watercourse
Lac *French,* Lake
Lacul *Romanian,* Lake
Lago *Italian, Portuguese, Spanish,* Lake

Laguna *Spanish,* Lagoon, Lake
Laht *Estonian,* Bay
Laut *Indonesian,* Sea
Lembalemba *Malagasy,* Plateau
Lerr *Armenian,* Mountain
Lerrnashght'a *Armenian,* Mountain range
Les *Czech,* Forest
Lich *Armenian,* Lake
Liqeni *Albanian,* Lake
Lumi *Albanian,* River
Lyman *Ukrainian,* Estuary

M

Mae Nam *Thai,* River
-mägi *Estonian,* Hill
Maja *Albanian,* Mountain
-man *Korean,* Bay
Marios *Lithuanian,* Lake
-meer *Dutch,* Lake
Melkosopochnik *Russian,* Plain
-meri *Estonian,* Sea
Mifraz *Hebrew,* Bay
Monkhafad *Arabic,* Depression
Mont(s) *French,* Mountain(s)
Monte *Italian, Portuguese,* Mountain
More *Russian,* Sea
Mörön *Mongolian,* River

N

Nagor'ye *Russian,* Upland
Naȷal *Hebrew,* River
Nahr *Arabic,* River
Nam *Laotian,* River
Nehri *Turkish,* River
Nevado *Spanish,* Mountain (snow-capped)
Nisoi *Greek,* Islands
Nizmennost' *Russian,* Lowland, plain
Nosy *Malagasy,* Island
Nur *Mongolian,* Lake
Nuruu *Mongolian,* Mountains
Nuur *Mongolian,* Lake
Nyzovyna *Ukrainian,* Lowland, plain

O

Ostrov(a) *Russian,* Island(s)
Oued *Arabic,* Watercourse
-oy *Faeroese,* Island
-øy(a) *Norwegian,* Island
Oya *Sinhala,* River
Ozero *Russian, Ukrainian,* Lake

P

Passo *Italian,* Pass
Pegunungan *Indonesian, Malay,* Mountain range
Pelagos *Greek,* Sea
Penisola *Italian,* Peninsula
Peski *Russian,* Sands
Phanom *Thai,* Mountain
Phou *Laotian,* Mountain
Pic *Catalan,* Peak
Pico *Portuguese, Spanish,* Peak
Pik *Russian,* Peak
Planalto *Portuguese,* Plateau
Planina, Planini *Bulgarian, Macedonian, Serbian, Croatian,* Mountain range
Ploskogor'ye *Russian,* Upland
Poluostrov *Russian,* Peninsula
Potamos *Greek,* River
Proliv *Russian,* Strait
Pulau *Indonesian, Malay,* Island
Pulu *Malay,* Island
Punta *Portuguese, Spanish,* Point

Q

Qá' *Arabic,* Depression
Qolleh *Persian,* Mountain

R

Raas *Somali,* Cape
-rags *Latvian,* Cape
Ramlat *Arabic,* Sands
Ra's *Arabic,* Cape, point, headland
Ravnina *Bulgarian, Russian,* Plain
Récif *French,* Reef
Represa (Rep.) *Spanish, Portuguese,* Reservoir
-rettó *Japanese,* Island chain
Riacho *Spanish,* Stream
Riban' *Malagasy,* Mountains
Rio *Portuguese,* River
Río *Spanish,* River
Riu *Catalan,* River
Rivier *Dutch,* River
Rivière *French,* River
Rowd *Pashtu,* River
Rúd *Persian,* River
Rudohorie *Slovak,* Mountains
Ruisseau *French,* Stream

S

Sabkhat *Arabic,* Salt marsh
Şaḥrá' *Arabic,* Desert
Samudra *Sinhala,* Reservoir
-san *Japanese, Korean,* Mountain
-sanchi *Japanese,* Mountains
-sanmaek *Korean,* Mountains
Sarír *Arabic,* Desert
Sebkha, Sebkhet *Arabic,* Salt marsh, depression
See *German,* Lake
Selat *Indonesian,* Strait
-selkä *Finnish,* Ridge
Selseleh *Persian,* Mountain range
Serra *Portuguese,* Mountain
Serranía *Spanish,* Mountain
Sha'íb *Arabic,* Watercourse
Shamo *Chinese,* Desert
Shan *Chinese,* Mountain(s)
Shan-mo *Chinese,* Mountain range
Shaṭṭ *Arabic,* Distributary
-shima *Japanese,* Island
Shui-tao *Chinese,* Channel
Sierra *Spanish,* Mountains
Sòn *Vietnamese,* Mountain
Sông *Vietnamese,* River
-spitze *German,* Peak
Štít *Slovak,* Peak
Stoeng *Cambodian,* River
Stretto *Italian,* Strait
Su Anbarı *Azerbaijani,* Reservoir
Sungai *Indonesian, Malay,* River
Suu *Turkish,* River

T

Tal *Mongolian,* Plain
Tandavan' *Malagasy,* Mountain range
Tangorombohitr' *Malagasy,* Mountain massif
Tao *Chinese,* Island
Tassili *Berber,* Plateau, mountain
Tau *Russian,* Mountain(s)
Taungdan *Burmese,* Mountain range

Teluk *Indonesian, Malay,* Bay
Terara *Amharic,* Mountain
Tog *Somali,* Valley
Tônlé *Cambodian,* Lake
Top *Dutch,* Peak
-tunturi *Finnish,* Mountain
Tur'at *Arabic,* Channel

V

Väin *Estonian,* Strait
-vatn *Icelandic,* Lake
-vesi *Finnish,* Lake
Vinh *Vietnamese,* Bay
Vodokhranilishche (Vdkhr.) *Russian,* Reservoir
Vodoskhovyshche (Vdskh.) *Ukrainian,* Reservoir
Volcán *Spanish,* Volcano
Vozvyshennost' *Russian,* Upland, plateau
Vrh *Macedonian,* Peak
Vysochyna *Ukrainian,* Upland
Vysočina *Czech,* Upland

W

Waadi *Somali,* Watercourse
Wâdí *Arabic,* Watercourse
Wâhat, Wâhat *Arabic,* Oasis
Wald *German,* Forest
Wan *Chinese,* Bay
Wyżyna *Polish,* Upland

X

Xé *Laotian,* River

Y

Yarımadası *Azerbaijani,* Peninsula
Yazovir *Bulgarian,* Reservoir
Yoma *Burmese,* Mountains
Yu *Chinese,* Islet

Z

Zaliv *Bulgarian, Russian,* Bay
Zatoka *Ukrainian,* Bay
Zemlya *Russian,* Land

Continental factfile

North & Central America

Total area:
9,400,000 sq miles
(24,346,000 sq km)

Total number of countries: 23

Total population:
512 million

Largest city with population: Mexico City, Mexico 20.1 million

Country with highest population density: Barbados 1807 people per sq mile (698 people per sq km)

Largest country:
Canada 3,855,171 sq miles
(9,984,670 sq km)

Smallest country:
St. Kitts & Nevis 101 sq miles
(261 sq km)

Largest lake: Lake Superior, Canada/ USA 32,151 sq miles (83,270 sq km)

Longest river: Mississippi-Missouri, USA 3710 miles (5969 km)

Highest point: Mt. McKinley (Denali), Alaska, USA 20,322 ft (6194 m)

lowest point: Death Valley, California, USA 282 ft (86 m) below sea level

South America

Total area:
6,880,000 sq miles
(17,819,000 sq km)

Total number of countries: 12

Total population:
375 million

Largest city with population: São Paulo, Brazil 19.6 million

Country with highest population density: Ecuador 138 people per sq mile (53 people per sq km)

Largest country:
Brazil 3,286,470 sq miles
(8,511,965 sq km)

Smallest country:
Suriname 63,039 sq miles
(163,270 sq km)

Largest lake: Lake Titicaca, Bolivia/Peru 3220 sq miles (8340 sq km)

Longest river: Amazon, Brazil 4049 miles (6516 km)

Highest point: Cerro Aconcagua, Argentina 22,831 ft (6959 m)

Lowest point: Laguna del Carbón, Argentina 344 ft (105 m) below sea level

Africa

Total area:
11,677,250 sq miles
(30,244,050 sq km)

Total number of countries: 57

Total population:
910 million

Largest city with population: Cairo, Egypt 11.4 million

Country with highest population density: Mauritius 1811 people per sq mile (699 people per sq km)

Largest country:
Algeria 919,590 sq miles
(2,381,740 sq km)

Smallest country:
Seychelles 176 sq miles
(455 sq km)

Largest lake: Lake Victoria, Uganda, Kenya, Tanzania 26,828 sq miles (69,484 sq km)

Longest river: Nile, Uganda/Sudan/Egypt 4160 miles (6695 km)

Highest point: Kilimanjaro, Tanzania 19,340 ft (5895 m)

Lowest point: Lac', Assal, Djibouti 512 ft (156 m) below sea level

Europe

Total area:
4,809,200 sq miles
(12,456,000 sq km)

Total number of countries: 46

Total population:
697 million

Largest city with population: Moscow, Euro Russia 11.5 million

Country with highest population density: Monaco 40,680 people per sq mile (15,641 people per sq km)

Largest country: European Russia 1,527,341 sq miles (3,955,818 sq km)

Smallest country:
Vatican City, Italy 0.17 sq miles
(0.44 sq km)

Largest lake: Ladoga, European Russia 7100 sq miles (18,390 sq km)

Longest river: Volga, European Russia 2290 miles (3688 km)

Highest point: El'brus, Caucasus Mts, European Russia 18,510 ft (5642 m)

Lowest point: Volga Delta, Caspian Sea, European Russia 92 ft (28 m) below sea level

North & West Asia

 Total area:
9,585,500 sq miles
(24,826,600 sq km)

 Total number of
countries: 24

 Total population:
398 million

 Largest city with
population: Tehran, Iran
8.4 million

 Country with highest
population density: Bahrain
4762 people per sq mile
(1841 people per sq km)

 Largest country: Asiatic
Russia 5,065,471 sq miles
(13,119,582 sq km)

 Smallest country:
Bahrain 239 sq miles
(620 sq km)

 Largest lake:
Caspian Sea 142,243 sq miles
(371,000 sq km)

 Longest river: Ob'-Irtysh,
Asiatic Russia 3461 miles
(5570 km)

 Highest point: Pik Pobedy,
Kyrgyzstan/China 24,408 ft
(7439 m)

 Lowest point: Dead Sea,
Israel/Jordan 1388 ft
(423 m) below sea level

South & East Asia

 Total area:
7,936,200 sq miles
(20,554,700 sq km)

 Total number of
countries: 24

 Total population:
3979 million

 Largest city with
population: Tokyo,
Japan 36.9 million

 Country with highest
population density: Singapore
22,034 people per sq mile
(8525 people per sq km)

 Largest country:
China 3,705,386 sq miles
(9,596,960 sq km)

 Smallest country:
Maldives 116 sq miles
(300 sq km)

 Largest lake: Tonle Sap,
Cambodia 1000 sq miles
(2850 sq km)

 Longest river: Chang Jiang
(Yangtze) 3965 miles
(6380 km)

 Highest point:
Mount Everest, Nepal
29,035 ft (8850 m)

 Lowest point: Turpan Hami,
(Turfan basin), China 505 ft
(154 m) below sea level

Australasia & Oceania

 Total area:
3,376,700 sq miles
(8,745,750 sq km)

 Total number of
countries: 14

 Total population:
32 million

 Largest city with
population: Sydney,
Australia 4.4 million

 Country with highest
population density: Nauru
1670 people per sq mile
(644 people per sq km)

 Largest country:
Australia 2,967,893 sq miles
(7,686,850 sq km)

 Smallest country:
Nauru 8 sq miles
(21 sq km)

 Largest lake: Lake Eyre,
Australia 3700 sq miles
(9583 sq km)

 Longest river: Murray-
Darling, Australia
2330 miles (3750 km)

 Highest point: Mt. Wilhelm,
Papua New Guinea 14,795 ft
(4509 m)

 Lowest point: Lake Eyre,
Australia 52 ft
(16 m) below sea level

Antarctica

 Total area: 5,450,500 sq miles (14,000,000 sq km)
of which approx. 324,300 sq miles
(840,000 sq km) is ice-free.

 Total number of countries: The Antarctic Treaty has
30 participating nations and 14 with observer status.
Claims by Australia, France, New Zealand, Norway,
Argentina, Chile, and the UK are not recognized by
other member states.

 Total Population: No indigenous population.
74 research stations, (42 are staffed all year-round).
Population varies between about 1000 (winter)
and 4000 (summer).

 Total volume of ice:
7,200,000 cu miles (30,000,000 cu km):
contains 90% of Earth's fresh water

 Sea ice: 1,158,300 sq miles (3,000,000
sq km) in February. 7,722,000 sq miles
(20,000,000 sq km) in October

 Lowest temperature: Vostok station
-89.5°C (-129°F)

 Highest point: Vinson Massif
16,072 ft (4897 m)

 Lowest Point: Coastline 0ft/m

Geographical comparisons

Largest countries

Russ. Fed. .... 6,592,735 sq miles ....(17,075,200 sq km)
Canada ....3,855,171 sq miles .....(9,984,670 sq km)
USA .... 3,717,792 sq miles .... (9,629,091 sq km)
China ....3,705,386 sq miles .....(9,596,960 sq km)
Brazil ....3,286,470 sq miles .....(8,511,965 sq km)
Australia ....2,967,893 sq miles .....(7,686,850 sq km)
India ....1,269,339 sq miles .....(3,287,590 sq km)
Argentina ....1,068,296 sq miles .....(2,766,890 sq km)
Kazakhstan ....1,049,150 sq miles .....(2,717,300 sq km)
Algeria .... 919,590 sq miles .....(2,381,740 sq km)

Smallest countries

Vatican City .... 0.17 sq miles ....(0.44 sq km)
Monaco .... 0.75 sq miles ....(1.95 sq km)
Nauru .... 8 sq miles ....(21 sq km)
Tuvalu .... 10 sq miles ....(26 sq km)
San Marino .... 24 sq miles ....(61 sq km)
Liechtenstein............. 62 sq miles ....(160 sq km)
Marshall Islands......... 70 sq miles ....(181 sq km)
St. Kitts & Nevis .... 101 sq miles ....(261 sq km)
Maldives................... 116 sq miles ....(300 sq km)
Malta....................... 124 sq miles ....(320 sq km)

Largest islands

Greenland...............849,400 sq miles (2,200,000 sq km)
New Guinea .... 312,000 sq miles (808,000 sq km)
Borneo ....292,222 sq miles (757,050 sq km)
Madagascar ....229,300 sq miles (594,000 sq km)
Sumatra....................202,300 sq miles (524,000 sq km)
Baffin Island ....183,800 sq miles (476,000 sq km)
Honshu .... 88,800 sq miles (230,000 sq km)
Britain.......................... 88,700 sq miles (229,800 sq km)
Victoria Island.............81,900 sq miles (212,000 sq km)
Ellesmere Island ....75,700 sq miles (196,000 sq km)

Richest countries (GNI per capita, in US$)

Monaco 188,150
Liechtenstein....................................137,070
Norway..88,890
Qatar...80,440
Luxembourg 78,130
Switzerland..76,380
Denmark..60,390
Sweden 52,230
Netherlands.......................................49,730
Kuwait..48,900

Poorest countries (GNI per capita, in US$)

Congo, Dem. Rep.................... 190
Liberia 240
Burundi 250
Sierra Leone. 340
Malawi 340
Niger...................................... 360
Ethiopia 400
Afghanistan 400
Madagascar 430
Eritrea 430

Most populous countries

China......................................1,347,300,000
India 1,240,000,000
USA..314,500,000
Indonesia...............................237,600,000
Brazil......................................193,300,000
Pakistan.................................180,800,000
Nigeria...................................166,500,000
Bangladesh 152,500,000
Russian Federation.................143,200,000
Japan.....................................127,500,000

Least populous countries

Vatican City 821
Nauru 9,378
Tuvalu 10,619
Palau 21,032
Monaco 30,510
San Marino 32,140
Liechtenstein.....................................36,713
St. Kitts & Nevis 50,726
Marshall Islands.................................64,480
Dominica 73,126

Most densely populated countries

Monaco ....40,680 people per sq mile (15,641 per sq km)
Singapore ....22,034 people per sq mile (8525 per sq km)
Vatican City......... 4918 people per sq mile (1900 per sq km)
Bahrain.................. 4762 people per sq mile (1841 per sq km)
Maldives................ 3400 people per sq mile (1315 per sq km)
Malta..................... 3226 people per sq mile (1250 per sq km)
Bangladesh .... 2911 people per sq mile (1124 per sq km)
Taiwan .... 1860 people per sq mile (718 per sq km)
Mauritius............... 1811 people per sq mile (699 per sq km)
Barbados .... 1807 people per sq mile (698 per sq km)

Most sparsely populated countries

Mongolia.........5 people per sq mile......... (2 per sq km)
Namibia...........7 people per sq mile......... (3 per sq km)
Australia...........8 people per sq mile......... (3 per sq km)
Suriname.........8 people per sq mile......... (3 per sq km)
Iceland ....8 people per sq mile......... (3 per sq km)
Mauritania ......9 people per sq mile......... (4 per sq km)
Botswana.........9 people per sq mile......... (4 per sq km)
Libya ....9 people per sq mile......... (4 per sq km)
Canada ....10 people per sq mile......... (4 per sq km)
Guyana ....11 people per sq mile......... (4 per sq km)

Most widely spoken languages

1. Chinese (Mandarin)	6. Arabic
2. English	7. Bengali
3. Hindi	8. Portuguese
4. Spanish	9. Malay-Indonesian
5. Russian	10. French

Largest conurbations

Tokyo 36,900,000
Delhi..21,900,000
Mexico City 20,100,000
New York - Newark 20,100,000
São Paulo..19,600,000
Shanghai...19,500,000
Mumbai...19,400,000
Beijing 15,000,000
Dhaka 14,900,000
Kolkata..14,300,000
Karachi..13,500,000
Buenos Aires 13,400,000
Los Angeles 13,200,000
Rio de Janeiro...11,800,000
Manilla..11,600,000
Moscow...11,500,000
Osaka 11,400,000
Cairo...11,400,000
Istanbul 10,900,000
Lagos 10,800,000
Paris 10,500,000
Guangzhou..10,500,000
Shenzhen 10,200,000
Seoul 9,700,000
Chongqing 9,700,000

Longest rivers

Nile (NE Africa) ....4160 miles ...... (6695 km)
Amazon (South America) ....4049 miles ...... (6516 km)
Yangtze (China).........................3915 miles ...... (6299 km)
Mississippi/Missouri (USA).........3710 miles........(5969 km)
Ob'-Irtysh (Russ. Fed.) ....3461 miles........(5570 km)
Yellow River (China) ....3395 miles ...... (5464 km)
Congo (Central Africa) ....2900 miles ...... (4667 km)
Mekong (Southeast Asia) ....2749 miles...... (4425 km)
Lena (Russian Federation)........2734 miles...... (4400 km)
Mackenzie (Canada) ....2640 miles....... (4250 km)
Yenisey (Russ. Federation) ......2541 miles...... (4090 km)

Highest mountains (Height above sea level)

Everest ....29,029 ft .... (8848 m)
K2 ....28,253 ft .... (8611 m)
Kanchenjunga I..........................28,210 ft .... (8598 m)
Makalu I ....27,767 ft .... (8463 m)
Cho Oyu ....26,907 ft .... (8201 m)
Dhaulagiri I................................26,796 ft .... (8167 m)
Manaslu I ....26,783 ft .... (8163 m)
Nanga Parbat I...........................26,661 ft .... (8126 m)
Annapurna I ....26,547 ft .... (8091 m)
Gasherbrum I ....26,471 ft .... (8068 m)

Largest bodies of inland water (Area & depth)

Caspian Sea
    143,243 sq miles (371,000 sq km).......3215 ft (980 m)
Lake Superior
    32,151 sq miles (83,270 sq km).......1289 ft (393 m)
Lake Victoria
    26,560 sq miles (68,880 sq km).........328 ft (100 m)
Lake Huron
    23,436 sq miles (60,700 sq km).........751 ft (229 m)
Lake Michigan
    22,402 sq miles (58,020 sq km).........922 ft (281 m)
Lake Tanganyika
    12,703 sq miles (32,900 sq km).... 4700 ft (1435 m)
Great Bear Lake
    12,274 sq miles (31,790 sq km)...... 1047 ft (319 m)
Lake Baikal
    11,776 sq miles (30,500 sq km).... 5712 ft (1741 m)
Great Slave Lake
    10,981 sq miles (28,440 sq km).........459 ft (140 m)
Lake Erie
    9915 sq miles (25,680 sq km)...........197 ft (60 m)

......continued on page 166

Geographical comparisons continued

Deepest ocean features

Challenger Deep, Mariana Trench (Pacific)
36,201 ft .... (11,034 m)
Vityaz III Depth, Tonga Trench (Pacific)
35,704 ft .... (10,882 m)
Vityaz Depth, Kurile-Kamchatka Trench (Pacific)
34,588 ft .... (10,542 m)
Cape Johnson Deep, Philippine Trench (Pacific)
34,441 ft .... (10,497 m)
Kermadec Trench (Pacific)
32,964 ft .... (10,047 m)
Ramapo Deep, Japan Trench (Pacific)
32,758 ft .... (9984 m)
Milwaukee Deep, Puerto Rico Trench (Atlantic)
30,185 ft .... (9200 m)
Argo Deep, Torres Trench (Pacific)
30,070 ft .... (9165 m)
Meteor Depth, South Sandwich Trench (Atlantic)
30,000 ft .... (9144 m)
Planet Deep, New Britain Trench (Pacific)
29,988 ft .... (9140 m)

Greatest waterfalls
(Mean flow of water)

Boyoma (D.R. Congo) ..... 600,400 cu. ft/sec (17,000 cu.m/sec)
Khône (Laos/Cambodia) ... 410,000 cu. ft/sec (11,600 cu.m/sec)
Niagara (USA/Canada) .... 195,000 cu. ft/sec (5500 cu.m/sec)
Grande, Salto (Uruguay) ..... 160,000 cu. ft/sec (4500 cu.m/sec)
Paulo Afonso (Brazil) .... 100,000 cu. ft/sec(2800 cu.m/sec)
Urubupungá (Brazil) .... 97,000 cu. ft/sec (2750 cu.m/sec)
Iguaçu (Argentina/Brazil) .... 62,000 cu. ft/sec (1700 cu.m/sec)
Maribondo (Brazil) .... 53,000 cu. ft/sec (1500 cu.m/sec)
Victoria (Zimbabwe) .... 39,000 cu. ft/sec (1100 cu.m/sec)
Murchison Falls (Uganda) ..... 42,000 cu. ft/sec (1200 cu.m/sec)
Churchill (Canada) .... 35,000 cu. ft/sec (1000 cu.m/sec)
Kaveri Falls (India) .... 33,000 cu. ft/sec (900 cu.m/sec)

Highest waterfalls

Angel (Venezuela) .... 3212 ft .... (979 m)
Tugela (South Africa) .... 3110 ft .... (948 m)
Utigard (Norway) .... 2625 ft .... (800 m)
Mongefossen (Norway) .... 2539 ft .... (774 m)
Mtarazi (Zimbabwe) .... 2500 ft .... (762 m)
Yosemite (USA) .... 2425 ft .... (739 m)
Ostre Mardola Foss (Norway) ..... 2156 ft .... (657 m)
Tyssestrengane (Norway) .... 2119 ft .... (646 m)
*Cuquenan (Venezuela) .... 2001 ft .... (610 m)
Sutherland (New Zealand) .... 1903 ft .... (580 m)
*Kjellfossen (Norway) .... 1841 ft .... (561 m)

indicates that the total height is a single leap

Largest deserts

Sahara .... 3,450,000 sq miles (9,065,000 sq km)
Gobi .... 500,000 sq miles (1,295,000 sq km)
Ar Rub al Khali ...... 289,600 sq miles (750,000 sq km)
Great Victorian ..... 249,800 sq miles (647,000 sq km)
Sonoran .... 120,000 sq miles (311,000 sq km)
Kalahari .... 120,000 sq miles (310,800 sq km)
Kara Kum .... 115,800 sq miles (300,000 sq km)
Takla Makan .... 100,400 sq miles (260,000 sq km)
Namib .... 52,100 sq miles (135,000 sq km)
Thar .... 33,670 sq miles (130,000 sq km)

*NB – Most of Antarctica is a polar desert, with only
2 inches (50 mm) of precipitation annually*

Hottest inhabited places

Djibouti (Djibouti) .... 86.0°F .... (30.0°C)
Tombouctou (Mali) .... 84.7°F .... (29.3°C)
Tirunelveli (India) .... 84.7°F .... (29.3°C)
Tuticorin (India) .... 84.7°F .... (29.3°C)
Nellore (India) .... 84.5°F .... (29.2°C)
Santa Marta (Colombia) .... 84.5°F .... (29.2°C)
Aden (Yemen) .... 84.0°F .... (29.0°C)
Madurai (India) .... 84.0°F .... (29.0°C)
Niamey (Niger) .... 84.0°F .... (29.0°C)

Driest inhabited places

Aswân (Egypt) .... 0.02 in .... (0.5 mm)
Luxor (Egypt) .... 0.03 in .... (0.7 mm)
Arica (Chile) .... 0.04 in .... (1.1 mm)
Ica (Peru) .... 0.10 in .... (2.3 mm)
Antofagasta (Chile) .... 0.20 in .... (4.9 mm)
El Minya (Egypt) .... 0.20 in .... (5.1 mm)
Asyut (Egypt) .... 0.20 in .... (5.2 mm)
Callao (Peru) .... 0.50 in ..... (12.0 mm)
Trujillo (Peru) .... 0.55 in ..... (14.0 mm)
Al Fayyum (Egypt) .... 0.80 in ..... (19.0 mm)

Wettest inhabited places

Mawsynram (India) .... 467 in .. (11,862 mm)
Mt Waialeale (Hawaii, USA) .... 460 in .. (11,684 mm)
Cherrapunji (India) .... 450 in .. (11,430 mm)
Cape Debundsha (Cameroon) ... 405 in .. (10,290 mm)
Quibdo (Colombia) .... 354 in .... (8892 mm)
Buenaventura (Colombia) .... 265 in .... (6743 mm)
Monrovia (Liberia) .... 202 in .... (5131 mm)
Pago Pago (American Samoa) .... 196 in .... (4990 mm)
Moulmein (Myanmar) .... 191 in .... (4852 mm)
Lae (Papua New Guinea) .... 183 in .... (4645 mm)

GLOSSARY OF ABBREVIATIONS
This Glossary provides a comprehensive guide to the abbreviations used in this Atlas, and in the Index.

A
abbrev. abbreviated
Afr. Afrikaans
Alb. Albanian
Amh. Amharic
anc. ancient
Ar. Arabic
Arm. Armenian
Az. Azerbaijani

B
Basq. Basque
Bel. Belorussian
Ben. Bengali
Bibl. Biblical
Bret. Breton
Bul. Bulgarian
Bur. Burmese

C
Cam. Cambodian
Cant. Cantonese
Cast. Castilian
Cat. Catalan
Chin. Chinese
Cro. Croat
Cz. Czech

D
Dan. Danish
Dut. Dutch

E
Eng. English
Est. Estonian
est. estimated

F
Faer. Faeroese
Fij. Fijian
Fin. Finnish
Flem. Flemish
Fr. French
Fris. Frisian

G
Geor. Georgian
Ger. German
Gk. Greek
Guj. Gujarati

H
Haw. Hawaiian
Heb. Hebrew
Hind. Hindi
hist. historical
Hung. Hungarian

I
Icel. Icelandic
Ind. Indonesian
In. Inuit
Ir. Irish
It. Italian

J
Jap. Japanese

K
Kaz. Kazakh
Kir. Kirghiz
Kor. Korean
Kurd. Kurdish

L
Lao. Laotian
Lapp. Lappish
Lat. Latin
Latv. Latvian

Lith. Lithanian
Lus. Lusatian

M
Mac. Macedonian
Mal. Malay
Malg. Malagasy
Malt. Maltese
Mon. Montenegro
Mong. Mongolian

N
Nepali. Nepali
Nor. Norwegian

O
off. officially

P
Pash. Pashtu
Per. Persian
Pol. Polish
Port. Portuguese
prev. previously

R
Rmsch. Romansch
Roman. Romanian
Rus. Russian

S
SCr. Serbo - Croatian
Serb. Serbian
Slvk. Slovak
Slvn. Slovene
Som. Somali
Sp. Spanish
Swa. Swahili
Swe. Swedish

T
Taj. Tajik
Th. Thai
Tib. Tibetan
Turk. Turkish
Turkm. Turkmenistan

U
Uigh. Uighur
Ukr. Ukrainian
Uzb. Uzbek

V
var. variant
Vtn. Vietnamese

W
Wel. Welsh

X
Xh. Xhosa

Key to country factboxes within the Index:

Formation
Date of independence

Population
Total population / population density - based on total land area .

Calorie consumption
Average number of calories consumed daily per person.

A
Aa see Gauja
Aachen 94 A4 Dut. Aken, Fr. Aix-la-Chapelle; anc. Aquae Grani, Aquisgranum. Nordrhein-Westfalen, W Germany
Aaiún see Laâyoune
Aalborg 85 B7 var. Ålborg, Ålborg-Nørresundby; anc. Alburgum. Nordjylland, N Denmark
Aalen 95 B6 Baden-Württemberg, S Germany
Aalsmeer 86 C3 Noord-Holland, C Netherlands
Aalst 87 B6 Oost-Vlaanderen, C Belgium
Aalten 86 E4 Gelderland, E Netherlands
Aalter 87 B5 Oost-Vlaanderen, NW Belgium
Aanaarjävri see Inarijärvi
Äänekoski 85 D5 Länsi-Suomi, W Finland
Aar see Aare
Aare 95 A7 var. Aar. river W Switzerland
Aarhus see Århus
Aarlen see Arlon
Aat see Ath
Aba 77 E5 Orientale, NE Dem. Rep. Congo
Aba 75 G5 Abia, S Nigeria
Abā as Su'ūd see Najrān
Abaco Island see Great Abaco, N Bahamas
Ābādān 120 C4 Khūzestān, SW Iran
Abadan 122 C3 prev. Bezmein, Büzmeýin, Rus. Byuzmeyin. Ahal Welaýaty, C Turkmenistan
Abai see Blue Nile
Abakan 114 D4 Respublika Khakasiya, S Russian Federation
Abancay 60 D4 Apurímac, SE Peru
Abariringa see Kanton
Abashiri 130 D2 var. Abasiri. Hokkaidō, NE Japan
Abasiri see Abashiri
Åbay Wenz see Blue Nile
Abbaia see Ābaya Hāyk'
Abbatis Villa see Abbeville
Abbazia see Opatija
Abbeville 90 C2 anc. Abbatis Villa. Somme, N France
'Abd al 'Azīz, Jabal 118 D2 mountain range NE Syria
Abéché 76 C3 var. Abécher, Abeshr. Ouaddaï, SE Chad
Abécher see Abéché
Abela see Ávila
Abellinum see Avellino
Abemama 144 D2 var. Apamama; prev. Roger Simpson Island. atoll Tungaru, W Kiribati
Abengourou 75 E5 E Côte d'Ivoire
Aberbrothock see Arbroath
Abercorn see Mbala
Aberdeen 88 D3 anc. Devana. NE Scotland, United Kingdom
Aberdeen 45 E2 South Dakota, N USA
Aberdeen 46 B2 Washington, NW USA
Abergwaun see Fishguard
Abertawe see Swansea
Aberystwyth 89 C6 W Wales, United Kingdom
Abeshr see Abéché
Abhā 121 B6 'Asīr, SW Saudi Arabia
Abidavichy 107 D7 Rus. Obidovichi. Mahilyowskaya Voblasts', E Belarus
Abidjan 75 E5 S Côte d'Ivoire
Abilene 49 F3 Texas, SW USA
Abingdon see Pinta, Isla
Åbo see Turku
Aboisso 75 E5 SE Côte d'Ivoire
Abo, Massif d' 76 B1 mountain range NW Chad
Abomey 75 F5 S Benin
Abou-Déïa 76 C3 Salamat, SE Chad
Aboudouhour see Abū aḍ Ḑuhūr
Abou Kémal see Abū Kamāl
Abrantes 92 B3 var. Abrántes. Santarém, C Portugal
Abrashlare see Brezovo
Abrolhos Bank 56 E4 undersea bank W Atlantic Ocean
Abrova 107 B6 Rus. Obrovo. Brestskaya Voblasts', SW Belarus
Abrud 108 B4 Ger. Gross-Schlatten, Hung. Abrudbánya. Alba, SW Romania
Abrudbánya see Abrud

Abruzzese, Appennino 96 C4 mountain range C Italy
Absaroka Range 44 B2 mountain range Montana/Wyoming, NW USA
Abū aḍ Ḑuhūr 118 B3 Fr. Aboudouhour. Idlib, NW Syria
Abu Hamed 72 C3 River Nile, N Sudan
Abū Ḩardān 118 E3 var. Hajîne. Dayr az Zawr, E Syria
Abuja 75 G4 country capital (Nigeria) Federal Capital District, C Nigeria
Abū Kamāl 118 E3 Fr. Abou Kémal. Dayr az Zawr, E Syria
Abula see Ávila
Abunã, Rio 62 C2 var. Río Abuná. river Bolivia/Brazil
Abut Head 151 B6 headland South Island, New Zealand
Abuye Meda 72 D4 mountain C Ethiopia
Abū Ẓaby 121 C5 var. Abū Ẓabī, Eng. Abu Dhabi. country capital (United Arab Emirates) Abū Ẓaby, C United Arab Emirates
Abū Ẓabī see Abū Ẓaby
Abyad, Al Baḩr al see White Nile
Abyei Area 73 B5 disputed region Southern Kordofan, S Sudan
Abyla see Ávila
Abyssinia see Ethiopia
Acalayong 77 A5 SW Equatorial Guinea
Acaponeta 50 D4 Nayarit, C Mexico
Acapulco 51 E5 var. Acapulco de Juárez. Guerrero, S Mexico
Acapulco de Juárez see Acapulco
Acarai Mountains 59 F4 Sp. Serra Acaraí. mountain range Brazil/Guyana
Acaraí, Serra see Acarai Mountains
Acarigua 58 D2 Portuguesa, N Venezuela
Accra 75 E5 country capital (Ghana) SE Ghana
Achacachi 61 E4 La Paz, W Bolivia
Ach'ara 117 F2 prev. Achara, var. Ajaria. autonomous republic SW Georgia
Achara see Ach'ara
Acklins Island 54 C2 island SE Bahamas
Aconcagua, Cerro 64 B4 mountain W Argentina
Açores/Açores, Arquipélago dos/ Açores, Ilhas dos see Azores
A Coruña 92 B1 Cast. La Coruña, Eng. Corunna; anc. Caronium. Galicia, NW Spain
Acre 62 C2 off. Estado do Acre. state W Brazil
Acre 62 C2 off. Estado do Acre. region W Brazil
Açu see Assu
Acunum Acusio see Montélimar
Ada 100 D3 Vojvodina, N Serbia
Ada 49 G2 Oklahoma, C USA
Ada Bazar see Adapazarı
Adalia see Antalya
Adalia, Gulf of see Antalya Körfezi
Adama see Nazrēt
'Adan 121 B7 Eng. Aden. SW Yemen
Adana 116 D4 var. Seyhan. Adana, S Turkey
Adâncata see Horlivka
Adapazarı 116 B2 prev. Ada Bazar. Sakarya, NW Turkey
Adare, Cape 154 B4 cape Antarctica
Ad Dahna 120 C4 desert E Saudi Arabia
Ad Dakhla 70 A4 var. Dakhla. SW Western Sahara
Ad Dalanj see Dilling
Ad Damar see Ed Damer
Ad Damazin see Ed Damazin
Ad Dāmir see Ed Damer
Ad Dammām 120 C4 var. Dammām. Ash Sharqiyah, NE Saudi Arabia
Ad Dāmūr see Damoûr
Ad Dawḩah 120 C4 Eng. Doha. country capital (Qatar) C Qatar
Aḑ Ḑiffah see Libyan Plateau
Addis Ababa see Ādīs Ābeba
Addoo Atoll see Addu Atoll
Addu Atoll 132 A5 var. Addoo Atoll, Seenu Atoll. atoll S Maldives
Adelaide 149 B6 state capital South Australia
Adelsberg see Postojna
Aden see 'Adan
Aden, Gulf of 121 C7 gulf SW Arabian Sea
Adige 96 C2 Ger. Etsch. river N Italy
Adirondack Mountains 41 F2 mountain range New York, NE USA

Ādīs Ābeba 73 C5 Eng. Addis Ababa. country capital (Ethiopia) Ādīs Ābeba, C Ethiopia
Adıyaman 117 E4 Adıyaman, SE Turkey
Adjud 108 C4 Vrancea, E Romania
Admiralty Islands 144 B3 island group N Papua New Guinea
Adra 93 E5 Andalucía, S Spain
Adrar 70 D3 C Algeria
Adrian 40 C3 Michigan, N USA
Adrianople/Adrianopolis see Edirne
Adriatico, Mare see Adriatic Sea
Adriatic Sea 112 B2 Alb. Deti Adriatik, It. Mare Adriatico, SCr. Jadransko More, Slvn. Jadransko Morje. sea N Mediterranean Sea
Adriatik, Deti see Adriatic Sea
Adycha 115 F2 river NE Russian Federation
Aegean Sea 105 C5 Gk. Aigaíon Pelagos, Aigaío Pélagos, Turk. Ege Denizi. sea NE Mediterranean Sea
Aegviidu 106 D2 Ger. Charlottenhof. Harjumaa, NW Estonia
Aegyptus see Egypt
Aelana see Al 'Aqabah
Aelok see Ailuk Atoll
Aelōnlaplap see Ailinglaplap Atoll
Aemona see Ljubljana
Aeolian Islands 97 C6 var. Isole Lipari, Eng. Aeolian Islands, Lipari Islands. island group S Italy
Aeolian Islands see Eolie, Isole
Æsernia see Isernia
Afar Depression see Danakil Desert
Afars et des Issas, Territoire Français des see Djibouti
Afghānestān, Dowlat-e Eslāmī-ye see Afghanistan
Afghanistan 122 C4 off. Islamic Republic of Afghanistan, Per. Dowlat-e Eslāmī-ye Afghānestān; prev. Republic of Afghanistan. country C Asia

AFGHANISTAN
Central Asia

Official name The Islamic Republic of Afghanistan
Formation 1919 / 1919
Capital Kabul
Population 32.4 million / 129 people per sq mile (50 people per sq km)
Total area 250,000 sq. miles (647,500 sq. km)
Languages Pashtu*, Tajik, Dari*, Farsi, Uzbek, Turkmen
Religions Sunni Muslim 80%, Shi'a Muslim 19%, Other 1%
Ethnic mix Pashtun 38%, Tajik 25%, Hazara 19%, Uzbek and Turkmen 15%, Other 3%
Government Nonparty system
Currency Afghani = 100 puls
Literacy rate 28%
Calorie consumption 1539 kilocalories

Afmadow 73 D6 Jubbada Hoose, S Somalia
Africa 68 continent
Africa, Horn of 68 E4 physical region Ethiopia/Somalia
Africana Seamount 141 A6 seamount SW Indian Ocean
'Afrīn 118 B2 Ḥalab, N Syria
Afyon 116 B3 var. Afyonkarahisar. Afyon, W Turkey
Agadès see Agadez
Agadez 75 G3 prev. Agadès. Agadez, C Niger
Agadir 70 B3 SW Morocco
Agana/Agaña see Hagåtña
Ágaro 73 C5 Oromīya, C Ethiopia
Agassiz Fracture Zone 143 G5 fracture zone S Pacific Ocean
Agatha see Agde
Agathónisi 105 D6 island Dodekánisa, Greece, Aegean Sea
Agde 91 C6 anc. Agatha. Hérault, S France
Agedabia see Ajdābiyā
Agen 91 B5 anc. Aginnum. Lot-et-Garonne, SW France
Agendicum see Sens
Aghri Dagh see Büyükağrı Dağı
Agiá 104 B4 var. Ayiá. Thessalía, C Greece
Agialoúsa see Yenierenköy

Agía Marína 105 E6 Léros, Dodekánisa, Greece, Aegean Sea
Aginnum see Agen
Ágios Efstrátios 104 D4 var. Áyios Evstrátios, Hagios Evstrátios. island E Greece
Ágios Nikólaos 105 D8 var. Áyios Nikólaos. Kríti, Greece, E Mediterranean Sea
Āgra 134 D3 Uttar Pradesh, N India
Agra and Oudh, United Provinces of see Uttar Pradesh
Agram see Zagreb
Ağrı 117 F3 var. Karaköse; prev. Karakılısse. Ağrı, NE Turkey
Agri Dagi see Büyükağrı Dağı
Agrigento 97 C7 Gk. Akragas; prev. Girgenti. Sicilia, Italy, C Mediterranean Sea
Agriovótano 105 C5 Évvoia, C Greece
Agropoli 97 D5 Campania, S Italy
Aguachica 58 B2 Cesar, N Colombia
Aguadulce 53 F5 Coclé, S Panama
Agua Prieta 50 B1 Sonora, NW Mexico
Aguascalientes 50 D4 Aguascalientes, C Mexico
Aguaytía 60 C3 Ucayali, C Peru
Aguilas 93 E4 Murcia, SE Spain
Aguililla 50 D4 Michoacán, SW Mexico
Agulhas Basin 69 D8 undersea basin SW Indian Ocean
Agulhas Plateau 67 D6 undersea plateau SW Indian Ocean
Ahaggar 75 F2 high plateau region SE Algeria
Ahlen 94 B4 Nordrhein-Westfalen, W Germany
Ahmadābād 134 C4 var. Ahmedabad. Gujarāt, W India
Ahmadnagar 134 C5 var. Ahmednagar. Mahārāshtra, W India
Ahmedabad see Ahmadābād
Ahmednagar see Ahmadnagar
Ahuachapán 52 B3 Ahuachapán, W El Salvador
Ahvāz 120 C4 var. Ahwāz; prev. Nāsiri. Khūzestān, SW Iran
Ahvenanmaa see Åland
Ahwāz see Ahvāz
Aigaíon Pelagos/Aigaío Pélagos see Aegean Sea
Aígina 105 C6 var. Aíyina, Egina. Aígina, C Greece
Aígio 105 B5 var. Egio; prev. Aíyion. Dytikí Elláda, S Greece
Aiken 43 E2 South Carolina, SE USA
Ailinglaplap Atoll 144 D2 var. Aelōnlaplap. atoll Ralik Chain, S Marshall Islands
Ailuk Atoll 144 D1 var. Aelok. atoll Ratak Chain, NE Marshall Islands
Ainaži 106 D3 Est. Heinaste, Ger. Hainasch. N Latvia
'Aïn Ben Tili 74 D1 Tiris Zemmour, N Mauritania
Aintab see Gaziantep
Aïoun el Atrous/Aïoun el Atroûss see 'Ayoûn el 'Atroûs
Aiquile 61 F4 Cochabamba, C Bolivia
Aïr see Aïr, Massif de l'
Air du Azbine see Aïr, Massif de l'
Aïr, Massif de l' 75 G2 var. Aïr, Air du Azbine, Asben. mountain range NC Niger
Aiud 108 B4 Ger. Strassburg, Hung. Nagyenyed; prev. Engeten. Alba, SW Romania
Aix see Aix-en-Provence
Aix-en-Provence 91 D6 var. Aix; anc. Aquae Sextiae. Bouches-du-Rhône, SE France
Aix-la-Chapelle see Aachen
Aíyina see Aígina
Aíyion see Aígio
Aizkraukle 106 C4 S Latvia
Ajaccio 91 E7 Corse, France, C Mediterranean Sea
Ajaria see Ach'ara
Ajastan see Armenia
Aj Bogd Uul 126 D2 mountain SW Mongolia
Ajdābiyā 71 G2 var. Agedabia, Ajdābiyah. NE Libya
Ajdābiyah see Ajdābiyā
Ajjinena see El Geneina
Ajmer 134 D3 var. Ajmere. Rājasthān, N India
Ajo 48 A3 Arizona, SW USA

Akaba see Al 'Aqabah
Akamagaseki see Shimonoseki
Akasha 72 B3 Northern, N Sudan
Akchâr 74 C2 desert W Mauritania
Aken see Aachen
Akermanceaster see Bath
Akhaltsikhe 117 F2 prev. Akhalts'ikhe. SW Georgia
Akhalts'ikhe see Akhaltsikhe
Akhisar 116 A3 Manisa, W Turkey
Akhmīm 72 B2 var. Akhmim; anc. Panopolis. C Egypt
Akhtubinsk 111 C7 Astrakhanskaya Oblast', SW Russian Federation
Akhtyrka see Okhtyrka
Akimiski Island 38 C3 island Nunavut, C Canada
Akinovka 109 F4 Zaporiz'ka Oblast', S Ukraine
Akita 130 D4 Akita, Honshū, C Japan
Akjoujt 74 C2 prev. Fort-Repoux. Inchiri, W Mauritania
Akkeshi 130 E2 Hokkaidō, NE Japan
Aklavik 36 D3 Northwest Territories, NW Canada
Akmola see Astana
Akmolinsk see Astana
Aknavásár see Târgu Ocna
Akpatok Island 39 E1 island Nunavut, E Canada
Akragas see Agrigento
Akron 40 D4 Ohio, N USA
Akrotiri see Akrotírion
Akrotírion 102 C5 var. Akrotiri. UK air base S Cyprus
Aksai Chin 124 B2 Chin. Aksayqin. disputed region China/India
Aksaray 116 C4 Aksaray, C Turkey
Aksayqin see Aksai Chin
Akşehir 116 B4 Konya, W Turkey
Aktash see Oqtosh
Aktau 114 A4 Kaz. Aqtaū; prev. Shevchenko. Mangistau, W Kazakhstan
Aktjubinsk/Aktyubinsk see Aktobe
Aktobe 114 B4 Kaz. Aqtöbe; prev. Aktjubinsk, Aktyubinsk. Aktyubinsk, NW Kazakhstan
Aktsyabrski 107 C7 Rus. Oktyabr'skiy; prev. Karpilovka. Homyel'skaya Voblasts', SE Belarus
Aktyubinsk see Aktobe
Akula 77 C5 Equateur, NW Dem. Rep. Congo
Akureyri 83 E4 Nordhurland Eystra, N Iceland
Akyab see Sittwe
Alabama 42 C2 off. State of Alabama, also known as Camellia State, Heart of Dixie, The Cotton State, Yellowhammer State. state S USA
Alabama River 42 C3 river Alabama, S USA
Alaca 116 C3 Çorum, N Turkey
Alagoas 63 G2 off. Estado de Alagoas. region E Brazil
Alagoas 63 G2 off. Estado de Alagoas. state E Brazil
Alais see Alès
Alajuela 53 E4 Alajuela, C Costa Rica
Alakanuk 36 C2 Alaska, USA
Al 'Alamayn 72 B1 var. El 'Alamein. N Egypt
Al 'Amārah 120 C3 var. Amara. Maysān, E Iraq
Alamo 47 D6 Nevada, W USA
Alamogordo 48 D3 New Mexico, SW USA
Alamosa 44 C5 Colorado, C USA
Åland Islands 85 C6 var. Aland Islands, Fin. Ahvenanmaa. island group SW Finland
Åland Islands see Åland
Åland Sea 85 C6 var. Aland Sea. strait Baltic Sea/Gulf of Bothnia
Aland Sea see Ålands Hav
Alanya 116 C4 Antalya, S Turkey
Alappuzha 132 C3 prev. Alleppey. Kerala, SW India
Al 'Aqabah 119 B8 var. Akaba, Aqaba, 'Aqaba; anc. Aelana, Elath. Al 'Aqabah, SW Jordan
Al 'Arabīyah as Su'ūdīyah see Saudi Arabia
Alasca, Golfo de see Alaska, Gulf of
Alaşehir 116 A4 Manisa, W Turkey
Al'Ashārah 118 E3 var. Ashara. Dayr az Zawr, E Syria

Alaska 36 C3 off. State of Alaska, also known as Land of the Midnight Sun, The Last Frontier, Seward's Folly; prev. Russian America. state NW USA
Alaska, Gulf of 36 C4 var. Golfo de Alasca. gulf Canada/USA
Alaska Peninsula 36 C3 peninsula Alaska, USA
Alaska Range 34 B2 mountain range Alaska, USA
Al-Asnam see Chlef
Alattio see Alta
Al Awaynāt see Al 'Uwaynāt
Alaykel'/Alay-Kuu see Kēk-Art
Al 'Aynā 119 B7 Al Karak, W Jordan
Alazeya 115 G2 river NE Russian Federation
Al Bāb 118 B2 Ḥalab, N Syria
Albacete 93 E3 Castilla-La Mancha, C Spain
Al Baghdādī 120 B3 var. Khān al Baghdādī. Al Anbār, SW Iraq
Al Bāha see Al Bāḥah
Al Bāḥah 121 B5 var. Al Bāha. Al Bāḥah, SW Saudi Arabia
Al Baḥrayn see Bahrain
Alba Iulia 108 B4 Ger. Weissenburg, Hung. Gyulafehérvár; prev. Bălgrad, Karlsburg, Károly-Fehérvár. Alba, W Romania
Albania 101 C7 off. Republic of Albania, Alb. Republika e Shqipërisë, Shqipëria; prev. People's Socialist Republic of Albania. country SE Europe

ALBANIA
Southeast Europe

Official name Republic of Albania
Formation 1912 / 1921
Capital Tirana
Population 3.2 million / 302 people per sq mile (117 people per sq km)
Total area 11,100 sq. miles (28,748 sq. km)
Languages Albanian*, Greek
Religions Sunni Muslim 70%, Albanian Orthodox 20%, Roman Catholic 10%
Ethnic mix Albanian 98%, Greek 1%, Other 1%
Government Parliamentary system
Currency Lek = 100 qindarka (qintars)
Literacy rate 96%
Calorie consumption 2903 kilocalories

Albania see Aubagne
Albany 147 B7 Western Australia
Albany 42 D3 Georgia, SE USA
Albany 41 F3 state capital New York, NE USA
Albany 46 B3 Oregon, NW USA
Albany 38 C3 river Ontario, S Canada
Alba Regia see Székesfehérvár
Al Bāridah 118 C4 var. Bāridah. Ḥimṣ, C Syria
Al Baṣrah 120 C3 Eng. Basra, hist. Busra, Bussora. Al Baṣrah, SE Iraq
Al Batrūn see Batroûn
Al Bayḍā' 71 G2 var. Beida. NE Libya
Albemarle Island see Isabela, Isla
Albemarle Sound 43 G1 inlet W Atlantic Ocean
Albergaria-a-Velha 92 B2 Aveiro, N Portugal
Albert 90 C3 Somme, N France
Alberta 37 E4 province SW Canada
Albert Edward Nyanza see Edward, Lake
Albert, Lake 73 B6 var. Albert Nyanza, Lac Mobutu Sese Seko. lake Uganda/Dem. Rep. Congo
Albert Lea 45 F3 Minnesota, N USA
Albert Nyanza see Albert, Lake
Albertville see Kalemie
Albi 91 C6 anc. Albiga. Tarn, S France
Albiga see Albi
Ålborg see Aalborg
Ålborg-Norresundby see Aalborg
Albuquerque 48 D2 New Mexico, SW USA
Al Burayqah see Marsá al Burayqah
Alburgum see Aalborg
Albury 149 C7 New South Wales, SE Australia
Alcácer do Sal 92 B4 Setúbal, W Portugal
Alcalá de Henares 93 E3 Ar. Alkal'a; anc. Complutum. Madrid, C Spain
Alcamo 97 C7 Sicilia, Italy, C Mediterranean Sea
Alcañiz 93 F2 Aragón, NE Spain

Alcántara, Embalse de *92 C3 reservoir* W Spain
Alcaudete *92 D4* Andalucía, S Spain
Alcázar *see* Ksar-el-Kebir
Alcazarquivir *see* Ksar-el-Kebir
Alcoi *see* Alcoy
Alcoy *93 F4 Cat.* Alcoi. Valenciana, E Spain
Aldabra Group *79 G2 island group* SW Seychelles
Aldan *115 F3 river* NE Russian Federation
al Dar al Baida *see* Rabat
Alderney *90 A2 island* Channel Islands
Aleg *74 C3* Brakna, SW Mauritania
Aleksandriya *see* Oleksandriya
Aleksandropol' *see* Gyumri
Aleksandrovka *see* Oleksandrivka
Aleksandrovsk *see* Zaporizhzhya
Aleksin *111 B5* Tul'skaya Oblast', W Russian Federation
Aleksinac *100 E4* Serbia, SE Serbia
Alençon *90 B3* Orne, N France
Alenquer *63 E2* Pará, NE Brazil
Alep/Aleppo *see* Ḥalab
Alert *37 F1* Ellesmere Island, Nunavut, N Canada
Alès *91 C6 prev.* Alais. Gard, S France
Aleşd *108 B3 Hung.* Élesd. Bihor, SW Romania
Alessandria *96 B2 Fr.* Alexandrie. Piemonte, N Italy
Ålesund *85 A5* Møre og Romsdal, S Norway
Aleutian Basin *113 G3 undersea basin* Bering Sea
Aleutian Islands *36 A3 island group* Alaska, USA
Aleutian Range *34 A2 mountain range* Alaska, USA
Aleutian Trench *113 H3 trench* S Bering Sea
Alexander Archipelago *36 D4 island group* Alaska, USA
Alexander City *42 D2* Alabama, S USA
Alexander Island *154 A3 island* Antarctica
Alexander Range *see* Kirghiz Range
Alexandra *151 B7* Otago, South Island, New Zealand
Alexándreia *104 B4 var.* Alexándria. Kentrikí Makedonía, N Greece
Alexandretta *see* İskenderun
Alexandretta, Gulf of *see* İskenderun Körfezi
Alexandria *72 B1 Ar.* Al Iskandarīyah. N Egypt
Alexandria *108 C5* Teleorman, S Romania
Alexandria *42 B3* Louisiana, S USA
Alexandria *45 F2* Minnesota, N USA
Alexándria *see* Alexándreia
Alexandrie *see* Alessandria
Alexandroúpoli *104 D3 var.* Alexandroúpolis, *Turk.* Dedeağaç, Dedeagach. Anatolikí Makedonía kai Thráki, NE Greece
Alexandroúpolis *see* Alexandroúpoli
Al Fāshir *see* El Fasher
Alfatar *104 E1* Silistra, NE Bulgaria
Alfeiós *105 B6 prev.* Alfiós; *anc.* Alpheius, Alpheus. *river* S Greece
Alfiós *see* Alfeiós
Alföld *see* Great Hungarian Plain
Al-Furāt *see* Euphrates
Alga *114 B4 Kaz.* Algha. Aktyubinsk, NW Kazakhstan
Algarve *92 B4 cultural region* S Portugal
Algeciras *92 C5* Andalucía, SW Spain
Algemesí *93 F3* Valenciana, E Spain
Al-Genain *see* El Geneina
Alger *71 E1 var.* Algiers, El Djazaïr, Al Jazair. *country capital* (Algeria) N Algeria
Algeria *70 C3 off.* Democratic and Popular Republic of Algeria. *country* N Africa

ALGERIA
North Africa

Official name People's Democratic Republic of Algeria
Formation 1962 / 1962
Capital Algiers
Population 36 million / 39 people per sq mile (15 people per sq km)
Total area 919,590 sq. miles (2,381,740 sq. km)

ALGERIA
(continued)

Languages Arabic*, Tamazight (Kabyle, Shawia, Tamashek), French
Religions Sunni Muslim 99%, Christian and Jewish 1%
Ethnic mix Arab 75%, Berber 24%, European and Jewish 1%
Government Presidential system
Currency Algerian dinar = 100 centimes
Literacy rate 75%
Calorie consumption 3239 kilocalories

Algeria, Democratic and Popular Republic of *see* Algeria
Algerian Basin *80 C5 var.* Balearic Plain. *undersea basin* W Mediterranean Sea
Algha *see* Alga
Al Ghābah *121 E5 var.* Ghaba. C Oman
Alghero *97 A5* Sardegna, Italy, C Mediterranean Sea
Al Ghurdaqah *72 C2 var.* Ghurdaqah, Hurghada. E Egypt
Algiers *see* Alger
Al Golea *see* El Goléa
Algona *45 F3* Iowa, C USA
Al Hajar al Gharbī *121 D5 mountain range* N Oman
Al Hamad *see* Syrian Desert
Al Ḥasakah *118 D2 var.* Al Hasijah, El Haseke, Fr. Hassetché. Al Ḥasakah, NE Syria
Al Hasijah *see* Al Ḥasakah
Al Ḥillah *120 B3 var.* Hilla. Bābil, C Iraq
Al Ḥisā *119 B7* Aṭ Ṭafīlah, W Jordan
Al Ḥudaydah *121 B6 Eng.* Hodeida. W Yemen
Al Hufūf *120 C4 var.* Hofuf. Ash Sharqīyah, NE Saudi Arabia
Aliákmon *see* Aliákmonas
Aliákmonas *104 B4 prev.* Aliákmon; *anc.* Haliacmon. *river* N Greece
Aliártos *105 C5* Stereá Elláda, C Greece
Alicante *93 F4 Cat.* Alacant, *Lat.* Lucentum. Valenciana, SE Spain
Alice *49 G5* Texas, SW USA
Alice Springs *148 A4* Northern Territory, C Australia
Alifu Atoll *see* Ari Atoll
Aligandí *53 G4* Kuna Yala, NE Panama
Alíki *see* Alykí
Alima *77 B6 river* C Congo
Al Imārāt al 'Arabīyahal Muttaḥidah *see* United Arab Emirates
Alindao *76 C4* Basse-Kotto, S Central African Republic
Aliquippa *40 D4* Pennsylvania, NE USA
Al Iskandarīyah *see* Alexandria
Al Ismā'īlīya *72 B1 var.* Ismailia, Ismā'īlīya. N Egypt
Alistráti *104 C3* Kentrikí Makedonía, NE Greece
Alivéri *105 C5 var.* Alivérion. Évvoia, C Greece
Alivérion *see* Alivéri
Al Jabal al Akhḍar *71 G2 mountain range* NE Libya
Al Jafr *119 B7* Ma'ān, S Jordan
Al Jaghbūb *71 H3* NE Libya
Al Jahrā' *120 C4 var.* Al Jahrah, Jahra. C Kuwait
Al Jahrah *see* Al Jahrā'
Al Jamāhīrīyah al 'Arabīyah al Lībīyah ash Sha'bīyah al Ishtirākīy *see* Libya
Al Jawf *120 B4 off.* Jauf. Al Jawf, NW Saudi Arabia
Al Jawlān *see* Golan Heights
Al Jazair *see* Alger
Al Jazirah *118 E2 physical region* Iraq/Syria
Al Jīzah *see* Giza
Al Junaynah *see* El Geneina
Alkal'a *see* Alcalá de Henares
Al Karak *119 B7 var.* El Kerak, Karak, Kerak; *anc.* Kir Moab, Kir of Moab. Al Karak, W Jordan
Al-Kasr al-Kebir *see* Ksar-el-Kebir
Al Khalil *see* Hebron
Al Khārijah *72 B2 var.* El Khârga. C Egypt
Al Khums *71 F2 var.* Homs, Khoms, Khums. NW Libya
Alkmaar *86 C2* Noord-Holland, NW Netherlands
Al Kūt *120 C3 var.* Kūt al 'Amārah, Kut al Imara. Wāsiṭ, E Iraq

Al-Kuwait *see* Al Kuwayt
Al Kuwayt *120 C4 var.* Al-Kuwait, *Eng.* Kuwait, Kuwait City; *prev.* Qurein. *country capital* (Kuwait) E Kuwait
Al Lādhiqīyah *118 A3 Eng.* Latakia, *Fr.* Lattaquié; *anc.* Laodicea, Laodicea ad Mare. Al Lādhiqīyah, W Syria
Allahābād *135 E3* Uttar Pradesh, N India
Allanmyo *see* Aunglan
Allegheny Plateau *41 E3 mountain range* New York/Pennsylvania, NE USA
Allenstein *see* Olsztyn
Allentown *41 F4* Pennsylvania, NE USA
Alleppey *see* Alappuzha
Alliance *44 D3* Nebraska, C USA
Al Līth *121 B5* Makkah, SW Saudi Arabia
Al Lubnān *see* Lebanon
Alma-Ata *see* Almaty
Almada *92 B4* Setúbal, W Portugal
Al Madīnah *121 A5 Eng.* Medina. Al Madīnah, W Saudi Arabia
Al Mafraq *119 B6 var.* Mafraq. Al Mafraq, N Jordan
Al Mahdīyah *see* Mahdia
Al Mahrah *121 C6 mountain range* E Yemen
Al Majma'ah *120 B4* Ar Riyāḍ, C Saudi Arabia
Al Mālikīyah *118 E1 var.* Malkiye. Al Ḥasakah, N Syria
Almalyk *see* Olmaliq
Al Mamlakah *see* Morocco
Al Mamlaka al Urdunīya al Hashemīyah *see* Jordan
Al Manāmah *120 C4 Eng.* Manama. *country capital* (Bahrain) N Bahrain
Al Manāṣif *118 E3 mountain range* E Syria
Almansa *93 F4* Castilla-La Mancha, C Spain
Al-Mariyya *see* Almería
Al Marj *71 G2 var.* Barka, *It.* Barce. NE Libya
Almaty *114 C5 var.* Alma-Ata. Almaty, SE Kazakhstan
Al Mawṣil *120 B2 Eng.* Mosul. Nīnawá, N Iraq
Al Mayādīn *118 D3 var.* Mayadin, *Fr.* Meyadine. Dayr az Zawr, E Syria
Al Mazra' *see* Al Mazra'ah
Al Mazra'ah *119 B6 var.* Al Mazra', Mazra'a. Al Karak, W Jordan
Almelo *86 E3* Overijssel, E Netherlands
Almendra, Embalse de *92 C2 reservoir* Castilla y León, NW Spain
Almendralejo *92 C4* Extremadura, W Spain
Almere *86 D3 var.* Almere-stad. Flevoland, C Netherlands
Almere-stad *see* Almere
Almería *93 E5 Ar.* Al-Mariyya; *anc.* Unci, *Lat.* Portus Magnus. Andalucía, S Spain
Al Mīnā' *see* El Mina
Al Minyā *72 B2 var.* El Minya, Minya. C Egypt
Almirante *53 E4* Bocas del Toro, NW Panama
Al Mudawwarah *119 B8* Ma'ān, SW Jordan
Al Mukallā *121 C6 var.* Mukalla. SE Yemen
Al Obayyid *see* El Obeid
Alofi *145 F4 dependent territory capital* (Niue) W Niue
Aloha State *see* Hawai'i
Aloja *106 D3* N Latvia
Alónnisos *105 C5 island* Vóreies Sporádes, Greece, Aegean Sea
Álora *92 D5* Andalucía, S Spain
Alor, Kepulauan *139 E5 island group* E Indonesia
Al Oued *see* El Oued
Alpen *see* Alps
Alpena *40 D2* Michigan, N USA
Alpes *see* Alps
Alpha Cordillera *155 B3 var.* Alpha Ridge. *seamount range* Arctic Ocean
Alpha Ridge *see* Alpha Cordillera
Alpheius *see* Alfeiós
Alphen *see* Alphen aan den Rijn
Alphen aan den Rijn *86 C3 var.* Alphen. Zuid-Holland, C Netherlands
Alpheus *see* Alfeiós
Alpi *see* Alps
Alpine *49 E4* Texas, SW USA

Alps *102 C1 Fr.* Alpes, *Ger.* Alpen, *It.* Alpi. *mountain range* C Europe
Al Qaḍārif *see* Gedaref
Al Qāhirah *see* Cairo
Al Qāmishlī *118 E1 var.* Kamishli, Qamishly. Al Ḥasakah, NE Syria
Al Qaşrayn *see* Kasserine
Al Qayrawān *see* Kairouan
Al-Qsar al-Kbir *see* Ksar-el-Kebir
Al Qubayyāt *see* Qoubaïyât
Al Quds/Al Quds ash Sharīf *see* Jerusalem
Alqueva, Barragem do *92 C4 reservoir* Portugal/Spain
Al Qunayṭirah *119 B5 var.* El Kuneitra, El Quneitra, Kuneira, Qunaytra. Al Qunayṭirah, SW Syria
Al Quşayr *118 B4 var.* El Quseir, Quşayr, *Fr.* Kousseir. Ḥimş, W Syria
Al Quwayrah *119 B8 var.* El Quweira. Al 'Aqabah, SW Jordan
Alsace *90 E3 Eng.* Alsatia; *anc.* Alsatia. *cultural region* NE France
Alsatia *see* Alsace
Alsdorf *94 A4* Nordrhein-Westfalen, W Germany
Alt *see* Olt
Alta *84 D2 Fin.* Alattio. Finnmark, N Norway
Altai *see* Altai Mountains
Altai Mountains *126 C2 var.* Altai, *Chin.* Altay Shan, *Rus.* Altay. *mountain range* Asia/Europe
Altamaha River *43 E3 river* Georgia, SE USA
Altamira *63 E2* Pará, NE Brazil
Altamura *97 E5 anc.* Lupatia. Puglia, SE Italy
Altar, Desierto de *50 A1 var.* Sonoran Desert. *desert* Mexico/USA
Altar, Desierto de *see* Sonoran Desert
Altay *126 C2* Xinjiang Uygur Zizhiqu, NW China
Altay *126 D2 prev.* Yösönbulag. Govĭ-Altay, W Mongolia
Altay *see* Altai Mountains, Asia/Europe
Altay Shan *see* Altai Mountains
Altbetsche *see* Bečej
Altenburg *see* Bucureşti, Romania
Altın Köprü *120 B3 var.* Altun Kupri. At Ta'mīm, N Iraq
Altiplano *61 F4 physical region* W South America
Altkancisha *see* Kanjiža
Alton *40 B5* Illinois, N USA
Alton *40 B4* Missouri, C USA
Altoona *41 E4* Pennsylvania, NE USA
Alto Paraná *see* Paraná
Altpazua *see* Stara Pazova
Alt-Schwanenburg *see* Gulbene
Altsohl *see* Zvolen
Altun Kupri *see* Altın Köprü
Altun Shan *126 C3 var.* Altyn Tagh. *mountain range* NW China
Altus *49 F2* Oklahoma, C USA
Altyn Tagh *see* Altun Shan
Al Ubayyiḍ *see* El Obeid
Alūksne *106 D3 Ger.* Marienburg. NE Latvia
Al 'Ulā *120 A4* Al Madīnah, NW Saudi Arabia
Al 'Umari *119 C6* 'Ammān, E Jordan
Alupka *109 F5* Avtonomna Respublika Krym, S Ukraine
Al Uqsur *see* Luxor
Al Urdunn *see* Jordan
Alushta *109 F5* Avtonomna Respublika Krym, S Ukraine
Al 'Uwaynāt *71 F4 var.* Al Awaynāt. SW Libya
Alva *49 F1* Oklahoma, C USA
Alvarado *51 F4* Veracruz-Llave, E Mexico
Alvin *49 H4* Texas, SW USA
Al Wajh *120 A4* Tabūk, NW Saudi Arabia
Alwar *134 D3* Rājasthān, N India
Al Warī'ah *120 C4* Ash Sharqīyah, N Saudi Arabia
Al Yaman *see* Yemen
Alykí *104 C4 var.* Alíki. Thásos, N Greece
Alytus *107 B5 Pol.* Olita. Alytus, S Lithuania
Alzette *87 D8 river* S Luxembourg
Amadeus, Lake *147 D5 seasonal lake* Northern Territory, C Australia
Amadi *73 B5* Western Equatoria, SW South Sudan

Amadjuak Lake 37 G3 *lake* Baffin Island, Nunavut, N Canada
Amakusa-nada 131 A7 *gulf* SW Japan
Åmål 85 B6 Västra Götaland, S Sweden
Amami-gunto 130 A3 *island group* SW Japan
Amami-o-shim 130 A3 *island* S Japan
Amantea 97 D6 Calabria, SW Italy
Amapá 63 E1 *off.* Estado de Amapá; *prev.* Território de Amapá. *region* NE Brazil
Amapá 63 E1 *off.* Estado de Amapá; *prev.* Território de Amapá. *state* NE Brazil
Amapá, Estado de *see* Amapá
Amapá, Território de *see* Amapá
Amara *see* Al 'Amārah
Amarapura 136 B3 Mandalay, C Myanmar (Burma)
Amarillo 49 E2 Texas, SW USA
Amay 87 C6 Liège, E Belgium
Amazon 63 E1 *Sp.* Amazonas. *river* Brazil/Peru
Amazonas *see* Amazon
Amazon Basin 62 D2 *basin* N South America
Amazon, Mouths of the 63 F1 *delta* NE Brazil
Ambam 77 B5 Sud, S Cameroon
Ambanja 79 G2 Antsirañana, N Madagascar
Ambarchik 115 G2 Respublika Sakha (Yakutiya), NE Russian Federation
Ambato 60 B1 Tungurahua, C Ecuador
Ambérieu-en-Bugey 91 D5 Ain, E France
Ambianum *see* Amiens
Amboasary 79 F4 Toliara, S Madagascar
Amboina *see* Ambon
Ambon 139 F4 *prev.* Amboina, Amboyna. Pulau Ambon, E Indonesia
Ambositra 79 G3 Fianarantsoa, SE Madagascar
Amboyna *see* Ambon
Ambracia *see* Árta
Ambre, Cap d' *see* Bobaomby, Tanjona
Ambrim *see* Ambrym
Ambriz 78 A1 Bengo, NW Angola
Ambrym 144 D4 *var.* Ambrim. *island* C Vanuatu
Amchitka Island 36 A2 *island* Aleutian Islands, Alaska, USA
Amdo 126 C5 Xizang Zizhiqu, W China
Ameland 86 D1 *Fris.* It Amelân. *island* Waddeneilanden, N Netherlands
Amelân, It *see* Ameland
America *see* United States of America
America-Antarctica Ridge 67 C7 *undersea ridge* S Atlantic Ocean
America in Miniature *see* Maryland
American Falls Reservoir 46 E4 *reservoir* Idaho, NW USA
American Samoa 145 E4 *US unincorporated territory* W Polynesia
Amersfoort 86 D3 Utrecht, C Netherlands
Ames 45 F3 Iowa, C USA
Amfilochía 105 A5 *var.* Amfilokhía. Dytikí Elláda, C Greece
Amfilokhía *see* Amfilochía
Amga 115 F3 *river* NE Russian Federation
Amherst 39 F4 Nova Scotia, SE Canada
Amherst *see* Kyaikkami
Amida *see* Diyarbakir
Amiens 90 C3 *anc.* Ambianum, Samarobriva. Somme, N France
Amíndaion/Amindeo *see* Amýntaion
Amindivi Islands 132 A2 *island group* Lakshadweep, India, N Indian Ocean
Amirante Islands 79 G1 *var.* Amirantes Group. *island group* C Seychelles
Amirantes Group *see* Amirante Islands
Amistad, Presa de la *see* Amistad Reservoir
Amistad Reservoir 49 F4 *var.* Presa de la Amistad. *reservoir* Mexico/USA
Amisus *see* Samsun
Ammaia *see* Portalegre
'Amman 119 B6 *var.* Amman; *anc.* Philadelphia, *Bibl.* Rabbah Ammon, Rabbath Ammon. *country capital* (Jordan) 'Ammān, NW Jordan
Ammassalik 82 D4 *var.* Angmagssalik. Tunu, S Greenland
Ammóchostos *see* Gazimağusa
Ammóchostos, Kólpos *see* Gazimağusa Körfezi
Amnok-kang *see* Yalu

Amoea *see* Portalegre
Amoentai *see* Amuntai
Āmol 120 D2 *var.* Amul. Māzandarān, N Iran
Amorgós 105 D6 Amorgós, Kykládes, Greece, Aegean Sea
Amorgós 105 D6 *island* Kykládes, Greece, Aegean Sea
Amos 38 D4 Québec, SE Canada
Amourj 74 D3 Hodh ech Chargui, SE Mauritania
Amoy *see* Xiamen
Ampato, Nevado 61 E4 *mountain* S Peru
Amposta 93 F2 Cataluña, NE Spain
Amraoti *see* Amrāvati
Amrāvati 134 D4 *prev.* Amraoti. Mahārāshtra, C India
Amritsar 134 D2 Punjab, N India
Amstelveen 86 C3 Noord-Holland, C Netherlands
Amsterdam 86 C3 *country capital* (Netherlands) Noord-Holland, C Netherlands
Amsterdam Island 141 C6 *island* NE French Southern and Antarctic Territories
Am Timan 76 C3 Salamat, SE Chad
Amu Darya 122 D2 *Rus.* Amudar'ya, *Taj.* Dar"yoi Amu, *Turkm.* Amyderya, *Uzb.* Amudaryo; *anc.* Oxus. *river* C Asia
Amu-Dar'ya *see* Amyderýa
Amudar'ya/Amudaryo/Amu, Dar"yoi *see* Amu Darya
Amul *see* Āmol
Amund Ringnes Island 37 F2 *Island* Nunavut, N Canada
Amundsen Basin *see* Fram Basin
Amundsen Plain 154 A4 *abyssal plain* S Pacific Ocean
Amundsen-Scott 154 B3 *US research station* Antarctica
Amundsen Sea 154 A4 *sea* S Pacific Ocean
Amuntai 138 D4 *prev.* Amoentai. Borneo, C Indonesia
Amur 115 G4 *Chin.* Heilong Jiang. *river* China/Russian Federation
Amvrosiyevka *see* Amvrosiyivka
Amvrosiyivka 109 H3 *Rus.* Amvrosiyevka. Donets'ka Oblast', SE Ukraine
Amyderýa 123 E3 *Rus.* Amu-Dar'ya. Lebap Welaýaty, NE Turkmenistan
Amyderya *see* Amu Darya
Amýntaio 104 B4 *var.* Amindeo; *prev.* Amíndaion. Dytikí Makedonía, N Greece
Anabar 115 E2 *river* NE Russian Federation
An Abhainn Mhór *see* Blackwater
Anaco 59 E2 Anzoátegui, NE Venezuela
Anaconda 44 B2 Montana, NW USA
Anacortes 46 B1 Washington, NW USA
Anadolu Dağları *see* Doğu Karadeniz Dağları
Anadyr' 115 H1 Chukotskiy Avtonomnyy Okrug, NE Russian Federation
Anadyr' 115 G1 *river* NE Russian Federation
Anadyr, Gulf of 115 H1 *Eng.* Gulf of Anadyr. *gulf* NE Russian Federation
Anadyr, Gulf of *see* Anadyrskiy Zaliv
Anáfi 105 D7 *anc.* Anaphe. *island* Kykládes, Greece, Aegean Sea
'Ānah *see* 'Annah
Anaheim 46 E2 California, W USA
Anaiza *see* 'Unayzah
Analalava 79 G2 Mahajanga, NW Madagascar
Anamur 116 C5 İçel, S Turkey
Anantapur 132 C2 Andhra Pradesh, S India
Anaphe *see* Anáfi
Anápolis 63 F3 Goiás, C Brazil
Anār 120 D3 Kermān, C Iran
Anatolia 116 C4 *plateau* C Turkey
Anatom *see* Aneityum
Añatuya 64 C3 Santiago del Estero, N Argentina
An Bhearú *see* Barrow
Anchorage 36 C3 Alaska, USA
Ancona 96 C3 Marche, C Italy
Ancud 65 B6 *prev.* San Carlos de Ancud. Los Lagos, S Chile
Ancyra *see* Ankara
Åndalsnes 85 A5 Møre og Romsdal, S Norway

Andalucía 92 D4 *cultural region* S Spain
Andalusia 42 C3 Alabama, S USA
Andaman Islands 124 B4 *island group* India, NE Indian Ocean
Andaman Sea 124 C4 *sea* NE Indian Ocean
Andenne 87 C6 Namur, SE Belgium
Anderlues 87 B7 Hainaut, S Belgium
Anderson 40 C4 Indiana, N USA
Andes 64 B3 *mountain range* W South America
Andhra Pradesh 135 E5 *cultural region* E India
Andijon 123 F2 *Rus.* Andizhan. Andijon Viloyati, E Uzbekistan
Andikíthira *see* Antikýthira
Andipaxi *see* Antípaxoi
Andípsara *see* Antípsara
Ándissa *see* Ántissa
Andizhan *see* Andijon
Andkhvóy 122 D3 *prev.* Andkhvoy. Fāryāb, N Afghanistan
Andorra 91 A7 *off.* Principality of Andorra, *Cat.* Valls d'Andorra. *Fr.* Vallée d'Andorre. *country* SW Europe

ANDORRA
Southwest Europe

Official name Principality of Andorra
Formation 1278 / 1278
Capital Andorra la Vella
Population 85,082 / 473 people per sq mile (183 people per sq km)
Total area 181 sq. miles (468 sq. km)
Languages Spanish, Catalan*, French, Portuguese
Religions Roman Catholic 94%, Other 6%
Ethnic mix Spanish 46%, Andorran 28%, Other 18%, French 8%
Government Parliamentary system
Currency Euro = 100 cents
Literacy rate 99%
Calorie consumption Not available

Andorra *see* Andorra la Vella
Andorra la Vella 91 A8 *var.* Andorra, *Fr.* Andorre la Vielle, *Sp.* Andorra la Vieja. *country capital* (Andorra) C Andorra
Andorra la Vieja *see* Andorra la Vella
Andorra, Principality of *see* Andorra
Andorra, Valls d'/Andorra, Vallée d' *see* Andorra
Andorre la Vielle *see* Andorra la Vella
Andover 89 D7 S England, United Kingdom
Andøya 84 C2 *island* C Norway
Andreanof Islands 36 A3 *island group* Aleutian Islands, Alaska, USA
Andrews 49 E3 Texas, SW USA
Andrew Tablemount 140 A4 *var.* Gora Andryu. *seamount* W Indian Ocean
Andria 97 D5 Puglia, SE Italy
An Droichead Nua *see* Newbridge
Andropov *see* Rybinsk
Ándros 105 D6 Ándros, Kykládes, Greece, Aegean Sea
Ándros 105 C6 *island* Kykládes, Greece, Aegean Sea
Andros 54 B2 *island* NW Bahamas
Andros Town 54 C1 Andros Island, NW Bahamas
Andryu, Gora *see* Andrew Tablemount
Aneityum 144 D5 *var.* Anatom; *prev.* Kéamu. *island* S Vanuatu
Ánewetak *see* Enewetak Atoll
Angara 115 E4 *river* C Russian Federation
Angarsk 115 E4 Irkutskaya Oblast', S Russian Federation
Ånge 85 C5 Västernorrland, C Sweden
Ángel de la Guarda, Isla 50 B2 *island* NW Mexico
Angeles 139 E1 *off.* Angeles City. Luzon, N Philippines
Angeles City *see* Angeles
Angel Falls 59 E3 *Eng.* Angel Falls. *waterfall* E Venezuela
Angel Falls *see* Ángel, Salto
Angerburg *see* Węgorzewo
Ångermanälven 84 C4 *river* N Sweden
Angermünde 94 D3 Brandenburg, NE Germany
Angers 90 B4 *anc.* Juliomagus. Maine-et-Loire, NW France
Anglesey 89 C5 *island* NW Wales, United Kingdom

Anglet 91 A6 Pyrénées-Atlantiques, SW France
Angleton 49 H4 Texas, SW USA
Anglia *see* England
Anglo-Egyptian Sudan *see* Sudan
Angmagssalik *see* Ammassalik
Ang Nam Ngum 136 C4 *lake* C Laos
Angola 78 B2 *off.* Republic of Angola; *prev.* People's Republic of Angola, Portuguese West Africa. *country* SW Africa

ANGOLA
Southern Africa

Official name Republic of Angola
Formation 1975 / 1975
Capital Luanda
Population 16.9 million / 41 people per sq mile (16 people per sq km)
Total area 481,351 sq. miles (1,246,700 sq. km)
Languages Portuguese*, Umbundu, Kimbundu, Kikongo
Religions Roman Catholic 68%, Protestant 20%, Indigenous beliefs 12%
Ethnic mix Ovimbundu 37%, Other 25%, Kimbundu 25%, Bakongo 13%
Government Presidential system
Currency Readjusted kwanza = 100 lwei
Literacy rate 70%
Calorie consumption 2079 kilocalories

Angola Basin 69 B5 *undersea basin* E Atlantic Ocean
Angola, People's Republic of *see* Angola
Angola, Republic of *see* Angola
Angora *see* Ankara
Angostura *see* Ciudad Bolívar
Angostura, Presa de la 51 G5 *reservoir* SE Mexico
Angoulême 91 B5 *anc.* Iculisma. Charente, W France
Angoumois 91 B5 *cultural region* W France
Angra Pequena *see* Lüderitz
Angren 123 F2 Toshkent Viloyati, E Uzbekistan
Anguilla 55 G3 *UK dependent territory* E West Indies
Anguilla Cays 54 B2 *islets* SW Bahamas
Anhui 128 C5 *var.* Anhui Sheng, Anhwei, Wan. *province* E China
AnhuiSheng/Anhwei Wan *see* Anhui
Anicium *see* le Puy
Anina 108 A4 *Ger.* Steierdorf, *Hung.* Stájerlakanina; *prev.* Staierdorf-Anina, Steierdorf-Anina, Steyerlak-Anina. Caraş-Severin, SW Romania
Anjou 90 B4 *cultural region* NW France
Anjouan *see* Nzwani
Ankara 116 C3 *prev.* Angora; *anc.* Ancyra. *country capital* (Turkey) Ankara, C Turkey
Ankeny 45 F3 Iowa, C USA
Anklam 94 D2 Mecklenburg-Vorpommern, NE Germany
Annaba 21 F1 *prev.* Bône. NE Algeria
An Nafud 120 B4 *desert* NW Saudi Arabia
'Annah 120 B3 *var.* 'Ānah. Al Anbār, NW Iraq
An Najaf 120 B3 *var.* Najaf. An Najaf, S Iraq
Annamite Mountains 136 D4 *var.* annamescordillera, *Fr.* Chaîne Annamitique, *Lao.* Phou Louang. *mountain range* C Laos
Annamitique, Chaîne *see* Annamite Mountains
Annamses Cordillera *see* Annamite Mountains
Annapolis 41 F4 *state capital* Maryland, NE USA
Annapurna 135 E3 *mountain* C Nepal
Ann Arbor 40 C3 Michigan, N USA
An Nāsiriyah 120 C3 *var.* Nasiriya. Dhī Qār, SE Iraq
Anneciacum *see* Annecy
Annecy 91 D5 *anc.* Anneciacum. Haute-Savoie, E France
An Nil al Abyaḍ *see* White Nile
An Nil al Azraq *see* Blue Nile
Anniston 42 D2 Alabama, S USA
Annotto Bay 54 B4 C Jamaica
An Ómaigh *see* Omagh

Anqing 128 D5 Anhui, E China
Anse La Raye 55 F1 NW Saint Lucia
Anshun 128 B6 Guizhou, S China
Ansongo 75 E3 Gao, E Mali
An Srath Bán *see* Strabane
Antakya 116 D4 *anc.* Antioch,
  Antiochia. Hatay, S Turkey
Antalaha 79 G2 Antsirañana,
  NE Madagascar
Antalya 116 B4 *prev.* Adalia; *anc.*
  Attaleia, *Bibl.* Attalia. Antalya,
  SW Turkey
Antalya, Gulf of 116 B4 *var.* Gulf of
  Adalia, *Eng.* Gulf of Antalya. *gulf*
  SW Turkey
Antalya, Gulf of *see* Antalya Körfezi
Antananarivo 79 G3 *prev.* Tananarive.
  country capital (Madagascar)
  Antananarivo, C Madagascar
Antarctica 154 B3 *continent*
Antarctic Peninsula 154 A2 *peninsula*
  Antarctica
Antep *see* Gaziantep
Antequera 92 D5 *anc.* Anticaria,
  Antiquaria. Andalucía, S Spain
Antequera *see* Oaxaca
Antibes 91 D6 *anc.* Antipolis. Alpes-
  Maritimes, SE France
Anticaria *see* Antequera
Anticosti, Île d' 39 F3 *Eng.* Anticosti
  Island. *island* Québec, E Canada
Anticosti Island *see* Anticosti, Île d'
Antigua 55 G3 *island* S Antigua and
  Barbuda, Leeward Islands
Antigua and Barbuda 55 G3 *country*
  E West Indies

ANTIGUA & BARBUDA
West Indies

Official name Antigua and Barbuda
Formation 1981 / 1981
Capital St. John's
Population 89,018 / 524 people
  per sq mile (202 people per sq km)
Total area 170 sq. miles (442 sq. km)
Languages English*, English patois
Religions Anglican 45%, Other Protestant
  42%, Roman Catholic 10%, Other 2%,
  Rastafarian 1%
Ethnic mix Black African 95%, Other 5%
Government Parliamentary system
Currency Eastern Caribbean dollar
  = 100 cents
Literacy rate 99%
Calorie consumption 2373 kilocalories

Antikythira 105 B7 *var.* Andikíthira.
  island S Greece
Anti-Lebanon 84 H4 *var.* Jebel esh
  Sharqi, *Ar.* Al Jabal ash Sharqī, *Fr.* Anti-
  Liban. *mountain range* Lebanon/Syria
Anti-Liban *see* Anti-Lebanon
Antioch *see* Antakya
Antiochia *see* Antakya
Antípaxoi 105 A5 *var.* Andípaxi.
  island Iónia Nisiá, Greece,
  C Mediterranean Sea
Antipodes Islands 142 D5 *island group*
  S New Zealand
Antípsara 105 D5 *var.* Andípsara.
  island E Greece
Antiquaria *see* Antequera
Ántissa 105 D5 *var.* Ándissa. Lésvos,
  E Greece
An tIúr *see* Newry
Antivari *see* Bar
Antofagasta 64 B2 Antofagasta,
  N Chile
Antony 90 E2 Hauts-de-Seine,
  N France
An tSionainn *see* Shannon
Antsirabe 79 G2 *province*
  N Madagascar
Antsohihy 79 G2 Mahajanga,
  NW Madagascar
An-tung *see* Dandong
Antwerpen 87 C5 *Eng.* Antwerp, *Fr.*
  Anvers. Antwerpen, N Belgium
Anuradhapura 132 D3 North Central
  Province, C Sri Lanka
Anvers *see* Antwerpen
Anyang 128 C4 Henan, C China
A'nyêmaqên Shan 126 D4 *mountain
  range* C China
Anykščiai 106 C4 Utena,
  E Lithuania
Anzio 97 C5 Lazio, C Italy

Ao Krung Thep 137 C5 *var.* Krung Thep
  Mahanakhon, *Eng.* Bangkok. *country
  capital* (Thailand) Bangkok, C Thailand
Aomen *see* Macao
Aomori 130 D3 Aomori, Honshū,
  C Japan
Aóos *see* Vjosës, Lumi i
Aoraki 151 B6 *prev.* Aorangi, Mount
  Cook. *mountain* South Island, New
  Zealand
Aorangi *see* Aoraki
Aosta 96 A1 *anc.* Augusta Praetoria.
  Valle d'Aosta, NW Italy
Aoukâr 74 D3 *var.* Aouker. *plateau*
  C Mauritania
Aouk, Bahr 76 C4 *river* Central African
  Republic/Chad
Aouker *see* Aoukâr
Aozou 76 C1 Borkou-Ennedi-Tibesti,
  N Chad
Apalachee Bay 42 D3 *bay* Florida,
  SE USA
Apalachicola River 42 D3 *river* Florida,
  SE USA
Apamama *see* Abemama
Apaporis, Río 58 C4 *river* Brazil/
  Colombia
Apatity 110 C2 Murmanskaya Oblast',
  NW Russian Federation
Ape 106 D3 NE Latvia
Apeldoorn 86 D3 Gelderland,
  E Netherlands
Apennines 96 E2 *Eng.* Apennines.
  mountain range Italy/San Marino
Apennines *see* Appennino
Āpia 145 F4 *country capital* (Samoa)
  Upolu, SE Samoa
Apkhazeti 117 E1 *var.* Abkhazia; *prev.*
  Ap'khazet'i. *autonomous republic*
  NW Georgia
Ap'khazet'i *see* Apkhazeti
Apoera 59 G3 Sipaliwini,
  NW Suriname
Apostle Islands 40 B1 *island group*
  Wisconsin, N USA
Appalachian Mountains 35 D5
  mountain range E USA
Appingedam 86 E1 Groningen,
  NE Netherlands
Appleton 40 B2 Wisconsin, N USA
Apulia *see* Puglia
Apure, Río 58 C2 *river* W Venezuela
Apurímac, Río 60 D3 *river* S Peru
Apuseni, Munții 108 A4 *mountain range*
  W Romania
Aqaba/'Aqaba *see* Al 'Aqabah
Aqaba, Gulf of 120 A4 *var.* Gulf of
  Elat, *Ar.* Khalīj al 'Aqabah; *anc.* Sinus
  Aelaniticus. *gulf* NE Red Sea
'Aqabah, Khalīj al *see* Aqaba, Gulf of
Āqcheh 123 E3 *var.* Āqcheh. Jowzjān,
  N Afghanistan
Āqcheh *see* Āqchah
Aqmola *see* Astana
Aqtöbe *see* Aktobe
Aquae Augustae *see* Dax
Aquae Calidae *see* Bath
Aquae Flaviae *see* Chaves
Aquae Grani *see* Aachen
Aquae Sextiae *see* Aix-en-Provence
Aquae Solis *see* Bath
Aquae Tarbelicae *see* Dax
Aquidauana 63 E4 Mato Grosso do
  Sul, S Brazil
Aquila/Aquila degli Abruzzi *see*
  L'Aquila
Aquisgranum *see* Aachen
Aquitaine 91 B6 *cultural region*
  SW France
'Arabah, Wadi al 119 B7 *Heb.* Ha'Arava.
  dry watercourse Israel/Jordan
Arabian Basin 124 A4 *undersea basin*
  N Arabian Sea
Arabian Desert *see* Sahara el Sharqīya
Arabian Peninsula 121 B5 *peninsula*
  SW Asia
Arabian Sea 124 A3 *sea* NW Indian
  Ocean
Arabicus, Sinus *see* Red Sea
'Arabi, Khalīj al *see* Persian Gulf
**'Arabiyah as Su'ūdīyah, Al Mamlakah
  al** *see* Saudi Arabia
'Arabīyah Jumhūrīyah, Mişr al *see* Egypt
Arab Republic of Egypt *see* Egypt
Aracaju 63 G3 *state capital* Sergipe,
  E Brazil
Araçuaí 63 F3 Minas Gerais, SE Brazil
Arad 119 B7 Southern, S Israel
Arad 108 A4 Arad, W Romania

Arafura Sea 142 A3 *Ind.* Laut Arafuru.
  sea W Pacific Ocean
Arafuru, Laut *see* Arafura Sea
Aragón 93 E2 *autonomous community*
  E Spain
Araguaia, Río 63 E3 *var.* Araguaya.
  river C Brazil
Araguari 63 F3 Minas Gerais, SE Brazil
Araguaya *see* Araguaia, Río
Ara Jovis *see* Aranjuez
Arāk 120 C3 *prev.* Sultānābād. Markazī,
  W Iran
Arakan Yoma 136 A3 *mountain range*
  W Myanmar (Burma)
Araks/Arak's *see* Aras
Aral *see* Aralsk, Kazakhstan
Aral Sea 122 C1 *Kaz.* Aral Tengizi, *Rus.*
  Aral'skoye More, *Uzb.* Orol Dengizi.
  inland sea Kazakhstan/Uzbekistan
Aral'sk 114 B4 *Kaz.* Aral. Kzylorda,
  SW Kazakhstan
Aral'skoye More/Aral Tengizi *see*
  Aral Sea
Aranda de Duero 92 D2 Castilla y León,
  N Spain
Arandelovac 100 D4 *prev.* Arandjelovac.
  Serbia, C Serbia
Arandjelovac *see* Arandelovac
Aranjuez 92 D3 *anc.* Ara Jovis. Madrid,
  C Spain
Araouane 75 E2 Tombouctou, N Mali
'Ar'ar 120 B3 Al Ḥudūd ash Shamālīyah,
  NW Saudi Arabia
Mount Ararat 117 F3 *var.* Aghri Dagh,
  Agri Dagi, Koh I Noh, Masis, *Eng.*
  Great Ararat, Mount Ararat. *mountain*
  E Turkey
Ararat, Mount *see* Büyükağrı Dağı
Aras 117 G3 *Arm.* Arak's, *Az.* Araz
  Nehri, *Per.* Rūd-e Aras, *Rus.* Araks;
  prev. Araxes. *river* SW Asia
Aras, Rūd-e *see* Aras
Arauca 58 C2 Arauca, NE Colombia
Arauca 58 C2 *river* Colombia/
  Venezuela
Arausio *see* Orange
Araxes *see* Aras
Araz Nehri *see* Aras
Arbela *see* Arbil
Arbil 120 B2 *var.* Erbil, Irbil, *Kurd.*
  Hawlêr; *anc.* Arbela. Arbil, N Iraq
Arbroath 88 D3 *anc.* Aberbrothock.
  E Scotland, United Kingdom
Arbuzinka *see* Arbuzynka
Arbuzynka 109 E3 *Rus.* Arbuzinka.
  Mykolayivs'ka Oblast', S Ukraine
Arcachon 91 B5 Gironde, SW France
Arcae Remorum *see*
  Châlons-en-Champagne
Arcata 46 A4 California, W USA
Archangel Bay *see* Arkhangel'sk
Archangel'skaya Guba *see*
  Chëshskaya Guba
Archidona 92 D5 Andalucía, S Spain
Arco 96 C2 Trentino-Alto Adige,
  N Italy
Arctic Mid Oceanic Ridge *see* Nansen
  Cordillera
Arctic Ocean 155 B3 *ocean*
Arda 104 C3 *var.* Ardhas, *Gk.* Ardas.
  river Bulgaria/Greece
Ardabil 120 C2 *var.* Ardebil. Ardabīl,
  NW Iran
Ardakān 120 D3 Yazd, C Iran
Ardas 104 D3 *var.* Ardhas, *Bul.* Arda.
  river Bulgaria/Greece
Arḍ aş Şawwān 119 C7 *var.* Ardh es
  Suwwān. *plain* S Jordan
Ardeal *see* Transylvania
Ardebil *see* Ardabil
Ardèche 91 C5 *cultural region* E France
Ardennes 87 C8 *physical region*
  Belgium/France
Ardhas *see* Arda/Ardas
Ardh es Suwwān *see* Arḍ aş Şawwān
Ardino 104 C3 Kürdzhali, S Bulgaria
Ard Mhacha *see* Armagh
Ardmore 49 G2 Oklahoma, C USA
Arel *see* Arlon
Arelas/Arelate *see* Arles
Arendal 85 A6 Aust-Agder, S Norway
Arensburg *see* Kuressaare
Arenys de Mar 93 G2 Cataluña,
  NE Spain
Areópoli 105 B7 *prev.* Areópolis.
  Pelopónnisos, S Greece
Areópolis *see* Areópoli
Arequipa 61 E4 Arequipa, SE Peru
Arezzo 96 C3 *anc.* Arretium. Toscana,
  C Italy

Argalastí 105 C5 Thessalía, C Greece
Argenteuil 90 D1 Val-d'Oise,
  N France
Argentina 65 B5 *off.* Argentine Republic.
  country S South America

ARGENTINA
South America

Official name The Argentine Republic
Formation 1816 / 1816
Capital Buenos Aires
Population 40.8 million / 39 people
  per sq mile (15 people per sq km)
Total area 1,068,296 sq. miles
  (2,766,890 sq. km)
Languages Spanish*, Italian,
  Amerindian languages
Religions Roman Catholic 70%,
  Other 18%, Protestant 9%,
  Muslim 2%, Jewish 2%
Ethnic mix Indo-European 97%,
  Mestizo 2%, Amerindian 1%
Government Presidential system
Currency Argentine peso = 100 centavos
Literacy rate 98%
Calorie consumption 2918 kilocalories

Argentina Basin *see* Argentine Basin
Argentine Basin 57 C7 *var.* Argentina
  Basin. *undersea basin* SW Atlantic
  Ocean
Argentine Republic *see* Argentina
Argentine Rise *see* Falkland Plateau
Argentoratum *see* Strasbourg
Darya-ye Arghandab 123 E5 *river*
  SE Afghanistan
Argirocastro *see* Gjirokastër
Argo 72 B3 Northern, N Sudan
Argo Fracture Zone 141 C5 *tectonic
  feature* C Indian Ocean
Árgos 105 B6 Pelopónnisos, S Greece
Argostóli 105 A5 *var.* Argostólion.
  Kefallinía, Iónia Nisiá, Greece,
  C Mediterranean Sea
Argostólion *see* Argostóli
Argun 125 E1 *Chin.* Ergun He, *Rus.*
  Argun'. *river* China/Russian Federation
Argyrokastron *see* Gjirokastër
Århus 85 B7 *var.* Aarhus. Midtjylland,
  C Denmark
Aria *see* Herāt
Ari Atoll 132 A4 *var.* Alifu Atoll. *atoll*
  C Maldives
Arica 64 B1 *hist.* San Marcos de Arica.
  Arica y Parinacota, N Chile
Aridaía 104 B3 *var.* Aridea, Aridhaía.
  Dytikí Makedonía, N Greece
Aridea *see* Aridaía
Aridhaía *see* Aridaía
Arīḥā 118 B3 Al Karak, W Jordan
Arīḥā *see* Jericho
Ariminum *see* Rimini
Arinsal 91 A7 NW Andorra Europe
Arizona 48 A2 *off.* State of Arizona, *also
  known as* Copper State, Grand Canyon
  State. *state* SW USA
Arkansas 42 A1 *off.* State of Arkansas,
  also known as The Land of Opportunity.
  state S USA
Arkansas City 45 F5 Kansas, C USA
Arkansas River 49 G1 *river* C USA
Arkhangel'sk 114 B2 *Eng.* Archangel.
  Arkhangel'skaya Oblast', NW Russian
  Federation
Arkoí 105 E6 *island* Dodekánisa, Greece,
  Aegean Sea
Arles 91 D6 *var.* Arles-sur-Rhône; *anc.*
  Arelas, Arelate. Bouches-du-Rhône,
  SE France
Arles-sur-Rhône *see* Arles
Arlington 49 G2 Texas, SW USA
Arlington 41 E4 Virginia, NE USA
Arlon 87 D8 *Dut.* Aarlen, *Ger.* Arel, *Lat.*
  Orolaunum. Luxembourg, SE Belgium
Armagh 89 B5 Ír. Ard Mhacha.
  S Northern Ireland, United Kingdom
Armagnac 91 B6 *cultural region* S France
Armenia 58 B3 Quindío, W Colombia
Armenia 117 F3 *off.* Republic of
  Armenia, *var.* Ajastan, *Arm.* Hayastani
  Hanrapetut'yun; *prev.* Armenian Soviet
  Socialist Republic. *country* SW Asia

ARMENIA
Southwest Asia

Official name Republic of Armenia
Formation 1991 / 1991

ARMENIA
(continued)

Capital Yerevan
Population 3.1 million / 269 people
per sq mile (104 people per sq km)
Total area 11,506 sq. miles (29,800 sq. km)
Languages Armenian*, Azeri, Russian
Religions Armenian Apostolic Church
(Orthodox) 88%, Other 6%, Armenian
Catholic Church 6%, Other 6%
Ethnic mix Armenian 98%, Other 1%,
Yezidi 1%
Government Parliamentary system
Currency Dram = 100 luma
Literacy rate 99%
Calorie consumption 2806 kilocalories

Armenian Soviet Socialist Republic
see Armenia
Armenia, Republic of see Armenia
Armidale 149 D6 New South Wales,
SE Australia
Armstrong 38 B3 Ontario, S Canada
Armyans'k 109 F4 Rus. Armyansk.
Avtonomna Respublika Krym,
S Ukraine
Arnaía 104 C4 Cont. Arnea. Kentrikí
Makedonía, N Greece
Arnaud 82 A3 river Québec, E Canada
Arnea see Arnaía
Arnedo 93 E2 La Rioja, N Spain
Arnhem 86 D4 Gelderland,
SE Netherlands
Arnhem Land 148 A2 physical region
Northern Territory, N Australia
Arno 96 B3 river C Italy
Arnold 45 G4 Missouri, C USA
Arnswalde see Choszczno
Aroe Islands see Aru, Kepulauan
Arorae 145 E3 atoll Tungaru,
W Kiribati
Arrabona see Győr
Ar Rahad see Er Rahad
Ar Ramādī 120 B3 var. Ramadi,
Rumadiya. Al Anbār, SW Iraq
Ar Rāmī 118 C4 Ḥimṣ, C Syria
Ar Ramthā 119 B5 var. Ramtha. Irbid,
N Jordan
Arran, Isle of 88 C4 island SW Scotland,
United Kingdom
Ar Raqqah 118 C2 var. Rakka; anc.
Nicephorium. Ar Raqqah, N Syria
Arras 90 C2 anc. Nemetocenna. Pas-de-
Calais, N France
Ar Rawḍatayn 120 C4 var. Raudhatain.
N Kuwait
Arretium see Arezzo
Arriaca see Guadalajara
Arriaga 51 G5 Chiapas, SE Mexico
Ar Riyāḍ 121 C5 Eng. Riyadh. country
capital (Saudi Arabia) Ar Riyāḍ,
C Saudi Arabia
Ar Rub 'al Khali 121 C6 Eng. Empty
Quarter, Great Sandy Desert. desert
SW Asia
Ar Rustāq 121 E5 var. Rostak, Rustaq.
N Oman
Ar Ruṭbah 120 B3 var. Rutba. Al Anbār,
SW Iraq
Árta 105 A5 anc. Ambracia. Ípeiros,
W Greece
Artashat 117 F3 S Armenia
Artemisa 54 B2 La Habana, W Cuba
Artesia 48 D3 New Mexico, SW USA
Arthur's Pass 151 C6 pass South Island,
New Zealand
Artigas 64 D3 prev. San Eugenio,
San Eugenio del Cuareim. Artigas,
N Uruguay
Art'ik 117 F2 W Armenia
Artois 90 C2 cultural region N France
Artsiz see Artsyz
Artsyz 108 D4 Rus. Artsiz. Odes'ka
Oblast', SW Ukraine
Artvin 117 F2 Artvin, NE Turkey
Arua 73 B6 NW Uganda
Aruba 58 C1 var. Oruba. Dutch
autonomous region S West Indies
Aru Islands see Aru, Kepulauan
Aru, Kepulauan 139 G4 Eng. Aru
Islands; prev. Aroe Islands. island
group E Indonesia
Arunāchal Pradesh 135 G3 prev. North
East Frontier Agency, North East
Frontier Agency of Assam. cultural
region NE India
Arusha 73 C7 Arusha, N Tanzania

Arviat 37 G4 prev. Eskimo Point.
Nunavut, C Canada
Arvidsjaur 84 C4 Norrbotten, N Sweden
'Arys' 114 B5 prev. Arys'. Yuzhnyy
Kazakhstan, S Kazakhstan
Arys' see 'Arys'
Asadābād 123 F4 var. Asadābād; prev.
Chaghasarāy. Kunar, E Afghanistan
Asadābād see Asadābād
Asahi-dake 130 D2 mountain Hokkaidō,
N Japan
Asahikawa 130 D2 Hokkaidō, N Japan
Asamankese 75 E5 SE Ghana
Āsansol 135 F4 West Bengal, NE India
Asben see Aïr, Massif de l'
Ascension Fracture Zone 69 A5 tectonic
Feature C Atlantic Ocean
Ascension Island 67 C5 dependency of
St.Helena C Atlantic Ocean
Ascoli Piceno 96 C4 anc. Asculum
Picenum. Marche, C Italy
Asculum Picenum see Ascoli Piceno
'Aseb 72 D4 var. Assab, Amh. Āseb.
SE Eritrea
A Serra de Outes 92 B1 Galicia,
NW Spain
Aşgabat 122 C3 prev. Ashgabat,
Ashkhabad, Poltoratsk. country
capital (Turkmenistan) Ahal Welaýaty,
C Turkmenistan
Ashara see Al 'Ashārah
Ashburton 151 C6 Canterbury, South
Island, New Zealand
Ashburton River 146 A4 river Western
Australia
Ashdod 119 A6 anc. Azotos, Lat. Azotus.
Central, W Israel
Asheville 43 E1 North Carolina, SE USA
Ashgabat see Aşgabat
Ashkelon 119 A6 prev. Ashqelon.
Southern, C Israel
Ashkhabad see Aşgabat
Ashland 46 B4 Oregon, NW USA
Ashland 40 B1 Wisconsin, N USA
Ashmore and Cartier Islands 142 A3
Australian external territory E Indian
Ocean
Ashmyany 107 C5 Rus. Oshmyany.
Hrodzyenskaya Voblasts', W Belarus
Ashqelon see Ashkelon
Ash Shaddādah 118 D2 var. Ash
Shaddādah, Jisr ash Shadadi, Shaddādī,
Shedadi, Tell Shedadi. Al Ḥasakah,
NE Syria
Ash Shaddādah see Ash Shaddādah
Ash Sharah 119 B7 var. Esh Sharā.
mountain range W Jordan
Ash Shāriqah 120 D4 Eng. Sharjah. Ash
Shāriqah, NE United Arab Emirates
Ash Shawbak 119 B7 Ma'ān, W Jordan
Ash Shiḥr 121 C6 SE Yemen
Asia 112 continent
Asinara 96 A4 island W Italy
Asipovichy 107 D6 Rus. Osipovichi.
Mahilyowskaya Voblasts', E Belarus
Aşkale 117 E3 Erzurum, NE Turkey
Askersund 85 C6 Örebro, C Sweden
Asmara see Asmera
Asmera 72 C4 var. Asmara. country
capital (Eritrea) C Eritrea
Aspadana see Eşfahān
Asphaltites, Lacus see Dead Sea
Aspinwall see Colón
Assab see 'Aseb
As Sabkhah 118 D2 var. Sabkha. Ar
Raqqah, NE Syria
Assad, Lake 118 C2 Eng. Lake Assad.
lake N Syria
Assad, Lake see Assad, Buḥayrat al
Aş Şafāwī 119 C6 Al Mafraq, N Jordan
Aş Şahrā' ash Sharqīyah see Sahara el
Sharqíya
As Salamīyah see Salamīyah
'Assal, Lac 68 E4 lake Y Djibouti
As Salṭ 119 B6 var. Salt. Al Balqā',
NW Jordan
Assamaka see Assamakka
Assamakka 75 F2 var. Assamaka.
Agadez, NW Niger
As Samāwah 120 B3 var. Samawa. Al
Muthanná, S Iraq
Assenede 87 B5 Oost-Vlaanderen,
NW Belgium
Assiout see Asyūṭ
Assiut see Asyūṭ
Assling see Jesenice
Assouan see Aswān
Assu 63 G2 var. Açu. Rio Grande do
Norte, E Brazil

Assuan see Aswān
As Sukhnah 118 C3 var. Sukhne, Fr.
Soukhné. Ḥimṣ, C Syria
As Sulaymānīyah 120 C3 var.
Sulaimaniya, Kurd. Slēmāni. As
Sulaymānīyah, NE Iraq
As Sulayyil 121 B5 Ar Riyāḍ, S Saudi
Arabia
Aş Şuwār 118 D2 var. Şuwār. Dayr az
Zawr, E Syria
As Suwaydā' 119 B5 var. El Suweida,
Es Suweida, Suweida, Fr. Soueida. As
Suwaydā', SW Syria
As Suways see Suez
Asta Colonia see Asti
Astacus see İzmit
Astana 114 C4 prev. Akmola,
Akmolinsk, Tselinograd, Aqmola.
country capital (Kazakhstan) Akmola,
N Kazakhstan
Asta Pompeia see Asti
Astarabad see Gorgān
Asterābād see Gorgān
Asti 96 A2 anc. Asta Colonia, Asta
Pompeia, Hasta Colonia, Hasta
Pompeia. Piemonte, NW Italy
Astigi see Écija
Astipálaia see Astypálaia
Astorga 92 C1 anc. Asturica Augusta.
Castilla y León, N Spain
Astrabad see Gorgān
Astrakhan' 111 C7 Astrakhanskaya
Oblast', SW Russian Federation
Asturias 92 C1 autonomous community
NW Spain
Asturias see Oviedo
Asturica Augusta see Astorga
Astypálaia 105 D7 var. Astipálaia, It.
Stampalia. island Kykládes, Greece,
Aegean Sea
Asunción 64 D2 country capital
(Paraguay) Central, S Paraguay
Aswān 72 B2 var. Assouan, Assuan,
Aswān; anc. Syene. SE Egypt
Aswān see Aswān
Asyūṭ 72 B2 var. Assiout, Assiut, Asyût,
Siut; anc. Lycopolis. C Egypt
Asyûṭ see Asyūṭ
Atacama Desert 64 B2 Eng. Atacama
Desert. desert N Chile
Atacama Desert see Atacama, Desierto de
Atafu 145 E3 island NW Tokelau
Atamyrat 122 D3 prev. Kerki. Lebap
Welaýaty, E Turkmenistan
Atâr 74 C2 Adrar, W Mauritania
Atas Bogd 126 D3 mountain
SW Mongolia
Atascadero 47 B7 California, W USA
Atatürk Baraji 117 E4 reservoir
S Turkey
Atbara 72 C3 var. 'Aṭbārah. River Nile,
NE Sudan
'Aṭbārah/'Aṭbarah, Nahr see Atbara
Atbasar 114 C4 Akmola,
N Kazakhstan
Atchison 45 F4 Kansas, C USA
Ath 87 B6 var. Aat. Hainaut, SW Belgium
Athabasca 37 E5 Alberta, SW Canada
Athabasca 37 E5 var. Athabaska. river
Alberta, SW Canada
Athabasca, Lake 37 F4 lake Alberta/
Saskatchewan, SW Canada
Athabaska see Athabasca
Athenae see Athína
Athens 43 E2 Georgia, SE USA
Athens 40 D1 Ohio, N USA
Athens 49 G3 Texas, SW USA
Athens see Athína
Atherton 148 D3 Queensland,
NE Australia
Athína 105 C6 Eng. Athens, prev.
Athínai; anc. Athenae. country capital
(Greece) Attikí, C Greece
Athínai see Athína
Athlone 89 B5 Ir. Baile Átha Luain.
C Ireland
Ath Thawrah see Madīnat ath Thawrah
Ati 76 C3 Batha, C Chad
Atikokan 38 B4 Ontario, S Canada
Atka 115 G3 Magadanskaya Oblast',
E Russian Federation
Atka 36 A3 Atka Island, Alaska, USA
Atlanta 42 D2 state capital Georgia,
SE USA
Atlanta 49 H2 Texas, SW USA
Atlantic City 41 F4 New Jersey, NE USA
Atlantic-Indian Basin 67 D7 undersea
basin SW Indian Ocean

Atlantic-Indian Ridge 69 B8 undersea
ridge SW Indian Ocean
Atlantic Ocean 66 B4 ocean
Atlas Mountains 70 C2 mountain range
NW Africa
Atlasovo 115 H3 Kamchatskiy Kray,
E Russian Federation
Atlas, Tell 102 C3 Eng. Tell Atlas.
mountain range N Algeria
Atlas, Tell see Atlas Tellien
Atlin 36 D4 British Columbia, W Canada
Aṭ Ṭafīlah 119 B7 var. Et Tafila, Tafila.
Aṭ Ṭafīlah, W Jordan
Aṭ Ṭafīlah see Aṭ Ṭafīlah
Aṭ Ṭā'if 121 B5 Makkah, W Saudi Arabia
Attaleia/Attalia see Antalya
At Tall al Abyaḍ 118 C2 var. Tall al
Abyaḍ, Tell Abyad, Fr. Tell Abiad. Ar
Raqqah, N Syria
Aṭ Ṭanf 118 D4 Ḥimṣ, S Syria
Attapu 137 E5 var. Attopeu, Samakhixai.
Attapu, S Laos
Attawapiskat 38 C3 Ontario, C Canada
Attawapiskat 38 C3 river Ontario,
S Canada
At Tibnī 118 D2 var. Tibnī. Dayr az
Zawr, NE Syria
Attopeu see Attapu
Attu Island 36 A2 island Aleutian
Islands, Alaska, USA
Atyrau 114 B4 prev. Gur'yev. Atyrau,
W Kazakhstan
Aubagne 91 D6 anc. Albania. Bouches-
du-Rhône, SE France
Aubange 87 D8 Luxembourg,
SE Belgium
Aubervilliers 90 E1 Seine-St-Denis,
Île-de-France, N France Europe
Auburn 46 B2 Washington, NW USA
Auch 91 B6 Lat. Augusta Auscorum,
Elimberrum. Gers, S France
Auckland 150 D2 Auckland, North
Island, New Zealand
Auckland Islands 142 C5 island group
S New Zealand
Audern see Audru
Audincourt 90 E4 Doubs, E France
Audru 106 D2 Ger. Audern. Pärnumaa,
SW Estonia
Augathella 149 D5 Queensland,
E Australia
Augsbourg see Augsburg
Augsburg 95 C6 Fr. Augsbourg; anc.
Augusta Vindelicorum. Bayern,
S Germany
Augusta 147 A7 Western Australia
Augusta 43 E2 Georgia, SE USA
Augusta 41 G2 state capital Maine,
NE USA
Augusta see London
Augusta Auscorum see Auch
Augusta Emerita see Mérida
Augusta Praetoria see Aosta
Augusta Trajana see Stara Zagora
Augusta Treverorum see Trier
Augusta Vangionum see Worms
Augusta Vindelicorum see Augsburg
Augustobona Tricassium see Troyes
Augustodurum see Bayeux
Augustoritum Lemovicensium see
Limoges
Augustów 98 E2 Rus. Avgustov.
Podlaskie, NE Poland
Aulie Ata/Auliye-Ata see Taraz
Aunglan 136 B4 var. Allanmyo, Myaydo.
Magway, C Myanmar (Burma)
Auob 78 B4 var. Oup. river Namibia/
South Africa
Aurangābād 134 D5 Mahārāshtra,
C India
Auray 90 A3 Morbihan, NW France
Aurelia Aquensis see Baden-Baden
Aurelianum see Orléans
Aurès, Massif de l' 102 C4 mountain
range NE Algeria
Aurillac 91 C5 Cantal, C France
Aurium see Ourense
Aurora 59 F2 NW Guyana
Aurora 44 D4 Colorado, C USA
Aurora 40 B3 Illinois, N USA
Aurora 45 G5 Missouri, C USA
Aurora see Maéwo, Vanuatu
Aus 78 B4 Karas, SW Namibia
Ausa see Vic
Aussig see Ústí nad Labem
Austin 45 G3 Minnesota, N USA
Austin 49 G3 state capital Texas, SW USA
Australes, Archipel des see Australes, Îles
**Australes et Antarctiques Françaises,
Terres** see French Southern and
Antarctic Territories

Australes, Îles 143 F4 var. Archipel des Australes, Îles Tubuai, Tubuai Islands, Eng. Austral Islands. island group SW French Polynesia
Austral Fracture Zone 143 H4 tectonic feature S Pacific Ocean
Australia 142 A4 off. Commonwealth of Australia. country

AUSTRALIA
Australasia & Oceania

Official name Commonwealth of Australia
Formation 1901 / 1901
Capital Canberra
Population 22.6 million / 8 people per sq mile (3 people per sq km)
Total area 2,967,893 sq. miles (7,686,850 sq. km)
Languages English*, Italian, Cantonese, Greek, Arabic, Vietnamese, Aboriginal languages
Religions Roman Catholic 26%, Nonreligious 19%, Anglican 19%, Other 17%, Other Christian 13%, United Church 6%
Ethnic mix European 92%, Asian 7%, Aboriginal and other 1%
Government Parliamentary system
Currency Australian dollar = 100 cents
Literacy rate 99%
Calorie consumption 3261 kilocalories

Australia, Commonwealth of see Australia
Australian Alps 149 C7 mountain range SE Australia
Australian Capital Territory 149 D7 prev. Federal Capital Territory. territory SE Australia
Australie, Bassin Nord de l' see North Australian Basin
Austral Islands see Australes, Îles
Austrava see Ostrov
Austria 95 D7 off. Republic of Austria, Ger. Österreich. country C Europe

AUSTRIA
Central Europe

Official name Republic of Austria
Formation 1918 / 1919
Capital Vienna
Population 8.4 million / 263 people per sq mile (102 people per sq km)
Total area 32,378 sq. miles (83,858 sq. km)
Languages German*, Croatian, Slovenian, Hungarian (Magyar)
Religions Roman Catholic 78%, Nonreligious 9%, Other (including Jewish and Muslim) 8%, Protestant 5%
Ethnic mix Austrian 93%, Croat, Slovene, and Hungarian 6%, Other 1%
Government Parliamentary system
Currency Euro = 100 cents
Literacy rate 99%
Calorie consumption 3800 kilocalories

Austria, Republic of see Austria
Autesiodorum see Auxerre
Autissiodorum see Auxerre
Autricum see Chartres
Auvergne 91 C5 cultural region C France
Auxerre 90 C4 anc. Autesiodorum, Autissiodorum. Yonne, C France
Avaricum see Bourges
Avarua 145 G5 dependent territory capital (Cook Islands) Rarotonga, S Cook Islands
Avasfelsőfalu see Negreşti-Oaş
Ávdira 104 C3 Anatoliki Makedonía kai Thráki, NE Greece
Aveiro 92 B2 anc. Talabriga. Aveiro, W Portugal
Avela see Ávila
Avellino 97 D5 anc. Abellinum. Campania, S Italy
Avenio see Avignon
Avesta 85 C6 Dalarna, C Sweden
Aveyron 91 C5 river S France
Avezzano 96 C4 Abruzzo, C Italy
Avgustov see Augustów
Aviemore 88 C3 N Scotland, United Kingdom
Avignon 91 D6 anc. Avenio. Vaucluse, SE France

Ávila 92 D3 var. Avila; anc. Abela, Abula, Abyla, Avela. Castilla y León, C Spain
Avilés 92 C1 Asturias, NW Spain
Avranches 90 B3 Manche, N France
Avveel see Ivalo, Finland
Avvil see Ivalo
Awaji-shima 131 C6 island SW Japan
Āwash 73 D5 Āfar, NE Ethiopia
Awbārī 71 F3 SW Libya
Ax see Dax
Axel 87 B5 Zeeland, SW Netherlands
Axel Heiberg Island 37 E1 var. Axel Heiburg. island Nunavut, N Canada
Axel Heiburg see Axel Heiberg Island
Axiós see Vardar
Ayacucho 60 D4 Ayacucho, S Peru
Ayagoz 114 C5 var. Ayaguz, Kaz. Ayakoz. river E Kazakhstan
Ayamonte 92 C4 Andalucía, S Spain
Ayaviri 61 E4 Puno, S Peru
Aydarko'l Ko'li 123 E2 Rus. Ozero Aydarkul'. lake C Uzbekistan
Aydarkul', Ozero see Aydarko'l Ko'li
Aydın 116 A4 var. Aidin; anc. Tralles Aydin. Aydın, SW Turkey
Ayers Rock see Uluru
Ayeyarwady see Irrawaddy
Ayiá see Agiá
Áyios Evstrátios see Ágios Efstrátios
Áyios Nikólaos see Ágios Nikólaos
Ayorou 75 E3 Tillabéri, W Niger
'Ayoûn el 'Atroûs 74 D3 var. Aîoun el Atrous, Aïoun el Atroûss. Hodh el Gharbi, SE Mauritania
Ayr 88 C4 W Scotland, United Kingdom
Ayteke Bi 114 B4 Kaz. Zhangaqazaly; prev. Novokazalinsk. Kyzylorda, SW Kazakhstan
Aytos 104 E2 Burgas, E Bulgaria
Ayutthaya 137 C5 var. Phra Nakhon Si Ayutthaya. Phra Nakhon Si Ayutthaya, C Thailand
Ayvalık 116 A3 Balıkesir, W Turkey
Azahar, Costa del 93 F3 coastal region E Spain
Azaouâd 75 E3 desert C Mali
Azärbaycan/Azärbaycan Respublikasï see Azerbaijan
A'zâz 118 B2 Ḥalab, NW Syria
Azerbaijan 117 G2 off. Azerbaijani Republic, Az. Azärbaycan/Azärbaycan Respublikasï; prev. Azerbaijan SSR. country SE Asia

AZERBAIJAN
Southwest Asia

Official name Republic of Azerbaijan
Formation 1991 / 1991
Capital Baku
Population 9.3 million / 278 people per sq mile (107 people per sq km)
Total area 33,436 sq. miles (86,600 sq. km)
Languages Azeri*, Russian
Religions Shi'a Muslim 68%, Sunni Muslim 26%, Russian Orthodox 3%, Armenian Apostolic Church (Orthodox) 2%, Other 1%
Ethnic mix Azeri 91%, Other 3%, Lazs 2%, Armenian 2%, Russian 2%
Government Presidential system
Currency New manat = 100 gopik
Literacy rate 99%
Calorie consumption 3072 kilocalories

Azerbaijani Republic see Azerbaijan
Azerbaijan SSR see Azerbaijan
Azimabad see Patna
Azizie see Telish
Azogues 60 B2 Cañar, S Ecuador
Azores 92 A4 var. Açores, Ilhas dos Açores, Port. Arquipélago dos Açores. island group Portugal, NE Atlantic Ocean
Azores-Biscay Rise 80 A3 undersea rise E Atlantic Ocean
Azotos/Azotus see Ashdod
Azoum, Bahr 76 C3 seasonal river SE Chad
Azov, Sea of 103 H1 Rus. Azovskoye More, Ukr. Azovs'ke More. sea NE Black Sea
Azovs'ke More/Azovskoye More see Azov, Sea of
Azraq, Wāḥat al 119 C6 oasis N Jordan
Aztec 48 C1 New Mexico, SW USA
Azuaga 92 C4 Extremadura, W Spain

Azuero, Península de 53 F5 peninsula S Panama
Azul 65 D5 Buenos Aires, E Argentina
Azur, Côte d' 91 E6 coastal region SE France
'Azza see Gaza
Az Zaqāzīq 72 B1 var. Zagazig. N Egypt
Az Zarqā' 119 B6 var. Zarqa. Az Zarqā', NW Jordan
Az Zāwiyah 71 F2 var. Zawia. NW Libya
Az Zilfī 120 B4 N Riyāḍ, N Saudi Arabia

B

Baalbek 118 B4 var. Ba'labakk; anc. Heliopolis. E Lebanon
Baardheere 73 D6 var. Bardere, It. Bardera. Gedo, SW Somalia
Baarle-Hertog 87 C5 Antwerpen, N Belgium
Baarn 86 C3 Utrecht, C Netherlands
Babadag 108 D5 Tulcea, SE Romania
Babahoyo 60 B2 prev. Bodegas. Los Ríos, C Ecuador
Bābā, Kūh-e 123 E4 mountain range C Afghanistan
Babayevo 110 B4 Vologodskaya Oblast', NW Russian Federation
Babeldaob 144 A1 var. Babeldaop, Babelthuap. island N Palau
Babeldaop see Babeldaob
Bab el Mandeb 121 B7 strait Gulf of Aden/Red Sea
Babelthuap see Babeldaob
Babian Jiang see Black River
Babruysk 107 D7 Rus. Bobruysk. Mahilyowskaya Voblasts', E Belarus
Babuyan Channel 139 E1 channel N Philippines
Babuyan Islands 139 E1 island group N Philippines
Bacabal 63 F2 Maranhão, E Brazil
Bacău 108 C4 Hung. Bákó. Bacău, NE Romania
Băc Bô, Vinh see Tongking, Gulf of
Băc Giang 136 D3 Ha Băc, N Vietnam
Bačka Palanka 100 D3 prev. Palanka. Serbia, NW Serbia
Bačka Topola 100 D3 Hung. Topolya; prev. Hung. Bácstopolya. Vojvodina, N Serbia
Bac Liêu 137 D6 var. Vinh Loi. Minh Hai, S Vietnam
Bacolod 125 E4 off. Bacolod City. Negros, C Philippines
Bacolod City see Bacolod
Bácsszenttamás see Srbobran
Bácstopolya see Bačka Topola
Bactra see Balkh
Badajoz 92 C4 anc. Pax Augusta. Extremadura, W Spain
Baden-Baden 95 B6 anc. Aurelia Aquensis. Baden-Württemberg, SW Germany
Bad Freienwalde 94 D3 Brandenburg, NE Germany
Badger State see Wisconsin
Bad Hersfeld 94 B4 Hessen, C Germany
Bad Homburg see Bad Homburg vor der Höhe
Bad Homburg vor der Höhe 95 B5 var. Bad Homburg. Hessen, W Germany
Bad Ischl 95 D7 Oberösterreich, N Austria
Bad Krozingen 95 A6 Baden-Württemberg, SW Germany
Badlands 44 D2 physical region North Dakota/South Dakota, N USA
Badu Island 148 C1 island Queensland, NE Australia
Bad Vöslau 95 E6 Niederösterreich, NE Austria
Baeterrae/Baeterrae Septimanorum see Béziers
Baetic Cordillera/Baetic Mountains see Béticos, Sistemas
Bafatá 74 C4 C Guinea-Bissau
Baffin Bay 37 G2 bay Canada/Greenland
Baffin Island 37 G2 island Nunavut, NE Canada
Bafing 74 C3 river W Africa
Bafoussam 76 A4 Ouest, W Cameroon
Bafra 116 D2 Samsun, N Turkey
Bāft 120 D4 Kermān, S Iran

Bagaces 52 D4 Guanacaste, NW Costa Rica
Bagdad see Baghdad
Bagé 63 E5 Rio Grande do Sul, S Brazil
Baghdad 120 B3 var. Bagdad, Eng. Baghdad. country capital (Iraq) Baghdād, C Iraq
Baghdad see Baghdad
Baghlān 123 E3 Baghlān, NE Afghanistan
Bago 136 B4 var. Pegu. Bago, SW Myanmar (Burma)
Bagoé 74 D4 river Côte d'Ivoire/Mali
Bagrationovsk 106 A4 Ger. Preussisch Eylau. Kaliningradskaya Oblast', W Russian Federation
Bagrax Hu see Bosten Hu
Baguio 139 E1 off. Baguio City. Luzon, N Philippines
Baguio City see Baguio
Bagzane, Monts 75 F3 mountain N Niger
Bahama Islands see Bahamas
Bahamas 54 C2 off. Commonwealth of the Bahamas. country N West Indies
Bahamas 35 D6 var. Bahama Islands. island group N West Indies

BAHAMAS
West Indies

Official name Commonwealth of the Bahamas
Formation 1973 / 1973
Capital Nassau
Population 300,000 / 78 people per sq mile (30 people per sq km)
Total area 5382 sq. miles (13,940 sq. km)
Languages English*, English Creole, French Creole
Religions Baptist 32%, Anglican 20%, Roman Catholic 19%, Other 17%, Methodist 6%, Church of God 6%
Ethnic mix Black African 85%, Other 15%
Government Parliamentary system
Currency Bahamian dollar = 100 cents
Literacy rate 96%
Calorie consumption 2750 kilocalories

Bahamas, Commonwealth of the see Bahamas
Baharly 122 C3 var. Bäherden, Rus. Bakharden; prev. Bakherden. Ahal Welaýaty, C Turkmenistan
Bahāwalpur 122 C3 Punjab, E Pakistan
Bäherden see Baharly
Bahia 63 F3 off. Estado da Bahia. state E Brazil
Bahia 63 E3 off. Estado da Bahia. region E Brazil
Bahía Blanca 65 C5 Buenos Aires, E Argentina
Bahia, Estado da see Bahia
Bahir Dar 72 C4 var. Bahr Dar, Bahrdar Giyorgis. Āmara, N Ethiopia
Bahraich 135 E3 Uttar Pradesh, N India
Bahrain 120 C4 off. State of Bahrain, Dawlat al Bahrayn, Ar. Al Baḥrayn, prev. anc. Tylos, Tyros. country SW Asia

BAHRAIN
Southwest Asia

Official name Kingdom of Bahrain
Formation 1971 / 1971
Capital Manama
Population 1.3 million / 4762 people per sq mile (1841 people per sq km)
Total area 239 sq. miles (620 sq. km)
Languages Arabic
Religions Muslim (mainly Shi'a) 99%, Other 1%
Ethnic mix Bahraini 63%, Asian 19%, Other Arab 10%, Iranian 8%
Government Mixed monarchical–parliamentary system
Currency Bahraini dinar = 1000 fils
Literacy rate 91%
Calorie consumption not available

Bahrain, State of see Bahrain
Bahrayn, Dawlat al see Bahrain
Bahr Dar/Bahrdar Giyorgis see Bahir Dar
Bahrein see Bahrain
Bahr el, Azraq see Blue Nile
Bahr Tabariya, Sea of see Tiberias, Lake
Bahushewsk 107 E6 Rus. Bogushëvsk. Vitsyebskaya Voblasts', NE Belarus

173

Baia Mare 108 B3 Ger. Frauenbach, Hung. Nagybánya; prev. Neustadt. Maramureş, NW Romania
Baia Sprie 108 B3 Ger. Mittelstadt, Hung. Felsőbánya. Maramureş, NW Romania
Baïbokoum 76 B4 Logone-Oriental, SW Chad
Baidoa see Baydhabo
Baie-Comeau 39 E3 Québec, SE Canada
Baikal, Lake 115 E4 Eng. Lake Baikal. lake S Russian Federation
Baikal, Lake see Baykal, Ozero
Baile Átha Cliath see Dublin
Baile Átha Luain see Athlone
Bailén 92 D4 Andalucía, S Spain
Baile na Mainistreach see Newtownabbey
Băileşti 108 B5 Dolj, SW Romania
Ba Illi 76 B3 Chari-Baguirmi, SW Chad
Bainbridge 42 D3 Georgia, SE USA
Ba'ir see Bāyir
Baireuth see Bayreuth
Bairiki 144 D2 country capital (Kiribati) Tarawa, NW Kiribati
Bairnsdale 149 C7 Victoria, SE Australia
Baishan 129 E3 prev. Hunjiang. Jilin, NE China
Baiyin 128 B4 Gansu, C China
Baja 99 C7 Bács-Kiskun, S Hungary
Baja California Norte 50 B2 state NW Mexico
Bajo Boquete see Boquete
Bajram Curri 101 D5 Kukës, N Albania
Bakala 76 C4 Ouaka, C Central African Republic
Bakan see Shimonoseki
Baker 46 C3 Oregon, NW USA
Baker and Howland Islands 145 E2 US unincorporated territory W Polynesia
Baker Lake 37 F3 var. Qamanittuaq. Nunavut, N Canada
Bakersfield 47 C7 California, W USA
Bakharden see Baharly
Bakhchisaray see Bakhchysaray
Bakhchysaray 109 F5 Rus. Bakhchisaray. Avtonomna Respublika Krym, S Ukraine
Bakherden see Baharly
Bakhmach 109 F1 Chernihivs'ka Oblast', N Ukraine
Bäkhtärän see Kermänshäh
Bakı 117 H2 Eng. Baku. country capital (Azerbaijan) E Azerbaijan
Bákó see Bacău
Bakony 99 C7 Eng. Bakony Mountains, Ger. Bakonywald. mountain range W Hungary
Bakony Mountains/Bakonywald see Bakony
Baku see Bakı
Bakwanga see Mbuji-Mayi
Balabac Island 129 C8 island W Philippines
Balabac, Selat see Balabac Strait
Balabac Strait 138 D2 var. Selat Balabac. strait Malaysia/Philippines
Ba'labakk see Baalbek
Balaguer 93 F2 Cataluña, NE Spain
Balakovo 111 C6 Saratovskaya Oblast', W Russian Federation
Bălă Morghāb see Bālā Murghāb
Bālā Murghāb 122 D4 prev. Bālă Morghāb. Laghmān, NW Afghanistan
Balashov 111 B6 Saratovskaya Oblast', W Russian Federation
Balasore see Bāleshwar
Balaton, Lake 99 C7 var. Lake Balaton, Ger. Plattensee. lake W Hungary
Balaton, Lake see Balaton
Balbina, Represa 62 D1 reservoir NW Brazil
Balboa 53 G4 Panamá, C Panama
Balcarce 65 D5 Buenos Aires, E Argentina
Balclutha 151 B7 Otago, South Island, New Zealand
Baldy Mountain 44 C1 mountain Montana, NW USA
Bâle see Basel
Balearic Plain see Algerian Basin
Baleares Major see Mallorca
Balearic Islands 93 G3 Eng. Balearic Islands. island group Spain, W Mediterranean Sea
Balearic Islands see Baleares, Islas
Balearis Minor see Menorca
Baleine, Rivière à la 39 E2 river Québec, E Canada
Balen 87 C5 Antwerpen, N Belgium

Bāleshwar 135 F4 prev. Balasore. Orissa, E India
Bálgrad see Alba Iulia
Bali 138 D5 island C Indonesia
Balıkesir 116 A3 Balıkesir, W Turkey
Balīkh, Nahr 118 C2 river N Syria
Balikpapan 138 D4 Borneo, C Indonesia
Balkanabat 122 B2 Rus. Nebitdag.
Balkan Welayäty, W Turkmenistan
Balkan Mountains 104 C2 Bul./ SCr. Stara Planina. mountain range Bulgaria/Serbia
Balkash 114 C5 Kaz. Balqash; prev. Balkhash. Karagandy, SE Kazakhstan
Balkash, Ozero 114 C5 Eng. Lake Balkhash, Kaz. Balqash; prev. Ozero Balkhash. lake SE Kazakhstan
Balkh 123 E3 anc. Bactra. Balkh, N Afghanistan
Balkhash see Balkash
Balkhash, Lake see Balkash, Ozero
Balkhash, Ozero see Balkash, Ozero
Balladonia 147 C6 Western Australia
Ballarat 149 C7 Victoria, SE Australia
Balleny Islands 154 B5 island group Antarctica
Ballinger 49 F3 Texas, SW USA
Balochistan 134 B3 prev. Baluchistan, Beluchistan. province SW Pakistan
Balqash see Balkhash/Balkhash, Ozero
Balş 108 B5 Olt, S Romania
Balsas 63 F2 Maranhão, E Brazil
Balsas, Río 51 E5 var. Río Mexcala. river S Mexico
Bal'shavik 107 D7 Rus. Bol'shevik. Homyel'skaya Voblasts', SE Belarus
Balta 108 D3 Odes'ka Oblast', SW Ukraine
Bălţi 108 D3 Rus. Bel'tsy. N Moldova
Baltic Port see Paldiski
Baltic Sea 85 C7 Ger. Ostee, Rus. Baltiskoye More. sea N Europe
Baltimore 41 F4 Maryland, NE USA
Baltischport/Baltiski see Paldiski
Baltiskoye More see Baltic Sea
Baltkrievija see Belarus
Baluchistan see Balochistan
Balvi 106 D4 NE Latvia
Balykchy 123 G2 Kir. Ysyk-Köl; prev. Issyk-Kul', Rybach'ye. Issyk-Kul'skaya Oblast', NE Kyrgyzstan
Balzers 94 E2 S Liechtenstein
Bam 120 E4 Kermän, SE Iran
Bamako 74 D4 country capital (Mali) Capital District, SW Mali
Bambari 76 C4 Ouaka, C Central African Republic
Bamberg 95 C5 Bayern, SE Germany
Bamenda 76 A4 Nord-Ouest, W Cameroon
Banaba 144 D2 var. Ocean Island. island Tungaru, W Kiribati
Banaras see Vārānasi
Banda Aceh 138 A3 var. Banda Atjeh; prev. Koetaradja, Kutaradja, Kutaraja. Sumatera, W Indonesia
Banda Atjeh see Banda Aceh
Banda, Laut see Banda Sea
Bandama 74 D5 var. Bandama Fleuve. river S Côte d'Ivoire
Bandama Fleuve see Bandama
Bandar 'Abbās see Bandar-e 'Abbās
Bandarbeyla 73 E5 var. Bender Beila, Bender Beyla. Bari, NE Somalia
Bandar-e-'Abbās 120 D4 var. Bandar 'Abbās; prev. Gombroon. Hormozgān, S Iran
Bandar-e Kängän 120 D4 var. Kängän. Büshehr, S Iran
Bandar-e Khamïr 120 D4 Hormozgān, S Iran
Bandar-e Langeh see Bandar-e Lengeh
Bandar-e Lengeh 120 D4 var. Bandar-e Langeh, Lingeh. Hormozgān, S Iran
Bandar Kassim see Boosaaso
Bandar Lampung 138 C4 var. Bandarlampung, Tanjungkarang-Telukbetung; prev. Tandjoengkarang, Tanjungkarang, Teloekbetoeng, Telukbetung. Sumatera, W Indonesia
Bandarlampung see Bandar Lampung
Bandar Maharani see Muar
Bandar Masulipatnam see Machilipatnam
Bandar Penggaram see Batu Pahat
Bandar Seri Begawan 138 D3 prev. Brunei Town. country capital (Brunei) N Brunei

Banda Sea 139 F5 var. Laut Banda. sea E Indonesia
Bandiagara 75 E3 Mopti, C Mali
Bandırma 116 A3 var. Penderma. Balıkesir, NW Turkey
Bandjarmasin see Banjarmasin
Bandoeng see Bandung
Bandundu 77 C6 prev. Banningville. Bandundu, W Dem. Rep. Congo
Bandung 138 C5 prev. Bandoeng. Jawa, C Indonesia
Bangalore 132 C2 var. Bengalooru. state capital Karnātaka, S India
Bangassou 76 D4 Mbomou, SE Central African Republic
Banggai, Kepulauan 139 E4 island group C Indonesia
Banghāzï 71 G2 Eng. Bengazi, Benghazi, It. Bengasi. NE Libya
Bangka, Pulau 138 C4 island W Indonesia
Bangkok see Ao Krung Thep
Bangkok, Bight of see Krung Thep, Ao
Bangladesh 135 G3 off. People's Republic of Bangladesh; prev. East Pakistan. republic S Asia

BANGLADESH		
South Asia		
Official name People's Republic of Bangladesh		
Formation 1971 / 1971		
Capital Dhaka		
Population 150 million / 2911 people per sq mile (1124 people per sq km)		
Total area 55,598 sq. miles (144,000 sq. km)		
Languages Bengali*, Urdu, Chakma, Marma (Magh), Garo, Khasi, Santhali, Tripuri, Mro		
Religions Muslim (mainly Sunni) 88%, Hindu 11%, Other 1%		
Ethnic mix Bengali 98%, Other 2%		
Government Parliamentary system		
Currency Taka = 100 poisha		
Literacy rate 56%		
Calorie consumption 2481 kilocalories		

Bangladesh, People's Republic of see Bangladesh
Ba Ngoi see Cam Ranh
Bangor 89 C6 NW Wales, United Kingdom
Bangor 89 B5 Ir. Beannchar. E Northern Ireland, United Kingdom
Bangor 41 G2 Maine, NE USA
Bang Pla Soi see Chon Buri
Bangui 77 B5 country capital (Central African Republic) Ombella-Mpoko, SW Central African Republic
Bangweulu, Lake 73 B8 var. Lake Bengwelu. lake N Zambia
Ban Hat Yai see Hat Yai
Ban Hin Heup 136 C4 Viangchan, C Laos
Ban Houayxay/Ban Houei Sai see Houayxay
Ban Hua Hin 137 C6 var. Hua Hin. Prachuap Khiri Khan, SW Thailand
Bani 74 D3 river S Mali
Banias see Bāniyās
Banijska Palanka see Glina
Beni Suwayf 72 B2 var. Beni Suef. N Egypt
Bāniyās 118 B3 var. Banias, Baniyas, Paneas. Tartūs, W Syria
Banjak, Kepulauan see Banyak, Kepulauan
Banja Luka 100 B3 Republika Srpska, NW Bosnia and Herzegovina
Banjarmasin 138 D4 prev. Bandjarmasin. Borneo, C Indonesia
Banjul 74 B3 prev. Bathurst. country capital (Gambia) W Gambia
Banks, Îles see Banks Islands
Banks Island 37 E2 island Northwest Territories, NW Canada
Banks Islands 144 D4 Fr. Îles Banks. island group N Vanuatu
Banks Lake 46 B1 reservoir Washington, NW USA
Banks Peninsula 151 C6 peninsula South Island, New Zealand
Banks Strait 149 C8 strait SW Tasman Sea
Bānkura 135 F4 West Bengal, NE India
Ban Mak Khaeng see Udon Thani

Banmo see Bhamo
Banningville see Bandundu
Bañolas see Banyoles
Ban Pak Phanang see Pak Phanang
Ban Sichon see Sichon
Banská Bystrica 99 C6 Ger. Neusohl, Hung. Besztercebánya. Banskobystricky Kraj, C Slovakia
Bantry Bay 89 A7 Ir. Bá Bheanntraí. bay SW Ireland
Banya 104 E2 Burgas, E Bulgaria
Banyak, Kepulauan 138 A3 prev. Kepulauan Banjak. island group NW Indonesia
Banyo 76 B4 Adamaoua, NW Cameroon
Banyoles 93 G2 var. Bañolas. Cataluña, NE Spain
Banzare Seamounts 141 C7 seamount range S Indian Ocean
Banzart see Bizerte
Baoji 128 B4 var. Pao-chi, Paoki. Shaanxi, C China
Baoro 76 B4 Nana-Mambéré, W Central African Republic
Baoshan 128 A6 var. Pao-shan. Yunnan, SW China
Baotou 127 F3 var. Pao-t'ou, Paotow. Nei Mongol Zizhiqu, N China
Ba'qübah 120 B3 var. Qubba. Diyālá, C Iraq
Baquerizo Moreno see Puerto Baquerizo Moreno
Bar 101 C5 It. Antivari. S Montenegro
Baraawe 73 D6 It. Brava. Shabeellaha Hoose, S Somalia
Bārāmati 134 C5 Mahārāshtra, W India
Baranavichy 107 B6 Pol. Baranowicze, Rus. Baranovichi. Brestskaya Voblasts', SW Belarus
Baranovichi/Baranowicze see Baranavichy
Barbados 55 G1 country SE West Indies

BARBADOS		
West Indies		
Official name Barbados		
Formation 1966 / 1966		
Capital Bridgetown		
Population 300,000 / 1807 people per sq mile (698 people per sq km)		
Total area 166 sq. miles (430 sq. km)		
Languages Bajan (Barbadian English), English*		
Religions Anglican 40%, Other 24%, Nonreligious 17%, Pentecostal 8%, Methodist 7%, Roman Catholic 4%		
Ethnic mix Black African 92%, White 3%, Other 3%, Mixed race 2%		
Government Parliamentary system		
Currency Barbados dollar = 100 cents		
Literacy rate 99%		
Calorie consumption 3021 kilocalories		

Barbastro 93 F2 Aragón, NE Spain
Barbate de Franco 92 C5 Andalucía, S Spain
Barbuda 55 G3 island N Antigua and Barbuda
Barcaldine 148 C4 Queensland, E Australia
Barcarozsnyó see Râşnov
Barcău see Berettyó
Barce see Al Marj
Barcelona 93 G2 anc. Barcino, Barcinona. Cataluña, E Spain
Barcelona 59 E2 Anzoátegui, NE Venezuela
Barcino/Barcinona see Barcelona
Barcoo see Cooper Creek
Barcs 99 C7 Somogy, SW Hungary
Bardaï 76 C1 Borkou-Ennedi-Tibesti, N Chad
Bardejov 99 D5 Ger. Bartfeld, Hung. Bártfa. Presovský Kraj, E Slovakia
Bardera/Bardere see Baardheere
Barduli see Barletta
Bareilly 135 E3 var. Bareli. Uttar Pradesh, N India
Bareli see Bareilly
Barendrecht 86 C4 Zuid-Holland, SW Netherlands
Barentin 90 C3 Seine-Maritime, N France
Barentsburg 83 G2 Spitsbergen, W Svalbard
Barentsevo More/Barents Havet see Barents Sea
Barentsøya 83 G2 island E Svalbard

Barents Sea *110 C2 Nor.* Barents Havet, *Rus.* Barentsevo More. *sea* Arctic Ocean
Bar Harbor *41 H2* Mount Desert Island, Maine, NE USA
Bari *97 E5 var.* Bari delle Puglie; *anc.* Barium. Puglia, SE Italy
Bari delle Puglie *see* Bari
Bāridah *see* Al Bāridah
Bari delle Puglie *see* Bari
Barikot *see* Barīkowṭ
Barīkowṭ *123 F4 var.* Barikot. Kunar, NE Afghanistan
Barillas *52 A2 var.* Santa Cruz Barillas. Huehuetenango, NW Guatemala
Barinas *58 C2* Barinas, W Venezuela
Barisal *135 G4* Barisal, S Bangladesh
Barisan, Pegunungan *138 B4 mountain range* Sumatera, W Indonesia
Barito, Sungai *138 D4 river* Borneo, C Indonesia
Barium *see* Bari
Barka *see* Al Marj
Barkly Tableland *148 B3 plateau* Northern Territory/Queensland, N Australia
Bârlad *108 D4 prev.* Bîrlad. Vaslui, E Romania
Barlavento, Ilhas de *74 A2 var.* Windward Islands. *island group* N Cape Verde
Bar-le-Duc *90 D3 var.* Bar-sur-Ornain. Meuse, NE France
Barlee, Lake *147 B6 lake* Western Australia
Barlee Range *146 A4 mountain range* Western Australia
Barletta *97 D5 anc.* Barduli. Puglia, SE Italy
Barlinek *98 B3 Ger.* Berlinchen. Zachodnio-pomorskie, NW Poland
Barmen-Elberfeld *see* Wuppertal
Barmouth *89 C6* NW Wales, United Kingdom
Barnaul *114 D4* Altayskiy Kray, C Russian Federation
Barnet *89 A7* United Kingdom
Barnstaple *89 C7* SW England, United Kingdom
Baroda *see* Vadodara
Baroghil Pass *123 F3 var.* Kowtal-e Barowghil. *pass* Afghanistan/Pakistan
Baron'ki *107 E7 Rus.* Boron'ki. Mahilyowskaya Voblasts', E Belarus
Barowghil, Kowtal-e *see* Baroghil Pass
Barquisimeto *58 C2* Lara, NW Venezuela
Barra *88 B3 island* NW Scotland, United Kingdom
Barra de Río Grande *53 E3* Región Autónoma Atlántico Sur, E Nicaragua
Barranca *60 C3* Lima, W Peru
Barrancabermeja *58 B2* Santander, N Colombia
Barranquilla *58 B1* Atlántico, N Colombia
Barreiro *92 B4* Setúbal, W Portugal
Barrier Range *149 C6 hill range* New South Wales, SE Australia
Barrow *36 D2* Alaska, USA
Barrow *89 B6 Ir.* An Bhearú. *river* SE Ireland
Barrow-in-Furness *89 C5* NW England, United Kingdom
Barrow Island *146 A4 island* Western Australia
Barstow *47 C7* California, W USA
Bar-sur-Ornain *see* Bar-le-Duc
Bartang *123 F3 river* SE Tajikistan
Bartenstein *see* Bartoszyce
Bártfa/Bartfeld *see* Bardejov
Bartica *59 F3* N Guyana
Bartın *116 C2* Bartın, NW Turkey
Bartlesville *49 G1* Oklahoma, C USA
Bartoszyce *98 D2 Ger.* Bartenstein. Warmińsko-mazurskie, NE Poland
Baruun-Urt *127 F2* Sühbaatar, E Mongolia
Barú, Volcán *53 E5 var.* Volcán de Chiriquí. *volcano* W Panama
Barwon River *149 D5 river* New South Wales, SE Australia
Barysaw *107 D6 Rus.* Borisov. Minskaya Voblasts', NE Belarus
Basarabeasca *108 D4 Rus.* Bessarabka. SE Moldova
Basel *95 A7 var.* Basle, *Fr.* Bâle. Basel Stadt, NW Switzerland
Basilan *139 E3 island* Sulu Archipelago, SW Philippines

Basle *see* Basel
Basra *see* Al Başrah
Bassano del Grappa *96 C2* Veneto, NE Italy
Bassein *see* Pathein
Basseterre *55 G4 country capital* (Saint Kitts and Nevis) Saint Kitts, Saint Kitts and Nevis
Basse-Terre *55 G3 dependent territory capital* (Guadeloupe) Basse Terre, SW Guadeloupe
Basse Terre *55 G4 island* W Guadeloupe
Bassikounou *74 D3* Hodh ech Chargui, SE Mauritania
Bass, Îlots de *see* Marotiri
Bass Strait *149 C7 strait* SE Australia
Bassum *94 B3* Niedersachsen, NW Germany
Bastia *91 E7* Corse, France, C Mediterranean Sea
Bastogne *87 D7* Luxembourg, SE Belgium
Bastrop *42 B2* Louisiana, S USA
Bastyn' *107 B7 Rus.* Bostyn'. Brestskaya Voblasts', SW Belarus
Basuo *see* Dongfang
Basutoland *see* Lesotho
Bata *77 A5* NW Equatorial Guinea
Batae Coritanorum *see* Leicester
Batajnica *100 D3* Vojvodina, N Serbia
Batangas *139 E2 off.* Batangas City. Luzon, N Philippines
Batangas City *see* Batangas
Batavia *see* Jakarta
Bătdâmbâng *137 C5 prev.* Battambang. Bătdâmbâng, NW Cambodia
Batéké, Plateaux *77 B6 plateau* S Congo
Bath *89 D7 hist.* Akermanceaster; *anc.* Aquae Calidae, Aquae Solis. SW England, United Kingdom
Bathinda *134 D2* Punjab, NW India
Bathsheba *55 G1* E Barbados
Bathurst *149 D6* New South Wales, SE Australia
Bathurst *39 F4* New Brunswick, SE Canada
Bathurst *see* Banjul
Bathurst Island *146 D2 island* Northern Territory, N Australia
Bathurst Island *37 F2 island* Parry Islands, Nunavut, N Canada
Wadi al Batin *120 C4 dry watercourse* SW Asia
Batman *117 E4 var.* Iluh. Batman, SE Turkey
Batna *71 E2* NE Algeria
Baton Rouge *42 B3 state capital* Louisiana, S USA
Batroûn *118 A4 var.* Al Batrūn. N Lebanon
Battambang *see* Bătdâmbâng
Batticaloa *132 D3* Eastern Province, E Sri Lanka
Battipaglia *97 D5* Campania, S Italy
Batumi *117 F2* W Georgia
Batu Pahat *138 B3 prev.* Bandar Penggaram. Johor, Peninsular Malaysia
Bauchi *75 G4* Bauchi, NE Nigeria
Bauer Basin *153 F3 undersea basin* E Pacific Ocean
Bauska *106 C3 Ger.* Bauske. S Latvia
Bauske *see* Bauska
Bautzen *94 D4 Lus.* Budyšin. Sachsen, E Germany
Bauzanum *see* Bolzano
Bavaria *see* Bayern
Bavarian Alps *95 C7 Ger.* Bayrische Alpen. *mountain range* Austria/Germany
Bavière *see* Bayern
Bavispe, Río *50 C2 river* NW Mexico
Bawīţi *72 B2 var.* Bawīṭī. N Egypt
Bawīṭī *see* Bawīṭī
Bawku *75 E4* N Ghana
Bayamo *54 C3* Granma, E Cuba
Bayan Har Shan *126 D4 var.* Bayan Khar. *mountain range* C China
Bayanhongor *126 D2* Bayanhongor, C Mongolia
Bayan Khar *see* Bayan Har Shan
Bayano, Lago *53 G4 lake* E Panama
Bay City *40 C3* Michigan, N USA
Bay City *49 G4* Texas, SW USA
Baydhabo *73 D6 var.* Baydhowa, Isha Baydhabo, *It.* Baidoa. Bay, SW Somalia
Baydhowa *see* Baydhabo
Bayern *95 C6 Eng.* Bavaria, *Fr.* Bavière. *state* SE Germany

Bayeux *90 B3 anc.* Augustodurum. Calvados, N France
Bâyir *119 C7 var.* Bā'ir. Ma'ān, S Jordan
Bay Islands *52 C1 Eng.* Bay Islands. *island group* N Honduras
Bay Islands *see* Bahía, Islas de la
Baymak *111 D6* Respublika Bashkortostan, W Russian Federation
Bayonne *91 A6 anc.* Lapurdum. Pyrénées-Atlantiques, SW France
Bayou State *see* Mississippi
Bayram-Ali *see* Baýramaly
Baýramaly *122 D3 var.* Bayramaly; *prev.* Bayram-Ali. Mary Welaýaty, S Turkmenistan
Bayreuth *95 C5 var.* Baireuth. Bayern, SE Germany
Bayrische Alpen *see* Bavarian Alps
Bayrūt *see* Beyrouth
Bay State *see* Massachusetts
Baysun *see* Boysun
Bayt Laḥm *see* Bethlehem
Bayt *see* Bethlehem
Baza *93 E4* Andalucía, S Spain
Bazargic *see* Dobrich
Bazin *see* Pezinok
Beagle Channel *65 C8 channel* Argentina/Chile
Béal Feirste *see* Belfast
Beannchar *see* Bangor, Northern Ireland, UK
Bear Island *see* Bjørnøya
Bear Lake *46 E4 lake* Idaho/Utah, NW USA
Beas de Segura *93 E4* Andalucía, S Spain
Beata, Isla *55 E3 island* SW Dominican Republic
Beatrice *45 F4* Nebraska, C USA
Beaufort Sea *154 D3 sea* Arctic Ocean
Beaufort West *78 C5 Afr.* Beaufort-Wes. Western Cape, South Africa
Beaufort-Wes *see* Beaufort West
Beaumont *49 H3* Texas, SW USA
Beaune *90 D4* Côte d'Or, C France
Beauvais *90 C3 anc.* Bellovacum, Caesaromagus. Oise, N France
Beaver Island *40 C2 island* Michigan, N USA
Beaver Lake *49 H1 reservoir* Arkansas, C USA
Beaver River *49 F1 river* Oklahoma, C USA
Beaver State *see* Oregon
Beāwar *134 C3* Rājasthān, N India
Bečej *100 D3 Ger.* Altbetsche, *Hung.* Óbecse, Rácz-Becse; *prev.* Magyar-Becse, Stari Bečej. Vojvodina, N Serbia
Béchar *70 D2 prev.* Colomb-Béchar. W Algeria
Beckley *40 D5* West Virginia, NE USA
Bécs *see* Wien
Bedford *89 D6* E England, United Kingdom
Bedum *86 E1* Groningen, NE Netherlands
Beehive State *see* Utah
Be'er Menuha *119 B7 prev.* Be'ér Menuḥa. Southern, S Israel
Be'ér Menuḥa *see* Be'er Menuha
Beernem *87 A5* West-Vlaanderen, NW Belgium
Beersheba *see* Be'er Sheva
Be'er Sheva *119 A7 var.* Beersheba, *Ar.* Bir es Saba; *prev.* Be'ér Sheva'. Southern, S Israel
Be'ér Sheva' *see* Be'er Sheva
Beesel *87 D5* Limburg, SE Netherlands
Beeville *49 G4* Texas, SW USA
Bega *149 D7* New South Wales, SE Australia
Begoml' *see* Byahoml'
Begovat *see* Bekobod
Behagle *see* Laï
Behar *see* Bihār
Beibu Wan *see* Tongking, Gulf of
Beida *see* Al Bayḍā'
Beihai *128 B6* Guangxi Zhuangzu Zizhiqu, S China
Beijing *128 C3 var.* Pei-ching, *Eng.* Peking; *prev.* Pei-p'ing. *country capital* (China) Beijing Shi, E China
Beira *79 E3* Sofala, C Mozambique
Beirut *see* Beyrouth
Beit Lekhem *see* Bethlehem
Beiuş *108 B3 Hung.* Belényes. Bihor, NW Romania
Beja *92 B4 anc.* Pax Julia. Beja, SE Portugal

Béjar *92 C3* Castilla y León, N Spain
Bejraburi *see* Phetchaburi
Bekabad *see* Bekobod
Békás *see* Bicaz
Bek-Budi *see* Qarshi
Békéscsaba *99 D7 Rom.* Bichiş-Ciaba. Békés, SE Hungary
Bekobod *123 E2 Rus.* Bekabad; *prev.* Begovat. Toshkent Viloyati, E Uzbekistan
Bela Crkva *100 D3 Ger.* Weisskirchen, *Hung.* Fehértemplom. Vojvodina, W Serbia
Belarus *107 B6 off.* Republic of Belarus, *var.* Belorussia, *Latv.* Baltkrievija; *prev.* Belorussian SSR, *Rus.* Belorusskaya SSR. *country* E Europe

Belarus, Republic of *see* Belarus
Belau *see* Palau
Belaya Tserkov' *see* Bila Tserkva
Bełchatów *98 C4 var.* Belchatow. Łódzski, C Poland
Belchatow *see* Bełchatów
Belcher, Îles *see* Belcher Islands
Belcher Islands *38 C2 Fr.* Îles Belcher. *island group* Nunavut, SE Canada
Beledweyne *73 D5 var.* Belet Huen, *It.* Belet Uen. Hiiraan, C Somalia
Belém *63 F1 var.* Pará. *state capital* Pará, N Brazil
Belén *52 D4* Rivas, SW Nicaragua
Belen *48 D2* New Mexico, SW USA
Belényes *see* Beiuş
Belet Huen/Belet Uen *see* Beledweyne
Belfast *89 B5 Ir.* Béal Feirste. *national capital* E Northern Ireland, United Kingdom
Belfield *44 D2* North Dakota, N USA
Belfort *90 E4* Territoire-de-Belfort, E France
Belgard *see* Białogard
Belgaum *132 B1* Karnātaka, W India
Belgian Congo *see* Congo (Democratic Republic of)
België/Belgique *see* Belgium
Belgium *87 B6 off.* Kingdom of Belgium, *Dut.* België, *Fr.* Belgique. *country* NW Europe

Belgium, Kingdom of *see* Belgium
Belgorod *111 A6* Belgorodskaya Oblast', W Russian Federation
Belgrano II *154 A2 Argentinian research station* Antarctica
Belice *see* Belize/Belize City
Beligrad *see* Berat
Beli Manastir *100 C3 Hung.* Pélmonostor; *prev.* Monostor. Osijek-Baranja, NE Croatia

Bélinga *77 B5* Ogooué-Ivindo, NE Gabon
Belitung, Pulau *138 C4 island*
W Indonesia
Belize *52 B1 Sp.* Belice; *prev.* British
Honduras, Colony of Belize. *country*
Central America

BELIZE
Central America

Official name Belize
Formation 1981 / 1981
Capital Belmopan
Population 294,385 / 33 people
per sq mile (13 people per sq km) / 48%
Total area 8867 sq. miles (22,966 sq. km)
Languages English*, English Creole,
Spanish, Mayan, Garifuna (Carib)
Religions Roman Catholic 62%,
Other 13%, Anglican 12%,
Methodist 6%, Mennonite 4%,
Seventh-day Adventist 3%
Ethnic mix Mestizo 49%, Creole 25%,
Maya 11%, Other 6%, Garifuna 6%,
Asian Indian 3%
Government Parliamentary system
Currency Belizean dollar = 100 cents
Literacy rate 75%
Calorie consumption 2869 kilocalories

Belize *52 B1 river* Belize/Guatemala
Belize *see* Belize City
Belize City *52 C1 var.* Belize, *Sp.* Belice.
Belize, NE Belize
Belize, Colony of *see* Belize
Beljak *see* Villach
Belkofski *39 B3* Alaska, USA
Belle Île *90 A4 island* NW France
Belle Isle, Strait of *39 G3 strait*
Newfoundland and Labrador, E Canada
Bellenz *see* Bellinzona
Belleville *40 B4* Illinois, N USA
Belleville *45 F4* Iowa, C USA
Bellevue *46 B2* Washington, NW USA
Bellingham *46 B1* Washington, NW USA
Belling Hausen Mulde *see* Southeast
Pacific Basin
Bellingshausen Abyssal Plain *see*
Bellingshausen Plain
Bellingshausen Plain *153 F5 var.*
Bellingshausen Abyssal Plain. *abyssal
plain* SE Pacific Ocean
Bellingshausen Sea *154 A3 sea*
Antarctica
Bellinzona *95 B8 Ger.* Bellenz. Ticino,
S Switzerland
Bello *58 B2* Antioquia, W Colombia
Bello Horizonte *see* Belo Horizonte
Bellovacum *see* Beauvais
Bellville *78 B5* Western Cape, SW South
Africa
Belmopan *52 C1 country capital* (Belize)
Cayo, C Belize
Belogradchik *104 B1* Vidin,
NW Bulgaria
Belo Horizonte *63 F4 prev.* Bello
Horizonte. *state capital* Minas Gerais,
SE Brazil
Belomorsk *110 B3* Respublika Kareliya,
NW Russian Federation
Beloretsk *111 D6* Respublika
Bashkortostan, W Russian Federation
Belorussia/Belorussian SSR *see* Belarus
Belorusskaya Gryada *see* Byelaruskaya
Hrada
Belorusskaya SSR *see* Belarus
Beloshchel'ye *see* Nar'yan-Mar
Belostok *see* Białystok
Belovár *see* Bjelovar
Belozërsk *110 B4* Vologodskaya Oblast',
NW Russian Federation
Belton *49 G3* Texas, SW USA
Bel'tsy *see* Bălți
Beluchistan *see* Balochistan
Belukha, Gora *114 D5 mountain*
Kazakhstan/Russian Federation
Belynichi *see* Byalynichy
Belyy, Ostrov *114 D2 island* N Russian
Federation
Bemaraha *79 F3 var.* Plateau du
Bemaraha. *mountain range*
W Madagascar
Bemaraha, Plateau du *see* Bemaraha
Bemidji *45 F1* Minnesota, N USA
Bemmel *86 D4* Gelderland,
SE Netherlands
Benaco *see* Garda, Lago di
Benares *see* Vārānasi
Benavente *92 D2* Castilla y León, N Spain

Bend *46 B3* Oregon, NW USA
Bender *see* Tighina
Bender Beila/Bender Beyla *see*
Bandarbeyla
Bender Cassim/Bender Qaasim *see*
Boosaaso
Bendern *94 E1* NW Liechtenstein Europe
Bendery *see* Tighina
Bendigo *149 C7* Victoria, SE Australia
Beneschau *see* Benešov
Beneški Zaliv *see* Venice, Gulf of
Benešov *99 B5 Ger.* Beneschau.
Středočeský Kraj, W Czech Republic
Benevento *97 D5 anc.* Beneventum,
Malventum. Campania, S Italy
Beneventum *see* Benevento
Bengal, Bay of *124 C4 bay* N Indian
Ocean
Bengalooru *see* Bangalore
Bengasi *see* Banghāzī
Bengazi *see* Banghāzī
Bengbu *128 D5 var.* Peng-pu. Anhui,
E China
Benghazi *see* Banghāzī
Bengkulu *138 B4 prev.* Bengkoeloe,
Benkoelen, Benkulen. Sumatera,
W Indonesia
Benguela *78 A2 var.* Benguella.
Benguela, W Angola
Benguella *see* Benguela
Bengweulu, Lake *see* Bangweulu, Lake
Ben Hope *88 B2 mountain* N Scotland,
United Kingdom
Beni *77 E5* Nord-Kivu, NE Dem. Rep.
Congo
Benidorm *93 F4* Valenciana, SE Spain
Beni-Mellal *70 C2* C Morocco
Benin *75 F4 off.* Republic of Benin; *prev.*
Dahomey. *country* W Africa

BENIN
West Africa

Official name Republic of Benin
Formation 1960 / 1960
Capital Porto-Novo
Population 9.1 million / 213 people
per sq mile (82 people per sq km)
Total area 43,483 sq. miles (112,620 sq. km)
Languages Fon, Bariba, Yoruba, Adja,
Houeda, Somba, French*
Religions Indigenous beliefs and
Voodoo 50%, Christian 30%, Muslim 20%
Ethnic mix Fon 41%, Other 21%, Adja 16%,
Yoruba 12%, Bariba 10%
Government Presidential system
Currency CFA franc = 100 centimes
Literacy rate 42%
Calorie consumption 2592 kilocalories

Benin, Bight of *75 F5 gulf* W Africa
Benin City *75 F5* Edo, SW Nigeria
Benin, Republic of *see* Benin
Beni, Río *61 E3 river* N Bolivia
Beni Suef *see* Banī Suwayf
Ben Nevis *88 C3 mountain* N Scotland,
United Kingdom
Bénoué *see* Benue
Benson *48 B3* Arizona, SW USA
Bent Jbaïl *119 A5 var.* Bint Jubayl.
S Lebanon
Benton *42 B1* Arkansas, C USA
Benue *76 A4 Fr.* Bénoué. *river*
Cameroon/Nigeria
Beograd *100 D3 Eng.* Belgrade. Serbia,
N Serbia
Berane *101 D5 prev.* Ivangrad.
E Montenegro
Berat *101 C6 var.* Berati, *SCr.* Beligrad.
Berat, C Albania
Berātku *see* Berat
Berati *see* Berat
Berau, Teluk *139 G4 var.* MacCluer
Gulf. *bay* Papua, E Indonesia
Berbera *72 D4* Woqooyi Galbeed,
NW Somalia
Berbérati *77 B5* Mambéré-Kadéï,
SW Central African Republic
Berck-Plage *90 C2* Pas-de-Calais,
N France
Berdichev *see* Berdychiv
Berdyans'k *109 G4 Rus.* Berdyansk;
prev. Osipenko. Zaporiz'ka Oblast',
SE Ukraine
Berdychiv *108 D2 Rus.* Berdichev.
Zhytomyrs'ka Oblast', N Ukraine
Beregovo/Beregszász *see* Berehove
Berehove *108 B3 Cz.* Berehovo,
Hung. Beregszász, *Rus.* Beregovo.
Zakarpats'ka Oblast', W Ukraine

Berehovo *see* Berehove
Bereket *122 B2 prev. Rus.* Gazandzhyk,
Kazandzhik, *Turkm.* Gazanjyk. Balkan
Welaýaty, W Turkmenistan
Beretău *see* Berettyó
Berettyó *99 D7 Rom.* Barcău; *prev.*
Berătău, Beretău. *river* Hungary/
Romania
Berettyóújfalu *99 D6* Hajdú-Bihar,
E Hungary
Berezhany *108 C2 Pol.* Brzeżany.
Ternopil's'ka Oblast', W Ukraine
Berezina *see* Byarezina
Berezniki *111 D5* Permskiy Kray,
NW Russian Federation
Berga *93 G2* Cataluña, NE Spain
Bergamo *96 B2 anc.* Bergomum.
Lombardia, N Italy
Bergara *93 E1* País Vasco, N Spain
Bergen *94 D2* Mecklenburg-
Vorpommern, NE Germany
Bergen *86 C2* Noord-Holland,
NW Netherlands
Bergen *85 A5* Hordaland, S Norway
Bergen *see* Mons
Bergerac *91 B5* Dordogne, SW France
Bergeyk *87 C5* Noord-Brabant,
S Netherlands
Bergomum *see* Bergamo
Bergse Maas *86 D4 river* S Netherlands
Beringen *87 C5* Limburg,
NE Belgium
Beringov Proliv *see* Bering Strait
Bering Sea *36 A2 sea* N Pacific Ocean
Bering Strait *36 C2 Rus.* Beringov Proliv.
strait Bering Sea/Chukchi Sea
Berja *93 E5* Andalucía, S Spain
Berkeley *47 B6* California, W USA
Berkner Island *154 A2 island* Antarctica
Berkovitsa *104 C2* Montana,
NW Bulgaria
Berlin *94 D3 country capital* (Germany)
Berlin, NE Germany
Berlin *41 G2* New Hampshire, NE USA
Berlinchen *see* Barlinek
Bermejo, Río *64 C2 river* N Argentina
Bermeo *93 E1* País Vasco, N Spain
Bermuda *35 E6 var.* Bermuda Islands,
Bermudas; *prev.* Somers Islands. *UK
crown colony* NW Atlantic Ocean
Bermuda Islands *see* Bermuda
Bermuda Rise *35 E6 undersea rise*
C Sargasso Sea
Bermudas *see* Bermuda
Bern *95 A7 Fr.* Berne. *country capital*
(Switzerland) Bern, W Switzerland
Bernau *94 D3* Brandenburg,
NE Germany
Bernburg *94 C4* Sachsen-Anhalt,
C Germany
Berne *see* Bern
Berner Alpen *95 A7 var.* Berner
Oberland, *Eng.* Bernese Oberland.
mountain range SW Switzerland
Berner Oberland/Bernese Oberland *see*
Berner Alpen
Bernier Island *147 A5 island* Western
Australia
Beroea *see* Ḥalab
Berry *90 C4 cultural region* C France
Berry Islands *54 C1 island group*
N Bahamas
Bertoua *77 B5* Est, E Cameroon
Beru *145 E2 var.* Peru. *atoll* Tungaru,
W Kiribati
Berwick-upon-Tweed *88 D4* N England,
United Kingdom
Berytus *see* Beyrouth
Besançon *90 D4 anc.* Besontium,
Vesontio. Doubs, E France
Beskra *see* Biskra
Besontium *see* Besançon
Bessarabka *see* Basarabeasca
Bezterece *see* Bistrița
Besztercebánya *see* Banská Bystrica
Betafo *79 G3* Antananarivo,
C Madagascar
Betanzos *92 B1* Galicia, NW Spain
Bethlehem *78 D4* Free State, C South
Africa
Bethlehem *119 B6 var.* Beit Lekhem,
Ar. Bayt Laḥm, *Heb.* Bet Leḥem.
C West Bank
Béticos, Sistema *92 D4 var.* Sistema
Penibético, *Eng.* Baetic Cordillera,
Baetic Mountains. *mountain range*
S Spain
Bet Leḥem *see* Bethlehem
Bétou *77 C5* Likouala, N Congo

Bette, Pic *see* Bette, Picco
Bette, Picco *71 G4 var.* Bīkkū Bīttī, Pic
Bette. *mountain* S Libya
Beulah *40 C2* Michigan, N USA
Beuthen *see* Bytom
Beveren *87 B5* Oost-Vlaanderen,
N Belgium
Beverley *89 D5* E England, United
Kingdom
Bexley *89 B8* Bexley, SE England, United
Kingdom
Beyla *74 D4* SE Guinea
Beyrouth *118 A4 var.* Bayrūt, *Eng.*
Beirut; *anc.* Berytus. *country capital*
(Lebanon) W Lebanon
Beyşehir *116 B4* Konya, SW Turkey
Beyşehir Gölü *116 B4 lake* C Turkey
Béziers *91 C6 anc.* Baeterrae, Baeterrae
Septimanorum, Julia Beterrae. Hérault,
S France
Bezmein *see* Abadan
Bezwada *see* Vijayawāda
Bhadrāvati *132 C2* Karnātaka,
SW India
Bhāgalpur *135 F3* Bihār, NE India
Bhaktapur *135 F3* Central, C Nepal
Bhamo *136 B2 var.* Banmo. Kachin
State, N Myanmar (Burma)
Bhārat *see* India
Bharūch *134 C4* Gujarāt, W India
Bhaunagar *see* Bhāvnagar
Bhāvnagar *134 C4 prev.* Bhaunagar.
Gujarāt, W India
Bheanttraí, Bá *see* Bantry Bay
Bhopāl *134 D4 state capital* Madhya
Pradesh, C India
Bhubaneshwar *135 F5 prev.*
Bhubaneswar, Bhuvaneshwar. *state
capital* Orissa, E India
Bhubaneswar *see* Bhubaneshwar
Bhuket *see* Phuket
Bhusaval *see* Bhusāwal
Bhusāwal *134 D4 prev.* Bhusaval.
Mahārāshtra, C India
Bhutan *135 G3 off.* Kingdom of Bhutan,
var. Druk-yul. *country* S Asia

BHUTAN
South Asia

Official name Kingdom of Bhutan
Formation 1656 / 1865
Capital Thimphu
Population 700,000 / 39 people
per sq mile (15 people per sq km)
Total area 18,147 sq. miles (47,000 sq. km)
Languages Dzongkha*, Nepali, Assamese
Religions Mahayana Buddhist 75%,
Hindu 25%
Ethnic mix Bhutanese 50%,
Nepalese 35%, Other 15%
Government Mixed monarchical–
parliamentary system
Currency Ngultrum = 100 chetrum
Literacy rate 56%
Calorie consumption Not available

Bhutan, Kingdom of *see* Bhutan
Bhuvaneshwar *see* Bhubaneshwar
Biak, Pulau *139 G4 island* E Indonesia
Biała Podlaska *98 E3* Lubelskie,
E Poland
Białogard *98 B2 Ger.* Belgard.
Zachodnio-pomorskie, NW Poland
Białystok *98 E3 Rus.* Belostok, Bielostok.
Podlaskie, NE Poland
Bianco, Monte *see* Blanc, Mont
Biarritz *91 A6* Pyrénées-Atlantiques,
SW France
Bicaz *108 C3 Hung.* Békás. Neamț,
NE Romania
Bichiș-Ciaba *see* Békéscsaba
Biddeford *41 G2* Maine, NE USA
Bideford *89 C7* SW England, United
Kingdom
Biel *95 A7 Fr.* Bienne. Bern,
W Switzerland
Bielefeld *94 B4* Nordrhein-Westfalen,
NW Germany
Bielitz/Bielitz-Biala *see* Bielsko-Biała
Bielostok *see* Białystok
Bielsko-Biała *99 C5 Ger.* Bielitz, Bielitz-
Biala. Śląskie, S Poland
Bielsk Podlaski *97 E3* Białystok,
E Poland
Bien Bien *see* Điện Biên Phủ
Biên Đông *see* South China Sea
Biên Hoa *137 E6* Đồng Nai, S Vietnam
Bienne *see* Biel

Bienville, Lac 38 D2 *lake* Québec, C Canada
Bié Plateau 78 B2 *var.* Bié Plateau. *plateau* C Angola
Bié Plateau *see* Bié, Planalto do
Big Cypress Swamp 43 E5 *wetland* Florida, SE USA
Bigge Island 146 C2 *island* Western Australia
Bighorn Mountains 44 C2 *mountain range* Wyoming, C USA
Bighorn River 44 C2 *river* Montana/ Wyoming, NW USA
Bignona 74 B3 SW Senegal
Bigorra *see* Tarbes
Bigosovo *see* Bihosava
Big Sioux River 45 E2 *river* Iowa/South Dakota, N USA
Big Spring 49 E3 Texas, SW USA
Bihać 100 B3 Federacija Bosna I Hercegovina, NW Bosnia and Herzegovina
Bihār 135 F3 *prev.* Behar. *cultural region* N India
Bihār *see* Bihār Sharīf
Biharamulo 73 B7 Kagera, NW Tanzania
Bihār Sharīf 135 F3 *var.* Bihār. Bihār, N India
Bihosava 107 D5 *Rus.* Bigosovo. Vitsyebskaya Voblasts', NW Belarus
Bijeljina 100 C3 Republika Srpska, NE Bosnia and Herzegovina
Bijelo Polje 101 D5 E Montenegro
Bīkāner 134 C3 Rājasthān, NW India
Bikin 115 G4 Khabarovskiy Kray, SE Russian Federation
Bikini Atoll 144 C1 *var.* Pikinni. *atoll* Ralik Chain, NW Marshall Islands
Bikkū Bīttī *see* Bette, Picco
Bilāspur 135 E4 Chhattīsgarh, C India
Biläsuvar 117 H3 *Rus.* Bilyasuvar; *prev.* Pushkino. SE Azerbaijan
Bila Tserkva 109 E2 *Rus.* Belaya Tserkov'. Kyyivs'ka Oblast', N Ukraine
Bilauktaung Range 137 C6 *var.* Thanintari Taungdan. *mountain range* Myanmar (Burma)/Thailand
Bilbao 93 E1 *Basq.* Bilbo. País Vasco, N Spain
Bilbo *see* Bilbao
Bilecik 116 B3 Bilecik, NW Turkey
Billings 44 C2 Montana, NW USA
Bilma, Grand Erg de 75 H3 *desert* NE Niger
Biloela 148 D4 Queensland, E Australia
Biloxi 42 C3 Mississippi, S USA
Biltine 76 C3 Biltine, E Chad
Bilwi *see* Puerto Cabezas
Bilyasuvar *see* Biläsuvar
Bilzen 87 D6 Limburg, NE Belgium
Bimini Islands 54 C1 *island group* W Bahamas
Binche 87 B7 Hainaut, S Belgium
Bindloe Island *see* Marchena, Isla
Bin Ghalfan, Jazā'ir *see* Ḩalāniyāt, Juzur al
Binghamton 41 F3 New York, NE USA
Bingöl 117 E3 Bingöl, E Turkey
Bint Jubayl *see* Bent Jbaïl
Bintulu 138 D3 Sarawak, East Malaysia
Binzhou 128 D4 Shandong, E China
Bío Bío, Río 65 B5 *river* C Chile
Bioco, Isla de 77 A5 *var.* Bioko, Eng. Fernando Po, *Sp.* Fernando Póo; *prev.* Macías Nguema Biyogo. *island* NW Equatorial Guinea
Bioko *see* Bioco, Isla de
Birāk 71 F3 *var.* Brak. C Libya
Birao 76 D3 Vakaga, NE Central African Republic
Birātnagar 135 F3 Eastern, SE Nepal
Bir es Saba *see* Be'er Sheva
Birjand 120 E3 Khorāsān-e Janūbī, E Iran
Birkenfeld 95 A5 Rheinland-Pfalz, SW Germany
Birkenhead 89 C5 NW England, United Kingdom
Birlad *see* Bârlad
Birmingham 89 C6 C England, United Kingdom
Birmingham 42 C2 Alabama, S USA
Bir Moghrein *see* Bîr Mogreïn
Bîr Mogreïn 74 C1 *var.* Bir Moghrein; *prev.* Fort-Trinquet. Tiris Zemmour, N Mauritania
Birnie Island 145 E3 *atoll* Phoenix Islands, C Kiribati
Birnin Konni 75 F3 *var.* Birni-Nkonni. Tahoua, SW Niger

Birni-Nkonni *see* Birnin Konni
Birobidzhan 115 G4 Yevreyskaya Avtonomnaya Oblast', SE Russian Federation
Birsen *see* Biržai
Birsk 111 D5 Respublika Bashkortostan, W Russian Federation
Biržai 106 C4 *Ger.* Birsen. Panevėžys, NE Lithuania
Biržebbuġa 102 B5 SE Malta
Bisanthe *see* Tekirdağ
Bisbee 48 B3 Arizona, SW USA
Biscaia, Baía de *see* Biscay, Bay of
Biscay, Bay of 80 B4 *Sp.* Golfo de Vizcaya, *Port.* Baía de Biscaia. *bay* France/Spain
Biscay Plain 80 B3 *abyssal plain* SE Bay of Biscay
Bischofsburg *see* Biskupiec
Bishah, Wadi 121 B5 *dry watercourse* C Saudi Arabia
Bishkek 123 G2 *var.* Pishpek; *prev.* Frunze. *country capital* (Kyrgyzstan) Chuyskaya Oblast', N Kyrgyzstan
Bishop's Lynn *see* King's Lynn
Bishri, Jabal 118 D3 *mountain range* E Syria
Biskara *see* Biskra
Biskra 71 E2 *var.* Beskra, Biskara. NE Algeria
Biskupiec 98 D2 *Ger.* Bischofsburg. Warmińsko-Mazurskie, NE Poland
Bislig 139 F2 Mindanao, S Philippines
Bismarck 45 E2 *state capital* North Dakota, N USA
Bismarck Archipelago 144 B3 *island group* NE Papua New Guinea
Bismarck Sea 144 B3 *sea* W Pacific Ocean
Bisnulok *see* Phitsanulok
Bissau 74 B4 *country capital* (Guinea-Bissau) W Guinea-Bissau
Bistriţa 108 B3 *Ger.* Bistritz, *Hung.* Beszterce; *prev.* Nösen. Bistriţa-Năsăud, N Romania
Bistritz *see* Bistriţa
Bitam 77 B5 Woleu-Ntem, N Gabon
Bitburg 95 A5 Rheinland-Pfalz, SW Germany
Bitlis 117 F3 Bitlis, SE Turkey
Bitoeng *see* Bitung
Bitola 101 D6 *Turk.* Monastir; *prev.* Bitolj. S FYR Macedonia
Bitolj *see* Bitola
Bitonto 97 D5 *anc.* Butuntum. Puglia, SE Italy
Bitterroot Range 46 D2 *mountain range* Idaho/Montana, NW USA
Bitung 139 F3 *prev.* Bitoeng. Sulawesi, C Indonesia
Biu 75 H4 Borno, E Nigeria
Biwa-ko 131 C6 *lake* Honshū, SW Japan
Bizerta *see* Bizerte
Bizerte 71 E1 *Ar.* Banzart, *Eng.* Bizerta. N Tunisia
Bjelovar 102 B2 Hung. Belovár. Bjelovar-Bilogora, N Croatia
Bjeshkët e Namuna *see* North Albanian Alps
Björneborg *see* Pori
Bjørnøya 83 F3 *Eng.* Bear Island. *island* N Norway
Blackall 148 C4 Queensland, E Australia
Black Drin 101 D6 *Alb.* Lumi i Drinit të Zi, *SCr.* Crni Drim. *river* Albania/FYR Macedonia
Blackfoot 46 E4 Idaho, NW USA
Black Forest 95 B6 *Eng.* Black Forest. *mountain range* SW Germany
Black Forest *see* Schwarzwald
Black Hills 44 D3 *mountain range* South Dakota/Wyoming, N USA
Blackpool 89 C5 NW England, United Kingdom
Black Range 48 C2 *mountain range* New Mexico, SW USA
Black River 54 A5 W Jamaica
Black River 136 C3 *Chin.* Babian Jiang, Lixian Jiang, *Fr.* Rivière Noire, *Vtn.* Sông Đa. *river* China/Vietnam
Black Rock Desert 47 C5 *desert* Nevada, W USA
Black Sand Desert *see* Garagum
Black Sea 116 B1 *var.* Euxine Sea, *Bul.* Cherno More, *Rom.* Marea Neagră, *Rus.* Chernoye More, *Turk.* Karadeniz, *Ukr.* Chorne More. *sea* Asia/Europe

Black Sea Lowland 109 E4 *Ukr.* Prychornomor'ska Nyzovyna. *depression* SE Europe
Black Volta 75 E4 *var.* Borongo, Mouhoun, Moun Hou, *Fr.* Volta Noire. *river* W Africa
Blackwater 89 A6 *Ir.* An Abhainn Mhór. *river* S Ireland
Blackwater State *see* Nebraska
Blagoevgrad 104 C3 *prev.* Gorna Dzhumaya. Blagoevgrad, W Bulgaria
Blagoveshchensk 115 G4 Amurskaya Oblast', SE Russian Federation
Blake Plateau 35 D6 *var.* Blake Terrace. *undersea plateau* W Atlantic Ocean
Blake Terrace *see* Blake Plateau
Blanca, Bahía 65 C5 *bay* E Argentina
Blanca, Costa 93 F4 *physical region* SE Spain
Blanche, Lake 149 B5 *lake* South Australia
Blanc, Mont 91 D5 *It.* Monte Bianco. *mountain* France/Italy
Blanco, Cape 46 A4 *headland* Oregon, NW USA
Blanes 93 G2 Cataluña, NE Spain
Blankenberge 87 A5 West-Vlaanderen, NW Belgium
Blankenheim 95 A5 Nordrhein-Westfalen, W Germany
Blanquilla, Isla 59 E1 *var.* La Blanquilla. *island* N Venezuela
Blanquilla, La *see* Blanquilla, Isla
Blantyre 79 E2 *var.* Blantyre-Limbe. Southern, S Malawi
Blantyre-Limbe *see* Blantyre
Blaricum 86 C3 Noord-Holland, C Netherlands
Blatnitsa *see* Durankulak
Blenheim 151 C5 Marlborough, South Island, New Zealand
Blesae *see* Blois
Blida 70 D2 *var.* El Boulaïda, El Boulaïda. N Algeria
Bloemfontein 78 D4 *var.* Mangaung. *country capital* (South Africa-judicial capital) Free State, C South Africa
Blois 90 C4 *anc.* Blesae. Loir-et-Cher, C France
Bloomfield 48 C1 New Mexico, SW USA
Bloomington 40 B4 Illinois, N USA
Bloomington 40 C4 Indiana, N USA
Bloomington 45 F2 Minnesota, N USA
Bloomsbury 148 D3 Queensland, NE Australia
Bluefield 40 D5 West Virginia, NE USA
Bluefields 53 E3 Región Autónoma Atlántico Sur, SE Nicaragua
Bluegrass State *see* Kentucky
Blue Hen State *see* Delaware
Blue Law State *see* Connecticut
Blue Mountain Peak 54 B5 *mountain* E Jamaica
Blue Mountains 46 C3 *mountain range* Oregon/Washington, NW USA
Blue Nile 72 C4 *var.* Abai, Bahr el, Azraq, *Amh.* Ābay Wenz, *Ar.* An Nil al Azraq. *river* Ethiopia/Sudan
Blumenau 63 E5 Santa Catarina, S Brazil
Blythe 47 D8 California, W USA
Blytheville 42 C1 Arkansas, C USA
Bo 74 C4 S Sierra Leone
Boaco 52 D3 Boaco, S Nicaragua
Boa Vista 62 D1 *state capital* Roraima, NW Brazil
Boa Vista 74 A3 *island* Ilhas de Barlavento, E Cape Verde
Bobaomby, Tanjona 79 G2 *Fr.* Cap d'Ambre. *headland* N Madagascar
Bobigny 90 E1 Seine-St-Denis, N France
Bobo-Dioulasso 74 D4 SW Burkina Faso
Bobrinets *see* Bobrynets'
Bobruysk *see* Babruysk
Bobrynets' 109 E3 *Rus.* Bobrinets. Kirovohrads'ka Oblast', C Ukraine
Boca Raton 43 F5 Florida, SE USA
Bocay 52 D2 Jinotega, N Nicaragua
Bocheykovo *see* Bacheykava
Bocholt 94 A4 Nordrhein-Westfalen, W Germany
Bochum 94 A4 Nordrhein-Westfalen, W Germany
Boçsa 108 A4 *Ger.* Bokschen, *Hung.* Boksánbánya. Caraş-Severin, SW Romania
Bodegas *see* Babahoyo

Boden 84 D4 Norrbotten, N Sweden
Bodensee *see* Constance, Lake, C Europe
Bodmin 89 C7 SW England, United Kingdom
Bodo 84 C3 Nordland, C Norway
Bodrum 116 A4 Muğla, SW Turkey
Boeloekoemba *see* Bulukumba
Boende 77 C5 Equateur, C Dem. Rep. Congo
Boeroe *see* Buru, Pulau
Boetoeng *see* Buton, Pulau
Bogale 136 B4 Ayeyarwady, SW Myanmar (Burma)
Bogalusa 42 B3 Louisiana, S USA
Bogatynia 98 B4 *Ger.* Reichenau. Dolnośląskie, SW Poland
Boğazlıyan 116 D3 Yozgat, C Turkey
Bogendorf *see* Łuków
Bogor 138 C5 *Dut.* Buitenzorg. Jawa, C Indonesia
Bogotá 58 B3 *prev.* Santa Fe, Santa Fe de Bogotá. *country capital* (Colombia) Cundinamarca, C Colombia
Boguchany *see* Boguchany
Boguslav *see* Bohuslav
Bo Hai 128 D4 *var.* Gulf of Chihli. *gulf* NE China
Bohemia 99 A5 *Cz.* Čechy, *Ger.* Böhmen. W Czech Republic
Bohemian Forest 95 C5 *Cz.* Český Les, *Šumava, Ger.* Böhmerwald. *mountain range* C Europe
Böhmen *see* Bohemia
Böhmerwald *see* Bohemian Forest
Böhmisch-Krumau *see* Český Krumlov
Bohol Sea 139 E2 *var.* Mindanao Sea. *sea* S Philippines
Bohuslav 109 E2 *Rus.* Boguslav. Kyyivs'ka Oblast', N Ukraine
Boise 46 D3 *var.* Boise City. *state capital* Idaho, NW USA
Boise City 49 E1 Oklahoma, C USA
Boise City *see* Boise
Bois, Lac des *see* Woods, Lake of the
Bois-le-Duc *see* 's-Hertogenbosch
Boizenburg 94 C3 Mecklenburg-Vorpommern, N Germany
Bojador *see* Boujdour
Bojnürd 120 D2 *var.* Bujnurd. Khorāsān-e Shemālī, N Iran
Bokāro 135 F4 Jhārkhand, N India
Boké 74 C4 W Guinea
Bokhara *see* Buxoro
Bokonbayevo 123 G2 *Kir.* Kajisay; *prev.* Kadzhi-Say. Issyk-Kul'skaya Oblast', NE Kyrgyzstan
Boksánbánya/Bokschen *see* Boçsa
Bol 76 B3 Lac, W Chad
Bolgatanga 75 E4 N Ghana
Bolgrad *see* Bolhrad
Bolhrad 108 D4 *Rus.* Bolgrad. Odes'ka Oblast', SW Ukraine
Bolívar, Pico 58 C2 *mountain* W Venezuela
Bolivia 61 F3 *off.* Republic of Bolivia. *country* W South America

BOLIVIA
South America

Official name Plurinational State of Bolivia
Formation 1825 / 1938
Capital La Paz (administrative); Sucre (judicial)
Population 10.1 million / 24 people per sq mile (9 people per sq km)
Total area 424,162 sq. miles (1,098,580 sq. km)
Languages Aymara*, Quechua*, Spanish*
Religions Roman Catholic 93%, Other 7%
Ethnic mix Quechua 37%, Aymara 32%, Mixed race 13%, European 10%, Other 8%
Government Presidential system
Currency Boliviano = 100 centavos
Literacy rate 91%
Calorie consumption 2172 kilocalories

Bolivia, Republic of *see* Bolivia
Bollène 91 D6 Vaucluse, SE France
Bollnäs 85 C5 Gävleborg, C Sweden
Bollon 149 D5 Queensland, C Australia
Bologna 96 C3 Emilia-Romagna, N Italy
Bol'shevik *see* Bal'shavik
Bol'shevik, Ostrov 115 E2 *island* Severnaya Zemlya, N Russian Federation

Bol'shezemel'skaya Tundra *110 E3 physical region* NW Russian Federation
Bol'shoy Lyakhovskiy, Ostrov *115 F2 island* NE Russian Federation
Bolton *89 D5 prev.* Bolton-le-Moors. NW England, United Kingdom
Bolton-le-Moors *see* Bolton
Bolu *116 B3* Bolu, NW Turkey
Bolungarvík *83 E4* Vestfirðhir, NW Iceland
Bolyarovo *104 D3 prev.* Pashkeni. Yambol, E Bulgaria
Bolzano *96 C1 Ger.* Bozen; *anc.* Bauzanum. Trentino-Alto Adige, N Italy
Boma *77 B6* Bas-Congo, W Dem. Rep. Congo
Bombay *see* Mumbai
Bomu *76 D4 var.* Mbomou, Mbomu, M'Bomu. *river* Central African Republic/Dem. Rep. Congo
Bonaire *55 F5 island* Lesser Antilles
Bonanza *52 D2* Región Autónoma Atlántico Norte, NE Nicaragua
Bonaparte Archipelago *146 C2 island group* Western Australia
Bon, Cap *102 D3 headland* N Tunisia
Bonda *77 B6* Ogooué-Lolo, C Gabon
Bondoukou *75 E4* E Côte d'Ivoire
Bône *see* Annaba, Algeria
Bone, Teluk *139 E4 bay* Sulawesi, C Indonesia
Bongaigaon *135 G3* Assam, NE India
Bongo, Massif des *76 D4 var.* Chaîne des Mongos. *mountain range* NE Central African Republic
Bongor *76 B3* Mayo-Kébbi, SW Chad
Bonifacio *91 E7* Corse, France, C Mediterranean Sea
Bonifacio, Bocche de/Bonifacio, Bouches de *see* Bonifacio, Strait of
Bonifacio, Strait of *96 A4 Fr.* Bouches de Bonifacio, *It.* Bocche di Bonifacio. *strait* C Mediterranean Sea
Bonn *95 A5* Nordrhein-Westfalen, W Germany
Bononia *see* Vidin, Bulgaria
Bononia *see* Boulogne-sur-Mer, France
Boosaaso *72 E4 var.* Bandar Kassim, Bender Qaasim, Bosaso, *It.* Bender Cassim. Bari, N Somalia
Boothia Felix *see* Boothia Peninsula
Boothia, Gulf of *37 F2 gulf* Nunavut, NE Canada
Boothia Peninsula *37 F2 prev.* Boothia Felix. *peninsula* Nunavut, NE Canada
Boppard *95 A5* Rheinland-Pfalz, W Germany
Boquete *53 E5 var.* Bajo Boquete. Chiriquí, W Panama
Boquillas *50 D2 var.* Boquillas del Carmen. Coahuila, NE Mexico
Boquillas del Carmen *see* Boquillas
Bor *100 E4* Serbia, E Serbia
Bor *73 B5* Jonglei, E South Sudan
Borås *85 B7* Västra Götaland, S Sweden
Borbetomagus *see* Worms
Borborema, Planalto da *56 E3 plateau* NE Brazil
Bordeaux *91 B5 anc.* Burdigala. Gironde, SW France
Bordj Omar Driss *71 E3* E Algeria
Borgå *see* Porvoo
Børgefjell *84 C4 mountain range* C Norway
Borger *86 E2* Drenthe, NE Netherlands
Borger *49 E1* Texas, SW USA
Borgholm *85 C7* Kalmar, S Sweden
Borgo Maggiore *96 E1* NW San Marino
Borislav *see* Boryslav
Borisoglebsk *111 B6* Voronezhskaya Oblast', W Russian Federation
Borisov *see* Barysaw
Borlänge *85 C6* Dalarna, C Sweden
Borne *86 E3* Overijssel, E Netherlands
Borneo *138 C4 island* Brunei/Indonesia/Malaysia
Bornholm *85 B8 island* E Denmark
Borohoro Shan *126 B2 mountain range* NW China
Borongo *see* Black Volta
Boron'ki *see* Baron'ki
Borosjenő *see* Ineu
Borovan *104 C2* Vratsa, NW Bulgaria
Borovichi *110 B4* Novgorodskaya Oblast', W Russian Federation
Borovo *100 C3* Vukovar-Srijem, NE Croatia

Borriana *93 F3 var.* Burriana. Valenciana, E Spain
Borşa *108 C3 Hung.* Borsa. Maramureş, N Romania
Boryslav *108 B2 Pol.* Borysław, *Rus.* Borislav. L'vivs'ka Oblast', NW Ukraine
Borysław *see* Boryslav
Bosanska Dubica *100 B3 var.* Kozarska Dubica. Republika Srpska, NW Bosnia and Herzegovina
Bosanska Gradiška *100 B3 var.* Gradiška. Republika Srpska, N Bosnia and Herzegovina
Bosanski Novi *100 B3 var.* Novi Grad. Republika Srpska, NW Bosnia and Herzegovina
Bosanski Šamac *100 C3 var.* Šamac. Republika Srpska, N Bosnia and Herzegovina
Bosaso *see* Boosaaso
Bösing *see* Pezinok
Boskovice *99 B5 Ger.* Boskowitz. Jihomoravský Kraj, SE Czech Republic
Boskowitz *see* Boskovice
Bosna *100 C4 river* N Bosnia and Herzegovina

Bosnia and Herzegovina *100 B3 off.* Republic of Bosnia and Herzegovina. *country* SE Europe

BOSNIA & HERZEGOVINA
Southeast Europe

Official name Bosnia and Herzegovina
Formation 1992 / 1992
Capital Sarajevo
Population 3.8 million / 192 people per sq mile (74 people per sq km)
Total area 19,741 sq. miles (51,129 sq. km)
Languages Bosnian*, Serbian*, Croatian*
Religions Muslim (mainly Sunni) 40%, Orthodox Christian 31%, Roman Catholic 15%, Other 10%, Protestant 4%
Ethnic mix Bosniak 48%, Serb 34%, Croat 16%, Other 2%
Government Parliamentary system
Currency Marka = 100 pfeninga
Literacy rate 98%
Calorie consumption 3070 kilocalories

Bosnia and Herzegovina, Republic of *see* Bosnia and Herzegovina
Boso-hanto *131 D6 peninsula* Honshū, S Japan
Bosphorus/Bosporus *see* Istanbul Boğazı
Bosporus *116 B2 var.* Bosporus Thracius, *Eng.* Bosphorus, Bosporus, *Turk.* Karadeniz Boğazı. *strait* NW Turkey
Bosporus Cimmerius *see* Kerch Strait
Bosporus Thracius *see* Istanbul Boğazı
Bossangoa *76 C4* Ouham, C Central African Republic
Bossembélé *76 C4* Ombella-Mpoko, C Central African Republic
Bossier City *42 A2* Louisiana, S USA
Bosten Hu *126 C3 var.* Bagrax Hu. *lake* NW China
Boston *89 E6 prev.* St.Botolph's Town. E England, United Kingdom
Boston *41 G3 state capital* Massachusetts, NE USA
Boston Mountains *42 B1 mountain range* Arkansas, C USA
Bostyn' *see* Bastyn'
Botany *148 E2* New South Wales, E Australia
Botany Bay *148 E2 inlet* New South Wales, SE Australia
Boteti *78 C3 var.* Botletle. *river* N Botswana
Bothnia, Gulf of *85 D5 Fin.* Pohjanlahti, *Swe.* Bottniska Viken. *gulf* N Baltic Sea
Botletle *see* Boteti
Botoşani *108 C3 Hung.* Botosány. Botoşani, NE Romania
Botosány *see* Botoşani
Botou *128 C4 prev.* Bozhen. Hebei, E China
Botrange *87 D6 mountain* E Belgium
Botswana *78 C3 off.* Republic of Botswana. *country* S Africa

BOTSWANA
Southern Africa

Official name Republic of Botswana
Formation 1966 / 1966
Capital Gaborone

BOTSWANA
(continued)

Population 2 million / 9 people per sq mile (4 people per sq km)
Total area 231,803 sq. miles (600,370 sq. km)
Languages Setswana, English*, Shona, San, Khoikhoi, isiNdebele
Religions Christian 70%, Nonreligious 20%, Traditional beliefs 6%, Other 4%
Ethnic mix Tswana 79%, Kalanga 11%, Other 10%
Government Presidential system
Currency Pula = 100 thebe
Literacy rate 84%
Calorie consumption 2164 kilocalories

Botswana, Republic of *see* Botswana
Bottniska Viken *see* Bothnia, Gulf of
Bouar *76 B4* Nana-Mambéré, W Central African Republic
Bou Craa *70 B3 var.* Bu Craa. NW Western Sahara
Bougainville Island *142 B3 island* NE Papua New Guinea
Bougaroun, Cap *102 C3 headland* NE Algeria
Bougouni *74 D4* Sikasso, SW Mali
Boujdour *70 A3 var.* Bojador. W Western Sahara
Boulder *44 C4* Colorado, C USA
Boulder *44 B2* Montana, NW USA
Boulogne *see* Boulogne-sur-Mer
Boulogne-Billancourt *90 D1* Île-de-France, N France
Boulogne-sur-Mer *90 C2 var.* Boulogne; *anc.* Bononia, Gesoriacum, Gessoriacum. Pas-de-Calais, N France
Boümdeïd *74 C3 var.* Boumdeït. Assaba, S Mauritania
Boumdeït *see* Boümdeïd
Boundiali *74 D4* N Côte d'Ivoire
Bountiful *44 B4* Utah, W USA
Bounty Basin *see* Bounty Trough
Bounty Islands *142 D5 island group* S New Zealand
Bounty Trough *152 C5 var.* Bounty Basin. *trough* S Pacific Ocean
Bourbonnais *90 C4 cultural region* C France
Bourbon Vendée *see* la Roche-sur-Yon
Bourg *see* Bourg-en-Bresse
Bourgas *see* Burgas
Bourge-en-Bresse *see* Bourg-en-Bresse
Bourg-en-Bresse *91 D5 var.* Bourg, Bourge-en-Bresse. Ain, E France
Bourges *90 C4 anc.* Avaricum. Cher, C France
Bourgogne *90 C4 Eng.* Burgundy. *cultural region* E France
Bourke *149 C5* New South Wales, SE Australia
Bournemouth *89 D7* S England, United Kingdom
Boutilimit *74 C3* Trarza, SW Mauritania
Bouvet Island *67 D7 Norwegian dependency* S Atlantic Ocean
Bowen *148 D3* Queensland, NE Australia
Bowling Green *40 B5* Kentucky, S USA
Bowling Green *40 C3* Ohio, N USA
Boxmeer *86 D4* Noord-Brabant, SE Netherlands
Boyarka *109 E2* Kyyivs'ka Oblast', N Ukraine
Boysun *123 E3 Rus.* Baysun. Surkhondaryo Viloyati, S Uzbekistan
Bozeman *44 B2* Montana, NW USA
Bozen *see* Bolzano
Bozhen *see* Botou
Bozüyük *116 B3* Bilecik, NW Turkey
Brač *100 B4 var.* Brach, *It.* Brazza; *anc.* Brattia. *island* S Croatia
Bracara Augusta *see* Braga
Brach *see* Brač
Brades *55 G3 de facto country capital,* (Montserrat) *(de jure capital, Plymouth, destroyed by volcano in 1995)* SW Montserrat
Bradford *89 D5* N England, United Kingdom
Brady *49 F3* Texas, SW USA
Braga *92 B2 anc.* Bracara Augusta. Braga, NW Portugal
Bragança *92 C2 Eng.* Braganza; *anc.* Julio Briga. Bragança, NE Portugal
Braganza *see* Bragança
Brahestad *see* Raahe

Brahmanbaria *135 G4* Chittagong, E Bangladesh
Brahmapur *135 F5* Orissa, E India
Brahmaputra *135 H3 var.* Padma, Tsangpo, *Ben.* Jamuna, *Chin.* Yarlung Zangbo Jiang, *Ind.* Bramaputra, Dihang, Siang. *river* S Asia
Brăila *108 D4* Brăila, E Romania
Braine-le-Comte *87 B6* Hainaut, SW Belgium
Brainerd *45 F2* Minnesota, N USA
Brak *see* Birāk
Bramaputra *see* Brahmaputra
Brampton *38 D5* Ontario, S Canada
Branco, Rio *56 C3 river* N Brazil
Brandberg *78 A3 mountain* NW Namibia
Brandenburg *94 C3 var.* Brandenburg an der Havel. Brandenburg, NE Germany
Brandenburg an der Havel *see* Brandenburg
Brandon *37 F5* Manitoba, S Canada
Braniewo *98 D2 Ger.* Braunsberg. Warmińsko-mazurskie, N Poland
Brasil *see* Brazil
Brasília *63 F3 country capital* (Brazil) Distrito Federal, C Brazil
Brasil, República Federativa do *see* Brazil
Braşov *108 C4 Ger.* Kronstadt, *Hung.* Brassó; *prev.* Oraşul Stalin. Braşov, C Romania
Brassó *see* Braşov
Bratislava *99 C6 Ger.* Pressburg, *Hung.* Pozsony. *country capital* (Slovakia) Bratislavský Kraj, W Slovakia
Bratsk *115 E4* Irkutskaya Oblast', C Russian Federation
Brattia *see* Brač
Braunsberg *see* Braniewo
Braunschweig *94 C4 Eng./Fr.* Brunswick. Niedersachsen, N Germany
Brava *see* Baraawe
Brava, Costa *93 H2 coastal region* NE Spain
Bravo del Norte, Río/Bravo, Río *see* Grande, Rio
Bravo, Río *50 C1 river* Mexico/USA North America
Brawley *47 D8* California, W USA
Brazil *62 C2 off.* Federative Republic of Brazil, *Port.* República Federativa do Brasil, *Sp.* Brasil; *prev.* United States of Brazil. *country* South America

BRAZIL
South America

Official name Federative Republic of Brazil
Formation 1822 / 1828
Capital Brasília
Population 197 million / 60 people per sq mile (23 people per sq km)
Total area 3,286,470 sq. miles (8,511,965 sq. km)
Languages Portuguese*, German, Italian, Spanish, Polish, Japanese, Amerindian languages
Religions Roman Catholic 74%, Protestant 15%, Atheist 7%, Other 4%
Ethnic mix White 54%, Mixed race 38%, Black 6%, Other 2%
Government Presidential system
Currency Real = 100 centavos
Literacy rate 90%
Calorie consumption 3173 kilocalories

Brazil Basin *56 C5 var.* Brazilian Basin, Brazil'skaya Kotlovina. *undersea basin* W Atlantic Ocean
Brazil, Federative Republic of *see* Brazil
Brazilian Basin *see* Brazil Basin
Brazilian Highlands *63 F3 var.* Brazilian Highlands. *mountain range* E Brazil
Brazilian Highlands *see* Central, Planalto
Brazil'skaya Kotlovina *see* Brazil Basin
Brazil, United States of *see* Brazil
Brazos River *49 G3 river* Texas, SW USA
Brazza *see* Brač
Brazzaville *77 B6 country capital* (Congo) Capital District, S Congo
Brčko *100 C3* Republika Srpska, NE Bosnia and Herzegovina
Brecht *87 C5* Antwerpen, N Belgium
Brecon Beacons *89 C6 mountain range* S Wales, United Kingdom

Breda 86 C4 Noord-Brabant, S Netherlands
Bree 87 D5 Limburg, NE Belgium
Bregalnica 101 E6 river E FYR Macedonia
Bregenz 57 B7 anc. Brigantium. Vorarlberg, W Austria
Bregovo 104 B1 Vidin, NW Bulgaria
Bremen 94 B3 Fr. Brême. Bremen, NW Germany
Bremerhaven 94 B3 Bremen, NW Germany
Bremerton 46 B2 Washington, NW USA
Brenham 49 G3 Texas, SW USA
Brenner, Col du/Brennero, Passo del see Brenner Pass
Brenner Pass 96 C1 var. Brenner Sattel, Fr. Col du Brenner, Ger. Brennerpass, It. Passo del Brennero. pass Austria/Italy
Brennerpass see Brenner Pass
Brenner Sattel see Brenner Pass
Brescia 96 B2 anc. Brixia. Lombardia, N Italy
Breslau see Wrocław
Bressanone 96 C1 Ger. Brixen. Trentino-Alto Adige, N Italy
Brest 107 A6 Pol. Brześć nad Bugiem, Rus. Brest-Litovsk; prev. Brześć Litewski. Brestskaya Voblasts', SW Belarus
Brest 90 A3 Finistère, NW France
Brest-Litovsk see Brest
Bretagne 90 A3 Eng. Brittany, Lat. Britannia Minor. cultural region NW France
Brewster, Kap see Kangikajik
Brewton 42 C3 Alabama, S USA
Brezhnev see Naberezhnyye Chelny
Brezovo 104 D2 prev. Abrashlare. Plovdiv, C Bulgaria
Bria 76 D4 Haute-Kotto, C Central African Republic
Briançon 91 D5 anc. Brigantio. Hautes-Alpes, SE France
Bricgstow see Bristol
Bridgeport 41 F3 Connecticut, NE USA
Bridgetown 55 G2 country capital (Barbados) SW Barbados
Bridlington 89 D5 E England, United Kingdom
Bridport 89 D7 S England, United Kingdom
Brieg see Brzeg
Brig 95 A7 Fr. Brigue, It. Briga. Valais, SW Switzerland
Briga see Brig
Brigantio see Briançon
Brigantium see Bregenz
Brigham City 44 B3 Utah, W USA
Brighton 89 E7 SE England, United Kingdom
Brighton 44 D4 Colorado, C USA
Brigue see Brig
Brindisi 97 E5 anc. Brundisium, Brundusium. Puglia, SE Italy
Briovera see St-Lô
Brisbane 149 E5 state capital Queensland, E Australia
Bristol 89 D7 anc. Bricgstow. SW England, United Kingdom
Bristol 41 F3 Connecticut, NE USA
Bristol 40 D5 Tennessee, S USA
Bristol Bay 36 B3 bay Alaska, USA
Bristol Channel 89 C7 inlet England/Wales, United Kingdom
Britain 80 C3 var. Great Britain. island United Kingdom
Britannia Minor see Bretagne
British Columbia 36 D4 Fr. Colombie-Britannique. province SW Canada
British Guiana see Guyana
British Honduras see Belize
British Indian Ocean Territory 141 B5 UK dependent territory C Indian Ocean
British Isles 89 island group NW Europe
British North Borneo see Sabah
British Solomon Islands Protectorate see Solomon Islands
British Virgin Islands 55 F3 var. Virgin Islands. UK dependent territory E West Indies
Brittany see Bretagne
Briva Curreta see Brive-la-Gaillarde
Briva Isarae see Pontoise
Brive see Brive-la-Gaillarde
Brive-la-Gaillarde 91 C5 prev. Brive; anc. Briva Curretia. Corrèze, C France
Brixen see Bressanone

Brixia see Brescia
Brno 99 B5 Ger. Brünn. Jihomoravský Kraj, SE Czech Republic
Bročeni 106 B3 SW Latvia
Brod/Bród see Slavonski Brod
Brodeur Peninsula 37 F2 peninsula Baffin Island, Nunavut, NE Canada
Brod na Savi see Slavonski Brod
Brodnica 98 C3 Ger. Buddenbrock. Kujawski-pomorskie, C Poland
Broek-in-Waterland 86 C3 Noord-Holland, C Netherlands
Broken Arrow 49 G1 Oklahoma, C USA
Broken Bay 148 E1 bay New South Wales, SE Australia
Broken Hill 149 B6 New South Wales, SE Australia
Broken Ridge 141 D6 undersea plateau S Indian Ocean
Bromberg see Bydgoszcz
Bromley 89 B8 United Kingdom
Brookhaven 42 B3 Mississippi, S USA
Brookings 45 F3 South Dakota, N USA
Brooks Range 36 D2 mountain range Alaska, USA
Brookton 147 B6 Western Australia
Broome 146 B3 Western Australia
Broomfield 44 D4 Colorado, C USA
Broucsella see Brussel/Bruxelles
Brovary 109 E2 Kyyivs'ka Oblast', N Ukraine
Brownfield 49 E2 Texas, SW USA
Brownsville 49 G5 Texas, SW USA
Brownwood 49 F3 Texas, SW USA
Brozha 107 D7 Mahilyowskaya Voblasts', E Belarus
Bruges see Brugge
Brugge 87 A5 Fr. Bruges. West-Vlaanderen, NW Belgium
Brummen 86 D3 Gelderland, E Netherlands
Brundisium/Brundusium see Brindisi
Brunei 138 D3 off. Brunei Darussalam, Mal. Negara Brunei Darussalam. country SE Asia

BRUNEI
Southeast Asia

Official name Brunei Darussalam
Formation 1984 / 1984
Capital Bandar Seri Begawan
Population 400,000 / 197 people per sq mile (76 people per sq km)
Total area 2228 sq. miles (5770 sq. km)
Languages Malay*, English, Chinese
Religions Muslim (mainly Sunni) 66%, Buddhist 14%, Christian 10%, Other 10%
Ethnic mix Malay 67%, Chinese 16%, Other 11%, Indigenous 6%
Government Monarchy
Currency Brunei dollar = 100 cents
Literacy rate 95%
Calorie consumption 3088 kilocalories

Brunei Darussalam see Brunei
Brunei Town see Bandar Seri Begawan
Brünn see Brno
Brunner, Lake 151 C5 lake South Island, New Zealand
Brunswick 43 E3 Georgia, SE USA
Brunswick see Braunschweig
Brusa see Bursa
Brus Laguna 52 D2 Gracias a Dios, E Honduras
Brussa see Bursa
Brussel 87 C6 var. Brussels, Fr. Bruxelles, Ger. Brüssel; anc. Broucsella. country capital (Belgium) Brussels, C Belgium
Brüssel/Brussels see Brussel/Bruxelles
Brüx see Most
Bruxelles see Brussel
Bryan 49 G3 Texas, SW USA
Bryansk 111 A5 Bryanskaya Oblast', W Russian Federation
Brzeg 98 C4 Ger. Brieg; anc. Civitas Altae Ripae. Opolskie, S Poland
Brześć Litewski/Brześć nad Bugiem see Brest
Brzeżany see Berezhany
Bucaramanga 58 B2 Santander, N Colombia
Buchanan 74 C5 prev. Grand Bassa. SW Liberia
Buchanan, Lake 49 F3 reservoir Texas, SW USA
Bucharest see București
Buckeye State see Ohio

Bu Craa see Bou Craa
București 108 C5 Eng. Bucharest, Ger. Bukarest, prev. Altenburg; anc. Cetatea Dâmbovița. country capital (Romania) București, S Romania
Buda-Kashalyova 107 D7 Rus. Buda-Koshelëvo. Homyel'skaya Voblasts', SE Belarus
Buda-Koshelëvo see Buda-Kashalyova
Budapest 99 C6 off. Budapest Főváros, SCr. Budimpešta. country capital (Hungary) Pest, N Hungary
Budapest Főváros see Budapest
Budaun 134 D3 Uttar Pradesh, N India
Buddenbrock see Brodnica
Budimpešta see Budapest
Budweis see České Budějovice
Budyšin see Bautzen
Buena Park 46 E2 California, W USA
Buenaventura 58 A3 Valle del Cauca, W Colombia
Buena Vista 61 G4 Santa Cruz, C Bolivia
Buena Vista 93 H5 S Gibraltar Europe
Buena Vista 93 H5 S Gibraltar Europe
Buenavista 93 H5 Baja California, NW Mexico
Buenavista 93 H5 Sonora, NW Mexico
Buena Vista 93 H5 Cerro Largo, Uruguay
Buena Vista 93 H5 Colorado, C USA
Buena Vista 93 H5 Georgia, SE USA
Buena Vista 93 H5 Virginia, NE USA
Buenos Aires 64 D4 hist. Santa Maria del Buen Aire. country capital (Argentina) Buenos Aires, E Argentina
Buenos Aires 53 E5 Puntarenas, SE Costa Rica
Buenos Aires, Lago 65 B6 var. Lago General Carrera. lake Argentina/Chile
Buffalo 41 E3 New York, NE USA
Buffalo Narrows 37 F4 Saskatchewan, C Canada
Buff Bay 54 B5 E Jamaica
Buftea 108 C5 Ilfov, S Romania
Bug 81 B3 Bel. Zakhodni Buh, Eng. Western Bug, Rus. Zapadnyy Bug, Ukr. Zakhidnyy Buh. river E Europe
Buga 58 B3 Valle del Cauca, W Colombia
Bughotu see Santa Isabel
Buguruslan 111 D6 Orenburgskaya Oblast', W Russian Federation
Buitenzorg see Bogor
Bujalance 92 D4 Andalucía, S Spain
Bujanovac 101 E5 SE Serbia
Bujnurd see Bojnūrd
Bujumbura 73 B7 prev. Usumbura. country capital (Burundi) W Burundi
Bukarest see București
Bukavu 77 E6 prev. Costermansville. Sud-Kivu, E Dem. Rep. Congo
Bukhara see Buxoro
Bukoba 73 B6 Kagera, NW Tanzania
Bülach 95 B7 Zürich, NW Switzerland
Bulawayo 78 D3 Matabeleland North, SW Zimbabwe
Bulgan 127 E2 Bulgan, N Mongolia
Bulgaria 104 C2 off. Republic of Bulgaria, Bul. Bŭlgariya; prev. People's Republic of Bulgaria. country SE Europe

BULGARIA
Southeast Europe

Official name Republic of Bulgaria
Formation 1908 / 1947
Capital Sofia
Population 7.4 million / 173 people per sq mile (67 people per sq km)
Total area 42,822 sq. miles (110,910 sq. km)
Languages Bulgarian*, Turkish, Romani
Religions Bulgarian Orthodox 83%, Muslim 12%, Other 4%, Roman Catholic 1%
Ethnic mix Bulgarian 84%, Turkish 9%, Roma 5%, Other 2%
Government Parliamentary system
Currency Lev = 100 stotinki
Literacy rate 98%
Calorie consumption 2791 kilocalories

Bulgaria, People's Republic of see Bulgaria
Bulgaria, Republic of see Bulgaria
Bŭlgariya see Bulgaria
Bullion State see Missouri
Bull Shoals Lake 42 B1 reservoir Arkansas/Missouri, C USA

Bulukumba 139 E4 prev. Boeloekoemba. Sulawesi, C Indonesia
Bumba 77 D5 Equateur, N Dem. Rep. Congo
Bunbury 147 A7 Western Australia
Bundaberg 148 E4 Queensland, E Australia
Bungo-suido 131 B7 strait SW Japan
Bunia 77 E5 Orientale, NE Dem. Rep. Congo
Bünyan 116 D3 Kayseri, C Turkey
Buraida see Buraydah
Buraydah 120 B4 var. Buraida. Al Qaşīm, N Saudi Arabia
Burdigala see Bordeaux
Burdur 116 B4 var. Buldur. Burdur, SW Turkey
Burdur Gölü 116 B4 salt lake SW Turkey
Burë 72 C4 Āmara, N Ethiopia
Burgas 104 E2 var. Bourgas. Burgas, E Bulgaria
Burgaski Zaliv 104 E2 gulf E Bulgaria
Burgos 92 D2 Castilla y León, N Spain
Burgundy see Bourgogne
Burhan Budai Shan 126 D4 mountain range C China
Buriram 137 D5 var. Buri Ram, Puriramya. Buri Ram, E Thailand
Buri Ram see Buriram
Burjassot 93 F3 Valenciana, E Spain
Burkburnett 49 F2 Texas, SW USA
Burketown 148 B3 Queensland, NE Australia
Burkina see Burkina Faso
Burkina Faso 75 E4 off. Burkina Faso; var. Burkina, prev. Upper Volta. country W Africa

BURKINA FASO
West Africa

Official name Burkina Faso
Formation 1960 / 1960
Capital Ouagadougou
Population 17 million / 161 people per sq mile (62 people per sq km)
Total area 105,869 sq. miles (274,200 sq. km)
Languages Mossi, Fulani, French*, Tuareg, Dyula, Songhai
Religions Muslim 55%, Christian 25%, Traditional beliefs 20%
Ethnic mix Mossi 48%, Other 21%, Peul 10%, Lobi 7%, Bobo 7%, Mandé 7%
Government Presidential system
Currency CFA franc = 100 centimes
Literacy rate 29%
Calorie consumption 2647 kilocalories

Burley 46 D4 Idaho, NW USA
Burlington 45 G4 Iowa, C USA
Burlington 41 F2 Vermont, NE USA
Burma 136 A3 off. Union of Myanmar. country SE Asia. See also Myanmar
Burnie 149 C8 Tasmania, SE Australia
Burns 46 C3 Oregon, NW USA
Burnside 37 F3 river Nunavut, NW Canada
Burnsville 45 F2 Minnesota, N USA
Burrel 101 C6 var. Burreli. Dibër, C Albania
Burreli see Burrel
Burriana see Borriana
Bursa 116 B3 var. Brussa, prev. Brusa; anc. Prusa. Bursa, NW Turkey
Bür Sa'īd 72 B1 var. Port Said. N Egypt
Burtnieks Ezers 106 C3 var. Burtnieks. lake N Latvia
Burtnieks Ezers see Burtnieks
Burundi 73 B7 off. Republic of Burundi; prev. Kingdom of Burundi, Urundi. country C Africa

BURUNDI
Central Africa

Official name Republic of Burundi
Formation 1962 / 1962
Capital Bujumbura
Population 8.6 million / 868 people per sq mile (335 people per sq km)
Total area 10,745 sq. miles (27,830 sq. km)
Languages Kirundi*, French*, Kiswahili
Religions Roman Catholic 62%, Traditional beliefs 23%, Muslim 10%, Protestant 5%
Ethnic mix Hutu 85%, Tutsi 14%, Twa 1%
Government Presidential system

BURUNDI
(continued)

Currency Burundian franc = 100 centimes
Literacy rate 67%
Calorie consumption 1604 kilocalories

Burundi, Kingdom of *see* Burundi
Burundi, Republic of *see* Burundi
Buru, Pulau *139 F4 prev.* Boeroe. *island*
  E Indonesia
Busan *129 E4 off.* Pusan-gwangyöksi,
  var. Vusan; *prev.* Pusan, *Jap.* Fusan.
  SE South Korea
Buşayrah *118 D3* Dayr az Zawr, E Syria
Büshehr/Bushire *see* Bandar-e Büshehr
Busra *see* Al Başrah, Iraq
Busselton *147 A7* Western Australia
Bussora *see* Al Başrah
Buta *77 D5* Orientale, N Dem. Rep.
  Congo
Butembo *77 E5* Nord-Kivu, N Dem.
  Rep. Congo
Butler *41 E4* Pennsylvania, NE USA
Buton, Pulau *139 E4 var.* Pulau Butung;
  prev. Boetoeng. *island* C Indonesia
Bütow *see* Bytów
Butte *44 B2* Montana, NW USA
Butterworth *138 B3* Pinang, Peninsular
  Malaysia
Button Islands *39 E1 island group*
  Nunavut, NE Canada
Butuan *139 F2 off.* Butuan City.
  Mindanao, S Philippines
Butuan City *see* Butuan
Butung, Pulau *see* Buton, Pulau
Bututntum *see* Bitonto
Buulobarde *73 D5 var.* Buulo Berde.
  Hiiraan, C Somalia
Buulo Berde *see* Buulobarde
Buur Gaabo *73 D6* Jubbada Hoose,
  S Somalia
Buxoro *122 D2 var.* Bokhara,
  Rus. Bukhara. Buxoro Viloyati,
  C Uzbekistan
Buynaksk *111 B8* Respublika Dagestan,
  SW Russian Federation
Büyükmenderes Nehri *116 A4 river*
  SW Turkey
Buzău *108 C4* Buzău, SE Romania
Büzmeyin *see* Abadan
Buzuluk *111 D6* Orenburgskaya Oblast',
  W Russian Federation
Byahoml' *107 D5 Rus.* Begoml'.
  Vitsyebskaya Voblasts', N Belarus
Byalynichy *107 D6 Rus.* Belynichi.
  Mahilyowskaya Voblasts', E Belarus
Byan Tumen *see* Choybalsan
Byarezina *107 D6 prev.* Byerezino, *Rus.*
  Berezina. *river* C Belarus
Bydgoszcz *98 C3 Ger.* Bromberg.
  Kujawski-pomorskie, C Poland
Byelaruskaya Hrada *107 B6 Rus.*
  Belorusskaya Gryada. *ridge* N Belarus
Byerezino *see* Byarezina
Byron Island *see* Nikunau
Bystrovka *see* Kemin
Bytča *99 C5* Žilinský Kraj, N Slovakia
Bytom *99 C5 Ger.* Beuthen. Śląskie,
  S Poland
Bytów *98 C2 Ger.* Bütow. Pomorskie,
  N Poland
Byuzmeyin *see* Abadan
Byval'ki *107 D8* Homyel'skaya Voblasts',
  SE Belarus
Byzantium *see* Istanbul

C

Caála *78 B2 var.* Kaala, Robert Williams,
  Port. Vila Robert Williams. Huambo,
  C Angola
Caazapá *64 D3* Caazapá, S Paraguay
Caballo Reservoir *48 C3 reservoir* New
  Mexico, SW USA
Cabanaquinta *92 D1* Asturias, N Spain
Cabanatuan *139 E1 off.* Cabanatuan
  City. Luzon, N Philippines
Cabanatuan City *see* Cabanatuan
Cabillonum *see* Chalon-sur-Saône
Cabimas *58 C1* Zulia, NW Venezuela
Cabinda *78 A1 var.* Kabinda. Cabinda,
  NW Angola
Cabinda *78 A1 var.* Kabinda. *province*
  NW Angola
Lake Cabora Bassa *78 D2 var.*
  Lake Cabora Bassa. *reservoir*
  NW Mozambique

Cabora Bassa, Lake *see* Cahora Bassa,
  Albufeira de
Caborca *50 B1* Sonora, NW Mexico
Cabot Strait *39 G4 strait* E Canada
Cabo Verde, Ilhas do *see* Cape Verde
Cabras, Ilha das *76 E2 island*
  S Sao Tome and Principe, Africa,
  E Atlantic Ocean
Cabrera *93 G3 river* NW Spain
Cáceres *92 C3 Ar.* Qazris. Extremadura,
  W Spain
Cachimbo, Serra do *63 E2 mountain
  range* C Brazil
Caconda *78 B2* Huíla, C Angola
Cadca *99 C5 Hung.* Csaca. Žilinský Kraj,
  N Slovakia
Cadillac *40 C2* Michigan, N USA
Cadiz *139 E2 off.* Cadiz City. Negros,
  C Philippines
Cádiz *92 C5 anc.* Gades, Gadier, Gadir,
  Gadire. Andalucía, SW Spain
Cadiz City *see* Cadiz
Gulf of Cadiz *92 B5 Eng.* Gulf of Cadiz.
  gulf Portugal/Spain
Cadiz, Gulf of *see* Cádiz, Golfo de
Cadurcum *see* Cahors
Caen *90 B3* Calvados, N France
Caene/Caenepolis *see* Qinâ
Caerdydd *see* Cardiff
Caer Glou *see* Gloucester
Caer Gybi *see* Holyhead
Caerleon *see* Chester
Caer Luel *see* Carlisle
Caesaraugusta *see* Zaragoza
Caesarea Mazaca *see* Kayseri
Caesarobriga *see* Talavera de la Reina
Caesarodunum *see* Tours
Caesaromagus *see* Beauvais
Caesena *see* Cesena
Cafayate *64 C2* Salta, N Argentina
Cagayan de Oro *139 E2 off.* Cagayan de
  Oro City. Mindanao, S Philippines
Cagayan de Oro City *see* Cagayan de Oro
Cagliari *97 A6 anc.* Caralis. Sardegna,
  Italy, C Mediterranean Sea
Caguas *55 F3* E Puerto Rico
Cahors *91 C5 anc.* Cadurcum. Lot,
  S France
Cahul *108 D4 Rus.* Kagul. S Moldova
Caicos Passage *54 D2 strait* Bahamas/
  Turks and Caicos Islands
Caiffa *see* Hefa
Cailungo *96 E1* N San Marino
Caiphas *see* Hefa
Cairns *148 D3* Queensland,
  NE Australia
Cairo *72 B2 var.* El Qâhira, *Ar.* Al
  Qâhirah. *country capital* (Egypt)
  N Egypt
Caislean an Bharraigh *see* Castlebar
Cajamarca *60 B3 prev.* Caxamarca.
  Cajamarca, NW Peru
Čakovec *100 B2 Ger.* Csakathurn, *Hung.*
  Csáktornya; *prev. Ger.* Tschakathurn.
  Medimurje, N Croatia
Calabar *75 G5* Cross River, S Nigeria
Calabozo *58 D2* Guárico, C Venezuela
Calafat *108 B5* Dolj, SW Romania
Calafate *see* El Calafate
Calahorra *93 E2* La Rioja, N Spain
Calais *90 C2* Pas-de-Calais, N France
Calais *41 H2* Maine, NE USA
Calais, Pas de *see* Dover, Strait of
Calama *64 B2* Antofagasta, N Chile
Călăras *108 D3 var.* Călăras, *Rus.*
  Kalarash. C Moldova
Călăraşi *108 C5* Călăraşi, SE Romania
Calatayud *93 E2* Aragón, NE Spain
Calbayog *139 E2 off.* Calbayog City.
  Samar, C Philippines
Calbayog City *see* Calbayog
Calcutta *135 G4* West Bengal, N India
Caldas da Rainha *92 B3* Leiria,
  W Portugal
Caldera *64 B3* Atacama, N Chile
Caldwell *46 C3* Idaho, NW USA
Caledonia *52 C1* Corozal, N Belize
Caleta Olivia *65 B6* Santa Cruz,
  SE Argentina
Calgary *37 E5* Alberta, SW Canada
Cali *58 B3* Valle del Cauca, W Colombia
Calicut *see* Kozhikode
California *47 B7 off.* State of California,
  also known as El Dorado, The Golden
  State. *state* W USA
Gulf of California *50 B2 Eng.* Gulf of
  California; *prev.* Sea of Cortez. *gulf*
  W Mexico

California, Gulf of *see* California,
  Golfo de
Călimăneşti *108 B4* Vâlcea, SW Romania
Calisia *see* Kalisz
Callabonna, Lake *149 B5 lake* South
  Australia
Callao *60 C4* Callao, W Peru
Callatis *see* Mangalia
Callosa de Segura *93 F4* Valenciana,
  E Spain
Calmar *see* Kalmar
Caloundra *149 E5* Queensland,
  E Australia
Caltanissetta *97 C7* Sicilia, Italy,
  C Mediterranean Sea
Caluula *72 E4* Bari, NE Somalia
Camabatela *78 B1* Cuanza Norte,
  NW Angola
Camacupa *78 B2 var.* General Machado,
  Port. Vila General Machado. Bié,
  C Angola
Camagüey *54 C2 prev.* Puerto Príncipe.
  Camagüey, C Cuba
Camagüey, Archipiélago de *54 C2
  island group* C Cuba
Camana *60 D4 var.* Camaná. Arequipa,
  SW Peru
Camargue *91 D6 physical region*
  SE France
Ca Mau *137 D6 var.* Quan Long. Minh
  Hai, S Vietnam
Cambay, Gulf of *see* Khambhât, Gulf of
Camberia *see* Chambéry
Cambodia *137 D5 off.* Kingdom
  of Cambodia, *var.* Democratic
  Kampuchea, Roat Kampuchea, *Cam.*
  Kampuchea; *prev.* People's Democratic
  Republic of Kampuchea. *country*
  SE Asia

CAMBODIA
Southeast Asia

Official name Kingdom of Cambodia
Formation 1953 / 1953
Capital Phnom Penh
Population 14.3 million / 210 people
per sq mile (81 people per sq km)
Total area 69,900 sq. miles (181,040 sq. km)
Languages Khmer*, French, Chinese,
Vietnamese, Cham
Religions Buddhist 93%, Muslim 6%,
Christian 1%
Ethnic mix Khmer 90%, Other 5%,
Vietnamese 4%, Chinese 1%
Government Parliamentary system
Currency Riel = 100 sen
Literacy rate 74%
Calorie consumption 2382 kilocalories

Cambodia, Kingdom of *see* Cambodia
Cambrai *90 C2 Flem.* Kambryk, *anc.*
  Cambray; *anc.* Cameracum. Nord,
  N France
Cambray *see* Cambrai
Cambrian Mountains *89 C6 mountain
  range* C Wales, United Kingdom
Cambridge *54 A4* W Jamaica
Cambridge *150 D3* Waikato, North
  Island, New Zealand
Cambridge *89 E6 Lat.* Cantabrigia.
  E England, United Kingdom
Cambridge *41 F4* Maryland, NE USA
Cambridge *40 D4* Ohio, NE USA
Cambridge Bay *37 F3 var.* Ikaluktutiak.
  Victoria Island, Nunavut, NW Canada
Camden *42 B2* Arkansas, C USA
Camellia State *see* Alabama
Cameracum *see* Cambrai
Cameroon *76 A4 off.* Republic of
  Cameroon, *Fr.* Cameroun. *country*
  W Africa

CAMEROON
Central Africa

Official name Republic of Cameroon
Formation 1960 / 1961
Capital Yaoundé
Population 20 million / 111 people
per sq mile (43 people per sq km)
Total area 183,567 sq. miles
(475,400 sq. km)
Languages Bamileke, Fang, Fulani,
French*, English*
Religions Roman Catholic 35%,
Traditional beliefs 25%, Muslim 22%,
Protestant 18%
Ethnic mix Cameroon highlanders 31%,

CAMEROON
(continued)

Other 21%, Equatorial Bantu 19%, Kirdi 11%,
Fulani 10%, Northwestern Bantu 8%
Government Presidential system
Currency CFA franc = 100 centimes
Literacy rate 71%
Calorie consumption 2457 kilocalories

Cameroon, Republic of *see* Cameroon
Cameroun *see* Cameroon
Camocim *63 F2* Ceará, E Brazil
Camopi *59 H3* E French Guiana
Campamento *52 C2* Olancho,
  C Honduras
Campania *97 D5 Eng.* Champagne.
  region S Italy
Campbell, Cape *151 D5 headland* South
  Island, New Zealand
Campbell Island *142 D5 island* S New
  Zealand
Campbell Plateau *142 D5 undersea
  plateau* SW Pacific Ocean
Campbell River *36 D5* Vancouver
  Island, British Columbia, SW Canada
Campeche *51 G4* Campeche, SE Mexico
Bay of Campeche *51 F4 Eng.* Bay of
  Campeche. *bay* E Mexico
Campeche, Bay of *see* Campeche,
  Bahía de
Câm Pha *136 E3* Quang Ninh,
  N Vietnam
Câmpina *108 C4 prev.* Cîmpina.
  Prahova, SE Romania
Campina Grande *63 G2* Paraíba, E Brazil
Campinas *63 F4* São Paulo, S Brazil
Campobasso *97 D5* Molise, C Italy
Campo Criptana *see* Campo de Criptana
Campo de Criptana *93 E3 var.* Campo
  Criptana. Castilla-La Mancha, C Spain
Campo Grande *63 E4 state capital* Mato
  Grosso do Sul, SW Brazil
Campos dos Goytacazes *63 F4* Rio de
  Janeiro, SE Brazil
Câmpulung *108 B4 prev.* Câmpulung-
  Muşcel, Cîmpulung. Argeş, S Romania
Câmpulung-Muşcel *see* Câmpulung
Campus Stellae *see* Santiago de
  Compostela
Cam Ranh *137 E6 prev.* Ba Ngoi. Khanh
  Hoa, S Vietnam
Canada *34 B4 country* N North America

CANADA
North America

Official name Canada
Formation 1867 / 1949
Capital Ottawa
Population 34.3 million / 10 people
per sq mile (4 people per sq km)
Total area 3,854,085 sq. miles
(9,984,670 sq. km)
Languages English*, French*, Chinese,
Italian, German, Ukrainian, Portuguese,
Inuktitut, Cree
Religions Roman Catholic 44%,
Protestant 29%, Other and
nonreligious 27%
Ethnic mix European 66%, Other 32%,
Amerindian 2%
Government Parliamentary system
Currency Canadian dollar = 100 cents
Literacy rate 99%
Calorie consumption 3399 kilocalories

Canada Basin *34 C2 undersea basin*
  Arctic Ocean
Canadian River *49 E2 river* SW USA
Çanakkale *116 A3 var.* Dardanelli; *prev.*
  Chanak, Kale Sultanie. Çanakkale,
  W Turkey
Cananea *50 B1* Sonora, NW Mexico
Canarreos, Archipiélago de los *54 B2
  island group* W Cuba
Canary Islands *70 A2 Eng.* Canary
  Islands. *island group* Spain,
  NE Atlantic Ocean
Canary Islands *see* Canarias, Islas
Cañas *52 D4* Guanacaste, NW Costa Rica
Canaveral, Cape *43 E4 headland* Florida,
  SE USA
Canavieiras *63 G3* Bahia, E Brazil
Canberra *142 C4 country capital*
  (Australia) Australian Capital Territory,
  SE Australia
Cancún *51 H3* Quintana Roo, SE Mexico
Candia *see* Irákleio

Canea see Chaniá
Cangzhou 128 D4 Hebei, E China
Caniapiscau 39 E2 river Québec, E Canada
Caniapiscau, Réservoir de 38 D3 reservoir Québec, C Canada
Canik Dağları 116 D2 mountain range N Turkey
Canillo 91 A7 Canillo, C Andorra Europe
Çankırı 116 C3 var. Chankiri; anc. Gangra, Germanicopolis. Çankırı, N Turkey
Cannanore see Kannur
Cannes 91 D6 Alpes-Maritimes, SE France
Canoas 63 E5 Rio Grande do Sul, S Brazil
Canon City 44 C5 Colorado, C USA
Cantabria 92 D1 autonomous community N Spain
Cantábrica, Cordillera 92 C1 mountain range N Spain
Cantabrigia see Cambridge
Cantaura 59 E2 Anzoátegui, NE Venezuela
Canterbury 89 E7 hist. Cantwaraburh; anc. Durovernum, Lat. Cantuaria. SE England, United Kingdom
Canterbury Bight 151 C6 bight South Island, New Zealand
Canterbury Plains 151 C6 plain South Island, New Zealand
Cân Thơ 137 E6 Cân Tho, S Vietnam
Canton 42 B2 Mississippi, S USA
Canton 40 D4 Ohio, N USA
Canton see Guangzhou
Canton Island see Kanton
Cantuaria/Cantwaraburh see Canterbury
Canyon 49 E2 Texas, SW USA
Cao Bằng 136 D3 var. Caobang. Cao Bằng, N Vietnam
Caobang see Cao Bằng
Cap-Breton, Île du see Cape Breton Island
Cape Barren Island 149 C8 island Furneaux Group, Tasmania, SE Australia
Cape Basin 69 B7 undersea basin S Atlantic Ocean
Cape Breton Island 39 G4 Fr. Île du Cap-Breton. island Nova Scotia, SE Canada
Cape Charles 41 F5 Virginia, NE USA
Cape Coast 75 E5 prev. Cape Coast Castle. S Ghana
Cape Coast Castle see Cape Coast
Cape Girardeau 45 H5 Missouri, C USA
Capelle aan den IJssel 86 C4 Zuid-Holland, SW Netherlands
Cape Palmas see Harper
Cape Saint Jacques see Vung Tau
Cape Town 78 B5 var. Ekapa, Afr. Kaapstad, Kapstad. country capital (South Africa-legislative capital) Western Cape, SW South Africa
Cape Verde 74 A2 off. Republic of Cape Verde, Port. Cabo Verde, Ilhas do Cabo Verde. country E Atlantic Ocean

---

CAPE VERDE
Atlantic Ocean

Official name Republic of Cape Verde
Formation 1975 / 1975
Capital Praia
Population 500,000 / 321 people per sq mile (124 people per sq km)
Total area 1557 sq. miles (4033 sq. km)
Languages Portuguese Creole, Portuguese*
Religions Roman Catholic 97%, Other 2%, Protestant (Church of the Nazarene) 1%
Ethnic mix Mestiço 71%, African 28%, European 1%
Government Mixed presidential–parliamentary system
Currency Cape Verde escudo = 100 centavos
Literacy rate 85%
Calorie consumption 2644 kilocalories

Cape Verde Basin 66 C4 undersea basin E Atlantic Ocean
Cape Verde Plain 66 C4 abyssal plain E Atlantic Ocean
Cape Verde, Republic of see Cape Verde
Cape York Peninsula 148 C2 peninsula Queensland, N Australia

Cap-Haïtien 54 D3 var. Le Cap. N Haiti
Capira 53 G5 Panamá, C Panama
Capitán Arturo Prat 154 A2 Chilean research station South Shetland Islands, Antarctica
Capitán Pablo Lagerenza 64 D1 var. Mayor Pablo Lagerenza. Chaco, N Paraguay
Capodistria see Koper
Capri 97 C5 island S Italy
Caprivi Concession see Caprivi Strip
Caprivi Strip 78 C3 Ger. Caprivizipfel; prev. Caprivi Concession. cultural region NE Namibia
Caprivizipfel see Caprivi Strip
Cap Saint-Jacques see Vung Tau
Caquetá, Río 58 C5 var. Rio Japurá, Yapurá. river Brazil/Colombia
Caquetá, Río see Japurá, Rio
CAR see Central African Republic
Caracal 108 B5 Olt, S Romania
Caracaraí 62 D1 Rondônia, W Brazil
Caracas 58 D1 country capital (Venezuela) Distrito Federal, N Venezuela
Caralis see Cagliari
Caratasca, Laguna de 53 E2 lagoon NE Honduras
Carballiño see O Carballiño
Carbondale 40 B5 Illinois, N USA
Carbon, Laguna del 64 B7 depression S Argentina
Carbonia 97 A6 var. Carbonia Centro. Sardegna, Italy, C Mediterranean Sea
Carbonia Centro see Carbonia
Carcaso see Carcassonne
Carcassonne 91 C6 anc. Carcaso. Aude, S France
Cardamomes, Chaîne des see Krâvanh, Chuŏr Phnum
Cardamom Mountains see Krâvanh, Chuŏr Phnum
Cárdenas 54 B2 Matanzas, W Cuba
Cardiff 89 C7 Wel. Caerdydd. national capital S Wales, United Kingdom
Cardigan Bay 89 C6 bay W Wales, United Kingdom
Carei 108 B3 Ger. Gross-Karol, Karol, Hung. Nagykároly; prev. Careii-Mari. Satu Mare, NW Romania
Careii-Mari see Carei
Carey, Lake 147 B6 lake Western Australia
Cariaco 59 E1 Sucre, NE Venezuela
Caribbean Sea 54 C4 sea W Atlantic Ocean
Caribrod see Dimitrovgrad
Carlisle 88 C4 anc. Caer Luel, Luguvallium, Luguvallum. NW England, United Kingdom
Carlow 89 B6 Ir. Ceatharlach. SE Ireland
Carlsbad 48 D3 New Mexico, SW USA
Carlsbad see Karlovy Vary
Carlsberg Ridge 140 B4 undersea ridge S Arabian Sea
Carlsruhe see Karlsruhe
Carmana/Carmania see Kermān
Carmarthen 89 C6 SW Wales, United Kingdom
Carmaux 91 C6 Tarn, S France
Carmel 40 C4 Indiana, N USA
Carmelita 52 B1 Petén, N Guatemala
Carmen 51 G4 var. Ciudad del Carmen. Campeche, SE Mexico
Carmona 92 C4 Andalucía, S Spain
Carmona see Uíge
Carnaro see Kvarner
Carnarvon 147 A5 Western Australia
Carnegie, Lake 147 B5 salt lake Western Australia
Car Nicobar 133 F3 island Nicobar Islands, India, NE Indian Ocean
Caroço, Ilha 76 E1 island N Sao Tome and Principe, Africa, E Atlantic Ocean
Carolina 63 F2 Maranhão, E Brazil
Caroline Island see Millennium Island
Caroline Islands 144 B2 island group C Micronesia
Carolopois see Châlons-en-Champagne
Caroní, Río 59 E3 river E Venezuela
Caronium see A Coruña
Carora 58 C1 Lara, N Venezuela
Carpathian Mountains 81 E4 var. Carpathians, Cz./Pol. Karpaty, Ger. Karpaten. mountain range E Europe
Carpathians see Carpathian Mountains
Carpatho/Carpathus see Kárpathos
Carpaţii Sudici see Carpaţii Meridionali
Carpentaria, Gulf of 148 B2 gulf N Australia

Carpi 96 C2 Emilia-Romagna, N Italy
Carrara 96 B3 Toscana, C Italy
Carson City 47 C5 state capital Nevada, W USA
Carson Sink 47 C5 salt flat Nevada, W USA
Carstensz, Puntjak see Jaya, Puncak
Cartagena 58 B1 var. Cartagena de los Indes. Bolívar, NW Colombia
Cartagena 93 F4 anc. Carthago Nova. Murcia, SE Spain
Cartagena de los Indes see Cartagena
Cartago 53 E4 Cartago, C Costa Rica
Carthage 45 F5 Missouri, C USA
Carthago Nova see Cartagena
Cartwright 39 F2 Newfoundland and Labrador, E Canada
Carúpano 59 E1 Sucre, NE Venezuela
Carusbur see Cherbourg
Caruthersville 45 H5 Missouri, C USA
Cary 43 F1 North Carolina, SE USA
Casablanca 70 C2 Ar. Dar-el-Beida. NW Morocco
Casa Grande 48 B2 Arizona, SW USA
Cascade Range 46 B3 mountain range Oregon/Washington, NW USA
Cascadia Basin 34 A4 undersea basin NE Pacific Ocean
Cascais 92 B4 Lisboa, C Portugal
Caserta 97 D5 Campania, S Italy
Casey 154 D4 Australian research station Antarctica
Cáslav 99 B5 Ger. Tschaslau. Střední Čechy, C Czech Republic
Casper 44 C3 Wyoming, C USA
Caspian Depression 111 B7 Kaz. Kaspiy Mangy Oypaty, Rus. Prikaspiyskaya Nizmennost'. depression Kazakhstan/Russian Federation
Caspian Sea 114 A4 Az. Xäzär Dänizi, Kaz. Kaspiy Tengizi, Per. Baḥr-e Khazar, Daryā-ye Khazar, Rus. Kaspiyskoye More. inland sea Asia/Europe
Cassai see Kasai
Cassel see Kassel
Castamoni see Kastamonu
Casteggio 96 B2 Lombardia, N Italy
Castelló de la Plana see Castellón de la Plana
Castellón see Castellón de la Plana
Castellón de la Plana 93 F3 var. Castellón, Cat. Castelló de la Plana. Valenciana, E Spain
Castelo Branco 92 C3 Castelo Branco, C Portugal
Castelsarrasin 91 B6 Tarn-et-Garonne, S France
Castelvetrano 97 C7 Sicilia, Italy, C Mediterranean Sea
Castilla-La Mancha 93 E3 autonomous community NE Spain
Castilla y León 92 C2 var. Castillia Leon. autonomous community NW Spain
Castillia Leon see Castilla y León
Castlebar 89 A5 Ir. Caisleán an Bharraigh. W Ireland
Castleford 89 D5 N England, United Kingdom
Castle Harbour 42 B5 inlet Bermuda, NW Atlantic Ocean
Castra Regina see Regensburg
Castricum 86 C3 Noord-Holland, W Netherlands
Castries 55 F1 country capital (Saint Lucia) N Saint Lucia
Castro 65 B6 Los Lagos, W Chile
Castrovillari 97 D6 Calabria, SW Italy
Castuera 92 D4 Extremadura, W Spain
Caswell Sound 151 A7 sound South Island, New Zealand
Catacamas 52 D2 Olancho, C Honduras
Catacaos 60 B3 Piura, NW Peru
Catalan Bay 93 H4 bay E Gibraltar, Mediterranean Sea
Cataluña 93 G2 N Spain
Catamarca see San Fernando del Valle de Catamarca
Catania 97 D7 Sicilia, Italy, C Mediterranean Sea
Catanzaro 97 D6 Calabria, SW Italy
Catarroja 93 F3 Valenciana, E Spain
Cat Island 54 C1 island E Bahamas
Catskill Mountains 41 F3 mountain range New York, NE USA
Cattaro see Kotor
Cauca, Río 58 B2 river N Colombia

Caucasia 58 B2 Antioquia, NW Colombia
Caucasus 81 G4 Rus. Kavkaz. mountain range Georgia/Russian Federation
Caura, Río 59 E3 river C Venezuela
Cavaia see Kavajë
Cavalla 74 D5 var. Cavally, Cavally Fleuve. river Côte d'Ivoire/Liberia
Cavally/Cavally Fleuve see Cavalla
Caviana de Fora, Ilha 63 E1 var. Ilha Caviana. island N Brazil
Caviana, Ilha see Caviana de Fora, Ilha
Cawnpore see Kānpur
Caxamarca see Cajamarca
Caxito 78 B1 Bengo, NW Angola
Cayenne 59 H3 dependent territory/ arrondissement capital (French Guiana) NE French Guiana
Cayes 54 D3 var. Les Cayes. SW Haiti
Cayman Brac 54 B3 island E Cayman Islands
Cayman Islands 54 B3 UK dependent territory W West Indies
Cayo see San Ignacio
Cay Sal 54 B2 islet SW Bahamas
Cazin 100 B3 Federacija Bosna I Hercegovina, NW Bosnia and Herzegovina
Cazorla 93 E4 Andalucía, S Spain
Ceadăr-Lunga see Ciadır-Lunga
Ceará 63 F2 off. Estado do Ceará. region C Brazil
Ceará 63 F2 off. Estado do Ceará. state C Brazil
Ceará see Fortaleza
Ceará Abyssal Plain see Ceará Plain
Ceará, Estado do see Ceará
Ceará Plain 56 F3 var. Ceara Abyssal Plain. abyssal plain W Atlantic Ocean
Ceatharlach see Carlow
Cébaco, Isla 53 F5 island SW Panama
Cebu 139 E2 off. Cebu City. Cebu, C Philippines
Cebu City see Cebu
Čechy see Bohemia
Cecina 96 B3 Toscana, C Italy
Cedar City 44 A5 Utah, W USA
Cedar Falls 45 G3 Iowa, C USA
Cedar Lake 38 A2 lake Manitoba, C Canada
Cedar Rapids 45 G3 Iowa, C USA
Cedros, Isla 50 A2 island W Mexico
Ceduna 149 A6 South Australia
Cefalù 97 C7 anc. Cephaloedium. Sicilia, Italy, C Mediterranean Sea
Celebes 139 E4 Eng. Celebes. island C Indonesia
Celebes see Sulawesi
Celebes Sea 139 E3 Ind. Laut Sulawesi. sea Indonesia/Philippines
Celje 95 E7 Ger. Cilli. C Slovenia
Celldömölk 99 C6 Vas, W Hungary
Celle 94 B3 var. Zelle. Niedersachsen, N Germany
Celovec see Klagenfurt
Celtic Sea 89 B7 Ir. An Mhuir Cheilteach. sea SW British Isles
Celtic Shelf 80 B3 continental shelf E Atlantic Ocean
Cenderawasih, Teluk 139 G4 var. Teluk Irian, Teluk Sarera. bay W Pacific Ocean
Cenon 91 B5 Gironde, SW France
Centennial State see Colorado
Centrafricaine, République see Central African Republic
Central African Republic 76 C4 var. République Centrafricaine, abbrev. CAR; prev. Ubangi-Shari, Oubangui-Chari, Territoire de l'Oubangui-Chari. country C Africa

---

CENTRAL AFRICAN REPUBLIC
Central Africa

Official name Central African Republic
Formation 1960 / 1960
Capital Bangui
Population 4.5 million / 19 people per sq mile (7 people per sq km)
Total area 240,534 sq. miles (622,984 sq. km)
Languages Sango, Banda, Gbaya, French*
Religions Traditional beliefs 35%, Roman Catholic 25%, Protestant 25%, Muslim 15%
Ethnic mix Baya 33%, Banda 27%, Other 17%, Mandjia 13%, Sara 10%
Government Presidential system

CENTRAL AFRICAN REPUBLIC
(continued)

Currency CFA franc = 100 centimes
Literacy rate 55%
Calorie consumption 2181 kilocalories

Central, Cordillera *58 B3 mountain range* W Colombia
Cordillera Central *55 E3 mountain range* C Dominican Republic
Cordillera Central *53 F5 mountain range* C Panama
Central, Cordillera *139 E1 mountain range* Luzon, N Philippines
Central Group *see* Inner Islands
Centralia *46 B2* Washington, NW USA
Central Indian Ridge *see* Mid-Indian Ridge
Central Makran Range *134 A3 mountain range* W Pakistan
Central Pacific Basin *142 D1 undersea basin* C Pacific Ocean
Central Provinces and Berar *see* Madhya Pradesh
Central Range *144 B3 mountain range* NW Papua New Guinea
Central Russian Upland *109 G1 Eng.* Central Russian Upland. *mountain range* W Russian Federation
Central Russian Upland *see* Srednerusskaya Vozvyshennost'
Central Siberian Plateau *114 D3 var.* Central Siberian Uplands, *Eng.* Central Siberian Plateau. *mountain range* N Russian Federation
Central Siberian Plateau/Central Siberian Uplands *see* Srednesibirskoye Ploskogor'ye
Central, Sistema *92 D3 mountain range* C Spain
Central Valley *47 B6 valley* California, W USA
Centum Cellae *see* Civitavecchia
Ceos *see* Tziá
Cephaloedium *see* Cefalù
Ceram *see* Seram, Pulau
Ceram Sea *see* Seram, Laut
Cerasus *see* Giresun
Cereté *58 B2* Córdoba, NW Colombia
Cergy-Pontoise *see* Pontoise
Cerignola *97 D5* Puglia, SE Italy
Çerkes *116 C2* Çankırı, N Turkey
Cernăuţi *see* Chernivtsi
Cernay *90 E4* Haut-Rhin, NE France
Cerro de Pasco *60 C3* Pasco, C Peru
Cervera *93 F2* Cataluña, NE Spain
Cervino, Monte *see* Matterhorn
Cesena *96 C3 anc.* Caesena. Emilia-Romagna, N Italy
Cēsis *106 D3 Ger.* Wenden. C Latvia
Česká Republika *see* Czech Republic
České Budějovice *99 B5 Ger.* Budweis. Jihočeský Kraj, S Czech Republic
Český Krumlov *99 A5 var.* Böhmisch-Krumau, *Ger.* Krummau. Jihočeský Kraj, S Czech Republic
Český Les *see* Bohemian Forest
Cetatea Damboviţei *see* Bucureşti
Cetinje *101 C5 It.* Cettigne. S Montenegro
Cette *see* Sète
Cettigne *see* Cetinje
Ceuta *70 C2 enclave* Spain, N Africa
Cévennes *91 C6 mountain range* S France
Ceyhan *116 D4* Adana, S Turkey
Ceylanpınar *117 E4* Şanlıurfa, SE Turkey
Ceylon *see* Sri Lanka
Ceylon Plain *124 B4 abyssal plain* N Indian Ocean
Ceyre to the Caribs *see* Marie-Galante
Chachapoyas *60 B2* Amazonas, NW Peru
Chachevichy *107 D6 Rus.* Chechevichi. Mahilyowskaya Voblasts', E Belarus
Chaco *see* Gran Chaco
Chad *76 C3 off.* Republic of Chad, *Fr.* Tchad. *country* C Africa

CHAD
Central Africa

Official name Republic of Chad
Formation 1960 / 1960
Capital N'Djamena
Population 11.5 million / 24 people per sq mile (9 people per sq km)
Total area 495,752 sq. miles

CHAD
(continued)

(1,284,000 sq. km)
Languages French*, Sara, Arabic*, Maba
Religions Muslim 51%, Christian 35%, Animist 7%, Traditional beliefs 7%
Ethnic mix Other 30%, Sara 28%, Mayo-Kebbi 12%, Arab 12%, Ouaddai 9%, Kanem-Bornou 9%
Government Presidential system
Currency CFA franc = 100 centimes
Literacy rate 34%
Calorie consumption 2074 kilocalories

Chad, Lake *76 B3 Fr.* Lac Tchad. *lake* C Africa
Chad, Republic of *see* Chad
Chadron *44 D3* Nebraska, C USA
Chadyr-Lunga *see* Ciadir-Lunga
Chagai Hills *134 A2 var.* Chāh Gay. *mountain range* Afghanistan/Pakistan
Chaghasarāy *see* Asadābād
Chagos-Laccadive Plateau *124 B4 undersea plateau* N Indian Ocean
Chagos Trench *141 C5 trench* N Indian Ocean
Chāh Gay *see* Chāgai Hills
Chaillu, Massif du *77 B6 mountain range* C Gabon
Chain Ridge *140 B4 undersea ridge* W Indian Ocean
Chajul *52 B2* Quiché, W Guatemala
Chakhānsūr *122 D5* Nīmrōz, SW Afghanistan
Chala *60 D4* Arequipa, SW Peru
Chalatenango *52 C3* Chalatenango, N El Salvador
Chalcidice *see* Chalkidikí
Chalcis *see* Chalkída
Chalki *105 E7 island* Dodekánisa, Greece, Aegean Sea
Chalkída *105 C5 var.* Halkida, *prev.* Khalkís; *anc.* Chalcis. Evvoia, E Greece
Chalkidikí *104 C4 var.* Khalkidhikí; *anc.* Chalcidice. *peninsula* NE Greece
Challans *90 B4* Vendée, NW France
Challapata *61 F4* Oruro, SW Bolivia
Challenger Deep *152 B3 trench* W Pacific Ocean
Challenger Deep *see* Mariana Trench
Challenger Fracture Zone *153 F4 tectonic feature* SE Pacific Ocean
Châlons-en-Champagne *90 D3 prev.* Châlons-sur-Marne, *hist.* Arcae Remorum; *anc.* Carolopois. Marne, NE France
Châlons-sur-Marne *see* Châlons-en-Champagne
Chalon-sur-Saône *90 D4 anc.* Cabillonum. Saône-et-Loire, C France
Cha Mai *see* Thung Song
Chaman *134 B2* Baluchistān, SW Pakistan
Chambéry *91 D5 anc.* Camberia. Savoie, E France
Champagne *90 D3 cultural region* N France
Champagne *see* Campania
Champaign *40 B4* Illinois, N USA
Champasak *137 D5* Champasak, S Laos
Champlain, Lake *41 F2 lake* Canada/USA
Champotón *51 G4* Campeche, SE Mexico
Chanak *see* Çanakkale
Chañaral *64 B3* Atacama, N Chile
Chan-chiang/Chanchiang *see* Zhanjiang
Chandeleur Islands *42 C3 island group* Louisiana, S USA
Chandīgarh *134 D2 state capital* Punjab, N India
Chandrapur *135 E5* Mahārāshtra, C India
Changan *see* Xi'an, Shaanxi, C China
Changane *79 E3 river* S Mozambique
Changchun *128 D3 var.* Ch'angch'un, Ch'ang-ch'un; *prev.* Hsinking. *province capital* Jilin, NE China
Ch'angch'un/Ch'ang-ch'un *see* Changchun
Chang Jiang *128 A5 Eng.* Yangtze. *river* SW China
Changkiakow *see* Zhangjiakou
Chang, Ko *137 C6 island* S Thailand
Changsha *128 C6 var.* Ch'angsha, Ch'ang-sha. *province capital* Hunan, S China

Ch'angsha/Ch'ang-sha *see* Changsha
Changzhi *128 C4* Shanxi, C China
Chaniá *105 C7 var.* Hania, Khaniá, *Eng.* Canea; *anc.* Cydonia. Kríti, Greece, E Mediterranean Sea
Chañi, Nevado de *64 B2 mountain* NW Argentina
Chankırı *see* Çankırı
Channel Islands *89 C8 Fr.* Iles Normandes. *island group* S English Channel
Channel Islands *47 B8 island group* California, W USA
Channel-Port aux Basques *39 G4* Newfoundland and Labrador, SE Canada
Channel, The *see* English Channel
Channel Tunnel *90 C2 tunnel* France/United Kingdom
Chantabun/Chantaburi *see* Chanthaburi
Chantada *92 C1* Galicia, NW Spain
Chanthaburi *137 C6 var.* Chantabun, Chantaburi. Chantaburi, S Thailand
Chanute *45 F5* Kansas, C USA
Chaouèn *see* Chefchaouen
Chaoyang *128 D3* Liaoning, NE China
Chapala, Lago de *50 D4 lake* C Mexico
Chapan, Gora *122 B3 mountain* C Turkmenistan
Chapayevsk *111 C6* Samarskaya Oblast', W Russian Federation
Chaplynka *109 F4* Khersons'ka Oblast', S Ukraine
Chapra *see* Chhapra
Charcot Seamounts *80 B3 seamount range* E Atlantic Ocean
Chardzhev *see* Türkmenabat
Chardzhou/Chardzhui *see* Türkmenabat
Charente *91 B5 cultural region* W France
Charente *91 B5 river* W France
Chari *76 B3 var.* Shari. *river* Central African Republic/Chad
Chārīkār *123 E4* Parwān, NE Afghanistan
Charity *59 F2* NW Guyana
Chärjew *see* Türkmenabat
Charkhlik/Charkhliq *see* Ruoqiang
Charleroi *87 C7* Hainaut, S Belgium
Charlesbourg *39 E4* Québec, SE Canada
Charles de Gaulle *90 E1* (Paris) Seine-et-Marne, N France
Charles Island *38 D1 island* Nunavut, NE Canada
Charles Island *see* Santa María, Isla
Charleston *43 F2* South Carolina, SE USA
Charleston *40 D5 state capital* West Virginia, NE USA
Charleville *149 D5* Queensland, E Australia
Charleville-Mézières *90 D3* Ardennes, N France
Charlie-Gibbs Fracture Zone *66 C2 tectonic feature* N Atlantic Ocean
Charlotte *43 E1* North Carolina, SE USA
Charlotte Amalie *55 F3 prev.* Saint Thomas. *dependent territory capital* (Virgin Islands (US)) Saint Thomas, N Virgin Islands (US)
Charlotte Harbor *43 E5 inlet* Florida, SE USA
Charlottenhof *see* Aegviidu
Charlottesville *41 E5* Virginia, NE USA
Charlottetown *39 F4 province capital* Prince Edward Island, Prince Edward Island, SE Canada
Charlotte Town *see* Roseau, Dominica
Charsk *see* Shar
Charters Towers *148 D3* Queensland, NE Australia
Chartres *90 C3 anc.* Autricum, Civitas Carnutum. Eure-et-Loir, C France
Chashniki *107 D5* Vitsyebskaya Voblasts', N Belarus
Châteaubriant *90 B4* Loire-Atlantique, NW France
Châteaudun *90 C3* Eure-et-Loir, C France
Châteauroux *90 C4 prev.* Indreville. Indre, C France
Château-Thierry *90 C3* Aisne, N France
Châtelet *87 C7* Hainaut, S Belgium
Châtelherault *see* Châtellerault
Châtellerault *90 B4 var.* Châtelherault. Vienne, W France

Chatham Rise *142 D5 var.* Chatham Island Rise. *undersea rise* S Pacific Ocean
Chatkal Range *123 F2 Rus.* Chatkal'skiy Khrebet. *mountain range* Kyrgyzstan/Uzbekistan
Chatkal'skiy Khrebet *see* Chatkal Range
Chāttagām *see* Chittagong
Chattahoochee River *42 D3 river* SE USA
Chattanooga *42 D1* Tennessee, S USA
Chatyr-Tash *123 G2* Narynskaya Oblast', C Kyrgyzstan
Châu Đốc *137 D6 var.* Chauphu, Chau Phu. An Giang, S Vietnam
Chauk *136 A3* Magway, W Myanmar (Burma)
Chaumont *90 D4 prev.* Chaumont-en-Bassigny. Haute-Marne, N France
Chaumont-en-Bassigny *see* Chaumont
Chau Phu *see* Châu Đốc
Chausy *see* Chavusy
Chaves *92 C2 anc.* Aquae Flaviae. Vila Real, N Portugal
Chávez, Isla *see* Santa Cruz, Isla
Chavusy *107 E6 Rus.* Chausy. Mahilyowskaya Voblasts', E Belarus
Chaykovskiy *111 D5* Permskiy Kray, NW Russian Federation
Cheb *99 A5 Ger.* Eger. Karlovarský Kraj, W Czech Republic
Cheboksary *111 C5* Chuvashskaya Respublika, W Russian Federation
Cheboygan *40 C2* Michigan, N USA
Chechaouèn *see* Chefchaouen
Chech, Erg *74 D1 desert* Algeria/Mali
Chechevichi *see* Chachevichy
Che-chiang *see* Zhejiang
Cheduba Island *136 A4 island* W Myanmar (Burma)
Chefchaouen *70 C2 var.* Chaouèn, Chechaouèn, *Sp.* Xauen. N Morocco
Chefoo *see* Yantai
Cheju-do *see* Jeju-do
Cheju Strait *see* Jeju Strait
Chekiang *see* Zhejiang
Cheleken *see* Hazar
Chelkar *see* Shalkar
Chelm *98 E4 Rus.* Kholm. Lubelskie, SE Poland
Chelmno *98 D3 Ger.* Culm, Kulm. Kujawski-pomorskie, C Poland
Chełmża *98 C3 Ger.* Culmsee, Kulmsee. Kujawski-pomorskie, C Poland
Cheltenham *89 D6* C England, United Kingdom
Chelyabinsk *114 C3* Chelyabinskaya Oblast', C Russian Federation
Chemnitz *94 D4 prev.* Karl-Marx-Stadt. Sachsen, E Germany
Chemulpo *see* Incheon
Chenāb *134 C2 river* India/Pakistan
Chengchiatun *see* Liaoyuan
Ch'eng-chou/Chengchow *see* Zhengzhou
Chengde *128 D3 var.* Jehol. Hebei, E China
Chengdu *128 B5 var.* Chengtu, Ch'eng-tu. *province capital* Sichuan, C China
Chenghsien *see* Zhengzhou
Chengtu/Ch'eng-tu *see* Chengdu
Chennai *132 D2 prev.* Madras. *state capital* Tamil Nādu, S India
Chenstokhov *see* Częstochowa
Chen Xian/Chenxian/Chen Xiang *see* Chenzhou
Chenzhou *128 C6 var.* Chenxian, Chen Xian, Chen Xiang. Hunan, S China
Chepelare *104 C3* Smolyan, S Bulgaria
Chepén *60 B3* La Libertad, C Peru
Cher *90 C4 river* C France
Cherbourg *90 B3 anc.* Carusbur. Manche, N France
Cherepovets *110 B4* Vologodskaya Oblast', NW Russian Federation
Chergui, Chott ech *70 D2 salt lake* NW Algeria
Cherikov *see* Cherykaw
Cherkassy *see* Cherkasy
Cherkasy *109 E2 Rus.* Cherkassy. Cherkas'ka Oblast', C Ukraine
Cherkessk *111 B7* Karachayevo-Cherkesskaya Respublika, SW Russian Federation
Chernigov *see* Chernihiv
Chernihiv *109 E1 Rus.* Chernigov. Chernihivs'ka Oblast', NE Ukraine
Chernivtsi *108 C3 Ger.* Czernowitz, *Rom.* Cernăuţi, *Rus.* Chernovtsy. Chernivets'ka Oblast', W Ukraine

Cherno More *see* Black Sea
Chernomorskoye *see* Chornomors'ke
Chernovtsy *see* Chernivtsi
Chernoye More *see* Black Sea
Chernyakhovsk *106 A4 Ger.* Insterburg.
　Kaliningradskaya Oblast', W Russian
　Federation
Cherry Hill *41 F4* New Jersey, NE USA
Cherski Range *see* Cherskogo, Khrebet
Cherskiy *115 G2* Respublika Sakha
　(Yakutiya), NE Russian Federation
Cherskogo, Khrebet *115 F2 var.* Cherski
　Range. *mountain range* NE Russian
　Federation
Cherso *see* Cres
Cherven' *see* Chervyen'
Chervonograd *see* Chervonohrad
Chervonohrad *108 C2 Rus.*
　Chervonograd. L'vivs'ka Oblast',
　NW Ukraine
Chervyen' *107 D6 Rus.* Cherven'.
　Minskaya Voblasts', C Belarus
Cherykaw *107 E7 Rus.* Cherikov.
　Mahilyowskaya Voblasts', E Belarus
Chesapeake Bay *41 F5 inlet* NE USA
Chesha Bay *see* Chëshskaya Guba
Chëshskaya Guba *155 D5 var.*
　Archangel Bay, Chesha Bay, Dvina
　Bay. *bay* NW Russian Federation
Chester *89 C6 Wel.* Caerleon, *hist.*
　Legaceaster, *Lat.* Deva, Devana Castra.
　C England, United Kingdom
Chetumal *51 H4 var.* Payo Obispo.
　Quintana Roo, SE Mexico
Cheviot Hills *88 D4 hill range* England/
　Scotland, United Kingdom
Cheyenne *44 D4 state capital* Wyoming,
　C USA
Cheyenne River *44 D3 river* South
　Dakota/Wyoming, N USA
Chezdi-Oşorheiu *see* Târgu Secuiesc
Chhapra *135 F3 prev.* Chapra. Bihār,
　N India
Chhattisgarh *135 E4 cultural region*
　E India
Chia-i *see* Jiayi
Chiai *see* Jiayi
Chiang-hsi *see* Jiangxi
Chiang Mai *136 B4 var.* Chiangmai,
　Chiengmai, Kiangmai. Chiang Mai,
　NW Thailand
Chiangmai *see* Chiang Mai
Chiang Rai *136 C3 var.* Chianpai,
　Chienrai, Muang Chiang Rai. Chiang
　Rai, NW Thailand
Chiang-su *see* Jiangsu
Chianning/Chian-ning *see* Nanjing
Chianpai *see* Chiang Rai
Chianti *96 C3 cultural region* C Italy
Chiapa *see* Chiapa de Corzo
Chiapa de Corzo *51 G5 var.* Chiapa.
　Chiapas, SE Mexico
Chiayi *see* Jiayi
Chiba *130 B1 var.* Tiba. Chiba, Honshū,
　S Japan
Chibougamau *38 D3* Québec, SE Canada
Chicago *40 B3* Illinois, N USA
Ch'i-ch'i-ha-erh *see* Qiqihar
Chickasha *49 G2* Oklahoma, C USA
Chiclayo *60 B3* Lambayeque, NW Peru
Chico *47 B5* California, W USA
Chico, Río *60 B7 river* S Argentina
Chico, Río *65 B6 river* S Argentina
Chicoutimi *39 E4* Québec, SE Canada
Chiengmai *see* Chiang Mai
Chienrai *see* Chiang Rai
Chiesanuova *96 D2* SW San Marino
Chieti *96 D4 var.* Teate. Abruzzo, C Italy
Chifeng *127 G2 var.* Ulanhad. Nei
　Mongol Zizhiqu, N China
Chigirin *see* Chyhyryn
Chih-fu *see* Yantai
Chihli *see* Hebei
Chihli, Gulf of *see* Bo Hai
Chihuahua *50 C2* Chihuahua,
　NW Mexico
Childress *49 F2* Texas, SW USA
Chile *64 B3 off.* Republic of Chile.
　country SW South America

CHILE
South America

Official name Republic of Chile
Formation 1818 / 1883
Capital Santiago
Population 17.3 million / 60 people
　per sq mile (23 people per sq km)
Total area 292.258 sq. miles

CHILE
(continued)

　(756,950 sq. km)
Languages Spanish*,
　Amerindian languages
Religions Roman Catholic 89%,
　Other and nonreligious 11%
Ethnic mix Mestizo and European 90%,
　Other Amerindian 9%, Mapuche 1%
Government Presidential system
Currency Chilean peso = 100 centavos
Literacy rate 99%
Calorie consumption 2908 kilocalories

Chile Basin *57 A5 undersea basin*
　E Pacific Ocean
Chile Chico *65 B6* Aisén, W Chile
Chile, Republic of *see* Chile
Chile Rise *57 A7 undersea rise* SE Pacific
　Ocean
Chilia-Nouă *see* Kiliya
Chililabombwe *78 D2* Copperbelt,
　C Zambia
Chi-lin *see* Jilin
Chillán *65 B5* Bío Bío, C Chile
Chillicothe *40 D4* Ohio, N USA
Chill Mhantáin, Sléibhte *see* Wicklow
　Mountains
Chiloé, Isla de *65 A6 var.* Isla Grande de
　Chiloé. *island* W Chile
Chilpancingo *51 E5 var.* Chilpancingo
　de los Bravos. Guerrero, S Mexico
Chilpancingo de los Bravos *see*
　Chilpancingo
Chilung *see* Jilong
Chimán *53 G5* Panamá, E Panama
Chimbay *see* Chimboy
Chimborazo *60 A1 volcano* C Ecuador
Chimbote *60 C3* Ancash, W Peru
Chimboy *122 D1 Rus.* Chimbay.
　Qoraqalpog'iston Respublikasi,
　NW Uzbekistan
Chimkent *see* Shymkent
Chimoio *79 E3* Manica, C Mozambique
China *124 C2 off.* People's Republic
　of China, *Chin.* Chung-hua Jen-min
　Kung-ho-kuo, Zhonghua Renmin
　Gongheguo; *prev.* Chinese Empire.
　country E Asia

CHINA
East Asia

Official name People's Republic of China
Formation 960 / 1999
Capital Beijing
Population 1.35 billion / 374 people
　per sq mile (144 people per sq km)
Total area 3,705,386 sq. miles
　(9,596,960 sq. km)
Languages Mandarin*, Wu, Cantonese,
　Hsiang, Min, Hakka, Kan
Religions Nonreligious 59%, Traditional
　beliefs 20%, Other 13%, Buddhist 6%,
　Muslim 2%
Ethnic mix Han 92%, Other 4%, Hui 1%,
　Miao 1%, Manchu 1%, Zhuang 1%
Government One-party state
Currency Renminbi (known as yuan)
　= 10 jiao = 100 fen
Literacy rate 94%
Calorie consumption 3036 kilocalories

Chi-nan/Chinan *see* Jinan
Chinandega *52 C3* Chinandega,
　NW Nicaragua
China, People's Republic of *see* China
China, Republic of *see* Taiwan
Chincha Alta *60 D4* Ica, SW Peru
Chin-chiang *see* Quanzhou
Chin-chou/Chinchow *see* Jinzhou
Chindwin *see* Chindwinn
Chindwinn *136 B2 var.* Chindwin. *river*
　N Myanmar (Burma)
Chinese Empire *see* China
Chinghai *see* Qinghai
Ch'ing Hai *see* Qinghai Hu, China
Chingola *78 D2* Copperbelt, C Zambia
Ching-Tao/Ch'ing-tao *see* Qingdao
Chinguetti *74 C2 var.* Chinguetti. Adrar,
　C Mauritania
Chin Hills *136 A3 mountain range*
　W Myanmar (Burma)
Chinhsien *see* Jinzhou
Chinnereth *see* Tiberias, Lake
Chinook Trough *113 H4 trough*
　N Pacific Ocean

Chioggia *96 C2 anc.* Fossa Claudia.
　Veneto, NE Italy
Chíos *105 D5 var.* Hios, Khíos, *It.* Scio,
　Turk. Sakiz-Adasi. Chíos, E Greece
Chíos *105 D5 var.* Khíos. *island* E Greece
Chipata *78 D2 prev.* Fort Jameson.
　Eastern, E Zambia
Chiquián *60 C3* Ancash, W Peru
Chiquimula *52 B2* Chiquimula,
　SE Guatemala
Chīrāla *132 D1* Andhra Pradesh, E India
Chirchik *see* Chirchiq
Chirchiq *123 E2 Rus.* Chirchik.
　Toshkent Viloyati, E Uzbekistan
Chiriqui Gulf *53 E5 Eng.* Chiriqui Gulf.
　gulf SW Panama
Chiriqui Gulf *see* Chiriquí, Golfo de
Chiriquí, Laguna de *53 E5 var.* Barú, Volcán
　NW Panama
Chiriquí, Volcán de *see* Barú, Volcán
Chirripó, Cerro *see* Chirripó Grande,
　Cerro
Chirripó Grande, Cerro *52 D4 var.*
　Cerro Chirripó. *mountain* SE Costa
　Rica
Chisec *52 B2* Alta Verapaz,
　C Guatemala
Chisholm *45 F1* Minnesota, N USA
Chisimaio/Chisimayu *see* Kismaayo
Chişinău *108 D4 Rus.* Kishinev. *country
　capital* (Moldova) C Moldova
Chita *115 F4* Zabaykal'skiy Kray,
　S Russian Federation
Chitangwiza *see* Chitungwiza
Chitato *78 C1* Lunda Norte, NE Angola
Chitina *36 D3* Alaska, USA
Chitose *130 D2 var.* Titose. Hokkaidō,
　NE Japan
Chitré *53 F5* Herrera, S Panama
Chittagong *135 G4 Ben.* Chāttagām.
　Chittagong, SE Bangladesh
Chitungwiza *78 D3 prev.* Chitangwiza.
　Mashonaland East, NE Zimbabwe
Chkalov *see* Orenburg
Chlef *70 D2 var.* Ech Cheliff, Ech
　Cheliff; *prev.* Al-Asnam, El Asnam,
　Orléansville. NW Algeria
Chocolate Mountains *47 D8 mountain
　range* California, W USA
Chodorów *see* Khodoriv
Chodzież *98 C3* Wielkopolskie, C Poland
Choele Choel *65 C5* Río Negro,
　C Argentina
Choiseul *144 C3 var.* Lauru. *island*
　NW Solomon Islands
Chojnice *98 C2 Ger.* Konitz. Pomorskie,
　N Poland
Ch'ok'ē *72 C4 var.* Choke Mountains.
　mountain range NW Ethiopia
Choke Mountains *see* Ch'ok'ē
Cholet *90 B4* Maine-et-Loire, NW France
Choluteca *52 C3* Choluteca, S Honduras
Choluteca, Río *52 C3 river*
　SW Honduras
Choma *78 D2* Southern, S Zambia
Chomutov *98 A4 Ger.* Komotau.
　Ústecký Kraj, NW Czech Republic
Chona *113 E2 river* C Russian Federation
Chon Buri *137 C5 prev.* Bang Pla Soi.
　Chon Buri, S Thailand
Chone *60 A1* Manabí, W Ecuador
Ch'ŏngjin *129 E3* NE North Korea
Chongqing *128 B5 var.* Ch'ung-ching,
　Ch'ung-ch'ing, Chungking, Pahsien,
　Tchongking, Yuzhou. Chongqing
　Shi, C China
Chonnacht *see* Connaught
Chonos, Archipiélago de los *65 A6
　island group* S Chile
Chóra Sfakíon *105 C8 var.* Sfákia. Kríti,
　Greece, E Mediterranean Sea
Chorne More *see* Black Sea
Chornomors'ke *109 E4 Rus.*
　Chernomorskoye. Avtonomna
　Respublika Krym, S Ukraine
Chorokh/Chorokhi *see* Çoruh Nehri
Chortkiv *108 C2 Rus.* Chortkov.
　Ternopil's'ka Oblast', W Ukraine
Chortkov *see* Chortkiv
Chorzów *99 C5 Ger.* Königshütte; *prev.*
　Królewska Huta. Śląskie, S Poland
Chośebuz *see* Cottbus
Chōsen-kaikyō *see* Korea Strait
Chōshi *131 D5 var.* Tyôsi. Chiba,
　Honshū, S Japan
Chosŏn-minjujuŭi-inmin-kanghwaguk
　see North Korea
Choszczno *98 B3 Ger.* Arnswalde.
　Zachodnio-pomorskie, NW Poland

Chota Nagpur *135 E4 plateau* N India
Choûm *74 C2* Adrar, C Mauritania
Choybalsan *127 F2 prev.* Byan Tumen.
　Dornod, E Mongolia
Christchurch *151 C6* Canterbury, South
　Island, New Zealand
Christiana *54 B5* C Jamaica
Christiania *see* Oslo
Christiansand *see* Kristiansand
Christianshåb *see* Qasigiannguit
Christiansund *see* Kristiansund
Christmas Island *141 D5 Australian
　external territory* E Indian Ocean
Christmas Island *see* Kiritimati
Christmas Ridge *143 E1 undersea ridge*
　C Pacific Ocean
Chuan *see* Sichuan
Ch'uan-chou *see* Quanzhou
Chubek *see* Moskva
Chubut, Río *65 B6 river* SE Argentina
Chudskoye Ozero *see* Peipus, Lake
Chugoku-sanchi *131 B6 mountain range*
　Honshū, SW Japan
Chui *see* Chuy
Chukai *see* Cukai
Chukchi Plain *155 B2 abyssal plain*
　Arctic Ocean
Chukchi Plateau *34 C2 undersea plateau*
　Arctic Ocean
Chukchi Sea *34 B2 Rus.* Chukotskoye
　More. *sea* Arctic Ocean
Chukotskoye More *see* Chukchi Sea
Chula Vista *47 C8* California, W USA
Chulucanas *60 B2* Piura, NW Peru
Chulym *114 D4 river* C Russian
　Federation
Chumphon *137 C6 var.* Jumporn.
　Chumphon, SW Thailand
Chuncheon *129 E4 Jap.* Shunsen; *prev.*
　Ch'unch'ŏn. N South Korea
Ch'unch'ŏn *see* Chuncheon
Ch'ung-ch'ing/Ch'ung-ching *see*
　Chongqing
Chung-hua Jen-min Kung-ho-kuo
　see China
Chungking *see* Chongqing
Chunya *115 E3 river* C Russian
　Federation
Chuquicamata *64 B2* Antofagasta,
　N Chile
Chuquisaca *see* Sucre
Chur *95 B7 Fr.* Coire, *It.* Coira, *Rmsch.*
　Cuera, Quera; *anc.* Curia Rhaetorum.
　Graubünden, E Switzerland
Churchill *37 G4* Manitoba, C Canada
Churchill *38 B2 river* Manitoba/
　Saskatchewan, C Canada
Churchill *39 F2 river* Newfoundland and
　Labrador, E Canada
Chuska Mountains *48 C1 mountain
　range* Arizona/New Mexico, SW USA
Chusovoy *111 D5* Permskiy Kray,
　NW Russian Federation
Chust *see* Khust
Chuuk Islands *144 B2 var.* Hogoley
　Islands; *prev.* Truk Islands. *island
　group* Caroline Islands, C Micronesia
Chuy *64 E4 var.* Chuí. Rocha, E Uruguay
Chyhyryn *109 E2 Rus.* Chigirin.
　Cherkas'ka Oblast', N Ukraine
Ciadir-Lunga *108 D4 var.* Ceadâr-
　Lunga, Rus. Chadyr-Lunga. S Moldova
Cide *116 C2* Kastamonu, N Turkey
Ciechanów *98 D3 prev.* Zichenau.
　Mazowieckie, C Poland
Ciego de Ávila *54 C2* Ciego de Ávila,
　C Cuba
Ciénaga *58 B1* Magdalena, N Colombia
Cienfuegos *54 B2* Cienfuegos, C Cuba
Cieza *93 E4* Murcia, SE Spain
Çihanbeyli *116 C3* Konya, C Turkey
Cikobia *145 E4 prev.* Thikombia.
　island N Fiji
Cilacap *138 C5 prev.* Tjilatjap. Jawa,
　C Indonesia
Cill Airne *see* Killarney
Cill Chainnigh *see* Kilkenny
Cilli *see* Celje
Cill Mhantáin *see* Wicklow
Cîmpina *see* Câmpina
Cîmpulung *see* Câmpulung
Cina Selatan, Laut *see* South China Sea
Cincinnati *40 C4* Ohio, N USA
Ciney *87 C7* Namur, SE Belgium
Cinto, Monte *91 E7 mountain* Corse,
　France, C Mediterranean Sea
Cintra *see* Sintra
Cipolletti *65 B5* Río Negro, C Argentina

Cirebon *138 C4 prev.* Tjirebon. Jawa, S Indonesia
Cirkvenica *see* Crikvenica
Cirò Marina *97 E6* Calabria, S Italy
Cirquenizza *see* Crikvenica
Cisnădie *108 B4 Ger.* Heltau, *Hung.* Nagydisznód. Sibiu, SW Romania
Citharista *see* la Ciotat
Citlaltépetl *see* Orizaba, Volcán Pico de
Citrus Heights *47 B5* California, W USA
Ciudad Acuña *see* Villa Acuña
Ciudad Bolívar *59 E2 prev.* Angostura. Bolívar, E Venezuela
Ciudad Camargo *50 D2* Chihuahua, N Mexico
Ciudad Cortés *see* Cortés
Ciudad Dario *52 D3 var.* Dario. Matagalpa, W Nicaragua
Ciudad de Dolores Hidalgo *see* Dolores Hidalgo
Ciudad de Guatemala *52 B2 Eng.* Guatemala City; *prev.* Santiago de los Caballeros. *country capital* (Guatemala) Guatemala, C Guatemala
Ciudad del Carmen *see* Carmen
Ciudad del Este *64 E2 prev.* Ciudad Presidente Stroessner, Presidente Stroessner, Puerto Presidente Stroessner. Alto Paraná, SE Paraguay
Ciudad Delicias *see* Delicias
Ciudad de México *see* México
Ciudad de Panama *see* Panamá
Ciudad Guayana *59 E2 prev.* San Tomé de Guayana, Santo Tomé de Guayana. Bolívar, NE Venezuela
Ciudad Guzmán *50 D4* Jalisco, SW Mexico
Ciudad Hidalgo *51 G5* Chiapas, SE Mexico
Ciudad Juárez *50 C1* Chihuahua, N Mexico
Ciudad Lerdo *50 D3* Durango, C Mexico
Ciudad Madero *51 E3 var.* Villa Cecilia. Tamaulipas, C Mexico
Ciudad Mante *51 E3* Tamaulipas, C Mexico
Ciudad Miguel Alemán *51 E2* Tamaulipas, C Mexico
Ciudad Obregón *50 B2* Sonora, NW Mexico
Ciudad Ojeda *58 C1* Zulia, NW Venezuela
Ciudad Porfirio Díaz *see* Piedras Negras
Ciudad Presidente Stroessner *see* Ciudad del Este
Ciudad Quesada *see* Quesada
Ciudad Real *92 D3* Castilla-La Mancha, C Spain
Ciudad-Rodrigo *92 C3* Castilla y León, N Spain
Ciudad Trujillo *see* Santo Domingo
Ciudad Valles *51 E3* San Luis Potosí, C Mexico
Ciudad Victoria *51 E3* Tamaulipas, C Mexico
Ciutadella *93 H3 var.* Ciutadella de Menorca. Menorca, Spain, W Mediterranean Sea
Ciutadella Ciutadella de Menorca *see* Ciutadella
Civitanova Marche *96 D3* Marche, C Italy
Civitas Altae Ripae *see* Brzeg
Civitas Carnutum *see* Chartres
Civitas Eburovicum *see* Évreux
Civitavecchia *96 C4 anc.* Centum Cellae, Trajani Portus. Lazio, C Italy
Claremore *49 G1* Oklahoma, C USA
Clarence *151 C5* Canterbury, South Island, New Zealand
Clarence *151 C5 river* South Island, New Zealand
Clarence Town *54 D2* Long Island, C Bahamas
Clarinda *45 F4* Iowa, C USA
Clarion Fracture Zone *153 E2 tectonic feature* NE Pacific Ocean
Clarión, Isla *50 A5 island* W Mexico
Clark Fork *44 A1 river* Idaho/Montana, NW USA
Clark Hill Lake *43 E2 var.* J.Storm Thurmond Reservoir. *reservoir* Georgia/South Carolina, SE USA
Clarksburg *40 D4* West Virginia, NE USA
Clarksdale *42 B2* Mississippi, S USA
Clarksville *42 C1* Tennessee, S USA
Clausentum *see* Southampton

Clayton *49 E1* New Mexico, SW USA
Clearwater *43 E4* Florida, SE USA
Clearwater Mountains *46 D2 mountain range* Idaho, NW USA
Cleburne *49 G3* Texas, SW USA
Clermont *148 D4* Queensland, E Australia
Clermont-Ferrand *91 C5* Puy-de-Dôme, C France
Cleveland *40 D3* Ohio, N USA
Cleveland *42 D1* Tennessee, S USA
Clifton *48 C2* Arizona, SW USA
Clinton *42 B2* Mississippi, S USA
Clinton *49 F1* Oklahoma, C USA
Clipperton Fracture Zone *153 E3 tectonic feature* E Pacific Ocean
Clipperton Island *35 A7 French dependency* of French Polynesia E Pacific Ocean
Cloncurry *148 B3* Queensland, C Australia
Clonmel *89 B6 Ir.* Cluain Meala. S Ireland
Cloppenburg *94 B3* Niedersachsen, NW Germany
Cloquet *45 G2* Minnesota, N USA
Cloud Peak *44 C3 mountain* Wyoming, C USA
Clovis *49 E2* New Mexico, SW USA
Cluain Meala *see* Clonmel
Cluj *see* Cluj-Napoca
Cluj-Napoca *108 B3 Ger.* Klausenburg, *Hung.* Kolozsvár; *prev.* Cluj. Cluj, NW Romania
Clutha *151 B7 river* South Island, New Zealand
Clyde *88 C4 river* W Scotland, United Kingdom
Coari *62 D2* Amazonas, N Brazil
Coast Mountains *36 D4 Fr.* Chaîne Côtière. *mountain range* Canada/USA
Coast Ranges *46 A4 mountain range* W USA
Coats Island *37 G3 island* Nunavut, NE Canada
Coats Land *154 B2 physical region* Antarctica
Coatzacoalcos *51 G4 var.* Quetzalcoalco; *prev.* Puerto México. Veracruz-Llave, E Mexico
Cobán *52 B2* Alta Verapaz, C Guatemala
Cobar *149 C6* New South Wales, SE Australia
Cobija *61 E3* Pando, NW Bolivia
Coblence/Coblenz *see* Koblenz
Coburg *95 C5* Bayern, SE Germany
Cocanada *see* Kākināda
Cochabamba *61 F4 hist.* Oropeza. Cochabamba, C Bolivia
Cochin *see* Kochi
Cochrane *38 C4* Ontario, S Canada
Cochrane *65 B7* Aisén, S Chile
Cocibolca *see* Nicaragua, Lago de
Cockade State *see* Maryland
Cockburn Town *55 E2* San Salvador, E Bahamas
Cockpit Country, The *54 A4 physical region* W Jamaica
Cocobeach *77 A5* Estuaire, NW Gabon
Coconino Plateau *48 B1 plain* Arizona, SW USA
Coco, Río *53 E2 var.* Río Wanki, Segovia Wangkí. *river* Honduras/Nicaragua
Cocos Basin *124 C5 undersea basin* E Indian Ocean
Cocos Island Ridge *see* Cocos Ridge
Cocos Islands *141 D5 island group* E Indian Ocean
Cocos Ridge *35 C8 var.* Cocos Island Ridge. *undersea ridge* E Pacific Ocean
Cod, Cape *41 G3 headland* Massachusetts, NE USA
Codfish Island *151 A8 island* SW New Zealand
Codlea *108 C4 Ger.* Zeiden, *Hung.* Feketehalom. Braşov, C Romania
Cody *44 C2* Wyoming, C USA
Coeur d'Alene *46 C2* Idaho, NW USA
Coevorden *86 E2* Drenthe, NE Netherlands
Coffs Harbour *149 E6* New South Wales, SE Australia
Cognac *91 B5 anc.* Compniacum. Charente, W France
Cohalm *see* Rupea
Coiba, Isla de *53 E5 island* SW Panama
Coihaique *65 B6 var.* Coyhaique. Aisén, S Chile

Coimbatore *132 C3* Tamil Nādu, S India
Coimbra *92 B3 anc.* Conímbria, Conimbriga. Coimbra, W Portugal
Coín *92 D5* Andalucía, S Spain
Coira/Coire *see* Chur
Coirib, Loch *see* Corrib, Lough
Colby *45 E4* Kansas, C USA
Colchester *89 E6* Connecticut, NE USA
Coleman *49 F3* Texas, SW USA
Coleraine *88 B4 Ir.* Cúil Raithin. N Northern Ireland, United Kingdom
Colesberg *78 C5* Northern Cape, C South Africa
Colima *50 D4* Colima, S Mexico
Coll *88 B3 island* W Scotland, United Kingdom
College Station *49 G3* Texas, SW USA
Collie *147 A7* Western Australia
Collipo *see* Leiria
Colmar *90 E4 Ger.* Kolmar. Haut-Rhin, NE France
Côln *see* Köln
Cologne *see* Köln
Colomb-Béchar *see* Béchar
Colombia *58 B3 off.* Republic of Colombia. *country* N South America
COLOMBIA
South America
Official name Republic of Colombia
Formation 1819 / 1903
Capital Bogotá
Population 46.9 million / 117 people per sq mile (45 people per sq km) / 77%
Total area 439,733 sq. miles (1,138,910 sq. km)
Languages Spanish*, Wayuu, Páez, and other Amerindian languages
Religions Roman Catholic 95%, Other 5%
Ethnic mix Mestizo 58%, White 20%, European–American 14%, African 4%, African–Amerindian 3%, Amerindian 1%
Government Presidential system
Currency Colombian peso = 100 centavos
Literacy rate 93%
Calorie consumption 2717 kilocalories

Colombian Basin *56 A1 undersea basin* SW Caribbean Sea
Colombia, Republic of *see* Colombia
Colombie-Britannique *see* British Columbia
Colombo *132 C4 country capital* (Sri Lanka) Western Province, W Sri Lanka
Colón *53 G4 prev.* Aspinwall. Colón, C Panama
Colonia Agrippina *see* Köln
Colón Ridge *35 B8 undersea ridge* E Pacific Ocean
Colorado *44 C4 off.* State of Colorado, *also known as* Centennial State, Silver State. *state* C USA
Colorado City *49 F3* Texas, SW USA
Colorado Plateau *48 B1 plateau* W USA
Colorado, Río *65 C5 river* E Argentina
Colorado, Río *see* Colorado River
Colorado River *35 B5 var.* Río Colorado. *river* Mexico/USA
Colorado River *49 G4 river* Texas, SW USA
Colorado Springs *44 D5* Colorado, C USA
Columbia *41 E4* Maryland, NE USA
Columbia *45 G4* Missouri, C USA
Columbia *43 E2 state capital* South Carolina, SE USA
Columbia *42 C1* Tennessee, S USA
Columbia River *46 B3 river* Canada/USA
Columbia Plateau *46 C3 plateau* Idaho/Oregon, NW USA
Columbus *42 D2* Georgia, SE USA
Columbus *40 C4* Indiana, N USA
Columbus *42 C2* Mississippi, S USA
Columbus *45 F4* Nebraska, C USA
Columbus *40 D4 state capital* Ohio, N USA
Colville Channel *150 D2 channel* North Island, New Zealand
Colville River *36 D2 river* Alaska, USA
Comacchio *96 C3 var.* Commachio; *anc.* Comactium. Emilia-Romagna, N Italy
Comactium *see* Comacchio
Comalcalco *51 G4* Tabasco, SE Mexico
Coma Pedrosa, Pic de *91 A7 mountain* NW Andorra
Comarapa *61 F4* Santa Cruz, C Bolivia

Comayagua *52 C2* Comayagua, W Honduras
Comer See *see* Como, Lago di
Comilla *135 G4 Ben.* Kumillā. Chittagong, E Bangladesh
Comino *see* Kemmuna
Comitán *51 G5 var.* Comitán de Domínguez. Chiapas, SE Mexico
Comitán de Domínguez *see* Comitán
Commachio *see* Comacchio
Commissioner's Point *42 A5 headland* W Bermuda
Communism Peak *123 F3 prev.* Qullai Kommunizm. *mountain* E Tajikistan
Como *96 B2 anc.* Comum. Lombardia, N Italy
Como, Lake *96 B2 var.* Lario, *Eng.* Lake Como, *Ger.* Comer See. *lake* N Italy
Como, Lake *see* Como, Lago di
Comores, République Fédérale Islamique des *see* Comoros
Comoros *79 F2 off.* Federal Islamic Republic of the Comoros, *Fr.* République Fédérale Islamique des Comores. *country* W Indian Ocean
COMOROS
Indian Ocean
Official name Union of the Comoros
Formation 1975 / 1975
Capital Moroni
Population 800,000 / 929 people per sq mile (359 people per sq km)
Total area 838 sq. miles (2170 sq. km)
Languages Arabic*, Comoran*, French*
Religions Muslim (mainly Sunni) 98%, Other 1%, Roman Catholic 1%
Ethnic mix Comoran 97%, Other 3%
Government Presidential system
Currency Comoros franc = 100 centimes
Literacy rate 74%
Calorie consumption 2139 kilocalories

Comoros, Federal Islamic Republic of the *see* Comoros
Compiègne *90 C3* Oise, N France
Complutum *see* Alcalá de Henares
Compniacum *see* Cognac
Compostela *see* Santiago de Compostela
Comrat *108 D4 Rus.* Komrat. S Moldova
Comum *see* Como
Conakry *74 C4 country capital* (Guinea) SW Guinea
Conca *see* Cuenca
Concarneau *90 A3* Finistère, NW France
Concepción *61 G3* Santa Cruz, E Bolivia
Concepción *65 B5* Bío Bío, C Chile
Concepción *64 D2 var.* Villa Concepción. Concepción, C Paraguay
Concepción *see* La Concepción
Concepción de la Vega *see* La Vega
Conchos, Río *48 D4 river* NW Mexico
Conchos, Río *52 D2 river* C Mexico
Concord *41 G3 state capital* New Hampshire, NE USA
Concordia *64 D4* Entre Ríos, E Argentina
Concordia *45 E4* Kansas, C USA
Côn Đao Sơn *137 E7 var.* Con Son. *island* S Vietnam
Condate *see* Rennes, Ille-et-Vilaine, France
Condate *see* St-Claude, Jura, France
Condega *52 D3* Estelí, NW Nicaragua
Condivincum *see* Nantes
Confluentes *see* Koblenz
Công Hoa Xa Hôi Chu Nghia Viêt Nam *see* Vietnam
Congo *77 D5 off.* Republic of the Congo, *Fr.* Moyen-Congo; *prev.* Middle Congo. *country* C Africa
CONGO
Central Africa
Official name Republic of the Congo
Formation 1960 / 1960
Capital Brazzaville
Population 4.1 million / 31 people per sq mile (12 people per sq km)
Total area 132,046 sq. miles (342,000 sq. km)
Languages Kongo, Teke, Lingala, French*
Religions Traditional beliefs 50%, Roman Catholic 35%, Protestant 13%, Muslim 2%
Ethnic mix Bakongo 51%, Teke 17%, Other 16%, Mbochi 11%, Mbédé 5%

CONGO
(continued)

Government Presidential system
Currency CFA franc = 100 centimes
Literacy rate 87%
Calorie consumption 2056 kilocalories

Congo, Dem. Rep. 77 C6 *off.* Democratic Republic of Congo; *prev.* Zaire, Belgian Congo, Congo (Kinshasa). *country* C Africa

CONGO, DEM. REP.
Central Africa

Official name Democratic Republic of the Congo
Formation 1960 / 1960
Capital Kinshasa
Population 67.8 million / 77 people per sq mile (30 people per sq km)
Total area 905,563 sq. miles (2,345,410 sq. km)
Languages Kiswahili, Tshiluba, Kikongo, Lingala, French*
Religions Roman Catholic 50%, Protestant 20%, Traditional beliefs and other 10%, Muslim 10%, Kimbanguist 10%
Ethnic mix Other 55%, Mongo, Luba, Kongo, and Mangbetu-Azande 45%
Government Presidential system
Currency Congolese franc = 100 centimes
Literacy rate 67%
Calorie consumption 1585 kilocalories

Congo 77 C6 *var.* Kongo, *Fr.* Zaire. *river* C Africa
Congo Basin 77 C6 *drainage basin* W Dem. Rep. Congo
Congo/Congo (Kinshasa) *see* Congo (Democratic Republic of)
Coni *see* Cuneo
Conimbria/Conimbriga *see* Coimbra
Conjeeveram *see* Kānchipuram
Connacht *see* Connaught
Connaught 89 A5 *var.* Connacht, *Ir.* Chonnacht, Cúige. *province* W Ireland
Connecticut 41 F3 *off.* State of Connecticut, *also known as* Blue Law State, Constitution State, Land of Steady Habits, Nutmeg State. *state* NE USA
Connecticut 41 G3 *river* Canada/USA
Conroe 49 G3 Texas, SW USA
Consentia *see* Cosenza
Consolación del Sur 54 A2 Pinar del Río, W Cuba
Con Son *see* Côn Đao Sơn
Constance *see* Konstanz
Constance, Lake 95 B7 *Ger.* Bodensee. *lake* C Europe
Constanța 108 D5 *var.* Küstendje, *Eng.* Constanza, *Ger.* Konstanza, *Turk.* Küstence. Constanța, SE Romania
Constantia *see* Coutances
Constantia *see* Konstanz
Constantine 71 E2 *var.* Qacentina, *Ar.* Qoussantina. NE Algeria
Constantinople *see* Istanbul
Constantiola *see* Oltenița
Constanz *see* Konstanz
Constanza *see* Constanța
Constitution State *see* Connecticut
Coo *see* Kos
Coober Pedy 149 A5 South Australia
Cookeville 42 D1 Tennessee, S USA
Cook Islands 145 F4 *territory in free association with New Zealand* S Pacific Ocean
Cook, Mount *see* Aoraki
Cook Strait 151 D5 *var.* Raukawa. *strait* New Zealand
Cooktown 148 D2 Queensland, NE Australia
Coolgardie 147 B6 Western Australia
Cooma 149 D7 New South Wales, SE Australia
Coomassie *see* Kumasi
Coon Rapids 45 F2 Minnesota, N USA
Cooper Creek 148 C4 *var.* Barcoo, Cooper's Creek. *seasonal river* Queensland/South Australia
Cooper's Creek *see* Cooper Creek
Coos Bay 46 A3 Oregon, NW USA
Cootamundra 149 D6 New South Wales, SE Australia

Copacabana 61 E4 La Paz, W Bolivia
Copenhagen *see* København
Copiapó 64 B3 Atacama, N Chile
Copperas Cove 49 G3 Texas, SW USA
Coppermine *see* Kugluktuk
Copper State *see* Arizona
Coquilhatville *see* Mbandaka
Coquimbo 64 B3 Coquimbo, N Chile
Corabia 108 B5 Olt, S Romania
Coral Harbour 37 G3 *var.* Salliq. Southampton Island, Nunavut, NE Canada
Coral Sea 142 B3 *sea* SW Pacific Ocean
Coral Sea Islands 144 B4 *Australian external territory* SW Pacific Ocean
Corantijn Rivier *see* Courantyne River
Corcovado, Golfo 65 B6 *gulf* S Chile
Corcyra Nigra *see* Korčula
Cordele 42 D3 Georgia, SE USA
Córdoba 64 C3 Córdoba, C Argentina
Córdoba 51 F4 Veracruz-Llave, E Mexico
Córdoba 92 D4 *var.* Cordoba, *Eng.* Cordova; *anc.* Corduba. Andalucía, SW Spain
Cordova 36 C3 Alaska, USA
Cordova/Cordoba *see* Córdoba
Corduba *see* Córdoba
Corentyne River *see* Courantyne River
Corfu 104 A4 *var.* Kérkira, *Eng.* Corfu. *island* Iónia Nisiá, Greece, C Mediterranean Sea
Corfu *see* Kérkyra
Coria 92 C3 Extremadura, W Spain
Corinth 42 C1 Mississippi, S USA
Corinth *see* Kórinthos
Corinth, Gulf of 105 B5 *Eng.* Gulf of Corinth; *anc.* Corinthiacus Sinus. *gulf* C Greece
Corinth, Gulf of/Corinthiacus Sinus *see* Korinthiakós Kólpos
Corinthus *see* Kórinthos
Corinto 52 C3 Chinandega, NW Nicaragua
Cork 89 A6 *Ir.* Corcaigh. S Ireland
Çorlu 116 A2 Tekirdağ, NW Turkey
Corner Brook 39 G3 Newfoundland, Newfoundland and Labrador, E Canada
Corn Islands 53 E3 *var.* Corn Islands. *island group* SE Nicaragua
Corn Islands *see* Maíz, Islas del
Cornwallis Island 37 F2 *Island* Nunavut, N Canada
Coro 58 C1 *prev.* Santa Ana de Coro. Falcón, NW Venezuela
Corocoro 61 F4 La Paz, W Bolivia
Coromandel 150 D2 Waikato, North Island, New Zealand
Coromandel Coast 132 D2 *coast* E India
Coromandel Peninsula 150 D2 *peninsula* North Island, New Zealand
Coronado, Bahía de 52 D5 *bay* S Costa Rica
Coronel Dorrego 65 C5 Buenos Aires, E Argentina
Coronel Oviedo 64 D2 Caaguazú, SE Paraguay
Corozal 52 C1 Corozal, N Belize
Corpus Christi 49 G4 Texas, SW USA
Corrales 48 D2 New Mexico, SW USA
Corrib, Lough 89 A5 *Ir.* Loch Coirib. *lake* W Ireland
Corrientes 64 D3 Corrientes, NE Argentina
Corriza *see* Korçë
Corsica 91 E7 *Eng.* Corsica. *island* France, C Mediterranean Sea
Corsica *see* Corse
Corsicana 49 G3 Texas, SW USA
Cortegana 92 C4 Andalucía, S Spain
Cortés 53 E5 *var.* Ciudad Cortés. Puntarenas, SE Costa Rica
Cortez, Sea of *see* California, Golfo de
Cortina d'Ampezzo 96 C1 Veneto, NE Italy
Coruche 92 B3 Santarém, C Portugal
Çoruh Nehri 117 E3 *Geor.* Chorokh, *Rus.* Chorokhi. *river* Georgia/Turkey
Çorum 116 D3 *var.* Chorum. Çorum, N Turkey
Corunna *see* A Coruña
Corvallis 46 B3 Oregon, NW USA
Corvo 92 A4 *var.* Ilha do Corvo. *island* Azores, Portugal, NE Atlantic Ocean
Corvo, Ilha do *see* Corvo
Cos *see* Kos
Cosenza 97 D6 *anc.* Consentia. Calabria, SW Italy
Cosne-Cours-sur-Loire 90 C4 Nièvre, Bourgogne, C France Europe

Costa Mesa 46 D2 California, W USA North America
Costa Rica 53 E4 *off.* Republic of Costa Rica. *country* Central America

COSTA RICA
Central America

Official name Republic of Costa Rica
Formation 1838 / 1838
Capital San José
Population 4.7 million / 238 people per sq mile (92 people per sq km)
Total area 19,730 sq. miles (51,100 sq. km)
Languages Spanish*, English Creole, Bribri, Cabecar
Religions Roman Catholic 71%, Evangelical 14%, Nonreligious 11%, Other 4%
Ethnic mix Mestizo and European 94%, Black 3%, Other 1%, Chinese 1%, Amerindian 1%
Government Presidential system
Currency Costa Rican colón = 100 céntimos
Literacy rate 95%
Calorie consumption 2876 kilocalories

Costa Rica, Republic of *see* Costa Rica
Costermansville *see* Bukavu
Cotagaita 61 F5 Potosí, S Bolivia
Côte d'Ivoire 74 D4 *off.* Republic of Côte d'Ivoire; *Fr.* Républic de la Côte d'Ivoire, *Eng* Ivory Coast. *country* W Africa

CÔTE D'IVOIRE (IVORY COAST)
West Africa

Official name Republic of Côte d'Ivoire
Formation 1960 / 1960
Capital Yamoussoukro
Population 20.2 million / 165 people per sq mile (64 people per sq km)
Total area 124,502 sq. miles (322,460 sq. km)
Languages Akan, French*, Krou, Voltaique
Religions Muslim 38%, Traditional beliefs 25%, Roman Catholic 25%, Other 6%, Protestant 6%
Ethnic mix Akan 42%, Voltaique 18%, Mandé du Nord 17%, Krou 11%, Mandé du Sud 10%, Other 2%
Government Presidential system
Currency CFA franc = 100 centimes
Literacy rate 55%
Calorie consumption 2670 calories

Côte d'Ivoire, République de la *see* Côte d'Ivoire
Côte d'Or 90 D4 *cultural region* C France
Côte Française des Somalis *see* Djibouti
Côtière, Chaîne *see* Coast Mountains
Cotonou 75 F5 *var.* Kotonu. S Benin
Cotrone *see* Crotone
Cotswold Hills 89 D6 *var.* Cotswolds. *hill range* S England, United Kingdom
Cotswolds *see* Cotswold Hills
Cottbus 94 D4 *Lus.* Chośebuz; *prev.* Kottbus. Brandenburg, E Germany
Cotton State, The *see* Alabama
Cotyora *see* Ordu
Couentrey *see* Coventry
Council Bluffs 45 F4 Iowa, C USA
Courantyne River 59 G4 *var.* Corantijn Rivier, Corentyne River. *river* Guyana/Suriname
Courland Lagoon 106 A4 *Ger.* Kurisches Haff, *Rus.* Kurskiy Zaliv. *lagoon* Lithuania/Russian Federation
Courtrai *see* Kortrijk
Coutances 90 B3 *anc.* Constantia. Manche, N France
Couvin 87 C7 Namur, S Belgium
Coventry 89 D6 *anc.* Couentrey. C England, United Kingdom
Covilhã 92 C3 Castelo Branco, E Portugal
Cowan, Lake 147 B6 *lake* Western Australia
Coxen Hole *see* Roatán
Coxin Hole *see* Roatán
Coyhaique *see* Coihaique
Coyote State, The *see* South Dakota
Cozhê 126 C5 Xizang, W China
Cozumel, Isla 51 H3 *island* SE Mexico
Cracovia/Cracow *see* Kraków
Cradock 78 C5 Eastern Cape, S South Africa
Craig 44 C4 Colorado, C USA

Craiova 108 B5 Dolj, SW Romania
Cranbrook 37 E5 British Columbia, SW Canada
Crane *see* The Crane
Cranz *see* Zelenogradsk
Crawley 89 E7 SE England, United Kingdom
Cremona 96 B2 Lombardia, N Italy
Creole State *see* Louisiana
Cres 100 A3 *It.* Cherso; *anc.* Crexa. *island* W Croatia
Crescent City 46 A4 California, W USA
Crescent Group 128 C7 *island group* C Paracel Islands
Creston 45 F4 Iowa, C USA
Crestview 42 D3 Florida, SE USA
Crete 105 C7 *Eng.* Crete. *island* Greece, Aegean Sea
Créteil 90 E2 Val-de-Marne, N France
Sea of Crete 105 D7 *var.* Kretikon Delagos, *Eng.* Sea of Crete; *anc.* Mare Creticum. *sea* Greece, Aegean Sea
Crete, Sea of/Creticum, Mare *see* Kritikó Pélagos
Creuse 90 B4 *river* C France
Crewe 89 D6 C England, United Kingdom
Crexa *see* Cres
Crikvenica 100 A3 *It.* Cirquenizza; *prev.* Cirkvenica, Crikvenica. Primorje-Gorski Kotar, NW Croatia
Crimea 81 F4 *peninsula* SE Ukraine Europe
Cristóbal 53 G4 Colón, C Panama
Cristóbal Colón, Pico 58 B1 *mountain* N Colombia
Cristur/Cristuru Săcuiesc *see* Cristuru Secuiesc
Cristuru Secuiesc 108 C4 *prev.* Cristur, Cristuru Săcuiesc, Sitaş Cristuru, *Ger.* Kreutz, *Hung.* Székelykeresztúr, Szitás-Keresztúr. Harghita, C Romania
Crjkvenica *see* Crikvenica
Crna Gora *see* Montenegro
Crna Reka 101 D6 *river* S FYR Macedonia
Crni Drim *see* Black Drin
Croatia 100 B3 *off.* Republic of Croatia, *Ger.* Kroatien, *SCr.* Hrvatska. *country* SE Europe

CROATIA
Southeast Europe

Official name Republic of Croatia
Formation 1991 / 1991
Capital Zagreb
Population 4.4 million / 202 people per sq mile (78 people per sq km)
Total area 21,831 sq. miles (56,542 sq. km)
Languages Croatian*
Religions Roman Catholic 88%, Other 7%, Orthodox Christian 4%, Muslim 1%
Ethnic mix Croat 90%, Other 5%, Serb 5%
Government Parliamentary system
Currency Kuna = 100 lipa
Literacy rate 99%
Calorie consumption 3130 kilocalories

Croatia, Republic of *see* Croatia
Crocodile *see* Limpopo
Croia *see* Krujë
Croker Island 146 E2 *island* Northern Territory, N Australia
Cromwell 151 B7 Otago, South Island, New Zealand
Crooked Island 54 D2 *island* SE Bahamas
Crooked Island Passage 54 C2 *channel* SE Bahamas
Crookston 45 F1 Minnesota, N USA
Crossen *see* Krosno Odrzańskie
Croton/Crotona *see* Crotone
Crotone 97 E6 *var.* Cotrone; *anc.* Croton, Crotona. Calabria, SW Italy
Croydon 89 A8 SE England, United Kingdom
Crozet Basin 141 B6 *undersea basin* S Indian Ocean
Crozet Islands 141 B7 *island group* French Southern and Antarctic Territories
Crozet Plateau 141 B7 *var.* Crozet Plateaus. *undersea plateau* SW Indian Ocean
Crozet Plateaus *see* Crozet Plateau
Crystal Brook 149 B6 South Australia
Csaca *see* Čadca

Csakathurn/Csáktornya *see* Čakovec
Csíkszereda *see* Miercurea-Ciuc
Csorna 99 C6 Győr-Moson-Sopron, NW Hungary
Csurgó 99 C7 Somogy, SW Hungary
Cuando 78 C2 *var.* Kwando. *river* S Africa
Cuango 78 B1 *var.* Kwango. *river* Angola/Dem. Rep. Congo
Cuango *see* Kwango
Cuanza 78 B1 *var.* Kwanza. *river* C Angola
Cuauhtémoc 50 C2 Chihuahua, N Mexico
Cuautla 51 E4 Morelos, S Mexico
Cuba 54 B2 *off.* Republic of Cuba. *country* W West Indies

CUBA
West Indies

Official name Republic of Cuba
Formation 1902 / 1902
Capital Havana
Population 11.3 million / 264 people per sq mile (102 people per sq km) / 76%
Total area 42,803 sq. miles (110,860 sq. km)
Languages Spanish
Religions Nonreligious 49%, Roman Catholic 40%, Atheist 6%, Other 4%, Protestant 1%
Ethnic mix Mulatto (mixed race) 51%, White 37%, Black 11%, Chinese 1%
Government One-party state
Currency Cuban peso = 100 centavos
Literacy rate 99%
Calorie consumption 3258 kilocalories

Cubal 78 B2 Benguela, W Angola
Cubango 78 B2 *var.* Kuvango, *Port.* Vila Artur de Paiva, Vila da Ponte. Huíla, SW Angola
Cubango 78 B2 *var.* Kavango, Kavengo, Kubango, Okavango, Okavanggo. *river* S Africa
Cuba, Republic of *see* Cuba
Cúcuta 58 C2 *var.* San José de Cúcuta. Norte de Santander, N Colombia
Cuddapah 132 C2 Andhra Pradesh, S India
Cuenca 60 B2 Azuay, S Ecuador
Cuenca 93 E3 *anc.* Conca. Castilla-La Mancha, C Spain
Cuera *see* Chur
Cuernavaca 51 E4 Morelos, S Mexico
Cuiabá 63 E3 *prev.* Cuyabá. *state capital* Mato Grosso, SW Brazil
Cúige *see* Connaught
Cúige Laighean *see* Leinster
Cúige Mumhan *see* Munster
Cuijck 86 D4 Noord-Brabant, SE Netherlands
Cúil Raithin *see* Coleraine
Cuito 78 B2 *var.* Kwito. *river* SE Angola
Cukai 138 B3 *var.* Chukai, Kemaman. Terengganu, Peninsular Malaysia
Cularo *see* Grenoble
Culiacán 50 C3 *var.* Culiacán Rosales, Culiacán-Rosales. Sinaloa, C Mexico
Culiacán-Rosales/Culiacán Rosales *see* Culiacán
Cullera 93 F3 Valenciana, E Spain
Cullman 42 C2 Alabama, S USA
Culm *see* Chełmno
Culmsee *see* Chełmża
Cumaná 59 E1 Sucre, NE Venezuela
Cumbal, Nevado de 58 A4 *elevation* S Colombia
Cumberland 41 E4 Maryland, NE USA
Cumberland Plateau 42 D1 *plateau* E USA
Cumberland Sound 37 H3 *inlet* Baffin Island, Nunavut, NE Canada
Cumpas 50 B2 Sonora, NW Mexico
Cuneo 96 A2 *Fr.* Coni. Piemonte, NW Italy
Cunnamulla 149 C5 Queensland, E Australia
Ćuprija 100 E4 Serbia, E Serbia
Curaçao 55 E5 *prev.* Dutch West Indies. *Dutch autonomous region* S Caribbean Sea
Curaçao 55 E5 *island* Lesser Antilles
Curia Rhaetorum *see* Chur
Curicó 64 B4 Maule, C Chile
Curieta *see* Krk
Curitiba 63 E4 *prev.* Curytiba. *state capital* Paraná, S Brazil
Curtbunar *see* Tervel

Curtea de Argeş 108 C4 *var.* Curtea-de-Arges. Argeş, S Romania
Curtea-de-Arges *see* Curtea de Argeş
Curtici 108 A4 *Ger.* Kurtitsch, *Hung.* Kürtös. Arad, W Romania
Curtis Island 148 E4 *island* Queensland, SE Australia
Curytiba *see* Curitiba
Curzola *see* Korčula
Cusco 61 E4 *var.* Cuzco. Cusco, C Peru
Cusset 91 C5 Allier, C France
Cutch, Gulf of *see* Kachchh, Gulf of
Cuttack 135 F4 Orissa, E India
Cuvier Plateau 141 E6 *undersea plateau* E Indian Ocean
Cuxhaven 94 B2 Niedersachsen, NW Germany
Cuyabá *see* Cuiabá
Cuyuni, Río *see* Cuyuni River
Cuyuni River 59 F3 *var.* Río Cuyuni. *river* Guyana/Venezuela
Cuzco *see* Cusco
Cyclades 105 D6 *var.* Kikládhes, *Eng.* Cyclades. *island group* SE Greece
Cyclades *see* Kykládes
Cydonia *see* Chaniá
Cymru *see* Wales
Cyprus 102 C4 *off.* Republic of Cyprus, *Gk.* Kypros, *Turk.* Kıbrıs, Kıbrıs Cumhuriyeti. *country* E Mediterranean Sea

CYPRUS
Southeast Europe

Official name Republic of Cyprus
Formation 1960 / 1960
Capital Nicosia
Population 1.1 million / 308 people per sq mile (119 people per sq km)
Total area 3571 sq. miles (9250 sq. km)
Languages Greek*, Turkish*
Religions Orthodox Christian 78%, Muslim 18%, Other 4%
Ethnic mix Greek 81%, Turkish 11%, Other 8%
Government Presidential system
Currency Euro (Turkish lira in TRNC) = 100 cents (euro); 100 kurus (Turkish lira)
Literacy rate 98%
Calorie consumption 2678 kilocalories

Cyprus, Republic of *see* Cyprus
Cythnos *see* Kýthnos
Czech Republic 99 A5 *Cz.* Česká Republika. *country* C Europe

CZECH REPUBLIC
Central Europe

Official name Czech Republic
Formation 1993 / 1993
Capital Prague
Population 10.5 million / 345 people per sq mile (133 people per sq km)
Total area 30,450 sq. miles (78,866 sq. km)
Languages Czech*, Slovak, Hungarian (Magyar)
Religions Roman Catholic 39%, Atheist 38%, Other 18%, Protestant 3%, Hussite 2%
Ethnic mix Czech 90%, Other 4%, Moravian 4%, Slovak 2%
Government Parliamentary system
Currency Czech koruna = 100 haleru
Literacy rate 99%
Calorie consumption 3305 kilocalories

Czenstochau *see* Częstochowa
Czernowitz *see* Chernivtsi
Częstochowa 98 C4 *Ger.* Czenstochau, Tschenstochau, *Rus.* Chenstokhov. Śląskie, S Poland
Człuchów 98 C3 *Ger.* Schlochau. Pomorskie, N Poland

D

Dabajuro 58 C1 Falcón, NW Venezuela
Dabeiba 58 B2 Antioquia, NW Colombia
Dąbrowa Tarnowska 99 D5 Małopolskie, S Poland
Dabryn' 107 C8 *Rus.* Dobryn'. Homyel'skaya Voblasts', SE Belarus
Dacca *see* Dhaka
Daegu 129 E4 *Jap.* Taikyū; *prev.* Taegu. SE South Korea

Daejeon 129 E4 , *Jap.* Taiden; *prev.* Taejŏn. C South Korea
Dagana 74 B3 N Senegal
Dagda 106 D4 SE Latvia
Dagden *see* Hiiumaa
Dagenham 89 B8 United Kingdom
Dağlıq Quarabağ *see* Nagorno-Karabakh
Dagö *see* Hiiumaa
Dagupan 139 E1 *off.* Dagupan City. Luzon, N Philippines
Dagupan City *see* Dagupan
Dahm, Ramlat 121 B6 *desert* NW Yemen
Dahomey *see* Benin
Daihoku *see* T'aipei
Daimiel 92 D3 Castilla-La Mancha, C Spain
Daimonia 105 B7 Pelopónnisos, S Greece
Dainan *see* Tainan
Daingin, Bá an *see* Dingle Bay
Dairen *see* Dalian
Dakar 74 B3 *country capital* (Senegal) W Senegal
Dakhla *see* Ad Dakhla
Dakoro 75 G3 Maradi, S Niger
Đakovica *see* Gjakovë
Đakovo 100 C3 *var.* Djakovo, *Hung.* Diakovár. Osijek-Baranja, E Croatia
Dakshin *see* Deccan
Dalain Hob 126 D3 *var.* Ejin Qi. Nei Mongol Zizhiqu, N China
Dalai Nor *see* Hulun Nur
Dalaman 116 A4 Muğla, SW Turkey
Dalandzadgad 127 E3 Ömnögovi, S Mongolia
Đa Lat 137 E6 Lâm Đồng, S Vietnam
Dalby 149 D5 Queensland, E Australia
Dale City 41 E4 Virginia, NE USA
Dalhart 49 E1 Texas, SW USA
Dali 128 A6 *var.* Xiaguan. Yunnan, SW China
Dalian 128 D4 *var.* Dairen, Dalien, Jay Dairen, Lüda, Ta-lien, *Rus.* Dalny. Liaoning, NE China
Dalien *see* Dalian
Dallas 49 G2 Texas, SW USA
Dalmacija 100 B4 *Eng.* Dalmatia, *Ger.* Dalmatien, *It.* Dalmazia. *cultural region* S Croatia
Dalmatia/Dalmatien/Dalmazia *see* Dalmacija
Dalny *see* Dalian
Dalton 42 D1 Georgia, SE USA
Dálvvadis *see* Jokkmokk
Daly Waters 148 A2 Northern Territory, N Australia
Damachova 107 A6 *var.* Damachova, *Pol.* Domaczewo, *Rus.* Domachëvo. Brestskaya Voblasts', SW Belarus
Damachova *see* Damachova
Damān 134 C4 Damān and Diu, W India
Damara 76 C4 Ombella-Mpoko, S Central African Republic
Damas *see* Dimashq
Damasco *see* Dimashq
Damascus *see* Dimashq
Qolleh-ye Damavand 120 D3 *mountain* N Iran
Damietta *see* Dumyât
Dammām *see* Ad Dammām
Damoûr 119 A5 *var.* Ad Dāmūr. W Lebanon
Dampier 146 A4 Western Australia
Dampier, Selat 139 F4 *strait* Papua, E Indonesia
Damqawt 121 D6 *var.* Damqut. E Yemen
Damqut *see* Damqawt
Damxung 126 C5 *var.* Gongtang. Xizang Zizhiqu, W China
Danakil Desert 72 D4 *var.* Afar Depression, Danakil Plain. *desert* E Africa
Danakil Plain *see* Danakil Desert
Danané 74 D5 W Côte d'Ivoire
Đa Nẵng 137 E5 *prev.* Tourane. Quang Nam-Da Nẵng, C Vietnam
Danborg *see* Daneborg
Dandong 128 D3 *var.* Tan-tung; *prev.* An-tung. Liaoning, NE China
Daneborg 83 E3 *var.* Danborg. Tunu, N Greenland
Dänew *see* Galkynyş
Dangara *see* Danghara
Dangerous Archipelago *see* Tuamotu, Îles
Danghara 123 E3 *Rus.* Dangara. SW Tajikistan
Danghe Nanshan 126 D3 *mountain range* W China

Dang Raek, Phanom/Dangrek, Chaine des *see* Dângrêk, Chuôr Phnum
Chuor Phnum Dangrek 137 D5 *var.* Phanom Dang Raek, Phanom Dong Rak, *Fr.* Chaine des Dangrek. *mountain range* Cambodia/Thailand
Dangriga 52 C1 *prev.* Stann Creek. Stann Creek, E Belize
Danish West Indies *see* Virgin Islands (US)
Danlí 52 D2 El Paraíso, S Honduras
Danmark *see* Denmark
Danmarksstraedet *see* Denmark Strait
Dannenberg 94 C3 Niedersachsen, N Germany
Dannevirke 150 D4 Manawatu-Wanganui, North Island, New Zealand
Dantzig *see* Gdańsk
Danube 81 E4 *Bul.* Dunav, *Cz.* Dunaj, *Ger.* Donau, *Hung.* Duna, *Rom.* Dunărea. *river* C Europe
Danubian Plain 104 C2 *Eng.* Danubian Plain. *lowlands* N Bulgaria
Danubian Plain *see* Dunavska Ravnina
Danum *see* Doncaster
Danville 41 E5 Virginia, NE USA
Danxian/Dan Xian *see* Danzhou
Danzhou 128 C7 *prev.* Danxian, Dan Xian, Nada. Hainan, S China
Danzig *see* Gdańsk
Danziger Bucht *see* Danzig, Gulf of
Danzig, Gulf of 98 C2 *var.* Gulf of Gdańsk, *Ger.* Danziger Bucht, *Pol.* Zakota Gdańska, *Rus.* Gdan'skaya Bukhta. *gulf* N Poland
Daqm *see* Duqm
Đa'ã 119 B5 *var.* Der'a, *Fr.* Déraa. Dar'ā, SW Syria
Darabani 108 C3 Botoşani, NW Romania
Daraut-Kurgan *see* Daroot-Korgon
Dardanelles 116 A2 *Eng.* Dardanelles. *strait* NW Turkey
Dardanelles *see* Çanakkale Boğazı
Dardanelli *see* Çanakkale
Dar-el-Beida *see* Casablanca
Dar es Salaam 73 C7 Dar es Salaam, E Tanzania
Darfield 151 C6 Canterbury, South Island, New Zealand
Darfur 72 A4 *var.* Darfur Massif. *cultural region* W Sudan
Darfur Massif *see* Darfur
Darhan 127 E2 Darhan Uul, N Mongolia
Darién, Golfo del *see* Darién, Gulf of
Darién, Gulf of 54 A2 *Sp.* Golfo del Darién. *gulf* S Caribbean Sea
Darién, Isthmus of *see* Panama, Istmo de
Darién, Serranía del 53 H5 *mountain range* Colombia/Panama
Dario *see* Ciudad Darío
Darioriguum *see* Vannes
Darjeeling *see* Därjiling
Därjiling 135 F3 *prev.* Darjeeling. West Bengal, NE India
Darling River 149 C6 *river* New South Wales, SE Australia
Darlington 89 D5 N England, United Kingdom
Darmstadt 95 B5 Hessen, SW Germany
Darnah 71 G2 *var.* Dérna. NE Libya
Darnley, Cape 154 D2 *cape* Antarctica
Daroca 93 E2 Aragón, NE Spain
Daroot-Korgon 123 F3 *var.* Daraut-Kurgan. Oshskaya Oblast', SW Kyrgyzstan
Dartford 89 B8 SE England, United Kingdom
Dartmoor 89 C7 *moorland* SW England, United Kingdom
Dartmouth 39 F4 Nova Scotia, SE Canada
Darvaza *see* Derweze, Turkmenistan
Darwin 146 D2 *prev.* Palmerston, Port Darwin. *territory capital* Northern Territory, N Australia
Darwin, Isla 60 A4 *island* Galápagos, Galápagos Islands, W Ecuador
Dashhowuz *see* Daşoguz
Dashkovka 107 D6 *Rus.* Dashkovka. Mahilyowskaya Voblasts', E Belarus
Dashkovka *see* Dashkovka
Daşoguz 122 C2 *Rus.* Dashkhovuz, *Turkm.* Dashhowuz; *prev.* Daşhowuz, Dashhowuz, Tashauz. Daşoguz Welaýaty, N Turkmenistan
Đa, Sông *see* Black River
Datong 128 C3 *var.* Tatung, Ta-t'ung. Shanxi, C China
Daugava *see* Western Dvina

Daugavpils 106 D4 *Ger.* Dünaburg; *prev.*
Rus. Dvinsk. SE Latvia
Daung Kyun 137 B6 *island* S Myanmar
(Burma)
Dauphiné 91 D5 *cultural region* E France
Dāvangere 132 C2 Karnātaka, W India
Davao 139 F3 *off.* Davao City.
Mindanao, S Philippines
Davao City *see* Davao
Davao Gulf 139 F3 *gulf* Mindanao,
S Philippines
Davenport 45 G3 Iowa, C USA
David 53 E5 Chiriquí, W Panama
Davie Ridge 141 A5 *undersea ridge*
W Indian Ocean
Davis 154 D3 *Australian research station*
Antarctica
Davis Sea 154 D3 *sea* Antarctica
Davis Strait 82 B3 *strait* Baffin Bay/
Labrador Sea
Dawei 137 B5 *var.* Tavoy, Htawei.
Tanintharyi, S Myanmar (Burma)
Dawlat Qatar *see* Qatar
Dax 91 B6 *var.* Acqs. Aquae Augustae,
Aquae Tarbelicae. Landes, SW France
Dayr az Zawr 118 D3 *var.* Deir ez Zor.
Dayr az Zawr, E Syria
Dayton 40 C4 Ohio, N USA
Daytona Beach 43 E4 Florida, SE USA
De Aar 78 C5 Northern Cape, C South
Africa
Dead Sea 119 B6 *var.* Bahret Lut, Lacus
Asphaltites, *Ar.* Al Baḥr al Mayyit,
Baḥrat Lūṭ, *Heb.* Yam HaMelaḥ. *salt
lake* Israel/Jordan
Deán Funes 64 C3 Córdoba, C Argentina
Death Valley 47 C7 *valley* California,
W USA
Deatnu 84 D2 *Fin.* Tenojoki, *Nor.* Tana.
river Finland/Norway
Debar 101 D6 *var.* Dibra, *Turk.* Debre.
W FYR Macedonia
De Behagle *see* Laï
Dębica 99 D5 Podkarpackie, SE Poland
De Bildt *see* De Bilt
De Bilt 86 C3 *var.* De Bildt. Utrecht,
C Netherlands
Dębno 98 B3 Zachodnio-pomorskie,
NW Poland
Debre *see* Debar
Deggendorf 99 D6 *Ger.* Debreczin, *Rom.*
Debreţin; *prev.* Debreczen. Hajdú-
Bihar, E Hungary
Debreczen/Debreczin *see* Debrecen
Debreţin *see* Debrecen
Decatur 42 C1 Alabama, S USA
Decatur 40 B4 Illinois, N USA
Deccan 134 D5 *Hind.* Dakshin. *plateau*
C India
Děčín 98 B4 *Ger.* Tetschen. Ústecký Kraj,
NW Czech Republic
Dedeagač/Dedeagach *see* Alexandroúpoli
Dedemsvaart 86 E3 Overijssel,
E Netherlands
Dee 88 C3 *river* NE Scotland, United
Kingdom
Deering 36 C2 Alaska, USA
Deés *see* Dej
Deggendorf 95 D6 Bayern, SE Germany
Değirmenlik 102 C5 *Gk.* Kythréa.
N Cyprus
Deh Bīd *see* Şafāshahr
Dehli *see* Delhi
Deh Shū *see* Dīshū
Deinze 87 B5 Oost-Vlaanderen,
NW Belgium
Deir ez Zor *see* Dayr az Zawr
Deirgeirt, Loch *see* Derg, Lough
Dej 108 B3 *Hung.* Dés; *prev.* Deés. Cluj,
NW Romania
De Jouwer *see* Joure
Dekéleia *see* Dhekélia
Dékoa 76 C4 Kémo, C Central African
Republic
De Land 43 E4 Florida, SE USA
Delano 47 C7 California, W USA
Delārām *see* Dilārām
Delaware 40 D4 Ohio, N USA
Delaware 41 F4 *off.* State of Delaware,
also known as Blue Hen State, Diamond
State, First State. *state* NE USA
Delft 86 C4 Zuid-Holland,
W Netherlands
Delfzijl 86 E1 Groningen,
NE Netherlands
Delgo 72 B3 Northern, N Sudan
Delhi 134 D3 *var.* Dehli, *Hind.* Dilli, *hist.*
Shahjahanabad. *union territory capital*
Delhi, N India

Delicias 50 D2 *var.* Ciudad Delicias.
Chihuahua, N Mexico
Déli-Kárpátok *see* Carpaţii Meridionalii
Delmenhorst 94 B3 Niedersachsen,
NW Germany
Del Rio 49 F4 Texas, SW USA
Deltona 43 E4 Florida, SE USA
Demba 77 D6 Kasai-Occidental, C Dem.
Rep. Congo
Dembia 76 D4 Mbomou, SE Central
African Republic
Demchok 126 A5 *var.* Dêmqog. *disputed
region* China/India
Demerara Plain 56 C2 *abyssal plain*
W Atlantic Ocean
Deming 48 C3 New Mexico, SW USA
Demmin 94 C2 Mecklenburg-
Vorpommern, NE Germany
Demopolis 42 C2 Alabama, S USA
Dêmqog 126 A5 *var.* Demchok. China/
India
Denali *see* McKinley, Mount
Denau *see* Denov
Dender 87 B6 *Fr.* Dendre. *river*
W Belgium
Dendre *see* Dender
Denekamp 86 E3 Overijssel,
E Netherlands
Den Haag *see* 's-Gravenhage
Denham 147 A5 Western Australia
Den Ham 86 E3 Overijssel,
E Netherlands
Den Helder 86 C2 Noord-Holland,
NW Netherlands
Dénia 93 F4 Valenciana, E Spain
Deniliquin 149 C7 New South Wales,
SE Australia
Denison 45 F3 Iowa, C USA
Denison 49 G2 Texas, SW USA
Denizli 116 B4 Denizli, SW Turkey
Denmark 85 A7 *off.* Kingdom of
Denmark, *Dan.* Danmark; *anc.* Hafnia.
country N Europe

DENMARK
Northern Europe

Official name Kingdom of Denmark
Formation 950 / 1944
Capital Copenhagen
Population 5.6 million / 342 people
per sq mile (132 people per sq km)
Total area 16,639 sq. miles (43,094 sq. km)
Languages Danish
Religions Evangelical Lutheran 95%,
Roman Catholic 3%, Muslim 2%
Ethnic mix Danish 96%, Other
(including Scandinavian and Turkish) 3%,
Faeroese and Inuit 1%
Government Parliamentary system
Currency Danish krone = 100 øre
Literacy rate 99%
Calorie consumption 3378 kilocalories

Denmark, Kingdom of *see* Denmark
Denmark Strait 82 D4 *var.*
Danmarksstraedet. *strait* Greenland/
Iceland
Dennery 55 F1 E Saint Lucia
Denov 123 E3 *Rus.* Denau.
Surkhondaryo Viloyati, S Uzbekistan
Denpasar 138 D5 *prev.* Paloe. Bali,
C Indonesia
Denton 49 G2 Texas, SW USA
D'Entrecasteaux Islands 144 B3 *island
group* SE Papua New Guinea
Denver 44 D4 *state capital* Colorado,
C USA
Der'a/Derá/Déraa *see* Dar'ā
Dera Ghāzi Khān 134 C2 *var.* Dera
Ghāzikhān. Punjab, C Pakistan
Dera Ghāzikhān *see* Dera Ghāzi Khān
Đeravica *see* Gjeravicë
Derbent 111 B8 Respublika Dagestan,
SW Russian Federation
Derby 89 D6 C England, United
Kingdom
Dereli *see* Gönnoi
Dergachi *see* Derhachi
Derg, Lough 89 A6 *Ir.* Loch Deirgeirt.
lake W Ireland
Derhachi 109 G2 *Rus.* Dergachi.
Kharkiv'ska Oblast', E Ukraine
De Ridder 42 A3 Louisiana, S USA
Dérna *see* Darnah
Dertosa *see* Tortosa
Derventa 100 B3 Republika Srpska,
N Bosnia and Herzegovina

Derweze 122 C2 *Rus.* Darvaza. Ahal
Welaýaty, C Turkmenistan
Dés *see* Dej
Deschutes River 46 B3 *river* Oregon,
NW USA
Desē 72 C4 *var.* Desse, *It.* Dessie. Āmara,
N Ethiopia
Deseado, Río 65 B7 *river* S Argentina
Desertas, Ilhas 70 A2 *island group*
Madeira, Portugal, NE Atlantic Ocean
Deshu *see* Dīshū
Des Moines 45 F3 *state capital* Iowa,
C USA
Desna 109 E2 *river* Russian Federation/
Ukraine
Dessau 94 C4 Sachsen-Anhalt,
E Germany
Desse *see* Desē
Dessie *see* Desē
Destèrro *see* Florianópolis
Detroit 40 D3 Michigan, N USA
Detroit Lakes 45 F2 Minnesota, N USA
Deurne 87 D5 Noord-Brabant,
SE Netherlands
Deutschendorf *see* Poprad
Deutsch-Eylau *see* Iława
Deutsch Krone *see* Wałcz
Deutschland/Deutschland,
Bundesrepublik *see* Germany
Deutsch-Südwestafrika *see* Namibia
Deva 108 B4 *Ger.* Diemrich, *Hung.* Déva.
Hunedoara, W Romania
Déva *see* Deva
Deva *see* Chester
Devana *see* Aberdeen
Devana Castra *see* Chester
Đeventer 86 D3 Overijssel, E Netherlands
Devils Lake 45 E1 North Dakota, N USA
Devoll *see* Devollit, Lumi i
Devollit, Lumi i 101 D6 *var.* Devoll.
river SE Albania
Devon Island 37 F2 *prev.* North Devon
Island. *island* Parry Islands, Nunavut,
NE Canada
Devonport 149 C8 Tasmania,
SE Australia
Devrek 116 C2 Zonguldak, N Turkey
Dexter 45 H5 Missouri, C USA
Deynau *see* Galkynyş
Dezfūl 120 C3 *var.* Dizful. Khūzestān,
SW Iran
Dezhou 128 D4 Shandong, E China
Dhaka 135 G4 *prev.* Dacca. *country
capital* (Bangladesh) Dhaka,
C Bangladesh
Dhanbād 135 F4 Jhārkhand, NE India
Dhekélia 102 C5 *Eng.* Dhekelia, *Gk.*
Dekéleia. *UK air base* SE Cyprus
see Dhekélia
Dhidhimótikhon *see* Didymóteicho
Dhíkti Ori *see* Díkti
Dhodhekánisos *see* Dodekánisa
Dhomokós *see* Domokós
Dhráma *see* Dráma
Dhrepanon, Akrotírio *see* Drépano,
Akrotírio
Dhún na nGall, Bá *see* Donegal Bay
Dhuusa Marreeb 73 E5 *var.* Dusa
Marreb, *It.* Dusa Mareb. Galguduud,
C Somalia
Diakovár *see* Đakovo
Diamantina, Chapada 63 F3 *mountain
range* E Brazil
Diamantina Fracture Zone 141 E6
tectonic feature E Indian Ocean
Diamond State *see* Delaware
Diarbekr *see* Diyarbakır
Dibio *see* Dijon
Dibra *see* Debar
Dibrugarh 135 H3 Assam, NE India
Dickinson 44 D2 North Dakota, N USA
Dicle *see* Tigris
Didimotiho *see* Didymóteicho
Didymóteicho 104 D3 *var.*
Dhidhimótikhon, Didimotiho.
Anatolikí Makedonía kai Thráki,
NE Greece
Diedenhofen *see* Thionville
Diekirch 87 D7 Diekirch, C Luxembourg
Diemrich *see* Deva
Điện Biên *see* Điện Biên Phu
Điện Biên Phu 136 D3 *var.* Bien Bien,
Điện Biên. Lai Châu, N Vietnam
Diepenbeek 87 D6 Limburg, NE Belgium
Diepholz 94 B3 Niedersachsen,
NW Germany
Dieppe 90 C2 Seine-Maritime, N France
Dieren 86 D4 Gelderland, E Netherlands

Differdange 87 D8 Luxembourg,
SW Luxembourg
Digne 91 D6 *var.* Digne-les-Bains.
Alpes-de-Haute-Provence, SE France
Digne-les-Bains *see* Digne
Digoel *see* Digul, Sungai
Digoin 90 C4 Saône-et-Loire, C France
Digul, Sungai 139 H5 *prev.* Digoel. *river*
Papua, E Indonesia
Dihang *see* Brahmaputra
Dijlah *see* Tigris
Dijon 90 D4 *anc.* Dibio. Côte d'Or,
C France
Dikhil 72 D4 SW Djibouti
Dikson 114 D2 Krasnoyarskiy Kray,
N Russian Federation
Dikti 105 D8 *var.* Dhíkti Ori.
mountain range Kríti, Greece,
E Mediterranean Sea
Dilārām 122 D5 *prev.* Delārām. Nīmrōz,
SW Afghanistan
Dili 139 F5 *var.* Dilli, Dilly. *country
capital* (East Timor) N East Timor
Dilia 75 G3 *var.* Dilly. *river* SE Niger
Di Linh 137 E6 Lâm Đông, S Vietnam
Dilli *see* Dili, East Timor
Dilli *see* Delhi, India
Dillia *see* Dilia
Dilling 72 B4 *var.* Ad Dalanj. Southern
Kordofan, C Sudan
Dillon 44 B2 Montana, NW USA
Dilly *see* Dili
Dilolo 77 D7 Katanga, S Dem. Rep.
Congo
Dimashq 119 B5 *var.* Ash Shām, Esh
Sham, *Eng.* Damascus, *Fr.* Damas, *It.*
Damasco. *country capital* (Syria) Rif
Dimashq, SW Syria
Dimitrovgrad 104 D3 Khaskovo,
S Bulgaria
Dimitrovgrad 111 C6 *prev.* Caribrod.
Serbia, SE Serbia
Dimitrovo *see* Pernik
Dimovo 104 B1 Vidin, NW Bulgaria
Dinajpur 135 F3 Rajshahi,
NW Bangladesh
Dinan 90 B3 Côtes d'Armor,
NW France
Dinant 87 C7 Namur, S Belgium
Dinar 116 B4 Afyon, SW Turkey
Dinara *see* Dinaric Alps
Dinaric Alps 100 C4 *var.* Dinara.
mountain range Bosnia and
Herzegovina/Croatia
Dindigul 132 C3 Tamil Nādu, SE India
Dingle Bay 89 A6 *Ir.* Bá an Daingin. *bay*
SW Ireland
Dinguiraye 74 C4 N Guinea
Diourbel 74 B3 W Senegal
Dirê Dawa 73 D5 *var.* Dire Dawa. E Ethiopia
Dirk Hartog Island 147 A5 *island*
Western Australia
Dirschau *see* Tczew
Disappointment, Lake 146 C4 *salt lake*
Western Australia
Discovery Bay 54 B4 Middlesex,
Jamaica, Greater Antilles, C Jamaica
Caribbean Sea
Dīshū 122 C5 *var.* Deshu; *prev.* Deh Shū.
Helmand, S Afghanistan
Disko Bugt *see* Qeqertarsuup Tunua
Dispur 135 G3 *state capital* Assam,
NE India
Divinópolis 63 F4 Minas Gerais,
SE Brazil
Divo 74 D5 S Côte d'Ivoire
Divodurum Mediomatricum *see* Metz
Diyarbakır 117 F4 *var.* Diarbekr; *anc.*
Amida. Diyarbakır, SE Turkey
Dizful *see* Dezfūl
Djailolo *see* Halmahera, Pulau
Djajapura *see* Jayapura
Djakarta *see* Jakarta
Djakovo *see* Đakovo
Djambala 77 B6 Plateaux, C Congo
Djambi *see* Hari, Batang
Djambi *see* Jambi
Djanet 71 E4 *prev.* Fort Charlet.
SE Algeria
Djéblé *see* Jablah
Djéma 76 D4 Haut-Mbomou, E Central
African Republic
Djember *see* Jember
Djérablous *see* Jarābulus
Djerba *see* Jerba, Île de
Djerba 71 F4 *var.* Djerba, Jazīrat Jarbah.
island E Tunisia
Djerba *see* Jerba, Île de
Djérem 76 B4 *river* C Cameroon

Djevdjelija *see* Gevgelija
Djibouti 72 D4 *var.* Jibuti. *country capital* (Djibouti) E Djibouti
Djibouti 72 D4 *off.* Republic of Djibouti, *var.* Jibuti; *prev.* French Somaliland, French Territory of the Afars and Issas, *Fr.* Côte Française des Somalis, Territoire Français des Afars et des Issas. *country* E Africa

DJIBOUTI
East Africa

Official name Republic of Djibouti
Formation 1977 / 1977
Capital Djibouti
Population 900,000 / 101 people per sq mile (39 people per sq km)
Total area 8494 sq. miles (22,000 sq. km)
Languages Somali, Afar, French*, Arabic*
Religions Muslim (mainly Sunni) 94%, Christian 6%
Ethnic mix Issa 60%, Afar 35%, Other 5%
Government Presidential system
Currency Djibouti franc = 100 centimes
Literacy rate 70%
Calorie consumption 2419 kilocalories

Djibouti, Republic of *see* Djibouti
Djokjakarta *see* Yogyakarta
Djourab, Erg du 76 C2 *desert* N Chad
Djúpivogur 83 E5 Austurland, SE Iceland
Dmitriyevsk *see* Makiyivka
Dnepr *see* Dnieper
Dneprodzerzhinsk *see* Romaniv
Dneprodzerzhinskoye Vodokhranilishche *see* Dniprodzerzhyns'ke Vodoskhovyshche
Dnepropetrovsk *see* Dnipropetrovs'k
Dneprorudnoye *see* Dniprorudne
Dnestr *see* Dniester
Dnieper 81 F4 *Bel.* Dnyapro, *Rus.* Dnepr, *Ukr.* Dnipro. *river* E Europe
Dnieper Lowland 109 E2 *Bel.* Prydnyaprowskaya Nizina, *Ukr.* Prydniprovs'ka Nyzovyna. *lowlands* Belarus/Ukraine
Dniester 81 E4 *Rom.* Nistru, *Rus.* Dnestr, *Ukr.* Dnister; *anc.* Tyras. *river* Moldova/Ukraine
Dnipro *see* Dnieper
Dniprodzerzhyns'k *see* Romaniv
Dniprodzerzhyns'ke Vodoskhovyshche 109 F3 *Rus.* Dneprodzerzhinskoye Vodokhranilishche. *reservoir* C Ukraine
Dnipropetrovs'k 109 F3 *Rus.* Dnepropetrovsk; *prev.* Yekaterinoslav. Dnipropetrovs'ka Oblast', E Ukraine
Dniprorudne 109 F3 *Rus.* Dneprorudnoye. Zaporiz'ka Oblast', SE Ukraine
Dnister *see* Dniester
Dnyapro *see* Dnieper
Doba 76 C4 Logone-Oriental, S Chad
Döbeln 94 D4 Sachsen, E Germany
Doberai Peninsula 139 G4 *Dut.* Vogelkop. *peninsula* Papua, E Indonesia
Doboj 100 C3 Republika Srpska, N Bosnia and Herzegovina
Dobre Miasto 98 D2 *Ger.* Guttstadt. Warmińsko-mazurskie, NE Poland
Dobrich 104 E1 *Rom.* Bazargic; *prev.* Tolbukhin. Dobrich, NE Bulgaria
Dobrush 107 D7 Homyel'skaya Voblasts', SE Belarus
Dobryn' *see* Dabryn'
Dodecanese 105 D6 *var.* Nóties Sporádes, *Eng.* Dodecanese; *prev.* Dhodhekánisos, Dodekanisos. *island group* SE Greece
Dodecanese *see* Dodekánisa
Dodekanisos *see* Dodekánisa
Dodge City 45 E5 Kansas, C USA
Dodoma 69 D5 *country capital* (Tanzania) Dodoma, C Tanzania
Dogana 96 E1 NE San Marino Europe
Dogo 131 B6 *island* Oki-shotō, SW Japan
Dogondoutchi 75 F3 Dosso, SW Niger
Dogrular *see* Pravda
Doğubayazıt 117 F3 Ağrı, E Turkey
Doğu Karadeniz Dağları 117 E3 *var.* Anadolu Dağları. *mountain range* NE Turkey
Doha *see* Ad Dawḩah
Doire *see* Londonderry

Dokkum 86 D1 Fryslân, N Netherlands
Dokuchayevs'k 109 G3 *var.* Dokuchayevsk. Donets'ka Oblast', SE Ukraine
Dokuchayevsk *see* Dokuchayevs'k
Doldrums Fracture Zone 66 C4 *fracture zone* W Atlantic Ocean
Dôle 90 D4 Jura, E France
Dolina *see* Dolyna
Dolinskaya *see* Dolyns'ka
Dolisie 77 B6 *prev.* Loubomo. Niari, S Congo
Dolomites 96 C1 *var.* Dolomiti, *Eng.* Dolomites. *mountain range* NE Italy
Dolomites/Dolomiti *see* Dolomitiche, Alpi
Dolores 64 D4 Buenos Aires, E Argentina
Dolores 52 B1 Petén, N Guatemala
Dolores 64 D4 Soriano, SW Uruguay
Dolores Hidalgo 51 E4 *var.* Ciudad de Dolores Hidalgo. Guanajuato, C Mexico
Dolyna 108 B2 *Rus.* Dolina. Ivano-Frankivs'ka Oblast', W Ukraine
Dolyns'ka 109 F3 *Rus.* Dolinskaya. Kirovohrads'ka Oblast', S Ukraine
Domachëvo/Domaczewo *see* Damachava
Dombås 85 B5 Oppland, S Norway
Domel Island *see* Letsôk-aw Kyun
Domesnes, Cape *see* Kolkasrags
Domeyko 64 B3 Atacama, N Chile
Dominica 55 H4 *off.* Commonwealth of Dominica. *country* E West Indies

DOMINICA
West Indies

Official name Commonwealth of Dominica
Formation 1978 / 1978
Capital Roseau
Population 73,126 / 252 people per sq mile (98 people per sq km)
Total area 291 sq. miles (754 sq. km)
Languages French Creole, English*
Religions Roman Catholic 77%, Protestant 15%, Other 8%
Ethnic mix Black 87%, Mixed race 9%, Carib 3%, Other 1%
Government Parliamentary system
Currency East Caribbean dollar = 100 cents
Literacy rate 88%
Calorie consumption 3147 kilocalories

Dominica Channel *see* Martinique Passage
Dominica, Commonwealth of *see* Dominica
Dominican Republic 55 E2 *country* C West Indies

DOMINICAN REPUBLIC
West Indies

Official name Dominican Republic
Formation 1865 / 1865
Capital Santo Domingo
Population 10.1 million / 541 people per sq mile (209 people per sq km)
Total area 18,679 sq. miles (48,380 sq. km)
Languages Spanish*, French Creole
Religions Roman Catholic 95%, Other and nonreligious 5%
Ethnic mix Mixed race 73%, European 16%, African 11%
Government Presidential system
Currency Dominican Republic peso = 100 centavos
Literacy rate 88%
Calorie consumption 2491 kilocalories

Domokós 105 B5 *var.* Dhomokós. Stereá Elláda, C Greece
Don 111 B6 *var.* Duna, Tanais. *river* SW Russian Federation
Donau *see* Danube
Donauwörth 95 C6 Bayern, S Germany
Don Benito 92 C3 Extremadura, W Spain
Doncaster 89 D5 *anc.* Danum. N England, United Kingdom
Dondo 78 B1 Cuanza Norte, NW Angola
Donegal 89 B5 *Ir.* Dún na nGall. Donegal, NW Ireland
Donegal Bay 89 A5 *Ir.* Bá Dhún na nGall. *bay* NW Ireland
Donets 109 G2 *river* Russian Federation/Ukraine

Donets'k 109 G3 *Rus.* Donetsk; *prev.* Stalino. Donets'ka Oblast', E Ukraine
Dongfang 128 B7 *var.* Basuo. Hainan, S China
Dongguan 128 C6 Guangdong, S China
Đông Ha 136 E4 Quang Tri, C Vietnam
Dong Hai *see* East China Sea
Đông Hơi 136 D4 Quang Binh, C Vietnam
Dongliao *see* Liaoyuan
Dongola 72 B3 *var.* Donqola, Dunqulah. Northern, N Sudan
Dongou 77 C5 Likouala, NE Congo
Dong Rak, Phanom *see* Dângrêk, Chuôr Phnum
Dongting Hu 128 C5 *var.* Tung-t'ing Hu. *lake* S China
Donostia/San Sebastián 93 E1 País Vasco, N Spain
Donqola *see* Dongola
Doolow 73 D5 Sumalē, E Ethiopia
Doornik *see* Tournai
Door Peninsula 40 C2 *peninsula* Wisconsin, N USA
Dooxo Nugaaleed 73 E5 *var.* Nogal Valley. *valley* E Somalia
Dordogne 91 B5 *cultural region* SW France
Dordogne 91 B5 *river* W France
Dordrecht 86 C4 *var.* Dordt, Dort. Zuid-Holland, SW Netherlands
Dordt *see* Dordrecht
Dorohoi 108 C3 Botoşani, NE Romania
Dorotea 84 C4 Västerbotten, N Sweden
Dorpat *see* Tartu
Dorre Island 147 A5 *island* Western Australia
Dort *see* Dordrecht
Dortmund 94 A4 Nordrhein-Westfalen, W Germany
Dos Hermanas 92 C4 Andalucía, S Spain
Dospad Dagh *see* Rhodope Mountains
Dospat 104 C3 Smolyan, S Bulgaria
Dothan 42 D3 Alabama, S USA
Dotnuva 106 B4 Kaunas, C Lithuania
Douai 90 C2 *prev.* Douay; *anc.* Duacum. Nord, N France
Douala 77 A5 *var.* Duala. Littoral, W Cameroon
Douay *see* Douai
Douglas 89 C5 *dependent territory capital* (Isle of Man) E Isle of Man
Douglas 48 C3 Arizona, SW USA
Douglas 44 D3 Wyoming, C USA
Douma *see* Dūmā
Douro *see* Duero
Douvres *see* Dover
Dover 89 E7 *Fr.* Douvres, *Lat.* Dubris Portus. SE England, United Kingdom
Dover 41 F4 *state capital* Delaware, NE USA
Dover, Strait of 90 C2 *var.* Straits of Dover, *Fr.* Pas de Calais. *strait* England, United Kingdom/France
Dover, Straits of *see* Dover, Strait of
Dovrefjell 85 B5 *plateau* S Norway
Downpatrick 89 B5 *Ir.* Dún Pádraig. SE Northern Ireland, United Kingdom
Dozen 131 B6 *island* Oki-shotō, SW Japan
Dråa, Hammada du *see* Dra, Hamada du
Drač/Draç *see* Durrës
Drachten 86 D2 Fryslân, N Netherlands
Drăgăşani 108 B5 Vâlcea, SW Romania
Dragoman 104 B2 Sofiya, W Bulgaria
Dra, Hamada du 70 C3 *var.* Hammada du Dråa, Haut Plateau du Dra. *plateau* W Algeria
Dra, Haut Plateau du *see* Dra, Hamada du
Drahichyn 107 B6 *Pol.* Drohiczyn Poleski, *Rus.* Drogichin. Brestskaya Voblasts', SW Belarus
Drakensberg 78 D5 *mountain range* Lesotho/South Africa
Drake Passage 57 B8 *passage* Atlantic Ocean/Pacific Ocean
Dralfa 104 D2 Türgovishte, N Bulgaria
Dráma 104 C3 *var.* Dhráma. Anatoliki Makedonía kai Thráki, NE Greece
Dramburg *see* Drawsko Pomorskie
Drammen 85 B6 Buskerud, S Norway
Drau *see* Drava
Drava 100 C3 *var.* Drau, Eng. Drave, Hung. Dráva. *river* C Europe
Dráva/Drave *see* Drava
Drawsko Pomorskie 98 B3 *Ger.* Dramburg. Zachodnio-pomorskie, NW Poland

Drépano, Akrotírio 104 C4 *var.* Akrotírio Dhrepanon. *headland* N Greece
Drepanum *see* Trapani
Dresden 94 D4 Sachsen, E Germany
Drin *see* Drinit, Lumi i
Drina 100 C3 *river* Bosnia and Herzegovina/Serbia
Drinit, Lumi i 101 D5 *var.* Drin. *river* NW Albania
Drinit të Zi, Lumi i *see* Black Drin
Drissa *see* Drysa
Drobeta-Turnu Severin 108 B5 *prev.* Turnu Severin. Mehedinţi, SW Romania
Drogheda 89 B5 *Ir.* Droichead Átha. NE Ireland
Drogichin *see* Drahichyn
Drogobych *see* Drohobych
Drohiczyn Poleski *see* Drahichyn
Drohobych 108 B2 *Pol.* Drohobycz, *Rus.* Drogobych. L'vivs'ka Oblast', NW Ukraine
Drohobycz *see* Drohobych
Droichead Átha *see* Drogheda
Drôme 91 D5 *cultural region* E France
Dronning Maud Land 154 B2 *physical region* Antarctica
Drontheim *see* Trondheim
Drug *see* Durg
Druk-yul *see* Bhutan
Drummondville 39 E4 Québec, SE Canada
Druskieniki *see* Druskininkai
Druskininkai 107 B5 *Pol.* Druskieniki. Alytus, S Lithuania
Dryden 38 B3 Ontario, C Canada
Drysa 107 D5 *Rus.* Drissa. *river* N Belarus
Duacum *see* Douai
Duala *see* Douala
Dubai *see* Dubayy
Dubăsari 108 D3 *Rus.* Dubossary. NE Moldova
Dubawnt 37 F4 *river* Nunavut, NW Canada
Dubayy 120 D4 *Eng.* Dubai. Dubayy, NE United Arab Emirates
Dubbo 149 D6 New South Wales, SE Australia
Dublin 89 B5 *Ir.* Baile Átha Cliath; *anc.* Eblana. *country capital* (Ireland) Dublin, E Ireland
Dublin 43 E2 Georgia, SE USA
Dubno 108 C2 Rivnens'ka Oblast', NW Ukraine
Dubossary *see* Dubăsari
Dubris Portus *see* Dover
Dubrovnik 101 B5 *It.* Ragusa. Dubrovnik-Neretva, SE Croatia
Dubuque 45 G3 Iowa, C USA
Dudelange 87 D8 *var.* Forge du Sud, *Ger.* Dudelingen. Luxembourg, S Luxembourg
Dudelingen *see* Dudelange
Duero 92 D2 *Port.* Douro. *river* Portugal/Spain
Duesseldorf *see* Düsseldorf
Duffel 87 C5 Antwerpen, C Belgium
Dugi Otok 100 A4 *var.* Isola Grossa, *It.* Isola Lunga. *island* W Croatia
Duinekerke *see* Dunkerque
Duisburg 94 A4 *prev.* Duisburg-Hamborn. Nordrhein-Westfalen, W Germany
Duisburg-Hamborn *see* Duisburg
Duiven 86 D4 Gelderland, E Netherlands
Duk Faiwil 73 B5 Jonglei, E South Sudan
Dulan 126 D4 *var.* Qagan Us. Qinghai, C China
Dulce, Golfo 53 E5 *gulf* S Costa Rica
Dulce, Golfo *see* Izabal, Lago de
Dülmen 94 A4 Nordrhein-Westfalen, W Germany
Dulovo 104 E1 Silistra, NE Bulgaria
Duluth 45 G2 Minnesota, N USA
Dūmā 119 B5 *Fr.* Douma. Rif Dimashq, SW Syria
Dumas 49 E1 Texas, SW USA
Dumfries 88 C4 S Scotland, United Kingdom
Dumont d'Urville 154 C4 *French research station* Antarctica
Dumyāt 72 B1 *var.* Dumyât, *Eng.* Damietta. N Egypt
Duna *see* Danube, C Europe
Düna *see* Western Dvina
Duna *see* Don, Russian Federation
Dünaburg *see* Daugavpils

Dunaj see Wien, Austria
Dunaj see Danube, C Europe
Dunapentele see Dunaújváros
Dunárea see Danube
Dunaújváros 99 C7 prev. Dunapentele, Sztálinváros. Fejér, C Hungary
Dunav see Danube
Duncan 49 G2 Oklahoma, C USA
Dundalk 89 B5 Ir. Dún Dealgan. Louth, NE Ireland
Dún Dealgan see Dundalk
Dundee 78 D4 KwaZulu/Natal, E South Africa
Dundee 88 C4 E Scotland, United Kingdom
Dunedin 151 B7 Otago, South Island, New Zealand
Dunfermline 88 C4 C Scotland, United Kingdom
Dungu 77 E5 Orientale, NE Dem. Rep. Congo
Dungun 138 B3 var. Kuala Dungun. Terengganu, Peninsular Malaysia
Dunholme see Durham
Dunkerque 90 C2 Eng. Dunkirk, Flem. Duinekerke; prev. Dunquerque. Nord, N France
Dunkirk see Dunkerque
Dún Laoghaire 89 B6 Eng. Dunleary; prev. Kingstown. E Ireland
Dunleary see Dún Laoghaire
Dún Pádraig see Downpatrick
Dunquerque see Dunkerque
Dunqulah see Dongola
Dupnitsa 104 C2 prev. Marek, Stanke Dimitrov. Kyustendil, W Bulgaria
Duqm 121 E5 var. Daqm. E Oman
Durance 91 D6 river SE France
Durango 50 D3 var. Victoria de Durango. Durango, W Mexico
Durango 44 C5 Colorado, C USA
Durankulak 104 E1 Rom. Răcari; prev. Blatnitsa, Duranulac. Dobrich, NE Bulgaria
Durant 49 G2 Oklahoma, C USA
Duranulac see Durankulak
Durazzo see Durrës
Durban 78 D4 var. Port Natal. KwaZulu/Natal, E South Africa
Durbe 106 B3 Ger. Durben. W Latvia
Durben see Durbe
Durg 135 E4 prev. Drug. Chhattisgarh, C India
Durham 89 D5 hist. Dunholme. N England, United Kingdom
Durham 43 F1 North Carolina, SE USA
Durocortorum see Reims
Durostorum see Silistra
Durovernum see Canterbury
Durrës 101 C6 var. Durrësi, Dursi, It. Durazzo, SCr. Drač, Turk. Draç. Durrës, W Albania
Durrësi see Durrës
Dursi see Durrës
Durūz, Jabal ad 119 C5 mountain SW Syria
D'Urville Island 150 C4 island C New Zealand
Dusa Mareb/Dusa Marreb see Dhuusa Marreeb
Dushanbe 123 E3 var. Dyushambe; prev. Stalinabad, Taj. Stalinobod. country capital (Tajikistan) W Tajikistan
Düsseldorf 94 A4 var. Duesseldorf. Nordrhein-Westfalen, W Germany
Düstí 123 E3 Rus. Dusti. SW Tajikistan
Dutch East Indies see Indonesia
Dutch Guiana see Suriname
Dutch Harbor 36 B3 Unalaska Island, Alaska, USA
Dutch New Guinea see Papua
Dutch West Indies see Curaçao
Duzdab see Zāhedān
Dvina Bay see Chëshskaya Guba
Dvinsk see Daugavpils
Dyanev see Galkynyş
Dyersburg 42 C1 Tennessee, S USA
Dyushambe see Dushanbe
Dza Chu see Mekong
Dzaudzhikau see Vladikavkaz
Dzerzhinsk 111 C5 Nizhegorodskaya Oblast', W Russian Federation
Dzerzhinskiy see Nar'yan-Mar
Dzhalal-Abad 123 F2 Kir. Jalal-Abad. Dzhalal-Abadskaya Oblast', W Kyrgyzstan
Dzhambul see Taraz

Dzhankoy 109 F4 Avtonomna Respublika Krym, S Ukraine
Dzharkurgan see Jarqo'rg'on
Dzhelandy 123 F3 SE Tajikistan
Dzhergalan 123 G2 Kir. Jyrgalan. Issyk-Kul'skaya Oblast', NE Kyrgyzstan
Dzhezkazgan see Zhezkazgan
Dzhizak see Jizzax
Dzhugdzhur, Khrebet 115 G3 mountain range E Russian Federation
Dzhusaly see Zhosaly
Działdowo 98 D3 Warmińsko-Mazurskie, C Poland
Dzuunmod 127 E2 Töv, C Mongolia
Dzüün Soyoni Nuruu see Vostochnyy Sayan
Dzvina see Western Dvina

E

Eagle Pass 49 F4 Texas, SW USA
East Açores Fracture Zone see East Azores Fracture Zone
East Antarctica 154 C3 prev. Greater Antarctica. physical region Antarctica
East Australian Basin see Tasman Basin
East Azores Fracture Zone 66 C3 var. East Açores Fracture Zone. tectonic feature E Atlantic Ocean
Eastbourne 89 E7 SE England, United Kingdom
East Cape 150 E3 headland North Island, New Zealand
East China Sea 125 E2 Chin. Dong Hai. sea W Pacific Ocean
Easter Fracture Zone 153 G4 tectonic feature E Pacific Ocean
Easter Island 153 F4 var. Rapa Nui, Easter Island. island E Pacific Ocean
Easter Island see Pascua, Isla de
Eastern Desert 68 D3 var. Aş Şaḥrā' ash Sharqīyah, Eng. Arabian Desert, Eastern Desert. desert E Egypt
Eastern Desert see Sahara el Sharqîya
Eastern Ghats 124 B3 mountain range SE India
Eastern Sayans see Vostochnyy Sayan
Eastern Sierra Madre see Madre Oriental, Sierra
East Falkland 65 D8 var. Isla Soledad. island E Falkland Islands
East Frisian Islands 94 A3 Eng. East Frisian Islands. island group NW Germany
East Frisian Islands see Ostfriesische Inseln
East Grand Forks 45 E1 Minnesota, N USA
East Indiaman Ridge 141 D6 undersea ridge E Indian Ocean
East Indies 152 A3 island group SE Asia
East Kilbride 88 C4 S Scotland, United Kingdom
East Korea Bay 129 E3 bay E North Korea
Eastleigh 89 D7 S England, United Kingdom
East London 78 D5 Afr. Oos-Londen; prev. Emonti, Port Rex. Eastern Cape, S South Africa
Eastmain 38 D3 river Québec, C Canada
East Mariana Basin 142 B1 undersea basin W Pacific Ocean
East Novaya Zemlya Trough 112 C1 var. Novaya Zemlya Trough. trough W Kara Sea
East Pacific Rise 153 F4 undersea rise E Pacific Ocean
East Pakistan see Bangladesh
East Saint Louis 40 B4 Illinois, N USA
East Scotia Basin 67 C7 undersea basin SE Scotia Sea
East Sea 130 A4 var. Sea of Japan, Rus. Yapanskoye More. Sea NW Pacific Ocean
East Siberian Sea 115 F1 Eng. East Siberian Sea. sea Arctic Ocean
East Siberian Sea see Vostochno-Sibirskoye More
East Timor 139 F5 var. Loro Sae; prev. Portuguese Timor, Timor Timur. country S Indonesia

EAST TIMOR
Southeast Asia

Official name Democratic Republic of Timor-Leste
Formation 2002 / 2002

EAST TIMOR
(continued)

Capital Dili
Population 1.2 million / 213 people per sq mile (82 people per sq km)
Total area 5756 sq. miles (14,874 sq. km)
Languages Tetum (Portuguese/ Austronesian)*, Bahasa Indonesia, Portuguese*
Religions Roman Catholic 95%, Other (including Muslim and Protestant) 5%
Government Parliamentary system
Currency US dollar = 100 cents
Literacy rate 51%
Calorie consumption 2076 kilocalories

Eau Claire 40 A2 Wisconsin, N USA
Eau Claire, Lac à L' see St. Clair, Lake
Eauripik Rise 142 B2 undersea rise W Pacific Ocean
Ebensee 95 D6 Oberösterreich, N Austria
Eberswalde-Finow 94 D3 Brandenburg, E Germany
Ebetsu 130 D2 var. Ebetu. Hokkaidō, NE Japan
Ebetu see Ebetsu
Eblana see Dublin
Ebolowa 77 A5 Sud, S Cameroon
Ebon Atoll 144 D2 var. Epoon. atoll Ralik Chain, S Marshall Islands
Ebora see Évora
Eboracum see York
Ebro 93 E2 river NE Spain
Eburacum see York
Ebusus see Eivissa
Ebusus see Eivissa
Ebusus see Eivissa
Ecbatana see Hamadān
Ech Cheliff/Ech Chleff see Chlef
Echo Bay 37 E3 Northwest Territories, NW Canada
Echt 87 D5 Limburg, SE Netherlands
Ecija 92 D4 anc. Astigi. Andalucía, SW Spain
Eckengraf see Viesīte
Ecuador 60 B1 off. Republic of Ecuador. country NW South America

ECUADOR
South America

Official name Republic of Ecuador
Formation 1830 / 1942
Capital Quito
Population 14.7 million / 138 people per sq mile (53 people per sq km)
Total area 109,483 sq. miles (283,560 sq. km)
Languages Spanish*, Quechua, other Amerindian languages
Religions Roman Catholic 95%, Protestant, Jewish, and other 5%
Ethnic mix Mestizo 77%, White 11%, Amerindian 7%, Black 5%
Government Presidential system
Currency US dollar = 100 cents
Literacy rate 84%
Calorie consumption 2267 kilocalories

Ecuador, Republic of see Ecuador
Ed Da'ein 72 A4 Southern Darfur, W Sudan
Ed Damazin 72 C4 var. Ad Damazīn. Blue Nile, E Sudan
Ed Damer 72 C4 var. Ad Dāmir, Ad Damar. River Nile, NE Sudan
Ed Debba 72 B3 Northern, N Sudan
Ede 86 D4 Gelderland, C Netherlands
Ede 75 F5 Osun, SW Nigeria
Edéa 77 A5 Littoral, SW Cameroon
Edessa see Şanlıurfa
Edfu see Idfū
Edgeoya 83 G2 island S Svalbard
Edgware 89 A7 Harrow, SE England, United Kingdom
Edinburg 49 G5 Texas, SW USA
Edinburgh 88 C4 national capital S Scotland, United Kingdom
Edingen see Enghien
Edirne 116 A2 Eng. Adrianople; anc. Adrianopolis, Hadrianopolis. Edirne, NW Turkey
Edmonds 46 B2 Washington, NW USA
Edmonton 37 E5 province capital Alberta, SW Canada

Edmundston 39 E4 New Brunswick, SE Canada
Edna 49 G4 Texas, SW USA
Edolo 96 B1 Lombardia, N Italy
Edremit 116 A3 Balıkesir, NW Turkey
Edward, Lake 77 E1 var. Albert Edward Nyanza, Edward Nyanza, Lac Idi Amin, Lake Rutanzige. lake Uganda/ Dem. Rep. Congo
Edward Nyanza see Edward, Lake
Edwards Plateau 49 F3 plain Texas, SW USA
Edzo 53 E4 prev. Rae-Edzo. Northwest Territories, NW Canada
Eeklo 87 B5 var. Eekloo. Oost-Vlaanderen, NW Belgium
Eekloo see Eeklo
Eems see Ems
Eersel 87 C5 Noord-Brabant, S Netherlands
Eesti Vabariik see Estonia
Efate 144 D4 var. Efate, Fr. Vaté; prev. Sandwich Island. island C Vanuatu
Éfaté see Efate
Effingham 40 B4 Illinois, N USA
Eforie-Sud 108 D5 Constanţa, E Romania
Egadi Is. 97 B7 island group S Italy
Ege Denizi see Aegean Sea
Eger 99 D6 Ger. Erlau. Heves, NE Hungary
Eger see Cheb, Czech Republic
Egeria Fracture Zone 141 C5 tectonic feature W Indian Ocean
Éghezée 87 C6 Namur, C Belgium
Egina see Aígina
Egio see Aígio
Egmont see Taranaki, Mount
Egmont, Cape 150 C4 headland North Island, New Zealand
Egoli see Johannesburg
Egypt 72 B2 off. Arab Republic of Egypt, Ar. Jumhūrīyah Miṣr al 'Arabīyah, prev. United Arab Republic; anc. Aegyptus. country NE Africa

EGYPT
North Africa

Official name Arab Republic of Egypt
Formation 1936 / 1982
Capital Cairo
Population 82.5 million / 215 people per sq mile (83 people per sq km)
Total area 386,660 sq. miles (1,001,450 sq. km)
Languages Arabic*, French, English, Berber
Religions Muslim (mainly Sunni) 90%, Coptic Christian and other 10%
Ethnic mix Egyptian 99%, Nubian, Armenian, Greek, and Berber 1%
Government Transitional regime
Currency Egyptian pound = 100 piastres
Literacy rate 72%
Calorie consumption 3349 kilocalories

Eibar 93 E1 País Vasco, N Spain
Eibergen 86 E3 Gelderland, E Netherlands
Eidfjord 85 A5 Hordaland, S Norway
Eier-Berg see Suur Munamägi
Eifel 95 A5 plateau W Germany
Eiger 95 B7 mountain C Switzerland
Eigg 88 B3 island W Scotland, United Kingdom
Eight Degree Channel 132 B3 channel India/Maldives
Eighty Mile Beach 146 B4 beach Western Australia
Eijsden 87 D6 Limburg, SE Netherlands
Eilat see Elat
Eindhoven 87 D5 Noord-Brabant, S Netherlands
Eipel see Ipel'
Éire see Ireland
Éireann, Muir see Irish Sea
Eisenhüttenstadt 94 D4 Brandenburg, E Germany
Eisenmarkt see Hunedoara
Eisenstadt 95 E6 Burgenland, E Austria
Eisleben 94 C4 Sachsen-Anhalt, C Germany
Eivissa 93 G3 var. Iviza, Cast. Ibiza; anc. Ebusus. Ibiza, Spain, W Mediterranean Sea
Eivissa 93 G3 var. Iviza, Cast. Ibiza; anc. Ebusus. Ibiza, Spain, W Mediterranean Sea

Eivissa 93 G3 *var.* Iviza, *Cast.*
 Ibiza; *anc.* Ebusus. Ibiza, Spain,
 W Mediterranean Sea
Ejea de los Caballeros 93 E2 Aragón,
 NE Spain
Ejin Qi *see* Dalain Hob
Ekapa *see* Cape Town
Ekaterinodar *see* Krasnodar
Ekiatapskiy Khrebet *see* Ekvyvatapskiy
 Khrebet
Ekvyvatapskiy Khrebet 115 G1 *prev.*
 Ekiatapskiy Khrebet. *mountain range*
 NE Russian Federation
El 'Alamein *see* Al 'Alamayn
El Asnam *see* Chlef
Elat 119 B8 *var.* Eilat, Elath. Southern,
 S Israel
Elat, Gulf of *see* Aqaba, Gulf of
Elath *see* Elat, Israel
Elath *see* Al 'Aqabah, Jordan
El'Atrun 72 B3 Northern Darfur,
 NW Sudan
Elâzığ 117 E3 *var.* Elâzig, Eláziz. Elâzığ,
 E Turkey
Elba 96 B4 *island* Archipelago Toscano,
 C Italy
Elbasan 101 D6 *var.* Elbasani. Elbasan,
 C Albania
Elbasani *see* Elbasan
Elbe 80 D3 *Cz.* Labe. *river* Czech
 Republic/Germany
Elbert, Mount 44 C4 *mountain*
 Colorado, C USA
Elbing *see* Elbląg
Elbląg 98 C2 *var.* Elblag, *Ger.* Elbing.
 Warmińsko-Mazurskie, NE Poland
El Boulaida/El Boulaïda *see* Blida
El'brus 111 A8 *var.* Gora El'brus.
 mountain SW Russian Federation
El'brus, Gora *see* El'brus
El Burgo de Osma 93 E2 Castilla y
 León, C Spain
Elburz Mountains 120 C2 *Eng.* Elburz
 Mountains. *mountain range* N Iran
Elburz Mountains *see* Alborz, Reshteh-ye
 Kūhhā-ye
El Cajon 47 C8 California, W USA
El Calafate 65 B7 *var.* Calafate. Santa
 Cruz, S Argentina
El Callao 59 E2 Bolívar, E Venezuela
El Campo 49 G4 Texas, SW USA
El Carmen de Bolívar 58 B2 Bolívar,
 NW Colombia
El Cayo *see* San Ignacio
El Centro 47 D8 California, W USA
Elche 93 F4 *Cat.* Elx; *anc.* Ilici, *Lat.* Illicis.
 Valenciana, E Spain
Elda 93 F4 Valenciana, E Spain
El Djazaïr *see* Alger
El Djelfa *see* Djelfa
Eldorado 64 E3 Misiones, NE Argentina
El Dorado 50 C3 Sinaloa, C Mexico
El Dorado 42 B2 Arkansas, C USA
El Dorado 45 F5 Kansas, C USA
El Dorado 59 F2 Bolívar, E Venezuela
El Dorado *see* California
Eldoret 73 C6 Rift Valley, W Kenya
Elektrostal' 111 B5 Moskovskaya
 Oblast', W Russian Federation
Elemi Triangle 73 B5 *disputed region*
 Kenya/Sudan
Elephant Butte Reservoir 48 C2
 reservoir New Mexico, SW USA
Élesd *see* Aleşd
Eleuthera Island 54 C1 *island*
 N Bahamas
El Fasher 72 A4 *var.* Al Fāshir. Northern
 Darfur, W Sudan
El Ferrol/El Ferrol del Caudillo *see*
 Ferrol
El Gedaref *see* Gedaref
El Geneina 72 A4 *var.* Ajjinena, Al-
 Genain, Al Junaynah. Western Darfur,
 W Sudan
Elgin 88 C3 NE Scotland, United
 Kingdom
Elgin 40 B3 Illinois, N USA
El Giza *see* Giza
El Goléa 70 D3 *var.* Al Golea. C Algeria
El Hank 74 D1 *cliff* N Mauritania
El Haseke *see* Al Ḥasakah
Elimberrum *see* Auch
Eliocroca *see* Lorca
Élisabethville *see* Lubumbashi
Elista 111 B7 Respublika Kalmykiya,
 SW Russian Federation
Elizabeth 149 B6 South Australia
Elizabeth City 43 G1 North Carolina,
 SE USA

Elizabethtown 40 C5 Kentucky, S USA
El-Jadida 70 C2 *prev.* Mazagan.
 W Morocco
Elk 98 E2 *Ger.* Lyck. Warmińsko-
 mazurskie, NE Poland
Elk City 49 F1 Oklahoma, C USA
El Khalil *see* Hebron
El Khârga *see* Al Khārijah
Elkhart 40 C3 Indiana, N USA
El Khartûm *see* Khartoum
Elk River 45 F2 Minnesota, N USA
El Kuneitra *see* Al Qunayţirah
Ellás *see* Greece
Ellef Ringnes Island 37 E1 *island*
 Nunavut, N Canada
Ellen, Mount 44 B5 *mountain* Utah,
 W USA
Ellensburg 46 B2 Washington, NW USA
Ellesmere Island 37 F1 *island* Queen
 Elizabeth Islands, Nunavut, N Canada
Ellesmere, Lake 151 C6 *lake* South
 Island, New Zealand
Ellice Islands *see* Tuvalu
Elliston 149 A6 South Australia
Ellsworth Land 154 A3 *physical region*
 Antarctica
El Mahbas 70 B3 *var.* Mahbés.
 SW Western Sahara
El Mina 118 B4 *var.* Al Mīnāʾ.
 N Lebanon
El Minya *see* Al Minyā
Elmira 41 F3 New York, NE USA
El Mreyyé 74 D2 *desert* E Mauritania
Elmshorn 94 B3 Schleswig-Holstein,
 N Germany
El Muglad 72 B4 Southern Kordofan,
 C Sudan
El Obeid 72 B4 *var.* Al Obayyid, Al
 Ubayyiḍ. Northern Kordofan, C Sudan
El Ouâdi *see* El Oued
El Oued 71 E2 *var.* Al Oued, El Ouâdi, El
 Wad. NE Algeria
Eloy 48 B2 Arizona, SW USA
El Paso 48 D3 Texas, SW USA
El Porvenir 53 G4 Kuna Yala, N Panama
El Progreso 52 C2 Yoro, NW Honduras
El Puerto de Santa María 92 C5
 Andalucía, S Spain
El Qâhira *see* Cairo
El Quneitra *see* Al Qunayţirah
El Quseir *see* Al Quşayr
El Quweira *see* Al Quwayrah
El Rama 53 E3 Región Autónoma
 Atlántico Sur, SE Nicaragua
El Real 53 H5 *var.* El Real de Santa María.
 Darién, SE Panama
El Real de Santa María *see* El Real
El Reno 49 F1 Oklahoma, C USA
El Salvador 52 B3 *off.* Republica de El
 Salvador. *country* Central America

EL SALVADOR
Central America

Official name Republic of El Salvador
Formation 1841 / 1841
Capital San Salvador
Population 6.2 million / 755 people
per sq mile (299 people per sq km)
Total area 8124 sq. miles (21,040 sq. km)
Languages Spanish
Religions Roman Catholic 80%,
Evangelical 18%, Other 2%
Ethnic mix Mestizo 90%,
White 9%, Amerindian 1%
Government Presidential system
Currency Salvadorean colón & US dollar =
100 centavos (colón); 100 cents (US dollar)
Literacy rate 84%
Calorie consumption 2574 kilocalories

El Salvador, Republica de *see* El Salvador
Elsass *see* Alsace
El Sáuz 50 C2 Chihuahua, N Mexico
El Serrat 91 A7 N Andorra Europe
Elst 86 D4 Gelderland, E Netherlands
El Sueco 50 C2 Chihuahua, N Mexico
El Suweida *see* As Suwaydāʾ
El Suweis *see* Suez
Eltanin Fracture Zone 153 E5 *tectonic
 feature* SE Pacific Ocean
El Tigre 59 E2 Anzoátegui, NE Venezuela
Elvas 92 C4 Portalegre, C Portugal
El Vendrell 93 G2 Cataluña, NE Spain
El Vigía 58 C2 Mérida, NW Venezuela
El Wad *see* El Oued
Elwell, Lake 44 B1 *reservoir* Montana,
 NW USA
Elx *see* Elche

Ely 47 D5 Nevada, W USA
El Yopal *see* Yopal
Emajõgi 106 D3 *Ger.* Embach. *river*
 SE Estonia
Emāmrūd *see* Shāhrūd
Emāmshahr *see* Shāhrūd
Emba 114 B4 *Kaz.* Embi. Aktyubinsk,
 W Kazakhstan
Embach *see* Emajõgi
Embi *see* Emba
Emden 94 A3 Niedersachsen,
 NW Germany
Emerald 148 D4 Queensland,
 E Australia
Emerald Isle *see* Montserrat
Emesa *see* Ḥimş
Emmaste 106 C2 Hiiumaa, W Estonia
Emmeloord 86 D2 Flevoland,
 N Netherlands
Emmen 86 E2 Drenthe, NE Netherlands
Emmendingen 95 A6 Baden-
 Württemberg, SW Germany
Emona *see* Ljubljana
Emonti *see* East London
Emory Peak 49 E4 *mountain* Texas,
 SW USA
Empalme 50 B2 Sonora, NW Mexico
Emperor Seamounts 113 G3 *seamount
 range* NW Pacific Ocean
Empire State of the South *see* Georgia
Emporia 45 F5 Kansas, C USA
Empty Quarter *see* Ar Rubʿ al Khālī
Ems 94 A3 *Dut.* Eems. *river*
 NW Germany
Enareträsk *see* Inarijärvi
Encamp 91 A8 Encamp, C Andorra
 Europe
Encarnación 64 D3 Itapúa, S Paraguay
Encinitas 47 C8 California, W USA
Encs 99 D6 Borsod-Abaúj-Zemplén,
 NE Hungary
Endeavour Strait 148 C1 *strait*
 Queensland, NE Australia
Enderbury Island 145 F3 *atoll* Phoenix
 Islands, C Kiribati
Enderby Land 154 D2 *physical region*
 Antarctica
Enderby Plain 154 D2 *abyssal plain*
 S Indian Ocean
Endersdorf *see* Jędrzejów
Enewetak Atoll 144 C1 *var.* Ānewetak,
 Eniwetok. *atoll* Ralik Chain,
 W Marshall Islands
Enfield 89 A7 United Kingdom
Engeten *see* Aiud
Enghien 87 B6 *Dut.* Edingen. Hainaut,
 SW Belgium
England 89 D5 *Lat.* Anglia. *cultural
 region* England, United Kingdom
Englewood 44 D4 Colorado, C USA
English Channel 89 D8 *var.* The
 Channel, *Fr.* La Manche. *channel*
 NW Europe
Engure 106 C3 W Latvia
Engures Ezers 106 B3 *lake* NW Latvia
Enguri 117 F1 *Rus.* Inguri. *river*
 NW Georgia
Enid 49 F1 Oklahoma, C USA
Enikale Strait *see* Kerch Strait
Eniwetok *see* Enewetak Atoll
En Nâqoûra 119 A5 *var.* An Nāqūrah.
 SW Lebanon
En Nazira *see* Naẕerat
Ennedi 76 D2 *plateau* E Chad
Ennis 89 A6 *Ir.* Inis. Clare, W Ireland
Ennis 49 G3 Texas, SW USA
Enniskillen 89 B5 *var.* Inniskilling, *Ir.*
 Inis Ceithleann. SW Northern Ireland,
 United Kingdom
Enns 95 D6 *river* C Austria
Enschede 86 E3 Overijssel, E Netherlands
Ensenada 50 A1 Baja California Norte,
 NW Mexico
Entebbe 73 B6 S Uganda
Entroncamento 92 B3 Santarém,
 C Portugal
Enugu 75 G5 Enugu, S Nigeria
Epanomi 104 B4 Kentrikí Makedonía,
 N Greece
Epéna 77 B5 Likouala, NE Congo
Eperies/Eperjes *see* Prešov
Epi 144 D4 *var.* Épi. *island* C Vanuatu
Épi *see* Epi
Épinal 90 D4 Vosges, NE France
Epiphania *see* Ḥamāh
Epitoli *see* Tshwane
Epoon *see* Ebon Atoll
Epsom 89 A8 United Kingdom
Equality State *see* Wyoming
Equatorial Guinea 77 A5 *off.* Equatorial
 Guinea, Republic of. *country* C Africa

EQUATORIAL GUINEA
Central Africa

Official name Republic of
Equatorial Guinea
Formation 1968 / 1968
Capital Malabo
Population 700,000 / 65 people
per sq mile (25 people per sq km)
Total area 10,830 sq. miles (28,051 sq. km)
Languages Spanish*, Fang, Bubi, French*
Religions Roman Catholic 90%,
Other 10%
Ethnic mix Fang 85%, Other 11%, Bubi 4%
Government Presidential system
Currency CFA franc = 100 centimes
Literacy rate 93%
Calorie consumption Not available

Equatorial Guinea, Republic of *see*
 Equatorial Guinea
Erautini *see* Johannesburg
Erbil *see* Arbil
Erciş 117 F3 Van, E Turkey
Erdély *see* Transylvania
Erdélyi-Havasok *see* Carpaţii
 Meridionalii
Erdenet 127 E2 Orhon, N Mongolia
Erdi 76 C2 *plateau* NE Chad
Erdi Ma 76 D2 *desert* NE Chad
Erebus, Mount 154 B4 *volcano* Ross
 Island, Antarctica
Ereğli 116 C4 Konya, S Turkey
Erenhot 127 F1 *var.* Erlian. Nei Mongol
 Zizhiqu, NE China
Erfurt 94 C4 Thüringen, C Germany
Ergene Çayı *see* Ergene Irmaği
Ergene Irmaği 116 A2 *var.* Ergene Çayı.
 river NW Turkey
Ergun 127 F1 *var.* Labudalin; *prev.* Ergun
 Youqi. Nei Mongol Zizhiqu, N China
Ergun He *see* Argun
Ergun Youqi *see* Ergun
Erie 40 D3 Pennsylvania, NE USA
Érié, Lac *see* Erie, Lake
Erie, Lake 40 D3 *Fr.* Lac Érié. *lake*
 Canada/USA
Eritrea 72 C4 *off.* State of Eritrea, Ertra.
 country E Africa

ERITREA
East Africa

Official name State of Eritrea
Formation 1993 / 2002
Capital Asmara
Population 5.4 million / 119 people
per sq mile (46 people per sq km)
Total area 46,842 sq. miles (121,320 sq. km)
Languages Tigrinya*, English*, Tigre,
Afar, Arabic*, Saho, Bilen, Kunama,
Nara, Hadareb
Religions Christian 50%, Muslim 48%,
Other 2%
Ethnic mix Tigray 50%, Tigre 31%, Other
9%, Afar 5%, Saho 5%
Government Transitional regime
Currency Nakfa = 100 cents
Literacy rate 67%
Calorie consumption 1640 kilocalories

Eritrea, State of *see* Eritrea
Erivan *see* Yerevan
Erlangen 95 C5 Bayern, S Germany
Erlau *see* Eger
Erlian *see* Erenhot
Ermelo 86 D3 Gelderland, C Netherlands
Ermióni 105 C6 Pelopónnisos, S Greece
Ermoúpoli 105 D6 *var.* Hermoupolis;
 prev. Ermoúpolis. Sýyros, Kykládes,
 Greece, Aegean Sea
Ermoúpolis *see* Ermoúpoli
Ernākulam 132 C3 Kerala, SW India
Erode 132 C2 Tamil Nādu, SE India
Erquelinnes 87 B7 Hainaut, S Belgium
Er-Rachidia 70 C2 *var.* Ksar al Soule.
 E Morocco
Er Rahad 72 B4 *var.* Ar Rahad. Northern
 Kordofan, C Sudan
Erromango 144 D4 *island* S Vanuatu
Ertis *see* Irtysh, C Asia
Êrtra *see* Eritrea
Erzerum *see* Erzurum
Erzincan 117 E3 *var.* Erzinjan. Erzincan,
 E Turkey
Erzinjan *see* Erzincan
Erzurum 117 E3 *prev.* Erzerum.
 Erzurum, NE Turkey

Esbjerg 85 A7 Syddtjylland, W Denmark
Esbo see Espoo
Escaldes 91 A8 Escaldes Engordany, C Andorra Europe
Escanaba 40 C2 Michigan, N USA
Escaut see Scheldt
Esch-sur-Alzette 87 D8 Luxembourg, S Luxembourg
Esclaves, Grand Lac des see Great Slave Lake
Escondido 47 C8 California, W USA
Escuinapa 50 D3 var. Escuinapa de Hidalgo. Sinaloa, C Mexico
Escuinapa de Hidalgo see Escuinapa
Escuintla 52 B2 Escuintla, S Guatemala
Escuintla 51 G5 Chiapas, SE Mexico
Esenguly 122 B3 Rus. Gasan-Kuli. Balkan Welaýaty, W Turkmenistan
Eşfahān 120 C3 Eng. Isfahan; anc. Aspadana. Eşfahān, C Iran
Esh Sharā see Ash Sharāh
Esil see Ishim, Kazakhstan/Russian Federation
Eskimo Point see Arviat
Eskişehir 116 B3 var. Eskishehr. Eskişehir, W Turkey
Eskishehr see Eskişehir
Eslāmābād see Eslāmābād-e Gharb
Eslāmābād-e Gharb 120 C3 var. Eslāmābād; prev. Harunabad, Shāhābād. Kermānshāhān, W Iran
Esmeraldas 60 A1 Esmeraldas, N Ecuador
Esna see Isnā
España see Spain
Espanola 48 D1 New Mexico, SW USA
Esperance 147 B7 Western Australia
Esperanza 50 B2 Sonora, NW Mexico
Esperanza 154 A2 Argentinian research station Antarctica
Espinal 58 B3 Tolima, C Colombia
Espinhaço, Serra do 56 D4 mountain range SE Brazil
Espírito Santo 63 F4 off. Estado do Espírito Santo. state E Brazil
Espírito Santo 63 F4 off. Estado do Espírito Santo. region E Brazil
Espíritu Santo, Estado do see Espírito Santo
Espiritu Santo 144 C4 var. Santo. island W Vanuatu
Espoo 85 D6 Swe. Esbo. Etelä-Suomi, S Finland
Esquel 65 B6 Chubut, SW Argentina
Essaouira 70 B2 prev. Mogador. W Morocco
Esseg see Osijek
Es Semara see Smara
Essen 87 C5 Antwerpen, N Belgium
Essen 94 A4 var. Essen an der Ruhr. Nordrhein-Westfalen, W Germany
Essen an der Ruhr see Essen
Essequibo River 59 F3 river C Guyana
Es Suwecīda see As Suwaydā'
Estacado, Llano 49 E2 plain New Mexico/Texas, SW USA
Estados, Isla de los 65 C8 prev. Eng. Staten Island. island S Argentina
Estância 63 G3 Sergipe, E Brazil
Esteli 52 D3 Esteli, NW Nicaragua
Estella 93 E1 Bas. Lizarra. Navarra, N Spain
Estepona 92 D5 Andalucía, S Spain
Estevan 37 F5 Saskatchewan, S Canada
Estland see Estonia
Estonia 106 D2 off. Republic of Estonia, Est. Eesti Vabariik, Ger. Estland, Latv. Igaunija; prev. Estonian SSR, Rus. Estonskaya SSR. country NE Europe

ESTONIA
Northeast Europe

Official name Republic of Estonia
Formation 1991 / 1991
Capital Tallinn
Population 1.3 million / 75 people per sq mile (29 people per sq km)
Total area 17,462 sq. miles (45,226 sq. km)
Languages Estonian*, Russian
Religions Evangelical Lutheran 56%, Orthodox Christian 25%, Other 19%
Ethnic mix Estonian 69%, Russian 25%, Other 4%, Ukrainian 2%
Government Parliamentary system
Currency Euro = 100 cents
Literacy rate 99%
Calorie consumption 3163 kilocalories

Estonian SSR see Estonia
Estonia, Republic of see Estonia
Estonskaya SSR see Estonia
Estrela, Serra da 92 C3 mountain range C Portugal
Estremadura see Extremadura
Estremoz 92 C4 Évora, S Portugal
Eszék see Osijek
Esztergom 99 C6 Ger. Gran; anc. Strigonium. Komárom-Esztergom, N Hungary
Étalle 87 D8 Luxembourg, SE Belgium
Etāwah 134 D3 Uttar Pradesh, N India
Ethiopia 73 C5 off. Federal Democratic Republic of Ethiopia; prev. Abyssinia, People's Democratic Republic of Ethiopia. country E Africa

ETHIOPIA
East Africa

Official name Federal Democratic Republic of Ethiopia
Formation 1896 / 2002
Capital Addis Ababa
Population 84.7 million / 198 people per sq mile (76 people per sq km)
Total area 435,184 sq. miles (1,127,127 sq. km)
Languages Amharic*, Tigrinya, Galla, Sidamo, Somali, English, Arabic
Religions Orthodox Christian 40%, Muslim 40%, Traditional beliefs 15%, Other 5%
Ethnic mix Oromo 40%, Amhara 25%, Other 13%, Sidama 9%, Tigray 7%, Somali 6%
Government Parliamentary system
Currency Ethiopian birr = 100 cents
Literacy rate 36%
Calorie consumption 2097 kilocalories

Ethiopia, Federal Democratic Republic of see Ethiopia
Ethiopian Highlands 73 C5 var. Ethiopian Plateau. plateau N Ethiopia
Ethiopian Plateau see Ethiopian Highlands
Ethiopia, People's Democratic Republic of see Ethiopia
Mount Etna 97 C7 Eng. Mount Etna. volcano Sicilia, Italy, C Mediterranean Sea
Etna, Mount see Etna, Mount
Etosha Pan 78 B3 salt lake N Namibia
Etoumbi 77 B5 Cuvette Ouest, NW Congo
Etsch see Adige
Et Tafila see Aţ Ţafilah
Ettelbrück 87 D8 Diekirch, C Luxembourg
'Eua 145 E5 prev. Middleburg Island. island Tongatapu Group, SE Tonga
Euboea 105 C5 Lat. Euboea. island C Greece
Euboea see Évvoia
Eucla 147 D6 Western Australia
Euclid 40 D3 Ohio, N USA
Eufaula Lake 49 G1 var. Eufaula Reservoir. reservoir Oklahoma, C USA
Eufaula Reservoir see Eufaula Lake
Eugene 46 B3 Oregon, NW USA
Eumolpias see Plovdiv
Eupen 87 D6 Liège, E Belgium
Euphrates 112 B4 Ar. Al-Furāt, Turk. Fırat Nehri. river SW Asia
Eureka 47 A5 California, W USA
Eureka 44 A1 Montana, NW USA
Europa Point 93 H5 headland S Gibraltar
Europe 80 continent
Eutin 94 C2 Schleswig-Holstein, N Germany
Euxine Sea see Black Sea
Evansdale 45 G3 Iowa, C USA
Evanston 40 B3 Illinois, N USA
Evanston 44 B4 Wyoming, C USA
Evansville 40 B5 Indiana, N USA
Eveleth 45 G1 Minnesota, N USA
Everard, Lake 147 A6 salt lake South Australia
Everest, Mount 126 D5 Chin. Qomolangma Feng, Nep. Sagarmāthā. mountain China/Nepal
Everett 46 B2 Washington, NW USA
Everglades, The 43 F5 wetland Florida, SE USA
Evje 85 A6 Aust-Agder, S Norway
Evmolpia see Plovdiv

Évora 92 B4 anc. Ebora, Lat. Liberalitas Julia. Évora, C Portugal
Évreux 90 C3 anc. Civitas Eburovicum. Eure, N France
Évros see Maritsa
Évry 90 E2 Essonne, N France
Ewarton 54 B5 C Jamaica
Excelsior Springs 45 F4 Missouri, C USA
Exe 89 C7 river SW England, United Kingdom
Exeter 89 C7 anc. Isca Damnoniorum. SW England, United Kingdom
Exmoor 89 C7 moorland SW England, United Kingdom
Exmouth 146 A4 Western Australia
Exmouth 89 C7 SW England, United Kingdom
Exmouth Gulf 146 A4 gulf Western Australia
Exmouth Plateau 141 E5 undersea plateau E Indian Ocean
Extremadura 92 C3 var. Estremadura. autonomous community W Spain
Exuma Cays 54 C1 islets C Bahamas
Exuma Sound 54 C1 sound C Bahamas
Eyre Mountains 151 A7 mountain range South Island, New Zealand
Eyre North, Lake 149 A5 salt lake South Australia
Eyre Peninsula 149 A6 peninsula South Australia
Eyre South, Lake 149 A5 salt lake South Australia
Ezo see Hokkaidō

F

Faadhippolhu Atoll 132 B4 var. Fadiffolu, Lhaviyani Atoll. atoll N Maldives
Fabens 48 D3 Texas, SW USA
Fada 76 C2 Borkou-Ennedi-Tibesti, E Chad
Fada-Ngourma 75 E4 E Burkina Faso
Fadiffolu see Faadhippolhu Atoll
Faenza 96 C3 anc. Faventia. Emilia-Romagna, N Italy
Faeroe-Iceland Ridge 80 C1 undersea ridge NW Norwegian Sea
Faeroe Islands 83 E5 Dan. Færøerne, Faer. Føroyar. Danish external territory N Atlantic Ocean
Færøerne see Faeroe Islands
Faeroe-Shetland Trough 80 C2 trough NE Atlantic Ocean
Faetano 96 E2 E San Marino
Făgăraş 108 C4 Ger. Fogarasch, Hung. Fogaras. Brașov, C Romania
Fagibina, Lake see Faguibine, Lac
Fagne 87 C7 hill range S Belgium
Faguibine, Lac 75 E3 var. Lake Fagibina. lake NW Mali
Fahlun see Falun
Fahraj 120 E4 Kermān, SE Iran
Faial 92 A5 var. Ilha do Faial. island Azores, Portugal, NE Atlantic Ocean
Faial, Ilha do see Faial
Faifo see Hôi An
Fairbanks 36 D3 Alaska, USA
Fairfield 47 B6 California, W USA
Fair Isle 88 D2 island NE Scotland, United Kingdom
Fairlie 151 B6 Canterbury, South Island, New Zealand
Fairmont 45 F3 Minnesota, N USA
Faisalābād 134 C2 prev. Lyallpur. Punjab, NE Pakistan
Faizābād 135 E3 Uttar Pradesh, N India
Faizabad/Faizābād see Feyzābād
Fakaofo Atoll 145 F3 island SE Tokelau
Falam 136 A3 Chin State, W Myanmar (Burma)
Falconara Marittima 96 C3 Marche, C Italy
Falkenau an der Eger see Sokolov
Falkland Islands 65 D7 var. Falklands, Islas Malvinas. UK dependent territory SW Atlantic Ocean
Falkland Plateau 57 D7 var. Argentine Rise. undersea feature SW Atlantic Ocean
Falklands see Falkland Islands
Falknov nad Ohří see Sokolov
Fallbrook 47 C8 California, W USA
Falmouth 54 A4 W Jamaica
Falmouth 89 C7 SW England, United Kingdom

Falster 85 B8 island SE Denmark
Fălticeni 108 C3 Hung. Falticsén. Suceava, NE Romania
Falticsén see Fălticeni
Falun 85 C6 var. Fahlun. Kopparberg, C Sweden
Famagusta see Gazimağusa
Famagusta Bay 102 C5 var. Famagusta Bay, Gk. Kólpos Ammóchostos. bay E Cyprus
Famagusta Bay see Gazimağusa Körfezi
Famenne 87 C7 physical region SE Belgium
Fang 136 C3 Chiang Mai, NW Thailand
Fanning Island see Tabuaeran
Fanø 96 C5 island W Denmark
Farafangana 79 G4 Fianarantsoa, SE Madagascar
Farāh 122 D4 var. Farah, Fararud. Farāh, W Afghanistan
Farah Rud 122 D4 river W Afghanistan
Faranah 74 C4 Haute-Guinée, S Guinea
Fararud see Farāh
Farasan, Jaza'ir 121 A6 island group SW Saudi Arabia
Farewell, Cape 150 C4 headland South Island, New Zealand
Farewell, Cape see Nunap Isua
Fargo 45 F2 North Dakota, N USA
Farg'ona 123 F2 Rus. Fergana; prev. Novyy Margilan. Farg'ona Viloyati, E Uzbekistan
Faribault 45 F2 Minnesota, N USA
Farīdābād 134 D3 Haryāna, N India
Farkhor 123 E3 Rus. Parkhar. SW Tajikistan
Farmington 45 G5 Missouri, C USA
Farmington 48 C1 New Mexico, SW USA
Faro 92 B5 Faro, S Portugal
Farquhar Group 79 G2 island group S Seychelles
Fars, Khalij-e see Persian Gulf
Farvel, Kap see Nunap Isua
Fastiv 109 E2 Rus. Fastov. Kyyivs'ka Oblast', NW Ukraine
Fastov see Fastiv
Fauske 84 C3 Nordland, C Norway
Faventia see Faenza
Faxa Bay see Faxaflói
Faxaflói 82 D5 Eng. Faxa Bay. bay W Iceland
Faya 76 C2 prev. Faya-Largeau, Largeau. Borkou-Ennedi-Tibesti, N Chad
Faya-Largeau see Faya
Fayetteville 42 A1 Arkansas, C USA
Fayetteville 43 F1 North Carolina, SE USA
Fdérick see Fdérik
Fdérik 74 C2 var. Fdérick, Fr. Fort Gouraud. Tiris Zemmour, NW Mauritania
Fear, Cape 43 F2 headland Bald Head Island, North Carolina, SE USA
Fécamp 90 B3 Seine-Maritime, N France
Fédala see Mohammedia
Federal Capital Territory see Australian Capital Territory
Fehérgyarmat 99 E6 Szabolcs-Szatmár-Bereg, E Hungary
Fehértemplom see Bela Crkva
Fehmarn 94 C2 island N Germany
Fehmarn Belt 94 C2 Dan. Femern Bælt, Ger. Fehmarnbelt. strait Denmark / Germany
Fehmarnbelt see Fehmarn Belt/Femer Bælt
Feijó 62 C2 Acre, W Brazil
Feilding 150 D4 Manawatu-Wanganui, North Island, New Zealand
Feira see Feira de Santana
Feira de Santana 63 G3 var. Feira. Bahia, E Brazil
Feizābād 123 F3 var. Faizabad, Faizābād, Feyzābād, Feyzad; prev. Feyzābād. Badakhshān, NE Afghanistan
Feketehalom see Codlea
Felanitx 93 G3 Mallorca, Spain, W Mediterranean Sea
Felidhu Atoll 132 B4 atoll C Maldives
Felipe Carrillo Puerto 51 H4 Quintana Roo, SE Mexico
Felixstowe 89 E6 E England, United Kingdom
Fellin see Viljandi
Felsőbánya see Baia Sprie
Felsőmuzslya see Mužlja
Femunden 85 B5 lake S Norway
Fénérive see Fenoarivo Atsinanana

Fengcheng 128 D3 var. Feng-cheng, Fenghwangcheng. Liaoning, NE China
Feng-cheng see Fengcheng
Fenghwangcheng see Fengcheng
Fengtien see Liaoning, China
Fengtien see Shenyang, China
Fenoarivo Atsinanana 79 G3 prev./Fr. Fénérive. Toamasina, E Madagascar
Fens, The 89 E6 wetland E England, United Kingdom
Feodosiya 109 F5 var. Kefe, It. Kaffa; anc. Theodosia. Avtonomna Respublika Krym, S Ukraine
Ferdinand see Montana, Bulgaria
Ferdinandsberg see Oțelu Roșu
Féres 104 D3 Anatolikí Makedonía kai Thráki, NE Greece
Fergana see Farg'ona
Fergus Falls 45 F2 Minnesota, N USA
Ferizaj 101 D5 Serb. Uroševac. C Kosovo
Ferkessédougou 74 D4 N Côte d'Ivoire
Fermo 96 C4 anc. Firmum Picenum. Marche, C Italy
Fernandina, Isla 60 A5 var. Narborough Island. island Galápagos Islands, Ecuador, E Pacific Ocean
Fernando de Noronha 63 H2 island E Brazil
Fernando Po/Fernando Póo see Bioco, Isla de
Ferrara 96 C2 anc. Forum Alieni. Emilia-Romagna, N Italy
Ferreñafe 60 B3 Lambayeque, W Peru
Ferro see Hierro
Ferrol 92 B1 var. El Ferrol; prev. El Ferrol del Caudillo. Galicia, NW Spain
Fertő see Neusiedler See
Ferwerd see Ferwert
Ferwert 86 D1 Dutch. Ferwerd. Fryslân, N Netherlands
Fès 70 C2 Eng. Fez. N Morocco
Feteşti 108 D5 Ialomiţa, SE Romania
Fethiye 116 B4 Muğla, SW Turkey
Fetlar 88 D1 island NE Scotland, United Kingdom
Feyzābād see Feyẕābād
Feyẕābād see Feyẕābād
Fez see Fès
Fianarantsoa 79 F3 Fianarantsoa, C Madagascar
Fianga 76 B4 Mayo-Kébbi, SW Chad
Fier 101 C6 var. Fieri. Fier, SW Albania
Fieri see Fier
Figeac 91 C5 Lot, S France
Figig see Figuig
Figueira da Foz 92 B3 Coimbra, W Portugal
Figueres 93 G2 Cataluña, E Spain
Figuig 70 D2 var. Figig. E Morocco
Fiji 145 E5 off. Sovereign Democratic Republic of Fiji, Fij. Viti. country SW Pacific Ocean

---

FIJI
Australasia & Oceania

Official name Republic of the Fiji Islands
Formation 1970 / 1970
Capital Suva
Population 900,000 / 128 people per sq mile (49 people per sq km)
Total area 7054 sq. miles (18,270 sq. km)
Languages Fijian, English*, Hindi, Urdu, Tamil, Telugu
Religions Hindu 38%, Methodist 37%, Roman Catholic 9%, Muslim 8%, Other 8%
Ethnic mix Melanesian 51%, Indian 44%, Other 5%
Government Transitional regime
Currency Fiji dollar = 100 cents
Literacy rate 94%
Calorie consumption 2996 kilocalories

Fiji, Sovereign Democratic Republic of see Fiji
Filadelfia 52 D4 Guanacaste, W Costa Rica
Filiaşi 108 B5 Dolj, SW Romania
Filipstad 85 B6 Värmland, C Sweden
Finale Ligure 96 A3 Liguria, NW Italy
Finchley 89 A7 United Kingdom
Findlay 40 C4 Ohio, N USA
Finike 116 B4 Antalya, SW Turkey
Finland 84 D4 off. Republic of Finland, Fin. Suomen Tasavalta, Suomi. country N Europe

---

FINLAND
Northern Europe

Official name Republic of Finland
Formation 1917 / 1947
Capital Helsinki
Population 5.4 million / 46 people per sq mile (18 people per sq km)
Total area 130,127 sq. miles (337,030 sq. km)
Languages Finnish*, Swedish*, Sámi
Religions Evangelical Lutheran 83%, Other 15%, Orthodox Christian 1%, Roman Catholic 1%
Ethnic mix Finnish 93%, Other (including Sámi) 7%
Government Parliamentary system
Currency Euro = 100 cents
Literacy rate 99%
Calorie consumption 3240 kilocalories

Finland, Gulf of 85 D6 Est. Soome Laht, Fin. Suomenlahti, Ger. Finnischer Meerbusen, Rus. Finskiy Zaliv, Swe. Finska Viken. gulf E Baltic Sea
Finland, Republic of see Finland
Finnischer Meerbusen see Finland, Gulf of
Finnmarksvidda 84 D2 physical region N Norway
Finska Viken/Finskiy Zaliv see Finland, Gulf of
Finsterwalde 94 D4 Brandenburg, E Germany
Fiordland 151 A7 physical region South Island, New Zealand
Fiorina 96 E1 NE San Marino
Firat Nehri see Euphrates
Firenze 96 C3 Eng. Florence; anc. Florentia. Toscana, C Italy
Firmum Picenum see Fermo
First State see Delaware
Fischbacher Alpen 95 E7 mountain range E Austria
Fischhausen see Primorsk
Fish 78 B4 var. Vis. river S Namibia
Fishguard 89 C6 Wel. Abergwaun. SW Wales, United Kingdom
Fisterra, Cabo 92 B1 headland NW Spain
Fitzroy Crossing 146 C3 Western Australia
Fitzroy River 146 C3 river Western Australia
Fiume see Rijeka
Flagstaff 48 B2 Arizona, SW USA
Flanders see Vlaanderen
Flandre see Vlaanderen
Flathead Lake 44 B1 lake Montana, NW USA
Flat Island 128 C8 island NE Spratly Islands
Flatts Village 42 B5 var. The Flatts Village. C Bermuda
Flensburg 94 B2 Schleswig-Holstein, N Germany
Flessingue see Vlissingen
Flickertail State see North Dakota
Flinders Island 149 C8 island Furneaux Group, Tasmania, SE Australia
Flinders Ranges 149 B6 mountain range South Australia
Flinders River 148 C3 river Queensland, NE Australia
Flin Flon 37 F5 Manitoba, C Canada
Flint 40 C3 Michigan, N USA
Flint Island 145 G4 island Line Islands, E Kiribati
Floreana, Isla see Santa María, Isla
Florence 42 C1 Alabama, S USA
Florence 43 F2 South Carolina, SE USA
Florence see Firenze
Florencia 58 B4 Caquetá, S Colombia
Florentia see Firenze
Flores 52 B1 Petén, N Guatemala
Flores 139 E5 island Nusa Tenggara, C Indonesia
Flores 92 A5 island Azores, Portugal, NE Atlantic Ocean
Flores, Laut see Flores Sea
Flores Sea 138 D5 Ind. Laut Flores. sea C Indonesia
Floriano 63 F2 Piauí, E Brazil
Florianópolis 63 F5 prev. Destêrro. state capital Santa Catarina, S Brazil
Florida 64 D4 Florida, S Uruguay
Florida 43 E4 off. State of Florida, also known as Peninsular State, Sunshine State. state SE USA

Florida Bay 43 E5 bay Florida, SE USA
Florida Keys 43 E5 island group Florida, SE USA
Florida, Straits of 54 B1 strait Atlantic Ocean/Gulf of Mexico
Flórina 104 B4 var. Phlórina. Dytikí Makedonía, N Greece
Florissant 45 G4 Missouri, C USA
Floúda, Akrotírio 105 D7 headland Astypálaia, Kykládes, Greece, Aegean Sea
Flushing see Vlissingen
Flylân see Vlieland
Foča 100 C4 var. Srbinje. SE Bosnia and Herzegovina
Focşani 108 C4 Vrancea, E Romania
Fogaras/Fogarasch see Făgăraş
Foggia 97 D5 Puglia, SE Italy
Fogo 74 A3 island Ilhas de Sotavento, SW Cape Verde
Foix 91 B6 Ariège, S France
Folégandros 105 C7 island Kykládes, Greece, Aegean Sea
Foleyet 38 C4 Ontario, S Canada
Foligno 96 C4 Umbria, C Italy
Folkestone 89 E7 SE England, United Kingdom
Fond du Lac 40 B2 Wisconsin, N USA
Fongafale 145 E3 var. Funafuti. country capital (Tuvalu) Funafuti Atoll, SE Tuvalu
Fonseca, Golfo de see Fonseca, Gulf of
Fonseca, Gulf of 52 C3 Sp. Golfo de Fonseca. gulf C Central America
Fontainebleau 90 C4 Seine-et-Marne, N France
Fontenay-le-Comte 90 B4 Vendée, NW France
Fontvieille 91 B8 SW Monaco Europe
Fonyód 99 C7 Somogy, W Hungary
Foochow see Fuzhou
Foochow see Fuzhou
Forchheim 95 C5 Bayern, SE Germany
Forel, Mont 82 D4 mountain SE Greenland
Forfar 88 C3 E Scotland, United Kingdom
Forge du Sud see Dudelange
Forlì 96 C3 anc. Forum Livii. Emilia-Romagna, N Italy
Formentera 93 G4 anc. Ophiusa, Lat. Frumentum. island Islas Baleares, Spain, W Mediterranean Sea
Formosa 64 D2 Formosa, NE Argentina
Formosa/Formo'sa see Taiwan
Formosa, Serra 63 E3 mountain range C Brazil
Formosa Strait see Taiwan Strait
Føroyar see Faeroe Islands
Forrest City 42 B1 Arkansas, C USA
Fort Albany 38 C3 Ontario, C Canada
Fortaleza 61 F2 Pando, N Bolivia
Fortaleza 63 G2 prev. Ceará. state capital Ceará, NE Brazil
Fort-Archambault see Sarh
Fort-Bayard see Zhanjiang
Fort-Cappolani see Tidjikja
Fort Charlet see Djanet
Fort-Chimo see Kuujjuaq
Fort Collins 44 D4 Colorado, C USA
Fort-Crampel see Kaga Bandoro
Fort Davis 49 E3 Texas, SW USA
Fort-de-France 55 H4 prev. Fort-Royal. dependent territory capital (Martinique) W Martinique
Fort Dodge 45 F3 Iowa, C USA
Fortescue River 146 A4 river Western Australia
Fort-Foureau see Kousséri
Fort Frances 38 B4 Ontario, S Canada
Fort Good Hope 37 E3 var. Rádeyilikóé. Northwest Territories, NW Canada
Fort Gouraud see Fdérik
Forth 88 C4 river C Scotland, United Kingdom
Forth, Firth of 88 C4 estuary E Scotland, United Kingdom
Fortín General Eugenio Garay see General Eugenio A. Garay
Fort Jameson see Chipata
Fort-Lamy see Ndjamena
Fort Lauderdale 43 F5 Florida, SE USA
Fort Liard 37 E4 var. Liard. Northwest Territories, W Canada
Fort Madison 45 G4 Iowa, C USA
Fort McMurray 37 E4 Alberta, C Canada
Fort McPherson 36 D3 var. McPherson. Northwest Territories, NW Canada
Fort Morgan 44 D4 Colorado, C USA

Fort Myers 43 E5 Florida, SE USA
Fort Nelson 37 E4 British Columbia, W Canada
Fort Peck Lake 44 C1 reservoir Montana, NW USA
Fort Pierce 43 F4 Florida, SE USA
Fort Providence 37 E4 var. Providence. Northwest Territories, W Canada
Fort-Repoux see Akjoujt
Fort Rosebery see Mansa
Fort Rousset see Owando
Fort-Royal see Fort-de-France
Fort St. John 37 E4 British Columbia, W Canada
Fort Scott 45 F5 Kansas, C USA
Fort Severn 38 C2 Ontario, C Canada
Fort-Shevchenko 114 A4 Mangistau, W Kazakhstan
Fort-Sibut see Sibut
Fort Simpson 37 E4 var. Simpson. Northwest Territories, W Canada
Fort Smith 37 E4 Northwest Territories, W Canada
Fort Smith 42 B1 Arkansas, C USA
Fort Stockton 49 E3 Texas, SW USA
Fort-Trinquet see Bîr Mogreïn
Fort Vermilion 37 E4 Alberta, W Canada
Fort Victoria see Masvingo
Fort Walton Beach 42 C3 Florida, SE USA
Fort Wayne 40 C4 Indiana, N USA
Fort William 88 C3 N Scotland, United Kingdom
Fort Worth 49 G2 Texas, SW USA
Fort Yukon 36 D3 Alaska, USA
Forum Alieni see Ferrara
Forum Livii see Forlì
Fossa Claudia see Chioggia
Fougamou 77 A6 Ngounié, C Gabon
Fougères 90 B3 Ille-et-Vilaine, NW France
Fou-hsin see Fuxin
Foulwind, Cape 151 B5 headland South Island, New Zealand
Foumban 76 A4 Ouest, NW Cameroon
Fou-shan see Fushun
Foveaux Strait 151 A8 strait S New Zealand
Foxe Basin 37 G3 sea Nunavut, N Canada
Fox Glacier 151 B6 West Coast, South Island, New Zealand
Fraga 93 F2 Aragón, NE Spain
Fram Basin 155 C3 var. Amundsen Basin. undersea basin Arctic Ocean
France 90 B4 off. French Republic, It./Sp. Francia; prev. Gaul, Gaule, Lat. Gallia. country W Europe

---

FRANCE
Western Europe

Official name French Republic
Formation 987 / 1919
Capital Paris
Population 63.1 million / 297 people per sq mile (115 people per sq km)
Total area 211,208 sq. miles (547,030 sq. km)
Languages French*, Provençal, German, Breton, Catalan, Basque
Religions Roman Catholic 88%, Muslim 8%, Protestant 2%, Buddhist 1%, Jewish 1%
Ethnic mix French 90%, North African (mainly Algerian) 6%, German (Alsace) 2%, Breton 1%, Other (including Corsicans) 1%
Government Mixed presidential–parliamentary system
Currency Euro = 100 cents
Literacy rate 99%
Calorie consumption 3531 kilocalories

Franceville 77 B6 var. Massoukou, Masuku. Haut-Ogooué, E Gabon
Francfort see Frankfurt am Main
Franche-Comté 90 D4 cultural region E France
Francia see France
Francis Case, Lake 45 E3 reservoir South Dakota, N USA
Francisco Escárcega 51 G4 Campeche, SE Mexico
Francistown 78 D3 North East, NE Botswana
Franconian Jura see Fränkische Alb
Frankenalb see Fränkische Alb

Frankenstein/Frankenstein in Schlesien see Ząbkowice Śląskie
Frankfort 40 C5 state capital Kentucky, S USA
Frankfort on the Main see Frankfurt am Main
Frankfurt see Frankfurt am Main, Germany
Frankfurt see Słubice, Poland
Frankfurt am Main 95 B5 var. Frankfurt, Fr. Francfort; prev. Eng. Frankfort on the Main. Hessen, SW Germany
Frankfurt an der Oder 94 D3 Brandenburg, E Germany
Fränkische Alb 95 C6 var. Frankenalb, Eng. Franconian Jura. mountain range S Germany
Franklin 42 C1 Tennessee, S USA
Franklin D. Roosevelt Lake 46 C1 reservoir Washington, NW USA
Franz Josef Land 114 D1 Eng. Franz Josef Land. island group N Russian Federation
Franz Josef Land see Frantsa-Iosifa, Zemlya
Fraserburgh 88 D3 NE Scotland, United Kingdom
Fraser Island 148 E4 var. Great Sandy Island. island Queensland, E Australia
Frauenbach see Baia Mare
Frauenburg see Saldus, Latvia
Fredericksburg 41 E5 Virginia, NE USA
Fredericton 39 F4 province capital New Brunswick, SE Canada
Frederikshåb see Paamiut
Frederikshald see Halden
Fredrikstad 85 B6 Østfold, S Norway
Freeport 54 C1 Grand Bahama Island, N Bahamas
Freeport 49 H4 Texas, SW USA
Free State see Maryland
Freetown 74 C4 country capital (Sierra Leone) W Sierra Leone
Freiburg see Freiburg im Breisgau, Germany
Freiburg im Breisgau 95 A6 var. Freiburg, Fr. Fribourg-en-Brisgau. Baden-Württemberg, SW Germany
Freiburg in Schlesien see Świebodzice
Fremantle 147 A6 Western Australia
Fremont 45 F4 Nebraska, C USA
French Guiana 59 H3 var. Guiana, Guyane. French overseas department N South America
French Guinea see Guinea
French Polynesia 143 F4 French overseas territory S Pacific Ocean
French Republic see France
French Somaliland see Djibouti
French Southern and Antarctic Territories 141 B7 Fr. Terres Australes et Antarctiques Françaises. French overseas territory S Indian Ocean
French Sudan see Mali
French Territory of the Afars and Issas see Djibouti
French Togoland see Togo
Fresnillo 50 D3 var. Fresnillo de González Echeverría. Zacatecas, C Mexico
Fresnillo de González Echeverría see Fresnillo
Fresno 47 C6 California, W USA
Frías 64 C3 Catamarca, N Argentina
Fribourg-en-Brisgau see Freiburg im Breisgau
Friedek-Mistek see Frýdek-Místek
Friedrichshafen 95 B7 Baden-Württemberg, S Germany
Friendly Islands see Tonga
Frisches Haff see Vistula Lagoon
Frobisher Bay 82 B3 inlet Baffin Island, Nunavut, NE Canada
Frobisher Bay see Iqaluit
Frohavet 84 B4 sound C Norway
Frome, Lake 149 B6 salt lake South Australia
Frontera 51 G4 Tabasco, SE Mexico
Frontignan 91 C6 Hérault, S France
Frostviken see Kvarnbergsvattnet
Frøya 84 A4 island W Norway
Frumentum see Formentera
Frunze see Bishkek
Frýdek-Místek 99 C5 Ger. Friedek-Mistek. Moravskoslezský Kraj, E Czech Republic
Fu-chien see Fujian
Fu-chou see Fuzhou

Fu-chou see Fuzhou
Fuengirola 92 D5 Andalucía, S Spain
Fuerte Olimpo 64 D2 var. Olimpo. Alto Paraguay, NE Paraguay
Fuerte, Río 48 C5 river C Mexico
Fuerteventura 70 B3 island Islas Canarias, Spain, NE Atlantic Ocean
Fuhkien see Fujian
Fu-hsin see Fuxin
Fuji 131 D6 var. Huzi. Shizuoka, Honshū, S Japan
Fujian 128 D6 var. Fu-chien, Fuhkien, Fukien, Min, Fujian Sheng. province SE China
Fujian Sheng see Fujian
Mount Fuji 131 C6 var. Fujiyama, Eng. Mount Fuji. mountain Honshū, SE Japan
Fuji, Mount/Fujiyama see Fuji-san
Fukang 126 C2 Xinjiang Uygur Zizhiqu, W China
Fukien see Fujian
Fukui 131 C6 var. Hukui. Fukui, Honshū, SW Japan
Fukuoka 131 A7 var. Hukuoka, hist. Najima. Fukuoka, Kyūshū, SW Japan
Fukushima 130 D4 var. Hukusima. Fukushima, Honshū, C Japan
Fulda 95 B5 Hessen, C Germany
Funafuti see Fongafale
Funafuti Atoll 145 E3 atoll C Tuvalu
Funchal 70 A2 Madeira, Portugal, NE Atlantic Ocean
Fundy, Bay of 39 F5 bay Canada/USA
Fünen see Fyn
Fünfkirchen see Pécs
Furnes see Veurne
Fürth 95 C5 Bayern, S Germany
Furukawa 130 D4 var. Hurukawa, Ōsaki. Miyagi, Honshū, C Japan
Fusan see Busan
Fushë Kosovë 101 D5 Serb. Kosovo Polje. C Kosovo
Fushun 128 D3 var. Fou-shan, Fu-shun. Liaoning, NE China
Fu-shun see Fushun
Fusin see Fuxin
Füssen 95 C7 Bayern, S Germany
Futog 100 D3 Vojvodina, NW Serbia
Futuna, Île 145 E4 island S Wallis and Futuna
Fuxin 128 D3 var. Fou-hsin, Fu-hsin, Fusin. Liaoning, NE China
Fuzhou 128 D3 var. Foochow, Fu-chou. province capital Fujian, SE China
Fuzhou 128 D6 var. Foochow, Fu-chou. province capital Fujian, SE China
Fyn 85 B8 Ger. Fünen. island C Denmark
FYR Macedonia/FYROM see Macedonia, FYR
Fyzabad see Feizābād

G

Gaafu Alifu Atoll see North Huvadhu Atoll
Gaalkacyo 73 E5 var. Galka'yo, It. Galcaio. Mudug, C Somalia
Gabela 78 B2 Cuanza Sul, W Angola
Gaberones see Gaborone
Gabès 71 E2 var. Qābis. E Tunisia
Gabès, Golfe de 71 F2 Ar. Khalij Qābis. gulf E Tunisia
Gabon 77 B6 off. Gabonese Republic. country C Africa

GABON
Central Africa

Official name Gabonese Republic
Formation 1960 / 1960
Capital Libreville
Population 1.5 million / 15 people per sq mile (6 people per sq km)
Total area 103,346 sq. miles (267,667 sq. km)
Languages Fang, French*, Punu, Sira, Nzebi, Mpongwe
Religions Christian (mainly Roman Catholic) 55%, Traditional beliefs 40%, Other 4%, Muslim 1%
Ethnic mix Fang 26%, Shira-punu 24%, Other 16%, Foreign residents 15%, Nzabi-duma 11%, Mbédé-Teke 8%
Government Presidential system
Currency CFA franc = 100 centimes
Literacy rate 88%
Calorie consumption 2745 kilocalories

Gabonese Republic see Gabon
Gaborone 78 C4 prev. Gaberones. country capital (Botswana) South East, SE Botswana
Gabrovo 104 D2 Gabrovo, N Bulgaria
Gadag 132 C1 Karnātaka, W India
Gades/Gadier/Gadir/Gadire see Cádiz
Gadsden 42 D2 Alabama, S USA
Gaeta 97 C5 Lazio, C Italy
Gaeta, Gulf of 97 C5 var. Gulf of Gaeta. gulf C Italy
Gaeta, Gulf of see Gaeta, Golfo di
Gäfle see Gävle
Gafsa 71 E2 var. Qafşah. W Tunisia
Gagnoa 74 D5 C Côte d'Ivoire
Gagra 117 E1 NW Georgia
Gaillac 91 C6 var. Gaillac-sur-Tarn. Tarn, S France
Gaillac-sur-Tarn see Gaillac
Gaillimh see Galway
Gaillimhe, Cuan na see Galway Bay
Gainesville 43 E3 Florida, SE USA
Gainesville 42 D2 Georgia, SE USA
Gainesville 49 G2 Texas, SW USA
Lake Gairdner 149 A6 salt lake South Australia
Gaizina Kalns see Gaiziņkalns
Gaiziņkalns 106 C3 var. Gaizina Kalns. mountain E Latvia
Galán, Cerro 64 B3 mountain NW Argentina
Galanta 99 C6 Hung. Galánta. Trnavský Kraj, W Slovakia
Galapagos Fracture Zone 153 E3 tectonic feature E Pacific Ocean
Galápagos Islands 153 F3 var. Islas de los Galápagos, Eng. Galapagos Islands, Tortoise Islands. island group Ecuador, E Pacific Ocean
Galápagos Islands see Colón, Archipiélago de
Galápagos, Islas de los see Colón, Archipiélago de
Galapagos Rise 153 F3 undersea rise E Pacific Ocean
Galashiels 88 C4 SE Scotland, United Kingdom
Galaţi 108 D4 Ger. Galatz. Galaţi, E Romania
Galatz see Galaţi
Galcaio see Gaalkacyo
Galesburg 40 B3 Illinois, N USA
Galicia 92 B1 anc. Gallaecia. autonomous community NW Spain
Galicia Bank 80 B4 undersea bank E Atlantic Ocean
Galilee, Sea of see Tiberias, Lake
Galka'yo see Gaalkacyo
Galkynyş 122 D3 prev. Rus. Deynau, Dyanev, Turkm. Däneav. Lebap Welaýaty, NE Turkmenistan
Gallaecia see Galicia
Galle 132 D4 prev. Point de Galle. Southern Province, SW Sri Lanka
Gallego Rise 153 F3 undersea rise E Pacific Ocean
Gallegos see Río Gallegos
Gallia see France
Gallipoli 97 E6 Puglia, SE Italy
Gällivare 84 C3 Lapp. Váhtjer. Norrbotten, N Sweden
Gallup 48 C1 New Mexico, SW USA
Galtat-Zemmour 70 B3 C Western Sahara
Galveston 49 H4 Texas, SW USA
Galway 89 A5 Ir. Gaillimh. W Ireland
Galway Bay 89 A6 Ir. Cuan na Gaillimhe. bay W Ireland
Gámas see Kaamanen
Gambell 36 C2 Saint Lawrence Island, Alaska, USA
Gambia 74 B3 off. Republic of The Gambia, The Gambia. country W Africa

GAMBIA
West Africa

Official name Republic of the Gambia
Formation 1965 / 1965
Capital Banjul
Population 1.8 million / 466 people per sq mile (180 people per sq km)
Total area 4363 sq. miles (11,300 sq. km)
Languages Mandinka, Fulani, Wolof, Jola, Soninke, English*
Religions Sunni Muslim 90%, Christian 8%, Traditional beliefs 2%
Ethnic mix Mandinka 42%, Fulani 18%,

GAMBIA
(continued)

Wolof 16%, Jola 10%, Serahuli 9%, Other 5%
Government Presidential system
Currency Dalasi = 100 butut
Literacy rate 46%
Calorie consumption 2643 kilocalories

Gambia 74 C3 Fr. Gambie. river W Africa
Gambia, Republic of The see Gambia
Gambia, The see Gambia
Gambie see Gambia
Gambier, Îles 143 G4 island group E French Polynesia
Gamboma 77 B6 Plateaux, E Congo
Gamlakarleby see Kokkola
Gan 132 B5 Addu Atoll, C Maldives
Gan see Gansu, China
Gan see Jiangxi, China
Ganaane see Juba
Gäncä 117 G2 Rus. Gyandzha; prev. Kirovabad, Yelisavetpol. W Azerbaijan
Gand see Gent
Gandajika 77 D7 Kasai-Oriental, S Dem. Rep. Congo
Gander 39 G3 Newfoundland and Labrador, SE Canada
Gāndhīdhām 134 C4 Gujarāt, W India
Gandia 93 F3 prev. Gandía. Valenciana, E Spain
Gandía see Gandia
Ganges 135 F3 Ben. Padma. river Bangladesh/India
Ganges Cone see Ganges Fan
Ganges Fan 140 D3 var. Ganges Cone. undersea fan N Bay of Bengal
Ganges, Mouths of the 135 G4 delta Bangladesh/India
Gangra see Çankırı
Gangtok 135 F3 state capital Sikkim, N India
Gansos, Lago dos see Goose Lake
Gansu 128 B4 var. Gan, Gansu Sheng, Kansu. province N China
Gansu Sheng see Gansu
Gantsevichi see Hantsavichy
Ganzhou 128 C6 Jiangxi, S China
Gao 75 E3 Gao, E Mali
Gaocheng see Litang
Gaoual 74 C4 N Guinea
Gaoxiong 128 D6 var. Kaohsiung, Jap. Takao, Takow. S Taiwan
Gap 91 D5 anc. Vapincum. Hautes-Alpes, SE France
Gaplaňgyr Platosy 122 C2 Rus. Plato Kaplangky. ridge Turkmenistan/ Uzbekistan
Gar see Gar Xincun
Garabil Belentligi 122 D3 Rus. Vozvyshennost' Karabil'. mountain range S Turkmenistan
Garabogaz Aylagy 122 B2 Rus. Zaliv Kara-Bogaz-Gol. bay NW Turkmenistan
Garachiné 53 G5 Darién, SE Panama
Garagum 122 C3 var. Garagumy, Qara Qum, Eng. Black Sand Desert, Kara Kum; prev. Peski Karakumy. desert C Turkmenistan
Garagum Canal 122 D3 var. Kara Kum Canal, Rus. Karagumskiy Kanal, Karakumskiy Kanal. canal C Turkmenistan
Garagumy see Garagum
Gara Khitrino 104 D2 Shumen, NE Bulgaria
Gárassavon see Kaaresuvanto
Garda, Lake 96 C2 var. Benaco, Eng. Lake Garda, Ger. Gardasee. lake NE Italy
Garda, Lake see Garda, Lago di
Gardasee see Garda, Lago di
Garden City 45 E5 Kansas, C USA
Garden State, The see New Jersey
Gardner Island see Nikumaroro
Garegegasnjárga see Karigasniemi
Gargždai 106 B3 Klaipėda, W Lithuania
Garissa 73 D6 Coast, E Kenya
Garland 49 G2 Texas, SW USA
Garoe see Garoowe
Garonne 91 B5 anc. Garumna. river S France
Garoowe 73 E5 var. Garoe. Nugaal, N Somalia
Garoua 76 B4 var. Garua. Nord, N Cameroon

Garry Lake *37 F3 lake* Nunavut, N Canada
Garsen *73 D6* Coast, S Kenya
Garua *see* Garoua
Garumna *see* Garonne
Garwolin *98 D4* Mazowieckie, E Poland
Gar Xincun *126 A4 prev.* Gar. Xizang Zizhiqu, W China
Gary *40 B3* Indiana, N USA
Garzón *58 B4* Huila, S Colombia
Gasan-Kuli *see* Esenguly
Gascogne *91 B6 Eng.* Gascony. *cultural region* S France
Gascony *see* Gascogne
Gascoyne River *147 A5 river* Western Australia
Gaspé *39 F3* Québec, SE Canada
Gaspé, Péninsule de *39 E4 var.* Péninsule de la Gaspésie. *peninsula* Québec, SE Canada
Gaspésie, Péninsule de la *see* Gaspé, Péninsule de
Gastonia *43 E1* North Carolina, SE USA
Gastoúni *105 B6* Dytikí Elláda, S Greece
Gatchina *110 B4* Leningradskaya Oblast', NW Russian Federation
Gatineau *38 D4* Québec, SE Canada
Gatooma *see* Kadoma
Gatún, Lake *53 F4 reservoir* C Panama
Gauháti *see* Guwāhāti
Gauja *106 D3 Ger.* Aa. *river* Estonia/Latvia
Gaul/Gaule *see* France
Gauteng *see* Johannesburg, South Africa
Gávbandi *120 D4* Hormozgān, S Iran
Gávdos *105 C8 island* SE Greece
Gavere *87 B6* Oost-Vlaanderen, NW Belgium
Gävle *85 C6 var.* Gäfle; *prev.* Gefle. Gävleborg, C Sweden
Gawler *149 B6* South Australia
Gaya *135 F3* Bihār, N India
Gaya *see* Kyjov
Gayndah *149 E5* Queensland, E Australia
Gaysin *see* Haysyn
Gaza *119 A6 Ar.* Ghazzah, *Heb.* 'Azza. NE Gaza Strip
Gaz-Achak *see* Gazojak
Gazandzhyk/Gazanjyk *see* Bereket
Gaza Strip *119 A7 Ar.* Qita Ghazzah. *disputed region* SW Asia
Gaziantep *116 D4 var.* Gazi Antep; *prev.* Aintab, Antep. Gaziantep, S Turkey
Gazi Antep *see* Gaziantep
Gazimağusa *102 D5 var.* Famagusta, *Gk.* Ammóchostos. E Cyprus
Gazli *122 D2* Buxoro Viloyati, C Uzbekistan
Gazojak *122 D2 Rus.* Gaz-Achak. Lebap Welaýaty, NE Turkmenistan
Gbanga *74 D5 var.* Gbarnga. N Liberia
Gbarnga *see* Gbanga
Gdańsk *98 C2 Fr.* Dantzig, *Ger.* Danzig. Pomorskie, N Poland
Gdan'skaya Bukhta/Gdańsk, Gulf of *see* Danzig, Gulf of
Gdańska, Zakota *see* Danzig, Gulf of
Gdingen *see* Gdynia
Gdynia *98 C2 Ger.* Gdingen. Pomorskie, N Poland
Gedaref *72 C4 var.* Al Qaḍārif, El Gedaref. Gedaref, E Sudan
Gediz *116 B3* Kütahya, W Turkey
Gediz Nehri *116 A3 river* W Turkey
Geel *87 C5 var.* Gheel. Antwerpen, N Belgium
Geelong *149 C7* Victoria, SE Australia
Ge'e'mu *see* Golmud
Gefle *see* Gävle
Geilo *85 A5* Buskerud, S Norway
Gejiu *128 B6 var.* Kochiu. Yunnan, S China
Gëkdepe *see* Gökdepe
Gela *97 C7 prev.* Terranova di Sicilia. Sicilia, Italy, C Mediterranean Sea
Geldermalsen *86 C4* Gelderland, C Netherlands
Geleen *87 D6* Limburg, SE Netherlands
Gelib *see* Jilib
Gellinsoor *73 E5* Galguduud, C Somalia
Gembloux *87 C6* Namur, Belgium
Gemena *77 C5* Equateur, NW Dem. Rep. Congo
Gem of the Mountains *see* Idaho
Gemona del Friuli *96 D2* Friuli-Venezia Giulia, NE Italy
Genalē Wenz *see* Juba
Genck *see* Genk

General Alvear *64 B4* Mendoza, W Argentina
General Carrera, Lago *see* Buenos Aires, Lago
General Eugenio A. Garay *64 C1 var.* Fortín General Eugenio Garay; *prev.* Yrendagüé. Nueva Asunción, NW Paraguay
General José F.Uriburu *see* Zárate
General Machado *see* Camacupa
General Santos *139 F3 off.* General Santos City. Mindanao, S Philippines
General Santos City *see* General Santos
Gênes *see* Genova
Geneva *see* Genève
Geneva, Lake *95 A7 Fr.* Lac de Genève, Lac Léman, le Léman, *Ger.* Genfer See. *lake* France/Switzerland
Genève *95 A7 Eng.* Geneva, *Ger.* Genf, *It.* Ginevra. Genève, SW Switzerland
Genève, Lac de *see* Geneva, Lake
Genf *see* Genève
Genfer See *see* Geneva, Lake
Genichesk *see* Heniches'k
Genk *87 D6 var.* Genck. Limburg, NE Belgium
Gennep *86 D4* Limburg, SE Netherlands
Genoa *see* Genova
Genoa, Gulf of *96 A3 Eng.* Gulf of Genoa. *gulf* NW Italy
Genoa, Gulf of *see* Genova, Golfo di
Genova *102 D1 Eng.* Genoa; *anc.* Genua, *Fr.* Gênes. Liguria, NW Italy
Genovesa, Isla *58 B5 var.* Tower Island. *island* Galápagos Islands, Ecuador, E Pacific Ocean
Gent *87 B5 Eng.* Ghent, *Fr.* Gand. Oost-Vlaanderen, NW Belgium
Genua *see* Genova
Geok-Tepe *see* Gökdepe
George *78 C5* Western Cape, S South Africa
George *82 A4 river* Newfoundland and Labrador/Québec, E Canada
George, Lake *43 E3 lake* Florida, SE USA
Georgenburg *see* Jurbarkas
Georges Bank *35 D5 undersea bank* W Atlantic Ocean
George Sound *151 A7 sound* South Island, New Zealand
Georges River *148 D2 river* New South Wales, E Australia
Georgetown *59 F2 country capital* (Guyana) (Guyana) N Guyana
George Town *54 C2* Great Exuma Island, C Bahamas
George Town *54 B3 var.* Georgetown. *dependent territory capital* (Cayman Islands) Grand Cayman, SW Cayman Islands
George Town *138 B3 var.* Penang, Pinang. Pinang, Peninsular Malaysia
Georgetown *43 F2* South Carolina, SE USA
Georgetown *see* George Town
George V Land *154 C4 physical region* Antarctica
Georgia *117 F2 off.* Republic of Georgia, *Geor.* Sak'art'velo, *Rus.* Gruzinskaya SSR, Gruziya. *country* SW Asia

GEORGIA
Southwest Asia

Official name Georgia
Formation 1991 / 1991
Capital Tbilisi
Population 4.3 million / 160 people per sq mile (62 people per sq km)
Total area 26,911 sq. miles (69,700 sq. km)
Languages Georgian*, Russian, Azeri, Armenian, Mingrelian, Ossetian, Abkhazian* *(in Abkhazia)*
Religions Georgian Orthodox 74%, Muslim 10%, Russian Orthodox 10%, Armenian Apostolic Church (Orthodox) 4%, Other 2%
Ethnic mix Georgian 84%, Armenian 6%, Azeri 6%, Russian 2%, Ossetian 1%, Other 1%
Government Presidential system
Currency Lari = 100 tetri
Literacy rate 99%
Calorie consumption 2743 kilocalories

Georgia *42 D2 off.* State of Georgia, *also known as* Empire State of the South, Peach State. *state* SE USA

Georgian Bay *40 D2 lake bay* Ontario, S Canada
Georgia, Republic of *see* Georgia
Georgia, Strait of *46 A1 strait* British Columbia, W Canada
Georgi Dimitrov *see* Kostenets
Georgiu-Dezh *see* Liski
Georg von Neumayer *154 A2 German research station* Antarctica
Gera *94 C4* Thüringen, E Germany
Geráki *105 B6* Pelopónnisos, S Greece
Geraldine *151 B6* Canterbury, South Island, New Zealand
Geraldton *147 A6* Western Australia
Geral, Serra *57 D5 mountain range* S Brazil
Gerede *116 C2* Bolu, N Turkey
Gereshk *122 D5* Helmand, SW Afghanistan
Gering *44 D3* Nebraska, C USA
German East Africa *see* Tanzania
Germanicopolis *see* Çankırı
Germanicum, Mare/German Ocean *see* North Sea
German Southwest Africa *see* Namibia
Germany *94 B4 off.* Federal Republic of Germany, Bundesrepublik Deutschland, *Ger.* Deutschland. *country* N Europe

GERMANY
Northern Europe

Official name Federal Republic of Germany
Formation 1871 / 1990
Capital Berlin
Population 82.2 million / 609 people per sq mile (235 people per sq km)
Total area 137,846 sq. miles (357,021 sq. km)
Languages German*, Turkish
Religions Protestant 34%, Roman Catholic 33%, Other 30%, Muslim 3%
Ethnic mix German 92%, Other European 3%, Other 3%, Turkish 2%
Government Parliamentary system
Currency Euro = 100 cents
Literacy rate 99%
Calorie consumption 3549 kilocalories

Germany, Federal Republic of *see* Germany
Geroliménas *105 B7* Pelopónnisos, S Greece
Gerona *see* Girona
Gerpinnes *87 C7* Hainaut, S Belgium
Gerunda *see* Girona
Gerze *116 D2* Sinop, N Turkey
Gesoriacum *see* Boulogne-sur-Mer
Gessoriacum *see* Boulogne-sur-Mer
Getafe *92 D3* Madrid, C Spain
Gevaş *117 F3* Van, SE Turkey
Gevgeli *see* Gevgelija
Gevgelija *101 E6 var.* Ðevdelija, Djevdjelija, *Turk.* Gevgeli. SE Macedonia
Ghaba *see* Al Ghābah
Ghana *75 E5 off.* Republic of Ghana. *country* W Africa

GHANA
West Africa

Official name Republic of Ghana
Formation 1957 / 1957
Capital Accra
Population 20 million / 281 people per sq mile (109 people per sq km)
Total area 92,100 sq. miles (238,540 sq. km)
Languages Twi, Fanti, Ewe, Ga, Adangbe, Gurma, Dagomba (Dagbani), English*
Religions Christian 69%, Muslim 16%, Traditional beliefs 9%, Other 6%
Ethnic mix Akan 49%, Mole-Dagbani 17%, Ewe 13%, Other 9%, Ga and Ga-Adangbe 8%, Guan 4%
Government Presidential system
Currency Cedi = 100 pesewas
Literacy rate 67%
Calorie consumption 2934 kilocalories

Ghanzi *78 C3 var.* Khanzi. Ghanzi, W Botswana
Gharandal *119 B7* Al'Aqabah, SW Jordan
Gharbt, Jabal al *see* Liban, Jebel
Ghardaïa *70 D2* N Algeria
Gharvān *see* Gharyān

Gharyān *71 F2 var.* Gharvān. NW Libya
Ghawdex *see* Gozo
Ghazni *123 E4 var.* Ghazni. Ghaznī, E Afghanistan
Ghazzah *see* Gaza
Gheel *see* Geel
Ghent *see* Gent
Gheorgheni *108 C4 prev.* Gheorghieni, Sîn-Miclăuş, *Ger.* Niklasmarkt, *Hung.* Gyergyószentmiklós. Harghita, C Romania
Gheorghieni *see* Gheorgheni
Ghōriān *122 D4 prev.* Ghūriān. Herāt, W Afghanistan
Ghūdara *123 F3 var.* Gudara, *Rus.* Kudara. SE Tajikistan
Ghurdaqah *see* Al Ghurdaqah
Ghūriān *see* Ghōriān
Giamame *see* Jamaame
Giannitsá *104 B4 var.* Yiannitsá. Kentrikí Makedonía, N Greece
Gibraltar *93 G4 UK dependent territory* SW Europe
Gibraltar, Bay of *93 G5 bay* Gibraltar/SpainMediterranean Sea Atlantic Ocean
Gibraltar, Détroit de/Gibraltar, Estrecho de *see* Gibraltar, Strait of
Gibraltar, Strait of *92 C5 Fr.* Détroit de Gibraltar, *Sp.* Estrecho de Gibraltar. *strait* Atlantic Ocean/Mediterranean Sea
Gibson Desert *147 B5 desert* Western Australia
Giebnegáisi *see* Kebnekaise
Giedraičiai *107 C5* Utena, E Lithuania
Giessen *95 B5* Hessen, W Germany
Gifu *131 C6 var.* Gihu. Gifu, Honshū, SW Japan
Giganta, Sierra de la *50 B3 mountain range* NW Mexico
Gihu *see* Gifu
G'ijduvon *122 D2 Rus.* Gizhduvon. Buxoro Viloyati, C Uzbekistan
Gijón *92 D1 var.* Xixón. Asturias, NW Spain
Gila River *48 A2 river* Arizona, SW USA
Gilbert Islands *see* Tungaru
Gilbert River *148 C3 river* Queensland, NE Australia
Gilf Kebir Plateau *see* Haḍabat al Jilf al Kabīr
Gillette *44 D3* Wyoming, C USA
Gilolo *see* Halmahera, Pulau
Gilroy *47 B6* California, W USA
Gimie, Mount *55 F1 mountain* C Saint Lucia
Gimma *see* Jīma
Ginevra *see* Genève
Gingin *147 A6* Western Australia
Giohar *see* Jawhar
Gipeswic *see* Ipswich
Girardot *58 B3* Cundinamarca, C Colombia
Giresun *117 E2 var.* Kerasunt; *anc.* Cerasus, Pharnacia. Giresun, NE Turkey
Girgenti *see* Agrigento
Girin *see* Jilin
Girne *102 C5 Gk.* Kerýneia, Kyrenia. N Cyprus
Giron *see* Kiruna
Girona *93 G2 var.* Gerona; *anc.* Gerunda. Cataluña, NE Spain
Gisborne *150 E3* Gisborne, North Island, New Zealand
Gissar Range *123 E3 Rus.* Gissarskiy Khrebet. *mountain range* Tajikistan/Uzbekistan
Gissarskiy Khrebet *see* Gissar Range
Githio *see* Gýtheio
Giulianova *96 D4* Abruzzi, C Italy
Giumri *see* Gyumri
Giurgiu *108 C5* Giurgiu, S Romania
Giza *72 B1 var.* Al Jīzah, El Gîza, Gizeh. E Egypt
Gizhduvon *see* G'ijduvon
Giżycko *98 D2 Ger.* Lötzen. Warmińsko-Mazurskie, NE Poland
Gjakovë *101 D5 Serb.* Đakovica. W Kosovo
Gjeravicë *101 D5 Serb.* Đeravica. *mountain* S Serbia
Gjilan *101 D5 Serb.* Gnjilane. E Kosovo
Gjinokastër *see* Gjirokastër
Gjirokastër *101 C7 var.* Gjirokastra; *prev.* Gjinokastër, *Gk.* Argyrokastron, *It.* Argirocastro. Gjirokastër, S Albania
Gjirokastra *see* Gjirokastër
Gjoa Haven *37 F3 var.* Uqsuqtuuq. King William Island, Nunavut, NW Canada

Gjøvik 85 B5 Oppland, S Norway
Glace Bay 39 G4 Cape Breton Island, Nova Scotia, SE Canada
Gladstone 148 E4 Queensland, E Australia
Gláma 85 B5 var. Glommen. river S Norway
Glasgow 88 C4 S Scotland, United Kingdom
Glavn'a Morava see Velika Morava
Glazov 111 D5 Udmurtskaya Respublika, NW Russian Federation
Gleiwitz see Gliwice
Glendale 48 B2 Arizona, SW USA
Glendive 44 D2 Montana, NW USA
Glens Falls 41 F3 New York, NE USA
Glevum see Gloucester
Glina 100 B3 var. Banijska Palanka. Sisak-Moslavina, NE Croatia
Glittertind 85 A5 mountain S Norway
Gliwice 99 C5 Ger. Gleiwitz. Śląskie, S Poland
Globe 48 B2 Arizona, SW USA
Globino see Hlobyne
Glogau see Głogów
Głogów 98 B4 Ger. Glogau, Glogow. Dolnośląskie, SW Poland
Glogow see Głogów
Glomma see Gláma
Glommen see Gláma
Gloucester 89 D6 hist. Caer Glou, Lat. Glevum. C England, United Kingdom
Głowno 98 D4 Łódź, C Poland
Glubokoye see Hlybokaye
Glukhov see Hlukhiv
Gnesen see Gniezno
Gniezno 98 C3 Ger. Gnesen. Weilkopolskie, C Poland
Gnjilane see Gjilan
Gobabis 78 B3 Omaheke, E Namibia
Gobi 126 D3 desert China/Mongolia
Gobō 131 C6 Wakayama, Honshū, SW Japan
Godavari 124 B3 var. Godavari. river C India
Godavari see Godāvari
Godhavn see Qeqertarsuaq
Godhra 134 C4 Gujarāt, W India
Göding see Hodonín
Godoy Cruz 64 B4 Mendoza, W Argentina
Godthaab/Godthåb see Nuuk
Godwin Austen, Mount see K2
Goede Hoop, Kaap de see Good Hope, Cape of
Goeie Hoop, Kaap die see Good Hope, Cape of
Goeree 86 B4 island SW Netherlands
Goes 87 B5 Zeeland, SW Netherlands
Goettingen see Göttingen
Gogebic Range 40 B1 hill range Michigan/Wisconsin, N USA
Goiânia 63 E3 prev. Goyania. state capital Goiás, C Brazil
Goiás 63 E3 off. Estado de Goiás; prev. Goiaz, Goyaz. region C Brazil
Goiás 63 E3 off. Estado de Goiás; prev. Goiaz, Goyaz. state C Brazil
Goiás, Estado de see Goiás
Goiaz see Goiás
Goidhoo Atoll see Horsburgh Atoll
Gojōme 130 D4 Akita, Honshū, NW Japan
Gökçeada 104 D4 var. Imroz Adasi, Gk. Imbros. island NW Turkey
Gökdepe 122 C3 Rus. Gekdepe, Geok-Tepe. Ahal Welaýaty, C Turkmenistan
Göksun 116 D4 Kahramanmaraş, C Turkey
Gol 85 A5 Buskerud, S Norway
Golan Heights 119 B5 Ar. Al Jawlān, Heb. HaGolan. mountain range SW Syria
Golaya Pristan see Hola Prystan'
Gołdap 98 E2 Ger. Goldap. Warmińsko-Mazurskie, NE Poland
Gold Coast 149 E5 cultural region Queensland, E Australia
Golden Bay 150 C4 bay South Island, New Zealand
Golden State, The see California
Goldingen see Kuldīga
Goldsboro 43 F1 North Carolina, SE USA
Goleniów 98 B3 Ger. Gollnow. Zachodnio-pomorskie, NW Poland
Gollnow see Goleniów
Golmo see Golmud

Golmud 126 D4 var. Ge'e'mu, Golmo, Chin. Ko-erh-mu. Qinghai, C China
Golovanevsk see Holovanivs'k
Golub-Dobrzyń 98 C3 Kujawski-pomorskie, C Poland
Goma 77 E6 Nord-Kivu, NE Dem. Rep. Congo
Gombi 75 H4 Adamawa, E Nigeria
Gombroon see Bandar-e 'Abbās
Gomel' see Homyel'
Gomera 70 A3 island Islas Canarias, Spain, NE Atlantic Ocean
Gómez Palacio 50 D3 Durango, C Mexico
Gonaïves 54 D3 var. Les Gonaïves. N Haiti
Gonâve, Île de la 54 D3 island C Haiti
Gondar see Gonder
Gonder 72 C4 var. Gondar. Āmara, NW Ethiopia
Gondia 135 E4 Mahārāshtra, C India
Gonggar 126 C5 var. Gyixong. Xizang Zizhiqu, W China
Gongola 75 G4 river E Nigeria
Gongtang see Damxung
Gonni/Gónnos see Gónnoi
Gónnoi 104 B4 var. Gonni, Gónnos; prev. Derelí. Thessalía, C Greece
Good Hope, Cape of 78 B5 Afr. Kaap de Goede Hoop, Kaap die Goeie Hoop. headland SW South Africa
Goodland 44 D4 Kansas, C USA
Goondiwindi 149 D5 Queensland, E Australia
Goor 86 E3 Overijssel, E Netherlands
Goose Green 65 D7 var. Prado del Ganso. East Falkland, Falkland Islands
Goose Lake 46 B4 var. Lago dos Gansos. lake California/Oregon, W USA
Gopher State see Minnesota
Göppingen 95 B6 Baden-Württemberg, SW Germany
Góra Kalwaria 114 D4 Mazowieckie, C Poland
Gorakhpur 135 E3 Uttar Pradesh, N India
Gorany see Harany
Goražde 100 C4 Federacija Bosna I Hercegovina, SE Bosnia and Herzegovina
Gorbovichi see Harbavichy
Goré 76 C4 Logone-Oriental, S Chad
Gorē 73 C5 Oromīya, C Ethiopia
Gore 151 B7 Southland, South Island, New Zealand
Gorgān 120 D2 var. Astarabad, Astrabad, Gurgan, prev. Asterābād; anc. Hyrcania. Golestán, N Iran
Gori 117 F2 C Georgia
Gorinchem 86 C4 var. Gorkum. Zuid-Holland, C Netherlands
Goris 117 G3 SE Armenia
Gorki see Horki
Gor'kiy see Nizhniy Novgorod
Gorkum see Gorinchem
Görlitz 94 D4 Sachsen, E Germany
Görlitz see Zgorzelec
Gorlovka see Horlivka
Gorna Dzhumaya see Blagoevgrad
Gornja Mužlja see Mužlja
Gornji Milanovac 100 C4 Serbia, C Serbia
Gorodets see Haradzyets
Gorodishche see Horodyshche
Gorodnya see Horodnya
Gorodok see Haradok
Gorodok/Gorodok Yagellonski see Horodok
Gorontalo 139 E4 Sulawesi, C Indonesia
Gorontalo, Teluk see Tomini, Teluk
Gorssel 86 D3 Gelderland, E Netherlands
Goryn see Horyn'
Gorzów Wielkopolski 98 B3 Ger. Landsberg, Landsberg an der Warthe. Lubuskie, W Poland
Gosford 149 D6 New South Wales, SE Australia
Goshogawara 130 D3 var. Gosyogawara. Aomori, Honshū, C Japan
Gospić 100 A3 Lika-Senj, C Croatia
Gostivar 101 D6 W FYR Macedonia
Gosyogawara see Goshogawara
Göteborg 85 B7 Eng. Gothenburg. Västra Götaland, S Sweden
Gotel Mountains 75 G5 mountain range E Nigeria
Gotha 94 C4 Thüringen, C Germany
Gothenburg see Göteborg
Gotland 85 C7 island SE Sweden

Goto-retto 131 A7 island group SW Japan
Gotska Sandön 106 B1 island SE Sweden
Gōtsu 131 B6 var. Gôtu. Shimane, Honshū, SW Japan
Göttingen 94 B4 var. Goettingen. Niedersachsen, C Germany
Gottschee see Kočevje
Gottwaldov see Zlín
Gôtu see Gōtsu
Gouda 86 C4 Zuid-Holland, C Netherlands
Gough Fracture Zone 67 C6 tectonic feature S Atlantic Ocean
Gough Island 69 B8 island Tristan da Cunha, S Atlantic Ocean
Gouin, Réservoir 38 D4 reservoir Québec, SE Canada
Goulburn 149 D6 New South Wales, SE Australia
Goundam 75 E3 Tombouctou, NW Mali
Gouré 75 G3 Zinder, SE Niger
Goverla, Gora see Hoverla, Hora
Governador Valadares 63 F4 Minas Gerais, SE Brazil
Govi Altayn Nuruu 127 E3 mountain range S Mongolia
Goya 64 D3 Corrientes, NE Argentina
Goyania see Goiânia
Goyaz see Goiás
Goz Beïda 76 C3 Ouaddaï, SE Chad
Gozo 97 C8 var. Ghawdex. island N Malta
Graciosa 92 A5 var. Ilha Graciosa. island Azores, Portugal, NE Atlantic Ocean
Graciosa, Ilha see Graciosa
Gradačac 100 C3 Federacija Bosna I Hercegovina, N Bosnia and Herzegovina
Gradaús, Serra dos 63 E3 mountain range C Brazil
Gradiška see Bosanska Gradiška
Grafton 149 E5 New South Wales, SE Australia
Grafton 45 E1 North Dakota, N USA
Graham Land 154 A2 physical region Antarctica
Grajewo 98 E3 Podlaskie, NE Poland
Grampian Mountains 88 C3 mountain range C Scotland, United Kingdom
Gran see Esztergom
Granada 52 D3 Granada, SW Nicaragua
Granada 92 D5 Andalucía, S Spain
Gran Canaria 70 A3 var. Grand Canary. island Islas Canarias, Spain, NE Atlantic Ocean
Gran Chaco 64 D2 var. Chaco. lowland plain South America
Grand Bahama Island 54 B1 island N Bahamas
Grand Banks of Newfoundland 34 E4 undersea basin NW Atlantic Ocean
Grand Bassa see Buchanan
Grand Canary see Gran Canaria
Grand Canyon 48 A1 canyon Arizona, SW USA
Grand Canyon State see Arizona
Grand Cayman 54 B3 island SW Cayman Islands
Grand Duchy of Luxembourg see Luxembourg
Grande, Bahía 65 B7 bay S Argentina
Grande Comore see Ngazidja
Grande de Chiloé, Isla see Chiloé, Isla de
Grande Prairie 37 E4 Alberta, W Canada
Grand Erg Occidental 70 D3 desert W Algeria
Grand Erg Oriental 71 E3 desert Algeria/Tunisia
Rio Grande 51 E2 var. Río Bravo, Sp. Río Bravo del Norte, Bravo del Norte. river Mexico/USA
Grande Terre 55 G3 island E West Indies
Grand Falls 39 G3 Newfoundland, Newfoundland and Labrador, SE Canada
Grand Forks 45 E1 North Dakota, N USA
Grandichi see Hrandzichy
Grand Island 45 E4 Nebraska, C USA
Grand Junction 44 C4 Colorado, C USA
Grand Paradis see Gran Paradiso
Grand Rapids 40 C3 Michigan, N USA
Grand Rapids 45 F1 Minnesota, N USA
Grand-Saint-Bernard, Col du see Great Saint Bernard Pass
Grand-Santi 59 G3 W French Guiana
Granite State see New Hampshire
Gran Lago see Nicaragua, Lago de

Gran Malvina see West Falkland
Gran Paradiso 96 A2 Fr. Grand Paradis. mountain NW Italy
Gran San Bernardo, Passo di see Great Saint Bernard Pass
Gran Santiago see Santiago
Grants 48 C2 New Mexico, SW USA
Grants Pass 46 B4 Oregon, NW USA
Granville 90 B3 Manche, N France
Gratianopolis see Grenoble
Gratz see Graz
Graudenz see Grudziądz
Graulhet 91 C6 Tarn, S France
Grave 86 D4 Noord-Brabant, SE Netherlands
Grayling 36 C2 Alaska, USA
Graz 95 E7 prev. Gratz. Steiermark, SE Austria
Great Abaco 54 C1 var. Abaco Island. island N Bahamas
Great Alfold see Great Hungarian Plain
Great Ararat see Büyükağrı Dağı
Great Australian Bight 147 D7 bight S Australia
Great Barrier Island 150 D2 island N New Zealand
Great Barrier Reef 148 D2 reef Queensland, NE Australia
Great Basin 47 C5 basin W USA
Great Bear Lake 37 E3 Fr. Grand Lac de l'Ours. lake Northwest Territories, NW Canada
Great Belt 85 B8 var. Store Bælt, Eng. Great Belt, Storebelt. channel Baltic Sea/Kattegat
Great Belt see Storebælt
Great Bend 45 E5 Kansas, C USA
Great Britain see Britain
Great Dividing Range 148 D4 mountain range NE Australia
Greater Antilles 54 D3 island group West Indies
Greater Caucasus 117 G2 mountain range Azerbaijan/Georgia/Russian Federation Asia/Europe
Greater Sunda Islands 124 D5 var. Sunda Islands. island group Indonesia
Great Exhibition Bay 150 C1 inlet North Island, New Zealand
Great Exuma Island 54 C2 island C Bahamas
Great Falls 44 B1 Montana, NW USA
Great Grimsby see Grimsby
Great Hungarian Plain 99 C7 var. Great Alfold, Plain of Hungary, Hung. Alföld. plain SE Europe
Great Inagua 54 D2 var. Inagua Islands. island S Bahamas
Great Indian Desert see Thar Desert
Great Khingan Range 127 G1 Eng. Great Khingan Range. mountain range NE China
Great Khingan Range see Da Hinggan Ling
Great Lake see Tônlé Sap
Great Lakes 35 C5 lakes Ontario, Canada/USA
Great Lakes State see Michigan
Great Meteor Seamount see Great Meteor Tablemount
Great Meteor Tablemount 66 B3 var. Great Meteor Seamount. seamount E Atlantic Ocean
Great Nicobar 133 G3 island Nicobar Islands, India, NE Indian Ocean
Great Plain of China 125 E2 plain E China
Great Plains 45 E3 var. High Plains. plains Canada/USA
Great Rift Valley 73 C5 var. Rift Valley. depression Asia/Africa
Great Ruaha 73 C7 river S Tanzania
Great Saint Bernard Pass 96 A1 Fr. Col du Grand-Saint-Bernard, It. Passo del Gran San Bernardo. pass Italy/Switzerland
Great Salt Desert see Kavir, Dasht-e
Great Salt Lake 44 A3 salt lake Utah, W USA
Great Salt Lake Desert 44 A4 plain Utah, W USA
Great Sand Sea 71 H3 desert Egypt/Libya
Great Sandy Desert 146 C4 desert Western Australia
Great Sandy Desert see Ar Rub' al Khālī
Great Sandy Island see Fraser Island
Great Slave Lake 37 E4 Fr. Grand Lac des Esclaves. lake Northwest Territories, NW Canada

Great Socialist People's Libyan Arab Jamahiriya *see* Libya
Great Sound *42 A5 sound* Bermuda, NW Atlantic Ocean
Great Victoria Desert *147 C5 desert* South Australia/Western Australia
Great Wall of China *128 C4 ancient monument* N China Asia
Great Yarmouth *89 E6 var.* Yarmouth. E England, United Kingdom
Grebenka *see* Hrebinka
Gredos, Sierra de *92 D3 mountain range* W Spain
Greece *105 A5 off.* Hellenic Republic, *Gk.* Ellás; *anc.* Hellas. *country* SE Europe

GREECE
Southeast Europe

Official name Hellenic Republic
Formation 1829 / 1947
Capital Athens
Population 11.4 million / 226 people per sq mile (87 people per sq km)
Total area 50,942 sq. miles (131,940 sq. km)
Languages Greek*, Turkish, Macedonian, Albanian
Religions Orthodox Christian 98%, Muslim 1%, Other 1%
Ethnic mix Greek 98%, Other 2%
Government Parliamentary system
Currency Euro = 100 cents
Literacy rate 97%
Calorie consumption 3661 kilocalories

Greeley *44 D4* Colorado, C USA
Green Bay *40 B2* Wisconsin, N USA
Green Bay *40 B2 lake bay* Michigan/Wisconsin, N USA
Greeneville *43 E1* Tennessee, S USA
Greenland *82 D3 Dan.* Grønland, *Inuit* Kalaallit Nunaat. *Danish external territory* NE North America
Greenland Sea *83 F2 sea* Arctic Ocean
Green Mountains *41 G2 mountain range* Vermont, NE USA
Green Mountain State *see* Vermont
Greenock *88 C4* W Scotland, United Kingdom
Green River *44 B3* Wyoming, C USA
Green River *40 C5 river* Kentucky, C USA
Greensboro *43 F1* North Carolina, SE USA
Greenville *42 B2* Mississippi, S USA
Greenville *43 F1* North Carolina, SE USA
Greenville *43 F1* South Carolina, SE USA
Greenville *49 G2* Texas, SW USA
Greenwich *89 B8* United Kingdom
Greenwood *42 B2* Mississippi, S USA
Greenwood *43 E2* South Carolina, SE USA
Gregory Range *148 C3 mountain range* Queensland, E Australia
Greifenberg/Greifenberg in Pommern *see* Gryfice
Greifswald *94 D2* Mecklenburg-Vorpommern, NE Germany
Grenada *42 C2* Mississippi, S USA
Grenada *55 G5 country* SE West Indies

GRENADA
West Indies

Official name Grenada
Formation 1974 / 1974
Capital St. George's
Population 109,011 / 832 people per sq mile (321 people per sq km)
Total area 131 sq. miles (340 sq. km)
Languages English*, English Creole
Religions Roman Catholic 68%, Anglican 17%, Other 15%
Ethnic mix Black African 82%, Mulatto (mixed race) 13%, East Indian 3%, Other 2%
Government Parliamentary system
Currency East Caribbean dollar = 100 cents
Literacy rate 96%
Calorie consumption 2456 kilocalories

Grenadines, The *55 H4 island group* Grenada/St Vincent and the Grenadines
Grenoble *91 D5 anc.* Cularo, Gratianopolis. Isère, E France
Gresham *46 B3* Oregon, NW USA

Grevená *104 B4* Dytikí Makedonía, N Greece
Grevenmacher *87 E8* Grevenmacher, E Luxembourg
Greymouth *151 B5* West Coast, South Island, New Zealand
Grey Range *149 C5 mountain range* New South Wales/Queensland, E Australia
Greytown *see* San Juan del Norte
Griffin *42 D2* Georgia, SE USA
Grimari *76 C4* Ouaka, C Central African Republic
Grimsby *89 E5 prev.* Great Grimsby. E England, United Kingdom
Grobin *see* Grobiņa
Grobiņa *106 B3 Ger.* Grobin. W Latvia
Gródek Jagielloński *see* Horodok
Grodno *see* Hrodna
Grodzisk Wielkopolski *98 B3* Wielkopolskie, C Poland
Groesbeek *86 D4* Gelderland, SE Netherlands
Grójec *98 D4* Mazowieckie, C Poland
Groningen *86 E1* Groningen, NE Netherlands
Grønland *see* Greenland
Groote Eylandt *148 B2 island* Northern Territory, N Australia
Grootfontein *78 B3* Otjozondjupa, N Namibia
Groot Karasberge *78 B4 mountain range* S Namibia
Gros Islet *55 F1* N Saint Lucia
Grossa, Isola *see* Dugi Otok
Grossbetschkerek *see* Zrenjanin
Grosse Morava *see* Velika Morava
Grosser Sund *see* Suur Väin
Grosseto *96 B4* Toscana, C Italy
Grossglockner *95 C7 mountain* W Austria
Grosskanizsa *see* Nagykanizsa
Gross-Karol *see* Carei
Grosskikinda *see* Kikinda
Grossmichel *see* Michalovce
Gross-Schlatten *see* Abrud
Grosswardein *see* Oradea
Grozny *111 B8* Chechenskaya Respublika, SW Russian Federation
Grudovo *see* Sredets
Grudziądz *98 C3 Ger.* Graudenz. Kujawsko-pomorskie, C Poland
Grums *85 B6* Värmland, C Sweden
Grünberg/Grünberg in Schlesien *see* Zielona Góra
Grüneberg *see* Zielona Góra
Gruzinskaya SSR/Gruziya *see* Georgia
Gryazi *111 B6* Lipetskaya Oblast', W Russian Federation
Gryfice *98 B2 Ger.* Greifenberg, Greifenberg in Pommern. Zachodnio-pomorskie, NW Poland
Guabito *53 E4* Bocas del Toro, NW Panama
Guadalajara *50 D4* Jalisco, C Mexico
Guadalajara *93 E3 Ar.* Wad Al-Hajarah; *anc.* Arriaca. Castilla-La Mancha, C Spain
Guadalcanal *144 C3 island* C Solomon Islands
Guadalquivir *92 D4 river* W Spain
Guadalupe *50 D3* Zacatecas, C Mexico
Guadalupe Peak *48 D3 mountain* Texas, SW USA
Guadalupe River *49 G4 river* SW USA
Guadarrama, Sierra de *93 E2 mountain range* C Spain
Guadeloupe *55 H3 French overseas department* E West Indies
Guadiana *92 C4 river* Portugal/Spain
Guadix *93 E4* Andalucía, S Spain
Guaimaca *52 C2* Francisco Morazán, C Honduras
Guajira, Península de la *58 B1 peninsula* N Colombia
Gualaco *52 D2* Olancho, C Honduras
Gualán *52 B2* Zacapa, C Guatemala
Gualdicciolo *96 D1* NW San Marino
Gualeguaychú *64 D4* Entre Ríos, E Argentina
Guam *144 B1 US unincorporated territory* W Pacific Ocean
Guamúchil *50 C3* Sinaloa, C Mexico
Guanabacoa *54 B2* La Habana, W Cuba
Guanajuato *51 E4* Guanajuato, C Mexico
Guanare *58 C2* Portuguesa, N Venezuela
Guanare, Río *58 D2 river* W Venezuela
Guangdong *128 C6 var.* Guangdong Sheng, Kuang-tung, Kwangtung, Yue. *province* S China

Guangdong Sheng *see* Guangdong
Guangju *see* Gwangju
Guangxi *see* Guangxi Zhuangzu Zizhiqu
Guangxi Zhuangzu Zizhiqu *128 C6 var.* Guangxi, Gui, Kuang-hsi, Kwangsi, *Eng.* Kwangsi Chuang Autonomous Region. *autonomous region* S China
Guangyuan *128 B5 var.* Kuang-yuan, Kwangyuan. Sichuan, C China
Guangzhou *128 C6 var.* Kuang-chou, Kwangchow, *Eng.* Canton. *province capital* Guangdong, S China
Guantánamo *54 D3* Guantánamo, SE Cuba
Guantánamo, Bahia de *54 D3 Eng.* Guantanamo Bay. *US military base* SE Cuba
Guantanamo Bay *see* Guantánamo, Bahia de
Guaporé, Rio *62 D3 var.* Río Iténez. *river* Bolivia/Brazil
Guarda *92 C3* Guarda, N Portugal
Guarumal *53 F5* Veraguas, S Panama
Guasave *50 C3* Sinaloa, C Mexico
Guatemala *52 A2 off.* Republic of Guatemala. *country* Central America

GUATEMALA
Central America

Official name Republic of Guatemala
Formation 1838 / 1838
Capital Guatemala City
Population 14.8 million / 354 people per sq mile (136 people per sq km)
Total area 42,042 sq. miles (108,890 sq. km)
Languages Quiché, Mam, Cakchiquel, Kekchí, Spanish*
Religions Roman Catholic 65%, Protestant 33%, Other and nonreligious 2%
Ethnic mix Amerindian 60%, Mestizo 30%, Other 10%
Government Presidential system
Currency Quetzal = 100 centavos
Literacy rate 74%
Calorie consumption 2219 kilocalories

Guatemala Basin *35 B7 undersea basin* E Pacific Ocean
Guatemala City *see* Ciudad de Guatemala
Guatemala, Republic of *see* Guatemala
Guaviare *56 B2 off.* Comisaría Guaviare. *province* S Colombia
Guaviare, Comisaría de *see* Guaviare
Guaviare, Río *58 D3 river* E Colombia
Guayana, Macizo de las *see* Guiana Highlands
Guayaquil *60 A2 var.* Santiago de Guayaquil. Guayas, SW Ecuador
Guayaquil, Gulf of *60 A2 var.* Gulf of Guayaquil. *gulf* SW Ecuador
Guayaquil, Gulf of *see* Guayaquil, Golfo de
Guaymas *50 B2* Sonora, NW Mexico
Gubadag *122 C2 Turkm.* Tel'man; *prev.* Tel'mansk. Daşoguz Welaýaty, N Turkmenistan
Guben *94 D4 var.* Wilhelm-Pieck-Stadt. Brandenburg, E Germany
Gudara *see* Ghūdara
Gudauta *117 E1 prev.* Gudaut'a. NW Georgia
Gudaut'a *see* Gudauta
Guéret *90 C4* Creuse, C France
Guerrero Negro *50 A2* Baja California Sur, NW Mexico
Gui *see* Guangxi Zhuangzu Zizhiqu
Guiana *see* French Guiana
Guiana Highlands *62 D1 var.* Macizo de las Guayanas. *mountain range* N South America
Guiba *see* Juba
Guidder *see* Guider
Guider *76 B4 var.* Guidder. Nord, N Cameroon
Guidimouni *75 G3* Zinder, S Niger
Guildford *89 D7* SE England, United Kingdom
Guilin *128 C6 var.* Kuei-lin, Kweilin. Guangxi Zhuangzu Zizhiqu, S China
Guimarães *92 B2 var.* Guimaráes. Braga, N Portugal
Guimaráes *see* Guimarães

Guinea *74 C4 off.* Republic of Guinea, *var.* Guinée; *prev.* French Guinea, People's Revolutionary Republic of Guinea. *country* W Africa

GUINEA
West Africa

Official name Republic of Guinea
Formation 1958 / 1958
Capital Conakry
Population 10.2 million / 107 people per sq mile (41 people per sq km)
Total area 94,925 sq. miles (245,857 sq. km)
Languages Pulaar, Malinké, Soussou, French
Religions Muslim 85%, Christian 8%, Traditional beliefs 7%
Ethnic mix Peul 40%, Malinké 30%, Soussou 20%, Other 10%
Government Transitional regime
Currency Guinea franc = 100 centimes
Literacy rate 40%
Calorie consumption 2652 kilocalories

Guinea Basin *69 A5 undersea basin* E Atlantic Ocean
Guinea-Bissau *74 B4 off.* Republic of Guinea-Bissau, *Fr.* Guinée-Bissau, *Port.* Guiné-Bissau; *prev.* Portuguese Guinea. *country* W Africa

GUINEA-BISSAU
West Africa

Official name Republic of Guinea-Bissau
Formation 1974 / 1974
Capital Bissau
Population 1.5 million / 138 people per sq mile (53 people per sq km)
Total area 13,946 sq. miles (36,120 sq. km)
Languages Portuguese Creole, Balante, Fulani, Malinké, Portuguese*
Religions Traditional beliefs 50%, Muslim 40%, Christian 10%
Ethnic mix Balante 30%, Fulani 20%, Other 16%, Mandyako 14%, Mandinka 13%, Papel 7%
Government Transitional regime
Currency CFA franc = 100 centimes
Literacy rate 52%
Calorie consumption 2476 kilocalories

Guinea-Bissau, Republic of *see* Guinea-Bissau
Guinea, Gulf of *68 B4 Fr.* Golfe de Guinée. *gulf* E Atlantic Ocean
Guinea, People's Revolutionary Republic of *see* Guinea
Guiné-Bissau *see* Guinea-Bissau
Guinée *see* Guinea
Guinée-Bissau *see* Guinea-Bissau
Guinée, Golfe de *see* Guinea, Gulf of
Güiria *59 E1* Sucre, NE Venezuela
Guiyang *128 B6 var.* Kuei-Yang, Kuei-yang, Kueiyang, Kweiyang; *prev.* Kweichu. *province capital* Guizhou, S China
Guizhou *128 B6* Guangdong, SE China
Gujarāt *134 C4 var.* Gujerat. *cultural region* W India
Gujerat *see* Gujarāt
Gujrānwāla *134 D2* Punjab, NE Pakistan
Gujrāt *134 D2* Punjab, E Pakistan
Gulbarga *132 C1* Karnātaka, C India
Gulbene *106 D3 Ger.* Alt-Schwanenburg. NE Latvia
Gulf of Liaotung *see* Liaodong Wan
Gulfport *42 C3* Mississippi, S USA
Gulistan *see* Guliston
Guliston *123 E2 Rus.* Gulistan. Sirdaryo Viloyati, E Uzbekistan
Gulja *see* Yining
Gulkana *36 D3* Alaska, USA
Gulu *73 B6* N Uganda
Gulyantsi *104 C1* Pleven, N Bulgaria
Guma *see* Pishan
Gumbinnen *see* Gusev
Gumpolds *see* Humpolec
Gümülcine/Gümüljina *see* Komotiní
Gümüşhane *117 E3 var.* Gümüşane, Gumushkhane. Gümüşhane, NE Turkey
Gumushkhane *see* Gümüşhane
Güney Doğu Toroslar *117 E4 mountain range* SE Turkey

Gunnbjørn Fjeld *82 D4 var.* Gunnbjörns Bjerge. *mountain* C Greenland
Gunnbjörns Bjerge *see* Gunnbjørn Fjeld
Gunnedah *149 D6* New South Wales, SE Australia
Gunnison *44 C5* Colorado, C USA
Gurbansoltan Eje *122 C2 prev.* Ýylanly, *Rus.* Il'yaly. Daşoguz Welaýaty, N Turkmenistan
Gurbantünggüt Shamo *126 B2 desert* W China
Gurgan *see* Gorgān
Guri, Embalse de *59 E2 reservoir* E Venezuela
Gurkfeld *see* Krško
Gurktaler Alpen *95 D7 mountain range* S Austria
Gürün *116 D3* Sivas, C Turkey
Gur'yev/Gur'yevskaya Oblast' *see* Atyrau
Gusau *75 G4* Zamfara, NW Nigeria
Gusev *106 B4 Ger.* Gumbinnen. Kaliningradskaya Oblast', W Russian Federation
Gustavus *36 D4* Alaska, USA
Güstrow *94 C3* Mecklenburg-Vorpommern, NE Germany
Guta/Gúta *see* Kolárovo
Gütersloh *94 B4* Nordrhein-Westfalen, W Germany
Gutta *see* Kolárovo
Guttstadt *see* Dobre Miasto
Guwāhāti *135 G3 prev.* Gauhāti. Assam, NE India
Guyana *59 F3 off.* Co-operative Republic of Guyana; *prev.* British Guiana. *country* N South America

---

GUYANA
South America

Official name Cooperative Republic of Guyana
Formation 1966 / 1966
Capital Georgetown
Population 800,000 / 11 people per sq mile (4 people per sq km)
Total area 83,000 sq. miles (214,970 sq. km)
Languages English Creole, Hindi, Tamil, Amerindian languages, English*
Religions Christian 57%, Hindu 28%, Muslim 10%, Other 5%
Ethnic mix East Indian 43%, Black African 30%, Mixed race 17%, Amerindian 9%, Other 1%
Government Presidential system
Currency Guyanese dollar = 100 cents
Literacy rate 99%
Calorie consumption 2718 kilocalories

Guyana, Co-operative Republic of *see* Guyana
Guyane *see* French Guiana
Guymon *49 E1* Oklahoma, C USA
Güzelyurt *102 C5 Gk.* Kólpos Mórfu, Morphou. W Cyprus
Gvardeysk *106 A4 Ger.* Tapaiu. Kaliningradskaya Oblast', W Russian Federation
Gwādar *134 A3 var.* Gwadur. Baluchistān, SW Pakistan
Gwadur *see* Gwādar
Gwalior *134 D3* Madhya Pradesh, C India
Gwanda *78 D3* Matabeleland South, SW Zimbabwe
Gwangju *129 E4 off.* Kwangju-gwangyŏksi, *var.* Guangju, Kwangchu; *prev.* Kwangju, *Jap.* Kōshū. SW South Korea
Gwy *see* Wye
Gyandzha *see* Gäncä
Gyangzê *126 C5* Xizang Zizhiqu, W China
Gyaring Co *126 C5 lake* W China
Gyêgu *see* Yushu
Gyergyószentmiklós *see* Gheorgheni
Gyixong *see* Gonggar
Gympie *149 E5* Queensland, E Australia
Gyomaendrőd *99 D7* Békés, SE Hungary
Gyöngyös *99 D6* Heves, NE Hungary
Győr *99 C6 Ger.* Raab, *Lat.* Arrabona. Győr-Moson-Sopron, NW Hungary
Gytheio *105 B6 var.* Githio; *prev.* Yíthion. Pelopónnisos, S Greece
Gyulafehérvár *see* Alba Iulia

Gyumri *117 F2 var.* Giumri, *Rus.* Kumayri; *prev.* Aleksandropol', Leninakan. W Armenia
Gyzyrlabat *see* Serdar

H

Haabai *see* Ha'apai Group
Haacht *87 C6* Vlaams Brabant, C Belgium
Haaksbergen *86 E3* Overijssel, E Netherlands
Ha'apai Group *145 F4 var.* Haabai. *island group* C Tonga
Haapsalu *106 D2 Ger.* Hapsal. Läänemaa, W Estonia
Ha'Arava *see* 'Arabah, Wādī al
Haarlem *86 C3 prev.* Harlem. Noord-Holland, W Netherlands
Haast *151 B6* West Coast, South Island, New Zealand
Hachijo-jima *131 D6 island* Izu-shotō, SE Japan
Hachinohe *130 D3* Aomori, Honshū, C Japan
Hacıqabal *117 H3 prev.* Qazimämmäd. SE Azerbaijan
Hadabat al Jilf al Kabīr *72 A2 var.* Gilf Kebir Plateau. *plateau* SW Egypt
Hadama *see* Nazrēt
Hadejia *75 G4* Jigawa, N Nigeria
Hadejia *75 G3 river* N Nigeria
Hadera *119 A6 var.* Khadera; *prev.* Ḥadera. Haifa, N Israel
Ḥadera *see* Hadera
Hadhdhunmathi Atoll *132 A5 atoll* S Maldives
Ha Đông *136 D3 var.* Hadong. Ha Tây, N Vietnam
Hadong *see* Ha Đông
Hadramaut *121 C6 Eng.* Hadramaut. *mountain range* S Yemen
Hadramaut *see* Ḥadramawt
Hadrianopolis *see* Edirne
Haerbin/Haerhpin/Ha-erh-pin *see* Harbin
Hafnia *see* Denmark
Hafnia *see* København
Hafren *see* Severn
Hafun, Ras *see* Xaafuun, Raas
Hagåtña *144 B1 , var.* Agaña. *dependent territory capital* (Guam) NW Guam
Hagerstown *41 E4* Maryland, NE USA
Ha Giang *136 D3* Ha Giang, N Vietnam
Hagios Evstrátios *see* Ágios Efstrátios
HaGolan *see* Golan Heights
Hagondange *90 E3* Moselle, NE France
Haguenau *90 E3* Bas-Rhin, NE France
Haibowan *see* Wuhai
Haicheng *128 C3* Liaoning, NE China
Haidarabad *see* Hyderābād
Haifa *see* Hefa
Haifa, Bay of *see* Mifrats Hefa
Haifong *see* Hai Phong
Haikou *128 C7 var.* Hai-k'ou, Hoihow, *Fr.* Hoï-Hao. *province capital* Hainan, S China
Hai-k'ou *see* Haikou
Ḥā'il *120 B4* Ḥā'il, NW Saudi Arabia
Hailuoto *84 D4 Swe.* Karlö. *island* W Finland
Hainan *128 B7 var.* Hainan Sheng, Qiong. *province* S China
Hainan Dao *128 C7 island* S China
Hainan Sheng *see* Hainan
Hainasch *see* Ainaži
Haines *36 D4* Alaska, USA
Hainichen *94 D4* Sachsen, E Germany
Hai Phong *136 D3 var.* Haifong, Haiphong. N Vietnam
Haiphong *see* Hai Phong
Haiti *54 D3 off.* Republic of Haiti. *country* C West Indies

---

HAITI
West Indies

Official name Republic of Haiti
Formation 1804 / 1844
Capital Port-au-Prince
Population 10.1 million / 949 people per sq mile (366 people per sq km)
Total area 10,714 sq. miles (27,750 sq. km)
Languages French Creole*, French*
Religions Roman Catholic 55%, Protestant 28%, Other (including Voodoo) 16%, Nonreligious 1%
Ethnic mix Black African 95%,

HAITI
(continued)

Mulatto (mixed race) and European 5%
Government Presidential system
Currency Gourde = 100 centimes
Literacy rate 62%
Calorie consumption 1979 kilocalories

Haiti, Republic of *see* Haiti
Haiya *72 C3* Red Sea, NE Sudan
Hajdúhadház *99 D6* Hajdú-Bihar, E Hungary
Hajine *see* Abū Ḥardān
Hajnówka *98 E3 Ger.* Hermhausen. Podlaskie, NE Poland
Hakodate *130 D3* Hokkaidō, NE Japan
Hal *see* Halle
Ḥalab *118 B2 Eng.* Aleppo, *Fr.* Alep; *anc.* Beroea. Ḥalab, NW Syria
Hala'ib Triangle *72 C3 region* SE Egypt
Ḥalānīyāt, Juzur al *121 D6 var.* Jazā'ir Bin Ghalfān, *Eng.* Kuria Muria Islands. *island group* S Oman
Halberstadt *94 C4* Sachsen-Anhalt, C Germany
Halden *85 B6 prev.* Fredrikshald. Østfold, S Norway
Halfmoon Bay *151 A8 var.* Oban. Stewart Island, Southland, New Zealand
Haliacmon *see* Aliákmonas
Halifax *39 F4 province capital* Nova Scotia, SE Canada
Halkida *see* Chalkída
Halle *87 B6 Fr.* Hal. Vlaams Brabant, C Belgium
Halle *94 C4 var.* Halle an der Saale. Sachsen-Anhalt, C Germany
Halle an der Saale *see* Halle
Halle-Neustadt *94 C4* Sachsen-Anhalt, C Germany
Halley *154 B2* UK research station Antarctica
Hall Islands *142 B2 island group* C Micronesia
Halls Creek *146 C3* Western Australia
Halmahera, Laut *139 F4 Eng.* Halmahera Sea. *sea* E Indonesia
Halmahera, Pulau *139 F4 var.* Djailolo, Gilolo, Jailolo. *island* E Indonesia
Halmahera Sea *see* Halmahera, Laut
Halmstad *85 B7* Halland, S Sweden
Ha Long *136 E3 prev.* Hông Gai, *var.* Hon Gai, Hongay. Quang Ninh, N Vietnam
Hälsingborg *see* Helsingborg
Hamada *131 B6* Shimane, Honshū, SW Japan
Hamadān *120 C3 anc.* Ecbatana. Hamadān, W Iran
Ḥamāh *118 B3 var.* Hama; *anc.* Epiphania, *Bibl.* Hamath. Ḥamāh, W Syria
Hamamatsu *131 D6 var.* Hamamatu. Shizuoka, Honshū, S Japan
Hamamatu *see* Hamamatsu
Hamar *85 B5 prev.* Storhammer. Hedmark, S Norway
Hamath *see* Ḥamāh
Hamburg *94 B3* Hamburg, N Germany
Hamd, Wadi al *120 A4 dry watercourse* W Saudi Arabia
Hämeenlinna *85 D5 Swe.* Tavastehus. Etelä-Suomi, S Finland
HaMela h, Yam *see* Dead Sea
Hamersley Range *146 A4 mountain range* Western Australia
Hamhŭng *129 E3* C North Korea
Hami *126 C3 var.* Ha-mi, Uigh. Kumul, Qomul. Xinjiang Uygur Zizhiqu, NW China
Ha-mi *see* Hami
Hamilton *42 A5 dependent territory capital* (Bermuda) C Bermuda
Hamilton *38 D5* Ontario, S Canada
Hamilton *150 D3* Waikato, North Island, New Zealand
Hamilton *88 C4* S Scotland, United Kingdom
Hamilton *42 C2* Alabama, S USA
Hamim, Wadi al *71 G2 var.* Wādī NE Libya
Hamm *94 B4 var.* Hamm in Westfalen. Nordrhein-Westfalen, W Germany
Ḥammāmāt, Khalīj al *see* Hammamet, Golfe de
Hammamet, Golfe de *102 D3 Ar.* Khalīj al Ḥammāmāt. *gulf* NE Tunisia

Hammar, Hawr al *120 C3 lake* SE Iraq
Hamm in Westfalen *see* Hamm
Hampden *151 B7* Otago, South Island, New Zealand
Hampstead *89 A7* Maryland, USA
Hamrun *102 B5* C Malta
Hāmūn, Daryācheh-ye *see* Şāberī, Hāmūn-e/Sīstān, Daryācheh-ye
Hamwih *see* Southampton
Hânceşti *see* Hînceşti
Hancewicze *see* Hantsavichy
Handan *128 C4 var.* Han-tan. Hebei, E China
Haneda *130 A2* (Tōkyō) Tōkyō, Honshū, S Japan
Hanford *47 C6* California, W USA
Hangayn Nuruu *126 D2 mountain range* C Mongolia
Hang-chou/Hangchow *see* Hangzhou
Hangö *see* Hanko
Hangzhou *128 D5 var.* Hang-chou, Hangchow. *province capital* Zhejiang, SE China
Hania *see* Chaniá
Hanka, Lake *see* Khanka, Lake
Hanko *85 D6 Swe.* Hangö. Etelä-Suomi, SW Finland
Han-kou/Han-k'ou/Hankow *see* Wuhan
Hanmer Springs *151 C5* Canterbury, South Island, New Zealand
Hannibal *45 G4* Missouri, C USA
Hannover *94 B3 Eng.* Hanover. Niedersachsen, NW Germany
Hanöbukten *85 B7 bay* S Sweden
Ha Nôi *136 D3 Eng.* Hanoi, *Fr.* Hanoï. *country capital* (Vietnam) N Vietnam
Hanover *see* Hannover
Han Shui *127 E4 river* C China
Han-tan *see* Handan
Hantsavichy *107 B6 Pol.* Hancewicze, *Rus.* Gantsevichi. Brestskaya Voblasts', SW Belarus
Hanyang *see* Wuhan
Hanzhong *128 B5* Shaanxi, C China
Hāora *135 F4 prev.* Howrah. West Bengal, NE India
Haparanda *84 D4* Norrbotten, N Sweden
Hapsal *see* Haapsalu
Haradok *107 E5 Rus.* Gorodok. Vitsyebskaya Voblasts', N Belarus
Haradzyets *107 B6 Rus.* Gorodets. Brestskaya Voblasts', SW Belarus
Haramachi *130 D4* Fukushima, Honshū, E Japan
Harany *107 D5 Rus.* Gorany. Vitsyebskaya Voblasts', N Belarus
Harare *78 D3 prev.* Salisbury. *country capital* (Zimbabwe) Mashonaland East, NE Zimbabwe
Harbavichy *107 E6 Rus.* Gorbovichi. Mahilyowskaya Voblasts', E Belarus
Harbel *74 C5* W Liberia
Harbin *129 E2 var.* Haerbin, Ha-erh-pin, Kharbin; *prev.* Haerhpin, Pingkiang, Pinkiang. *province capital* Heilongjiang, NE China
Hardangerfjorden *85 A6 fjord* S Norway
Hardangervidda *85 A6 plateau* S Norway
Hardenberg *86 E3* Overijssel, E Netherlands
Harelbeke *87 A6 var.* Harlebeke. West-Vlaanderen, W Belgium
Harem *see* Ḥārim
Haren *86 E2* Groningen, NE Netherlands
Härer *73 D5* E Ethiopia
Hargeysa *73 D5 var.* Hargeisa. Woqooyi Galbeed, NW Somalia
Hariana *see* Haryāna
Hari, Batang *138 B4 prev.* Djambi. *river* Sumatera, W Indonesia
Ḥārim *118 B2 var.* Harem. Idlib, N Syria
Harima-nada *131 B6 sea* S Japan
Harirud *123 E4 var.* Tedzhen, *Turkm.* Tejen. *river* Afghanistan/Iran
Harlan *45 F3* Iowa, C USA
Harlebeke *see* Harelbeke
Harlem *see* Haarlem
Harlingen *86 D2 Fris.* Harns. Fryslân, N Netherlands
Harlingen *49 G5* Texas, SW USA
Harlow *89 E6* E England, United Kingdom
Harney Basin *46 B4 basin* Oregon, NW USA
Härnösand *85 C5 var.* Hernösand. Västernorrland, C Sweden

Harns see Harlingen
Harper 74 D5 var. Cape Palmas.
NE Liberia
Harricana 38 D3 river Québec,
SE Canada
Harris 88 B3 physical region
NW Scotland, United Kingdom
Harrisburg 41 E4 state capital
Pennsylvania, NE USA
Harrisonburg 41 E4 Virginia, NE USA
Harrison, Cape 39 F2 headland
Newfoundland and Labrador, E Canada
Harris Ridge see Lomonosov Ridge
Harrogate 89 D5 N England, United
Kingdom
Hârșova 108 D5 prev. Hîrșova.
Constanța, SE Romania
Harstad 84 C2 Troms, N Norway
Hartford 41 G3 state capital Connecticut,
NE USA
Hartlepool 89 D5 N England, United
Kingdom
Harunabad see Eslāmābād-e Gharb
Har Us Gol 126 C2 lake Hovd,
W Mongolia
Har Us Nuur 126 C2 lake
NW Mongolia
Harwich 89 E6 E England, United
Kingdom
Haryāna 134 D2 var. Hariana. cultural
region N India
Hashemite Kingdom of Jordan see
Jordan
Hasselt 87 C6 Limburg, NE Belgium
Hassetché see Al Ḥasakah
Hasta Colonia/Hasta Pompeia see Asti
Hastings 150 E4 Hawke's Bay, North
Island, New Zealand
Hastings 89 E7 SE England, United
Kingdom
Hastings 45 E4 Nebraska, C USA
Hațeg 108 B4 Ger. Wallenthal, Hung.
Hátszeg; prev. Hatzeg, Hötzing.
Hunedoara, SW Romania
Hátszeg see Hațeg
Hattem 86 D3 Gelderland, E Netherlands
Hatteras, Cape 43 G1 headland North
Carolina, SE USA
Hatteras Plain 35 D6 abyssal plain
W Atlantic Ocean
Hattiesburg 42 C3 Mississippi, S USA
Hatton Bank see Hatton Ridge
Hatton Ridge 80 B2 var. Hatton Bank.
undersea ridge N Atlantic Ocean
Hat Yai 137 C7 var. Ban Hat Yai.
Songkhla, SW Thailand
Hatzeg see Hațeg
Hatzfeld see Jimbolia
Haugesund 85 A6 Rogaland, S Norway
Haukeligrend 85 A6 Telemark,
S Norway
Haukivesi 85 E5 lake SE Finland
Hauraki Gulf 150 D2 gulf North Island,
N New Zealand
Hauroko, Lake 151 A7 lake South
Island, New Zealand
Hautes Fagnes 87 D6 Ger. Hohes Venn.
mountain range E Belgium
Hauts Plateaux 70 D2 plateau Algeria/
Morocco
Hauzenberg 95 D6 Bayern, SE Germany
Havana 35 D6 Illinois, N USA
Havana see la Habana
Havant 89 D7 S England, United
Kingdom
Havelock 43 F1 North Carolina, SE USA
Havelock North 150 E4 Hawke's Bay,
North Island, New Zealand
Haverfordwest 89 C6 SW Wales, United
Kingdom
Havířov 99 C5 Moravskoslezský Kraj,
E Czech Republic
Havre 44 C1 Montana, NW USA
Havre see le Havre
Havre-St-Pierre 39 F3 Québec,
E Canada
Hawai'i 47 A8 off. State of Hawai'i,
also known as Aloha State, Paradise
of the Pacific, var. Hawaii. state USA,
C Pacific Ocean
Hawai'i 47 B8 var. Hawaii. island
Hawaiian Islands, USA, C Pacific Ocean
Hawai'ian Islands 152 D2 prev.
Sandwich Islands. island group
Hawaii, USA
Hawaiian Ridge 152 H4 undersea ridge
N Pacific Ocean
Hawea, Lake 151 B6 lake South Island,
New Zealand

Hawera 150 D4 Taranaki, North Island,
New Zealand
Hawick 88 C4 SE Scotland, United
Kingdom
Hawke Bay 150 E4 bay North Island,
New Zealand
Hawkeye State see Iowa
Hawlēr see Arbil
Hawthorne 47 C6 Nevada, W USA
Hay 149 C6 New South Wales,
SE Australia
HaYarden see Jordan
Hayastani Hanrapetut'yun see Armenia
Hayes 38 B2 river Manitoba, C Canada
Hay River 37 E4 Northwest Territories,
W Canada
Hays 45 E5 Kansas, C USA
Haysyn 108 D3 Rus. Gaysin. Vinnyts'ka
Oblast', C Ukraine
Hazar 122 B2 prev. Rus. Cheleken.
Balkan Welaýaty, W Turkmenistan
Heard and McDonald Islands 141 B7
Australian external territory S Indian
Ocean
Hearst 38 C4 Ontario, S Canada
Heart of Dixie see Alabama
Heathrow 89 A8 (London) SE England,
United Kingdom
Hebei 128 C4 var. Hebei Sheng, Hopeh,
Hopei, Ji; prev. Chihli. province
E China
Hebei Sheng see Hebei
Hebron 119 A6 var. Al Khalīl, El Khalil,
Heb. Hevron; anc. Kiriath-Arba.
S West Bank
Heemskerk 86 C3 Noord-Holland,
W Netherlands
Heerde 86 D3 Gelderland, E Netherlands
Heerenveen 86 D2 Fris. It Hearrenfean.
Fryslân, N Netherlands
Heerhugowaard 86 C2 Noord-Holland,
NW Netherlands
Heerlen 87 D6 Limburg, SE Netherlands
Heerwegen see Polkowice
Hefa 119 A5 var. Haifa, hist. Caiffa,
Caiphas; anc. Sycaminum. Haifa,
N Israel
Ḥefa, Mifraz see Mifrats Hefa
Hefei 128 D5 var. Hofei, hist. Luchow.
province capital Anhui, E China
Hegang 129 E2 Heilongjiang, NE China
Hei see Heilongjiang
Heide 94 B2 Schleswig-Holstein,
N Germany
Heidelberg 95 B5 Baden-Württemberg,
SW Germany
Heidenheim see Heidenheim an der
Brenz
Heidenheim an der Brenz 95 B6 var.
Heidenheim. Baden-Württemberg,
S Germany
Hei-ho see Nagqu
Heilbronn 95 B5 Baden-Württemberg,
SW Germany
Heiligenbeil see Mamonovo
Heilongjiang 128 D2 var. Hei,
Heilongjiang Sheng, Hei-lung-chiang,
Heilungkiang. province NE China
Heilong Jiang see Amur
Heilongjiang Sheng see Heilongjiang
Heiloo 86 C3 Noord-Holland,
NW Netherlands
Heilsberg see Lidzbark Warmiński
Hei-lung-chiang/Heilungkiang see
Heilongjiang
Heimdal 85 B5 Sør-Trøndelag, S Norway
Heinaste see Ainaži
Hekimhan 116 D3 Malatya, C Turkey
Helena 44 B2 state capital Montana,
NW USA
Helensville 150 D2 Auckland, North
Island, New Zealand
Helgoland Bay see Helgoländer Bucht
Helgoländer Bucht 94 A2 var.
Helgoland Bay, Heligoland Bight. bay
NW Germany
Heligoland Bight see Helgoländer Bucht
Heliopolis see Baalbek
Hellas see Greece
Hellenic Republic see Greece
Hellevoetsluis 86 B4 Zuid-Holland,
SW Netherlands
Hellín 93 E4 Castilla-La Mancha,
C Spain
Darya-ye Helmand 122 D5 var. Rūd-e
Hīrmand. river Afghanistan/Iran
Helmantica see Salamanca
Helmond 87 D5 Noord-Brabant,
S Netherlands

Helsingborg 85 B7 prev. Hälsingborg.
Skåne, S Sweden
Helsingfors see Helsinki
Helsinki 85 D6 Swe. Helsingfors.
country capital (Finland) Etelä-Suomi,
S Finland
Heltau see Cisnădie
Helvetia see Switzerland
Henan 128 C5 var. Henan Sheng,
Honan, Yu. province C China
Henderson 40 B5 Kentucky, S USA
Henderson 47 D7 Nevada, W USA
Henderson 49 H3 Texas, SW USA
Hendŭ Kosh see Hindu Kush
Hengchow see Hengyang
Hengduan Shan 128 A5 mountain range
SW China
Hengelo 86 E3 Overijssel, E Netherlands
Hengnan see Hengyang
Hengyang 128 C5 var. Hengnan, Heng-
yang; prev. Hengchow. Hunan, S China
Heng-yang see Hengyang
Heniches'k 109 F4 Rus. Genichesk.
Khersons'ka Oblast', S Ukraine
Hennebont 90 A3 Morbihan, NW France
Henrique de Carvalho see Saurimo
Henzada see Hinthada
Herakleion see Irákleio
Herāt 122 D4 var. Herat; anc. Aria.
Herāt, W Afghanistan
Heredia 53 E4 Heredia, C Costa Rica
Hereford 49 E2 Texas, SW USA
Herford 94 B4 Nordrhein-Westfalen,
NW Germany
Herk-de-Stad 87 C6 Limburg,
NE Belgium
Herlen Gol/Herlen He see Kerulen
Hermannstadt see Sibiu
Hermansverk 85 A5 Sogn Og Fjordane,
S Norway
Hermhausen see Hajnówka
Hermiston 46 C2 Oregon, NW USA
Hermon, Mount 119 B5 Ar. Jabal ash
Shaykh. mountain S Syria
Hermosillo 50 B2 Sonora, NW Mexico
Hernösand see Härnösand
Herrera del Duque 92 D3 Extremadura,
W Spain
Herselt 87 C5 Antwerpen, C Belgium
Herstal 87 D6 Fr. Héristal. Liège,
E Belgium
Herzogenbusch see 's-Hertogenbosch
Hesse see Hessen
Hessen 95 B5 Eng./Fr. Hesse. state
C Germany
Hevron see Hebron
Heydebrech see Kędzierzyn-Kozle
Heydekrug see Šilutė
Heywood Islands 146 C3 island group
Western Australia
Hibbing 45 F1 Minnesota, N USA
Hibernia see Ireland
Hidalgo del Parral 50 C2 var. Parral.
Chihuahua, N Mexico
Hida-sanmyaku 131 C5 mountain range
Honshū, S Japan
Hierosolyma see Jerusalem
Hierro 70 A3 var. Ferro. island Islas
Canarias, Spain, NE Atlantic Ocean
High Atlas 70 C2 Eng. High Atlas.
mountain range C Morocco
High Atlas see Haut Atlas
High Plains see Great Plains
High Point 43 E1 North Carolina,
SE USA
Hiiumaa 106 C2 Ger. Dagden, Swe.
Dagö. island W Estonia
Hikurangi 150 D2 Northland, North
Island, New Zealand
Hildesheim 94 B4 Niedersachsen,
N Germany
Hilla see Al Ḥillah
Hillaby, Mount 55 G1 mountain
N Barbados
Hill Bank 52 C1 Orange Walk, N Belize
Hillegom 86 C3 Zuid-Holland,
W Netherlands
Hilo 47 B8 Hawaii, USA, C Pacific Ocean
Hilton Head Island 43 E2 South
Carolina, SE USA
Hilversum 86 C3 Noord-Holland,
C Netherlands
Himalaya/Himalaya Shan see Himalayas
Himalayas 135 E2 var. Himalaya, Chin.
Himalaya Shan. mountain range S Asia
Himeji 131 C6 var. Himezi. Hyōgo,
Honshū, SW Japan

Himezi see Himeji
Ḥimş 118 B4 var. Homs; anc. Emesa.
Ḥimş, C Syria
Hîncești 108 D4 var. Hâncești; prev.
Kotovsk. C Moldova
Hinchinbrook Island 148 D3 island
Queensland, NE Australia
Hinds 151 C6 Canterbury, South Island,
New Zealand
Hindu Kush 123 F4 Per. Hendŭ Kosh.
mountain range Afghanistan/Pakistan
Hinesville 43 E3 Georgia, SE USA
Hinnøya 84 C3 Lapp. Iinnasuolu. island
C Norway
Hinson Bay 42 A5 bay W Bermuda
W Atlantic Ocean
Hinthada 136 B4 var. Henzada.
Ayeyarwady, SW Myanmar (Burma)
Híos see Chíos
Hirfanlı Barajı 116 C3 reservoir
C Turkey
Hirmand, Rūd-e see Helmand, Daryā-ye
Hirosaki 130 D3 Aomori, Honshū,
C Japan
Hiroshima 131 B6 var. Hirosima.
Hiroshima, Honshū, SW Japan
Hirosima see Hiroshima
**Hirschberg/Hirschberg im
Riesengebirge/Hirschberg in
Schlesien** see Jelenia Góra
Hirson 90 D3 Aisne, N France
Hîrșova see Hârșova
Hispalis see Sevilla
Hispana/Hispania see Spain
Hispaniola 56 B1 island Dominion
Republic/Haiti
Hitachi 131 D5 var. Hitati. Ibaraki,
Honshū, S Japan
Hitati see Hitachi
Hitra 84 A4 prev. Hittern. island
S Norway
Hitteren see Hitra
Hjälmaren 85 C6 Eng. Lake Hjalmar.
lake C Sweden
Hjalmar, Lake see Hjälmaren
Hjørring 85 B7 Nordjylland, N Denmark
Hkakabo Razi 136 B1 mountain
Myanmar (Burma)/China
Hlobyne 109 F2 Rus. Globino.
Poltavs'ka Oblast', NE Ukraine
Hlukhiv 109 F1 Rus. Glukhov. Sums'ka
Oblast', NE Ukraine
Hlybokaye 107 D5 Rus. Glubokoye.
Vitsyebskaya Voblasts', N Belarus
Hoa Binh 136 D3 Hoa Binh, N Vietnam
Hoang Lien Son 136 D3 mountain range
N Vietnam
Hobart 149 C8 prev. Hobarton, Hobart
Town. state capital Tasmania,
SE Australia
Hobarton/Hobart Town see Hobart
Hobbs 49 E3 New Mexico, SW USA
Hobro 85 A7 Nordjylland, N Denmark
Hô Chi Minh 137 E6 var. Ho Chi Minh
City; prev. Saigon. S Vietnam
Ho Chi Minh City see Hô Chi Minh
Hodeida see Al Ḥudaydah
Hódmezővásárhely 99 D7 Csongrád,
SE Hungary
Hodna, Chott El 102 C4 var. Chott
el-Hodna, Ar. Shatt al-Hodna. salt
lake N Algeria
Hodna, Chott el-/Hodna, Shatt al- see
Hodna, Chott El
Hodonín 99 C5 Ger. Göding.
Jihomoravský Kraj, SE Czech Republic
Hoei see Huy
Hoey see Huy
Hof 95 C5 Bayern, SE Germany
Hofei see Hefei
Hōfu 131 B7 Yamaguchi, Honshū,
SW Japan
Hofuf see Al Hufūf
Hogoley Islands see Chuuk Islands
Hohensalza see Inowrocław
Hohenstadt see Zábřeh
Hohes Venn see Hautes Fagnes
Hohe Tauern 95 C7 mountain range
W Austria
Hohhot 127 F3 var. Huhehot,
Huhohaote, Mong. Kukukhoto; prev.
Kweisui, Kwesui. Nei Mongol Zizhiqu,
N China
Hôi An 137 E5 prev. Faifo. Quang Nam-
Đa Nâng, C Vietnam
Hoi-Hao/Hoihow see Haikou
Hokianga Harbour 150 C2 inlet
SE Tasman Sea
Hokitika 151 B5 West Coast, South
Island, New Zealand

Hokkaido 130 C2 prev. Ezo, Yeso, Yezo. island NE Japan
Hola Prystan' 109 E4 Rus. Golaya Pristan. Khersons'ka Oblast', S Ukraine
Holbrook 48 B2 Arizona, SW USA
Holetown 55 G1 prev. Jamestown. W Barbados
Holguín 54 C2 Holguín, SE Cuba
Holin Gol 127 G2 prev. Hulingol. Nei Mongol Zizhiqu, N China
Hollabrunn 95 E6 Niederösterreich, NE Austria
Holland see Netherlands
Hollandia see Jayapura
Holly Springs 42 C1 Mississippi, S USA
Holman 37 E3 Victoria Island, Northwest Territories, N Canada
Holmsund 84 D4 Västerbotten, N Sweden
Holon 119 A6 var. Kholon; prev. Ḥolon. Tel Aviv, C Israel
Ḥolon see Holon
Holovanivs'k 109 E3 Rus. Golovanevsk. Kirovohrads'ka Oblast', C Ukraine
Holstebro 85 A7 Midtjylland, W Denmark
Holsteinborg/Holsteinsborg/ Holstenborg/Holstensborg see Sisimiut
Holyhead 89 C5 Wel. Caer Gybi. NW Wales, United Kingdom
Hombori 75 E3 Mopti, S Mali
Homs see Al Khums, Libya
Homs see Ḥimṣ
Homyel' 107 D7 Rus. Gomel'. Homyel'skaya Voblasts', SE Belarus
Honan see Henan, China
Honan see Luoyang, China
Hondo 49 F4 Texas, SW USA
Hondo see Honshū
Honduras 52 C2 off. Republic of Honduras. country Central America

HONDURAS
Central America

Official name Republic of Honduras
Formation 1838 / 1838
Capital Tegucigalpa
Population 7.8 million / 181 people per sq mile (70 people per sq km)
Total area 43,278 sq. miles (112,090 sq. km)
Languages Spanish*, Garífuna (Carib), English Creole
Religions Roman Catholic 97%, Protestant 3%
Ethnic mix Mestizo 90%, Black 5%, Amerindian 4%, White 1%
Government Presidential system
Currency Lempira = 100 centavos
Literacy rate 84%
Calorie consumption 2694 kilocalories

Honduras, Golfo de see Honduras, Gulf of
Honduras, Gulf of 52 C2 Sp. Golfo de Honduras. gulf W Caribbean Sea
Honduras, Republic of see Honduras
Hønefoss 85 B6 Buskerud, S Norway
Honey Lake 47 B5 lake California, W USA
Hon Gai see Ha Long
Hongay see Ha Long
Hồng Gai see Ha Long
Hồng Hà, Sông see Red River
Hong Kong 128 A1 Chin. Xianggang. Hong Kong, S China
Hong Kong Island 128 B2 island S China Asia
Honiara 144 C3 country capital (Solomon Islands) Guadalcanal, C Solomon Islands
Honjō 130 D4 var. Honzyô, Yurihonjô. Akita, Honshū, C Japan
Honolulu 47 A8 state capital O'ahu, Hawaii, USA, C Pacific Ocean
Honshu 131 E5 var. Hondo, Honsyû. island SW Japan
Honsyû see Honshū
Honte see Westerschelde
Honzyô see Honjō
Hoogeveen 86 E2 Drenthe, NE Netherlands
Hoogezand-Sappemeer 86 E2 Groningen, NE Netherlands
Hoorn 86 C2 Noord-Holland, NW Netherlands
Hoosier State see Indiana
Hopa 117 E2 Artvin, NE Turkey

Hope 36 C3 British Columbia, SW Canada
Hopedale 39 F2 Newfoundland and Labrador, NE Canada
Hopeh/Hopei see Hebei
Hopkinsville 40 B5 Kentucky, S USA
Horasan 117 F3 Erzurum, NE Turkey
Horizon Deep 152 D4 trench W Pacific Ocean
Horki 107 E6 Rus. Gorki. Mahilyowskaya Voblasts', E Belarus
Horlivka 109 G3 Rom. Adâncata, Rus. Gorlovka. Donets'ka Oblast', E Ukraine
Hormoz, Tangeh-ye see Hormuz, Strait of
Hormuz, Strait of 120 D4 var. Strait of Ormuz, Per. Tangeh-ye Hormoz. strait Iran/Oman
Cape Horn 65 C8 Eng. Cape Horn. headland S Chile
Horn, Cape see Hornos, Cabo de
Hornsby 148 E1 New South Wales, SE Australia
Horodnya 109 E1 Rus. Gorodnya. Chernihivs'ka Oblast', NE Ukraine
Horodok 108 B2 Pol. Gródek Jagielloński, Rus. Gorodok, Gorodok Yagellonski. L'vivs'ka Oblast', NW Ukraine
Horodyshche 109 E2 Rus. Gorodishche. Cherkas'ka Oblast', C Ukraine
Horoshiri-dake 130 D2 var. Horosiri Dake. mountain Hokkaidō, N Japan
Horosiri Dake see Horoshiri-dake
Horsburgh Atoll 132 A4 var. Goidhoo Atoll. atoll N Maldives
Horseshoe Bay 42 A5 bay W Bermuda W Atlantic Ocean
Horseshoe Seamounts 80 A4 seamount range E Atlantic Ocean
Horsham 149 B7 Victoria, SE Australia
Horst 87 D5 Limburg, SE Netherlands
Horten 85 B6 Vestfold, S Norway
Horyn' 107 B7 Rus. Goryn. river NW Ukraine
Hosingen 87 D7 Diekirch, NE Luxembourg
Hospitalet see L'Hospitalet de Llobregat
Hotan 126 B4 var. Khotan, Chin. Ho-t'ien. Xinjiang Uygur Zizhiqu, NW China
Ho-t'ien see Hotan
Hoting 84 C4 Jämtland, C Sweden
Hot Springs 42 B1 Arkansas, C USA
Hötzing see Hațeg
Houayxay 136 C3 var. Ban Houayxay. Bokèo, N Laos
Houghton 40 B1 Michigan, N USA
Houilles 91 B5 Yvelines, Île-de-France, N France Europe
Houlton 41 H1 Maine, NE USA
Houma 42 B3 Louisiana, S USA
Houston 49 H4 Texas, SW USA
Hovd 126 C2 var. Khovd, Kobdo; prev. Jirgalanta. Hovd, W Mongolia
Hove 89 E7 SE England, United Kingdom
Hoverla, Hora 108 C3 Rus. Gora Goverla. mountain W Ukraine
Hovsgol, Lake see Hövsgöl Nuur
Hövsgöl Nuur 126 D1 var. Lake Hovsgol. lake N Mongolia
Howa, Ouadi see Howar, Wādi
Howar, Wādi 72 A3 var. Ouadi Howa. river Chad/Sudan
Howrah see Hāora
Hoy 88 C2 island N Scotland, United Kingdom
Hoyerswerda 94 D4 Lus. Wojerecy. Sachsen, E Germany
Hpa-an 136 B4 var. Pa-an. Kayin State, S Myanmar (Burma)
Hpyu see Phyu
Hradec Králové 94 B5 Ger. Königgrätz. Královéhradecký Kraj, N Czech Republic
Hrandzichy 107 B5 Rus. Grandichi. Hrodzyenskaya Voblasts', W Belarus
Hranice 95 C5 Ger. Mährisch-Weisskirchen. Olomoucký Kraj, E Czech Republic
Hrebinka 109 F2 Rus. Grebenka. Poltavs'ka Oblast', NE Ukraine
Hrodna 107 B5 Pol. Grodno. Hrodzyenskaya Voblasts', W Belarus
Hrvatska see Croatia
Hsia-men see Xiamen

Hsiang-t'an see Xiangtan
Hsi Chiang see Xi Jiang
Hsing-K'ai Hu see Khanka, Lake
Hsi-ning/Hsining see Xining
Hsinking see Changchun
Hsin-yang see Xinyang
Hsu-chou see Xuzhou
Htawei see Dawei
Huacho 60 C4 Lima, W Peru
Hua Hin see Ban Hua Hin
Huaihua 128 C5 Hunan, S China
Huailai 128 C3 var. Shacheng. Hebei, E China
Huainan 128 D5 var. Huai-nan, Hwainan. Anhui, E China
Huai-nan see Huainan
Huajuapan 51 F5 var. Huajuapan de León. Oaxaca, SE Mexico
Huajuapan de León see Huajuapan
Hualapai Peak 48 A2 mountain Arizona, SW USA
Huallaga, Río 60 C3 river N Peru
Huambo 78 B2 Port. Nova Lisboa. Huambo, C Angola
Huancavelica 60 D4 Huancavelica, SW Peru
Huancayo 60 D3 Junín, C Peru
Huang Hai see Yellow Sea
Huangshi 128 C5 var. Huang-shih, Hwangshih. Hubei, C China
Huang-shih see Huangshi
Huanta 60 D4 Ayacucho, C Peru
Huánuco 60 C3 Huánuco, C Peru
Huanuni 61 F4 Oruro, W Bolivia
Huaral 60 C4 Lima, W Peru
Huarás see Huaraz
Huaraz 60 C3 var. Huarás. Ancash, W Peru
Huarmey 60 C3 Ancash, W Peru
Huatabampo 50 C2 Sonora, NW Mexico
Hubli 124 B3 Karnātaka, SW India
Huddersfield 89 D5 N England, United Kingdom
Hudiksvall 85 C5 Gävleborg, C Sweden
Hudson Bay 37 G4 bay NE Canada
Hudson, Détroit d' see Hudson Strait
Hudson Strait 37 H3 Fr. Détroit d'Hudson. strait Northwest Territories/Québec, NE Canada
Hudur see Xuddur
Huê 136 E4 Th. a Thiên-Huê, C Vietnam
Huehuetenango 52 A2 Huehuetenango, W Guatemala
Huelva 92 C4 anc. Onuba. Andalucía, SW Spain
Huesca 93 F2 anc. Osca. Aragón, NE Spain
Huéscar 93 E4 Andalucía, S Spain
Hughenden 148 C3 Queensland, NE Australia
Hugo 49 G2 Oklahoma, C USA
Huhehot/Huhehaote see Hohhot
Huíla Plateau 78 B2 plateau S Angola
Huixtla 51 G5 Chiapas, SE Mexico
Hulingol see Holin Gol
Hull 38 D4 Québec, SE Canada
Hull see Kingston upon Hull
Hull Island see Orona
Hulst 87 B5 Zeeland, SW Netherlands
Hulun see Hulun Buir
Hulun Buir 127 F1 var. Hailar; prev. Hulun. Nei Mongol Zizhiqu, N China
Hulun Nur 127 F1 var. Hu-lun Ch'ih; prev. Dalai Nor. lake N China
Hu-lun Ch'ih see Hulun Nur
Humaitá 62 D2 Amazonas, N Brazil
Humboldt River 47 C5 river Nevada, W USA
Humphreys Peak 48 B1 mountain Arizona, SW USA
Humpolec 99 B5 Ger. Gumpolds, Humpoletz. Vysočina, C Czech Republic
Humpoletz see Humpolec
Hunan 128 C6 var. Hunan Sheng, Xiang. province S China
Hunan Sheng see Hunan
Hunedoara 108 B4 Ger. Eisenmarkt, Hung. Vajdahunyad. Hunedoara, SW Romania
Hünfeld 95 B5 Hessen, C Germany
Hungarian People's Republic see Hungary
Hungary 99 C6 off. Republic of Hungary, Ger. Ungarn, Hung. Magyarország, Rom. Ungaria, SCr. Mađarska, Ukr. Uhorshchyna; prev. Hungarian People's Republic. country C Europe

HUNGARY
Central Europe

Official name Republic of Hungary
Formation 1918 / 1947
Capital Budapest
Population 10 million / 280 people per sq mile (108 people per sq km)
Total area 35,919 sq. miles (93,030 sq. km)
Languages Hungarian (Magyar)*
Religions Roman Catholic 52%, Calvinist 16%, Orthodox 15%, Nonreligious 14%, Lutheran 3%
Ethnic mix Magyar 90%, Roma 4%, German 3%, Serb 2%, Other 1%
Government Parliamentary system
Currency Forint = 100 fillér
Literacy rate 99%
Calorie consumption 3477 kilocalories

Hungary, Plain of see Great Hungarian Plain
Hungary, Republic of see Hungary
Hunjiang see Baishan
Hunter Island 149 B8 island Tasmania, SE Australia
Huntington 40 D4 West Virginia, NE USA
Huntington Beach 47 B8 California, W USA
Huntly 150 D3 Waikato, North Island, New Zealand
Huntsville 42 D1 Alabama, S USA
Huntsville 49 G3 Texas, SW USA
Hurghada see Al Ghurdaqah
Huron 45 E3 South Dakota, N USA
Huron, Lake 40 D2 lake Canada/USA
Hurukawa see Furukawa
Hurunui 151 C5 river South Island, New Zealand
Húsavík 83 E4 Norðurland Eystra, NE Iceland
Husté see Khust
Husum 94 B2 Schleswig-Holstein, N Germany
Huszt see Khust
Hutchinson 45 E5 Kansas, C USA
Hutchinson Island 43 F4 island Florida, SE USA
Huy 87 C6 Dut. Hoei, Hoey. Liège, E Belgium
Huzi see Fuji
Hvannadalshnúkur 83 E5 volcano S Iceland
Hvar 100 B4 It. Lesina; anc. Pharus. island S Croatia
Hwainan see Huainan
Hwange 78 D3 prev. Wankie. Matabeleland North, W Zimbabwe
Hwang-Hae see Yellow Sea
Hwangshih see Huangshi
Hyargas Nuur 126 C2 lake NW Mongolia
Hyderābād 134 D5 var. Haidarabad. state capital Andhra Pradesh, C India
Hyderābād 134 B3 var. Haidarabad. Sind, SE Pakistan
Hyères 91 D6 Var, SE France
Hyères, Îles d' 91 D6 island group S France
Hypanis see Kuban'
Hyrcania see Gorgān
Hyvinge see Hyvinkää
Hyvinkää 85 D5 Swe. Hyvinge. Etelä-Suomi, S Finland

I

Iader see Zadar
Ialomița 108 C5 river SE Romania
Iaşi 108 D3 Ger. Jassy. Iaşi, NE Romania
Ibadan 75 F5 Oyo, SW Nigeria
Ibagué 58 B3 Tolima, C Colombia
Ibar see Iber
Ibarra 60 B1 var. San Miguel de Ibarra. Imbabura, N Ecuador
Ibēr 100 D4 Serb. Ibar. river C Serbia
Iberia see Spain
Iberian Mountains see Ibérico, Sistema
Iberian Peninsula 80 B4 physical region Portugal/Spain
Iberian Plain 80 B4 abyssal plain E Atlantic Ocean
Ibérica, Cordillera see Ibérico, Sistema
Ibérico, Sistema 93 E2 var. Cordillera Ibérica, Eng. Iberian Mountains. mountain range NE Spain

Ibiza *see* Eivissa
Ibo *see* Sassandra
Ica 60 D4 Ica, SW Peru
Icaria *see* Ikaría
Içá, Rio 62 C2 *var.* Río Putumayo. *river* NW South America
Içá, Rio *see* Putumayo, Río
İçel *see* Mersin
Iceland 83 E4 *off.* Republic of Iceland, *Dan.* Island, *Icel.* Ísland. *country* N Atlantic Ocean

ICELAND
Northwest Europe

Official name Republic of Iceland
Formation 1944 / 1944
Capital Reykjavík
Population 300,000 / 8 people per sq mile (3 people per sq km)
Total area 39,768 sq. miles (103,000 sq. km)
Languages Icelandic*
Religions Evangelical Lutheran 84%, Other (mostly Christian) 10%, Roman Catholic 3%, Nonreligious 3%
Ethnic mix Icelandic 94%, Other 5%, Danish 1%
Government Parliamentary system
Currency Icelandic króna = 100 aurar
Literacy rate 99%
Calorie consumption 3376 kilocalories

Iceland Basin 80 B1 *undersea basin* N Atlantic Ocean
Icelandic Plateau *see* Iceland Plateau
Iceland Plateau 155 B6 *var.* Icelandic Plateau. *undersea plateau* S Greenland Sea
Iceland, Republic of *see* Iceland
Iconium *see* Konya
Iculisma *see* Angoulême
Idabel 49 H2 Oklahoma, C USA
Idaho 46 D3 *off.* State of Idaho, *also known as* Gem of the Mountains, Gem State. *state* NW USA
Idaho Falls 46 E3 Idaho, NW USA
Idensalmi *see* Iisalmi
Idfû 72 B2 *var.* Edfu. SE Egypt
Idi Amin, Lac *see* Edward, Lake
Idini 74 B2 Trarza, W Mauritania
Idlib 118 B3 Idlib, NW Syria
Idre 85 B5 Dalarna, C Sweden
Iecava 106 C3 S Latvia
Ieper 87 A6 Fr. Ypres. West-Vlaanderen, W Belgium
Ierápetra 105 D8 Kríti, Greece, E Mediterranean Sea
Ierisós *see* Ierissós
Ierissós 104 C4 *var.* Ierisós. Kentrikí Makedonía, N Greece
Iferouâne 75 G2 Agadez, N Niger
Ifôghas, Adrar des 75 E2 *var.* Adrar des Iforas. *mountain range* NE Mali
Iforas, Adrar des *see* Ifôghas, Adrar des
Igarka 114 D3 Krasnoyarskiy Kray, N Russian Federation
Igaunija *see* Estonia
Iglau/Iglawa *see* Jihlava
Iglesias 97 A5 Sardegna, Italy, C Mediterranean Sea
Igloolik 37 G2 Nunavut, N Canada
Igoumenítsa 104 A4 Ípeiros, W Greece
Iguaçu, Rio 63 E4 *Sp.* Río Iguazú. *river* Argentina/Brazil
Iguaçu, Salto do 63 E4 *Sp.* Cataratas del Iguazú; *prev.* Victoria Falls. *waterfall* Argentina/Brazil
Iguala 51 E4 *var.* Iguala de la Independencia. Guerrero, S Mexico
Iguala de la Independencia *see* Iguala
Iguazú, Cataratas del *see* Iguaçu, Salto do
Iguazú, Río *see* Iguaçu, Rio
Iguid, Erg *see* Iguidi, 'Erg
Iguidi, 'Erg 70 C3 *var.* Erg Iguid. *desert* Algeria/Mauritania
Ihavandippolhu Atoll 132 A3 *var.* Ihavandiffulu Atoll. *atoll* N Maldives
Ihavandiffulu Atoll *see* Ihavandippolhu Atoll
Ihosy 79 F4 Fianarantsoa, S Madagascar
Iinnasuolu *see* Hinnøya
Iisalmi 84 E4 *var.* Idensalmi. Itä-Suomi, C Finland
IJmuiden 86 C3 Noord-Holland, W Netherlands
IJssel 86 D3 *var.* Yssel. *river* Netherlands
IJsselmeer 86 C2 *prev.* Zuider Zee. *lake* N Netherlands

IJsselmuiden 86 D3 Overijssel, E Netherlands
Ijzer 87 A6 *river* W Belgium
Ikahauk *see* Sachs Harbour
Ikaluktutiak *see* Cambridge Bay
Ikaría 105 D6 *var.* Kariot, Nicaria, Nikaria; *anc.* Icaria. *island* Dodekánisa, Greece, Aegean Sea
Ikela 77 D6 Équateur, C Dem. Rep. Congo
Iki 131 A7 *island* SW Japan
Ilagan 129 E1 Luzon, N Philippines
Ilave 61 E4 Puno, S Peru
Iława 98 D3 Ger. Deutsch-Eylau. Warmińsko-Mazurskie, NE Poland
Ilebo 77 C6 *prev.* Port-Francqui. Kasai-Occidental, W Dem. Rep. Congo
Île-de-France 90 C3 *cultural region* N France
Ilerda *see* Lleida
Ilfracombe 89 C7 SW England, United Kingdom
Ílhavo 92 B2 Aveiro, N Portugal
Iliamna Lake 36 C3 *lake* Alaska, USA
Il'ichevsk *see* Illichivs'k, Ukraine
Ilici *see* Elche
Iligan 139 E2 *off.* Iligan City. Mindanao, S Philippines
Iligan City *see* Iligan
Illapel 64 B4 Coquimbo, C Chile
Illichivs'k 109 E4 *Rus.* Il'ichevsk. Odes'ka Oblast', SW Ukraine
Illicis *see* Elche
Illinois 40 A4 *off.* State of Illinois, *also known as* Prairie State, Sucker State. *state* C USA
Illinois River 40 B4 *river* Illinois, N USA
Illurco *see* Lorca
Illuro *see* Mataró
Ilo 61 E4 Moquegua, SW Peru
Iloilo 139 E2 *off.* Iloilo City. Panay Island, C Philippines
Iloilo City *see* Iloilo
Ilorin 75 F4 Kwara, W Nigeria
Ilovlya 111 B6 Volgogradskaya Oblast', SW Russian Federation
Iluh *see* Batman
Il'yaly *see* Gurbansoltan Eje
Imatra 85 E5 Etelä-Suomi, SE Finland
Imbros *see* Gökçeada
Imishli *see* İmişli
İmişli 117 H3 *Rus.* Imishli. C Azerbaijan
Imola 96 C3 Emilia-Romagna, N Italy
Imperatriz 63 F2 Maranhão, NE Brazil
Imperia 96 A3 Liguria, NW Italy
Impfondo 77 C5 Likouala, NE Congo
Imphâl 135 H3 *state capital* Manipur, NE India
Imroz Adası *see* Gökçeada
Inagua Islands *see* Little Inagua
Inagua Islands *see* Great Inagua
Inarijärvi 84 D2 *Lapp.* Aanaarjävri, *Swe.* Enareträsk. *lake* N Finland
Iñau *see* Ineu
Inawashiro-ko 131 D5 *var.* Inawasiro Ko. *lake* Honshū, C Japan
Inawasiro Ko *see* Inawashiro-ko
Íncesu 116 D3 Kayseri, Turkey Asia
Incheon 129 E4 *Jap.* Jinsen; *prev.* Chemulpo, Inch'ŏn. NW South Korea
Inch'ŏn *see* Incheon
Incudine, Monte 91 E7 *mountain* Corse, France, C Mediterranean Sea
Indefatigable Island *see* Santa Cruz, Isla
Independence 45 F4 Missouri, C USA
Independence Fjord 83 E1 *fjord* N Greenland
Independence Island *see* Malden Island
Independence Mountains 46 C4 *mountain range* Nevada, W USA
India 124 B3 *off.* Republic of India, *var.* Indian Union, Union of India, *Hind.* Bhārat. *country* S Asia

INDIA
South Asia

Official name Republic of India
Formation 1947 / 1947
Capital New Delhi
Population 1.24 billion / 1081 people per sq mile (418 people per sq km)
Total area 1,269,338 sq. miles (3,287,590 sq. km)
Languages Hindi*, English*, Urdu, Bengali, Marathi, Telugu, Tamil, Bihari, Gujarati, Kanarese
Religions Hindu 81%, Muslim 13%, Christian 2%, Sikh 2%, Buddhist 1%,

INDIA
South Asia

Other 1%
Ethnic mix Indo-Aryan 72%, Dravidian 25%, Mongoloid and other 3%
Government Parliamentary system
Currency Indian rupee = 100 paise
Literacy rate 66%
Calorie consumption 2321 kilocalories

India *see* Indija
Indiana 40 B4 *off.* State of Indiana, *also known as* Hoosier State. *state* N USA
Indianapolis 40 C4 *state capital* Indiana, N USA
Indian Church 52 C1 Orange Walk, N Belize
Indian Desert *see* Thar Desert
Indianola 45 F4 Iowa, C USA
Indian Union *see* India
India, Republic of *see* India
India, Union of *see* India
Indigirka 115 F2 *river* NE Russian Federation
Indija 100 D3 *Hung.* India; *prev.* Indjija. Vojvodina, N Serbia
Indira Point 132 G3 *headland* Andaman and Nicobar Island, India, NE Indian Ocean
Indjija *see* Indija
Indomed Fracture Zone 141 B6 *tectonic feature* SW Indian Ocean
Indonesia 138 B4 *off.* Republic of Indonesia, *Ind.* Republik Indonesia; *prev.* Dutch East Indies, Netherlands East Indies, United States of Indonesia. *country* SE Asia

INDONESIA
Southeast Asia

Official name Republic of Indonesia
Formation 1949 / 1999
Capital Jakarta
Population 242 million / 349 people per sq mile (135 people per sq km)
Total area 741,096 sq. miles (1,919,440 sq. km)
Languages Javanese, Sundanese, Madurese, Bahasa Indonesian*, Dutch
Religions Sunni Muslim 86%, Protestant 6%, Roman Catholic 3%, Hindu 2%, Other 2%, Buddhist 1%
Ethnic mix Javanese 41%, Other 28%, Sundanese 15%, Coastal Malays 12%, Madurese 3%
Government Presidential system
Currency Rupiah = 100 sen
Literacy rate 92%
Calorie consumption 2646 kilocalories

Indonesian Borneo *see* Kalimantan
Indonesia, Republic of *see* Indonesia
Indonesia, Republik *see* Indonesia
Indonesia, United States of *see* Indonesia
Indore 134 D4 Madhya Pradesh, C India
Indreville *see* Châteauroux
Indus 134 C2 *Chin.* Yindu He; *prev.* Yin-tu Ho. *river* S Asia
Indus Cone *see* Indus Fan
Indus Fan 112 C5 *var.* Indus Cone. *undersea fan* N Arabian Sea
Indus, Mouths of the 134 B4 *delta* S Pakistan
İnebolu 116 C2 Kastamonu, N Turkey
Ineu 108 A4 *Hung.* Borosjenő; *prev.* Iñau. Arad, W Romania
Infiernillo, Presa del 51 E4 *reservoir* S Mexico
Inglewood 46 D2 California, W USA
Ingolstadt 95 C6 Bayern, S Germany
Ingulets *see* Inhulets'
Inguri *see* Enguri
Inhambane 79 E4 Inhambane, SE Mozambique
Inhulets' 109 F3 *Rus.* Ingulets. Dnipropetrovs'ka Oblast', E Ukraine
I-ning *see* Yining
Inis *see* Ennis
Inis Ceithleann *see* Enniskillen
Inn 95 C6 *river* C Europe
Innaanganeq 82 C1 *var.* Kap York. *headland* NW Greenland

Inner Hebrides 88 B4 *island group* W Scotland, United Kingdom
Inner Islands 79 H1 *var.* Central Group. *island group* NE Seychelles
Innisfail 148 D3 Queensland, NE Australia
Inniskilling *see* Enniskillen
Innsbruch *see* Innsbruck
Innsbruck 95 C7 *var.* Innsbruch. Tirol, W Austria
Inoucdjouac *see* Inukjuak
Inowazław *see* Inowrocław
Inowrocław 98 C3 *Ger.* Hohensalza; *prev.* Inowrazław. Kujawski-pomorskie, C Poland
I-n-Sakane, 'Erg 75 E2 *desert* N Mali
I-n-Salah 70 D3 *var.* In Salah. C Algeria
Insterburg *see* Chernyakhovsk
Insula *see* Lille
Inta 110 E3 Respublika Komi, NW Russian Federation
Interamna *see* Teramo
Interamna Nahars *see* Terni
International Falls 45 F1 Minnesota, N USA
Inukjuak 38 D2 *var.* Inoucdjouac; *prev.* Port Harrison. Québec, NE Canada
Inuuvik *see* Inuvik
Inuvik 36 D3 *var.* Inuuvik. Northwest Territories, NW Canada
Invercargill 151 A7 Southland, South Island, New Zealand
Inverness 88 C3 N Scotland, United Kingdom
Investigator Ridge 141 D5 *undersea ridge* E Indian Ocean
Investigator Strait 149 B7 *strait* South Australia
Inyangani 78 D3 *mountain* NE Zimbabwe
Ioánnina 104 A4 *var.* Janina, Yannina. Ípeiros, W Greece
Iola 45 F5 Kansas, C USA
Ionia Basin *see* Ionian Basin
Ionian Basin 80 D5 *var.* Ionia Basin. *undersea basin* Ionian Sea, C Mediterranean Sea
Ionian Sea 83 E3 *Gk.* Iónio Pélagos, *It.* Mar Ionio. *sea* C Mediterranean Sea
Iónioi Nísoi 105 A5 *Eng.* Ionian Islands. *region* W Greece
Ionio, Mar/Iónio Pélagos *see* Ionian Sea
Íos 105 D6 *var.* Nio. *island* Kykládes, Greece, Aegean Sea
Íos 105 D6 *var.* Nio. *island* Kykládes, Greece, Aegean Sea
Íos 105 D6 *var.* Nio. *island* Kykládes, Greece, Aegean Sea
Ioulís 105 C6 *prev.* Kéa. Tziá, Kykládes, Greece, Aegean Sea
Iowa 45 F3 *off.* State of Iowa, *also known as* Hawkeye State. *state* C USA
Iowa City 45 G3 Iowa, C USA
Iowa Falls 45 G3 Iowa, C USA
Ipel' 99 C6 *var.* Ipoly, *Ger.* Eipel. *river* Hungary/Slovakia
Ipiales 58 A4 Nariño, SW Colombia
Ipoh 138 B3 Perak, Peninsular Malaysia
Ipoly *see* Ipel'
Ippy 76 C4 Ouaka, C Central African Republic
Ipswich 149 E5 Queensland, E Australia
Ipswich 89 E6 *hist.* Gipeswic. E England, United Kingdom
Iqaluit 37 H3 *prev.* Frobisher Bay. *province capital* Baffin Island, Nunavut, NE Canada
Iquique 64 B1 Tarapacá, N Chile
Iquitos 60 C1 Loreto, N Peru
Iráklaio 105 D7 *var.* Herakleion, *Eng.* Candia; *prev.* Iráklion. Kríti, Greece, E Mediterranean Sea
Iráklion *see* Iráklaio
Iran 120 C3 *off.* Islamic Republic of Iran; *prev.* Persia. *country* SW Asia

IRAN
Southwest Asia

Official name Islamic Republic of Iran
Formation 1502 / 1990
Capital Tehran
Population 74.8 million / 118 people per sq mile (46 people per sq km)
Total area 636,293 sq. miles (1,648,000 sq. km)
Languages Farsi*, Azeri, Luri, Gilaki, Mazanderani, Kurdish, Turkmen,

IRAN
(continued)

Arabic, Baluchi
Religions Shi'a Muslim 89%,
Sunni Muslim 9%, Other 2%
Ethnic mix Persian 51%, Azari 24%,
Other 10%, Lur and Bakhtiari 8%,
Kurdish 7%
Government Islamic theocracy
Currency Iranian rial = 100 dinars
Literacy rate 85%
Calorie consumption 3143 kilocalories

Iranian Plateau 120 D3 var. Plateau of
Iran. *plateau* N Iran
Iran, Islamic Republic of *see* Iran
Iran, Plateau of *see* Iranian Plateau
Irapuato 51 E4 Guanajuato, C Mexico
Iraq 120 B3 off. Republic of Iraq, Ar.
'Irâq. *country* SW Asia

IRAQ
Southwest Asia

Official name Republic of Iraq
Formation 1932 / 1990
Capital Baghdad
Population 32.7 million / 194 people
per sq mile (75 people per sq km)
Total area 168,753 sq. miles
(437,072 sq. km)
Languages Arabic*, Kurdish*, Turkic
languages, Armenian, Assyrian
Religions Shi'a Muslim 60%,
Sunni Muslim 35%, Other (including
Christian) 5%
Ethnic mix Arab 80%, Kurdish 15%,
Turkmen 3%, Other 2%
Government Parliamentary system
Currency New Iraqi dinar = 1000 fils
Literacy rate 78%
Calorie consumption 2197 kilocalories

'Irâq *see* Iraq
Iraq, Republic of *see* Iraq
Irbid 119 B5 Irbid, N Jordan
Irbil *see* Arbil
Ireland 80 A5 off. Republic of Ireland, Ir.
Éire. *country* NW Europe

IRELAND
Northwest Europe

Official name Ireland
Formation 1922 / 1922
Capital Dublin
Population 4.5 million / 169 people
per sq mile (65 people per sq km)
Total area 27,135 sq. miles (70,280 sq. km)
Languages English*, Irish Gaelic*
Religions Roman Catholic 87%,
Other and nonreligious 10%, Anglican 3%
Ethnic mix Irish 99%, Other 1%
Government Parliamentary system
Currency Euro = 100 cents
Literacy rate 99%
Calorie consumption 3617 kilocalories

Ireland 80 C3 Lat. Hibernia. *island*
Ireland/United Kingdom
Ireland, Republic of *see* Ireland
Irian *see* New Guinea
Irian Barat *see* Papua
Irian Jaya *see* Papua
Irian, Teluk *see* Cenderawasih, Teluk
Iringa 73 C7 Iringa, C Tanzania
Iriomote-jima 130 A4 *island* Sakishima-
shotō, SW Japan
Iriona 52 D2 Colón, NE Honduras
Irish Sea 89 C5 Ir. Muir Éireann. *sea*
C British Isles
Irkutsk 115 E4 Irkutskaya Oblast',
S Russian Federation
Irminger Basin *see* Reykjanes Basin
Iroise 90 A3 *sea* NW France
Iron Mountain 40 B2 Michigan, N USA
Ironwood 40 B1 Michigan, N USA
Irrawaddy 136 B4 var. Ayeyarwady.
river W Myanmar (Burma)
Irrawaddy, Mouths of the 137 A5 *delta*
SW Myanmar (Burma)
Irtish *see* Yertis
Irtysh *see* Yertis
Irun 93 E1 Cast. Irún. País Vasco,
N Spain
Irún *see* Irun
Iruña *see* Pamplona

Isabela, Isla 60 A5 var. Albemarle Island.
island Galápagos Islands, Ecuador,
E Pacific Ocean
Isaccea 108 D4 Tulcea, E Romania
Isachsen 37 F1 Ellef Ringnes Island,
Nunavut, N Canada
Ísafjördhur 83 E4 Vestfirdhir,
NW Iceland
Isbarta *see* Isparta
Isca Damnoniorum *see* Exeter
Ise 131 C6 Mie, Honshū, SW Japan
Iseghem *see* Izegem
Isère 91 D5 *river* E France
Isernia 97 D5 var. Æsernia. Molise,
C Italy
Ise-wan 131 C6 *bay* S Japan
Isfahan *see* Eşfahān
Isha Baydhabo *see* Baydhabo
Ishigaki-jima 130 A4 *island* Sakishima-
shotō, SW Japan
Ishikari-wan 130 C2 *bay* Hokkaidō,
NE Japan
Ishim 114 C4 Tyumenskaya Oblast',
C Russian Federation
Ishim 114 C4 var. Isinomaki.
Miyagi, Honshū, C Japan
Ishkashim *see* Ishkoshim
Ishkoshim 123 F3 Rus. Ishkashim.
S Tajikistan
Isinomaki *see* Ishinomaki
Isiro 77 E5 Orientale, NE Dem. Rep.
Congo
Iskär *see* Iskŭr
İskenderun 116 D4 Eng. Alexandretta.
Hatay, S Turkey
İskenderun Körfezi 118 A2 Eng. Gulf of
Alexandretta. *gulf* S Turkey
Iskŭr 104 C2 var. Iskår. *river*
NW Bulgaria
Yazovir Iskur 104 B2 prev. Yazovir
Stalin. *reservoir* W Bulgaria
Isla Cristina 92 C4 Andalucía, S Spain
Isla de León *see* San Fernando
Islāmābād 134 C1 *country capital*
(Pakistan) Federal Capital Territory
Islāmābād, NE Pakistan
Island/Ísland *see* Iceland
Islay 88 B4 *island* SW Scotland, United
Kingdom
Isle 91 B5 *river* W France
Isle of Man 89 B5 UK crown dependency
NW Europe
Isles of Scilly 89 B8 *island group*
SW England, United Kingdom
Ismailia *see* Al Ismā'īlīya
Ismâ'ilîya *see* Al Ismā'īlīya
Ismid *see* İzmit
Isnā 72 B2 var. Esna. SE Egypt
Isoka 78 D1 Northern, NE Zambia
Isparta 116 B4 var. Isbarta. Isparta,
SW Turkey
Ispir 117 E3 Erzurum, NE Turkey
Israel 119 A7 off. State of Israel, var.
Medinat Israel, Heb. Yisrael, Yisra'el.
country SW Asia

ISRAEL
Southwest Asia

Official name State of Israel
Formation 1948 / 1994
Capital Jerusalem (not internationally
recognized)
Population 7.6 million / 968 people
per sq mile (374 people per sq km)
Total area 8019 sq. miles (20,770 sq. km)
Languages Hebrew*, Arabic*,
Yiddish, German, Russian, Polish,
Romanian, Persian
Religions Jewish 76%, Muslim (mainly
Sunni) 16%, Other 4%, Druze 2%,
Christian 2%
Ethnic mix Jewish 76%, Arab 20%,
Other 4%
Government Parliamentary system
Currency Shekel = 100 agorot
Literacy rate 99%
Calorie consumption 3569 kilocalories

Israel, State of *see* Israel
Issa *see* Vis
Issiq Köl *see* Issyk-Kul', Ozero
Issoire 91 C5 Puy-de-Dôme, C France
Issyk-Kul' *see* Balykchy
Issyk-Kul', Ozero 123 G2 var. Issiq Köl,
Kir. Ysyk-Köl. *lake* E Kyrgyzstan
İstanbul 116 B2 Bul. Tsarigrad, Eng.
Istanbul, prev. Constantinople; anc.
Byzantium. İstanbul, NW Turkey

Istarska Županija *see* Istra
Istra 100 A3 off. Istarska Županija.
province NW Croatia
Istra 100 A3 Eng. Istria, Ger. Istrien.
cultural region NW Croatia
Istria/Istrien *see* Istra
Itabuna 63 G3 Bahia, E Brazil
Itagüí 58 B3 Antioquia, W Colombia
Itaipú, Represa de 63 E4 *reservoir* Brazil/
Paraguay
Itaituba 63 E2 Pará, NE Brazil
**Italia/Italiana, Republica/Italian
Republic, The** *see* Italy
Italian Somaliland *see* Somalia
Italy 96 C3 off. The Italian Republic, It.
Italia, Repubblica Italiana. *country*
S Europe

ITALY
Southern Europe

Official name Italian Republic
Formation 1861 / 1947
Capital Rome
Population 60.8 million / 536 people
per sq mile (207 people per sq km)
Total area 116,305 sq. miles
(301,230 sq. km)
Languages Italian*, German, French,
Rhaeto-Romanic, Sardinian
Religions Roman Catholic 85%,
Other and nonreligious 13%, Muslim 2%
Ethnic mix Italian 94%, Other 4%,
Sardinian 2%
Government Parliamentary system
Currency Euro = 100 cents
Literacy rate 99%
Calorie consumption 3627 kilocalories

Iténez, Río *see* Guaporé, Rio
Ithaca 41 E3 New York, NE USA
It Hearrenfean *see* Heerenveen
Itoigawa 131 C5 Niigata, Honshū,
C Japan
Itseqqortoormiit *see* Ittoqqortoormiit
Ittoqqortoormiit 83 F3 var.
Itseqqortoormiit, Dan. Scoresbysund,
Eng. Scoresby Sound. Tunu,
C Greenland
Iturup, Ostrov 130 E1 *island* Kuril'skiye
Ostrova, SE Russian Federation
Itzehoe 94 B2 Schleswig-Holstein,
N Germany
Ivalo 84 D2 Lapp. Avveel, Avvil. Lappi,
N Finland
Ivanava 107 B7 Pol. Janów, Janów
Poleski, Rus. Ivanovo. Brestskaya
Voblasts', SW Belarus
Ivanhoe 149 C6 New South Wales,
SE Australia
Ivano-Frankivs'k 108 C2 Ger. Stanislau,
Pol. Stanisławów, Rus. Ivano-
Frankovsk; prev. Stanislav. Ivano-
Frankivs'ka Oblast', W Ukraine
Ivano-Frankovsk *see* Ivano-Frankivs'k
Ivanovo 111 B5 Ivanovskaya Oblast',
W Russian Federation
Ivanovo *see* Ivanava
Ivantsevichi/Ivatsevichi *see* Ivatsevichy
Ivatsevichy 107 B6 Pol. Iwacewicze, Rus.
Ivantsevichi, Ivatsevichi. Brestskaya
Voblasts', SW Belarus
Ivigtut *see* Ivittuut
Ivittuut 82 B4 var. Ivigtut. Kitaa,
S Greenland
Iviza *see* Eivissa\Ibiza
Ivory Coast *see* Côte d'Ivoire
Ivory Coast, Republic of the *see* Côte
d'Ivoire
Ivujivik 38 D1 Québec, NE Canada
Iwacewicze *see* Ivatsevichy
Iwaki 131 D5 Fukushima, Honshū,
N Japan
Iwakuni 131 B7 Yamaguchi, Honshū,
SW Japan
Iwanai 130 C2 Hokkaidō, NE Japan
Iwate 130 D3 Iwate, Honshū, N Japan
Ixtapa 51 E5 Guerrero, S Mexico
Ixtepec 51 F5 Oaxaca, SE Mexico
Iyo-nada 131 B7 *sea* S Japan
Izabal, Lago de 52 B2 prev. Golfo Dulce.
lake E Guatemala
Izad Khvāst 120 D3 Fārs, C Iran
Izegem 87 A6 prev. Iseghem. West-
Vlaanderen, W Belgium
Izhevsk 111 D5 prev. Ustinov.
Udmurtskaya Respublika, NW Russian
Federation

Izmail *see* Izmayil
Izmayil 108 D4 Rus. Izmail. Odes'ka
Oblast', SW Ukraine
İzmir 116 A3 prev. Smyrna. İzmir,
W Turkey
İzmit 116 B2 var. Ismid; anc. Astacus.
Kocaeli, NW Turkey
İznik Gölü 116 B3 *lake* NW Turkey
Izu-hanto 131 D6 *peninsula* Honshū,
S Japan
Izu Shichito *see* Izu-shotō
Izu-shotō 131 D6 var. Izu Shichito.
island group S Japan
Izvor 104 B2 Pernik, W Bulgaria
Izyaslav 108 C2 Khmel'nyts'ka Oblast',
W Ukraine
Izyum 109 G2 Kharkivs'ka Oblast',
E Ukraine

J

Jabal ash Shifa 120 A4 *desert* NW Saudi
Arabia
Jabalpur 135 E4 prev. Jubbulpore.
Madhya Pradesh, C India
Jabbūl, Sabkhat al 118 B2 *sabkha*
NW Syria
Jablah 118 A3 var. Jeble, Fr. Djéblé. Al
Lādhiqiyah, W Syria
Jaca 93 F1 Aragón, NE Spain
Jacaltenango 52 A2 Huehuetenango,
W Guatemala
Jackson 42 B2 *state capital* Mississippi,
S USA
Jackson 45 H5 Missouri, C USA
Jackson 42 C1 Tennessee, S USA
Jackson Head 151 A6 *headland* South
Island, New Zealand
Jacksonville 43 E3 Florida, SE USA
Jacksonville 40 B4 Illinois, N USA
Jacksonville 43 F1 North Carolina,
SE USA
Jacksonville 49 G3 Texas, SW USA
Jacmel 54 D3 var. Jaquemel. S Haiti
Jacob *see* Nkayi
Jacobābād 134 B3 Sind, SE Pakistan
Jadotville *see* Likasi
Jadransko More/Jadransko Morje *see*
Adriatic Sea
Jaén 60 B2 Cajamarca, N Peru
Jaén 92 D4 Andalucía, SW Spain
Jaffna 132 D3 Northern Province,
N Sri Lanka
Jagannath *see* Puri
Jagdalpur 135 E5 Chhattisgarh, C India
Jagdaqi 127 G1 Nei Mongol Zizhiqu,
N China
Jagodina 100 D4 prev. Svetozarevo.
Serbia, C Serbia
Jahra *see* Al Jahrā'
Jailolo *see* Halmahera, Pulau
Jaipur 134 D3 prev. Jeypore. *state capital*
Rājasthān, N India
Jaisalmer 134 C3 Rājasthān, NW India
Jajce 100 B3 Federacija Bosna
I Hercegovina, W Bosnia and
Herzegovina
Jakarta 138 C5 prev. Djakarta, Dut.
Batavia. *country capital* (Indonesia)
Jawa, C Indonesia
Jakobstad 84 D4 Fin. Pietarsaari. Länsi-
Suomi, W Finland
Jakobstadt *see* Jēkabpils
Jalālābād 123 F4 var. Jalalabad,
Jelalabad. Nangarhār, E Afghanistan
Jalal-Abad *see* Dzhalal-Abad, Dzhalal-
Abadskaya Oblast', Kyrgyzstan
Jalandhar 134 D2 prev. Jullundur.
Punjab, N India
Jalapa 52 D3 Nueva Segovia,
NW Nicaragua
Jalpa 50 D4 Zacatecas, C Mexico
Jālū 71 G3 var. Jālā. NE Libya
Jaluit Atoll 144 D2 var. Jālwōj. *atoll*
Ralik Chain, S Marshall Islands
Jālwōj *see* Jaluit Atoll
Jamaame 73 D6 It. Giamame; prev.
Margherita. Jubbada Hoose, S Somalia
Jamaica 54 A4 *country* W West Indies

JAMAICA
West Indies

Official name Jamaica
Formation 1962 / 1962
Capital Kingston
Population 2.8 million / 670 people
per sq mile (259 people per sq km)

JAMAICA
(continued)

Total area 4243 sq. miles (10,990 sq. km)
Languages English Creole, English*
Religions Other and nonreligious 45%, Other Protestant 20%, Church of God 18%, Baptist 10%, Anglican 7%
Ethnic mix Black African 91%, Mulatto (mixed race) 7%, East Indian 1%, European and Chinese 1%
Government Parliamentary system
Currency Jamaican dollar = 100 cents
Literacy rate 86%
Calorie consumption 2807 kilocalories

Jamaica *56 A1 island* W West Indies
Jamaica Channel *54 D3 channel* Haiti/ Jamaica
Jamālpur *135 F3* Bihār, NE India
Jambi *138 B4 var.* Telanaipura; *prev.* Djambi. Sumatera, W Indonesia
Jamdena *see* Yamdena, Pulau
James Bay *38 C3 bay* Ontario/Québec, E Canada
James River *45 E2 river* North Dakota/ South Dakota, N USA
James River *41 E5 river* Virginia, NE USA
Jamestown *41 E3* New York, NE USA
Jamestown *45 E2* North Dakota, N USA
Jamestown *see* Holetown
Jammu *134 D2 prev.* Jummoo. *state capital* Jammu and Kashmir, NW India
Jammu and Kashmir *134 D1 disputed region* India/Pakistan
Jāmnagar *134 C4 prev.* Navanagar. Gujarāt, W India
Jamshedpur *135 F4* Jhārkhand, NE India
Jamuna *see* Brahmaputra
Janaúba *63 F3* Minas Gerais, SE Brazil
Janesville *40 B3* Wisconsin, N USA
Janina *see* Ioánnina
Janischken *see* Joniškis
Jankovac *see* Jánoshalma
Jan Mayen *83 F4 Norwegian dependency* N Atlantic Ocean
Jánoshalma *99 C7 SCr.* Jankovac. Bács-Kiskun, S Hungary
Janów *see* Ivanava, Belarus
Janow/Janów *see* Jonava, Lithuania
Janów Poleski *see* Ivanava
Japan *130 C4 var.* Nippon, *Jap.* Nihon. *country* E Asia

JAPAN
East Asia

Official name Japan
Formation 1590 / 1972
Capital Tokyo
Population 126 million / 870 people per sq mile (336 people per sq km)
Total area 145,882 sq. miles (377,835 sq. km)
Languages Japanese*, Korean, Chinese
Religions Shinto and Buddhist 76%, Buddhist 16%, Other (including Christian) 8%
Ethnic mix Japanese 99%, Other (mainly Korean) 1%
Government Parliamentary system
Currency Yen = 100 sen
Literacy rate 99%
Calorie consumption 2723 kilocalories

Japan, Sea of *130 A4 var.* East Sea, *Rus.* Yapanskoye More. *sea* NW Pacific Ocean
Japan Trench *125 F1 trench* NW Pacific Ocean
Japen *see* Yapen, Pulau
Japiim *62 C2 var.* Máncio Lima. Acre, W Brazil
Japurá, Rio *62 C2 var.* Río Caquetá, Yapurá. *river* Brazil/Colombia
Japurá, Rio *see* Caquetá, Río
Jaque *53 G5* Darién, SE Panama
Jaquemel *see* Jacmel
Jarablos *see* Jarābulus
Jarābulus *118 C2 var.* Jarablos, Jerablus, *Fr.* Djérablous. Ḥalab, N Syria
Jarbah, Jazīrat *see* Jerba, Île de
Jardines de la Reina, Archipiélago de los *54 B2 island group* C Cuba
Jarid, Shaṭṭ al *see* Jerid, Chott el
Jarocin *98 C4* Wielkopolskie, C Poland
Jaroslau *see* Jarosław

Jarosław *99 E5 Ger.* Jaroslau, *Rus.* Yaroslav. Podkarpackie, SE Poland
Jarqo'rg'on *123 E3 Rus.* Dzharkurgan. Surkhondaryo Viloyati, S Uzbekistan
Jarvis Island *145 G2 US unincorporated territory* C Pacific Ocean
Jasło *99 D5* Podkarpackie, SE Poland
Jastrzębie-Zdrój *99 C5* Śląskie, S Poland
Jataí *63 E3* Goiás, C Brazil
Jativa *see* Xàtiva
Jauf *see* Al Jawf
Jaunpiebalga *106 D3* NE Latvia
Jaunpur *135 E3* Uttar Pradesh, N India
Java *152 A3* South Dakota, N USA
Javalambre *93 E3 mountain* E Spain
Java Sea *138 D4 Ind.* Laut Jawa. *sea* W Indonesia
Java Trench *124 D5 var.* Sunda Trench. *trench* E Indian Ocean
Jawa, Laut *see* Java Sea
Jawhar *73 D6 var.* Jowhar, *It.* Giohar. Shabeellaha Dhexe, S Somalia
Jaworów *see* Yavoriv
Jaya, Puncak *139 G4 prev.* Puntjak Carstensz, Puntjak Sukarno. *mountain* Papua, E Indonesia
Jayapura *139 H4 var.* Djajapura, *Dut.* Hollandia; *prev.* Kotabaru, Sukarnapura. Papua, E Indonesia
Jay Dairen *see* Dalian
Jayhawker State *see* Kansas
Jaz Murian, Hamun-e *120 E4 lake* SE Iran
Jebba *75 F4* Kwara, W Nigeria
Jebel, Bahr el *see* White Nile
Jeble *see* Jablah
Jedda *see* Jiddah
Jędrzejów *98 D4 Ger.* Endersdorf. Świętokrzyskie, C Poland
Jefferson City *45 G5 state capital* Missouri, C USA
Jega *75 F4* Kebbi, NW Nigeria
Jehol *see* Chengde
Jeju-do *129 E4 Jap.* Saishū; *prev.* Cheju-do, Quelpart. *island* S South Korea
Jeju Strait *129 E4 prev.* Cheju Strait. *strait* S South Korea
Jēkabpils *106 D4 Ger.* Jakobstadt. S Latvia
Jelalabad *see* Jalālābād
Jelenia Góra *98 B4 Ger.* Hirschberg, Hirschberg im Riesengebirge, Hirschberg in Riesengebirge, Hirschberg in Schlesien. Dolnośląskie, SW Poland
Jelgava *106 C3 Ger.* Mitau. C Latvia
Jemappes *87 B6* Hainaut, S Belgium
Jember *138 D5 prev.* Djember. Jawa, C Indonesia
Jena *94 C4* Thüringen, C Germany
Jenin *119 A6* N West Bank
Jerablus *see* Jarābulus
Jerada *70 D2* NE Morocco
Jérémie *54 D3* SW Haiti
Jerez *see* Jeréz de la Frontera, Spain
Jerez de la Frontera *92 C5 var.* Jerez; *prev.* Xeres. Andalucía, SW Spain
Jerez de los Caballeros *92 C4* Extremadura, W Spain
Jericho *119 B6 Ar.* Arīḥā, *Heb.* Yeriḥo. E West Bank
Jerid, Chott el *71 E2 var.* Shaṭṭ al Jarīd. *salt lake* SW Tunisia
Jersey *89 D8 uk crown dependency* Channel Islands, NW Europe
Jerusalem *103 H4 Ar.* Al Quds, Al Quds ash Sharif, *Heb.* Yerushalayim; *anc.* Hierosolyma. *country capital* (Israel) Jerusalem, NE Israel
Jesenice *95 D7 Ger.* Assling. NW Slovenia
Jesselton *see* Kota Kinabalu
Jessore *135 G4* Khulna, W Bangladesh
Jesús María *64 C3* Córdoba, C Argentina
Jeypore *see* Jaipur, Rājasthān, India
Jhānsi *134 D3* Uttar Pradesh, N India
Jhārkhand *135 F4 cultural region* NE India
Jhelum *134 C2* Punjab, NE Pakistan
Ji *see* Hebei, China
Ji *see* Jilin, China
Jiangmen *128 C6* Guangdong, S China
Jiangsu *128 D4 var.* Chiang-su, Jiangsu Sheng, Kiangsu, Su. *province* E China
Jiangsu *see* Nanjing
Jiangsu Sheng *see* Jiangsu
Jiangxi *128 C6 var.* Chiang-hsi, Gan, Jiangxi Sheng, Kiangsi. *province* S China

Jiangxi Sheng *see* Jiangxi
Jiaxing *128 D5* Zhejiang, SE China
Jiayi *128 D6 var.* Chia-i, Chiai, Chiayi, Kiayi, *Jap.* Kagi. C Taiwan
Jibuti *see* Djibouti
Jiddah *121 A5 Eng.* Jedda. (Saudi Arabia) Makkah, W Saudi Arabia
Jih-k'a-tse *see* Xigazê
Jihlava *99 B5 Ger.* Iglau, *Pol.* Iglawa. Vysocina, S Czech Republic
Jilib *73 D6* It. Gelib. Jubbada Dhexe, S Somalia
Jilin *128 E3 var.* Chi-lin, Girin, Kirin; *prev.* Yungki, Yunki. Jilin, NE China
Jilin *128 E3 var.* Chi-lin, Girin, Ji, Jilin Sheng, Kirin. *province* NE China
Jilin Sheng *see* Jilin
Jilong *128 D6 var.* Keelung, *Jap.* Kirun, Kirun', *prev.* Chilung, *prev. Sp.* Santissima Trinidad. N Taiwan
Jima *73 C5 var.* Jimma, *It.* Gimma. Oromīya, C Ethiopia
Jimbolia *108 A4 Ger.* Hatzfeld, *Hung.* Zsombolya. Timiş, W Romania
Jiménez *50 D2* Chihuahua, N Mexico
Jimma *see* Jima
Jimsar *126 C3* Xinjiang Uygur Zizhiqu, NW China
Jin *see* Shanxi
Jin *see* Tianjin Shi
Jinan *128 C4 var.* Chinan, Chi-nan, Tsinan. *province capital* Shandong, E China
Jingdezhen *128 C5* Jiangxi, S China
Jinghong *128 A6 var.* Yunjinghong. Yunnan, SW China
Jinhua *128 D5* Zhejiang, SE China
Jining *127 F3* Shandong, E China
Jinja *73 C6* S Uganda
Jinotega *52 D3* Jinotega, NW Nicaragua
Jinotepe *52 D3* Carazo, SW Nicaragua
Jinsen *see* Incheon
Jinzhong *128 C4 var.* Yuci. Shanxi, C China
Jinzhou *128 D3 var.* Chin-chou, Chinchow; *prev.* Chinhsien. Liaoning, NE China
Jirgalanta *see* Hovd
Jisr ash Shadadi *see* Ash Shadādah
Jiu *108 B5 Ger.* Schil, Schyl, *Hung.* Zsil, Zsily. *river* S Romania
Jiujiang *128 C5* Jiangxi, S China
Jixi *128 E2* Heilongjiang, NE China
Jīzān *121 B6 var.* Qīzān. Jīzān, SW Saudi Arabia
Jizzax *123 E2 Rus.* Dzhizak. Jizzax Viloyati, C Uzbekistan
João Belo *see* Xai-Xai
João Pessoa *63 G2 prev.* Paraíba. *state capital* Paraíba, E Brazil
Joazeiro *see* Juazeiro
Job'urg *see* Johannesburg
Jo-ch'iang *see* Ruoqiang
Jodhpur *134 C3* Rājasthān, NW India
Joensuu *85 E5* Itä-Suomi, SE Finland
Jõetsu *131 C5 var.* Zyôetu. Niigata, Honshū, C Japan
Jogjakarta *see* Yogyakarta
Johannesburg *78 D4 var.* Egoli, Erautini, Gauteng, *abbrev.* Job'urg. Gauteng, NE South Africa
Johannisburg *see* Pisz
John Day River *46 C3 river* Oregon, NW USA
John o'Groats *88 D7* N Scotland, United Kingdom
Johnston Atoll *143 E1 US unincorporated territory* C Pacific Ocean
Johor Baharu *see* Johor Bahru
Johor Bahru *138 B3 var.* Johor Baharu, Johore Bahru. Johor, Peninsular Malaysia
Johore Bahru *see* Johor Bahru
Johore Strait *138 A1 strait* Johor, Peninsular Malaysia, Malaysia/ Singapore Asia Andaman Sea/South China Sea
Joinville *see* Joinville
Joinville *63 E4 var.* Joinvile. Santa Catarina, S Brazil
Jokkmokk *84 C3 Lapp.* Dálvvadis. Norrbotten, N Sweden
Jokyakarta *see* Yogyakarta
Joliet *40 B3* Illinois, N USA
Jonava *106 B4 Ger.* Janow, *Pol.* Janów. Kaunas, C Lithuania
Jonesboro *42 B1* Arkansas, C USA

Joniškis *106 C3 Ger.* Janischken. Šiauliai, N Lithuania
Jönköping *85 B7* Jönköping, S Sweden
Jonquière *39 E4* Québec, SE Canada
Joplin *45 F5* Missouri, C USA
Jordan *119 B6 off.* Hashemite Kingdom of Jordan, *Ar.* Al Mamlaka al Urdunīya al Hashemīyah, Al Urdunn; *prev.* Transjordan. *country* SW Asia

JORDAN
Southwest Asia

Official name Hashemite Kingdom of Jordan
Formation 1946 / 1967
Capital Amman
Population 6.3 million / 183 people per sq mile (71 people per sq km)
Total area 35,637 sq. miles (92,300 sq. km)
Languages Arabic*
Religions Muslim (mainly Sunni) 92%, Christian 6%, Other 2%
Ethnic mix Arab 98%, Circassian 1%, Armenian 1%
Government Monarchy
Currency Jordanian dinar = 1000 fils
Literacy rate 92%
Calorie consumption 2977 kilocalories

Jordan *119 B5 Ar.* Urdunn, *Heb.* HaYarden. *river* SW Asia
Jorhāt *135 H3* Assam, NE India
Jos *75 G4* Plateau, C Nigeria
Joseph Bonaparte Gulf *146 D2 gulf* N Australia
Jos Plateau *75 G4 plateau* C Nigeria
Jotunheimen *85 A5 mountain range* S Norway
Joûnié *118 A4 var.* Junīyah. W Lebanon
Joure *86 D2 Fris.* De Jouwer. Fryslân, N Netherlands
Joutseno *85 E5* Etelä-Suomi, SE Finland
Jowhar *see* Jawhar
J.Storm Thurmond Reservoir *see* Clark Hill Lake
Juan Aldama *50 D3* Zacatecas, C Mexico
Juan de Fuca, Strait of *46 A1 strait* Canada/USA
Juan Fernandez Islands *57 A6 Eng.* Juan Fernandez Islands. *island group* W Chile
Juan Fernandez Islands *see* Juan Fernández, Islas
Juazeiro *63 G2 prev.* Joazeiro. Bahia, E Brazil
Juazeiro do Norte *63 G2* Ceará, E Brazil
Juba *73 B5 var.* Jūbā. *country capital* (South Sudan) Central Equatoria, S South Sudan
Juba *73 D6 Amh.* Genalē Wenz, *It.* Guiba, *Som.* Ganaane, Webi Jubba. *river* Ethiopia/Somalia
Jubba, Webi *see* Juba
Jubbulpore *see* Jabalpur
Júcar *93 E3 var.* Jucar. *river* C Spain
Juchitán *51 F5 var.* Juchitán de Zaragosa. Oaxaca, SE Mexico
Juchitán de Zaragosa *see* Juchitán
Judayyidat Hāmir *120 B3* Al Anbār, S Iraq
Judenburg *95 D7* Steiermark, C Austria
Jugoslavija *see* Serbia
Juigalpa *52 D3* Chontales, S Nicaragua
Juiz de Fora *63 F4* Minas Gerais, SE Brazil
Jujuy *see* San Salvador de Jujuy
Jūlā *see* Jālū, Libya
Julia Beterrae *see* Béziers
Juliaca *61 E4* Puno, SE Peru
Juliana Top *59 G3 mountain* C Suriname
Julianehåb *see* Qaqortoq
Julio Briga *see* Bragança
Juliobriga *see* Logroño
Juliomagus *see* Angers
Jullundur *see* Jalandhar
Jumilla *93 E4* Murcia, SE Spain
Jummoo *see* Jammu
Jumna *see* Yamuna
Jumporn *see* Chumphon
Junction City *45 F4* Kansas, C USA
Juneau *36 D4 state capital* Alaska, USA
Junín *64 C4* Buenos Aires, E Argentina
Junīyah *see* Joûnié
Junkseylon *see* Phuket
Jur *73 B5 river* W South Sudan
Jura *90 D4 cultural region* E France
Jura *95 A7 var.* Jura Mountains. *mountain range* France/Switzerland

Jura 88 B4 *island* SW Scotland, United Kingdom
Jura Mountains *see* Jura
Jurbarkas 106 B4 *Ger.* Georgenburg, Jurburg. Tauragė, W Lithuania
Jurburg *see* Jurbarkas
Jūrmala 106 C3 C Latvia
Juruá, Rio 62 C2 *var.* Río Yuruá. *river* Brazil/Peru
Juruena, Rio 62 D3 *river* W Brazil
Jutiapa 52 B2 Jutiapa, S Guatemala
Juticalpa 52 D2 Olancho, C Honduras
Jutland *see* Jylland
Juvavum *see* Salzburg
Južna Morava 101 E5 *Ger.* Südliche Morava. *river* SE Serbia
Jwaneng 78 C4 Southern, S Botswana
Jylland 85 A7 *Eng.* Jutland. *peninsula* W Denmark
Jyrgalan *see* Dzhergalan
Jyväskylä 85 D5 Länsi-Suomi, C Finland

K

K2 126 A4 *Chin.* Qogir Feng, *Eng.* Mount Godwin Austen. *mountain* China/Pakistan
Kaafu Atoll *see* Male' Atoll
Kaaimanston 59 G3 Sipaliwini, N Suriname
Kaakhka *see* Kaka
Kaala *see* Caála
Kaamanen 84 D2 *Lapp.* Gámas. Lappi, N Finland
Kaapstad *see* Cape Town
Kaaresuvanto 84 C3 *Lapp.* Gárassavon. Lappi, N Finland
Kabale 73 B6 SW Uganda
Kabinda 77 D7 Kasai-Oriental, SE Dem. Rep. Congo
Kabinda *see* Cabinda
Kabol *see* Kabul
Kabompo 78 C2 *river* W Zambia
Kābul 123 E4 *prev.* Kābol. *country capital* (Afghanistan) Kābul, E Afghanistan
Kabul 123 E4 *var.* Daryā-ye Kābul. *river* Afghanistan/Pakistan
Kābul, Daryā-ye *see* Kabul
Kabwe 78 D2 Central, C Zambia
Kachchh, Gulf of 134 B4 *var.* Gulf of Cutch, Gulf of Kutch. *gulf* W India
Kachchh, Rann of 134 B4 *var.* Rann of Kachh, Rann of Kutch. *salt marsh* India/Pakistan
Kachh, Rann of *see* Kachchh, Rann of
Kadan Kyun 137 B5 *prev.* King Island. *island* Mergui Archipelago, S Myanmar (Burma)
Kadavu 145 E4 *prev.* Kandavu. *island* S Fiji
Kadoma 78 D3 *prev.* Gatooma. Mashonaland West, C Zimbabwe
Kadugli 72 B4 Southern Kordofan, S Sudan
Kaduna 75 G4 Kaduna, C Nigeria
Kadzhi-Say *see* Bokonbayevo
Kaédi 74 C3 Gorgol, S Mauritania
Kaffa *see* Feodosiya
Kafue 78 D2 Lusaka, SE Zambia
Kafue 78 C2 *river* C Zambia
Kaga Bandoro 76 C4 *prev.* Fort-Crampel. Nana-Grébizi, C Central African Republic
Kagan *see* Kogon
Kâghet 74 D1 *var.* Karet. *physical region* N Mauritania
Kagi *see* Jiayi
Kagoshima 131 B8 *var.* Kagosima. Kagoshima, Kyūshū, SW Japan
Kagoshima-wan 131 A8 *bay* SW Japan
Kagosima *see* Kagoshima
Kagul *see* Cahul
Darya-ye Kahmard 123 E4 *prev.* Darya-i-surkhab. *river* NE Afghanistan
Kahramanmaraş 116 D4 *var.* Kahraman Maraş, Maraş, Marash. Kahramanmaraş, S Turkey
Kaiapoi 151 C6 Canterbury, South Island, New Zealand
Kaifeng 128 C4 Henan, C China
Kai, Kepulauan 139 F4 *prev.* Kei Islands. *island group* Maluku, SE Indonesia
Kaikohe 150 C2 Northland, North Island, New Zealand
Kaikoura 151 C5 Canterbury, South Island, New Zealand

Kaikoura Peninsula 151 C5 *peninsula* South Island, New Zealand
Kainji Lake *see* Kainji Reservoir
Kainji Reservoir 75 F4 *var.* Kainji Lake. *reservoir* W Nigeria
Kaipara Harbour 150 C2 *harbour* North Island, New Zealand
Kairouan 71 E2 *var.* Al Qayrawān. E Tunisia
Kaisaria *see* Kayseri
Kaiserslautern 95 A5 Rheinland-Pfalz, SW Germany
Kaišiadorys 107 B5 Kaunas, S Lithuania
Kaitaia 150 C2 Northland, North Island, New Zealand
Kajaani 84 E4 *Swe.* Kajana. Oulu, C Finland
Kajan *see* Kayan, Sungai
Kajana *see* Kajaani
Kajisay *see* Bokonbayevo
Kaka 122 C2 *Rus.* Kaakhka. Ahal Welayaty, S Turkmenistan
Kake 36 D4 Kupreanof Island, Alaska, USA
Kakhovka 109 F4 Khersons'ka Oblast', S Ukraine
Kakhovs'ke Vodoskhovyshche 109 F4 *Rus.* Kakhovskoye Vodokhranilishche. *reservoir* SE Ukraine
Kakhovskoye Vodokhranilishche *see* Kakhovs'ke Vodoskhovyshche
Kākināda 132 D1 *prev.* Cocanada. Andhra Pradesh, E India
Kakshaal-Too, Khrebet *see* Kokshaal-Tau
Kaktovik 36 D2 Alaska, USA
Kalaallit Nunaat *see* Greenland
Kalahari Desert 78 B4 *desert* Southern Africa
Kalaikhum *see* Qal'aikhum
Kálamai *see* Kalámata
Kalamariá 104 B4 Kentrikí Makedonía, N Greece
Kalamás 104 A4 *var.* Thíamis; *prev.* Thýamis. *river* W Greece
Kalámata 105 B6 *prev.* Kalámai. Pelopónnisos, S Greece
Kalamazoo 40 C3 Michigan, N USA
Kalambaka *see* Kalampáka
Kalamos 105 C5 Attikí, C Greece
Kalampáka 104 B4 *var.* Kalambaka. Thessalía, C Greece
Kalanchak 109 F4 Khersons'ka Oblast', S Ukraine
Kalarash *see* Călăraşi
Kalasin 136 D4 *var.* Muang Kalasin. Kalasin, E Thailand
Kālat 134 B2 *var.* Kelat, Khelat. Baluchistān, SW Pakistan
Kalāt *see* Qalāt
Kalbarri 147 A5 Western Australia
Kalecik 116 C3 Ankara, N Turkey
Kalemie 77 E6 *prev.* Albertville. Katanga, SE Dem. Rep. Congo
Kale Sultanie *see* Çanakkale
Kalgan *see* Zhangjiakou
Kalgoorlie 147 B6 Western Australia
Kalima 77 D6 Maniema, E Dem. Rep. Congo
Kalimantan 138 D4 *Eng.* Indonesian Borneo. *geopolitical region* Borneo, C Indonesia
Kalinin *see* Tver'
Kaliningrad 106 A4 Kaliningradskaya Oblast', W Russian Federation
Kaliningrad *see* Kaliningradskaya Oblast'
Kaliningradskaya Oblast' 106 B4 *var.* Kaliningrad. *province and enclave* W Russian Federation
Kalinkavichy 107 C7 *Rus.* Kalinkovichi. Homyel'skaya Voblasts', SE Belarus
Kalinkovichi *see* Kalinkavichy
Kalisch/Kalish *see* Kalisz
Kalispell 44 B1 Montana, NW USA
Kalisz 98 C4 *Ger.* Kalisch, *Rus.* Kalish; *anc.* Calisia. Wielkopolskie, C Poland
Kalix 84 D4 Norrbotten, N Sweden
Kalixälven 84 D3 *river* N Sweden
Kallaste 106 E3 *Ger.* Krasnogor. Tartumaa, SE Estonia
Kallavesi 85 E5 *lake* SE Finland
Kalloní 105 D5 Lésvos, E Greece
Kalmar 85 C7 *var.* Calmar. Kalmar, S Sweden
Kalmthout 87 C5 Antwerpen, N Belgium
Kalpáki 104 A4 Ípeiros, W Greece
Kalpeni Island 132 B3 *island* Lakshadweep, India, N Indian Ocean
Kaltdorf *see* Pruszków

Kaluga 111 B5 Kaluzhskaya Oblast', W Russian Federation
Kalush 108 C2 *Pol.* Kałusz. Ivano-Frankivs'ka Oblast', W Ukraine
Kałusz *see* Kalush
Kalutara 132 D4 Western Province, SW Sri Lanka
Kalvarija 107 B5 *Pol.* Kalwaria. Marijampolė, S Lithuania
Kalwaria *see* Kalvarija
Kalyān 134 C5 Mahārāshtra, W India
Kálymnos 105 D6 *var.* Kálimnos. *island* Dodekánisa, Greece, Aegean Sea
Kama 110 D4 *river* NW Russian Federation
Kamarang 59 F3 W Guyana
Kambryk *see* Cambrai
Kamchatka 115 G3 *Eng.* Kamchatka. *peninsula* E Russian Federation
Kamchatka *see* Kamchatka, Poluostrov
Kamenets-Podol'skiy *see* Kam"yanets'-Podil's'kyy
Kamenka Dneprovskaya *see* Kam"yanka-Dniprovs'ka
Kamenskoye *see* Romaniv
Kamensk-Shakhtinskiy 111 B6 Rostovskaya Oblast', SW Russian Federation
Kamina 77 D7 Katanga, S Dem. Rep. Congo
Kamishli *see* Al Qāmishlī
Kamloops 37 E5 British Columbia, SW Canada
Kammu Seamount 152 C2 *guyot* N Pacific Ocean
Kampala 73 B6 *country capital* (Uganda) S Uganda
Kâmpóng Cham 137 D6 *prev.* Kompong Cham. Kâmpóng Cham, C Cambodia
Kâmpóng Chhnăng 137 D6 *prev.* Kompong. Kâmpóng Chhnăng, C Cambodia
Kâmpóng Saôm *see* Sihanoukville
Kâmpóng Spoe 137 D6 *prev.* Kompong Speu. Kâmpóng Spoe, S Cambodia
Kâmpóng Thum 137 D5 *var.* Trâpeăng Vêng. Kâmpóng Thum, C Cambodia
Kâmpóng Trâbêk 137 D6 *prev.* Phumĭ Kâmpóng Trâbêk, Phum Kompong Trabek. Kâmpóng Thum, C Cambodia
Kâmpôt 137 D6 Kâmpôt, SW Cambodia
Kampuchea *see* Cambodia
Kampuchea, Democratic *see* Cambodia
Kampuchea, People's Democratic Republic of *see* Cambodia
Kamenets-Podol'skiy. Khmel'nyts'ka Oblast', W Ukraine
Kam"yanka-Dniprovs'ka 109 F3 *Rus.* Kamenka Dneprovskaya. Zaporiz'ka Oblast', SE Ukraine
Kamyshin 111 B6 Volgogradskaya Oblast', SW Russian Federation
Kanaky *see* New Caledonia
Kananga 77 D6 *prev.* Luluabourg. Kasai-Occidental, S Dem. Rep. Congo
Kanara *see* Karnātaka
Kanash 111 C5 Chuvashskaya Respublika, W Russian Federation
Kanazawa 131 C5 Ishikawa, Honshū, SW Japan
Kanbe 136 B4 Yangon, SW Myanmar (Burma)
Kānchipuram 132 C2 *prev.* Conjeeveram. Tamil Nādu, SE India
Kandahār 123 E5 *Per.* Qandahār. Kandahār, S Afghanistan
Kandalakša *see* Kandalaksha
Kandalaksha 110 B2 *var.* Kandalakša, *Fin.* Kantalahti. Murmanskaya Oblast', NW Russian Federation
Kandangan 138 D4 Borneo, C Indonesia
Kandau *see* Kandava
Kandava 106 C3 *Ger.* Kandau. W Latvia
Kandavu *see* Kadavu
Kandi 75 F4 N Benin
Kandy 132 D3 Central Province, C Sri Lanka
Kane Fracture Zone 66 B4 *fracture zone* NW Atlantic Ocean
Kāne'ohe 47 A8 *var.* Kaneohe. O'ahu, Hawaii, USA, C Pacific Ocean
Kanestron, Akrotírio *see* Palioúri, Akrotírio
Kanëv *see* Kaniv
Kanevskoye Vodokhranilishche *see* Kanivs'ke Vodoskhovyshche
Kangân *see* Bandar-e Kangân

Kangaroo Island 149 A7 *island* South Australia
Kangertittivaq 83 E4 *Dan.* Scoresby Sund. *fjord* E Greenland
Kangikajik 83 E4 *var.* Kap Brewster. *headland* E Greenland
Kaniv 109 E2 *Rus.* Kanëv. Cherkas'ka Oblast', C Ukraine
Kanivs'ke Vodoskhovyshche 109 E2 *Rus.* Kanevskoye Vodokhranilishche. *reservoir* C Ukraine
Kanjiža 100 D2 *Ger.* Altkanischa, *Hung.* Magyarkanizsa, Ókanizsa; *prev.* Stara Kanjiža. N Serbia
Kankaanpää 85 D5 Länsi-Suomi, SW Finland
Kankakee 40 B3 Illinois, N USA
Kankan 74 D4 E Guinea
Kannur 132 B2 *prev.* Cannanore, Jagatsinghapur. Kerala, SW India
Kano 75 G4 Kano, N Nigeria
Kānpur 135 E3 *Eng.* Cawnpore. Uttar Pradesh, N India
Kansas 45 F5 *off.* State of Kansas, *also known as* Jayhawker State, Sunflower State. *state* C USA
Kansas City 45 F4 Kansas, C USA
Kansas City 45 F4 Missouri, C USA
Kansas River 45 F5 *river* Kansas, C USA
Kansk 115 E4 Krasnoyarskiy Kray, S Russian Federation
Kansu *see* Gansu
Kantalahti *see* Kandalaksha
Kántanos 105 C7 Kríti, Greece, E Mediterranean Sea
Kantemirovka 111 B6 Voronezhskaya Oblast', W Russian Federation
Kantipur *see* Kathmandu
Kanton 145 F3 *var.* Abariringa, Canton Island; *prev.* Mary Island. *atoll* Phoenix Islands, C Kiribati
Kanye 78 C4 Southern, SE Botswana
Kaohsiung *see* Gaoxiong
Kaolack 74 B3 *var.* Kaolak. W Senegal
Kaolak *see* Kaolack
Kaolan *see* Lanzhou
Kaoma 78 C2 Western, W Zambia
Kapelle 87 B5 Zeeland, SW Netherlands
Kapellen 87 C5 Antwerpen, N Belgium
Kapka, Massif du 76 C2 *mountain range* E Chad
Kaplangky, Plato *see* Gaplañgyr Platosy
Kapoeas *see* Kapuas, Sungai
Kapoeta 73 C5 Eastern Equatoria, SE South Sudan
Kaposvár 99 C7 Somogy, SW Hungary
Kappeln 94 B2 Schleswig-Holstein, N Germany
Kaproncza *see* Koprivnica
Kapstad *see* Cape Town
Kapsukas *see* Marijampolė
Kaptsevichy 107 C7 *Rus.* Koptsevichi. Homyel'skaya Voblasts', SE Belarus
Kapuas, Sungai 138 C4 *prev.* Kapoeas. *river* Borneo, C Indonesia
Kapuskasing 38 C4 Ontario, S Canada
Kapyl' 107 C6 *Rus.* Kopyl'. Minskaya Voblasts', C Belarus
Kara-Balta 123 F2 Chuyskaya Oblast', N Kyrgyzstan
Karabil', Vozvyshennost' *see* Garabil Belentligi
Kara-Bogaz-Gol, Zaliv *see* Garabogaz Aylagy
Karabük 116 C2 Karabük, NW Turkey
Kārāchi 134 B3 Sind, SE Pakistan
Karácsonkő *see* Piatra-Neamţ
Karadeniz *see* Black Sea
Karadeniz Boğazı *see* İstanbul Boğazı
Karaferiye *see* Véroia
Karaganda *see* Karagandy
Karagandy 114 C4 *Kaz.* Qaraghandy; *prev.* Karaganda. Karagandy, C Kazakhstan
Karaginskiy, Ostrov 115 H2 *island* E Russian Federation
Karagumskiy Kanal *see* Garagum Kanaly
Karak *see* Al Karak
Karakax *see* Moyu
Karakilisse *see* Ağrı
Karakol 123 G2 *var.* Karakolka. Issyk-Kul'skaya Oblast', NE Kyrgyzstan
Karakol 123 G2 *prev.* Przheval'sk. Issyk-Kul'skaya Oblast', NE Kyrgyzstan
Karakolka *see* Karakol
Karakoram Range 134 D1 *mountain range* C Asia
Karaköse *see* Ağrı
Karakul' *see* Qarokül, Tajikistan

Kara Kum *see* Garagum
Kara Kum Canal/Karakumskiy Kanal
  see Garagum Kanaly
Karakumy, Peski *see* Garagum
Karamai *see* Karamay
Karaman *116 C4* Karaman, S Turkey
Karamay *126 B2 var.* Karamai,
  Kelamayi; *prev. Chin.* K'o-la-ma-i.
  Xinjiang Uygur Zizhiqu, NW China
Karamea Bight *151 B5 gulf* South Island,
  New Zealand
Karapelit *104 E1 Rom.* Stejarul.
  Dobrich, NE Bulgaria
Kara-Say *123 G2* Issyk-Kul'skaya
  Oblast', NE Kyrgyzstan
Karasburg *78 D4* Karas, S Namibia
Kara Sea *114 D2 Eng.* Kara Sea. *sea*
  Arctic Ocean
Kara Sea *see* Karskoye More
Kara Strait *110 E2 Eng.* Kara Strait.
  strait N Russian Federation
Kara Strait *see* Karskiye Vorota, Proliv
Karatau *114 C5 Kaz.* Qarataū. Zhambyl,
  S Kazakhstan
Karavás *105 B7* Kýthira, S Greece
Karbalā' *120 B3 var.* Kerbala, Kerbela.
  Karbalā', S Iraq
Kardeljevo *see* Ploče
Kardhítsa *see* Kardítsa
Kardítsa *105 B5 var.* Kardhítsa.
  Thessalía, C Greece
Kärdla *106 C2 Ger.* Kertel. Hiiumaa,
  W Estonia
Karet *see* Kâghet
Kargı *116 C2* Çorum, N Turkey
Kargilik *see* Yecheng
Kariba *78 D2* Mashonaland West,
  N Zimbabwe
Kariba, Lake *78 D3 reservoir* Zambia/
  Zimbabwe
Karibib *78 B3* Erongo, C Namibia
Karies *see* Karyés
Karigasniemi *84 D2 Lapp.*
  Garegegasnjárga. Lappi, N Finland
Karimata, Selat *138 C4 strait*
  W Indonesia
Karimnagar *134 D5* Andhra Pradesh,
  C India
Karin *72 D4* Woqooyi Galbeed,
  N Somalia
Kariot *see* Ikaría
Káristos *see* Kárystos
Karkinits'ka Zatoka *109 E4 Rus.*
  Karkinitskiy Zaliv. *gulf* S Ukraine
Karkinitskiy Zaliv *see* Karkinits'ka
  Zatoka
Karkük *see* Kirkük
Karleby *see* Kokkola
Karl-Marx-Stadt *see* Chemnitz
Karlō *see* Hailuoto
Karlovac *100 B3 Ger.* Karlstadt, *Hung.*
  Károlyváros. C Croatia
Karlovy Vary *99 A5 Ger.* Karlsbad;
  prev. Eng. Carlsbad. Karlovarský Kraj,
  W Czech Republic
Karlsbad *see* Karlovy Vary
Karlsburg *see* Alba Iulia
Karlskrona *85 C7* Blekinge, S Sweden
Karlsruhe *95 B6 var.* Carlsruhe. Baden-
  Württemberg, SW Germany
Karlstad *85 B6* Värmland, C Sweden
Karlstadt *see* Karlovac
Karnāl *134 D2* Haryāna, N India
Karnātaka *132 C1 var.* Kanara; *prev.*
  Maisur, Mysore. *cultural region*
  W India
Karnobat *104 D2* Burgas, E Bulgaria
Karnul *see* Kurnool
Karol *see* Carei
Károly-Fehérvár *see* Alba Iulia
Károlyváros *see* Karlovac
Karpaten *see* Carpathian Mountains
Kárpathos *105 E7* Kárpathos, SE Greece
Kárpathos *105 E7 It.* Scarpanto;
  anc. Carpathos, Carpathus. *island*
  SE Greece
Karpaty *see* Carpathian Mountains
Karpenísi *105 B5 prev.* Karpenísion.
  Stereá Elláda, C Greece
Karpenision *see* Karpenísi
Karpilovka *see* Aktsyabrski
Kars *117 F2 var.* Qars. Kars,
  NE Turkey
Karsau *see* Kârsava
Kârsava *106 D4 Ger.* Karsau; *prev. Rus.*
  Korsovka. E Latvia
Karshi *see* Qarshi, Uzbekistan
Karyés *104 C4 var.* Karíes. Ágion Óros,
  N Greece

Kárystos *105 C6 var.* Káristos. Évvoia,
  C Greece
Kasai *77 C6 var.* Cassai, Kassai. *river*
  Angola/Dem. Rep. Congo
Kasaji *77 D7* Katanga, S Dem. Rep.
  Congo
Kasama *78 D1* Northern, N Zambia
Kasan *see* Koson
Kāsaragod *132 B2* Kerala, SW India
Kaschau *see* Košice
Kāshān *120 C3* Eşfahān, C Iran
Kashgar *see* Kashi
Kashi *126 A3 Chin.* Kaxgar, K'o-shih,
  Uigh. Kashgar. Xinjiang Uygur Zizhiqu,
  NW China
Kasi *see* Vārānasi
Kasongo *77 D6* Maniema, E Dem.
  Rep. Congo
Kasongo-Lunda *77 C7* Bandundu,
  SW Dem. Rep. Congo
Kásos *105 D7 island* S Greece
Kaspiy Mangy Oypaty *see* Caspian
  Depression
Kaspiysk *111 B8* Respublika Dagestan,
  SW Russian Federation
Kaspiyskoye More/Kaspiy Tengizi *see*
  Caspian Sea
Kassa *see* Košice
Kassai *see* Kasai
Kassala *72 C4* Kassala, E Sudan
Kassel *94 B4 prev.* Cassel. Hessen,
  C Germany
Kasserine *71 E2 var.* Al Qaşrayn.
  W Tunisia
Kastamonu *116 C2 var.* Castamoni,
  Kastamuni. Kastamonu, N Turkey
Kastamuni *see* Kastamonu
Kastaneá *see* Kastaniá
Kastaniá *104 B4 prev.* Kastaneá. Kentrikí
  Makedonía, N Greece
Kastélli *see* Kíssamos
Kastoría *104 B4* Dytikí Makedonía,
  N Greece
Kástro *105 C6* Sífnos, Kykládes, Greece,
  Aegean Sea
Kastsyukovichy *107 E7 Rus.*
  Kostyukovichi. Mahilyowskaya
  Voblasts', E Belarus
Kastsyukowka *107 D7 Rus.*
  Kostyukovka. Homyel'skaya Voblasts',
  SE Belarus
Kasulu *73 B7* Kigoma, W Tanzania
Kasumiga-ura *131 D5 lake* Honshū,
  S Japan
Katahdin, Mount *41 G1 mountain*
  Maine, NE USA
Katalla *36 C3* Alaska, USA
Katana *see* Qaţanā
Katanning *147 B7* Western Australia
Katawaz *see* Zarghūn Shahr
Katchall Island *133 F3 island* Nicobar
  Islands, India, NE Indian Ocean
Kateríni *104 B4* Kentrikí Makedonía,
  N Greece
Katha *136 B2* Sagaing, N Myanmar
  (Burma)
Katherine *148 A2* Northern Territory,
  N Australia
Kathmandu *124 C3 prev.* Kantipur.
  country capital (Nepal) Central,
  C Nepal
Katikati *150 D3* Bay of Plenty, North
  Island, New Zealand
Katima Mulilo *78 C3* Caprivi,
  NE Namibia
Katiola *74 D4* C Côte d'Ivoire
Káto Achaḯa *105 B5 var.* Kato Ahaia,
  Káto Akhaḯa. Dytikí Elláda, S Greece
Kato Ahaia/Káto Akhaía *see* Káto Achaḯa
Katoúna *105 A5* Dytikí Elláda,
  C Greece
Katowice *99 C5 Ger.* Kattowitz. Śląskie,
  S Poland
Katsina *75 G3* Katsina, N Nigeria
Kattakurgan *see* Kattaqo'rg'on
Kattaqo'rg'on *123 E2 Rus.* Kattakurgan.
  Samarqand Viloyati, C Uzbekistan
Kattavía *105 E7* Ródos, Dodekánisa,
  Greece, Aegean Sea
Kattegat *85 B7 Dan.* Kattegatt. *strait*
  N Europe
Kattegatt *see* Kattegat
Kattowitz *see* Katowice
Kaua'i *47 A7 var.* Kauai. *island*
  Hawaiian Islands, Hawai'i, USA,
  C Pacific Ocean
Kauai *see* Kaua'i
Kauen *see* Kaunas
Kaufbeuren *95 C6* Bayern, S Germany

Kaunas *106 B4 Ger.* Kauen, *Pol.* Kowno;
  prev. Rus. Kovno. Kaunas, C Lithuania
Kavadar *see* Kavadarci
Kavadarci *101 E6 Turk.* Kavadar.
  C Macedonia
Kavaja *see* Kavajë
Kavajë *101 C6 It.* Cavaia, Kavaja.
  Tiranë, W Albania
Kavakli *see* Topolovgrad
Kavála *104 C3 prev.* Kaválla. Anatolikí
  Makedonía kai Thráki, NE Greece
Kāvali *132 D2* Andhra Pradesh, E India
Kaválla *see* Kavála
Kavango *see* Cubango/Okavango
Kavaratti Island *132 A3 island*
  Lakshadweep, Lakshadweep, SW India
  Asia N Indian Ocean
Kavarna *104 E2* Dobrich, NE Bulgaria
Kavengo *see* Cubango/Okavango
Kavir, Dasht-e *120 D3 var.* Great Salt
  Desert. *salt pan* N Iran
Kavkaz *see* Caucasus
Kawagoe *131 D5* Saitama, Honshū,
  S Japan
Kawasaki *130 A2* Kanagawa, Honshū,
  S Japan
Kawerau *150 E3* Bay of Plenty, North
  Island, New Zealand
Kaxgar *see* Kashi
Kaya *75 E3* C Burkina Faso
Kayan *136 B4* Yangon, SW Myanmar
  (Burma)
Kayan, Sungai *138 D3 prev.* Kajan. *river*
  Borneo, C Indonesia
Kayes *74 C3* Kayes, W Mali
Kayseri *116 D3 var.* Kaisaria; *anc.*
  Caesarea Mazaca, Mazaca. Kayseri,
  C Turkey
Kazach'ye *115 F2* Respublika Sakha
  (Yakutiya), NE Russian Federation
**Kazakhskaya SSR/Kazakh Soviet
  Socialist Republic** *see* Kazakhstan
Kazakhstan *114 B4 off.* Republic of
  Kazakhstan, *var.* Kazakstan, *Kaz.*
  Qazaqstan, Qazaqstan Respublikasy;
  prev. Kazakh Soviet Socialist Republic,
  Rus. Kazakhskaya SSR. *country* C Asia

Kazakhstan, Republic of *see* Kazakhstan
Kazakh Uplands *114 C4 Eng.* Kazakh
  Uplands, Kirghiz Steppe. *uplands*
  C Kazakhstan
Kazakh Uplands *see* Saryarka
Kazakstan *see* Kazakhstan
Kazan' *111 C5* Respublika Tatarstan,
  W Russian Federation
Kazandzhik *see* Bereket
Kazanlik *see* Kazanlŭk
Kazanlŭk *104 D2 prev.* Kazanlik. Stara
  Zagora, C Bulgaria
Kazatin *see* Kozyatyn
Kazbegi *see* Kazbek
Kazbek *117 F1 var.* Kazbegi, *Geor.*
  Mqinvartsveri. *mountain* N Georgia
Käzerün *120 D4* Fārs, S Iran
Kazvin *see* Qazvin
Kéa *see* Tziá
Kéa *see* Ioulís
Kea, Mauna *47 B8 mountain* Hawai'i,
  USA
Kéamu *see* Aneityum
Kearney *45 E4* Nebraska, C USA
Keban Barajı *117 E3 reservoir* C Turkey
Kebkabiya *72 A4* Northern Darfur,
  W Sudan
Kebnekaise *84 C3 Lapp.* Giebnegáisi.
  mountain N Sweden

Kecskemét *99 D7* Bács-Kiskun,
  C Hungary
Kediri *138 D5* Jawa, C Indonesia
Kędzierzyn-Kozle *99 C5 Ger.*
  Heydebrech. Opolskie, S Poland
Keelung *see* Jilong
Keetmanshoop *78 B4* Karas, S Namibia
Kefallinía *see* Kefallonía
Kefallonía *105 A5 var.* Kefallinía.
  island Iónia Nisiá, Greece,
  C Mediterranean Sea
Kefe *see* Feodosiya
Kegel *see* Keila
Kehl *95 A6* Baden-Württemberg,
  SW Germany
Kei Islands *see* Kai, Kepulauan
Keijō *see* Seoul
Keila *106 D2 Ger.* Kegel. Harjumaa,
  NW Estonia
Keïta *75 F3* Tahoua, C Niger
Keith *149 B7* South Australia
Kēk-Art *123 G2 prev.* Alaykel', Alay-
  Kuu. Oshskaya Oblast', SW Kyrgyzstan
Kékes *99 C6 mountain* N Hungary
Kelamayi *see* Karamay
Kelang *see* Klang
Kelat *see* Kālat
Kelifskiy Uzboy *see* Kelif Uzboÿ
Kelif Uzboÿy *122 D3 Rus.* Kelifskiy
  Uzboy. *salt marsh* E Turkmenistan
Kelkit Çayı *117 E3 river* N Turkey
Kelmė *106 B4* Šiauliai, C Lithuania
Kélo *76 B4* Tandjilé, SW Chad
Kelowna *37 E5* British Columbia,
  SW Canada
Kelso *46 B2* Washington, NW USA
Keltsy *see* Kielce
Keluang *138 B3 var.* Kluang. Johor,
  Peninsular Malaysia
Kem' *110 B3* Respublika Kareliya,
  NW Russian Federation
Kemah *117 E3* Erzincan, E Turkey
Kemaman *see* Cukai
Kemerovo *114 D4 prev.* Shcheglovsk.
  Kemerovskaya Oblast', C Russian
  Federation
Kemi *84 D4* Lappi, NW Finland
Kemijärvi *84 D3 Swe.* Kemiträsk. Lappi,
  N Finland
Kemijoki *84 D3 river* NW Finland
Kemin *123 G2 prev.* Bystrovka.
  Chuyskaya Oblast', N Kyrgyzstan
Kemins Island *see* Nikumaroro
Kemiträsk *see* Kemijärvi
Kemmuna *102 A5 var.* Comino. *island*
  C Malta
Kempele *84 D4* Oulu, C Finland
Kempten *95 B7* Bayern, S Germany
Kendal *89 D5* NW England, United
  Kingdom
Kendari *139 E4* Sulawesi, C Indonesia
Kenedy *49 G4* Texas, SW USA
Kenema *74 C4* SE Sierra Leone
Këneürgench *see* Köneürgenç
Kenge *77 C6* Bandundu, SW Dem.
  Rep. Congo
Kengtung *136 C3* Shan State, E Myanmar
  (Burma)
Kénitra *70 C2 prev.* Port-Lyautey.
  NW Morocco
Kennett *45 H5* Missouri, C USA
Kennewick *46 C2* Washington, NW USA
Kenora *38 A3* Ontario, S Canada
Kenosha *40 B3* Wisconsin, N USA
Kentau *114 B5* Yuzhnyy Kazakhstan,
  S Kazakhstan
Kentucky *40 C5 off.* Commonwealth
  of Kentucky, *also known as* Bluegrass
  State. *state* C USA
Kentucky Lake *40 B5 reservoir*
  Kentucky/Tennessee, S USA
Kenya *73 C6 off.* Republic of Kenya.
  country E Africa

KENYA
(continued)

Luhya 14%, Luo 14%, Kalenjin 11%,
Kamba 11%
Government Mixed Presidential–
Parliamentary system
Currency Kenya shilling = 100 cents
Literacy rate 87%
Calorie consumption 2090 kilocalories

Kenya, Mount *see* Kirinyaga
Kenya, Republic of *see* Kenya
Keokuk *45 G4* Iowa, C USA
Kéos *see* Tziá
Kępno *98 C4* Wielkopolskie,
  C Poland
Keppel Island *see* Niuatoputapu
Kerak *see* Al Karak
Kerala *132 C2 cultural region* S India
Kerasunt *see* Giresun
Keratéa *105 C6 var.* Keratea. Attikí,
  C Greece
Keratea *see* Keratéa
Kerbala/Kerbela *see* Karbalāʾ
Kerch *109 G5 Rus.* Kerchʹ. Avtonomna
  Respublika Krym, SE Ukraine
Kerchʹ *see* Kerch
**Kerchensʹka Protska/Kerchenskiy
  Proliv** *see* Kerch Strait
Kerch Strait *109 G4 var.* Bosporus
  Cimmerius, Enikale Strait, *Rus.*
  Kerchenskiy Proliv, *Ukr.* Kerchensʹka
  Protska. *strait* Black Sea/Sea of Azov
Keremitlik *see* Lyulyakovo
Kerguelen *141 C7 island* C French
  Southern and Antarctic Territories
Kerguelen Plateau *141 C7 undersea
  plateau* S Indian Ocean
Kerí *105 A6* Zákynthos, Iónia Nisiá,
  Greece, C Mediterranean Sea
Kerikeri *150 D2* Northland, North
  Island, New Zealand
Kerkenah, Îles de *102 D4 var.* Kerkenna
  Islands, *Ar.* Juzur Qarqannah. *island
  group* E Tunisia
Kerkenna Islands *see* Kerkenah, Îles de
Kerki *see* Atamyrat
Kérkira *see* Kérkyra
Kerkrade *87 D6* Limburg,
  SE Netherlands
Kerkuk *see* Kirkūk
Kérkyra *104 A4 var.* Kérkira, *Eng.*
  Corfu. Kérkyra, Iónia Nisiá, Greece,
  C Mediterranean Sea
Kermadec Islands *152 C4 island group*
  New Zealand, SW Pacific Ocean
Kermadec Trench *143 E4 trench*
  SW Pacific Ocean
Kermān *120 D3 var.* Kirman; *anc.*
  Carmana. Kermān, C Iran
Kermānshāh *120 C3 var.*
  Qahremānshahr; *prev.* Bākhtarān.
  Kermānshāhān, W Iran
Kerrville *49 F4* Texas, SW USA
Kertel *see* Kärdla
Kerulen *127 E2 Chin.* Herlen He, *Mong.*
  Herlen Gol. *river* China/Mongolia
Kerýneia *see* Girne
Kesennuma *130 D4* Miyagi, Honshū,
  C Japan
Keszthely *99 C7* Zala, SW Hungary
Ketchikan *36 D4* Revillagigedo Island,
  Alaska, USA
Kętrzyn *98 D2 Ger.* Rastenburg.
  Warmińsko-Mazurskie, NE Poland
Kettering *89 D6* C England, United
  Kingdom
Kettering *40 C4* Ohio, N USA
Keupriya *see* Primorsko
Keuruu *85 D5* Länsi-Suomi, C Finland
Keweenaw Peninsula *40 B1 peninsula*
  Michigan, N USA
Key Largo *43 F5* Key Largo, Florida,
  SE USA
Keystone State *see* Pennsylvania
Key West *43 E5* Florida Keys, Florida,
  SE USA
Kezdivásárhely *see* Târgu Secuiesc
Khabarovsk *115 G4* Khabarovskiy Kray,
  SE Russian Federation
Khachmas *see* Xaçmaz
Khadera *see* Hadera
Khairpur *134 B3* Sind, SE Pakistan
Khalij as Suways *72 B2 var.* Suez, Gulf
  of. *gulf* NE Egypt
Khalkidhikí *see* Chalkidikí
Khalkís *see* Chalkída

Gulf of Khambhat *134 C4 Eng.* Gulf of
  Cambay. *gulf* W India
Khamis Mushayṭ *121 B6 var.* Hamīs
  Musait. ʿAsīr, SW Saudi Arabia
Khānābād *123 E3* Kunduz,
  NE Afghanistan
Khān al Baghdādī *see* Al Baghdādī
Khandwa *134 D4* Madhya Pradesh,
  C India
Khanh Hung *see* Soc Trăng
Khaniá *see* Chaniá
Khanka, Lake *129 E2 var.* Hsing-Kʹai
  Hu, Lake Hanka, *Chin.* Xingkai Hu,
  Rus. Ozero Khanka. *lake* China/
  Russian Federation
Khanka, Ozero *see* Khanka, Lake
Khankendi *see* Xankändi
Khanthabouli *see* Savannakhét
Khanty-Mansiysk *114 C3 prev.*
  Ostyako-Vogulsʹk. Khanty-Mansiyskiy
  Avtonomnyy Okrug-Yugra, C Russian
  Federation
Khān Yūnis *119 A7 var.* Khān Yūnus.
  S Gaza Strip
Khān Yūnus *see* Khān Yūnis
Khanzi *see* Ghanzi
Kharagpur *135 F4* West Bengal,
  NE India
Kharbin *see* Harbin
Kharkiv *109 G2 Rus.* Kharʹkov.
  Kharkivsʹka Oblastʹ, NE Ukraine
Kharʹkov *see* Kharkiv
Kharmanli *104 D3* Khaskovo, S Bulgaria
Khartoum *72 B4 var.* El Khartûm,
  Khartum. *country capital* (Sudan)
  Khartoum, C Sudan
Khartum *see* Khartoum
Khasavyurt *111 B8* Respublika Dagestan,
  SW Russian Federation
Khash, Dasht-e *122 D5 Eng.* Khash
  Desert. *desert* SW Afghanistan
Khash Desert *see* Khāsh, Dasht-e
Khashim Al Qirba/Khashm al Qirbah
  see Khashm el Girba
Khashm el Girba *72 C4 var.* Khashim
  Al Qirba, Khashm al Qirbah. Kassala,
  E Sudan
Khaskovo *104 D3* Khaskovo, S Bulgaria
Khaybar, Kowtal-e *see* Khyber Pass
Khaydarkan *123 F2 var.* Khaydarken.
  Batkenskaya Oblastʹ, SW Kyrgyzstan
Khaydarken *see* Khaydarkan
Khazar, Baḥr-e/Khazar, Daryā-ye *see*
  Caspian Sea
Khelat *see* Kālat
Kherson *109 E4* Khersonsʹka Oblastʹ,
  S Ukraine
Kheta *115 E2 river* N Russian Federation
Khíos *see* Chíos
Khirbet et ʿAuja et Taḥtā *119 E7* E West
  Bank Asia
Khiva/Khiwa *see* Xiva
Khmelʹnitskiy *see* Khmelʹnytsʹkyy
Khmelʹnytsʹkyy *108 D2 Rus.*
  Khmelʹnitskiy; *prev.* Proskurov.
  Khmelʹnytsʹka Oblastʹ, W Ukraine
Khodasy *107 E6 Rus.* Khodosy.
  Mahilyowskaya Voblastsʹ, E Belarus
Khodoriv *108 C2 Pol.* Chodorów,
  Rus. Khodorov. Lʹvivsʹka Oblastʹ,
  NW Ukraine
Khodorov *see* Khodoriv
Khodosy *see* Khodasy
Khodzhent *see* Khujand
Khoi *see* Khvoy
Khojend *see* Khujand
Khokand *see* Qoʹqon
Kholm *see* Khulm
Kholm *see* Chełm
Kholon *see* Holon
Khoms *see* Al Khums
Khong Sedone *see* Muang Khôngxédôn
Khon Kaen *136 D4 var.* Muang Khon
  Kaen. Khon Kaen, E Thailand
Khor *115 G4* Khabarovskiy Kray,
  SE Russian Federation
Khorog *see* Khorugh
Khorat *see* Nakhon Ratchasima
Khorugh *123 F3 Rus.* Khorog.
  S Tajikistan
Khöst *123 F4 prev.* Khowst. Khōst,
  E Afghanistan
Khotan *see* Hotan
Khouribga *70 B2* C Morocco
Khovd *see* Hovd
Khoy *see* Khvoy
Khoyniki *107 D8* Homyelʹskaya
  Voblastsʹ, SE Belarus
Khudzhand *see* Khujand

Khujand *123 E2 var.* Khodzhent,
  Khojend, *Rus.* Khudzhand; *prev.*
  Leninabad, *Taj.* Leninobod.
  N Tajikistan
Khulm *123 E3 var.* Tashqurghan; *prev.*
  Kholm. Balkh, N Afghanistan
Khulna *135 G4* Khulna, SW Bangladesh
Khums *see* Al Khums
Khust *108 B3 var.* Husté, *Cz.* Chust,
  Hung. Huszt. Zakarpatsʹka Oblastʹ,
  W Ukraine
Khvoy *120 C2 var.* Khoi, Khoy.
  Āzarbāyjān-e Bākhtarī, NW Iran
Khyber Pass *134 C1 var.* Kowtal-e
  Khaybar. *pass* Afghanistan/Pakistan
Kiangmai *see* Chiang Mai
Kiang-ning *see* Nanjing
Kiangsi *see* Jiangxi
Kiangsu *see* Jiangsu
Kiáto *105 B6 prev.* Kiáton. Pelopónnisos,
  S Greece
Kiáton *see* Kiáto
Kiayi *see* Jiayi
Kibangou *77 B6* Niari, SW Congo
Kibombo *77 D6* Maniema, E Dem.
  Rep. Congo
Kıbrıs/Kıbrıs Cumhuriyeti *see* Cyprus
Kičevo *101 D6* SW FYR Macedonia
Kidderminster *89 D6* C England, United
  Kingdom
Kiel *94 B2* Schleswig-Holstein,
  N Germany
Kielce *98 D4 Rus.* Keltsy. Świętokrzyskie,
  C Poland
Kieler Bucht *94 B2 bay* N Germany
Kiev *see* Kyyiv
Kiev Reservoir *109 E1 Eng.* Kiev
  Reservoir, *Rus.* Kiyevskoye
  Vodokhranilishche. *reservoir*
  N Ukraine
Kiev Reservoir *see* Kyyivsʹke
  Vodoskhovyshche
Kiffa *74 C3* Assaba, S Mauritania
Kigali *77 B6 country capital* (Rwanda)
  C Rwanda
Kigoma *73 B7* Kigoma, W Tanzania
Kihnu *106 C2 var.* Kihnu Saar, *Ger.*
  Kühnö. *island* SW Estonia
Kihnu Saar *see* Kihnu
Kii-suido *131 C7 strait* S Japan
Kikinda *100 D3 Ger.* Grosskikinda,
  Hung. Nagykikinda; *prev.* Velika
  Kikinda. Vojvodina, N Serbia
Kikládhes *see* Kykládes
Kikwit *77 C6* Bandundu, W Dem.
  Rep. Congo
Kilien Mountains *see* Qilian Shan
Kilimane *see* Quelimane
Kilimanjaro *69 E5 region* E Tanzania
Kilimanjaro *73 C7 var.* Uhuru Peak.
  volcano NE Tanzania
Kilingi-Nõmme *106 D2 Ger.* Kurkund.
  Pärnumaa, SW Estonia
Kilis *116 D4* Kilis, S Turkey
Kiliya *108 D4 Rom.* Chilia-Nouă.
  Odesʹka Oblastʹ, SW Ukraine
Kilkenny *89 B6 Ir.* Cill Chainnigh.
  Kilkenny, S Ireland
Kilkís *104 B3* Kentrikí Makedonía,
  N Greece
Killarney *89 A6 Ir.* Cill Airne. Kerry,
  SW Ireland
Killeen *49 G3* Texas, SW USA
Kilmain *see* Quelimane
Kilmarnock *88 C4* W Scotland, United
  Kingdom
Kilwa *see* Kilwa Kivinje
Kilwa Kivinje *73 C7 var.* Kilwa. Lindi,
  SE Tanzania
Kimberley *78 C4* Northern Cape,
  C South Africa
Kimberley Plateau *146 C3 plateau*
  Western Australia
Kimchʹaek *129 E3 prev.* Sŏngjin.
  E North Korea
Kími *see* Kými
Kinabalu, Gunung *138 D3 mountain*
  East Malaysia
Kindersley *37 F5* Saskatchewan,
  S Canada
Kindia *74 C4* Guinée-Maritime,
  SW Guinea
Kindley Field *42 A4 air base*
  E Bermuda
Kindu *77 D6 prev.* Kindu-Port-Empain.
  Maniema, C Dem. Rep. Congo
Kindu-Port-Empain *see* Kindu
Kineshma *111 C5* Ivanovskaya Oblastʹ,
  W Russian Federation

King Charles Islands *see* Kong Karls
  Land
King Christian IX Land *see* Kong
  Christian IX Land
King Frederik VI Coast *see* Kong
  Frederik VI Kyst
King Frederik VIII Land *see* Kong
  Frederik VIII Land
King Island *149 B8 island* Tasmania,
  SE Australia
King Island *see* Kadan Kyun
Kingissepp *see* Kuressaare
Kingman *48 A1* Arizona, SW USA
Kingman Reef *145 E2 US territory*
  C Pacific Ocean
Kingsford Smith *148 E2* (Sydney) New
  South Wales, SE Australia
King's Lynn *89 E6 var.* Bishop's Lynn,
  Kings Lynn, Lynn, Lynn Regis.
  E England, United Kingdom
Kings Lynn *see* King's Lynn
King Sound *146 B3 sound* Western
  Australia
Kingsport *43 E1* Tennessee,
  S USA
Kingston *54 B5 country capital*
  (Jamaica) E Jamaica
Kingston *38 D5* Ontario, SE Canada
Kingston *41 F3* New York, NE USA
Kingston upon Hull *89 D5 var.* Hull.
  E England, United Kingdom
Kingston upon Thames *89 A8*
  SE England, United Kingdom
Kingstown *55 H4 country capital*
  (Saint Vincent and the Grenadines)
  Saint Vincent, Saint Vincent and the
  Grenadines
Kingstown *see* Dún Laoghaire
Kingsville *49 G5* Texas, SW USA
King William Island *37 F3 island*
  Nunavut, N Canada
Kinneret, Yam *see* Tiberias, Lake
Kinrooi *87 D5* Limburg, NE Belgium
Kinshasa *77 B6 prev.* Léopoldville.
  country capital (Dem. Rep. Congo)
  Kinshasa, W Dem. Rep. Congo
Kintyre *88 B4 peninsula* W Scotland,
  United Kingdom
Kinyeti *73 B5 mountain* S South Sudan
Kiparissía *see* Kyparissía
Kipili *73 B7* Rukwa, W Tanzania
Kipushi *77 D8* Katanga, SE Dem. Rep.
  Congo
Kirdzhali *see* Kŭrdzhali
Kirghizia *see* Kyrgyzstan
Kirghiz Range *123 F2 Rus.* Kirgizskiy
  Khrebet; *prev.* Alexander Range.
  mountain range Kazakhstan/
  Kyrgyzstan
Kirghiz SSR *see* Kyrgyzstan
Kirghiz Steppe *see* Saryarka
Kirgizskaya SSR *see* Kyrgyzstan
Kirgizskiy Khrebet *see* Kirghiz Range
Kiriath-Arba *see* Hebron
Kiribati *145 F2 off.* Republic of Kiribati.
  country C Pacific Ocean

KIRIBATI
Australasia & Oceania

Official name Republic of Kiribati
Formation 1979 / 1979
Capital Bairiki (Tarawa Atoll)
Population 101,998 / 372 people
per sq mile (144 people per sq km)
Total area 277 sq. miles (717 sq. km)
Languages English*, Kiribati
Religions Roman Catholic 55%,
Kiribati Protestant Church 36%, Other 9%
Ethnic mix Micronesian 99%, Other 1%
Government Nonparty system
Currency Australian dollar = 100 cents
Literacy rate 99%
Calorie consumption 2866 kilocalories

Kiribati, Republic of *see* Kiribati
Kırıkhan *116 D4* Hatay, S Turkey
Kırıkkale *116 C3 province* C Turkey
Kirin *see* Jilin
Kirinyaga *73 C6 prev.* Mount Kenya.
  volcano C Kenya
Kirishi *110 B4 var.* Kirisi.
  Leningradskaya Oblastʹ, NW Russian
  Federation
Kirisi *see* Kirishi
Kiritimati *145 G2 prev.* Christmas
  Island. *atoll* Line Islands, E Kiribati
Kirkenes *84 E2 Fin.* Kirkkoniemi.
  Finnmark, N Norway

Kirk-Kilissa see Kırklareli
Kirkkoniemi see Kirkenes
Kirkland Lake 38 D4 Ontario, S Canada
Kırklareli 116 A2 prev. Kirk-Kilissa.
  Kırklareli, NW Turkey
Kirkpatrick, Mount 154 B3 mountain
  Antarctica
Kirksville 45 G4 Missouri, C USA
Kirkūk 120 B3 var. Karkūk, Kerkuk. At
  Ta'mím, N Iraq
Kirkwall 88 C2 NE Scotland, United
  Kingdom
Kirkwood 45 G4 Missouri, C USA
Kir Moab/Kir of Moab see Al Karak
Kirov 111 C5 prev. Vyatka. Kirovskaya
  Oblast', NW Russian Federation
Kirovabad see Gäncä
Kirovakan see Vanadzor
Kirovo-Chepetsk 111 D5 Kirovskaya
  Oblast', NW Russian Federation
Kirovohrad 109 E3 Rus. Kirovograd;
  prev. Kirovo, Yelizavetgrad,
  Zinov'yevsk. Kirovohrads'ka Oblast',
  C Ukraine
Kirovo/Kirovograd see Kirovohrad
Kirthar Range 134 B3 mountain range
  S Pakistan
Kiruna 84 C3 Lapp. Giron. Norrbotten,
  N Sweden
Kirun/Kirun' see Jilong
Kisalföld see Little Alföld
Kisangani 77 D5 prev. Stanleyville.
  Orientale, NE Dem. Rep. Congo
Kishinev see Chişinău
Kislovodsk 111 B7 Stavropol'skiy Kray,
  SW Russian Federation
Kismaayo 73 D6 var. Chisimayu,
  Kismayu, It. Chisimaio. Jubbada
  Hoose, S Somalia
Kismayu see Kismaayo
Kíssamos 105 C7 prev. Kastélli. Kríti,
  Greece, E Mediterranean Sea
Kissidougou 74 C4 Guinée-Forestière,
  S Guinea
Kissimmee, Lake 43 E4 lake Florida,
  SE USA
Kistna see Krishna
Kisumu 73 C6 prev. Port Florence.
  Nyanza, W Kenya
Kisvárda 99 E6 Ger. Kleinwardein.
  Szabolcs-Szatmár-Bereg, E Hungary
Kita 74 D3 Kayes, W Mali
Kitab see Kitob
Kitakyūshū 131 A7 var. Kitakyûsyû.
  Fukuoka, Kyūshū, SW Japan
Kitakyûsyû see Kitakyūshū
Kitami 130 D2 Hokkaidō, NE Japan
Kitchener 38 C5 Ontario, S Canada
Kíthnos see Kýthnos
Kitimat 36 D4 British Columbia,
  SW Canada
Kitinen 84 D3 river N Finland
Kitob 123 E3 Rus. Kitab. Qashqadaryo
  Viloyati, S Uzbekistan
Kitwe 78 D2 var. Kitwe-Nkana.
  Copperbelt, C Zambia
Kitwe-Nkana see Kitwe
Kitzbüheler Alpen 95 C7 mountain
  range W Austria
Kivalina 36 C2 Alaska, USA
Kivalo 84 D3 ridge C Finland
Kívertsi 108 C1 Pol. Kiwerce, Rus.
  Kivertsy. Volyns'ka Oblast',
  NW Ukraine
Kivertsy see Kívertsi
Kivu, Lac see Kivu, Lake
Kivu, Lake 77 E6 Fr. Lac Kivu. lake
  Rwanda/Dem. Rep. Congo
Kiwerce see Kívertsi
Kiyev see Kyyiv
Kiyevskoye Vodokhranilishche see
  Kyyivs'ke Vodoskhovyshche
Kızıl Irmak 116 C3 river C Turkey
Kizil Kum see Kyzyl Kum
Kizyl-Arvat see Serdar
Kjølen see Kölen
Kladno 99 A5 Středočeský, NW Czech
  Republic
Klagenfurt 95 D7 Slvn. Celovec.
  Kärnten, S Austria
Klaipėda 106 B3 Ger. Memel. Klaipeda,
  NW Lithuania
Klamath Falls 46 B4 Oregon, NW USA
Klamath Mountains 46 A4 mountain
  range California/Oregon, W USA
Klang 138 B3 var. Kelang; prev. Port
  Swettenham. Selangor, Peninsular
  Malaysia
Klarälven 85 B6 river Norway/Sweden

Klatovy 99 A5 Ger. Klattau. Plzeňský
  Kraj, W Czech Republic
Klattau see Klatovy
Klausenburg see Cluj-Napoca
Klazienaveen 86 E2 Drenthe,
  NE Netherlands
Kleines Ungarisches Tiefland see
  Little Alföld
Klein Karas 78 B4 Karas, S Namibia
Kleinwardein see Kisvárda
Kleisoúra 105 A5 Ípeiros, W Greece
Klerksdorp 78 D4 North-West, N South
  Africa
Klimavichy 107 E7 Rus. Klimovichi.
  Mahilyowskaya Voblasts', E Belarus
Klimovichi see Klimavichy
Klintsy 111 A5 Bryanskaya Oblast',
  W Russian Federation
Klisura 104 C2 Plovdiv, C Bulgaria
Ključ 100 B3 Federacija Bosna I
  Hercegovina, NW Bosnia and
  Herzegovina
Klobuck 98 C4 Śląskie, S Poland
Klosters 95 B7 Graubünden,
  SE Switzerland
Kluang see Keluang
Kluczbork 98 C4 Ger. Kreuzburg,
  Kreuzburg in Oberschlesien. Opolskie,
  S Poland
Klyuchevskaya Sopka, Vulkan 115 H3
  volcano E Russian Federation
Knin 100 B4 Šibenik-Knin, S Croatia
Knjaževac 100 E4 Serbia, E Serbia
Knokke-Heist 87 A5 West-Vlaanderen,
  NW Belgium
Knoxville 42 D1 Tennessee, S USA
Knud Rasmussen Land 82 D1 physical
  region N Greenland
Kobdo see Hovd
Kōbe 131 C6 Hyōgo, Honshū,
  SW Japan
København 85 B7 Eng. Copenhagen;
  anc. Hafnia. country capital (Denmark)
  Sjælland, København, E Denmark
Kobenni 74 D3 Hodh el Gharbi,
  S Mauritania
Koblenz 95 A5 prev. Coblenz, Fr.
  Coblence; anc. Confluentes. Rheinland-
  Pfalz,-W Germany
Kobrin see Kobryn
Kobryn 107 A6 Rus. Kobrin. Brestskaya
  Voblasts', SW Belarus
Kobuleti 117 F2 prev. K'obulet'i.
  W Georgia
K'obulet'i see Kobuleti
Kočani 101 E6 NE FYR Macedonia
Kočevje 95 D8 Ger. Gottschee. S Slovenia
Koch Bihār 135 G3 West Bengal,
  NE India
Kochchi see Kochi
Kochi 132 C3 prev. Cochin, var. Kochchi.
  Kerala, SW India
Kōchi 131 B7 var. Kôti. Kōchi, Shikoku,
  SW Japan
Kochiu see Gejiu
Kodiak 36 C3 Kodiak Island, Alaska,
  USA
Kodiak Island 36 C3 island Alaska, USA
Koedoes see Kudus
Koeln see Köln
Koepang see Kupang
Ko-erh-mu see Golmud
Koetai see Mahakam, Sungai
Koetaradja see Banda Aceh
Kōfu 131 D5 var. Kôhu. Yamanashi,
  Honshū, S Japan
Kogarah 148 E3 New South Wales,
  E Australia
Kogon 122 D2 Rus. Kagan. Buxoro
  Viloyati, C Uzbekistan
Kōhalom see Rupea
Kohima 135 H3 state capital Nāgāland,
  E India
Koh I Noh see Büyükağrı Dağı
Kohtla-Järve 106 E2 Ida-Virumaa,
  NE Estonia
Kôhu see Kōfu
Kokand see Qo'qon
Kokchetav see Kokshetau
Kokkola 84 D4 Swe. Karleby; prev. Swe.
  Gamlakarleby. Länsi-Suomi, W Finland
Koko 75 F4 Kebbi, W Nigeria
Kokomo 40 C4 Indiana, N USA
Koko Nor see Qinghai Hu, China
Koko Nor see Qinghai, China
Kokrines 36 C2 Alaska, USA
Kokshaal-Tau 123 G2 Rus. Khrebet
  Kakshaal-Too. mountain range China/
  Kyrgyzstan

Kokshetau 114 C4 Kaz. Kökshetaü; prev.
  Kokchetav. Kokshetau, N Kazakhstan
Kökshetaü see Kokshetau
Koksijde 87 A5 West-Vlaanderen,
  W Belgium
Koksoak 38 D2 river Québec, E Canada
Kokstad 78 D5 KwaZulu/Natal, E South
  Africa
Kolaka 139 E4 Sulawesi, C Indonesia
K'o-la-ma-i see Karamay
Kola Peninsula 110 C2 Eng. Kola
  Peninsula. peninsula NW Russian
  Federation
Kola Peninsula see Kol'skiy Poluostrov
Kolari 84 D3 Lappi, NW Finland
Kolárovo 99 C6 Ger. Gutta; prev.
  Guta, Hung. Gúta. Nitriansky Kraj,
  SW Slovakia
Kolberg see Kołobrzeg
Kolda 74 C3 S Senegal
Kolding 85 A7 Syddanmark, C Denmark
Kölen 81 E1 Nor. Kjølen. mountain
  range Norway/Sweden
Kolguyev, Ostrov 110 C2 island
  NW Russian Federation
Kolhāpur 132 B1 Mahārāshtra, SW India
Kolhumadulu 132 A5 var. Thaa Atoll.
  atoll S Maldives
Kolín 99 B5 Ger. Kolin. Střední Čechy,
  C Czech Republic
Kolka 106 C2 NW Latvia
Kolkasrags 106 C2 prev. Eng. Cape
  Domesnes. headland NW Latvia
Kollam 132 C3 prev. Quilon. Kerala,
  SW India
Kolmar see Colmar
Köln 94 A4 var. Koeln, Eng./Fr. Cologne;
  prev. Cöln; anc. Colonia Agrippina,
  Oppidum Ubiorum. Nordrhein-
  Westfalen, W Germany
Koło 98 C3 Wielkopolskie, C Poland
Kołobrzeg 98 B2 Ger. Kolberg.
  Zachodnio-pomorskie, NW Poland
Kolokani 74 D3 Koulikoro, W Mali
Kolomea see Kolomyya
Kolomna 111 B5 Moskovskaya Oblast',
  W Russian Federation
Kolomyya 108 C3 Ger. Kolomea. Ivano-
  Frankivs'ka Oblast', W Ukraine
Kolosjoki see Nikel'
Kolozsvár see Cluj-Napoca
Kolpa 100 A2 Ger. Kulpa, SCr. Kupa.
  river Croatia/Slovenia
Kolpino 110 B4 Leningradskaya Oblast',
  NW Russian Federation
Kólpos Mórfu see Güzelyurt
Kolwezi 77 D7 Katanga, S Dem. Rep.
  Congo
Kolyma 115 G2 river NE Russian
  Federation
Komárno 99 C6 Ger. Komorn, Hung.
  Komárom. Nitriansky Kraj, SW Slovakia
Komárom see Komárno
Komatsu 131 C5 var. Komatu. Ishikawa,
  Honshū, SW Japan
Komatu see Komatsu
Kommunizm, Qullai see Ismoili Somoní,
  Qullai
Komoé 75 E4 var. Komoé Fleuve. river
  E Côte d'Ivoire
Komoé Fleuve see Komoé
Komotau see Chomutov
Komotiní 104 D3 var. Gümüljina, Turk.
  Gümülcine. Anatolikí Makedonía kai
  Thráki, NE Greece
Kompong see Kâmpóng Chhnăng
Kompong Cham see Kâmpóng Cham
Kompong Som see Sihanoukville
Kompong Speu see Kâmpóng Spœ
Komrat see Comrat
Komsomolets, Ostrov 115 E1 island
  Severnaya Zemlya, N Russian
  Federation
Komsomol'sk-na-Amure 115 G4
  Khabarovskiy Kray, SE Russian
  Federation
Kondolovo 104 E3 Burgas, E Bulgaria
Kondopoga 110 B3 Respublika Kareliya,
  NW Russian Federation
Kondoz see Kunduz
Köneürgench 122 C2 var. Köneürgench,
  Rus. Këneurgench; prev. Kunya-
  Urgench. Daşoguz Welaýaty,
  N Turkmenistan
Konga 152 C2 var. Köneürgench,
  [text] Köneurgench; prev. Kunya-
  Urgench. [text]
Kong Christian IX Land 82 D4 Eng.
  King Christian IX Land. physical region
  SE Greenland
Kong Christian X Land 82 D3 Eng.
  King Christian X Land. physical region
  SE Greenland
Kong Frederik IX Land 82 C3 physical
  region SW Greenland
Kong Frederik VIII Land 83 E2 Eng.
  King Frederik VIII Land. physical
  region NE Greenland

Kong Frederik VI Kyst 82 C4 Eng. King
  Frederik VI Coast. physical region
  SE Greenland
Kong Karls Land 83 G2 Eng. King
  Charles Islands. island group
  SE Svalbard
Kongo see Congo (river)
Kongolo 77 D6 Katanga, E Dem. Rep.
  Congo
Kongor 73 B5 Jonglei, E South Sudan
Kong Oscar Fjord 83 E3 fjord
  E Greenland
Kongsberg 85 B6 Buskerud, S Norway
Kông, Tônlé 137 E5 var. Xê Kong. river
  Cambodia/Laos
Kong, Xê see Kông, Tônlé
Königgrätz see Hradec Králové
Königshütte see Chorzów
Konin 98 C3 Ger. Kuhnau.
  Weilkopolskie, C Poland
Koninkrijk der Nederlanden see
  Netherlands
Konispol 101 C7 var. Konispoli. Vlorë,
  S Albania
Konispoli see Konispol
Kónitsa 104 A4 Ípeiros, W Greece
Konitz see Chojnice
Konjic 100 C4 Federacija Bosna I
  Hercegovina, S Bosnia and
  Herzegovina
Konosha 110 C4 Arkhangel'skaya
  Oblast', NW Russian Federation
Konotop 109 F1 Sums'ka Oblast',
  NE Ukraine
Konstantinovka see Kostyantynivka
Konstanz 95 B7 var. Constanz, Eng.
  Constance, hist. Kostnitz; anc.
  Constantia. Baden-Württemberg,
  S Germany
Konstanza see Constanţa
Konya 116 C4 var. Konieh; prev. Konia;
  anc. Iconium. Konya, C Turkey
Kopaonik 101 D5 mountain range
  S Serbia
Kopar see Koper
Koper 95 D8 It. Capodistria; prev. Kopar.
  SW Slovenia
Köpetdag Gershi 122 C3 mountain
  range Iran/Turkmenistan
Köpetdag Gershi/Kopetdag, Khrebet
  see Koppeh Dāgh
Koppeh Dagh 120 D2 Rus. Khrebet
  Kopetdag, Turkm. Köpetdag Gershi.
  mountain range Iran/Turkmenistan
Kopreinitz see Koprivnica
Koprivnica 100 B2 Ger. Kopreinitz,
  Hung. Kaproncza. Koprivnica-
  Križevci, N Croatia
Köprülü see Veles
Koptsevichi see Kaptsevichy
Kopyl' see Kapyl'
Korat see Nakhon Ratchasima
Korat Plateau 136 D4 plateau
  E Thailand
Korba 135 E4 Chhattīsgarh, C India
Korça see Korçë
Korçë 101 D6 var. Korça, Gk. Korytsa,
  It. Corriza; prev. Koritsa. Korçë,
  SE Albania
Korčula 100 B4 It. Curzola; anc. Corcyra
  Nigra. island S Croatia
Korea Bay 127 G3 bay China/North
  Korea
**Korea, Democratic People's Republic
  of** see North Korea
Korea, Republic of see South Korea
Korea Strait 131 A7 Jap. Chōsen-kaikyō,
  Kor. Taehan-haehyŏp. channel Japan/
  South Korea
Korhogo 74 D4 N Côte d'Ivoire
Kórinthos 105 B6 anc. Corinthus Eng.
  Corinth. Pelopónnisos, S Greece
Koritsa see Korçë
Kōriyama 131 D5 Fukushima, Honshū,
  C Japan
Korla 126 C3 Chin. K'u-erh-lo. Xinjiang
  Uygur Zizhiqu, NW China
Körmend 99 B7 Vas, W Hungary
Koróni 105 B6 Pelopónnisos,
  S Greece
Koror 144 A2 (Palau) Oreor, N Palau
Körös see Križevci
Korosten' 108 D1 Zhytomyrs'ka Oblast',
  NW Ukraine
Koro Toro 76 C2 Borkou-Ennedi-
  Tibesti, N Chad
Korsovka see Kārsava
Kortrijk 87 A6 Fr. Courtrai. West-
  Vlaanderen, W Belgium

Koryak Range 115 H2 *var.* Koryakskiy Khrebet, *Eng.* Koryak Range. *mountain range* NE Russian Federation
Koryak Range *see* Koryakskoy e Nagor'ye
Koryakskiy Khrebet *see* Koryakskoye Nagor'ye
Koryazhma 110 C4 Arkhangel'skaya Oblast', NW Russian Federation
Korytsa *see* Korçë
Kos 105 E6 Kos, Dodekánisa, Greece, Aegean Sea
Kos 105 E6 *It.* Coo; *anc.* Cos. *island* Dodekánisa, Greece, Aegean Sea
Ko-saki 131 A7 *headland* Nagasaki, Tsushima, SW Japan
Kościan 98 B4 Ger. Kosten. Wielkopolskie, C Poland
Kościerzyna 98 C2 Pomorskie, NW Poland
Kosciusko, Mount *see* Kosciuszko, Mount
Kosciuszko, Mount 149 C7 *prev.* Mount Kosciusko. *mountain* New South Wales, SE Australia
K'o-shih *see* Kashi
Koshikijima-retto 131 A8 *var.* Kosikizima Rettō. *island group* SW Japan
Kōshū *see* Gwangju
Košice 99 D6 *Ger.* Kaschau, *Hung.* Kassa. Košický Kraj, E Slovakia
Kosikizima Rettō *see* Koshikijima-rettō
Köslin *see* Koszalin
Koson 123 E3 *Rus.* Kasan. Qashqadaryo Viloyati, S Uzbekistan
Kosovo 101 D5 *prev.* Autonomous Province of Kosovo and Metohija. *country* SE Europe

KOSOVO (not yet fully recognized)
Southeast Europe

Official name Republic of Kosovo
Formation 2008 / 2008
Capital Priishtinë
Population 1.73 million / 412 people per sq mile (159 people per sq km)
Total area 4212 sq miles (10,908 sq km)
Languages Albanian*, Serbian*, Bosniak, Gorani, Roma, Turkish
Religions Muslim 92%, Roman Catholic 4%, Orthodox Christian 4%
Ethnic mix Albanian 92%, Serb 4%, Bosniak and Gorani 2%, Turkish 1%, Roma 1%
Government Parliamentary system
Currency Euro = 100 cents
Literacy rate 92%
Calorie consumption Not available

Kosovo and Metohija, Autonomous Province of *see* Kosovo
Kosovo Polje *see* Fushë Kosovë
Kosovska Mitrovica *see* Mitrovicë
Kosrae 144 C2 *prev.* Kusaie. *island* Caroline Islands, E Micronesia
Kossou, Lac de 74 D5 *lake* C Côte d'Ivoire
Kostanay 114 C4 *var.* Kustanay, *Kaz.* Qostanay. Kostanay, N Kazakhstan
Kosten *see* Kościan
Kostenets 104 C2 *prev.* Georgi Dimitrov. Sofiya, W Bulgaria
Kostnitz *see* Konstanz
Kostroma 110 B4 Kostromskaya Oblast', NW Russian Federation
Kostyantynivka 109 G3 *Rus.* Konstantinovka. Donets'ka Oblast', SE Ukraine
Kostyukovichi *see* Kastsyukovichy
Kostyukovka *see* Kastsyukowka
Koszalin 98 B2 *Ger.* Köslin. Zachodnio-pomorskie, NW Poland
Kota 134 D3 *prev.* Kotah. Rājasthān, N India
Kota Baharu *see* Kota Bharu
Kota Bahru *see* Kota Bharu
Kotabaru *see* Jayapura
Kota Bharu 138 B3 *var.* Kota Baharu, Kota Bahru. Kelantan, Peninsular Malaysia
Kotaboemi *see* Kotabumi
Kotabumi 138 B4 *prev.* Kotaboemi. Sumatera, W Indonesia
Kotah *see* Kota
Kota Kinabalu 138 D3 *prev.* Jesselton. Sabah, East Malaysia

Kotel'nyy, Ostrov 115 E2 *island* Novosibirskiye Ostrova, N Russian Federation
Kotka 85 E5 Etelä-Suomi, S Finland
Kotlas 110 C4 Arkhangel'skaya Oblast', NW Russian Federation
Kotonu *see* Cotonou
Kotor 101 C5 *It.* Cattaro. SW Montenegro
Kotovs'k 108 D3 *Rus.* Kotovsk. Odes'ka Oblast', SW Ukraine
Kotovsk *see* Hîncești
Kottbus *see* Cottbus
Kotto 76 D4 *river* Central African Republic/Dem. Rep. Congo
Kotuy 115 E2 *river* N Russian Federation
Koudougou 75 E4 C Burkina Faso
Koulamoutou 77 B6 Ogooué-Lolo, C Gabon
Koulikoro 74 D3 Koulikoro, SW Mali
Koumra 76 C4 Moyen-Chari, S Chad
Kourou 59 H3 N French Guiana
Kousséir *see* Al Quşayr
Kousséri 76 B3 *prev.* Fort-Foureau. Extrême-Nord, NE Cameroon
Koutiala 74 D4 Sikasso, S Mali
Kouvola 85 E5 Etelä-Suomi, S Finland
Kovel' 108 C1 *Pol.* Kowel. Volyns'ka Oblast', NW Ukraine
Kovno *see* Kaunas
Koweit *see* Kuwait
Kowel *see* Kovel'
Kowloon 128 A2 Hong Kong, S China
Kowno *see* Kaunas
Kozáni 104 B4 Dytikí Makedonía, N Greece
Kozara 100 B3 *mountain range* NW Bosnia and Herzegovina
Kozarska Dubica *see* Bosanska Dubica
Kozhikode 132 C2 *var.* Calicut. Kerala, SW India
Kozu-shima 131 D6 *island* E Japan
Kozyatyn 108 D2 *Rus.* Kazatin. Vinnyts'ka Oblast', C Ukraine
Kpalimé 75 E5 *var.* Palimé. SW Togo
Krâchéh 137 D6 *prev.* Kratie. Krâchéh, E Cambodia
Kragujevac 100 D4 Serbia, C Serbia
Krainburg *see* Kranj
Kra, Isthmus of 137 B6 *isthmus* Malaysia/Thailand
Krakau *see* Kraków
Kraków 99 D5 *Eng.* Cracow, *Ger.* Krakau; *anc.* Cracovia. Małopolskie, S Poland
Králänh 137 D5 Siĕmréab, NW Cambodia
Kralendijk 100 D4 *dependent territory capital* (Netherlands) Bonaire
Kraljevo 100 D4 Serbia, C Serbia
Kramators'k 109 G3 *Rus.* Kramatorsk. Donets'ka Oblast', SE Ukraine
Kramatorsk *see* Kramators'k
Kramfors 85 C5 Västernorrland, C Sweden
Kranéa *see* Kraniá
Kraniá 104 B4 *var.* Kranéa. Dytikí Makedonía, N Greece
Kranj 95 D7 *Ger.* Krainburg. NW Slovenia
Kranz *see* Zelenogradsk
Kráslava 106 D4 SE Latvia
Krasnaye 107 C5 *Rus.* Krasnoye. Minskaya Voblasts', C Belarus
Krasnoarmeysk 111 C6 Saratovskaya Oblast', W Russian Federation
Krasnodar 111 A7 *prev.* Ekaterinodar, Yekaterinodar. Krasnodarskiy Kray, SW Russian Federation
Krasnodon 109 H3 Luhans'ka Oblast', E Ukraine
Krasnogor *see* Kallaste
Krasnogvardeyskoye *see* Kotshnvardiys'ke
Krasnohvardiys'ke 109 F4 *Rus.* Krasnogvardeyskoye. Avtonomna Respublika Krym, S Ukraine
Krasnokamsk 115 F4 Zabaykal'skiy Kray, S Russian Federation
Krasnokamsk 111 D5 Permskiy Kray, W Russian Federation
Krasnoperekops'k 109 F4 *Rus.* Krasnoperekopsk. Avtonomna Respublika Krym, S Ukraine
Krasnoperekopsk *see* Krasnoperekops'k
Krasnostav *see* Krasnystaw
Krasnovodsk *see* Türkmenbaşy

Krasnovodskiy Zaliv *see* Türkmenbaşy Aylagy
Krasnowodsk Aylagy *see* Türkmenbaşy Aylagy
Krasnoyarsk 114 D4 Krasnoyarskiy Kray, S Russian Federation
Krasnoye *see* Krasnaye
Krasnystaw 98 E4 *Rus.* Krasnostav. Lubelskie, SE Poland
Krasnyy Kut 111 C6 Saratovskaya Oblast', W Russian Federation
Krasnyy Luch 109 H3 *prev.* Krindachevka. Luhans'ka Oblast', E Ukraine
Kratie *see* Krâchéh
Kràvanh, Chuŏr Phnum 137 C6 *Eng.* Cardamom Mountains, *Fr.* Chaîne des Cardamomes. *mountain range* W Cambodia
Krefeld 94 A4 Nordrhein-Westfalen, W Germany
Kreisstadt *see* Krosno Odrzańskie
Kremenchug *see* Kremenchuk
Kremenchugskoye Vodokhranilishche/ Kremenchuk Reservoir *see* Kremenchuts'ke Vodoskhovyshche
Kremenchuk 109 F2 *Rus.* Kremenchug. Poltavs'ka Oblast', NE Ukraine
Kremenchuk Reservoir 109 F2 *Eng.* Kremenchuk Reservoir, *Rus.* Kremenchugskoye Vodokhranilishche. *reservoir* C Ukraine
Kremenets' 108 C2 *Pol.* Krzemieniec, *Rus.* Kremenets. Ternopil's'ka Oblast', W Ukraine
Kremennaya *see* Kreminna
Kreminna 109 G2 *Rus.* Kremennaya. Luhans'ka Oblast', E Ukraine
Kresena *see* Kresna
Kresna 104 C3 *var.* Kresena. Blagoevgrad, SW Bulgaria
Kretikon Delagos *see* Kritikó Pélagos
Kretinga 106 B3 *Ger.* Krottingen. Klaipėda, NW Lithuania
Kreutz *see* Cristuru Secuiesc
Kreuz *see* Križevci, Croatia
Kreuz *see* Risti, Estonia
Kreuzburg/Kreuzburg in Oberschlesien *see* Kluczbork
Krichëv *see* Krychaw
Krievija *see* Russian Federation
Krindachevka *see* Krasnyy Luch
Krishna 132 C1 *prev.* Kistna. *river* C India
Krishnagiri 132 C2 Tamil Nādu, SE India
Kristiania *see* Oslo
Kristiansand 85 A6 *var.* Christiansand. Vest-Agder, S Norway
Kristianstad 85 B7 Skåne, S Sweden
Kristiansund 84 A4 *var.* Christiansund. Møre og Romsdal, S Norway
Krivoy Rog *see* Kryvyy Rih
Križevci 100 B2 *Ger.* Kreuz, *Hung.* Kőrös. Varaždin, NE Croatia
Krk 100 A3 *It.* Veglia; *anc.* Curieta. *island* NW Croatia
Kroatien *see* Croatia
Krolevets' 109 F1 *Rus.* Krolevets. Sums'ka Oblast', NE Ukraine
Krolevets *see* Krolevets'
Królewska Huta *see* Chorzów
Kronach 95 C5 Bayern, E Germany
Kronstadt *see* Braşov
Kroonstad 78 D4 Free State, C South Africa
Kropotkin 111 A7 Krasnodarskiy Kray, SW Russian Federation
Krosno 99 D5 *Ger.* Krossen. Podkarpackie, SE Poland
Krosno Odrzańskie 98 B3 *Ger.* Crossen, Kreisstadt. Lubuskie, W Poland
Krossen *see* Krosno
Krottingen *see* Kretinga
Krško 95 E8 *Ger.* Gurkfeld; *prev.* Videm-Krško. E Slovenia
Kruglaye 107 D6 *Rus.* Krugloye. Mahilyowskaya Voblasts', E Belarus
Krugloye *see* Kruglaye
Kruja *see* Krujë
Krujë 101 C6 *var.* Kruja, *It.* Croia. Durrës, C Albania
Krummau *see* Český Krumlov
Krung Thep, Ao 137 C5 *var.* Bight of Bangkok. *bay* S Thailand
Krung Thep Mahanakhon *see* Ao Krung Thep
Krupki 107 D6 Minskaya Voblasts', C Belarus

Krušné Hory *see* Erzgebirge
Krychaw 107 E7 *Rus.* Krichëv. Mahilyowskaya Voblasts', E Belarus
Kryms'ki Hory 109 F5 *mountain range* S Ukraine
Kryms'kyy Pivostriv 109 F5 *peninsula* S Ukraine
Krynica 99 D5 *Ger.* Tannenhof. Małopolskie, S Poland
Kryve Ozero 109 E3 Odes'ka Oblast', SW Ukraine
Kryvyy Rih 109 F3 *Rus.* Krivoy Rog. Dnipropetrovs'ka Oblast', SE Ukraine
Krzemieniec *see* Kremenets'
Ksar al Kabir *see* Ksar-el-Kebir
Ksar al Soule *see* Er-Rachidia
Ksar-el-Kebir 70 C2 *var.* Alcázar, Ksar al Kabir, Ksar-el-Kébir, *Ar.* Al-Ksar al-Kebir, Al-Qsar al-Kbir, *Sp.* Alcazarquivir. NW Morocco
Ksar-el-Kébir *see* Ksar-el-Kebir
Kuala Dungun *see* Dungun
Kuala Lumpur 138 B3 *country capital* (Malaysia) Kuala Lumpur, Peninsular Malaysia
Kuala Terengganu 138 B3 *var.* Kuala Trengganu. Terengganu, Peninsular Malaysia
Kualatungkal 138 B4 Sumatera, W Indonesia
Kuang-chou *see* Guangzhou
Kuang-hsi *see* Guangxi Zhuangzu Zizhiqu
Kuang-tung *see* Guangdong
Kuang-yuan *see* Guangyuan
Kuantan 138 B3 Pahang, Peninsular Malaysia
Kuba *see* Quba
Kuban' 109 G5 *var.* Hypanis. *river* SW Russian Federation
Kubango *see* Cubango/Okavango
Kuching 138 C3 *prev.* Sarawak. Sarawak, East Malaysia
Küchnay Darwëshän 122 D5 *prev.* Küchnay Darweyshän. Helmand, S Afghanistan
Küchnay Darweyshän *see* Küchnay Darwëshän
Kuçova *see* Kuçovë
Kuçovë 101 C6 *var.* Kuçova; *prev.* Qyteti Stalin. Berat, C Albania
Kudara *see* Ghūdara
Kudus 138 C5 *prev.* Koedoes. Jawa, C Indonesia
Kuei-lin *see* Guilin
Kuei-Yang/Kuei-yang *see* Guiyang
K'u-erh-lo *see* Korla
Kueyang *see* Guiyang
Kugaaruk 37 G3 *prev.* Pelly Bay. Nunavut, N Canada
Kugluktuk 53 E3 *var.* Qurlurtuuq; *prev.* Coppermine. Nunavut, NW Canada
Kuhmo 84 E4 Oulu, E Finland
Kuhnau *see* Konin
Kŭhnō *see* Kihnu
Kuibyshev *see* Kuybyshevskoye Vodokhranilishche
Kuito 78 B2 Port. Silva Porto. Bié, C Angola
Kuji 130 D3 *var.* Kuzi. Iwate, Honshū, C Japan
Kukës 101 D5 *var.* Kukësi. Kukës, NE Albania
Kukësi *see* Kukës
Kukong *see* Shaoguan
Kukukhoto *see* Hohhot
Kula Kangri 135 G3 *var.* Kulhakangri. *mountain* Bhutan/China
Kuldiga 106 B3 *Ger.* Goldingen. W Latvia
Kuldja *see* Yining
Kulhakangri *see* Kula Kangri
Kullorsuaq 82 D2 *var.* Kuvdlorssuak. Kitaa, C Greenland
Kulm *see* Chełmno
Kulmsee *see* Chełmza
Kŭlob 123 F3 *Rus.* Kulyab. SW Tajikistan
Kulpa *see* Kolpa
Kulu 116 C3 Konya, W Turkey
Kulunda Steppe *see* Ravnina Kulyndy
Kulundinskaya Ravnina *see* Ravnina Kulyndy
Kulyab *see* Kŭlob
Kum *see* Qom
Kuma 111 B7 *river* SW Russian Federation
Kumamoto 131 A7 Kumamoto, Kyūshū, SW Japan
Kumanovo *see* Kumanovo

Kumanovo 101 E5 Turk. Kumanova.
N Macedonia
Kumasi 75 E5 prev. Coomassie. C Ghana
Kumayri see Gyumri
Kumba 77 A5 Sud-Ouest, W Cameroon
Kumertau 111 D6 Respublika
Bashkortostan, W Russian Federation
Kumillā see Comilla
Kumo 75 G4 Gombe, E Nigeria
Kumon Range 136 B2 mountain range
N Myanmar (Burma)
Kumul see Hami
Kunashiri see Kunashir, Ostrov
Kunashir, Ostrov 130 E1 var. Kunashiri.
island Kuril'skiye Ostrova, SE Russian
Federation
Kunda 106 E2 Lääne-Virumaa,
NE Estonia
Kunduz 123 E3 prev. Kondoz. province
NE Afghanistan
Kunene 69 C6 var. Kunene. river
Angola/Namibia
Kunene see Cunene
Kungsbacka 85 B7 Halland, S Sweden
Kungur 111 D5 Permskiy Kray,
NW Russian Federation
Kunlun Mountains see Kunlun Shan
Kunlun Shan 126 B4 Eng. Kunlun
Mountains. mountain range NW China
Kunming 128 B6 var. K'un-ming; prev.
Yunnan. province capital Yunnan,
SW China
K'un-ming see Kunming
Kununurra 146 D3 Western Australia
Kunya-Urgench see Köneürgenç
Kuopio 85 E5 Itä-Suomi, C Finland
Kupa see Kolpa
Kupang 139 E5 prev. Koepang. Timor,
C Indonesia
Kup"yans'k 109 G2 Rus. Kupyansk.
Kharkivs'ka Oblast', E Ukraine
Kupyansk see Kup"yans'k
Kür see Kura
Kura 117 H3 Az. Kür, Geor. Mtkvari,
Turk. Kura Nehri. river SW Asia
Kura Nehri see Kura
Kurashiki 131 B6 var. Kurasiki.
Okayama, Honshū, SW Japan
Kurasiki see Kurashiki
Kurdistan 117 F4 cultural region SW Asia
Kürdzhali 104 D3 var. Kirdzhali.
Kürdzhali, S Bulgaria
Kure 131 B7 Hiroshima, Honshū,
SW Japan
Küre Dağları 116 C2 mountain range
T Turkey
Kuressaare 106 C2 Ger. Arensburg; prev.
Kingissepp. Saaremaa, W Estonia
Kureyka 112 D2 river N Russian
Federation
Kurgan-Tyube see Qürghonteppa
Kuria Muria Islands see Ḩalāniyāt,
Juzur al
Kurile Islands 115 H4 Eng. Kurile
Islands. island group SE Russian
Federation
Kurile Islands see Kuril'skiye Ostrova
Kurile-Kamchatka Depression see
Kurile Trench
Kurile Trench 113 F3 var. Kurile-
Kamchatka Depression. trench
NW Pacific Ocean
Kuril'sk 130 E1 Jap. Shana. Kuril'skiye
Ostrova, Sakhalinskaya Oblats',
SE Russian Federation
Ku-ring-gai 148 E1 New South Wales,
E Australia
Kurisches Haff see Courland Lagoon
Kurkund see Kilingi-Nõmme
Kurnool 132 C1 var. Karnul. Andhra
Pradesh, S India
Kursk 111 A6 Kurskaya Oblast',
W Russian Federation
Kurskiy Zaliv see Courland Lagoon
Kuršumlija 101 D5 Serbia, S Serbia
Kurtbunar see Tervel
Kurtitsch/Kürtös see Curtici
Kuruktag 126 C3 mountain range
NW China
Kurume 131 A7 Fukuoka, Kyūshū,
SW Japan
Kurupukari 59 F3 C Guyana
Kusaie see Kosrae
Kushiro 130 D2 var. Kusiro. Hokkaidō,
NE Japan
Kushka see Serhetabat
Kusiro see Kushiro
Kuskokwim Mountains 36 C3
mountain range Alaska, USA

Kustanay see Kostanay
Küstence/Küstendje see Constanţa
Kütahya 116 B3 prev. Kutaia. Kütahya,
W Turkey
Kutai see Mahakam, Sungai
Kutaisi 117 F2 W Georgia
Kūt al 'Amārah see Al Kūt
Kut al Imara see Al Kūt
Kutaradja/Kutaraja see Banda Aceh
Kutch, Gulf of see Kachchh, Gulf of
Kutch, Rann of see Kachchh, Rann of
Kutina 100 B3 Sisak-Moslavina,
NE Croatia
Kutno 98 C3 Łódzkie, C Poland
Kuujjuaq 39 E2 prev. Fort-Chimo.
Québec, E Canada
Kuusamo 84 E3 Oulu, E Finland
Kuvango see Cubango
Kuvdlorssuak see Kullorsuaq
Kuwait 120 C4 off. State of Kuwait, var.
Dawlat al Kuwait, Koweit, Kuwet.
country SW Asia

KUWAIT
Southwest Asia

Official name State of Kuwait
Formation 1961 / 1961
Capital Kuwait City
Population 2.8 million / 407 people
per sq mile (157 people per sq km) / 96%
Total area 6880 sq. miles (17,820 sq. km)
Languages Arabic*, English
Religions Sunni Muslim 45%, Shi'a
Muslim 40%, Christian, Hindu,
and other 15%
Ethnic mix Kuwaiti 45%, Other Arab 35%,
South Asian 9%, Other 7%, Iranian 4%
Government Monarchy
Currency Kuwaiti dinar = 1000 fils
Literacy rate 94%
Calorie consumption 3681 kilocalories

Kuwait see Al Kuwayt
Kuwait City see Al Kuwayt
Kuwait, Dawlat al see Kuwait
Kuwait, State of see Kuwait
Kuwajleen see Kwajalein Atoll
Kuwayt 120 C3 Maysān, E Iraq
Kuweit see Kuwait
Kuybyshev see Samara
Kuybyshev Reservoir 111 C5 var.
Kuibyshev, Eng. Kuybyshev Reservoir.
reservoir W Russian Federation
Kuybyshev Reservoir see
Kuybyshevskoye Vodokhranilishche
Kuytun 126 B2 Xinjiang Uygur Zizhiqu,
NW China
Kuzi see Kuji
Kuznetsk 111 B6 Penzenskaya Oblast',
W Russian Federation
Kuźnica 98 E2 Białystok, NE Poland
Europe
Kvaløya 84 C2 island N Norway
Kvarnbergsvattnet 84 B4 var.
Frostviken. lake N Sweden
Kvarner 100 A3 var. Carnaro, It.
Quarnero. gulf W Croatia
Kvitøya 83 G1 island NE Svalbard
Kwajalein Atoll 144 C1 var. Kuwajleen.
atoll Ralik Chain, C Marshall Islands
Kwando see Cuando
Kwangchow see Guangzhou
Kwangchu see Gwangju
Kwangju see Gwangju
Kwangju-gwangyŏksi see Gwangju
Kwango 77 C7 Port. Cuango. river
Angola/Dem. Rep. Congo
Kwango see Cuango
Kwangsi/Kwangsi Chuang
Autonomous Region see Guangxi
Zhuangzu Zizhiqu
Kwangtung see Guangdong
Kwangyuan see Guangyuan
Kwanza see Cuanza
Kweichu see Guiyang
Kweilin see Guilin
Kweisui see Hohhot
Kweiyang see Guiyang
Kwesui see Hohhot
Kwidzyń 98 C2 Ger. Marienwerder.
Pomorskie, N Poland
Kwigillingok 36 C3 Alaska,
USA
Kwilu 77 C6 river W Dem. Rep. Congo
Kwito see Cuito
Kyabé 76 C4 Moyen-Chari, S Chad

Kyaikkami 137 B5 prev. Amherst. Mon
State, S Myanmar (Burma)
Kyaiklat 136 B4 Ayeyarwady,
SW Myanmar (Burma)
Kyaikto 136 B4 Mon State, S Myanmar
(Burma)
Kyakhta 115 E5 Respublika Buryatiya,
S Russian Federation
Kyaukse 136 B3 Mandalay, C Myanmar
(Burma)
Kyjov 99 C5 Ger. Gaya. Jihomoravský
Kraj, SE Czech Republic
Kými 105 C5 prev. Kími. Évvoia,
C Greece
Kyŏngsŏng see Seoul
Kyōto 131 C6 Kyōto, Honshū, SW Japan
Kyparissía 105 B6 var. Kiparissía.
Pelopónnisos, S Greece
Kypros see Cyprus
Kyrá Panagía 105 C5 island Vóreies
Sporádes, Greece, Aegean Sea
Kyrenia see Girne
Kyrgyz Republic see Kyrgyzstan
Kyrgyzstan 123 F2 off. Kyrgyz Republic,
var. Kirghizia; prev. Kirgizskaya SSR,
Kirghiz SSR, Republic of Kyrgyzstan.
country C Asia

KYRGYZSTAN
Central Asia

Official name Kyrgyz Republic
Formation 1991 / 1991
Capital Bishkek
Population 5.4 million / 70 people
per sq mile (27 people per sq km) / 34%
Total area 76,641 sq. miles (198,500 sq. km)
Languages Kyrgyz*, Russian*, Uzbek,
Tatar, Ukrainian
Religions Muslim (mainly Sunni) 70%,
Orthodox Christian 30%
Ethnic mix Kyrgyz 69%, Uzbek 14%,
Russian 9%, Other 6%, Dungan 1%,
Uighur 1%
Government Presidential system
Currency Som = 100 tyiyn
Literacy rate 99%
Calorie consumption 2791 kilocalories

Kyrgyzstan, Republic of see Kyrgyzstan
Kythira 105 C7 var. Kíthira, It. Cerigo,
Lat. Cythera. island S Greece
Kýthnos 105 C6 Kínythnos, Kykládes,
Greece, Aegean Sea
Kythnos 105 C6 var. Kíthnos, Thermiá,
It. Termia; anc. Cythnos. island
Kykládes, Greece, Aegean Sea
Kythréa see Değirmenlik
Kyushu 131 B7 var. Kyūsyū. island
SW Japan
Kyushu-Palau Ridge 125 F3 var.
Kyusyu-Palau Ridge. undersea ridge
W Pacific Ocean
Kyustendil 104 B2 anc. Pautalia.
Kyustendil, W Bulgaria
Kyūsyū see Kyūshū
Kyusyu-Palau Ridge see Kyushu-Palau
Ridge
Kyyiv 109 E2 Eng. Kiev, Rus. Kiyev.
country capital (Ukraine) Kyyivs'ka
Oblast', N Ukraine
Kyzyl 114 D4 Respublika Tyva, C Russian
Federation
Kyzyl Kum 122 D2 var. Kizil Kum,
Qizil Qum, Uzb. Qizilqum. desert
Kazakhstan/Uzbekistan
Kyzylorda 114 B5 var. Kzyl-Orda, Qizil
Orda, Qyzylorda; prev. Kyzylorda,
Perovsk. Kyzylorda, S Kazakhstan
Kyzylrabot see Qizilrabot
Kyzyl-Suu 123 G2 prev. Pokrovka.
Issyk-Kul'skaya Oblast', NE Kyrgyzstan
Kzyl-Orda see Kyzylorda
Kzylorda see Kyzylorda

L

Laaland see Lolland
La Algaba 92 C4 Andalucía, S Spain
Laarne 87 B5 Oost-Vlaanderen,
NW Belgium
La Asunción 59 E1 Nueva Esparta,
NE Venezuela
Laatokka see Ladozhskoye, Ozero
Laâyoune 70 B3 var. Aaiún. country
capital (Western Sahara)
NW Western Sahara
La Banda Oriental see Uruguay

la Baule-Escoublac 90 A4 Loire-
Atlantique, NW France
Labé 74 C4 NW Guinea
Labe see Elbe
Laborca see Laborec
Laborec 99 E5 Hung. Laborca. river
E Slovakia
Labrador 39 F2 cultural region
Newfoundland and Labrador,
SW Canada
Labrador Basin 34 E3 var. Labrador Sea
Basin. undersea basin Labrador Sea
Labrador Sea 82 A4 sea NW Atlantic
Ocean
Labrador Sea Basin see Labrador Basin
Labudalin see Ergun
Labutta 137 A5 Ayeyarwady,
SW Myanmar (Burma)
Laç 101 C6 var. Laci. Lezhë, C Albania
La Calera 64 B4 Valparaíso, C Chile
La Carolina 92 D4 Andalucía, S Spain
Laccadive Islands 132 A3 Eng. Laccadive
Islands. island group India, N Indian
Ocean
**Laccadive Islands/Laccadive Minicoy
and Amindivi Islands, the** see
Lakshadweep
La Ceiba 52 D2 Atlántida, N Honduras
Lachanás 104 B3 Kentrikí Makedonía,
N Greece
La Chaux-de-Fonds 95 A7 Neuchâtel,
W Switzerland
Lachlan River 149 C6 river New South
Wales, SE Australia
Laci see Laç
la Ciotat 91 D6 anc. Citharista. Bouches-
du-Rhône, SE France
Lacobriga see Lagos
La Concepción 53 E5 var. Concepción.
Chiriquí, W Panama
La Concepción 58 C1 Zulia,
NW Venezuela
La Condamine 91 C8 W Monaco
Laconia 41 G2 New Hampshire, NE USA
La Crosse 40 A2 Wisconsin, N USA
La Cruz 52 D4 Guanacaste, NW Costa
Rica
Lake Ladoga 110 B3 Eng. Lake Ladoga,
Fin. Laatokka. lake NW Russian
Federation
Ladoga, Lake see Ladozhskoye, Ozero
Ladysmith 40 B2 Wisconsin, N USA
Lae 144 B3 Morobe, W Papua New
Guinea
La Esperanza 52 C2 Intibucá,
SW Honduras
Lafayette 40 C4 Indiana, N USA
Lafayette 42 B3 Louisiana, S USA
La Fé 54 A2 Pinar del Río, W Cuba
Lafia 75 G4 Nassarawa, C Nigeria
la Flèche 90 B4 Sarthe, NW France
Lagdo, Lac de 76 B4 lake N Cameroon
Laghouat 70 D2 N Algeria
Lagos 75 F5 Lagos, SW Nigeria
Lagos 92 B5 anc. Lacobriga. Faro,
S Portugal
Lagos de Moreno 51 E4 Jalisco,
SW Mexico
Lagouira 70 A4 SW Western Sahara
La Grande 46 C3 Oregon, NW USA
La Guaira 66 B4 Distrito Federal,
N Venezuela
Lagunas 64 B1 Tarapacá, N Chile
Lagunillas 61 G4 Santa Cruz, SE Bolivia
La Habana 54 B2 var. Havana. country
capital (Cuba) Ciudad de La Habana,
W Cuba
Lahat 138 B4 Sumatera, W Indonesia
La Haye see 's-Gravenhage
Laholm 85 B7 Halland, S Sweden
Lahore 134 D2 Punjab, NE Pakistan
Lahr 95 A6 Baden-Württemberg,
S Germany
Lahti 85 D5 Swe. Lahtis. Etelä-Suomi,
S Finland
Lahtis see Lahti
Lai 76 B4 prev. Behagle, De Behagle.
Tandjilé, S Chad
Laibach see Ljubljana
Lai Châu 136 D3 Lai Châu, N Vietnam
Laila see Laylā
La Junta 44 D5 Colorado, C USA
Lake Charles 42 A3 Louisiana, S USA
Lake City 43 E3 Florida, SE USA
Lake District 89 C5 physical region
NW England, United Kingdom
Lake Havasu City 48 A2 Arizona,
SW USA
Lake Jackson 49 H4 Texas, SW USA

Lakeland *43 E4* Florida, SE USA
Lakeside *47 C8* California, W USA
Lake State *see* Michigan
Lakewood *44 D4* Colorado, C USA
Lakhnau *see* Lucknow
Lakonikós Kólpos *105 B7 gulf*
  S Greece
Lakselv *84 D2 Lapp.* Leavdnja.
  Finnmark, N Norway
la Laon *see* Laon
Lalibela *72 C4* Āmara, Ethiopia
La Libertad *52 B1* Petén, N Guatemala
La Ligua *64 B4* Valparaíso, C Chile
Lalín *92 C1* Galicia, NW Spain
Lalitpur *135 F3* Central, C Nepal
La Louvière *87 B6* Hainaut, S Belgium
la Maddalena *96 A4* Sardegna, Italy,
  C Mediterranean Sea
la Manche *see* English Channel
Lamar *44 D5* Colorado, C USA
La Marmora, Punta *97 A5 mountain*
  Sardegna, Italy, C Mediterranean Sea
la Massana *91 A8* La Massana,
  W Andorra Europe
Lambaréné *77 A6* Moyen-Ogooué,
  W Gabon
Lamego *92 C2* Viseu, N Portugal
Lamesa *49 E3* Texas, SW USA
Lamezia Terme *97 D6* Calabria, SE Italy
Lamía *105 B5* Stereá Elláda, C Greece
Lamoni *45 F4* Iowa, C USA
Lampang *136 C4 var.* Muang Lampang.
  Lampang, NW Thailand
Lámpeia *105 B6* Dytikí Elláda, S Greece
Lanbi Kyun *137 B6 prev.* Sullivan Island.
  island Mergui Archipelago, S Myanmar
  (Burma)
Lancang Jiang *see* Mekong
Lancaster *89 D5* NW England, United
  Kingdom
Lancaster *47 C7* California, W USA
Lancaster *41 F4* Pennsylvania, NE USA
Lancaster Sound *37 F2 sound* Nunavut,
  N Canada
Lan-chou/Lan-chow/Lanchow *see*
  Lanzhou
Landao *see* Lantau Island
Landen *87 C6* Vlaams Brabant,
  C Belgium
Lander *44 C3* Wyoming, C USA
Landerneau *90 A3* Finistère, NW France
Landes *91 B5 cultural region* SW France
Land of Enchantment *see* New Mexico
The Land of Opportunity *see* Arkansas
Land of Steady Habits *see* Connecticut
Land of the Midnight Sun *see* Alaska
Landsberg *see* Gorzów Wielkopolski,
  Lubuskie, Poland
Landsberg an der Warthe *see* Gorzów
  Wielkopolski
Land's End *89 B8 headland* SW England,
  United Kingdom
Landshut *95 C6* Bayern, SE Germany
Langar *123 E2 Rus.* Lyangar. Navoiy
  Viloyati, C Uzbekistan
Langfang *128 D4* Hebei, E China
Langkawi, Pulau *137 B7 island*
  Peninsular Malaysia
Langres *90 D4* Haute-Marne, N France
Langsa *138 A3* Sumatera, W Indonesia
Lang Shan *127 E3 mountain range*
  N China
Lang Sơn *136 D3 var.* Langson. Lang
  Sơn, N Vietnam
Langson *see* Lang Sơn
Lang Suan *137 B6* Chumphon,
  SW Thailand
Languedoc *91 C6 cultural region* S France
Länkäran *117 H3 Rus.* Lenkoran'.
  S Azerbaijan
Lansing *40 C3 state capital* Michigan,
  N USA
Lanta, Ko *137 B7 island* S Thailand
Lantau Island *128 A2 Cant.* Tai Yue
  Shan, *Chin.* Landao. *island* Hong
  Kong, S China
Lan-ts'ang Chiang *see* Mekong
Lantung, Gulf of *see* Liaodong Wan
Lanzarote *70 B3 island* Islas Canarias,
  Spain, NE Atlantic Ocean
Lanzhou *128 B4 var.* Lan-chou,
  Lanchow, Lan-chow; *prev.* Kaolan.
  province capital Gansu, C China
Lao Cai *136 D3* Lao Cai, N Vietnam
Laodicea/Laodicea ad Mare *see* Al
  Lādhiqīyah
Laoet *see* Laut, Pulau
Laon *90 D3 var.* la Laon; *anc.* Laudunum.
  Aisne, N France

Lao People's Democratic Republic
  see Laos
La Orchila, Isla *58 D1 island*
  N Venezuela
La Oroya *60 C4* Junín, C Peru
Laos *136 D4 off.* Lao People's Democratic
  Republic. *country* SE Asia

LAOS
Southeast Asia

Official name Lao People's Democratic
  Republic
Formation 1953 / 1953
Capital Vientiane
Population 6.3 million / 71 people
  per sq mile (27 people per sq km)
Total area 91,428 sq. miles
  (236,800 sq. km)
Languages Lao*, Mon-Khmer, Yao,
  Vietnamese, Chinese, French
Religions Buddhist 65%, Other
  (including animist) 34%, Christian 1%
Ethnic mix Lao Loum 66%, Lao
  Theung 30%, Lao Soung 2%, Other 2%
Government One-party state
Currency New kip = 100 at
Literacy rate 73%
Calorie consumption 2377 kilocalories

La Palma *53 G5* Darién, SE Panama
La Palma *70 A3 island* Islas Canarias,
  Spain, NE Atlantic Ocean
La Paz *61 F4 var.* La Paz de Ayacucho.
  country capital (Bolivia-legislative
  and administrative capital) La Paz,
  W Bolivia
La Paz *50 B3* Baja California Sur,
  NW Mexico
La Paz, Bahía de *50 B3 bay* NW Mexico
La Paz de Ayacucho *see* La Paz
La Pérouse Strait *130 D1 Jap.* Sōya-
  kaikyō, *Rus.* Proliv Laperuza. *strait*
  Japan/Russian Federation
Laperuza, Proliv *see* La Pérouse Strait
Lápithos *see* Lapta
Lapland *84 D3 Fin.* Lappi, *Swe.*
  Lappland. *cultural region* N Europe
La Plata *64 D4* Buenos Aires,
  E Argentina
La Plata *see* Sucre
La Pola *92 D1 prev.* Pola de Lena.
  Asturias, N Spain
Lappeenranta *85 E5 Swe.* Villmanstrand.
  Etelä-Suomi, SE Finland
Lappi/Lappland *see* Lapland
Lappo *see* Lapua
Lapta *102 C5 Gk.* Lápithos. NW Cyprus
Laptev Sea *115 E2 Eng.* Laptev Sea. *sea*
  Arctic Ocean
Laptev Sea *see* Laptevykh, More
Lapua *85 D5 Swe.* Lappo. Länsi-Suomi,
  W Finland
Lapurdum *see* Bayonne
Łapy *98 E3* Podlaskie, NE Poland
La Quiaca *64 C2* Jujuy, N Argentina
L'Aquila *96 C4 var.* Aquila, Aquila degli
  Abruzzi. Abruzzo, C Italy
Laracha *92 B1* Galicia, NW Spain
Laramie *44 C4* Wyoming, C USA
Laramie Mountains *44 C3 mountain*
  range Wyoming, C USA
Laredo *93 E1* Cantabria, N Spain
Laredo *49 F5* Texas, SW USA
La Réunion *see* Réunion
Largeau *see* Faya
Largo *43 E4* Florida, SE USA
Largo, Cayo *54 B2 island* W Cuba
Lario *see* Como, Lago di
La Rioja *64 C3* La Rioja, NW Argentina
La Rioja *93 E2 autonomous community*
  N Spain
La Unión *52 C2* Valdivia, C Honduras
La Unión *93 F4* Murcia, SE Spain
Lárisa *104 B4 var.* Larissa. Thessalía,
  C Greece
Larissa *see* Lárisa
Lärkäna *134 B3 var.* Larkhana. Sind,
  SE Pakistan
Larkhana *see* Lärkäna
Larnaca *see* Lárnaca
Lárnaca *102 C5 var.* Larnaca, Larnax.
  SE Cyprus
Larnax *see* Lárnaca
La Rochelle *90 B4 anc.* Rupella.
  Charente-Maritime, W France
la Roche-sur-Yon *90 B4 prev.* Bourbon
  Vendée, Napoléon-Vendée. Vendée,
  NW France
La Roda *93 E3* Castilla-La Mancha,
  C Spain

La Romana *55 E3* E Dominican Republic
Larvotto *91 C8* N Monaco Europe
La-sa *see* Lhasa
Las Cabezas de San Juan *92 C5*
  Andalucía, S Spain
Las Cruces *48 D3* New Mexico, SW USA
La Serena *64 B3* Coquimbo, C Chile
La Seu d'Urgell *93 G1 var.* La Seu
  d'Urgell; *prev.* Seo de Urgel. Cataluña,
  NE Spain
La Seu d'Urgell *see* La Seu d'Urgell
La Seyne-sur-Mer *91 D6* Var, SE France
Lashio *136 B3* Shan State, E Myanmar
  (Burma)
Lashkar Gāh *122 D5 var.* Lash-Kar-Gar'.
  Helmand, S Afghanistan
Lash-Kar-Gar' *see* Lashkar Gāh
La Sila *97 D6 mountain range* SW Italy
La Sirena *52 D3* Región Autónoma
  Atlántico Sur, E Nicaragua
Łask *98 C4* Łódzkie, C Poland
Las Lomitas *64 D2* Formosa,
  N Argentina
La Solana *93 E4* Castilla-La Mancha,
  C Spain
Las Palmas *70 A3 var.* Las Palmas de
  Gran Canaria. Gran Canaria, Islas
  Canarias, Spain, NE Atlantic Ocean
Las Palmas de Gran Canaria *see* Las
  Palmas
La Spezia *96 B3* Liguria, NW Italy
Lassa *see* Lhasa
Las Tablas *53 F5* Los Santos, S Panama
Last Frontier, The *see* Alaska
Las Tunas *54 C2 var.* Victoria de las
  Tunas. Las Tunas, E Cuba
La Suisse *see* Switzerland
Las Vegas *47 D7* Nevada, W USA
Latacunga *60 B1* Cotopaxi, C Ecuador
La Teste *91 B5* Gironde, SW France
Latina *97 C5 prev.* Littoria. Lazio, C Italy
La Tortuga, Isla *59 E1 var.* Isla Tortuga.
  island N Venezuela
La Tuque *39 E4* Québec, SE Canada
Latvia *106 C3 off.* Republic of Latvia,
  Ger. Lettland, *Latv.* Latvija, Latvijas
  Republika; *prev.* Latvian SSR, *Rus.*
  Latviyskaya SSR. *country* NE Europe

LATVIA
Northeast Europe

Official name Republic of Latvia
Formation 1991 / 1991
Capital Riga
Population 2.2 million / 88 people
  per sq mile (34 people per sq km)
Total area 24,938 sq. miles (64,589 sq. km)
Languages Latvian*, Russian
Religions Other 43%, Lutheran 24%,
  Roman Catholic 18%, Orthodox
  Christian 15%
Ethnic mix Latvian 59%, Russian 28%,
  Belarussian 4%, Other 4%, Ukrainian 3%,
  Polish 2%
Government Parliamentary system
Currency Lats = 100 santimi
Literacy rate 99%
Calorie consumption 2923 kilocalories

Latvian SSR/Latvija/Latvijas
  Republika/Latviyskaya SSR *see* Latvia
Latvia, Republic of *see* Latvia
Laudunum *see* Laon
Laudus *see* St-Lô
Lauenburg/Lauenburg in Pommern
  see Lębork
Lau Group *145 E4 island group* E Fiji
Lauis *see* Lugano
Launceston *149 C8* Tasmania,
  SE Australia
La Unión *52 C2* Valdivia, C Honduras
La Unión *93 F4* Murcia, SE Spain
Laurel *42 C3* Mississippi, S USA
Laurel *44 C2* Montana, NW USA
Laurentian Highlands *see* Laurentian
  Mountains
Laurentian Mountains *39 E3 var.*
  Laurentian Highlands, *Fr.* Les
  Laurentides. *plateau* Newfoundland
  and Labrador/Québec, Canada
Laurentides, Les *see* Laurentian
  Mountains
Lauria *97 D6* Basilicata, S Italy
Laurinburg *43 F1* North Carolina,
  SE USA
Lauru *see* Choiseul
Lausanne *95 A7 It.* Losanna. Vaud,
  SW Switzerland

Laut, Pulau *138 D4 prev.* Laoet. *island*
  Borneo, C Indonesia
Laval *38 D4* Québec, SE Canada
Laval *90 B3* Mayenne, NW France
La Vall d'Uixó *93 F3 var.* Vall D'Uxó.
  Valenciana, E Spain
La Vega *55 E3 var.* Concepción de la
  Vega. C Dominican Republic
La Vila Joiosa *see* Villajoyosa
Lávrio *105 C6 prev.* Lávrion. Attikí,
  C Greece
Lávrion *see* Lávrio
Lawrence *41 G3* Massachusetts, NE USA
Lawrenceburg *42 C1* Tennessee, S USA
Lawton *49 F2* Oklahoma, C USA
La Yarada *61 E4* Tacna, SW Peru
Laylā *121 C5 var.* Laila. Ar Riyāḍ,
  C Saudi Arabia
Lazarev Sea *154 B1 sea* Antarctica
Lázaro Cárdenas *51 E5* Michoacán,
  SW Mexico
Leal *see* Lihula
Leamhcán *see* Lucan
Leamington *38 C5* Ontario, S Canada
Leavdnja *see* Lakselv
Lebak *139 E3* Mindanao, S Philippines
Lebanese Republic *see* Lebanon
Lebanon *45 G5* Missouri, C USA
Lebanon *41 G2* New Hampshire,
  NE USA
Lebanon *46 B3* Oregon, NW USA
Lebanon *118 A4 off.* Lebanese Republic,
  Ar. Al Lubnān, *Fr.* Liban. *country*
  SW Asia

LEBANON
Southwest Asia

Official name Republic of Lebanon
Formation 1941 / 1941
Capital Beirut
Population 4.3 million / 1089 people
  per sq mile (420 people per sq km)
Total area 4015 sq. miles (10,400 sq. km)
Languages Arabic*, French,
  Armenian, Assyrian
Religions Muslim 60%, Christian 39%,
  Other 1%
Ethnic mix Arab 95%, Armenian 4%,
  Other 1%
Government Parliamentary system
Currency Lebanese pound = 100 piastres
Literacy rate 90%
Calorie consumption 3153 kilocalories

Lebanon, Mount *see* Liban, Jebel
Lebap *122 D2* Lebapskiy Velayat,
  NE Turkmenistan
Lebedin *see* Lebedyn
Lebedyn *109 F2 Rus.* Lebedin. Sums'ka
  Oblast', NE Ukraine
Lębork *98 C2 var.* Lębórk, *Ger.*
  Lauenburg, Lauenburg in Pommern.
  Pomorskie, N Poland
Lebrija *92 C5* Andalucía, S Spain
Lebu *65 A5* Bío Bío, C Chile
le Cannet *91 D6* Alpes-Maritimes,
  SE France
Le Cap *see* Cap-Haïtien
Lecce *97 E6* Puglia, SE Italy
Lechainá *105 B6 var.* Lehena, Lekhainá.
  Dytikí Elláda, S Greece
Ledo Salinarius *see* Lons-le-Saunier
Leduc *37 E5* Alberta, SW Canada
Leech Lake *45 F2 lake* Minnesota, N USA
Leeds *89 D5* N England, United Kingdom
Leek *86 E2* Groningen, NE Netherlands
Leer *94 A3* Niedersachsen, NW Germany
Leeuwarden *86 D1 Fris.* Ljouwert.
  Fryslân, N Netherlands
Leeuwin, Cape *142 A5 headland*
  Western Australia
Leeward Islands *55 G3 island group*
  E West Indies
Leeward Islands *see* Sotavento, Ilhas de
Lefkáda *105 A5 prev.* Levkás.
  Lefkáda, Iónia Nisiá, Greece,
  C Mediterranean Sea
Lefkáda *105 A5 It.* Santa Maura, *prev.*
  Levkás; *anc.* Leucas. *island* Iónia Nisiá,
  Greece, C Mediterranean Sea
Lefká Óri *105 C7 mountain range* Kríti,
  Greece, E Mediterranean Sea
Lefkímmi *105 A5 var.* Levkímmi.
  Kérkyra, Iónia Nisiá, Greece,
  C Mediterranean Sea
Lefkosia/Lefkoşa *see* Nicosia
Legaceaster *see* Chester
Legaspi *see* Legazpi City

Leghorn see Livorno
Legnica 98 B4 Ger. Liegnitz.
Dolnośląskie, SW Poland
le Havre 90 B3 Eng. Havre; prev. le
Havre-de-Grâce. Seine-Maritime,
N France
le Havre-de-Grâce see le Havre
Lehena see Lechainá
Leicester 89 D6 Lat. Batae Coritanorum.
C England, United Kingdom
Leiden 86 B3 prev. Leyden; anc.
Lugdunum Batavorum. Zuid-Holland,
W Netherlands
Leie 90 D2 Fr. Lys. river Belgium/France
Leinster 89 B6 Ir. Cúige Laighean.
cultural region E Ireland
Leipsic see Leipzig
Leipsoí 105 E6 island Dodekánisa,
Greece, Aegean Sea
Leipzig 94 C4 Pol. Lipsk, hist. Leipsic;
anc. Lipsia. Sachsen, E Germany
Leiria 92 B3 anc. Collipo. Leiria,
C Portugal
Leirvik 85 A6 Hordaland, S Norway
Lek 86 C4 river SW Netherlands
Lekhainá see Lechainá
Lekhchevo 104 C2 Montana,
NW Bulgaria
Leksand 85 C5 Dalarna, C Sweden
Lel'chitsy see Lyel'chytsy
le Léman see Geneva, Lake
Lelystad 86 D3 Flevoland, C Netherlands
Léman, Lac see Geneva, Lake
le Mans 90 B3 Sarthe, NW France
Lemberg see L'viv
Lemesós 102 C5 var. Limassol.
SW Cyprus
Lemhi Range 46 D3 mountain range
Idaho, C USA North America
Lemnos see Límnos
Lemovices see Limoges
Lena 113 F3 river NE Russian Federation
Lena Tablemount 141 B7 seamount
S Indian Ocean
Len Dao 128 C8 island S Spratly Islands
Leninabad see Khujand
Leninakan see Gyumri
Lenine 109 G5 Rus. Lenino. Avtonomna
Respublika Krym, S Ukraine
Leningor see Leninogorsk
Leningrad see Sankt-Peterburg
Leningradskaya 154 B4 Russian research
station Antarctica
Lenino see Lenine, Ukraine
Leninobod see Khujand
Leninogorsk see Ridder
Leninpol' 123 F2 Talasskaya Oblast',
NW Kyrgyzstan
Lenin-Turkmenski see Türkmenabat
Lenkoran' see Länkäran
Lenti 99 B7 Zala, SW Hungary
Lentia see Linz
Leoben 95 E7 Steiermark, C Austria
León 51 E4 var. León de los Aldamas.
Guanajuato, C Mexico
León 52 C3 León, NW Nicaragua
León 92 D1 Castilla y León, NW Spain
León de los Aldamas see León
Leonídi see Leonídio
Leonídio 105 B6 var. Leonídi.
Pelopónnisos, S Greece
Léopold II, Lac see Mai-Ndombe, Lac
Léopoldville see Kinshasa
Lepe 92 C4 Andalucía, S Spain
Lepel' see Lyepyel'
le Portel 90 C2 Pas-de-Calais, N France
Le Puglie see Puglia
le Puy 91 C5 prev. le Puy-en-Velay, hist.
Anicium, Podium Anicensis. Haute-
Loire, C France
le Puy-en-Velay see le Puy
Léré 76 B4 Mayo-Kébbi, SW Chad
Lérida see Lleida
Lerma 92 D2 Castilla y León, N Spain
Leros 105 D6 island Dodekánisa, Greece,
Aegean Sea
Lerrnayin Gharabakh see
Nagorno-Karabakh
Lerwick 88 D1 NE Scotland, United
Kingdom
Lesbos 116 A3 anc. Lesbos. island
E Greece
Lesbos see Lésvos
Les Cayes see Cayes
Les Gonaïves see Gonaïves
Leshan 128 B5 Sichuan, C China
les Herbiers 90 B4 Vendée, NW France
Lesh/Leshi see Lezhë
Lesina see Hvar

Leskovac 101 E5 Serbia, SE Serbia
Lesnoy 114 C3 Sverdlovskaya Oblast',
C Russian Federation
Lesotho 78 D4 off. Kingdom of Lesotho;
prev. Basutoland. country S Africa

LESOTHO
Southern Africa

Official name Kingdom of Lesotho
Formation 1966 / 1966
Capital Maseru
Population 2.2 million / 188 people
per sq mile (72 people per sq km)
Total area 11,720 sq. miles (30,355 sq. km)
Languages English*, Sesotho*, isiZulu
Religions Christian 90%, Traditional
beliefs 10%
Ethnic mix Sotho 99%, European
and Asian 1%
Government Parliamentary system
Currency Loti & South African rand =
100 lisente
Literacy rate 90%
Calorie consumption 2371 kilocalories

Lesotho, Kingdom of see Lesotho
les Sables-d'Olonne 90 B4 Vendée,
NW France
Lesser Antarctica see West Antarctica
Lesser Antilles 55 G4 island group
E West Indies
Lesser Caucasus 117 F2 Rus. Malyy
Kavkaz. mountain range SW Asia
Lesser Khingan Range see Xiao Hinggan
Ling
Lesser Sunda Islands 139 E5 Eng.
Lesser Sunda Islands. island group
C Indonesia
Lesser Sunda Islands see Nusa Tenggara
Leszno 98 B4 Ger. Lissa. Wielkopolskie,
C Poland
Lethbridge 37 E5 Alberta, SW Canada
Lethem 59 F3 S Guyana
Leti, Kepulauan 139 F5 island group
E Indonesia
Letpadan 136 B4 Bago, SW Myanmar
(Burma)
Letsôk-aw Kyun 137 B6 var. Letsutan
Island; prev. Domel Island. island
Mergui Archipelago, S Myanmar
(Burma)
Letsutan Island see Letsôk-aw Kyun
Lettland see Latvia
Lëtzebuerg see Luxembourg
Leucas see Lefkáda
Leuven 87 C6 Fr. Louvain, Ger. Löwen.
Vlaams Brabant, C Belgium
Leuze-en-Hainaut 87 B6 var. Leuze.
Hainaut, SW Belgium
Léva see Levice
Levanger 84 B4 Nord-Trøndelag,
C Norway
Levelland 49 E2 Texas, SW USA
Leverkusen 94 A4 Nordrhein-Westfalen,
W Germany
Levice 99 C6 Ger. Lewentz, Hung. Léva,
Lewenz. Nitriansky Kraj, SW Slovakia
Levin 150 D4 Manawatu-Wanganui,
North Island, New Zealand
Levkás see Lefkáda
Levkímmi see Lefkímmi
Lewentz/Lewenz see Levice
Lewis, Isle of 88 B2 island NW Scotland,
United Kingdom
Lewis Range 44 B1 mountain range
Montana, NW USA
Lewiston 46 C2 Idaho, NW USA
Lewiston 41 G2 Maine, NE USA
Lewistown 44 C1 Montana,
NW USA
Lexington 40 C5 Kentucky, S USA
Lexington 45 E4 Nebraska, C USA
Leyden see Leiden
Leyte 139 F2 island C Philippines
Lezajsk 99 E5 Podkarpackie, SE Poland
Lezha see Lezhë
Lezhë 101 C6 var. Lezha; prev. Lesh,
Leshi. Lezhë, NW Albania
Lhasa 126 C5 var. La-sa, Lassa. Xizang
Zizhiqu, W China
Lhaviyani Atoll see Faadhippolhu Atoll
Lhazê 126 C5 var. Quxar. Xizang
Zizhiqu, China E Asia
L'Hospitalet de Llobregat 93 G2 var.
Hospitalet. Cataluña, NE Spain
Liancourt Rocks 131 A5 island group
Japan/South Korea

Lianyungang 128 D4 var. Xinpu.
Jiangsu, E China
Liao see Liaoning
Liaodong Wan 127 G3 Eng. Gulf of
Lantung, Gulf of Liaotung. gulf
NE China
Liao He 125 E1 river NE China
Liaoning 128 D3 var. Liao, Liaoning
Sheng, Shengking, hist. Fengtien,
Shenking. province NE China
Liaoning Sheng see Liaoning
Liaoyuan 129 E3 var. Dongliao, Shuang-
liao, Jap. Chengchiatun. Jilin, NE China
Liard see Fort Liard
Liban see Lebanon
Liban, Jebel 118 B4 Ar. Jabal al Gharbt,
Jabal Lubnân, Eng. Mount Lebanon.
mountain range C Lebanon
Libau see Liepāja
Libby 44 A1 Montana, NW USA
Liberal 45 E5 Kansas, C USA
Liberalitas Julia see Évora
Liberec 98 B4 Ger. Reichenberg.
Liberecký Kraj, N Czech Republic
Liberia 52 D4 Guanacaste, NW Costa
Rica
Liberia 74 C5 off. Republic of Liberia.
country W Africa

LIBERIA
West Africa

Official name Republic of Liberia
Formation 1847 / 1847
Capital Monrovia
Population 4.1 million / 110 people
per sq mile (43 people per sq km)
Total area 43,000 sq. miles (111,370 sq. km)
Languages Kpelle, Vai, Bassa, Kru, Grebo,
Kissi, Gola, Loma, English*
Religions Christian 40%, Traditional
beliefs 40%, Muslim 20%
Ethnic mix Indigenous tribes (12 groups)
49%, Kpelle 20%, Bassa 16%,
Gio 8%, Krou 7%
Government Presidential system
Currency Liberian dollar = 100 cents
Literacy rate 59%
Calorie consumption 2261 kilocalories

Liberia, Republic of see Liberia
Libian Desert see Libyan Desert
Libiyah, Aş Şahrā' al see Libyan Desert
Libourne 91 B5 Gironde, SW France
Libreville 77 A5 country capital (Gabon)
Estuaire, NW Gabon
Libya 71 F3 prev. Great Socialist People's
Libyan Arab Jamahiriya, Al Jamāhīrīya
al 'Arabīyah al Lībīyah ash Sha'bīyah
al Ishtirākīy, Libyan Arab Republic.
country N Africa

LIBYA
North Africa

Official name Libya
Formation 1951 / 1951
Capital Tripoli
Population 6.4 million / 9 people
per sq mile (4 people per sq km)
Total area 679,358 sq. miles
(1,759,540 sq. km)
Languages Arabic*, Tuareg
Religions Muslim (mainly Sunni) 97%,
Other 3%
Ethnic mix Arab and Berber 97%,
Other 3%
Government Transitional regime
Currency Libyan dinar = 1000 dirhams
Literacy rate 89%
Calorie consumption 3157 kilocalories

Libyan Arab Republic see Libya
Libyan Desert 71 H4 var. Libian Desert,
Ar. Aş Şahrā' al Lībīyah. desert N Africa
Libyan Plateau 103 F4 var. Ad Diffah.
plateau Egypt/Libya
Lichtenfels 95 C5 Bayern, SE Germany
Lichtenvoorde 86 E4 Gelderland,
E Netherlands
Lichuan 128 C5 Hubei, C China
Lida 107 B5 Hrodzyenskaya Voblasts',
W Belarus
Lidhoríkion see Lidoríki
Lidköping 85 B6 Västra Götaland,
S Sweden
Lidokhorikion see Lidoríki
Lidoríki 105 B5 prev. Lidhorikíon,
Lidokhorikion. Stereá Elláda, C Greece

Lidzbark Warmiński 98 D2 Ger.
Heilsberg. Olsztyn, N Poland
Liechtenstein 94 D1 off. Principality of
Liechtenstein. country C Europe

LIECHTENSTEIN
Central Europe

Official name Principality of
Liechtenstein
Formation 1719 / 1719
Capital Vaduz
Population 36,713 / 592 people
per sq mile (229 people per sq km)
Total area 62 sq. miles (160 sq. km)
Languages German*, Alemannish
dialect, Italian
Religions Roman Catholic 79%,
Other 13%, Protestant 8%
Ethnic mix Liechtensteiner 66%,
Other 12%, Swiss 10%, Austrian 6%,
German 3%, Italian 3%
Government Parliamentary system
Currency Swiss franc = 100 rappen/
centimes
Literacy rate 99%
Calorie consumption Not available

Liechtenstein, Principality of see
Liechtenstein
Liège 87 D6 Dut. Luik, Ger. Lüttich.
Liège, E Belgium
Liegnitz see Legnica
Lienz 95 D7 Tirol, W Austria
Liepāja 106 B3 Ger. Libau. W Latvia
Lietuva see Lithuania
Lievenhof see Līvāni
Liezen 95 D7 Steiermark, C Austria
Liffey 89 B6 river Ireland
Lifou 144 D5 island Îles Loyauté, E New
Caledonia
Liger see Loire
Ligure, Appennino 96 A2 Eng. Ligurian
Mountains. mountain range NW Italy
Ligure, Mar see Ligurian Sea
Ligurian Mountains see Ligure,
Appennino
Ligurian Sea 96 A3 Fr. Mer
Ligurienne, It. Mar Ligure. sea
N Mediterranean Sea
Ligurienne, Mer see Ligurian Sea
Lihu'e 47 A7 var. Lihue. Kaua'i,
Hawaii, USA
Lihue see Lihu'e
Lihula 106 D2 Ger. Leal. Läänemaa,
W Estonia
Liivi Laht see Riga, Gulf of
Likasi 77 D7 prev. Jadotville. Shaba,
SE Dem. Rep. Congo
Liknes 85 A6 Vest-Agder, S Norway
Lille 90 C2 var. l'Isle, Dut. Rijssel, Flem.
Ryssel, prev. Lisle; anc. Insula. Nord,
N France
Lillehammer 85 B5 Oppland, S Norway
Lillestrøm 85 B6 Akershus, S Norway
Lilongwe 79 E2 country capital (Malawi)
Central , W Malawi
Lilybaeum see Marsala
Lima 60 C4 country capital (Peru)
Lima, W Peru
Limanowa 99 D5 Małopolskie, S Poland
Limassol see Lemesós
Limerick 89 A6 Ir. Luimneach. Limerick,
SW Ireland
Limín Vathéos see Sámos
Límnos 103 F3 anc. Lemnos. island
E Greece
Limoges 91 C5 anc. Augustoritum
Lemovicensium, Lemovices. Haute-
Vienne, C France
Limón 53 E4 var. Puerto Limón. Limón,
E Costa Rica
Limón 52 D2 Colón, NE Honduras
Limonum see Poitiers
Limousin 91 C5 cultural region C France
Limoux 91 C6 Aude, S France
Limpopo 78 D3 var. Crocodile. river
S Africa
Linares 64 B4 Maule, C Chile
Linares 51 E3 Nuevo León, NE Mexico
Linares 92 D4 Andalucía, S Spain
Lincoln 89 D5 anc. Lindum, Lindum
Colonia. E England, United Kingdom
Lincoln 41 H2 Maine, NE USA
Lincoln 45 F4 state capital Nebraska, C
USA
Lincoln Sea 34 D2 sea Arctic Ocean
Linden 59 F3 E Guyana
Líndhos see Líndos

Lindi 73 D8 Lindi, SE Tanzania
Líndos 105 E7 var. Líndhos. Ródos, Dodekánisa, Greece, Aegean Sea
Lindum/Lindum Colonia see Lincoln
Line Islands 145 G3 island group E Kiribati
Lingeh see Bandar-e Lengeh
Lingen 94 A3 var. Lingen an der Ems. Niedersachsen, NW Germany
Lingen an der Ems see Lingen
Lingga, Kepulauan 138 B4 island group W Indonesia
Lingling 129 C6 prev. Yongzhou, Zhishan. Hunan, S China
Linköping 85 C6 Östergötland, S Sweden
Linz 95 D6 anc. Lentia. Oberösterreich, N Austria
Lion, Gulf of 91 C7 Eng. Gulf of Lion, Gulf of Lions; anc. Sinus Gallicus. gulf S France
Lion, Gulf of/Lions, Gulf of see Lion, Golfe du
Liozno see Lyozna
Lipari 97 D6 island Isole Eolie, S Italy
Lipari Islands/Lipari, Isole see Eolie, Isole
Lipetsk 111 B5 Lipetskaya Oblast', W Russian Federation
Lipno 98 C3 Kujawsko-pomorskie, C Poland
Lipova 108 A4 Hung. Lippa. Arad, W Romania
Lipovets' see Lypovets'
Lippa see Lipova
Lipsia/Lipsk see Leipzig
Lira 73 B6 N Uganda
Lisala 77 C5 Equateur, N Dem. Rep. Congo
Lisboa 92 B4 Eng. Lisbon; anc. Felicitas Julia, Olisipo. country capital (Portugal) Lisboa, W Portugal
Lisbon see Lisboa
Lisichansk see Lysychans'k
Lisieux 90 B3 anc. Noviomagus. Calvados, N France
Liski 111 B6 prev. Georgiu-Dezh. Voronezhskaya Oblast', W Russian Federation
Lisle/l'Isle see Lille
Lismore 149 E5 New South Wales, SE Australia
Lissa see Vis, Croatia
Lissa see Leszno, Poland
Lisse 86 C3 Zuid-Holland, W Netherlands
Litang 128 A5 var. Gaocheng. Sichuan, C China
Litani, Nahr el 119 B5 var. Nahr al Litant. river C Lebanon
Litant, Nahr al see Litani, Nahr el
Litauen see Lithuania
Lithgow 149 D6 New South Wales, SE Australia
Lithuania 106 B4 off. Republic of Lithuania, Ger. Litauen, Lith. Lietuva, Pol. Litwa, Rus. Litva; prev. Lithuanian SSR, Rus. Litovskaya SSR. country NE Europe

LITHUANIA
Northeast Europe

Official name Republic of Lithuania
Formation 1991 / 1991
Capital Vilnius
Population 3.3 million / 131 people per sq mile (51 people per sq km)
Total area 25,174 sq. miles (65,200 sq. km)
Languages Lithuanian*, Russian
Religions Roman Catholic 79%, Other 16%, Russian Orthodox 4%, Protestant 2%
Ethnic mix Lithuanian 85%, Polish 6%, Russian 5%, Other 3%, Belarussian 1%
Government Parliamentary system
Currency Litas = 100 centu
Literacy rate 99%
Calorie consumption 3486 kilocalories

Lithuanian SSR see Lithuania
Lithuania, Republic of see Lithuania
Litóchoro 104 B4 var. Litohoro, Litókhoron. Kentrikí Makedonía, N Greece
Litohoro/Litókhoron see Litóchoro
Litovskaya SSR see Lithuania

Little Alföld 99 C6 Ger. Kleines Ungarisches Tiefland, Hung. Kisalföld, Slvk. Podunajská Rovina. plain Hungary/Slovakia
Little Andaman 133 F2 island Andaman Islands, India, NE Indian Ocean
Little Barrier Island 150 D2 island N New Zealand
Little Bay 93 H5 bay Alboran Sea, Mediterranean Sea
Little Cayman 54 B3 island E Cayman Islands
Little Falls 45 F2 Minnesota, N USA
Littlefield 49 E2 Texas, SW USA
Little Inagua 54 D2 var. Inagua Islands. island S Bahamas
Little Minch, The 88 B3 strait NW Scotland, United Kingdom
Little Missouri River 44 D2 river NW USA
Little Nicobar 133 G3 island Nicobar Islands, India, NE Indian Ocean
Little Rhody see Rhode Island
Little Rock 42 B1 state capital Arkansas, C USA
Little Saint Bernard Pass 91 D5 Fr. Col du Petit St-Bernard, It. Colle del Piccolo San Bernardo. pass France/Italy
Little Sound 42 A5 bay Bermuda, NW Atlantic Ocean
Littleton 44 D4 Colorado, C USA
Littoria see Latina
Litva/Litwa see Lithuania
Liu-chou/Liuchow see Liuzhou
Liuzhou 128 C6 var. Liu-chou, Liuchow. Guangxi Zhuangzu Zizhiqu, S China
Livanátai see Livanátes
Livanátes 105 B5 prev. Livanátai. Stereá Elláda, C Greece
Līvāni 106 D4 Ger. Lievenhof. SE Latvia
Liverpool 39 F5 Nova Scotia, SE Canada
Liverpool 89 C5 NW England, United Kingdom
Livingston 44 B2 Montana, NW USA
Livingston 49 H4 Texas, SW USA
Livingstone 49 H3 var. Maramba. Southern, S Zambia
Livingstone 78 C3 var. Maramba. Southern, S Zambia
Livingstone Mountains 151 A7 mountain range South Island, New Zealand
Livno 100 B4 Federicija Bosna I Hercegovina, SW Bosnia and Herzegovina
Livojoki 84 D4 river C Finland
Livonia 40 D3 Michigan, N USA
Livorno 96 B3 Eng. Leghorn. Toscana, C Italy
Lixian Jiang see Black River
Lixoúri 105 A5 prev. Lixoúrion. Kefallinía, Iónia Nisiá, Greece, C Mediterranean Sea
Lixoúrion see Lixoúri
Lizarra see Estella
Ljouwert see Leeuwarden
Ljubelj see Loibl Pass
Ljubljana 95 D7 Ger. Laibach, It. Lubiana; anc. Aemona, Emona. country capital (Slovenia) C Slovenia
Ljungby 85 B7 Kronoberg, S Sweden
Ljusdal 85 C5 Gävleborg, C Sweden
Ljusnan 85 C5 river C Sweden
Llanelli 89 C6 prev. Llanelly. SW Wales, United Kingdom
Llanelly see Llanelli
Llanes 92 D1 Asturias, N Spain
Llanos 58 D2 physical region Colombia/Venezuela
Lleida 93 F2 Cast. Lérida; anc. Ilerda. Cataluña, NE Spain
Llucmajor 93 G3 Mallorca, Spain, W Mediterranean Sea
Loaita Island 128 C8 island W Spratly Islands
Loanda see Luanda
Lobatse 78 C4 var. Lobatsi. Kgatleng, SE Botswana
Lobatsi see Lobatse
Löbau 94 D4 Sachsen, E Germany
Lobito 78 B2 Benguela, W Angola
Lob Nor see Lop Nur
Lobositz see Lovosice
Loburi see Lop Buri
Locarno 95 B8 Ger. Luggarus. Ticino, S Switzerland
Lochem 86 E3 Gelderland, E Netherlands
Lockport 41 E3 New York, NE USA

Lodja 77 D6 Kasai-Oriental, C Dem. Rep. Congo
Lodwar 73 C6 Rift Valley, NW Kenya
Łódź 98 D4 Rus. Lodz. Łódź, C Poland
Loei 136 C4 var. Loey, Muang Loei. Loei, C Thailand
Loey see Loei
Lofoten 84 B3 var. Lofoten Islands. island group C Norway
Lofoten Islands see Lofoten
Logan 44 B3 Utah, W USA
Logan, Mount 36 D3 mountain Yukon Territory, W Canada
Logroño 93 E1 anc. Vareia, Lat. Juliobriga. La Rioja, N Spain
Loibl Pass 95 D7 Ger. Loiblpass, Slvn. Ljubelj. pass Austria/Slovenia
Loiblpass see Loibl Pass
Loikaw 136 B4 Kayah State, C Myanmar (Burma)
Loire 90 B4 var. Liger. river C France
Loja 60 B2 Loja, S Ecuador
Lokitaung 73 C5 Rift Valley, NW Kenya
Lokoja 75 G4 Kogi, C Nigeria
Loksa 106 E2 Ger. Loxa. Harjumaa, NW Estonia
Lolland 85 B8 prev. Laaland. island S Denmark
Lom 104 C1 prev. Lom-Palanka. Montana, NW Bulgaria
Lomami 77 D6 river C Dem. Rep. Congo
Lomas 60 D4 Arequipa, SW Peru
Lomas de Zamora 64 D4 Buenos Aires, E Argentina
Lombardia 96 B2 Eng. Lombardy. region N Italy
Lombardy see Lombardia
Lombok, Pulau 138 D5 island Nusa Tenggara, C Indonesia
Lomé 75 F5 country capital (Togo) S Togo
Lomela 77 D6 Kasai-Oriental, C Dem. Rep. Congo
Lommel 87 C5 Limburg, N Belgium
Lomond, Loch 88 B4 lake C Scotland, United Kingdom
Lomonosov Ridge 155 B3 var. Harris Ridge, Rus. Khrebet Homosova. undersea ridge Arctic Ocean
Lomonosova, Khrebet see Lomonosov Ridge
Lom-Palanka see Lom
Lompoc 47 B7 California, W USA
Lom Sak 136 C4 var. Muang Lom Sak. Phetchabun, C Thailand
Łomża 98 D3 Rus. Lomzha. Podlaskie, NE Poland
Lomzha see Łomża
Loncoche 65 B5 Araucanía, C Chile
Londinium see London
London 89 A7 anc. Augusta, Lat. Londinium. country capital (United Kingdom) SE England, United Kingdom
London 38 C5 Ontario, S Canada
London 40 C5 Kentucky, S USA
Londonderry 88 B4 var. Derry, Ir. Doire. NW Northern Ireland, United Kingdom
Londonderry, Cape 146 C2 cape Western Australia
Londrina 63 E4 Paraná, S Brazil
Lone Star State see Texas
Long Bay 43 F2 bay W Jamaica
Long Beach 47 C7 California, W USA
Longford 89 B5 Ir. An Longfort. Longford, C Ireland
Long Island 54 D2 island C Bahamas
Long Island 41 G4 island New York, NE USA
Longlac 38 C3 Ontario, S Canada
Longmont 44 D4 Colorado, C USA
Longreach 148 C4 Queensland, E Australia
Long Strait 115 G1 Eng. Long Strait. strait NE Russian Federation
Long Strait see Longa, Proliv
Longview 49 H3 Texas, SW USA
Longview 46 B2 Washington, NW USA
Long Xuyên 137 D6 var. Longxuyen. An Giang, S Vietnam
Longxuyen see Long Xuyên
Long Xuyen see Long Xuyên
Longyan 128 D6 Fujian, SE China
Longyearbyen 83 G2 dependent territory capital (Svalbard) Spitsbergen, W Svalbard
Lons-le-Saunier 90 D4 anc. Ledo Salinarius. Jura, E France
Lop Buri 137 C5 var. Loburi. Lop Buri, C Thailand

Lop Nor see Lop Nur
Lop Nur 126 C3 var. Lob Nor, Lop Nor, Lo-pu Po. seasonal lake NW China
Loppersum 86 E1 Groningen, NE Netherlands
Lo-pu Po see Lop Nur
Lorca 93 E4 Ar. Lurka; anc. Eliocroca, Lat. Illurco. Murcia, S Spain
Lord Howe Island 142 C4 island E Australia
Lord Howe Rise 142 C4 undersea rise SW Pacific Ocean
Loreto 50 B3 Baja California Sur, NW Mexico
Lorient 90 A3 prev. l'Orient. Morbihan, NW France
l'Orient see Lorient
Lorn, Firth of 88 B4 inlet W Scotland, United Kingdom
Loro Sae see East Timor
Lörrach 95 A7 Baden-Württemberg, S Germany
Lorraine 90 D3 cultural region NE France
Los Alamos 48 C1 New Mexico, SW USA
Los Amates 52 B2 Izabal, E Guatemala
Los Ángeles 65 B5 Bío Bío, C Chile
Los Angeles 47 C7 California, W USA
Losanna see Lausanne
Lošinj 100 A3 Ger. Lussin, It. Lussino. island W Croatia
Loslau see Wodzisław Śląski
Los Mochis 50 C3 Sinaloa, C Mexico
Losonc/Losontz see Lučenec
Los Roques, Islas 58 D1 island group N Venezuela
Lot 91 B5 cultural region S France
Lot 91 B5 river S France
Lotagipi Swamp 73 C5 wetland Kenya/Sudan
Lötzen see Giżycko
Loualaba see Lualaba
Louangnamtha 136 C3 var. Luong Nam Tha. Louang Namtha, N Laos
Louangphabang 124 D3 var. Louangphrabang, Luang Prabang. Louangphabang, N Laos
Louangphrabang see Louangphabang
Loubomo see Dolisie
Loudéac 90 A3 Côtes d'Armor, NW France
Loudi 128 C5 Hunan, S China
Louga 74 B3 NW Senegal
Louisiade Archipelago 144 B4 island group SE Papua New Guinea
Louisiana 42 A2 off. State of Louisiana, also known as Creole State, Pelican State. state S USA
Louisville 40 C5 Kentucky, S USA
Louisville Ridge 143 E4 undersea ridge S Pacific Ocean
Loup River 45 E4 river Nebraska, C USA
Lourdes 91 B6 Hautes-Pyrénées, S France
Lourenço Marques see Maputo
Louth 89 E5 E England, United Kingdom
Loutrá 104 C4 Kentrikí Makedonía, N Greece
Louvain see Leuven
Louvain-la Neuve 87 C6 Walloon Brabant, C Belgium
Louviers 90 C3 Eure, N France
Lovech 104 C2 Lovech, N Bulgaria
Loveland 44 D4 Colorado, C USA
Lovosice 98 A4 Ger. Lobositz. Ústecký Kraj, NW Czech Republic
Lóvua 78 C1 Moxico, E Angola
Lowell 41 G3 Massachusetts, NE USA
Löwen see Leuven
Lower California 48 A4 Eng. Lower California. peninsula NW Mexico
Lower California see Baja California
Lower Hutt 151 D5 Wellington, North Island, New Zealand
Lower Lough Erne 89 A5 lake SW Northern Ireland, United Kingdom
Lower Red Lake 45 F1 lake Minnesota, N USA
Lower Rhine see Neder Rijn
Lower Tunguska 115 E3 Eng. Lower Tunguska. river N Russian Federation
Lower Tunguska see Nizhnyaya Tunguska
Lowestoft 89 E6 E England, United Kingdom
Loxa see Loksa
Loyauté, Îles 144 D5 island group S New Caledonia
Loyev see Loyew

Loyew *107 D8 Rus.* Loyev. Homyel'skaya Voblasts', SE Belarus
Loznica *100 C3* Serbia, W Serbia
Lu *see* Shandong, China
Lualaba *77 D6 Fr.* Loualaba. *river* SE Dem. Rep. Congo
Luanda *78 A1 var.* Loanda, *Port.* São Paulo de Loanda. *country capital* (Angola) Luanda, NW Angola
Luang Prabang *see* Louangphabang
Luang, Thale *137 C7 lagoon* S Thailand
Luangua, Rio *see* Luangwa
Luangwa *73 B8 var.* Aruängua, Rio Luangua. *river* Mozambique/Zambia
Luanshya *78 D2* Copperbelt, C Zambia
Luarca *92 C1* Asturias, N Spain
Lubaczów *99 E5 var.* Lúbaczów. Podkarpackie, SE Poland
L'uban' *98 B4* Leningradskaya Oblast', Russian Federation
Lubānas Ezers *see* Lubāns
Lubango *78 B2 Port.* Sá da Bandeira. Huíla, SW Angola
Lubāns *106 D4 var.* Lubānas Ezers. *lake* E Latvia
Lubao *77 D6* Kasai-Oriental, C Dem. Rep. Congo
Lübben *94 D4* Brandenburg, E Germany
Lübbenau *94 D4* Brandenburg, E Germany
Lubbock *49 E2* Texas, SW USA
Lübeck *94 C2* Schleswig-Holstein, N Germany
Lubelska, Wyżyna *98 E4 plateau* SE Poland
Lüben *see* Lubin
Lubiana *see* Ljubljana
Lubin *98 B4 Ger.* Lüben. Dolnośląskie, SW Poland
Lublin *98 E4 Rus.* Lyublin. Lubelskie, E Poland
Lubliniec *98 C4* Śląskie, S Poland
Lubnān, Jabal *see* Liban, Jebel
Lubny *109 F2* Poltavs'ka Oblast', NE Ukraine
Lubsko *98 B4 Ger.* Sommerfeld. Lubuskie, W Poland
Lubumbashi *77 E8 prev.* Élisabethville. Shaba, SE Dem. Rep. Congo
Lubutu *77 D6* Maniema, E Dem. Rep. Congo
Luca *see* Lucca
Lucan *89 B5 Ir.* Leamhcán. Dublin, E Ireland
Lucanian Mountains *see* Lucano, Appennino
Lucano, Appennino *97 D5 Eng.* Lucanian Mountains. *mountain range* S Italy
Lucapa *78 C1 var.* Lukapa. Lunda Norte, NE Angola
Lucca *96 B3 anc.* Luca. Toscana, C Italy
Lucea *54 A4* W Jamaica
Lucena *139 E1 off.* Lucena City. Luzon, N Philippines
Lucena *92 D4* Andalucía, S Spain
Lucena City *see* Lucena
Lučenec *99 D6 Ger.* Losontz, *Hung.* Losoncz. Banskobystrický Kraj, C Slovakia
Lucentum *see* Alicante
Lucerna/Lucerne *see* Luzern
Luchow *see* Hefei
Łuck *see* Luts'k
Lucknow *135 E3 var.* Lakhnau. *state capital* Uttar Pradesh, N India
Lüda *see* Dalian
Luda Kamchiya *104 D2 river* E Bulgaria
Ludasch *see* Luduş
Lüderitz *78 B4 prev.* Angra Pequena. Karas, SW Namibia
Ludhiāna *134 D2* Punjab, N India
Ludington *40 C2* Michigan, N USA
Ludsan *see* Ludza
Luduş *108 B4 Ger.* Ludasch, *Hung.* Marosludas. Mureş, C Romania
Ludvika *85 C6* Dalarna, C Sweden
Ludwigsburg *95 B6* Baden-Württemberg, SW Germany
Ludwigsfelde *94 D3* Brandenburg, NE Germany
Ludwigshafen *95 B5 var.* Ludwigshafen am Rhein. Rheinland-Pfalz, W Germany
Ludwigshafen am Rhein *see* Ludwigshafen
Ludwigslust *94 C3* Mecklenburg-Vorpommern, N Germany
Ludza *106 D4 Ger.* Ludsan. E Latvia

Luebo *77 C6* Kasai-Occidental, SW Dem. Rep. Congo
Luena *78 C2 var.* Lwena, *Port.* Luso. Moxico, E Angola
Lufira *77 E7 river* SE Dem. Rep. Congo
Lufkin *49 H3* Texas, SW USA
Luga *110 A4* Leningradskaya Oblast', NW Russian Federation
Lugano *95 B8 Ger.* Lauis. Ticino, S Switzerland
Lugansk *see* Luhans'k
Lugdunum *see* Lyon
Lugdunum Batavorum *see* Leiden
Lugenda, Rio *79 E2 river* N Mozambique
Luggarus *see* Locarno
Lugh Ganana *see* Luuq
Lugo *92 C1 anc.* Lugus Augusti. Galicia, NW Spain
Lugoj *108 A4 Ger.* Lugosch, *Hung.* Lugos. Timiş, W Romania
Lugos/Lugosch *see* Lugoj
Lugus Augusti *see* Lugo
Luguvallium/Luguvallum *see* Carlisle
Luhans'k *109 H3 Rus.* Lugansk; *prev.* Voroshilovgrad. Luhans'ka Oblast', E Ukraine
Luimneach *see* Limerick
Lukapa *see* Lucapa
Lukenie *77 C6 river* C Dem. Rep. Congo
Lukovit *104 C2* Lovech, N Bulgaria
Łuków *98 E4 Ger.* Bogendorf. Lubelskie, E Poland
Lukuga *77 D7 river* SE Dem. Rep. Congo
Luleå *84 D4* Norrbotten, N Sweden
Luleälven *84 C3 river* N Sweden
Lulonga *77 C5 river* NW Dem. Rep. Congo
Lulua *77 D7 river* S Dem. Rep. Congo
Luluabourg *see* Kananga
Lumber State *see* Dugi Otok
Lumbo *79 F2* Nampula, NE Mozambique
Lumsden *151 A7* Southland, South Island, New Zealand
Lund *85 B7* Skåne, S Sweden
Lüneburg *94 C3* Niedersachsen, N Germany
Lunga, Isola *see* Dugi Otok
Lungkiang *see* Qiqihar
Lungué-Bungo *78 C2 var.* Lungwebungu. *river* Angola/Zambia
Lungwebungu *see* Lungué-Bungo
Luninets *see* Luninyets
Łuniniec *see* Luninyets
Luninyets *107 B7 Pol.* Łuniniec, *Rus.* Luninets. Brestskaya Voblasts', SW Belarus
Lunteren *86 D4* Gelderland, C Netherlands
Luong Nam Tha *see* Louangnamtha
Luoyang *128 C4 var.* Honan, Lo-yang. Henan, C China
Lupatia *see* Altamura
Lúrio *79 F2* Nampula, NE Mozambique
Lúrio, Rio *79 E2 river* NE Mozambique
Lurka *see* Lorca
Lusaka *78 D2 country capital* (Zambia) Lusaka, SE Zambia
Lushnja *see* Lushnjë
Lushnjë *101 C6 var.* Lushnja. Fier, C Albania
Luso *see* Luena
Lussin/Lussino *see* Lošinj
Lūt, Baḥrat/Lut, Bahret *see* Dead Sea
Lut, Dasht-e *120 D3 var.* Kavīr-e Lūt. *desert* E Iran
Lutetia/Lutetia Parisiorum *see* Paris
Lūt, Kavīr-e *see* Lut, Dasht-e
Luton *89 D6* E England, United Kingdom
Łutselk'e *37 F4 prev.* Snowdrift. Northwest Territories, W Canada
Luts'k *108 C1 Pol.* Łuck, *Rus.* Lutsk. Volyns'ka Oblast', NW Ukraine
Lutsk *see* Luts'k
Lüttich *see* Liège
Lutzow-Holm Bay *154 C2 var.* Lutzow-Holm Bay. *bay* Antarctica
Lützow-Holm Bay *see* Lützow Holmbukta
Luuq *73 D6 It.* Lugh Ganana. Gedo, SW Somalia
Luvua *77 D7 river* SE Dem. Rep. Congo
Luwego *73 C8 river* S Tanzania
Luxembourg *87 D8 country capital* (Luxembourg) Luxembourg, S Luxembourg
Luxembourg *87 D8 off.* Grand Duchy of Luxembourg, *var.* Lëtzebuerg, Luxemburg. *country* NW Europe

LUXEMBOURG
Northwest Europe

Official name Grand Duchy of Luxembourg
Formation 1867 / 1867
Capital Luxembourg-Ville
Population 500,000 / 501 people per sq mile (193 people per sq km)
Total area 998 sq. miles (2586 sq. km)
Languages Luxembourgish*, German*, French*
Religions Roman Catholic 97%, Protestant, Orthodox Christian, and Jewish 3%
Ethnic mix Luxembourger 62%, Foreign residents 38%
Government Parliamentary system
Currency Euro = 100 cents
Literacy rate 99%
Calorie consumption 3637 kilocalories

Luxemburg *see* Luxembourg
Luxor *72 B2 Ar.* Al Uqsur. E Egypt
Luza *110 C4* Kirovskaya Oblast', NW Russian Federation
Luz, Costa de la *92 C5 coastal region* SW Spain
Luzern *95 B7 Fr.* Lucerne, *It.* Lucerna. Luzern, C Switzerland
Luzon *139 E1 island* N Philippines
Luzon Strait *125 E3 strait* Philippines/ Taiwan
L'viv *108 B2 Ger.* Lemberg, *Pol.* Lwów, *Rus.* L'vov. L'vivs'ka Oblast', W Ukraine
L'vov *see* L'viv
Lwena *see* Luena
Lwów *see* L'viv
Lyakhavichy *107 B6 Rus.* Lyakhovichi. Brestskaya Voblasts', SW Belarus
Lyakhovichi *see* Lyakhavichy
Lyallpur *see* Faisalābād
Lyangar *see* Langar
Lyck *see* Ełk
Lycksele *84 C4* Västerbotten, N Sweden
Lycopolis *see* Asyūt
Lyel'chytsy *107 C7 Rus.* Lel'chitsy. Homyel'skaya Voblasts', SE Belarus
Lyepyel' *107 D5 Rus.* Lepel'. Vitsyebskaya Voblasts', N Belarus
Lyme Bay *89 C7 bay* S England, United Kingdom
Lynchburg *41 E5* Virginia, NE USA
Lynn *see* King's Lynn
Lynn Lake *37 F4* Manitoba, C Canada
Lynn Regis *see* King's Lynn
Lyon *91 D5 Eng.* Lyons; *anc.* Lugdunum. Rhône, E France
Lyons *see* Lyon
Lyozna *107 E6 Rus.* Liozno. Vitsyebskaya Voblasts', NE Belarus
Lypovets' *108 D2 Rus.* Lipovets. Vinnyts'ka Oblast', C Ukraine
Lys *see* Leie
Lysychans'k *109 H3 Rus.* Lisichansk. Luhans'ka Oblast', E Ukraine
Lyttelton *151 C6* South Island, New Zealand
Lyublin *see* Lublin
Lyubotin *see* Lyubotyn
Lyubotyn *109 G2 Rus.* Lyubotin. Kharkivs'ka Oblast', E Ukraine
Lyulyakovo *104 E2 prev.* Keremitlik. Burgas, E Bulgaria
Lyusina *107 B6 Rus.* Lyusino. Brestskaya Voblasts', SW Belarus
Lyusino *see* Lyusina

M

Maale *see* Male'
Ma'ān *119 B7* Ma'ān, SW Jordan
Maardu *106 D2 Ger.* Maart. Harjumaa, NW Estonia
Ma'aret-en-Nu'man *see* Ma'arrat an Nu'mān
Ma'arrat an Nu'mān *118 B3 var.* Ma'aret-en-Nu'man, *Fr.* Maarret enn Naamâne. Idlib, NW Syria
Maarret enn Naamâne *see* Ma'arrat an Nu'mān
Maart *see* Maardu
Maas *see* Meuse
Maaseik *87 D5 prev.* Maeseyck. Limburg, NE Belgium

Maastricht *87 D6 var.* Maestricht; *anc.* Traiectum ad Mosam, Traiectum Tungorum. Limburg, SE Netherlands
Macao *129 C6 Chin.* Aomen, *Port.* Macau. Guangdong, SE China
Macapá *63 E1 state capital* Amapá, N Brazil
Macarsca *see* Makarska
Macassar *see* Makassar
Macău *see* Makó, Hungary
Macau *see* Macao
MacCluer Gulf *see* Berau, Teluk
Macdonnell Ranges *146 D4 mountain range* Northern Territory, C Australia
Macedonia *see* Macedonia, FYR
Macedonia, FYR *101 D6 off.* the Former Yugoslav Republic of Macedonia, *var.* Macedonia, *Mac.* Makedonija, *abbrev.* FYR Macedonia, FYROM. *country* SE Europe

MACEDONIA
Southeast Europe

Official name Republic of Macedonia
Formation 1991 / 1991
Capital Skopje
Population 2.1 million / 212 people per sq mile (82 people per sq km)
Total area 9781 sq. miles (25,333 sq. km)
Languages Macedonian*, Albanian*, Turkish, Romani, Serbian
Religions Orthodox Christian 65%, Muslim 29%, Roman Catholic 4%, Other 2%
Ethnic mix Macedonian 64%, Albanian 25%, Turkish 4%, Roma 3%, Serb 2%, Other 2%
Government Mixed presidential–parliamentary system
Currency Macedonian denar = 100 deni
Literacy rate 97%
Calorie consumption 2983 kilocalories

Macedonia, the Former Yugoslav Republic of *see* Macedonia, FYR
Maceió *63 G3 state capital* Alagoas, E Brazil
Machachi *60 B1* Pichincha, C Ecuador
Machala *60 B2* El Oro, SW Ecuador
Machanga *79 E3* Sofala, E Mozambique
Machilipatnam *132 D1 var.* Bandar Masulipatnam. Andhra Pradesh, E India
Machiques *58 C2* Zulia, NW Venezuela
Macías Nguema Biyogo *see* Bioco, Isla de
Măcin *108 D5* Tulcea, SE Romania
Mackay *148 D4* Queensland, NE Australia
Mackay, Lake *146 C4 salt lake* Northern Territory/Western Australia
Mackenzie *37 E3 river* Northwest Territories, NW Canada
Mackenzie Bay *154 D3 bay* Antarctica
Mackenzie Mountains *36 D3 mountain range* Northwest Territories, NW Canada
Macleod, Lake *146 A4 lake* Western Australia
Macomb *40 A4* Illinois, N USA
Macomer *97 A5* Sardegna, Italy, C Mediterranean Sea
Mâcon *91 D5 anc.* Matisco, Matisco Ædourum. Saône-et-Loire, C France
Macon *42 D2* Georgia, SE USA
Macon *45 G4* Missouri, C USA
Macquarie Ridge *154 C5 undersea ridge* SW Pacific Ocean
Macuspana *51 G4* Tabasco, SE Mexico
Ma'dabā *119 B6 var.* Mādabā, Madeba; *anc.* Medeba. Ma'dabā, NW Jordan
Mādabā *see* Ma'dabā
Madagascar *79 F3 off.* Democratic Republic of Madagascar, *Malg.* Madagasikara; *prev.* Malagasy Republic. *country* W Indian Ocean

MADAGASCAR
Indian Ocean

Official name Republic of Madagascar
Formation 1960 / 1960
Capital Antananarivo
Population 21.3 million / 95 people per sq mile (37 people per sq km)
Total area 226,656 sq. miles (587,040 sq. km)
Languages Malagasy*, French*, English*
Religions Traditional beliefs 52%,

MADAGASCAR
(continued)

Christian (mainly Roman Catholic) 41%, Muslim 7%
Ethnic mix Other Malay 46%, Merina 26%, Betsimisaraka 15%, Betsileo 12%, Other 1%
Government Transitional regime
Currency Ariary = 5 iraimbilanja
Literacy rate 64%
Calorie consumption 2117 kilocalories

Madagascar 79 F3 *island* W Indian Ocean
Madagascar Basin 69 E7 *undersea basin* W Indian Ocean
Madagascar, Democratic Republic of *see* Madagascar
Madagascar Plateau 69 E7 *var.* Madagascar Ridge, Madagascar Rise, *Rus.* Madagaskarskiy Khrebet. *undersea plateau* W Indian Ocean
Madagascar Rise/Madagascar Ridge *see* Madagascar Plateau
Madagasikara *see* Madagascar
Madagaskarskiy Khrebet *see* Madagascar Plateau
Madang 144 B3 Madang, N Papua New Guinea
Madaniyīn *see* Médenine
Madarska *see* Hungary
Made 86 C4 Noord-Brabant, S Netherlands
Madeba *see* Ma'dabā
Madeira 70 A2 *var.* Ilha de Madeira. *island* Madeira, Portugal, NE Atlantic Ocean
Madeira, Ilha de *see* Madeira
Madeira Plain 66 C3 *abyssal plain* E Atlantic Ocean
Madeira, Rio 62 D2 *var.* Río Madera. *river* Bolivia/Brazil
Madeleine, Îles de la 39 F4 *Eng.* Magdalen Islands. *island group* Québec, E Canada
Madera 47 B6 California, W USA
Madera, Río *see* Madeira, Rio
Madhya Pradesh 135 E4 *prev.* Central Provinces and Berar. *cultural region* C India
Madīnat ath Thawrah 118 C2 *var.* Ath Thawrah. Ar Raqqah, N Syria
Madioen *see* Madiun
Madison 45 F3 South Dakota, N USA
Madison 40 B3 *state capital* Wisconsin, N USA
Madiun 138 D5 *prev.* Madioen. Jawa, C Indonesia
Madoera *see* Madura, Pulau
Madona 106 D4 *Ger.* Modohn. E Latvia
Madras *see* Tamil Nādu
Madras *see* Chennai
Madre de Dios, Río 61 E3 *river* Bolivia/Peru
Madre del Sur, Sierra 51 E5 *mountain range* S Mexico
Madre, Laguna 51 F3 *lagoon* NE Mexico
Madre, Laguna 49 G5 *lagoon* Texas, SW USA
Madre Occidental, Sierra 50 C3 *var.* Western Sierra Madre. *mountain range* C Mexico
Madre Oriental, Sierra 51 E3 *var.* Eastern Sierra Madre. *mountain range* C Mexico
Madre, Sierra 52 B2 *var.* Sierra de Soconusco. *mountain range* Guatemala/Mexico
Madrid 92 D3 *country capital* (Spain) Madrid, C Spain
Madura *see* Madurai
Madurai 132 C3 *prev.* Madura, Mathurai. Tamil Nādu, S India
Madura, Pulau 138 D5 *prev.* Madoera. *island* C Indonesia
Maebashi 131 G5 *var.* Maebasi, Mayebashi. Gunma, Honshū, S Japan
Maebasi *see* Maebashi
Mae Nam Khong *see* Mekong
Mae Nam Nan 136 C4 *river* NW Thailand
Mae Nam Yom 136 C4 *river* W Thailand
Maeseyck *see* Maaseik
Maestricht *see* Maastricht
Maéwo 144 D4 *var.* Aurora. *island* C Vanuatu
Mafia 73 D7 *island* E Tanzania

Mafraq/Muḥāfaẓat al Mafraq *see* Al Mafraq
Magadan 115 G3 Magadanskaya Oblast', E Russian Federation
Magallanes *see* Punta Arenas
Magallanes, Estrecho de *see* Magellan, Strait of
Magangué 58 B2 Bolívar, N Colombia
Magdalena 61 F3 El Beni, N Bolivia
Magdalena 50 B1 Sonora, NW Mexico
Isla Magdalena 50 B3 *island* NW Mexico
Magdalena, Río 58 B2 *river* C Colombia
Magdalen Islands *see* Madeleine, Îles de la
Magdeburg 94 C4 Sachsen-Anhalt, C Germany
Magelang 138 C5 Jawa, C Indonesia
Magellan, Strait of 65 B8 *Sp.* Estrecho de Magallanes. *strait* Argentina/Chile
Magerøy *see* Magerøya
Magerøya 84 D1 *var.* Magerøy, *Lapp.* Máhkarávju. *island* N Norway
Maggiore, Lago *see* Maggiore, Lake
Maggiore, Lake 96 B1 *It.* Lago Maggiore. *lake* Italy/Switzerland
Maglaj 100 C3 Federacija Bosna I Hercegovina, N Bosnia and Herzegovina
Maglie 97 E6 Puglia, SE Italy
Magna 44 B4 Utah, W USA
Magnesia *see* Manisa
Magnitogorsk 114 B4 Chelyabinskaya Oblast', C Russian Federation
Magnolia State *see* Mississippi
Magta' Lahjar 74 C3 *var.* Magta Lahjar, Magta' Lahjar, Magtá Lahjar. Brakna, SW Mauritania
Magway 136 A3 *var.* Magwe. Magway, W Myanmar (Burma)
Magwe *see* Magway
Magyar-Becse *see* Bečej
Magyarkanizsa *see* Kanjiža
Magyarország *see* Hungary
Mahajanga 79 F2 *var.* Majunga. Mahajanga, NW Madagascar
Mahakam, Sungai 138 D4 *var.* Koetai, Kutai. *river* Borneo, C Indonesia
Mahalapye 78 D3 *var.* Mahalatswe. Central, SE Botswana
Mahalatswe *see* Mahalapye
Māhān 120 D3 Kermān, E Iran
Mahanādi 135 F4 *river* E India
Mahārāshtra 134 D5 *cultural region* W India
Mahbés *see* El Mahbas
Mahbūbnagar 134 D5 Andhra Pradesh, C India
Mahdia 71 F2 *var.* Al Mahdīyah, Mehdia. NE Tunisia
Mahé 79 H1 *island* Inner Islands, NE Seychelles
Mahia Peninsula 150 E4 *peninsula* North Island, New Zealand
Mahilyow 107 D6 *Rus.* Mogilëv. Mahilyowskaya Voblasts', E Belarus
Máhkarávju *see* Magerøya
Mahmūd-e 'Erāqī *see* Mahmūd-e Rāqī
Mahmūd-e Rāqī 123 E4 *var.* Mahmūd-e 'Erāqī. Kāpīsā, NE Afghanistan
Mahón *see* Maó
Mähren *see* Moravia
Mährisch-Weisskirchen *see* Hranice
Maicao 58 C1 La Guajira, N Colombia
Mai Ceu/Mai Chio *see* Maych'ew
Maïdān Shahr 123 E4 *var.* Maydān Shahr; *prev.* Meydān Shahr. Wardak, E Afghanistan
Maidstone 89 E7 SE England, United Kingdom
Maiduguri 75 H4 Borno, NE Nigeria
Mailand *see* Milano
Maimāna *see* Maïmanah
Maïmanah 122 D3 *var.* Maimāna, Maymana; *prev.* Maymaneh. Fāryāb, NW Afghanistan
Main 95 B5 *river* C Germany
Mai-Ndombe, Lac 77 C6 *prev.* Lac Léopold II. *lake* W Dem. Rep. Congo
Maine 41 G2 *off.* State of Maine, *also known as* Lumber State, Pine Tree State. *state* NE USA
Maine 90 B3 *cultural region* NW France
Maine, Gulf of 41 H2 *gulf* NE USA
Mainland 88 C2 *island* N Scotland, United Kingdom
Mainland 88 D1 *island* NE Scotland, United Kingdom
Mainz 95 B5 *Fr.* Mayence. Rheinland-Pfalz, SW Germany

Maio 74 A3 *var.* Mayo. *island* Ilhas de Sotavento, SE Cape Verde
Maisur *see* Mysore, India
Maisur *see* Karnātaka, India
Maizhokunggar 126 C5 Xizang Zizhiqu, W China
Majorca 93 G3 *Eng.* Majorca; *anc.* Baleares Major. *island* Islas Baleares, Spain, W Mediterranean Sea
Majorca *see* Mallorca
Mājro *see* Majuro Atoll
Majunga *see* Mahajanga
Majuro Atoll 144 D2 *var.* Mājro. *atoll* Ratak Chain, SE Marshall Islands
Makale *see* Mek'elē
Makarov Basin 155 B3 *undersea basin* Arctic Ocean
Makarska 100 B4 *It.* Macarsca. Split-Dalmacija, SE Croatia
Makasar *see* Makassar
Makasar, Selat *see* Makassar Straits
Makassar 139 E4 *var.* Macassar, Makasar; *prev.* Ujungpandang. Sulawesi, C Indonesia
Makassar Straits 138 D4 *Ind.* Makasar Selat. *strait* C Indonesia
Makay 79 F3 *var.* Massif du Makay. *mountain range* SW Madagascar
Makay, Massif du *see* Makay
Makedonija *see* Macedonia, FYR
Makeni 74 C4 C Sierra Leone
Makeyevka *see* Makiyivka
Makhachkala 114 A4 *prev.* Petrovsk-Port. Respublika Dagestan, SW Russian Federation
Makin 144 D2 *prev.* Pitt Island. *atoll* Tungaru, W Kiribati
Makira *see* San Cristobal
Makiyivka 109 G3 *Rus.* Makeyevka; *prev.* Dmitriyevsk. Donets'ka Oblast', E Ukraine
Makkah 121 A5 *Eng.* Mecca. Makkah, W Saudi Arabia
Makkovik 39 F2 Newfoundland and Labrador, NE Canada
Makó 99 D7 *Rom.* Macău. Csongrád, SE Hungary
Makoua 77 B5 Cuvette, C Congo
Makran Coast 120 E4 *coastal region* SE Iran
Makrany 107 A6 *Rus.* Mokrany. Brestskaya Voblasts', SW Belarus
Mākū 120 B2 Āzarbāyjān-e Gharbī, NW Iran
Makurdi 75 G4 Benue, C Nigeria
Mala *see* Malaita, Solomon Islands
Malabār Coast 132 B3 *coast* SW India
Malabo 77 A5 *prev.* Santa Isabel. *country capital* (Equatorial Guinea) Isla de Bioco, NW Equatorial Guinea
Malaca *see* Málaga
Malacca, Strait of 138 B3 *Ind.* Selat Malaka. *strait* Indonesia/Malaysia
Malacka *see* Malacky
Malacky 99 C6 *Hung.* Malacka. Bratislavský Kraj, W Slovakia
Maladzyechna 107 C5 *Pol.* Molodeczno, *Rus.* Molodechno. Minskaya Voblasts', C Belarus
Málaga 92 D5 *anc.* Malaca. Andalucía, S Spain
Malagarasi River 73 B7 *river* W Tanzania Africa
Malagasy Republic *see* Madagascar
Malaita 144 C3 *var.* Mala. *island* N Solomon Islands
Malakal 73 B5 Upper Nile, NE South Sudan
Malakula *see* Malekula
Malang 138 D5 Jawa, C Indonesia
Malange *see* Malanje
Malanje 78 B1 *var.* Malange. Malanje, NW Angola
Mälaren 85 C6 *lake* C Sweden
Malatya 117 E4 *anc.* Melitene. Malatya, SE Turkey
Mala Vyska 109 E3 *Rus.* Malaya Viska. Kirovohrads'ka Oblast', S Ukraine
Malawi 79 E1 *off.* Republic of Malawi; *prev.* Nyasaland, Nyasaland Protectorate. *country* S Africa

MALAWI
Southern Africa

Official name Republic of Malawi
Formation 1964 / 1964
Capital Lilongwe
Population 15.4 million / 424 people

MALAWI
(continued)

per sq mile (164 people per sq km)
Total area 45,745 sq. miles (118,480 sq. km)
Languages Chewa, Lomwe, Yao, Ngoni, English*
Religions Protestant 55%, Roman Catholic 20%, Muslim 20%, Traditional beliefs 5%
Ethnic mix Bantu 99%, Other 1%
Government Presidential system
Currency Malawi kwacha = 100 tambala
Literacy rate 74%
Calorie consumption 2318 kilocalories

Malawi, Lake *see* Nyasa, Lake
Malaŵi, Republic of *see* Malawi
Malaya Viska *see* Mala Vyska
Malay Peninsula 124 D4 *peninsula* Malaysia/Thailand
Malaysia 138 B3 *off.* Malaysia, *var.* Federation of Malaysia; *prev.* separate territories of Federation of Malaya, Sarawak and Sabah (North Borneo) and Singapore. *country* SE Asia

MALAYSIA
Southeast Asia

Official name Federation of Malaysia
Formation 1963 / 1965
Capital Kuala Lumpur; Putrajaya (administrative)
Population 28.9 million / 228 people per sq mile (88 people per sq km)
Total area 127,316 sq. miles (329,750 sq. km)
Languages Bahasa Malaysia*, Malay, Chinese, Tamil, English
Religions Muslim (mainly Sunni) 61%, Buddhist 19%, Christian 9%, Hindu 6%, Other 5%
Ethnic mix Malay 53%, Chinese 26%, Indigenous tribes 12%, Indian 8%, Other 1%
Government Parliamentary system
Currency Ringgit = 100 sen
Literacy rate 93%
Calorie consumption 2902 kilocalories

Malaysia, Federation of *see* Malaysia
Malbork 98 C2 *Ger.* Marienburg, Marienburg in Westpreussen. Pomorskie, N Poland
Malchin 94 C3 Mecklenburg-Vorpommern, N Germany
Malden 45 H5 Missouri, C USA
Malden Island 145 G3 *prev.* Independence Island. *atoll* E Kiribati
Maldives 132 A4 *off.* Maldivian Divehi, Republic of Maldives. *country* N Indian Ocean

MALDIVES
Indian Ocean

Official name Republic of Maldives
Formation 1965 / 1965
Capital Male'
Population 394,491 / 3400 people per sq mile (1315 people per sq km)
Total area 116 sq. miles (300 sq. km)
Languages Dhivehi (Maldivian)*, Sinhala, Tamil, Arabic
Religions Sunni Muslim 100%
Ethnic mix Arab–Sinhalese–Malay 100%
Government Presidential system
Currency Rufiyaa = 100 laari
Literacy rate 97%
Calorie consumption 2720 kilocalories

Maldives, Republic of *see* Maldives
Maldivian Divehi *see* Maldives
Male' 132 B4 *Div.* Male. *country capital* (Maldives) Male' Atoll, C Maldives
Male' Atoll 132 A4 *var.* Kaafu Atoll. *atoll* C Maldives
Malekula 144 D4 *var.* Malakula; *prev.* Mallicolo. *island* W Vanuatu
Malesína 105 C5 Stereá Elláda, E Greece
Malheur Lake 46 C3 *lake* Oregon, NW USA
Mali 75 E3 *off.* Republic of Mali, *Fr.* République du Mali; *prev.* French Sudan, Sudanese Republic. *country* W Africa

MALI
West Africa

Official name Republic of Mali
Formation 1960 / 1960
Capital Bamako
Population 15.8 million / 34 people
per sq mile (13 people per sq km)
Total area 478,764 sq. miles
(1,240,000 sq. km)
Languages Bambara, Fulani, Senufo,
Soninke, French*
Religions Muslim (mainly Sunni) 90%,
Traditional beliefs 6%, Christian 4%
Ethnic mix Bambara 52%, Other 14%,
Fulani 11%, Saracolé 7%, Soninka 7%,
Tuareg 5%, Mianka 4%
Government Transitional regime
Currency CFA franc = 100 centimes
Literacy rate 23%
Calorie consumption 2624 kilocalories

Malik, Wadi al *see* Milk, Wadi el
Mali Kyun 137 B5 *var.* Tavoy Island.
  island Mergui Archipelago, S Myanmar
  (Burma)
Malin *see* Malyn
Malindi 73 D7 Coast, SE Kenya
Malines *see* Mechelen
Mali, Républic of *see* Mali
Mali, République du *see* Mali
Malkiye *see* Al Mālikīyah
Malko Tŭrnovo 104 E3 Burgas,
  E Bulgaria
Mallaig 88 B3 N Scotland, United
  Kingdom
Mallawi 72 B2 *var.* Mallawi. C Egypt
Mallawi *see* Mallawi
Mallicolo *see* Malekula
Malmberget 84 C3 *Lapp.* Malmivaara.
  Norrbotten, N Sweden
Malmédy 87 D6 Liège, E Belgium
Malmivaara *see* Malmberget
Malmö 85 B7 Skåne, S Sweden
Maloelap *see* Maloelap Atoll
Maloelap Atoll 144 D1 *var.* Maḷoeḷap.
  atoll E Marshall Islands
Małopolska, Wyżyna 98 D4 *plateau*
  S Poland
Malozemel'skaya Tundra 110 D3
  physical region NW Russian Federation
Malta 106 D4 SE Latvia
Malta 44 C1 Montana, NW USA
Malta 97 C8 *off.* Republic of Malta.
  country C Mediterranean Sea

MALTA
Southern Europe

Official name Republic of Malta
Formation 1964 / 1964
Capital Valletta
Population 400,000 / 3226 people
per sq mile (1250 people per sq km)
Total area 122 sq. miles (316 sq. km)
Languages Maltese*, English*
Religions Roman Catholic 98%,
Other and nonreligious 2%
Ethnic mix Maltese 96%, Other 4%
Government Parliamentary system
Currency Euro = 100 cents
Literacy rate 92%
Calorie consumption 3438 kilocalories

Malta 97 C8 *island* Malta,
  C Mediterranean Sea
Malta, Canale di *see* Malta Channel
Malta Channel 97 C8 *It.* Canale di Malta.
  strait Italy/Malta
Malta, Republic of *see* Malta
Maluku, Laut *see* Molucca Sea
Malung 85 B6 Dalarna, C Sweden
Malventum *see* Benevento
Malvina, Isla Gran *see* West Falkland
Malvinas, Islas *see* Falkland Islands
Malyn 108 D2 *Rus.* Malin. Zhytomyrs'ka
  Oblast', N Ukraine
Malyy Kavkaz *see* Lesser Caucasus
Mamberamo, Sungai 139 H4 *river*
  Papua, E Indonesia
Mambij *see* Manbij
Mamonovo 106 A4 *Ger.* Heiligenbeil.
  Kaliningradskaya Oblast', W Russian
  Federation
Mamoré, Rio 61 F3 *river* Bolivia/Brazil
Mamou 74 C4 W Guinea
Mamoudzou 79 F2 *dependent territory
  capital* (Mayotte) C Mayotte

Mamuno 78 C3 Ghanzi, W Botswana
Manacor 93 G3 Mallorca, Spain,
  W Mediterranean Sea
Manado 139 F3 *prev.* Menado. Sulawesi,
  C Indonesia
Managua 52 D3 *country capital*
  (Nicaragua) Managua, W Nicaragua
Managua, Lake 52 C3 *var.* Xolotlán. *lake*
  W Nicaragua
Manakara 79 G4 Fianarantsoa,
  SE Madagascar
Manama *see* Al Manāmah
Mananjary 79 G3 Fianarantsoa,
  SE Madagascar
Manáos *see* Manaus
Manapouri, Lake 151 A7 *lake* South
  Island, New Zealand
Manar *see* Mannar
Manas, Gora 123 E2 *mountain*
  Kyrgyzstan/Uzbekistan
Manaus 62 D2 *prev.* Manáos. *state
  capital* Amazonas, NW Brazil
Manavgat 116 B4 Antalya, SW Turkey
Manbij 118 C2 *var.* Mambij, *Fr.*
  Membidj. Ḥalab, N Syria
Manchester 89 D5 *Lat.* Mancunium.
  NW England, United Kingdom
Manchester 41 G3 New Hampshire,
  NE USA
Man-chou-li *see* Manzhouli
Manchurian Plain 125 E1 *plain*
  NE China
Máncio Lima *see* Japiim
Mancunium *see* Manchester
Mand *see* Mand, Rūd-e
Mandalay 136 B3 Mandalay, C Myanmar
  (Burma)
Mandan 45 E2 North Dakota,
  N USA
Mandeville 54 B5 C Jamaica
Mándra 105 C6 Attikí, C Greece
Rud-e Mand 120 D4 *var.* Mand. *river*
  S Iran
Mandurah 147 A6 Western Australia
Manduria 97 E5 Puglia, SE Italy
Mandya 122 C2 Karnātaka, C India
Manfredonia 97 D5 Puglia, SE Italy
Mangai 77 C6 Bandundu, W Dem.
  Rep. Congo
Mangaia 145 G5 *island group* S Cook
  Islands
Mangalia 108 D5 *anc.* Callatis.
  Constanța, SE Romania
Mangalmé 76 C3 Guéra, SE Chad
Mangalore 132 B2 Karnātaka,
  W India
Mangaung *see* Bloemfontein
Mango *see* Sansanné-Mango, Togo
Mangoky 79 F3 *river* W Madagascar
Manhattan 45 F4 Kansas, C USA
Manicouagan, Réservoir 38 D3 *lake*
  Québec, E Canada
Manihiki 145 G4 *atoll* N Cook Islands
Manihiki Plateau 143 E3 *undersea
  plateau* C Pacific Ocean
Maniitsoq 82 C3 *var.* Manītsoq, *Dan.*
  Sukkertoppen. Kitaa, S Greenland
Manila 116 A3 *var.* Manissa, *prev.*
  Saruhan; *anc.* Magnesia. Manisa,
  W Turkey
Manissa *see* Manisa
Manitoba 37 F5 *province* S Canada
Manitoba, Lake 37 F5 *lake* Manitoba,
  S Canada
Manitoulin Island 38 C4 *island* Ontario,
  S Canada
Maniitsoq *see* Maniitsoq
Manizales 58 B3 Caldas, W Colombia
Manjimup 147 A7 Western Australia
Mankato 45 F3 Minnesota, N USA
Manlleu 93 G2 Cataluña, NE Spain
Manly 148 E1 Iowa, C USA
Manmād 134 C5 Mahārāshtra, W India
Mannar 132 C3 *var.* Manar. Northern
  Province, NW Sri Lanka
Mannar, Gulf of 132 C3 *gulf* India/
  Sri Lanka
Mannheim 95 B5 Baden-Württemberg,
  SW Germany
Manono 77 E7 Shaba, SE Dem. Rep.
  Congo
Manosque 91 D6 Alpes-de-Haute-
  Provence, SE France
Manra 145 F3 *prev.* Sydney Island. *atoll*
  Phoenix Islands, C Kiribati

Mansa 78 D2 *prev.* Fort Rosebery.
  Luapula, N Zambia
Mansel Island 37 G3 *island* Nunavut,
  NE Canada
Mansfield 40 D4 Ohio, N USA
Manta 60 A2 Manabí, W Ecuador
Manteca 47 B6 California, W USA
Mantoue *see* Mantova
Mantova 96 B2 *Eng.* Mantua, *Fr.*
  Mantoue. Lombardia, NW Italy
Mantua *see* Mantova
Manuae 145 G4 *island* S Cook Islands
Manukau *see* Manukau
Manurewa 150 D3 *var.* Manukau.
  Auckland, North Island, New Zealand
Manzanares 93 E3 Castilla-La Mancha,
  C Spain
Manzanillo 54 C3 Granma, E Cuba
Manzanillo 50 D4 Colima, SW Mexico
Manzhouli 127 F1 *var.* Man-chou-li. Nei
  Mongol Zizhiqu, N China
Mao 76 B3 Kanem, W Chad
Maó 93 H3 *Cast.* Mahón, *Eng.* Port
  Mahon; *anc.* Portus Magonis. Menorca,
  Spain, W Mediterranean Sea
Maoke, Pegunungan 139 H4 *Dut.*
  Sneeuw-gebergte, *Eng.* Snow
  Mountains. *mountain range* Papua,
  E Indonesia
Maoming 128 C6 Guangdong, S China
Mapmaker Seamounts 125 H2
  seamount range N Pacific Ocean
Maputo 78 D4 *prev.* Lourenço Marques.
  country capital (Mozambique) Maputo,
  S Mozambique
Marabá 63 F2 Pará, NE Brazil
Maracaibo 58 C1 Zulia, NW Venezuela
Maracaibo, Gulf of *see* Venezuela,
  Golfo de
Maracaibo, Lake 58 C2 *var.* Lake
  Maracaibo. *inlet* NW Venezuela
Maracaibo, Lake *see* Maracaibo, Lago de
Maracay 58 D2 Aragua, N Venezuela
Marada *see* Marādah
Marādah 71 G3 *var.* Marada. N Libya
Maradi 75 G3 Maradi, S Niger
Maragha *see* Marāgheh
Marāgheh 120 C2 *var.* Maragha.
  Āžarbāyjān-e Khāvarī, NW Iran
Marajó, Baía de 63 F1 *bay* N Brazil
Marajó, Ilha de 63 E1 *island* N Brazil
Marakesh *see* Marrakech
Maramba *see* Livingstone
Maramba *see* Livingstone
Maranhão 63 F2 *off.* Estado do
  Maranhão. *state* E Brazil
Maranhão 63 F2 *off.* Estado do
  Maranhão. *region* E Brazil
Maranhão, Estado do *see* Maranhão
Marañón, Rio 60 B2 *river* N Peru
Marathon 38 C4 Ontario, S Canada
Marathón *see* Marathónas
Marathónas 105 C5 *prev.* Marathón.
  Attikí, C Greece
Märäzä *see* Qobustan
Marbella 92 D5 Andalucía, S Spain
Marble Bar 146 B4 Western Australia
Marburg *see* Marburg an der Lahn,
  Germany
Marburg *see* Maribor, Slovenia
Marburg an der Lahn 94 B4 *hist.*
  Marburg. Hessen, W Germany
March *see* Morava
Marche 96 C3 *Eng.* Marches. *region*
  C Italy
Marche 91 C5 *cultural region* C France
Marche-en-Famenne 87 C7
  Luxembourg, SE Belgium
Marchena, Isla 60 B5 *var.* Bindloe
  Island. *island* Galápagos Islands,
  Ecuador, E Pacific Ocean
Marches *see* Marche
Mar Chiquita, Laguna 64 C3 *lake*
  C Argentina
Marcounda *see* Markounda
Mardān 134 C1 Khyber Pakhtunkhwa,
  N Pakistan
Mar del Plata 65 D5 Buenos Aires,
  E Argentina
Mardin 117 E4 Mardin, SE Turkey
Maré 144 D5 *island* Îles Loyauté, E New
  Caledonia
Marea Neagră *see* Black Sea
Mareeba 148 D3 Queensland,
  NE Australia
Marek *see* Dupnitsa
Marganets *see* Marhanets'
Margarita, Isla de 59 E1 *island*
  N Venezuela

Margate 89 E7 *prev.* Mergate.
  SE England, United Kingdom
Margherita *see* Jamaame
Margherita, Lake 73 C5 *Eng.*
  Lake Margherita, *It.* Abbaia. *lake*
  SW Ethiopia
Margherita, Lake *see* Ābaya Hāyk'
Marghita 108 B3 *Hung.* Margitta. Bihor,
  NW Romania
Margitta *see* Marghita
Marhanets' 109 F3 *Rus.* Marganets.
  Dnipropetrovs'ka Oblast', E Ukraine
María Cleofas, Isla 50 C4 *island*
  C Mexico
Maria Island 149 C8 *island* Tasmania,
  SE Australia
María Madre, Isla 50 C4 *island*
  C Mexico
María Magdalena, Isla 50 C4 *island*
  C Mexico
Mariana Trench 125 G4 *var.* Challenger
  Deep. *trench* W Pacific Ocean
Mariánské Lázně 99 A5 *Ger.* Marienbad.
  Karlovarský Kraj, W Czech Republic
Marias, Islas 50 C4 *island group*
  C Mexico
Maria-Theresiopel *see* Subotica
Maribor 95 E7 *Ger.* Marburg.
  NE Slovenia
Marica *see* Maritsa
Maridi 73 B5 Western Equatoria,
  SW South Sudan
Marie Byrd Land 154 A3 *physical region*
  Antarctica
Marie-Galante 55 G4 *var.* Ceyre to the
  Caribs. *island* SE Guadeloupe
Marienbad *see* Mariánské Lázně
Marienburg *see* Alūksne, Latvia
Marienburg *see* Malbork, Poland
Marienburg in Westpreussen *see*
  Malbork
Marienhausen *see* Viḷaka
Mariental 78 B4 Hardap, SW Namibia
Marienwerder *see* Kwidzyń
Mariestad 85 B6 Västra Götaland,
  S Sweden
Marietta 42 D2 Georgia, SE USA
Marijampolė 106 B4 *prev.* Kapsukas.
  Marijampolė, S Lithuania
Marília 63 E4 São Paulo, S Brazil
Marín 93 B1 Galicia, NW Spain
Mar'ina Gorka *see* Mar"ina Horka
Mar"ina Horka 107 C6 *Rus.* Mar'ina
  Gorka. Minskaya Voblasts',
  C Belarus
Maringá 63 E4 Paraná, S Brazil
Marion 45 G3 Iowa, C USA
Marion 40 D4 Ohio, N USA
Marion, Lake 43 E2 *reservoir* South
  Carolina, SE USA
Mariscal Estigarribia 64 D2 Boquerón,
  NW Paraguay
Maritsa 104 D3 *var.* Marica, *Gk.* Évros,
  Turk. Meriç; *anc.* Hebrus. *river*
  SW Europe
Maritzburg *see* Pietermaritzburg
Mariupol' 109 G4 *prev.* Zhdanov.
  Donets'ka Oblast', SE Ukraine
Marka 73 D6 *var.* Merca. Shabeellaha
  Hoose, S Somalia
Markham, Mount 154 B4 *mountain*
  Antarctica
Markounda 76 C4 *var.* Marcounda.
  Ouham, NW Central African Republic
Marktredwitz 95 C5 Bayern, E Germany
Marlborough 148 D4 Queensland,
  E Australia
Marmande *see* Marmande
Marmande 91 B5 *anc.* Marmanda. Lot-
  et-Garonne, SW France
Sea of Marmara 116 A2 *Eng.* Sea of
  Marmara. *sea* NW Turkey
Marmara, Sea of *see* Marmara Denizi
Marmaris 116 A4 Muğla, SW Turkey
Marne 90 C3 *cultural region* N France
Marne 90 D3 *river* N France
Maro 76 C4 Moyen-Chari, S Chad
Maroantsetra 79 G2 Toamasina,
  NE Madagascar
Maromokotro 79 G2 *mountain*
  N Madagascar
Maroni 79 G2 *var.* Marowijne. *river*
  French Guiana/Suriname
Marosheviz *see* Luduș
Marosludas *see* Luduș
Marosvásárhely *see* Târgu Mureș
Marotiri 143 F4 *var.* Îlots de Bass,
  Morotiri. *island group* Îles Australes,
  SW French Polynesia

Maroua 76 B3 Extrême-Nord,
  N Cameroon
Marowijne see Maroni
Marquesas Fracture Zone 153 E3
  fracture zone E Pacific Ocean
Marquette 40 B1 Michigan, N USA
Marrakech 70 C2 var. Marakesh, Eng.
  Marrakesh; prev. Morocco. W Morocco
Marrakesh see Marrakech
Marrawah 149 C8 Tasmania,
  SE Australia
Marree 149 B5 South Australia
Marsá al Burayqah 71 G3 var. Al
  Burayqah. N Libya
Marsabit 73 C6 Eastern, N Kenya
Marsala 97 B7 anc. Lilybaeum. Sicilia,
  Italy, C Mediterranean Sea
Marsberg 94 B4 Nordrhein-Westfalen,
  W Germany
Marseille 91 D6 Eng. Marseilles;
  anc. Massilia. Bouches-du-Rhône,
  SE France
Marseilles see Marseille
Marshall 45 F2 Minnesota, N USA
Marshall 49 H2 Texas, SW USA
Marshall Islands 144 C1 off. Republic of
  the Marshall Islands. country W Pacific
  Ocean

MARSHALL ISLANDS
Australasia & Oceania

Official name Republic of
the Marshall Islands
Formation 1986 / 1986
Capital Majuro
Population 68,480 / 978 people
per sq mile (378 people per sq km)
Total area 70 sq. miles (181 sq. km)
Languages Marshallese*, English*,
Japanese, German
Religions Protestant 90%,
Roman Catholic 8%, Other 2%
Ethnic mix Micronesian 90%, Other 10%
Government Presidential system
Currency US dollar = 100 cents
Literacy rate 91%
Calorie consumption Not available

Marshall Islands, Republic of the see
  Marshall Islands
Marshall Seamounts 125 H3 seamount
  range SW Pacific Ocean
Marsh Harbour 54 C1 Great Abaco,
  W Bahamas
Martaban see Mottama
Martha's Vineyard 41 G3 island
  Massachusetts, NE USA
Martigues 91 D6 Bouches-du-Rhône,
  SE France
Martin 99 C5 Ger. Sankt Martin, Hung.
  Turócszentmárton; prev. Turčiansky
  Svätý Martin. Žilinský Kraj,
  N Slovakia
Martinique 55 G4 French overseas
  department E West Indies
Martinique Channel see Martinique
  Passage
Martinique Passage 55 G4 var.
  Dominica Channel, Martinique
  Channel. channel Dominica/
  Martinique
Marton 150 D4 Manawatu-Wanganui,
  North Island, New Zealand
Martos 92 D4 Andalucía, S Spain
Marungu 77 E7 mountain range SE Dem.
  Rep. Congo
Mary 122 D3 prev. Merv. Mary
  Welaýaty, S Turkmenistan
Maryborough 149 D4 Queensland,
  E Australia
Maryborough see Port Laoise
Mary Island see Kanton
Maryland 41 E5 off. State of Maryland,
  also known as America in Miniature,
  Cockade State, Free State, Old Line
  State. state NE USA
Maryland, State of see Maryland
Maryville 45 F4 Missouri, C USA
Maryville 42 D1 Tennessee, S USA
Masai Steppe 73 C7 grassland
  NW Tanzania
Masaka 73 B6 SW Uganda
Masallı 117 H3 Rus. Masally.
  S Azerbaijan
Masally see Masallı
Masasi 73 C8 Mtwara, SE Tanzania
Masawa/Massawa see Mits'iwa
Masaya 52 D3 Masaya, W Nicaragua

Mascarene Basin 141 B5 undersea basin
  W Indian Ocean
Mascarene Islands 79 H4 island group
  W Indian Ocean
Mascarene Plain 141 B5 abyssal plain
  W Indian Ocean
Mascarene Plateau 141 B5 undersea
  plateau W Indian Ocean
Maseru 78 D4 country capital (Lesotho)
  W Lesotho
Mas-ha 119 D7 W West Bank Asia
Mashhad 120 E2 var. Meshed.
  Khorāsān-Razavī, NE Iran
Masindi 73 B6 W Uganda
Masira see Maşīrah, Jazīrat
Masira, Gulf of 121 E5 var. Gulf of
  Masira. bay E Oman
Masira, Gulf of see Maşīrah, Khalīj
Maşīrah, Jazīrat 121 E5 var. Masira.
  island E Oman
Masis see Büyükağrı Dağı
Maskat see Masqaţ
Mason City 45 F3 Iowa, C USA
Masqaţ 121 E5 var. Maskat, Eng. Muscat.
  country capital (Oman) NE Oman
Massa 96 B3 Toscana, C Italy
Massachusetts 41 G3 off.
  Commonwealth of Massachusetts, also
  known as Bay State, Old Bay State, Old
  Colony State. state NE USA
Massenya 76 B3 Chari-Baguirmi,
  SW Chad
Massif Central 91 C5 plateau
  C France
Massilia see Marseille
Massoukou see Franceville
Mastanli see Momchilgrad
Masterton 151 D5 Wellington, North
  Island, New Zealand
Masty 107 B5 Rus. Mosty.
  Hrodzyenskaya Voblasts', W Belarus
Masuda 131 B6 Shimane, Honshū,
  SW Japan
Masuku see Franceville
Masvingo 78 D3 prev. Fort Victoria,
  Nyanda, Victoria. Masvingo,
  SE Zimbabwe
Maşyāf 118 B3 Fr. Misiaf. Ḥamāh,
  C Syria
Matadi 77 B6 Bas-Congo, W Dem.
  Rep. Congo
Matagalpa 52 D3 Matagalpa,
  C Nicaragua
Matale 132 D3 Central Province,
  C Sri Lanka
Matam 74 C3 NE Senegal
Matamata 150 D3 Waikato, North
  Island, New Zealand
Matamoros 50 D3 Coahuila, NE Mexico
Matamoros 51 E2 Tamaulipas, C Mexico
Matane 39 E4 Québec, SE Canada
Matanzas 54 B2 Matanzas, NW Cuba
Matara 132 D4 Southern Province,
  S Sri Lanka
Mataram 138 D5 Pulau Lombok,
  C Indonesia
Mataró 93 G2 anc. Illuro. Cataluña,
  E Spain
Mataura 151 B7 Southland, South Island,
  New Zealand
Mataura 151 B7 river South Island,
  New Zealand
Mata Uta see Matā'utu
Matā'utu 145 E4 var. Mata Uta.
  dependent territory capital (Wallis and
  Futuna) Île Uvea, Wallis and Futuna
Matera 97 E5 Basilicata, S Italy
Mathurai see Madurai
Matianus see Orūmīyeh, Daryācheh-ye
Matías Romero 51 F5 Oaxaca,
  SE Mexico
Matisco/Matisco Ædourum see Mâcon
Mato Grosso 63 E3 off. Estado de Mato
  Grosso; prev. Matto Grosso. state
  W Brazil
Mato Grosso 63 E3 off. Estado de Mato
  Grosso; prev. Matto Grosso. region
  W Brazil
Mato Grosso do Sul 63 E4 off. Estado de
  Mato Grosso do Sul. state S Brazil
Mato Grosso do Sul 63 E4 off. Estado de
  Mato Grosso do Sul. region S Brazil
Mato Grosso do Sul, Estado de see Mato
  Grosso do Sul
Mato Grosso, Estado de see Mato Grosso
Mato Grosso, Planalto de 56 C4 plateau
  C Brazil
Matosinhos 92 B2 prev. Matozinhos.
  Porto, NW Portugal

Matozinhos see Matosinhos
Matsue 131 B6 var. Matsuye, Matue.
  Shimane, Honshū, SW Japan
Matsumoto 131 C5 var. Matumoto.
  Nagano, Honshū, S Japan
Matsuyama 131 B7 var. Matuyama.
  Ehime, Shikoku, SW Japan
Matsuye see Matsue
Matterhorn 95 A8 It. Monte Cervino.
  mountain Italy/Switzerland
Matthews Ridge 59 F2 N Guyana
Matthew Town 54 D2 Great Inagua,
  S Bahamas
Matto Grosso see Mato Grosso
Matucana 60 C4 Lima, W Peru
Matue see Matsue
Matumoto see Matsumoto
Maturín 59 E2 Monagas, NE Venezuela
Matuyama see Matsuyama
Mau 135 E3 var. Maunāth Bhanjan.
  Uttar Pradesh, N India
Maui 47 B8 island Hawai'i, USA,
  C Pacific Ocean
Maun 78 C3 North-West, C Botswana
Maunāth Bhanjan see Mau
Mauren 94 E1 NE Liechtenstein Europe
Maurice see Mauritius
Mauritania 74 C2 off. Islamic Republic of
  Mauritania, Ar. Mūrītānīyah. country
  W Africa

MAURITANIA
West Africa

Official name Islamic Republic
of Mauritania
Formation 1960 / 1960
Capital Nouakchott
Population 3.5 million / 9 people
per sq mile (3 people per sq km)
Total area 397,953 sq. miles
(1,030,700 sq. km)
Languages Hassaniyah Arabic*,
Wolof, French
Religions Sunni Muslim 100%
Ethnic mix Maure 81%, Wolof 7%,
Tukolor 5%, Other 4%, Soninka 3%
Government Presidential system
Currency Ouguiya = 5 khoums
Literacy rate 58%
Calorie consumption 2856 kilocalories

Mauritania, Islamic Republic of see
  Mauritania
Mauritius 79 H3 off. Republic of
  Mauritius, Fr. Maurice. country
  W Indian Ocean

MAURITIUS
Indian Ocean

Official name Republic of Mauritius
Formation 1968 / 1968
Capital Port Louis
Population 1.3 million / 1811 people
per sq mile (699 people per sq km)
Total area 718 sq. miles (1860 sq. km)
Languages French Creole, Hindi, Urdu,
Tamil, Chinese, English*, French
Religions Hindu 48%, Roman Catholic
24%, Muslim 17%, Protestant 10%,
Other 2%
Ethnic mix Indo-Mauritian 68%,
Creole 27%, Sino-Mauritian 3%,
Franco-Mauritian 2%
Government Parliamentary system
Currency Mauritian rupee = 100 cents
Literacy rate 88%
Calorie consumption 2993 kilocalories

Mauritius 141 B5 island
  W Indian Ocean
Mauritius, Republic of see Mauritius
Mawlamyaing see Mawlamyine
Mawlamyine 136 B4 var. Mawlamyaing,
  Moulmein. Mon State, S Myanmar
  (Burma)
Mawson 154 D2 Australian research
  station Antarctica
Mayadin see Al Mayādīn
Mayaguana 51 D2 island SE Bahamas
Mayaguana Passage 54 D2 passage
  SE Bahamas
Mayagüez 55 F3 W Puerto Rico
Mayamey 120 D2 Semnān, N Iran
Maya Mountains 52 B2 Sp. Montañas
  Mayas. mountain range Belize/
  Guatemala
Mayas, Montañas see Maya Mountains

Maych'ew 72 C4 var. Mai Chio, It. Mai
  Ceu. Tigray, N Ethiopia
Maydān Shahr see Maīdān Shahr
Mayebashi see Maebashi
Mayence see Mainz
Mayfield 151 B6 Canterbury, South
  Island, New Zealand
Maykop 111 A7 Respublika Adygeya,
  SW Russian Federation
Maymana see Maïmanah
Maymyo see Pyin-Oo-Lwin
Mayo see Maio
Mayor Island 150 D3 island NE New
  Zealand
Mayor Pablo Lagerenza see Capitán
  Pablo Lagerenza
Mayotte 79 F2 French territorial
  collectivity E Africa
May Pen 54 B5 C Jamaica
Mayyit, Al Bahr al see Dead Sea
Mazabuka 78 D2 Southern, S Zambia
Mazaca see Kayseri
Mazagan see El-Jadida
Mazār-e Sharīf 123 E3 var. Mazār-i
  Sharif. Balkh, N Afghanistan
Mazār-i Sharif see Mazār-e Sharīf
Mazatlán 50 C3 Sinaloa, C Mexico
Mažeikiai 106 B3 Telšiai,
  NW Lithuania
Mazirbe 106 C2 NW Latvia
Mazra'a see Al Mazra'ah
Mazury 98 D3 physical region NE Poland
Mazyr 107 C7 Rus. Mozyr'.
  Homyel'skaya Voblasts', SE Belarus
Mbabane 78 D4 country capital
  (Swaziland) NW Swaziland
Mbacké see Mbaké
Mbaïki 77 C5 var. M'Baiki. Lobaye,
  SW Central African Republic
M'Baiki see Mbaïki
Mbaké 74 B3 var. Mbacké. W Senegal
Mbala 78 D1 prev. Abercorn. Northern,
  NE Zambia
Mbale 73 C6 E Uganda
Mbandaka 77 C5 prev. Coquilhatville.
  Equateur, NW Dem. Rep. Congo
M'Banza Congo 78 B1 var. Mbanza
  Congo; prev. São Salvador, São
  Salvador do Congo. Dem. Rep. Congo,
  NW Angola
Mbanza-Ngungu 77 B6 Bas-Congo,
  W Dem. Rep. Congo
Mbarara 73 B6 SW Uganda
Mbé 76 B4 Nord, N Cameroon
Mbeya 73 C7 Mbeya, SW Tanzania
Mbomou/M'Bomu/Mbomu see Bomu
Mbour 74 B3 W Senegal
Mbuji-Mayi 77 D7 prev. Bakwanga.
  Kasai-Oriental, S Dem. Rep. Congo
McAlester 49 G2 Oklahoma, C USA
McAllen 49 G5 Texas, SW USA
McCamey 49 E3 Texas, SW USA
McComb 42 B3 Mississippi, S USA
McCook 45 E4 Nebraska, C USA
McKean Island 145 E3 island Phoenix
  Islands, C Kiribati
Mount McKinley 36 C3 var. Denali.
  mountain Alaska, USA
McKinley Park 36 C3 Alaska, USA
M'Clintock Channel 37 F2 channel
  Nunavut, N Canada
McMinnville 46 B3 Oregon, NW USA
McMurdo 154 B4 US research station
  Antarctica
McPherson 45 E5 Kansas, C USA
McPherson see Fort McPherson
Mdantsane 78 D5 Eastern Cape,
  SE South Africa
Mead, Lake 47 D6 reservoir Arizona/
  Nevada, W USA
Mecca see Makkah
Mechelen 87 C5 Eng. Mechlin, Fr.
  Malines. Antwerpen, C Belgium
Mechlin see Mechelen
Mecklenburger Bucht 94 C2 bay
  N Germany
Mecsek 99 C7 mountain range
  SW Hungary
Medan 138 B3 Sumatera, E Indonesia
Medeba see Ma'dabā
Medellín 58 B3 Antioquia,
  NW Colombia
Médenine 71 F2 var. Madanīyīn.
  SE Tunisia
Medeshamstede see Peterborough
Medford 46 B4 Oregon, NW USA
Medgidia 108 D5 Constanța,
  SE Romania
Medgyes see Mediaș

Mediaş 108 B4 Ger. Mediasch, Hung. Medgyes. Sibiu, C Romania
Mediasch see Mediaş
Medicine Hat 37 F5 Alberta, SW Canada
Medina see Al Madinah
Medinaceli 93 E2 Castilla y León, N Spain
Medina del Campo 92 D2 Castilla y León, N Spain
Medinat Israel see Israel
Mediolanum see Saintes, France
Mediolanum see Milano, Italy
Mediomatrica see Metz
Mediterranean Sea 102 D3 Fr. Mer Méditerranée. sea Africa/Asia/Europe
Méditerranée, Mer see Mediterranean Sea
Médoc 91 B5 cultural region SW France
Medvezh'yegorsk 110 B3 Respublika Kareliya, NW Russian Federation
Meekatharra 147 B5 Western Australia
Meemu Atoll see Mulakatholhu
Meerssen 87 D6 var. Mersen. Limburg, SE Netherlands
Meerut 134 D2 Uttar Pradesh, N India
Megáli Préspa, Límni see Prespa, Lake
Meghālaya 113 G3 cultural region NE India
Mehdia see Mahdia
Meheso see Mi'ēso
Me Hka see Nmai Hka
Mehrīz 120 D3 Yazd, C Iran
Mehtar Lām 123 F4 var. Mehtarlām, Meterlam, Methariam, Metharlam. Laghmān, E Afghanistan
Mehtarlām see Mehtar Lām
Meiktila 136 B3 Mandalay, C Myanmar (Burma)
Méjico see Mexico
Mejillones 64 B2 Antofagasta, N Chile
Mek'elē 72 C4 var. Makale. Tigray, N Ethiopia
Mékhé 74 B3 NW Senegal
Mekong 124 D3 var. Lan-ts'ang Chiang, Cam. Mékôngk, Chin. Lancang Jiang, Lao. Mènam Khong, Nam Khong, Th. Mae Nam Khong, Tib. Dza Chu, Vtn. Sông Tiên Giang. river SE Asia
Mékôngk see Mekong
Mekong, Mouths of the 137 E6 delta S Vietnam
Melaka 138 B3 var. Malacca. Melaka, Peninsular Malaysia
Melaka, Selat see Malacca, Strait of
Melanesia 144 D3 island group W Pacific Ocean
Melanesian Basin 142 C2 undersea basin W Pacific Ocean
Melbourne 149 C7 state capital Victoria, SE Australia
Melbourne 43 E4 Florida, SE USA
Meleda see Mljet
Melghir, Chott 71 E2 var. Chott Melrhir. salt lake E Algeria
Melilla 80 B5 anc. Rusaddir, Russadir. Melilla, Spain, N Africa
Melilla 70 D2 enclave Spain, N Africa
Melita 37 F5 Manitoba, S Canada
Melita see Mljet
Melitene see Malatya
Melitopol' 109 F4 Zaporiz'ka Oblast', SE Ukraine
Melle 87 B5 Oost-Vlaanderen, NW Belgium
Mellerud 85 B6 Västra Götaland, S Sweden
Mellieha 102 B5 E Malta
Mellizo Sur, Cerro 65 A7 mountain S Chile
Melo 64 E4 Cerro Largo, NE Uruguay
Melodunum see Melun
Melrhir, Chott see Melghir, Chott
Melsungen 94 B4 Hessen, C Germany
Melun 90 C3 anc. Melodunum. Seine-et-Marne, N France
Melville Bay/Melville Bugt see Qimusseriarsuaq
Melville Island 146 D2 island Northern Territory, N Australia
Melville Island 37 E2 island Parry Islands, Northwest Territories, NW Canada
Melville, Lake 39 F2 lake Newfoundland and Labrador, E Canada
Melville Peninsula 37 G3 peninsula Nunavut, NE Canada
Melville Sound see Viscount Melville Sound
Membidj see Manbij

Memel see Neman, NE Europe
Memel see Klaipeda, Lithuania
Memmingen 95 B6 Bayern, S Germany
Memphis 42 C1 Tennessee, S USA
Menaam see Menaldum
Menado see Manado
Ménaka 75 F3 Goa, E Mali
Menaldum 86 D1 Fris. Menaam. Fryslân, N Netherlands
Mènam Khong see Mekong
Mendaña Fracture Zone 153 F4 fracture zone E Pacific Ocean
Mende 91 C5 anc. Mimatum. Lozère, S France
Mendeleyev Ridge 155 B2 undersea ridge Arctic Ocean
Mendocino Fracture Zone 152 D2 fracture zone NE Pacific Ocean
Mendoza 64 B4 Mendoza, W Argentina
Menemen 116 A3 İzmir, W Turkey
Menengiyn Tal 127 F2 plain E Mongolia
Menongue 78 B2 var. Vila Serpa Pinto, Port. Serpa Pinto. Cuando Cubango, C Angola
Mentawai, Kepulauan 138 A4 island group W Indonesia
Meppel 86 D2 Drenthe, NE Netherlands
Meran see Merano
Merano 96 C1 Ger. Meran. Trentino-Alto Adige, N Italy
Merca see Marka
Mercedes 64 D3 Corrientes, NE Argentina
Mercedes 64 D4 Soriano, SW Uruguay
Meredith, Lake 49 E1 reservoir Texas, SW USA
Merefa 109 G2 Kharkiv'ska Oblast', E Ukraine
Mergate see Margate
Mergui see Myeik
Mergui Archipelago see Myeik Archipelago
Mérida 51 H3 Yucatán, SW Mexico
Mérida 92 C4 anc. Augusta Emerita. Extremadura, W Spain
Mérida 58 C2 Mérida, W Venezuela
Meridian 42 C2 Mississippi, S USA
Mérignac 91 B5 Gironde, SW France
Merin, Laguna see Mirim Lagoon
Merkulovichi see Myerkulavichy
Merowe 72 B3 Northern, N Sudan
Merredin 147 B6 Western Australia
Mersen see Meerssen
Mersey 89 D5 river NW England, United Kingdom
Mersin 116 C4 var. İçel. İçel, S Turkey
Mērsrags 106 C3 NW Latvia
Meru 73 C6 Eastern, C Kenya
Merv see Mary
Merzifon 116 D2 Amasya, N Turkey
Merzig 95 A5 Saarland, SW Germany
Mesa 48 B2 Arizona, SW USA
Meseritz see Międzyrzecz
Meshed see Mashhad
Mesopotamia 57 C5 var. Mesopotamia Argentina. physical region NE Argentina
Mesopotamia Argentina see Mesopotamia
Messalo, Rio 79 E2 var. Mualo. river NE Mozambique
Messana 97 D7 var. Messana, Messene; anc. Zancle. Sicilia, Italy, C Mediterranean Sea
Messina see Musina
Messina, Strait of 97 D7 Eng. Strait of Messina. strait SW Italy
Messina, Strait of see Messina, Stretto di
Messíni 105 B6 Pelopónnisos, S Greece
Mesta see Néstos
Mestghanem see Mostaganem
Mest'ia F11 prev. Mestia, var. Mestiya. N Georgia
Mestia see Mest'ia
Mestiya see Mest'ia
Mestre 96 C2 Veneto, NE Italy
Metairie 42 B3 Louisiana, S USA
Metán 64 C2 Salta, N Argentina
Metapán 52 B2 Santa Ana, NW El Salvador
Meta, Río 58 D3 river Colombia/Venezuela
Meterlam see Mehtar Lām
Metharriam/Metharlam see Mehtar Lām
Metis see Metz
Metković 100 B4 Dubrovnik-Neretva, SE Croatia

Métsovo 104 B4 prev. Métsovon. Ípeiros, C Greece
Métsovon see Métsovo
Metz 90 D3 anc. Divodurum Mediomatricum, Mediomatrica, Metis. Moselle, NE France
Meulaboh 138 A3 Sumatera, W Indonesia
Meuse 87 C6 Dut. Maas. river W Europe
Mexcala, Río see Balsas, Río
Mexicali 50 A1 Baja California Norte, NW Mexico
Mexicanos, Estados Unidos see Mexico
México 51 E4 var. Ciudad de México, Eng. Mexico City. country capital (Mexico) México, C Mexico
Mexico 45 G4 Missouri, C USA
Mexico 50 C3 off. United Mexican States, var. Méjico, Mexico, Sp. Estados Unidos Mexicanos. country N Central America

MEXICO
North America

Official name United Mexican States
Formation 1836 / 1848
Capital Mexico City
Population 115 million / 156 people per sq mile (60 people per sq km)
Total area 761,602 sq. miles (1,972,550 sq. km)
Languages Spanish*, Nahuatl, Mayan, Zapotec, Mixtec, Otomi, Totonac, Tzotzil, Tzeltal
Religions Roman Catholic 77%, Other 14%, Protestant 6%, Nonreligious 3%
Ethnic mix Mestizo 60%, Amerindian 30%, European 9%, Other 1%
Government Presidential system
Currency Mexican peso = 100 centavos
Literacy rate 93%
Calorie consumption 3146 kilocalories

México see Mexico
Mexico City see Mexico
México, Golfo de see Mexico, Gulf of
Mexico, Gulf of 51 F2 Sp. Golfo de México. gulf W Atlantic Ocean
Meyadine see Al Mayādīn
Meydān Shahr see Maidān Shahr
Meymaneh see Maimana
Mezen' 110 D3 river NW Russian Federation
Mezőtúr 99 D7 Jász-Nagykun-Szolnok, E Hungary
Mġarr 102 A5 Gozo, N Malta
Miadzioł Nowy see Myadzyel
Miahuatlán 51 F5 var. Miahuatlán de Porfirio Díaz. Oaxaca, SE Mexico
Miahuatlán de Porfirio Díaz see Miahuatlán
Miami 43 F5 Florida, SE USA
Miami 49 G1 Oklahoma, C USA
Miami Beach 43 F5 Florida, SE USA
Miāneh 120 C2 var. Miyāneh. Āzarbāyjān-e Sharqī, NW Iran
Mianyang 128 B5 Sichuan, C China
Miastko 98 C2 Ger. Rummelsburg in Pommern. Pomorskie, N Poland
Mi Chai see Nong Khai
Michalovce 99 E5 Ger. Grossmichel, Hung. Nagymihály. Košický Kraj, E Slovakia
Michigan 40 C1 off. State of Michigan, also known as Great Lakes State, Lake State, Wolverine State. state N USA
Michigan, Lake 40 C2 lake N USA
Michurin see Tsarevo
Michurinsk 111 B5 Tambovskaya Oblast', W Russian Federation
Micoud 55 F2 SE Saint Lucia
Micronesia 144 B1 off. Federated States of Micronesia. country W Pacific Ocean
Micronesia 144 C1 island group W Pacific Ocean

MICRONESIA
Australasia & Oceania

Official name Federated States of Micronesia
Formation 1986 / 1986
Capital Palikir (Pohnpei Island)
Population 106,487 / 393 people per sq mile (152 people per sq km)
Total area 271 sq. miles (702 sq. km)
Languages Trukese, Pohnpeian,

MICRONESIA
(continued)

Kosraean, Yapese, English*
Religions Roman Catholic 50%, Protestant 47%, Other 3%
Ethnic mix Chuukese 49%, Pohnpeian 24%, Other 14%, Kosraean 6%, Yapese 5%, Asian 2%
Government Nonparty system
Currency US dollar = 100 cents
Literacy rate 81%
Calorie consumption Not available

Micronesia, Federated States of see Micronesia
Mid-Atlantic Cordillera see Mid-Atlantic Ridge
Mid-Atlantic Ridge 66 C3 var. Mid-Atlantic Cordillera, Mid-Atlantic Rise, Mid-Atlantic Swell. undersea ridge Atlantic Ocean
Mid-Atlantic Rise/Mid-Atlantic Swell see Mid-Atlantic Ridge
Middelburg 87 B5 Zeeland, SW Netherlands
Middelharnis 86 B4 Zuid-Holland, SW Netherlands
Middelkerke 87 A5 West-Vlaanderen, W Belgium
Middle America Trench 35 B7 trench E Pacific Ocean
Middle Andaman 133 F2 island Andaman Islands, India, NE Indian Ocean
Middle Atlas 70 C2 Eng. Middle Atlas. mountain range N Morocco
Middle Atlas see Moyen Atlas
Middleburg Island see 'Eua
Middle Congo see Congo (Republic of)
Middlesboro 40 C5 Kentucky, S USA
Middlesbrough 89 D5 N England, United Kingdom
Middletown 41 F4 New Jersey, NE USA
Middletown 41 F3 New York, NE USA
Mid-Indian Basin 141 C5 undersea basin N Indian Ocean
Mid-Indian Ridge 141 C5 var. Central Indian Ridge. undersea ridge C Indian Ocean
Midland 38 D5 Ontario, S Canada
Midland 40 C3 Michigan, N USA
Midland 49 E3 Texas, SW USA
Mid-Pacific Mountains 152 C2 var. Mid-Pacific Seamounts. seamount range NW Pacific Ocean
Mid-Pacific Seamounts see Mid-Pacific Mountains
Midway Islands 152 D2 US territory C Pacific Ocean
Miechów 99 D5 Małopolskie, S Poland
Międzyrzec Podlaski 98 E3 Lubelskie, E Poland
Międzyrzecz 98 B3 Ger. Meseritz. Lubuskie, W Poland
Mielec 99 D5 Podkarpackie, SE Poland
Miercurea-Ciuc 108 C4 Ger. Szeklerburg, Hung. Csíkszereda. Harghita, C Romania
Mieres del Camín 92 D1 var. Mieres del Camino. Asturias, NW Spain
Mieres del Camino see Mieres del Camín
Mi'ēso 73 D5 var. Meheso, Miesso. Oromiya, C Ethiopia
Miesso see Mi'ēso
Mifrats Hefa 119 A5 Eng. Bay of Haifa; prev. MifraẓḤefa. bay N Israel
Miguel Asua 50 D3 var. Miguel Auza. Zacatecas, C Mexico
Miguel Auza see Miguel Asua
Mijdrecht 86 C3 Utrecht, C Netherlands
Mikashevichi see Mikashevichy
Mikashevichy 107 C7 Pol. Mikaszewicze, Rus. Mikashevichi. Brestskaya Voblasts', SW Belarus
Mikaszewicze see Mikashevichy
Mikhaylograd see Montana
Mikhaylovka 111 B6 Volgogradskaya Oblast', SW Russian Federation
Míkonos see Mýkonos
Mikre 104 C2 Lovech, N Bulgaria
Mikun' 110 D4 Respublika Komi, NW Russian Federation
Mikuni-sanmyaku 131 D5 mountain range Honshū, N Japan Asia
Mikura-jima 131 D6 island E Japan
Milagro 60 B2 Guayas, SW Ecuador
Milan see Milano

Milange *79 E2* Zambézia,
NE Mozambique
Milano *96 B2 Eng.* Milan, *Ger.* Mailand;
anc. Mediolanum. Lombardia, N Italy
Milas *116 A4* Muğla, SW Turkey
Milashavichy *107 C7 Rus.* Milashevichi.
Homyel'skaya Voblasts', SE Belarus
Milashevichi *see* Milashavichy
Mildura *149 C6* Victoria, SE Australia
Mile *see* Mili Atoll
Miles *149 D5* Queensland, E Australia
Miles City *44 C2* Montana, NW USA
Milford *see* Milford Haven
Milford Haven *89 C6 prev.* Milford.
SW Wales, United Kingdom
Milford Sound *151 A6* Southland, South
Island, New Zealand
Milford Sound *151 A6 inlet* South
Island, New Zealand
Milḥ, Baḥr al *see* Razāzah, Buḥayrat ar
Mili Atoll *144 D2 var.* Mile. *atoll* Ratak
Chain, SE Marshall Islands
Mil'kovo *115 H3* Kamchatskiy Kray,
E Russian Federation
Milk River *37 E5* Alberta, SW Canada
Milk River *44 C1 river* Montana,
NW USA
Milk, Wadi el *88 B4 var.* Wadi al Malik.
river C Sudan
Milledgeville *43 E2* Georgia, SE USA
Mille Lacs Lake *45 F2 lake* Minnesota,
N USA
Millennium Island *143 F3 prev.*
Caroline Island, Thornton Island. *atoll*
Line Islands, E Kiribati
Millerovo *111 B6* Rostovskaya Oblast',
SW Russian Federation
Mílos *105 C6 island* Kykládes, Greece,
Aegean Sea
Mílos *105 C6 island* Kykládes, Greece,
Aegean Sea
Mílos *105 C7 island* Kykládes, Greece,
Aegean Sea
Milton *151 B7* Otago, South Island,
New Zealand
Milton Keynes *89 D6* SE England,
United Kingdom
Milwaukee *40 B3* Wisconsin, N USA
Mimatum *see* Mende
Min *see* Fujian
Minā' Qābūs *140 B3* NE Oman
Minas Gerais *63 F3 off.* Estado de Minas
Gerais. *state* E Brazil
Minas Gerais *63 F3 off.* Estado de Minas
Gerais. *region* E Brazil
Minas Gerais, Estado de *see* Minas Gerais
Minatitlán *51 F4* Veracruz-Llave,
E Mexico
Minbu *136 A3* Magway, W Myanmar
(Burma)
Minch, The *88 B3 var.* North Minch.
strait NW Scotland, United Kingdom
Mindanao *139 F2 island* S Philippines
Mindanao Sea *see* Bohol Sea
Mindelheim *95 C6* Bayern, S Germany
Mindello *see* Mindelo
Mindelo *74 A2 var.* Mindello; *prev.* Porto
Grande. São Vicente, N Cape Verde
Minden *94 B4 anc.* Minthun. Nordrhein-
Westfalen, NW Germany
Mindoro *139 E2 island* N Philippines
Mindoro Strait *139 E2 strait*
W Philippines
Mineral Wells *49 F2* Texas, SW USA
Mingäçevir *117 G2 Rus.* Mingechaur,
Mingechevir. C Azerbaijan
Mingáora *see* Saidu
Mingechaur/Mingechevir *see*
Mingäçevir
Mingora *see* Saidu
Minho *92 B2 former province* N Portugal
Minho *92 B2 Sp.* Miño. *river* Portugal/
Spain
Minho, Rio *see* Miño
Minicoy Island *132 B3 island* SW India
Minius *see* Miño
Minna *75 G4* Niger, C Nigeria
Minneapolis *45 F2* Minnesota, N USA
Minnesota *45 F2 off.* State of Minnesota,
also known as Gopher State, New
England of the West, North Star State.
state N USA
Mino *92 B2 var.* Mino, Minius, Port. Rio
Minho. *river* Portugal/Spain
Miño *see* Minho, Rio
Minorca *93 H3 Eng.* Minorca; *anc.*
Balearis Minor. *island* Islas Baleares,
Spain, W Mediterranean Sea
Minorca *see* Menorca

Minot *45 E1* North Dakota, N USA
Minsk *107 C6 country capital* (Belarus)
Minskaya Voblasts', C Belarus
Minskaya Wzvyshsha *107 C6 mountain
range* C Belarus
Mińsk Mazowiecki *98 D3 var.* Nowo-
Minsk. Mazowieckie, C Poland
Minthun *see* Minden
Minto, Lac *38 D2 lake* Québec, C Canada
Minya *see* Al Minyā
Miraflores *50 C3* Baja California Sur,
NW Mexico
Miranda de Ebro *93 E1* La Rioja,
N Spain
Mirgorod *see* Myrhorod
Miri *138 D3* Sarawak, East Malaysia
Mirim Lagoon *63 E5 var.* Lake Mirim,
Sp. Laguna Merín. *lagoon* Brazil/
Uruguay
Mirim, Lake *see* Mirim Lagoon
Mírina *see* Mýrina
Mīrjāveh *120 E4* Sīstān va Balūchestān,
SE Iran
Mirny *154 C3 Russian research station*
Antarctica
Mirnyy *115 F3* Respublika Sakha
(Yakutiya), NE Russian Federation
Mīrpur Khās *134 B3* Sind, SE Pakistan
Mirtoan Sea *105 C6 Eng.* Mirtoan Sea;
anc. Myrtoum Mare. *sea* S Greece
Mirtoan Sea *see* Mirtóo Pélagos
Misiaf *see* Maşyāf
Miskito Coast *see* La Mosquitia
Miskitos, Cayos *53 E2 island group*
NE Nicaragua
Miskolc *99 D6* Borsod-Abaúj-Zemplén,
NE Hungary
Misool, Pulau *139 F4 island* Maluku,
E Indonesia
Mişrātah *71 F2 var.* Misurata. NW Libya
Mission *49 G5* Texas, SW USA
Mississippi *42 B2 off.* State of
Mississippi, *also known as* Bayou State,
Magnolia State. *state* SE USA
Mississippi Delta *42 B4 delta* Louisiana,
S USA
Mississippi River *35 C6 river* C USA
Missoula *44 B1* Montana, NW USA
Missouri *45 F5 off.* State of Missouri,
also known as Bullion State, Show Me
State. *state* C USA
Missouri River *45 E3 river* C USA
Mistassini, Lac *38 D3 lake* Québec,
SE Canada
Mistelbach an der Zaya *95 E6*
Niederösterreich, NE Austria
Misti, Volcán *61 E4 volcano* S Peru
Misurata *see* Mişrātah
Mitau *see* Jelgava
Mitchell *149 D5* Queensland, E Australia
Mitchell *45 E3* South Dakota, N USA
Mitchell, Mount *43 E1 mountain* North
Carolina, SE USA
Mitchell River *148 C2 river* Queensland,
NE Australia
Mi Tho *see* My Tho
Mitilíni *see* Mytilíni
Mito *131 D5* Ibaraki, Honshū, S Japan
Mitrovica/Mitrovicë *see* Kosovska
Mitrovica, Serbia
Mitrovica/Mitrowitz *see* Sremska
Mitrovica, Serbia
Mitrovicë *101 D5 Serb.* Mitrovica,
Kosovska Mitrovica, Titova Mitrovica.
N Kosovo
Mits'iwa *72 C4 var.* Masawa, Massawa.
E Eritrea
Mitspe Ramon *119 A7 prev.* Mizpe
Ramon. Southern, S Israel
Mittelstadt *see* Baia Sprie
Mitú *58 C4* Vaupés, SE Colombia
Mitumba, Chaîne des/Mitumba Range
see Mitumba, Monts
Mitumba Range *77 E7 var.* Chaîne des
Mitumba, Mitumba Range. *mountain
range* E Dem. Rep. Congo
Miueru Wantipa, Lake *77 E7 lake*
N Zambia
Miyake-jima *131 D6 island* Sakishima-
shotō, SW Japan
Miyako *130 D4* Iwate, Honshū, C Japan
Miyakonojō *131 D8 var.* Miyakonzyo.
Miyazaki, Kyūshū, SW Japan
Miyakonzyō *see* Miyakonojō
Miyāneh *see* Mīāneh
Miyazaki *131 B8* Miyazaki, Kyūshū,
SW Japan
Mizil *108 C5* Prahova, SE Romania
Miziya *104 C1* Vratsa, NW Bulgaria

Mizpe Ramon *see* Mitspe Ramon
Mjøsa *85 B6 var.* Mjøsen. *lake* S Norway
Mjøsen *see* Mjøsa
Mladenovac *100 D4* Serbia, C Serbia
Mława *98 D3* Mazowieckie, C Poland
Mljet *101 B5 It.* Meleda; *anc.* Melita.
island S Croatia
Mmabatho *78 C4* North-West, N South
Africa
Moab *44 B5* Utah, W USA
Moa Island *148 C1 island* Queensland,
NE Australia
Moanda *77 B6 var.* Mouanda. Haut-
Ogooué, SE Gabon
Moba *77 E7* Katanga, E Dem. Rep. Congo
Mobay *see* Montego Bay
Mobaye *77 C5* Basse-Kotto, S Central
African Republic
Moberly *45 G4* Missouri, C USA
Mobile *42 C3* Alabama, S USA
Mobutu Sese Seko, Lac *see* Albert, Lake
Moçâmedes *see* Namibe
Mochudi *78 C4* Kgatleng,
SE Botswana
Mocímboa da Praia *79 F2 var.* Vila de
Mocímboa da Praia. Cabo Delgado,
N Mozambique
Môco *78 B2 var.* Morro de Môco.
mountain W Angola
Mocoa *58 A4* Putumayo, SW Colombia
Môco, Morro de *see* Môco
Mocuba *79 E3* Zambézia,
NE Mozambique
Modena *96 B3 anc.* Mutina. Emilia-
Romagna, N Italy
Modesto *47 B6* California, W USA
Modica *97 C7 anc.* Motyca. Sicilia, Italy,
C Mediterranean Sea
Modimolle *78 D4 prev.* Nylstroom.
Limpopo, NE South Africa
Modohn *see* Madona
Modriča *100 C3* Republika Srpska,
N Bosnia and Herzegovina
Moe *149 C7* Victoria, SE Australia
Møen *see* Møn, Denmark
Moero, Lac *see* Mweru, Lake
Moeskroen *see* Mouscron
Mogadiscio/Mogadishu *see* Muqdisho
Mogador *see* Essaouira
Mogilëv *see* Mahilyow
Mogilev-Podol'skiy *see*
Mohyliv-Podil's'kyy
Mogilno *98 C3* Kujawsko-pomorskie,
C Poland
Mohammadābād-e Rīgān *120 E4*
Kermān, SE Iran
Mohammedia *70 C2 prev.* Fédala.
NW Morocco
Mohave, Lake *47 D7 reservoir* Arizona/
Nevada, W USA
Mohawk River *41 F3 river* New York,
NE USA
Mohéli *see* Mwali
Mohns Ridge *83 F3 undersea ridge*
Greenland Sea/Norwegian Sea
Moho *61 E4* Puno, SE Peru
Mohoro *73 C7* Pwani, E Tanzania
Mohyliv-Podil's'kyy *108 D3 Rus.*
Mogilev-Podol'skiy. Vinnyts'ka
Oblast', C Ukraine
Moi *85 A6* Rogaland, S Norway
Moili *see* Mwali
Mo i Rana *84 C3* Nordland, C Norway
Mõisaküla *106 D3 Ger.* Moiseküll.
Viljandimaa, S Estonia
Moiseküll *see* Mõisaküla
Moissac *91 B6* Tarn-et-Garonne,
S France
Mojácar *93 E5* Andalucía, S Spain
Mojave Desert *47 D7 plain* California,
W USA
Mokrany *see* Makrany
Moktama *see* Mottama
Mol *87 C5 prev.* Moll. Antwerpen,
N Belgium
Moldavia *see* Moldova
Moldavian SSR/Moldavskaya SSR *see*
Moldova
Molde *85 A5* Møre og Romsdal,
S Norway
Moldotau, Khrebet *see* Moldo-Too,
Khrebet
Moldo-Too, Khrebet *123 G2 prev.*
Khrebet Moldotau. *mountain range*
C Kyrgyzstan
Moldova *108 D3 off.* Republic of
Moldova, *var.* Moldavia; *prev.*
Moldavian SSR, *Rus.* Moldavskaya SSR.
country SE Europe

MOLDOVA
Southeast Europe

Official name Republic of Moldova
Formation 1991 / 1991
Capital Chisinau
Population 3.5 million / 269 people
per sq mile (104 people per sq km)
Total area 13,067 sq. miles (33,843 sq. km)
Languages Moldovan*, Ukrainian,
Russian
Religions Orthodox Christian 93%, Other
6%, Baptist 1%
Ethnic mix Moldovan 84%, Ukrainian 7%,
Gagauz 5%, Russian 2%, Bulgarian 1%,
Other 1%
Government Parliamentary system
Currency Moldovan leu = 100 bani
Literacy rate 99%
Calorie consumption 2707 kilocalories

Moldova Nouă *108 A4 Ger.*
Neumoldowa, *Hung.* Újmoldova.
Caraş-Severin, SW Romania
Moldova, Republic of *see* Moldova
Moldoveanul *see* Vârful Moldoveanu
Molfetta *97 E5* Puglia, SE Italy
Moll *see* Mol
Mollendo *61 E4* Arequipa, SW Peru
Mölndal *85 B7* Västra Götaland,
S Sweden
Molochans'k *109 G4 Rus.* Molochansk.
Zaporiz'ka Oblast', SE Ukraine
Molodechno/Molodeczno *see*
Maladzyechna
Molodezhnaya *154 C2 Russian research
station* Antarctica
Moloka'i *47 B8 var.* Molokai. *island*
Hawaiian Islands, Hawai'i, USA
Molokai Fracture Zone *153 E2 tectonic
feature* NE Pacific Ocean
Molopo *78 C4 seasonal river* Botswana/
South Africa
Mólos *105 B5* Stereá Elláda,
C Greece
Molotov *see* Severodvinsk,
Arkhangel'skaya Oblast', Russian
Federation
Molotov *see* Perm', Permskaya Oblast',
Russian Federation
Moluccas *139 F4 Dut.* Molukken, *Eng.*
Moluccas; *prev.* Spice Islands. *island
group* E Indonesia
Molucca Sea *139 F4 Ind.* Laut Maluku.
sea E Indonesia
Molukken *see* Maluku
Mombasa *73 D7* Coast, SE Kenya
Mombetsu *see* Monbetsu
Momchilgrad *104 D3 prev.* Mastanli.
Kŭrdzhali, S Bulgaria
Møn *85 B8 prev.* Möen. *island*
SE Denmark
Mona, Canal de la *see* Mona Passage
Monaco *91 C7 var.* Monaco-Ville; *anc.*
Monoecus. *country capital* (Monaco)
S Monaco
Monaco *91 E6 off.* Principality of
Monaco. *country* W Europe

MONACO
Southern Europe

Official name Principality of Monaco
Formation 1861 / 1861
Capital Monaco-Ville
Population 30,510 / 40,680 people per
sq mile (15,646 people per sq km)
Total area 0.75 sq. miles (1.95 sq. km)
Languages French*, Italian,
Monégasque, English
Religions Roman Catholic 89%,
Protestant 6%, Other 5%
Ethnic mix French 47%, Other 21%,
Italian 16%, Monégasque 16%
Government Mixed monarchical–
parliamentary system
Currency Euro = 100 cents
Literacy rate 99%
Calorie consumption Not available

Monaco *see* München
Monaco, Port de *91 C8 bay* S Monaco
W Mediterranean Sea
Monaco, Principality of *see* Monaco
Monaco-Ville *see* Monaco
Monahans *49 E3* Texas,
SW USA
Mona, Isla *55 E3 island* W Puerto Rico

Mona Passage *55 E3 Sp.* Canal de la Mona. *channel* Dominican Republic/ Puerto Rico
Monastir *see* Bitola
Monbetsu *130 D2 var.* Mombetsu, Monbetu. Hokkaidō, NE Japan
Monbetu *see* Monbetsu
Moncalieri *96 A2* Piemonte, NW Italy
Monchegorsk *110 C2* Murmanskaya Oblast', NW Russian Federation
Monclova *50 D2* Coahuila, NE Mexico
Moncton *39 F4* New Brunswick, SE Canada
Mondovì *96 A2* Piemonte, NW Italy
Monfalcone *96 D2* Friuli-Venezia Giulia, NE Italy
Monforte de Lemos *92 C1* Galicia, NW Spain
Mongo *76 C3* Guéra, C Chad
Mongolia *126 C2 Mong.* Mongol Uls. *country* E Asia

MONGOLIA
East Asia

Official name Mongolia
Formation 1924 / 1924
Capital Ulan Bator
Population 2.8 million / 5 people per sq mile (2 people per sq km)
Total area 604,247 sq. miles (1,565,000 sq. km)
Languages Khalkha Mongolian*, Kazakh, Chinese, Russian
Religions Tibetan Buddhist 50%, Nonreligious 40%, Shamanist and Christian 6%, Muslim 4%
Ethnic mix Khalkh 95%, Kazakh 4%, Other 1%
Government Mixed presidential– parliamentary system
Currency Tugrik (tögrög) = 100 möngö
Literacy rate 98%
Calorie consumption 2434 kilocalories

Mongolia, Plateau of *124 D1 plateau* E Mongolia
Mongol Uls *see* Mongolia
Mongora *see* Saidu
Mongos, Chaine des *see* Bongo, Massif des
Mongu *78 C2* Western, W Zambia
Monkchester *see* Newcastle upon Tyne
Monkey Bay *79 E2* Southern, SE Malawi
Monkey River *see* Monkey River Town
Monkey River Town *52 C2 var.* Monkey River. Toledo, SE Belize
Monoecus *see* Monaco
Mono Lake *47 C6 lake* California, W USA
Monostor *see* Beli Manastir
Monóvar *93 F4 Cat.* Monòver. Valenciana, E Spain
Monòver *see* Monóvar
Monroe *42 B2* Louisiana, S USA
Monrovia *74 C5 country capital* (Liberia) W Liberia
Mons *87 B6 Dut.* Bergen. Hainaut, S Belgium
Monselice *96 C2* Veneto, NE Italy
Montana *104 C2 prev.* Ferdinand, Mikhaylovgrad. Montana, NW Bulgaria
Montana *44 B1 off.* State of Montana, *also known as* Mountain State, Treasure State. *state* NW USA
Montargis *90 C4* Loiret, C France
Montauban *91 B6* Tarn-et-Garonne, S France
Montbéliard *90 D4* Doubs, E France
Mont Cenis, Col du *91 D5 pass* E France
Mont-de-Marsan *91 B6* Landes, SW France
Monteagudo *61 G4* Chuquisaca, S Bolivia
Montecarlo *61 C8* Misiones, NE Argentina
Monte Caseros *64 D3* Corrientes, NE Argentina
Monte Cristi *54 D3 var.* San Fernando de Monte Cristi. NW Dominican Republic
Monte Croce Carnico, Passo di *see* Plöcken Pass
Montegiardino *96 E2* SE San Marino
Montego Bay *54 A4 var.* Mobay. W Jamaica
Montélimar *91 D5 anc.* Acunum Acusio, Montilium Adhemari. Drôme, E France

Montemorelos *51 E3* Nuevo León, NE Mexico
Montenegro *101 C5 Serb.* Crna Gora. *country* SW Europe

MONTENEGRO
Southeast Europe

Official name Montenegro
Formation 2006 / 2006
Capital Podgorica
Population 600,000 / 113 people per sq mile (43 people per sq km)
Total area 5332 sq. miles (13,812 sq. km)
Languages Montenegrin*, Serbian, Albanian, Bosniak, Croatian
Religions Orthodox Christian 74%, Muslim 18%, Roman Catholic 4%, Other 4%
Ethnic mix Montenegrin 43%, Serb 32%, Other 12%, Bosniak 8%, Albanian 5%
Government Parliamentary system
Currency Euro = 100 cents
Literacy rate 98%
Calorie consumption 2887

Monte Patria *64 B3* Coquimbo, N Chile
Monterey *47 B6* California, W USA
Monterey *see* Monterrey
Monterey Bay *47 A6 bay* California, W USA
Montería *58 B2* Córdoba, NW Colombia
Montero *61 G4* Santa Cruz, C Bolivia
Monterrey *51 E3 var.* Monterey. Nuevo León, NE Mexico
Montes Claros *63 F3* Minas Gerais, SE Brazil
Montevideo *64 D4 country capital* (Uruguay) Montevideo, S Uruguay
Montevideo *45 F2* Minnesota, N USA
Montgenèvre, Col de *91 D5 pass* France/Italy
Montgomery *42 D2 state capital* Alabama, S USA
Montgomery *see* Sāhīwāl
Monthey *95 A7* Valais, SW Switzerland
Montilium Adhemari *see* Montélimar
Montluçon *90 C4* Allier, C France
Montoro *92 D4* Andalucía, S Spain
Montpelier *41 G2 state capital* Vermont, NE USA
Montpellier *91 C6* Hérault, S France
Montréal *39 F4 Eng.* Montreal. Québec, SE Canada
Montrose *88 D3* E Scotland, United Kingdom
Montrose *44 C5* Colorado, C USA
Montserrat *55 G3 var.* Emerald Isle. *UK dependent territory* E West Indies
Monywa *136 B3* Sagaing, C Myanmar (Burma)
Monza *96 B2* Lombardia, N Italy
Monze *78 D2* Southern, S Zambia
Monzón *93 F2* Aragón, NE Spain
Moonie *149 D5* Queensland, E Australia
Moon-Sund *see* Väinameri
Moora *147 A6* Western Australia
Moore *49 G1* Oklahoma, C USA
Moore, Lake *147 B6 lake* Western Australia
Moorhead *45 F2* Minnesota, N USA
Moose *38 C3 river* Ontario, S Canada
Moosehead Lake *41 G1 lake* Maine, NE USA
Moosonee *38 C3* Ontario, SE Canada
Mopti *75 E3* Mopti, C Mali
Moquegua *61 E4* Moquegua, SE Peru
Mora *85 C5* Dalarna, C Sweden
Morales *52 C2* Izabal, E Guatemala
Morant Bay *54 B5* E Jamaica
Moratalla *93 E4* Murcia, SE Spain
Morava *99 C5 var.* March. *river* C Europe
Morava *see* Moravia, Czech Republic
Morava *see* Velika Morava, Serbia
Moravia *99 B5 Cz.* Morava, *Ger.* Mähren. *cultural region* E Czech Republic
Moray Firth *88 C3 inlet* N Scotland, United Kingdom
Morea *see* Pelopónnisos
Moreau River *44 D2 river* South Dakota, N USA
Moree *149 D5* New South Wales, SE Australia
Morelia *51 E4* Michoacán, S Mexico
Morena, Sierra *92 C4 mountain range* S Spain
Moreni *108 C5* Dâmboviţa, S Romania

Morgan City *42 B3* Louisiana, S USA
Morghāb, Daryā-ye *see* Murgap
Morioka *130 D4* Iwate, Honshū, C Japan
Morlaix *90 A3* Finistère, NW France
Mormon State *see* Utah
Mornington Abyssal Plain *67 A7 abyssal plain* SE Pacific Ocean
Mornington Island *148 B2 island* Wellesley Islands, Queensland, N Australia
Morocco *70 B3 off.* Kingdom of Morocco, *Ar.* Al Mamlakah. *country* N Africa

MOROCCO
North Africa

Official name Kingdom of Morocco
Formation 1956 / 1969
Capital Rabat
Population 32.3 million / 187 people per sq mile (72 people per sq km)
Total area 172,316 sq. miles (446,300 sq. km)
Languages Arabic*, Tamazight (Berber), French, Spanish
Religions Muslim (mainly Sunni) 99%, Other (mostly Christian) 1%
Ethnic mix Arab 70%, Berber 29%, European 1%
Government Mixed monarchical– parliamentary system
Currency Moroccan dirham = 100 centimes
Literacy rate 56%
Calorie consumption 3264 kilocalories

Morocco *see* Marrakech
Morocco, Kingdom of *see* Morocco
Morogoro *73 C7* Morogoro, E Tanzania
Moro Gulf *139 E3 gulf* S Philippines
Morón *54 C2* Ciego de Ávila, C Cuba
Mörön *126 D2* Hövsgöl, N Mongolia
Morondava *79 F3* Toliara, W Madagascar
Moroni *79 F2 country capital* (Comoros) Grande Comore, NW Comoros
Morotai, Pulau *139 F3 island* Maluku, E Indonesia
Morotiri *see* Marotiri
Morphou *see* Güzelyurt
Morrinsville *150 D3* Waikato, North Island, New Zealand
Morris *45 F2* Minnesota, N USA
Morris Jesup, Kap *83 E1 headland* N Greenland
Morvan *90 D4 physical region* C France
Moscow *46 C2* Idaho, NW USA
Moscow *see* Moskva
Mosel *95 A5 Fr.* Moselle. *river* W Europe
Mosel *see* Moselle
Moselle *87 E8 Ger.* Mosel. *river* W Europe
Moselle *see* Mosel
Mosgiel *151 B7* Otago, South Island, New Zealand
Moshi *73 C7* Kilimanjaro, NE Tanzania
Mosjøen *84 B4* Nordland, C Norway
Moskovskiy *see* Moskva
Moskva *111 B5 Eng.* Moscow. *country capital* (Russian Federation) Gorod Moskva, W Russian Federation
Moskva *123 E3 Rus.* Moskovskiy; *prev.* Chubek. SW Tajikistan
Moson and Magyaróvár *see* Mosonmagyaróvár
Mosonmagyaróvár *99 C6 Ger.* Wieselburg-Ungarisch-Altenburg; *prev.* Moson and Magyaróvár, *Ger.* Wieselburg and Ungarisch-Altenburg. Győr-Moson-Sopron, NW Hungary
Mosquito Coast *53 E3 var.* Miskito Coast, *Eng.* Mosquitia. *coastal region* E Nicaragua
Mosquito Coast *see* La Mosquitia
Mosquito Gulf *53 F4 Eng.* Mosquito Gulf. *gulf* N Panama
Mosquito Gulf *see* Mosquitos, Golfo de los
Moss *85 B6* Østfold, S Norway
Mossâmedes *see* Namibe
Mosselbaai *78 C5 var.* Mosselbaai, *Eng.* Mossel Bay. Western Cape, SW South Africa
Mosselbai/Mossel Bay *see* Mosselbaai
Mossendjo *77 B6* Niari, SW Congo

Mossoró *63 G2* Rio Grande do Norte, NE Brazil
Most *98 A4 Ger.* Brüx. Ústecký Kraj, NW Czech Republic
Mosta *102 B5 var.* Musta. C Malta
Mostaganem *70 D2 var.* Mestghanem. NW Algeria
Mostar *100 C4* Federacija Bosna I Hercegovina, S Bosnia and Herzegovina
Mosty *see* Masty
Mosul *see* Al Mawşil
Mota del Cuervo *93 E3* Castilla-La Mancha, C Spain
Motagua, Río *52 B2 river* Guatemala/ Honduras
Mother of Presidents/Mother of States *see* Virginia
Motril *92 D5* Andalucía, S Spain
Motru *108 B4* Gorj, SW Romania
Mottama *136 B4 var.* Martaban, Moktama. Mon State, S Myanmar (Burma)
Motueka *151 C5* Tasman, South Island, New Zealand
Motul *51 H3 var.* Motul de Felipe Carrillo Puerto. Yucatán, SE Mexico
Motul de Felipe Carrillo Puerto *see* Motul
Motyca *see* Modica
Mouanda *see* Moanda
Mouhoun *see* Black Volta
Mouila *77 A6* Ngounié, C Gabon
Moukden *see* Shenyang
Mould Bay *37 E2* Prince Patrick Island, Northwest Territories, N Canada
Moulins *90 C4* Allier, C France
Moulmein *see* Mawlamyine
Moundou *76 B4* Logone-Occidental, SW Chad
Moŭng Roessei *137 D5* Bătdâmbâng, W Cambodia
Moun Hou *see* Black Volta
Mountain Home *42 B1* Arkansas, C USA
Mountain State *see* Montana
Mountain State *see* West Virginia
Mount Cook *151 B6* Canterbury, South Island, New Zealand
Mount Desert Island *41 H2 island* Maine, NE USA
Mount Gambier *149 B7* South Australia
Mount Isa *148 B3* Queensland, C Australia
Mount Magnet *147 B5* Western Australia
Mount Pleasant *45 G4* Iowa, C USA
Mount Pleasant *40 C3* Michigan, N USA
Mount Vernon *40 B5* Illinois, N USA
Mount Vernon *46 B1* Washington, NW USA
Mourdi, Dépression du *76 C2 desert lowland* Chad/Sudan
Mouscron *87 A6 Dut.* Moeskroen. Hainaut, W Belgium
Mouse River *see* Souris River
Moussoro *76 B3* Kanem, W Chad
Moyen-Congo *see* Congo (Republic of)
Mo'ynoq *122 C1 Rus.* Muynak. Qoraqalpog'iston Respublikasi, NW Uzbekistan
Moyobamba *60 B2* San Martín, NW Peru
Moyu *126 B3 var.* Karakax. Xinjiang Uygur Zizhiqu, NW China
Moynkum, Peski *123 F1 Kaz.* Moyynqum. *desert* S Kazakhstan
Moyynqum *see* Moyynkum, Peski
Mozambika, Lakandranon'i *see* Mozambique Channel
Mozambique *79 E3 off.* Republic of Mozambique; *prev.* People's Republic of Mozambique, Portuguese East Africa. *country* S Africa

MOZAMBIQUE
Southern Africa

Official name Republic of Mozambique
Formation 1975 / 1975
Capital Maputo
Population 23.9 million / 79 people per sq mile (30 people per sq km)
Total area 309,494 sq. miles (801,590 sq. km)
Languages Makua, Xitsonga, Sena, Lomwe, Portuguese*
Religions Traditional beliefs 56%, Christian 30%, Muslim 14%
Ethnic mix Makua Lomwe 47%, Tsonga 23%, Malawi 12%, Shona 11%,

MOZAMBIQUE
(continued)

Yao 4%, Other 3%
Government Presidential system
Currency New metical = 100 centavos
Literacy rate 55%
Calorie consumption 2112 kilocalories

Mozambique Basin see Natal Basin
Mozambique, Canal de see Mozambique Channel
Mozambique Channel 79 E3 *Fr.* Canal de Mozambique, *Mal.* Lakandranon' i Mozambika. *strait* W Indian Ocean
Mozambique, People's Republic of see Mozambique
Mozambique Plateau 69 D7 *var.* Mozambique Rise. *undersea plateau* SW Indian Ocean
Mozambique, Republic of see Mozambique
Mozambique Rise see Mozambique Plateau
Mozyr' see Mazyr
Mpama 77 B6 *river* C Congo
Mpika 78 D2 Northern, NE Zambia
Mqinvartsveri see Kazbek
Mragowo 98 D2 *Ger.* Sensburg. Warmińsko-Mazurskie, NE Poland
Mthatha 78 D5 *prev.* Umtata. Eastern Cape, SE South Africa
Mtkvari see Kura
Mtwara 73 D8 Mtwara, SE Tanzania
Mualo see Messalo, Rio
Muang Chiang Rai see Chiang Rai
Muang Kalasin see Kalasin
Muang Khammouan see Thakhèk
Muang Không 137 D5 Champasak, S Laos
Muang Khôngxédôn 137 D5 *var.* Khong Sedone. Salavan, S Laos
Muang Khon Kaen see Khon Kaen
Muang Lampang see Lampang
Muang Loei see Loei
Muang Lom Sak see Lom Sak
Muang Nakhon Sawan see Nakhon Sawan
Muang Namo 136 C3 Oudômxai, N Laos
Muang Nan see Nan
Muang Phalan 136 D4 *var.* Muang Phalane. Savannakhét, S Laos
Muang Phalane see Muang Phalan
Muang Phayao see Phayao
Muang Phitsanulok see Phitsanulok
Muang Phrae see Phrae
Muang Roi Et see Roi Et
Muang Sakon Nakhon see Sakon Nakhon
Muang Samut Prakan see Samut Prakan
Muang Sing 136 C3 Louang Namtha, N Laos
Muang Ubon see Ubon Ratchathani
Muang Xaignabouri see Xaignabouli
Muar 138 B3 *var.* Bandar Maharani. Johor, Peninsular Malaysia
Mucojo 79 F2 Cabo Delgado, N Mozambique
Mudanjiang 129 E3 *var.* Mu-tan-chiang. Heilongjiang, NE China
Mudon 137 B5 Mon State, S Myanmar (Burma)
Muenchen see München
Muenster see Münster
Mufulira 78 D2 Copperbelt, C Zambia
Mughla see Muğla
Muğla 116 A4 *var.* Mughla. Muğla, SW Turkey
Muḥ, Sabkhat al 118 C3 *lake* C Syria
Muhu Väin see Väinameri
Muisne 60 A1 Esmeraldas, NW Ecuador
Mukacheve 108 B3 *Hung.* Munkács, *Rus.* Mukachevo. Zakarpats'ka Oblast', W Ukraine
Mukachevo see Mukacheve
Mukalla see Al Mukallā
Mukden see Shenyang
Mula 93 E4 Murcia, SE Spain
Mulakatholhu 132 B4 *var.* Meemu Atoll, Mulaku Atoll. *atoll* C Maldives
Mulaku Atoll see Mulakatholhu
Muleshoe 49 E2 Texas, SW USA
Mulhacén 93 E5 *var.* Cerro de Mulhacén. *mountain* S Spain
Mulhacén, Cerro de see Mulhacén
Mülhausen see Mulhouse

Mülheim 95 A6 *var.* Mulheim an der Ruhr. Nordrhein-Westfalen, W Germany
Mulheim an der Ruhr see Mülheim
Mulhouse 90 E4 *Ger.* Mülhausen. Haut-Rhin, NE France
Müller-gerbergte see Muller, Pegunungan
Muller, Pegunungan 138 D4 *Dut.* Müller-gerbergte. *mountain range* Borneo, C Indonesia
Mull, Isle of 88 B4 *island* W Scotland, United Kingdom
Mulongo 77 D7 Katanga, SE Dem. Rep. Congo
Multān 134 C2 Punjab, E Pakistan
Mumbai 134 C5 *prev.* Bombay. *state capital* Mahārāshtra, W India
Munamägi see Suur Munamägi
Münchberg 95 C5 Bayern, E Germany
München 95 C6 *var.* Munich, *Eng.* Munich, *It.* Monaco. Bayern, SE Germany
Muncie 40 C4 Indiana, N USA
Mungbere 77 E5 Orientale, NE Dem. Rep. Congo
Mu Nggava see Rennell
Munich see München
Munkács see Mukacheve
Münster 94 A4 *var.* Muenster, Münster in Westfalen. Nordrhein-Westfalen, W Germany
Munster 89 A6 *Ir.* Cúige Mumhan. *cultural region* S Ireland
Münster in Westfalen see Münster
Muong Xiang Ngeun 136 C4 *var.* Xieng Ngeun. Louangphabang, N Laos
Muonio 84 D3 Lappi, N Finland
Muonioälv/Muoniojoki see Muoniojoki
Muonionjoki 84 D3 *var.* Muoniojoki, *Swe.* Muonioälv. *river* Finland/Sweden
Muqāt 119 C5 Al Mafraq, E Jordan
Muqdisho 73 D6 *Eng.* Mogadishu, *It.* Mogadiscio. *country capital* (Somalia) Banaadir, S Somalia
Mur 95 E7 *SCr.* Mura. *river* C Europe
Mura see Mur
Muradiye 117 F3 Van, E Turkey
Murapara see Murupara
Murata 96 E2 S San Marino
Murchison River 147 A5 *river* Western Australia
Murcia 93 F4 Murcia, SE Spain
Murcia 93 E4 *autonomous community* SE Spain
Mureş 108 A4 *river* Hungary/Romania
Murfreesboro 42 D1 Tennessee, S USA
Murgab see Murghob
Murgap 122 D3 Mary Welaýaty, S Turkmenistan
Murgap 122 D3 *var.* Deryasi Murgap, Murghab, *Pash.* Daryā-ye Morghāb, *Rus.* Murgab. *river* Afghanistan/Turkmenistan
Murghob 123 F3 *Rus.* Murgab. SE Tajikistan
Murgon 149 E5 Queensland, E Australia
Müritäniyah see Mauritania
Müritz 94 C3 *var.* Müritzee. *lake* NE Germany
Müritzee see Müritz
Murmansk 110 C2 Murmanskaya Oblast', NW Russian Federation
Murmashi 110 C2 Murmanskaya Oblast', NW Russian Federation
Murom 111 B5 Vladimirskaya Oblast', W Russian Federation
Muroran 130 D3 Hokkaidō, NE Japan
Muros 92 B1 Galicia, NW Spain
Murray Fracture Zone 153 E2 *fracture zone* NE Pacific Ocean
Murray Range see Murray Ridge
Murray Ridge 112 C5 *var.* Murray Range. *undersea ridge* N Arabian Sea
Murray River 149 B6 *river* SE Australia
Murrumbidgee River 149 C6 *river* New South Wales, SE Australia
Murska Sobota 95 E7 *Ger.* Olsnitz. NE Slovenia
Murupara 150 D3 *var.* Murapara. Bay of Plenty, North Island, New Zealand
Murviedro see Sagunto
Murwāra 135 E4 Madhya Pradesh, N India
Murwillumbah 149 E5 New South Wales, SE Australia
Murzuq, Edeyin see Murzuq, Idhān
Murzuq, Idhān 71 F4 *var.* Edeyin Murzuq. *desert* SW Libya

Mürzzuschlag 95 E7 Steiermark, E Austria
Muş 117 F3 *var.* Mush. Muş, E Turkey
Musa, Gebel 72 C2 *var.* Gebel Mûsa. *mountain* NE Egypt
Mûsa, Gebel see Mûsá, Jabal
Musala 104 B3 *mountain* W Bulgaria
Muscat see Masqaţ
Muscat and Oman see Oman
Muscatine 45 G3 Iowa, C USA
Musgrave Ranges 147 D5 *mountain range* South Australia
Musina 78 D3 *prev.* Messina. Limpopo, NE South Africa
Muskegon 40 C3 Michigan, N USA
Muskogean see Tallahassee
Muskogee 49 G1 Oklahoma, C USA
Musoma 73 C6 Mara, N Tanzania
Musta see Mosta
Mustafa-Pasha see Svilengrad
Musters, Lago 65 B6 *lake* S Argentina
Muswellbrook 149 D6 New South Wales, SE Australia
Mut 116 C4 İçel, S Turkey
Mu-tan-chiang see Mudanjiang
Mutare 78 D3 *var.* Mutari; *prev.* Umtali. Manicaland, E Zimbabwe
Mutari see Mutare
Mutina see Modena
Mutsu-wan 130 D3 *bay* N Japan
Muttonbird Islands 151 A8 *island group* SW New Zealand
Mu Us Shadi 127 E3 *var.* Ordos Desert; *prev.* Mu Us Shamo. *desert* N China
Mu Us Shamo see Mu Us Shadi
Muy Muy 52 D3 Matagalpa, C Nicaragua
Muynak see Mo'ynoq
Mužlja 100 D3 *Hung.* Felsőmuzslya; *prev.* Gornja Mužlja. Vojvodina, N Serbia
Mwali 79 F2 *var.* Moili, *Fr.* Mohéli. *island* S Comoros
Mwanza 73 B6 Mwanza, NW Tanzania
Mweka 77 C6 Kasai-Occidental, C Dem. Rep. Congo
Mwene-Ditu 77 D7 Kasai-Oriental, S Dem. Rep. Congo
Mweru, Lake 77 D7 *var.* Lac Moero. *lake* Dem. Rep. Congo/Zambia
Myadel' see Myadzyel
Myadzyel 107 C5 *prev.* Myadel, *Rus.* Myadel'. Minskaya Voblasts', N Belarus
Myanaung 136 B4 Ayeyarwady, SW Myanmar (Burma)
Myanmar 136 A3 *off.* Union of Myanmar. *country* SE Asia. *See also* Burma

MYANMAR (BURMA)
Southeast Asia

Official name Union of Myanmar
Formation 1948 / 1948
Capital Nay Pyi Taw
Population 48.3 million / 190 people per sq mile (73 people per sq km)
Total area 261,969 sq. miles (678,500 sq. km)
Languages Burmese*, Shan, Karen, Rakhine, Chin, Yangbye, Kachin, Mon
Religions Buddhist 89%, Christian 4%, Muslim 4%, Other 2%, Animist 1%
Ethnic mix Burman (Bamah) 68%, Other 12%, Shan 9%, Karen 7%, Rakhine 4%
Government Presidential system
Currency Kyat = 100 pyas
Literacy rate 92%
Calorie consumption 2493 calories

Myaungmya 136 A4 Ayeyarwady, SW Myanmar (Burma)
Myaydo see Aunglan
Myeik 137 B6 *var.* Mergui. Tanintharyi, S Myanmar (Burma)
Myeik Archipelago see Mergui Archipelago. *island group* S Myanmar (Burma)
Myerkulavichy 107 D7 *Rus.* Merkulovichi. Homyel'skaya Voblasts', SE Belarus
Myingyan 136 B3 Mandalay, C Myanmar (Burma)
Myitkyina 136 B2 Kachin State, N Myanmar (Burma)
Mykolayiv 109 E4 *Rus.* Nikolayev. Mykolayivs'ka Oblast', S Ukraine
Mykonos 105 D6 *var.* Míkonos. *island* Kykládes, Greece, Aegean Sea

Myrhorod 109 F2 *Rus.* Mirgorod. Poltavs'ka Oblast', NE Ukraine
Mýrina 104 D4 *var.* Mírina. Límnos, SE Greece
Myrtle Beach 43 F2 South Carolina, SE USA
Mýrtos 105 D8 Kríti, Greece, E Mediterranean Sea
Myrtoum Mare see Mirtóo Pélagos
Myślibórz 98 B3 Zachodnio-pomorskie, NW Poland
Mysore 132 C2 *var.* Maisur. Karnātaka, W India
Mysore see Karnātaka
My Tho 137 E6 *var.* Mi Tho. Tiền Giang, S Vietnam
Mytilene see Mytilíni
Mytilíni 105 D5 *var.* Mitilíni; *anc.* Mytilene. Lésvos, E Greece
Mzuzu 79 E2 Northern, N Malawi

N

Naberezhnyye Chelny 111 D5 *prev.* Brezhnev. Respublika Tatarstan, W Russian Federation
Nablus 119 A6 *var.* Nābulus, *Heb.* Shekhem; *anc.* Neapolis, *Bibl.* Shechem. N West Bank
Nābulus see Nablus
Nacala 79 F2 Nampula, NE Mozambique
Na-Ch'ii see Nagqu
Nada see Danzhou
Nadi 145 E4 *prev.* Nandi. Viti Levu, W Fiji
Nadur 102 A5 Gozo, N Malta
Nadvirna 108 C3 *Pol.* Nadwórna, *Rus.* Nadvornaya. Ivano-Frankivs'ka Oblast', W Ukraine
Nadvoitsy 110 B3 Respublika Kareliya, NW Russian Federation
Nadvornaya/Nadwórna see Nadvirna
Nadym 114 D3 Yamalo-Nenetskiy Avtonomnyy Okrug, N Russian Federation
Náfpaktos 105 B5 *var.* Návpaktos. Dytikí Elláda, C Greece
Náfplio 105 B6 *prev.* Návplion. Peloponnísos, S Greece
Naga 139 E2 *off.* Naga City; *prev.* Nueva Caceres. Luzon, N Philippines
Naga City see Naga
Nagano 131 C5 Nagano, Honshū, S Japan
Nagaoka 131 D5 Niigata, Honshū, C Japan
Nagara Pathom see Nakhon Pathom
Nagara Sridharmaraj see Nakhon Si Thammarat
Nagara Svarga see Nakhon Sawan
Nagasaki 131 A7 Nagasaki, Kyūshū, SW Japan
Nagato 131 A7 Yamaguchi, Honshū, SW Japan
Nāgercoil 132 C3 Tamil Nādu, SE India
Nagorno-Karabakh 117 G3 *var.* Nagorno- Karabakhskaya Avtonomnaya Oblast. *Arm.* Lerrnayin Gharabakh, *Az.* Dağlıq Quarabağ, *Rus.* Nagornyy Karabakh. *former autonomous region* SW Azerbaijan
Nagorno- Karabakhskaya Avtonomnaya Oblast see Nagorno-Karabakh
Nagornyy Karabakh see Nagorno-Karabakh
Nagoya 131 C6 Aichi, Honshū, SW Japan
Nägpur 134 D4 Mahārāshtra, C India
Nagqu 126 C5 Chin. Na-Ch'ii; *prev.* Hei-ho. Xizang Zizhiqu, W China
Nagybánya see Baia Mare
Nagybecskerek see Zrenjanin
Nagydisznód see Cisnădie
Nagyenyed see Aiud
Nagykálló 99 E6 Szabolcs-Szatmár-Bereg, E Hungary
Nagykanizsa 99 C7 *Ger.* Grosskanizsa. Zala, SW Hungary
Nagykároly see Carei
Nagykikinda see Kikinda
Nagykőrös 99 D7 Pest, C Hungary
Nagymihály see Michalovce
Nagysurány see Šurany
Nagyszalonta see Salonta
Nagyszeben see Sibiu
Nagyszentmiklós see Sânnicolau Mare
Nagyszöllős see Vynohradiv
Nagyszombat see Trnava
Nagytapolcsány see Topoľčany

Nagyvárad *see* Oradea
Naha *130 A3* Okinawa, Okinawa, SW Japan
Nahariya *119 A5 prev.* Nahariyya. Northern, N Israel
Nahariyya *see* Nahariya
Nahuel Huapi, Lago *65 B5 lake* W Argentina
Nain *39 F2* Newfoundland and Labrador, NE Canada
Nā'īn *120 D3* Eşfahān, C Iran
Nairobi *69 E5 country capital* (Kenya) Nairobi Area, S Kenya
Nairobi *73 C6* Nairobi Area, S Kenya
Naissus *see* Niš
Najaf *see* An Najaf
Najima *see* Fukuoka
Najin *129 E3* NE North Korea
Najrān *121 B6 var.* Abā as Su'ūd. Najrān, S Saudi Arabia
Nakambé *see* White Volta
Nakamura *131 B7 var.* Shimanto. Kōchi, Shikoku, SW Japan
Nakatsugawa *131 C6 var.* Nakatugawa. Gifu, Honshū, SW Japan
Nakatugawa *see* Nakatsugawa
Nakhichevan' *see* Naxçıvan
Nakhodka *115 G5* Primorskiy Kray, SE Russian Federation
Nakhon Pathom *137 C5 var.* Nagara Pathom, Nakorn Pathom. Nakhon Pathom, W Thailand
Nakhon Ratchasima *137 C5 var.* Khorat, Korat. Nakhon Ratchasima, E Thailand
Nakhon Sawan *137 C5 var.* Muang Nakhon Sawan, Nagara Svarga. Nakhon Sawan, W Thailand
Nakhon Si Thammarat *137 C7 var.* Nagara Sridharmaraj, Nakhon Sithammaraj. Nakhon Si Thammarat, SW Thailand
Nakhon Sithammaraj *see* Nakhon Si Thammarat
Nakorn Pathom *see* Nakhon Pathom
Nakuru *73 C6* Rift Valley, SW Kenya
Nal'chik *111 B8* Kabardino-Balkarskaya Respublika, SW Russian Federation
Nālūt *71 F2* NW Libya
Namakan Lake *40 A1 lake* Canada/ USA
Namangan *123 F2* Namangan Viloyati, E Uzbekistan
Nambala *78 D2* Central, C Zambia
Nam Co *126 C5 lake* W China
Nam Đinh *136 D3* Nam Ha, N Vietnam
Namib Desert *78 B3 desert* N Namibia
Namibe *78 A2 Port.* Moçâmedes, Mossâmedes. Namibe, SW Angola
Namibia *78 B3 off.* Republic of Namibia, *var.* South West Africa, *Afr.* Suidwes-Afrika, *Ger.* Deutsch-Südwestafrika; *prev.* German Southwest Africa, South-West Africa. *country* S Africa

---

NAMIBIA
Southern Africa

Official name Republic of Namibia
Formation 1990 / 1994
Capital Windhoek
Population 2.3 million / 7 people per sq mile (3 people per sq km)
Total area 318,694 sq. miles (825,418 sq. km)
Languages Ovambo, Kavango, English*, Bergdama, German, Afrikaans
Religions Christian 90%, Traditional beliefs 10%
Ethnic mix Ovambo 50%, Other tribes 22%, Kavango 9%, Damara 7%, Herero 7%, Other 5%
Government Presidential system
Currency Namibian dollar & South African rand = 100 cents
Literacy rate 88%
Calorie consumption 2151 kilocalories

Namibia, Republic of *see* Namibia
Nam Khong *see* Mekong
Namnetes *see* Nantes
Namo *see* Namu Atoll
Nam Ou *136 C3 river* N Laos
Nampa *46 D3* Idaho, NW USA
Nampula *79 E2* Nampula, NE Mozambique
Namsos *84 B4* Nord-Trøndelag, C Norway
Nam Tha *136 C4 river* N Laos

Namu Atoll *144 D2 var.* Namo. *atoll* Ralik Chain, C Marshall Islands
Namur *87 C6 Dut.* Namen. Namur, SE Belgium
Namyit Island *128 C8 island* S Spratly Islands
Nan *136 C4 var.* Muang Nan. Nan, NW Thailand
Nanaimo *36 D5* Vancouver Island, British Columbia, SW Canada
Nanchang *128 C5 var.* Nan-ch'ang, Nanch'ang-hsien. *province capital* Jiangxi, S China
Nan-ch'ang *see* Nanchang
Nanch'ang-hsien *see* Nanchang
Nan-ching *see* Nanjing
Nancy *90 D3* Meurthe-et-Moselle, NE France
Nandaime *52 D3* Granada, SW Nicaragua
Nanded *134 D5* Mahārāshtra, C India
Nandi *see* Nadi
Nándorhegy *see* Oţelu Roşu
Nandyāl *132 C1* Andhra Pradesh, E India
Nan Hai *see* South China Sea
Naniwa *see* Ōsaka
Nanjing *128 C5 var.* Nan-ching, Nanking; *prev.* Chianning, Chian-ning, Kiang-ning, Jiangsu. *province capital* Jiangsu, E China
Nanking *see* Nanjing
Nanning *128 B6 var.* Nan-ning; *prev.* Yung-ning. Guangxi Zhuangzu Zizhiqu, S China
Nan-ning *see* Nanning
Nanortalik *82 C5* Kitaa, S Greenland
Nanpan Jiang *136 D2 river* S China
Nanping *128 D6 var.* Nan-p'ing; *prev.* Yenping. Fujian, SE China
Nan-p'ing *see* Nanping
Nansei Syotō Trench *see* Ryukyu Trench
Nansen Basin *155 C4 undersea basin* Arctic Ocean
Nansen Cordillera *155 B3 var.* Arctic Mid Oceanic Ridge, Nansen Ridge. *seamount range* Arctic Ocean
Nansen Ridge *see* Nansen Cordillera
Nansha Qundao *see* Spratly Islands
Nanterre *90 D1* Hauts-de-Seine, N France
Nantes *90 B4 Bret.* Naoned; *anc.* Condivincum, Namnetes. Loire-Atlantique, NW France
Nantucket Island *41 G3 island* Massachusetts, NE USA
Nanumaga *145 E3 var.* Nanumanga. *atoll* NW Tuvalu
Nanumanga *see* Nanumaga
Nanumea Atoll *145 E3 atoll* NW Tuvalu
Nanyang *128 C5 var.* Nan-yang. Henan, C China
Nan-yang *see* Nanyang
Naoned *see* Nantes
Napa *47 B6* California, W USA
Napier *150 E4* Hawke's Bay, North Island, New Zealand
Naples *43 E5* Florida, SE USA
Naples *see* Napoli
Napo *56 A3 province* NE Ecuador
Napoléon-Vendée *see* la Roche-sur-Yon
Napoli *97 C5 Eng.* Naples, *Ger.* Neapel; *anc.* Neapolis. Campania, S Italy
Napo, Río *60 C2 river* Ecuador/Peru
Naracoorte *149 B7* South Australia
Naradhivas *see* Narathiwat
Narathiwat *137 C7 var.* Naradhivas. Narathiwat, SW Thailand
Narbada *see* Narmada
Narbo Martius *see* Narbonne
Narbonne *91 C6 anc.* Narbo Martius. Aude, S France
Narborough Island *see* Fernandina, Isla
Nares Abyssal Plain *see* Nares Plain
Nares Plain *35 E6 var.* Nares Abyssal Plain. *abyssal plain* NW Atlantic Ocean
Nares Stræde *see* Nares Strait
Nares Strait *82 D1 Dan.* Nares Stræde. *strait* Canada/Greenland
Narew *98 E3 river* E Poland
Narmada *124 B3 var.* Narbada. *river* C India
Narova *see* Narva
Narovlya *see* Narowlya
Narowlya *107 C8 Rus.* Narovlya. Homyel'skaya Voblasts', SE Belarus
Närpes *85 D5 Fin.* Närpiö. Länsi-Suomi, W Finland
Närpiö *see* Närpes

Narrabri *149 D6* New South Wales, SE Australia
Narrogin *147 B6* Western Australia
Narva *106 E2* Ida-Virumaa, NE Estonia
Narva *106 E2 prev.* Narova. *river* Estonia/Russian Federation
Narva Bay *106 E2 Est.* Narva Laht, *Ger.* Narwa-Bucht, *Rus.* Narvskiy Zaliv. *bay* Estonia/Russian Federation
Narva Laht *see* Narva Bay
Narva Reservoir *106 E2 Est.* Narva Veehoidla, *Rus.* Narvskoye Vodokhranilishche. *reservoir* Estonia/ Russian Federation
Narva Veehoidla *see* Narva Reservoir
Narvik *84 C3* Nordland, C Norway
Narvskiy Zaliv *see* Narva Bay
Narvskoye Vodokhranilishche *see* Narva Reservoir
Narwa-Bucht *see* Narva Bay
Nar'yan-Mar *110 D3 prev.* Beloshchel'ye, Dzerzhinsky. Nenetskiy Avtonomnyy Okrug, NW Russian Federation
Naryn *123 G2* Narynskaya Oblast', C Kyrgyzstan
Nassau *54 C1 country capital* (Bahamas) New Providence, N Bahamas
Năsăud *108 B3 Ger.* Nussdorf, *Hung.* Naszód. Bistriţa-Năsăud, N Romania
Nase *see* Naze
Nāshik *134 C5 prev.* Nāsik. Mahārāshtra, W India
Nashua *41 G3* New Hampshire, NE USA
Nashville *42 C1 state capital* Tennessee, S USA
Näsijärvi *85 D5 lake* SW Finland
Nāsik *see* Nāshik
Nasir, Buhayrat/Nâşir,Buheiret *see* Nasser, Lake
Nāsiri *see* Ahvāz
Nasiriya *see* An Nāşirīyah
Nasser, Lake *72 B3 var.* Buhayrat Nasir, Buhayrat Nâşir, Buheiret Nâşir. *lake* Egypt/Sudan
Naszód *see* Năsăud
Nata *78 C3* Central, NE Botswana
Natal *63 G2 state capital* Rio Grande do Norte, E Brazil
Natal Basin *141 A6 var.* Mozambique Basin. *undersea basin* W Indian Ocean
Natanya *see* Netanya
Natchez *42 B3* Mississippi, S USA
Natchitoches *42 A2* Louisiana, S USA
Nathanya *see* Netanya
Natitingou *75 F4* NW Benin
Natsrat *see* Natzrat
Natuna Islands *see* Natuna, Kepulauan
Natuna, Kepulauan *124 D4 var.* Natuna Islands. *island group* W Indonesia
Naturaliste Plateau *141 E6 undersea plateau* E Indian Ocean
Natzrat *119 A5 var.* Natsrat, *Ar.* En Nazira, *Eng.* Nazareth; *prev.* Nazerat. Northern, N Israel
Naugard *see* Nowogard
Naujamiestis *106 C4* Panevėžys, C Lithuania
Nauru *144 D2 off.* Republic of Nauru; *prev.* Pleasant Island. *country* W Pacific Ocean

---

NAURU
Australasia & Oceania

Official name Republic of Nauru
Formation 1968 / 1968
Capital Yaren District
Population 9378 / 1158 people per sq mile (447 people per sq km)
Total area 8.1 sq. miles (21 sq. km)
Languages Nauruan*, Kiribati, Chinese, Tuvaluan, English
Religions Nauruan Congregational Church 60%, Roman Catholic 35%, Other 5%
Ethnic mix Nauruan 93%, Chinese 5%, European 1%, Other Pacific islanders 1%
Government Nonparty system
Currency Australian dollar = 100 cents
Literacy rate 95%
Calorie consumption Not available

Nauru, Republic of *see* Nauru
Nauta *60 C2* Loreto, N Peru
Navahrudak *107 C6 Pol.* Nowogródek, *Rus.* Novogrudok. Hrodzyenskaya Voblasts', W Belarus
Navanagar *see* Jāmnagar

Navapolatsk *107 D5 Rus.* Novopolotsk. Vitsyebskaya Voblasts', N Belarus
Navarra *93 E2 Eng./Fr.* Navarre. *autonomous community* N Spain
Navarre *see* Navarra
Navassa Island *54 C3 US unincorporated territory* C West Indies
Navoi *see* Navoiy
Navoiy *123 E2 Rus.* Navoi. Navoiy Viloyati, C Uzbekistan
Navojoa *50 C2* Sonora, NW Mexico
Navolat *see* Navolato
Navolato *50 C3 var.* Navolat. Sinaloa, C Mexico
Návpaktos *see* Náfpaktos
Návplion *see* Náfplio
Nawabashah *see* Nawābshāh
Nawābshāh *134 B3 var.* Nawabashah. Sind, S Pakistan
Naxçıvan *117 G3 Rus.* Nakhichevan'. SW Azerbaijan
Náxos *105 D6 var.* Naxos. Náxos, Kykládes, Greece, Aegean Sea
Náxos *105 D6 island* Kykládes, Greece, Aegean Sea
Nayoro *130 D2* Hokkaidō, NE Japan
Nay Pyi Taw *136 B4 country capital* (Myanmar (Burma)) Mandalay, C Myanmar (Burma)
Nazareth *see* Natzrat
Nazca *60 D4* Ica, S Peru
Nazca Ridge *57 A5 undersea ridge* E Pacific Ocean
Naze *130 B3 var.* Nase. Kagoshima, Amami-ōshima, SW Japan
Nazerat *see* Natzrat
Nazilli *116 A4* Aydın, SW Turkey
Nazrēt *73 A var.* Adama, Hadama. Oromiya, C Ethiopia
N'Dalatando *78 B1 Port.* Salazar, Vila Salazar. Cuanza Norte, NW Angola
Ndélé *76 C4* Bamingui-Bangoran, N Central African Republic
Ndendé *77 B6* Ngounié, S Gabon
Ndindi *77 A6* Nyanga, S Gabon
Ndjamena *76 B3 var.* N'Djamena; *prev.* Fort-Lamy. *country capital* (Chad) Chari-Baguirmi, W Chad
N'Djamena *see* Ndjamena
Ndjolé *77 A5* Moyen-Ogooué, W Gabon
Ndola *78 D2* Copperbelt, C Zambia
Ndzouani *see* Nzwani
Neagh, Lough *89 B5 lake* E Northern Ireland, United Kingdom
Néa Moudania *104 C4 var.* Néa Moudhaniá. Kentrikí Makedonía, N Greece
Néa Moudhaniá *see* Néa Moudania
Neapel *see* Napoli
Neápoli *104 B4 prev.* Neápolis. Dytikí Makedonía, N Greece
Neápoli *105 D8* Kríti, Greece, E Mediterranean Sea
Neápoli *105 C7* Pelopónnisos, S Greece
Neápolis *see* Neápoli, Greece
Neapolis *see* Napoli, Italy
Neapolis *see* Nablus, West Bank
Near Islands *35 A2 island group* Aleutian Islands, Alaska, USA
Néa Zíkhni *104 C3 var.* Néa Zíkhni; *prev.* Néa Zíkhna. Kentrikí Makedonía, NE Greece
Néa Zíkhna/Néa Zíkhni *see* Néa Zíchni
Nebaj *52 B2* Quiché, W Guatemala
Nebitdag *see* Balkanabat
Neblina, Pico da *62 C1 mountain* NW Brazil
Nebraska *44 D4 off.* State of Nebraska, *also known as* Blackwater State, Cornhusker State, Tree Planters State. *state* C USA
Nebraska City *45 F4* Nebraska, C USA
Neches River *49 H3 river* Texas, SW USA
Neckar *95 B6 river* SW Germany
Necochea *65 D5* Buenos Aires, E Argentina
Nederland *see* Netherlands
Neder Rijn *86 D4 Eng.* Lower Rhine. *river* C Netherlands
Nederweert *87 D5* Limburg, SE Netherlands
Neede *86 E3* Gelderland, E Netherlands
Neerpelt *87 D5* Limburg, NE Belgium
Neftekamsk *111 D5* Bashkortostan, W Russian Federation
Neftezavodsk *see* Seýdi
Negara Brunei Darussalam *see* Brunei
Negēlē *73 D5 var.* Negelli, *It.* Neghelli. Oromiya, C Ethiopia

Negelli see Negēlē
Negev 119 A7 Eng. Negev. desert S Israel
Negev see HaNegev
Neghelli see Negēlē
Negomane 79 E2 var. Negomano. Cabo Delgado, N Mozambique
Negomano see Negomane
Negombo 132 C3 Western Province, SW Sri Lanka
Negotin 100 E4 Serbia, E Serbia
Negra, Punto 60 A3 headland NW Peru
Negreşti see Negreşti-Oaş
Negreşti-Oaş 108 B3 Hung. Avasfelsőfalu; prev. Negreşti. Satu Mare, NE Romania
Negro, Río 65 C5 river E Argentina
Negro, Río 62 D1 river N South America
Negro, Río 64 river Brazil/Uruguay
Negros 139 E2 island C Philippines
Nehbandān 120 E3 Khorāsān, E Iran
Neijiang 128 B5 Sichuan, C China
Neiva 58 B3 Huila, S Colombia
Nellore 132 D2 Andhra Pradesh, E India
Nelson 37 G4 river Manitoba, C Canada
Nelson 151 C5 Nelson, South Island, New Zealand
Nelson 37 G4 river Manitoba, C Canada
Néma 74 D3 Hodh ech Chargui, SE Mauritania
Neman 106 B4 Ger. Ragnit. Kaliningradskaya Oblast', W Russian Federation
Neman 106 A4 Bel. Nyoman, Ger. Memel, Lith. Nemunas, Pol. Niemen. river NE Europe
Nemausus see Nîmes
Neméa 105 B6 Pelopónnisos, S Greece
Nemetocenna see Arras
Nemours 90 C3 Seine-et-Marne, N France
Nemunas see Neman
Nemuro 130 E2 Hokkaidō, NE Japan
Neochóri 105 B5 Dytikí Elláda, C Greece
Nepal 135 E3 off. Nepal. country S Asia

NEPAL
South Asia

Official name Nepal
Formation 1769 / 1769
Capital Kathmandu
Population 30.5 million / 577 people per sq mile (223 people per sq km)
Total area 54,363 sq. miles (140,800 sq. km)
Languages Nepali*, Maithili, Bhojpuri
Religions Hindu 81%, Buddhist 11%, Muslim 4%, Other (including Christian) 4%
Ethnic mix Other 52%, Chhetri 16%, Hill Brahman 13%, Tharu 7%, Magar 7%, Tamang 5%
Government Transitional regime
Currency Nepalese rupee = 100 paisa
Literacy rate 59%
Calorie consumption 2443 kilocalories

Nepal see Nepal
Nereta 106 C4 S Latvia
Neretva 100 C4 river Bosnia and Herzegovina/Croatia
Neris 107 C5 Bel. Viliya, Pol. Wilia; prev. Pol. Wilja. river Belarus/Lithuania
Neris see Viliya
Nerva 92 C4 Andalucía, S Spain
Neryungri 115 F4 Respublika Sakha (Yakutiya), NE Russian Federation
Neskaupstadhur 83 E5 Austurland, E Iceland
Ness, Loch 88 C3 lake N Scotland, United Kingdom
Nesterov see Zhovkva
Néstos 104 C3 Bul. Mesta, Turk. Kara Su. river Bulgaria/Greece
Nesvizh see Nyasvizh
Netanya 119 A6 var. Natanya, Nathanya. Central, C Israel
Netherlands 86 C3 off. Kingdom of the Netherlands, var. Holland, Dut. Koninkrijk der Nederlanden. country NW Europe

NETHERLANDS
Northwest Europe

Official name Kingdom of the Netherlands
Formation 1648 / 1839
Capital Amsterdam; The Hague (administrative)
Population 16.7 million / 1275 people

NETHERLANDS
(continued)

per sq mile (492 people per sq km)
Total area 16,033 sq. miles (41,526 sq. km)
Languages Dutch*, Frisian
Religions Roman Catholic 36%, Other 34%, Protestant 27%, Muslim 3%
Ethnic mix Dutch 82%, Other 12%, Surinamese 2%, Turkish 2%, Moroccan 2%
Government Parliamentary system
Currency Euro = 100 cents
Literacy rate 99%
Calorie consumption 3261 kilocalories

Netherlands East Indies see Indonesia
Netherlands Guiana see Suriname
Netherlands, Kingdom of the see Netherlands
Netherlands New Guinea see Papua
Nettilling Lake 37 G3 lake Baffin Island, Nunavut, N Canada
Netze see Noteć
Neu Amerika see Pulawy
Neubrandenburg 94 D3 Mecklenburg-Vorpommern, NE Germany
Neuchâtel 95 A7 Ger. Neuenburg. Neuchâtel, W Switzerland
Neuchâtel, Lac de 95 A7 Ger. Neuenburger See. lake W Switzerland
Neuenburg see Neuchâtel
Neuenburger See see Neuchâtel, Lac de
Neufchâteau 87 D8 Luxembourg, SE Belgium
Neugradisk see Nova Gradiška
Neuhof see Zgierz
Neukuhren see Pionerskiy
Neumarkt see Târgu Secuiesc, Covasna, Romania
Neumarkt see Târgu Mureş
Neumoldowa see Moldova Nouă
Neumünster 94 B2 Schleswig-Holstein, N Germany
Neunkirchen 95 A5 Saarland, SW Germany
Neuquén 65 B5 Neuquén, SE Argentina
Neuruppin 94 C3 Brandenburg, NE Germany
Neusalz an der Oder see Nowa Sól
Neu Sandec see Nowy Sącz
Neusatz see Novi Sad
Neusiedler See 95 E6 Hung. Fertő. lake Austria/Hungary
Neusohl see Banská Bystrica
Neustadt see Baia Mare, Maramureş, Romania
Neustadt an der Haardt see Neustadt an der Weinstrasse
Neustadt an der Weinstrasse 95 B5 prev. Neustadt an der Haardt, hist. Niewenstat; anc. Nova Civitas. Rheinland-Pfalz, SW Germany
Neustadtl see Novo mesto
Neustettin see Szczecinek
Neustrelitz 94 D3 Mecklenburg-Vorpommern, NE Germany
Neutra see Nitra
Neu-Ulm 95 B6 Bayern, S Germany
Neuwied 95 A5 Rheinland-Pfalz, W Germany
Neuzen see Terneuzen
Nevada 47 C5 off. State of Nevada, also known as Battle Born State, Sagebrush State, Silver State. state W USA
NevadaSierra 92 C5 mountain range S Spain
Nevada, Sierra 47 C6 mountain range W USA
Nevers 90 C4 anc. Noviodunum. Nièvre, C France
Neves 76 E2 São Tomé, S Sao Tome and Principe, Africa
Nevinnomyssk 111 B7 Stavropol'skiy Kray, SW Russian Federation
Nevşehir 116 C3 var. Nevshehr. Nevşehir, C Turkey
Newala 73 C8 Mtwara, SE Tanzania
New Albany 40 C5 Indiana, N USA
New Amsterdam 59 G3 E Guyana
Newark 41 F4 New Jersey, NE USA
New Bedford 41 G3 Massachusetts, NE USA
Newberg 46 B3 Oregon, NW USA
New Bern 43 F1 North Carolina, SE USA
New Braunfels 49 G4 Texas, SW USA
Newbridge 89 B6 Ir. An Droichead Nua. Kildare, C Ireland
New Britain 144 B3 island E Papua New Guinea

New Brunswick 39 E4 Fr. Nouveau-Brunswick. province SE Canada
New Caledonia 144 D4 var. Kanaky, Fr. Nouvelle-Calédonie. French overseas territory SW Pacific Ocean
New Caledonia 144 C5 island SW Pacific Ocean
New Caledonia Basin 142 C4 undersea basin W Pacific Ocean
Newcastle 149 D6 New South Wales, SE Australia
Newcastle see Newcastle upon Tyne
Newcastle upon Tyne 88 D4 var. Newcastle, hist. Monkchester, Lat. Pons Aelii. NE England, United Kingdom
New Delhi 134 D3 country capital (India) Delhi, N India
New England of the West see Minnesota
Newfoundland 39 G3 Fr. Terre-Neuve. island Newfoundland and Labrador, SE Canada
Newfoundland and Labrador 39 F2 Fr. Terre Neuve. province E Canada
Newfoundland Basin 66 B3 undersea feature NW Atlantic Ocean
New Georgia Islands 144 C3 island group NW Solomon Islands
New Glasgow 39 F4 Nova Scotia, SE Canada
New Goa see Panaji
New Guinea 144 A3 Dut. Nieuw Guinea, Ind. Irian. island Indonesia/Papua New Guinea
New Hampshire 41 F2 off. State of New Hampshire, also known as Granite State. state NE USA
New Haven 41 G3 Connecticut, NE USA
New Hebrides see Vanuatu
New Iberia 42 B3 Louisiana, S USA
New Ireland 144 C3 island NE Papua New Guinea
New Jersey 41 F4 off. State of New Jersey, also known as The Garden State. state NE USA
Newman 146 B4 Western Australia
Newmarket 89 E6 E England, United Kingdom
New Mexico 48 C2 off. State of New Mexico, also known as Land of Enchantment, Sunshine State. state SW USA
New Orleans 42 B3 Louisiana, S USA
New Plymouth 150 C4 Taranaki, North Island, New Zealand
Newport 89 D7 S England, United Kingdom
Newport 89 C7 SE Wales, United Kingdom
Newport 40 C4 Kentucky, S USA
Newport 41 G2 Vermont, NE USA
Newport News 41 F5 Virginia, NE USA
New Providence 54 C1 island N Bahamas
Newquay 89 C7 SW England, United Kingdom
Newry 89 B5 Ir. An tIúr. SE Northern Ireland, United Kingdom
New Sarum see Salisbury
New Siberian Islands 115 F1 Eng. New Siberian Islands. island group N Russian Federation
New Siberian Islands see Novosibirskiye Ostrova
New South Wales 149 C6 state SE Australia
Newton 45 G3 Iowa, C USA
Newton 45 F5 Kansas, C USA
Newtownabbey 89 B5 Ir. Baile na Mainistreach. E Northern Ireland, United Kingdom
New Ulm 45 F2 Minnesota, N USA
New York 41 F4 New York, NE USA
New York 41 F3 state NE USA
New Zealand 150 A4 country SW Pacific Ocean

NEW ZEALAND
Australasia & Oceania

Official name New Zealand
Formation 1947 / 1947
Capital Wellington
Population 4.4 million / 42 people per sq mile (16 people per sq km)
Total area 103,737 sq. miles (268,680 sq. km)
Languages English*, Maori*
Religions Anglican 24%, Other 22%, Presbyterian 18%, Nonreligious 16%,

NEW ZEALAND
(continued)

Roman Catholic 15%, Methodist 5%
Ethnic mix European 75%, Maori 15%, Other 7%, Samoan 3%
Government Parliamentary system
Currency New Zealand dollar = 100 cents
Literacy rate 99%
Calorie consumption 3172 kilocalories

Neyveli 132 C2 Tamil Nādu, SE India
Nezhin see Nizhyn
Ngangze Co 126 B5 lake W China
Ngaoundéré 76 B4 var. N'Gaoundéré. Adamaoua, N Cameroon
N'Gaoundéré see Ngaoundéré
Ngazidja 79 F2 Fr. Grande Comore, var. Njazidja. island W Comoros
N'Giva 78 B3 var. Ondjiva, Port. Vila Pereira de Eça. Cunene, S Angola
Ngo 77 B6 Plateaux, SE Congo
Ngoko 77 B5 river Cameroon/Congo
Ngourti 75 H3 Diffa, E Niger
Nguigmi 75 H3 var. N'Guigmi. Diffa, SE Niger
N'Guigmi see Nguigmi
N'Gunza see Sumbe
Nguru 75 G3 Yobe, NE Nigeria
Nha Trang 137 E6 Khanh Hoa, S Vietnam
Niagara Falls 38 D5 Ontario, S Canada
Niagara Falls 41 E3 New York, NE USA
Niagara Falls 40 D3 waterfall Canada/USA
Niamey 75 F3 country capital (Niger) Niamey, SW Niger
Niangay, Lac 75 E3 lake E Mali
Nia-Nia 77 E5 Orientale, NE Dem. Rep. Congo
Nias, Pulau 138 A3 island W Indonesia
Nicaea see Nice
Nicaragua 52 D3 off. Republic of Nicaragua. country Central America

NICARAGUA
Central America

Official name Republic of Nicaragua
Formation 1838 / 1838
Capital Managua
Population 5.9 million / 129 people per sq mile (50 people per sq km)
Total area 49,998 sq. miles (129,494 sq. km)
Languages Spanish*, English Creole, Miskito
Religions Roman Catholic 80%, Protestant Evangelical 17%, Other 3%
Ethnic mix Mestizo 69%, White 17%, Black 9%, Amerindian 5%
Government Presidential system
Currency Córdoba oro = 100 centavos
Literacy rate 80%
Calorie consumption 2517 kilocalories

Lake Nicaragua 52 D4 var. Cocibolca, Gran Lago, Eng. Lake Nicaragua. lake S Nicaragua
Nicaragua, Lake see Nicaragua, Lago de
Nicaragua, Republic of see Nicaragua
Nicaria see Ikaría
Nice 91 D6 It. Nizza; anc. Nicaea. Alpes-Maritimes, SE France
Nicephorium see Ar Raqqah
Nicholas II Land see Severnaya Zemlya
Nicholls Town 54 C1 Andros Island, NW Bahamas
Nicobar Islands 124 B4 island group India, E Indian Ocean
Nicosia 102 C5 Gk. Lefkosía, Turk. Lefkoşa. country capital (Cyprus) C Cyprus
Nicoya 52 D4 Guanacaste, W Costa Rica
Nicoya, Golfo de 52 D5 gulf W Costa Rica
Nicoya, Península de 52 D4 peninsula NW Costa Rica
Nida 106 A3 Ger. Nidden. Klaipėda, SW Lithuania
Nidaros see Trondheim
Nidden see Nida
Nidzica 98 D3 Ger. Niedenburg. Warmińsko-Mazurskie, NE Poland
Niedenburg see Nidzica
Niedere Tauern 99 A6 mountain range C Austria
Niemen see Neman
Nieśwież see Nyasvizh

Nieuw Amsterdam 59 G3 Commewijne, NE Suriname
Nieuw-Bergen 86 D4 Limburg, SE Netherlands
Nieuwegein 86 C4 Utrecht, C Netherlands
Nieuw Guinea see New Guinea
Nieuw Nickerie 59 G3 Nickerie, NW Suriname
Niewenstat see Neustadt an der Weinstrasse
Niğde 116 C4 Niğde, C Turkey
Niger 75 F3 off. Republic of Niger. country W Africa

NIGER
West Africa

Official name Republic of Niger
Formation 1960 / 1960
Capital Niamey
Population 16.1 million / 33 people per sq mile (13 people per sq km)
Total area 489,188 sq. miles (1,267,000 sq. km)
Languages Hausa, Djerma, Fulani, Tuareg, Teda, French*
Religions Muslim 99%, Other (including Christian) 1%
Ethnic mix Hausa 53%, Djerma and Songhai 21%, Tuareg 11%, Fulani 7%, Kanuri 6%, Other 2%
Government Presidential system
Currency CFA franc = 100 centimes
Literacy rate 30%
Calorie consumption 2489 kilocalories

Niger 75 F4 river W Africa
Nigeria 75 F4 off. Federal Republic of Nigeria. country W Africa

NIGERIA
West Africa

Official name Federal Republic of Nigeria
Formation 1960 / 1961
Capital Abuja
Population 162 million / 462 people per sq mile (178 people per sq km)
Total area 356,667 sq. miles (923,768 sq. km)
Languages Hausa, English*, Yoruba, Ibo
Religions Muslim 50%, Christian 40%, Traditional beliefs 10%
Ethnic mix Other 29%, Hausa 21%, Yoruba 21%, Ibo 18%, Fulani 11%
Government Presidential system
Currency Naira = 100 kobo
Literacy rate 61%
Calorie consumption 2711 kilocalories

Nigeria, Federal Republic of see Nigeria
Niger, Mouths of the 75 F5 delta S Nigeria
Niger, Republic of see Niger
Nihon see Japan
Niigata 131 D5 Niigata, Honshū, C Japan
Niihama 131 B7 Ehime, Shikoku, SW Japan
Ni'ihau 47 A7 var. Niihau. island Hawai'i, USA, C Pacific Ocean
Nii-jima 131 D6 island E Japan
Nijkerk 86 D3 Gelderland, C Netherlands
Nijlen 87 C5 Antwerpen, N Belgium
Nijmegen 86 D4 Ger. Nimwegen; anc. Noviomagus. Gelderland, SE Netherlands
Nikaria see Ikaría
Nikel' 110 C2 Finn. Kolosjoki. Murmanskaya Oblast', NW Russian Federation
Nikiniki 139 E5 Timor, S Indonesia
Niklasmarkt see Gheorgheni
Nikolainkaupunki see Vaasa
Nikolayev see Mykolayiv
Nikol'sk see Ussuriysk
Nikol'sk-Ussuriyskiy see Ussuriysk
Nikopol' 109 F3 Dnipropetrovs'ka Oblast', SE Ukraine
Nikšić 101 C5 C Montenegro
Nikumaroro 145 E3 ; prev. Gardner Island. atoll Phoenix Islands, C Kiribati
Nikunau 145 E3 var. Nukunau; prev. Byron Island. atoll Tungaru, W Kiribati
Nile 72 B2 former province NW Uganda
Nile 68 D3 Ar. Nahr an Nīl. river N Africa

Nile Delta 72 B1 delta N Egypt
Nīl, Nahr an see Nile
Nîmes 91 C6 anc. Nemausus, Nismes. Gard, S France
Nimwegen see Nijmegen
Nine Degree Channel 132 B3 channel India/Maldives
Ninetyeast Ridge 141 D5 undersea feature E Indian Ocean
Ninety Mile Beach 150 C1 beach North Island, New Zealand
Ningbo 128 D5 var. Ning-po, Yin-hsien; prev. Ninghsien. Zhejiang, SE China
Ning-hsia see Ningxia
Ninghsien see Ningbo
Ning-po see Ningbo
Ningsia/Ningsia Hui/Ningsia Hui Autonomous Region see Ningxia
Ningxia 128 B4 off. Ningxia Huizu Zizhiqu, var. Ning-hsia, Ningsia, Eng. Ningsia Hui, Ningsia Hui Autonomous Region. autonomous region N China
Ningxia Huizu Zizhiqu see Ningxia
Nio see Íos
Niobrara River 45 E3 river Nebraska/Wyoming, C USA
Nioro 74 D3 var. Nioro du Sahel. Kayes, W Mali
Nioro du Sahel see Nioro
Niort 90 B4 Deux-Sèvres, W France
Nipigon 38 B4 Ontario, S Canada
Nipigon, Lake 38 B3 lake Ontario, S Canada
Nippon see Japan
Niš 101 E5 Eng. Nish, Ger. Nisch; anc. Naissus. Serbia, SE Serbia
Nişab 120 B4 Al Ḩudūd ash Shamālīyah, N Saudi Arabia
Nisch/Nish see Niš
Nisibin see Nusaybin
Nísiros see Nísyros
Nisko 98 E4 Podkarpackie, SE Poland
Nismes see Nîmes
Nistru see Dniester
Nísyros 105 E7 var. Nisiros. island Dodekánisa, Greece, Aegean Sea
Nitra 99 C6 Ger. Neutra, Hung. Nyitra. Nitriansky Kraj, SW Slovakia
Nitra 99 C6 Ger. Neutra, Hung. Nyitra. river W Slovakia
Niuatobutabu see Niuatoputapu
Niuatoputapu 145 E4 var. Niuatobutabu; prev. Keppel Island. island N Tonga
Niue 145 F4 self-governing territory in free association with New Zealand S Pacific Ocean
Niulakita 145 E3 var. Nurakita. atoll S Tuvalu
Niutao 145 E3 atoll NW Tuvalu
Nivernais 90 C4 cultural region C France
Nizāmābād 134 D5 Andhra Pradesh, C India
Nizhnegorskiy see Nyzhn'ohirs'kyy
Nizhnekamsk 111 C5 Respublika Tatarstan, W Russian Federation
Nizhnevartovsk 114 D3 Khanty-Mansiyskiy Avtonomnyy Okrug-Yugra, C Russian Federation
Nizhniy Novgorod 111 C5 prev. Gor'kiy. Nizhegorodskaya Oblast', W Russian Federation
Nizhniy Odes 110 D4 Respublika Komi, NW Russian Federation
Nizhyn 109 E1 Rus. Nezhin. Chernihivs'ka Oblast', NE Ukraine
Nizza see Nice
Njazidja see Ngazidja
Njombe 73 C8 Iringa, S Tanzania
Nkayi 77 B6 prev. Jacob. Bouenza, S Congo
Nkongsamba 76 A4 var. N'Kongsamba. Littoral, W Cameroon
N'Kongsamba see Nkongsamba
Nmai Hka 136 B2 var. Me Hka. river N Myanmar (Burma)
Nobeoka 131 B7 Miyazaki, Kyūshū, SW Japan
Noboribetsu 130 D3 var. Noboribetu. Hokkaidō, NE Japan
Noboribetu see Noboribetsu
Nogales 50 B1 Sonora, NW Mexico
Nogales 48 B3 Arizona, SW USA
Nogal Valley see Dooxo Nugaaleed
Noire, Rivi`ere see Black River
Nokia 85 D5 Länsi-Suomi, W Finland
Nokou 76 B3 Kanem, W Chad

Nola 77 B5 Sangha-Mbaéré, SW Central African Republic
Nolinsk 111 C5 Kirovskaya Oblast', NW Russian Federation
Nongkaya see Nong Khai
Nong Khai 136 C4 var. Mi Chai, Nongkaya. Nong Khai, E Thailand
Nonouti 144 D2 prev. Sydenham Island. atoll Tungaru, W Kiribati
Noord-Beveland 86 B4 var. North Beveland. island SW Netherlands
Noordwijk aan Zee 86 C3 Zuid-Holland, W Netherlands
Noordzee see North Sea
Nora 85 C6 Örebro, C Sweden
Norak 123 E3 Rus. Nurek. W Tajikistan
Nord 83 F1 Avannaarsua, N Greenland
Nordaustlandet 83 G1 island NE Svalbard
Norden 94 A3 Niedersachsen, NW Germany
Norderstedt 94 B3 Schleswig-Holstein, N Germany
Nordfriesische Inseln see North Frisian Islands
Nordhausen 94 C4 Thüringen, C Germany
Nordhorn 94 A3 Niedersachsen, NW Germany
Nord, Mer du see North Sea
Nord-Ouest, Territoires du see Northwest Territories
Nordsee/Nordsjøen/Nordsøen see North Sea
Norfolk 45 E3 Nebraska, C USA
Norfolk 41 F5 Virginia, NE USA
Norfolk Island 142 D4 Australian external territory SW Pacific Ocean
Norfolk Ridge 142 D4 undersea feature W Pacific Ocean
Norge see Norway
Norias 49 G5 Texas, SW USA
Noril'sk 114 D3 Krasnoyarskiy Kray, N Russian Federation
Norman 49 G1 Oklahoma, C USA
Normandes, Îles see Channel Islands
Normandie 90 B3 Eng. Normandy. cultural region N France
Normandy see Normandie
Normanton 148 C3 Queensland, NE Australia
Norrköping 85 C6 Östergötland, S Sweden
Norrtälje 85 C6 Stockholm, C Sweden
Norseman 147 B6 Western Australia
Norske Havet see Norwegian Sea
North Albanian Alps 101 C5 Alb. Bjeshkët e Namuna, SCr. Prokletije. mountain range SE Europe
Northallerton 89 D5 N England, United Kingdom
Northam 147 A6 Western Australia
North America 34 continent
Northampton 89 D6 C England, United Kingdom
North Andaman 133 F2 island Andaman Islands, India, NE Indian Ocean
North Bay 38 D4 Ontario, S Canada
North Beveland see Noord-Beveland
North Borneo see Sabah
North Cape 150 C1 headland North Island, New Zealand
North Cape 84 D1 Eng. North Cape. headland N Norway
North Cape see Nordkapp
North Carolina 43 E1 off. State of North Carolina, also known as Old North State, Tar Heel State, Turpentine State. state SE USA
North Channel 40 D2 lake channel Canada/USA
North Charleston 43 F2 South Carolina, SE USA
North Dakota 44 D2 off. State of North Dakota, also known as Flickertail State, Peace Garden State, Sioux State. state N USA
North Devon Island see Devon Island
North East Frontier Agency/North East Frontier Agency of Assam see Arunāchal Pradesh
Northeast Providence Channel 54 C1 channel N Bahamas

Northeim 94 B4 Niedersachsen, C Germany
Northern Cook Islands 145 F4 island group N Cook Islands
Northern Dvina 110 C4 var. Northern Dvina. river NW Russian Federation
Northern Dvina see Severnaya Dvina
Northern Ireland 88 B4 var. The Six Counties. cultural region Northern Ireland, United Kingdom
Northern Mariana Islands 142 B1 US commonwealth territory W Pacific Ocean
Northern Rhodesia see Zambia
Northern Sporades 105 C5 var. Vóreioi Sporádes, Vórioi Sporádhes, Eng. Northern Sporades. island group E Greece
Northern Sporades see Vóreies Sporádes
Northern Territory 144 A5 territory N Australia
North European Plain 81 E3 plain N Europe
Northfield 45 F2 Minnesota, N USA
North Fiji Basin 142 D3 undersea feature N Coral Sea
North Frisian Islands 94 B2 var. Nordfriesische Inseln. island group N Germany
North Huvadhu Atoll 132 B5 var. Gaafu Alifu Atoll. atoll S Maldives
North Island 150 B2 island N New Zealand
North Korea 129 E3 off. Democratic People's Republic of Korea, Kor. Chosŏn-minjujuŭi-inmin-kanghwaguk. country E Asia

NORTH KOREA
East Asia

Official name Democratic People's Republic of Korea
Formation 1948 / 1953
Capital Pyongyang
Population 24.5 million / 527 people per sq mile (203 people per sq km)
Total area 46,540 sq. miles (120,540 sq. km)
Languages Korean*
Religions Atheist 100%
Ethnic mix Korean 100%
Government One-party state
Currency North Korean won = 100 chon
Literacy rate 99%
Calorie consumption 2078 kilocalories

North Little Rock 42 B1 Arkansas, C USA
North Minch, The see Minch, The
North Mole 93 G4 harbour wall NW Gibraltar Europe
North Platte 45 E4 Nebraska, C USA
North Platte River 44 D4 river C USA
North Pole 155 B3 pole Arctic Ocean
North Saskatchewan 37 F5 river Alberta/Saskatchewan, S Canada
North Sea 80 D3 Dan. Nordsøen, Dut. Noordzee, Fr. Mer du Nord, Ger. Nordsee, Nor. Nordsjøen; prev. German Ocean, Lat. Mare Germanicum. sea NW Europe
North Siberian Lowland 115 E2 var. North Siberian Plain, Eng. North Siberian Lowland. lowlands N Russian Federation
North Siberian Lowland/North Siberian Plain see Severo-Sibirskaya Nizmennost'
North Star State see Minnesota
North Taranaki Bight 150 C3 gulf North Island, New Zealand
North Uist 88 B3 island NW Scotland, United Kingdom
Northwest Atlantic Mid-Ocean Canyon 34 E4 undersea feature N Atlantic Ocean
North West Highlands 88 C3 mountain range N Scotland, United Kingdom
Northwest Pacific Basin 113 G4 undersea feature NW Pacific Ocean
Northwest Territories 37 E3 Fr. Territoires du Nord-Ouest. territory NW Canada
Northwind Plain 155 B2 undersea feature Arctic Ocean
Norton Sound 36 C2 inlet Alaska, USA
Norway 85 A5 off. Kingdom of Norway, Nor. Norge. country N Europe

NORWAY
Northern Europe

Official name Kingdom of Norway
Formation 1905 / 1905
Capital Oslo
Population 4.9 million / 41 people
per sq mile (16 people per sq km)
Total area 125,181 sq. miles (324,220 sq. km)
Languages Norwegian* (Bokmål
"book language" and Nynorsk
"new Norsk"), Sámi
Religions Evangelical Lutheran 88%,
Other and nonreligious 8%, Muslim 2%,
Pentecostal 1%, Roman Catholic 1%
Ethnic mix Norwegian 93%, Other 6%,
Sámi 1%
Government Parliamentary system
Currency Norwegian krone = 100 øre
Literacy rate 99%
Calorie consumption 3453 kilocalories

Norway, Kingdom of see Norway
Norwegian Basin 83 F4 undersea feature
NW Norwegian Sea
Norwegian Sea 83 F4 var. Norske Havet.
sea NE Atlantic Ocean
Norwich 89 E6 E England, United
Kingdom
Nösen see Bistrița
Noshiro 130 D4 var. Nosiro; prev.
Noshirominato. Akita, Honshū,
C Japan
Noshirominato/Nosiro see Noshiro
Nosivka 109 E1 Rus. Nosovka.
Chernihivs'ka Oblast', NE Ukraine
Nosovka see Nosivka
Noşratābād 120 E3 Sīstān va
Balūchestān, E Iran
Nossob 78 C4 river E Namibia
Noteć 98 C3 Ger. Netze. river
NW Poland
Nóties Sporádes see Dodekánisa
Nottingham 89 D6 C England, United
Kingdom
Nouâdhibou 74 B2 prev. Port-Étienne.
Dakhlet Nouâdhibou, W Mauritania
Nouakchott 74 B2 country capital
(Mauritania) Nouakchott District,
SW Mauritania
Nouméa 144 C5 dependent territory
capital (New Caledonia) Province Sud,
S New Caledonia
Nouveau-Brunswick see New Brunswick
Nouvelle-Calédonie see New Caledonia
Nouvelle Écosse see Nova Scotia
Nova Civitas see Neustadt an der
Weinstrasse
Nova Gorica 95 D8 W Slovenia
Nova Gradiška 100 C3 Ger. Neugradisk,
Hung. Újgradiska. Brod-Posavina,
NE Croatia
Nova Iguaçu 63 F4 Rio de Janeiro,
SE Brazil
Nova Lisboa see Huambo
Novara 96 B2 anc. Novaria. Piemonte,
NW Italy
Novaria see Novara
Nova Scotia 39 F4 Fr. Nouvelle Écosse.
province SE Canada
Nova Scotia 35 E5 physical region
SE Canada
Novaya Sibir', Ostrov 115 F1 island
Novosibirskiye Ostrova, NE Russian
Federation
Novaya Zemlya 110 D1 island group
N Russian Federation
Novaya Zemlya Trough see East Novaya
Zemlya Trough
Novgorod see Velikiy Novgorod
Novi Grad see Bosanski Novi
Novi Iskŭr 104 C2 Sofiya-Grad,
W Bulgaria
Noviodunum see Nevers, Nièvre,
France
Noviomagus see Lisieux, Calvados,
France
Noviomagus see Nijmegen, Netherlands
Novi Pazar 101 D5 Turk. Yenipazar,
Serbia, S Serbia
Novi Sad 100 D3 Ger. Neusatz, Hung.
Újvidék. Vojvodina, N Serbia
Novoazovs'k 109 G4 Rus. Novoazovsk.
Donets'ka Oblast', E Ukraine
Novocheboksarsk 111 C5 Chuvashskaya
Respublika, W Russian Federation
Novocherkassk 111 B7 Rostovskaya
Oblast', SW Russian Federation

Novodvinsk 110 C3 Arkhangel'skaya
Oblast', NW Russian Federation
Novograd-Volynskiy see
Novohrad-Volyns'kyi
Novogrudok see Navahrudak
Novohrad-Volyns'kyy 108 D2 Rus.
Novograd-Volynskiy. Zhytomyrs'ka
Oblast', N Ukraine
Novokazalinsk see Ayteke Bi
Novokuznetsk 114 D4 prev. Stalinsk.
Kemerovskaya Oblast', S Russian
Federation
Novolazarevskaya 154 C2 Russian
research station Antarctica
Novo mesto 95 E8 Ger. Rudolfswert;
prev. Ger. Neustadtl. SE Slovenia
Novomoskovsk 111 B5 Tul'skaya
Oblast', W Russian Federation
Novomoskovs'k 109 F3 Rus.
Novomoskovsk. Dnipropetrovs'ka
Oblast', E Ukraine
Novopolotsk see Navapolatsk
Novoradomsk see Radomsko
Novo Redondo see Sumbe
Novorossiysk 111 A7 Krasnodarskiy
Kray, SW Russian Federation
Novoshakhtinsk 111 B6 Rostovskaya
Oblast', SW Russian Federation
Novosibirsk 114 D4 Novosibirskaya
Oblast', C Russian Federation
Novotroitsk 111 D6 Orenburgskaya
Oblast', W Russian Federation
Novotroitskoye see Novotroyits'ke,
Ukraine
Novotroyits'ke 109 F4 Rus.
Novotroitskoye. Khersons'ka Oblast',
S Ukraine
Novo-Urgench see Urganch
Novovolyns'k 108 C1 Rus. Novovolynsk.
Volyns'ka Oblast', NW Ukraine
Novy Dvor 107 B6 Rus. Novyy Dvor.
Hrodzyenskaya Voblasts', W Belarus
Novyy Bug see Novyy Buh
Novyy Buh 109 E3 Rus. Novyy Bug.
Mykolayivs'ka Oblast', S Ukraine
Novyy Dvor see Novy Dvor
Novyy Margilan see Farg'ona
Novyy Uzen' see Zhanaozen
Nowa Sól 98 B4 var. Nowasól, Ger.
Neusalz an der Oder. Lubuskie,
W Poland
Nowasól see Nowa Sól
Nowogard 98 B2 var. Nowógard, Ger.
Naugard. Zachodnio-pomorskie,
NW Poland
Nowogródek see Navahrudak
Nowo-Minsk see Mińsk Mazowiecki
Nowy Dwór Mazowiecki 98 D3
Mazowieckie, C Poland
Nowy Sącz 99 D5 Ger. Neu Sandec.
Małopolskie, S Poland
Nowy Tomyśl 98 B3 var. Nowy Tomysl.
Wielkopolskie, C Poland
Nowy Tomysl see Nowy Tomyśl
Noyon 90 C3 Oise, N France
Nsanje 79 E3 Southern, S Malawi
Nsawam 75 E5 SE Ghana
Ntomba, Lac 77 C6 var. Lac Tumba.
lake NW Dem. Rep. Congo
Nubian Desert 72 B3 desert
NE Sudan
Nu Chiang see Salween
Nu'eima 119 E7 E West Bank Asia
Nueva Caceres see Naga
Nueva Gerona 54 B2 Isla de la Juventud,
S Cuba
Nueva Rosita 50 D2 Coahuila,
NE Mexico
Nuevitas 54 C2 Camagüey, E Cuba
Nuevo, Bajo 53 G1 island NW Colombia
South America
Nuevas Casas Grandes 50 C1 Chihuahua,
N Mexico
Nuevo, Golfo 65 C6 gulf S Argentina
Nuevo Laredo 51 E2 Tamaulipas,
NE Mexico
Nui Atoll 145 E3 atoll W Tuvalu
Nu Jiang see Salween
Nûk see Nuuk
Nukha see Şäki
Nuku'alofa 145 E5 country capital
(Tonga) Tongatapu, S Tonga
Nukufetau Atoll 145 E3 atoll C Tuvalu
Nukulaelae Atoll 145 E3 var. Nukulailai.
atoll E Tuvalu
Nukulailai see Nukulaelae Atoll
Nukunau see Nikunau
Nukunonu Atoll 145 E3 island
C Tokelau

Nukus 122 C2 Qoraqalpog'iston
Respublikasi, W Uzbekistan
Nullarbor Plain 147 C6 plateau South
Australia/Western Australia
Nunap Isua 82 C5 var. Uummannarsuaq,
Dan. Kap Farvel, Eng. Cape Farewell.
cape S Greenland
Nunavut 37 F3 territory N Canada
Nuneaton 89 D6 C England, United
Kingdom
Nunivak Island 36 B2 island Alaska,
USA
Nunspeet 86 D3 Gelderland,
E Netherlands
Nuoro 97 A5 Sardegna, Italy,
C Mediterranean Sea
Nuquí 58 A3 Chocó, W Colombia
Nurakita see Niulakita
Nurata see Nurota
Nurek see Norak
Nuremberg see Nürnberg
Nurmes 84 E4 Itä-Suomi, E Finland
Nürnberg 95 C5 Eng. Nuremberg.
Bayern, S Germany
Nurota 123 E2 Rus. Nurata. Navoiy
Viloyati, C Uzbekistan
Nusaybin 117 F4 var. Nisibin. Manisa,
SE Turkey
Nussdorf see Näsåud
Nutmeg State see Connecticut
Nuuk 82 C4 var. Nûk, Dan. Godthaab,
Godthåb. dependent territory capital
(Greenland) Kitaa, SW Greenland
Nyagan' 114 C3 Khanty-Mansiyskiy
Avtonomnyy Okrug-Yugra, N Russian
Federation
Nyainqentanglha Shan 126 C5
mountain range W China
Nyala 72 A4 Southern Darfur, W Sudan
Nyamapanda 78 D3 Mashonaland East,
NE Zimbabwe
Nyamtumbo 73 C8 Ruvuma, S Tanzania
Nyanda see Masvingo
Nyandoma 110 C4 Arkhangel'skaya
Oblast', NW Russian Federation
Nyantakara 73 B7 Kagera, NW Tanzania
Nyasa, Lake 79 E2 var. Lake Malawi;
prev. Lago Nyassa. lake E Africa
Nyasaland/Nyasaland Protectorate
see Malawi
Nyassa, Lago see Nyasa, Lake
Nyasvizh 107 C6 Pol. Nieśwież, Rus.
Nesvizh. Minskaya Voblasts', C Belarus
Nyaunglebin 136 B4 Bago, SW Myanmar
(Burma)
Nyeri 73 C6 Central, C Kenya
Nyíregyháza 99 D6 Szabolcs-Szatmár-
Bereg, NE Hungary
Nyitra see Nitra
Nykøbing 85 B8 Sjælland, SE Denmark
Nyköping 85 C6 Södermanland,
S Sweden
Nylstroom see Modimolle
Nyngan 149 D6 New South Wales,
SE Australia
Nyoman see Neman
Nyurba 115 F3 Respublika Sakha
(Yakutiya), NE Russian Federation
Nyzhn'ohirs'kyy 109 F4 Rus.
Nizhnegorskiy. Avtonomna Respublika
Krym, S Ukraine
NZ see New Zealand
Nzega 73 C7 Tabora, C Tanzania
Nzérékoré 74 D4 SE Guinea
Nzwani 79 F2 Fr. Anjouan, var.
Ndzouani. island SE Comoros

O

Oa'hu 47 A7 var. Oahu. island Hawai'ian
Islands, Hawai'i, USA
Oak Harbor 46 B1 Washington,
NW USA
Oakland 47 B6 California, W USA
Oamaru 151 B7 Otago, South Island,
New Zealand
Oaxaca 51 F5 var. Oaxaca de Juárez; prev.
Antequera. Oaxaca, SE Mexico
Oaxaca de Juárez see Oaxaca
Ob' 112 C2 river C Russian Federation
Obal' 107 D5 Rus. Obol'. Vitsyebskaya
Voblasts', N Belarus
Oban 88 C4 W Scotland, United
Kingdom
Oban see Halfmoon Bay
Obando see Puerto Inírida
Obdorsk see Salekhard
Óbecse see Bečej

Obeliai 106 C4 Panevėžys, NE Lithuania
Oberhollabrunn see Tulln
Ob', Gulf of 114 D3 Eng. Gulf of Ob. gulf
N Russian Federation
Ob', Gulf of see Obskaya Guba
Obidovichi see Abidavichy
Obihiro 130 D2 Hokkaidō, NE Japan
Obo 76 D4 Haut-Mbomou, E Central
African Republic
Obock 72 D4 E Djibouti
Obol' see Obal'
Oborniki 98 C3 Wielkolpolskie,
W Poland
Obrovo see Abrova
Ob' Tablemount 141 B7 undersea
feature S Indian Ocean
Ocala 43 E4 Florida, SE USA
Ocaña 58 B2 Norte de Santander,
N Colombia
Ocaña 92 D3 Castilla-La Mancha,
C Spain
O Carballiño 92 C1 Cast. Carballiño.
Galicia, NW Spain
Occidental, Cordillera 58 B2 mountain
range W South America
Occidental, Cordillera 61 E4 mountain
range Bolivia/Chile
Ocean Falls 36 D5 British Columbia,
SW Canada
Ocean Island see Banaba
Oceanside 47 C8 California, W USA
Ocean State see Rhode Island
Ochakiv 109 E4 Rus. Ochakov.
Mykolayivs'ka Oblast', S Ukraine
Ochakov see Ochakiv
Ochamchira see Ochamchire
Ochamchire 117 E2 Rus. Ochamchira;
prev. Ochamchir'e. W Georgia
Och'amch'ire see Ochamchire
Ocho Rios 54 B4 C Jamaica
Ochrida see Ohrid
Ochrida, Lake see Ohrid, Lake
Ocotal 52 D3 Nueva Segovia,
NW Nicaragua
Ocozocuautla 51 G5 Chiapas, SE Mexico
October Revolution Island 115 E2
Eng. October Revolution Island.
island Severnaya Zemlya, N Russian
Federation
October Revolution Island see
Oktyabr'skoy Revolyutsii, Ostrov
Ocú 53 F5 Herrera, S Panama
Ōdate 130 D3 Akita, Honshū, C Japan
Oddur see Xuddur
Ödemiş 116 A4 Izmir, SW Turkey
Ödenburg see Sopron
Odenpäh see Otepää
Odense 85 B7 Syddtjylland, C Denmark
Oder 80 B3 Cz./Pol. Odra. river
C Europe
Oderhaff see Szczeciński, Zalew
Odesa 109 E4 Rus. Odessa. Odes'ka
Oblast', SW Ukraine
Odessa 49 E3 Texas, SW USA
Odessa see Odesa
Odessus see Varna
Odienné 74 D4 NW Côte d'Ivoire
Odisha see Orissa
Ódóngk 137 D6 Kâmpóng Spoe,
S Cambodia
Odoorn 86 E2 Drenthe, NE Netherlands
Odra see Oder
Oesel see Saaremaa
Of 117 E2 Trabzon, NE Turkey
Ofanto 97 D5 river S Italy
Offenbach 95 B5 var. Offenbach am
Main. Hessen, W Germany
Offenbach am Main see Offenbach
Offenburg 95 B6 Baden-Württemberg,
SW Germany
Ogaadeen see Ogaden
Ogaden 73 D5 Som. Ogaadeen. plateau
Ethiopia/Somalia
Ōgaki 131 C6 Gifu, Honshū, SW Japan
Ogallala 44 D4 Nebraska, C USA
Ogbomosho 75 F4 var. Ogmoboso. Oyo,
W Nigeria
Ogden 44 B4 Utah, W USA
Ogdensburg 41 F2 New York,
NE USA
Ogmoboso see Ogbomosho
Ogulin 100 A3 Karlovac, NW Croatia
Ohio 40 C4 off. State of Ohio, also known
as Buckeye State. state N USA
Ohio River 40 C4 river N USA
Ohlau see Oława
Ohri see Ohrid
Ohrid 101 D6 Turk. Ochrida, Ohri.
SW FYR Macedonia

Ohrid, Lake 101 D6 var. Lake Ochrida, Alb. Liqeni i Ohrit, Mac. Ohridsko Ezero. lake Albania/FYR Macedonia
Ohridsko Ezero/Ohrit, Liqeni i see Ohrid, Lake
Ohura 150 D3 Manawatu-Wanganui, North Island, New Zealand
Oirschot 87 C5 Noord-Brabant, S Netherlands
Oise 90 C3 river N France
Oistins 55 G2 S Barbados
Ōita 131 B7 Ōita, Kyūshū, SW Japan
Ojinaga 50 D2 Chihuahua, N Mexico
Ojos del Salado, Cerro 64 B3 mountain W Argentina
Okaihau 150 C2 Northland, North Island, New Zealand
Okanizsa see Kanjiža
Okāra 134 C2 Punjab, E Pakistan
Okavanggo see Cubango/Okavango
Okavango see Cubango
Okavango Delta 78 C3 wetland N Botswana
Okayama 131 B6 Okayama, Honshū, SW Japan
Okazaki 131 C6 Aichi, Honshū, C Japan
Okeechobee, Lake 43 E4 lake Florida, SE USA
Okefenokee Swamp 43 E3 wetland Georgia, SE USA
Okhotsk 115 G3 Khabarovskiy Kray, E Russian Federation
Okhotsk, Sea of 113 F3 sea NW Pacific Ocean
Okhtyrka 109 F2 Rus. Akhtyrka. Sums'ka Oblast', NE Ukraine
Oki-guntō see Oki-shotō
Okinawa 130 A3 island SW Japan
Okinawa-shoto 130 A3 island group Nansei-shotō, SW Japan Asia
Oki-shoto 131 B6 var. Oki-guntō. island group SW Japan
Oklahoma 49 F2 off. State of Oklahoma, also known as The Sooner State. state C USA
Oklahoma City 49 G1 state capital Oklahoma, C USA
Okmulgee 49 G1 Oklahoma, C USA
Oko, Wadi 72 C3 river NE Sudan
Oktyabr'skiy 111 D6 Volgogradskaya Oblast', SW Russian Federation
Oktyabr'skiy see Aktsyabrski
Okulovka 110 B4 var. Okulovka. Novgorodskaya Oblast', W Russian Federation
Okulovka see Okulovka
Okushiri-to 130 C3 var. Okusiri Tô. island NE Japan
Okusiri Tô see Okushiri-tô
Oláh-Toplicza see Topliţa
Öland 85 C7 island S Sweden
Olavarría 65 D5 Buenos Aires, E Argentina
Oława 98 C4 Ger. Ohlau. Dolnośląskie, SW Poland
Olbia 97 A5 prev. Terranova Pausania. Sardegna, Italy, C Mediterranean Sea
Old Bay State/Old Colony State see Massachusetts
Old Dominion see Virginia
Oldebroek 86 D3 Gelderland, E Netherlands
Oldenburg 94 B3 Niedersachsen, NW Germany
Oldenburg 94 C2 var. Oldenburg in Holstein. Schleswig-Holstein, N Germany
Oldenburg in Holstein see Oldenburg
Oldenzaal 86 E3 Overijssel, E Netherlands
Old Harbour 54 B5 C Jamaica
Old Line State see Maryland
Old North State see North Carolina
Olëkma 115 F4 river C Russian Federation
Olëkminsk 115 F3 Respublika Sakha (Yakutiya), NE Russian Federation
Oleksandrivka 109 E3 Rus. Aleksandrovka. Kirovohrads'ka Oblast', C Ukraine
Oleksandriya 109 F3 Rus. Aleksandriya. Kirovohrads'ka Oblast', C Ukraine
Olenegorsk 110 C2 Murmanskaya Oblast', NW Russian Federation
Olenëk 115 E3 Respublika Sakha (Yakutiya), NE Russian Federation
Olenëk 115 E3 river NE Russian Federation
Oléron, Île d' 91 A5 island W France

Olevs'k 108 D1 Rus. Olevsk. Zhytomyrs'ka Oblast', N Ukraine
Olevsk see Olevs'k
Ölgiy 126 C2 Bayan-Ölgiy, W Mongolia
Olhão 92 B5 Faro, S Portugal
Olifa 78 B3 Kunene, NW Namibia
Ólimbos see Ólympos
Olimpo see Fuerte Olimpo
Olisipo see Lisboa
Olita see Alytus
Oliva 93 F4 Valenciana, E Spain
Olivet 90 C4 Loiret, C France
Olmaliq 123 E2 Rus. Almalyk. Toshkent Viloyati, E Uzbekistan
Olmütz see Olomouc
Olomouc 99 C5 Ger. Olmütz, Pol. Ołomuniec. Olomoucký Kraj, E Czech Republic
Ołomuniec see Olomouc
Olonets 110 B3 Respublika Kareliya, NW Russian Federation
Olovyannaya 115 F4 Zabaykal'skiy Kray, S Russian Federation
Olpe 94 B4 Nordrhein-Westfalen, W Germany
Olshanka see Vil'shanka
Olsnitz see Murska Sobota
Olsztyn 98 D2 Ger. Allenstein. Warmińsko-Mazurskie, N Poland
Olt 108 B5 var. Oltul, Ger. Alt. river S Romania
Olteniţa 108 C5 prev. Eng. Oltenitsa; anc. Constantiola. Călăraşi, SE Romania
Oltenitsa see Olteniţa
Oltul see Olt
Olvera 92 D5 Andalucía, S Spain
Ol'viopol' see Pervomays'k
Olympia 46 B2 state capital Washington, NW USA
Olympic Mountains 46 A2 mountain range Washington, NW USA
Olympus, Mount 104 B4 var. Ólimbos, Eng. Mount Olympus. mountain N Greece
Omagh 89 B5 Ir. An Ómaigh. N Northern Ireland, United Kingdom
Omaha 45 F4 Nebraska, C USA
Oman 121 D6 off. Sultanate of Oman, Ar. Salţanat 'Umān; prev. Muscat and Oman. country SW Asia

OMAN
Southwest Asia

Official name	Sultanate of Oman
Formation	1951 / 1951
Capital	Muscat
Population	2.8 million / 34 people per sq mile (13 people per sq km)
Total area	82,031 sq. miles (212,460 sq. km)
Languages	Arabic*, Baluchi, Farsi, Hindi, Punjabi
Religions	Ibadi Muslim 75%, Other Muslim and Hindu 25%
Ethnic mix	Arab 88%, Baluchi 4%, Persian 3%, Indian and Pakistani 3%, African 2%
Government	Monarchy
Currency	Omani rial = 1000 baisa
Literacy rate	87%
Calorie consumption	Not available

Oman, Gulf of 120 E4 Ar. Khalīj 'Umān. gulf N Arabian Sea
Oman, Sultanate of see Oman
Omboué 77 A6 Ogooué-Maritime, W Gabon
Omdurman 72 B4 var. Umm Durmān. Khartoum, C Sudan
Ometepe, Isla de 52 D4 island S Nicaragua
Ommen 86 E3 Overijssel, E Netherlands
Omsk 114 C4 Omskaya Oblast', C Russian Federation
Ōmuta 131 A7 Fukuoka, Kyūshū, SW Japan
Onda 93 F3 Valenciana, E Spain
Ondjiva see Vil'shanka
Öndörhaan 127 E2 var. Undur Khan; prev. Tsetsen Khan. Hentiy, E Mongolia
Onega 110 C3 Arkhangel'skaya Oblast', NW Russian Federation
Onega 110 B4 river NW Russian Federation
Lake Onega 110 B4 Eng. Lake Onega. lake NW Russian Federation
Onega, Lake see Onezhskoye Ozero
Onex 95 A7 Genève, SW Switzerland
Ongole 132 D1 Andhra Pradesh, E India

Onitsha 75 G5 Anambra, S Nigeria
Onon Gol 127 E2 river N Mongolia
Onslow 146 A4 Western Australia
Onslow Bay 43 F1 bay North Carolina, E USA
Ontario 38 B3 province S Canada
Ontario, Lake 41 E3 lake Canada/USA
Onteniente see Ontinyent
Ontinyent 93 F4 var. Onteniente. Valenciana, E Spain
Ontong Java Rise 125 H4 undersea feature W Pacific Ocean
Onuba see Huelva
Oodeypore see Udaipur
Oos-Londen see East London
Oostakker 87 B5 Oost-Vlaanderen, NW Belgium
Oostburg 87 B5 Zeeland, SW Netherlands
Oostende 87 A5 Eng. Ostend, Fr. Ostende. West-Vlaanderen, NW Belgium
Oosterbeek 86 D4 Gelderland, SE Netherlands
Oosterhout 86 C4 Noord-Brabant, S Netherlands
Opatija 100 A2 It. Abbazia. Primorje-Gorski Kotar, NW Croatia
Opava 99 C5 Ger. Troppau. Moravskoslezský Kraj, E Czech Republic
Opazova see Stara Pazova
Opelika 42 D2 Alabama, S USA
Opelousas 42 B3 Louisiana, S USA
Ophiusa see Formentera
Opmeer 86 C2 Noord-Holland, NW Netherlands
Opochka 110 A4 Pskovskaya Oblast', W Russian Federation
Opole 98 C4 Ger. Oppeln. Opolskie, S Poland
Oporto see Porto
Opotiki 150 E3 Bay of Plenty, North Island, New Zealand
Oppeln see Opole
Oppidum Ubiorum see Köln
Oqtosh 123 E2 Rus. Aktash. Samarqand Viloyati, C Uzbekistan
Oradea 108 B3 prev. Oradea Mare, Ger. Grosswardein, Hung. Nagyvárad. Bihor, NW Romania
Oradea Mare see Oradea
Orahovac see Rahovec
Oral see Ural'sk
Oran 70 D2 var. Ouahran, Wahran. NW Algeria
Orange 149 D6 New South Wales, SE Australia
Orange 91 D6 anc. Arausio. Vaucluse, SE France
Orangeburg 43 E2 South Carolina, SE USA
Orange Cone see Orange Fan
Orange Fan 69 C7 var. Orange Cone. undersea feature SW Indian Ocean
Orange Mouth/Orangemund see Oranjemund
Orange River 78 B4 Afr. Oranjerivier. river S Africa
Orange Walk 52 C1 Orange Walk, N Belize
Oranienburg 94 D3 Brandenburg, NE Germany
Oranjemund 78 B4 var. Orangemund; prev. Orange Mouth. Karas, SW Namibia
Oranjerivier see Orange River
Oranjestad 55 E5 dependent territory capital (Aruba) W Aruba
Orany see Varėna
Oraşul Stalin see Braşov
Oravicabánya see Oraviţa
Oraviţa 108 A4 Ger. Orawitza, Hung. Oravicabánya. Caraş-Severin, SW Romania
Orawitza see Oraviţa
Orbetello 96 B4 Toscana, C Italy
Orcadas 154 A1 Argentinian research station South Orkney Islands, Antarctica
Orchard Homes 44 B1 Montana, NW USA
Ordino 91 A8 Ordino, NW Andorra Europe
Ordos Desert see Mu Us Shadi
Ordu 116 D2 anc. Cotyora. Ordu, N Turkey
Ordzhonikidze 109 F3 Dnipropetrovs'ka Oblast', E Ukraine

Ordzhonikidze see Vladikavkaz, Russian Federation
Ordzhonikidze see Yenakiyeve, Ukraine
Orealla 59 G3 E Guyana
Örebro 85 C6 Örebro, C Sweden
Oregon 46 B3 off. State of Oregon, also known as Beaver State, Sunset State, Valentine State, Webfoot State. state NW USA
Oregon City 46 B3 Oregon, NW USA
Oregon, State of see Oregon
Orekhov see Orikhiv
Orël 111 B5 Orlovskaya Oblast', W Russian Federation
Orem 44 B4 Utah, W USA
Ore Mountains 95 C5 Cz. Krušné Hory, Eng. Ore Mountains. mountain range Czech Republic/Germany
Ore Mountains see Erzgebirge/Krušné Hory
Orenburg 111 D6 prev. Chkalov. Orenburgskaya Oblast', W Russian Federation
Orense see Ourense
Orestiáda 104 D3 prev. Orestiás. Anatolikí Makedonía kai Thráki, NE Greece
Orestiás see Orestiáda
Organ Peak 48 D3 mountain New Mexico, SW USA
Orgeyev see Orhei
Orhei 108 D3 var. Orheiu, Rus. Orgeyev. N Moldova
Orheiu see Orhei
Oriental, Cordillera 60 D3 mountain range Bolivia/Peru
Oriental, Cordillera 58 B3 mountain range C Colombia
Orihuela 93 F4 Valenciana, E Spain
Orikhiv 109 G3 Rus. Orekhov. Zaporiz'ka Oblast', SE Ukraine
Orinoco, Río 59 E2 river Colombia/Venezuela
Orissa 134 F4 var. Odisha. cultural region NE India
Orissaar see Orissaare
Orissaare 106 C2 Ger. Orissaar. Saaremaa, W Estonia
Oristano 97 A5 Sardegna, Italy, C Mediterranean Sea
Orito 58 A4 Putumayo, SW Colombia
Orizaba, Volcán Pico de 35 C7 var. Citlaltépetl. mountain S Mexico
Orkney see Orkney Islands
Orkney Islands 88 C2 var. Orkney, Orkneys. island group N Scotland, United Kingdom
Orkneys see Orkney Islands
Orlando 43 E4 Florida, SE USA
Orléanais 90 C4 cultural region C France
Orléans 90 C4 anc. Aurelianum. Loiret, C France
Orléansville see Chlef
Orly 90 E2 (Paris) Essonne, N France
Orlya 107 B6 Hrodzyenskaya Voblasts', W Belarus
Ormsö see Vormsi
Ormuz, Strait of see Hormuz, Strait of
Örnsköldsvik 85 C5 Västernorrland, C Sweden
Orolaunum see Arlon
Orol Dengizi see Aral Sea
Oromocto 39 F4 New Brunswick, SE Canada
Orona 145 F3 prev. Hull Island. atoll Phoenix Islands, C Kiribati
Oropeza see Cochabamba
Orosirá Rodhópis see Rhodope Mountains
Orpington 89 B8 United Kingdom
Orschowa see Orşova
Orsha 107 E6 Vitsyebskaya Voblasts', NE Belarus
Orsk 114 B4 Orenburgskaya Oblast', W Russian Federation
Orşova 108 A4 Ger. Orschowa, Hung. Orsova. Mehedinţi, SW Romania
Ortelsburg see Szczytno
Orthez 91 B6 Pyrénées-Atlantiques, SW France
Ortona 96 D4 Abruzzo, C Italy
Oruba see Aruba
Oruro 61 F4 Oruro, W Bolivia
Oryokko see Yalu
Oss 86 D4 Noord-Brabant, S Netherlands
Ōsaka 131 C6 hist. Naniwa. Ōsaka, Honshū, SW Japan
Ōsaki see Furukawa

Osa, Península de *53 E5 peninsula* S Costa Rica
Osborn Plateau *141 D5 undersea feature* E Indian Ocean
Osca *see* Huesca
Ösel *see* Saaremaa
Osh *123 F2* Oshskaya Oblast', SW Kyrgyzstan
Oshawa *38 D5* Ontario, SE Canada
Oshikango *78 B3* Ohangwena, N Namibia
O-shima *131 D6 island* S Japan
Oshkosh *40 B2* Wisconsin, N USA
Oshmyany *see* Ashmyany
Osiek *see* Osijek
Osijek *100 C3 prev.* Osiek, Osjek, *Ger.* Esseg, *Hung.* Eszék. Osijek-Baranja, E Croatia
Osipenko *see* Berdyans'k
Osipovichi *see* Asipovichy
Osjek *see* Osijek
Oskaloosa *45 G4* Iowa, C USA
Oskarshamn *85 C7* Kalmar, S Sweden
Öskemen *see* Ust'-Kamenogorsk
Oskil *109 G2 Rus.* Oskil. *river* Russian Federation/Ukraine
Oskil *see* Oskil
Oslo *85 B6 prev.* Christiania, Kristiania. *country capital* (Norway) Oslo, S Norway
Osmaniye *116 D4* Osmaniye, S Turkey
Osnabrück *94 A3* Niedersachsen, NW Germany
Osogov Mountains *104 B3 var.* Osogovske Planine, Osogovski Planina, *Mac.* Osogovski Planini. *mountain range* Bulgaria/FYR Macedonia
Osogovske Planine/Osogovski Planina/ Osogovski Planini *see* Osogov Mountains
Oşorhei *see* Târgu Mureş
Osorno *65 B5* Los Lagos, C Chile
Ossa, Serra d' *92 C4 mountain range* SE Portugal
Ossora *115 H2* Krasnoyarskiy Kray, E Russian Federation
Ostee *see* Baltic Sea
Ostend/Ostende *see* Oostende
Oster *109 E1* Chernihivs'ka Oblast', N Ukraine
Östermyra *see* Seinäjoki
Osterode/Osterode in Ostpreussen *see* Ostróda
Österreich *see* Austria
Östersund *85 C5* Jämtland, C Sweden
Ostia Aterni *see* Pescara
Ostiglia *96 C2* Lombardia, N Italy
Ostrava *99 C5* Moravskoslezský Kraj, E Czech Republic
Ostróda *98 D3 Ger.* Osterode, Osterode in Ostpreussen. Warmińsko-Mazurskie, NE Poland
Ostrołęka *98 D3 Ger.* Wiesenhof, *Rus.* Ostrolenka. Mazowieckie, C Poland
Ostrolenka *see* Ostrołęka
Ostrov *110 A4 Latv.* Astrava. Pskovskaya Oblast', W Russian Federation
Ostrovets *see* Ostrowiec Świętokrzyski
Ostrovnoy *110 C2* Murmanskaya Oblast', NW Russian Federation
Ostrów *see* Ostrów Wielkopolski
Ostrowiec *see* Ostrowiec Świętokrzyski
Ostrowiec Świętokrzyski *98 D4 var.* Ostrowiec, *Rus.* Ostrovets. Świętokrzyskie, C Poland
Ostrów Mazowiecka *98 D3 var.* Ostrów Mazowiecki. Mazowieckie, NE Poland
Ostrów Mazowiecki *see* Ostrów Mazowiecka
Ostrowo *see* Ostrów Wielkopolski
Ostrów Wielkopolski *98 C4 var.* Ostrów, *Ger.* Ostrowo. Wielkopolskie, C Poland
Ostyako-Voguls'k *see* Khanty-Mansiysk
Osum *see* Osumit, Lumi i
Osumi-shoto *131 A8 island group* Kagoshima, Nansei-shotō, SW Japan Asia East China Sea Pacific Ocean
Osumit, Lumi i *101 D7 var.* Osum. *river* SE Albania
Osuna *92 D4* Andalucía, S Spain
Oswego *41 F2* New York, NE USA
Otago Peninsula *151 B7 peninsula* South Island, New Zealand
Otaki *150 D4* Wellington, North Island, New Zealand
Otaru *130 C2* Hokkaidō, NE Japan
Otavalo *60 B1* Imbabura, N Ecuador

Otavi *78 B3* Otjozondjupa, N Namibia
Oţelu Roşu *108 B4 Ger.* Ferdinandsberg, *Hung.* Nándorhgy. Caras-Severin, SW Romania
Otepää *106 D3 Ger.* Odenpäh. Valgamaa, SE Estonia
Oti *75 E4 river* N Togo
Otira *151 C6* West Coast, South Island, New Zealand
Otjiwarongo *78 B3* Otjozondjupa, N Namibia
Otorohanga *150 D3* Waikato, North Island, New Zealand
Otranto, Canale d' *see* Otranto, Strait of
Otranto, Strait of *101 C6 It.* Canale d'Otranto. *strait* Albania/Italy
Otrokovice *99 C5 Ger.* Otrokowitz. Zlínský Kraj, E Czech Republic
Otrokowitz *see* Otrokovice
Ōtsu *131 C6 var.* Ōtu. Shiga, Honshū, SW Japan
Ottawa *38 D5 country capital* (Canada) Ontario, SE Canada
Ottawa *40 B3* Illinois, N USA
Ottawa *45 F5* Kansas, C USA
Ottawa *41 E2 Fr.* Outaouais. *river* Ontario/Québec, SE Canada
Ottawa Islands *38 C1 island group* Nunavut, C Canada
Ottignies *87 C6* Walloon Brabant, C Belgium
Ottumwa *45 G4* Iowa, C USA
Ōtu *see* Ōtsu
Ouachita Mountains *42 A1 mountain range* Arkansas/Oklahoma, C USA
Ouachita River *42 B2 river* Arkansas/Louisiana, C USA
Ouagadougou *75 E4 var.* Wagadugu. *country capital* (Burkina Faso) C Burkina Faso
Ouahigouya *75 E3* NW Burkina Faso
Ouahran *see* Oran
Oualâta *74 D3 var.* Oualata. Hodh ech Chargui, SE Mauritania
Ouanary *59 H3* E French Guiana
Ouanda Djallé *76 D4* Vakaga, NE Central African Republic
Ouarâne *74 D2 desert* C Mauritania
Ouargla *71 E2 var.* Wargla. NE Algeria
Ouarzazate *70 C3* S Morocco
Oubangui *77 C5 Fr.* Oubangui. *river* C Africa
Oubangui *see* Ubangi
Oubangui-Chari *see* Central African Republic
Oubangui-Chari, Territoire de l' *see* Central African Republic
Oudjda *see* Oujda
Ouessant, Île d' *90 A3 Eng.* Ushant. *island* NW France
Ouésso *77 B5* Sangha, NW Congo
Oujda *70 D2 Ar.* Oudjda, Ujda. NE Morocco
Oujeft *74 C2* Adrar, C Mauritania
Oulu *84 D4 Swe.* Uleåborg. Oulu, C Finland
Oulujärvi *84 D4 Swe.* Uleträsk. *lake* C Finland
Oulujoki *84 D4 Swe.* Uleälv. *river* C Finland
Ounasjoki *84 D3 river* N Finland
Ounianga Kébir *76 C2* Borkou-Ennedi-Tibesti, N Chad
Oup *see* Auob
Oupeye *87 D6* Liège, E Belgium
Our *87 D6 river* NW Europe
Ourense *92 C1 Cast.* Orense, *Lat.* Aurium. Galicia, NW Spain
Ourique *92 B4* Beja, S Portugal
Ours, Grand Lac de l' *see* Great Bear Lake
Ouse *89 D5 river* E England, United Kingdom
Outaouais *see* Ottawa
Outer Hebrides *88 B3 var.* Western Isles. *island group* NW Scotland, United Kingdom
Outer Islands *79 G1 island group* SW Seychelles Africa W Indian Ocean
Ouvéa *144 D5 island* Îles Loyauté, NE New Calédonia
Ouyen *149 C6* Victoria, SE Australia
Ovalle *64 B3* Coquimbo, N Chile
Ovar *92 B2* Aveiro, N Portugal
Overflakkee *86 B4 island* SW Netherlands
Overijse *87 C6* Vlaams Brabant, C Belgium

Oviedo *92 C1 anc.* Asturias. Asturias, NW Spain
Ovilava *see* Wels
Ovruch *108 D1* Zhytomyrs'ka Oblast', N Ukraine
Owando *77 B5 prev.* Fort Rousset. Cuvette, C Congo
Owase *131 C6* Mie, Honshū, SW Japan
Owatonna *45 F3* Minnesota, N USA
Owen Fracture Zone *140 B4 tectonic feature* W Arabian Sea
Owen, Mount *151 C5 mountain* South Island, New Zealand
Owensboro *40 B5* Kentucky, S USA
Owen Stanley Range *144 B3 mountain range* S Papua New Guinea
Owerri *75 G5* Imo, S Nigeria
Owo *75 F5* Ondo, SW Nigeria
Owyhee River *46 C4 river* Idaho/Oregon, NW USA
Oxford *151 C6* Canterbury, South Island, New Zealand
Oxford *89 D6 Lat.* Oxonia. S England, United Kingdom
Oxkutzcab *51 H4* Yucatán, SE Mexico
Oxnard *47 B7* California, W USA
Oxonia *see* Oxford
Oxus *see* Amu Darya
Oyama *131 D5* Tochigi, Honshū, S Japan
Oyem *77 B5* Woleu-Ntem, N Gabon
Oyo *77 B6* Cuvette, C Congo
Oyo *75 F4* Oyo, W Nigeria
Ozark *42 D3* Alabama, S USA
Ozark Plateau *45 G5 plain* Arkansas/Missouri, C USA
Ozarks, Lake of the *45 F5 reservoir* Missouri, C USA
Ozbourn Seamount *152 D4 undersea feature* W Pacific Ocean
Ózd *99 D6* Borsod-Abaúj-Zemplén, NE Hungary
Ozieri *97 A5* Sardegna, Italy, C Mediterranean Sea

P

Paamiut *82 B4 var.* Pâmiut, *Dan.* Frederikshåb. S Greenland
Pa-an *see* Hpa-an
Pabianice *98 C4* Łódzki, Poland
Pabna *135 G4* Rajshahi, W Bangladesh
Pacaraima, Sierra/Pacaraim, Serra *see* Pakaraima Mountains
Pachuca *51 E4 var.* Pachuca de Soto. Hidalgo, C Mexico
Pachuca de Soto *see* Pachuca
Pacific-Antarctic Ridge *154 B5 undersea feature* S Pacific Ocean
Pacific Ocean *152 D3 ocean*
Padalung *see* Phatthalung
Padang *138 B4* Sumatera, W Indonesia
Paderborn *94 B4* Nordrhein-Westfalen, NW Germany
Padma *see* Brahmaputra
Padma *see* Ganges
Padova *96 C2 Eng.* Padua; *anc.* Patavium. Veneto, NE Italy
Padre Island *49 G5 island* Texas, SW USA
Padua *see* Padova
Paducah *40 B5* Kentucky, S USA
Paeroa *150 D3* Waikato, North Island, New Zealand
Páfos *102 C5 var.* Paphos. W Cyprus
Pag *48 B1* Arizona, SW USA
Pag *100 A3 It.* Pago. *island* Zadar, C Croatia
Page *48 B1* Arizona, SW USA
Pago *see* Pag
Pago Pago *145 F4 dependent territory capital* (American Samoa) Tutuila, W American Samoa
Pahiatua *150 D4* Manawatu-Wanganui, North Island, New Zealand
Pahsien *see* Chongqing
Paide *106 D2 Ger.* Weissenstein. Järvamaa, N Estonia
Paihia *150 D2* Northland, North Island, New Zealand
Päijänne *85 D5 lake* S Finland
Paine, Cerro *65 A7 mountain* S Chile
Painted Desert *48 B1 desert* Arizona, SW USA
Paisance *see* Piacenza
Paisley *88 C4* W Scotland, United Kingdom
País Vasco *93 E1 cultural region* N Spain
Paita *60 B3* Piura, NW Peru
Pakanbaru *see* Pekanbaru

Pakaraima Mountains *59 E3 var.* Serra Pacaraim, Sierra Pacaraima. *mountain range* N South America
Pakistan *134 A2 off.* Islamic Republic of Pakistan, *var.* Islami Jamhuriya e Pakistan. *country* S Asia

PAKISTAN
South Asia

Official name Islamic Republic of Pakistan
Formation 1947 / 1971
Capital Islamabad
Population 177 million / 594 people per sq mile (229 people per sq km)
Total area 310,401 sq. miles (803,940 sq. km)
Languages Punjabi, Sindhi, Pashtu, Urdu*, Baluchi, Brahui
Religions Sunni Muslim 77%, Shi'a Muslim 20%, Hindu 2%, Christian 1%
Ethnic mix Punjabi 56%, Pathan (Pashtun) 15%, Sindhi 14%, Mohajir 7%, Baluchi 4%, Other 4%
Government Presidential system
Currency Pakistani rupee = 100 paisa
Literacy rate 56%
Calorie consumption 2423 kilocalories

Pakistan, Islamic Republic of *see* Pakistan
Pakistan, Islami Jamhuriya e *see* Pakistan
Paknam *see* Samut Prakan
Pakokku *136 A3* Magway, C Myanmar (Burma)
Pak Phanang *137 C7 var.* Ban Pak Phanang. Nakhon Si Thammarat, SW Thailand
Pakruojis *106 C4* Šiauliai, N Lithuania
Paks *99 C7* Tolna, S Hungary
Paksé *see* Pakxé
Pakxé *137 D5 var.* Paksé. Champasak, S Laos
Palafrugell *93 G2* Cataluña, NE Spain
Palagruža *101 B5 It.* Pelagosa. *island* SW Croatia
Palaiá Epídavros *105 C6* Pelopónnisos, S Greece
Palaiseau *90 D2* Essonne, N France
Palamós *93 G2* Cataluña, NE Spain
Palamuse *106 E2 Ger.* Sankt-Bartholomäi. Jõgevamaa, E Estonia
Palanka *see* Bačka Palanka
Pālanpur *134 C4* Gujarāt, W India
Palantia *see* Palencia
Palapye *78 D3* Central, SE Botswana
Palau *144 A2 var.* Belau. *country* W Pacific Ocean

PALAU
Australasia & Oceania

Official name Republic of Palau
Formation 1994 / 1994
Capital Melekeok
Population 21,032 / 107 people per sq mile (41 people per sq km)
Total area 177 sq. miles (458 sq. km)
Languages Palauan*, English*, Japanese, Angaur, Tobi, Sonsorolese
Religions Christian 66%, Modekngei 34%
Ethnic mix Palauan 74%, Filipino 16%, Other 6%, Chinese and other Asian 4%
Government Nonparty system
Currency US dollar = 100 cents
Literacy rate 98%
Calorie consumption Not available

Palawan *139 E2 island* W Philippines
Palawan Passage *138 D2 passage* W Philippines
Paldiski *106 D2 prev.* Baltiski, *Eng.* Baltic Port, *Ger.* Baltischport. Harjumaa, NW Estonia
Palembang *138 B4* Sumatera, W Indonesia
Palencia *92 D2 anc.* Palantia, Pallantia. Castilla y León, NW Spain
Palerme *see* Palermo
Palermo *97 C7 Fr.* Palerme; *anc.* Panhormus, Panormus. Sicilia, Italy, C Mediterranean Sea
Pāli *134 C3* Rājasthān, N India
Palikir *144 C2 country capital* (Micronesia) Pohnpei, E Micronesia
Palimé *see* Kpalimé

Palioúri, Akrotírio 104 C4 *var.*
Akrotírio Kanestron. *headland*
N Greece
Palk Strait 132 C3 *strait* India/Sri Lanka
Pallantia *see* Palencia
Palliser, Cape 151 D5 *headland* North
Island, New Zealand
Palma 93 G3 *var.* Palma de Mallorca.
Mallorca, Spain, W Mediterranean Sea
Palma del Río 92 D4 Andalucía,
S Spain
Palma de Mallorca *see* Palma
Palmar Sur 53 E5 Puntarenas,
SE Costa Rica
Palma Soriano 54 C3 Santiago de Cuba,
E Cuba
Palm Beach 148 E1 New South Wales,
E Australia
Palmer 154 A2 *US research station*
Antarctica
Palmer Land 154 A3 *physical region*
Antarctica
Palmerston 145 F4 *island*
S Cook Islands
Palmerston *see* Darwin
Palmerston North 150 D4 Manawatu-
Wanganui, North Island, New Zealand
The Palmetto State *see* South Carolina
Palmi 97 D7 Calabria, SW Italy
Palmira 58 B3 Valle del Cauca,
W Colombia
Palm Springs 47 D7 California,
W USA
Palmyra *see* Tudmur
Palmyra Atoll 145 G2 *US privately
owned unincorporated territory*
C Pacific Ocean
Palo Alto 47 B6 California, W USA
Paloe *see* Denpasar, Bali, C Indonesia
Paloe *see* Palu
Palu 139 E4 *prev.* Paloe. Sulawesi,
C Indonesia
Pamiers 91 B6 Ariège, S France
Pamir 123 F3 *var.* Daryā-ye Pāmir, *Taj.*
Dar"yoi Pomir. *river* Afghanistan/
Tajikistan
Pāmir, Daryā-ye Pamir
Pamir/Pāmir, Daryā-ye *see* Pamirs
Pamirs 123 F3 *Pash.* Daryā-ye Pāmir,
Rus. Pamir. *mountain range* C Asia
Pāmiut *see* Paamiut
Pamlico Sound 43 G1 *sound* North
Carolina, SE USA
Pampa 49 E1 Texas, SW USA
Pampa Aullagas, Lago *see* Poopó, Lago
Pampas 64 C4 *plain* C Argentina
Pampeluna *see* Pamplona
Pamplona 58 C2 Norte de Santander,
N Colombia
Pamplona 93 E1 *Basq.* Iruña, *prev.*
Pampeluna; *anc.* Pompaelo. Navarra,
N Spain
Panaji 132 B1 *var.* Pangim, Panjim, New
Goa. *state capital* Goa, W India
Panamá 53 G4 *var.* Ciudad de Panama,
Eng. Panama City. *country capital*
(Panama) Panamá, C Panama
Panama 53 G5 *off.* Republic of Panama.
country Central America

PANAMA
Central America

Official name Republic of Panama
Formation 1903 / 1903
Capital Panama City
Population 3.6 million / 123 people
per sq mile (47 people per sq km)
Total area 30,193 sq. miles (78,200 sq. km)
Languages English Creole,
Spanish*, Amerindian languages,
Chibchan languages
Religions Roman Catholic 84%,
Protestant 15%, Other 1%
Ethnic mix Mestizo 70%, Black 14%,
White 10%, Amerindian 6%
Government Presidential system
Currency Balboa = 100 centésimos
Literacy rate 94%
Calorie consumption 2606 kilocalories

Panama Basin 35 C8 *undersea feature*
E Pacific Ocean
Panama Canal 53 F4 *canal* E Panama
Panama City 42 D3 Florida, SE USA
Panama City *see* Panamá
Gulf of Panama 53 G5 *var.* Gulf of
Panama. *gulf* S Panama
Panama, Gulf of *see* Panamá, Golfo de

Isthmus of Panama 53 G4 *Eng.* Isthmus
of Panama; *prev.* Isthmus of Darien.
isthmus E Panama
Panama, Isthmus of *see* Panama,
Istmo de
Panama, Republic of *see* Panama
Panay Island 139 E2 *island* C Philippines
Pančevo 100 D3 *Ger.* Pantschowa, *Hung.*
Pancsova. Vojvodina, N Serbia
Pancsova *see* Pančevo
Paneas *see* Bāniyās
Panevėžys 106 C4 Panevėžys,
C Lithuania
Pangim *see* Panaji
Pangkalpinang 138 C4 Pulau Bangka,
W Indonesia
Pang-Nga *see* Phang-Nga
Panhormus *see* Palermo
Panjim *see* Panaji
Panopolis *see* Akhmīm
Pánormos 105 C7 Kríti, Greece,
E Mediterranean Sea
Panormus *see* Palermo
Pantanal 63 A3 *var.* Pantanalmato-
Grossense. *swamp* SW Brazil
Pantanalmato-Grossense *see* Pantanal
Pantelleria, Isola di 97 B7 *island*
SW Italy
Pantschowa *see* Pančevo
Pánuco 51 E3 Veracruz-Llave,
E Mexico
Pao-chi/Paoki *see* Baoji
Paola 102 B5 E Malta
Pao-shan *see* Baoshan
Pao-t'ou/Paotow *see* Baotou
Papagayo, Golfo de 52 C4 *gulf*
NW Costa Rica
Papakura 150 D3 Auckland, North
Island, New Zealand
Papantla 51 F4 *var.* Papantla de Olarte.
Veracruz-Llave, E Mexico
Papantla de Olarte *see* Papantla
Papeete 145 H4 *dependent territory
capital* (French Polynesia) Tahiti,
W French Polynesia
Paphos *see* Páfos
Papilė 106 B3 Šiauliai, NW Lithuania
Papillion 45 F4 Nebraska, C USA
Papua 139 H4 *var.* Irian Barat, West
Irian, West New Guinea, West Papua;
prev. Dutch New Guinea, Irian Jaya,
Netherlands New Guinea. *province*
E Indonesia
Papua and New Guinea, Territory of *see*
Papua and New Guinea
Papua, Gulf of 144 B3 *gulf* S Papua
New Guinea
Papua New Guinea 144 B3 *off.*
Independent State of Papua New
Guinea; *prev.* Territory of Papua and
New Guinea. *country* NW Melanesia

PAPUA NEW GUINEA
Australasia & Oceania

Official name Independent State
of Papua New Guinea
Formation 1975 / 1975
Capital Port Moresby
Population 7 million / 40 people
per sq mile (15 people per sq km)
Total area 178,703 sq. miles
(462,840 sq. km)
Languages Pidgin English, Papuan,
English*, Motu, 800 (est.) native languages
Religions Protestant 60%, Roman
Catholic 37%, Other 3%
Ethnic mix Melanesian and mixed
race 100%
Government Parliamentary system
Currency Kina = 100 toea
Literacy rate 60%
Calorie consumption 2193 kilocalories

**Papua New Guinea, Independent State
of** *see* Papua New Guinea
Papuk 100 C3 *mountain range*
NE Croatia
Pará 63 E2 *off.* Estado do Pará. *state*
NE Brazil
Pará 63 E2 *off.* Estado do Pará. *region*
NE Brazil
Pará *see* Belém
Paracel Islands 125 E3 *disputed territory*
SE Asia
Paraćin 100 D4 Serbia, C Serbia
Paradise of the Pacific *see* Hawai'i
Pará, Estado do *see* Pará
Paragua, Río 59 E3 *river* SE Venezuela

Paraguay 64 C2 *country* C South
America

PARAGUAY
South America

Official name Republic of Paraguay
Formation 1811 / 1938
Capital Asunción
Population 6.6 million / 43 people
per sq mile (17 people per sq km)
Total area 157,046 sq. miles
(406,750 sq. km)
Languages Guaraní, Spanish*, German
Religions Roman Catholic 90%,
Protestant (including Mennonite) 10%
Ethnic mix Mestizo 91%, Other 7%,
Amerindian 2%
Government Presidential system
Currency Guaraní = 100 céntimos
Literacy rate 95%
Calorie consumption 2518 kilocalories

Paraguay 64 D2 *var.* Río Paraguay. *river*
C South America
Paraguay, Río *see* Paraguay
Paraíba 63 G2 *off.* Estado da Paraíba;
prev. Parahiba, Parahyba. *state* E Brazil
Paraíba 63 G2 *off.* Estado da Paraíba;
prev. Parahiba, Parahyba. *region*
E Brazil
Paraíba *see* João Pessoa
Paraíba, Estado da *see* Paraíba
Parakou 75 F4 C Benin
Paramaribo 59 G3 *country capital*
(Suriname) Paramaribo, N Suriname
Paramushir, Ostrov 115 H3 *island*
SE Russian Federation
Paraná 63 E4 Entre Ríos, E Argentina
Paraná 63 E5 *off.* Estado do Paraná.
state S Brazil
Paraná 63 E5 *off.* Estado do Paraná.
region S Brazil
Paraná 57 C5 *var.* Alto Paraná. *river*
C South America
Paraná, Estado do *see* Paraná
Paranésti 104 C3 *var.* Paranestio.
Anatolikí Makedonía kai Thráki,
NE Greece
Paranestio *see* Paranésti
Paraparaumu 151 D5 Wellington, North
Island, New Zealand
Parchim 94 C3 Mecklenburg-
Vorpommern, N Germany
Parczew 98 E4 Lubelskie, E Poland
Pardubice 99 B5 *Ger.* Pardubitz.
Pardubický Kraj, C Czech Republic
Pardubitz *see* Pardubice
Parechcha 107 B5 Pol. Porzecze, *Rus.*
Porech'ye. Hrodzyenskaya Voblasts',
W Belarus
Parecis, Chapada dos 62 D3 *var.* Serra
dos Parecis. *mountain range* W Brazil
Parecis, Serra dos *see* Parecis, Chapada
dos
Parenzo *see* Poreč
Parepare 139 E4 Sulawesi, C Indonesia
Pária, Golfo de *see* Paria, Gulf of
Paria, Gulf of 59 E1 *var.* Golfo de Paria.
gulf Trinidad and Tobago/Venezuela
Parika 59 F2 NE Guyana
Paris 90 D1 *anc.* Lutetia, Lutetia
Parisiorum, Parisii. *country capital*
(France) Paris, N France
Paris 49 G2 Texas, SW USA
Parisii *see* Paris
Parkersburg 40 D4 West Virginia,
NE USA
Parkes 149 D6 New South Wales,
SE Australia
Parkhar *see* Farkhor
Parma 96 B2 Emilia-Romagna, N Italy
Parnahyba *see* Parnaíba
Parnaíba 63 F2 *var.* Parnahyba. Piauí,
E Brazil
Pärnu 106 D2 *Ger.* Pernau, *Latv.*
Pērnava; *prev. Rus.* Pernov. Pärnumaa,
SW Estonia
Pärnu 106 D2 *var.* Parnu Jõgi, *Ger.*
Pernau. *river* SW Estonia
Pärnu-Jaaguppi 106 D2 *Ger.* Sankt-
Jakobi. Pärnumaa, SW Estonia
Parnu Jõgi *see* Pärnu
Pärnu Laht 106 D2 *Ger.* Pernauer Bucht.
bay SW Estonia
Paropamisus Range *see* Sefīd Kūh,
Selseleh-ye

Páros 105 C6 *island* Kykládes, Greece,
Aegean Sea
Parral 64 B4 Maule, C Chile
Parral *see* Hidalgo del Parral
Parramatta 148 D1 New South Wales,
SE Australia
Parras 50 D3 *var.* Parras de la Fuente.
Coahuila, NE Mexico
Parras de la Fuente *see* Parras
Parsons 45 F5 Kansas, C USA
Pasadena 47 C7 California, W USA
Pasadena 49 H4 Texas, SW USA
Pașcani 108 C3 *Hung.* Páskán. Iași,
NE Romania
Pasco 46 C2 Washington, NW USA
Pasewalk 94 D3 Mecklenburg-
Vorpommern, NE Germany
Pashkeni *see* Bolyarovo
Pasinler 117 F3 Erzurum, NE Turkey
Páskán *see* Pașcani
Pasłęk 98 D2 *Ger.* Preußisch Holland.
Warmińsko-Mazurskie, NE Poland
Pasni 134 A3 Baluchistān, SW Pakistan
Paso de Indios 65 B6 Chubut,
S Argentina
Passarowitz *see* Požarevac
Passau 95 D6 Bayern, SE Germany
Passo Fundo 63 E5 Rio Grande do
Sul, S Brazil
Pastavy 107 C5 Pol. Postawy, *Rus.*
Postavy. Vitsyebskaya Voblasts',
NW Belarus
Pastaza, Río 60 B2 *river* Ecuador/Peru
Pasto 58 A4 Nariño, SW Colombia
Pasvalys 106 C4 Panevėžys, N Lithuania
Patagonia 57 B7 *physical region*
Argentina/Chile
Patalung *see* Phatthalung
Patani *see* Pattani
Patavium *see* Padova
Patea 150 D4 Taranaki, North Island,
New Zealand
Paterson 41 F3 New Jersey, NE USA
Pathein 136 A4 *var.* Bassein.
Ayeyarwady, SW Myanmar (Burma)
Pátmos 105 D6 *island* Dodekánisa,
Greece, Aegean Sea
Patna 135 F3 *var.* Azimabad. *state capital*
Bihār, N India
Patnos 117 F3 Ağrı, E Turkey
Patos, Lagoa dos 63 E5 *lagoon*
S Brazil
Pátra 105 B5 *Eng.* Patras; *prev.* Pátrai.
Dytikí Elláda, S Greece
Pátrai/Patras *see* Pátra
Pattani 137 C7 *var.* Patani. Pattani,
SW Thailand
Pattaya 137 C5 Chon Buri, S Thailand
Patuca, Río 52 D2 *river* E Honduras
Pau 91 B6 Pyrénées-Atlantiques,
SW France
Paulatuk 37 E3 Northwest Territories,
NW Canada
Paungde 136 B4 Bago, C Myanmar
(Burma)
Pautalia *see* Kyustendil
Pavia 96 B2 *anc.* Ticinum. Lombardia,
N Italy
Pāvilosta 106 B3 W Latvia
Pavlikeni 104 D2 Veliko Tŭrnovo,
N Bulgaria
Pavlodar 114 C4 Pavlodar,
NE Kazakhstan
Pavlograd *see* Pavlohrad
Pavlohrad 109 G3 *Rus.* Pavlograd.
Dnipropetrovs'ka Oblast', E Ukraine
Pawai, Pulau 138 A2 *island*
SW Singapore Asia
Pawn, Nam 136 B3 *river* C Myanmar
(Burma)
Pax Augusta *see* Badajoz
Pax Julia *see* Beja
Paxoí 105 A5 *island* Iónia Nisiá, Greece,
C Mediterranean Sea
Payo Obispo *see* Chetumal
Paysandú 64 D4 Paysandú, W Uruguay
Pazar 117 F2 Rize, NE Turkey
Pazardzhik 104 C3 *prev.* Tatar
Pazardzhik. Pazardzhik, SW Bulgaria
Peace Garden State *see* North Dakota
Peach State *see* Georgia
Pearl Islands 53 G5 *Eng.* Pearl Islands.
island group SE Panama
Pearl Islands *see* Perlas, Archipiélago
de las
Pearl Lagoon 53 E3 *Eng.* Pearl Lagoon.
lagoon E Nicaragua
Pearl Lagoon *see* Perlas, Laguna de

Pearl River *42 B3 river* Louisiana/
Mississippi, S USA
Pearsall *49 F4* Texas, SW USA
Peawanuk *38 C2 river* Ontario, S Canada
Peč *see* Pejë
Pechora *110 D3* Respublika Komi,
NW Russian Federation
Pechora *110 D3 river* NW Russian
Federation
Pechora Sea *110 D2 Eng.* Pechora Sea.
sea NW Russian Federation
Pechora Sea *see* Pechorskoye More
Pecos *49 E3* Texas, SW USA
Pecos River *49 E3 river* New Mexico/
Texas, SW USA
Pécs *99 C7 Ger.* Fünfkirchen, *Lat.*
Sopianae. Baranya, SW Hungary
Pedra Lume *74 A3* Sal, NE Cape Verde
Pedro Cays *54 C3 island group* Greater
Antilles, S Jamaica North America
N Caribbean Sea W Atlantic Ocean
Pedro Juan Caballero *64 D2* Amambay,
E Paraguay
Peer *87 D5* Limburg, NE Belgium
Pegasus Bay *151 C6 bay* South Island,
New Zealand
Pegu *see* Bago
Pehuajó *64 C4* Buenos Aires, E Argentina
Pei-ching *see* Beijing/Beijing Shi
Peine *94 B3* Niedersachsen, C Germany
Pei-p'ing *see* Beijing/Beijing Shi
Peipsi Järv/Peipus-See *see* Peipus, Lake
Peipus, Lake *106 E3 Est.* Peipsi Järv, *Ger.*
Peipus-See, *Rus.* Chudskoye Ozero.
lake Estonia/Russian Federation
Peiraías *105 C6 prev.* Piraiévs, *Eng.*
Piraeus. Attikí, C Greece
Pejë *101 D5 Serb.* Peč. W Kosovo
Pèk *see* Phônsaven
Pekalongan *138 C4* Jawa, C Indonesia
Pekanbaru *138 B3 var.* Pakanbaru.
Sumatera, W Indonesia
Pekin *40 B4* Illinois, N USA
Peking *see* Beijing/Beijing Shi
Pelagie *97 B8 island group* SW Italy
Pelagosa *see* Palagruža
Pelican State *see* Louisiana
Pelly Bay *see* Kugaaruk
Pélmonostor *see* Beli Manastir
Peloponnese *105 B6 var.* Morea, *Eng.*
Peloponnese; *anc.* Peloponnesus.
peninsula S Greece
Peloponnese/Peloponnesus *see*
Pelopónnisos
Pematangsiantar *138 B3* Sumatera,
W Indonesia
Pemba *79 F2 prev.* Port Amelia,
Porto Amélia. Cabo Delgado,
NE Mozambique
Pemba *73 D7 island* E Tanzania
Pembroke *38 D4* Ontario, SE Canada
Penang *see* Pinang, Pulau, Peninsular
Malaysia
Penang *see* George Town
Penas, Golfo de *65 A7 gulf* S Chile
Penderma *see* Bandırma
Pendleton *46 C3* Oregon, NW USA
Pend Oreille, Lake *46 D2 lake* Idaho,
NW USA
Peneius *see* Pineiós
Peng-pu *see* Bengbu
Penibético, Sistema *see* Béticos, Sistemas
Peniche *92 B3* Leiria, W Portugal
Peninsular State *see* Florida
Pennine, Alpes/Pennine, Alpi *see*
Pennine Alps
Pennine Alps *95 A8 Fr.* Alpes Pennines,
It. Alpi Pennine, *Lat.* Alpes Penninae.
mountain range Italy/Switzerland
Pennine Chain *see* Pennines
Pennines *89 D5 var.* Pennine Chain.
mountain range N England, United
Kingdom
Pennines, Alpes *see* Pennine Alps
Pennsylvania *41 E4 off.* Commonwealth
of Pennsylvania, *also known as*
Keystone State. *state* NE USA
Penobscot River *41 G2 river* Maine,
NE USA
Penong *149 A6* South Australia
Penonomé *53 F5* Coclé, C Panamá
Penrhyn *145 G3 atoll* N Cook Islands
Penrhyn Basin *143 F3 undersea feature*
C Pacific Ocean
Penrith *148 D1* New South Wales,
SE Australia
Penrith *89 D5* NW England, United
Kingdom

Pensacola *42 C3* Florida, SE USA
Pentecost *144 D4 Fr.* Pentecôte. *island*
C Vanuatu
Pentecôte *see* Pentecost
Penza *111 C6* Penzenskaya Oblast',
W Russian Federation
Penzance *89 C7* SW England, United
Kingdom
Peoria *40 B4* Illinois, N USA
Perchtoldsdorf *95 E6* Niederösterreich,
NE Austria
Percival Lakes *146 C4 lakes* Western
Australia
Perdido, Monte *93 F1 mountain*
NE Spain
Perece Vela Basin *see* West Mariana
Basin
Pereira *58 B3* Risaralda, W Colombia
Peremyshl *see* Przemyśl
Pergamino *64 C4* Buenos Aires,
E Argentina
Périgueux *91 C5 anc.* Vesuna.
Dordogne, SW France
Perito Moreno *65 B6* Santa Cruz,
S Argentina
Perleberg *94 C3* Brandenburg,
N Germany
Perlepe *see* Prilep
Perm' *114 C3 prev.* Molotov. Permskiy
Kray, NW Russian Federation
Pernambuco *63 G2 off.* Estado de
Pernambuco. *region* E Brazil
Pernambuco *63 G2 off.* Estado de
Pernambuco. *state* E Brazil
Pernambuco *see* Recife
Pernambuco Abyssal Plain *see*
Pernambuco Plain
Pernambuco, Estado de *see*
Pernambuco
Pernambuco Plain *67 C5 var.*
Pernambuco Abyssal Plain. *undersea
feature* E Atlantic Ocean
Pernau *see* Pärnu
Pernauer Bucht *see* Pärnu Laht
Pērnava *see* Pärnu
Pernik *104 B2 prev.* Dimitrovo. Pernik,
W Bulgaria
Pernov *see* Pärnu
Perote *51 F4* Veracruz-Llave, E Mexico
Pérouse *see* Perugia
Perovsk *see* Kyzylorda
Perpignan *91 C6* Pyrénées-Orientales,
S France
Perryton *49 F1* Texas, SW USA
Perryville *45 H5* Missouri, C USA
Persia *see* Iran
Persian Gulf *120 C4 var.* Gulf, The,
Ar. Khalīj al 'Arabī, *Per.* Khalīj-e Fars.
gulf SW Asia
Perth *147 A6 state capital* Western
Australia
Perth *88 C4* C Scotland,
United Kingdom
Perth Basin *141 E6 undersea feature*
SE Indian Ocean
Peru *60 C3 off.* Republic of Peru. *country*
W South America

PERU
South America

Official name Republic of Peru
Formation 1824 / 1941
Capital Lima
Population 29.4 million / 59 people
per sq mile (23 people per sq km)
Total area 496,223 sq. miles
(1,285,200 sq. km)
Languages Spanish*, Quechua*, Aymara
Religions Roman Catholic 81%, Other 19%
Ethnic mix Amerindian 45%,
Mestizo 37%, White 15%, Other 3%
Government Presidential system
Currency New sol = 100 céntimos
Literacy rate 90%
Calorie consumption 2563 kilocalories

Peru *see* Beru
Peru Basin *67 A5 undersea feature*
E Pacific Ocean
Peru-Chile Trench *56 A4 undersea
feature* E Pacific Ocean
Perugia *96 C4 Fr.* Pérouse; *anc.* Perusia.
Umbria, C Italy
Perugia, Lake of *see* Trasimeno, Lago
Peru, Republic of *see* Peru
Perusia *see* Perugia
Péruwelz *87 B6* Hainaut, SW Belgium

Pervomays'k *109 E3 prev.* Ol'viopol'.
Mykolayivs'ka Oblast', S Ukraine
Pervyy Kuril'skiy Proliv *115 H3 strait*
E Russian Federation
Pesaro *96 C3 anc.* Pisaurum. Marche,
C Italy
Pescara *96 D4 anc.* Aternum, Ostia
Aterni. Abruzzo, C Italy
Peshāwar *134 C1* Khyber Pakhtunkhwa,
N Pakistan
Peshkopi *101 D6 var.* Peshkopia,
Peshkopija. Dibër, NE Albania
Peshkopia/Peshkopija *see* Peshkopi
Pessac *91 B5* Gironde, SW France
Petach-Tikva *see* Petah Tikva
Petah Tikva *119 A6 var.* Petach-Tikva,
Petah Tiqwa, Petah Tikva; *prev.* Petaẖ
Tiqwa. Tel Aviv, C Israel
Petaẖ Tiqwa *see* Petah Tikva
Petah Tikva/Petah Tiqwa *see* Petah
Tikva
Pétange *87 D8* Luxembourg,
SW Luxembourg
Petchaburi *see* Phetchaburi
Peterborough *149 B6* South Australia
Peterborough *38 D5* Ontario, SE Canada
Peterborough *89 E6 prev.*
Medeshamstede. E England, United
Kingdom
Peterhead *88 D3* NE Scotland, United
Kingdom
Peter I Øy *154 A3 Norwegian
dependency* Antarctica
Petermann Bjerg *83 E3 mountain*
C Greenland
Petersburg *41 E5* Virginia, NE USA
Peters Mine *59 F3 var.* Peter's Mine.
N Guyana
Petit St-Bernard, Col du *see* Little Saint
Bernard Pass
Peto *51 H4* Yucatán, SE Mexico
Petoskey *40 C2* Michigan, N USA
Petra *see* Wādī Mūsā
Petrich *104 C3* Blagoevgrad,
SW Bulgaria
Petrikau *see* Piotrków Trybunalski
Petrikov *see* Pyetrykaw
Petrinja *100 B3* Sisak-Moslavina,
C Croatia
Petroaleksandrovsk *see* To'rtko'l
Petrodvorets *110 A4 Fin.* Pietarhovi.
Leningradskaya Oblast', NW Russian
Federation
Petrograd *see* Sankt-Peterburg
Petrokov *see* Piotrków Trybunalski
Petropavl *see* Petropavlovsk
Petropavlovsk *114 C4 Kaz.* Petropavl.
Severnyy Kazakhstan, N Kazakhstan
Petropavlovsk-Kamchatskiy *115
H3* Kamchatskiy Kray, E Russian
Federation
Petroşani *108 B4 var.* Petroseni,
Ger. Petroschen, *Hung.* Petrozsény.
Hunedoara, W Romania
Petroschen/Petroşeni *see* Petroşani
Petroskoi *see* Petrozavodsk
Petrovgrad *see* Zrenjanin
Petrovsk-Port *see* Makhachkala
Petrozavodsk *114 B2 Fin.* Petroskoi.
Respublika Kareliya, NW Russian
Federation
Petrozsény *see* Petroşani
Pettau *see* Ptuj
Pevek *115 G1* Chukotskiy Avtonomnyy
Okrug, NE Russian Federation
Pezinok *99 C6 Ger.* Bösing, *Hung.* Bazin.
Bratislavský Kraj, W Slovakia
Pforzheim *95 B6* Baden-Württemberg,
SW Germany
Pfungstadt *95 B5* Hessen, W Germany
Phangan, Ko *137 C6 island* SW Thailand
Phang-Nga *137 B7 var.* Pang-Nga,
Phangnga. Phangnga, SW Thailand
Phangnga *see* Phang-Nga
Phan Rang/Phanrang *see* Phan Rang-
Thap Cham
Phan Rang-Thap Cham *137 E6 var.*
Phanrang, Phan Rang, Phan Rang
Thap Cham. Ninh Thuận, S Vietnam
Phan Thiết *137 E6* Bình Thuận,
S Vietnam
Pharnacia *see* Giresun
Pharus *see* Hvar
Phatthalung *137 C7 var.* Padalung,
Patalung. Phatthalung, SW Thailand
Phayao *136 C4 var.* Muang Phayao.
Phayao, NW Thailand
Phenix City *42 D2* Alabama, S USA
Phet Buri *see* Phetchaburi

Phetchaburi *137 C5 var.* Bejraburi,
Petchaburi, Phet Buri. Phetchaburi,
SW Thailand
Philadelphia *41 F4* Pennsylvania,
NE USA
Philadelphia *see* 'Ammān
Philippine Basin *125 F3 undersea
feature* W Pacific Ocean
Philippine Islands *139 E1 island group*
W Pacific Ocean
Philippines *139 E1 off.* Republic of the
Philippines. *country* SE Asia

PHILIPPINES
Southeast Asia

Official name Republic of the Philippines
Formation 1946 / 1946
Capital Manila
Population 84.9 million / 824 people
per sq mile (318 people per sq km)
Total area 115,830 sq. miles
(300,000 sq. km)
Languages Filipino, English, Tagalog,
Cebuano, Ilocano, Hiligaynon, many
other local languages
Religions Roman Catholic 81%,
Protestant 9%, Muslim 5%,
Other (including Buddhist) 5%
Ethnic mix Other 34%, Tagalog 28%,
Cebuano 13%, Ilocano 9%, Hiligaynon 8%,
Bisaya 8%
Government Presidential system
Currency Philippine peso = 100 centavos
Literacy rate 95%
Calorie consumption 2580 kilocalories

Philippine Sea *125 F3 sea* W Pacific
Ocean
Philippines, Republic of the *see*
Philippines
Philippine Trench *142 A1 undersea
feature* W Philippine Sea
Philippopolis *see* Plovdiv
Phitsanulok *136 C4 var.* Bisnulok,
Muang Phitsanulok, Pitsanulok.
Phitsanulok, C Thailand
Phlórina *see* Flórina
Phnom Penh *see* Phnum Penh
Phnum Penh *137 D6 var.* Phnom
Penh. *country capital* (Cambodia)
Phnum Penh,
S Cambodia
Phoenix *48 B2 state capital* Arizona,
SW USA
Phoenix Islands *145 E3 island group*
C Kiribati
Phôngsali *136 C3 var.* Phong Saly.
Phôngsali, N Laos
Phong Saly *see* Phôngsali
Phônsaven *136 D4 var.* Pèk, Xieng
Khouang; *prev.* Xiangkhoang.
Xiangkhoang, N Laos
Phou Louang *see* Annamite Mountains
Phrae *136 C4 var.* Muang Phrae, Prae.
Phrae, NW Thailand
Phra Nakhon Si Ayutthaya *see*
Ayutthaya
Phra Thong, Ko *137 B6 island*
SW Thailand
Phuket *137 B7 var.* Bhuket, Puket, *Mal.*
Ujung Salang; *prev.* Junkseylon, Salang.
Phuket, SW Thailand
Phuket, Ko *137 B7 island* SW Thailand
Phumĭ Kâmpóng Trâbêk *see* Kâmpóng
Trâbêk
Phumĭ Sâmraông *see* Sâmraông
Phum Kompong Trabek *see* Kâmpóng
Trâbêk
Phum Samrong *see* Sâmraông
Phu Vinh *see* Tra Vinh
Phyu *136 B4 var.* Hpyu, Pyu. Bago,
C Myanmar (Burma)
Piacenza *96 B2 Fr.* Paisance; *anc.*
Placentia. Emilia-Romagna, N Italy
Piatra-Neamţ *108 C4 Hung.*
Karácsonkő. Neamţ, NE Romania
Piauhy *see* Piauí
Piauí *63 F2 off.* Estado do Piauí; *prev.*
Piauhy. *state* E Brazil
Piauí *63 F2 off.* Estado do Piauí; *prev.*
Piauhy. *region* E Brazil
Piauí, Estado do *see* Piauí
Picardie *90 C3 Eng.* Picardy. *cultural
region* N France
Picardy *see* Picardie
Piccolo San Bernardo, Colle di *see* Little
Saint Bernard Pass
Pichilemu *64 B4* Libertador, C Chile

Pico *92 A5 var.* Ilha do Pico. *island*
Azores, Portugal, NE Atlantic Ocean
Pico, Ilha do *see* Pico
Picos *63 F2* Piauí, E Brazil
Picton *151 C5* Marlborough, South
Island, New Zealand
Piedmont *see* Piemonte
Piedras Negras *51 E2 var.* Ciudad
Porfirio Díaz. Coahuila, NE Mexico
Pielavesi *84 D4 lake* C Finland
Pielinen *84 E4 var.* Pielisjärvi. *lake*
E Finland
Pielisjärvi *see* Pielinen
Piemonte *96 A2 Eng.* Piedmont. *region*
NW Italy
Pierre *45 E3 state capital* South Dakota,
N USA
Piešt'any *99 C6 Ger.* Pistyan, *Hung.*
Pöstyén. Tranavský Kraj, W Slovakia
Pietarhovi *see* Petrodvorets
Pietari *see* Sankt-Peterburg
Pietarsaari *see* Jakobstad
Pietermaritzburg *78 C5 var.*
Maritzburg. KwaZulu/Natal, E South
Africa
Pietersburg *see* Polokwane
Bay of Pigs *54 B2 Eng.* Bay of Pigs. *bay*
SE Cuba
Pigs, Bay of *see* Cochinos, Bahía de
Pihkva Järv *see* Pskov, Lake
Pijijiapán *51 G5* Chiapas, SE Mexico
Pikes Peak *44 C5 mountain* Colorado,
C USA
Pikeville *40 D5* Kentucky, S USA
Pikinni *see* Bikini Atoll
Piła *98 B3 Ger.* Schneidemühl.
Wielkopolskie, C Poland
Pilar *64 D3 var.* Villa del Pilar.
Ñeembucú, S Paraguay
Pilcomayo, Rio *57 C5 river* C South
America
Pilos *see* Pýlos
Pilsen *see* Plzeň
Pilzno *see* Plzeň
Pinang *see* Pinang, Pulau, Peninsular
Malaysia
Pinang *see* George Town
Pinang, Pulau *138 B3 var.* Penang,
Pinang; *prev.* Prince of Wales Island.
island Peninsular Malaysia
Pinar del Río *54 A2* Pinar del Río,
W Cuba
Píndhos/Píndhos Óros *see* Píndos
Pindus Mountains *104 A4 var.* Píndhos
Óros, *Eng.* Pindus Mountains; *prev.*
Píndhos. *mountain range* C Greece
Pindus Mountains *see* Píndos
Pine Bluff *42 B2* Arkansas, C USA
Pine Creek *146 D2* Northern Territory,
N Australia
Pinega *110 C3 river* NW Russian
Federation
Pineiós *104 B4 var.* Piniós; *anc.* Peneius.
river C Greece
Pineland *49 H3* Texas, SW USA
Pínes, Akrotírio *104 C4 var.* Akrotírio
Pinnes. *headland* N Greece
Pines, The Isle of the *see* Juventud,
Isla de la
Pine Tree State *see* Maine
Pingdingshan *128 C4* Henan, C China
Pingkiang *see* Harbin
Ping, Mae Nam *136 B4 river* W Thailand
Piniós *see* Pineiós
Pinkiang *see* Harbin
Pinnes, Akrotírio *see* Pínes, Akrotírio
Pinos, Isla de *see* Juventud, Isla de la
Pinotepa Nacional *51 F5 var.* Santiago
Pinotepa Nacional. Oaxaca, SE Mexico
Pinsk *107 B7* Pol. Pińsk. Brestskaya
Voblasts', SW Belarus
Pinta, Isla *60 A5 var.* Abingdon. *island*
Galápagos Islands, Ecuador, E Pacific
Ocean
Piombino *96 B3* Toscana, C Italy
Pioneer Mountains *44 D3 mountain*
range Montana, N USA North America
Pionerskiy *106 A4 Ger.* Neukuhren.
Kaliningradskaya Oblast', W Russian
Federation
Piotrków Trybunalski *98 D4 Ger.*
Petrikau, *Rus.* Petrokov. Łodzkie,
C Poland
Piraeus/Piraiévs *see* Peiraiás
Pírgos *see* Pýrgos
Pirineos *see* Pyrenees
Piripiri *63 F2* Piauí, E Brazil
Pirna *94 D4* Sachsen, E Germany
Pirot *101 E5* Serbia, SE Serbia

Piryatin *see* Pyryatyn
Pisa *96 B3 var.* Pisae. Toscana, C Italy
Pisae *see* Pisa
Pisaurum *see* Pesaro
Pisco *60 D4* Ica, SW Peru
Písek *99 A5* Budějovický Kraj, S Czech
Republic
Pishan *126 A3 var.* Guma. Xinjiang
Uygur Zizhiqu, NW China
Pishpek *see* Bishkek
Pistoia *96 B3 anc.* Pistoria, Pistoriæ.
Toscana, C Italy
Pistoria/Pistoriæ *see* Pistoia
Pistyan *see* Piešt'any
Pisz *98 D3 Ger.* Johannisburg.
Warmińsko-Mazurskie, NE Poland
Pita *74 C4* NW Guinea
Pitalito *58 B4* Huila, S Colombia
Pitcairn Island *143 G4 island* S Pitcairn
Islands
Pitcairn Islands *143 G4 UK dependent*
territory C Pacific Ocean
Piteå *84 D4* Norrbotten, N Sweden
Pitești *108 B5* Argeș, S Romania
Pitsanulok *see* Phitsanulok
Pitt Island *see* Makin
Pittsburg *45 F5* Kansas, C USA
Pittsburgh *41 E4* Pennsylvania, NE USA
Pittsfield *41 F3* Massachusetts, NE USA
Piura *60 B2* Piura, NW Peru
Pivdennyy Buh *109 E3 Rus.* Yuzhnyy
Bug. *river* S Ukraine
Placentia *see* Piacenza
Placetas *54 B2* Villa Clara, C Cuba
Plainview *49 E2* Texas, SW USA
Planeta Rica *58 B2* Córdoba,
NW Colombia
Planken *94 E1* C Liechtenstein Europe
Plano *49 G2* Texas, SW USA
Plasencia *92 C3* Extremadura, W Spain
Plate, River *64 D4 var.* River Plate.
estuary Argentina/Uruguay
Plate, River *see* Plata, Río de la
Platinum *36 C3* Alaska, USA
Plattensee *see* Balaton
Platte River *45 E4 river* Nebraska, C USA
Plattsburgh *41 F2* New York, NE USA
Plauen *95 C5 var.* Plauen im Vogtland.
Sachsen, E Germany
Plauen im Vogtland *see* Plauen
Plauen im Vogtland *see* Plauen
Plāviņas *106 D4 Ger.* Stockmannshof.
C Latvia
Plây Cu *see* Plei Ku
Pleasant Island *see* Nauru
Plei Ku *137 E5 prev.* Plây Cu. Gia Lai,
C Vietnam
Plenty, Bay of *150 E3 bay* North Island,
New Zealand
Plérin *90 A3* Côtes d'Armor, NW France
Plesetsk *110 C3* Arkhangel'skaya Oblast',
NW Russian Federation
Pleshchenitsy *see* Plyeshchanitsy
Pleskau *see* Pskov
Pleskauer See *see* Pskov, Lake
Pleskava *see* Pskov
Pleszew *98 C4* Wielkopolskie, C Poland
Pleven *104 C2 prev.* Plevna. Pleven,
N Bulgaria
Plevlja/Plevlje *see* Pljevlja
Plevna *see* Pleven
Pljevlja *100 C4 prev.* Plevlja, Plevlje.
N Montenegro
Plocce *see* Ploče
Ploče *100 B4 It.* Plocce; *prev.* Kardeljevo.
Dubrovnik-Neretva, SE Croatia
Płock *98 D3 Ger.* Plozk. Mazowieckie,
C Poland
Plöcken Pass *95 C7 Ger.* Plöckenpass,
It. Passo di Monte Croce Carnico. *pass*
SW Austria
Plöckenpass *see* Plöcken Pass
Ploești *see* Ploiești
Ploiești *108 C5 prev.* Ploești. Prahova,
SE Romania
Plomári *105 D5 prev.* Plomárion.
Lésvos, E Greece
Plomárion *see* Plomári
Płońsk *98 D3* Mazowieckie, C Poland
Plovdiv *104 C3 prev.* Eumolpias;
anc. Evmolpia, Philippopolis, *Lat.*
Trimontium. Plovdiv, C Bulgaria
Plozk *see* Płock
Plungė *106 B3* Telšiai, W Lithuania
Plyeshchanitsy *107 D5 Rus.*
Pleshchenitsy. Minskaya Voblasts',
N Belarus
Plymouth *89 C7* SW England, United
Kingdom
Plymouth *see* Brades

Plzeň *99 A5 Ger.* Pilsen, *Pol.* Pilzno.
Plzeňský Kraj, W Czech Republic
Po *80 D4 river* N Italy
Pobedy, Pik *126 B3 Chin.* Tomür Feng.
mountain China/Kyrgyzstan
Po, Bocche del *see* Po, Foci del
Pocahontas *42 B1* Arkansas, C USA
Pocatello *46 E4* Idaho, NW USA
Pochinok *111 A5* Smolenskaya Oblast',
W Russian Federation
Pocking *95 D6* Bayern, SE Germany
Poděbrady *99 B5 Ger.* Podiebrad.
Středočeský Kraj, C Czech Republic
Podgorica *101 C5 prev.* Titograd.
country capital (Montenegro)
S Montenegro
Podiebrad *see* Poděbrady
Podil's'ka Vysochina *108 D3 plateau*
W Ukraine
Podium Anicensis *see* le Puy
Podol'sk *111 B5* Moskovskaya Oblast',
W Russian Federation
Podravska Slatina *see* Slatina
Podujevě *101 D5 Serb.* Podujevo.
N Kosovo
Podujevo *see* Podujevě
Podunajská Rovina *see* Little Alföld
Poetovio *see* Ptuj
Pogradec *101 D6 var.* Pogradeci. Korçë,
SE Albania
Pogradeci *see* Pogradec
Pohjanlahti *see* Bothnia, Gulf of
Pohnpei *144 C2 prev.* Ponape Ascension
Island. *island* E Micronesia
Poitiers *see* Poitiers
Poinsett, Cape *154 D4 headland*
Antarctica
Point de Galle *see* Galle
Pointe-à-Pitre *55 G3* Grande Terre,
C Guadeloupe
Pointe-Noire *77 B6* Kouilou, S Congo
Point Lay *36 C2* Alaska, USA
Poitiers *90 B4 prev.* Poictiers; *anc.*
Limonum. Vienne, W France
Poitou *90 B4 cultural region* W France
Pokhará *135 E3* Western, C Nepal
Pokrovka *123 G2* Rus. Pokrovskoye.
Dnipropetrovs'ka Oblast', E Ukraine
Pokrovskoye *see* Pokrovka
Pola *see* Pula
Pola de Lena *see* La Pola
Poland *98 B4 off.* Republic of Poland,
var. Polish Republic, *Pol.* Polska,
Rzeczpospolita Polska; *prev. Pol.* Polska
Rzeczpospolita Ludowa, 'The Polish
People's Republic'. *country* C Europe

POLAND
Northern Europe

Official name	Republic of Poland
Formation	1918 / 1945
Capital	Warsaw
Population	38.3 million / 326 people per sq mile (126 people per sq km)
Total area	120,728 sq. miles (312,685 sq km)
Languages	Polish*
Religions	Roman Catholic 93%, Other and nonreligious 5%, Orthodox Christian 2%
Ethnic mix	Polish 98%, Other 2%
Government	Parliamentary system
Currency	Zloty = 100 groszy
Literacy rate	99%
Calorie consumption	3392 kilocalories

Poland, Republic of *see* Poland
Polatlı *116 C3* Ankara, C Turkey
Polatsk *107 D5 Rus.* Polotsk.
Vitsyebskaya Voblasts', N Belarus
Pol-e Khomrī *see* Pul-e Khumrī
Poli *see* Pólis
Polikastro/Polikastron *see* Polýkastro
Polikrayshte *104 D2* Veliko Tŭrnovo,
N Bulgaria
Pólis *102 C5 var.* Poli. W Cyprus
Polish People's Republic, The *see*
Poland
Polish Republic *see* Poland
Polkowice *98 B4 Ger.* Heerwegen.
Dolnośląskie, SW Poland
Pollença *93 G3* Mallorca, Spain,
W Mediterranean Sea
Pologi *see* Polohy
Polohy *109 G3 Rus.* Pologi. Zaporiz'ka
Oblast', SE Ukraine
Polokwane *78 D4 prev.* Pietersburg.
Limpopo, NE South Africa

Polonne *108 D2 Rus.* Polonnoye.
Khmel'nyts'ka Oblast', NW Ukraine
Polonnoye *see* Polonne
Polotsk *see* Polatsk
Polska/Polska, Rzeczpospolita/Polska
Rzeczpospolita Ludowa *see* Poland
Polsko Kosovo *104 D2* Ruse, N Bulgaria
Poltava *109 F2* Poltavs'ka Oblast',
NE Ukraine
Poltoratsk *see* Aşgabat
Põlva *106 E3 Ger.* Pölwe. Põlvamaa,
SE Estonia
Pölwe *see* Põlva
Polyarnyy *110 C2* Murmanskaya Oblast',
NW Russian Federation
Polýkastro *104 B3 var.* Polikastro; *prev.*
Polikastron. Kentrikí Makedonía,
N Greece
Polynesia *143 F4 island group* C Pacific
Ocean
Pomeranian Bay *94 D2 Ger.*
Pommersche Bucht, *Pol.* Zatoka
Pomorska. *bay* Germany/Poland
Pommersche Bucht *see* Pomeranian Bay
Pomorska, Zatoka *see* Pomeranian Bay
Pomorskiy Proliv *110 D2 strait*
NW Russian Federation
Po, Mouth of the *96 C2 var.* Bocche del
Po. *river* NE Italy
Pompaelo *see* Pamplona
Pompano Beach *43 F5* Florida, SE USA
Ponape Ascension Island *see* Pohnpei
Ponca City *49 G1* Oklahoma, C USA
Ponce *55 F3* C Puerto Rico
Pondicherry *132 C2 var.* Puducherri,
Fr. Pondichéry. Pondicherry, SE India
Ponferrada *92 C1* Castilla y León,
NW Spain
Poniatowa *98 E4* Lubelskie, E Poland
Pons Aelii *see* Newcastle upon Tyne
Pons Vetus *see* Pontevedra
Ponta Delgada *92 B5* São Miguel,
Azores, Portugal, NE Atlantic Ocean
Ponta Grossa *63 E4* Paraná, S Brazil
Pontarlier *90 D4* Doubs, E France
Pontareas *92 B2* Galicia, NW Spain
Ponte da Barca *92 B2* Viana do Castelo,
N Portugal
Pontevedra *92 B1 anc.* Pons Vetus.
Galicia, NW Spain
Pontiac *40 D3* Michigan, N USA
Pontianak *138 C4* Borneo, C Indonesia
Pontisarae *see* Pontoise
Pontivy *90 A3* Morbihan, NW France
Pontoise *90 C3 anc.* Briva Isarae, Cergy-
Pontoise, Pontisarae. Val-d'Oise,
N France
Ponziane Island *97 C5 island* C Italy
Poole *89 D7* S England, United Kingdom
Poona *see* Pune
Poopó, Lago *61 F4 var.* Lago Pampa
Aullagas. *lake* W Bolivia
Popayán *58 B4* Cauca, SW Colombia
Poperinge *87 A6* West-Vlaanderen,
W Belgium
Poplar Bluff *45 G5* Missouri, C USA
Popocatépetl *51 E4 volcano* S Mexico
Popper *see* Poprad
Poprad *99 D5 Ger.* Deutschendorf,
Hung. Poprád. Prešovský Kraj,
E Slovakia
Poprád *99 D5 Ger.* Popper, *Hung.*
Poprád. *river* Poland/Slovakia
Porbandar *134 B4* Gujarāt, W India
Porcupine Plain *80 B3 undersea feature*
E Atlantic Ocean
Pordenone *96 C2 anc.* Portenau. Friuli-
Venezia Giulia, NE Italy
Poreč *100 A2 It.* Parenzo. Istra,
NW Croatia
Porech'ye *see* Parechcha
Pori *85 D5 Swe.* Björneborg. Länsi-
Suomi, SW Finland
Porirua *151 D5* Wellington, North
Island, New Zealand
Porkhov *110 A4* Pskovskaya Oblast',
W Russian Federation
Porlamar *59 E1* Nueva Esparta,
NE Venezuela
Póros *105 C5* Pelopónnisos, S Greece
Póros *105 A5* Kefallinía, Iónia Nisiá,
Greece, C Mediterranean Sea
Porsangenfjorden *84 D2 Lapp.*
Porsáŋgguvuotna. *fjord* N Norway
Porsáŋgguvuotna *see* Porsangenfjorden
Porsgrunn *85 B6* Telemark, S Norway
Portachuelo *61 G4* Santa Cruz, C Bolivia

Portadown 89 B5 *Ir.* Port An Dúnáin. S Northern Ireland, United Kingdom
Portalegre 92 C3 *anc.* Ammaia, Amoea. Portalegre, E Portugal
Port Alexander 36 D4 Baranof Island, Alaska, USA
Port Alfred 78 D5 Eastern Cape, S South Africa
Port Amelia *see* Pemba
Port An Dúnáin *see* Portadown
Port Angeles 46 B1 Washington, NW USA
Port Antonio 54 B5 NE Jamaica
Port Arthur 49 H4 Texas, SW USA
Port Augusta 149 B6 South Australia
Port-au-Prince 54 D3 *country capital* (Haiti) C Haiti
Port Blair 133 F2 Andaman and Nicobar Islands, SE India
Port Charlotte 43 E4 Florida, SE USA
Port Darwin *see* Darwin
Port d'Envalira 91 B8 E Andorra Europe
Port Douglas 148 D3 Queensland, NE Australia
Port Elizabeth 78 C5 Eastern Cape, S South Africa
Portenau *see* Pordenone
Porterville 47 C7 California, W USA
Port-Étienne *see* Nouâdhibou
Port Florence *see* Kisumu
Port-Francqui *see* Ilebo
Port-Gentil 77 A6 Ogooué-Maritime, W Gabon
Port Harcourt 75 G5 Rivers, S Nigeria
Port Hardy 36 C5 Vancouver Island, British Columbia, SW Canada
Port Harrison *see* Inukjuak
Port Hedland 146 B4 Western Australia
Port Huron 40 D3 Michigan, N USA
Portimão 92 B4 *var.* Vila Nova de Portimão. Faro, S Portugal
Port Jackson 148 E1 *harbour* New South Wales, E Australia
Portland 149 B7 Victoria, SE Australia
Portland 41 G2 Maine, NE USA
Portland 46 B3 Oregon, NW USA
Portland 49 G4 Texas, SW USA
Portland Bight 54 B5 *bay* S Jamaica
Portlaoighise *see* Port Laoise
Port Laoise 89 B6 *var.* Portlaoise, *Ir.* Portlaoighise; *prev.* Maryborough. C Ireland
Portlaoise *see* Port Laoise
Port Lavaca 49 G4 Texas, SW USA
Port Lincoln 149 A6 South Australia
Port Louis 79 H3 *country capital* (Mauritius) NW Mauritius
Port-Lyautey *see* Kénitra
Port Macquarie 149 E6 New South Wales, SE Australia
Port Mahon *see* Maó
Portmore 54 B5 C Jamaica
Port Moresby 144 B3 *country capital* (Papua New Guinea) Central/National Capital District, SW Papua New Guinea
Port Natal *see* Durban
Porto 92 B2 *Eng.* Oporto; *anc.* Portus Cale. NW Portugal
Porto Alegre 63 F5 *var.* Pôrto Alegre. *state capital* Rio Grande do Sul, S Brazil
Porto Alegre 76 E2 São Tomé, S Sao Tome and Principe, Africa
Porto Alegre 76 E2 São Tomé, S Sao Tome and Principe, Africa
Porto Alexandre *see* Tombua
Porto Amélia *see* Pemba
Porto Bello *see* Portobelo
Portobelo 53 G4 *var.* Porto Bello, Puerto Bello. Colón, N Panama
Port O'Connor 49 G4 Texas, SW USA
Porto Edda *see* Sarandë
Portoferraio 96 B4 Toscana, C Italy
Port-of-Spain 55 H5 *country capital* (Trinidad and Tobago) Trinidad, Trinidad and Tobago
Porto Grande *see* Mindelo
Portogruaro 96 C2 Veneto, NE Italy
Porto-Novo 75 F5 *country capital* (Benin) S Benin
Porto Rico *see* Puerto Rico
Porto Santo 70 A2 *var.* Ilha do Porto Santo. *island* Madeira, Portugal, NE Atlantic Ocean
Porto Santo *see* Porto Santo
Porto Torres 97 A5 Sardegna, Italy, C Mediterranean Sea

Porto Velho 62 D2 *var.* Velho. *state capital* Rondônia, W Brazil
Portoviejo 60 A2 *var.* Puertoviejo. Manabí, W Ecuador
Port Pirie 149 B6 South Australia
Port Rex *see* East London
Port Said *see* Būr Sa'īd
Portsmouth 89 D7 S England, United Kingdom
Portsmouth 41 G3 New Hampshire, NE USA
Portsmouth 40 D4 Ohio, N USA
Portsmouth 41 F5 Virginia, NE USA
Port Stanley *see* Stanley
Port Sudan 72 C3 Red Sea, NE Sudan
Port Swettenham *see* Klang/Pelabuhan Klang
Port Talbot 89 C7 S Wales, United Kingdom
Portugal 92 B3 *off.* Portuguese Republic. *country* SW Europe

---

PORTUGAL
Southwest Europe

Official name The Portuguese Republic
Formation 1139 / 1640
Capital Lisbon
Population 10.7 million / 301 people per sq mile (116 people per sq km)
Total area 35,672 sq. miles (92,391 sq. km)
Languages Portuguese*
Religions Roman Catholic 92%, Protestant 6%, Nonreligious 3%, Other 1%
Ethnic mix Portuguese 98%, African and other 2%
Government Parliamentary system
Currency Euro = 100 cents
Literacy rate 95%
Calorie consumption 3617 kilocalories

Portuguese East Africa *see* Mozambique
Portuguese Guinea *see* Guinea-Bissau
Portuguese Republic *see* Portugal
Portuguese Timor *see* East Timor
Portuguese West Africa *see* Angola
Portus Cale *see* Porto
Portus Magnus *see* Almería
Portus Magonis *see* Maó
Port-Vila 144 D4 *var.* Vila. *country capital* (Vanuatu) Éfaté, C Vanuatu
Porvenir 61 E3 Pando, NW Bolivia
Porvenir 65 B8 Magallanes, S Chile
Porvoo 85 E6 Swe. Borgå. Etelä-Suomi, S Finland
Porzecze *see* Parechcha
Posadas 64 D3 Misiones, NE Argentina
Poschega *see* Požega
Posen *see* Poznań
Posnania *see* Poznań
Postavy/Postawy *see* Pastavy
Posterholt 87 D5 Limburg, SE Netherlands
Postojna 95 D8 *Ger.* Adelsberg, *It.* Postumia. SW Slovenia
Postumia *see* Postojna
Pöstyén *see* Piešťany
Potamós 105 C7 Antikýthira, S Greece
Potentia *see* Potenza
Potenza 97 D5 *anc.* Potentia. Basilicata, S Italy
Poti 117 F2 *prev.* P'ot'i. W Georgia
P'ot'i *see* Poti
Potiskum 75 G4 Yobe, NE Nigeria
Potomac River 41 E5 *river* NE USA
Potosí 61 F4 Potosí, S Bolivia
Potsdam 94 D3 Brandenburg, NE Germany
Potwar Plateau 134 C2 *plateau* NE Pakistan
Poŭthĭsăt 137 D6 *prev.* Pursat. Poŭthĭsăt, W Cambodia
Po, Valle del *see* Po Valley
Po Valley 96 C2 *It.* Valle del Po. *valley* N Italy
Poverty Bay 150 E4 *inlet* North Island, New Zealand
Póvoa de Varzim 92 B2 Porto, NW Portugal
Powder River 44 D2 *river* Montana/ Wyoming, NW USA
Powell 44 C2 Wyoming, C USA
Powell, Lake 44 B5 *lake* Utah, W USA
Požarevac 100 D4 *Ger.* Passarowitz. Serbia, NE Serbia
Poza Rica 51 F4 *var.* Poza Rica de Hidalgo. Veracruz-Llave, E Mexico

Poza Rica de Hidalgo *see* Poza Rica
Požega 100 D4 *prev.* Slavonska Požega, *Ger.* Poschega, *Hung.* Pozsega. Požega-Slavonija, NE Croatia
Požega 100 D4 Serbia
Poznań 98 C3 *Ger.* Posen, Posnania. Wielkolpolskie, C Poland
Pozoblanco 92 D4 Andalucía, S Spain
Pozsega *see* Požega
Pozsony *see* Bratislava
Pozzallo 97 C8 Sicilia, Italy, C Mediterranean Sea
Prachatice 99 A5 *Ger.* Prachatitz. Jihočeský Kraj, S Czech Republic
Prachatitz *see* Prachatice
Prado del Ganso *see* Goose Green
Prae *see* Phrae
Prag/Praga/Prague *see* Praha
Praha 99 A5 *Eng.* Prague, *Ger.* Prag, *Pol.* Praga. *country capital* (Czech Republic) Středočeský Kraj, NW Czech Republic
Praia 74 A3 *country capital* (Cape Verde) Santiago, S Cape Verde
Prairie State *see* Illinois
Prathet Thai *see* Thailand
Prato 96 B3 Toscana, C Italy
Pratt 45 E5 Kansas, C USA
Prattville 42 D2 Alabama, S USA
Pravda 104 D1 *prev.* Dogrular. Silistra, NE Bulgaria
Pravia 92 C1 Asturias, N Spain
Preny *see* Prienai
Prenzlau 94 D3 Brandenburg, NE Germany
Prerau *see* Přerov
Přerov 99 C5 *Ger.* Prerau. Olomoucký Kraj, E Czech Republic
Preschau *see* Prešov
Prescott 48 B2 Arizona, SW USA
Prešov 101 D5 Serbia, SE Serbia
Presidente Epitácio 63 E4 São Paulo, S Brazil
Presidente Stroessner *see* Ciudad del Este
Prešov 99 D5 *var.* Preschau, *Ger.* Eperies, *Hung.* Eperjes. Prešovský Kraj, E Slovakia
Prespa, Lake 101 D6 *Alb.* Liqen i Prespës, *Gk.* Límni Megáli Préspa, Límni Prespa, *Mac.* Prespansko Ezero, *Serb.* Prespansko Jezero. *lake* SE Europe
Prespa, Limni/Prespansko Ezero/ Prespansko Jezero/Prespës, Liqen i *see* Prespa, Lake
Presque Isle 41 H1 Maine, NE USA
Pressburg *see* Bratislava
Preston 89 D5 NW England, United Kingdom
Prestwick 88 C4 W Scotland, United Kingdom
Pretoria 78 D4 *see also.* Tshwane. *country capital* (South Africa). (admin. capital) NE South Africa
Preussisch Eylau *see* Bagrationovsk
Preußisch Holland *see* Pasłęk
Preussisch-Stargard *see* Starogard Gdański
Préveza 105 A5 Ípeiros, W Greece
Pribilof Islands 36 A3 *island group* Alaska, USA
Priboj 100 C4 Serbia, W Serbia
Price 44 B4 Utah, W USA
Prichard 42 C3 Alabama, S USA
Priekule 106 B3 *Ger.* Prökuls. Klaipėda, W Lithuania
Prienai 107 B5 *Pol.* Preny. Kaunas, S Lithuania
Prieska 78 C4 Northern Cape, C South Africa
Prijedor 100 B3 Republika Srpska, NW Bosnia and Herzegovina
Prijepolje 100 D4 Serbia, W Serbia
Prikaspiyskaya Nizmennost' *see* Caspian Depression
Prilep 101 D6 *Turk.* Perlepe. S FYR Macedonia
Priluki *see* Pryluky
Primorsk 104 A4 *Ger.* Fischhausen. Kaliningradskaya Oblast', W Russian Federation
Primorsko 104 E2 *prev.* Keupriya. Burgas, E Bulgaria
Primorsk/Primorskoye *see* Prymors'k
Prince Albert 37 F5 Saskatchewan, S Canada
Prince Edward Island 39 F4 *Fr.* Île-du Prince-Édouard. *province* SE Canada

Prince Edward Islands 69 E8 *island group* S South Africa
Prince George 37 E5 British Columbia, SW Canada
Prince of Wales Island 148 B1 *island* Queensland, E Australia
Prince of Wales Island 37 F2 *island* Queen Elizabeth Islands, Nunavut, NW Canada
Prince of Wales Island *see* Pinang, Pulau
Prince Patrick Island 37 E2 *island* Parry Islands, Northwest Territories, NW Canada
Prince Rupert 36 D4 British Columbia, SW Canada
Prince's Island *see* Príncipe
Princess Charlotte Bay 148 C2 *bay* Queensland, NE Australia
Princess Elizabeth Land 154 D3 *physical region* Antarctica
Príncipe 77 A5 *var.* Príncipe Island, *Eng.* Prince's Island. *island* N Sao Tome and Principe
Príncipe Island *see* Príncipe
Prinzapolka 53 E3 Región Autónoma Atlántico Norte, NE Nicaragua
Pripet 107 C7 *Bel.* Prypyats', *Ukr.* Pryp"yat'. *river* Belarus/Ukraine
Pripet Marshes 107 B7 *wetland* Belarus/ Ukraine
Prishtinë 101 D5 *Serb.* Priština. C Kosovo
Priština *see* Prishtinë
Privas 91 D5 Ardèche, E France
Prizren 101 D5 S Kosovo
Probolinggo 138 D5 Jawa, C Indonesia
Probstberg *see* Wyszków
Progreso 51 H3 Yucatán, SE Mexico
Prokhladnyy 111 B8 Kabardino-Balkarskaya Respublika, SW Russian Federation
Prokletije *see* North Albanian Alps
Prökuls *see* Priekule
Prokuplje 101 D5 Serbia, SE Serbia
Prome *see* Pyay
Promyshlennyy 110 E3 Respublika Komi, NW Russian Federation
Prościejów *see* Prostějov
Proskurov *see* Khmel 'nyts'kyy
Prossnitz *see* Prostějov
Prostějov 99 C5 *Ger.* Prossnitz, *Pol.* Prościejów. Olomoucký Kraj, E Czech Republic
Provence 91 D6 *cultural region* SE France
Providence 41 G3 *state capital* Rhode Island, NE USA
Providence *see* Fort Providence
Providencia, Isla de 53 F3 *island* NW Colombia, Caribbean Sea
Provideniya 155 B1 Chukotskiy Avtonomnyy Okrug, NE Russian Federation
Provo 44 B4 Utah, W USA
Prudhoe Bay 36 D2 Alaska, USA
Prusa *see* Bursa
Pruszków 98 D3 *Ger.* Kaltdorf. Mazowieckie, C Poland
Prut 108 D4 *Ger.* Pruth. *river* E Europe
Pruth *see* Prut
Pružana *see* Pruzhany
Pruzhany 107 B6 *Pol.* Pružana. Brestskaya Voblasts', SW Belarus
Prychornomor'ska Nyzovyna *see* Black Sea Lowland
Prydniprovs'ka Nyzovyna/ Prydnyaprowskaya Nizina *see* Dnieper Lowland
Prydz Bay 154 D3 *bay* Antarctica
Pryluky 109 E2 *Rus.* Priluki. Chernihivs'ka Oblast', NE Ukraine
Prymors'k 109 G4 *Rus.* Primorsk; *prev.* Primorskoye. Zaporiz'ka Oblast', SE Ukraine
Pryp"yat'/Prypyats' *see* Pripet
Przemyśl 99 E5 *Rus.* Peremyshl. Podkarpackie, C Poland
Przheval'sk *see* Karakol
Psará 105 D5 *island* E Greece
Psel 109 F2 *Rus.* Psël. *river* Russian Federation/Ukraine
Psël *see* Psel
Pskov 114 B2 *Ger.* Pleskau, *Latv.* Pleskava. Pskovskaya Oblast', W Russian Federation
Pskov, Lake 106 E3 *Est.* Pihkva Järv, *Ger.* Pleskauer See, *Rus.* Pskovskoye Ozero. *lake* Estonia/Russian Federation
Pskovskoye Ozero *see* Pskov, Lake
Ptich' *see* Ptsich

Ptsich 107 C7 *Rus.* Ptich'. Homyel'skaya Voblasts', SE Belarus
Ptsich 107 C7 *Rus.* Ptich'. *river* SE Belarus
Ptuj 95 E7 *Ger.* Pettau; *anc.* Poetovio. NE Slovenia
Pucallpa 60 C3 Ucayali, C Peru
Puck 98 C2 Pomorskie, N Poland
Pudasjärvi 84 D4 Oulu, C Finland
Puebla 51 F4 *var.* Puebla de Zaragoza. Puebla, S Mexico
Puebla de Zaragoza *see* Puebla
Pueblo 44 D5 Colorado, C USA
Puerto Acosta 61 E4 La Paz, W Bolivia
Puerto Aisén 65 B6 Aisén, S Chile
Puerto Ángel 51 F5 Oaxaca, SE Mexico
Puerto Argentino *see* Stanley
Puerto Ayacucho 58 D3 Amazonas, SW Venezuela
Puerto Baquerizo Moreno 60 B5 *var.* Baquerizo Moreno. Galápagos Islands, Ecuador, E Pacific Ocean
Puerto Barrios 52 C2 Izabal, E Guatemala
Puerto Bello *see* Portobelo
Puerto Berrío 58 B2 Antioquia, C Colombia
Puerto Cabello 58 D1 Carabobo, N Venezuela
Puerto Cabezas 53 E2 *var.* Bilwi. Región Autónoma Atlántico Norte, NE Nicaragua
Puerto Carreño 58 D3 Vichada, E Colombia
Puerto Cortés 52 C2 Cortés, NW Honduras
Puerto Cumarebo 58 C1 Falcón, N Venezuela
Puerto Deseado 65 C7 Santa Cruz, SE Argentina
Puerto Escondido 51 F5 Oaxaca, SE Mexico
Puerto Gallegos *see* Río Gallegos
Puerto Inírida 58 D3 *var.* Obando. Guainía, E Colombia
Puerto La Cruz 59 E1 Anzoátegui, NE Venezuela
Puerto Lempira 53 E2 Gracias a Dios, E Honduras
Puerto Limón *see* Limón
Puertollano 92 D4 Castilla-La Mancha, C Spain
Puerto López 58 C1 La Guajira, N Colombia
Puerto Maldonado 61 E3 Madre de Dios, E Peru
Puerto México *see* Coatzacoalcos
Puerto Montt 65 B5 Los Lagos, C Chile
Puerto Natales 65 B7 Magallanes, S Chile
Puerto Obaldía 53 H5 Kuna Yala, NE Panama
Puerto Plata 55 E3 *var.* San Felipe de Puerto Plata. N Dominican Republic
Puerto Presidente Stroessner *see* Ciudad del Este
Puerto Princesa 117 A8 *off.* Puerto Princesa City. Palawan, W Philippines
Puerto Princesa City *see* Puerto Princesa
Puerto Príncipe *see* Camagüey
Puerto Rico 55 F3 *off.* Commonwealth of Puerto Rico; *prev.* Porto Rico. US *commonwealth territory* C West Indies
Puerto Rico 56 B1 *island* C West Indies
Puerto Rico, Commonwealth of *see* Puerto Rico
Puerto Rico Trench 56 B1 *trench* NE Caribbean Sea
Puerto San José *see* San José
Puerto San Julián 65 B7 *var.* San Julián. Santa Cruz, SE Argentina
Puerto Suárez 61 H4 Santa Cruz, E Bolivia
Puerto Vallarta 50 D4 Jalisco, SW Mexico
Puerto Varas 65 B5 Los Lagos, C Chile
Puerto Viejo 53 E4 Heredia, NE Costa Rica
Puertoviejo *see* Portoviejo
Puget Sound 46 B1 *sound* Washington, NW USA
Puglia 97 E5 *var.* Le Puglie, *Eng.* Apulia. *region* SE Italy
Pukaki, Lake 151 B6 *lake* South Island, New Zealand
Pukekohe 150 D3 Auckland, North Island, New Zealand

Puket *see* Phuket
Pukhavichy 107 C6 *Rus.* Pukhovichi. Minskaya Voblasts', C Belarus
Pukhovichi *see* Pukhavichy
Pula 100 A3 *It.* Pola; *prev.* Pulj. Istra, NW Croatia
Pulaski 40 D5 Virginia, NE USA
Puławy 98 E4 *Ger.* Neu Amerika. Lubelskie, E Poland
Pul-e Khumrī 123 E4 *prev.* Pol-e Khomrī. Baghlān, NE Afghanistan
Pulj *see* Pula
Pullman 46 C2 Washington, NW USA
Pułtusk 98 D3 Mazowieckie, C Poland
Puná, Isla 60 A2 *island* SW Ecuador
Pune 134 C5 *prev.* Poona. Mahārāshtra, W India
Punjab 134 C2 *prev.* West Punjab, Western Punjab. *province* E Pakistan
Puno 61 E4 Puno, SE Peru
Punta Alta 65 C5 Buenos Aires, E Argentina
Punta Arenas 65 B8 *prev.* Magallanes. Magallanes, S Chile
Punta Gorda 52 C2 Toledo, SE Belize
Punta Gorda 53 E4 Región Autónoma Atlántico Sur, SE Nicaragua
Puntarenas 52 D4 Puntarenas, W Costa Rica
Punto Fijo 58 C1 Falcón, N Venezuela
Pupuya, Nevado 61 E4 *mountain* W Bolivia
Puri 135 F5 *var.* Jagannath. Orissa, E India
Puriramya *see* Buriram
Purmerend 86 C3 Noord-Holland, C Netherlands
Pursat *see* Poŭthĭsăt, Poŭthĭsăt, W Cambodia
Purus, Rio 62 C2 *var.* Río Purús. *river* Brazil/Peru
Pusan *see* Busan
Pusan-gwangyŏksi *see* Busan
Pushkino *see* Bilăsuvar
Püspökladány 99 D6 Hajdú-Bihar, E Hungary
Putrajaya 138 B3 *country capital* (Malaysia) (administrative) Kuala Lumpur, Peninsular Malaysia
Puttalam 132 C3 North Western Province, W Sri Lanka
Puttgarden 94 C2 Schleswig-Holstein, N Germany
Putumayo, Río 58 B5 *var.* Içá, Rio. *river* NW South America
Putumayo, Río *see* Içá, Rio
Puurmani 106 D2 *Ger.* Talkhof. Jõgevamaa, E Estonia
Pyatigorsk 111 B7 Stavropol'skiy Kray, SW Russian Federation
Pyatikhatki *see* P"yatykhatky
P"yatykhatky 109 F3 *Rus.* Pyatikhatki. Dnipropetrovs'ka Oblast', E Ukraine
Pyay 136 B4 *var.* Prome, Pye. Bago, C Myanmar (Burma)
Pye *see* Pyay
Pyetrykaw 107 C7 *Rus.* Petrikov. Homyel'skaya Voblasts', SE Belarus
Pyin-Oo-Lwin 136 B3 *var.* Maymyo. Mandalay, C Myanmar (Burma)
Pýlos 105 B6 *var.* Pilos. Pelopónnisos, S Greece
P'yŏngyang 129 E3 *var.* P'yŏngyang-si, *Eng.* Pyongyang. *country capital* (North Korea) SW North Korea
P'yŏngyang-si *see* P'yŏngyang
Pyramid Lake 47 C5 *lake* Nevada, W USA
Pyrenaei Montes *see* Pyrenees
Pyrenees 102 B2 *Fr.* Pyrénées, *Sp.* Pirineos; *anc.* Pyrenaei Montes. *mountain range* SW Europe
Pýrgos 105 B6 *var.* Pírgos. Dytikí Elláda, S Greece
Pyritz *see* Pyrzyce
Pyryatyn 109 E2 *Rus.* Piryatin. Poltavs'ka Oblast', NE Ukraine
Pyrzyce 98 B3 *Ger.* Pyritz. Zachodnio-pomorskie, NW Poland
Pyu *see* Phyu
Pyuntaza 136 B4 Bago, SW Myanmar (Burma)

Q

Qā' al Jafr 119 C7 *lake* S Jordan
Qaanaaq 82 D1 *var.* Qânâq, *Dan.* Thule. Avannaarsua, N Greenland
Qabātiya 119 E6 N West Bank Asia
Qābis *see* Gabès
Qābis, Khalij *see* Gabès, Golfe de
Qacentina *see* Constantine
Qafsah *see* Gafsa
Qagan Us *see* Dulan
Qahremānshahr *see* Kermānshāh
Qaidam Pendi 126 C4 *basin* C China
Qal'aikhum 123 F3 *Rus.* Kalaikhum. S Tajikistan
Qalāt 123 E5 *Per.* Kalāt. Zābul, S Afghanistan
Qal'at Bīshah 121 B5 'Asīr, SW Saudi Arabia
Qalqīliya *see* Qalqilya
Qalqīlya 119 D6 *var.* Qalqiliya. Central, W West Bank Asia
Qamanittuaq *see* Baker Lake
Qamdo 126 D5 Xizang Zizhiqu, W China
Qamishly *see* Al Qāmishlī
Qānāq *see* Qaanaaq
Qaoqrtoq 82 C4 *Dan.* Julianehåb. Kitaa, S Greenland
Qaraghandy/Qaraghandy Oblysy *see* Karagandy
Qara Qum *see* Garagum
Qarataū *see* Karatau, Zhambyl, Kazakhstan
Qarkilik *see* Ruoqiang
Qarokūl 123 F3 *Rus.* Karakul'. E Tajikistan
Qarqannah, Juzur *see* Kerkenah, Îles de
Qars *see* Kars
Qarshi 123 E3 *Rus.* Karshi; *prev.* Bek-Budi. Qashqadaryo Viloyati, S Uzbekistan
Qasigiannguit *see* Qasigiannguit
Qasigiannguit 82 C3 *var.* Qasigiannguit, *Dan.* Christianshåb. Kitaa, C Greenland
Qasr Farāfirah 72 B2 *var.* Qasr Farāfra. W Egypt
Qasr Farāfra *see* Qasr al Farāfirah
Qaṭanā 119 B5 *var.* Katana. Rif Dimashq, S Syria
Qatar 120 C4 *off.* State of Qatar, *Ar.* Dawlat Qaṭar. *country* SW Asia

---

QATAR
Southwest Asia

Official name State of Qatar
Formation 1971 / 1971
Capital Doha
Population 1.9 million / 447 people per sq mile (173 people per sq km)
Total area 4416 sq miles (11,437 sq km)
Languages Arabic*
Religions Muslim (mainly Sunni) 95%, Other 5%
Ethnic mix Qatari 20%, Indian 20%, Other Arab 20%, Nepalese 13%, Filipino 10%, Other 10%, Pakistani 7%
Government Monarchy
Currency Qatar riyal = 100 dirhams
Literacy rate 95%
Calorie consumption Not available

Qatar, State of *see* Qatar
Qattara Depression 72 A1 *var.* Munkhafaḍ al Qaṭṭārah *var.* Monkhafad el Qattâra, *Eng.* Qattara Depression. *desert* NW Egypt
Qattara Depression/Qaṭṭārah, Munkhafaḍ al *see* Qaṭṭārah, Munkhafaḍ al
Qaṭṭāra, Monkhafad el *see* Qaṭṭārah, Munkhafaḍ al
Qausuittuq *see* Resolute
Qazaqstan/Qazaqstan Respublikasy *see* Kazakhstan
Qazimämmäd *see* Hacıqabal
Qazris *see* Cáceres
Qazvīn 120 C2 *var.* Kazvin. Qazvīn, N Iran
Qena *see* Qinā
Qeqertarsuaq *see* Qeqertarsuaq
Qeqertarsuaq 82 C3 *var.* Qeqertarsuaq, *Dan.* Godhavn. Kitaa, S Greenland
Qeqertarsuaq 82 C3 *island* W Greenland

Qeqertarsuup Tunua 82 C3 *Dan.* Disko Bugt. *inlet* W Greenland
Qerveh *see* Qorveh
Qeshm 120 D4 *var.* Jazīreh-ye Qeshm, Qeshm Island. *island* S Iran
Qeshm Island/Qeshm, Jazīreh-ye *see* Qeshm
Qilian Shan 126 D3 *var.* Kilien Mountains. *mountain range* N China
Qimusseriarsuaq 82 C2 *Dan.* Melville Bugt, *Eng.* Melville Bay. *bay* NW Greenland
Qinā 72 B2 *var.* Qena; *anc.* Caene, Caenepolis. E Egypt
Qing *see* Qinghai
Qingdao 128 D4 *var.* Ching-Tao, Ch'ing-tao, Tsingtao, Tsintao, *Ger.* Tsingtau. Shandong, E China
Qinghai 126 C4 *var.* Chinghai, Koko Nor, Qing, Qinghai Sheng, Tsinghai. *province* C China
Qinghai Hu 126 D4 *var.* Ch'ing Hai, Tsing Hai, *Mong.* Koko Nor. *lake* C China
Qinghai Sheng *see* Qinghai
Qinhuangdao 128 D3 Hebei, E China
Qinzhou 128 B6 Guangxi Zhuangzu Zizhiqu, S China
Qiong *see* Hainan
Qiqihar 128 D2 *var.* Ch'i-ch'i-ha-erh, Tsitsihar; *prev.* Lungkiang. Heilongjiang, NE China
Qira 126 B4 Xinjiang Uygur Zizhiqu, NW China
Qita Ghazzah *see* Gaza Strip
Qitai 126 C3 Xinjiang Uygur Zizhiqu, NW China
Qīzān *see* Jīzān
Qizil Orda *see* Kyzylorda
Qizil Qum/Qizilqum *see* Kyzyl Kum
Qizilrabot 123 G3 *Rus.* Kyzylrabot. SE Tajikistan
Qobustan 117 H2 *prev.* Märäzä. E Azerbaijan
Qogir Feng *see* K2
Qom 120 C3 *var.* Kum, Qum. Qom, N Iran
Qomolangma Feng *see* Everest, Mount
Qomul *see* Hami
Qo'qon 123 F2 *var.* Khokand, *Rus.* Kokand. Farg'ona Viloyati, E Uzbekistan
Qorveh 120 C3 *var.* Qerveh, Qurveh. Kordestān, W Iran
Qostanay/Qostanay Oblysy *see* Kostanay
Qoubaïyât 118 B4 *var.* Al Qubayyāt. N Lebanon
Qoussantina *see* Constantine
Quang Ngai 137 E5 *var.* Quangngai, Quang Nghia. Quang Ngai, C Vietnam
Quangngai *see* Quang Ngai
Quang Nghia *see* Quang Ngai
Quan Long *see* Ca Mau
Quanzhou 128 D6 *var.* Ch'uan-chou, Tsinkiang; *prev.* Chin-chiang. Fujian, SE China
Quanzhou 128 C6 Guangxi Zhuangzu Zizhiqu, S China
Qu'Appelle 37 F5 *river* Saskatchewan, S Canada
Quarles, Pegunungan 139 E4 *mountain range* Sulawesi, C Indonesia
Quarnero *see* Kvarner
Quartu Sant' Elena 97 A6 Sardegna, Italy, C Mediterranean Sea
Quba 117 H2 *Rus.* Kuba. N Azerbaijan
Qubba *see* Ba'qūbah
Québec 39 E4 *var.* Quebec. *province capital* Québec, SE Canada
Québec 38 D3 *var.* Quebec. *province* SE Canada
Queen Charlotte Islands 36 C5 *Fr.* Îles de la Reine-Charlotte. *island group* British Columbia, SW Canada
Queen Charlotte Sound 36 C5 *sea area* British Columbia, W Canada
Queen Elizabeth Islands 37 E1 *Fr.* Îles de la Reine-Élisabeth. *island group* Nunavut, N Canada
Queensland 148 B4 *state* N Australia
Queenstown 151 B7 Otago, South Island, New Zealand
Queenstown 78 D5 Eastern Cape, S South Africa
Quelimane 79 E3 *var.* Kilimane, Kilmain, Quilimane. Zambézia, NE Mozambique

Quelpart *see* Jeju-do
Quepos *53 E4* Puntarenas, S Costa Rica
Que Que *see* Kwekwe
Quera *see* Chur
Querétaro *51 E4* Querétaro de Arteaga,
C Mexico
Quesada *53 E4 var.* Ciudad Quesada,
San Carlos. Alajuela, N Costa Rica
Quetta *134 B2* Baluchistān,
SW Pakistan
Quetzalcoalco *see* Coatzacoalcos
Quezaltenango *52 A2 var.*
Quetzaltenango. Quezaltenango,
W Guatemala
Quibdó *58 A3* Chocó, W Colombia
Quilimane *see* Quelimane
Quillabamba *60 D3* Cusco, C Peru
Quilon *see* Kollam
Quimper *90 A3 anc.* Quimper Corentin.
Finistère, NW France
Quimper Corentin *see* Quimper
Quimperlé *90 A3* Finistère, NW France
Quincy *40 C4* Illinois, N USA
Qui Nhon/Quinhon *see* Quy Nhơn
Quissico *79 E4* Inhambane,
S Mozambique
Quito *60 B1 country capital* (Ecuador)
Pichincha, N Ecuador
Qulyndy Zhazyghy *see* Ravnina Kulyndy
Qum *see* Qom
Qurein *see* Al Kuwayt
Qūrghonteppa *123 E3 Rus.* Kurgan-
Tyube. SW Tajikistan
Qurlurtuuq *see* Kugluktuk
Qurveh *see* Qorveh
Quşayr *see* Lhazê
Quxar *see* Lhazê
Quy Nhơn *137 E5 var.* Quinhon, Qui
Nhon. Bình Định, C Vietnam
Qyteti Stalin *see* Kuçovë
Qyzylorda *see* Kyzylorda

R

Raab *100 B1 Hung.* Rába. *river* Austria/
Hungary
Raab *see* Rába
Raab *see* Győr
Raahe *84 D4 Swe.* Brahestad. Oulu,
W Finland
Raalte *86 D3* Overijssel, E Netherlands
Raamsdonksveer *86 C4* Noord-Brabant,
S Netherlands
Raasiku *106 D2 Ger.* Rasik. Harjumaa,
NW Estonia
Rába *99 B7 Ger.* Raab. *river* Austria/
Hungary
Rába *see* Raab
Rabat *70 C2 var.* al Dar al Baida. *country
capital* (Morocco) NW Morocco
Rabat *102 B5* W Malta
Rabat *see* Victoria
Rabbah Ammon/Rabbath Ammon
see 'Ammān
Rabinal *52 B2* Baja Verapaz,
C Guatemala
Rabka *99 D5* Małopolskie, S Poland
Râbniţa *see* Rîbniţa
Rabyanah Ramlat *71 G4 var.* Rebiana
Sand Sea, Şaḩrā' Rabyānah. *desert*
SE Libya
Rabyānah, Şaḥrā' *see* Rabyānah, Ramlat
Răcari *see* Durankulak
Race, Cape *39 H3 headland*
Newfoundland, Newfoundland and
Labrador, E Canada
Rach Gia *137 D6* Kiên Giang,
S Vietnam
Rach Gia, Vinh *137 D6 bay* S Vietnam
Racine *40 B3* Wisconsin, N USA
Rácz-Becse *see* Bečej
Rădăuţi *108 C3 Ger.* Radautz, *Hung.*
Rádóc. Suceava, N Romania
Radautz *see* Rădăuţi
Rădeyilikóé *see* Fort Good Hope
Rádóc *see* Rădăuţi
Radom *98 D4* Mazowieckie, C Poland
Radomsko *98 D4 Rus.* Novoradomsk.
Łódzkie, C Poland
Radomyshl' *108 D2* Zhytomyrs'ka
Oblast', N Ukraine
Radoviš *101 E6 prev.* Radovište.
E Macedonia
Radovište *see* Radoviš
Radviliškis *106 B4* Šiauliai, N Lithuania
Radzyń Podlaski *98 E4* Lubelskie,
E Poland
Rae-Edzo *see* Edzo

Raetihi *150 D4* Manawatu-Wanganui,
North Island, New Zealand
Rafa *see* Rafah
Rafaela *64 C3* Santa Fe, E Argentina
Rafah *119 A7 var.* Rafa, Rafaḩ, *Heb.*
Rafiaḥ, Raphiah. SW Gaza Strip
Rafḩah *120 B4* Al Ḥudūd ash
Shamālīyah, N Saudi Arabia
Rafiaḥ *see* Rafah
Raga *73 A5* Western Bahr el Ghazal,
W South Sudan
Ragged Island Range *54 C2 island group*
S Bahamas
Ragnit *see* Neman
Ragusa *97 C7* Sicilia, Italy,
C Mediterranean Sea
Ragusa *see* Dubrovnik
Rahachow *107 D7 Rus.* Rogachëv.
Homyel'skaya Voblasts', SE Belarus
Rahaeng *see* Tak
Rahaţ, Ḥarrat *121 B5 lava flow* W Saudi
Arabia
Rahimyār Khān *134 C3* Punjab,
SE Pakistan
Rahovec *101 D5 Serb.* Orahovac.
W Kosovo
Raiatea *145 G4 island* Îles Sous le Vent,
W French Polynesia
Raichur *132 C1* Karnātaka, C India
Raidestos *see* Tekirdağ
Rainier, Mount *34 A4 volcano*
Washington, NW USA
Rainy Lake *38 A4 lake* Canada/USA
Raipur *135 E4* Chhattīsgarh, C India
Rājahmundry *135 E5* Andhra Pradesh,
E India
Rajang *see* Rajang, Batang
Rajang, Batang *138 D3 var.* Rajang.
river East Malaysia
Rājapālaiyam *132 C3* Tamil Nādu,
SE India
Rājasthān *134 C3 cultural region*
NW India
Rājkot *134 C4* Gujarāt, W India
Rāj Nāndgaon *135 E4* Chhattīsgarh,
C India
Rajshahi *135 G3 prev.* Rampur Boalia.
Rajshahi, W Bangladesh
Rakahanga *145 F3 atoll* N Cook Islands
Rakaia *151 B6 river* South Island, New
Zealand
Rakka *see* Ar Raqqah
Rakke *106 E2* Lääne-Virumaa,
NE Estonia
Rakvere *106 E2 Ger.* Wesenberg. Lääne-
Virumaa, N Estonia
Raleigh *43 F1 state capital* North
Carolina, SE USA
Ralik Chain *144 D1 island group* Ralik
Chain, W Marshall Islands
Ramadi *see* Ar Ramādī
Râmnicul-Sărat *see* Râmnicu Sărat
Râmnicu Sărat *108 C4 prev.* Râmnicul-
Sărat, Rîmnicu-Sărat. Buzău,
E Romania
Râmnicu Vâlcea *108 B4 prev.* Rîmnicu
Vîlcea. Vâlcea, C Romania
Rampur Boalia *see* Rajshahi
Ramree Island *136 A4 island*
W Myanmar (Burma)
Ramtha *see* Ar Ramthā
Rancagua *64 B4* Libertador, C Chile
Rānchi *135 F4* Jhārkhand, N India
Randers *85 B7* Midtjylland, C Denmark
Rånes *see* Ringvassøya
Rangiora *151 C6* Canterbury, South
Island, New Zealand
Rangitikei *150 D4 river* North Island,
New Zealand
Rangoon *see* Yangon
Rangpur *135 G3* Rajshahi, N Bangladesh
Rankin Inlet *37 G3* Nunavut, C Canada
Ranong *137 B6* Ranong, SW Thailand
Rapa Nui *see* Pascua, Isla de
Raphiah *see* Rafah
Rapid City *44 D3* South Dakota, N USA
Räpina *106 E3 Ger.* Rappin. Põlvamaa,
SE Estonia
Rapla *106 D2 Ger.* Rappel. Raplamaa,
NW Estonia
Rappel *see* Rapla
Rappin *see* Räpina
Rarotonga *145 G5 island* S Cook Islands,
C Pacific Ocean
Ra's al Ain *see* Ra's al 'Ayn
Ra's al 'Ayn *118 D1 var.* Ras al'Ain. Al
Ḩasakah, N Syria
Ra's an Naqb *119 B7* Ma'ān, S Jordan

Raseiniai *106 B4* Kaunas, C Lithuania
Rasht *120 C2 var.* Resht. Gīlān, N Iran
Rasik *see* Raasiku
Râşnov *108 C4 prev.* Rîşno, Rozsnyó,
Hung. Barcarozsnyó. Braşov,
C Romania
Rastenburg *see* Kętrzyn
Ratak Chain *144 D1 island group* Ratak
Chain, E Marshall Islands
Ratān *85 C5* Jämtland, C Sweden
Rat Buri *see* Ratchaburi
Ratchaburi *137 C5 var.* Rat Buri.
Ratchaburi, W Thailand
Ratisbon/Ratisbona/Ratisbonne *see*
Regensburg
Rat Islands *36 A2 island group* Aleutian
Islands, Alaska, USA
Ratlām *134 D4 prev.* Rutlam. Madhya
Pradesh, C India
Ratnapura *132 D4* Sabaragamuwa
Province, S Sri Lanka
Raton *48 D1* New Mexico, SW USA
Rättvik *85 C5* Dalarna, C Sweden
Raudhatain *see* Ar Rawdatayn
Raufarhöfn *83 E4* Norðhurland Eystra,
NE Iceland
Raukawa *see* Cook Strait
Raukumara Range *150 E3 mountain
range* North Island, New Zealand
Rāulakela *see* Rourkela
Rauma *85 D5 Swe.* Raumo. Länsi-
Suomi, SW Finland
Raumo *see* Rauma
Rāurkela *135 F4 var.* Rāulakela,
Rourkela. Orissa, E India
Ravenna *96 C3* Emilia-Romagna,
N Italy
Ravi *134 C2 river* India/Pakistan
Ravnina Kulyndy *114 C4 prev.* Kulunda
Steppe, *Kaz.* Qulyndy Zhazyghy, *Rus.*
Kulundinskaya Ravnina. *grassland*
Kazakhstan/Russian Federation
Rāwalpindi *134 C1* Punjab, NE Pakistan
Rawa Mazowiecka *98 D4* Łódzkie,
C Poland
Rawicz *98 C4 Ger.* Rawitsch.
Wielkopolskie, C Poland
Rawitsch *see* Rawicz
Rawlins *44 C3* Wyoming, C USA
Rawson *65 C6* Chubut, SE Argentina
Rayak *118 B4 var.* Rayaq, Riyāq.
E Lebanon
Rayaq *see* Rayak
Rayong *137 C5* Rayong, S Thailand
Razazah, Buhayrat ar *120 B3 var.* Baḩr
al Milḩ. *lake* C Iraq
Razdolnoye *see* Rozdol'ne
Razelm, Lacul *see* Razim, Lacul
Razgrad *104 D2* Razgrad, N Bulgaria
Razim, Lacul *108 D5 prev.* Lacul Razelm.
lagoon NW Black Sea
Reading *89 D7* S England, United
Kingdom
Reading *41 F4* Pennsylvania, NE USA
Realicó *64 C4* La Pampa, C Argentina
Reăng Kesei *137 D5* Bătdâmbâng,
W Cambodia
Greater Antarctica *see* East Antarctica
Rebecca, Lake *147 C6 lake* Western
Australia
Rebiana Sand Sea *see* Rabyanah, Ramlat
Rebun-to *130 C2 island* NE Japan
Rechitsa *see* Rechytsa
Rechytsa *107 D7 Rus.* Rechitsa.
Brestskaya Voblasts', SW Belarus
Recife *63 G2 prev.* Pernambuco. *state
capital* Pernambuco, E Brazil
Recklinghausen *94 A4* Nordrhein-
Westfalen, W Germany
Recogne *87 C7* Luxembourg,
SE Belgium
Reconquista *64 D3* Santa Fe,
C Argentina
Red Deer *37 E5* Alberta, SW Canada
Redding *47 B5* California, W USA
Redon *90 A4* Ille-et-Vilaine, NW France
Red River *136 C2 var.* Yuan. Yuan
Jiang, *Vtn.* Sông Hồng Hà. *river* China/
Vietnam
Red River *45 F1 river* Canada/USA
Red River *42 B3 river* Louisiana, S USA
Red Sea *72 C3 var.* Sinus Arabicus. *sea*
Africa/Asia
Red Wing *45 G2* Minnesota, N USA
Reefton *151 C5* West Coast, South
Island, New Zealand
Reese River *47 C5 river* Nevada, W USA
Refahiye *117 E3* Erzincan, C Turkey

Regensburg *95 C6 Eng.* Ratisbon, *Fr.*
Ratisbonne, *hist.* Ratisbona; *anc.* Castra
Regina, Reginum. Bayern, SE Germany
Regenstauf *95 C6* Bayern, SE Germany
Régestân *122 D5 var.* Registan *prev.*
Rīgestān. S Afghanistan
Reggane *70 D3* C Algeria
Reggio *see* Reggio nell'Emilia
Reggio Calabria *see* Reggio di Calabria
Reggio di Calabria *97 D7 var.* Reggio
Calabria, *Gk.* Rhegion; *anc.* Regium,
Rhegium. Calabria, SW Italy
Reggio Emilia *see* Reggio nell'Emilia
Reggio nell'Emilia *96 B2 var.* Reggio
Emilia, *abbrev.* Reggio; *anc.* Regium
Lepidum. Emilia-Romagna, N Italy
Reghin *108 C4 Ger.* Sächsisch-Reen,
Hung. Szászrégen; *prev.* Reghinul
Săsesc, *Ger.* Sächsisch-Regen. Mureş,
C Romania
Reghinul Săsesc *see* Reghin
Regina *37 F5 province capital*
Saskatchewan, S Canada
Reginum *see* Regensburg
Registan *see* Régestân
Regium *see* Reggio di Calabria
Regium Lepidum *see* Reggio nell'Emilia
Rehoboth *78 B3* Hardap, C Namibia
Rehovot *119 A6; prev.* Reḩovot. Central,
C Israel
Reḩovot *see* Rehovot
Reichenau *see* Bogatynia, Poland
Reichenberg *see* Liberec
Reid *147 D6* Western Australia
Reikjavik *see* Reykjavík
Ré, Île de *90 A4 island* W France
Reims *90 D3 Eng.* Rheims; *anc.*
Durocortorum, Remi. Marne,
N France
Reindeer Lake *37 F4 lake* Manitoba/
Saskatchewan, C Canada
Reine-Charlotte, Îles de la *see* Queen
Charlotte Islands
Reine-Élisabeth, Îles de la *see* Queen
Elizabeth Islands
Reinga, Cape *150 C1 headland* North
Island, New Zealand
Reinosa *92 D1* Cantabria, N Spain
Reka *see* Rijeka
Rekhovot *see* Rehovot
Reliance *37 F4* Northwest Territories,
C Canada
Remi *see* Reims
Rendina *see* Rentína
Rendsburg *94 B2* Schleswig-Holstein,
N Germany
Rengat *138 B4* Sumatera, W Indonesia
Reni *108 D4* Odes'ka Oblast',
SW Ukraine
Rennell *144 C4 var.* Mu Nggava. *island*
S Solomon Islands
Rennes *90 B3 Bret.* Roazon; *anc.*
Condate. Ille-et-Vilaine, NW France
Reno *47 C5* Nevada, W USA
Renqiu *128 C4* Hebei, E China
Rentína *105 B5 var.* Rendina. Thessalía,
C Greece
Reps *see* Rupea
Repulse Bay *37 G3* Northwest
Terretories, N Canada
Reschitza *see* Reşiţa
Resht *see* Rasht
Resicabánya *see* Reşiţa
Resistencia *64 D3* Chaco, NE Argentina
Reşiţa *108 A4 Ger.* Reschitza, *Hung.*
Resicabánya. Caraş-Severin,
W Romania
Resolute *37 F2 Inuit* Qausuittuq.
Cornwallis Island, Nunavut, N Canada
Resolution Island *39 E1 island* Nunavut,
NE Canada
Resolution Island *151 A7 island*
SW New Zealand
Réunion *79 H4 off.* La Réunion. *French
overseas department* W Indian Ocean
Réunion *141 B5 island* W Indian Ocean
Reus *93 F2* Cataluña, E Spain
Reutlingen *95 B6* Baden-Württemberg,
S Germany
Reuver *87 D5* Limburg, SE Netherlands
Reval/Revel *see* Tallinn
Revillagigedo Island *50 B5 island*
Alexander Archipelago, Alaska, USA
Rexburg *46 E3* Idaho, NW USA
Reyes *61 F3* El Beni, NW Bolivia
Rey, Isla del *53 G5 island* Archipiélago
de las Perlas, SE Panama
Reykjanes Basin *82 C5 var.* Irminger
Basin. *undersea basin* N Atlantic Ocean

Reykjanes Ridge 80 A1 *undersea ridge*
N Atlantic Ocean
Reykjavík 83 E5 *var.* Reikjavik.
country capital (Iceland)
Höfudhborgarsvaedhi, W Iceland
Reynosa 51 E2 Tamaulipas, C Mexico
Rezā'iyeh, Daryācheh-ye *see* Orūmīyeh,
Daryācheh-ye
Rezé 90 A4 Loire-Atlantique,
NW France
Rēzekne 106 D4 Ger. Rositten; *prev. Rus.*
Rezhitsa. SE Latvia
Rezhitsa *see* Rēzekne
Rezovo 104 E3 Turk. Rezve. Burgas,
E Bulgaria
Rezve *see* Rezovo
Rhaedestus *see* Tekirdağ
Rhegion/Rhegium *see* Reggio di Calabria
Rheims *see* Reims
Rhein *see* Rhine
Rhine 94 A3 *var.* Rheine in Westfalen.
Nordrhein-Westfalen, W Germany
Rheine in Westfalen *see* Rheine
Rheinisches Schiefergebirge 95 A5 *var.*
Rhine State Uplands, *Eng.* Rhenish
Slate Mountains. *mountain range*
W Germany
Rhenish Slate Mountains *see* Rheinisches
Schiefergebirge
Rhin *see* Rhine
Rhine 80 D4 *Dut.* Rijn, *Fr.* Rhin, *Ger.*
Rhein. *river* W Europe
Rhinelander 40 B2 Wisconsin, N USA
Rhine State Uplands *see* Rheinisches
Schiefergebirge
Rho 96 B2 Lombardia, N Italy
Rhode Island 41 G3 *off.* State of Rhode
Island and Providence Plantations, *also
known as* Little Rhody, Ocean State.
state NE USA
Rhodes 105 E7 *var.* Ródhos, *Eng.*
Rhodes, *It.* Rodi; *anc.* Rhodos. *island*
Dodekánisa, Greece, Aegean Sea
Rhodes *see* Ródos
Rhodesia *see* Zimbabwe
Rhodope Mountains 104 C3 *var.*
Rodhópi Óri, *Bul.* Rhodope Planina,
Rodopi, *Gk.* Orosirá Rodhópis, *Turk.*
Dospad Dagh. *mountain range*
Bulgaria/Greece
Rhodope Planina *see* Rhodope
Mountains
Rhône 80 C4 *river* France/Switzerland
Rhum 88 B3 *var.* Rum. *island*
W Scotland, United Kingdom
Ribble 89 D5 *river* NW England, United
Kingdom
Ribeira *see* Santa Uxía de Ribeira
Ribeirão Preto 63 F4 São Paulo,
S Brazil
Riberalta 61 F2 El Beni, N Bolivia
Rîbniţa 108 D3 *var.* Rābniţa, *Rus.*
Rybnitsa. NE Moldova
Rice Lake 40 A2 Wisconsin, N USA
Richard Toll 74 B3 N Senegal
Richfield 44 B4 Utah, W USA
Richland 46 C2 Washington,
NW USA
Richmond 151 C5 Tasman, South Island,
New Zealand
Richmond 40 C5 Kentucky, S USA
Richmond 41 E5 *state capital* Virginia,
NE USA
Richmond Range 151 C5 *mountain
range* South Island, New Zealand
Ricobayo, Embalse de 92 C2 *reservoir*
NW Spain
Ricomagus *see* Riom
Ridder 114 D4 *prev.* Leninogorsk, *Kaz.*
Leningor. Vostochnyy Kazakhstan,
E Kazakhstan
Ridgecrest 47 C7 California, W USA
Ried *see* Ried im Innkreis
Ried im Innkreis 95 D6 *var.* Ried.
Oberösterreich, NW Austria
Riemst 87 D6 Limburg, NE Belgium
Riesa 94 D4 Sachsen, E Germany
Rift Valley *see* Great Rift Valley
Riga 106 C3 *Eng.* Riga. *country capital*
(Latvia) C Latvia
Rīgas Jūras Līcis *see* Riga, Gulf of
Rigestān *see* Rēgestān
Riia Laht *see* Riga, Gulf of
Riihimäki 85 D5 Etelä-Suomi, S Finland

Rijeka 100 A2 Ger. Sankt Veit am Flaum,
It. Fiume, *Slvn.* Reka; *anc.* Tarsatica.
Primorje-Gorski Kotar, NW Croatia
Rijn *see* Rhine
Rijssel *see* Lille
Rijssen 86 E3 Overijssel, E Netherlands
Rimah, Wadi ar 120 B4 *var.* Wādī ar
Rummah. *dry watercourse* C Saudi
Arabia
Rimini 96 C3 *anc.* Ariminum. Emilia-
Romagna, N Italy
Rîmnicu-Sărat *see* Râmnicu Sărat
Rîmnicu Vîlcea *see* Râmnicu Vâlcea
Rimouski 39 F4 Québec, SE Canada
Ringebu 85 B5 Oppland, S Norway
Ringen *see* Rõngu
Ringkøbing Fjord 85 A7 *fjord*
W Denmark
Ringvassøya 84 C2 Lapp. Ráneš. *island*
N Norway
Rio *see* Rio de Janeiro
Riobamba 60 B1 Chimborazo,
C Ecuador
Rio Branco 56 B3 *state capital* Acre,
W Brazil
Rio Branco, Território de *see* Roraima
Río Bravo 51 E2 Tamaulipas, C Mexico
Río Cuarto 64 C4 Córdoba, C Argentina
Rio de Janeiro 63 F4 *var.* Rio. *state*
capital Rio de Janeiro, SE Brazil
Río Gallegos 65 B7 *var.* Gallegos, Puerto
Gallegos. Santa Cruz, S Argentina
Rio Grande 63 E5 *var.* São Pedro do
Rio Grande do Sul. Rio Grande do
Sul, S Brazil
Río Grande 50 D3 Zacatecas, C Mexico
Rio Grande do Norte 63 G2 *off.* Estado
do Rio Grande do Norte. *state* E Brazil
Rio Grande do Norte 63 G2 *off.* Estado
do Rio Grande do Norte. *region* E Brazil
Rio Grande do Norte, Estado do *see* Rio
Grande do Norte
Rio Grande do Sul 63 E5 *off.* Estado do
Rio Grande do Sul. *state* S Brazil
Rio Grande do Sul 63 E5 *off.* Estado do
Rio Grande do Sul. *region* S Brazil
Rio Grande do Sul, Estado do *see* Rio
Grande do Sul
Rio Grande Plateau *see* Rio Grande Rise
Rio Grande Rise 57 E6 *var.* Rio Grande
Plateau. *undersea plateau* SW Atlantic
Ocean
Ríohacha 58 B1 La Guajira, N Colombia
Río Lagartos 51 H3 Yucatán, SE Mexico
Riom 91 C5 *anc.* Ricomagus. Puy-de-
Dôme, C France
Río Verde 51 E4 *var.* Rioverde. San Luis
Potosí, C Mexico
Rioverde *see* Río Verde
Ripoll 93 G2 Cataluña, NE Spain
Rishiri-to 130 C2 *var.* Risiri Tô. *island*
NE Japan
Risiri Tô *see* Rishiri-tô
Rişno *see* Râşnov
Risti 106 D2 Ger. Kreuz. Läänemaa,
W Estonia
Rivas 52 D4 Rivas, SW Nicaragua
Rivera 64 D3 Rivera, NE Uruguay
River Falls 40 A2 Wisconsin, N USA
Riverside 47 C7 California, W USA
Riverton 151 A7 Southland, South
Island, New Zealand
Riverton 44 C3 Wyoming, C USA
Rivière-du-Loup 39 E4 Québec,
SE Canada
Rivne 108 C2 Pol. Równe, *Rus.* Rovno.
Rivnens'ka Oblast', NW Ukraine
Rivoli 96 A2 Piemonte, NW Italy
Riyadh/Riyāḍ, Minţaqat ar *see* Ar Riyāḍ
Riyāq *see* Rayak
Rize 117 E2 Rize, NE Turkey
Rizhao 128 D4 Shandong, E China
Rizhskiy Zaliv *see* Riga, Gulf of
Rkîz 74 C3 Trarza, W Mauritania
Road Town 55 F3 *dependent territory
capital* (British Virgin Islands) Tortola,
C British Virgin Islands
Roanne 91 C5 *anc.* Rodunma. Loire,
E France
Roanoke 41 E5 Virginia, NE USA
Roanoke River 43 F1 *river* North
Carolina/Virginia, SE USA
Roatán 52 C2 *var.* Coxen Hole, Coxin
Hole. Isla de la Bahía, N Honduras
Roat Kampuchea *see* Cambodia
Roazon *see* Rennes
Robbie Ridge 143 E3 *undersea ridge*
W Pacific Ocean
Robert Williams *see* Caála

Robinson Range 147 B5 *mountain range*
Western Australia
Robson, Mount 37 E5 *mountain* British
Columbia, SW Canada
Robstown 49 G4 Texas, SW USA
Roca Partida, Isla 50 B5 *island*
W Mexico
Rocas, Atol das 63 G2 *island* E Brazil
Rochefort 87 C7 Namur, SE Belgium
Rochefort 90 B4 *var.* Rochefort sur Mer.
Charente-Maritime, W France
Rochefort sur Mer *see* Rochefort
Rochester 45 G3 Minnesota, N USA
Rochester 41 G2 New Hampshire,
NE USA
Rocheuses, Montagnes/Rockies *see*
Rocky Mountains
Rockall Bank 80 B2 *undersea bank*
N Atlantic Ocean
Rockall Trough 80 B2 *trough* N Atlantic
Ocean
Rockdale 148 E2 Texas, SW USA
Rockford 40 B3 Illinois, N USA
Rockhampton 148 D4 Queensland,
E Australia
Rock Hill 43 E1 South Carolina, SE USA
Rockingham 147 A6 Western Australia
Rock Island 40 B3 Illinois, N USA
Rock Sound 54 C1 Eleuthera Island,
C Bahamas
Rock Springs 44 C3 Wyoming, C USA
Rockstone 59 F3 C Guyana
Rocky Mount 43 F1 North Carolina,
SE USA
Rocky Mountains 34 B4 *var.* Rockies,
Fr. Montagnes Rocheuses. *mountain
range* Canada/USA
Roden 86 E2 Drenthe, NE Netherlands
Rodez 91 C5 *anc.* Segodunum. Aveyron,
S France
Rodhópi Óri *see* Rhodope Mountains
Ródhos/Rodi *see* Rhodes
Rodopi *see* Rhodope Mountains
Rodosto *see* Tekirdağ
Rodunma *see* Roanne
Roermond 87 D5 Limburg,
SE Netherlands
Roeselare 87 A6 Fr. Roulers; *prev.*
Rousselaere. West-Vlaanderen,
W Belgium
Rogachëv *see* Rahachow
Rogatica 100 C4 Republika Srpska,
SE Bosnia and Herzegovina
Rogers 42 A1 Arkansas, C USA
Roger Simpson Island *see* Abemama
Roi Ed *see* Roi Et
Roi Et 137 D5 *var.* Muang Roi Et, Roi
Ed. Roi Et, E Thailand
Roja 106 C2 NW Latvia
Rokiškis 106 C4 Panevėžys,
NE Lithuania
Rokycany 99 A5 Ger. Rokytzan.
Plzeňský Kraj, W Czech Republic
Rokytzan *see* Rokycany
Rôlas, Ilha das 76 E2 *island* S Sao Tome
and Principe, Africa, E Atlantic Ocean
Rolla 45 G5 Missouri, C USA
Rôm *see* Rømø
Roma 96 C4 Eng. Rome. *country capital*
(Italy) Lazio, C Italy
Roma 149 D5 Queensland, E Australia
Roman 104 C2 Vratsa, NW Bulgaria
Roman 108 C4 Hung. Románvásár.
Neamţ, NE Romania
Romania 108 B4 Bul. Rumūniya, Ger.
Rumänien, Hung. Románia, Rom.
România, SCr. Rumunjska, Ukr.
Rumuniya, *prev.* Republica Socialistă
România, Roumania, Rumania,
Socialist Republic of Romania, *prev.
Rom.* Romînia. *country* SE Europe

Roma 2%, Other 2%
Government Presidential system
Currency New Romanian leu = 100 bani
Literacy rate 98%
Calorie consumption 3487 kilocalories

România, Republica Socialistă *see*
Romania
Romania, Socialist Republic of *see*
Romania
Romanivka 109 F3 Rus. Dneprodzerzhinsk,
prev. Dniprodzerzhyns'k.; *prev.*
Kamenskoye. Dnipropetrovs'ka
Oblast', E Ukraine
Románvásár *see* Roman
Rome 42 D2 Georgia, SE USA
Rome *see* Roma
Rominia *see* Romania
Romny 109 F2 Sums'ka Oblast',
NE Ukraine
Rømø 85 A7 Ger. Röm. *island*
SW Denmark
Roncador, Serra do 56 D4 *mountain
range* C Brazil
Ronda 92 D5 Andalucía, S Spain
Rondônia 62 D3 *off.* Estado de
Rondônia; *prev.* Território de
Rondônia. *state* W Brazil
Rondônia 62 D3 *off.* Estado de
Rondônia; *prev.* Território de
Rondônia. *region* W Brazil
Rondônia, Estado de *see* Rondônia
Rondônia, Território de *see* Rondônia
Rondonópolis 63 E3 Mato Grosso,
W Brazil
Rongelap Atoll 144 D1 *var.* Rönlap.
atoll Ralik Chain, NW Marshall Islands
Rõngu 106 D3 Ger. Ringen. Tartumaa,
SE Estonia
Rönlap *see* Rongelap Atoll
Rønne 85 B8 Bornholm, E Denmark
Ronne Ice Shelf 154 A3 *ice shelf*
Antarctica
Roosendaal 87 C5 Noord-Brabant,
S Netherlands
Roosevelt Island 154 B4 *island*
Antarctica
Roraima 62 D1 *off.* Estado de Roraima;
prev. Território de Rio Branco,
Território de Roraima. *state* N Brazil
Roraima 62 D1 *off.* Estado de Roraima;
prev. Território de Rio Branco,
Território de Roraima. *region* N Brazil
Roraima, Estado de *see* Roraima
Roraima, Mount 59 E3 *mountain*
N South America
Roraima, Território de *see* Roraima
Røros 85 B5 Sør-Trøndelag, S Norway
Ross 151 B6 West Coast, South Island,
New Zealand
Rosa, Lake 54 D2 *lake* Great Inagua,
S Bahamas
Rosario 64 D4 Santa Fe, C Argentina
Rosario 64 D2 San Pedro, C Paraguay
Rosario *see* Rosarito
Rosarito 50 A1 *var.* Rosario. Baja
California Norte, NW Mexico
Roscianum *see* Rossano
Roscommon 40 C2 Michigan, N USA
Roseau 55 G4 *prev.* Charlotte
Town. *country capital* (Dominica)
SW Dominica
Roseburg 46 B4 Oregon, NW USA
Rosenau *see* Rožňava
Rosenberg 49 G4 Texas, SW USA
Rosenberg *see* Ružomberok, Slovakia
Rosengarten 94 B3 Niedersachsen,
N Germany
Rosenheim 95 C6 Bayern, S Germany
Rosia 93 H5 W Gibraltar Europe
Rosia Bay 93 H5 *bay* SW Gibraltar
Europe W Mediterranean Sea Atlantic
Ocean
Roşiori de Vede 108 B5 Teleorman,
S Romania
Rositten *see* Rēzekne
Roslavl' 111 A5 Smolenskaya Oblast',
W Russian Federation
Rosmalen 86 C4 Noord-Brabant,
S Netherlands
Rossano 97 E6 *anc.* Roscianum.
Calabria, SW Italy
Ross Ice Shelf 154 B4 *ice shelf* Antarctica
Rossiyskaya Federatsiya *see* Russian
Federation

ROMANIA
(continued)

ROMANIA
Southeast Europe

Official name	Romania
Formation	1878 / 1947
Capital	Bucharest
Population	21.4 million / 241 people per sq mile (93 people per sq km)
Total area	91,699 sq. miles (237,500 sq. km)
Languages	Romanian*, Hungarian (Magyar), Romani, German
Religions	Romanian Orthodox 87%, Protestant 10%, Roman Catholic 1%, Greek Orthodox 1%, Greek Catholic (Uniate) 1%, Other 1%
Ethnic mix	Romanian 89%, Magyar 7%,

Rosso *74 B3* Trarza, SW Mauritania
Rossosh' *111 B6* Voronezhskaya Oblast',
   W Russian Federation
Ross Sea *154 B4* *sea* Antarctica
Rostak *see* Ar Rustāq
Rostock *94 C2* Mecklenburg-
   Vorpommern, NE Germany
Rostov *see* Rostov-na-Donu
Rostov-na-Donu *111 B7 var.* Rostov,
   Eng. Rostov-on-Don. Rostovskaya
   Oblast', SW Russian Federation
Rostov-on-Don *see* Rostov-na-Donu
Roswell *48 D2* New Mexico,
   SW USA
Rota *144 B1* *island* S Northern Mariana
   Islands
Rotcher Island *see* Tamana
Rothera *154 A2* *UK research station*
   Antarctica
Rotomagus *see* Rouen
Rotorua *150 D3* Bay of Plenty, North
   Island, New Zealand
Rotorua, Lake *150 D3* *lake* North Island,
   New Zealand
Rotterdam *86 C4* Zuid-Holland,
   SW Netherlands
Rottweil *95 B6* Baden-Württemberg,
   S Germany
Rotuma *145 E4* *island* NW Fiji Oceania
   S Pacific Ocean
Roubaix *90 C2* Nord, N France
Rouen *90 C3 anc.* Rotomagus. Seine-
   Maritime, N France
Roulers *see* Roeselare
Roumania *see* Romania
Round Rock *49 G3* Texas, SW USA
Rourkela *see* Rāurkela
Rousselaere *see* Roeselare
Roussillon *91 C6* *cultural region*
   S France
Rouyn-Noranda *38 D4* Québec,
   SE Canada
Rovaniemi *84 D3* Lappi, N Finland
Rovigno *see* Rovinj
Rovigo *96 C2* Veneto, NE Italy
Rovinj *100 A3 It.* Rovigno. Istra,
   NW Croatia
Rovno *see* Rivne
Rovuma, Rio *79 F2 var.* Ruvuma. *river*
   Mozambique/Tanzania
Rovuma, Rio *see* Ruvuma
Równe *see* Rivne
Roxas City *139 E2* Panay Island,
   C Philippines
Royale, Isle *40 B1* *island* Michigan,
   N USA
Royan *91 B5* Charente-Maritime,
   W France
Rozdol'ne *109 F4 Rus.* Razdolnoye.
   Avtonomna Respublika Krym,
   S Ukraine
Rožňava *99 D6 Ger.* Rosenau, *Hung.*
   Rozsnyó. Košický Kraj,
   E Slovakia
Rózsahegy *see* Ružomberok
Rozsnyó *see* Râşnov, Romania
Rozsnyó *see* Rožňava, Slovakia
Ruanda *see* Rwanda
Ruapehu, Mount *150 D4* *volcano* North
   Island, New Zealand
Ruapuke Island *151 B8* *island*
   SW New Zealand
Ruatoria *150 E3* Gisborne, North Island,
   New Zealand
Ruawai *150 D2* Northland, North Island,
   New Zealand
Rubezhnoye *see* Rubizhne
Rubizhne *109 H3 Rus.* Rubezhnoye.
   Luhans'ka Oblast', E Ukraine
Ruby Mountains *47 D5* *mountain range*
   Nevada, W USA
Rucava *106 B3* SW Latvia
Rudensk *see* Rudzyensk
Rūdiškės *107 B5* Vilnius, S Lithuania
Rudnik *104 E2* Varna, E Bulgaria
Rudny *see* Rudnyy
Rudnyy *114 C4 var.* Rudny. Kostanay,
   N Kazakhstan
Rudolf, Lake *see* Turkana, Lake
Rudolfswert *see* Novo Mesto
Rudzyensk *107 C6 Rus.* Rudensk.
   Minskaya Voblasts', C Belarus
Rufiji *73 C7* *river* E Tanzania
Rufino *64 C4* Santa Fe, C Argentina
Rugāji *106 D4* E Latvia
Rügen *94 D2* *headland* NE Germany
Ruggell *94 E1* N Liechtenstein
   Europe
Ruhja *see* Rūjiena

Ruhnu *106 C2 var.* Ruhnu Saar, *Swe.*
   Runö. *island* SW Estonia
Ruhnu Saar *see* Ruhnu
Rujen *see* Rūjiena
Rūjiena *106 D3 Est.* Ruhja, *Ger.* Rujen.
   N Latvia
Rukwa, Lake *73 B7* *lake* SE Tanzania
Rum *see* Rhum
Ruma *100 D3* Vojvodina, N Serbia
Rumadīya *see* Ar Ramādī
Rumania/Rumänien *see* Romania
Rumbek *73 B5* El Buhayrat, C South
   Sudan
Rum Cay *54 D2* *island* C Bahamas
Rumia *98 C2* Pomorskie, N Poland
Rummah, Wādī ar *see* Rimah, Wādī ar
Rummelsburg in Pommern *see*
   Miastko
Rumuniya/Rumūniya/Rumunjska
   see Romania
Runanga *151 B5* West Coast, South
   Island, New Zealand
Rundu *78 C3 var.* Runtu. Okavango,
   NE Namibia
Runö *see* Ruhnu
Runtu *see* Rundu
Ruoqiang *126 C3 var.* Jo-ch'iang, *Uigh.*
   Charkhlik, Charkhliq, Qarkilik.
   Xinjiang Uygur Zizhiqu, NW China
Rupea *108 C4 Ger.* Reps, *Hung.*
   Kőhalom; *prev.* Cohalm. Braşov,
   C Romania
Rupel *87 B5* *river* N Belgium
Rupella *see* La Rochelle
Rupert, Rivière de *38 D3* *river* Québec,
   C Canada
Rusaddir *see* Melilla
Ruschuk/Rusçuk *see* Ruse
Ruse *104 D1 var.* Ruschuk, Rustchuk,
   Turk. Rusçuk. Ruse, N Bulgaria
Russadir *see* Melilla
Russellville *42 A1* Arkansas, C USA
Russia *see* Russian Federation
Russian America *see* Alaska
Russian Federation *112 D2 off.* Russian
   Federation, *var.* Russia, *Latv.* Krievija,
   Rus. Rossiyskaya Federatsiya. *country*
   Asia/Europe

RUSSIAN FEDERATION
Europe / Asia

Official name Russian Federation
Formation 1480 / 1991
Capital Moscow
Population 143 million / 22 people
per sq mile (8 people per sq km)
Total area 6,592,735 sq. miles
(17,075,200 sq. km)
Languages Russian*, Tatar, Ukrainian,
Chavash, various other national languages
Religions Orthodox Christian 75%,
Muslim 14%, Other 11%
Ethnic mix Russian 80%, Other 12%,
Tatar 4%, Ukrainian 2%, Bashkir 1%,
Chavash 1%
Government Mixed Presidential–
Parliamentary system
Currency Russian rouble = 100 kopeks
Literacy rate 99%
Calorie consumption 3172 kilocalories

Russian Federation *see* Russian
   Federation
Rustaq *see* Ar Rustāq
Rustavi *117 G2 prev.* Rust'avi.
   SE Georgia
Rust'avi *see* Rustavi
Rustchuk *see* Ruse
Ruston *42 B2* Louisiana, S USA
Rutanzige, Lake *see* Edward, Lake
Rutba *see* Ar Ruţbah
Rutlam *see* Ratlām
Rutland *41 F2* Vermont, NE USA
Rutog *126 A4 var.* Rutög, Rutok. Xizang
   Zizhiqu, W China
Rutok *see* Rutog
Ruvuma *69 E5 var.* Rio Rovuma. *river*
   Mozambique/Tanzania
Ruvuma *see* Rovuma, Rio
Ruwenzori *77 E5* *mountain range* Dem.
   Rep. Congo/Uganda
Ruzhany *107 B6* Brestskaya Voblasts',
   SW Belarus
Ružomberok *99 C5 Ger.* Rosenberg,
   Hung. Rózsahegy. Zilinský Kraj,
   N Slovakia
Rwanda *73 B6 off.* Rwandese Republic;
   prev. Ruanda. *country* C Africa

RWANDA
Central Africa

Official name Republic of Rwanda
Formation 1962 / 1962
Capital Kigali
Population 10.9 million / 1132 people
per sq mile (437 people per sq km)
Total area 10,169 sq. miles (26,338 sq. km)
Languages Kinyarwanda*, French*,
Kiswahili, English*
Religions Christian 94%, Muslim 5%,
Traditional beliefs 1%
Ethnic mix Hutu 85%, Tutsi 14%,
Other (including Twa) 1%
Government Presidential system
Currency Rwanda franc = 100 centimes
Literacy rate 71%
Calorie consumption 2188 kilocalories

Rwandese Republic *see* Rwanda
Ryazan' *111 B5* Ryazanskaya Oblast',
   W Russian Federation
Rybach'ye *see* Balykchy
Rybinsk *110 B4 prev.* Andropov.
   Yaroslavskaya Oblast', W Russian
   Federation
Rybnik *99 C5* Śląskie, S Poland
Rybnitsa *see* Rîbniţa
Ryde *148 E1* United Kingdom
Ryki *98 D4* Lubelskie, E Poland
Rykovo *see* Yenakiyeve
Rypin *98 C3* Kujawsko-pomorskie,
   C Poland
Ryssel *see* Lille
Rysy *99 C5* *mountain* S Poland
Ryukyu Islands *130 A2 Eng.* Ryukyu
   Islands. *island group* SW Japan
Ryukyu Islands *125 E3 Eng.* Ryukyu
   Islands. *island group* SW Japan
Ryukyu Islands *see* Nansei-shotō
Ryukyu Islands *see* Nansei-shotō
Ryukyu Trench *125 F3 var.* Nansei Syotō
   Trench. *trench* S East China Sea
Rzeszów *99 E5* Podkarpackie,
   SE Poland
Rzhev *110 B4* Tverskaya Oblast',
   W Russian Federation

S

Saale *94 C4* *river* C Germany
Saalfeld *95 C5 var.* Saalfeld an der Saale.
   Thüringen, C Germany
Saalfeld an der Saale *see* Saalfeld
Saarbrücken *95 A6 Fr.* Sarrebruck.
   Saarland, SW Germany
Sääre *102 C2 var.* Sjar. Saaremaa,
   W Estonia
Saare *see* Saaremaa
Saaremaa *106 C2 Ger.* Oesel, Ösel; *prev.*
   Saare. *island* W Estonia
Saariselkä *84 D2* Lapp. Suoločielgi.
   Lappi, N Finland
Sab' Ābār *118 C4 var.* Sab'a Biyar, Sa'b
   Bi'ār. Ḥimş, C Syria
Sab'a Biyar *see* Sab' Ābār
Šabac *100 D3* Serbia, W Serbia
Sabadell *93 G2* Cataluña, E Spain
Sabah *138 D3 prev.* British North
   Borneo, North Borneo. *state* East
   Malaysia
Sabanalarga *58 B1* Atlántico,
   N Colombia
Sabaneta *58 C1* Falcón, N Venezuela
Sabaria *see* Szombathely
Sab'atayn, Ramlat as *121 C6 desert*
   C Yemen
Sabaya *61 F4* Oruro, S Bolivia
Sa'b Bi'ār *see* Sab' Ābār
Saberi, Hamun-e *122 C5 var.*
   Daryācheh-ye Hāmun, Daryācheh-ye
   Sīstān. *lake* Afghanistan/Iran
Sabhā *71 F3* C Libya
Sabi *see* Save
Sabinas *51 E2* Coahuila, NE Mexico
Sabinas Hidalgo *51 E2* Nuevo León,
   NE Mexico
Sabine River *49 H3* *river* Louisiana/
   Texas, SW USA
Sabkha *see* As Sabkhah
Sable, Cape *43 E5* *headland* Florida,
   SE USA
Sable Island *39 G4* *island* Nova Scotia,
   SE Canada
Şabyā *121 B6* Jīzān, SW Saudi Arabia

Sabzawar *see* Sabzevār
Sabzevār *120 D2 var.* Sabzawar.
   Khorāsān-Razavī, NE Iran
Sachsen *94 D4 Eng.* Saxony, *Fr.* Saxe.
   state E Germany
Sachs Harbour *37 E2 var.* Ikaahuk.
   Banks Island, Northwest Territories,
   N Canada
Sächsisch-Reen/Sächsisch-Regen
   see Reghin
Sacramento *47 B5* *state capital*
   California, W USA
Sacramento Mountains *48 D2*
   mountain range New Mexico,
   SW USA
Sacramento River *47 B5* *river* California,
   W USA
Sacramento Valley *47 B5* *valley*
   California, W USA
Sá da Bandeira *see* Lubango
Şa'dah *121 B6* NW Yemen
Sado *see* Sado-shima
Sadoga-shima *131 C5 var.* Sado. *island*
   C Japan
Saena Julia *see* Siena
Safad *see* Tsefat
Şafāqis *see* Sfax
Şafāshahr *120 D3 var.* Deh Bīd. Fārs,
   C Iran
Safed *see* Tsefat
Säffle *85 B6* Värmland, C Sweden
Safford *48 C3* Arizona, SW USA
Safi *70 B2* W Morocco
Selseleh-ye Safīd Kūh *122 D4 Eng.*
   Paropamisus Range. *mountain range*
   W Afghanistan
Sagaing *136 B3* Sagaing, C Myanmar
   (Burma)
Sagami-nada *131 D6* *inlet* SW Japan
Sagan *see* Żagań
Sāgar *134 D4 prev.* Saugor. Madhya
   Pradesh, C India
Sagarmāthā *see* Everest, Mount
Sagebrush State *see* Nevada
Saghez *see* Saqqez
Saginaw *40 C3* Michigan, N USA
Saginaw Bay *40 D2* *lake bay* Michigan,
   N USA
Sagua la Grande *54 B2* Villa Clara,
   C Cuba
Sagunto *93 F3* Cat. Sagunt, *Ar.*
   Murviedro; *anc.* Saguntum.
   Valenciana, E Spain
Sagunt/Saguntum *see* Sagunto
Sahara *68 B3 desert* Libya/Algeria
Sahara el Gharbīya *see* Şaḥrā' al
   Gharbīyah
Saharan Atlas *70 D2 var.* Saharan Atlas.
   mountain range Algeria/Morocco
Sahel *74 D3 physical region* C Africa
Şāḥilīyah, Jibāl as *118 B3 mountain*
   range NW Syria
Sāhīwāl *134 C2 prev.* Montgomery.
   Punjab, E Pakistan
Saïda *119 A5 var.* Şaydā, Sayida; *anc.*
   Sidon. W Lebanon
Sa'īdābād *see* Sīrjān
Saidpur *135 G3 var.* Syedpur. Rajshahi,
   NW Bangladesh
Saidu *134 C1 var.* Mingora, Mongora;
   prev. Mingāora. Khyber Pakhtunkhwa,
   N Pakistan
Saigon *see* Hồ Chí Minh
Saimaa *85 E5* lake SE Finland
St Albans *89 E6 anc.* Verulamium.
   E England, United Kingdom
Saint Albans *40 D5* West Virginia,
   NE USA
St Andrews *88 C4* E Scotland, United
   Kingdom
Saint Anna Trough *see* Svyataya Anna
   Trough
St. Ann's Bay *54 B4* C Jamaica
St. Anthony *39 G3* Newfoundland and
   Labrador, SE Canada
Saint Augustine *43 E3* Florida,
   SE USA
St Austell *89 C7* SW England, United
   Kingdom
St.Botolph's Town *see* Boston
St-Brieuc *90 A3* Côtes d'Armor,
   NW France
St. Catharines *38 D5* Ontario, S Canada
St-Chamond *91 D5* Loire, E France
Saint Christopher and Nevis,
   Federation of *see* Saint Kitts and Nevis

Saint Christopher-Nevis *see* Saint Kitts and Nevis
Saint Clair, Lake *40 D3 var.* Lac à L'Eau Claire. *lake* Canada/USA
St-Claude *91 D5 anc.* Condate. Jura, E France
Saint Cloud *45 F2* Minnesota, N USA
Saint Croix *55 F3 island* S Virgin Islands (US)
Saint Croix River *40 A2 river* Minnesota/Wisconsin, N USA
St David's Island *42 B5 island* E Bermuda
St-Denis *79 G4 dependent territory capital* (Réunion) NW Réunion
St-Dié *90 E4* Vosges, NE France
St-Egrève *91 D5* Isère, E France
Sainte Marie, Cap *see* Vohimena, Tanjona
Saintes *91 B5 anc.* Mediolanum. Charente-Maritime, W France
St-Étienne *91 D5* Loire, E France
St-Flour *91 C5* Cantal, C France
St-Gall/Saint Gall/St. Gallen *see* Sankt Gallen
St-Gaudens *91 B6* Haute-Garonne, S France
Saint George *149 D5* Queensland, E Australia
St George *42 B4* N Bermuda
Saint George *44 A5* Utah, W USA
St. George's *55 G5 country capital* (Grenada) SW Grenada
St-Georges *39 E4* Québec, SE Canada
St-Georges *59 H3* E French Guiana
Saint George's Channel *89 B6 channel* Ireland/Wales, United Kingdom
St George's Island *42 B4 island* E Bermuda
Saint Helena *69 B6 UK dependent territory* C Atlantic Ocean
St Helier *89 D8 dependent territory capital* (Jersey) S Jersey, Channel Islands
St.Iago de la Vega *see* Spanish Town
Saint Ignace *40 C2* Michigan, N USA
St-Jean, Lac *39 E4 lake* Québec, SE Canada
Saint Joe River *46 D2 river* Idaho, NW USA North America
St. John *39 F4* New Brunswick, SE Canada
Saint-John *see* Saint John
Saint John River *41 H1 Fr.* Saint-John. *river* Canada/USA
St John's *55 G3 country capital* (Antigua and Barbuda) Antigua, Antigua and Barbuda
St. John's *39 H3 province capital* Newfoundland and Labrador, E Canada
Saint Joseph *45 F4* Missouri, C USA
St Julian's *see* San Giljan
St Kilda *88 A3 island* NW Scotland, United Kingdom
Saint Kitts and Nevis *55 F3 off.* Federation of Saint Christopher and Nevis, *var.* Saint Christopher-Nevis. *country* E West Indies

SAINT KITTS & NEVIS
West Indies

Official name Federation of Saint Christopher and Nevis
Formation 1983 / 1983
Capital Basseterre
Population 50,726 / 365 people per sq mile (141 people per sq km)
Total area 101 sq. miles (261 sq. km)
Languages English*, English Creole
Religions Anglican 33%, Methodist 29%, Other 22%, Moravian 9%, Roman Catholic 7%
Ethnic mix Black 95%, Mixed race 3%, White 1%, Other and Amerindian 1%
Government Parliamentary system
Currency Eastern Caribbean dollar = 100 cents
Literacy rate 98%
Calorie consumption 2546 kilocalories

St-Laurent *see* St-Laurent-du-Maroni
St-Laurent-du-Maroni *59 H3 var.* St-Laurent. NW French Guiana
St-Laurent, Fleuve *see* St. Lawrence
St. Lawrence *39 E4 Fr.* Fleuve St-Laurent. *river* Canada/USA

St. Lawrence, Gulf of *39 F3 gulf* NW Atlantic Ocean
Saint Lawrence Island *36 B2 island* Alaska, USA
St-Lô *90 B3 anc.* Briovera, Laudus. Manche, N France
St-Louis *90 E4* Haut-Rhin, NE France
Saint Louis *74 B3* NW Senegal
Saint Louis *45 G4* Missouri, C USA
Saint Lucia *55 E1 country* SE West Indies

SAINT LUCIA
West Indies

Official name Saint Lucia
Formation 1979 / 1979
Capital Castries
Population 162,178 / 687 people per sq mile (266 people per sq km)
Total area 239 sq. miles (620 sq. km)
Languages English*, French Creole
Religions Roman Catholic 90%, Other 10%
Ethnic mix Black 83%, Mulatto (mixed race) 13%, Asian 3%, Other 1%
Government Parliamentary system
Currency Eastern Caribbean dollar = 100 cents
Literacy rate 95%
Calorie consumption 2710 kilocalories

Saint Lucia Channel *55 H4 channel* Martinique/Saint Lucia
St-Malo *90 B3* Ille-et-Vilaine, NW France
St-Malo, Golfe de *90 A3 gulf* NW France
Saint Martin *see* Sint Maarten
St.Matthew's Island *see* Zadetkyi Kyun
St.Matthias Group *144 B3 island group* NE Papua New Guinea
St. Moritz *95 B7 Ger.* Sankt Moritz, *Rmsch.* San Murezzan. Graubünden, SE Switzerland
St-Nazaire *90 A4* Loire-Atlantique, NW France
Saint Nicholas *see* São Nicolau
Saint-Nicolas *see* Sint-Niklaas
St-Omer *90 C2* Pas-de-Calais, N France
Saint Paul *45 F2 state capital* Minnesota, N USA
St-Paul, Île *141 C6 var.* St.Paul Island. *island* Île St-Paul, NE French Southern and Antarctic Territories Antarctica Indian Ocea
St.Paul Island *see* St-Paul, Île
St Peter Port *89 D8 dependent territory capital* (Guernsey) C Guernsey, Channel Islands
Saint Petersburg *43 E4* Florida, SE USA
Saint Petersburg *see* Sankt-Peterburg
St-Pierre and Miquelon *39 G4 Fr.* Îles St-Pierre et Miquelon. *French territorial collectivity* NE North America
St-Quentin *90 C3* Aisne, N France
Saint Thomas *see* São Tomé, Sao Tome and Principe
Saint Thomas *see* Charlotte Amalie, Virgin Islands (US)
Saint Ubes *see* Setúbal
Saint Vincent *55 G4 island* N Saint Vincent and the Grenadines
Saint Vincent *see* São Vicente
Saint Vincent and the Grenadines *55 H4 country* SE West Indies

SAINT VINCENT & THE GRENADINES
West Indies

Official name Saint Vincent and the Grenadines
Formation 1979 / 1979
Capital Kingstown
Population 103,537 / 790 people per sq mile (305 people per sq km)
Total area 150 sq. miles (389 sq. km)
Languages English*, English Creole
Religions Anglican 47%, Methodist 28%, Roman Catholic 13%, Other 12%
Ethnic mix Black 66%, Mulatto (mixed race) 19%, Other 12%, Carib 2%, Asian 1%
Government Parliamentary system **Currency** Eastern Caribbean dollar = 100 cents
Literacy rate 88%
Calorie consumption 2914 kilocalories

Saint Vincent, Cape *see* São Vicente, Cabo de
Saint Vincent Passage *55 H4 passage* Saint Lucia/Saint Vincent and the Grenadines
Saint Yves *see* Setúbal
Saipan *142 B1 island/country capital* (Northern Mariana Islands) S Northern Mariana Islands
Saishū *see* Jeju-do
Sajama, Nevado *61 F4 mountain* W Bolivia
Sajószentpéter *99 D6* Borsod-Abaúj-Zemplén, NE Hungary
Sakākah *120 B4* Al Jawf, NW Saudi Arabia
Sakakawea, Lake *44 D1 reservoir* North Dakota, N USA
Sak'art'velo *see* Georgia
Sakata *130 D4* Yamagata, Honshū, C Japan
Sakhalin *115 G4 var.* Sakhalin. *island* SE Russian Federation
Sakhalin *see* Sakhalin, Ostrov
Sakhon Nakhon *see* Sakon Nakhon
Şäki *117 G2 Rus.* Sheki; *prev.* Nukha. NW Azerbaijan
Saki *see* Saky
Sakishima-shoto *130 A3 var.* Sakisima Syotō. *island group* SW Japan
Sakisima Syotō *see* Sakishima-shotō
Skiz *see* Saqqez
Skiz-Adasi *see* Chíos
Sakon Nakhon *136 D4 var.* Muang Sakon Nakhon, Sakhon Nakhon. Sakon Nakhon, E Thailand
Saky *109 F5 Rus.* Saki. Avtonomna Respublika Krym, S Ukraine
Sal *74 A3 island* Ilhas de Barlavento, NE Cape Verde
Sala *85 C6* Västmanland, C Sweden
Salacgriva *106 C3 Est.* Salatsi. N Latvia
Sala Consilina *97 D5* Campania, S Italy
Salado, Río *62 D5 river* E Argentina
Salado, Río *64 C3 river* C Argentina
Şalālah *121 D6* SW Oman
Salamá *52 B2* Baja Verapaz, C Guatemala
Salamanca *64 B4* Coquimbo, C Chile
Salamanca *92 D2 anc.* Helmantica, Salmantica. Castilla y León, NW Spain
Salamīyah *118 B3 var.* As Salamīyah. Ḥamāh, W Syria
Salang *see* Phuket
Salantai *106 B3* Klaipėda, NW Lithuania
Salatsi *see* Salacgrīva
Salavan *137 D5 var.* Saravan, Saravane. Salavan, S Laos
Salavat *111 D6* Respublika Bashkortostan, W Russian Federation
Sala y Gomez *153 F4 island* Chile, E Pacific Ocean
Sala y Gomez Fracture Zone *see* Sala y Gomez Ridge
Sala y Gomez Ridge *153 G4 var.* Sala y Gomez Fracture Zone. *fracture zone* SE Pacific Ocean
Salazar *see* N'Dalatando
Šalčininkai *107 C5* Vilnius, SE Lithuania
Salduba *see* Zaragoza
Saldus *106 B3 Ger.* Frauenburg. W Latvia
Sale *149 C7* Victoria, SE Australia
Salé *70 C2* NW Morocco
Salekhard *114 D3 prev.* Obdorsk. Yamalo-Nenetskiy Avtonomnyy Okrug, N Russian Federation
Salem *132 C2* Tamil Nādu, SE India
Salem *46 B3 state capital* Oregon, NW USA
Salerno *97 D5 anc.* Salernum. Campania, S Italy
Salerno, Gulf of *97 C5 Eng.* Gulf of Salerno. *gulf* S Italy
Salerno, Gulf of *see* Salerno, Golfo di
Salernum *see* Salerno
Salihorsk *107 C7 Rus.* Soligorsk. Minskaya Voblasts', S Belarus
Salima *79 E2* Central, C Malawi
Salina *45 E5* Kansas, C USA
Salina Cruz *51 F5* Oaxaca, SE Mexico
Salinas *60 A2* Guayas, W Ecuador
Salinas *47 B6* California, W USA
Salisbury *89 D7 var.* New Sarum. S England, United Kingdom
Salisbury *see* Harare
Salliq *see* Coral Harbour

Sallyana *see* Şalyän
Salmantica *see* Salamanca
Salmon River *46 D3 river* Idaho, NW USA
Salmon River Mountains *46 D3 mountain range* Idaho, NW USA
Salo *85 D6* Länsi-Suomi, SW Finland
Salon-de-Provence *91 D6* Bouches-du-Rhône, SE France
Salonica/Salonika *see* Thessaloníki
Salonta *108 A3 Hung.* Nagyszalonta. Bihor, W Romania
Sal'sk *111 B7* Rostovskaya Oblast', SW Russian Federation
Salt *see* As Salţ
Salta *64 C2* Salta, NW Argentina
Saltash *89 C7* SW England, United Kingdom
Saltillo *51 E3* Coahuila, NE Mexico
Salt Lake City *44 B4 state capital* Utah, W USA
Salto *64 D4* Salto, N Uruguay
Salton Sea *47 D8 lake* California, W USA
Salvador *63 G3 prev.* São Salvador. *state capital* Bahia, E Brazil
Salween *124 C2 Bur.* Thanlwin, *Chin.* Nu Chiang, Nu Jiang. *river* SE Asia
Şalyän *135 E3 var.* Sallyana. Mid Western, W Nepal
Salzburg *95 D6 anc.* Juvavum. Salzburg, N Austria
Salzgitter *94 C4 prev.* Watenstedt-Salzgitter. Niedersachsen, C Germany
Salzwedel *94 C3* Sachsen-Anhalt, N Germany
Šamac *see* Bosanski Šamac
Samakhixai *see* Attapu
Samalayuca *50 C1* Chihuahua, N Mexico
Samar *139 F2 island* C Philippines
Samara *114 B3 prev.* Kuybyshev. Samarskaya Oblast', W Russian Federation
Samarang *see* Semarang
Samarinda *138 D4* Borneo, C Indonesia
Samarkand *see* Samarqand
Samarkandski/Samarkandskoye *see* Temirtau
Samarobriva *see* Amiens
Samarqand *123 E2 Rus.* Samarkand. Samarqand Viloyati, C Uzbekistan
Samawa *see* As Samāwah
Sambalpur *135 F4* Orissa, E India
Sambava *79 G2* Antsiranana, NE Madagascar
Sambir *108 B2 Rus.* Sambor. L'vivs'ka Oblast', NW Ukraine
Sambor *see* Sambir
Sambre *90 D2 river* Belgium/France
Samfya *78 D2* Luapula, N Zambia
Saminatal *94 E2 valley* Austria/Liechtenstein Europe
Samnän *see* Semnän
Sam Neua *see* Xam Nua
Samoa *145 E4 off.* Independent State of Samoa, *var.* Sāmoa; *prev.* Western Samoa. *country* W Polynesia

SAMOA
Australasia & Oceania

Official name Independent State of Samoa
Formation 1962 / 1962
Capital Apia
Population 200,000 / 183 people per sq mile (71 people per sq km)
Total area 1104 sq. miles (2860 sq. km)
Languages Samoan*, English*
Religions Christian 99%, Other 1%
Ethnic mix Polynesian 91%, Euronesian 7%, Other 2%
Government Parliamentary system
Currency Tala = 100 sene
Literacy rate 99%
Calorie consumption 2997 kilocalories

Sāmoa *see* Samoa
Samoa Basin *143 E3 undersea basin* W Pacific Ocean
Samoa, Independent State of *see* Samoa
Samobor *100 A2* Zagreb, N Croatia
Sámos *105 E6 prev.* Limín Vathéos. Sámos, Dodekánisa, Greece, Aegean Sea
Sámos *105 D6 island* Dodekánisa, Greece, Aegean Sea
Samothrace *see* Samothráki

Samothráki 104 D4 Samothráki,
NE Greece
Samothraki 104 C4 anc. Samothrace.
island NE Greece
Sampit 138 C4 Borneo, C Indonesia
Sâmraông 137 D5 prev. Phumĭ
Sâmraông, Phum Samrong. Siěmréab,
NW Cambodia
Samsun 116 D2 anc. Amisus. Samsun,
N Turkey
Samt'redia 117 F2 prev. Samtredia.
W Georgia
Samtredia see Samt'redia
Samui, Ko 137 C6 island SW Thailand
Samut Prakan 137 C5 var. Muang Samut
Prakan, Paknam. Samut Prakan,
C Thailand
San 74 D3 Ségou, C Mali
San 99 E5 river SE Poland
Şan'a' 121 B6 Eng. Sana. country capital
(Yemen) W Yemen
Sana 100 B3 river NW Bosnia and
Herzegovina
Sanae 154 B2 South African research
station Antarctica
Sanaga 77 B5 river C Cameroon
San Ambrosio, Isla 57 A5 Eng. San
Ambrosio Island. island W Chile
San Ambrosio Island see San Ambrosio,
Isla
Sanandaj 120 C3 prev. Sinneh.
Kordestán, W Iran
San Andrés, Isla de 53 F3 island
NW Colombia, Caribbean Sea
San Andrés Tuxtla 51 F4 var. Tuxtla.
Veracruz-Llave, E Mexico
San Angelo 49 F3 Texas, SW USA
San Antonio 52 B2 Toledo, S Belize
San Antonio 64 B4 Valparaíso, C Chile
San Antonio 49 F4 Texas, SW USA
San Antonio Oeste 65 C5 Río Negro,
E Argentina
San Antonio River 49 G4 river Texas,
SW USA
Sanata Uxía de Ribeira 92 B1 var.
Ribeira. Galicia, NW Spain
Sanãw 121 C6 var. Sanaw. NE Yemen
San Benedicto, Isla 50 B4 island
W Mexico
San Benito 52 B1 Petén, N Guatemala
San Benito 49 G5 Texas, SW USA
San Bernardino 47 C7 California,
W USA
San Blas 50 C3 Sinaloa, C Mexico
San Blas, Cape 42 D3 headland Florida,
SE USA
San Blas, Cordillera de 53 G4 mountain
range NE Panama
San Carlos 52 D4 Río San Juan,
S Nicaragua
San Carlos 48 B2 Arizona, SW USA
San Carlos see Quesada, Costa Rica
San Carlos de Ancud see Ancud
San Carlos de Bariloche 65 B5 Río
Negro, SW Argentina
San Carlos del Zulia 58 C2 Zulia,
W Venezuela
San Clemente Island 47 B8 island
Channel Islands, California, W USA
San Cristóbal 58 C2 Táchira,
W Venezuela
San Cristóbal 144 C4 var. Makira. island
SE Solomon Islands
San Cristóbal see San Cristóbal de
Las Casas
San Cristóbal de Las Casas 51 G5 var.
San Cristóbal. Chiapas, SE Mexico
San Cristóbal, Isla 60 B5 var. Chatham
Island. island Galápagos Islands,
Ecuador, E Pacific Ocean
Sancti Spíritus 54 B2 Sancti Spíritus,
C Cuba
Sandakan 138 D3 Sabah, East Malaysia
Sandalwood Island see Sumba, Pulau
Sandanski 104 C3 prev. Sveti Vrach.
Blagoevgrad, SW Bulgaria
Sanday 88 D2 island NE Scotland, United
Kingdom
Sanders 48 C2 Arizona, SW USA
Sand Hills 44 D3 mountain range
Nebraska, C USA
San Diego 47 C8 California, W USA
Sandnes 85 A6 Rogaland, S Norway
Sandomierz 98 D4 Rus. Sandomir.
Świętokrzyskie, C Poland
Sandomir see Sandomierz
Sandoway see Thandwe

Sandpoint 46 C1 Idaho, NW USA
Sand Springs 49 G1 Oklahoma, C USA
Sandusky 40 D3 Ohio, N USA
Sandvika 85 A6 Akershus, S Norway
Sandviken 85 C6 Gävleborg, C Sweden
Sandwich Island see Efate
Sandwich Islands see Hawai'ian Islands
Sandy Bay 93 H5 Saskatchewan,
C Canada
Sandy City 44 B4 Utah, W USA
Sandy Lake 38 B3 lake Ontario,
C Canada
San Esteban 52 D2 Olancho, C Honduras
San Eugenio/San Eugenio del Cuareim
see Artigas
San Felipe 58 D1 Yaracuy,
NW Venezuela
San Felipe de Puerto Plata see Puerto
Plata
San Félix, Isla 57 A5 Eng. San Felix
Island. island W Chile
San Felix Island see San Félix, Isla
San Fernando 92 C5 prev. Isla de León.
Andalucía, S Spain
San Fernando 55 H5 Trinidad, Trinidad
and Tobago
San Fernando 46 D1 California,
W USA
San Fernando 58 D2 var. San Fernando
de Apure. Apure, C Venezuela
San Fernando de Apure see San
Fernando
San Fernando del Valle de Catamarca
64 C3 var. Catamarca. Catamarca,
NW Argentina
San Fernando de Monte Cristi see
Monte Cristi
San Francisco 47 B6 California, W USA
San Francisco del Oro 50 C2
Chihuahua, N Mexico
San Francisco de Macorís 55 E3
C Dominican Republic
San Fructuoso see Tacuarembó
San Gabriel 60 B1 Carchi, N Ecuador
San Gabriel Mountains 46 E1 mountain
range California, USA
Sangihe, Kepulauan see Sangir,
Kepulauan
San Giljan 102 B5 var. St Julian's.
N Malta
Sangir, Kepulauan 139 F3 var.
Kepulauan Sangihe. island group
N Indonesia
Sängli 132 B1 Mahārāshtra, W India
Sangmélima 77 B5 Sud, S Cameroon
Sangre de Cristo Mountains 48 D1
mountain range Colorado/New Mexico,
C USA
San Ignacio 52 B1 prev. Cayo, El Cayo.
Cayo, W Belize
San Ignacio 61 F3 El Beni, N Bolivia
San Ignacio 50 B2 Baja California Sur,
NW Mexico
San Joaquin Valley 47 B7 valley
California, W USA
San Jorge, Gulf of 65 C6 var. Gulf of
Jorge. gulf S Argentina
San Jorge, Gulf of see San Jorge, Golfo
San José 53 E4 country capital
(Costa Rica) San José,
C Costa Rica
San José 61 G3 var. San José de
Chiquitos. Santa Cruz, E Bolivia
San José 52 B3 var. Puerto San José.
Escuintla, S Guatemala
San José 47 B6 California, W USA
San José see San José del Guaviare,
Colombia
San José de Chiquitos see San José
San José de Cúcuta see Cúcuta
San José del Guaviare 58 C4 var. San
José. Guaviare, S Colombia
San Juan 64 B4 San Juan, W Argentina
San Juan 55 F3 dependent territory
capital (Puerto Rico) NE Puerto Rico
San Juan see San Juan de los Morros
San Juan Bautista 64 D3 Misiones,
S Paraguay
San Juan Bautista see Villahermosa
San Juan Bautista Tuxtepec see Tuxtepec
San Juan de Alicante see Sant Joan
d'Alacant
San Juan del Norte 53 E4 var. Greytown.
Río San Juan, SE Nicaragua
San Juan de los Morros 58 D2 var. San
Juan. Guárico, N Venezuela
San Juanito, Isla 50 C4 island C Mexico

San Juan Mountains 48 D1 mountain
range Colorado, C USA
San Juan, Río 53 E4 river Costa Rica/
Nicaragua
San Juan River 48 C1 river Colorado/
Utah, W USA
San Julián see Puerto San Julián
Sankt-Bartholomäi see Palamuse
Sankt Gallen 95 B7 var. St. Gallen, Eng.
Saint Gall, Fr. St-Gall. Sankt Gallen,
NE Switzerland
Sankt-Georgen see Sfântu Gheorghe
Sankt-Jakobi see Pärnu-Jaagupi,
Pärnumaa, Estonia
Sankt Martin see Martin
Sankt Moritz see St. Moritz
Sankt-Peterburg 110 B4 prev.
Leningrad, Petrograd, Eng.
Saint Petersburg, Fin. Pietari.
Leningradskaya Oblast', NW Russian
Federation
Sankt Pölten 95 E6 Niederösterreich,
N Austria
Sankt Veit am Flaum see Rijeka
Sankuru 77 D6 river C Dem. Rep. Congo
Şanlıurfa 117 E4 prev. Sanli Urfa, Urfa;
anc. Edessa. şanlıurfa, S Turkey
Sanli Urfa see Şanlıurfa
San Lorenzo 61 G5 Tarija, S Bolivia
San Lorenzo 60 A1 Esmeraldas,
N Ecuador
San Lorenzo, Isla 60 C4 island W Peru
Sanlúcar de Barrameda 92 C5
Andalucía, S Spain
San Luis 64 C4 San Luis, C Argentina
San Luis 52 B2 Petén, NE Guatemala
San Luis Obispo 47 B7 California,
W USA
San Luis Potosí 51 E3 San Luis Potosí,
C Mexico
San Luis Río Colorado 50 A1 var.
San Luis Río Colorado. Sonora,
NW Mexico
San Luis Río Colorado see San Luis Río
Colorado
San Marcos 52 A2 San Marcos,
W Guatemala
San Marcos 49 G4 Texas, SW USA
San Marcos de Arica see Arica
San Marino 96 E1 country capital (San
Marino) C San Marino
San Marino 96 D1 off. Republic of San
Marino. country S Europe

SAN MARINO
Southern Europe

Official name Republic of San Marino
Formation 1631 / 1631
Capital San Marino
Population 32,140 / 1539 people
per sq mile (527 people per sq km)
Total area 23.6 sq. miles (61 sq. km)
Languages Italian*
Religions Roman Catholic 93%,
Other and nonreligious 7%
Ethnic mix Sammarinese 88%,
Italian 10%, Other 2%
Government Parliamentary system
Currency Euro = 100 cents
Literacy rate 99%
Calorie consumption Not available

San Marino, Republic of see San Marino
San Martín 154 A2 Argentinian research
station Antarctica
San Mateo 59 E2 Anzoátegui,
NE Venezuela
San Matías 61 H3 Santa Cruz, E Bolivia
San Matías, Gulf of 65 C5 var. Gulf of
San Matías. gulf E Argentina
San Matías, Gulf of see San Matías, Golfo
Sanmenxia 128 C4 var. Shan Xian.
Henan, C China
San Miguel 52 C3 San Miguel,
SE El Salvador
San Miguel 50 D2 Coahuila,
N Mexico
San Miguel de Ibarra see Ibarra
San Miguel de Tucumán 64 C3 var.
Tucumán. Tucumán, N Argentina
San Miguelito 53 G4 Panamá, C Panama
San Miguel, Río 61 G3 river E Bolivia
San Murezzan see St. Moritz
Sannär see Sennar
Sânnicolau-Mare see Sânnicolau Mare

Sânnicolau Mare 108 A4 var.
Sânnicolau-Mare, Hung.
Nagyszentmiklós; prev. Sânnicláuş
Mare, Sínnicolau Mare. Timiş,
W Romania
Sanok 99 E5 Podkarpackie, SE Poland
San Pablo 61 F5 Potosí, S Bolivia
San Pedro 52 C1 Corozal, NE Belize
San-Pédro 74 D5 S Côte d'Ivoire
San Pedro 50 D3 var. San Pedro de las
Colonias. Coahuila, NE Mexico
San Pedro de la Cueva 50 C2 Sonora,
NW Mexico
San Pedro de las Colonias see San Pedro
San Pedro de Lloc 60 B3 La Libertad,
NW Peru
San Pedro Mártir, Sierra 50 A1
mountain range NW Mexico
San Pedro Sula 52 C2 Cortés,
NW Honduras
San Rafael 64 B4 Mendoza, W Argentina
San Rafael Mountains 47 C7 mountain
range California, W USA
San Ramón de la Nueva Orán 64 C2
Salta, N Argentina
San Remo 96 A3 Liguria, NW Italy
San Salvador 52 B3 country capital
(El Salvador) San Salvador,
SW El Salvador
San Salvador 54 D2 prev. Watlings
Island. island E Bahamas
San Salvador de Jujuy 64 C2 var. Jujuy.
Jujuy, N Argentina
San Salvador, Isla 60 A4 island Ecuador
Sansanné-Mango 75 E4 var. Mango.
N Togo
Sansepolcro 96 C3 Toscana, C Italy
San Severo 97 D5 Puglia, SE Italy
Santa Ana 61 F3 El Beni, N Bolivia
Santa Ana 52 B3 Santa Ana,
NW El Salvador
Santa Ana de Coro see Coro
Santa Ana Mountains 46 E2 mountain
range California, W USA
Santa Barbara 50 C2 Chihuahua,
N Mexico
Santa Barbara 47 C7 California, W USA
Santa Catalina de Armada 92 B1
Galicia, NW Spain
Santa Catalina Island 47 B8 island
Channel Islands, California, W USA
Santa Catarina 63 E5 off. Estado de
Santa Catarina. region S Brazil
Santa Catarina 63 E5 off. Estado de
Santa Catarina. state S Brazil
Santa Catarina, Estado de see Santa
Catarina
Santa Clara 54 B2 Villa Clara, C Cuba
Santa Clarita 46 D1 California, USA
Santa Cruz 76 E2 São Tomé, S Sao Tome
and Principe, Africa
Santa Cruz 61 G4 department E Bolivia
Santa Cruz Barillas see Barillas
Santa Cruz del Quiché 52 B2 Quiché,
W Guatemala
Santa Cruz de Tenerife 70 A3 Tenerife,
Islas Canarias, Spain, NE Atlantic Ocean
Santa Cruz, Isla 60 B5 var. Indefatigable
Island, Isla Chávez. island Galápagos
Islands, Ecuador, E Pacific Ocean
Santa Cruz Islands 144 D3 island group
E Solomon Islands
Santa Cruz, Río 65 B7 river S Argentina
Santa Elena 52 B1 Cayo, W Belize
Santa Fe 64 C4 Santa Fe, C Argentina
Santa Fe 48 D1 state capital New Mexico,
SW USA
Santa Fe see Bogotá
Santa Fe de Bogotá see Bogotá
Santa Genoveva 50 B3 mountain
NW Mexico
Santa Isabel 144 C3 var. Bughotu. island
N Solomon Islands
Santa Isabel see Malabo
Santa Lucia Range 47 B7 mountain
range California, W USA
Santa Margarita, Isla 50 B3 island
NW Mexico
Santa Maria 63 E5 Rio Grande do Sul,
S Brazil
Santa Maria 47 B7 California, USA
Santa Maria 92 A5 island Azores,
Portugal, NE Atlantic Ocean
Santa Maria del Buen Aire see Buenos
Aires

Santa María, Isla 60 A5 var. Isla
Floreana, Charles Island. island
Galápagos Islands, Ecuador, E Pacific
Ocean
Santa Marta 58 B1 Magdalena,
N Colombia
Santa Maura see Lefkáda
Santa Monica 46 D1 California,
W USA
Santana 76 E2 São Tomé, C Sao Tome
and Principe, Africa
Santander 92 D1 Cantabria, N Spain
Santarém 63 E2 Pará, N Brazil
Santarém 92 B3 anc. Scalabis. Santarém,
W Portugal
Santa Rosa 64 C4 La Pampa,
C Argentina
Santa Rosa see Santa Rosa de Copán
Santa Rosa de Copán 52 C2 var. Santa
Rosa. C Honduras
Santa Rosa Island 47 B8 island
California, W USA
Sant Carles de la Rápida see Sant Carles
de la Rápita
Sant Carles de la Ràpita 93 F3 var. Sant
Carles de la Rápida. Cataluña,
NE Spain
Santiago 64 B4 var. Santiago.
country capital (Chile) Santiago,
C Chile
Santiago 55 E3 var. Santiago de los
Caballeros. N Dominican Republic
Santiago 53 F5 Veraguas, S Panama
Santiago 74 A3 var. São Tiago. island
Ilhas de Sotavento, S Cape Verde
Santiago see Santiago de Cuba, Cuba
Santiago see Santiago de Compostela
Santiago de Compostela 92 B1 var.
Santiago, Eng. Compostella; anc.
Campus Stellae. Galicia, NW Spain
Santiago de Cuba 54 C3 var. Santiago.
Santiago de Cuba, E Cuba
Santiago de Guayaquil see Guayaquil
Santiago del Estero 64 C3 Santiago del
Estero, C Argentina
Santiago de los Caballeros see Santiago,
Dominican Republic
Santiago de los Caballeros see Ciudad de
Guatemala, Guatemala
Santiago Pinotepa Nacional see
Pinotepa Nacional
Santiago, Río 60 B2 river N Peru
Santi Quaranta see Sarandë
Santissima Trinidad see Jilong
Sant Joan d'Alacant 93 F4 Cast. San
Juan de Alicante. Valenciana,
E Spain
Sant Julià de Loria 91 A8 Sant Julià de
Lòria, SW Andorra Europe
Santo see Espíritu Santo
Santo Antão 74 A2 island Ilhas de
Barlavento, N Cape Verde
Santo António 76 E1 Príncipe,
N Sao Tome and Principe, Africa
Santo Domingo 55 D3 prev. Ciudad
Trujillo. country capital (Dominican
Republic) SE Dominican Republic
Santo Domingo de los Colorados 60 B1
Pichincha, NW Ecuador
Santo Domingo Tehuantepec see
Tehuantepec
San Tomé de Guayana see Ciudad
Guayana
Santos 63 F4 São Paulo, S Brazil
Santos Plateau 57 D5 undersea plateau
SW Atlantic Ocean
Santo Tomé 64 D3 Corrientes,
NE Argentina
Santo Tomé de Guayana see Ciudad
Guayana
San Valentín, Cerro 65 A6 mountain
S Chile
San Vicente 52 C3 San Vicente,
C El Salvador
São Francisco, Rio 63 F3 river E Brazil
São Hill 73 C7 Iringa, S Tanzania
São João da Madeira 92 B2 Aveiro,
N Portugal
São Jorge 92 A5 island Azores, Portugal,
NE Atlantic Ocean
São Luís 63 F2 state capital Maranhão,
NE Brazil
São Mandol see São Manuel, Rio
São Manuel, Rio 63 E3 var. São Mandol,
Teles Pirés. river C Brazil
São Marcos, Baía de 63 F1 bay
N Brazil

São Miguel 92 A5 island Azores,
Portugal, NE Atlantic Ocean
Saona, Isla 55 E3 island SE Dominican
Republic
Saône 91 D5 river E France
São Nicolau 74 A3 Eng. Saint Nicholas.
island Ilhas de Barlavento, N Cape
Verde
São Paulo 63 E4 state capital São Paulo,
S Brazil
São Paulo 63 E4 off. Estado de São
Paulo. region S Brazil
São Paulo 63 E4 off. Estado de São
Paulo. state S Brazil
São Paulo de Loanda see Luanda
São Paulo, Estado de see São Paulo
São Pedro do Rio Grande do Sul see
Rio Grande
São Roque, Cabo de 63 G2 headland
E Brazil
São Salvador see Salvador, Brazil
São Salvador/São Salvador do Congo
see M'Banza Congo, Angola
São Tiago see Santiago
São Tomé 77 A5 country capital
(Sao Tome and Principe)
São Tomé, S Sao Tome
and Principe
São Tomé 76 E2 Eng. Saint Thomas.
island S Sao Tome and Principe
Sao Tome and Principe 76 D1 off.
Democratic Republic of Sao Tome and
Principe. country E Atlantic Ocean

SÃO TOMÉ & PRÍNCIPE
West Africa

Official name The Democratic Republic
of Sao Tome and Principe
Formation 1975 / 1975
Capital São Tomé
Population 200,000 / 539 people
per sq mile (208 people per sq km)
Total area 386 sq. miles (1001 sq. km)
Languages Portuguese Creole,
Portuguese*
Religions Roman Catholic 84%, Other 16%
Ethnic mix Black 90%, Portuguese
and Creole 10%
Government Presidential system
Currency Dobra = 100 céntimos
Literacy rate 89%
Calorie consumption 2734 kilocalories

**Sao Tome and Principe, Democratic
Republic of** see Sao Tome and Principe
São Tomé, Pico de 76 D2 mountain
São Tomé, S Sao Tome and Principe,
Africa
São Vicente 74 A3 Eng. Saint Vincent.
island Ilhas de Barlavento, N Cape
Verde
São Vicente, Cabo de 92 B5 Eng.
Cape Saint Vincent, Port. Cabode São
Vicente. cape S Portugal
São Vicente, Cabo de see São Vicente,
Cabo de
Sápai see Sápes
Sapele 75 F5 Delta, S Nigeria
Sápes 104 C4 var. Sápai. Anatolikí
Makedonía kai Thráki, NE Greece
Sapir 119 B7 prev. Sappir. Southern,
S Israel
Sa Pobla 93 G3 Mallorca, Spain,
W Mediterranean Sea
Sappir see Sapir
Sapporo 130 D2 Hokkaidō,
NE Japan
Sapri 97 D6 Campania, S Italy
Sapulpa 49 G1 Oklahoma, C USA
Saqqez 120 C2 var. Saghez, Sakiz,
Saqqiz. Kordestān, NW Iran
Saqqiz see Saqqez
Sara Buri 137 C5 var. Saraburi. Saraburi,
C Thailand
Saraburi see Sara Buri
Saragossa see Zaragoza
Saragt see Sarahs
Saraguro 60 B2 Loja, S Ecuador
Sarahs 122 D3 var. Saragt, Rus. Serakhs.
Ahal Welaýaty, S Turkmenistan
Sarajevo 100 C4 country capital
(Bosnia and Herzegovina) Federacija
Bosna I Hercegovina, SE Bosnia and
Herzegovina
Sarakhs 120 E2 Khorāsān-Razavī,
NE Iran

Saraktash 111 D6 Orenburgskaya
Oblast', W Russian Federation
Saran' 114 C4 Kaz. Saran. Karagandy,
C Kazakhstan
Saranda see Sarandë
Sarandë 101 C7 var. Saranda, It. Porto
Edda; prev. Santi Quaranta. Vlorë,
S Albania
Saransk 111 C5 Respublika Mordoviya,
W Russian Federation
Sarasota 43 E4 Florida, SE USA
Saratov 114 B3 Saratovskaya Oblast',
W Russian Federation
Saravan/Saravane see Salavan
Sarawak 138 D3 state East Malaysia
Sarawak see Kuching
Sarcelles 90 D1 Val-d'Oise, Île-de-
France, N France Europe
Sardinia 97 A5 Eng. Sardinia. island
Italy, C Mediterranean Sea
Sardinia see Sardegna
Sarera, Teluk see Cenderawasih, Teluk
Sargasso Sea 66 B4 sea W Atlantic Ocean
Sargodha 134 C2 Punjab, NE Pakistan
Sarh 76 C4 prev. Fort-Archambault.
Moyen-Chari, S Chad
Sāri 120 D2 var. Sari, Sāri. Māzandarān,
N Iran
Saria 105 E7 island SE Greece
Sarıkamış 117 F3 Kars, NE Turkey
Sarikol Range 123 G3 Rus. Sarykol'skiy
Khrebet. mountain range China/
Tajikistan
Sark 89 D8 Fr. Sercq. island Channel
Islands
Şarkışla 116 D3 Sivas, C Turkey
Sarmiento 65 B6 Chubut, S Argentina
Sarnia 38 C5 Ontario, S Canada
Sarny 108 C1 Rivnens'ka Oblast',
NW Ukraine
Sarochyna 107 D5 Rus. Sorochino.
Vitsyebskaya Voblasts', N Belarus
Sarov 111 C5 prev. Sarova. Respublika
Mordoviya, SW Russian Federation
Sarova see Sarov
Sarpsborg 85 B6 Østfold, S Norway
Sarrebruck see Saarbrücken
Sartène 91 E7 Corse, France,
C Mediterranean Sea
Sarthe 90 B4 river N France
Sárti 104 C4 Kentrikí Makedonía,
N Greece
Saruhan see Manisa
Sarykol'skiy Khrebet see Sarikol Range
Sary-Tash 123 F2 Oshskaya Oblast',
SW Kyrgyzstan
Saryyesik-Atyrau, Peski 123 G1 desert
E Kazakhstan
Sasebo 131 A7 Nagasaki, Kyūshū,
SW Japan
Saskatchewan 37 F5 province
SW Canada
Saskatchewan 37 F5 river Manitoba/
Saskatchewan, C Canada
Saskatoon 37 F5 Saskatchewan,
S Canada
Sasovo 111 B5 Ryazanskaya Oblast',
W Russian Federation
Sassandra 74 D5 S Côte d'Ivoire
Sassandra 74 D5 var. Ibo, Sassandra
Fleuve. river S Côte d'Ivoire
Sassandra Fleuve see Sassandra
Sassari 97 A5 Sardegna, Italy,
C Mediterranean Sea
Sassenheim 86 C3 Zuid-Holland,
W Netherlands
Sassnitz 94 D2 Mecklenburg-
Vorpommern, NE Germany
Sathmar see Satu Mare
Sátoraljaújhely 99 D6 Borsod-Abaúj-
Zemplén, NE Hungary
Satpura Range 134 D4 mountain range
C India
Satsuma-Sendai 131 A8 Kagoshima,
Kyūshū, SW Japan
Satsunan-shoto 130 A3 island group
Nansei-shotō, SW Japan Asia
Sattanen 84 D3 Lappi, NE Finland
Satu Mare 108 B3 Ger. Sathmar,
Hung. Szatmárrnémeti. Satu Mare,
NW Romania
Sau see Sava
Saudi Arabia 121 B5 off. Kingdom
of Saudi Arabia, Ar. Al 'Arabīyah as
Su'ūdīyah, Ar. Al Mamlakah al
'Arabīyah as Su'ūdīyah. country
SW Asia

SAUDI ARABIA
Southwest Asia

Official name Kingdom of Saudi Arabia
Formation 1932 / 1932
Capital Riyadh
Population 28.1 million / 34 people
per sq mile (13 people per sq km)
Total area 756,981 sq. miles
(1,960,582 sq. km)
Languages Arabic*
Religions Sunni Muslim 85%,
Shi'a Muslim 15%
Ethnic mix Arab 72%, Foreign residents
(mostly south and southeast Asian) 20%,
Afro-Asian 8%
Government Monarchy
Currency Saudi riyal = 100 halalat
Literacy rate 86%
Calorie consumption 3076 kilocalories

Saudi Arabia, Kingdom of see Saudi
Arabia
Sauer see Sûre
Saugor see Sāgar
Saulkrasti 106 C3 C Latvia
Sault Sainte Marie 38 C4 Michigan,
N USA
Sault Sainte Marie 40 C1 Michigan,
N USA
Sault Ste. Marie 38 C4 Ontario,
S Canada
Saumur 90 B4 Maine-et-Loire,
NW France
Saurimo 78 C1 Port. Henrique de
Carvalho, Vila Henrique de Carvalho.
Lunda Sul, NE Angola
Sava 107 E6 Mahilyowskaya Voblasts',
E Belarus
Savá 52 D2 Colón, N Honduras
Savai'i 145 E4 island NW Samoa
Savannah 43 E2 Georgia, SE USA
Savannah River 43 E2 river Georgia/
South Carolina, SE USA
Savannakhét 136 D4 var. Khanthabouli.
Savannakhét, S Laos
Savanna-La-Mar 54 A5 W Jamaica
Savaria see Szombathely
Save 100 B3 Eng. Save, Ger. Sau, Hung.
Száva. river SE Europe
Save see Sava
Save, Rio 79 E3 var. Sabi. river
Mozambique/Zimbabwe
Saverne 90 E3 var. Zabern; anc. Tres
Tabernae. Bas-Rhin, NE France
Savigliano 96 A2 Piemonte, NW Italy
Savigsivik see Savissivik
Savinski see Savinskiy
Savinskiy 110 C3 var. Savinski.
Arkhangel'skaya Oblast', NW Russian
Federation
Savissivik 82 D1 var. Savigsivik.
Avannaarsua, N Greenland
Savoie 91 D5 cultural region E France
Savona 96 A2 Liguria, NW Italy
Savu Sea 139 E5 Ind. Laut Sawu. sea
S Indonesia
Sawakin see Suakin
Sawdirī see Sodiri
Sawhāj 72 B2 var. Sawhāj, var. Sohāg,
Suliag. C Egypt
Sawhāj see Sawhāj
Şawqirah 121 D6 var. Suqrah. S Oman
Sawu, Laut see Savu Sea
Saxe see Sachsen
Saxony see Sachsen
Sayaboury see Xaignabouli
Sayanskiy Khrebet 112 D3 mountain
range S Russian Federation
Saýat 122 D3 Rus. Sayat. Lebap
Welaýaty, E Turkmenistan
Sayaxché 52 B2 Petén, N Guatemala
Şaydā/Sayida see Saïda
Sayhūt 121 D6 E Yemen
Saynshand 127 E2 Dornogovĭ,
SE Mongolia
Sayre 41 E3 Pennsylvania, NE USA
Say'ūn 121 C6 var. Saywūn. C Yemen
Saywūn see Say'ūn
Scalabis see Santarém
Scandinavia 66 D2 geophysical region
NW Europe
Scarborough 89 D5 N England, United
Kingdom
Scarpanto see Kárpathos
Scebeli see Shebeli
Schaan 94 E1 W Liechtenstein Europe

Schaerbeek *87 C6* Brussels, C Belgium
Schaffhausen *95 B7* Fr. Schaffhouse.
  Schaffhausen, N Switzerland
Schaffhouse *see* Schaffhausen
Schagen *86 C2* Noord-Holland,
  NW Netherlands
Schaulen *see* Šiauliai
Schebschi Mountains *see* Shebshi
  Mountains
Scheessel *94 B3* Niedersachsen,
  NW Germany
Schefferville *39 E2* Québec, E Canada
Schelde *see* Scheldt
Scheldt *87 B5* Dut. Schelde, Fr. Escaut.
  river W Europe
Schell Creek Range *47 D5* mountain
  range Nevada, W USA
Schenectady *41 F3* New York, NE USA
Schertz *49 G4* Texas, SW USA
Schiermonnikoog *86 D1* Fris.
  Skiermûntseach. *island*
  Waddeneilanden, N Netherlands
Schijndel *86 D4* Noord-Brabant,
  S Netherlands
Schil *see* Jiu
Schiltigheim *90 E3* Bas-Rhin, NE France
Schivelbein *see* Świdwin
Schleswig *94 B2* Schleswig-Holstein,
  N Germany
Schleswig-Holstein *94 B2* state
  N Germany
Schlettstadt *see* Sélestat
Schlochau *see* Człuchów
Schneekoppe *see* Sněžka
Schneidemühl *see* Piła
Schoden *see* Skuodas
Schönebeck *94 C4* Sachsen-Anhalt,
  C Germany
Schönlanke *see* Trzcianka
Schooten *see* Schoten
Schoten *87 C5* var. Schooten.
  Antwerpen, N Belgium
Schouwen *86 B4* island SW Netherlands
Schwabenalb *see* Schwäbische Alb
Schwäbische Alb *95 B6* var.
  Schwabenalb, Eng. Swabian Jura.
  mountain range S Germany
Schwandorf *95 C5* Bayern, SE Germany
Schwaz *95 C7* Tirol, W Austria
Schweidnitz *see* Świdnica
Schweinfurt *95 B5* Bayern, SE Germany
Schweiz *see* Switzerland
Schwerin *94 C3* Mecklenburg-
  Vorpommern, N Germany
Schwertberg *see* Świecie
Schwiebus *see* Świebodzin
Schwyz *95 B7* var. Schwiz. Schwyz,
  C Switzerland
Schyl *see* Jiu
Scio *see* Chíos
Scoresby Sound/Scoresbysund *see*
  Ittoqqortoormiit
Scoresby Sund *see* Kangertittivaq
Scotia Sea *57 C8* sea SW Atlantic Ocean
Scotland *88 C3* cultural region Scotland,
  U K
Scott Base *154 B4* NZ research station
  Antarctica
Scott Island *154 B5* island Antarctica
Scottsbluff *44 D3* Nebraska, C USA
Scottsboro *42 D1* Alabama, S USA
Scottsdale *48 B2* Arizona, SW USA
Scranton *41 F3* Pennsylvania, NE USA
Scrobesbyrig' *see* Shrewsbury
Scupi *see* Skopje
Scutari *see* Shkodër
Scutari, Lake *101 C5* Alb. Liqeni i
  Shkodrës, SCr. Skadarsko Jezero. lake
  Albania/Montenegro
Scyros *see* Skýros
Searcy *42 B1* Arkansas, C USA
Seattle *46 B2* Washington, NW USA
Sébaco *52 D3* Matagalpa, W Nicaragua
Sebaste/Sebastia *see* Sivas
Sebastián Vizcaíno, Bahía *50 A2* bay
  NW Mexico
Sebastopol *see* Sevastopol'
Sebenico *see* Šibenik
Sechura, Bahía de *60 A3* bay NW Peru
Secunderābād *132 D6* var.
  Sikandarabad. Andhra Pradesh, C India
Sedan *90 D3* Ardennes, N France
Seddon *151 D5* Marlborough, South
  Island, New Zealand
Seddonville *151 C5* West Coast, South
  Island, New Zealand
Sédhiou *74 B3* SW Senegal

Sedlez *see* Siedlce
Sedona *48 B2* Arizona, SW USA
Sedunum *see* Sion
Seeland *see* Sjælland
Seenu Atoll *see* Addu Atoll
Seesen *94 B4* Niedersachsen, C Germany
Segestica *see* Sisak
Segezha *110 B3* Respublika Kareliya,
  NW Russian Federation
Seghedin *see* Szeged
Segna *see* Senj
Segodunum *see* Rodez
Ségou *74 D3* var. Segu. Ségou, C Mali
Segovia *92 D2* Castilla y León, C Spain
Segoviao Wangki *see* Coco, Río
Segu *see* Ségou
Séguédine *75 H2* Agadez, NE Niger
Seguin *49 G4* Texas, SW USA
Segura *93 E4* river S Spain
Seinäjoki *85 D5* Swe. Östermyra. Länsi-
  Suomi, W Finland
Seine *90 D1* river N France
Seine, Baie de la *90 B3* bay N France
Sekondi *see* Sekondi-Takoradi
Sekondi-Takoradi *75 E5* var. Sekondi.
  S Ghana
Selânik *see* Thessaloníki
Selenga *127 E1* Mong. Selenge Mörön.
  river Mongolia/Russian Federation
Selenge Mörön *see* Selenga
Sélestat *90 E4* Ger. Schlettstadt. Bas-
  Rhin, NE France
Seleucia *see* Silifke
Selfoss *83 E5* Suðhurland, SW Iceland
Sélibaby *74 C3* var. Sélibaby. Guidimaka,
  S Mauritania
Sélibaby *see* Sélibaby
Selma *47 C6* California, W USA
Selway River *46 D2* river Idaho,
  NW USA North America
Selwyn Range *148 B3* mountain range
  Queensland, C Australia
Selzaete *see* Zelzate
Semarang *138 C5* var. Samarang. Jawa,
  C Indonesia
Sembé *77 B5* Sangha, NW Congo
Semendria *see* Smederevo
Semey *114 D4* prev. Semipalatinsk.
  Vostochnyy Kazakhstan, E Kazakhstan
Semezhevo *see* Syemyezhava
Seminole *49 E3* Texas, SW USA
Seminole, Lake *42 D3* reservoir Florida/
  Georgia, SE USA
Semipalatinsk *see* Semey
Semnān *120 D3* var. Samnān. Semnān,
  N Iran
Semois *87 C8* river SE Belgium
Sendai *130 D4* Miyagi, Honshū,
  C Japan
Sendai-wan *130 D4* bay E Japan
Senec *99 C6* Ger. Wartberg, Hung. Szenc;
  prev. Szempcz. Bratislavský Kraj,
  W Slovakia
Senegal *74 B3* off. Republic of Senegal,
  Fr. Sénégal. country W Africa

SENEGAL
West Africa

Official name Republic of Senegal
Formation 1960 / 1960
Capital Dakar
Population 12.8 million / 172 people
  per sq mile (66 people per sq km)
Total area 75,749 sq. miles (196,190 sq. km)
Languages Wolof, Pulaar, Serer, Diola,
  Mandinka, Malinké, Soninké, French*
Religions Sunni Muslim 95%, Christian
  (mainly Roman Catholic) 4%, Traditional
  beliefs 1%
Ethnic mix Wolof 43%, Serer 15%,
  Peul 14%, Other 14%, Toucouleur 9%,
  Diola 5%
Government Presidential system
Currency CFA franc = 100 centimes
Literacy rate 50%
Calorie consumption 2479 kilocalories

Senegal *74 C3* Fr. Sénégal. river W Africa
Senegal, Republic of *see* Senegal
Senftenberg *94 D4* Brandenburg,
  E Germany
Senia *see* Senj
Senica *99 C6* Ger. Senitz, Hung. Szenice.
  Trnavský Kraj, W Slovakia
Senica *see* Sjenica
Senitz *see* Senica

Senj *100 A3* Ger. Zengg, It. Segna; anc.
  Senia. Lika-Senj, NW Croatia
Senja *84 C2* prev. Senjen. island
  N Norway
Senjen *see* Senja
Sejong City *128 E4* country capital
  (South Korea) (administrative)
  C South Korea
Senkaku-shoto *130 A3* island group
  SW Japan
Senlis *90 C3* Oise, N France
Sennar *72 C4* var. Sannār. Sinnar,
  C Sudan
Senones *see* Sens
Sens *90 C3* anc. Agendicum, Senones.
  Yonne, C France
Sensburg *see* Mrągowo
Sên, Stœng *137 D5* river C Cambodia
Senta *100 D3* Hung. Zenta. Vojvodina,
  N Serbia
Seo de Urgel *see* La Seu d'Urgell
Seoul *129 E4 , Jap. Keijō; prev.
  Kyŏngsŏng, Sŏul. country capital
  (South Korea) N South Korea
Şepşi-Sângeorz/Sepsiszentgyörgy *see*
  Sfântu Gheorghe
Sept-Îles *39 E3* Québec,
  SE Canada
Seraing *87 D6* Liège, E Belgium
Serakhs *see* Sarahs
Seram, Laut *139 F4* Eng. Ceram Sea. sea
  E Indonesia
Pulau Seram *139 F4* var. Serang,
  Eng. Ceram. island Maluku,
  E Indonesia
Serang *138 C5* Jawa, C Indonesia
Serang *see* Seram, Pulau
Serasan, Selat *138 C3* strait Indonesia/
  Malaysia
Serbia *100 D4* off. Federal Republic
  of Serbia; prev. Yugoslavia, SCr.
  Jugoslavija. country SE Europe

SERBIA
Southeast Europe

Official name Republic of Serbia
Formation 2006 / 2008
Capital Belgrade
Population 9.9 million / 331 people
  per sq mile (128 people per sq km)
Total area 29,905 sq miles (77,453 sq km)
Languages Serbian*, Hungarian (Magyar)
Religions Orthodox Christian 85%,
  Roman Catholic 6%, Other 6%,
  Muslim 3%
Ethnic mix Serb 83%, Other 10%,
  Magyar 4%, Bosniak 2%, Roma 1%
Government Parliamentary system
Currency Dinar = 100 para
Literacy rate 98%
Calorie consumption 2823 kilocalories

Serbia, Federal Republic of *see* Serbia
Serçq *see* Sark
Serdar *122 C2* prev. Rus. Gyzyrlabat,
  Kizyl-Arvat. Balkan Welaýaty,
  W Turkmenistan
Serdica *see* Sofiya
Serdobol' *see* Sortavala
Serenje *78 D2* Central, E Zambia
Seres *see* Sérres
Seret/Sereth *see* Siret
Serhetabat *122 D4* prev. Rus.
  Gushgy, Kushka. Mary Welaýaty,
  S Turkmenistan
Sérifos *105 C6* anc. Seriphos. island
  Kykládes, Greece, Aegean Sea
Seriphos *see* Sérifos
Serov *114 C3* Sverdlovskaya Oblast',
  C Russian Federation
Serowe *78 D3* Central, SE Botswana
Serpa Pinto *see* Menongue
Serpent's Mouth, The *59 F2* Sp. Boca
  de la Serpiente. strait Trinidad and
  Tobago/Venezuela
Serpiente, Boca de la *see* Serpent's
  Mouth, The
Serpukhov *111 B5* Moskovskaya Oblast',
  W Russian Federation
Sérrai *see* Sérres
Serrana, Cayo de *53 F2* island group
  NW Colombia South America
Serranilla, Cayo de *53 F2* island
  group NW Colombia South America
  Caribbean Sea
Serravalle *96 E1* N San Marino

Sérrai *104 C3* var. Seres; prev. Sérrai.
  Kentrikí Makedonía, NE Greece
Sesdlets *see* Siedlce
Sesto San Giovanni *96 B2* Lombardia,
  N Italy
Sesvete *100 B2* Zagreb, N Croatia
Setabis *see* Xàtiva
Sète *91 C6* prev. Cette. Hérault, S France
Setesdal *85 A6* valley S Norway
Sétif *71 E2* var. Stif. N Algeria
Setté Cama *77 A6* Ogooué-Maritime,
  SW Gabon
Setúbal *92 B4* Eng. Saint Ubes, Saint
  Yves. Setúbal, W Portugal
Setúbal, Baía de *92 B4* bay W Portugal
Seul, Lac *38 B3* lake Ontario, S Canada
Sevan *117 G2* C Armenia
Sevan, Lake *117 G3* Eng. Lake Sevan,
  Rus. Ozero Sevan. lake E Armenia
Sevan, Lake/Sevan, Ozero *see* Sevana
  Lich
Sevastopol' *109 F5* Eng. Sebastopol.
  Avtonomna Respublika Krym,
  S Ukraine
Severn *38 B2* river Ontario, S Canada
Severn *89 D6* Wel. Hafren. river
  England/Wales, United Kingdom
Severnaya Zemlya *115 E2* var. Nicholas
  II Land. island group N Russian
  Federation
Severnyy *110 E3* Respublika Komi,
  NW Russian Federation
Severodonetsk *see* Syeverodonets'k
Severodvinsk *110 C3* prev. Molotov,
  Sudostroy. Arkhangel'skaya Oblast',
  NW Russian Federation
Severomorsk *110 C2* Murmanskaya
  Oblast', NW Russian Federation
Seversk *114 D4* Tomskaya Oblast',
  C Russian Federation
Sevier Lake *44 A4* lake Utah,
  W USA
Sevilla *92 C4* Eng. Seville; anc. Hispalis.
  Andalucía, SW Spain
Seville *see* Sevilla
Sevlievo *104 D2* Gabrovo,
  N Bulgaria
Sevluš/Sevlyush *see* Vynohradiv
Seward's Folly *see* Alaska
Seychelles *79 G1* off. Republic of
  Seychelles. country W Indian Ocean

SEYCHELLES
Indian Ocean

Official name Republic of Seychelles
Formation 1976 / 1976
Capital Victoria
Population 90,024 /866 people
  per sq mile (333 people per sq km)
Total area 176 sq. miles (455 sq. km)
Languages French Creole*,
  English*, French*
Religions Roman Catholic 82%,
  Anglican 6%, Other (including Muslim)
  6%, Other Christian 3%, Hindu 1%
Ethnic mix Creole 89%, Indian 5%,
  Other 4%, Chinese 2%
Government Presidential system
Currency Seychelles rupee = 100 cents
Literacy rate 92%
Calorie consumption 2426 kilocalories

Seychelles, Republic of *see* Seychelles
Seydhisfjördhur *83 E5* Austurland,
  E Iceland
Seýdi *122 D2* Rus. Seydi; prev.
  Neftezavodsk. Lebap Welaýaty,
  E Turkmenistan
Seyhan *see* Adana
Sfákia *see* Chóra Sfakíon
Sfântu Gheorghe *108 C4* Ger. Sankt-
  Georgen, Hung. Sepsiszentgyörgy;
  prev. Şepşi-Sângeorz, Sfîntu Gheorghe.
  Covasna, C Romania
Sfax *71 F2* Ar. Şafāqis. E Tunisia
Sfîntu Gheorghe *see* Sfântu Gheorghe
's-Gravenhage *86 B4* var. Den Haag,
  Eng. The Hague, Fr. La Haye.
  country capital (Netherlands)
  (seat of government)
  Zuid-Holland,
  W Netherlands
's-Gravenzande *86 B4* Zuid-Holland,
  W Netherlands
Shaan/Shaanxi Sheng *see* Shaanxi

Shaanxi 128 B5 var. Shaan, Shaanxi Sheng, Shan-hsi, Shenshi, Shensi. province C China
Shabani see Zvishavane
Shabeelle, Webi see Shebeli
Shache 126 A3 var. Yarkant. Xinjiang Uygur Zizhiqu, NW China
Shacheng see Huailai
Shackleton Ice Shelf 154 D3 ice shelf Antarctica
Shaddādi see Ash Shadādah
Shāhābād see Eslāmābād-e Gharb
Sha Hi see Orūmīyeh, Daryācheh-ye
Shahjahanabad see Delhi
Shahr-e Kord 120 C3 var. Shahr Kord. Chahār Maḥall va Bakhtiārī, C Iran
Shahr Kord see Shahr-e Kord
Shāhrūd 120 D2 prev. Emāmrūd, Emāmshahr. Semnān, N Iran
Shalkar 114 B4 var. Chelkar. Aktyubinsk, W Kazakhstan
Shām, Bādiyat ash see Syrian Desert
Shana see Kuril'sk
Shandi see Shendi
Shandong 128 D4 var. Lu, Shandong Sheng, Shantung. province E China
Shandong Sheng see Shandong
Shanghai 128 D5 var. Shang-hai. Shanghai Shi, E China
Shangrao 128 D5 Jiangxi, S China
Shan-hsi see Shaanxi, China
Shan-hsi see Shanxi, China
Shannon 89 A6 Ir. An tSionainn. river W Ireland
Shan Plateau 136 B3 plateau E Myanmar (Burma)
Shansi see Shanxi
Shantar Islands see Shantarskiye Ostrova
Shantarskiye Ostrova 115 G3 Eng. Shantar Islands. island group E Russian Federation
Shantou 128 D6 var. Shan-t'ou, Swatow. Guangdong, S China
Shan-t'ou see Shantou
Shantung see Shandong
Shanxi 128 C4 var. Jin, Shan-hsi, Shansi, Shanxi Sheng. province C China
Shan Xian see Sanmenxia
Shanxi Sheng see Shanxi
Shaoguan 128 C6 var. Shao-kuan, Cant. Kukong; prev. Ch'u-chiang. Guangdong, S China
Shao-kuan see Shaoguan
Shaqrā' 120 B4 Ar Riyāḍ, C Saudi Arabia
Shaqrā see Shuqrah
Shar 114 D5 var. Charsk. Vostochnyy Kazakhstan, E Kazakhstan
Shari see Chari
Sharjah see Ash Shāriqah
Shark Bay 147 A5 bay Western Australia
Sharqi, Al Jabal ash/Sharqi, Jebel esh see Anti-Lebanon
Shashe 78 D3 var. Shashi. river Botswana/Zimbabwe
Shashi see Shashe
Shatskiy Rise 125 G1 undersea rise N Pacific Ocean
Shawnee 49 G1 Oklahoma, C USA
Shaykh, Jabal ash see Hermon, Mount
Shchadryn 107 D7 Rus. Shchedrin. Homyel'skaya Voblasts', SE Belarus
Shchedrin see Shchadryn
Shcheglovsk see Kemerovo
Shchëkino 111 B5 Tul'skaya Oblast', W Russian Federation
Shchors 109 E1 Chernihivs'ka Oblast', N Ukraine
Shchuchin see Shchuchyn
Shchuchinsk 114 C4 prev. Shchuchye. Akmola, N Kazakhstan
Shchuchye see Shchuchinsk
Shchuchyn 107 B5 Pol. Szczuczyn Nowogródzki, Rus. Shchuchin. Hrodzyenskaya Voblasts', W Belarus
Shebekino 111 A6 Belgorodskaya Oblast', W Russian Federation
Shebelē Wenz, Wabē see Shebeli
Shebeli 73 D5 Amh. Wabē Shebelē Wenz, It. Scebeli, Som. Webi Shabeelle. river Ethiopia/Somalia
Sheberghan see Shibirghān
Sheboygan 40 B2 Wisconsin, N USA

Shebshi Mountains 76 A4 var. Schebschi Mountains. mountain range E NIgeria
Shechem see Nablus
Shedadi see Ash Shadādah
Sheffield 89 D5 N England, United Kingdom
Shekhem see Nablus
Sheki see Şäki
Shelby 44 B1 Montana, NW USA
Sheldon 45 F3 Iowa, C USA
Shelekhov Gulf 115 G2 Eng. Shelekhov Gulf. gulf E Russian Federation
Shelekhov Gulf see Shelikhova, Zaliv
Shendi 72 C4 var. Shandi. River Nile, NE Sudan
Shengking see Liaoning
Shenking see Liaoning
Shenshi/Shensi see Shaanxi
Shenyang 128 D3 Chin. Shen-yang, Eng. Moukden, Mukden; prev. Fengtien. province capital Liaoning, NE China
Shen-yang see Shenyang
Shepetivka 108 D2 Rus. Shepetovka. Khmel'nyts'ka Oblast', NW Ukraine
Shepetovka see Shepetivka
Shepparton 149 C7 Victoria, SE Australia
Sherbrooke 39 E4 Québec, SE Canada
Shereik 72 C3 River Nile, N Sudan
Sheridan 44 C2 Wyoming, C USA
Sherman 49 G2 Texas, SW USA
's-Hertogenbosch 86 C4 Fr. Bois-le-Duc, Ger. Herzogenbusch. Noord-Brabant, S Netherlands
Shetland Islands 88 D1 island group NE Scotland, United Kingdom
Shevchenko see Aktau
Shibarghān see Shibirghān
Shiberghan/Shiberghān see Shibirghān
Shibetsu 130 D2 var. Sibetu. Hokkaidō, NE Japan
Shibh Jazīrat Sīnā' see Sinai
Shibirghān 123 E3 var. Shibarghān, Shiberghan, Shiberghān; prev. Sheberghan. Jowzjān, N Afghanistan
Shibushi-wan 131 B8 bay SW Japan
Shigatse see Xigazê
Shih-chia-chuang/Shihmen see Shijiazhuang
Shihezi 126 C2 Xinjiang Uygur Zizhiqu, NW China
Shiichi see Shyichy
Shijiazhuang 128 C4 var. Shih-chia-chuang; prev. Shihmen. province capital Hebei, E China
Shikārpur 134 B3 Sind, S Pakistan
Shikoku 131 C7 var. Sikoku. island SW Japan
Shikoku Basin 125 F2 var. Sikoku Basin. undersea basin N Philippine Sea
Shikotan, Ostrov 130 E2 Jap. Shikotan-tō. island NE Russian Federation
Shikotan-tō see Shikotan, Ostrov
Shilabo 73 D5 Sumalē, E Ethiopia
Shiliguri 135 F3 prev. Siliguri. West Bengal, NE India
Shilka 115 F4 river S Russian Federation
Shillong 135 G3 state capital Meghālaya, NE India
Shimanto see Nakamura
Shimbir Berris see Shimbiris
Shimbiris 72 E4 var. Shimbir Berris. mountain N Somalia
Shimoga 132 C2 Karnātaka, W India
Shimonoseki 131 A7 var. Simonoseki, hist. Akamagaseki, Bakan. Yamaguchi, Honshū, SW Japan
Shinano-gawa 131 C5 var. Sinano Gawa. river Honshū, C Japan
Shīndand 122 D4 prev. Shīndand. Herāt, W Afghanistan
Shīndand see Shīndand
Shingū 131 C6 var. Singū. Wakayama, Honshū, SW Japan
Shinjō 130 D4 var. Sinzyô. Yamagata, Honshū, C Japan
Shinyanga 73 C7 Shinyanga, NW Tanzania
Shiprock 48 C1 New Mexico, SW USA
Shīrāz 120 D4 var. Shīrāz. Fārs, S Iran
Shishchitsy see Shyshchytsy
Shivpuri 134 D3 Madhya Pradesh, C India
Shizugawa 130 D4 Miyagi, Honshū, NE Japan

Shizuoka 131 D6 var. Sizuoka. Shizuoka, Honshū, S Japan
Shklov see Shklow
Shklow 107 D6 Rus. Shklov. Mahilyowskaya Voblasts', E Belarus
Shkodër 101 C5 var. Shkodra, It. Scutari, SCr. Skadar. Shkodër, NW Albania
Shkodra see Shkodër
Shkodrës, Liqeni i see Scutari, Lake
Shkumbinit, Lumi i 101 C6 var. Shkumbî, Shkumbin. river C Albania
Shkumbi/Shkumbin see Shkumbinit, Lumi i
Sholāpur see Solāpur
Shostka 109 F1 Sums'ka Oblast', NE Ukraine
Show Low 48 B2 Arizona, SW USA
Show Me State see Missouri
Shpola 109 E3 Cherkas'ka Oblast', N Ukraine
Shqipëria/Shqipërisë, Republika e see Albania
Shreveport 42 A2 Louisiana, S USA
Shrewsbury 89 D6 hist. Scrobesbyrig'. W England, United Kingdom
Shu 114 C5 Kaz. Shū. Zhambyl, SE Kazakhstan
Shuang-liao see Liaoyuan
Shū, Kazakhstan see Shu
Shumagin Islands 36 B3 island group Alaska, USA
Shumen 104 D2 Shumen, NE Bulgaria
Shumilina 107 E5 Rus. Shumilino. Vitsyebskaya Voblasts', NE Belarus
Shumilino see Shumilina
Shunsen see Chuncheon
Shuqrah 121 B7 var. Shaqrā. SW Yemen
Shwebo 136 B3 Sagaing, C Myanmar (Burma)
Shyichy 107 C7 Rus. Shiichi. Homyel'skaya Voblasts', SE Belarus
Shymkent 114 B5 prev. Chimkent. Yuzhnyy Kazakhstan, S Kazakhstan
Shyshchytsy 107 C6 Rus. Shishchitsy. Minskaya Voblasts', C Belarus
Siam see Thailand
Siam, Gulf of see Thailand, Gulf of
Sian see Xi'an
Siang see Brahmaputra
Siangtan see Xiangtan
Šiauliai 106 B4 Ger. Schaulen. Šiauliai, N Lithuania
Siazan' see Siyäzän
Sibay 111 D6 Respublika Bashkortostan, W Russian Federation
Šibenik 100 B4 It. Sebenico. Šibenik-Knin, S Croatia
Siberia 115 E3 var. Siberia. physical region NE Russian Federation
Siberia see Sibir'
Siberoet see Siberut, Pulau
Siberut, Pulau 138 A4 prev. Siberoet. island Kepulauan Mentawai, W Indonesia
Sibi 134 B2 Baluchistān, SW Pakistan
Sibiti 77 B6 Lékoumou, S Congo
Sibiu 108 B4 Ger. Hermannstadt, Hung. Nagyszeben. Sibiu, C Romania
Sibolga 138 B3 Sumatera, W Indonesia
Sibu 138 D3 Sarawak, East Malaysia
Sibut 76 C4 prev. Fort-Sibut. Kémo, S Central African Republic
Sibuyan Sea 139 E2 sea W Pacific Ocean
Sichon 137 C6 var. Ban Sichon, Si Chon. Nakhon Si Thammarat, SW Thailand
Sichuan 128 B5 var. Chuan, Sichuan Sheng, Ssu-ch'uan, Szechuan, Szechwan. province C China
Sichuan Pendi 128 B5 basin C China
Sichuan Sheng see Sichuan
Sicilian Channel see Sicily, Strait of
Sicily 97 C7 Eng. Sicily; anc. Trinacria. island Italy, C Mediterranean Sea
Sicily, Strait of 97 B7 var. Sicilian Channel. strait C Mediterranean Sea
Sicuani 61 E4 Cusco, S Peru
Sidári 104 A4 Kérkyra, Iónia Nisiá, Greece, C Mediterranean Sea
Sidas 138 C4 Borneo, C Indonesia
Siderno 97 D7 Calabria, SW Italy
Sidhirókastron see Sidirókastro
Sîdî Barrâni 72 A1 NW Egypt
Sidi Bel Abbès 70 D2 var. Sidi bel Abbès, Sidi-Bel-Abbès. NW Algeria

Sidirókastro 104 C3 prev. Sidhirókastron. Kentrikí Makedonía, NE Greece
Sidley, Mount 154 D4 mountain Antarctica
Sidney 44 D1 Montana, NW USA
Sidney 44 D4 Nebraska, C USA
Sidney 40 C4 Ohio, N USA
Sidon see Saïda
Sidra see Surt
Sidra/Sidra, Gulf of see Surt, Khalij, N Libya
Siebenbürgen see Transylvania
Siedlce 98 E3 Ger. Sedlez, Rus. Sesdlets. Mazowieckie, C Poland
Siegen 94 B4 Nordrhein-Westfalen, W Germany
Siemiatycze 98 E3 Podlaskie, NE Poland
Siena 96 B3 Fr. Sienne; anc. Saena Julia. Toscana, C Italy
Sienne see Siena
Sieradz 98 C4 Sieradz, C Poland
Sierpc 98 D3 Mazowieckie, C Poland
Sierra Leone 74 C4 off. Republic of Sierra Leone. country W Africa

SIERRA LEONE	
West Africa	
Official name	Republic of Sierra Leone
Formation	1961 / 1961
Capital	Freetown
Population	6 million / 217 people per sq mile (84 people per sq km)
Total area	27,698 sq. miles (71,740 sq. km)
Languages	Mende, Temne, Krio, English*
Religions	Muslim 60%, Christian 30%, Traditional beliefs 10%
Ethnic mix	Mende 35%, Temne 32%, Other 21%, Limba 8%, Kuranko 4%
Government	Presidential system
Currency	Leone = 100 cents
Literacy rate	41%
Calorie consumption	2162 kilocalories

Sierra Leone Basin 66 C4 undersea basin E Atlantic Ocean
Sierra Leone, Republic of see Sierra Leone
Sierra Leone Ridge see Sierra Leone Rise
Sierra Leone Rise 66 C4 var. Sierra Leone Ridge, Sierra Leone Schwelle. undersea rise E Atlantic Ocean
Sierra Leone Schwelle see Sierra Leone Rise
Sierra Vista 48 B3 Arizona, SW USA
Sífnos 105 C6 anc. Siphnos. island Kykládes, Greece, Aegean Sea
Sigli 138 A3 Sumatera, W Indonesia
Siglufjördhur 83 E4 Nordhurland Vestra, N Iceland
Signal Peak 48 A2 mountain Arizona, SW USA
Signan see Xi'an
Signy 154 A2 UK research station South Orkney Islands, Antarctica
Siguatepeque 52 C2 Comayagua, W Honduras
Siguiri 74 D4 NE Guinea
Sihanoukville 137 D6 var. Kâmpóng Saôm; prev. Kompong Som. Kâmpóng Saôm, SW Cambodia
Siilinjärvi 84 E4 Itä-Suomi, C Finland
Siirt 117 F4 var. Sert; anc. Tigranocerta. Siirt, SE Turkey
Sikandarabad see Secunderābād
Sikasso 74 D4 Sikasso, S Mali
Sikeston 45 H5 Missouri, C USA
Sikhote-Alin', Khrebet 115 G4 mountain range SE Russian Federation
Siking see Xi'an
Siklós 99 C7 Baranya, SW Hungary
Sikoku see Shikoku
Sikoku Basin see Shikoku Basin
Šilalė 106 B4 Tauragė, W Lithuania
Silchar 135 G3 Assam, NE India
Silesia 98 B4 physical region SW Poland
Silifke 116 C4 anc. Seleucia. İçel, S Turkey
Siliguri see Shiliguri
Siling Co 126 C5 lake W China
Silinhot see Xilinhot
Silistra 104 E1 var. Silistria; anc. Durostorum. Silistra, NE Bulgaria
Silistria see Silistra
Sillamäe 106 E2 Ger. Sillamäggi. Ida-Virumaa, NE Estonia

Sillamäggi see Sillamäe
Sillein see Žilina
Šilutė *106 B4* Ger. Heydekrug. Klaipėda, W Lithuania
Silvan *117 E4* Diyarbakır, SE Turkey
Silva Porto see Kuito
Silver State see Colorado
Silver State see Nevada
Simanichy *107 C7* Rus. Simonichi. Homyel'skaya Voblasts', SE Belarus
Simav *116 B3* Kütahya, W Turkey
Simav Çayı *116 A3* river NW Turkey
Simbirsk see Ul'yanovsk
Simeto *97 C7* river Sicilia, Italy, C Mediterranean Sea
Simeulue, Pulau *138 A3* island NW Indonesia
Simferopol' *109 F5* Avtonomna Respublika Krym, S Ukraine
Simitla *104 C3* Blagoevgrad, SW Bulgaria
Şimlăul Silvaniei/Şimleul Silvaniei see Şimleu Silvaniei
Şimleu Silvaniei *108 B3* Hung. Szilágysomlyó; prev. Şimläul Silvaniei, Şimleul Silvaniei. Sălaj, NW Romania
Simonichi see Simanichy
Simonoseki see Shimonoseki
Simpelveld *87 D6* Limburg, SE Netherlands
Simplon Pass *95 B8* pass S Switzerland
Simpson see Fort Simpson
Simpson Desert *148 B4* desert Northern Territory/South Australia
Sinai *72 C2* var. Sinai Peninsula, Ar. Shibh Jazīrat Sīnā', Sīnā. physical region NE Egypt
Sinaia *108 C4* Prahova, SE Romania
Sinano Gawa see Shinano-gawa
Sinä/Sinai Peninsula see Sinai
Sincelejo *58 B2* Sucre, NW Colombia
Sind see Sindh
Sindelfingen *95 B6* Baden-Württemberg, SW Germany
Sindh *134 B3* prev. Sind. province SE Pakistan
Sindi *106 D2* Ger. Zintenhof. Pärnumaa, SW Estonia
Sines *92 B4* Setúbal, S Portugal
Singan see Xi'an
Singapore *138 B3* country capital (Singapore) (Singapore) S Singapore
Singapore *138 A1* off. Republic of Singapore. country SE Asia

SINGAPORE
Southeast Asia

Official name Republic of Singapore
Formation 1965 / 1965
Capital Singapore
Population 5.2 million / 22,034 people per sq mile (8525 people per sq km)
Total area 250 sq. miles (648 sq. km)
Languages Mandarin*, Malay*, Tamil*, English*
Religions Buddhist 55%, Taoist 22%, Muslim 16%, Hindu, Christian, and Sikh 7%
Ethnic mix Chinese 74%, Malay 14%, Indian 9%, Other 3%
Government Parliamentary system
Currency Singapore dollar = 100 cents
Literacy rate 95%
Calorie consumption Not available

Singapore, Republic of see Singapore
Singen *95 B6* Baden-Württemberg, S Germany
Singida *73 C7* Singida, C Tanzania
Singkang *139 E4* Sulawesi, C Indonesia
Singkawang *138 C3* Borneo, C Indonesia
Singora see Songkhla
Singū see Shingū
Sining see Xining
Siniscola *97 A5* Sardegna, Italy, C Mediterranean Sea
Sinj *100 B4* Split-Dalmacija, SE Croatia
Sinkiang/Sinkiang Uighur Autonomous Region see Xinjiang Uygur Zizhiqu
Sinnamarie see Sinnamary
Sinnamary *59 H3* var. Sinnamarie. N French Guiana
Sinneh see Sanandaj
Sinnicolau Mare see Sânnicolau Mare
Sinoe, Lacul see Sinoie, Lacul
Sinoie, Lacul *108 D5* prev. Lacul Sinoe. lagoon SE Romania

Sinop *116 D2* anc. Sinope. Sinop, N Turkey
Sinope see Sinop
Sinsheim *95 B6* Baden-Württemberg, SW Germany
Sint Maarten *55 G3* Eng. Saint Martin. Dutch autonomous region NE Caribbean Sea
Sint-Michielsgestel *86 C4* Noord-Brabant, S Netherlands
Sin-Miclăuş see Gheorgheni
Sint-Niklaas *87 B5* Fr. Saint-Nicolas. Oost-Vlaanderen, N Belgium
Sint-Pieters-Leeuw *87 B6* Vlaams Brabant, C Belgium
Sintra *92 B3* prev. Cintra. Lisboa, W Portugal
Sinŭiju *73 E5* Nugaal, NE Somalia
Sinus Aelaniticus see Aqaba, Gulf of
Sinus Gallicus see Lion, Golfe du
Sinyang see Xinyang
Sinzyō see Shinjō
Sion *95 A7* Ger. Sitten; anc. Sedunum. Valais, SW Switzerland
Sioux City *45 F3* Iowa, C USA
Sioux Falls *45 F3* South Dakota, N USA
Sioux State see North Dakota
Siphnos see Sifnos
Siping *128 D3* var. Ssu-p'ing, Szeping; prev. Ssu-p'ing-chieh. Jilin, NE China
Siple, Mount *154 A4* mountain Siple Island, Antarctica
Siquirres *53 E4* Limón, E Costa Rica
Siracusa *97 D7* Eng. Syracuse. Sicilia, Italy, C Mediterranean Sea
Sir Edward Pellew Group *148 B2* island group Northern Territory, NE Australia
Siret *108 C3* var. Siretul, Ger. Sereth, Rus. Seret. river Romania/Ukraine
Siretul see Siret
Siria see Syria
Sirikit Reservoir *136 C4* lake N Thailand
Sīrjān *120 D4* prev. Sa'īdābād. Kermān, S Iran
Sirna see Sýrna
Şırnak *117 F4* Şırnak, SE Turkey
Síros see Sýros
Sirte see Surt
Sirte, Gulf of *71 E2* Eng. Gulf of Sidra, Gulf of Sirti, Sidra. gulf N Libya
Sirti, Gulf of see Surt, Khalīj
Sisak *100 B3* var. Siscia, Ger. Sissek, Hung. Sziszek; anc. Segestica. Sisak-Moslavina, C Croatia
Siscia see Sisak
Sisimiut *82 C3* var. Holsteinborg, Holsteinsborg, Holstenborg, Holstensborg. Kitaa, S Greenland
Sissek see Sisak
Sistān, Daryācheh-ye see Şāberī, Hāmūn-e
Sitaş Cristuru see Cristuru Secuiesc
Siteía *105 D8* var. Sitía. Kríti, Greece, E Mediterranean Sea
Sitges *93 G2* Cataluña, NE Spain
Sitía see Siteía
Sittang see Sittoung
Sittard *87 D6* Limburg, SE Netherlands
Sitten see Sion
Sittoung *136 B4* var. Sittang. river S Myanmar (Burma)
Sittwe *136 A3* var. Akyab. Rakhine State, W Myanmar (Burma)
Siuna *52 D3* Región Autónoma Atlántico Norte, NE Nicaragua
Siut see Asyūţ
Sivas *116 D3* anc. Sebastia, Sebaste. Sivas, C Turkey
Siverek *117 E4* Şanlıurfa, S Turkey
Siwa see Sīwah
Sīwah *72 A2* var. Siwa. NW Egypt
Six Counties, The see Northern Ireland
Six-Fours-les-Plages *91 D6* Var, SE France
Siyäzän *117 H2* Rus. Siazan'. NE Azerbaijan
Sjar see Sääre
Sjenica *101 D5* Turk. Seniça. Serbia, SW Serbia
Skadar see Shkodër
Skadarsko Jezero see Scutari, Lake
Skagen see Skagerrak
Skagerrak *85 A6* var. Skagerak. channel N Europe

Skagit River *46 B1* river Washington, NW USA
Skalka *84 C3* Lapp. Skalkká. lake N Sweden
Skalkká see Skalka
Skarżysko-Kamienna *98 D4* Świętokrzyskie, C Poland
Skaudvilė *106 B4* Tauragė, SW Lithuania
Skegness *89 E6* E England, United Kingdom
Skellefteå *84 D4* Västerbotten, N Sweden
Skellefteälven *84 C4* river N Sweden
Ski *85 B6* Akershus, S Norway
Skíathos *105 C5* Skíathos, Vóreies Sporádes, Greece, Aegean Sea
Skidal' *107 B5* Rus. Skidel'. Hrodzyenskaya Voblasts', W Belarus
Skidel' see Skidal'
Skiermûntseach see Schiermonnikoog
Skierniewice *98 D3* Łódzkie, C Poland
Skíftet *106 C1* strait Finland Atlantic Ocean Baltic Sea Gulf of Bothnia/Gulf of Finland
Skíros see Skýros
Skópelos *105 C5* Skópelos, Vóreies Sporádes, Greece, Aegean Sea
Skopje *101 D6* var. Üsküb, Turk. Üsküp, prev. Skoplje; anc. Scupi. country capital (Macedonia) N FYR Macedonia
Skoplje see Skopje
Skovorodino *115 F4* Amurskaya Oblast', SE Russian Federation
Skudeneshavn see Skudenesfjord
Skudenesfjord *85 A6* S Norway
Skuodas *106 B3* Ger. Schoden, Pol. Szkudy. Klaipėda, NW Lithuania
Skye, Isle of *88 B3* island NW Scotland, United Kingdom
Skylge see Terschelling
Skýros *105 C5* var. Skíros. Skýros, Vóreies Sporádes, Greece, Aegean Sea
Skýros *105 C5* var. Skíros; anc. Scyros. island Vóreies Sporádes, Greece, Aegean Sea
Slagelse *85 B7* Sjælland, E Denmark
Slatina *100 C3* Hung. Szlatina; prev. Podravska Slatina. Virovitica-Podravina, NE Croatia
Slatina *108 B5* Olt, S Romania
Slavgorod see Slawharad
Slavonski Brod *100 C3* Ger. Brod, Hung. Bród; prev. Brod, Brod na Savi. Brod-Posavina, NE Croatia
Slavuta *108 C2* Khmel'nyts'ka Oblast', NW Ukraine
Slavyansk see Slov''yans'k
Slawharad *107 E7* Rus. Slavgorod. Mahilyowskaya Voblasts', E Belarus
Sławno *98 C2* Zachodnio-pomorskie, NW Poland
Slěmäni see As Sulaymānīyah
Sliema *102 B5* N Malta
Sligo *89 A5* Ir. Sligeach. Sligo, NW Ireland
Sliven *104 D2* var. Slivno. Sliven, C Bulgaria
Slivnitsa *104 B2* Sofiya, W Bulgaria
Slivno see Sliven
Slobozia *108 C5* Ialomiţa, SE Romania
Slonim *107 B6* Pol. Słonim. Hrodzyenskaya Voblasts', W Belarus
Słonim see Slonim
Slovakia *99 C6* off. Slovenská Republika, Ger. Slowakei, Hung. Szlovákia, Slvk. Slovensko. country C Europe

SLOVAKIA
Central Europe

Official name Slovak Republic
Formation 1993 / 1993
Capital Bratislava
Population 5.5 million / 290 people per sq mile (112 people per sq km)
Total area 18,859 sq. miles (48,845 sq. km)
Languages Slovak*, Hungarian (Magyar), Czech
Religions Roman Catholic 69%, Nonreligious 13%, Other 13%, Greek Catholic (Uniate) 4%, Orthodox Christian 1%
Ethnic mix Slovak 86%, Magyar 10%, Roma 2%, Czech 1%, Other 1%
Government Parliamentary system
Currency Euro = 100 cents
Literacy rate 99%
Calorie consumption 2881 kilocalories

Slovak Ore Mountains see Slovenské rudohorie
Slovenia *95 D8* off. Republic of Slovenia, Ger. Slowenien, Slvn. Slovenija. country SE Europe

SLOVENIA
Central Europe

Official name Republic of Slovenia
Formation 1991 / 1991
Capital Ljubljana
Population 2 million / 256 people per sq mile (99 people per sq km)
Total area 7820 sq. miles (20,253 sq. km)
Languages Slovenian*
Religions Roman Catholic 58%, Other 28%, Atheist 10%, Orthodox Christian 2%, Muslim 2%
Ethnic mix Slovene 83%, Other 12%, Serb 2%, Croat 2%, Bosniak 1%
Government Parliamentary system
Currency Euro = 100 cents
Literacy rate 99%
Calorie consumption 3275 kilocalories

Slovenia, Republic of see Slovenia
Slovenija see Slovenia
Slovenská Republika see Slovakia
Slovenské rudohorie *99 D6* Eng. Slovak Ore Mountains, Ger. Slowakisches Erzgebirge, Ungarisches Erzgebirge. mountain range C Slovakia
Slovensko see Slovakia
Slov''yans'k *109 G3* Rus. Slavyansk. Donets'ka Oblast', E Ukraine
Slowakei see Slovakia
Slowakisches Erzgebirge see Slovenské rudohorie
Slowenien see Slovenia
Słubice *98 B3* Ger. Frankfurt. Lubuskie, W Poland
Sluch *108 D1* river NW Ukraine
Słupsk *98 C2* Ger. Stolp. Pomorskie, N Poland
Slutsk *107 C6* Minskaya Voblasts', S Belarus
Smallwood Reservoir *39 F2* lake Newfoundland and Labrador, S Canada
Smara *70 B3* var. Es Semara. N Western Sahara
Smarhon' *107 C5* Pol. Smorgonie, Rus. Smorgon'. Hrodzyenskaya Voblasts', W Belarus
Smederevo *100 D4* Ger. Semendria. Serbia, N Serbia
Smederevska Palanka *100 D4* Serbia, C Serbia
Smela see Smila
Smila *109 E2* Rus. Smela. Cherkas'ka Oblast', C Ukraine
Smilten see Smiltene
Smiltene *106 D3* Ger. Smilten. N Latvia
Smøla *84 A4* island W Norway
Smolensk *111 A5* Smolenskaya Oblast', W Russian Federation
Smorgon'/Smorgonie see Smarhon'
Smyrna see İzmir
Snake *34 B4* river Yukon Territory, NW Canada
Snake River *46 C3* river NW USA
Snake River Plain *46 D4* plain Idaho, NW USA
Sneek *86 D2* Fris. Snits. Fryslân, N Netherlands
Sneeuw-gebergte see Maoke, Pegunungan
Snežka *98 B4* Ger. Schneekoppe, Pol. Śnieżka. mountain N Czech Republic/ Poland
Śniardwy, Jezioro *98 D2* Ger. Spirdingsee. lake NE Poland
Sniečkus see Visaginas
Śnieżka see Snežka
Snina *99 E5* Hung. Szinna. Prešovský Kraj, E Slovakia
Snits see Sneek
Snowdonia *89 C6* mountain range NW Wales, United Kingdom
Snowdrift see Łutselk'e
Snow Mountains see Maoke, Pegunungan
Snyder *49 F3* Texas, SW USA
Sobradinho, Barragem de see Sobradinho, Represa de
Sobradinho, Represa de *63 F2* var. Barragem de Sobradinho. reservoir E Brazil

Sochi *111 A7* Krasnodarskiy Kray, SW Russian Federation

Société, Îles de la/Society Islands *see* Société, Archipel de la

Society Islands *145 G4 var.* Archipel de Tahiti, Îles de la Société, *Eng.* Society Islands. *island group* W French Polynesia

Soconusco, Sierra de *see* Madre, Sierra

Socorro *48 D2* New Mexico, SW USA

Socorro, Isla *50 B5* island W Mexico

Socotra *121 C7 var.* Sokotra, *Eng.* Socotra. *island* SE Yemen

Socotra *see* Suquṭrā

Soc Trăng *137 D6 var.* Khanh Hung. Soc Trăng, S Vietnam

Socuéllamos *93 E3* Castilla-La Mancha, C Spain

Sodankylä *84 D3* Lappi, N Finland

Sodari *see* Sodiri

Söderhamn *85 C5* Gävleborg, C Sweden

Södertälje *85 C6* Stockholm, C Sweden

Sodiri *72 B4 var.* Sawdīrī, Sodari. Northern Kordofan, C Sudan

Soekaboemi *see* Sukabumi

Soemba *see* Sumba, Pulau

Soengaipenoeh *see* Sungaipenuh

Soerabaja *see* Surabaya

Soerakarta *see* Surakarta

Sofia *see* Sofiya

Sofiya *104 C2 var.* Sophia, *Eng.* Sofia, *Lat.* Serdica. *country capital (Bulgaria)* Sofiya-Grad, W Bulgaria

Sogamoso *58 B3* Boyacá, C Colombia

Sognefjorden *85 A5* fjord NE North Sea

Sohâg *see* Sawhāj

Sohar *see* Ṣuḥār

Sohm Plain *66 B3 abyssal plain* NW Atlantic Ocean

Sohrau *see* Żory

Sokal' *108 C2 Rus.* Sokal. L'vivs'ka Oblast', NW Ukraine

Söke *116 A4* Aydın, SW Turkey

Sokhumi *117 E1 Rus.* Sukhumi. NW Georgia

Sokodé *75 F4* C Togo

Sokol *110 C4* Vologodskaya Oblast', NW Russian Federation

Sokółka *98 E3* Podlaskie, NE Poland

Sokolov *99 A5 Ger.* Falkenau an der Eger; *prev.* Falknov nad Ohří. Karlovarský Kraj, W Czech Republic

Sokone *74 B3* W Senegal

Sokoto *75 F3* Sokoto, NW Nigeria

Sokoto *75 F4* river NW Nigeria

Sokotra *see* Suquṭrā

Solāpur *124 B3 var.* Sholāpur. Mahārāshtra, W India

Solca *108 C3 Ger.* Solka. Suceava, N Romania

Sol, Costa del *92 D5 coastal region* S Spain

Soldeu *91 B7* NE Andorra Europe

Solec Kujawski *98 C3* Kujawsko-pomorskie, C Poland

Soledad *58 B1* Atlántico, N Colombia

Isla Soledad *see* East Falkland

Soligorsk *see* Salihorsk

Solikamsk *114 C3* Permskiy Kray, NW Russian Federation

Sol'-Iletsk *111 D6* Orenburgskaya Oblast', W Russian Federation

Solingen *94 A4* Nordrhein-Westfalen, W Germany

Solka *see* Solca

Sollentuna *85 C6* Stockholm, C Sweden

Solo *see* Surakarta

Solok *138 B4* Sumatera, W Indonesia

Solomon Islands *144 C3 prev.* British Solomon Islands Protectorate. *country* W Solomon Islands N Melanesia W Pacific Ocean

SOLOMON ISLANDS
Australasia & Oceania

Official name Solomon Islands
Formation 1978 / 1978
Capital Honiara
Population 600,000 / 56 people per sq mile (21 people per sq km)
Total area 10,985 sq. miles (28,450 sq. km)
Languages English*, Pidgin English, Melanesian Pidgin, c.120 others
Religions Church of Melanesia (Anglican) 34%, Roman Catholic 19%, South Seas

SOLOMON ISLANDS
(continued)

Evangelical Church 17%, Methodist 11%, Seventh-day Adventist 10%, Other 9%
Ethnic mix Melanesian 93%, Polynesian 4%, Micronesian 2%, Other 1%
Government Parliamentary system
Currency Solomon Islands dollar = 100 cents
Literacy rate 77%
Calorie consumption 2439 kilocalories

Solomon Islands *144 C3 island group* Papua New Guinea/Solomon Islands

Solomon Sea *144 B3 sea* W Pacific Ocean

Soltau *94 B3* Niedersachsen, NW Germany

Sol'tsy *110 A4* Novgorodskaya Oblast', W Russian Federation

Solun *see* Thessaloníki

Solwezi *78 D2* North Western, NW Zambia

Sōma *130 D4* Fukushima, Honshū, C Japan

Somalia *73 D5 off.* Somali Democratic Republic, *Som.* Jamuuriyada Demuqraadiga Soomaaliyeed, Soomaaliya; *prev.* Italian Somaliland, Somaliland Protectorate. *country* E Africa

SOMALIA
East Africa

Official name The Somali Democratic Republic
Formation 1960 / 1960
Capital Mogadishu
Population 9.6 million / 40 people per sq mile (15 people per sq km)
Total area 246,199 sq. miles (637,657 sq. km)
Languages Somali*, Arabic*, English, Italian
Religions Sunni Muslim 99%, Christian 1%
Ethnic mix Somali 85%, Other 15%
Government Transitional regime
Currency Somali shilin = 100 senti
Literacy rate 24%
Calorie consumption 1762 kilocalories

Somali Basin *69 E5 undersea basin* W Indian Ocean

Somali Democratic Republic *see* Somalia

Somaliland *73 D5 disputed territory* N Somalia

Somaliland Protectorate *see* Somalia

Sombor *100 C3 Hung.* Zombor. Vojvodina, NW Serbia

Someren *87 D5* Noord-Brabant, SE Netherlands

Somerset *42 A5 var.* Somerset Village. W Bermuda

Somerset *40 C5* Kentucky, S USA

Somerset Island *42 A5 island* W Bermuda

Somerset Island *37 F2 island* Queen Elizabeth Islands, Nunavut, NW Canada

Somerset Village *see* Somerset

Somers Islands *see* Bermuda

Somerton *48 A2* Arizona, SW USA

Someş *108 B3* river Hungary/Romania Europe

Somme *90 C2* river N France

Sommerfeld *see* Lubsko

Somotillo *52 C3* Chinandega, NW Nicaragua

Somoto *52 D3* Madriz, NW Nicaragua

Songea *73 D4* Ruvuma, S Tanzania

Sŏngjin *see* Kimch'aek

Songkhla *137 C7 var.* Songkla, *Mal.* Singora. Songkhla, SW Thailand

Songkla *see* Songkhla

Sonoran Desert *48 A3 var.* Desierto de Altar. *desert* Mexico/USA

Sonsonate *52 B3* Sonsonate, W El Salvador

Soochow *see* Suzhou

Soomaaliya/Soomaaliyeed, Jamuuriyada Demuqraadiga *see* Somalia

Soome Laht *see* Finland, Gulf of

Sop Hao *136 D3* Houaphan, N Laos

Sophia *see* Sofiya

Sopianae *see* Pécs

Sopot *98 C2 Ger.* Zoppot. Pomorskie, N Poland

Sopron *99 B6 Ger.* Ödenburg. Győr-Moson-Sopron, NW Hungary

Sorau/Sorau in der Niederlausitz *see* Żary

Sorgues *91 D6* Vaucluse, SE France

Sorgun *116 D3* Yozgat, C Turkey

Soria *93 E2* Castilla y León, N Spain

Soroca *108 D3 Rus.* Soroki. N Moldova

Sorochino *see* Sarochyna

Soroki *see* Soroca

Sorong *139 F4* Papua, E Indonesia

Sørøy *see* Sørøya

Sørøya *84 C2 var.* Sørøy, *Lapp.* Sállan. *island* N Norway

Sortavala *110 B3 prev.* Serdobol'. Respublika Kareliya, NW Russian Federation

Sotavento, Ilhas de *74 A3 var.* Leeward Islands. *island group* S Cape Verde

Sotkamo *84 E4* Oulu, C Finland

Souanké *77 B5* Sangha, NW Congo

Soueida *see* As Suwaydā'

Souflí *104 D3 prev.* Souflíon. Anatolikí Makedonía kai Thráki, NE Greece

Souflíon *see* Souflí

Soufrière *55 F2* W Saint Lucia

Soukhné *see* As Sukhnah

Sŏul *see* Seoul

Soûr *119 A5 var.* Şūr; *anc.* Tyre. SW Lebanon

Souris River *45 E1 var.* Mouse River. river Canada/USA

Soúrpi *105 B5* Thessalía, C Greece

Sousse *71 F2 var.* Sūsah. NE Tunisia

South Africa *78 C4 off.* Republic of South Africa, *Afr.* Suid-Afrika. *country* S Africa

SOUTH AFRICA
Southern Africa

Official name Republic of South Africa
Formation 1934 / 1994
Capital Pretoria (Tshwane); Cape Town; Bloemfontein
Population 55 million / 117 people per sq mile (41 people per sq km)
Total area 471,008 sq. miles (1,219,912 sq. km)
Languages English, isiZulu, isiXhosa, Afrikaans, Sepedi, Setswana, Sesotho, Xitsonga, siSwati, Tshivenda, isiNdebele
Religions Christian 68%, Traditional beliefs and animist 29%, Muslim 2%, Hindu 1%
Ethnic mix Black 89%, White 9%, Asian 2%
Government Presidential system
Currency Rand = 100 cents
Literacy rate 89%
Calorie consumption 3017 kilocalories

South Africa, Republic of *see* South Africa

South America *56* continent

Southampton *89 D7 hist.* Hamwih, *Lat.* Clausentum. S England, United Kingdom

Southampton Island *37 G3 island* Nunavut, NE Canada

South Andaman *133 F2 island* Andaman Islands, India, NE Indian Ocean

South Australia *149 A5* state S Australia

South Australian Basin *142 B5 undersea basin* SW Indian Ocean

South Bend *40 C3* Indiana, N USA

South Beveland *see* Zuid-Beveland

South Bruny Island *149 C8 island* Tasmania, SE Australia

South Carolina *42 A2 off.* State of South Carolina, *also known as* The Palmetto State. *state* SE USA

South Carpathians *see* Carpaṭii Meridionali

South China Basin *125 E4 undersea basin* SE South China Sea

South China Sea *125 E4 Chin.* Nan Hai, *Ind.* Laut Cina Selatan, *Vtn.* Biển Đông. *sea* SE Asia

South Dakota *44 D2 off.* State of South Dakota, *also known as* The Coyote State, Sunshine State. *state* N USA

Southeast Indian Ridge *141 D7 undersea ridge* Indian Ocean/Pacific Ocean

Southeast Pacific Basin *153 E5 var.* Belling Hausen Mulde. *undersea basin* SE Pacific Ocean

South East Point *149 C7 headland* Victoria, S Australia

Southend-on-Sea *89 E6* E England, United Kingdom

Southern Alps *151 B6 mountain range* South Island, New Zealand

Southern Cook Islands *145 F4 island group* S Cook Islands

Southern Cross *147 B6* Western Australia

Southern Indian Lake *37 F4 lake* Manitoba, C Canada

Southern Ocean *67 B7 ocean* Atlantic Ocean/Indian Ocean/Pacific Ocean

Southern Uplands *88 C4 mountain range* S Scotland, United Kingdom

South Fiji Basin *142 D4 undersea basin* S Pacific Ocean

South Geomagnetic Pole *154 B3 pole* Antarctica

South Georgia *57 D8 island* South Georgia and the South Sandwich Islands, SW Atlantic Ocean

South Goulburn Island *146 E2 island* Northern Territory, N Australia

South Huvadhu Atoll *132 A5 atoll* S Maldives

South Indian Basin *141 D7 undersea basin* Indian Ocean/Pacific Ocean

South Island *151 C6 island* S New Zealand

South Korea *129 E4 off.* Republic of Korea, *Kor.* Taehan Min'guk. *country* E Asia

SOUTH KOREA
East Asia

Official name Republic of Korea
Formation 1948 / 1953
Capital Seoul; Sejong City
Population 48.4 million / 1270 people per sq mile (490 people per sq km)
Total area 38,023 sq. miles (98,480 sq. km)
Languages Korean*
Religions Mahayana Buddhist 47%, Protestant 38%, Roman Catholic 11%, Confucianist 3%, Other 1%
Ethnic mix Korean 100%
Government Presidential system
Currency South Korean won = 100 chon
Literacy rate 99%
Calorie consumption 3200 kilocalories

South Lake Tahoe *47 C5* California, W USA

South Orkney Islands *154 A2 island group* Antarctica

South Ossetia *117 F2 former autonomous region* SW Georgia

South Pacific Basin *see* Southwest Pacific Basin

South Platte River *44 D4* river Colorado/Nebraska, C USA

South Pole *154 B3 pole* Antarctica

South Sandwich Islands *57 D8 island group* SW Atlantic Ocean

South Sandwich Trench *57 E8 trench* SW Atlantic Ocean

South Shetland Islands *154 A2 island group* Antarctica

South Shields *88 D4* NE England, United Kingdom

South Sioux City *45 F3* Nebraska, C USA

South Sudan *73 B5 off.* Republic of South Sudan. *country* E Africa

SOUTH SUDAN
East Africa

Official name Republic of South Sudan
Formation 2011 / 2011
Capital Juba
Population 8.3 million / 33 people per sq mile (13 people per sq km)
Total area 248,777 sq. miles (644,329 sq. km)
Languages Arabic, Dinka, Nuer, Zande, Bari, Shilluk, Lotuko
Religions Over half of the population

SOUTH SUDAN
(continued)

follow Christian or traditional beliefs
Ethnic mix Dinka 40%, Nuer 15%,.
Bari 10%, Shilluk/Anwak 10%,
Azande 10%, Arab 10%, Other 5%
Government Transitional regime
Currency South Sudan pound = 100
piastres
Literacy rate 37%
Calorie consumption Not available

South Taranaki Bight 150 C4 *bight*
SE Tasman Sea
South Tasmania Plateau *see* Tasman
Plateau
South Uist 88 B3 *island* NW Scotland,
United Kingdom
South-West Africa/South West Africa
see Namibia
South West Cape 151 A8 *headland*
Stewart Island, New Zealand
Southwest Indian Ocean Ridge *see*
Southwest Indian Ridge
Southwest Indian Ridge 141 B6 *var.*
Southwest Indian Ocean Ridge.
undersea ridge SW Indian Ocean
Southwest Pacific Basin 143 E4 *var.*
South Pacific Basin. *undersea basin*
SE Pacific Ocean
Sovereign Base Area 102 C5 *uk military
installation* S Cyprus
Soweto 78 D4 Gauteng,
NE South Africa
Sōya-kaikyō *see* La Pérouse Strait
Spain 92 D3 *off.* Kingdom of Spain, *Sp.*
España; *anc.* Hispania, Iberia, *Lat.*
Hispana. *country* SW Europe

SPAIN
Southwest Europe

Official name Kingdom of Spain
Formation 1492 / 1713
Capital Madrid
Population 46.5 million / 241 people per
sq mile (93 people per sq km)
Total area 194,896 sq. miles
(2504,782 sq. km)
Languages Spanish*, Catalan*,
Galician*, Basque*
Religions Roman Catholic 96%, Other 4%
Ethnic mix Castilian Spanish 72%,
Catalan 17%, Galician 6%, Basque 2%,
Other 2%, Roma 1%
Government Parliamentary system
Currency Euro = 100 cents
Literacy rate 98%
Calorie consumption 3239 kilocalories

Spain, Kingdom of *see* Spain
Spalato *see* Split
Spanish Town 54 B5 *hist.* St.Iago de la
Vega. C Jamaica
Sparks 47 C5 Nevada, W USA
Sparta *see* Spárti
Spartanburg 43 E1 South Carolina,
SE USA
Spárti 105 B6 *Eng.* Sparta. Pelopónnisos,
S Greece
Spearfish 44 D2 South Dakota,
N USA
Speightstown 55 G1 NW Barbados
Spencer 45 F3 Iowa, C USA
Spencer Gulf 149 B6 *gulf* South Australia
Spey 88 C3 *river* NE Scotland, United
Kingdom
Spice Islands *see* Maluku
Spiess Seamount 67 C7 *seamount*
S Atlantic Ocean
Spijkenisse 86 B4 Zuid-Holland,
SW Netherlands
Spili 105 C8 Kríti, Greece,
E Mediterranean Sea
Spin Büldak 123 E5 *prev.* Spīn Būldak.
Kandahār, S Afghanistan
Spīn Būldak *see* Spin Büldak
Spirdingsee *see* Śniardwy, Jezioro
Spitsbergen 83 F2 *island* NW Svalbard
Split 100 B4 *It.* Spalato. Split-Dalmacija,
S Croatia
Spoği 106 D4 SE Latvia
Spokane 46 C2 Washington, NW USA
Spratly Islands 138 B2 *Chin.* Nansha
Qundao. *disputed territory* SE Asia
Spree 94 D4 *river* E Germany

Springfield 40 B4 *state capital* Illinois,
N USA
Springfield 11 G3 Massachusetts,
NE USA
Springfield 45 G5 Missouri, C USA
Springfield 40 C4 Ohio, N USA
Springfield 46 B3 Oregon, NW USA
Spring Garden 59 F2 NE Guyana
Spring Hill 43 E4 Florida, SE USA
Springs Junction 151 C5 West Coast,
South Island, New Zealand
Springsure 148 D4 Queensland,
E Australia
Sprottau *see* Szprotawa
Spruce Knob 41 E4 *mountain* West
Virginia, NE USA
Srbinje *see* Foča
Srbobran 100 D3 *var.* Bácsszenttamás,
Hung. Szenttamás. Vojvodina,
N Serbia
Srebrenica 100 C4 Republika Srpska,
E Bosnia and Herzegovina
Sredets 104 D2 *prev.* Syulemeshlii. Stara
Zagora, C Bulgaria
Sredets 104 E2 *prev.* Grudovo. Burgas,
E Bulgaria
Sremska Mitrovica 100 C3 *prev.*
Mitrovica, *Ger.* Mitrowitz. Vojvodina,
NW Serbia
Srepok, Sông *see* Srêpôk, Tônle
Srêpôk, Tônle 137 E5 *var.* Sông Srepok.
river Cambodia/Vietnam
Sri Aman 138 C3 Sarawak,
East Malaysia
Sri Jayewardenapura Kotte 132 D3
country capital (Sri Lanka) (legislative)
Western Province, W Sri Lanka
Srikākulam 135 F5 Andhra Pradesh,
E India
Sri Lanka 132 D3 *off.* Democratic
Socialist Republic of Sri Lanka; *prev.*
Ceylon. *country* S Asia

SRI LANKA
South Asia

Official name Democratic Socialist
Republic of Sri Lanka
Formation 1948 / 1948
Capital Colombo; Sri Jayewardenapura
Kotte
Population 21 million / 840 people
per sq mile (324 people per sq km)
Total area 25,332 sq. miles (65,610 sq. km)
Languages Sinhala*, Tamil*,
Sinhala-Tamil, English
Religions Buddhist 69%, Hindu 15%,
Muslim 8%, Christian 8%
Ethnic mix Sinhalese 74%, Tamil 18%,
Moor 7%, Other 1%
Government Mixed presidential–
parliamentary system
Currency Sri Lanka rupee = 100 cents
Literacy rate 91%
Calorie consumption 2426 kilocalories

**Sri Lanka, Democratic Socialist
Republic of** *see* Sri Lanka
Srinagarind Reservoir 137 C5 *lake*
W Thailand
Srpska, Republika 100 B3 *republic*
Bosnia and Herzegovina
Ssu-ch'uan *see* Sichuan
Ssu-p'ing/Ssu-p'ing-chieh *see* Siping
Stabroek 87 B5 Antwerpen,
N Belgium
Stade 94 B3 Niedersachsen,
NW Germany
Stadskanaal 86 E2 Groningen,
NE Netherlands
Stafford 89 D6 C England, United
Kingdom
Staicele 106 D3 N Latvia
Ştaierdorf-Anina *see* Anina
Stájerlakanina *see* Anina
Stakhanov 109 H3 Luhans'ka Oblast',
E Ukraine
Stalin *see* Varna
Stalinabad *see* Dushanbe
Stalingrad *see* Volgograd
Stalino *see* Donets'k
Stalinobod *see* Dushanbe
Stalinsk *see* Novokuznetsk
Stalinski Zaliv *see* Varnenski Zaliv
Stalin, Yazovir *see* Iskür, Yazovir
Stalowa Wola 98 E4 Podkarpackie,
SE Poland

Stamford 41 F3 Connecticut,
NE USA
Stampalla *see* Astypalaia
Stanislau *see* Ivano-Frankivs'k
Stanislav *see* Ivano-Frankivs'k
Stanisławów *see* Ivano-Frankivs'k
Stanke Dimitrov *see* Dupnitsa
Stanley 65 D7 *var.* Port Stanley, Puerto
Argentino. *dependent territory capital*
(Falkland Islands) East Falkland,
Falkland Islands
Stanleyville *see* Kisangani
Stann Creek *see* Dangriga
Stanovoy Khrebet 113 E3 *mountain
range* SE Russian Federation
Stanthorpe 149 D5 Queensland,
E Australia
Staphorst 86 D2 Overijssel,
E Netherlands
Starachowice 98 D4 Świętokrzyskie,
C Poland
Stara Kanjiža *see* Kanjiža
Stara Pazova 100 D3 *Ger.* Altpasua,
Hung. Ópazova. Vojvodina, N Serbia
Stara Planina *see* Balkan Mountains
Stara Zagora 104 D2 *var.* Stara Zagora,
Trajana. Stara Zagora, C Bulgaria
Starbuck Island 145 G3 *prev.* Volunteer
Island. *island* E Kiribati
Stargard in Pommern *see* Stargard
Szczeciński
Stargard Szczeciński 98 B3 *Ger.*
Stargard in Pommern. Zachodnio-
pomorskie, NW Poland
Stari Bečej *see* Bečej
Starobel'sk *see* Starobil's'k
Starobil's'k 109 H2 *Rus.* Starobel'sk.
Luhans'ka Oblast', E Ukraine
Starobin 107 C7 *var.* Starobyn.
Minskaya Voblasts', S Belarus
Starobyn *see* Starobin
Starogard Gdański 98 C2 *Ger.*
Preussisch-Stargard. Pomorskie,
N Poland
Starokonstantinov *see* Starokostyantyniv
Starokostyantyniv 108 D2 *Rus.*
Starokonstantinov. Khmel'nyts'ka
Oblast', NW Ukraine
Starominskaya 111 A7 Krasnodarskiy
Kray, SW Russian Federation
Staryya Darohi 107 C6 *Rus.* Staryye
Dorogi. Minskaya Voblasts', S Belarus
Staryye Dorogi *see* Staryya Darohi
Staryy Oskol 111 B6 Belgorodskaya
Oblast', W Russian Federation
State College 41 E4 Pennsylvania,
NE USA
Staten Island *see* Estados, Isla de los
Statesboro 43 E2 Georgia, SE USA
States, The *see* United States of America
Staunton 41 E5 Virginia, NE USA
Stavanger 85 A6 Rogaland, S Norway
Stavers Island *see* Vostok Island
Stavropol' 111 B7 *prev.* Voroshilovsk.
Stavropol'skiy Kray, SW Russian
Federation
Stavropol' *see* Tol'yatti
Steamboat Springs 44 C4 Colorado,
C USA
Steenwijk 86 D2 Overijssel,
N Netherlands
Steier *see* Steyr
Steierdorf/Steierdorf-Anina *see* Anina
Steinamanger *see* Szombathely
Steinkjer 84 B4 Nord-Trøndelag,
C Norway
Stejarul *see* Karapelit
Stendal 94 C3 Sachsen-Anhalt,
C Germany
Stepanakert *see* Xankändi
Stephenville 49 F3 Texas, SW USA
Sterling 44 D4 Colorado, C USA
Sterling 40 B3 Illinois, N USA
Sterlitamak 114 B3 Respublika
Bashkortostan, W Russian Federation
Stettin *see* Szczecin
Stettiner Haff *see* Szczeciński, Zalew
Stevenage 89 E6 E England, United
Kingdom
Stevens Point 40 B2 Wisconsin, N USA
Stewart Island 151 A8 *island* S New
Zealand
Steyerlak-Anina *see* Anina
Steyr 95 D6 *var.* Steier. Oberösterreich,
N Austria
St. Helena Bay 78 B5 *bay* SW South
Africa

Stif *see* Sétif
Stillwater 49 G1 Oklahoma, C USA
Štip 101 E6 E FYR Macedonia
Stirling 88 C4 C Scotland, United
Kingdom
Stjørdalshalsen 84 B4 Nord-Trøndelag,
C Norway
St-Maur-des-Fossés 90 E2 Val-de-
Marne, Île-de-France, N France Europe
Stockach 95 B6 Baden-Württemberg,
S Germany
Stockholm 85 C6 *country capital*
(Sweden) Stockholm, C Sweden
Stockmannshof *see* Pļaviņas
Stockton 47 B6 California, W USA
Stockton Plateau 49 E4 *plain* Texas,
SW USA
Stœng Trêng 137 D5 *prev.* Stung Treng.
Stœng Trêng, NE Cambodia
Stoke *see* Stoke-on-Trent
Stoke-on-Trent 89 D6 *var.* Stoke.
C England, United Kingdom
Stolbce *see* Stowbtsy
Stolbtsy *see* Stowbtsy
Stolp *see* Słupsk
Stolpmünde *see* Ustka
Stómio 104 B4 Thessalía, C Greece
Store Bælt *see* Storebælt
Storebelt *see* Storebælt
Støren 85 B5 Sør-Trøndelag,
S Norway
Storfjorden 83 G2 *fjord* S Norway
Storhammer *see* Hamar
Stornoway 88 B2 NW Scotland, United
Kingdom
Storsjön 85 B5 *lake* C Sweden
Storuman 84 C4 Västerbotten,
N Sweden
Storuman 84 C4 *lake* N Sweden
Stowbtsy 107 C6 *Pol.* Stolbce, *Rus.*
Stolbtsy. Minskaya Voblasts',
C Belarus
Strabane 89 B5 *Ir.* An Srath Bán.
W Northern Ireland, United Kingdom
Strakonice 99 A5 *Ger.* Strakonitz.
Jihočeský Kraj, S Czech Republic
Strakonitz *see* Strakonice
Stralsund 94 D2 Mecklenburg-
Vorpommern, NE Germany
Stranraer 89 C5 S Scotland, United
Kingdom
Strasbourg 90 E3 *Ger.* Strassburg; *anc.*
Argentoratum. Bas-Rhin, NE France
Strasburg *see* Aiud, Romania
Strășeni 108 D3 *var.* Strasheny.
C Moldova
Strasheny *see* Strășeni
Strasbourg *see* Strasbourg, France
Strassburg *see* Aiud, Romania
Stratford 150 D4 Taranaki, North Island,
New Zealand
Strathfield 148 E2 New South Wales,
E Australia
Straubing 95 C6 Bayern,
SE Germany
Strehaia 108 B5 Mehedinți,
SW Romania
Strelka 114 D4 Krasnoyarskiy Kray,
C Russian Federation
Strigonium *see* Esztergom
Strofilia 105 C5 *var.* Strofiliá. Évvoia,
C Greece
Strofiliá 105 C5 *var.* Strofilia. Évvoia,
C Greece
Stromboli 97 D6 *island* Isole Eolie,
S Italy
Stromeferry 88 C3 N Scotland, United
Kingdom
Strömstad 85 B6 Västra Götaland,
S Sweden
Strömsund 84 C4 Jämtland, C Sweden
Struga 101 D6 SW FYR Macedonia
Struma *see* Strymónas
Strumica 101 E6 E FYR Macedonia
Strumyani 104 C3 Blagoevgrad,
SW Bulgaria
Strymónas 104 C3 *Bul.* Struma. *river*
Bulgaria/Greece
Stryy 108 B2 L'vivs'ka Oblast',
NW Ukraine
Studholme 151 B6 Canterbury, South
Island, New Zealand
Stuhlweissenberg *see* Székesfehérvár
Stung Treng *see* Stœng Trêng
Sturgis 44 D3 South Dakota, N USA
Stuttgart 95 B6 Baden-Württemberg,
SW Germany
Stykkishólmur 83 E4 Vesturland,
W Iceland

Styr *108 C1 Rus.* Styr'. *river* Belarus/ Ukraine
Su *see* Jiangsu
Suakin *72 C3 var.* Sawakin. Red Sea, NE Sudan
Subačius *106 C4* Panevėžys, NE Lithuania
Subaykhān *118 E3* Dayr az Zawr, E Syria
Subotica *100 D2 Ger.* Maria-Theresiopel, *Hung.* Szabadka. Vojvodina, N Serbia
Suceava *108 C3 Ger.* Suczawa, *Hung.* Szucsava. Suceava, NE Romania
Su-chou *see* Suzhou
Suchow *see* Xuzhou, Jiangsu, China
Suchow *see* Suzhou, Jiangsu, China
Sucker State *see* Illinois
Sucre *61 F4 hist.* Chuquisaca, La Plata. *country capital* (Bolivia) (legal capital) Chuquisaca, S Bolivia
Suczawa *see* Suceava
Sudan *72 A4 off.* Republic of Sudan, *Ar.* Jumhuriyat as-Sudan; *prev.* Anglo-Egyptian Sudan. *country* N Africa

SUDAN
East Africa

Official name Republic of the Sudan
Formation 1956 / 2011
Capital Khartoum
Population 34 million / 47 people per sq mile (18 people per sq km)
Total area 718,722 sq. miles (1,861,481 sq. km)
Languages Arabic, Nubian, Beja, Fur
Religions Nearly the whole population is Muslim (mainly Sunni)
Ethnic mix Arab 60%, Other 18%, Nubian 10%, Beja 8%, Fur 3%, Zaghawa 1%
Government Presidential system
Currency New Sudanese pound = 100 piastres
Literacy rate 61%
Calorie consumption 2326 kilocalories

Sudanese Republic *see* Mali
Sudan, Jumhuriyat as- *see* Sudan
Sudan, Republic of *see* Sudan
Sudbury *38 C4* Ontario, S Canada
Sudd *73 B5 swamp region* C South Sudan
Sudeten *98 B4 var.* Sudetes, Sudetic Mountains, *Cz./Pol.* Sudety. *mountain range* Czech Republic/Poland
Sudetes/Sudetic Mountains/Sudety *see* Sudeten
Südkarpaten *see* Carpaţii Meridionalii
Südliche Morava *see* Južna Morava
Sudong, Pulau *138 A2 island* SW Singapore Asia
Sudostroy *see* Severodvinsk
Sue *73 B5 river* W South Sudan
Sueca *93 F3* Valenciana, E Spain
Sue Wood Bay *42 B5 bay* W Bermuda North America W Atlantic Ocean
Suez *72 B1 Ar.* As Suways, El Suweis. NE Egypt
Suez Canal *72 B1 Ar.* Qanāt as Suways. *canal* NE Egypt
Suez, Gulf of *see* Khalīj as Suways
Suğla Gölü *116 C4 lake* SW Turkey
Şuhār *121 D5 var.* Sohar. N Oman
Sühbaatar *127 E1* Selenge, N Mongolia
Suhl *95 C5* Thüringen, C Germany
Suicheng *see* Suixi
Suid-Afrika *see* South Africa
Suidwes-Afrika *see* Namibia
Suixi *128 C6 var.* Suicheng. Guangdong, S China
Sujāwal *134 B3* Sind, SE Pakistan
Sukabumi *138 C5 prev.* Soekaboemi. Jawa, C Indonesia
Sukagawa *131 D5* Fukushima, Honshū, C Japan
Sukarnapura *see* Jayapura
Sukarno, Puntjak *see* Jaya, Puncak
Sukhne *see* As Sukhnah
Sukhona *110 C4 var.* Tot'ma. *river* NW Russian Federation
Sukhumi *see* Sokhumi
Sukkertoppen *see* Maniitsoq
Sukkur *134 B3* Sind, SE Pakistan
Sukumo *131 B7* Kōchi, Shikoku, SW Japan

Sulaimaniya *see* As Sulaymānīyah
Sulaiman Range *134 C2 mountain range* C Pakistan
Sula, Kepulauan *139 E4 island group* C Indonesia
Sulawesi, Laut *see* Celebes Sea
Sulechów *98 B3 Ger.* Züllichau. Lubuskie, W Poland
Suliag *see* Sawhāj
Sullana *60 B2* Piura, NW Peru
Sullivan Island *see* Lanbi Kyun
Sulphur Springs *49 G2* Texas, SW USA
Sultānābād *see* Arāk
Sulu Archipelago *139 E3 island group* SW Philippines
Sülüktü *see* Sulyukta
Sulu, Laut *see* Sulu Sea
Sulu Sea *139 E2 var.* Laut Sulu. *sea* SW Philippines
Sulyukta *123 E2 Kir.* Sülüktü. Batkenskaya Oblast', SW Kyrgyzstan
Sumatra *137 B8 Eng.* Sumatra. *island* W Indonesia
Sumatra *see* Sumatera
Šumava *see* Bohemian Forest
Sumba, Pulau *139 E5 Eng.* Sandalwood Island; *prev.* Soemba. *island* Nusa Tenggara, C Indonesia
Sumba, Selat *139 E5 strait* Nusa Tenggara, S Indonesia
Sumbawanga *73 B7* Rukwa, W Tanzania
Sumbe *78 B2 var.* N'Gunza, *Port.* Novo Redondo. Cuanza Sul, W Angola
Sumeih *73 B5* Southern Darfur, S Sudan
Sumgait *see* Sumqayıt, Azerbaijan
Summer Lake *46 B4 lake* Oregon, NW USA
Summit *93 H5* Alaska, USA
Sumqayıt *117 H2 Rus.* Sumgait. E Azerbaijan
Sumy *109 F2* Sums'ka Oblast', NE Ukraine
Sunbury *149 C7* Victoria, SE Australia
Sunda Islands *see* Greater Sunda Islands
Sunda, Selat *138 B5 strait* Jawa/ Sumatera, SW Indonesia
Sunda Trench *see* Java Trench
Sunderland *88 D4 var.* Wearmouth. NE England, United Kingdom
Sundsvall *85 C5* Västernorrland, C Sweden
Sunflower State *see* Kansas
Sungaipenuh *138 B4 prev.* Soengaipenoeh. Sumatera, W Indonesia
Sunnyvale *47 A6* California, W USA
Sunset State *see* Oregon
Sunshine State *see* Florida
Sunshine State *see* New Mexico
Sunshine State *see* South Dakota
Suntar *115 F3* Respublika Sakha (Yakutiya), NE Russian Federation
Sunyani *75 E5* W Ghana
Suoločielgi *see* Saariselkä
Suomenlahti *see* Finland, Gulf of
Suomen Tasavalta/Suomi *see* Finland
Suomussalmi *84 E4* Oulu, E Finland
Suông *137 D6* Kâmpóng Cham, C Cambodia
Suoyarvi *110 B3* Respublika Kareliya, NW Russian Federation
Supe *60 C3* Lima, W Peru
Supérieur, Lac *see* Superior, Lake
Superior *40 A1* Wisconsin, N USA
Superior, Lake *40 B1 Fr.* Lac Supérieur. *lake* Canada/USA
Suqrah *see* Şawqirah
Şūr *121 E5* NE Oman
Şūr *see* Soûr
Surabaja *see* Surabaya
Surabaya *138 D5 prev.* Surabaja, Soerabaja. Jawa, C Indonesia
Surakarta *138 C5 Eng.* Solo; *prev.* Soerakarta. Jawa, S Indonesia
Šurany *99 C6 Hung.* Nagysurány. Nitriansky Kraj, SW Slovakia
Sūrat *134 C4* Gujarāt, W India
Suratdhani *see* Surat Thani
Surat Thani *137 C6 var.* Suratdhani. Surat Thani, SW Thailand
Surazh *107 E5* Vitsyebskaya Voblasts', NE Belarus
Surdulica *101 E5* Serbia, SE Serbia

Sûre *87 D7 var.* Sauer. *river* W Europe
Surendranagar *134 C4* Gujarāt, W India
Surfers Paradise *149 E5* Queensland, E Australia
Surgut *114 D3* Khanty-Mansiyskiy Avtonomnyy Okrug-Yugra, C Russian Federation
Surin *137 D5* Surin, E Thailand
Surinam *see* Suriname
Suriname *59 G3 off.* Republic of Suriname, *var.* Surinam; *prev.* Dutch Guiana, Netherlands Guiana. *country* N South America

SURINAME
South America

Official name Republic of Suriname
Formation 1975 / 1975
Capital Paramaribo
Population 500,000 / 8 people per sq mile (3 people per sq km)
Total area 63,039 sq. miles (163,270 sq. km)
Languages Sranan (Creole), Dutch*, Javanese, Sarnami Hindi, Saramaccan, Chinese, Carib
Religions Hindu 27%, Protestant 25%, Roman Catholic 23%, Muslim 20%, Traditional beliefs 5%
Ethnic mix East Indian 27%, Creole 18%, Black 15%, Javanese 15%, Mixed race 13%, Other 6%, Amerindian 4%, Chinese 2%
Government Parliamentary system
Currency Surinamese dollar = 100 cents
Literacy rate 95%
Calorie consumption 2548 kilocalories

Suriname, Republic of *see* Suriname
Sūriya/Sūriyah, Al-Jumhūriyah al-'Arabiyah as- *see* Syria
Surkhab, Darya-i- *see* Kahmard, Daryā-ye
Surkhob *123 F3 river* C Tajikistan
Surt *71 G2 var.* Sidra, Sirte. N Libya
Surtsey *83 E5 island* S Iceland
Suruga-wan *131 D6 bay* SE Japan
Susa *96 A2* Piemonte, NE Italy
Süsah *see* Sousse
Susanville *47 B5* California, W USA
Susitna *36 C3* Alaska, USA
Susteren *87 D5* Limburg, SE Netherlands
Susuman *115 G3* Magadanskaya Oblast', E Russian Federation
Sutlej *134 C2 river* India/Pakistan
Suur Munamägi *106 D3 var.* Munamägi, *Ger.* Eier-Berg. *mountain* SE Estonia
Suur Väin *106 C2 Ger.* Grosser Sund. *strait* W Estonia
Suva *145 E4 country capital* (Fiji) Viti Levu, W Fiji
Suvalkai/Suvalki *see* Suwałki
Suwałki *98 E2 Lith.* Suvalkai, *Rus.* Suvalki. Podlaskie, NE Poland
Suways, Qanāt as *see* Suez Canal
Suweida *see* As Suwaydā'
Suzhou *128 D5 var.* Soochow, Su-chou, Suchow; *prev.* Wuhsien. Jiangsu, E China
Svalbard *83 E1 Norwegian dependency* Arctic Ocean
Svartisen *84 C3 glacier* C Norway
Svay Riĕng *137 D6* Svay Riĕng, S Cambodia
Sveg *85 B5* Jämtland, C Sweden
Svenstavik *85 C5* Jämtland, C Sweden
Sverdlovsk *see* Yekaterinburg
Sverige *see* Sweden
Sveti Vrach *see* Sandanski
Svetlogorsk *see* Svyetlahorsk
Svetlograd *111 B7* Stavropol'skiy Kray, SW Russian Federation
Svetlovodsk *see* Svitlovods'k
Svetozarevo *see* Jagodina
Svilengrad *104 D3 prev.* Mustafa-Pasha. Khaskovo, S Bulgaria
Svitlovods'k *109 F3 Rus.* Svetlovodsk. Kirovohrads'ka Oblast', C Ukraine
Svizzera *see* Switzerland
Svobodnyy *115 G4* Amurskaya Oblast', SE Russian Federation
Svyataya Anna Trough *155 C4 var.* Saint Anna Trough. *trough* N Kara Sea
Svyetlahorsk *107 D7 Rus.* Svetlogorsk. Homyel'skaya Voblasts', SE Belarus
Swabian Jura *see* Schwäbische Alb
Swakopmund *78 B3* Erongo, W Namibia

Swan Islands *53 E1 island group* NE Honduras North America
Swansea *89 C7 Wel.* Abertawe. S Wales, United Kingdom
Swarzędz *98 C3* Poznań, W Poland
Swatow *see* Shantou
Swaziland *78 D4 off.* Kingdom of Swaziland. *country* S Africa

SWAZILAND
Southern Africa

Official name Kingdom of Swaziland
Formation 1968 / 1968
Capital Mbabane
Population 1.2 million / 181 people per sq mile (70 people per sq km)
Total area 6704 sq. miles (17,363 sq. km)
Languages English*, siSwati*, isiZulu, Xitsonga
Religions Traditional beliefs 40%, Other 30%, Roman Catholic 20%, Muslim 10%
Ethnic mix Swazi 97%, Other 3%
Government Monarchy
Currency Lilangeni = 100 cents
Literacy rate 87%
Calorie consumption 2249 kilocalories

Swaziland, Kingdom of *see* Swaziland
Sweden *84 B4 off.* Kingdom of Sweden, *Swe.* Sverige. *country* N Europe

SWEDEN
Northern Europe

Official name Kingdom of Sweden
Formation 1523 / 1921
Capital Stockholm
Population 9.4 million / 59 people per sq mile (23 people per sq km)
Total area 173,731 sq. miles (449,964 sq. km)
Languages Swedish*, Finnish, Sámi
Religions Evangelical Lutheran 75%, Other 13%, Muslim 5%, Other Protestant 5%, Roman Catholic 2%
Ethnic mix Swedish 86%, Foreign-born or first-generation immigrant 12%, Finnish and Sámi 2%
Government Parliamentary system
Currency Swedish krona = 100 öre
Literacy rate 99%
Calorie consumption 3125 kilocalories

Sweden, Kingdom of *see* Sweden
Sweetwater *49 F3* Texas, SW USA
Świdnica *98 B4 Ger.* Schweidnitz. Wałbrzych, SW Poland
Świdwin *98 B2 Ger.* Schivelbein. Zachodnio-pomorskie, NW Poland
Świebodzice *98 B4 Ger.* Freiburg in Schlesien, Swiebodzice. Wałbrzych, SW Poland
Świebodzin *98 B3 Ger.* Schwiebus. Lubuskie, W Poland
Świecie *98 C3 Ger.* Schwertberg. Kujawsko-pomorskie, C Poland
Swindon *89 D7* S England, United Kingdom
Swinemünde *see* Świnoujście
Świnoujście *98 B2 Ger.* Swinemünde. Zachodnio-pomorskie, NW Poland
Swiss Confederation *see* Switzerland
Switzerland *95 A7 off.* Swiss Confederation, *Fr.* La Suisse, *Ger.* Schweiz, *It.* Svizzera; *anc.* Helvetia. *country* C Europe

SWITZERLAND
Central Europe

Official name Swiss Confederation
Formation 1291 / 1857
Capital Bern
Population 7.7 million / 501 people per sq mile (194 people per sq km)
Total area 15,942 sq. miles (41,290 sq. km)
Languages German*, Swiss-German, French*, Italian*, Romansh
Religions Roman Catholic 42%, Protestant 35%, Other and nonreligious 19%, Muslim 4%
Ethnic mix German 64%, French 20%, Other 9.5%, Italian 6%, Romansch 0.5%

SWITZERLAND
(continued)

Government Parliamentary system
Currency Swiss franc = 100
rappen/centimes
Literacy rate 99%
Calorie consumption 3454 kilocalories

Sycaminum see Hefa
Sydenham Island see Nonouti
Sydney 148 D1 *state capital* New South
Wales, SE Australia
Sydney 39 G4 Cape Breton Island, Nova
Scotia, SE Canada
Sydney Island see Manra
Syedpur see Saidpur
Syemyezhava 107 C6 *Rus.* Semezhovo.
Minskaya Voblasts', C Belarus
Syene see Aswān
Syeverodonets'k 109 H3 *Rus.*
Severodonetsk. Luhans'ka Oblast',
E Ukraine
Syktyvkar 110 D4 *prev.* Ust'-Sysol'sk.
Respublika Komi, NW Russian
Federation
Sylhet 135 G3 Sylhet, NE Bangladesh
Synel'nykove 109 G3 Dnipropetrovs'ka
Oblast', E Ukraine
Syowa 154 C2 *Japanese research station*
Antarctica
Syracuse 41 E3 New York, NE USA
Syracuse see Siracusa
Syrdar'ya 114 B4 Sirdaryo Viloyati,
E Uzbekistan
Syria 118 B3 *off.* Syrian Arab Republic,
var. Siria, Syrie, *Ar.* Al-Jumhūrīyah
al-'Arabīyah as-Sūrīyah, Sūrīya.
country SW Asia

SYRIA
Southwest Asia

Official name Syrian Arab Republic
Formation 1941 / 1967
Capital Damascus
Population 20.8 million / 293 people
per sq mile (113 people per sq km)
Total area 114.9 sq. miles (184,180 sq. km)
Languages Arabic*, French, Kurdish,
Armenian, Circassian, Turkic languages,
Assyrian, Aramaic
Religions Sunni Muslim 74%, Alawi 12%,
Christian 10%, Druze 3%, Other 1%
Ethnic mix Arab 90%, Kurdish 9%,
Armenian, Turkmen, and Circassian 1%
Government One-party state
Currency Syrian pound = 100 piastres
Literacy rate 84%
Calorie consumption 3212 kilocalories

Syrian Arab Republic see Syria
Syrian Desert 119 D5 *Ar.* Al Hamad,
Bādiyat ash Shām. *desert* SW Asia
Syrie see Syria
Sýrna 105 E7 *var.* Sirna. *island* Kykládes,
Greece, Aegean Sea
Sýros 105 C6 *var.* Síros. *island* Kykládes,
Greece, Aegean Sea
Syulemeshlii see Sredets
Syvash, Zaliv see Syvash, Zatoka
Syvash, Zatoka 109 F4 *Rus.* Zaliv Syvash.
inlet S Ukraine
Syzran' 111 C6 Samarskaya Oblast',
W Russian Federation
Szabadka see Subotica
Szamotuły 98 B3 Poznań, W Poland
Százrégen see Reghin
Szatmárnémeti see Satu Mare
Száva see Sava
Szczecin 98 B3 *Eng./Ger.* Stettin.
Zachodnio-pomorskie, NW Poland
Szczecinek 98 B2 *Ger.* Neustettin.
Zachodnio-pomorskie, NW Poland
Szczeciński, Zalew 98 A2 *var.* Stettiner
Haff, *Ger.* Oderhaff. *bay* Germany/
Poland
Szczuczyn Nowogródzki see
Shchuchyn
Szczytno 98 D3 *Ger.* Ortelsburg.
Warmińsko-Mazurskie,
NE Poland
Szechuan/Szechwan see Sichuan
Szeged 99 D7 *Ger.* Szegedin, *Rom.*
Seghedin. Csongrád, SE Hungary
Szegedin see Szeged
Székelykeresztúr see Cristuru Secuiesc

Székesfehérvár 99 C6 *Ger.*
Stuhlweissenberg; *anc.* Alba Regia.
Fejér, W Hungary
Szeklerburg see Miercurea-Ciuc
Szekler Neumarkt see Târgu Secuiesc
Szekszárd 99 C7 Tolna, S Hungary
Szempcz/Szenc see Senec
Szenice see Senica
Szenttamás see Srbobran
Szeping see Siping
Szilágysomlyó see Şimleu Silvaniei
Szinna see Snina
Sziszek see Sisak
Szitás-Keresztúr see Cristuru Secuiesc
Szkudy see Skuodas
Szlatina see Slatina
Szlovákia see Slovakia
Szolnok 99 D6 Jász-Nagykun-Szolnok,
C Hungary
Szombathely 99 B6 *Ger.* Steinamanger;
anc. Sabaria, Savaria. Vas,
W Hungary
Szprotawa 98 B4 *Ger.* Sprottau.
Lubuskie, W Poland
Sztálinváros see Dunaújváros
Szucsava see Suceava

T

Tabariya, Bahrat see Tiberias, Lake
Table Rock Lake 49 G1 *reservoir*
Arkansas/Missouri, C USA
Tábor 99 B5 Jihočeský Kraj, S Czech
Republic
Tabora 73 B7 Tabora, W Tanzania
Tabriz 120 C2 *var.* Tebriz; *anc.* Tauris.
Āzarbāyjān-e Sharqī, NW Iran
Tabuaeran 145 G2 *prev.* Fanning Island.
atoll Line Islands, E Kiribati
Tabūk 120 A4 Tabūk, NW Saudi Arabia
Täby 85 C6 Stockholm, C Sweden
Tachau see Tachov
Tachov 99 A5 *Ger.* Tachau. Plveňský
Kraj, W Czech Republic
Tacloban 139 F2 *off.* Tacloban City.
Leyte, C Philippines
Tacloban City see Tacloban
Tacna 61 E4 Tacna, SE Peru
Tacoma 46 B2 Washington, NW USA
Tacuarembó 64 D4 *prev.* San Fructuoso.
Tacuarembó, C Uruguay
Tademait, Plateau du 70 D3 *plateau*
C Algeria
Tadmor/Tadmur see Tudmur
Tādpatri 132 C2 Andhra Pradesh,
E India
Tadzhikistan see Tajikistan
Taegu see Daegu
Taehan-haehyŏp see Korea Strait
Taehan Min'guk see South Korea
Taejŏn see Daejeon
Tafassâsset, Ténéré du 75 G2 *desert*
N Niger
Tafila/Ṭafilah, Muḩāfaẓat aṭ see Aṭ
Ṭafīlah
Taganrog 111 A7 Rostovskaya Oblast',
SW Russian Federation
Taganrog, Gulf of 109 G4 *Rus.*
Taganrogskiy Zaliv, *Ukr.* Tahanroz'ka
Zatoka. *gulf* Russian Federation/
Ukraine
Taganrogskiy Zaliv see Taganrog,
Gulf of
Taguatinga 63 F3 Tocantins,
C Brazil
Tagus 92 C3 *Port.* Rio Tejo, *Sp.* Río Tajo.
river Portugal/Spain
Tagus Plain 80 A4 *abyssal plain*
E Atlantic Ocean
Tahanroz'ka Zatoka see Taganrog,
Gulf of
Tahat 71 E4 *mountain* SE Algeria
Tahiti 145 H4 *island* Îles du Vent,
W French Polynesia
Tahiti, Archipel de see Société, Archipel
de la
Tahlequah 49 G1 Oklahoma,
C USA
Tahoe, Lake 47 B5 *lake* California/
Nevada, W USA
Tahoua 75 F3 Tahoua, W Niger
Taichū see Taizhong
T'aichung see Taizhong
Taiden see Daejeon

Taieri 151 B7 *river* South Island, New
Zealand
Taihape 150 D4 Manawatu-Wanganui,
North Island, New Zealand
Taihoku see T'aipei
Taikyū see Daegu
Tailem Bend 149 B7 South Australia
Tainan 128 D6 *prev.* Dainan, T'ainan.
S Taiwan
T'aipei 128 D6 *Jap.* Taihoku; *prev.*
Daihoku. *country capital* (Taiwan)
N Taiwan
Taiping 138 B3 Perak, Peninsular
Malaysia
Taiwan 128 D6 *off.* Republic of China,
var. Formosa, Formo'sa. *country*
E Asia

TAIWAN
East Asia

Official name Republic of China (ROC)
Formation 1949 / 1949
Capital Taipei
Population 23.2 million / 1860 people
per sq mile (718 people per sq km)
Total area 13,892 sq. miles (35,980 sq. km)
Languages Amoy Chinese, Mandarin
Chinese*, Hakka Chinese
Religions Buddhist, Confucianist, and
Taoist 93%, Christian 5%, Other 2%
Ethnic mix Han (pre-20th-century
migration) 84%, Han (20th-century
migration) 14%, Aboriginal 2%
Government Presidential system
Currency Taiwan dollar = 100 cents
Literacy rate 98%
Calorie consumption 2673 kilocalories

Taiwan see Taizhong
T'aiwan Haihsia/Taiwan Haixia see
Taiwan Strait
Taiwan Strait 128 D6 *var.* Formosa
Strait, *Chin.* T'aiwan Haihsia, Taiwan
Haixia. *strait* China/Taiwan
Taiyuan 128 C4 *var.* T'ai-yuan, T'ai-
yüan; *prev.* Yangku. *province capital*
Shanxi, C China
T'ai-yuan/T'ai-yüan see Taiyuan
Taizhong 128 D6 *Jap.* Taichū; *prev.*
T'aichung, Taiwan. C Taiwan
Ta'izz 121 B7 SW Yemen
Tajikistan 123 E3 *off.* Republic of
Tajikistan, *Rus.* Tadzhikistan, *Taj.*
Jumhurii Tojikiston; *prev.* Tajik S.S.R.
country C Asia

TAJIKISTAN
Central Asia

Official name Republic of Tajikistan
Formation 1991 / 1991
Capital Dushanbe
Population 7 million / 127 people
per sq mile (143,100 sq. km)
Total area 55,251 sq. miles (143,100 sq. km)
Languages Tajik*, Uzbek, Russian
Religions Sunni Muslim 95%,
Shi'a Muslim 3%, Other 2%
Ethnic mix Tajik 80%, Uzbek 15%,
Other 3%, Russian 1%, Kyrgyz 1%
Government Presidential system
Currency Somoni = 100 diram
Literacy rate 99%
Calorie consumption 2106 kilocalories

Tajikistan, Republic of see Tajikistan
Tajik S.S.R see Tajikistan
Tajo, Río see Tagus
Tak 136 C4 *var.* Rahaeng. Tak,
W Thailand
Takao see Gaoxiong
Takaoka 131 C5 Toyama, Honshū,
SW Japan
Takapuna 150 D2 Auckland, North
Island, New Zealand
Takhiatash see Taxiatosh
Takhtakupyr see Taxtako'pir
Takikawa 130 D2 Hokkaidō,
NE Japan
Takla Makan Desert 126 B3 *Eng.* Takla
Makan Desert. *desert* NW China
Takla Makan Desert see Taklimakan
Shamo
Takow see Gaoxiong
Takutea 145 G4 *island* S Cook Islands

Talabriga see Aveiro, Portugal
Talabriga see Talavera de la Reina,
Spain
Talachyn 107 D6 *Rus.* Tolochin.
Vitsyebskaya Voblasts', NE Belarus
Talamanca, Cordillera de 53 E5
mountain range S Costa Rica
Talara 60 B2 Piura, NW Peru
Talas 123 F2 Talasskaya Oblast',
NW Kyrgyzstan
Talaud, Kepulauan 139 F3 *island group*
E Indonesia
Talavera de la Reina 92 D3 *anc.*
Caesarobriga, Talabriga. Castilla-La
Mancha, C Spain
Talca 64 B4 Maule, C Chile
Talcahuano 65 B5 Bío Bío, C Chile
Taldykorgan 114 C5 *Kaz.* Taldyqorghan;
prev. Taldy-Kurgan. Taldykorgan,
SE Kazakhstan
Taldy-Kurgan/Taldyqorghan see
Taldykorgan
Ta-lien see Dalian
Taliq-an see Tāloqān
Tal'ka 107 C6 Minskaya Voblasts',
C Belarus
Talkhof see Puurmani
Tallahassee 42 D3 *prev.* Muskogean.
state capital Florida, SE USA
Tall al Abyaḍ see At Tall al Abyaḍ
Tallin see Tallinn
Tallinn 106 D2 *Ger.* Reval, *Rus.* Tallin;
prev. Revel. *country capital* (Estonia)
Harjumaa, NW Estonia
Tall Kalakh 118 B4 *var.* Tell Kalakh.
Ḥimş, C Syria
Tallulah 42 B2 Louisiana,
S USA
Talnakh 114 D3 Krasnoyarskiy Kray,
N Russian Federation
Tal'ne 109 E3 *Rus.* Tal'noye. Cherkas'ka
Oblast', C Ukraine
Tal'noye see Tal'ne
Taloga 49 F1 Oklahoma, C USA
Tāloqān 123 E3 *var.* Taliq-an. Takhār,
NE Afghanistan
Talsen see Talsi
Talsi 106 C3 *Ger.* Talsen.
NW Latvia
Taltal 64 B2 Antofagasta, N Chile
Talvik 84 D2 Finnmark, N Norway
Tamabo, Banjaran 138 D3 *mountain
range* East Malaysia
Tamale 75 E4 C Ghana
Tamana 145 E3 *prev.* Rotcher Island.
atoll Tungaru, W Kiribati
Tamanrasset 71 E4 *var.* Tamenghest.
S Algeria
Tamar 89 C7 *river* SW England, United
Kingdom
Tamar see Tudmur
Tamatave see Toamasina
Tamazunchale 51 E4 San Luis Potosí,
C Mexico
Tambacounda 74 C3 SE Senegal
Tambov 111 B6 Tambovskaya Oblast',
W Russian Federation
Tambura 73 B5 Western Equatoria,
SW South Sudan
Tamchaket see Tâmchekket
Tâmchekket 74 C3 *var.* Tamchaket.
Hodh el Gharbi, S Mauritania
Tamenghest see Tamanrasset
Tamil Nādu 132 C3 *prev.* Madras.
cultural region SE India
Tam Ky 137 E5 Quang Nam-fa Nâng,
C Vietnam
Tammerfors see Tampere
Tampa 43 E4 Florida, SE USA
Tampa Bay 43 E4 *bay* Florida,
SE USA
Tampere 85 D5 *Swe.* Tammerfors.
Länsi-Suomi, W Finland
Tampico 51 E3 Tamaulipas,
C Mexico
Tamworth 149 D6 New South Wales,
SE Australia
Tanabe 131 C7 Wakayama, Honshū,
SW Japan
Tana Bru 84 D2 Finnmark, N Norway
Tanais see Don
Lake Tana 72 C4 *var.* Lake Tana. *lake*
NW Ethiopia
Tana, Lake see T'ana Hāyk'

Tanami Desert 146 D3 *desert* Northern Territory, N Australia

Tananarive *see* Antananarivo

Țăndărei 108 D5 Ialomița, SE Romania

Tandil 65 D5 Buenos Aires, E Argentina

Tandjoengkarang *see* Bandar Lampung

Tanega-shima 131 B8 *island* Nanseishotō, SW Japan

Tanen Taunggyi *see* Tane Range

Tane Range 136 B4 *Bur.* Tanen Taunggyi. *mountain range* W Thailand

Tanezrouft 70 D4 *desert* Algeria/Mali

Țanf, Jabal at 118 D4 *mountain* SE Syria

Tanga 73 C7 Tanga, E Tanzania

Tanganyika and Zanzibar *see* Tanzania

Tanganyika, Lake 73 B7 *lake* E Africa

Tanger 70 C2 *var.* Tangiers, Tangier, *Fr./Ger.* Tangerk, *Sp.* Tánger; *anc.* Tingis. NW Morocco

Tangerk *see* Tanger

Tanggula Shan 126 C4 *mountain* W China

Tangier *see* Tanger

Tangiers *see* Tanger

Tangra Yumco 126 B5 *var.* Tangro Tso. *lake* W China

Tangro Tso *see* Tangra Yumco

Tangshan 128 D3 *var.* T'ang-shan. Hebei, E China

T'ang-shan *see* Tangshan

Tanimbar, Kepulauan 139 F5 *island group* Maluku, E Indonesia

Tanintharyi 137 B6 *var.* Tenasserim. Tanintharyi, S Myanmar (Burma)

Tanjungkarang/Tanjungkarang-Telukbetung *see* Bandar Lampung

Tanna 144 D4 *island* S Vanuatu

Tannenhof *see* Krynica

Tan-Tan 70 B3 SW Morocco

Tan-tung *see* Dandong

Tanzania 73 C7 *off.* United Republic of Tanzania, *Swa.* Jamhuri ya Muungano wa Tanzania; *prev.* German East Africa, Tanganyika and Zanzibar. *country* E Africa

---

TANZANIA
East Africa

Official name United Republic of Tanzania
Formation 1964 / 1964
Capital Dodoma
Population 46.2 million / 135 people per sq mile (52 people per sq km)
Total area 364,898 sq. miles (945,087 sq. km)
Languages Kiswahili*, Sukuma, Chagga, Nyamwezi, Hehe, Makonde, Yao, Sandawe, English*
Religions Christian 63%, Muslim 35%, Other 2%
Ethnic mix Native African (over 120 tribes) 99%, European, Asian, and Arab 1%
Government Presidential system
Currency Tanzanian shilling = 100 cents
Literacy rate 73%
Calorie consumption 2137 kilocalories

Tanzania, Jamhuri ya Muungano wa *see* Tanzania

Tanzania, United Republic of *see* Tanzania

Taoudenit *see* Taoudenni

Taoudenni 75 E2 *var.* Taoudenit. Tombouctou, N Mali

Tapa 106 E2 *Ger.* Taps. Lääne-Virumaa, NE Estonia

Tapachula 51 G5 Chiapas, SE Mexico

Tapaiu *see* Gvardeysk

Tapajós, Rio 63 E2 *var.* Tapajóz. *river* NW Brazil

Tapajóz *see* Tapajós, Rio

Taps *see* Tapa

Țarābulus 71 F2 *var.* Țarābulus al Gharb, *Eng.* Tripoli. *country capital* (Libya) NW Libya

Țarābulus al Gharb *see* Țarābulus

Țarābulus/Țarābulus ash Shām *see* Tripoli

Taraclia 108 D4 *Rus.* Tarakilya. S Moldova

Tarakilya *see* Taraclia

Mount Taranaki 150 C4 *var.* Egmont. *volcano* North Island, New Zealand

Tarancón 93 E3 Castilla-La Mancha, C Spain

Taranto 97 E5 *var.* Tarentum. Puglia, SE Italy

Taranto, Gulf of 97 E6 *Eng.* Gulf of Taranto. *gulf* S Italy

Taranto, Gulf of *see* Taranto, Golfo di

Tarapoto 60 C2 San Martín, N Peru

Tarare 91 D5 Rhône, E France

Tarascon 91 D6 Bouches-du-Rhône, SE France

Tarawa 144 D2 *atoll* Tungaru, W Kiribati

Taraz 114 C5 *prev.* Aulie Ata, Auliye-Ata, Dzhambul, Zhambyl. Zhambyl, S Kazakhstan

Tarazona 93 E2 Aragón, NE Spain

Tarbes 91 B6 *anc.* Bigorra. Hautes-Pyrénées, S France

Tarcoola 149 A6 South Australia

Taree 149 D6 New South Wales, SE Australia

Tarentum *see* Taranto

Târgoviște 108 C5 *prev.* Tîrgoviște. Dâmbovița, S Romania

Targu Jiu 108 B4 *prev.* Tîrgu Jiu. Gorj, W Romania

Târgul-Neamț *see* Târgu-Neamț

Târgul-Săcuiesc *see* Târgu Secuiesc

Târgu Mureș 108 B4 *prev.* Oșorhei, Tîrgu Mures, *Ger.* Neumarkt, *Hung.* Marosvásárhely. Mureș, C Romania

Târgu-Neamț 108 C3 *var.* Târgul-Neamț; *prev.* Tîrgu-Neamț. Neamț, NE Romania

Târgu Ocna 108 C4 *Hung.* Aknavásár; *prev.* Tîrgu Ocna. Bacău, E Romania

Târgu Secuiesc 108 C4 *Ger.* Neumarkt, Szekler Neumarkt, *Hung.* Kezdivásárhely; *prev.* Chezdi-Oșorheiu, Târgul-Săcuiesc, Tîrgu Secuiesc. Covasna, E Romania

Tar Heel State *see* North Carolina

Tarija 61 G5 Tarija, S Bolivia

Tarim 121 C6 C Yemen

Tarim Basin 124 C2 *Eng.* Tarim Basin. *basin* NW China

Tarim Basin *see* Tarim Pendi

Tarim He 126 B3 *river* NW China

Tarma 60 C3 Junín, C Peru

Tarn 91 C6 *cultural region* S France

Tarn 91 C6 *river* S France

Tarnobrzeg 98 D4 Podkarpackie, SE Poland

Tarnopol *see* Ternopil'

Tarnów 99 D5 Małopolskie, S Poland

Tarraco *see* Tarragona

Tarragona 93 G2 *anc.* Tarraco. Cataluña, E Spain

Tarrasa *see* Terrassa

Tàrrega 93 F2 *var.* Tarrega. Cataluña, NE Spain

Tarsatica *see* Rijeka

Tarsus 116 C4 İçel, S Turkey

Tartous/Tartouss *see* Țarțūs

Tartu 106 D3 *Ger.* Dorpat; *prev.* Rus. Yurev, Yury'ev. Tartumaa, SE Estonia

Țarțūs 118 A3 *off.* Muḥāfaẓat Țarțūs, *var.* Tartous, Tartus. *governorate* W Syria

Țarțūs, Muḥāfaẓat *see* Țarțūs

Ta Ru Tao, Ko 137 B7 *island* S Thailand Asia

Tarvisio 96 D2 Friuli-Venezia Giulia, NE Italy

Tarvisium *see* Treviso

Tashauz *see* Daşoguz

Tashi Chho Dzong *see* Thimphu

Tashkent *see* Toshkent

Tash-Kömür *see* Tash-Kumyr

Tash-Kumyr 123 F2 *Kir.* Tash-Kömür. Dzhalal-Abadskaya Oblast', W Kyrgyzstan

Tashqurghan *see* Khulm

Tasikmalaja *see* Tasikmalaya

Tasikmalaya 138 C5 *prev.* Tasikmalaja. Jawa, C Indonesia

Tasman Basin 142 C5 *var.* East Australian Basin. *undersea basin* S Tasman Sea

Tasman Bay 151 C5 *inlet* South Island, New Zealand

Tasmania 149 B8 *prev.* Van Diemen's Land. *state* SE Australia

Tasmania 152 B4 *island* SE Australia

Tasman Plateau 142 C5 *var.* South Tasmania Plateau. *undersea plateau* SW Tasman Sea

Tasman Sea 142 C5 *sea* SW Pacific Ocean

Tassili-n-Ajjer 71 E4 *plateau* E Algeria

Tatabánya 99 C6 Komárom-Esztergom, NW Hungary

Tatar Pazardzhik *see* Pazardzhik

Tathlith 121 B5 'Asīr, S Saudi Arabia

Tatra Mountains 99 D5 *Ger.* Tatra, *Hung.* Tátra, *Pol./Slvk.* Tatry. *mountain range* Poland/Slovakia

Tatra/Tátra *see* Tatra Mountains

Tatry *see* Tatra Mountains

Ta-t'ung/Tatung *see* Datong

Tatvan 117 F3 Bitlis, SE Turkey

Ta'ū 145 F4 *var.* Tau. *island* Manua Islands, E American Samoa

Taukum, Peski 123 G1 *desert* SE Kazakhstan

Taumarunui 150 D4 Manawatu-Wanganui, North Island, New Zealand

Taungdwingyi 136 B3 Magway, C Myanmar (Burma)

Taunggyi 136 B3 Shan State, C Myanmar (Burma)

Taungoo 136 B4 Bago, C Myanmar (Burma)

Taunton 89 C7 SW England, United Kingdom

Taupo 150 D3 Waikato, North Island, New Zealand

Taupo, Lake 150 D3 *lake* North Island, New Zealand

Tauragė 106 B4 *Ger.* Tauroggen. Tauragė, SW Lithuania

Tauranga 150 D3 Bay of Plenty, North Island, New Zealand

Tauris *see* Tabrīz

Taurisci *see* Tabrīz

Tauroggen *see* Tauragė

Taurus Mountains 116 C4 *Eng.* Taurus Mountains. *mountain range* S Turkey

Taurus Mountains *see* Toros Dağları

Tavas 116 B4 Denizli, SW Turkey

Tavastehus *see* Hämeenlinna

Tavira 92 C5 Faro, S Portugal

Tavoy *see* Dawei

Tavoy Island *see* Mali Kyun

Ta Waewae Bay 151 A7 *bay* South Island, New Zealand

Tawakoni, Lake 49 G2 *reservoir* Texas, SW USA

Tawau 138 D3 Sabah, East Malaysia

Țawkar *see* Tokar

Tawzar *see* Tozeur

Taxco 51 E4 *var.* Taxco de Alarcón. Guerrero, S Mexico

Taxco de Alarcón *see* Taxco

Taxiatosh 122 C2 *Rus.* Takhiatash. Qoraqalpog'iston Respublikasi, W Uzbekistan

Taxtako'pir 122 D1 *Rus.* Takhtakupyr. Qoraqalpog'iston Respublikasi, NW Uzbekistan

Tay 88 C3 *river* C Scotland, United Kingdom

Taylor 49 G3 Texas, SW USA

Taymā' 120 A4 Tabūk, NW Saudi Arabia

Taymyr, Ozero 115 E2 *lake* N Russian Federation

Taymyr, Poluostrov 115 E2 *peninsula* N Russian Federation

Taz 114 D3 *river* N Russian Federation

Tbilisi 117 G2 *Eng.* Tiflis. *country capital* (Georgia) SE Georgia

Tchad *see* Chad

Tchad, Lac *see* Chad, Lake

Tchien *see* Zwedru

Tchongking *see* Chongqing

Tczew 98 C2 *Ger.* Dirschau. Pomorskie, N Poland

Te Anau 151 A7 Southland, South Island, New Zealand

Te Anau, Lake 151 A7 *lake* South Island, New Zealand

Teapa 51 G4 Tabasco, SE Mexico

Teate *see* Chieti

Tebingtinggi 138 B3 Sumatera, N Indonesia

Tebriz *see* Tabrīz

Techirghiol 108 D5 Constanța, SE Romania

Tecomán 50 D4 Colima, SW Mexico

Tecpan 51 E5 *var.* Tecpan de Galeana. Guerrero, S Mexico

Tecpan de Galeana *see* Tecpan

Tecuci 108 C4 Galați, E Romania

Tedzhen *see* Harīrūd/Tejen

Tedzhen *see* Tejen

Tees 89 D5 *river* N England, United Kingdom

Tefé 62 D2 Amazonas, N Brazil

Tegal 138 C4 Jawa, C Indonesia

Tegelen 87 D5 Limburg, SE Netherlands

Tegucigalpa *see* Toncontín

Teheran *see* Tehrān

Tehrān 120 C3 *var.* Teheran. *country capital* (Iran) Tehrān, N Iran

Tehuacán 51 F4 Puebla, S Mexico

Tehuantepec 51 F5 *var.* Santo Domingo Tehuantepec. Oaxaca, SE Mexico

Gulf of Tehuantepec 51 F5 *var.* Gulf of Tehuantepec. *gulf* S Mexico

Tehuantepec, Gulf of *see* Tehuantepec, Golfo de

Isthmus of Tehuantepec 51 F5 *var.* Isthmus of Tehuantepec. *isthmus* SE Mexico

Tehuantepec, Isthmus of *see* Tehuantepec, Istmo de

Tejen 122 C3 *Rus.* Tedzhen. Ahal Welaýaty, S Turkmenistan

Tejen *see* Harīrūd

Tejo, Rio *see* Tagus

Te Kao 150 C1 Northland, North Island, New Zealand

Tekax 51 H4 *var.* Tekax de Álvaro Obregón. Yucatán, SE Mexico

Tekax de Álvaro Obregón *see* Tekax

Tekeli 114 C5 Almaty, SE Kazakhstan

Tekirdağ 116 A2 *It.* Rodosto; *anc.* Bisanthe, Raidestos, Rhaedestus. Tekirdağ, NW Turkey

Te Kuiti 150 D3 Waikato, North Island, New Zealand

Tela 52 C2 Atlántida, NW Honduras

Telanaipura *see* Jambi

Tel Aviv-Jaffa *see* Tel Aviv-Yafo

Tel Aviv-Yafo 119 A6 *var.* Tel Aviv-Jaffa. Tel Aviv, C Israel

Teles Pirés *see* São Manuel, Rio

Telish 104 C2 *prev.* Azizie. Pleven, N Bulgaria

Tell Abiad/Tell Abyad *see* At Tall al Abyaḍ

Tell Kalakh *see* Tall Kalakh

Tell Shedadi *see* Ash Shadādah

Tel'man/Tel'mansk *see* Gubadag

Teloekbetoeng *see* Bandar Lampung

Telo Martius *see* Toulon

Telschen *see* Telšiai

Telšiai 106 B3 *Ger.* Telschen. Telšiai, NW Lithuania

Telukbetung *see* Bandar Lampung

Temerin 100 D3 Vojvodina, N Serbia

Temeschburg/Temeschwar *see* Timișoara

Temesvár/Temeswar *see* Timișoara

Temirtau 114 C4 *prev.* Samarkandskii, Samarkandskoye. Karagandy, C Kazakhstan

Tempio Pausania 97 A5 Sardegna, Italy, C Mediterranean Sea

Temple 49 G3 Texas, SW USA

Temuco 65 B5 Araucanía, C Chile

Temuka 151 B6 Canterbury, South Island, New Zealand

Tenasserim *see* Tanintharyi

Ténenkou 74 D3 Mopti, C Mali

Ténéré 75 G3 *physical region* C Niger

Tenerife 70 A3 *island* Islas Canarias, Spain, NE Atlantic Ocean

Tengger Shamo 127 E3 *desert* N China

Tengréla 74 D4 *var.* Tingréla. N Côte d'Ivoire

Tenkodogo 75 E4 S Burkina Faso

Tennant Creek 148 A3 Northern Territory, C Australia

Tennessee 42 C1 off. State of Tennessee, also known as The Volunteer State. state SE USA
Tennessee River 42 C1 river S USA
Tenos see Tínos
Tepelena see Tepelenë
Tepelenë 101 C7 var. Tepelena, It. Tepeleni. Gjirokastër, S Albania
Tepeleni see Tepelenë
Tepic 50 D4 Nayarit, C Mexico
Teplice 98 A4 Ger. Teplitz; prev. Teplice-Šanov, Teplitz-Schönau. Ústecký Kraj, NW Czech Republic
Teplice-Šanov/Teplitz/Teplitz-Schönau see Teplice
Tequila 50 D4 Jalisco, SW Mexico
Teraina 145 G2 prev. Washington Island. atoll Line Islands, E Kiribati
Teramo 96 C4 anc. Interamna. Abruzzi, C Italy
Tercan 117 E3 Erzincan, NE Turkey
Terceira 92 A5 var. Ilha Terceira. island Azores, Portugal, NE Atlantic Ocean
Terceira, Ilha see Terceira
Terekhovka see Tsyerakhowka
Teresina 63 F2 var. Therezina. state capital Piauí, NE Brazil
Termez see Termiz
Termia see Kýthnos
Términos, Laguna de 51 G4 lagoon SE Mexico
Termiz 123 E3 Rus. Termez. Surkhondaryo Viloyati, S Uzbekistan
Termoli 96 D4 Molise, C Italy
Terneuzen 87 B5 var. Neuzen. Zeeland, SW Netherlands
Terni 96 C4 anc. Interamna Nahars. Umbria, C Italy
Ternopil' 108 C2 Pol. Tarnopol, Rus. Ternopol'. Ternopol's'ka Oblast', W Ukraine
Ternopol' see Ternopil'
Terracina 97 C5 Lazio, C Italy
Terranova di Sicilia see Gela
Terranova Pausania see Olbia
Terrassa 93 G2 Cast. Tarrasa. Cataluña, E Spain
Terre Adélie 154 C4 physical region Antarctica
Terre Haute 40 B4 Indiana, N USA
Terre Neuve see Newfoundland and Labrador
Terschelling 86 C1 Fris. Skylge. island Waddeneilanden, N Netherlands
Teruel 93 F3 anc. Turba. Aragón, E Spain
Tervel 104 E1 prev. Kurtbunar, Rom. Curtbunar. Dobrich, NE Bulgaria
Tervueren see Tervuren
Tervuren 87 C6 var. Tervueren. Vlaams Brabant, C Belgium
Teseney 72 C4 var. Tessenei. W Eritrea
Tessalit 75 E2 Kidal, NE Mali
Tessaoua 75 G3 Maradi, S Niger
Tessenderlo 87 C5 Limburg, NE Belgium
Tessenei see Teseney
Testigos, Islas los 59 E1 island group N Venezuela
Tete 79 E2 Tete, NW Mozambique
Teterow 94 D3 Mecklenburg-Vorpommern, NE Germany
Tétouan 70 C2 var. Tetouan, Tetuán. N Morocco
Tetovo 101 D5 Razgrad, N Bulgaria
Tetschen see Děčín
Tetuán see Tétouan
Teverya see Tverya
Te Waewae Bay 151 A7 bay South Island, New Zealand
Texarkana 42 A2 Arkansas, C USA
Texarkana 49 H2 Texas, SW USA
Texas 49 F3 off. State of Texas, also known as Lone Star State. state S USA
Texas City 49 H4 Texas, SW USA
Texel 86 C2 island Waddeneilanden, NW Netherlands
Texoma, Lake 49 G2 reservoir Oklahoma/Texas, C USA
Teziutlán 51 F4 Puebla, S Mexico
Thaa Atoll see Kolhumadulu
Thai, Ao see Thailand, Gulf of
Thai Bình 136 D3 Thai Bình, N Vietnam

Thailand 137 C5 off. Kingdom of Thailand, Th. Prathet Thai; prev. Siam. country SE Asia

THAILAND
Southeast Asia

Official name Kingdom of Thailand
Formation 1238 / 1907
Capital Bangkok
Population 69.5 million / 352 people per sq mile (136 people per sq km)
Total area 198,455 sq. miles (514,000 sq. km)
Languages Thai*, Chinese, Malay, Khmer, Mon, Karen, Miao
Religions Buddhist 95%, Muslim 4%, Other (including Christian) 1%
Ethnic mix Thai 83%, Chinese 12%, Malay 3%, Khmer and Other 2%
Government Parliamentary system
Currency Baht = 100 satang
Literacy rate 94%
Calorie consumption 2862 kilocalories

Thailand, Gulf of 137 C6 var. Gulf of Siam, Th. Ao Thai, Vtn. Vinh Thai Lan. gulf SE Asia
Thailand, Kingdom of see Thailand
Thai Lan, Vinh see Thailand, Gulf of
Thai Nguyên 136 D3 Bǎc Thai, N Vietnam
Thakhèk 136 D4 var. Muang Khammouan. Khammouan, C Laos
Thamarid see Thamarit
Thamarit 121 D6 var. Thamarīd, Thumrayt. SW Oman
Thames 150 D3 Waikato, North Island, New Zealand
Thames 89 B8 river S England, United Kingdom
Thandwe 136 A4 var. Sandoway. Rakhine State, W Myanmar (Burma)
Thanh Hoa 136 D3 Thanh Hoa, N Vietnam
Thanintari Taungdan see Bilauktaung Range
Thanlwin see Salween
Thar Desert 123 C4 var. Great Indian Desert, Indian Desert. desert India/Pakistan
Tharthar, Buhayrat ath 120 B3 lake C Iraq
Thásos 104 C4 Thásos, E Greece
Thásos 104 C4 island E Greece
Thaton 136 B4 Mon State, S Myanmar (Burma)
Thayetmyo 136 A4 Magway, C Myanmar (Burma)
The Crane 55 H2 var. Crane. S Barbados
The Dalles 46 B3 Oregon, NW USA
The Flatts Village see Flatts Village
The Hague see 's-Gravenhage
Theodosia see Feodosiya
The Pas 37 F5 Manitoba, C Canada
Therezina see Teresina
Thérma 105 D6 Ikaría, Dodekánisa, Greece, Aegean Sea
Thermaic Gulf 104 B4 Eng. Thermaic Gulf; anc. Thermaicus Sinus. gulf N Greece
Thermaic Gulf/Thermaicus Sinus see Thermaïkós Kólpos
Thermiá see Kýthnos
Thérmo 105 B5 Dytikí Elláda, C Greece
The Rock 93 H4 New South Wales, SE Australia
The Sooner State see Oklahoma
Thessaloníki 104 C3 Eng. Salonica, Salonika, SCr. Solun, Turk. Selânik. Kentrikí Makedonía, N Greece
The Valley 55 G3 dependent territory capital (Anguilla) E Anguilla
The Village 49 G1 Oklahoma, C USA
The Volunteer State see Tennessee
Thiamis see Kalamás
Thian Shan see Tien Shan
Thibet see Xizang Zizhiqu
Thief River Falls 45 F1 Minnesota, N USA
Thienen see Tienen
Thiers 91 C5 Puy-de-Dôme, C France

Thiès 74 B3 W Senegal
Thikombia see Cikobia
Thimbu see Thimphu
Thimphu 135 G3 var. Thimbu; prev. Tashi Chho Dzong. country capital (Bhutan) W Bhutan
Thionville 90 D3 Ger. Diedenhofen. Moselle, NE France
Thíra 105 D7 Santorini, Kykládes, Greece, Aegean Sea
Thíra 105 D7 Santorini, Kykládes, Greece, Aegean Sea
Thíra 105 D7 Santorini, Kykládes, Greece, Aegean Sea
Thiruvananthapuram 132 C3 prev. Trivandrum, var. Tiruvantapuram. state capital Kerala, SW India
Thitu Island 128 C8 island NW Spratly Islands
Tholen 86 B4 island SW Netherlands
Thomasville 42 D3 Georgia, SE USA
Thompson 37 F4 Manitoba, C Canada
Thonon-les-Bains 91 D5 Haute-Savoie, E France
Thorenburg see Turda
Thorlákshöfn 83 E5 Sudhurland, SW Iceland
Thorn see Toruń
Thornton Island see Millennium Island
Thorshavn see Tórshavn
Thospitis see Van Gölü
Thouars 90 B4 Deux-Sèvres, W France
Thoune see Thun
Thracian Sea 104 D4 Gk. Thrakikó Pélagos; anc. Thracium Mare. sea Greece/Turkey
Thracium Mare/Thrakikó Pélagos see Thracian Sea
Three Kings Islands 150 C1 island group N New Zealand
Thrissur 132 C3 prev. Trichūr. Kerala, SW India
Thuin 87 B7 Hainaut, S Belgium
Thule see Qaanaaq
Thumrayt see Thamarit
Thun 95 A7 Fr. Thoune. Bern, W Switzerland
Thunder Bay 38 B4 Ontario, S Canada
Thuner See 95 A7 lake C Switzerland
Thung Song 137 C7 var. Cha Mai. Nakhon Si Thammarat, SW Thailand
Thurso 88 C2 N Scotland, United Kingdom
Thýamis see Kalamás
Tianjin 128 D4 var. Tientsin. Tianjin Shi, E China
Tianjin see Tianjin Shi
Tianjin Shi 128 D4 var. Jin, Tianjin, T'ien-ching, Tientsin. municipality E China
Tian Shan see Tien Shan
Tianshui 128 B4 Gansu, C China
Tiba see Chiba
Tiber 96 C4 Eng. Tiber. river C Italy
Tiber see Tevere, Italy
Tiber see Tivoli, Italy
Tiberias see Tverya
Tiberias, Lake 119 B5 var. Chinnereth, Sea of Bahr Tabariya, Sea of Galilee, Ar. Bahrat Tabariya, Heb. Yam Kinneret. lake N Israel
Tibesti 76 C2 var. Tibesti Massif, Ar. Tibistī. mountain range N Africa
Tibesti Massif see Tibesti
Tibet see Xizang Zizhiqu
Tibetan Autonomous Region see Xizang Zizhiqu
Tibet, Plateau of 126 B4 var. Xizang Gaoyuan, Eng. Plateau of Tibet. plateau W China
Tibet, Plateau of see Qingzang Gaoyuan
Tibistī see Tibesti
Tibnī see At Tibnī
Tiburón 50 B2 var. Isla del Tiburón. island NW Mexico
Tiburón, Isla del see Tiburón, Isla
Tichau see Tychy
Tichît 74 D2 var. Tichitt. Tagant, C Mauritania
Tichitt see Tichît
Ticinum see Pavia
Ticul 51 H3 Yucatán, SE Mexico

Tidjikdja see Tidjikja
Tidjikja 74 C2 var. Tidjikdja; prev. Fort-Cappolani. Tagant, C Mauritania
T'ien-ching see Tianjin Shi
Tienen 87 C6 var. Thienen, Fr. Tirlemont. Vlaams Brabant, C Belgium
Tien Giang, Sông see Mekong
Tien Shan 126 B3 Chin. Thian Shan, Tian Shan, T'ien Shan, Rus. Tyan'-Shan'. mountain range C Asia
Tientsin see Tianjin
Tierp 85 C6 Uppsala, C Sweden
Tierra del Fuego 65 B8 island Argentina/Chile
Tiflis see Tbilisi
Tifton 42 D3 Georgia, SE USA
Tifu 139 F4 Pulau Buru, E Indonesia
Tighina 108 D4 Rus. Bendery; prev. Bender. E Moldova
Tigranocerta see Siirt
Tigris 120 B2 Ar. Dijlah, Turk. Dicle. river Iraq/Turkey
Tiguentourine 71 E3 E Algeria
Ti-hua/Tihwa see Ürümqi
Tijuana 50 A1 Baja California Norte, NW Mexico
Tikhoretsk 111 A7 Krasnodarskiy Kray, SW Russian Federation
Tikhvin 110 B4 Leningradskaya Oblast', NW Russian Federation
Tiki Basin 143 G3 undersea basin S Pacific Ocean
Tikirarjuaq see Whale Cove
Tiksi 115 F2 Respublika Sakha (Yakutiya), NE Russian Federation
Tilburg 86 C4 Noord-Brabant, S Netherlands
Tilimsen see Tlemcen
Tilio Martius see Toulon
Tillabéri 75 F3 var. Tillabéry. Tillabéri, W Niger
Tillabéry see Tillabéri
Tílos 105 E7 island Dodekánisa, Greece, Aegean Sea
Timan Ridge 110 D3 Eng. Timan Ridge. ridge NW Russian Federation
Timan Ridge see Timanskiy Kryazh
Timaru 151 B6 Canterbury, South Island, New Zealand
Timbaki/Timbákion see Tympáki
Timbedgha 74 D3 var. Timbédra. Hodh ech Chargui, SE Mauritania
Timbédra see Timbedgha
Timbuktu see Tombouctou
Timiş 108 A4 county SW Romania
Timişoara 108 A4 Ger. Temeschwar, Temeswar, Hung. Temesvár; prev. Temeschburg. Timiş, W Romania
Timmins 38 C4 Ontario, S Canada
Timor 125 F5 island Nusa Tenggara, C Indonesia
Timor Sea 125 F5 sea E Indian Ocean
Timor Timur see East Timor
Timor Trench see Timor Trough
Timor Trough 125 F5 var. Timor Trench. trough NE Timor Sea
Timrå 85 C5 Västernorrland, C Sweden
Tindouf 70 C3 W Algeria
Tineo 92 C1 Asturias, N Spain
Tingis see Tanger
Tingo María 60 C3 Huánuco, C Peru
Tingréla see Tengréla
Tinhosa Grande 76 E2 island N Sao Tome and Principe, Africa, E Atlantic Ocean
Tinhosa Pequena 76 E1 island N Sao Tome and Principe, Africa, E Atlantic Ocean
Tinian 144 B1 island S Northern Mariana Islands
Tínos 105 D6 Tínos, Kykládes, Greece, Aegean Sea
Tínos 105 D6 anc. Tenos. island Kykládes, Greece, Aegean Sea
Tip 101 E6 Papua, E Indonesia
Tipitapa 52 D3 Managua, W Nicaragua
Tip Top Mountain 38 C4 mountain Ontario, S Canada
Tirana see Tiranë
Tiranë 101 C6 var. Tirana. country capital (Albania) Tiranë, C Albania

Tiraspol *108 D4 Rus.* Tiraspol'.
E Moldova
Tiraspol' *see* Tiraspol
Tiree *88 B3 island* W Scotland,
United Kingdom
Tîrgoviște *see* Târgoviște
Tîrgu Jiu *see* Targu Jiu
Tîrgu Mureș *see* Târgu Mureș
Tîrgu-Neamţ *see* Târgu-Neamţ
Tîrgu Ocna *see* Târgu Ocna
Tîrgu Secuiesc *see* Târgu Secuiesc
Tîrlemont *see* Tienen
Tîrnavos *see* Týrnavos
Tîrnovo *see* Veliko Tŭrnovo
Tirol *95 C7 off.* Land Tirol, *var.* Tyrol, *It.*
Tirolo. *state* W Austria
Tirol, Land *see* Tirol
Tirolo *see* Tirol
Tirreno, Mare *see* Tyrrhenian Sea
Tiruchchirāppalli *132 C3 prev.*
Trichinopoly. Tamil Nādu,
SE India
Tiruppattūr *132 C2* Tamil Nādu,
SE India
Tiruvantapuram *see*
Thiruvananthapuram
Tisa *103 F1 Ger.* Theiss, *Rom./Slvn./*
SCr. Tisa, *Rus.* Tissa, *Ukr.* Tysa. *river*
SE Europe
Tisa *see* Tisza
Tiszakécske *99 D7* Bács-Kiskun,
C Hungary
Titano, Monte *96 E1 mountain*
C San Marino
Titicaca, Lake *61 E4 lake* Bolivia/
Peru
Titograd *see* Podgorica
Titose *see* Chitose
Titova Mitrovica *see* Mitrovicë
Titovo Užice *see* Užice
Titu *108 C5* Dâmbovița, S Romania
Titule *77 D5* Orientale, N Dem. Rep.
Congo
Tiverton *89 C7* SW England, United
Kingdom
Tivoli *96 C4 anc.* Tiber. Lazio,
C Italy
Tizimín *51 H3* Yucatán, SE Mexico
Tizi Ouzou *71 E1 var.* Tizi-Ouzou.
N Algeria
Tizi-Ouzou *see* Tizi Ouzou
Tiznit *70 B3* SW Morocco
Tjilatjap *see* Cilacap
Tjirebon *see* Cirebon
Tlaquepaque *50 D4* Jalisco,
C Mexico
Tlascala *see* Tlaxcala
Tlaxcala *51 F4 var.* Tlascala, Tlaxcala de
Xicohténcatl. Tlaxcala, C Mexico
Tlaxcala de Xicohténcatl *see* Tlaxcala
Tlemcen *70 D2 var.* Tilimsen, Tlemsen.
NW Algeria
Tlemsen *see* Tlemcen
Toamasina *79 G3 prev./Fr.* Tamatave.
Toamasina, E Madagascar
Toba, Danau *138 B3 lake* Sumatera,
W Indonesia
Tobago *55 H5 island* NE Trinidad and
Tobago
Toba Kakar Range *134 B2 mountain*
range NW Pakistan
Tobol *see* Tobyl
Tobol'sk *114 C3* Tyumenskaya Oblast',
C Russian Federation
Tobruch/Tobruk *see* Ţubruq
Tobyl *114 C4 prev.* Tobol. *river*
Kazakhstan/Russian Federation
Tocantins *63 E3 off.* Estado do
Tocantins. *state* C Brazil
Tocantins *63 E3 off.* Estado do
Tocantins. *region* C Brazil
Tocantins, Estado do *see* Tocantins
Tocantins, Rio *63 F2 river* N Brazil
Tocoa *52 D2* Colón, N Honduras
Tocopilla *64 B2* Antofagasta, N Chile
Todi *96 C4* Umbria, C Italy
Todos os Santos, Baía de *63 G3 bay*
E Brazil
Toetoes Bay *151 B8 bay* South Island,
New Zealand
Tofua *145 E4 island* Ha'apai Group,
C Tonga
Togo *75 E4 off.* Togolese Republic; *prev.*
French Togoland. *country* W Africa

TOGO
West Africa
Official name The Togolese Republic
Formation 1960 / 1960
Capital Lomé
Population 6.2 million / 295 people
per sq mile (114 people per sq km)
Total area 21,924 sq. miles (56,785 sq. km)
Languages Ewe, Kabye, Gurma, French*
Religions Christian 47%, Traditional
beliefs 33%, Muslim 14%, Other 6%
Ethnic mix Ewe 46%, Other African 41%,
Kabye 12%, European 1%
Government Presidential system
Currency CFA franc = 100 centimes
Literacy rate 57%
Calorie consumption 2363 kilocalories

Togolese Republic *see* Togo
Tojikiston, Jumhurii *see* Tajikistan
Tokanui *151 B7* Southland, South Island,
New Zealand
Tokar *72 C3 var.* Ţawkar. Red Sea,
NE Sudan
Tokat *116 D3* Tokat, N Turkey
Tokelau *145 E3 NZ overseas territory*
W Polynesia
Tokio *see* Tōkyō
Tokmak *109 G4 var.* Velykyy Tokmak.
Zaporiz'ka Oblast', SE Ukraine
Tokmak *see* Tomok
Tokoroa *150 D3* Waikato, North Island,
New Zealand
Tokounou *74 C4* C Guinea
Tokushima *131 C6 var.* Tokusima.
Tokushima, Shikoku, SW Japan
Tōkyō *130 A1 var.* Tokio. *country*
capital (Japan) Tōkyō, Honshū,
S Japan
Tōkyō-wan *130 A2 bay* S Japan
Tolbukhin *see* Dobrich
Toledo *92 D3 anc.* Toletum. Castilla-La
Mancha, C Spain
Toledo *40 D3* Ohio, N USA
Toledo Bend Reservoir *49 G3 reservoir*
Louisiana/Texas, SW USA
Toletum *see* Toledo
Toliara *79 F4 var.* Toliary; *prev.* Tuléar.
Toliara, SW Madagascar
Toliary *see* Toliara
Tolmein *see* Tolmin
Tolmin *95 D7 Ger.* Tolmein, *It.* Tolmino.
W Slovenia
Tolmino *see* Tolmin
Tolna *99 C7 Ger.* Tolnau. Tolna,
S Hungary
Tolnau *see* Tolna
Tolochin *see* Talachyn
Tolosa *93 E1* País Vasco, N Spain
Tolosa *see* Toulouse
Toluca *51 E4 var.* Toluca de Lerdo.
México, S Mexico
Toluca de Lerdo *see* Toluca
Tol'yatti *111 C6 prev.* Stavropol'.
Samarskaya Oblast', W Russian
Federation
Tomah *40 B2* Wisconsin,
N USA
Tomakomai *130 D2* Hokkaidō,
NE Japan
Tomar *92 B3* Santarém, W Portugal
Tomaschow *see* Tomaszów Mazowiecki
Tomaschow *see* Tomaszów Lubelski
Tomaszów *see* Tomaszów Mazowiecki
Tomaszów Lubelski *98 E4 Ger.*
Tomaschow. Lubelskie,
E Poland
Tomaszów Mazowiecka *see* Tomaszów
Mazowiecki
Tomaszów Mazowiecki *98 D4 var.*
Tomaszów Mazowiecka; *prev.*
Tomaszów, *Ger.* Tomaschow. Łódzkie,
C Poland
Tombigbee River *42 C3 river* Alabama/
Mississippi, S USA
Tombouctou *75 E3 Eng.* Timbuktu.
Tombouctou, N Mali
Tombua *78 A2 Port.* Porto Alexandre.
Namibe, SW Angola
Tomelloso *93 E3* Castilla-La Mancha,
C Spain
Tomini, Gulf of *see* Tomini, Teluk

Tomini, Teluk *139 E4 var.* Gulf of
Tomini; *prev.* Teluk Gorontalo. *bay*
Sulawesi, C Indonesia
Tomok *123 G2 prev.* Tokmak.
Chuyskaya Oblast', N Kyrgyzstan
Tomsk *114 D4* Tomskaya Oblast',
C Russian Federation
Tomür Feng *see* Pobedy, Pik
Toncontín *52 C3 prev.* Tegucigalpa.
country capital (Honduras) Francisco
Morazán, SW Honduras
Tonezh *see* Tonyezh
Tonga *145 E4 off.* Kingdom of Tonga,
var. Friendly Islands. *country*
SW Pacific Ocean

TONGA
Australasia & Oceania
Official name Kingdom of Tonga
Formation 1970 / 1970
Capital Nuku'alofa
Population 106,146 / 382 people
per sq mile (147 people per sq km)
Total area 289 sq. miles (748 sq. km)
Languages English*, Tongan*
Religions Free Wesleyan 41%, Other 17%,
Roman Catholic 16%, Church of Jesus
Christ of Latter-day Saints 14%,
Free Church of Tonga 12%
Ethnic mix Tongan 98%, Other 2%
Government Monarchy
Currency Pa'anga (Tongan dollar)
= 100 seniti
Literacy rate 99%
Calorie consumption Not available

Tonga, Kingdom of *see* Tonga
Tongatapu *145 E5 island* Tongatapu
Group, S Tonga
Tongatapu Group *145 E5 island group*
S Tonga
Tonga Trench *143 E3 trench* S Pacific
Ocean
Tongchuan *128 C4* Shaanxi,
C China
Tongeren *87 D6 Fr.* Tongres. Limburg,
NE Belgium
Tongking, Gulf of *128 B7 Chin.* Beibu
Wan, *Vtn.* Vinh Băc Bô. *gulf* China/
Vietnam
Tongliao *127 G2* Nei Mongol Zizhiqu,
N China
Tongres *see* Tongeren
Tongshan *see* Xuzhou, Jiangsu, China
Tongtian He *126 C4 var.* Zhi Qu. *river*
C China
Tonj *73 B5* Warap, W South Sudan
Tônlé Sap *137 D5 Eng.* Great Lake. *lake*
W Cambodia
Tonopah *47 C6* Nevada, W USA
Tonyezh *107 C7 Rus.* Tonezh.
Homyel'skaya Voblasts', SE Belarus
Tooele *44 B4* Utah, W USA
Toowoomba *149 E5* Queensland,
E Australia
Topeka *45 F4 state capital* Kansas,
C USA
Toplica *see* Topliţa
Topliţa *108 C3 Ger.* Töplitz, *Hung.*
Maroshévíz; *prev.* Topliţa Română,
Hung. Oláh-Toplicza, Toplicza.
Harghita, C Romania
Topliţa Română/Töplitz *see* Topliţa
Topolčany *99 C6 Hung.* Nagytapolcsány.
Nitriansky Kraj, W Slovakia
Topolovgrad *104 D3 prev.* Kavakli.
Khaskovo, S Bulgaria
Topolya *see* Bačka Topola
Top Springs Roadhouse *146 E3*
Northern Territory, N Australia
Torda *see* Turda
Torez *109 H3* Donets'ka Oblast',
SE Ukraine
Torgau *94 D4* Sachsen, E Germany
Torhout *87 A5* West-Vlaanderen,
W Belgium
Torino *96 A2 Eng.* Turin. Piemonte,
NW Italy
Tornacum *see* Tournai
Torneà *see* Tornio
Torneträsk *84 C3 lake* N Sweden
Tornio *84 D4 Swe.* Torneå. Lappi,
NW Finland
Tornionjoki *84 D3 river* Finland/Sweden

Tornionjoki *84 D3 river* Finland/
Sweden
Toro *92 D2* Castilla y León, N Spain
Toronto *38 D5 province capital* Ontario,
S Canada
Torquay *89 C7* SW England, United
Kingdom
Torrance *46 D2* California, W USA
Torre, Alto da *92 B3 mountain*
C Portugal
Torre del Greco *97 D5* Campania,
S Italy
Torrejón de Ardoz *93 E3* Madrid,
C Spain
Torrelavega *92 D1* Cantabria,
N Spain
Torrens, Lake *149 A6 salt lake* South
Australia
Torrent *93 F3 Cas.* Torrente, *var.*
Torrent de l'Horta. Valenciana,
E Spain
Torrent de l'Horta/Torrente *see*
Torrent
Torreón *50 D3* Coahuila, NE Mexico
Torres Strait *148 C1 strait* Australia/
Papua New Guinea
Torres Vedras *92 B3* Lisboa,
C Portugal
Torrington *44 D3* Wyoming,
C USA
Tórshavn *83 F5 Dan.* Thorshavn.
Dependent territory capital Faeroe
Islands
To'rtkok'l *122 D2 var.* Türtkül, *Rus.*
Turtkul'; *prev.* Petroaleksandrovsk.
Qoraqalpog'iston Respublikasi,
W Uzbekistan
Tortoise Islands *see* Colón,
Archipiélago de
Tortosa *93 F2 anc.* Dertosa. Cataluña,
E Spain
Tortue, Montagne *59 H3 mountain*
range C French Guiana
Tortuga, Isla *see* La Tortuga, Isla
Toruń *98 C3 Ger.* Thorn. Toruń,
Kujawsko-pomorskie, C Poland
Tõrva *106 D3 Ger.* Tõrwa. Valgamaa,
S Estonia
Tõrwa *see* Tõrva
Torzhok *110 B4* Tverskaya Oblast',
W Russian Federation
Tosa-wan *131 B7 bay* SW Japan
Toscana *96 B3 Eng.* Tuscany. *region*
C Italy
Toscano, Archipelago *96 B4 Eng.*
Tuscan Archipelago. *island group*
C Italy
Toshkent *123 E2 Eng./Rus.* Tashkent.
country capital (Uzbekistan) Toshkent
Viloyati, E Uzbekistan
Totana *93 E4* Murcia, SE Spain
Tot'ma *see* Sukhona
Totness *59 G3* Coronie, N Suriname
Tottori *131 B6* Tottori, Honshū,
SW Japan
Touâjîl *74 C2* Tiris Zemmour,
N Mauritania
Touggourt *71 E2* NE Algeria
Toukoto *74 C3* Kayes, W Mali
Toul *90 D3* Meurthe-et-Moselle,
NE France
Toulon *91 D6 anc.* Telo Martius, Tilio
Martius. Var, SE France
Toulouse *91 B6 anc.* Tolosa. Haute-
Garonne, S France
Toungoo *see* Taungoo
Touraine *90 B4 cultural region*
C France
Tourane *see* Đa Năng
Tourcoing *90 C2* Nord, N France
Tournai *87 A6 var.* Tournay, *Dut.*
Doornik; *anc.* Tornacum. Hainaut,
SW Belgium
Tournay *see* Tournai
Tours *90 B4 anc.* Caesarodunum,
Turoni. Indre-et-Loire, C France
Tovarkovskiy *111 B5* Tul'skaya Oblast',
W Russian Federation
Tower Island *see* Genovesa, Isla
Townsville *148 D3* Queensland,
NE Australia
Towoeti Meer *see* Towuti, Danau
Towraghoudī *122 D4* Herāt,
NW Afghanistan

Towson *41 F4* Maryland, NE USA
Towuti, Danau *139 E4 Dut.* Towoeti
Meer. *lake* Sulawesi, C Indonesia
Toyama *131 C5* Toyama, Honshū,
SW Japan
Toyama-wan *131 B5 bay* W Japan
Toyohara *see* Yuzhno-Sakhalinsk
Toyota *131 C6* Aichi, Honshū,
SW Japan
Tozeur *71 E2 var.* Tawzar. W Tunisia
Trâblous *see* Tripoli
Trabzon *117 E2 Eng.* Trebizond; *anc.*
Trapezus. Trabzon, NE Turkey
Traiectum ad Mosam/Traiectum
Tungorum *see* Maastricht
Traiskirchen *95 E6* Niederösterreich,
NE Austria
Trajani Portus *see* Civitavecchia
Trajectum ad Rhenum *see* Utrecht
Trakai *107 C5 Ger.* Traken, *Pol.* Troki.
Vilnius, SE Lithuania
Traken *see* Trakai
Tralee *89 A6 Ir.* Trá Lí. SW Ireland
Trá Lí *see* Tralee
Tralles Aydin *see* Aydın
Trang *137 C7* Trang, S Thailand
Transantarctic Mountains *154 B3*
mountain range Antarctica
Transilvania *see* Transylvania
Transilvaniei, Alpi *see* Carpaţii
Meridionalii
Transjordan *see* Jordan
Transsylvanische Alpen/
Transylvanian Alps *see* Carpaţii
Meridionalii
Transylvania *108 B4 Eng.* Ardeal,
Transilvania, *Ger.* Siebenbürgen, *Hung.*
Erdély. *cultural region* NW Romania
Transylvanian Alps *108 B4 var.* Alpi
Transilvaniei, Carpaţii Sudici, *Eng.*
South Carpathians, Transylvanian Alps,
Ger. Südkarpaten, Transsylvanische
Alpen, *Hung.* Déli-Kárpátok, Erdélyi-
Havasok. *mountain range* C Romania
Trapani *97 B7 anc.* Drepanum. Sicilia,
Italy, C Mediterranean Sea
Trâpeăng Vêng *see* Kâmpóng Thum
Trapezus *see* Trabzon
Traralgon *149 C7* Victoria, SE Australia
Trasimenischersee *see* Trasimeno, Lago
Trasimeno, Lago *96 C4 Eng.* Lake
of Perugia, *Ger.* Trasimenischersee.
lake C Italy
Traù *see* Trogir
Traverse City *40 C2* Michigan,
N USA
Tra Vinh *137 D6 var.* Phu Vinh. Tra
Vinh, S Vietnam
Travis, Lake *49 F3 reservoir* Texas,
SW USA
Travnik *100 C4* Federacija Bosna
I Hercegovina, C Bosnia and
Herzegovina
Trbovlje *95 E7 Ger.* Trifail. C Slovenia
Treasure State *see* Montana
Třebíč *99 B5 Ger.* Trebitsch. Vysočina,
C Czech Republic
Trebinje *101 C5* Republika Srpska,
S Bosnia and Herzegovina
Trebišov *99 D6 Hung.* Tőketerebes.
Košický Kraj, E Slovakia
Trebitsch *see* Třebíč
Trebnitz *see* Trzebnica
Tree Planters State *see* Nebraska
Trélazé *90 B4* Maine-et-Loire,
NW France
Trelew *65 C6* Chubut, SE Argentina
Tremelo *87 C5* Vlaams Brabant,
C Belgium
Trenčín *99 C5 Ger.* Trentschin,
Hung. Trencsén. Trenčiansky Kraj,
W Slovakia
Trencsén *see* Trenčín
Trengganu, Kuala *see*
Kuala Terengganu
Trenque Lauquen *64 C4* Buenos Aires,
E Argentina
Trent *see* Trento
Trento *96 C2 Eng.* Trent, *Ger.* Trient;
anc. Tridentum. Trentino-Alto Adige,
N Italy
Trenton *41 F4 state capital* New Jersey,
NE USA
Trentschin *see* Trenčín

Tres Arroyos *65 D5* Buenos Aires,
E Argentina
Treskavica *100 C4 mountain range*
SE Bosnia and Herzegovina
Tres Tabernae *see* Saverne
Treves/Trèves *see* Trier
Treviso *96 C2 anc.* Tarvisium. Veneto,
NE Italy
Trichinopoly *see* Tiruchchirāppalli
Trichūr *see* Thrissur
Tridentum/Trient *see* Trento
Trier *95 A5 Eng.* Treves, *Fr.* Trèves; *anc.*
Augusta Treverorum. Rheinland-Pfalz,
SW Germany
Triesen *94 E2* SW Liechtenstein Europe
Triesenberg *94 E2* SW Liechtenstein
Trieste *96 D2 Slvn.* Trst. Friuli-Venezia
Giulia, NE Italy
Trifail *see* Trbovlje
Tríkala *104 B4 prev.* Trikkala. Thessalía,
C Greece
Trikkala *see* Tríkala
Trimontium *see* Plovdiv
Trinacria *see* Sicilia
Trincomalee *132 D3 var.* Trinkomali.
Eastern Province, NE Sri Lanka
Trindade, Ilha da *67 C5 island* Brazil,
W Atlantic Ocean
Trinidad *61 F3* El Beni, N Bolivia
Trinidad *64 D4* Flores, S Uruguay
Trinidad *44 C5* Colorado, C USA
Trinidad *55 H5 island* C Trinidad and
Tobago
Trinidad and Tobago *55 H5 off.*
Republic of Trinidad and Tobago.
country SE West Indies

TRINIDAD & TOBAGO
West Indies

Official name Republic of Trinidad
and Tobago
Formation 1962 / 1962
Capital Port-of-Spain
Population 1.3 million / 656 people
per sq mile (253 people per sq km)
Total area 1980 sq. miles (5128 sq. km)
Languages English Creole, English*, Hindi,
French, Spanish
Religions Roman Catholic 26%,
Hindu 23%, Other and nonreligious 23%,
Anglican 8%, Baptist 7%, Pentecostal 7%,
Muslim 6%
Ethnic mix East Indian 40%, Black 38%,
Mixed race 20%, Other 2%
Government Parliamentary system
Currency Trinidad and Tobago dollar
= 100 cents
Literacy rate 99%
Calorie consumption 2751 kilocalories

Trinidad and Tobago, Republic of *see*
Trinidad and Tobago
Trinité, Montagnes de la *59 H3*
mountain range C French Guiana
Trinity River *49 G3 river* Texas, SW USA
Trinkomali *see* Trincomalee
Trípoli *105 B6 prev.* Trípolis.
Pelopónnisos, S Greece
Tripoli *118 B4 var.* Ţarābulus, Ţarābulus
ash Shām, Trâblous; *anc.* Tripolis.
N Lebanon
Tripoli *see* Ţarābulus
Trípolis *see* Trípoli, Greece
Tripolis *see* Tripoli, Lebanon
Tristan da Cunha *69 B7 dependency of*
Saint Helena SE Atlantic Ocean
Triton Island *128 B7 island* S Paracel
Islands
Trivandrum *see* Thiruvanathapuram
Trnava *99 C6 Ger.* Tyrnau, *Hung.*
Nagyszombat. Trnavský Kraj,
W Slovakia
Trnovo *see* Veliko Tŭrnovo
Trogir *100 B4 It.* Traù. Split-Dalmacija,
S Croatia
Troglav *100 B4 mountain* Bosnia and
Herzegovina/Croatia
Trois-Rivières *39 E4* Québec, SE Canada
Troki *see* Trakai
Trollhättan *85 B6* Västra Götaland,
S Sweden
Tromsø *84 C2 Fin.* Tromssa. Troms,
N Norway
Tromssa *see* Tromsø

Trondheim *84 B4 Ger.* Drontheim; *prev.*
Nidaros, Trondhjem. Sør-Trøndelag,
S Norway
Trondheimsfjorden *84 B4 fjord*
S Norway
Trondhjem *see* Trondheim
Troódos *102 C5 var.* Troodos
Mountains. *mountain range*
C Cyprus
Troodos Mountains *see* Troódos
Troppau *see* Opava
Troy *42 D3* Alabama, S USA
Troy *41 F3* New York, NE USA
Troyan *104 C2* Lovech, N Bulgaria
Troyes *90 D3 anc.* Augustobona
Tricassium. Aube, N France
Trst *see* Trieste
Trstenik *100 E4* Serbia, C Serbia
Trucial States *see* United Arab Emirates
Trujillo *52 D2* Colón, NE Honduras
Trujillo *60 B3* La Libertad, NW Peru
Trujillo *92 C3* Extremadura, W Spain
Truk Islands *see* Chuuk Islands
Trün *104 B2* Pernik, W Bulgaria
Truro *39 F4* Nova Scotia, SE Canada
Truro *89 C7* SW England, United
Kingdom
Trzcianka *98 B3 Ger.* Schönlanke. Pila,
Wielkopolskie, C Poland
Trzebnica *98 C4 Ger.* Trebnitz.
Dolnośląskie, SW Poland
Tsalka *117 F2* S Georgia Asia
Tsamkong *see* Zhanjiang
Tsangpo *see* Brahmaputra
Tsarevo *104 E2 prev.* Michurin. Burgas,
E Bulgaria
Tsarigrad *see* İstanbul
Tsaritsyn *see* Volgograd
Tschakathurn *see* Čakovec
Tschaslau *see* Čáslav
Tschenstochau *see* Częstochowa
Tsefat *119 B5 var.* Safad, *Ar.* Safad; *prev.*
Zefat. Northern, N Israel
Tselinograd *see* Astana
Tsetsen Khan *see* Öndörhaan
Tsetserleg *126 D2* Arhangay,
C Mongolia
Tshela *77 B6* Bas-Congo, W Dem.
Rep. Congo
Tshikapa *77 C7* Kasai-Occidental,
SW Dem. Rep. Congo
Tshuapa *77 D6 river* C Dem. Rep.
Congo
Tshwane *78 D4 var.* Epitoli; *see also.*
Pretoria. *country capital* (South Africa)
(administrative capital)
Gauteng, NE South Africa
Tsinan *see* Jinan
Tsing Hai *see* Qinghai Hu, China
Tsinghai *see* Qinghai, China
Tsingtao/Tsingtau *see* Qingdao
Tsinkiang *see* Quanzhou
Tsintao *see* Qingdao
Tsitsihar *see* Qiqihar
Tsu *131 C6 var.* Tsu. Mie, Honshū,
SW Japan
Tsugaru-kaikyo *130 C3 strait*
N Japan
Tsumeb *78 B3* Oshikoto, N Namibia
Tsuruga *131 C6 var.* Turuga. Fukui,
Honshū, SW Japan
Tsuruoka *130 D4 var.* Turuoka.
Yamagata, Honshū, C Japan
Tsushima *131 A7 var.* Tsushima-tō,
Tusima. *island group* SW Japan
Tsushima-tō *see* Tsushima
Tsyerakhowka *107 D8 Rus.* Terekhovka.
Homyel'skaya Voblasts', SE Belarus
Tsyurupinsk *see* Tsyurupyns'k
Tsyurupyns'k *109 E4 Rus.* Tsyurupinsk.
Khersons'ka Oblast', S Ukraine
Tu *see* Tsu
Tuamotu, Archipel des *see* Tuamotu, Îles
Tuamotu Fracture Zone *143 H3*
fracture zone E Pacific Ocean
Tuamotu Islands *145 H4 var.* Archipel
des Tuamotu, Dangerous Archipelago,
Tuamotu Islands. *island group*
N French Polynesia
Tuamotu Islands *see* Tuamotu, Îles
Tuapi *53 E2* Región Autónoma Atlántico
Norte, NE Nicaragua
Tuapse *111 A7* Krasnodarskiy Kray,
SW Russian Federation

Tuba City *48 B1* Arizona,
SW USA
Tubbergen *86 E3* Overijssel,
E Netherlands
Tubeke *see* Tubize
Tubize *87 B6 Dut.* Tubeke. Walloon
Brabant, C Belgium
Tubmanburg *74 C5* NW Liberia
Ţubruq *71 H2 Eng.* Tobruk, *It.* Tobruch.
NE Libya
Tubuai, Îles/Tubuai Islands *see*
Australes, Îles
Tucker's Town *42 B5* E Bermuda
Tuckum *see* Tukums
Tucson *48 B3* Arizona, SW USA
Tucumán *see* San Miguel de Tucumán
Tucumcari *49 E2* New Mexico, S
W USA
Tucupita *59 E2* Delta Amacuro,
NE Venezuela
Tucuruí, Represa de *63 F2 reservoir*
NE Brazil
Tudela *93 E2 Basq.* Tutera; *anc.* Tutela.
Navarra, N Spain
Tudmur *118 C3 var.* Tadmur, Tamar,
Gk. Palmyra, *Bibl.* Tadmor. Ḥimş,
C Syria
Tuguegarao *139 E1* Luzon,
N Philippines
Tuktoyaktuk *37 E3* Northwest
Territories, NW Canada
Tukums *106 C3 Ger.* Tuckum.
W Latvia
Tula *111 B5* Tul'skaya Oblast', W Russian
Federation
Tulancingo *51 E4* Hidalgo, C Mexico
Tulare Lake Bed *47 C7 salt flat*
California, W USA
Tulcán *60 B1* Carchi, N Ecuador
Tulcea *108 D5* Tulcea, E Romania
Tul'chin *see* Tul'chyn
Tul'chyn *108 D3 Rus.* Tul'chin.
Vinnyts'ka Oblast', C Ukraine
Tuléar *see* Toliara
Tulia *49 E2* Texas, SW USA
Tülkarm *119 D7* West Bank, Israel
Tulle *91 C5 anc.* Tutela. Corrèze,
C France
Tulln *95 E6 var.* Oberhollabrunn.
Niederösterreich, NE Austria
Tully *148 D3* Queensland,
NE Australia
Tulsa *49 G1* Oklahoma, C USA
Tuluá *58 B3* Valle del Cauca,
W Colombia
Tulun *115 E4* Irkutskaya Oblast',
S Russian Federation
Tumaco *58 A4* Nariño, SW Colombia
Tumba, Lac *see* Ntomba, Lac
Tumbes *60 A2* Tumbes, NW Peru
Tumkūr *132 C2* Karnātaka,
W India
Tumuc-Humac Mountains *63 E1 var.*
Serra Tumucumaque. *mountain range*
S South America
Tumucumaque, Serra *see* Tumuc-
Humac Mountains
Tunca Nehri *see* Tundzha
Tunduru *73 C8* Ruvuma,
S Tanzania
Tundzha *104 D3 Turk.* Tunca Nehri.
river Bulgaria/Turkey
Tungabhadra Reservoir *132 C2 lake*
S India
Tungaru *145 E2 prev.* Gilbert Islands.
island group W Kiribati
T'ung-shan *see* Xuzhou
Tungsten *36 D4* Northwest Territories,
W Canada
Tung-t'ing Hu *see* Dongting Hu
Tunis *71 E1 var.* Tūnis. *country capital*
(Tunisia) NE Tunisia
Tunis, Golfe de *102 D3 Ar.* Khalīj Tūnis.
gulf NE Tunisia
Tunisia *71 F2 off.* Tunisian Republic,
Ar. Al Jumhūrīyah at Tūnisīyah, *Fr.*
République Tunisienne. *country*
N Africa

TUNISIA
North Africa

Official name The Tunisian Republic
Formation 1956 / 1956
Capital Tunis

TUNISIA
(continued)

Population 10.6 million / 177 people per sq mile (68 people per sq km)
Total area 63,169 sq. miles (163,610 sq. km)
Languages Arabic*, French
Religions Muslim (mainly Sunni) 98%, Christian 1%, Jewish 1%
Ethnic mix Arab and Berber 98%, Jewish 1%, European 1%
Government Transitional regime
Currency Tunisian dinar = 1000 millimes
Literacy rate 78%
Calorie consumption 3314 kilocalories

Tunisian Republic see Tunisia
Tunisienne, République see Tunisia
Tûnisîyah, Al Jumhûrîyah at see Tunisia
Tûnis, Khalij see Tunis, Golfe de
Tunja 58 B3 Boyacá, C Colombia
Tuong Buong see Tương Đương
Tương Đương 136 D4 var. Tuong Buong. Nghệ An, N Vietnam
Tüp see Tyup
Tupelo 42 C2 Mississippi, S USA
Tupiza 61 G5 Potosí, S Bolivia
Turabah 121 B5 Makkah, W Saudi Arabia
Turangi 150 D4 Waikato, North Island, New Zealand
Turan Lowland 122 C2 var. Turan Plain, Kaz. Turan Oypaty, Rus. Turanskaya Nizmennost', Turk. Turan Pesligi, Uzb. Turan Pasttekisligi. plain C Asia
Turan Oypaty/Turan Pesligi/Turan Plain/Turanskaya Nizmennost' see Turan Lowland
Turan Pasttekisligi see Turan Lowland
Ţurayf 120 A3 Al Ḩudūd ash Shamālīyah, NW Saudi Arabia
Turba see Teruel
Turbat 134 A3 Baluchistān, SW Pakistan
Turčiansky Svätý Martin see Martin
Turda 108 B4 Ger. Thorenburg, Hung. Torda. Cluj, NW Romania
Turek 98 C3 Wielkopolskie, C Poland
Turfan see Turpan
Turin see Torino
Turkana, Lake 73 C6 var. Lake Rudolf. lake N Kenya
Turkestan see Turkistan
Turkey 116 B3 off. Republic of Turkey, Turk. Türkiye Cumhuriyeti. country SW Asia

TURKEY
Asia / Europe

Official name Republic of Turkey
Formation 1923 / 1939
Capital Ankara
Population 73.6 million / 248 people per sq mile (96 people per sq km)
Total area 301,382 sq. miles (780,580 sq. km)
Languages Turkish*, Kurdish, Arabic, Circassian, Armenian, Greek, Georgian, Ladino
Religions Muslim (mainly Sunni) 99%, Other 1%
Ethnic mix Turkish 70%, Kurdish 20%, Other 8%, Arab 2%
Government Parliamentary system
Currency new Turkish lira = 100 kurus
Literacy rate 91%
Calorie consumption 3666 kilocalories

Turkey, Republic of see Turkey
Turkish Republic of Northern Cyprus 102 D5 disputed territory Cyprus
Turkistan 114 B5 prev. Turkestan. Yuzhnyy Kazakhstan, S Kazakhstan
Türkiye Cumhuriyeti see Turkey
Türkmenabat 122 D3 prev. Rus. Chardzhev, Chardzhou, Chardzhui, Lenin-Turkmenski, Turkm. Chärjew. Lebap Welaýaty, E Turkmenistan
Türkmen Aylagy 122 B2 Rus. Turkmenskiy Zaliv. lake gulf W Turkmenistan
Türkmenbashi see Türkmenbaşy

Türkmenbaşy 122 B2 Rus. Turkmenbashi; prev. Krasnovodsk. Balkan Welaýaty, W Turkmenistan
Türkmenbaşy Aylagy 122 A2 prev. Rus. Krasnovodskiy Zaliv, Turkm. Krasnowodsk Aylagy. lake Gulf W Turkmenistan
Turkmenistan 122 B2 ; prev. Turkmenskaya Soviet Socialist Republic. country C Asia

TURKMENISTAN
Central Asia

Official name Turkmenistan
Formation 1991 / 1991
Capital Ashgabat
Population 5.1 million / 27 people per sq mile (10 people per sq km)
Total area 188,455 sq. miles (488,100 sq. km)
Languages Turkmen*, Uzbek, Russian, Kazakh, Tatar
Religions Sunni Muslim 89%, Orthodox Christian 9%, Other 2%
Ethnic mix Turkmen 85%, Other 6%, Uzbek 5%, Russian 4%
Government One-party state
Currency Manat = 100 tenge
Literacy rate 99%
Calorie consumption 2878 kilocalories

Turkmenskaya Soviet Socialist Republic see Turkmenistan
Turkmenskiy Zaliv see Türkmen Aylagy
Turks and Caicos Islands 55 E2 UK dependent territory N West Indies
Turku 85 D6 Swe. Åbo. Länsi-Suomi, SW Finland
Turlock 47 B6 California, W USA
Turnagain, Cape 150 D4 headland North Island, New Zealand
Turnau see Turnov
Turnhout 87 C5 Antwerpen, N Belgium
Turnov 98 B4 Ger. Turnau. Liberecký Kraj, N Czech Republic
Türnovo see Veliko Türnovo
Turnu Măgurele 108 B5 var. Turnu-Măgurele. Teleorman, S Romania
Turnu Severin see Drobeta-Turnu Severin
Turócszentmárton see Martin
Turoni see Tours
Turpan 126 C3 var. Turfan. Xinjiang Uygur Zizhiqu, NW China
Turpan Depression see Turpan Pendi
Turpan Pendi 126 C3 Eng. Turpan Depression. depression NW China
Turpentine State see North Carolina
Türtkül/Turtkul' see To'rtkok'l
Turuga see Tsuruga
Turuoka see Tsuruoka
Tuscaloosa 42 C2 Alabama, S USA
Tuscan Archipelago see Toscano, Archipelago
Tuscany see Toscana
Tusima see Tsushima
Tutela see Tulle, France
Tutela see Tudela, Spain
Tutera see Tudela
Tuticorin 132 C3 Tamil Nādu, SE India
Tutrakan 104 D1 Silistra, NE Bulgaria
Tutuila 145 F4 island W American Samoa
Tuvalu 145 E3 prev. Ellice Islands. country SW Pacific Ocean

TUVALU
Australasia & Oceania

Official name Tuvalu
Formation 1978 / 1978
Capital Fongafale, on Funafuti Atoll
Population 10,619 / 1062 people per sq mile (408 people per sq km)
Total area 10 sq. miles (26 sq. km)
Languages Tuvaluan, Kiribati, English*
Religions Church of Tuvalu 97%, Baha'i 1%, Seventh-day Adventist 1%, Other 1%
Ethnic mix Polynesian 96%, Micronesian 4%

TUVALU
(continued)

Government Nonparty system
Currency Australian dollar and Tuvaluan dollar = 100 cents
Literacy rate 98%
Calorie consumption Not available

Tuwayq, Jabal 121 C5 mountain range C Saudi Arabia
Tuxpan 50 D4 Jalisco, C Mexico
Tuxpan 50 D4 Nayarit, C Mexico
Tuxpán 51 F4 var. Tuxpán de Rodríguez Cano. Veracruz-Llave, E Mexico
Tuxpán de Rodríguez Cano see Tuxpán
Tuxtepec 51 F4 var. San Juan Bautista Tuxtepec. Oaxaca, S Mexico
Tuxtla 51 G5 var. Tuxtla Gutiérrez. Chiapas, SE Mexico
Tuxtla see San Andrés Tuxtla
Tuxtla Gutiérrez see Tuxtla
Tuy Hoa 137 E5 Phu Yên, S Vietnam
Tuz, Lake 116 C3 lake C Turkey
Tver' 110 B4 prev. Kalinin. Tverskaya Oblast', W Russian Federation
Tverya 119 B5 var. Tiberias; prev. Teverya. Northern, N Israel
Twin Falls 46 D4 Idaho, NW USA
Tyan'-Shan' see Tien Shan
Tychy 99 D5 Ger. Tichau. Śląskie, S Poland
Tyler 49 G3 Texas, SW USA
Tylos see Bahrain
Tympáki 105 C8 var. Timbaki; prev. Timbákion. Kriti, Greece, E Mediterranean Sea
Tynda 115 F4 Amurskaya Oblast', SE Russian Federation
Tyne 88 D4 river N England, United Kingdom
Tyôsi see Chōshi
Tyras see Dniester
Tyre see Soûr
Tyrnau see Trnava
Tyrnavos 104 B4 var. Tírnavos. Thessalía, C Greece
Tyrol see Tirol
Tyros see Bahrain
Tyrrhenian Sea 97 B6 It. Mare Tirreno. sea N Mediterranean Sea
Tyumen' 114 C3 Tyumenskaya Oblast', C Russian Federation
Tyup 123 G2 Kir. Tüp. Issyk-Kul'skaya Oblast', NE Kyrgyzstan
Tywyn 89 C6 W Wales, United Kingdom
Tzekung see Zigong
Tziá 105 C6 prev. Kéa, Kéos; anc. Ceos. island Kykládes, Greece, Aegean Sea

U

UAE see United Arab Emirates
Uanle Uen see Wanlaweyn
Uaupés, Rio see Vaupés, Río
Ubangi-Shari see Central African Republic
Ube 131 B7 Yamaguchi, Honshū, SW Japan
Ubeda 93 E4 Andalucía, S Spain
Uberaba 63 F4 Minas Gerais, SE Brazil
Uberlândia 63 F4 Minas Gerais, S E Brazil
Ubol Rajadhani/Ubol Ratchathani see Ubon Ratchathani
Ubon Ratchathani 137 D5 var. Muang Ubon, Ubol Rajadhani, Ubol Ratchathani, Udon Ratchathani, Ubon Ratchathani. E Thailand
Ubrique 92 D5 Andalucía, S Spain
Ubsu-Nur, Ozero see Uvs Nuur
Ucayali, Río 60 D3 river C Peru
Uchiura-wan 130 D3 bay NW Pacific Ocean
Uchkuduk see Uchquduq
Uchquduq 122 D2 Rus. Uchkuduk. Navoiy Viloyati, N Uzbekistan
Uchtagan Gumy/Uchtagan, Peski see Uçtagan Gumy

Uçtagan Gumy 122 C2 var. Uchtagan Gumy, Rus. Peski Uchtagan. desert NW Turkmenistan
Udaipur 134 C3 prev. Oodeypore. Rājasthān, N India
Uddevalla 85 B6 Västra Götaland, S Sweden
Udine 96 D2 anc. Utina. Friuli-Venezia Giulia, NE Italy
Udintsev Fracture Zone 154 A5 tectonic feature S Pacific Ocean
Udipi see Udupi
Udon Ratchathani see Ubon Ratchathani
Udon Thani 136 C4 var. Ban Mak Khaeng, Udorndhani. Udon Thani, N Thailand
Udorndhani see Udon Thani
Udupi 132 B2 var. Udipi. Karnātaka, SW India
Uele 77 D5 var. Welle. river NE Dem. Rep. Congo
Uelzen 94 C3 Niedersachsen, N Germany
Ufa 111 D6 Respublika Bashkortostan, W Russian Federation
Ugâle 106 C2 NW Latvia
Uganda 73 B6 off. Republic of Uganda. country E Africa

UGANDA
East Africa

Official name Republic of Uganda
Formation 1962 / 1962
Capital Kampala
Population 34.5 million / 448 people per sq mile (173 people per sq km)
Total area 91,135 sq. miles (236,040 sq. km)
Languages Luganda, Nkole, Chiga, Lango, Acholi, Teso, Lugbara, English*
Religions Christian 85%, Muslim (mainly Sunni) 12%, Other 3%
Ethnic mix Other 50%, Baganda 17%, Banyakole 10%, Basoga 9%, Iteso 7%, Bakiga 7%
Government Presidential system
Currency New Uganda shilling = 100 cents
Literacy rate 74%
Calorie consumption 2260 kilocalories

Uganda, Republic of see Uganda
Uhorshchyna see Hungary
Uhuru Peak see Kilimanjaro
Uíge 78 B1 Port. Carmona, Vila Marechal Carmona. Uíge, NW Angola
Uinta Mountains 44 B4 mountain range Utah, W USA
Uitenhage 78 C5 Eastern Cape, S South Africa
Uithoorn 86 C3 Noord-Holland, C Netherlands
Ujda see Oujda
Ujelang Atoll 144 C1 var. Wujlān. atoll Ralik Chain, W Marshall Islands
Újgradiska see Nova Gradiška
Újmoldova see Moldova Nouă
Ujungpandang see Makassar
Ujung Salang see Phuket
Újvidék see Novi Sad
UK see United Kingdom
Ukhta 111 C4 Respublika Komi, NW Russian Federation
Ukiah 47 B5 California, W USA
Ukmergé 106 C4 Pol. Wiłkomierz. Vilnius, C Lithuania
Ukraina see Ukraine
Ukraine 108 C2 off. Ukraine, Rus. Ukraina, Ukr. Ukrayina; prev. Ukrainian Soviet Socialist Republic, Ukrainskay S.S.R. country SE Europe

UKRAINE
Eastern Europe

Official name Ukraine
Formation 1991 / 1991
Capital Kiev
Population 45.2 million / 194 people per sq mile (75 people per sq km)
Total area 233,089 sq. miles (603,700 sq. km)
Languages Ukrainian*, Russian, Tatar
Religions Christian (mainly

UKRAINE
(continued)

Orthodox) 95%, Other 5%
Ethnic mix Ukrainian 78%, Russian 17%,
Other 5%
Government Presidential system
Currency Hryvna = 100 kopiykas
Literacy rate 99%
Calorie consumption 3198 kilocalories

Ukraine *see* Ukraine
Ukrainian Soviet Socialist Republic
see Ukraine
Ukrainskaya S.S.R/Ukrayina *see*
Ukraine
Ulaanbaatar *127 E2 Eng.* Ulan Bator;
prev. Urga. *country capital* (Mongolia)
Töv, C Mongolia
Ulaangom *126 C2* Uvs,
NW Mongolia
Ulan Bator *see* Ulaanbaatar
Ulanhad *see* Chifeng
Ulan-Ude *115 E4 prev.* Verkhneudinsk.
Respublika Buryatiya, S Russian
Federation
Uleälv *see* Oulujoki
Uleträsk *see* Oulujärvi
Ulft *86 E4* Gelderland, E Netherlands
Ullapool *88 C3* N Scotland, United
Kingdom
Ulm *95 B6* Baden-Württemberg,
S Germany
Ulsan *129 E4 Jap.* Urusan. SE South
Korea
Ulster *89 B5 province* Northern Ireland,
United Kingdom/Ireland
Ulungur Hu *126 B2 lake* NW China
Uluru *147 D5 var.* Ayers Rock. *monolith*
Northern Territory, C Australia
Ul'yanovka *109 E3* Kirovohrads'ka
Oblast', C Ukraine
Ul'yanovsk *111 C5 prev.* Simbirsk.
Ul'yanovskaya Oblast', W Russian
Federation
Umán *51 H3* Yucatán, SE Mexico
Uman' *109 E3 Rus.* Uman. Cherkas'ka
Oblast', C Ukraine
Uman *see* Uman'
Umanak/Umanaq *see* Uummannaq
'Umān, Khalīj *see* Oman, Gulf of
'Umān, Salţanat *see* Oman
Umbrian-Machigian Mountains *see*
Umbro-Marchigiano, Appennino
Umbro-Marchigiano, Appennino
96 C3 Eng. Umbrian-Machigian
Mountains. *mountain range* C Italy
Umeå *84 C4* Västerbotten, N Sweden
Umeälven *84 C4 river* N Sweden
Umiat *36 D2* Alaska, USA
Umm Buru *72 A4* Western Darfur,
W Sudan
Umm Durmān *see* Omdurman
Umm Ruwaba *72 C4 var.* Umm
Ruwābah, Um Ruwāba. Northern
Kordofan, C Sudan
Umm Ruwābah *see* Umm Ruwaba
Umnak Island *36 A3 island* Aleutian
Islands, Alaska, USA
Um Ruwāba *see* Umm Ruwaba
Umtali *see* Mutare
Umtata *see* Mthatha
Una *100 B3 river* Bosnia and
Herzegovina/Croatia
Unac *100 B3 river* W Bosnia and
Herzegovina
Unalaska Island *36 A3 island* Aleutian
Islands, Alaska, USA
'Unayzah *120 B4 var.* Anaiza. Al Qaşīm,
C Saudi Arabia
Unci *see* Almería
Uncía *61 F4* Potosí, C Bolivia
Uncompahgre Peak *44 B5 mountain*
Colorado, C USA
Undur Khan *see* Öndörhaan
Ungaria *see* Hungary
Ungarisches Erzgebirge *see* Slovenské
rudohorie
Ungarn *see* Hungary
Ungava Bay *39 E1 bay* Québec,
E Canada
Ungava Peninsula *38 D1 peninsula*
Québec, SE Canada
Ungeny *see* Ungheni

Ungheni *108 D3 Rus.* Ungeny.
W Moldova
Unguja *see* Zanzibar
Üngüz Angyrsyndaky Garagum *122 C2
Rus.* Zaunguzskiye Garagumy. *desert*
N Turkmenistan
Ungvár *see* Uzhhorod
Unimak Island *36 B3 island* Aleutian
Islands, Alaska, USA
Union *43 E1* South Carolina, SE USA
Union City *42 C1* Tennessee, S USA
Union of Myanmar *see* Burma
United Arab Emirates *121 C5 Ar.* Al
Imārāt al 'Arabīyah al Muttaḩidah,
abbrev. UAE; *prev.* Trucial States.
country SW Asia

UNITED ARAB EMIRATES
Southwest Asia

Official name United Arab Emirates
Formation 1971 / 1972
Capital Abu Dhabi
Population 7.9 million / 245 people
per sq mile (94 people per sq km)
Total area 32,000 sq. miles (82,880 sq. km)
Languages Arabic*, Farsi, Indian and
Pakistani languages, English
Religions Muslim (mainly Sunni) 96%,
Christian, Hindu, and other 4%
Ethnic mix Asian 60%, Emirian 25%,
Other Arab 12%, European 3%
Government Monarchy
Currency UAE dirham = 100 fils
Literacy rate 90%
Calorie consumption 3245 kilocalories

United Arab Republic *see* Egypt
United Kingdom *89 B5 off.* United
Kingdom of Great Britain and
Northern Ireland, *abbrev.* UK. *country*
NW Europe

UNITED KINGDOM
Northwest Europe

Official name United Kingdom of Great
Britain and Northern Ireland
Formation 1707 / 1922
Capital London
Population 62.4 million / 669 people
per sq mile (258 people per sq km)
Total area 94,525 sq. miles
(244,820 sq. km)
Languages English*, Welsh* (in Wales),
Scottish Gaelic, Irish Gaelic
Religions Anglican 45%, Other and
nonreligious 36%, Roman Catholic 9%,
Presbyterian 4%, Muslim 3%,
Methodist 2%, Hindu 1%
Ethnic mix English 80%, Scottish 9%,
West Indian, Asian, and other 5%,
Northern Irish 3%, Welsh 3%
Government Parliamentary system
Currency Pound sterling = 100 pence
Literacy rate 99%
Calorie consumption 3432 kilocalories

**United Kingdom of Great Britain and
Northern Ireland** *see*
United Kingdom
United Mexican States *see* Mexico
United Provinces *see* Uttar Pradesh
United States of America *35 B5 off.*
United States of America, *var.* America,
The States, *abbrev.* U.S., USA. *country*
North America

UNITED STATES
North America

Official name United States of America
Formation 1776 / 1959
Capital Washington D.C.
Population 313 million / 88 people
per sq mile (34 people per sq km)
Total area 3,717,792 sq. miles
(9,626,091 sq. km)
Languages English, Spanish, Chinese,
French, German, Tagalog, Vietnamese,
Italian, Korean, Russian, Polish
Religions Protestant 52%, Roman
Catholic 25%, Other and nonreligious
20%, Jewish 3%, Muslim 2%
Ethnic mix White 62%, Hispanic 13%,
Black American/African 13%, Other 7%,
Asian 4%, Native American 1%

UNITED STATES
(continued)

Government Presidential system
Currency US dollar = 100 cents
Literacy rate 99%
Calorie consumption 3688 kilocalories

United States of America *see* United
States of America
Unst *88 D1 island* NE Scotland, United
Kingdom
Ünye *116 D2* Ordu, W Turkey
Upala *52 D4* Alajuela, NW Costa Rica
Upata *59 E2* Bolívar, E Venezuela
Upemba, Lac *77 D7 lake* SE Dem.
Rep. Congo
Upernavik *82 C2 var.* Upernivik. Kitaa,
C Greenland
Upington *78 C4* Northern Cape,
W South Africa
'Upolu *145 F4 island* SE Samoa
Upper Klamath Lake *46 A4 lake*
Oregon, NW USA
Upper Lough Erne *89 A5 lake*
SW Northern Ireland, United
Kingdom
Upper Red Lake *45 F1 lake* Minnesota,
N USA
Upper Volta *see* Burkina Faso
Uppsala *85 C6* Uppsala, C Sweden
Uqsuqtuuq *see* Gjoa Haven
Ural *114 B4 Kaz.* Zayyq. *river*
Kazakhstan/Russian Federation
Ural Mountains *114 C3 var.* Ural'skiy
Khrebet, *Eng.* Ural Mountains.
mountain range Kazakhstan/Russian
Federation
Ural Mountains *see* Ural'skiye Gory
Ural'sk *114 B3 Kaz.* Oral. Zapadnyy
Kazakhstan, NW Kazakhstan
Ural'skiy Khrebet *see* Ural'skiye Gory
Uraricoera *62 D1* Roraima, N Brazil
Ura-Tyube *see* Ŭroteppa
Urbandale *45 F3* Iowa, C USA
Urdunn *see* Jordan
Uren' *111 C5* Nizhegorodskaya Oblast',
W Russian Federation
Urga *see* Ulaanbaatar
Urganch *122 D2 Rus.* Urgench; *prev.*
Novo-Urgench. Xorazm Viloyati,
W Uzbekistan
Urgench *see* Urganch
Urgut *123 E3* Samarqand Viloyati,
C Uzbekistan
Urmia, Lake *121 C2 var.* Matianus, Sha
Hi, Urumi Yeh, *Eng.* Lake Urmia; *prev.*
Daryācheh-ye Reẕā'īyeh. *lake*
NW Iran
Urmia, Lake *see* Orūmīyeh,
Daryācheh-ye
Uroševac *see* Ferizaj
Ŭroteppa *123 E2 Rus.* Ura-Tyube.
NW Tajikistan
Uruapan *51 E4 var.* Uruapan del
Progreso. Michoacán,
SW Mexico
Uruapan del Progreso *see* Uruapan
Uruguai, Rio *see* Uruguay
Uruguay *64 D4 off.* Oriental Republic
of Uruguay; *prev.* La Banda Oriental.
country E South America

URUGUAY
South America

Official name Eastern Republic
of Uruguay
Formation 1828 / 1828
Capital Montevideo
Population 3.4 million / 50 people
per sq mile (19 people per sq km)
Total area 68,039 sq. miles (176,220 sq. km)
Languages Spanish*
Religions Roman Catholic 66%, Other
and nonreligious 30%,
Jewish 2%, Protestant 2%
Ethnic mix White 90%, Mestizo 6%,
Black 4%
Government Presidential system
Currency Uruguayan peso
= 100 centésimos
Literacy rate 98%
Calorie consumption 2808 kilocalories

Uruguay *64 D3 var.* Rio Uruguai, Río
Uruguay. *river* E South America
Uruguay, Oriental Republic of *see*
Uruguay
Uruguay, Rio *see* Uruguay
Urumchi *see* Ürümqi
Urumi Yeh *see* Orūmīyeh, Daryācheh-ye
Ürümqi *126 C3 var.* Tihwa, Urumchi,
Urumqi, Urumtsi, Wu-lu-k'o-mu-shi,
Wu-lu-mu-ch'i; *prev.* Ti-hua. Xinjiang
Uygur Zizhiqu, NW China
Urumtsi *see* Ürümqi
Urundi *see* Burundi
Urup, Ostrov *115 H4 island* Kuril'skiye
Ostrova, SE Russian Federation
Urusan *see* Ulsan
Urziceni *108 C5* Ialomiţa,
SE Romania
Usa *110 E3 river* NW Russian
Federation
Uşak *116 B3 prev.* Ushak. Uşak,
W Turkey
Ushak *see* Uşak
Ushant *see* Ouessant, Île d'
Ushuaia *65 B8* Tierra del Fuego,
S Argentina
Usinsk *110 E3* Respublika Komi,
NW Russian Federation
Üsküb/Üsküp *see* Skopje
Usmas Ezers *106 B3 lake* NW Latvia
Usol'ye-Sibirskoye *115 E4* Irkutskaya
Oblast', C Russian Federation
Ussel *91 C5* Corrèze, C France
Ussuriysk *115 G5 prev.* Nikol'sk,
Nikol'sk-Ussuriyskiy, Voroshilov.
Primorskiy Kray, SE Russian
Federation
Ustica *97 B6 island* S Italy
Ust'-Ilimsk *115 E4* Irkutskaya Oblast',
C Russian Federation
Ústí nad Labem *98 A4 Ger.* Aussig.
Ústecký Kraj, NW Czech Republic
Ustinov *see* Izhevsk
Ustka *98 C2 Ger.* Stolpmünde.
Pomorskie, N Poland
Ust'-Kamchatsk *115 H2* Kamchatskiy
Kray, E Russian Federation
Ust'-Kamenogorsk *114 D5 Kaz.*
Öskemen. Vostochnyy Kazakhstan,
E Kazakhstan
Ust'-Kut *115 E4* Irkutskaya Oblast',
C Russian Federation
Ust'-Olenëk *115 E3* Respublika Sakha
(Yakutiya), NE Russian Federation
Ustrzyki Dolne *99 E5* Podkarpackie,
SE Poland
Ust'-Sysol'sk *see* Syktyvkar
Ust Urt *see* Ustyurt Plateau
Ustyurt Plateau *122 B1 var.* Ust
Urt, *Uzb.* Ustyurt Platosi. *plateau*
Kazakhstan/Uzbekistan
Ustyurt Platosi *see* Ustyurt Plateau
Usulután *52 C3* Usulután,
SE El Salvador
Usumacinta, Rio *52 B1 river*
Guatemala/Mexico
Usumbura *see* Bujumbura
U.S./USA *see* United States of America
Utah *44 B4 off.* State of Utah, *also known
as* Beehive State, Mormon State. *state*
W USA
Utah Lake *44 B4 lake* Utah,
W USA
Utena *106 C4* Utena, E Lithuania
Utica *41 F3* New York, NE USA
Utina *see* Udine
Utrecht *86 C4 Lat.* Trajectum ad
Rhenum. Utrecht, C Netherlands
Utsunomiya *131 D5 var.* Utunomiya.
Tochigi, Honshū, S Japan
Uttarakhand *135 E2 cultural region*
N India
Uttar Pradesh *135 E3 prev.* United
Provinces, United Provinces of Agra
and Oudh. *cultural region* N India
Utunomiya *see* Utsunomiya
Uulu *106 D2* Pärnumaa, SW Estonia
Uummannaq *82 C3 var.* Umanak,
Umanaq. Kitaa, C Greenland
Uummannarsuaq *see* Nunap Isua
Uvalde *49 F4* Texas,
SW USA
Uvaravichy *107 D7 Rus.* Uvarovichi.
Homyel'skaya Voblasts', SE Belarus

Uvarovichi see Uvarovichy
Uvea, Île 145 E4 island N Wallis and
 Futuna
Uvs Nuur 126 C1 var. Ozero Ubsu-Nur.
 lake Mongolia/Russian Federation
'Uwaynāt, Jabal al 88 A3 var. Jebel
 Uweinat. mountain Libya/Sudan
Uweinat, Jebel see 'Uwaynāt, Jabal al
Uyo 75 G5 Akwa Ibom, S Nigeria
Uyuni 61 F5 Potosí, W Bolivia
Uzbekistan 122 D2 off. Republic of
 Uzbekistan. country C Asia

UZBEKISTAN
Central Asia

Official name Republic of Uzbekistan
Formation 1991 / 1991
Capital Tashkent
Population 27.8 million / 161 people
 per sq mile (62 people per sq km)
Total area 172,741 sq. miles
 (447,400 sq. km)
Languages Uzbek*, Russian, Tajik, Kazakh
Religions Sunni Muslim 88%,
 Orthodox Christian 9%, Other 3%
Ethnic mix Uzbek 80%, Russian 6%,
 Other 6%, Tajik 5%, Kazakh 3%
Government Presidential system
Currency Som = 100 tiyin
Literacy rate 99%
Calorie consumption 2618 kilocalories

Uzbekistan, Republic of see Uzbekistan
Uzhgorod see Uzhhorod
Uzhhorod 108 B2 Rus. Uzhgorod;
 prev. Ungvár. Zakarpats'ka Oblast',
 W Ukraine
Užice 100 D4 prev. Titovo Užice. Serbia,
 W Serbia

V

Vaal 78 D4 river C South Africa
Vaals 87 D6 Limburg, SE Netherlands
Vaasa 85 D5 Swe. Vasa; prev.
 Nikolainkaupunki. Länsi-Suomi,
 W Finland
Vaassen 86 D3 Gelderland,
 E Netherlands
Vác 99 C6 Ger. Waitzen. Pest,
 N Hungary
Vadodara 134 C4 prev. Baroda. Gujarāt,
 W India
Vaduz 94 E2 country capital
 (Liechtenstein) W Liechtenstein
Vág see Váh
Vágbeszterce see Považská Bystrica
Váh 99 C5 Ger. Waag, Hung. Vág. river
 W Slovakia
Váhtjer see Gällivare
Väinameri 106 C2 prev. Muhu Väin,
 Ger. Moon-Sund. sea E Baltic Sea
Vajdahunyad see Hunedoara
Valachia see Wallachia
Valday 110 B4 Novgorodskaya Oblast',
 W Russian Federation
Valdecañas, Embalse de 92 D3 reservoir
 W Spain
Valdepeñas 93 E4 Castilla-La Mancha,
 C Spain
Valdés, Península 65 C6 peninsula
 SE Argentina
Valdez 36 C3 Alaska, USA
Valdia see Weldiya
Valdivia 65 B5 Los Ríos, C Chile
Val-d'Or 38 D4 Québec, SE Canada
Valdosta 43 E3 Georgia, SE USA
Valence 91 D5 anc. Valentia, Valentia
 Julia, Ventia. Drôme, E France
Valencia 93 F3 Valenciana,
 E Spain
Valencia 46 D1 California, USA
Valencia 58 D1 Carabobo,
 N Venezuela
Valencia, gulf of 93 F3 var. Gulf of
 Valencia. gulf E Spain
Valencia, Gulf of see Valencia, Golfo de
Valenciana 93 F3 var. Valencia, Cat.
 València; anc. Valentia. autonomous
 community NE Spain
Valencia/València see Valenciana
Valenciennes 90 D2 Nord,
 N France

Valentia see Valence, France
Valentia see Valenciana
Valentia Julia see Valence
Valentine State see Oregon
Valera 58 C2 Trujillo, NW Venezuela
Valetta see Valletta
Valga 106 D3 Ger. Walk, Latv. Valka.
 Valgamaa, S Estonia
Valira 91 A8 river Andorra/Spain
Valjevo 100 C4 Serbia, W Serbia
Valjok see Válljohka
Valka 106 D3 Ger. Walk. N Latvia
Valka see Valga
Valkenswaard 87 D5 Noord-Brabant,
 S Netherlands
Valladolid 51 H3 Yucatán, SE Mexico
Valladolid 92 D2 Castilla y León,
 NW Spain
Vall D'Uxó see La Vall d'Uixó
Valle de La Pascua 58 D2 Guárico,
 N Venezuela
Valledupar 58 B1 Cesar, N Colombia
Vallejo 47 B6 California, W USA
Vallenar 64 B3 Atacama, N Chile
Valletta 97 C8 prev. Valetta. country
 capital (Malta) E Malta
Valley City 45 E2 North Dakota,
 N USA
Válljohka 84 D2 var. Valjok. Finnmark,
 N Norway
Valls 93 G2 Cataluña, NE Spain
Valmiera 106 D3 Est. Volmari, Ger.
 Wolmar. N Latvia
Valona see Vlorë
Valozhyn 107 C5 Pol. Wołożyn, Rus.
 Volozhin. Minskaya Voblasts',
 C Belarus
Valparaíso 64 B4 Valparaíso,
 C Chile
Valparaiso 40 C3 Indiana, N USA
Valverde del Camino 92 C4 Andalucía,
 S Spain
Van 117 F3 Van, E Turkey
Vanadzor 117 F2 prev. Kirovakan.
 N Armenia
Vancouver 36 D5 British Columbia,
 SW Canada
Vancouver 46 B3 Washington,
 NW USA
Vancouver Island 36 D5 island British
 Columbia, SW Canada
Vanda see Vantaa
Van Diemen Gulf 146 D2 gulf Northern
 Territory, N Australia
Van Diemen's Land see Tasmania
Vaner, Lake see Vänern
Vänern 85 B6 Eng. Lake Vaner; prev.
 Lake Vener. lake S Sweden
Vangaindrano 79 G4 Fianarantsoa,
 SE Madagascar
Van Horn 48 D3 Texas, SW USA
Lake Van 117 F3 Eng. Lake Van; anc.
 Thospitis. salt lake E Turkey
Van, Lake var. Van Gölü
Vannes 90 A3 anc. Dariorigum.
 Morbihan, NW France
Vantaa 85 D6 Swe. Vanda. Etelä-Suomi,
 S Finland
Vanua Levu 145 E4 island N Fiji
Vanuatu 144 C4 off. Republic of
 Vanuatu; prev. New Hebrides. country
 SW Pacific Ocean

VANUATU
Australasia & Oceania

Official name Republic of Vanuatu
Formation 1980 / 1980
Capital Port Vila
Population 200,000 / 42 people
 per sq mile (16 people per sq km)
Total area 4710 sq. miles (12,200 sq. km)
Languages Bislama* (Melanesian
 pidgin), English*, French*, other
 indigenous languages
Religions Presbyterian 37%, Other 19%,
 Anglican 15%, Roman Catholic 15%,
 Traditional beliefs 8%, Seventh-day
 Adventist 6%
Ethnic mix ni-Vanuatu 94%,
 European 4%, Other 2%
Government Parliamentary system
Currency Vatu = 100 centimes
Literacy rate 74%
Calorie consumption 2841 kilocalories

Vanuatu, Republic of see Vanuatu
Van Wert 40 C4 Ohio, N USA
Vapincum see Gap
Varakļāni 106 D4 C Latvia
Vārānasi 135 E3 prev. Banaras, Benares,
 hist. Kasi. Uttar Pradesh, N India
Varangerfjorden 84 E2 Lapp.
 Várjjatvuotna. fjord N Norway
Varangerhalvøya 84 D2 Lapp.
 Várnjárga. peninsula N Norway
Varannó see Vranov nad Topl'ou
Varasd see Varaždin
Varaždin 100 B2 Ger. Warasdin, Hung.
 Varasd. Varaždin, N Croatia
Varberg 85 B7 Halland, S Sweden
Vardar 101 E6 Gk. Axiós. river
 FYR Macedonia/Greece
Varde 85 A7 Syddtjylland,
 W Denmark
Vareia see Logroño
Varēna 107 B5 Pol. Orany. Alytus,
 S Lithuania
Varese 96 B2 Lombardia, N Italy
Vârful Moldoveanu 108 B4 var.
 Moldoveanul; prev. Vîrful Moldoveanu.
 mountain C Romania
Várjjatvuotna see Varangerfjorden
Varkaus 85 E5 Itä-Suomi, C Finland
Varna 104 E2 prev. Stalin; anc. Odessus.
 Varna, E Bulgaria
Varnenski Zaliv 104 E2 prev. Stalinski
 Zaliv. bay E Bulgaria
Várnjárga see Varangerhalvøya
Varshava see Warszawa
Vasa see Vaasa
Vasilikí 105 A5 Lefkáda, Iónia Nisiá,
 Greece, C Mediterranean Sea
Vasilishki 107 B5 Pol. Wasiliszki.
 Hrodzyenskaya Voblasts',
 W Belarus
Vasil'kov see Vasyl'kiv
Vaslui 108 D4 Vaslui, C Romania
Västerås 85 C6 Västmanland,
 C Sweden
Vasyl'kiv 109 E2 var. Vasil'kov.
 Kyyivs'ka Oblast', N Ukraine
Vaté see Efate
Vatican City 95 A7 off. Vatican City.
 country S Europe

VATICAN CITY
Southern Europe

Official name State of the Vatican City
Formation 1929 / 1929
Capital Vatican City
Population 836 / 4918 people per sq mile
 (1900 people per sq km)
Total area 0.17 sq. miles (0.44 sq. km)
Languages Italian*, Latin*
Religions Roman Catholic 100%
Ethnic mix The current pope is German,
 though most popes for the last 500 years
 have been Italian. Cardinals are from
 many nationalities, but Italians form the
 largest group. Most of the resident lay
 persons are Italian
Government Papal state
Currency Euro = 100 cents
Literacy rate 99%
Calorie consumption Not available

Vatican City see Vatican City
Vatnajökull 83 E5 glacier
 SE Iceland
Vatter, Lake see Vättern
Vättern 85 B6 Eng. Lake Vatter; prev.
 Lake Vetter. lake S Sweden
Vaughn 48 D2 New Mexico,
 SW USA
Vaupés 56 C4 var. Rio Uaupés.
 river Brazil/Colombia
Vava'u Group 145 E4 island group
 N Tonga
Vavuniya 132 D3 Northern Province,
 N Sri Lanka
Vawkavysk 107 B6 Pol. Wołkowysk,
 Rus. Volkovysk. Hrodzyenskaya
 Voblasts', W Belarus
Växjö 85 C7 var. Vexiö. Kronoberg,
 S Sweden
Vaygach, Ostrov 110 E2 island
 NW Russian Federation
Veendam 86 E2 Groningen,
 NE Netherlands

Veenendaal 86 D4 Utrecht,
 C Netherlands
Vega 84 B4 island C Norway
Veglia see Krk
Veisiejai 107 B5 Alytus, S Lithuania
Vejer de la Frontera 92 C5 Andalucía,
 S Spain
Veldhoven 87 D5 Noord-Brabant,
 S Netherlands
Velebit 100 A3 mountain range
 C Croatia
Velenje 95 E7 Ger. Wöllan.
 N Slovenia
Veles 101 E6 Turk. Köprülü. C
 FYR Macedonia
Velho see Porto Velho
Velika Kikinda see Kikinda
Velika Morava 100 D4 var. Glavn'a
 Morava, Morava, Ger. Grosse
 Morava. river C Serbia
Velikaya 113 G2 river NE Russian
 Federation
Veliki Bečkerek see Zrenjanin
Velikiye Luki 110 A4 Pskovskaya
 Oblast', W Russian Federation
Velikiy Novgorod 110 B4 prev.
 Novgorod. Novgorodskaya Oblast',
 W Russian Federation
Veliko Tŭrnovo 104 D2 prev. Tirnovo,
 Trnovo, Tŭrnovo. Veliko Tŭrnovo,
 N Bulgaria
Velingrad 104 C3 Pazardzhik,
 C Bulgaria
Vel'ký Krtíš 99 D6 Banskobystrický
 Kraj, C Slovakia
Vellore 132 C2 Tamil Nādu, SE India
Velobriga see Viana do Castelo
Velsen see Velsen-Noord
Velsen-Noord 86 C3 var. Velsen.
 Noord-Holland, W Netherlands
Vel'sk 110 C4 var. Velsk.
 Arkhangel'skaya Oblast', NW Russian
 Federation
Velykyy Tokmak see Tokmak
Vendôme 90 C4 Loir-et-Cher,
 C France
Venedig see Venezia
Vener, Lake see Vänern
Venetia see Venezia
Venezia 96 C2 Eng. Venice, Fr. Venise,
 Ger. Venedig; anc. Venetia. Veneto,
 NE Italy
Venezia, Golfo di see Venice, Gulf of
Venezuela 58 D2 off. Republic of
 Venezuela; prev. Estados Unidos de
 Venezuela, United States of Venezuela.
 country N South America

VENEZUELA
South America

Official name Bolivarian Republic of
 Venezuela
Formation 1830 / 1830
Capital Caracas
Population 29.4 million / 86 people
 per sq mile (33 people per sq km)
Total area 352,143 sq. miles
 (912,050 sq. km)
Languages Spanish*,
 Amerindian languages
Religions Roman Catholic 96%,
 Protestant 2%, Other 2%
Ethnic mix Mestizo 69%, White 20%,
 Black 9%, Amerindian 2%
Government Presidential system
Currency Bolívar fuerte = 100 céntimos
Literacy rate 93%
Calorie consumption 3014 kilocalories

Venezuela, Estados Unidos de see
 Venezuela
Venezuela, Gulf of 58 C1 Eng. Gulf of
 Maracaibo, Gulf of Venezuela. gulf
 NW Venezuela
Venezuela, Gulf of see Venezuela,
 Golfo de
Venezuelan Basin 56 B1 undersea basin
 E Caribbean Sea
Venezuela, Republic of see
 Venezuela
Venezuela, United States of see
 Venezuela
Venice 42 C4 Louisiana, S USA
Venice see Venezia

Venice, Gulf of *96 C2* It. Golfo di Venezia, Slvn. Beneški Zaliv. *gulf* N Adriatic Sea
Venise see Venezia
Venlo *87 D5* prev. Venloo. Limburg, SE Netherlands
Venloo see Venlo
Venta *106 B3* Ger. Windau. *river* Latvia/ Lithuania
Venta Belgarum see Winchester
Ventia see Valence
Ventimiglia *96 A3* Liguria, NW Italy
Ventspils *106 B2* Ger. Windau. NW Latvia
Vera *64 D3* Santa Fe, C Argentina
Veracruz *51 F4* var. Veracruz Llave. Veracruz-Llave, E Mexico
Veracruz Llave see Veracruz
Vercellae see Vercelli
Vercelli *96 A2* anc. Vercellae. Piemonte, NW Italy
Verdal see Verdalsøra
Verdalsøra *84 B4* var. Verdal. Nord-Trøndelag, C Norway
Verde, Cabo see Cape Verde
Verde, Costa *92 D1* coastal region N Spain
Verden *94 B3* Niedersachsen, NW Germany
Veria see Véroia
Verkhnedvinsk see Vyerkhnyadzvinsk
Verkhneudinsk see Ulan-Ude
Verkhoyanskiy Khrebet *115 F3 mountain range* NE Russian Federation
Vermillion *45 F3* South Dakota, N USA
Vermont *41 F2* off. State of Vermont, also known as Green Mountain State. *state* NE USA
Vernal *44 B4* Utah, W USA
Vernon *49 F2* Texas, SW USA
Verőcze see Virovitica
Véroia *104 B4* var. Veria, Vérroia, Turk. Karaferiye. Kentrikí Makedonía, N Greece
Verona *96 C2* Veneto, NE Italy
Vérroia see Véroia
Versailles *90 D1* Yvelines, N France
Versecz see Vršac
Verulamium see St Albans
Verviers *87 D6* Liège, E Belgium
Vesdre *87 D6* river E Belgium
Veselinovo *104 D2* Shumen, NE Bulgaria
Vesontio see Besançon
Vesoul *90 D4* anc. Vesulium, Vesulum. Haute-Saône, E France
Vesterålen *84 B2* island group N Norway
Vestfjorden *84 C3* fjord C Norway
Vestmannaeyjar *83 E5* Sudhurland, S Iceland
Vesulium/Vesulum see Vesoul
Vesuna see Périgueux
Vesuvio *97 D5* Eng. Vesuvius. volcano S Italy
Vesuvius see Vesuvio
Veszprém *99 C7* Ger. Veszprim. Veszprém, W Hungary
Veszprim see Veszprém
Vetrino *104 E2* Varna, E Bulgaria
Vetrino see Vyetryna
Vetter, Lake see Vättern
Veurne *87 A5* var. Furnes. West-Vlaanderen, W Belgium
Vexió see Växjö
Viacha *61 F4* La Paz, W Bolivia
Viana de Castelo see Viana do Castelo
Viana do Castelo *92 B2* var. Viana de Castelo; anc. Velobriga. Viana do Castelo, NW Portugal
Vianen *86 C4* Utrecht, C Netherlands
Viangchan *136 C4* Eng./Fr. Vientiane. country capital (Laos) C Laos
Viangphoukha *136 C3* var. Vieng Pou Kha. Louangnamtha, N Laos
Viareggio *96 B3* Toscana, C Italy
Viborg *83 A7* Midtjylland, NW Denmark
Vic *93 G2* var. Vich; anc. Ausa, Vicus Ausonensis. Cataluña, NE Spain
Vicentia see Vicenza
Vicenza *96 C2* anc. Vicentia. Veneto, NE Italy

Vich see Vic
Vichy *91 C5* Allier, C France
Vicksburg *42 B2* Mississippi, S USA
Victoria *79 H1* country capital (Seychelles) Mahé, SW Seychelles
Victoria *36 D5* province capital Vancouver Island, British Columbia, SW Canada
Victoria *102 A5* var. Rabat. Gozo, NW Malta
Victoria *49 G4* Texas, SW USA
Victoria *149 C7* state SE Australia
Victoria see Masvingo, Zimbabwe
Victoria Bank see Vitória Seamount
Victoria de Durango see Durango
Victoria de las Tunas see Las Tunas
Victoria Falls *78 C3* Matabeleland North, W Zimbabwe
Victoria Falls *78 C2* waterfall Zambia/ Zimbabwe
Victoria Falls see Iguaçu, Salto do
Victoria Island *37 F3* island Northwest Territories/Nunavut, NW Canada
Victoria, Lake *73 B6* var. Victoria Nyanza. lake E Africa
Victoria Land *154 C4* physical region Antarctica
Victoria Nyanza see Victoria, Lake
Victoria River *146 D3* river Northern Territory, N Australia
Victorville *47 C7* California, W USA
Vicus Ausonensis see Vic
Vicus Elbii see Viterbo
Vidalia *43 E2* Georgia, SE USA
Videm-Krško see Krško
Viden see Wien
Vidin *104 B1* anc. Bononia. Vidin, NW Bulgaria
Vidzy *107 C5* Vitsyebskaya Voblasts', NW Belarus
Viedma *65 C5* Río Negro, E Argentina
Vieja, Sierra *48 D3* mountain range Texas, SW USA
Vieng Pou Kha see Viangphoukha
Vienna see Wien, Austria
Vienna see Vienne, France
Vienne *91 D5* anc. Vienna. Isère, E France
Vienne *90 B4* river W France
Vientiane see Viangchan
Vientos, Paso de los see Windward Passage
Vierzon *90 C4* Cher, C France
Viesīte *106 C4* Ger. Eckengraf. S Latvia
Vietnam *136 D4* off. Socialist Republic of Vietnam, Vtn. Công Hoa Xa Hôi Chu Nghia Viêt Nam. country SE Asia

---

VIETNAM
Southeast Asia

Official name Socialist Republic of Vietnam
Formation 1976 / 1976
Capital Hanoi
Population 88.8 million / 707 people per sq mile (273 people per sq km)
Total area 127,243 sq. miles (329,560 sq. km)
Languages Vietnamese*, Chinese, Thai, Khmer, Muong, Nung, Miao, Yao, Jarai
Religions Buddhist 55%, Christian 8%, Other 29%, Cao Dai 3%, Hoa Hao 3%, Muslim 1%, Protestant 1%
Ethnic mix Vietnamese 86%, Other 8%, Muong 2%, Tay 2%, Thai 2%
Government One-party state
Currency Dông = 10 hao = 100 xu
Literacy rate 93%
Calorie consumption 2690 kilocalories

Vietnam, Socialist Republic of see Vietnam
Vietri see Viêt Tri
Viêt Tri *136 D3* var. Vietri. Vinh Phu, N Vietnam
Vieux Fort *55 F2* S Saint Lucia
Vigo *92 B2* Galicia, NW Spain
Viipuri see Vyborg
Vijayawada *132 D1* prev. Bezwada. Andhra Pradesh, SE India
Vila see Port-Vila
Vila Artur de Paiva see Cubango
Vila da Ponte see Cubango

Vila de João Belo see Xai-Xai
Vila de Mocímboa da Praia see Mocímboa da Praia
Vila do Conde *92 B2* Porto, NW Portugal
Vila do Zumbo *78 D2* prev. Vila do Zumbu, Zumbo. Tete, NW Mozambique
Vila do Zumbu see Vila do Zumbo
Vilafranca del Penedès *93 G2* var. Villafranca del Panadés. Cataluña, NE Spain
Vila General Machado see Camacupa
Vila Henrique de Carvalho see Saurimo
Viļaka *106 D4* Ger. Marienhausen. NE Latvia
Vilalba *92 C1* Galicia, NW Spain
Vila Marechal Carmona see Uíge
Vila Nova de Gaia *92 B2* Porto, NW Portugal
Vila Nova de Portimão see Portimão
Vila Pereira de Eça see N'Giva
Vila Real *92 C2* var. Vila Rial. Vila Real, N Portugal
Vila Rial see Vila Real
Vila Robert Williams see Caála
Vila Salazar see N'Dalatando
Vila Serpa Pinto see Menongue
Vileyka see Vilyeyka
Vilhelmina *84 C4* Västerbotten, N Sweden
Vilhena *62 D3* Rondônia, W Brazil
Viliya *107 C5* Lith. Neris. river W Belarus
Viliya see Neris
Viljandi *106 D2* Ger. Fellin. Viljandimaa, S Estonia
Vilkaviškis *106 B4* Pol. Wyłkowyszki. Marijampolė, SW Lithuania
Villa Acuña *50 D2* var. Ciudad Acuña. Coahuila, NE Mexico
Villa Bella *61 F2* El Beni, N Bolivia
Villacarrillo *93 E4* Andalucía, S Spain
Villa Cecilia see Ciudad Madero
Villach *95 D7* Slvn. Beljak. Kärnten, S Austria
Villacidro *97 A5* Sardegna, Italy, C Mediterranean Sea
Villa Concepción see Concepción
Villa del Pilar see Pilar
Villafranca de los Barros *92 C4* Extremadura, W Spain
Villafranca del Panadés see Vilafranca del Penedès
Villahermosa *51 G4* prev. San Juan Bautista. Tabasco, SE Mexico
Villajoyosa *93 F4* Cat. La Vila Joíosa. Valenciana, E Spain
Villa María *64 C4* Córdoba, C Argentina
Villa Martín *61 F5* Potosí, SW Bolivia
Villa Mercedes *64 C4* var. Mercedes. San Luis, C Argentina
Villanueva *50 D3* Zacatecas, C Mexico
Villanueva de la Serena *92 C3* Extremadura, W Spain
Villanueva de los Infantes *93 E4* Castilla-La Mancha, C Spain
Villarrica *64 D2* Guairá, SE Paraguay
Villavicencio *58 B3* Meta, C Colombia
Villaviciosa *92 D1* Asturias, N Spain
Villazón *61 G5* Potosí, S Bolivia
Villena *93 F4* Valenciana, E Spain
Villeurbanne *91 D5* Rhône, E France
Villingen-Schwenningen *95 B6* Baden-Württemberg, S Germany
Villmanstrand see Lappeenranta
Vilna see Vilnius
Vilnius *107 C5* Pol. Wilno, Ger. Wilna; prev. Rus. Vilna. country capital (Lithuania) Vilnius, SE Lithuania
Vil'shanka *109 E3* Rus. Olshanka. Kirovohrads'ka Oblast', C Ukraine
Vilvoorde *87 C6* Fr. Vilvorde. Vlaams Brabant, C Belgium
Vilvorde see Vilvoorde
Vilyeyka *107 C5* Pol. Wilejka, Rus. Vileyka. Minskaya Voblasts', NW Belarus

Vilyuy *115 F3* river NE Russian Federation
Viña del Mar *64 B4* Valparaíso, C Chile
Vinaròs *93 F3* Valenciana, E Spain
Vincennes *40 B4* Indiana, N USA
Vindhya Mountains see Vindhya Range
Vindhya Range *134 D4* var. Vindhya Mountains. mountain range N India
Vindobona see Wien
Vineland *41 F4* New Jersey, NE USA
Vinh *136 D4* Nghê An, N Vietnam
Vinh Loi see Bac Liêu
Vinishte *104 C2* Montana, NW Bulgaria
Vinita *49 G1* Oklahoma, C USA
Vinkovci *100 C3* Ger. Winkowitz, Hung. Vinkovce. Vukovar-Srijem, E Croatia
Vinkovce see Vinkovci
Vinnitsa see Vinnytsya
Vinnytsya *108 D2* Rus. Vinnitsa. Vinnyts'ka Oblast', C Ukraine
Vinogradov see Vynohradiv
Vinson Massif *154 A3* mountain Antarctica
Viranşehir *117 E4* Şanlıurfa, SE Turkey
Vîrful Moldoveanu see Vârful Moldoveanu
Virginia *45 G1* Minnesota, N USA
Virginia *41 E5* off. Commonwealth of Virginia, also known as Mother of Presidents, Mother of States, Old Dominion. state NE USA
Virginia Beach *41 F5* Virginia, NE USA
Virgin Islands see British Virgin Islands
Virgin Islands (US) *55 F3* var. Virgin Islands of the United States; prev. Danish West Indies. US unincorporated territory E West Indies
Virgin Islands of the United States see Virgin Islands (US)
Vîrôchey *137 E5* Rôtânôkiri, NE Cambodia
Virovitica *100 C2* Ger. Virovititz, Hung. Verőcze; prev. Ger. Werowitz. Virovitica-Podravina, NE Croatia
Virovititz see Virovitica
Virton *87 D8* Luxembourg, SE Belgium
Virtsu *106 D2* Ger. Werder. Läänemaa, W Estonia
Vis *100 B4* It. Lissa; anc. Issa. island S Croatia
Vis see Fish
Visaginas *106 C4* prev. Sniečkus. Utena, E Lithuania
Visākhapatnam *135 E5* var. Vishakhapatnam. Andhra Pradesh, SE India
Visalia *47 C6* California, W USA
Visby *85 C7* Ger. Wisby. Gotland, SE Sweden
Viscount Melville Sound *37 F2* prev. Melville Sound. sound Northwest Territories, N Canada
Visé *87 D6* Liège, E Belgium
Viseu *92 C2* prev. Vizeu. Viseu, N Portugal
Vishakhapatnam see Visākhapatnam
Vislinskiy Zaliv see Vistula Lagoon
Visoko *100 C4* Federacija Bosna I Hercegovina, C Bosnia and Herzegovina
Visttasjohka *84 D3* river N Sweden
Vistula *98 C2* Eng. Vistula, Ger. Weichsel. river C Poland
Vistula see Wisła
Vistula Lagoon *98 C2* Ger. Frisches Haff, Pol. Zalew Wiślany, Rus. Vislinskiy Zaliv. lagoon Poland/Russian Federation
Vitebsk see Vitsyebsk
Viterbo *96 C4* anc. Vicus Elbii. Lazio, C Italy
Viti see Fiji
Viti Levu *145 E4* island W Fiji
Vitim *115 F4* river C Russian Federation
Vitória *63 F4* state capital Espírito Santo, SE Brazil
Vitoria see Vitoria-Gasteiz
Vitória Bank see Vitória Seamount
Vitória da Conquista *63 F3* Bahia, E Brazil

Vitoria-Gasteiz *93 E1 var.* Vitoria, *Eng.*
Vittoria. País Vasco, N Spain
Vitória Seamount *67 B5 var.* Victoria
Bank, Vitoria Bank. *seamount*
C Atlantic Ocean
Vitré *90 B3* Ille-et-Vilaine, NW France
Vitsyebsk *107 E5 Rus.* Vitebsk.
Vitsyebskaya Voblasts', NE Belarus
Vittoria *97 C7* Sicilia, Italy,
C Mediterranean Sea
Vittoria *see* Vitoria-Gastei
Vizcaya, Golfo de *see* Biscay, Bay of
Vizianagaram *135 E5 var.* Vizianagram.
Andhra Pradesh, E India
Vizianagram *see* Vizianagaram
Vjosës, Lumi i *101 C7 var.* Vijosa,
Vijosë, *Gk.* Aóos. *river* Albania/
Greece
Vlaanderen *87 A6 Eng.* Flanders, *Fr.*
Flandre. *cultural region* Belgium/
France
Vlaardingen *86 B4* Zuid-Holland,
SW Netherlands
Vladikavkaz *111 B8 prev.* Dzaudzhikau,
Ordzhonikidze. Respublika Severnaya
Osetiya, SW Russian Federation
Vladimir *111 B5* Vladimirskaya Oblast',
W Russian Federation
Vladimirovka *see* Yuzhno-Sakhalinsk
Vladimir-Volynskiy *see*
Volodymyr-Volyns'kyy
Vladivostok *115 C5* Primorskiy Kray,
SE Russian Federation
Vlagtwedde *86 E2* Groningen,
NE Netherlands
Vlasotince *101 E5* Serbia, SE Serbia
Vlieland *86 C1 Fris.* Flylân. *island*
Waddeneilanden, N Netherlands
Vlijmen *86 C4* Noord-Brabant,
S Netherlands
Vlissingen *87 B5 Eng.* Flushing, *Fr.*
Flessingue. Zeeland, SW Netherlands
Vlodava *see* Włodawa
Vlonë/Vlora *see* Vlorë
Vlorë *101 C7 prev.* Vlonë, *It.* Valona,
Vlora. Vlorë, SW Albania
Vlotslavsk *see* Włocławek
Vöcklabruck *95 D6* Oberösterreich,
NW Austria
Vogelkop *see* Doberai, Jazirah
Vohimena, Tanjona *79 F4 Fr.* Cap
Sainte Marie. *headland*
S Madagascar
Voiron *91 D5* Isère, E France
Vojvodina *100 D3 Ger.* Wojwodina.
Vojvodina, N Serbia
Volga *111 B7 river* NW Russian
Federation
Volga Uplands *81 G3 var.* Volga
Uplands. *mountain range*
W Russian Federation
Volga Uplands *see* Privolzhskaya
Vozvyshennost'
Volgodonsk *111 B7* Rostovskaya Oblast',
SW Russian Federation
Volgograd *111 B7 prev.* Stalingrad,
Tsaritsyn. Volgogradskaya Oblast',
SW Russian Federation
Volkhov *110 B4* Leningradskaya Oblast',
NW Russian Federation
Volkovysk *see* Vawkavysk
Volmari *see* Valmiera
Volnovakha *109 G3* Donets'ka Oblast',
SE Ukraine
Volodymyr-Volyns'kyy *108 C1 Pol.*
Włodzimierz, *Rus.* Vladimir-Volynskiy.
Volyns'ka Oblast', NW Ukraine
Vologda *110 B4* Vologodskaya Oblast',
W Russian Federation
Vólos *105 B5* Thessalía, C Greece
Volozhin *see* Valozhyn
Vol'sk *111 C6* Saratovskaya Oblast',
W Russian Federation
Volta *75 E5 river* E Ghana
Volta Blanche *see* White Volta
Volta, Lake *75 E5 reservoir* SE Ghana
Volta Noire *see* Black Volta
Volturno *97 D5 river* S Italy
Volunteer Island *see* Starbuck Island
Volzhskiy *111 B6* Volgogradskaya
Oblast', SW Russian Federation
Võnnu *106 E3 Ger.* Wendau. Tartumaa,
SE Estonia
Voorst *86 D3* Gelderland, E Netherlands

Voranava *107 C5 Pol.* Werenów, *Rus.*
Voronovo. Hrodzyenskaya Voblasts',
W Belarus
Vorderrhein *95 B7 river* SE Switzerland
Vóreioi Sporádes *see* Vóries Sporádes
Vórioi Sporádhes *see* Vóries Sporádes
Vorkuta *114 C2* Respublika Komi,
NW Russian Federation
Vormsi *106 C2 var.* Vormsi Saar,
Ger. Worms, *Swed.* Ormsö. *island*
W Estonia
Vormsi Saar *see* Vormsi
Voronezh *111 B6* Voronezhskaya
Oblast', W Russian Federation
Voronovo *see* Voranava
Voroshilov *see* Ussuriysk
Voroshilovgrad *see* Luhans'k, Ukraine
Voroshilovsk *see* Stavropol', Russian
Federation
Võru *106 D3 Ger.* Werro. Võrumaa,
SE Estonia
Vosges *90 E4 mountain range*
NE France
Vostochnyy Sayan *115 E4 Eng.* Eastern
Sayans, *Mong.* Dzüün Soyonï Nuruu.
mountain range Mongolia/Russian
Federation
Vostock Island *see* Vostok Island
Vostok *154 C3 Russian research station*
Antarctica
Vostok Island *145 G3 var.* Vostock
Island; *prev.* Stavers Island. *island* Line
Islands, SE Kiribati
Voznesens'k *109 E3 Rus.* Voznesensk.
Mykolayivs'ka Oblast', S Ukraine
Vranje *101 E5* Serbia, SE Serbia
Vranov *see* Vranov nad Topl'ou
Vranov nad Topl'ou *99 D5 var.* Vranov,
Hung. Varannó. Prešovský Kraj,
E Slovakia
Vratsa *104 C2* Vratsa, NW Bulgaria
Vrbas *100 C3* Vojvodina, NW Serbia
Vrbas *100 C3 river* N Bosnia and
Herzegovina
Vršac *100 E3 Ger.* Werschetz, *Hung.*
Versecz. Vojvodina, NE Serbia
Vsetín *99 C5 Ger.* Wsetin. Zlínský Kraj,
E Czech Republic
Vučitrn *see* Vushtrri
Vukovar *100 C3 Hung.* Vukovár.
Vukovar-Srijem, E Croatia
Vulcano, Isola *97 C7 island* Isole
Eolie, S Italy
Vung Tau *127 E6 prev.* Fr. Cape Saint
Jacques, Cap Saint-Jacques. Ba Ria-
Vung Tau, S Vietnam
Vusan *see* Busan
Vushtrri *101 D5 Serb.* Vučitrn.
N Kosovo
Vyatka *111 C5 river* NW Russian
Federation
Vyatka *see* Kirov
Vyborg *110 B3 Fin.* Viipuri.
Leningradskaya Oblast', NW Russian
Federation
Vyerkhnyadzvinsk *107 D5 Rus.*
Verkhnedvinsk. Vitsyebskaya
Voblasts', N Belarus
Vyetryna *107 D5 Rus.* Vetrino.
Vitsyebskaya Voblasts', N Belarus
Vynohradiv *108 B3 Cz.* Sevluš, *Hung.*
Nagyszőllős, *Rus.* Vinogradov; *prev.*
Sevlyush. Zakarpats'ka Oblast',
W Ukraine

W

Wa *75 E4* NW Ghana
Waag *see* Váh
Waagbistritz *see* Považská Bystrica
Waal *86 C4 river* S Netherlands
Wabash *40 C4* Indiana, N USA
Wabash River *40 B5 river* N USA
Waco *49 G3* Texas, SW USA
Wad Al-Hajarah *see* Guadalajara
Waddān *71 F3* NW Libya
Waddenzee *86 C1 var.* Wadden Zee.
sea SE North Sea
Wadden Zee *see* Waddenzee
Waddington, Mount *36 D5 mountain*
British Columbia, SW Canada
Wādī as Sīr *119 B6 var.* Wadi es Sir.
'Ammān, NW Jordan

Wadi es Sir *see* Wādī as Sīr
Wadi Halfa *72 B3 var.* Wādī Ḥalfā'.
Northern, N Sudan
Wādī Mūsā *119 B7 var.* Petra. Ma'ān,
S Jordan
Wad Madani *see* Wad Medani
Wad Medani *72 C4 var.* Wad Madanī.
Gezira, C Sudan
Waflia *139 F4* Pulau Buru, E Indonesia
Wagadugu *see* Ouagadougou
Wagga Wagga *149 C7* New South Wales,
SE Australia
Wagin *147 B7* Western Australia
Wāh *134 C1* Punjab, NE Pakistan
Wahai *139 F4* Pulau Seram,
E Indonesia
Wahaybah, Ramlat Al *see* Wahībah,
Ramlat Āl
Wahiawā *47 A8 var.* Wahiawa. O'ahu,
Hawaii, USA, C Pacific Ocean
Wahibah, Ramlat Ahl *see* Wahībah,
Ramlat Āl
Wahībah Sands *121 E5 var.* Ramlat Ahl
Wahībah, Ramlat Al Wahaybah, *Eng.*
Wahībah Sands. *desert* N Oman
Wahibah Sands *see* Wahibah, Ramlat Āl
Wahpeton *45 F2* North Dakota,
N USA
Wahran *see* Oran
Waiau *151 A7 river* South Island, New
Zealand
Waigeo, Pulau *139 G4 island* Maluku,
E Indonesia
Waikaremoana, Lake *150 E4 lake*
North Island, New Zealand
Wailuku *47 B8* Maui, Hawaii, USA,
C Pacific Ocean
Waimate *151 B6* Canterbury, South
Island, New Zealand
Waiouru *150 D4* Manawatu-Wanganui,
North Island, New Zealand
Waipara *151 C6* Canterbury, South
Island, New Zealand
Waipawa *150 E4* Hawke's Bay, North
Island, New Zealand
Waipukurau *150 D4* Hawke's Bay,
North Island, New Zealand
Wairau *151 C5 river* South Island, New
Zealand
Wairoa *150 E4* Hawke's Bay, North
Island, New Zealand
Wairoa *150 D2 river* North Island, New
Zealand
Waitaki *151 B6 river* South Island, New
Zealand
Waitara *150 D4* Taranaki, North Island,
New Zealand
Waitzen *see* Vác
Waiuku *150 D3* Auckland, North Island,
New Zealand
Wakasa-wan *131 C6 bay* C Japan
Wakatipu, Lake *151 A7 lake* South
Island, New Zealand
Wakayama *131 C6* Wakayama, Honshū,
SW Japan
Wake Island *152 C2 US unincorporated
territory* NW Pacific Ocean
Wake Island *142 D1 atoll* NW Pacific
Ocean
Wakkanai *130 C1* Hokkaidō, NE Japan
Walachei/Walachia *see* Wallachia
Wałbrzych *98 B4 Ger.* Waldenburg,
Waldenburg in Schlesien. Dolnośląskie,
SW Poland
Walcourt *87 C7* Namur, S Belgium
Wałcz *98 B3 Ger.* Deutsch Krone.
Zachodnio-pomorskie, NW Poland
Waldenburg/Waldenburg in Schlesien
see Wałbrzych
Waldia *see* Weldiya
Wales *36 C2* Alaska, USA
Wales *89 C6 Wel.* Cymru. *cultural region*
Wales, United Kingdom
Walgett *149 D5* New South Wales,
SE Australia
Walk *see* Valga, Estonia
Walk *see* Valka, Latvia
Walker Lake *47 C5 lake* Nevada,
W USA
Wallachia *108 B5 var.* Walachia, *Ger.*
Walachei, *Rom.* Valachia. *cultural
region* S Romania
Walla Walla *46 C2* Washington,
NW USA

Wallenthal *see* Hațeg
Wallis and Futuna *145 E4 Fr.* Territoire
de Wallis et Futuna. *French overseas
territory* C Pacific Ocean
Wallis et Futuna, Territoire de *see*
Wallis and Futuna
Walnut Ridge *42 B1* Arkansas,
C USA
Waltenberg *see* Zalău
Walthamstow *89 B7* Waltham Forest,
SE England, United Kingdom
Walvisbaai *see* Walvis Bay
Walvis Bay *78 A4 Afr.* Walvisbaai.
Erongo, NW Namibia
Walvis Ridge *69 B7 var.* Walvish Ridge.
undersea ridge E Atlantic Ocean
Wan *see* Anhui
Wanaka *151 B6* Otago, South Island,
New Zealand
Wanaka, Lake *151 A6 lake* South Island,
New Zealand
Wanchuan *see* Zhangjiakou
Wandel Sea *83 E1 sea* Arctic Ocean
Wandsworth *89 A8* Wandsworth,
SE England, United Kingdom
Wanganui *150 D4* Manawatu-
Wanganui, North Island,
New Zealand
Wangaratta *149 C7* Victoria,
SE Australia
Wankie *see* Hwange
Wanki, Río *see* Coco, Río
Wanlaweyn *73 D6 var.* Wanle Weyn,
It. Uanle Uen. Shabeellaha Hoose,
SW Somalia
Wanle Weyn *see* Wanlaweyn
Wanxian *see* Wanzhou
Wanzhou *128 B5 var.* Wanxian.
Chongqing Shi, C China
Warangal *135 E5* Andhra Pradesh,
C India
Warasdin *see* Varaždin
Warburg *94 B4* Nordrhein-Westfalen,
W Germany
Ware *37 E4* British Columbia,
W Canada
Waremme *87 C6* Liège, E Belgium
Waren *94 C3* Mecklenburg-
Vorpommern, NE Germany
Wargla *see* Ouargla
Warkworth *150 D2* Auckland, North
Island, New Zealand
Warnemünde *94 C2* Mecklenburg-
Vorpommern, NE Germany
Warner *49 G1* Oklahoma, C USA
Warnes *61 G4* Santa Cruz, C Bolivia
Warrego River *149 C5 seasonal river*
New South Wales/Queensland,
E Australia
Warren *40 D3* Michigan, N USA
Warren *40 D3* Ohio, N USA
Warren *41 E3* Pennsylvania,
NE USA
Warri *75 F5* Delta, S Nigeria
Warrnambool *149 B7* Victoria,
SE Australia
Warsaw/Warschau *see* Warszawa
Warszawa *98 D3 Eng.* Warsaw,
Ger. Warschau, *Rus.* Varshava.
country capital (Poland) Mazowieckie,
C Poland
Warta *98 B3 Ger.* Warthe. *river*
W Poland
Wartberg *see* Senec
Warthe *see* Warta
Warwick *149 E5* Queensland,
E Australia
Washington *44 A2* NE England, United
Kingdom
Washington DC *41 E4 country capital*
(USA) District of Columbia, NE USA
Washington Island *see* Teraina
Washington, Mount *41 G2 mountain*
New Hampshire, NE USA
Wash, The *89 E6 inlet* E England, United
Kingdom
Wasiliszki *see* Vasilishki
Waspam *53 E2 var.* Waspán. Región
Autónoma Atlántico Norte,
NE Nicaragua
Waspán *see* Waspam
Watampone *139 E4 var.* Bone. Sulawesi,
C Indonesia

Watenstedt-Salzgitter *see* Salzgitter
Waterbury *41 F3* Connecticut,
NE USA
Waterford *89 B6 Ir.* Port Láirge.
Waterford, S Ireland
Waterloo *45 G3* Iowa, C USA
Watertown *41 F2* New York,
NE USA
Watertown *45 F2* South Dakota,
N USA
Waterville *41 G2* Maine, NE USA
Watford *89 A7* E England, United
Kingdom
Watlings Island *see* San Salvador
Watsa *77 E5* Orientale, NE Dem. Rep.
Congo
Watts Bar Lake *42 D1 reservoir*
Tennessee, S USA
Wau *73 B5 var.* Wāw. Western Bahr el
Ghazal, W South Sudan
Waukegan *40 B3* Illinois, N USA
Waukesha *40 B3* Wisconsin, N USA
Wausau *40 B2* Wisconsin, N USA
Waverly *45 G3* Iowa, C USA
Wavre *87 C6* Walloon Brabant,
C Belgium
Wāw *see* Wau
Wawa *38 C4* Ontario, S Canada
Waycross *43 E3* Georgia, SE USA
Wearmouth *see* Sunderland
Webfoot State *see* Oregon
Webster City *45 F3* Iowa, C USA
Weddell Plain *154 A2 abyssal plain*
SW Atlantic Ocean
Weddell Sea *154 A2 sea* SW Atlantic
Ocean
Weener *94 A3* Niedersachsen,
NW Germany
Weert *87 D5* Limburg, SE Netherlands
Weesp *86 C3* Noord-Holland,
C Netherlands
Wegorzewo *98 D2 Ger.* Angerburg.
Warmińsko-Mazurskie, NE Poland
Weichsel *see* Wisła
Weimar *94 C4* Thüringen, C Germany
Weissenburg *see* Alba Iulia, Romania
Weissenburg in Bayern *95 C6* Bayern,
SE Germany
Weissenstein *see* Paide
Weisskirchen *see* Bela Crkva
Weiswampach *87 D7* Diekirch,
N Luxembourg
Wejherowo *98 C2* Pomorskie,
NW Poland
Welchman Hall *55 G1* C Barbados
Weldiya *72 C4 var.* Waldia. *It.* Valdia.
Āmara, N Ethiopia
Welkom *78 D4* Free State,
C South Africa
Welle *see* Uele
Wellesley Islands *148 B2 island group*
Queensland, N Australia
Wellington *151 D5 country capital*
(New Zealand) Wellington, North
Island, New Zealand
Wellington *45 F5* Kansas, C USA
Wellington *see* Wellington, Isla
Wellington, Isla *65 A7 var.* Wellington.
island S Chile
Wells *46 D4* Nevada, W USA
Wellsford *150 D2* Auckland, North
Island, New Zealand
Wells, Lake *147 C5 lake* Western
Australia
Wels *95 D6 anc.* Ovilava. Oberösterreich,
N Austria
Wembley *89 A8* Alberta, W Canada
Wemmel *87 B6* Vlaams Brabant,
C Belgium
Wenatchee *46 B2* Washington,
NW USA
Wenchi *75 E4* W Ghana
Wen-chou/Wenchow *see* Wenzhou
Wendau *see* Võnnu
Wenden *see* Cēsis
Wenzhou *128 D5 var.* Wen-chou,
Wenchow. Zhejiang, SE China
Werda *78 C4* Kgalagadi, S Botswana
Werder *see* Virtsu
Werenöw *see* Voranava
Werkendam *86 C4* Noord-Brabant,
S Netherlands
Werowitz *see* Virovitica
Werro *see* Võru

Werschetz *see* Vršac
Wesenberg *see* Rakvere
Weser *94 B3 river* NW Germany
Wessel Islands *148 B1 island group*
Northern Territory, N Australia
West Antarctica *see* Wharton
Basin
West Antarctica *154 A3 prev.* Lesser
Antarctica. *physical region* Antarctica
West Australian Basin *see* Wharton
Basin
West Bank *119 A6 disputed region*
SW Asia
West Bend *40 B3* Wisconsin, N USA
West Bengal *135 F4 cultural region*
NE India
West Cape *151 A7 headland* South
Island, New Zealand
West Des Moines *45 F3* Iowa, C USA
Westerland *94 B2* Schleswig-Holstein,
N Germany
Western Australia *146 B4 state*
W Australia
Western Bug *see* Bug
Western Carpathians *99 E7 mountain
range* W Romania Europe
Western Desert *72 B2 var.* Sahara el
Gharbīya, *Eng.* Western Desert. *desert*
C Egypt
Western Desert *see* Şaḥrā' al Gharbīyah
Western Dvina *85 E7 Bel.* Dzvina, *Ger.*
Düna, *Latv.* Daugava, *Rus.* Zapadnaya
Dvina. *river* W Europe
Western Ghats *134 C5 mountain range*
SW India
Western Isles *see* Outer Hebrides
Western Punjab *see* Punjab
Western Sahara *70 B3 disputed territory*
N Africa
Western Samoa *see* Samoa
Western Sayans *114 D4 Eng.* Western
Sayans. *mountain range* S Russian
Federation
Western Sayans *see* Zapadnyy Sayan
Western Scheldt *87 B5 Eng.* Western
Scheldt; *prev.* Honte. *inlet* S
North Sea
Western Scheldt *see* Westerschelde
Western Sierra Madre *see* Madre
Occidental, Sierra
West Falkland *65 C7 var.* Gran Malvina,
Isla Gran Malvina. *island* W Falkland
Islands
West Fargo *45 F2* North Dakota,
N USA
West Frisian Islands *86 C1 Eng.*
West Frisian Islands. *island group*
N Netherlands
West Frisian Islands *see*
Waddeneilanden
West Irian *see* Papua
Westliche Morava *see* Zapadna Morava
West Mariana Basin *142 B1 var.* Perece
Vela Basin. *undersea feature* W Pacific
Ocean
West Memphis *42 B1* Arkansas,
C USA
West New Guinea *see* Papua
Weston-super-Mare *89 D7* SW England,
United Kingdom
West Palm Beach *43 F4* Florida,
SE USA
West Papua *see* Papua
Westport *151 C5* West Coast, South
Island, New Zealand
West Punjab *see* Punjab
West River *see* Xi Jiang
West Siberian Plain *114 C3 Eng.*
West Siberian Plain. *plain* C Russian
Federation
West Siberian Plain *see* Zapadno-
Sibirskaya Ravnina
West Virginia *40 D4 off.* State of West
Virginia, *also known as* Mountain State.
state NE USA
Wetar, Pulau *139 F5 island* Kepulauan
Damar, E Indonesia
Wetzlar *95 B5* Hessen, W Germany
Wevok *36 C2 var.* Wewuk. Alaska,
USA
Wewuk *see* Wevok
Wexford *89 B6 Ir.* Loch Garman.
SE Ireland
Weyburn *37 F5* Saskatchewan, S Canada
Weymouth *89 D7* S England, United
Kingdom

Wezep *86 D3* Gelderland,
E Netherlands
Whakatane *150 E3* Bay of Plenty,
North Island, New Zealand
Whale Cove *37 G3 var.* Tikirarjuaq.
Nunavut, C Canada
Whangarei *150 D2* Northland, North
Island, New Zealand
Wharton Basin *141 D5 var.* West
Australian Basin. *undersea feature*
E Indian Ocean
Whataroa *151 B6* West Coast, South
Island, New Zealand
Wheatland *44 D3* Wyoming, C USA
Wheeler Peak *48 D1 mountain* New
Mexico, SW USA
Wheeling *40 D4* West Virginia,
NE USA
Whitby *89 D5* N England, United
Kingdom
Whitefish *44 B1* Montana, NW USA
Whitehaven *89 C5* NW England,
United Kingdom
Whitehorse *36 D4 territory capital*
Yukon Territory, W Canada
White Nile *72 B4 Ar.* Al Baḥr al Abyaḍ,
An Nīl al Abyaḍ, Bahr el Jebel. *river*
NE South Sudan
White Nile *72 B4 var.* Bahr el Jebel.
river S Sudan
White River *44 D3 river* South Dakota,
N USA
White Sea *110 C3 Eng.* White Sea. *sea*
NW Russian Federation
White Sea *see* Beloye More
White Volta *75 E4 var.* Nakambé, *Fr.*
Volta Blanche. *river* Burkina Faso/
Ghana
Whitianga *150 D2* Waikato, North
Island, New Zealand
Whitney, Mount *47 C6 mountain*
California, W USA
Whitsunday Group *148 D3 island group*
Queensland, E Australia
Whyalla *149 B6* South Australia
Wichita *45 F5* Kansas, C USA
Wichita Falls *49 F2* Texas, SW USA
Wichita River *49 F2 river* Texas,
SW USA
Wickenburg *48 B2* Arizona, SW USA
Wicklow *89 B6 Ir.* Cill Mhantáin. *county*
E Ireland
Wicklow Mountains *89 B6 Ir.* Sléibhte
Chill Mhantáin. *mountain range*
E Ireland
Wieliczka *99 D5* Małopolskie, S Poland
Wieluń *98 C4* Sieradz, C Poland
Wien *95 E6 Eng.* Vienna, *Hung.*
Bécs, *Slvk.* Videň, *Slvn.* Dunaj; *anc.*
Vindobona. *country capital* (Austria)
Wien, NE Austria
Wiener Neustadt *95 E6*
Niederösterreich, E Austria
Wierden *86 E3* Overijssel,
E Netherlands
Wiesbaden *95 B5* Hessen,
W Germany
**Wieselburg and Ungarisch-Altenburg/
Wieselburg-Ungarisch-Altenburg**
see Mosonmagyaróvár
Wiesenhof *see* Ostrołęka
Wight, Isle of *89 D7 island* United
Kingdom
Wigorna Ceaster *see* Worcester
Wijchen *86 D4* Gelderland,
SE Netherlands
Wijk bij Duurstede *86 D4* Utrecht,
C Netherlands
Wilcannia *149 C6* New South Wales,
SE Australia
Wilejka *see* Vilyeyka
Wilhelm, Mount *144 B3 mountain*
C Papua New Guinea
Wilhelm-Pieck-Stadt *see* Guben
Wilhelmshaven *94 B3* Niedersachsen,
NW Germany
Wilia/Wilja *see* Neris
Wilkes Barre *41 F3* Pennsylvania,
NE USA
Wilkes Land *154 C4 physical region*
Antarctica
Wilkomierz *see* Ukmergė
Willard *48 D2* New Mexico,
SW USA

Willcox *48 C3* Arizona, SW USA
Willebroek *87 B5* Antwerpen,
C Belgium
Willemstad *55 E5 dependent territory
capital* (Netherlands) Curaçao
Williston *44 D1* North Dakota,
N USA
Wilmington *41 F4* Delaware,
NE USA
Wilmington *43 F2* North Carolina,
SE USA
Wilmington *40 C4* Ohio, N USA
Wilna/Wilno *see* Vilnius
Wilrijk *87 C5* Antwerpen, N Belgium
Winchester *89 D7 hist.* Wintanceaster,
Lat. Venta Belgarum. S England,
United Kingdom
Winchester *41 E4* Virginia, NE USA
Windau *see* Ventspils, Latvia
Windau *see* Venta, Latvia/Lithuania
Windhoek *78 B3 Ger.* Windhuk.
country capital (Namibia) Khomas,
C Namibia
Windhuk *see* Windhoek
Windorah *148 C4* Queensland,
C Australia
Windsor *38 C5* Ontario, S Canada
Windsor *89 D7* S England, United
Kingdom
Windsor *41 G3* Connecticut,
NE USA
Windward Islands *55 H4 island group*
E West Indies
Windward Islands *see* Barlavento,
Ilhas de, Cape Verde
Windward Passage *54 D3 Sp.* Paso de
los Vientos. *channel* Cuba/Haiti
Winisk *38 C2 prev.* Winisk. Ontario,
C Canada
Winisk *see* Winisk
Winkowitz *see* Vinkovci
Winnebago, Lake *40 B2 lake*
Wisconsin, N USA
Winnemucca *47 C5* Nevada, W USA
Winnipeg *37 G5 province capital*
Manitoba, S Canada
Winnipeg, Lake *37 G5 lake* Manitoba,
C Canada
Winnipegosis, Lake *38 A3 lake*
Manitoba, C Canada
Winona *45 G3* Minnesota, N USA
Winschoten *86 E2* Groningen,
NE Netherlands
Winsen *94 B3* Niedersachsen,
N Germany
Winston Salem *43 E1* North Carolina,
SE USA
Winsum *86 D1* Groningen,
NE Netherlands
Wintanceaster *see* Winchester
Winterswijk *86 E4* Gelderland,
E Netherlands
Winterthur *95 B7* Zürich,
NE Switzerland
Winton *148 C4* Queensland,
E Australia
Winton *151 A7* Southland,
South Island, New Zealand
Wisby *see* Visby
Wisconsin *40 A2 off.* State of
Wisconsin, *also known as*
Badger State. *state* N USA
Wisconsin Rapids *40 B2* Wisconsin,
N USA
Wisconsin River *40 B3 river*
Wisconsin, N USA
Wiślany, Zalew *see* Vistula Lagoon
Wismar *94 C2* Mecklenburg-
Vorpommern, N Germany
Wittenberge *94 C3* Brandenburg,
N Germany
Wittlich *95 A5* Rheinland-Pfalz,
SW Germany
Wittstock *94 C3* Brandenburg,
NE Germany
W. J. van Blommesteinmeer *59 G3
reservoir* E Suriname
Władysławowo *98 C2* Pomorskie,
N Poland
Włocławek *98 C3 Ger./Rus.* Vlotslavsk.
Kujawsko-pomorskie, C Poland
Włodawa *98 E4 Rus.* Vlodava. Lubelskie,
SE Poland
Włodzimierz *see* Volodymyr-Volyns'kyy

Wlotzkasbaken *78 B3* Erongo, W Namibia
Wodonga *149 C7* Victoria, SE Australia
Wodzisław Śląski *99 C5* Ger. Loslau. Śląskie, S Poland
Wojerecy *see* Hoyerswerda
Wōjjä *see* Wotje Atoll
Wojwodina *see* Vojvodina
Woking *89 D7* SE England, United Kingdom
Wolf, Isla *60 A4 island* Galápagos, Galápagos Islands, W Ecuador South America
Wolfsberg *95 D7* Kärnten, SE Austria
Wolfsburg *94 C3* Niedersachsen, N Germany
Wolgast *94 D2* Mecklenburg-Vorpommern, NE Germany
Wołkowysk *see* Vawkavysk
Wöllan *see* Velenje
Wollaston Lake *37 F4* Saskatchewan, C Canada
Wollongong *149 D6* New South Wales, SE Australia
Wolmar *see* Valmiera
Wołożyn *see* Valozhyn
Wolvega *86 D2* Fris. Wolvegea. Fryslân, N Netherlands
Wolvegea *see* Wolvega
Wolverhampton *89 D6* C England, United Kingdom
Wolverine State *see* Michigan
Wŏnsan *129 E3* SE North Korea
Woodburn *46 B3* Oregon, NW USA
Woodland *47 B5* California, W USA
Woodruff *40 B2* Wisconsin, N USA
Woods, Lake of the *38 A3 Fr.* Lac des Bois. *lake* Canada/USA
Woodville *150 D4* Manawatu-Wanganui, North Island, New Zealand
Woodward *49 F1* Oklahoma, C USA
Worcester *78 C5* Western Cape, SW South Africa
Worcester *89 D6 hist.* Wigorna Ceaster. W England, United Kingdom
Worcester *41 G3* Massachusetts, NE USA
Workington *89 C5* NW England, United Kingdom
Worland *44 C3* Wyoming, C USA
Wormatia *see* Worms
Worms *95 B5 anc.* Augusta Vangionum, Borbetomagus, Wormatia. Rheinland-Pfalz, SW Germany
Worms *see* Vormsi
Worthington *45 F3* Minnesota, N USA
Wotje Atoll *144 D2 var.* Wōjjä. *atoll* Ratak Chain, E Marshall Islands
Woudrichem *86 C4* Noord-Brabant, S Netherlands
Wrangel Island *115 F1 Eng.* Wrangel Island. *island* NE Russian Federation
Wrangel Island *see* Vrangelya, Ostrov
Wrangel Plain *155 B2 undersea feature* Arctic Ocean
Wrocław *98 C4 Eng./Ger.* Breslau. Dolnośląskie, SW Poland
Września *98 C3* Wielkopolskie, C Poland
Wsetin *see* Vsetín
Wuchang *see* Wuhan
Wuday'ah *121 C6 spring/well* S Saudi Arabia
Wuhai *127 E3 var.* Haibowan. Nei Mongol Zizhiqu, N China
Wuhan *128 C5 var.* Han-kou, Han-k'ou, Hanyang, Wuchang, Wu-han; *prev.* Hankow. *province capital* Hubei, C China
Wu-han *see* Wuhan
Wuhsien *see* Suzhou
Wuhsi/Wu-hsi *see* Wuxi
Wuhu *128 D5 var.* Wu-na-mu. Anhui, E China
Wujlān *see* Ujelang Atoll
Wukari *75 G4* Taraba, E Nigeria
Wuliang Shan *128 A6 mountain range* SW China

Wu-lu-k'o-mu-shi/Wu-lu-mu-ch'i *see* Ürümqi
Wu-na-mu *see* Wuhu
Wuppertal *94 A4 prev.* Barmen-Elberfeld. Nordrhein-Westfalen, W Germany
Würzburg *95 B5* Bayern, SW Germany
Wusih *see* Wuxi
Wuxi *128 D5 var.* Wuhsi, Wu-hsi, Wusih. Jiangsu, E China
Wuyi Shan *125 E3 mountain range* SE China
Wye *89 C6 Wel.* Gwy. *river* England/Wales, United Kingdom
Wyłkowyszki *see* Vilkaviškis
Wyndham *146 D3* Western Australia
Wyoming *40 C3* Michigan, N USA
Wyoming *44 B3 off.* State of Wyoming, *also known as* Equality State. *state* C USA
Wyszków *98 D3 Ger.* Probstberg. Mazowieckie, NE Poland

X

Xaafuun, Raas *72 E4 var.* Ras Hafun. *cape* NE Somalia
Xaçmaz *117 H2 Rus.* Khachmas. N Azerbaijan
Xaignabouli *136 C4 prev.* Muang Xaignabouri, *Fr.* Sayaboury. Xaignabouli, N Laos
Xai-Xai *79 E4 prev.* João Belo, Vila de João Belo. Gaza, S Mozambique
Xalapa *51 F4* Veracruz-Llave, Mexico
Xam Nua *136 D3 var.* Sam Neua. Houaphan, N Laos
Xankändi *117 G3 Rus.* Khankendi; *prev.* Stepanakert. SW Azerbaijan
Xánthi *104 C3* Anatolikí Makedonía kai Thráki, NE Greece
Xàtiva *93 F3 Cas.* Xàtiva; *anc.* Setabis, *var.* Jativa. Valencia, E Spain
Xauen *see* Chefchaouen
Xäzär Dänizi *see* Caspian Sea
Xeres *see* Jerez de la Frontera
Xiaguan *see* Dali
Xiamen *128 D6 var.* Hsia-men; *prev.* Amoy. Fujian, SE China
Xi'an *128 C4 var.* Changan, Sian, Signan, Siking, Singan, Xian. *province capital* Shaanxi, C China
Xiang *see* Hunan
Xianggang *see* Hong Kong
Xiangkhoang *see* Phônsaven
Xiangtan *128 C5 var.* Hsiang-t'an, Siangtan. Hunan, S China
Xiao Hinggan Ling *128 D2 Eng.* Lesser Khingan Range. *mountain range* NE China
Xichang *128 B5* Sichuan, C China
Xieng Khouang *see* Phônsaven
Xieng Ngeun *see* Muong Xiang Ngeun
Xigazê *126 C5 var.* Jih-k'a-tse, Shigatse, Xigaze. Xizang Zizhiqu, W China
Xi Jiang *124 D3 var.* Hsi Chiang, *Eng.* West River. *river* S China
Xilinhot *127 F2 var.* Silinhot. Nei Mongol Zizhiqu, N China
Xilokastro *see* Xylókastro
Xin *see* Xinjiang Uygur Zizhiqu
Xingkai Hu *see* Khanka, Lake
Xingu, Rio *63 E2 river* C Brazil
Xingxingxia *126 D3* Xinjiang Uygur Zizhiqu, NW China
Xining *127 E4 var.* Hsining, Hsi-ning, Sining. *province capital* Qinghai, C China
Xinjiang *see* Xinjiang Uygur Zizhiqu
Xinjiang Uygur Zizhiqu *126 B3 var.* Sinkiang, Sinkiang Uighur Autonomous Region, Xin, Xinjiang. *autonomous region* NW China
Xinpu *see* Lianyungang
Xinxiang *128 C4* Henan, C China
Xinyang *128 C5 var.* Hsin-yang, Sinyang. Henan, C China
Xinzo de Limia *92 C2* Galicia, NW Spain
Xiqing Shan *124 D2 mountain range* C China
Xiva *122 D2 Rus.* Khiva, Khiwa. Xorazm Viloyati, W Uzbekistan

Xixón *see* Gijón
Xizang *see* Xizang Zizhiqu
Xizang Gaoyuan *see* Qingzang Gaoyuan
Xizang Zizhiqu *126 B4 var.* Thibet, Tibetan Autonomous Region, Xizang, *Eng.* Tibet. *autonomous region* W China
Xolotlán *see* Managua, Lago de
Xucheng *see* Xuwen
Xuddur *73 D5 var.* Hudur, *It.* Oddur. Bakool, SW Somalia
Xuwen *128 C7 var.* Xucheng. Guangdong, S China
Xuzhou *128 D4 var.* Hsu-chou, Suchow, Tongshan; *prev.* T'ung-shan. Jiangsu, E China
Xylókastro *105 B5 var.* Xilokastro. Pelopónnisos, S Greece

Y

Ya'an *128 B5 var.* Yaan. Sichuan, C China
Yabēlo *73 C5* Oromīya, C Ethiopia
Yablis *53 E2* Región Autónoma Atlántico Norte, NE Nicaragua
Yablonovyy Khrebet *115 F4 mountain range* S Russian Federation
Yabrai Shan *127 E3 mountain range* NE China
Yafran *71 F2* NW Libya
Yaghan Basin *67 B7 undersea feature* SE Pacific Ocean
Yagotin *see* Yahotyn
Yahualica *50 D4* Jalisco, SW Mexico
Yakima *46 B2* Washington, NW USA
Yakima River *46 B2 river* Washington, NW USA
Yakoruda *104 C3* Blagoevgrad, SW Bulgaria
Yaku-shima *131 B8 island* Nansei-shotō, SW Japan
Yakutat *36 D4* Alaska, USA
Yakutsk *115 F3* Respublika Sakha (Yakutiya), NE Russian Federation
Yala *137 C7* Yala, SW Thailand
Yalizava *107 D6 Rus.* Yelizovo. Mahilyowskaya Voblasts', E Belarus
Yalong Jiang *128 A5 river* C China
Yalova *116 B3* Yalova, NW Turkey
Yalpug, Ozero *see* Yalpuh, Ozero
Yalpuh, Ozero *108 D4 Rus.* Ozero Yalpug. *lake* SW Ukraine
Yalta *109 F5* Avtonomna Respublika Krym, S Ukraine
Yalu *125 E2 Chin.* Yalu Jiang, *Jap.* Oryokko, *Kor.* Amnok-kang. *river* China/North Korea
Yalu Jiang *see* Yalu
Yamaguchi *131 B7 var.* Yamaguti. Yamaguchi, Honshū, SW Japan
Yamal, Poluostrov *114 D2 peninsula* N Russian Federation
Yamanīyah, Al Jumhūrīyah al *see* Yemen
Yambio *73 B5 var.* Yambiyo. Western Equatoria, S South Sudan
Yambiyo *see* Yambio
Yambol *104 D2 Turk.* Yanboli. Yambol, E Bulgaria
Yamdena, Pulau *139 G5 prev.* Jamdena. *island* Kepulauan Tanimbar, E Indonesia
Yamoussoukro *74 D5 country capital* (Côte d'Ivoire) C Côte d'Ivoire
Yamuna *134 D3 prev.* Jumna. *river* N India
Yana *115 F2 river* NE Russian Federation
Yanboli *see* Yambol
Yanbu' al Baḩr *121 A5* Al Madīnah, W Saudi Arabia
Yangambi *77 D5* Orientale, N Dem. Rep. Congo
Yangchow *see* Yangzhou
Yangiyo'l *123 E2 Rus.* Yangiyul'. Toshkent Viloyati, E Uzbekistan
Yangiyul' *see* Yangiyo'l
Yangon *136 B4 Eng.* Rangoon. Yangon, S Myanmar (Burma)

Yangtze *128 B5 var.* Yangtze Kiang, *Eng.* Yangtze. *river* C China
Yangtze *see* Chang Jiang/Jinsha Jiang
Yangtze *see* Chang Jiang
Yangtze Kiang *see* Chang Jiang
Yangzhou *128 D5 var.* Yangchow. Jiangsu, E China
Yankton *45 E3* South Dakota, N USA
Yannina *see* Ioánnina
Yanskiy Zaliv *113 F2 bay* N Russian Federation
Yantai *128 D4 var.* Yan-t'ai; *prev.* Chefoo, Chih-fu. Shandong, E China
Yaoundé *77 B5 var.* Yaunde. *country capital* (Cameroon) Centre, S Cameroon
Yap *144 A1 island* Caroline Islands, W Micronesia
Yapanskoye More East Sea/ Japan, Sea of
Yapen, Pulau *139 G4 prev.* Japen. *island* E Indonesia
Yap Trench *142 B2 var.* Yap Trough. *undersea feature* SE Philippine Sea
Yap Trough *see* Yap Trench
Yapurá *see* Caquetá, Río, Brazil/ Colombia
Yapurá *see* Japurá, Río, Brazil/ Colombia
Yaqui, Río *50 C2 river* NW Mexico
Yaransk *111 C5* Kirovskaya Oblast', NW Russian Federation
Yarega *110 D4* Respublika Komi, NW Russian Federation
Yarkant *see* Shache
Yarlung Zangbo Jiang *see* Brahmaputra
Yarmouth *39 F5* Nova Scotia, SE Canada
Yarmouth *see* Great Yarmouth
Yaroslav *see* Jaroslaw
Yaroslavl' *110 B4* Yaroslavskaya Oblast', W Russian Federation
Yarumal *58 B2* Antioquia, NW Colombia
Yasyel'da *107 B7 river* Brestskaya Voblasts', SW Belarus Europe
Yatsushiro *131 A7 var.* Yatusiro. Kumamoto, Kyūshū, SW Japan
Yatusiro *see* Yatsushiro
Yaunde *see* Yaoundé
Yavari *see* Javari, Río
Rio Yavari *62 C2 var.* Yavarí. *river* Brazil/Peru
Yaviza *53 H5* Darién, SE Panama
Yavorív *108 B2 Pol.* Jaworów, *Rus.* Yavorov. L'vivs'ka Oblast', NW Ukraine
Yavorov *see* Yavorív
Yazd *120 D3 var.* Yezd. Yazd, C Iran
Yazoo City *42 B2* Mississippi, S USA
Yding Skovhøj *85 A7 hill* C Denmark
Ýdra *105 C6 var.* Ídhra. *island* Ýdra, S Greece
Ye *137 B5* Mon State, S Myanmar (Burma)
Yecheng *126 A3 var.* Kargilik. Xinjiang Uygur Zizhiqu, NW China
Yefremov *111 B5* Tul'skaya Oblast', W Russian Federation
Yekaterinburg *114 C3 prev.* Sverdlovsk. Sverdlovskaya Oblast', C Russian Federation
Yekaterinodar *see* Krasnodar
Yekaterinoslav *see* Dnipropetrovs'k
Yelets *111 B5* Lipetskaya Oblast', W Russian Federation
Yelisavetpol *see* Gäncä
Yelizavetgrad *see* Kirovohrad
Yelizovo *see* Yalizava
Yell *88 D1 island* NE Scotland, United Kingdom
Yellowhammer State *see* Alabama
Yellowknife *37 E4 territory capital* Northwest Territories, W Canada
Yellow River *128 C4 var.* Yellow River. *river* C China
Yellow River *see* Huang He
Yellow Sea *128 D4 Chin.* Huang Hai, *Kor.* Hwang-Hae. *sea* E Asia

Key to map pages

North & West Asia 112-113

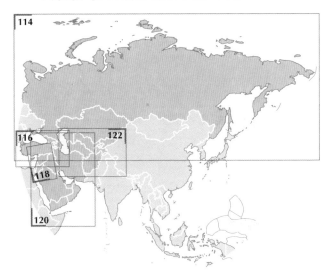

114
116
122
118
120

South & East Asia 124-125

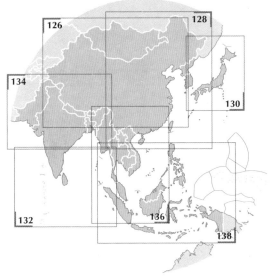

126
128
134
130
132
136
138

Yellowstone River *44 C2 river* Montana/
Wyoming, NW USA
Yel'sk *107 C7* Homyel'skaya Voblasts',
SE Belarus
Yelwa *75 F4* Kebbi, W Nigeria
Yemen *121 C7 off.* Republic of Yemen,
Ar. Al Jumhuriyah al Yamaniyah, Al
Yaman. *country* SW Asia

YEMEN
Southwest Asia

Official name Republic of Yemen
Formation 1990 / 1990
Capital Sana
Population 24.8 million / 114 people
per sq mile (44 people per sq km)
Total area 203,849 sq. miles
(527,970 sq. km)
Languages Arabic*
Religions Sunni Muslim 55%, Shi'a
Muslim 42%, Christian, Hindu, and
Jewish 3%
Ethnic mix Arab 99%, Afro-Arab, Indian,
Somali, and European 1%
Government Transitional regime
Currency Yemeni rial = 100 fils
Literacy rate 62%
Calorie consumption 2109 kilocalories

Yemen, Republic of *see* Yemen
Yemva *110 D4 prev.* Zheleznodorozhnyy.
Respublika Komi, NW Russian
Federation
Yenakiyeve *109 G3 Rus.* Yenakiyevo;
prev. Ordzhonikidze, Rykovo.
Donets'ka Oblast', E Ukraine
Yenakiyevo *see* Yenakiyeve
Yenangyaung *136 A3* Magway,
W Myanmar (Burma)
Yendi *75 E4* NE Ghana
Yengisar *126 A3* Xinjiang Uygur
Zizhiqu, NW China
Yenierenköy *102 D4 var.* Yialousa, *Gk.*
Agialoúsa. NE Cyprus
Yenipazar *see* Novi Pazar
Yenisey *114 D3 river* Mongolia/Russian
Federation
Yenping *see* Nanping
Yeovil *89 D7* SW England, United
Kingdom
Yeppoon *148 D4* Queensland,
E Australia
Yerevan *117 F3 Eng.* Erivan. *country
capital* (Armenia) C Armenia
Yeriho *see* Jericho
Yertis *114 C4 var.* Irtish, *Kaz.* Ertis; *prev.*
Irtysh. *river* C Asia
Yesil' *114 C4 Kaz.* Esil. *river*
Kazakhstan/Russian Federation
Yeso *see* Hokkaidō
Yeu, Île d' *90 A4 island* NW France
Yevlakh *see* Yevlax
Yevlax *117 G2 Rus.* Yevlakh.
C Azerbaijan
Yevpatoriya *109 F5* Avtonomna
Respublika Krym, S Ukraine
Yeya *109 H4 river* SW Russian
Federation
Yezerishche *see* Yezyaryshcha
Yezo *see* Hokkaidō
Yezyaryshcha *107 E5 Rus.* Yezerishche.
Vitsyebskaya Voblasts',
NE Belarus
Yialousa *see* Yenierenköy
Yiannitsá *see* Giannitsá
Yichang *128 C5* Hubei, C China
Yıldızeli *116 D3* Sivas, N Turkey
Yinchuan *128 B4 var.* Yinch'uan,
Yin-ch'uan, Yinchwan.
province capital Ningxia,
N China
Yinchwan *see* Yinchuan
Yindu He *see* Indus
Yin-hsien *see* Ningbo
Yining *126 B2 var.* I-ning, *Uigh.* Gulja,
Kuldja. Xinjiang Uygur Zizhiqu,
NW China
Yin-tu Ho *see* Indus
Yisrael/Yisra'el *see* Israel
Yíthion *see* Gýtheio
Yogyakarta *138 C5 prev.* Djokjakarta,
Jogjakarta, Jokyakarta. Jawa,
C Indonesia

Yokohama *131 D5* Aomori, Honshū,
C Japan
Yokohama *130 A2* Kanagawa, Honshū,
S Japan
Yokote *130 D4* Akita, Honshū,
C Japan
Yonago *131 B6* Tottori, Honshū,
SW Japan
Yong'an *128 D6 var.* Yongan. Fujian,
SE China
Yongzhou *see* Lingling
Yonkers *41 F3* New York,
NE USA
Yonne *90 C4 river* C France
Yopal *58 C3 var.* El Yopal. Casanare,
C Colombia
York *89 D5 anc.* Eboracum,
Eburacum. N England,
United Kingdom
York *45 E4* Nebraska, C USA
York, Cape *148 C1 headland*
Queensland, NE Australia
York, Kap *see* Innaanganeq
Yorkton *37 F5* Saskatchewan,
S Canada
Yoro *52 C2* Yoro, C Honduras
Yoshkar-Ola *111 C5* Respublika Mariy
El, W Russian Federation
Yösönbulag *see* Altay
Youngstown *40 D4* Ohio, N USA
Youth, Isle of *54 A2 var.* Isla de Pinos,
Eng. Isle of Youth; *prev.* The Isle of the
Pines. *island* W Cuba
Youth, Isle of *see* Juventud, Isla de la
Ypres *see* Ieper
Yreka *46 B4* California, W USA
Yrendagüé *see*
General Eugenio A. Garay
Yssel *see* IJssel
Ysyk-Köl *see* Issyk-Kul', Ozero
Ysyk-Köl *see* Balykchy
Yu *see* Henan
Yuan *see* Red River
Yuan Jiang *see* Red River
Yuba City *47 B5* California, W USA
Yucatán, Canal de *see*
Yucatan Channel
Yucatan Channel *51 H3 Sp.* Canal de
Yucatán. *channel* Cuba/Mexico
Yucatan Peninsula *35 C7 Eng.* Yucatan
Peninsula. *peninsula* Guatemala/
Mexico
Yucatán Peninsula *see* Yucatán,
Península de
Yuci *see* Jinzhong
Yue *see* Guangdong
Yue Shan, Tai *see* Lantau Island
Yueyang *128 C5* Hunan, S China
Yugoslavia *see* Serbia
Yukhavichy *107 D5 Rus.* Yukhovichi.
Vitsyebskaya Voblasts', N Belarus
Yukhovichi *see* Yukhavichy
Yukon *see* Yukon Territory
Yukon River *36 C2 river*
Canada/USA
Yukon, Territoire du *see* Yukon
Territory
Yukon Territory *36 D3 var.* Yukon,
Fr. Territoire du Yukon. *territory*
NW Canada
Yulin *128 C6* Guangxi Zhuangzu
Zizhiqu, S China
Yuma *48 A2* Arizona, SW USA
Yumendong *128 A3 prev.* Laojunmiao.
Gansu, N China
Yun *see* Yunnan
Yungki *see* Jilin
Yung-ning *see* Nanning
Yunjinghong *see* Jinghong
Yunki *see* Jilin
Yunnan *128 A6 var.* Yun, Yunnan
Sheng, Yünnan, Yun-nan. *province*
SW China
Yunnan *see* Kunming
Yunnan Sheng *see* Yunnan
Yünnan/Yun-nan *see* Yunnan
Yurev *see* Tartu
Yurihonjo *see* Honjō
Yuruá, Río *see* Juruá, Rio
Yury'ev *see* Tartu
Yushu *126 D4 var.* Gyêgu. Qinghai,
C China
Yuty *64 D3* Caazapá, S Paraguay

Yuzhno-Sakhalinsk *115 H4 Jap.*
Toyohara; *prev.* Vladimirovka. Ostrov
Sakhalin, Sakhalinskaya Oblast',
SE Russian Federation
Yuzhnyy Bug *see* Pivdennyy Buh
Yuzhou *see* Chongqing
Ýylanly *see* Gurbansoltan Eje

Z

Zaandam *see* Zaanstad
Zaanstad *86 C3 prev.* Zaandam. Noord-
Holland, C Netherlands
Zabaykal'sk *115 F5* Zabaykal'skiy Kray,
S Russian Federation
Zabern *see* Saverne
Zabid *121 B7* W Yemen
Żabinka *see* Zhabinka
Ząbkowice *see* Ząbkowice Śląskie
Ząbkowice Śląskie *98 B4 var.*
Ząbkowice, *Ger.* Frankenstein,
Frankenstein in Schlesien.
Dolnośląskie, SW Poland
Zábřeh *99 C5 Ger.* Hohenstadt.
Olomoucký Kraj, E Czech Republic
Zacapa *52 B2* Zacapa, E Guatemala
Zacatecas *50 D3* Zacatecas, C Mexico
Zacatepec *51 E4* Morelos, S Mexico
Zacháro *105 B6 var.* Zaharo, Zakháro.
Dytikí Elláda, S Greece
Zadar *100 A3 It.* Zara; *anc.* Iader.
Zadar, SW Croatia
Zadetkyi Kyun *137 B6 var.* St.Matthew's
Island. *island* Mergui Archipelago,
S Myanmar (Burma)
Zafra *92 C4* Extremadura, W Spain
Żagań *98 B4 var.* Zagań, Żegań, *Ger.*
Sagan. Lubuskie, W Poland
Zagazig *see* Az Zaqāziq
Zágráb *see* Zagreb
Zagreb *100 B2 Ger.* Agram, *Hung.*
Zágráb. *country capital* (Croatia)
Zagreb, N Croatia
Zagros Mountains *120 C3 Eng.* Zagros
Mountains. *mountain range* W Iran
Zagros Mountains *see* Zágros, Kühhā-ye
Zaharo *see* Zacháro
Zähedän *120 E4 var.* Zahidan; *prev.*
Duzdab. Sīstān va Balūchestān,
SE Iran
Zahidan *see* Zähedän
Zahlah *see* Zahlé
Zahlé *118 B4 var.* Zaḥlah. C Lebanon
Záhony *99 E6* Szabolcs-Szatmár-Bereg,
NE Hungary
Zaire *see* Congo (river)
Zaire *see* Congo (Democratic Republic of)
Zaječar *100 E4* Serbia, E Serbia
Zakataly *see* Zaqatala
Zakháro *see* Zacháro
Zakhidnyy Buh/Zakhodni Buh *see* Bug
Zákhö *120 B2 var.* Zákhü. Dahūk, N Iraq
Zákhü *see* Zákhö
Zakopane *99 D5* Małopolskie, S Poland
Zákynthos *105 A6 var.* Zákinthos, *It.*
Zante. *island* Iónia Nísoi, Greece,
C Mediterranean Sea
Zalaegerszeg *99 B7* Zala, W Hungary
Zalău *108 B3 Ger.* Waltenberg, *Hung.*
Zilah; *prev. Ger.* Zillenmarkt. Sălaj,
NW Romania
Zalim *121 B5* Makkah, W Saudi Arabia
Zambesi/Zambeze *see* Zambezi
Zambezi *78 C2* North Western,
W Zambia
Zambezi *78 D2 var.* Zambesi, *Port.*
Zambeze. *river* S Africa
Zambia *78 C2 off.* Republic of Zambia;
prev. Northern Rhodesia. *country*
S Africa

ZAMBIA
Southern Africa

Official name Republic of Zambia
Formation 1964 / 1964
Capital Lusaka
Population 13.5 million / 47 people
per sq mile (18 people per sq km)
Total area 290,584 sq. miles
(752,614 sq. km)
Languages Bemba, Tonga, Nyanja, Lozi,
Lala-Bisa, Nsenga, English*
Religions Christian 63%, Traditional

ZAMBIA
(continued)

beliefs 36%, Muslim and Hindu 1%
Ethnic mix Bemba 34%, Other
African 26%, Tonga 16%, Nyanja 14%,
Lozi 9%, European 1%
Government Presidential system
Currency Zambian kwacha = 100 ngwee
Literacy rate 71%
Calorie consumption 1879 kilocalories

Zambia, Republic of *see* Zambia
Zamboanga *139 E3 off.* Zamboanga City.
Mindanao, S Philippines
Zamboanga City *see* Zamboanga
Zambrów *98 E3* Łomża, E Poland
Zamora *92 D2* Castilla y León,
NW Spain
Zamora de Hidalgo *50 D4* Michoacán,
SW Mexico
Zamość *98 E4 Rus.* Zamoste. Lubelskie,
E Poland
Zamoste *see* Zamość
Zancle *see* Messina
Zanda *126 A4* Xizang Zizhiqu, W China
Zanesville *40 D4* Ohio, N USA
Zanjān *120 C2 var.* Zenjan, Zinjan.
Zanjān, NW Iran
Zante *see* Zákynthos
Zanthus *147 C6* Western Australia,
S Australia Oceania
Zanzibar *73 D7* Zanzibar, E Tanzania
Zanzibar *73 C7 Swa.* Unguja. *island*
E Tanzania
Zaozhuang *128 D4* Shandong,
E China
Zapadna Morava *100 D4 Ger.* Westliche
Morava. *river* C Serbia
Zapadnaya Dvina *110 A4* Tverskaya
Oblast', W Russian Federation
Zapadnaya Dvina *see* Western Dvina
Zapadnyy Bug *see* Bug
Zapala *65 B5* Neuquén, W Argentina
Zapiola Ridge *67 B6 undersea feature*
SW Atlantic Ocean
Zapolyarnyy *110 C2* Murmanskaya
Oblast', NW Russian Federation
Zaporizhzhya *109 F3 Rus.* Zaporozh'ye;
prev. Aleksandrovsk. Zaporiz'ka
Oblast', SE Ukraine
Zaporozh'ye *see* Zaporizhzhya
Zapotiltic *50 D4* Jalisco, SW Mexico
Zaqatala *117 G2 Rus.* Zakataly.
NW Azerbaijan
Zara *116 D3* Sivas, C Turkey
Zara *see* Zadar
Zarafshan *see* Zarafshon
Zarafshon *122 D2 Rus.* Zarafshan.
Navoiy Viloyati, N Uzbekistan
Zarafshon *see* Zeravshan
Zaragoza *93 F2 Eng.* Saragossa; *anc.*
Caesaraugusta, Salduba. Aragón,
NE Spain
Zarand *120 D3* Kermān, C Iran
Zaranj *122 D5* Nīmrōz, SW Afghanistan
Zarasai *106 C4* Utena, E Lithuania
Zárate *64 D4 prev.* General José
F.Uriburu. Buenos Aires, E Argentina
Zarautz *93 E1 var.* Zarauz. País Vasco,
N Spain
Zarauz *see* Zarautz
Zaraza *59 E2* Guárico, N Venezuela
Zarghūn Shahr *123 E4 var.* Katawaz.
Paktikā, SE Afghanistan
Zaria *75 G4* Kaduna, C Nigeria
Zarós *105 D8* Kríti, Greece,
E Mediterranean Sea
Zarqa *see* Az Zarqā'
Żary *98 B4 Ger.* Sorau, Sorau in der
Niederlausitz. Lubuskie, W Poland
Zaunguzskiye Garagumy *see* Üngüz
Angyrsyndaky Garagum
Zavertse *see* Zawiercie
Zavet *104 D1* Razgrad, NE Bulgaria
Zavidovići *100 C3* Federacija Bosna
I Hercegovina, N Bosnia and
Herzegovina
Zawiercie *98 D4 Rus.* Zavertse. Śląskie,
S Poland
Zawilah *71 F3 var.* Zuwaylah, *It.* Zueila.
C Libya
Zaysan Köl *see* Zaysan, Ozero